ELEMENTS OF PSYCHOLOGY

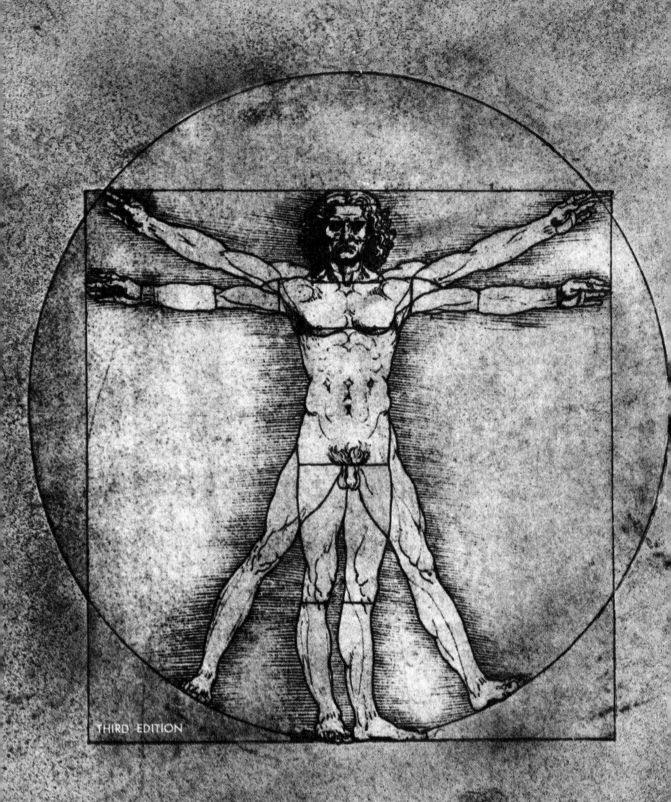
THIRD EDITION

ELEMENTS OF PSYCHOLOGY

DAVID KRECH AND RICHARD S. CRUTCHFIELD
University of California, Berkeley

NORMAN LIVSON
California State University, Hayward

With the collaboration of **WILLIAM A. WILSON, JR.**
University of Connecticut

ALFRED A. KNOPF   NEW YORK

TO THOSE WHO WOULD GLADLY TEACH AND GLADLY LEARN

THIS IS A BORZOI BOOK
PUBLISHED BY ALFRED A. KNOPF, INC.

Third Edition

98765432

Library of Congress Cataloging in Publication Data

Krech, David.
  Elements of psychology.

  Bibliography: p.
  1. Psychology. I. Crutchfield, Richard S.,
joint author. II. Livson, Norman, 1924-   joint author.
III. Title. [DNLM: 1. Psychology.
BF121 K91e 1974]
BF121.K73 1974   150   73-21864
ISBN 0-394-31768-8
ISBN 0-394-49223-4

Manufactured in the United States of America

IN APPRECIATION OF OUR CONTRIBUTORS

We owe an unusual debt to the ten teachers and scholars who worked with us in our effort to create a credible textbook in general psychology. Whereas (in our previous two editions) we believed that a few authors could reasonably undertake to write such a textbook, we have been forced to recognize the folly (and irresponsibility) of attempting to do so today without substantial assistance from many specialists in many fields of psychology. The enormous growth of psychology, both in the scope of the problems with which it contends and in the technical sophistication required by its greater depth of inquiry, now demands a fund of expertise beyond the capabilities of a few authors.

In recognition of this, we have sought help not only from scholars of high technical competence in their chosen areas of research but also from those who could meet the additional requirement that they be active and experienced teachers. Only such persons, we believed, could make effective contributions to what we were attempting: the creation of a scientifically sound account of contemporary psychology *and* a pedagogically effective textbook.

Our contributors, in most instances, prepared working papers to cover the one or more units within their areas of specialization. These papers served the four authors of this book, and served us well, as points of departure in our efforts to forge a coherent and seriously intended textbook—one that possesses a unity of purpose, an orientation, and a style of presentation that can come only from the close collaboration of a limited number of psychologist-teachers of like mind. We did not wish to present either a symposium or a "professional writer's" rewriting of the work of disparate experts. But the drafts of our consultants have in every case been carefully reviewed, reworked, and rewritten by us, and then integrated with all the other contributions. Some contributors indeed may no longer recognize their original materials (or may even not wish to); we absolve them of responsibility for any faults that we may have introduced.

We thank them all. In the order in which their areas appear in our Table of Contents, they are:

I. Michael Lerner	GENETICS
Robert M. Olton	THINKING AND PROBLEM SOLVING
Daniel I. Slobin	LANGUAGE DEVELOPMENT
Marjorie P. Honzik	MENTAL ABILITIES
John M. Kennedy	PERCEPTION
Jerome Smith	LEARNING, MEMORY
Charles T. Tart	ALTERED STATES OF CONSCIOUSNESS
Robert W. Moulton	MENTAL DISORDERS, PSYCHOTHERAPY, THEORIES OF PERSONALITY
Georgia Babladelis	PERSONALITY
Joan Sieber	SOCIAL PSYCHOLOGY

PREFACE
TO THE FIRST EDITION

The preface of a book usually turns out to be the most pleasant chapter to write. This is not only because, in the inverted and realistic logic of book-making, it is the last chapter which needs to be written, but primarily because it is the one chapter where the authors can make explicit their debt to the many people who have helped make the book possible.

We cannot hope to name all who deserve our thanks, but we can, at the very least, indicate those of our friends and colleagues who contributed well beyond the normal call of friendship and good will.

Of course no book is completely the work of the authors whose names are listed on the title page, and the unnamed authors of this book, as is true of any scientific enterprise, are legion. First among these are the research workers in psychology and the cognate sciences upon whose findings we have attempted to build a systematic approach to the science of human behavior. Since this book is not only a presentation of a body of scientific knowledge and speculation, but is also a teaching instrument, it reflects, we hope, all that we have learned from our students—at Swarthmore College, Bryn Mawr College, Mount Holyoke College, Harvard University, the University of Oslo, the University of Colorado, and the University of California—where we have been privileged to teach and to share with these students the adventure of examining anew, every year, what man has learned about man.

Most immediately, we are indebted to several friends who have read and criticized the first draft of the manuscript incorporated in this book. Among them is Professor Leo Postman who carefully and painstakingly went over large sections of our manuscript, especially those dealing with perception and learning, and whose helpful criticism has not only saved us from a number of errors, but whose sound scholarship has helped make this book so much the better. Professor Mark R. Rosenzweig has read, and made suggestions relating to, the chapters on physiology and neurology, and has been most generous in helping to design the anatomical illustrations used in those chapters. Professor Edwin E. Ghiselli, through his rare combination of a basic familiarity with the "pure" science of psychology and a mastery of industrial psychology, has made many valuable suggestions which we have not hesitated to incorporate. Professors Paul H. Mussen and John P. McKee have reviewed in a critical and sympathetic manner our chapters on child development, and we have profited from their reviews. Professor Rheem F. Jarrett has gone over our chapter on statistics, and has made several contributions to it. Professor Hans Wallach read and made a number of helpful comments on our chapters on perception, as did Professor Mason Haire, whose interest and kind enthusiasm have encouraged us greatly. And finally, as have so many others, we have profited from the wisdom and encouragement of Professor Robert B. MacLeod.

We have attempted to present in this book an effective teaching instrument. If we have been successful, a large part of the credit properly belongs to the illustrators and draftsmen who strove to put a number of our notions into interesting, clear, and pleasing graphic form. Mr. Walter Schwarz, the scientific illustrator, has shown infinite patience, a perceptive intelligence, and his usual high order of skill in his execution of the anatomical drawings. Mr. Wolfgang Lederer helped us by his imaginative capacity to translate the "write-ups" of experimental procedure into charming and clear illustrations, and Mrs. Katherine Eardley, who is responsible for the charts, graphs, and some of the line drawings of the book, has always been a friend and colleague upon whose patience, talent, and imagination we have drawn liberally. Mr. Herbert Kling, technician of our laboratory, has done yeoman's service in his able photographic and reproductive work.

Miss Jean Pierce was responsible for typing the many, many versions of our manuscript. Her interest, skill, and intelligence made her not only our typist, but our first critical reader and editor. She has helped enormously. Finally, it is with gratitude that we acknowledge our indebtedness to Dr. Ray Ginger, Editor of the College Department of Alfred A. Knopf, Inc., whose careful and sensitive readings improved both how we have had our say, and, at many points, what we have had to say.

We have been most fortunate in the generosity of many individuals who have made available to us original figures, photographs, and manuscripts: Professors Wilder Penfield, Heinrich Klüver, Donald B. Lindsley, Raúl Hernández-Peón, and Per Saugstad.

We wish also to express our most sincere appreciation to the following journals, publishers, and individuals who have granted permission to reproduce tables, figures, illustrations, and excerpts:

American Journal of Psychology
American Philosophical Society
American Psychological Association
Appleton-Century-Crofts, Inc.
Archives of Psychology
Mrs. Madison Bentley
British Journal of Psychology
Dodd, Mead & Co.
Dover Publications, Inc.
Genetic Psychology Monographs
Ginn & Company
Harper & Brothers
Henry Holt & Co., Inc.
Houghton Mifflin Company
Journal of Comparative Psychology
Journal of Electroencephalography and
    Clinical Neurophysiology
Journal of Experimental Psychology
Journal of General Psychology
Journal of Genetic Psychology
Journal of Speech and Hearing Disorders
Liveright Publishing Corp.
The Macmillan Co.
McGraw-Hill Book Co.
W. W. Norton & Company, Inc.
Perception Demonstration Center of
    Princeton University
Princeton University Press
Psychological Monographs
Psychological Review
Science
Scientific American
Scientific Publishing Company
The Technology Press
University of California Press
University of Chicago Press
University of Wichita Press
D. Van Nostrand Co., Inc.
The Viking Press, Inc.
John Wiley & Sons, Inc.
Yale University Press

David Krech / Richard S. Crutchfield
Berkeley, California
September, 1957

PREFACE
TO THE THIRD EDITION

The first edition of *Elements of Psychology* was published in 1958; the second edition, in 1969. The need for the present edition after a lapse of only half the interval between the earlier ones tells us something important about the state of the science of psychology. That there are today many more psychologists than in 1969 (about 5,000 more, according to the membership of the American Psychological Association) implies only growth in size. That the number of research papers reported in *Psychological Abstracts* has grown nearly 50 percent in the same period tells us somewhat more: The message is that the study of behavior is growing at an enormous rate; it requires attention to the work of many more investigators not only from within psychology but also from other scientific disciplines. Clearly, a textbook in general psychology for the mid-seventies must look at and strive to make some coherent sense of a burgeoning body of ever-changing data. With the assistance of a number of expert contributors, we have attempted just that task in the third edition.

The result is a thoroughgoing revision, considerably more extensive than we had thought necessary when we started to work on this edition. Not only has the total number of research references increased significantly but a large proportion is new to this edition. In part this increase in new material reflects the increase in scope and the rapidity of change of psychology today, as we have just noted. But to

a substantial extent it can also be traced to our decision to pay closer attention to the redistribution of emphases that has come about in psychology in recent years. In our decision to provide more intensive coverage of certain previously treated areas and in our introduction of some wholly new ones, we have been guided by our scientific conscience and goaded by the hundreds of questions, comments, and criticisms from instructors and students who have read the second edition. We are grateful to them all.

What *is* new and different in this third edition? We can point here to only a few of the major differences: (1) a new, extensive unit on altered states of consciousness; (2) a significantly expanded consideration of psychological disorders and of the psychotherapies that have been developed to cope with them; (3) a fresh and broader look at the field of social psychology; (4) a restated treatment of developmental psycholinguistics, reflecting the intellectual ferment within this very "hot" area of research; (5) an interweaving of behavior genetics data throughout the text in the several units where this increasingly fertile area can contribute to our understanding of psychological phenomena.

Our treatments of perception and the physiological bases of behavior are briefer but extensively updated. The developmental theme (already a focus in the second edition) has been further emphasized, not by lengthening the unit on development but by integrating many new developmental data, where pertinent and useful, into our consideration of each psychological function. To our treatment of mental abilities we have added what we believe to be a candid assessment of the data and polemic on "IQ and race."

But enough. Those of you who read the book will see for yourselves where we have evolved along new and different lines, and how well we have done so. If the verdict is favorable, that will be largely the result of the counsel freely given by those colleagues to whom we turned in the troubled moments that plague authors. We shall not name them, but we are grateful. We happily also acknowledge the "without whom" role so skillfully played by Susan Thatcher. Transforming scrawled drafts into legible type; somehow keeping track of the innum-

erable bits and pieces of which textbooks are made; checking our list of references—all these things and many more were hers to do, and she did them well. We owe an extra measure of gratitude for her uncompromising marginal notes: "This just doesn't make sense!" We hope it now does.

Elaine Rosenberg, of Alfred A. Knopf, has seen us through these labors with patience, necessary persistence, and editorial skill. We have been a difficult, often mutinous, crew, but somehow she has helped see us safely to port.

David Krech/Richard S. Crutchfield/
Norman Livson
Berkeley, California
William A. Wilson, Jr.
Storrs, Connecticut
January, 1974

CONTENTS

PART ONE | ORIGINS, GROWTH, AND DEVELOPMENT

PART TWO | THINKING AND LANGUAGE

PART THREE | INTELLIGENCE

PART FOUR | PERCEPTION

PART FIVE | CONDITIONING, LEARNING, AND MEMORY

PART SIX | MOTIVATION AND EMOTION

PART SEVEN | CONFLICT AND ADJUSTMENT

PART EIGHT | PERSONALITY

PART NINE | INDIVIDUAL IN SOCIETY

INTRODUCTION
THE STUDY OF HUMANKIND

The study of psychology, by its very nature, is afflicted with certain special problems that rarely, if ever, fall upon other areas of scientific inquiry. These problems result from the fact that, barring a few unreflective souls, each of us, in the course of living, inevitably evolves a more or less articulate set of notions about the nature of humankind.

Few of us would be presumptuous enough to attempt, untutored and on our own, to provide explanations of gravity, exploding stars, or chemical reactions. More of us might embark upon explanations of historical events, of political change, or of economic trends—but, confronted by an expert who possessed appropriate academic credentials, we would usually defer to her superior knowledge and experience. Not so in psychology. In this field we encounter—and with some justification—the argument that all of us live and grow in human societies and that, in the process, much that is true is learned about psychological phenomena.

Proverbs and homilies that lay claim to an understanding and explanation of human behavior abound. Literature of all forms has never shied away from psychological interpretation—nor have politicians, theologians, philosophers, artists, doctors, or businessmen.

Faced with this array of opinion on matters psychological, the psychologist has a double responsibility; he must lay to rest incorrect beliefs and at the same time replace them with what, at the moment, he feels are the correct ones. The mythology that has grown up around human behavior is endless, so that some of the things we shall discuss in this book may challenge highly cherished, long-held, but frequently altogether incompatible sets of beliefs. Thus, both "Clothes make the man" and "You can't make a silk purse out of a sow's ear" have considerable truth in them, but it is up to psychological investigation to establish the degree to which, and under what circumstances, external factors can determine and change personality and under what circumstances genetic factors underlying personality override environmental forces.

Much of popular psychology is true. For example: We all know that children, human and animal, form close attachments to their parents and, quite early in life, gain an awareness of their own kind. But in such "obvious truths" as this the psychologist finds a host of challenging problems. For example, when and under what circumstances do these close attachments form (see Box I.1, p. xvi)?

Psychology, more than other sciences, is also afflicted with a number of taboo topics—dark corners that the psychologist, perhaps as much as the layman, is reluctant to investigate. There are a number of admittedly important research areas within psychology that, to a lesser

BOX I.1

A MOMENT OF IMPRINTING,
A LIFETIME OF LOYALTY

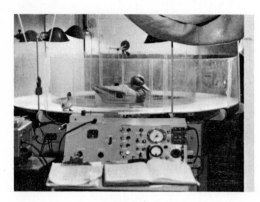

Imprinting is a curious form of early learning that, for many species, appears to play a key role in the formation of strong attachments of the very young. Perhaps the most distinctive feature of imprinting is its tendency to occur very early in life and within rather narrow age limits known as the "critical period." Specifically, an animal is imprinted when, on the basis of brief exposure to a particular object during its critical period, it thereafter behaves toward that object in a number of ways that indicate a deep and enduring attachment to it.

Some evidence for imprinting has been found in dogs, sheep, guinea pigs, even buffalo. But imprinting finds its most clear-cut expression in birds of various species. Perhaps the most popular species for work in imprinting is the mallard duckling, and a good deal of our knowledge of the imprinting process in this bird comes from the research of Eckhard Hess, a psychologist at the University of Chicago. On the basis of a number of experiments, Hess has demonstrated that a duckling becomes imprinted upon an object (usually a wooden decoy of a male mallard) after following that object for a short time— ten minutes can be enough time for imprinting to take place (see photograph). This imprinting is most easily achieved at about fourteen hours after hatching but can occur—with decreasing ease—through the first day or two of life. Thereafter, perhaps because the duckling has by that time developed a fear of new and strange objects, imprinting is difficult if not impossible. Once imprinted on an object, the duckling tends to follow that object, even under discouraging circumstances or in the presence of a more natural object of its affection; for example, it will remain loyal to the male decoy and resist the attractions of a live female mallard.

Not all objects are equally qualified for imprinting. Some animals imprint only upon members of their own species or upon closely related ones; others can range more widely in imprintability; thus, ducklings and other birds have been successfully imprinted on human beings. One factor that has been shown to affect attractiveness of an imprinting object is its general perceptual liveliness. Working with baby chicks, P. H. Klopfer and J. P. Hailman found that the chicks were much more likely to follow a visually striking mallard duck decoy (yellow, covered

or greater extent, are researched with probably less vigor than they deserve and that seem to elicit from the scientific community something more than the usual and desirable degree of criticism.

Among these topics are the experiences of love (as distinct from sex) and of dying (and the subject of death generally). But there are exceptions, as we shall see throughout this book and as illustrated by Boxes I.2, page xviii, and I.3, page xix. Parapsychological phenomena—including ESP and mental telepathy—are also typically assigned an outlaw status (see Box I.4, p. xx).

This avoidance of certain problems as legitimate concerns for psychological research is a dangerous practice, particularly when important human phenomena are involved. Self-censorship is a crippling and perverse indulgence for any science but, particularly for psychology, what we choose *not* to look at may very well be those areas that are avoided precisely because they are the most threatening. Hence, aversion to certain areas may possibly most hamper our full development as individuals. Such indeed is the reasoning of those who, for example, advocate intensive and rigorous investigation of altered states of consciousness, once

with multicolored patches and stripes) than to follow a plain white one. Chicks that were initially exposed, during the critical period, to the plain decoy subsequently tended to follow the vividly colored decoy rather than the plain one.

The process of imprinting—once regarded as a rather unitary one in which the young animal defined its mother, discovered its own kind, and identified the target of its later sexual advance—is beginning to appear somewhat more complex. F. Schutz, working in the laboratory of Konrad Lorenz—a German zoologist and naturalist who has made many contributions to the understanding of imprinting and similar phenomena—has reported that ducks of various species show somewhat different critical periods for different aspects of a general imprinting process. Their primary attachment to a "mother" occurs first and quite early, but not until five or six weeks of age does the duckling identify with its species. If the duckling is exposed to one species for the first three weeks of life and then to another species, the latter species is chosen for mating when sexual maturity is achieved.

More recently, English biologists G. Horn, S. P. R. Rose, and P. P. G. Bateson have presented new data and reviewed the available evidence for specific biochemical changes in the nervous system of various species accompanying very early experiences, changes distinguishable from those following the same experiences occurring at later stages of development. Their work contains hints that may lead to an understanding of the profoundly rapid learning that characterizes the imprinting processes in terms of the much greater plasticity of the nervous system in subhuman newborns.

A question that has not yet been answered is whether or not anything like imprinting takes place in human infants. A baby certainly does develop, somewhere about six months of age, an unmistakable and discriminating attachment to the person, usually the mother, who takes care of him, and some psychologists have suggested that these six months define the critical period for humans. This view is supported by the fact that babies also begin to show fear of strangers at about this age, and such fear responses may signal the end of the critical period. Although this hypothesis merits—and is obtaining—research attention, we must beware of making too easy a translation of this sort. All species do develop attachments and a sense of their own kind, however, and this process does seem to occur later for more slowly developing species. This fact makes adaptive sense, as imprinting—if it is to occur—should have a critical period well within the time during which the infant remains dependent. The result would be to ensure that, barring the intervention of manipulative psychologists, every animal would be in the presence of its own species during its critical period. Otherwise, the rambling lamb might choose a casually encountered wolf as its mother, with obvious and strikingly maladaptive consequences.

E. H. HESS. Imprinting in birds. *Science*, 1964, **146**, 1128–1139.
P. H. KLOPFER & J. P. HAILMAN. Perceptual preferences and imprinting in chicks. *Science*, 1964, **145**, 1333–1334.
F. SCHUTZ. Sexuelle Prägung bei anatiden. *Z. Tierpsychol.*, 1965, **22**, 50–103.
G. HORN, S. P. R. ROSE, & P. P. G. BATESON. Experience and plasticity in the central nervous system. *Science*, 1973, **181**, 506–514.
Photo courtesy E. H. Hess, the University of Chicago.

a taboo topic. We have chosen in this edition to devote a full unit to this rapidly growing area of research (Unit 21).

Fortunately, many taboo areas are beginning to yield to irresistible human curiosity, and psychology is fast approaching the fulfillment of its logical credo: Nothing that is human can be alien to the Compleat Psychologist.

ANALYSIS AND SYNTHESIS

In studying humankind, we psychologists resort to a convenient bit of science fiction. We know perfectly well that we cannot study a person in piecemeal fashion without losing sight of his unity as an individual. But we also know that we cannot achieve an understanding of people unless we proceed as if people could be studied piecemeal. We have no choice, for the person-as-a-whole is just too big a piece for any scientist to handle with the instruments and concepts now available. But this bit of science fiction has proved to be profitable, not only for psychology but for all sciences. Taking a whole, breaking it down into parts, and studying each part intensively constitute a common method of science. It is the method of *analysis*.

BOX I.2

...THY KINSMEN ARE NO STOP TO ME

With love's light wings did I o'erperch these walls;
For stony limits cannot hold love out,
And what love can do, that dares love attempt.
Therefore thy kinsmen are no stop to me.

Thus spake Romeo Montague when, having scaled the walls surrounding the home of Juliet Capulet, he is reminded by his lady love (from her balcony) that "this place is death, considering who thou art, if any of my kinsmen find thee here." The theme is a familiar one: Love laughs at locksmiths, and generally overcomes whatever stop (hindrance) an insensitive and unsentimental world places in the path of romance. Could it be, however, that love not only overcomes but, even more, is nurtured by and thrives upon opposition? Ancient love and myths subscribe to the Romeo and Juliet effect. Thus Edith Hamilton observes, in recounting the Roman myth of Pyramus and Thisbe: "They longed to marry, but their parents forbade it. Love, however, cannot be forbidden. The more the flame is covered up, the hotter it burns." All of this accords with contemporary psychological theory that predicts intensified striving when access to a highly desired goal is blocked.

Psychologists R. Driscoll, K. E. Davis, and M. E. Lipetz, of the University of Colorado, put this very question to empirical test, as one part of a broader investigation of the nature and course of love and marriage. Their hypothesis is directly stated: "Parental interference in a love relationship intensifies the feelings of romantic love between members of a couple." One test of this hypothesis was provided by comparing changes in reported love and degree of parental interference for twenty-nine young couples. The twenty-nine couples first completed questionnaires (including a "feelings questionnaire") exploring these (and many other) topics when their romance had, on the average, already lasted several months; the same questionnaires were filled out again some six to ten months later (during which interval some of the couples had married). Measures of both love and parental interference (derived from the responses to the questionnaire) provide the data for testing the hypothesis.

The results seem decisive: Greater expressions of interference and opposition by one or both sets of parents were accompanied by increased love between the pairs of couples. This held true for the nine couples who had married as well as for the twenty couples who had not. For each group separately and for the total group, the correlations between increased parental interference and increased love are larger than .30. (See Appendix, p. 831, for a discussion of the correlation statistic.)

The fact that two measures are positively correlated does not by itself tell us which is the chicken and which the egg. Perhaps partners became more involved with one another because of their families, or perhaps the parents interfered more because they perceived that the romantic attachment was growing more serious. Driscoll et al., after further statistical analyses, have come to the conclusion that, for the most part, heightened parental opposition is the cause of the intensification of love.

Why did parents place themselves in opposition? The parents' reasons, as reported by the couples, were highly varied. Some of the opposition derived from socioeconomic, religious, and racial differences between the two young people; some parents felt that their offspring should finish school first or could "do better"; some parents objected to the manner, dress, and life style of the partner, and so on. A paradoxical effect of parental opposition was observed: Though the young lovers fell more deeply in love, at the same time they reported becoming less trustful and more critical of one another. The investigators suggest that this might have been because of parental interference "making the couples more dependent upon each other for love and emotional support, and yet at the same time less certain that the relationship [could] survive the stress." Love and doubt can both feed on parental opposition. The increased doubts may reflect the partners' taking to heart and beginning to share the doubts expressed by their families; the increased love may be necessary to provide reassurance to the lovers that they have made the right choice.

So the course of love, after all, may not be so ephemeral as to elude scientific inquiry; neither is it so fragile as to wilt under the gaze of sensitive scrutiny.

W. SHAKESPEARE. *Romeo and Juliet* (Act II, Scene 2).
E. HAMILTON. *Mythology*. New York: New American Library of World Literature, 1942.
R. DRISCOLL, K. E. DAVIS, & M. E. LIPETZ. Parental interference and romantic love: The Romeo and Juliet effect. *Journal of Personality and Social Psychology*, 1972, **24**, 1–10.

BOX I.3

ON DEATH AND DYING

Elisabeth Kübler-Ross, a Chicago physician, has prepared a sensitive clinical report which distills her experiences from years of working with dying hospital patients. Her approach is described in her book preface:

> We have asked [the dying patient] . . . to be our teacher so that we may learn more about the final stages of life with all its anxieties, fears, and hopes. I am simply telling the stories of my patients who shared their agonies, their expectations, and their frustrations with us. It is hoped that it will encourage others not to shy away from the "hopelessly" sick but to get closer to them, as they can help them much during their final hours. The few who can do this will also discover that it can be a mutually gratifying experience; they will learn much about the functioning of the human mind, the unique human aspects of our existence, and will emerge from the experience enriched and perhaps with fewer anxieties about their own finality.

Kübler-Ross interviewed over 200 dying patients in the course of her study—a study that, when read, convincingly demonstrates that in this instance the subjects were direct beneficiaries of the research process, as well as indispensable sources of rare data. Great resistance was encountered in arranging these interviews, but it came in largest measure from the physicians in charge. Nine of ten physicians, when first approached for permission to talk with their dying patients, reacted with "discomfort, annoyance, or overt or covert hostility." Though there were few outright refusals of permission, there was massive resistance, and a variety of excuses. Some even denied having any terminally ill patients under their care, when this was not the case. This denial was often accompanied by a parallel attitude: to not tell the patient that she was dying. Kübler-Ross observes that "the [patient's] need for denial is in direct proportion with the doctor's need for denial."

But denial and a self-imposed psychological isolation are clearly the initial stages in a patient who has learned of her impending death. Kübler-Ross asserts that it is a necessary stage, granting her a buffer against overwhelming fear and time to collect her thoughts and resources.

Denial cannot, with rare exceptions, be maintained throughout the time of dying. Kübler-Ross offers a sequence of subsequent stages that she has commonly observed: After denial often comes anger at one's fate and envy of others' good health and good fortune. This stage is sometimes followed by a brief period of bargaining—somehow, through promises to become a better person, to appease inexorable fate and thus gain at least a temporary reprieve. Then, inevitably, comes the stage of depression, but there are two kinds. At first the patient is depressed, and for good reason, over his physical deterioration, the anxiety and disruption caused his family, etc. This, to some extent and sometimes with surprising success, can be alleviated and reassurances and practical steps taken to handle practical problems (the financial burden of his hospitalization, for example). But the second, later form of depression is not—and Kübler-Ross argues, *should* not be —dissipated by reassurance and helpful deeds. Why not? Because, she believes, it provides the patient with the opportunity to contemplate his own death— it is a *necessary* preparation for death. At this stage the patient typically seeks solitude and, ironically, any attempts to cheer the patient or even his family only deepen his grief. When he is seeking to make peace with himself, such efforts increase his inner turmoil.

If the patient has had enough time and sensitive help in working through the earlier stages he may achieve an acceptance of his death. In a sense, he is now done with mourning—mourning for his impending loss of loved ones and for himself. It is a time of relative inner peace, though one almost devoid of feelings. But, for friends and family, it may be a particularly difficult time since the patient often has already withdrawn from life and has little need to communicate with them. However, their quiet presence is often deeply welcomed during this terminal period.

There is much to be gained in looking closely at death: For dying patients, their families, and for observers and students (as we all are) of the human condition.

E. KÜBLER-ROSS. *On Death and Dying.* New York: Macmillan, 1970. Paperback edition.

In studying people, then, we break down our inquiry into nine different parts.

(1) We analyze first the operation of *hereditary mechanisms* and their interaction with environmental factors in order to determine the course of the individual's *growth and development.*

(2) We next examine how people think,

how they solve problems, and how they acquire that peculiarly human ability—*language.*

(3) *Intelligence* is our next order of business—how we measure its development and account for the enormous variations in human mental abilities.

(4) Then we turn to the study of *perception*—how we see, hear, smell, taste, and feel the

---

BOX I.4

A CENSORED SENSE?

One of the most prominent researchers in the field of extrasensory perception (ESP)—and one who has tried to have psychology keep an open mind on this controversial phenomenon—is Gardner Murphy of the Menninger Foundation. In his assessment of the reasons for the status of ESP and of the whole field of parapsychology as a taboo topic, he begins with a telling anecdote. He relates the incident of a scientist who, prior to the turn of the century, presented before a meeting of the British Association for the Advancement of Science some new experimental findings concerning ESP or, as it was then commonly called, "mental telepathy." Hermann Ludwig Ferdinand von Helmholtz, one of the principal scientific figures of the day, was present at the meeting and is reported to have declared, "Neither the testimony of all the members of the British Association for the Advancement of Science, nor my own testimony from what my own eyes recorded, could convince me of telepathy, since it is manifestly impossible."

The crux of the scientific objection to this research area is indicated by its very name—"extrasensory perception"—a term that implies that perception occurs without known receptor structures and processes. The implied lack of a physical basis for ESP is emphasized by other alleged phenomena of parapsychology: clairvoyance (the ability to perceive future events) and psychokinesis (the ability to move objects through thought alone). The argument, as Helmholtz said, is that the events claimed by parapsychology are impossible because they require us to abandon a keystone of all scientific thought: that all events must ultimately have some

material basis that can be observed and measured and that can find a place within our physically oriented notion of the nature of reality.

Quite possibly a physical basis for ESP and similar phenomena will eventually be discovered; if and when it is, scientists will gladly reverse their present verdict of incredibility. Some of the more ardent proponents of ESP deny that it need have a physical basis and assert that it is indeed "extra"-sensory. Most, however, acknowledge that a physical basis should be sought but meanwhile are determined to continue collecting data on something for which our present knowledge provides no explanation.

An important indication that there is some lifting of the cloud of suspicion regarding ESP in the scientific community was the sponsorship by the American Association for the Advancement of Science (AAAS), in 1970, of a symposium on this general topic. Considerable new research, most of it seemingly inexplicable by currently acceptable theories, was reported at this meeting, including a careful, world-ranging study of the effect of distance on the effectiveness of ESP (it declined with distance). With the formal affiliation of the Parapsychological Association with the AAAS (in 1969) we may expect a continuation of this necessary open-forum attitude toward such challenging phenomena.

Science has come up with many wrong answers in the course of its history, and it will continue to do so. Continual experimentation, however, provides the ready and reliable remedy for error. Wrong answers there may be, but forbidden questions there cannot be if psychology is ever to complete its study of man.

G. MURPHY. Parapsychology. In N. L. Farberow (Ed.), *Taboo Topics.* New York: Atherton, 1966.
Techniques and status of modern parapsychology. A symposium at the annual meeting of the American Association for the Advancement of Science, Chicago, 1970.

world about us. In part we deal with the senses separately, but the human organism is far more complex. Almost immediately we become impressed with the interactions among the senses, which permit us a unified impression of the world of objects. This interaction and unity of the senses is nowhere more dramatically illus-

processes involve our nervous system.

(6) Next we concern ourselves with the *motives* and *emotions* of people—our needs, desires, aspirations, fears, and loves—and how intimately these interact with other psychological and physiological processes.

(7) Life is fraught with frustration and

A   B   C

FIGURE I.1 Sculpture by the blind. A—This bust is the work of the Italian sculptor, Gonnelli. He was blinded in his twenties, by which time he had already become a skilled sculptor. The quality of this work must therefore owe something to his previous visual experience. B—This is the work of the Tyrolean sculptor, Kleinhans, who was blinded at age four. From that time on he could barely distinguish light from dark. He characteristically worked by tactually examining his artistic subjects in great detail, and he was able to translate this information into accurate and impressive visual form. C—This crude face is by an amateur blind sculptor, convincingly portraying in visual terms his impression of a person in a state of terror.

D. Katz. *Psychological Atlas.* New York: Philosophical Library, 1948.

trated than in the capacity of a person to experience an object with one sense, say touch, and translate that experience in terms of another sense, say vision (see Figure I.1).

(5) We then examine the various ways that we *learn*, remember (and forget), and we present an account of the growing understanding that is rapidly being achieved of how these

conflict. How we respond to this—adaptively or, in the case of *mental disorders*, maladaptively— is the theme of the next part of our study. The varied and ever-growing area of *psychotherapeutic techniques* is discussed.

(8) All of us know what personality is. Or do we? The many and differing definitions of personality and the varieties of its measurement

are presented, together with an overview of the many different forces that influence its development.

(9) Finally, we look at how people perceive and judge one another and how *social behavior* is regulated in a functioning society. A glimpse of the effects of social groups on individual behavior (and vice versa) completes our presentation.

These are the parts (and Parts of the book) into which we have chosen to analyze the person-as-a-whole. But what the psychologist tears asunder, the psychologist seeks to join together. We use not only the method of analysis but also the method of *synthesis*; we put the parts together to re-create an abstract but scientific facsimile of the original whole. We have indicated throughout the text how this synthesis may be attempted, if not altogether achieved. Emotion affects perception (and vice versa), personality affects learning (and vice versa), and so on.

TO STUDY THE BOOK

In this book, we have sought to go beyond a simple organization of facts, observations, theories, and speculations on psychology; we have attempted to uncover whatever inherent harmony may exist within the data of psychology. We have at the same time attempted to make this book an effective teaching instrument. To further this objective we have included several devices intended to aid the student in her study of the material:

1. Each unit opens with a number of provocative *questions* relevant to the topic about to be considered. Their purpose is twofold: to inform you, more comprehensively than the unit title can, of what will be discussed; and to help you see connections between what you may be curious about and what psychology is discovering that may satisfy your curiosity. At times you will find the questions specifically answered within the unit; at times we will explore the question but confess that a final answer cannot yet be given.

2. The *Summaries* at the end of each unit

are quite detailed, sufficiently so that you may readily review the material. But they do not condense all that is useful in the unit.

The *Glossaries* are qualified by the same caution: They provide useful definitions of the new concepts and technical terms presented in the unit, but they are not meant to stand alone. (The General Glossary, p. 849, alphabetically lists all the terms defined in the unit glossaries and makes it possible to locate immediately the definition of any term without having to remember the unit in which it was presented.)

3. The *Boxes* contain material of various types. Some of the Boxes supplement the main discussion in a unit; some contain further illustrative material; some provide the student with an opportunity to carry out his own demonstration experiments; but most of them present research evidence for the generalizations stated in the text.

The last may be of particular interest. No science is sounder than its research, and, if the reader of this book is to achieve a *critical understanding* of the science of psychology, he must become familiar not only with the as-of-now answers of psychology but also with the research behind these generalizations. This knowledge will enable him to understand the answers better and to evaluate them critically. The Boxes present enough detail to acquaint the student with the reasoning, methods, and difficulties of research in psychology. We have chosen to include classic studies that have continued over many years to hold an important place in psychology. In this way we indicate not only the essential continuity of scientific progress but present some of the fascinating history of our field of inquiry.

4. In our *Statistical Appendix* we present what we consider to be an essential minimum of information for an understanding of the quantitative techniques employed in psychological research. Much of the material in the text will simply be *non-sense* unless you make sense of this.

Finally, in Box I.5, we present our reasons for a bit of textbook unorthodoxy we have chosen to commit—an unorthodoxy that you may indeed already have noted.

BOX 1.5

A NOTE ON GENDER

"Trust in God; She will help you!" the ardent suffragette said to a discouraged young woman during the first woman's liberation movement.

The humor here lies in the unexpected use of the word "She." Incidentally, of course, the joke makes fun of the fanatic feminist who takes for granted that God would have to be a woman; and since God has always been called "He," one is startled to hear God referred to as "She." In this book we have sought to achieve the same sort of shock value by sometimes using the word "she" where standard usage makes the reader expect—almost demand—the word "he" as the referent for "person." Some may find this confusing, even disturbing, for throughout we have used "she" and "he" interchangeably and haphazardly. We have tried to jar the reader into thinking afresh about the fact that, traditionally, the synonym for "person" has been "man." We want each reader to realize the further fact that, when you refer to people in general as *men*, you unwittingly reinforce the concept that woman is a sort of subspecies of man.

We are not suggesting that the unorthodox way we refer, in this book, to "her" and "him" become standard usage. A better solution will probably emerge. But through our unconventional use of language, by using "she" and "he" interchangeably, we remind our readers from time to time that the attitudes, reactions, responses, and experiences described in this book are shared, in common, by men and women; that the times "they is a-changin' "; and that language has always changed and evolved with the times. With sex roles and sexual stereotypes now undergoing such dramatic modifications, new words and new forms of speech are bound to evolve.

Neither as authors nor as psychologists is it our primary purpose to coin new words or usages. But we hope that, by speaking and writing in this new way, we can jolt our readers and perhaps hasten (if only a little) new ways of feeling about "him" and "her"; of behaving toward "her" and "him"; and inspire the working out of more satisfactory, mutually beneficial relations between the sexes.

For a footnote to this position, see Box 1.6.

BOX 1.6

FOOLISH CONSISTENCY IS THE HOBGOBLIN . . .

Admittedly our proposed solution for the appropriate gender of the second person pronoun when referring to a person (sex unspecified) is awkward. However, when one adheres consistently to the approved form: *Use the masculine gender in all cases when referring to people, and use the word "man" as the species designation for human beings,* some extraordinary things can happen. A case in point: In *Science*, 1928, Volume 68, page 453, appears an article which reports a study of intermenstrual bleeding in a woman. The article, by Miriam E. Simpson and Herbert M. Evans, carries the title: "Occurrence of Faint Bleeding on a Definite Inter-menstrual Day in Man."

In the very first sentence of this article occurs the following phrase: ". . . we were at work on a study of the vaginal smear in man. . . ." (!)

ELEMENTS OF PSYCHOLOGY

origins, growth, and development

heredity and environment

DO YOU KNOW...

- *why humankind as a species survives?*

- *how the hereditary mechanism works, and how it can guarantee that virtually every person is genetically unique?*

- *how identical and fraternal twins come about, and how you can tell these two kinds of twins apart?*

- *what is meant by saying that a gene is dominant or that it is recessive?*

- *whether conditions in the prenatal environment can affect the behavior of the organism long after birth?*

- *why it is pointless to ask whether heredity or environment is the factor responsible for any given trait?*

- *for which traits of animal behavior selective breeding has been successful?*

- *how widespread are various physical and mental disorders associated with defects in single genes and enzymes?*

- *where to get professional advice on the possibilities of genetic defects occurring in your children?*

unit
1

CONTENTS

We start our inquiry into the nature of humankind by hoisting a banner with the motto "Cherish Diversity!" To this banner all biological scientists — and especially geneticists, evolutionists, and psychologists—can well repair. As you become more familiar with biology and psychology you will see more clearly why, if humankind is to survive on this earth, we must all learn—above all else—to cherish and nurture diversity.

The permissible range of variation for many of humanity's characteristics is so broad that we rarely know where the limits actually lie. On the need for oxygen there is a limiting level and we know it: A few minutes of total deprivation, and a man or woman is dead. But what of the limits on human intelligence, on human skills, on human feelings and experience? Here it is only the uninformed or the arrogant who dare specify how far people can go. We need only contrast our lives today with those of people living a few decades ago to see how quickly the impossible becomes the commonplace in man's achievement and behavior. Or we can glance now at the lives of people throughout the world and immediately confront the seemingly endless variation among human societies in how the "average person" feels, thinks, and acts.

Certainly, we have come a long way not only from our animal ancestors but also from our own origin as a distinct species. In evolution those new species that were able to adapt to the environmental conditions of their time were able to survive, reproduce, and—for a time —flourish. If conditions remain the same, then a species should forever endure. But conditions change. Even if cataclysmic changes in the physical environment, an Ice Age for example, did not occur, less dramatic but nevertheless significant modifications in the conditions of life might come about. Previously abundant natural food supplies may suddenly disappear or species competing for the same resources may invade the territory. New species may then evolve and old ones disappear.

Who survives? *Within* a species, those individuals who are best able to adapt to the new conditions of life: the strong, when strength can save the day; the fleet, when escape means survival; the intelligent, when intelligence can discover a solution to the new environmental problems. Thus the species continues, although its average characteristics change to reflect the increasing importance of now this quality and now that. *Among* species, those that produce sufficient individuals that can adapt will survive. Thus, raise the temperature of a lake, and some trout and some frogs (those that can best tolerate increased heat) will survive and reproduce; future generations in this lake will have increasingly high proportions of individuals able to tolerate warmer water. But drain the lake, and, as no trout can survive aridity, all the trout species in that lake become extinct. Some frogs, however, may jump as far as another nearby lake and survive. In short, adaptability is the inexorable *sine qua non* for survival. Species, as well as their individual members, cannot evade this law of life.

HUMAN DIVERSITY AND ADAPTABILITY

Judged by this standard, humankind is today preeminent. Our ability as a species to adapt to new conditions, and through technology to change even the conditions themselves, has no near rival. Fish swim, birds fly, and animals roam the land; we do all three. What is more, people are to be found living among ice floes, in dense jungle, in scorching desert, and—perhaps most impressive of all—in the concrete-and-steel cities we have created (see Figure 1.1A–F). People have broader limits than other species on the ranges of temperature, aridity, altitude, and food sources within which they can survive and function effectively. But we must consider humankind's extensive adaptability as separable into two components: What a *person* can do and what *people* can do. Or, put another way, we are doubly blessed—in the range of environments to which a given individual can learn to adapt and in our diversity. Each person has her limits, and they are necessarily narrower

than those of her species. Sea-level dwellers, even after rigorous training, can rarely climb the highest mountain, yet the Sherpas of the Himalayas live and work at such altitudes.

Thus, what one man cannot do or learn to do his distant brother often can—and it is in such differences among humankind that its viability as a species and its hope for survival lie. As we said at the outset, we do not yet know the limits on what any one person can become nor on what humankind can become, given the full potential of the species for variation among its individual members. But we do know something about how a man comes to be what he is and how he comes to be different from his fellows. Individuals are what they are because of their particular heredity and environment.

HEREDITARY MECHANISMS

In sketching our portrait of humankind as an evolving species of enormous diversity and adaptability, we have not considered in detail the mechanisms by which successive generations are linked one to the other. Does it matter that the more adaptive members of a species tend to survive and to procreate if their progeny do not manifest their critical adaptive characteristics?

The picture of hereditary transmission, as it has been unveiled so far, is not described by the simple formula "Like begets like." The facts of the genetic mechanism demand that there be not only resemblances between parents and offspring but also differences. This is why members of a species, while sharing adaptive properties, also are able to maintain their wide diversity.

The Individual Begins

Individuality begins when a **sperm cell** from the father penetrates the wall of an **ovum** (or egg) from the mother and fertilizes it. Each sperm cell contains twenty-three **chromosomes**, the carriers of heredity. This sperm derives from a germ cell in the father. Each mature germ cell of the father has twenty-three pairs of chromosomes, or a total of forty-six—the normal number of chromosomes found in all human cells

8

A

FIGURE 1.1 Man can adapt to nearly every environment in which he finds himself, such as A—the extreme heights of the Peruvian Andes, where the oxygen content of the air is extremely low; B—Philippine caves; C—the Arctic wastes, where he may live in an igloo; D—the dry desert of the Cameroons, where he must dig for water; E—the over-crowded conditions of Hong Kong, where a houseboat on the water is the only available space; and F—even in the cold, impersonal glass-and-steel canyons of New York City.

A—Photo by Paul Conklin/Courtesy, Peace Corps; B—Photo by John Launois/Black Star; C—Photo by Paul Baich; D—Courtesy, United Nations; E—Courtesy, BOAC; and F—Photo by Ken Heyman.

B

C

E

D

F

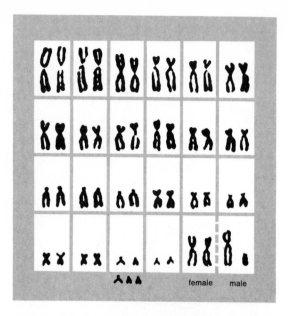

FIGURE 1.2 Paired human chromosomes. The first twenty-two pairs are found in both men and women. The last pair is XX for a woman or XY for a man. Occasionally, instead of the normal two chromosomes found, there occur three chromosomes (as shown for pair 21 in the colored margin). When this occurs the individual suffers from a condition known as trisomy-21 (also known as Down's syndrome, or mongolism, a condition producing severe mental deficiency).

Courtesy, Margery W. Shaw, M.D., Department of Human Genetics, the University of Michigan, Ann Arbor, Michigan, and the Upjohn Company, Kalamazoo, Michigan.

(see Figure 1.2). When the germ cell reaches full maturity it undergoes division into two sperm cells. During such division, half the chromosomes go to one sperm and half to the other sperm. Which member of each pair of chromosomes goes to the particular sperm is generally a random matter. As there are twenty-three different pairs of chromosomes, the number of genetically different sperm that a single human male can produce is 2^{23}, or approximately 8 million.

In a similar manner, ova develop by division of mature germ cells in the mother. And following the same reasoning as above, a single human female can also produce approximately 8 million genetically different ova.

Thus, when the sperm penetrates the ovum the resulting **zygote** has its full comple-

ment of twenty-three pairs of chromosomes, one of each pair coming from the father and the other from the mother (see Figure 1.3). In a single mating, therefore, any one of the 8 million different chromosome patterns of the sperm might combine with any of the 8 million different chromosome patterns of the ovum to form a single zygote. This means that the particular zygote that a particular father and a particular mother produce is one of more than 60 trillion different possible ones.

Relatives Are the Same and Different

Each chromosome bears many sets of deoxyribonucleic acid (DNA) molecules. These sets of DNA molecules are called **genes**. And it is the genes that determine inherited characteristics. The genes do not always stay in their own chromosomes. There is a phenomenon known as **crossing-over**, which refers to the fact that, occasionally, when the germ cell divides, one segment of a chromosome will break off and be exchanged with a corresponding segment from a homologous chromosome (see Figure 1.4). The fact that chromosomes can exchange genes increases tremendously the already astronomically large number of genetically different zygotes that can be produced from human matings. The number of possible combinations of chromosomes in the zygote is practically infinite, and our reproductive system virtually guarantees that, except in the case of identical twins, who develop from a single zygote, no brothers or sisters can ever be genetically the same. Put more generally, it is extremely unlikely (except for identical twins) that there are now or have ever been in the vast sea of humanity two people with the same genetic make-up. Heredity implies individual differences.

On the other hand, no matter which combination of chromosomes ends up in the zygote, nothing can be there that was not contributed by one of the parents. In this sense, there is a definite limit to the individual differences possible in a family. For this reason, the offspring of a single set of parents will necessarily be

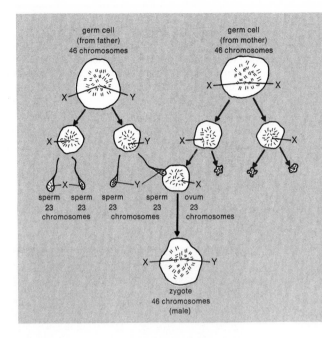

FIGURE 1.3   Relation between the mature parental germ cells and the zygote. Each mature germ cell of both the father and mother (top of illustration) has the full number of chromosomes (twenty-three pairs, or forty-six chromosomes). When these germ cells reach full maturity, they undergo division and become ova (for the female) and sperm (for the male). Typically, only one of the ova is fully developed and can be fertilized; the others are not functional.

During such division the chromosomes are assorted so that each sperm (and ovum) has only one member of each pair, that is, twenty-three chromosomes. When one sperm enters through the cell body of one ovum, a zygote is formed, and the zygote, of course, will have the full forty-six chromosomes. From the zygote a new organism develops.

One pair of the chromosomes is of a special kind—consisting of the X and Y chromosomes. The male cell has one X and one Y chromosome; the female cell has two X chromosomes. When the male germ cell divides into sperm, one of the resulting sperm receives the X and the other the Y. Each ovum, of course, receives an X. If the sperm with the Y chromosome happens to unite with the ovum, the zygote will have an XY pair (as in the illustration); if the sperm with the X chromosome fertilizes the ovum, then the zygote will have an XX pair. A zygote with an XY pair will develop into a male; a zygote with an XX pair will develop into a female. The zygote in the illustration will thus develop into a male. Occasionally irregularities in sperm or egg formation occur and abnormal individuals with XXY or XO or other chromosomal constitutions arise.

more alike on the average than will unrelated individuals. Heredity also implies similarity.

Identical twins   Because they are genetically identical, **identical twins** are of great interest to the psychologist concerned with the problem of heredity. How do identical twins come about?

The zygote multiplies by division. It first divides into two daughter cells, each of which is a complete and faithful replica of the other. We have seen that the single zygote has within it the full complement of chromosomes. This means that each daughter cell has within it the potentialities of becoming a complete individual. In most cases, however, this cell division does not mean cell separation. The two cells remain as parts of a single organism. If the two cells remain together, each one divides and subdivides until the 10 trillion cells of a human being have been formed (see Box 1.1, p. 12). As the

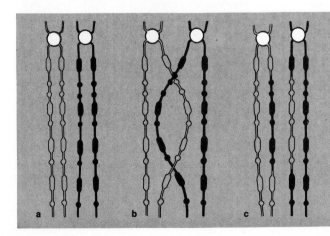

FIGURE 1.4   At one period of development of the mature germ cell, the two members of a pair of chromosomes (see a) approach each other and become intimately intertwined (see b). During this period one section of one chromosome may be exchanged with a corresponding section of the other chromosome, so that when the pair is separated again (see c) we have a recombination of genes in the two chromosomes (compare a and c). This phenomenon is called "crossing-over."

ders are composed of four chemical substances, which can be paired in specific ways, and this four-letter alphabet seems capable of storing or coding the full genetic endowment of an individual. The sequence of five photographs illustrates the

BOX 1.1

OUT OF ONE, MANY: DNA AND RNA

Until 1953 scientists could say only that in some way the full complement of forty-six chromosomes found in the fertilized ovum—the first cell of human life—was duplicated in the trillions of cells that eventually constitute a human organism. Furthermore, there was equal mystery concerning the process by which the genetic information carried within these chromosomes guided the development of the innumerable structures constituting a developed individual. But in that year three scientists—an American (J. D. Watson) and two Englishmen (F. H. C. Crick and M. H. F. Wilkins)—deduced the molecular structure of a chemical substance that is in all genetic material; this achievement quickened the pace of research that contributes to an understanding of the growth of living things and won for them the 1962 Nobel Prize in Medicine and Physiology. That substance is DNA (deoxyribonucleic acid), and its discovery lies at the heart of the new science of molecular biology.

The idea that a chemical mechanism is involved in storage and transfer of genetic information from one cell generation to the next and from an individual to his offspring had long been in the air. Watson and Crick were able to construct a model of DNA structure, explaining how this occurred. Very roughly, DNA is a molecule composed of two ladders intertwining with each other around a single, common axis. When a cell divides, the two ladders of the DNA molecule it contains come apart; each ladder then duplicates its complement, so that each of the two new cells contains a complete DNA molecule identical with the one in the parent cell. Furthermore, the rungs of the lad-

deoxyribose	large ball
phosphate	plum ball
cytosine	small white ball
guanine	large white ball
adenine	large light plum ball
thymine	small light plum ball

A

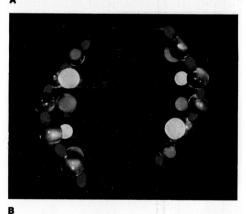

B

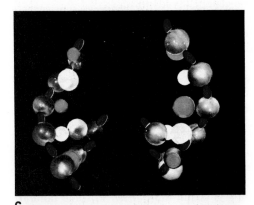

C

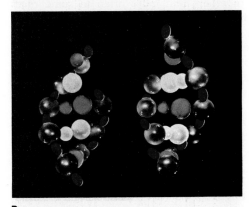

D

E

DNA molecule in the process of duplication. From a resting state (A) the DNA fiber separates (B), and new complementary ladders swing into place (C, D). Each of the two completed DNA fibers (E) contains one-half the original fiber.

There are also other closely related molecules participating in the hereditary processes. They are the RNA molecules (ribonucleic acid). One of them, messenger RNA, is synthesized by the DNA molecule, which itself remains in the nucleus of the cell. It then carries the information to the protein factories of the body. The second, transfer RNA, is responsible for the transfer of the raw materials that form the protein structures constituting the organism and for the assembly of these building blocks according to the specifications contained in the DNA blueprint. In this way, with differing arrangements dictated by the particular code present in the DNA molecule, the trillions of cells in a human being are formed, and a human life is created from a single fertilized ovum.

But, despite the brilliant discoveries in molecular biology, the reader must be cautioned that biochemical knowledge of the hereditary process has not by any means led us to a full understanding of what we are. Perhaps a fair assessment at this time is the opinion of the biologist George Gaylord Simpson, who asserts that

. . . nothing that has so far been learned about DNA has helped significantly to understand the nature of man or of any other whole organism. It certainly is necessary for such understanding to examine what is inherited, how it is expressed in the developing individual, how it evolves in populations, and so on. Up to now the triumphs of DNA research have had virtually no effect on our understanding of those subjects. In due course molecular biology will undoubtedly become more firmly connected with the biology of whole organisms and with evolution, and then it will become of greater concern for those more interested in the nature of man than in the nature of molecules.

G. G. SIMPSON. The biological nature of man. *Science*, 1966, **152**, 472–478. Photos courtesy, Margery W. Shaw, M.D., Department of Human Genetics, the University of Michigan, Ann Arbor, Michigan, and the Upjohn Company, Kalamazoo, Michigan.

total number of cells increases, the mass of sub-divided cells begins to become differentiated into bone cells, nerve cells, skin cells, and so forth. The **embryo**, which at first resembles an expanding ball, begins to take shape, and the first suggestions of a head, eyes, trunk, and limbs appear; eventually, it develops (at about six to eight weeks after conception) into the more differentiated **fetus**.

In some instances, however, daughter cells do not stay together but actually separate. Now the two separate embryos can develop into two distinct individuals through the division process occurring separately in the two daughter cells. Indeed, this actual separation can continue, so that three or four or more individuals can develop (see Figure 1.5). These individuals are known as identical twins, identical triplets, and so on, because, as can readily be seen, they have

developed from the same zygote and therefore must be genetically identical.

Fraternal twins   The mother may sometimes produce more than one functional ovum at a time. If she produces two and each is fertilized (by two different sperm, of course), then genetically the twins are different individuals no more similar than any combination of brothers or sisters. They are known as **fraternal twins**.

According to available statistics, twins occur in the United States about once in eighty-six births. Identical twins are rarer than fraternal twins, numbering about one-third of all twins. Twinning is found more often in some families than in others and more often in some races than in others. Women in their thirties are more likely to give birth to fraternal twins than are women of any other age; also, the greater the number of children a woman has previously borne, the higher the frequency of such twins (Bulmer, 1970).

If twins are of the same sex it may not be easy to determine whether they are identical or fraternal from their external appearance alone. Although identical twins of course look alike, so do many fraternal twins of the same sex. (For a situation in which this very difficulty in distinguishing between identical and fraternal twins is a crucial advantage in research on "heredity versus environment" problems, see the Freedman-Keller study reported in Unit 28.)

There are a great many usable criteria for distinguishing between fraternal and identical twins. Three of the several possible tests to be met before we can assume that a pair of like-sex twins is identical are, first, that the two children must have the same blood type; second, that they must have similar (but not identical) fingerprints; and, third, that they must show identical kinds of various serum proteins that are genetically determined. There does exist a highly accurate test as to whether twins are identical or not, but this test is not generally applied to human beings. It is known that genetically identical individuals have a much higher rate of successful skin transplantation. If the skin from one twin is transplanted to the skin of the other and if the transplanted skin is accepted and continues to grow in the host twin, then we have

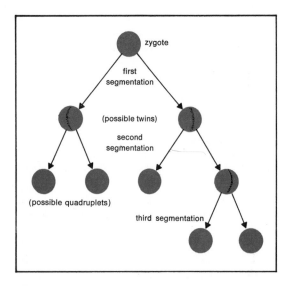

FIGURE 1.5 This figure is a diagram of the process by which identical multiple births may occur. If the zygote, during the first cell division, does not segment, only one child will develop. If, at the first division, actual segmentation takes place, so that there are now two zygotes, and if no further actual separation occurs, then identical twins will develop. If, however, at the first cell division of these two identical zygotes, another separation takes place, there is the possibility of more than two identical children. The figure shows the process up to the point at which identical quintuplets become possible. Indeed, this is the suggested scheme for the origin of the famed Dionne quintuplets.

powerful evidence that the donor twin and the host twin are genetically identical.

Gene Action and Interaction

We have said that genes determine inherited traits or characteristics (e.g., eye color, hair structure, body length). But this does not mean that one gene is responsible for each trait. Actually, any one gene, although producing only one substance, does produce a multitude of effects, and each trait is determined by the interaction of many factors from several genes—often from genes found in separate chromosomes. The multifactorial determination of traits is, as we shall see, of major importance in understanding the inheritance of abilities in man.

A form of gene interaction is demonstrated by the phenomenon of dominance and recessiveness. Every gene in any one chromosome has its corresponding partner in the paired chromosome. Thus gene A in chromosome 1 will have gene a in chromosome 1', gene B will have its partner b, and so on. The two members of any pair may have opposite influences in determining a particular trait. For example, one of the sets of genes that plays an important part in determining whether a person is normal or an albino may be found in the following pairs for different individuals: AA, aa, or Aa. In the first, AA, either gene is such as to produce normal skin color. As both genes are the same, the person is said to be **homozygous** for this gene.

In the second combination, aa, we again have a homozygous state. Now both genes cause albinism. Therefore the individual will be an albino, and if her mate is also homozygous for this gene, all their progeny will be albino.

In the third combination, Aa, A tends to produce normal color; a, on the other hand, tends to produce albinism. Genetically, the individual is a mixture of the two kinds of determiners. Such a person is said to be **heterozygous** for this gene. But A is dominant over a (it suppresses the expression of a), and therefore the person will develop normal pigmentation. But he continues to carry within his germ cells the a genes. Now suppose an Aa father and an Aa mother (both of whom must be normal) mate. Any of the progeny who receive both an a from

the father and an a from the mother, that is, aa, will be albino, even though both parents were normal.

Recently a catalog of known human genes was compiled (McKusick, 1971). In it 415 dominant and 365 recessive inherited characteristics are described. In addition, 86 other genes known to be carried on the X-chromosome are described, as well as 1,010 still other properties suspected to be determined by single genes.

But we must emphasize that very few traits are determined by single genes. We must consider that, for most human traits, dominance and recessiveness are only relative terms, since some genes are incompletely dominant. Furthermore, because psychological traits, as the term is commonly understood, typically involve determination by many sets of genes, it is highly unlikely that such traits will exhibit clear-cut dominant-recessive properties. However, a single gene pair *may* exert a profound influence upon the psychological characteristics of an individual. Certain psychologically pervasive traits have a relatively simple genetic basis. For example, as noted below, many dominant genes control production of specific chemical substances essential for normal functioning: Individuals homozygous for the recessive form will display a variety of types of mental deficiencies.

One point that should be immediately clear from our discussion of dominance and recessiveness is that the person's **phenotype** (his observable characteristics) is only a partial manifestation of his **genotype**—the genes he possesses and can transmit to his offspring. More complexity is added when we consider that each chromosome of the organism, perhaps even each gene in the zygote, may influence the whole body. And each part of the process is influenced by all the others. Genetics teaches us the same lesson as does psychology—the individual is a complex, interrelated unity of parts.

The Continuity of Humankind

The inherited characteristics that are produced by genes are passed along unchanged, with relatively rare exceptions, from one generation to another. The rare exceptions occur when genes themselves are changed through a chemical accident or through stimulation by such radiant energies as x-rays and cosmic rays. These genetic changes are called **mutations**, and they provide the raw materials for evolutionary changes in organisms.

However, the psychological experiences of an individual cannot be passed on to her progeny by heredity. Only genes are passed on, and they remain unchanged by life experiences.

ENVIRONMENT

Each fertilized egg, then, carries within it hereditary determinants from the father and the mother, and each zygote almost surely differs from all other zygotes at the very moment of conception. These differences become magnified and more easily detectable as an individual grows in her mother's womb, as she is born, and as she enters into the activities of the outside world. The continuous unity that is a woman is an ever-changing one.

These changes, however, do not take place in a biological organism suspended in a vacuum. From the very moment of fertilization, through the development of the zygote, the embryo, and the fetus, the organism is immersed in an environment that is unique to him. Just as it is nearly certain that each zygote differs from all other zygotes, we can assert with equal confidence that the *environment* of each zygote differs from that of every other zygote.

We have known for a long time that the conditions prevailing in the zygote's environment—the uterus—can have profound effects upon the physical development of the organism. Our knowledge of some of the conditions that interfere with normal development is extensive, and we are continually learning more about this subject. By now, all physicians and most mothers know that German measles around the third month of pregnancy can interfere seriously with the course of growth *in utero* and can lead to defective offspring. Certain commonly used drugs, some antibiotics for example, have been shown to have enduring effects on the developing organism. The tragic results of taking the drug thalidomide during pregnancy—gross physical deformities in the child—have alerted us all

to the by now obvious facts that the uterus is indeed a relevant environment and that the embryo and later the fetus does not grow and develop in a vacuum during the forty weeks of pregnancy. As more research focuses upon the effects of various externally controllable conditions in the uterus during pregnancy, we shall be better able to avoid, or to treat, conditions that are, in the broad sense, toxic to normal development.

But of late we have come to know something quite new about the influence of the zygote's environment, something that to many seems most surprising. It is the increasing evidence that the later *behavior* of the organism is affected by the prenatal environment. Such effects are perhaps surprising because they seem to confirm, in a very general sense, some of the old wives' tales. Psychologists have *not* found that assiduous concert going during pregnancy leads to musically gifted offspring, but they have found, for example, that emotional upset during pregnancy can affect the emotional characteristics of offspring (see Box 1.2).

Whatever the significance of such prenatal environmental effects, it is after birth, of course, that the environment can begin to exert its colossal influence on behavior. Throughout life, the two broad sets of factors contribute to the distinctions among organisms: heredity and environment. And both play their roles—sometimes interacting with each other—from the very moment of conception.

FORMULATION OF THE NATURE-NURTURE PROBLEM

The recognition that our behavioral traits result from the interaction of heredity and environment has changed the formulation of the nature-nurture problem. We no longer speak of the nature-nurture controversy (heredity *versus* environment). The questions we ask assume, at the outset, that both heredity and environment are involved. The three questions of concern to research workers in the field are: First, what proportion of variation in any given trait in a group of individuals is determined by heredity and

BOX 1.2

PRENATAL INFLUENCES ON OFFSPRING

W. R. Thompson at Wesleyan University has tested the hypothesis that emotional upset undergone by female rats during pregnancy can affect the emotional characteristics of the offspring.

Thompson trained five female rats in a double-compartment shuttlebox first to expect strong shock at the sound of a buzzer and then to avoid the shock by opening a door between the compartments and running through to the safe side. When the rats had learned this lesson, they were mated. As soon as they became pregnant, they were exposed to the buzzer three times every day in the shock side of the shuttlebox, but with the shock turned off and the door to the safe side locked. This procedure was continued until the females gave birth to their pups. During pregnancy, the mother rats were thus exposed to an anxiety-arousing situation, but their accustomed means to escape was blocked. Thompson's assumption was that this exposure would generate strong free-floating anxiety in the pregnant females and that any resulting endocrine changes would be transmitted via the bloodstream to the fetuses. Would this anxiety create emotional offspring?

The emotionality of the offspring (there were thirty of them) was measured by two tests given at 30 to 40 and at 130 to 140 days of age and compared with results for thirty offspring of control animals who had not been subjected to this stress. In test A, the offspring of the experiment and control animals were placed in a large open area for three daily sessions of 10 min each, and their activity was measured on the assumption that, the more timid or emotional the animal, the less the activity in an open area. In test B, emotionality was measured by the time elapsing before the rat left the home cage to reach food at the end of an alley leading from the cage. For this test the animals were first deprived of food for 24 hrs. Both these tests (especially test A, which is sometimes called the "open-field test") are used fairly commonly to measure emotionality in rats.

The results are shown in the table. It is clear that the offspring of the experimental animals differ strikingly from offspring of the control animals. Furthermore, it appears that these differences persist, to a great extent, into adulthood.

	Test A	Test B
	Amount of Activity (Distance Moved)	*Time to Leave Home Cage (Minutes)*
	Tests given at age 30 to 40 days	
Experimental	86.0	14.9
Control	134.5	5.2
	Tests given at age 130 to 140 days	
Experimental	114.5	4.8
Control	162.3	2.1

Although these differences are statistically reliable, there is some ambiguity regarding their cause. It is possible that the buzzer was strong enough to act on the fetuses directly rather than indirectly by causing release of hormones in the mother. For this reason, Thompson concludes cautiously, ". . . there are some grounds for supposing that prenatal maternal anxiety does actually increase the emotionality of offspring."

Later research with mice supports Thompson's findings and makes his conclusion less tentative. Recent research, however, introduces some complications into the finding that prenatal stress in the mother leads to greater emotionality in her offspring. J. C. DeFries (1964), for example, finds that there are important strain differences in this effect; that is, the effects of the stress are different depending upon the particular strain or breed of mouse that is tested. Even further, not only the genotype of the mother but also that of the fetal offspring is a factor. Clearly, then, broad generalizations of these findings to all species are highly risky, and research will have to discover the precise mechanisms involved in the operation of prenatal influences before we can say more.

Whatever the mechanism is finally shown to be, however, it seems that differences in the prenatal environments of the rats can cause differences in later behavior.

W. R. THOMPSON. Influence of prenatal maternal anxiety on emotionality in young rats. *Science*, 1957, **125**, 698–699. Table adapted by permission of the American Association for the Advancement of Science.
J. C. DeFRIES. Prenatal maternal stress in mice: Differential effects on behavior. *Journal of Heredity*, 1964, **55**, 289–295.

what proportion by environment? Second, what is the specific nature of the genetic mechanism responsible for the inheritance of behavior tendencies or traits? Third, how much difference can variations in the environment make in traits that are partly determined by heredity?

With regard to the first question, the relative importance of heredity and environment is seen in terms of the average contribution of each factor in a population living in a particular environment. Let us elaborate on this point. Within a given individual the relative importance of heredity or environment can be very far from the average value. Thus, whatever we know regarding this value with respect, say, to intelligence, is utterly irrelevant to an individual who is unfortunate enough to possess the single extra chromosome that has been found to be responsible for the severe mental retardation known as "trisomy-21." Here, heredity plays a massive dominant role, and the child is doomed to be intellectually defective. Yet, even aside from such extreme cases, it is clear that hereditary intellectual endowments, as well as intelligence-stimulating environments, vary enormously in the general population, so that, for a given person, we are unable to say to what extent his intellectual attainment is attributable to heredity on one hand and to environment on the other.

Furthermore, rarely can we pinpoint, as in the case of trisomy-21, the exact genetic element that is responsible for a given behavioral outcome, particularly in human beings. Our inability to do so does not preclude experimental investigation of the genetic influence upon various behavioral phenomena, as we shall see in the following discussion of behavior genetics.

The answer to the third question is implicit in the preceding discussion. Again, we must caution that whatever result we obtain can apply only to a certain population of organisms in general. Take the realm of personality as a broad example. Without going into details concerning the influence of heredity upon various personality traits (this topic is discussed in Unit 28), the potential influence of environmental variation on a given facet of personality depends heavily upon the hereditary base on

which this variation impinges. Thus, as we shall see in Unit 24, the interaction between an inherited potential for schizophrenia and the environmental forces that can prevent or promote the emergence of this disorder is crucial. Lacking the supposed hereditary susceptibility, even the worst of psychological environments will not result in a schizophrenic breakdown. But, given the genetic potential, some people will become schizophrenic, and others will not, depending upon the stress present in their environments. Thus, when we speak of genetic influences on behavior, it is critical to remember that, apart from hereditary defects resulting from the presence of trisomy-21 or of specific genes that cause extreme mental deficiency, most hereditary traits are not exhibited in an all-or-none fashion. Generally, genetic factors are predisposing elements; any behavioral outcome is necessarily a varying blend of what was given at conception and the environmental forces that have since operated upon it. The organism's inheritance at times may set limits—often quite broad ones—on how widely a trait can range but only very rarely does its presence determine its precise nature.

This theme of continual interaction between nature and nurture, with its almost inevitable guarantee against a rigid link between genes and behavior, is a fortunate, and even an indispensable, aspect of man's development as an individual and as a species. Most changes that have been observed in the nature of humankind's existence on earth throughout written history are the outcome more of extraordinary environmental modifications than of genetic factors. As the geneticist Dobzhansky (1967) has observed:

> The preponderance of cultural over biological evolution will continue or increase in the foreseeable future. We would not wish this to be otherwise: adaptation to environment by culture is more rapid and efficient than biological adaptation. Moreover, control of the cultural evolution is achievable probably more easily than control of the biological evolution.

This is not to assume that we have ceased to evolve biologically and that all cultural evolution builds upon the same distribution of genotypes as existed at our beginnings. Even if no other factors were operative, the simple fact that each new set of parents throughout time represents a potential for new and unique genetic combinations would ensure continuing biological change. The relation of genetic potential to expressed behavior poses many interesting questions; the field of **behavior genetics** has undertaken their investigation.

Animal Behavior Genetics

The experimental study of animal behavior genetics, though now very active, has a rather short history. The first extensive experiment in psychology was that of Tryon, who initiated his now classic **selective breeding** experiment with rats in 1927.

Selective breeding consists of mating animals that display certain traits in a very high or low degree, selecting from among their offspring those that express the trait in a similar high or low degree, and then breeding from those offspring. If the trait is regulated by heredity, continued selection for a number of generations may result in a strain that breeds more or less true for that trait.

Tryon's results were clear: Bright mazelearners produce bright progeny; dull mazelearners produce dull progeny (see Box 1.3, p. 20). Many other experimenters have corroborated and greatly extended Tryon's results. Selective breeding for behavioral traits is by no means confined to maze learning or to a single species of rats.

Among invertebrates, for instance, the geneticists' favorite experimental animal, the fruit fly (*Drosophila*), has been used for the study of behavioral genetics. For example, it has been successfully bred for strength of attraction to light (Hirsch & Boudreau, 1958; Hadler, 1964). The same species has also been shown to have a substantial genetic basis for geotaxis, the tendency to move with or against gravitational pull (see Figures 1.6 and 1.7).

Normally, the flour beetle (*Tribolium*) crawls, but when starved it "flies," that is, it takes short hops. Through continued selective breeding of those beetles showing the most readiness to "fly," the proportion of beetles en-

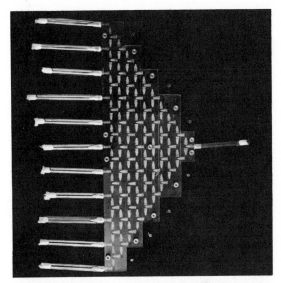

FIGURE 1.6 This vertical ten-unit plastic maze facing a fluorescent tube (not shown here) is an apparatus to measure geotaxis in fruit flies. Squads of fruit flies (*Drosophila*) are introduced to the maze through the vial at right and are collected from the several vials at left. The flies are induced to go through the maze by the light, to which they are attracted, and by a pervasive odor of food. Successive selected breeding of flies that tend to crawl either upward or downward as they pass through the maze results eventually in two strains of fruit fly, one tending to oppose gravitational pull and one tending to go with gravity.

J. Hirsch. Behavior genetics and individuality understood. *Science*, **142**, 1436–1442; copyright 1963 by the American Association for the Advancement of Science; reprinted by permission.

gaging in hopping behavior (during a 24-hr test period) rose dramatically from 2 to 50 percent in a mere six generations, with a high proportion of these beetles actually being able to *fly* across the room (Lerner & Inouye, 1969).

Currently, molecular biologists, attempting to harness genetic techniques to understand basic neurophysiological processes on which behavior is based, choose to experiment with even simpler vertebrates. For instance, they study roundworms, which have an elementary 200-cell nervous system as compared with man's 10 billion neurons (see Unit 3). On a scale of mere microseconds they thus explore RNA and protein synthesis to elucidate the processes of nerve conduction, stimulation, memory, etc.

BOX 1.3

INHERITANCE OF LEARNING ABILITY

The purpose of R. C. Tryon's experiment at the University of California was to establish, by selective breeding, a line of maze-bright and a line of maze-dull rats.

Tryon started with a parental generation of 142 male and female rats. Each animal was run for nineteen trials through a seventeen-unit maze. The brightest animals made a total of approximately fourteen errors in learning the maze, the dullest about 174. The bright females were then mated with the bright males, the dull females with the dull males; the other animals were discarded. Then the offspring of these matings were tested on the same maze. On the basis of their performance, the brightest rats within each of the bright litters were mated, and the dullest within each of the dullest litters were mated. This testing and selective breeding procedure was followed for eighteen generations. The results are summarized in the distribution curves of the figure, which shows the errors made by the parental group, the third generation (F₂), the seventh generation (F₆), and the ninth generation (F₈). With successive generations the two strains of rats pulled apart, until by the F₈ generation the dullest of the bright rats was about as bright as or brighter than the brightest of the dull rats.

Rigorous environmental controls were employed in this experiment. All animals were given identical care. In some cases, indeed, a dull mother would be given the pups of a bright mother to raise, and a bright mother would be given the pups of a dull mother. This mixing was intended to rule out the possibility of different maternal care as an environmental factor. The maze was highly reliable, and the errors were scored automatically by an electrical recorder, so as to eliminate any possible unconscious bias of the experimenter in scoring the rats.

A number of years later, L. V. Searle, working in Tryon's laboratory, tested the two strains on

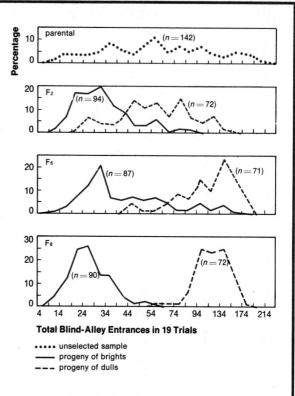

Total Blind-Alley Entrances in 19 Trials

· · · · · unselected sample
——— progeny of brights
– – – progeny of dulls

various other learning tests. He did not find that the brights were bright on everything or that the dulls were altogether dull. Instead, the rats from each strain showed different patterns of abilities.

No matter how the question of the generality of the learning ability of Tryon's two strains will eventually be answered—and research is continuing on this question—the minimal conclusion is clear: Some kinds of learning ability can be inherited.

R. C. TRYON. Genetic differences in maze learning in rats. In National Society for the Study of Education, *The Thirty-ninth Yearbook*. Bloomington, Ill.: Public School Publishing Co., 1940. Figure adapted by permission of National Society for the Study of Education.
L. V. SEARLE. The organization of hereditary maze-brightness and maze-dullness. *Genetic Psychology Monographs*, 1949, **39**, 279–325.

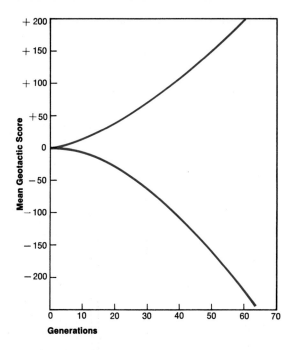

FIGURE 1.7 The results of selection in *Drosophila* for positive geotaxis and negative geotaxis over sixty-five generations (cumulative curves).

Adapted from Erlenmeyer-Kimling et al., 1962.

Moving up the scale of complexity to chickens, selective breeding has been found successful for aggressive behavior and social dominance (the so-called pecking order). And so too for mating frequency, sexual behavior that is mediated by hormone make-up. In mice and rats, a wide range of behaviors has been selected for, including among others emotionality (measured by nervousness in an open-field situation), hoarding, tameness versus wildness, and alcohol preference, a behavioral phenotype perhaps based in part on genetic differences in level of a liver enzyme that aids in the metabolic breakdown of alcohol. Many single-gene neurological mutants have also been isolated, for example, mice that are uncoordinated waltzers, or twisters, or reelers, that is, suffering from a genetic wiring defect in the cerebellum.

One of the most extensive investigations in mammalian behavior genetics is reported by Scott and Fuller (1965). Their main theme is the social behavior, broadly defined, of dogs. In a study lasting more than a dozen years they carefully observed the behavior of purebred and crossbred dogs of five breeds, selected in part for their characteristic behavioral differences: African basenjis, beagles, cocker spaniels, fox terriers, and Shetland sheepdogs. These dogs, about 500 of them, were tested at various times over their first year of life in about thirty standardized situations designed to elicit data on such characteristics as emotional reactivity, trainability, and problem-solving skills. By comparing the performances of the purebreds with those of the crossbreds of various kinds and degrees, Scott and Fuller were often able to detect the genetic bases of various behavioral traits existing among the five kinds of dogs studied.

Aside from its many contributions to the science of behavior genetics, the Scott and Fuller study has had some eminently practical side effects. Trainers of guide dogs for the blind have made extensive use of these findings, as have breeders seeking to select dogs for different kinds of work, for example, hunting versus guarding versus sheepherding.

The general picture in animal behavior genetics is one of rapid progress. But what of man?

Human Behavior Genetics

Selective breeding of human beings is, for obvious reasons, not the experimental method of choice in this area. Rather, psychologists and others have had to turn to comparisons of abilities and behavior among identical and fraternal twins, among brothers and sisters, and among parents and their children. In other words, family resemblances in various traits and abilities have been investigated. One immediately apparent difficulty with this general approach is that families not only are linked genetically but also typically share the same environments over long periods. For this reason, instances of twins reared in different homes and children placed for adoption and reared by foster parents have been eagerly analyzed for research purposes in the field of human behavior genetics.

Most investigations in this area have dealt with the extent of genetic contributions to intelligence; these findings are more appropriately presented in our general discussion of the sources of variation in mental ability (see Unit 10). The heritability of various emotional, temperamental, and personality traits has fairly recently also become a topic of considerable research; again, we defer presentation of specific findings to the broader treatment of individual determinants of these traits (see Units 20 and 28).

As we shall see in Unit 24, the evidence argues strongly for a genetic factor in schizophrenia, though this by no means implies a simple hereditary explanation. The role of genetic factors in this important and pervasive mental disorder is obviously complex and not yet well understood. But there are certain other behavior disorders in which the genetic source is clearer and simpler. In McKusick's catalog (see p. 15) of 1876 human phenotypes identified with single genes, approximately 150 are genes associated with behavior pathologies. Of 103 specific enzyme deficiencies that are listed, many have behavioral effects, mostly in various forms of mental retardation.

In *phenylketonuria* (PKU), for instance, an enzyme deficiency leads to accumulation in the bloodstream of phenylalanine, which is toxic to the central nervous system. Severe mental retardation results, the IQ range of PKU children being roughly 20 to 80. Treatment consists of a diet low in phenylalanine; to be effective the treatment must begin early in life. One study found that fourteen out of seventeen PKU babies on the diet had normal IQs, whereas no children started on the diet as late as six years showed improvement. It would appear that we have here a case of successful nutritional management of a genetically caused defect.

Another fascinating behavioral anomaly associated with a single-gene defect is the *testicular feminization syndrome*. It is found in biological (XY) males who produce male hormone (androgen) but whose somatic cells are for genetic reasons insensitive to it. Consequently, the XY individual develops into a phenotypic female, having female breasts and certain other female body characteristics, but with a blind vagina

and no ovaries or menstruation. Behaviorally, these individuals adopt the female sex role (in conventional female occupations, for example) and, interestingly, in cognitive abilities they tend to score higher on verbal than on spatial tests, just as XX females do.

Certain gross abnormalities of the chromosomes are also known to result in aberrant behavior. In Figure 1.2, page 10, we have already referred to trisomy-21, a condition of severe mental deficiency (mongolism) caused by a mutation in which an extra, a third chromosome, occurs in pair 21. Trisomy-21 occurs in about one out of 650 births; among institutionalized mental defectives perhaps 10 to 15 percent have this disorder.

Considerable interest has recently been aroused by the suggestion that some forms of antisocial behavior in males may be related to the occurrence of an extra X or Y in the sex chromosomes, resulting in an XXY or an XYY individual. British studies find two to three times as many XXY males as others among institutionalized patients exhibiting excessive violent or aggressive and criminal behavior. Other studies also seem to find pronounced aggressiveness in XXY males. But the case is far from proven. Perhaps the aggressiveness merely goes with the typical taller stature of these individuals; XYY males have been found to be unusually tall. (Another form of chromosomal abnormality, involving a single instead of two X chromosomes, produces the so-called Turner syndrome. See Unit 10.)

Genetic counseling The remarkable advances in our knowledge of human genetic variation have raised concern for the welfare of the individual and society. A result has been the emergence of the new field and profession of **genetic counseling**, which provides information to parents and others about the diagnosis, prognosis, and treatment of individuals carrying defective genes. The most common sort of advice sought is that by parents who have produced abnormal children asking about the probability that subsequent children would suffer from the same abnormality; or by couples about to be married where one of them has a family history of genetic abnormality. Lerner (1968) reports that a

University of Michigan genetic counselor was visited by a Roman Catholic mother:

one of whose children had the phenotypic symptoms of trisomy-21. The woman wanted to encourage one of her other children to become a priest. She went to the counselor because she thought that if any of her sons were a carrier of the abnormality . . . he should be the one to enter this celibate profession and, thus, avoid passing on the defect to the next generation. . . . The counselor was able to sort out the normal and abnormal offspring by looking at their chromosomes.

According to the most recent directory of genetic services (Lynch, 1971), there are now 680 genetic counseling centers in the world. Of these, 62 (32 in the United States) offer advice on behavior genetics.

One factor contributing to the rapid growth of the field is the development of powerful new techniques for the diagnosis of genetic defects in the individual. These techniques relate, among other problems, to the fundamental issue of identification of embryos and fetuses that will be grossly defective at birth. It is now feasible by extraction and analysis of amniotic fluid from the pregnant mother to determine many genetic characteristics of the fetus and should the fetus be diagnosed as hopelessly aberrant, to induce an abortion if that is legally permissible. Incidentally, the same technique can be used to diagnose the sex of the unborn child.

The field of genetic counseling is also extended by new possibilities of treatment of genetic disorders. For example, a proper diet can be crucial in warding off mental retardation effects of such disorders as PKU (see p. 22), or *galactosemia* (inability to utilize sugar in maternal milk), or, presumably, of still other enzymatic deficiencies.

On the horizon are far-reaching methods of so-called genetic engineering, which may be able to correct genetic defects by manipulating genotypes. This possibility is still in the future. But it is important to realize that we are no longer dealing with science fiction. Genetic manipulation of one kind or another is an eventuality that calls for our attention now. The methods of harnessing it to human welfare, including full utilization of genetic counseling, must be considered by all concerned with the future of humankind. This problem is seen by the geneticist I. M. Lerner as an ethical and moral problem—and one for which we do not have an adequate set of guidelines:

Clearly, whatever biological problems the wonders of euphenics [the improvement of the *phenotype* by medical or other biological means] and genetical engineering may solve, they will create many unprecedented social and ethical problems, for the solution of which much collective wisdom will be needed. The requisite wisdom is unlikely to come from the genetical engineers alone, because it involves moral issues on which they are not experts. The traditional ethical guidelines have come from religion, but the new religion of science and technology that is arising, with its hierarchy of scientists instead of priests, with its sacred language of mathematics instead of Latin, with its sacrifices of traffic casualties instead of heretics, and with space-exploration for its Crusades, is as yet not capable of providing any. (Lerner, 1968)

SUMMARY

1. The evolution of humankind has involved a greatly increasing diversity and an expanded flexibility for adaptation to a wide range of environmental challenges. The process of evolution, roughly speaking, has as its fundamental governing mechanism the phenomenon of natural selection. Species more able to adapt to changed environmental demands tend to survive; within species, those individuals best able to cope with these demands are more likely to remain alive and to procreate, thus passing on their particular genetic endowments. In ability to adapt, humankind today is preeminent.

2. At conception, a human individual starts off with one particular combination, among more than 60 trillion possible combinations, of twenty-three chromosomes from each parent. This fact, together with the phenomenon of crossing-over of genes from one chromosome to another, practically guarantees that, except for identical twins, no two people ever have the same genetic make-up.

3. Identical twins are two distinct individuals who develop from a single zygote and hence are genetically identical. In contrast, fraternal twins arise from two different ova and consequently are no more genetically similar than any other combination of brothers or sisters. From external appearance alone it is often difficult to tell whether a set of twins is identical or fraternal, but there are available highly developed tests that can differentiate between the two types.

4. The genes are DNA molecules that constitute the chromosome. It is the genes that are the determiners of inherited characteristics. An important form of gene interaction is dominance and recessiveness, one reason why a person's phenotype (his observed characteristics) is only a partial manifestation of his genotype (the genes he possesses and transmits unchanged except for mutations to his offspring). Although it is true that certain psychologically important traits, such as forms of mental deficiency, may have a relatively simple genetic basis, more typically traits are determined by many sets of genes, and thus it is unlikely that such traits will exhibit clear-cut dominant-recessive properties.

5. The expression of genetic determinants is substantially influenced by environmental factors from the moment of conception onward; intrauterine conditions affect development of the embryo and fetus, and environmental influences on maturation and development obviously become even greater after birth.

6. There are three major inquiries pursued by research workers concerned with the nature-nurture issue: (1) What proportion of the variation in any given trait in a group of individuals is determined by heredity and what proportion by environment? (2) What is the specific nature of the genetic mechanism responsible for the inheritance of behavior tendencies or traits? (3) How much difference can variations in the environment make in traits that are partly determined by heredity?

7. In behavior genetics, selective breeding experiments with animals of widely varying levels of complexity and for a great variety of traits are providing new information and insights on the nature-nurture question for behavior as well as for physical characteristics. At the human level, studies of relatives—twins, siblings, parents, and children—are beginning to provide comparable information regarding genetic and environmental determinants of behavior, particularly with respect to intelligence, personality, and mental disorder.

8. The newly emerging profession of genetic counseling provides information to parents and others about the diagnosis and treatment of individuals carrying defective genes. Powerful new techniques are being developed to enable the identification of embryos and fetuses that will be grossly defective at birth. New possibilities for the treatment of genetic disorders, such as through diet, are also being explored. Future methods of genetic engineering, which may be able to correct genetic defects by manipulating genotypes, raise concern for the welfare of the individual and society among those working in the fields of medicine, law, theology, and the behavioral sciences, including psychology.

GLOSSARY

behavior genetics   The field of genetics, closely associated with psychology, which is concerned with study of the genetic factors in behavior. Behavior genetics deals with both animals and people.

chromosomes   Threadlike bodies of different sizes and shapes appearing in like pairs, found within animal cell bodies. Normal human cells seem to contain twenty-three pairs of chromosomes each, or a total of forty-six chromosomes. Chromosomes carry the genes.

crossing-over of genes   Refers to the fact that one segment of a chromosome may break off and be exchanged with a corresponding segment from the paired chromosome. Genes thus do not always remain in their original chromosomes.

embryo   A young animal during the early stages within its mother's body. For man the term "embryo" is used to describe the developing individual up to the end of the seventh week after conception.

fetus   Refers to the young of an animal in the womb, especially in its later stages.

fraternal twins   Two individuals who have developed from two different fertilized ova (zygotes). They are to be contrasted with identical twins. Fraternal twins may be both male, both female, or one of each. Fraternal twins are no more genetically similar than are any two brothers or sisters.

gene   A stretch of DNA in the chromosome that codes for production of a specific part of a protein. The gene, as it reacts with the environment and other genes, is a factor in determining the hereditary traits and structures of the developing individual.

genetic counseling   The profession that provides information, interpretation, and advice to parents and others about the diagnosis, prognosis, and treatment of defective genes that individuals may carry.

genotype   The genetic potential that an individual possesses and can in part transmit to his offspring. This potential may be only partially expressed in his phenotype.

heterozygous state   The state in which the individual has a pair of genes that differ in their effects on any one hereditary trait, for example, one dominant and one recessive gene (Aa).

homozygous state   The state in which the individual has a pair of genes that are identical in their effects on any one hereditary trait, for example, two dominant genes (AA) or two recessive genes (aa).

identical twins   Two complete individuals who have developed from one segmented, fertilized ovum (zygote). They are to be contrasted with fraternal twins. Identical twins are therefore genetically identical and are of great interest to the psychologist who is concerned with the problem of the hereditary factors in behavior.

mutation   A change in genes that causes a sudden departure from the parent type, as when an individual is found to carry a gene that neither of his parents had.

ovum (egg)   The female germ (or reproductive) cell produced by the ovaries. The ovum contains within it one member of each pair of chromosomes from the mother, or a total of twenty-three chromosomes. After fertilization by the sperm the ovum can develop into a new individual.

phenotype   The observable characteristics of an individual that are only partial manifestations of his genetic potential, or genotype.

selective breeding   A technique used in experimental genetics. It consists of mating animals that display certain traits and selecting for breeding from among their offspring those that express the trait. If the trait is regulated by heredity, continued selection for a number of generations may result in a strain that breeds true for that trait.

sperm   The male germ (or reproductive) cell produced by the testes. The sperm carries within it one member of each pair of chromosomes from the father, or a total of twenty-three chromosomes.

zygote   The fertilized ovum, or the cell produced by the union of an ovum and a sperm. The normal human zygote contains twenty-three complete pairs of chromosomes (or forty-six chromosomes), one member of each pair coming from the ovum, the other from the sperm.

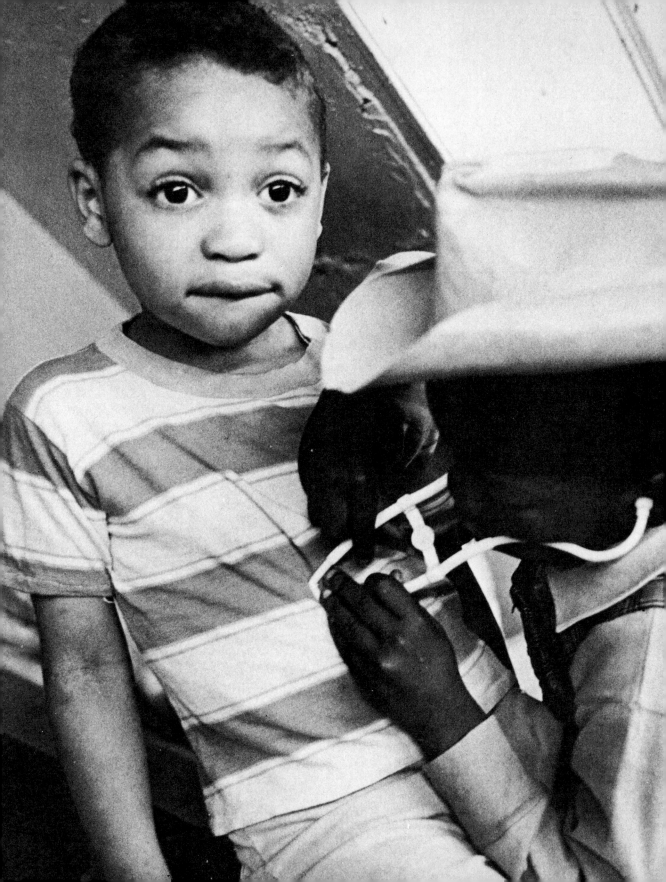

growth and development

DO YOU KNOW…

- why it is that studying true developmental change requires observing the same person over time, which few psychologists do?

- whether children who grow fastest at first end up, as adults, being larger?

- whether you can believe what a mother reports about how she raised her child?

- whether there has really been a change in adolescent personality over the past generation?

- that girls a hundred years ago matured sexually four or five years later than they do today?

- that black infants develop motor skills considerably more rapidly than whites during their first year?

- what we mean when we speak of being ready to learn a particular skill?

- why it is difficult to define when it is that an individual ends his adolescence and becomes, psychologically, an adult?

- whether retirement should be a period of disengagement or one of continued (even if new) activity and involvement?

Photo by Henry Monroe

CONTENTS

In a very real sense almost every field of psychology might properly be classed under the rubric "human development." No matter which topic we consider—perception, learning, motivation and emotion, intelligence, personality, or social behavior—it inevitably raises developmental questions.

What does an infant perceive of the world about him, and what is the course of growth of the perceptual function from its rudimentary beginnings at birth to its highly efficient state in the adult? What can a baby learn, and when and through what means does he come to achieve the impressive learning abilities of the average adult? At the start of life, are the motives that drive the infant's behavior adult motives, and are his emotional reactions to his environment as rich and as varied as our own? Is personality the same in the infant, in the preschool child, in the adolescent, in the adult? If not, what accounts for whatever continuity is found, and what factors are responsible for personality change? We hardly expect or find what can be called truly social behavior in the newborn, not to mention the highly articulated social beliefs and attitudes of the mature adult. Add to these questions those related to the opposite end of the developmental process—as the adult begins to age—and we have spanned the full course of human life without ever abandoning the developmental orientation.

Throughout this text, data and discussion on developmental phenomena are to be found in the units dealing with various specific topics. For this reason we will focus here only on broad developmental issues and tend to emphasize biological growth and development.

All is change, at least in the psychology of man. Change takes place as new experiences impinge upon and modify the psychological self, which is each of us at any given moment—a self derived from what we are, genetically and constitutionally, and all that we have up until that moment seen and learned and felt. This self is therefore in a continual process of re-creation.

What psychology typically does and what we shall for the most part do in this text is to freeze and study the individual at a single point in time. Rarely (and we will discuss some of those rare events) does the psychologist observe a given individual on more than one occasion. What is more, the psychologist must treat various psychological functions separately, and, even further, the psychologist's research most often attends to the behavior that occurs *on the average* in any given circumstance. Through these simplifying devices the psychologist studies perception, learning, and so forth, as they describe and explain the behavior of the average person. We can glimpse the developmental histories of each of these functions by comparing investigations of the same phenomenon in different age groups. The rare exception to this strategy is the longitudinal method, to be discussed later, in which the same persons are studied repeatedly throughout their life spans.

THE DEVELOPMENTAL PROCESS

Perhaps we can best begin by pointing out that the terms "growth" and "development," though technically distinguishable, are essentially synonymous for our purposes. Strictly speaking, growth refers to an increase in magnitude—in bodily size, in muscular strength, in intellectual ability, or even in social poise. Not all development is growth in this sense, for, with increasing age, some things decrease. Certain motor reflexes present at birth and in infancy rapidly disappear, for example, and even certain organs, like the thymus gland (see Figure 2.6, p. 42), shrink and atrophy after adolescence. A more general term, "development," may be broadly defined as referring to any sequential and continuous process of change, both quantitative and qualitative, in any physical structure or function and in any direction.

Change is sometimes understood to connote gradualness, the notion that what exists at time 2 is only a bit different from what was there at time 1. For many physical and behavioral characteristics this notion is indeed valid; our growth in height is the total of infinitesimal increments. Yet there are exceptions to this kind of change. Certain psychological phenomena show abrupt transitions. A meaningless conglomeration of blotches is instantly transformed into a perceptually meaningful picture; a totally impossible problem is solved in what seems an instantaneous flash of insight. Sometimes, of course, what appears to be abrupt and discontinuous is the result of other invisible processes that may have proceeded gradually. The blinding insight may be the end product of a continuing evaluation of evidence and a testing of hypotheses.

So it is with many aspects of human development. The attainment of menarche, or first menstruation, is for the adolescent girl an abrupt event, yet we know that it is the necessary result of a host of gradual physiological changes. So with learning to read at school or, for that matter, the acquiring of any skill. For long periods, training and practice seem to lead to little if any improvement, but then, with apparent abruptness, printed words become meaningful and bicycles become ridable.

Hereditary characteristics also often convey a sense of developmental discontinuity. As we see in Unit 1, an individual's genetic make-up is fully determined at the moment of conception, yet the physical or behavioral expression of these built-in potentials is not usually evident until a considerable time after birth. But, nevertheless, development according to the blueprint set down by genes proceeds continuously and sequentially.

Intelligence, which is to some extent hereditary, exhibits this apparent delayed-action effect. As Honzik (1963) has shown, significant parent-child resemblance in intelligence does not occur until about age three in girls and age five in boys, reflecting the generally faster maturation rate of females.

Parameters of Development

The course of all developmental processes can be described by just a few general characteristics. These characteristics may be quickly summarized as follows.

Rate of development   This term refers simply to a rate of change with time. This rate need not be—and in fact rarely is—constant throughout the entire period of development. Taking

A

B

E

A—Photo by Kingsley Fairbridge; B—Photo by Shelly Rusten; C—Photo by Melissa Shook; D—Photo by Marion Bernstein; E—Photo by Van Bucher/Photo Researchers, Inc.; F—Photo by Marion Bernstein; and G—Photo by Yvonne Freund.

C

D

G

F

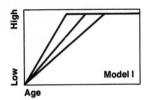 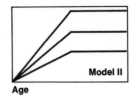 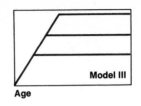 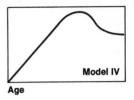

FIGURE 2.1   Models of the developmental process.

J. Loevinger. Models and measures of developmental variation. *Annals of the New York Academy of Sciences*, 1966, **134**, 589–590; adapted by permission.

height as an example, growth is extremely rapid within the first year or two of life, then slows down to a relatively moderate rate, only to experience an abrupt spurt sometime in the adolescent years (see Figure 2.2, p. 37). And, typical of height and most other characteristics, the developmental rate tapers off as the individual approaches maturity with respect to a given function.

Timing   Not all characteristics begin to develop, at least observably, at birth but get started at different times and reach mature levels at different times. The ability to walk is an example, and even language development can be so classified. These two points in time are not necessarily related; an individual may start late but be no later than others in completing the developmental process. Whether or not she catches up is of course a function of rate of growth.

Ceiling   Quite apart from when a developmental process begins and is completed and quite apart from its rate, the parameter of ceiling refers to the culminating characteristics for a particular function. To take an obvious example: We all eventually attain different heights. Each of these culminating heights (e.g., 5 ft 6 in., 6 ft 5 in.) is at the ceiling. These mature heights are quite independent of the previous course of our growth curves. The same can be said of intellectual development—some children are slow starters in the educational process, but their ultimate achievement level will not necessarily be lower.

Differentiation and stages of development   Certain parameters of development—**differentiation**

and **stages of development**—cannot be cast in simple quantitative terms. They are essentially changes in the *nature* of the behavior. Intellectual or cognitive development is characterized by this kind of development. For an excellent example of this, the reader is referred to the discussion of Jean Piaget's elaborate scheme of developmental stages, which encompasses intelligence and thinking and even language development (see Unit 4). The achievement of sexual maturity is another example of a qualitative change in the course of a developmental process.

Models of Developmental Variation

These few parameters can be employed to construct different models of development, and with only a few such models we can encompass a large number of physical and psychological developmental processes. Loevinger (1966) has done just this, and our presentation is largely drawn from her proposals (see Figure 2.1). Model I refers to developmental processes in which all persons ultimately attain the same ceiling, starting at the same time but proceeding at different rates. Bone development is a prime example of this kind of process; gradual ossification of the epiphyses (the regions lying between adjacent bones) is a continual phenomenon, beginning at the start of life and proceeding at different rates until the epiphyses are closed and the skeletal structure has reached its mature state. Various motor skills (from becoming toilet-trained to being able to walk effectively) show much the same pattern.

Model II portrays a varying rate of development of a characteristic that differs in ceiling, or ultimate level. Here, perhaps, intelligence is the best example, for mental development does proceed at different paces, does reach different final levels, and—most important—does seem to level off, no matter what the ceiling value, at about the same age (sometime during adolescence). This characterization is somewhat oversimplified, but it is true that, at least as measured by conventional tests, persons seem to reach their mature levels of intellectual ability at approximately the same time.

Model III is difficult to illustrate by a pure example: It includes processes in which society prescribes a fixed rate of progression but allows variation at terminal levels. One's educational career would illustrate this model as, by and large, advancement from grade to grade goes according to a rather fixed schedule, but individuals do drop out at various points along the way. Verbal ability to some extent follows this model, at least in its earliest stage, where children show much the same increase in their vocabularies over a period of years, only to have some children level off at certain points while others go on to different, higher ones.

Model IV is the only one in which the assumption of an enduring ceiling level is discarded. To some extent, many of the characteristics we have been discussing show some decrease from peak level with time, but it is usually minor. Intelligence provides particularly illuminating data for this case. If we look at different aspects of intelligence (they are fully discussed in Unit 9), we find that some intellectual abilities follow Model II, whereas others are best described by Model IV. For the former model, we have such abilities as vocabulary and information. They do not decrease with age, and, indeed, there is some evidence that this sort of intelligence actually increases as we grow older, especially among those who were initially quite gifted (Bayley & Oden, 1955).

Other intellectual and cognitive functions, however, decay markedly as we advance in age. They include performances that require a certain cognitive flexibility, an ability to solve novel and complex problems rapidly. In fact, any task for which sheer speed of response is an important factor tends to be more difficult as we grow older. Cattell (1963) recognizes these

differences when he draws a distinction between intelligence-test items that show no age decline (he sees them as measuring "crystallized intelligence") and those that decay, often quite rapidly, with advancing age (measuring "fluid intelligence").

These models are, of course, simplifications gleaned from a survey of many different developmental processes. There are possible variations on these models. Our purpose here is only to alert the reader to the fact that development is not a unitary, general process but can follow many routes.

ALTERNATE METHODS OF STUDYING DEVELOPMENT

The necessary (but for certain questions insufficient) requirement for a developmental investigation is simply that we have measures of the characteristic under study at a number of different ages spotted throughout the span of its development. We can obtain our measures in a number of ways: First, at a given time we can measure groups of individuals of different ages; second, we can measure individuals at a certain age but obtain information on previous ages through the subjects' reports; third, we can measure the same individuals at various ages as they develop. The first of these methods is called **cross-sectional studies;** the second, **retrospective studies;** and the last, **longitudinal studies.** We shall consider what can and what cannot be reliably discovered by each.

Cross-Sectional Studies

Most data currently available on physical and psychological development are obtained by the cross-sectional method. The investigator, at a given time, collects comparative data on a particular characteristic from children, adolescents, young adults, and so on; computes the average values; and then plots these values to yield a developmental curve. This method is certainly a convenient one and, for many purposes, is adequate. It can and does accurately portray average trends, except for characteristics that are subject to **secular change,** that is, to change with time (not age) as a function of environmental factors of one sort or another.

Secular change is not an insignificant factor in mapping the developmental trends of a psychological characteristic such as intelligence or a physical characteristic such as height. For example, Jones and Conrad (1933) tested the intelligence of almost all persons living in a small New England town in order to discover the age trends in a number of different aspects of intellectual ability. One factor that tended to exaggerate the general developmental decline in intelligence arose from a secular change: On the average, the older the person, the less formal schooling he had had. Because some aspects of intellectual performance are enhanced by formal schooling, it follows that at least some of the intellectual decline that apparently accompanies aging is not a developmental decline at all but, instead, is a result of a secular change, namely, an increase in educational opportunity in more recent years and therefore increased schooling for younger people.

Height shows the same effect. For some time it has been widely assumed that height, which reaches mature levels sometime in late adolescence or in the early twenties, begins to decrease somewhat later on, perhaps in the fifties or sixties. Damon (1965), from his own research and that of others, concludes that this decline in height may to a very large extent be due to a secular change: Mature adult height has been increasing over the course of many decades. For example, in a recent study men whose average age was over eighty were 2.4 in. shorter than a group of men in their twenties. Do these data indicate that a shrinkage in stature of more than 2 in. occurs in the course of six decades of mature adulthood? By no means. *All* of the apparent developmental decline in height could be attributable to the simple fact that men born more recently grow taller than those born several decades ago.

This is not to deny that there is indeed a small degree of body shrinkage with advanced age, which shows in certain bodily characteristics and in certain individuals. The point being made here is that secular change in a given characteristic can distort its apparent developmental

trend when the data used are derived from cross-sectional studies.

Retrospective Studies

Quite simply, the essential design of retrospective studies is that current measurements are compared with *recalled* values for such measurements, going back to various previous points in time for the same individual with such data. Presumably, we could then describe developmental processes free of the errors inherent in secular change. Logically, this method should work; psychologically, it does not. Human memory is just too fallible. Data supporting this conclusion come from longitudinal studies, which actually measure an individual throughout his development. These studies are unanimous in their finding of substantial errors of recall, even when the information requested would seem to be of a highly memorable nature and when only a relatively short period of time intervened between the actual event and the moment of recall.

A pioneer study on this question, and one that focuses upon presumably memorable events, is by Pyles, Stolz, and Macfarlane (1935). They compared mothers' reports on items relating to pregnancy, birth, and early development for 252 children with the true data on these events ascertained at the time of their occurrence. The mothers' reports were obtained when the children were twenty-one months of age, and so, in the case of some of the recalled items, like the infant's weight at age twelve months, less than a year had elapsed between the events and their recall. In the case of this particular item, to take one example, the average error of recall (ignoring whether the mother tended to over- or underestimate her baby's weight) was approximately 19 oz—and at a time when average infant weight was only 23 lb. Perhaps more startling is the comparison between the actual duration of the mother's labor (8.6 hr, on the average) and its average error of recall (3.5 hr), a 41 percent error. Other items showed equally unreliable reporting. There was little more than chance correspondence between mothers' reports of their physical health during pregnancy and their actual health, as established from physicians' records. The occurrence of illness in the infant during its first year of life was somewhat better reported, but thirty mothers whose children had suffered relatively severe illnesses at some point during this period reported, when the child was twenty-one months of age, *no illnesses at all.*

When we consider such more equivocal events as the child-rearing practices of the mother throughout the first few years of life and when we increase the interval of recall, retrospection is shown to be even more untrustworthy. Robbins (1963) reports from a longitudinal study in which data were collected on actual infant behavior at three-month intervals during the first year and six-month intervals thereafter. When the children were three years old, parents were asked to recall a number of child behaviors and child-rearing practices. Overall accuracy was low, although mothers were somewhat less in error than were fathers. Robbins also points out:

> Inaccuracies were greatest for items dealing with the age of weaning and toilet training, the occurrence of thumbsucking, and demand feeding. Inaccuracies tended to be in the direction of the recommendations of experts in child-rearing, especially on the part of the mothers.

The last sentence points to at least one important determinant of retrospective inaccuracy—a bias toward reporting things as better than they actually were. This distortion is a real one, in the sense that the parents were, for the most part, not deliberately lying in order to make a more favorable impression; an *earlier* study (when the elapsed time between the event and the parents' reports was much shorter) of these same parents found a high degree of accuracy (Chess et al., 1960). Apparently, recall must fade and memories become more ambiguous before what we may wish to remember is transformed into what we honestly do remember and report.

A more recent study (Yarrow, Campbell, & Burton, 1970) confirms this finding of rosy recall of developmental events that adds the observation that psychologically warmer mothers are more prone to this. Also reported was a tendency for *children's* recall of the same events to resemble their mothers' recollections more than reality, leading the investigators to suggest that "mothers have a significant role in determining the folklore of the family and, by extension, shaping the nature of the findings in retrospective investigation."

Many psychological investigations present provocative relations between later personality characteristics of children and various aspects of their early child-rearing and development of their early personalities, as reported by parents and by the now-adult children themselves after an elapsed interval of ten, fifteen, or more years. But with the results of these investigations on the preceding pages in mind, the studies based on later recall leave themselves open to doubt.

Longitudinal Studies

The essential feature of a longitudinal study is that it observes and measures the same group of individuals repeatedly over the period of development being investigated. This method, aside from avoiding hazards of the cross-sectional and retrospective methods, is also the *only possible* method for certain kinds of questions. As Kodlin and Thompson (1958), in their thorough appraisal of the longitudinal method, have pointed out:

> The longitudinal approach is the *only* approach which gives a complete description of the growth phenomenon. . . . The cross-sectional approach never can satisfy the objective of a study which requires the measurement of the change in a trait through time on a given individual. This means that when the objective of the growth study is to arrive at *predictions of individual growth*, or to establish the *correlation between measurements* obtained at successive ages, it is necessary to employ the longitudinal approach.

Even if secular change were not a problem, cross-sectional studies can yield only *group* averages, not *individual* development curves. Such individual records are necessary if we are to find the variation in the rate of change among individuals for a given characteristic over a certain period. Cross-sectional studies can tell us as well as longitudinal studies that, for example, boys on the average experience their most rapid growth sometime between their thirteenth and fifteenth birthdays and that the amount grown during that two-year interval is, again on the average, a little more than 3 in. But only a longitudinal study can tell us that some boys undergo their periods of most rapid growth as early as age ten, others as late as age seventeen (Nicolson & Hanley, 1953); indeed, the actual increase in height during this two-year period of most rapid growth, whenever it occurs, is considerably more than 3 in., and inspection of individual growth records demonstrates that it can be as much as 12 in. And the abruptness and magnitude of this growth spurt, over the two-year period, are the greater the earlier it begins.

Not only does longitudinal study provide us with our only access to directly measurable individual developmental changes, but it is also the only avenue to prediction of the future from the past. Whether psychologists are attempting to predict height, intelligence, emotional adjustment, or adult occupational achievement, such predictions require that we obtain measures, on the individuals whose behavior is being predicted, at two points in time at least. (For a possible exception, see Box 2.1, p. 38).

For many reasons, longitudinal studies of development are rare, although they have recently begun to increase in number. Aside from the obvious need for money and patience in the conduct of such studies, there are other pitfalls that make them risky. First, there is sample attrition. With increasing duration of the study, subjects are lost for a variety of reasons. Some die, some move from the community, some refuse to cooperate, some no longer can participate because of illness. Second, there is repeated measurement. There is always the risk that continual study of individuals may affect the course of their development or at least the validity of some of the measures obtained. Third, there is time-limited generality. Secular changes inevitably confuse longitudinal research. For example, Woodruff and Birren (1972) compared the results on the same personality test for a group who were studied both at adolescence (in 1944) and at middle age (in 1969). Personality change, thus measured over a twenty-five-year span, was very slight, *but* a new group of young people, also tested in 1969, showed substantial differences from the 1944 data. Were we to base a description of today's adolescent personality on the earlier data we would be seriously in error. Along the same lines, what is discovered concerning, say, the influence of parental disciplinary practices in the 1940s upon the development of conscience in now-adult children, conceivably may not hold for a sample of children born today. Historical events and cultural change may alter the social and psychological context in which children develop, so that a parental practice that led to one effect decades ago may lead to quite another if it is used now. Wars, economic upheavals, changes in educational quality and standards—all these factors may affect the applicability of a relation obtained in a decades-old longitudinal study to the development of today's children.

DEVELOPMENT IN INFANCY AND CHILDHOOD

We must recognize that the child is not an adult in miniature; the child is a different biological organism from the adult. His skeletal structure is differently proportioned, his nervous system is different, his hormonal and biochemical make-up is different. And these differences are significant enough to prevent our generalizing from the behavior of the adult to the behavior of the child. Out of the studies of the differences have come several developmental principles relating function to structure.

Overall Growth Rates

Data on the overall bodily growth rate of man have been accumulating for many years, and the general shape of the physical growth curve is well established. The overall mental growth rate has also been studied, and comparison between bodily and mental growth is now possible.

The two simplest measures of overall bodily growth in man are total height and total weight. These measures tell similar stories. Figure 2.2 depicts the growth of man as repre-

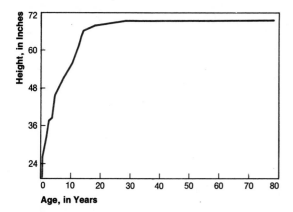

FIGURE 2.2   Average growth in height of American males from birth to eighty years of age.

N. Bayley. Development and maturation. In H. Helson (Ed.), *Theoretical Foundations of Psychology*; copyright 1951 by D. Van Nostrand Company, Inc.; adapted by permission.

sented by total height. The most rapid changes —those occurring during the prenatal period, from conception to birth—are not indicated in the figure. Immediately after birth the growth rate continues to be rapid, more so than at any other time after birth. Sometime during the second year of life the child has attained one-half her adult height. Toward the end of childhood, there is another spurt of growth that lasts into the adolescent years. After **puberty,** the rate of growth slows down considerably until the final height is reached. Then comes a fairly stable period, after which there may begin an actual slight shrinking in overall height and body size—senescence has begun.

As longitudinal data have shown us, there are large individual variations from this average picture, in terms of both the age at which puberty is reached and the maximum growth attained. Some girls reach their adult height by the time they are fourteen years old, some boys not until they are twenty-two or twenty-three years old.

Factors influencing rate of growth include nutritional level, physical and psychological health, and, of course, heredity (Tanner, 1970). Children's rate of growth is slowed during periods of severe malnutrition, as in wartime famine, but it generally catches up once normal

diets are resumed. However, when a population is chronically malnourished its adult members never fully achieve their growth potential. Severe illness shows much the same short-term result, and extreme psychological stress may also, at least for a time, tend to stunt growth. There are even seasonal variations: Growth in height during spring months is almost twice that in the fall. Within the normal range of experience, genetic factors are by far the most potent influence on growth rate and ultimate size. Livson, McNeill, and Thomas (1962), collating evidence from several longitudinal studies, find increasing parent-child resemblances in height as the child develops toward maturity, reaching correlations of about .5—easily large enough to permit reasonably accurate prediction of children's heights from those of their parents.

There have been profound secular changes in the rate of physical maturation. Age of attaining menarche, a critical milestone in sexual maturation, has shown a remarkable shift in the last hundred years or so (see Figure 2.3, p. 40). Most recent evidence suggests that the trend is continuing; data from a variety of sources place the average age of menarche, at least in certain well-nourished populations, as early as age twelve.

Differential Growth Rates

An overall-growth rate is the sum of several quite different growth rates. The different parts of the body do not grow at the same speed. The head, the trunk, and the legs, for example, lengthen at different times and at different rates. Some of the organs of the body grow very rapidly at first, then slow down; others start off slowly, then accelerate.

Because of these differences in rates of growth and varying times of maturation of parts, it might be expected that psychological development would also progress at differential rates. Such is indeed the case.

Developmental direction   One of the most striking characteristics of the growing human body is the change in the form and proportions of its various parts (Figures 2.4, p. 40, and 2.5, p.

BOX 2.1

PERCEPTIONS OF THINGS PAST

It is the rare psychological phenomenon that has not been studied developmentally. For most of the standard visual illusions, for example, we have data, typically gathered by the cross-sectional method, on how the magnitude of the illusion varies with age, at least from childhood to the adult years. H. W. Leibowitz, M. Parrish, and R. M. Lundy, at Pennsylvania State University, carried out such investigations on the Ponzo illusion (Figure A—the left vertical line appears longer but is not) and on the Poggendorff illusion (Figure B—the diagonal bar appears discontinuous but actually runs straight through the rectangular block). Their results, which show quite different developmental changes for the two illusions, provided the basis for an ingenious experiment with startling implications.

This experiment set out to test the phenomenon of hypnotic age regression. This phenomenon is defined as the ability of a person, when hypnotized and instructed to go back in time, to reproduce responses typical of an earlier age but that he has not shown for a long time and that, under normal circumstances, he could not evoke at will no matter how hard he tried. An example would be to recall accurately, when you are adult, the names of all your classmates in the first grade when you have not seen or thought about them for many years. Most such studies have been open to criticism on methodological grounds; they have been criticized, for example, for not having fully ensured that the subject had not had opportunities during the intervening time span to have reexperienced or rehearsed what he is able to recall in the hypnotic, age-regressed state. Another frequent criticism is of the failure to ensure that the subject, if he tried hard enough, could not in fact remember the same things *without* hypnosis.

The Parrish-Lundy-Leibowitz experiment was designed to be free of these dangers: It was certainly unlikely that their subjects had practiced the Ponzo and Poggendorff illusions or had ever been exposed to them during their lifetimes. Also,

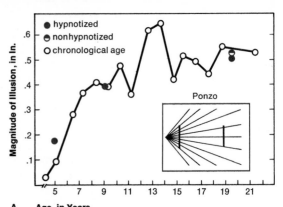

A   **Age, in Years**

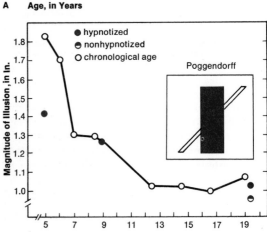

B   **Age, in Years**

as we shall see, they set up a control condition that tested the possibility that their results could have been gotten just as easily without hypnosis.

Ten nineteen-year-old volunteer undergraduates, who by prior procedures had been shown to be readily hypnotizable, were the subjects. Each subject's susceptibility to each of the two illusions was tested under four conditions (in random order), three of which required that they be in a hypnotic state: No Hypnosis, Hypnosis–No Regression, Hypnosis–Regression to Age Nine, Hypnosis–Regression to Age Five. In both of the age-regression conditions subjects, after being hypnotized, were carried back to the appropriate earlier age by a series of questions designed to elicit recall of a variety of experiences from that age (a birthday party, school events, etc.). The point of these questions was *not* to test recall but to help the subject regress to nine or five years old. What were the results, and what do they mean?

Figures A and B tell the story. Previous research with children and adults had indicated that the strength of the Ponzo illusion clearly increased with age, as indicated by the open-circle graph in Figure A. College-age subjects had been shown to be highly susceptible; so also were the nineteen-year-olds in this experiment when they were tested either in their normal, that is, nonhypnotized, state or hypnotized but not instructed to age-regress. Merely being in a state of hypnosis, then, did not alter their behavior. *But when age-regressed to age nine and to age five they showed a magnitude of Ponzo illusion almost identical with actual nine- and five-year-old children.*

So far, so good. But maybe—just maybe—these age-regressed subjects might somehow have guessed that children were less susceptible to visual illusions and, being highly suggestible, reported weaker illusions. The data for the Poggendorff illusion eliminates this alternate possibility (see Figure B). There, previous research had clearly indicated that the magnitude of the illusion *decreased* with age. And, once again the age-regressed subjects behaved quite like younger children actually had. It could hardly be argued that, somehow, age-regressed subjects could make an opposite (and accurate) guess as to how children would respond to this different illusion.

But now a new alternate explanation arises. Perhaps the results could be reproduced by nonhypnotized subjects attempting to function as nine- and five-year-olds; if so, then hypnotic age-regression would not necessarily have been demonstrated. The experimenters therefore tested another group of subjects who were not hypnotized but were instructed and helped to age-regress in a manner identical to the subjects in the two hypnotized–age-regressed groups. For both the Ponzo and Poggendorff illusions these subjects showed a substantial increase in magnitude (from what would normally be expected of college-age subjects—and from their own mean values when they were tested without the age-regression instructions). Apparently pretending increases the reported illusion—and there-

fore it cannot account for main results, which show an increase or decrease, depending on the illusion.

How then can we account for these results? To explain them by attributing them to age regression does not tell us what mechanisms are involved. The investigators merely suggest that: "Age regression facilitates the use or nonuse of visual cues in a manner appropriate to earlier stages of perceptual development." What are these cues and precisely how does hypnotic age regression modify their use? We do not yet know. But though the mystery may persist for some time, the findings from this experiment hold an important promise for the methodology of developmental research. In the area of perceptual development, at least, it suggests that longitudinal studies (tests at different ages) can be conducted at a single point in time. No need to test subjects repeatedly throughout their lives (and the lives of short-lived experimenters).

An investigation as striking in its results as this one deserves a corroboratory investigation. L. M. Ascher, T. X. Barber, and N. P. Spanos of the Medfield Foundation repeated the experiment with the same stimuli and procedures, but using nurses as subjects. This repetition had the active cooperation of Leibowitz and his colleagues. Ascher et al. failed to reproduce the original results. Why? Leibowitz has some thoughts on the matter, but he by no means feels he can fully account for the contradictory outcome: "In my opinion there are several possible bases for the differences between Barber and us. . . . One should note that Barber's subjects are nurses [and also] not volunteers. On the other hand, our subjects were enthusiastic volunteers from elementary psychology classes." He also observes that one of his colleagues, Parrish, is an unusually effective hypnotist; Barber's subjects, on the other hand, may have been less deeply hypnotized.

In any event, the implications of this investigation and their importance, both theoretically and methodologically, clearly indicate the need for further research.

M. PARRISH, R. M. LUNDY, & H. W. LEIBOWITZ. Effect of hypnotic age regression on the magnitude of the Ponzo and Poggendorff illusions. *Journal of Abnormal Pyschology*, 1969, **74**, 693–698. Copyright 1969 by The American Psychological Association. Reprinted by permission.
L. M. ASCHER, T. X. BARBER, & N. P. SPANOS. Two attempts to replicate the Parrish-Lundy-Leibowitz experiment on hypnotic age regression. Unpublished manuscript from the Medfield Foundation, Harding, Mass., 1970.
H. W. LEIBOWITZ. Personal communication, 1973.

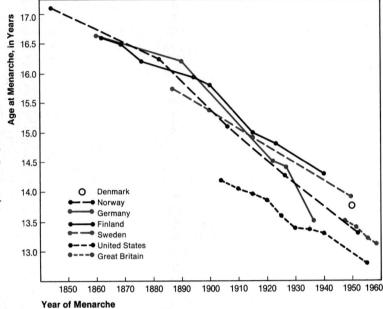

FIGURE 2.3 Secular changes in age of menarche for seven Western countries.

J. M. Tanner. *Growth at Adolescence*, 2nd ed.; adapted by permission of Blackwell Scientific Publications, Ltd., 1962.

41). At two months after conception you were about 50 percent head. At birth you were 25 percent head and the rest evenly divided between trunk and legs. Eventually, you have developed into the average adult, whose length is 50 percent legs, about one-third trunk, and only about 12–14 percent head (see Figure 2.4). (Here again we must make allowances for individual differences. Look around you at your neighbors.)

These changes come about through very different growth rates for the different parts of the body. The head starts growing at a very rapid rate almost immediately after conception. By the time the baby is born, the head has already achieved more than 60 percent of its adult size (see Figure 2.5). The trunk is next in growth rate, and by the end of the second year it has reached a point halfway to its final

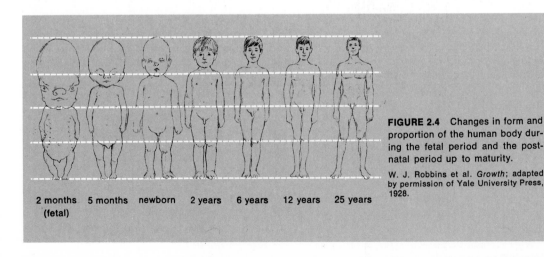

2 months (fetal)   5 months   newborn   2 years   6 years   12 years   25 years

FIGURE 2.4 Changes in form and proportion of the human body during the fetal period and the postnatal period up to maturity.

W. J. Robbins et al. *Growth*; adapted by permission of Yale University Press, 1928.

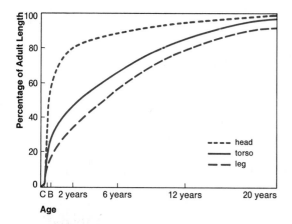

FIGURE 2.5 Differential growth of the human head, torso, and legs from conception to maturity. C stands for conception, B for birth.

length. During the second year, the legs and arms begin to grow in earnest, reaching the 50 percent point at about the fourth year. This progressive growth—first the head, then the trunk, then the legs—has been designated by the term **cephalocaudal direction** (head-to-foot).

While the body has been growing in length, it has also been growing in a **proximodistal direction,** that is, from the central part out to the peripheral part. For example, the trunk and shoulders develop first, and then the arms, fingers, and toes begin their real growth.

Correlated with these physical-growth directions, the sensorimotor behavior of the infant also shows a head-to-foot and center-to-periphery development. Nursing is the earliest and best-organized behavior in the neonate. It is, of course, primarily localized in the head. The normal infant shows the following sequence of **sensorimotor development** (Gesell & Amatruda, 1947):

4 weeks—control of eye movements; ability to follow an object visually, and so forth
16 weeks—ability to balance head
28 weeks—ability to use the hands for grasping and manipulating objects
40 weeks—control of the trunk, enabling the child to sit and crawl
52 weeks—control of the legs and feet, enabling the child to stand and cruise about

It is clear that we have here a cephalocaudal direction of development. In the development of locomotion and movement the proximodistal direction is also apparent. At first the child's purposeful movements stem from the shoulder and pelvic girdles. Later in infancy, movements appear at the elbows, wrists, knees, and ankles. For example, in reaching for something, the infant first moves his shoulders and elbows toward the object and only later does he begin to use his wrists and fingers.

A recent comparative study of motor development, contrasting American infants born in the 1960s with those born almost thirty years earlier, finds—as have many studies—the same developmental sequences and very little, if any, secular change in average age of occurrence of various motor skills within the first year (Bayley, 1965).

However, Bayley does find a substantial racial difference among her more recently born infants: Black children show distinctly more rapid motor development within the first year of life. Other investigations in the United States have reported the same finding, as have some studies of black African infants (e.g., Geber, 1958; Ainsworth, 1967). Both latter investigators attribute at least part of this precocious motor development to environmental factors, specifically to the considerable freedom of movement permitted these infants and the unusual degree of physical contact provided by their mothers. However, observations of motor reflexes at birth argue that, to some extent at least, this superiority of black infants is genetically based. [That environmental stimulation can be made to play a role in motor precocity is supported by the Zelazo et al. (1972) data reported in Box 2.3, p. 48.] Whatever the cause, sensorimotor development is subject to considerable variation in timing, but not in sequence.

Differences among organs Not only do the chief divisions of the body (head, trunk, and limbs) show variable growth rates, but so also do the different organs within the body. Furthermore, the different parts within the individual organ grow at different rates. A consideration of both these differential growth patterns—among organs and within organs—will lead us to other important developmental principles.

The various organs of man can be grouped into four different growth types, as shown in Figure 2.6. The genital organs show a positive acceleration: very slow growth during childhood and then extremely rapid acceleration at puberty. The opposite is true of the brain and its parts. Here we have a negatively accelerated growth curve, with rapid growth during the first few years of life and then a sharp slowing down. (Since by far the major portion of brain development occurs in a rather narrow time span around birth, we can understand why it is that malnutrition of the fetus and during early infancy might impede mental development, as discussed in Unit 22.)

The lymphoid group shows a growth reversal, increasing very rapidly at first, then actually decreasing in size. Finally, the general type shows an S-shaped curve—starting and ending with rapid growth periods separated by a long period of very little gain.

Differences within organs   Different parts of some of the endocrine glands (especially of the pituitary) develop at different rates. Perhaps the most interesting and important example of differential growth within a single organ is provided by the cerebral cortex.

At birth the cortex has all the neural cells it is ever going to have. As the body grows, however, certain changes occur in the brain. Among them are changes in the size and chemical composition of the nerve cells and in the length and state of development of the nerve fibers. These changes occur at different rates for different areas of the cortex. For example, the pyramidal Betz cells (important for motor control) are more advanced in overall development than is any other type of cell in the cortex from birth to the age of six months. During the first six months of life the circumference, length, structural compactness, and protective covering of the nerve fibers in the primary motor and sensory areas are far advanced over the fibers in the rest of the brain. Only later

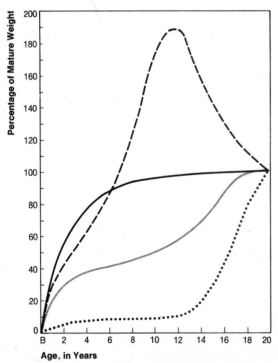

FIGURE 2.6   Curves showing growth rates of the four major categories of organs or tissue types in the human body. Examples of each category are listed.

R. E. Scammon. The measurement of the body in childhood. In J. A. Harris et al., *The Measurement of Man*; copyright 1930 by the University of Minnesota; adapted by permission of the University of Minnesota Press.

– – **Lymphoid Type**
thymus, lymph nodes, intestinal lymphoid masses

—— **Neural Type**
brain and its parts, spinal cord, and so on

—— **General Type**
respiratory and digestive organs, kidneys, musculature as a whole, skeleton as a whole

•••• **Genital Type**
testis, ovary, uterine tube, prostate, seminal vesicles

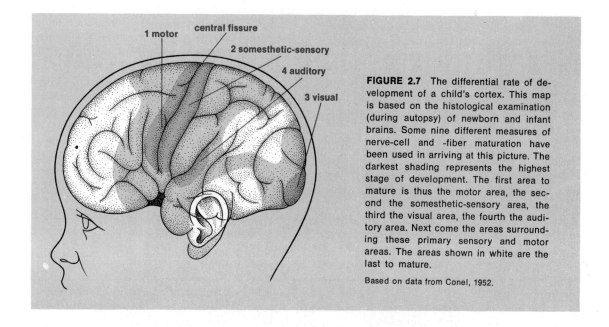

FIGURE 2.7 The differential rate of development of a child's cortex. This map is based on the histological examination (during autopsy) of newborn and infant brains. Some nine different measures of nerve-cell and -fiber maturation have been used in arriving at this picture. The darkest shading represents the highest stage of development. The first area to mature is thus the motor area, the second the somesthetic-sensory area, the third the visual area, the fourth the auditory area. Next come the areas surrounding these primary sensory and motor areas. The areas shown in white are the last to mature.

Based on data from Conel, 1952.

do the other areas of the brain develop to the mature level (see Figure 2.7).

The human infant is born with a brain whose parts and functions mature at different rates. The sensory and motor areas can begin to function relatively early, and simple conditioning may be possible, but the association areas (presumably those importantly involved in complex perception and problem solving) are just not ready to go to work until some later time. Recent evidence, reviewed in Unit 18, page 434, suggests that brain growth is influenced, at least in animals, by early experience.

Maturation and Learning

The story of bodily growth suggests that the development of behavior will show a successive unfolding of functions and capacities as their underlying bodily structures develop. If we were to ask, therefore, why the behavior of the older child is much more complex than that of the infant, we could not merely answer learning or experience. The recognition of this point has led to the following **maturation-learning principle:** The development of behavior reflects **maturation**

through growth, as well as the cumulative effects of learning through experience.

But what can the infant learn?

Learning in the newborn and in the infant   Attempts to demonstrate some form of learning in the newborn—say in the first week or so of life—have met with inconsistent success and have led to considerable controversy over theoretical and methodological fine points. The newborn does show habituation, that is, he shows a decrease in response to initially innately arousing stimuli when they are repeated over and over again (Kessen, Haith, & Salapatek, 1970). For example, a certain sound may at first elicit a variety of behaviors in the newborn, indicating that he is aware of the stimulus, but, upon repetition, this responsiveness wanes. Habituation is the most primitive form of learning (see Unit 15, p. 360), if it is indeed learning; it does not require a new response, but rather ceasing from an unlearned one. Somewhat higher forms of learning, such as classical conditioning (Unit 15) and instrumental learning (Unit 16), have sometimes been demonstrated for the newborn. For the former we have the example of sucking to a specific sound that has been paired with feeding (Lipsitt & Kage, 1964); for the latter we have the example of newborn infants learning to turn their heads when rewarded by administration of a sugar solution (Sigueland & Lipsitt, 1966). And the fact that, within the first few weeks of life, the infant apparently learns to produce voluntarily an initially reflex response may also be taken as evidence of newborn learning (see Box 2.3, p. 48).

When we recall that the cortex of the newborn is quite undeveloped and that we do not even have clear evidence that her cortical cells can conduct impulses at all, the blankness of the newborn becomes understandable. The most impatient of parents must wait for growth. Furthermore, we must remember that as the child grows older her cortex first becomes a motor cortex, then a motor-sensory one, and only later do the various association areas mature.

But learning, of various forms rapidly becomes more evident after only several weeks of life. In part this is the result of the rapid development of the central nervous system during this period; in part it is the result of the number of things the infant has already learned, which facilitates further and more complex learning.

There is no debate as to whether the infant is capable of learning once he is well launched into the first year of life. Proud parents by then firmly believe that they are dealing with a responsive human being—and a potential adult. What can be, and are, debated are a number of issues concerning what is learned, how and when it is best to learn, and even—in a special sense—*why* learning takes place. (For a provocative view of the "why" of some learning, see Box 2.2, p. 46). The issue of *when* best to learn, as it relates to the maturational progress of the human infant, has obvious practical implications and thus has long been a popular one.

Readiness for training   The maturation-learning principle suggests that certain training should not be undertaken until the child is specifically ready for it. It might then be thought that the child psychologist could draw up a list of the ages at which the child becomes ready for different kinds of training and that this list could be used to guide both parents and teacher. Some lists have been attempted, but two major considerations limit the applicability of such readiness guides.

First, although some performances develop despite restricted stimulation, the amount and kinds of general stimulation may in fact speed up some of the innate growth factors. For example, some data suggest that the continued transmission of impulses through the nervous system speeds up the maturation of the nerve fibers. Thus it is thought that the very attempt to learn and the stimulation of the child in that attempt may speed up the maturation process. The animal data on anatomical and biochemical modifications of the cortex caused by early experience strongly support this idea (see Unit 18).

Second, there are large individual differences in maturation rates. This statement holds true whether we use such measures as body weight or sensitivity to various emotional, social, and intellectual situations (see Figure 2.8). The maturation-learning principle, as a guide to the educational program for a child, must be applied with full allowance for such individual differences. From a wide range of research reports, it can be estimated that when a first-grade teacher meets her class of youngsters, all about six years of age, she is in fact confronted with an array of children who, on various abilities, in fact vary in readiness from ages three to eleven. Within a single child there may be a variation of several years in readiness, depending upon the particular aspects of learning considered. Thus the proper timing for effective training requires sensitive and subtle judgment —and a great deal more research of the sort found in Box 2.3, page 48.

Differentiation of Structure and Function

As the major parts of the body, its organs and its systems, develop, greater and greater precision of function within any one system becomes possible. For example, at first the entire upper half of the child's body—starting with the

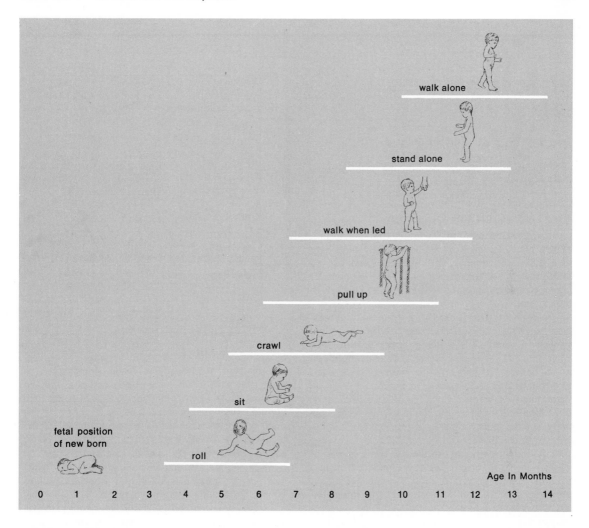

FIGURE 2.8   One indication of the extent of individual differences in maturation rate is seen in the development of walking. Although the *order* in which children progress from one stage to another is similar, the *age* at which the different stages are reached varies greatly. Shown here are the age *zones* within which 95 percent of a group of 215 infants studied at a well-known baby clinic in Rochester, Minnesota, reached the various stages of performance. In general, there was more than a four-month spread for any one stage. For example, some children were able to stand alone at about eight and a half months; others were not able to stand alone until thirteen months.

Data from Aldrich & Norval, 1946.

shoulder region and involving the arms, hands, and fingers—moves spasmodically and excitedly toward a desired object. With development, more and more limited movements are used until finally only the fingers—or even only one finger—may languidly and surely stretch out to retrieve the object.

This gradual narrowing down or differentiation of behavior from a massive, all-inclusive pattern to several precise, limited, and relatively independent ones has been observed at all levels of analysis. It summarizes the difference between the behavior of the newborn and that of early childhood. It is apparent in the growth

BOX 2.2

SMILING, COOING, AND "THE GAME"

"The Game" is not important to the infant because people play it, but rather people become important to the infant because they play "The Game."

With those words John S. Watson, a psychologist at the University of California (Berkeley), concludes his proposal of a hypothesis that may help to explain why infants learn. Further (and not so incidentally), he suggests how in this process of learning they also learn to become involved with human beings.

What is "The Game"? As it naturally occurs, it is a certain kind of interaction between an adult, typically a parent, and a young infant. Watson gives some familiar examples of adults' initiating such interactions: "They touch [the infant's] nose each time he widens his eyes, or they bounce him on their knee each time he bobs his head, or they blow on his belly each time he jiggles his legs, or they make sounds after he makes a sound." What is the general principle here? The infant is being provided with an opportunity to experience some sense of control over a feature in his environment by having a certain behavior of the adult become contingent upon a bit of his own behavior (e.g., his head bob leads to a knee bounce). As the particular game is repeated over and over again, the infant gradually becomes aware of this clear contingency—of his ability to have some adult behavior *reliably* happen on his behavioral say-so. And with this awareness he begins to smile and coo enthusiastically at the human face hovering over him. At this point, Watson asserts, a rudimentary social reaction has been learned to a stimulus (the face) that initially had power to elicit neither a smile nor a coo.

What led Watson to this hypothesis? As is so often the case in research in general, the idea evolved as a by-product of a number of experiments on two rather different questions. We will discuss only a few of these experiments. First there are the findings from his own studies and those of

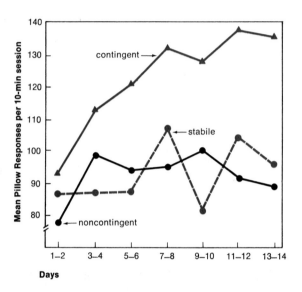

Days

others that infants in the early months of life rapidly develop a tendency to smile vigorously at a front view of a silent human face and that they so respond most of all when the face is vertical and upright. That infants should become happy at the presence of a face seems sensible enough since faces in his environment are typically attached to people, primarily to his mother, who is the source of good things for him. But why should the infant smile most at an *upright* face? If you observe mother-infant interactions, Watson suggests, it is *not* the case that the mother is characteristically face-to-face with the infant at the moments when she is dispensing food and succor to her baby. So, wondered Watson, during what kind of interaction with an infant is the adult usually face-to-face with him? His answer: "When the adult is playing 'The Game.'"

But what earlier experimental evidence was there that, in fact, becoming aware of the power to control elicited smiling and cooing in the infant? J. McV. Hunt and I. Uzgiris of the University of Illinois noticed this response first, reporting that a few infants who learned to control the movements of a mobile attached to their cribs by jiggling their bodies tended to act out the following sequence: jiggling, watching the resultant movement of the mobile, *and smiling and cooing at the effect.*

Hunt and Uzgiris drew a different interpretation from these observations, one that need not concern us here. However, in another experiment—and this was part of the second, quite different, direction mentioned earlier—Watson and C. Ramey made a similar observation. Their investigation set out to determine whether infants (eighteen of them) could learn to control the movements of an overhead mobile. The mobile was rigged to turn for 1 sec when, and only when, they pressed their heads down on a pillow specially designed to activate it (see photo). This apparatus was installed in the homes of these eighteen infants (the Contingent group), and they had a 10-min experience with it daily for two weeks, beginning at age eight weeks.

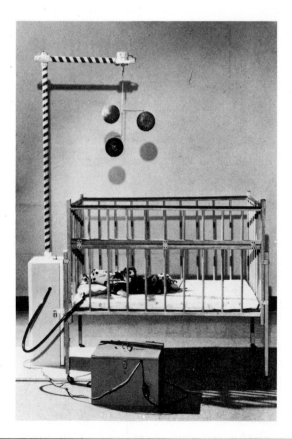

Two control groups were used, each with eleven additional infants: (1) the Stabile group for whom the mobile always remained immobile and (2) the Noncontingent group for whom the mobile moved but not in response to their head movements. The figure clearly demonstrates that only the Contingent-group infants showed an increase in pillow-pressing responses. What the figure does not show but is reported by Watson and Ramey is that "the mothers of the infants with contingent mobiles almost unanimously reported the appearance of vigorous smiling and cooing in their infants [starting] on approximately the third or fourth day of exposure." Mothers of control infants reported very much less smiling.

Thus Watson and Ramey found the same results as Hunt and Uzgiris but with the important addition that smiling and cooing were directly and systematically related to a specific experience. But Watson's interpretation of this phenomenon is a unique one: He is proposing that an infant begins learning its essential attachment to the human family because it happens to be a human being who plays "The Game" first and most frequently. In this way, the infant's earliest signs of attachment—smiling and cooing—accidentally become expressed toward members of its own species. Watson would insist that an infant would start becoming attached to any mechanical contrivance if such a contrivance happened to be the most reliable source of a contingent response. But he would also insist that the accident is no accident but rather a necessarily evolved mechanism through which "we are normally guaranteed to begin vigorous smiling and cooing at fellow species members."

So, to complete the circle, " 'The Game' is *not* important to the infant because people play it, but rather people become important to the infant because they play 'The Game.' "

J. S. WATSON. Smiling, cooing, and "the game." *Merrill-Palmer Quarterly*, 1972, **18**, 323–339.
Photo courtesy of John S. Watson.
J. S. WATSON. Perception of object orientation in infants. *Merrill-Palmer Quarterly*, 1966, **12**, 73–94.
J. HUNT & I. UZGIRIS. Cathexis from recognitive familiarity: An exploratory study. Paper presented at the annual meeting of the American Psychological Association, Los Angeles, 1964.
J. S. WATSON & C. RAMEY. Reactions to response contingent stimulation in early infancy. Revision of paper presented at the biennial meeting of the Society for Research in Child Development, Santa Monica, Cal., 1969.

BOX 2.3

WHAT'S THE RUSH?

The maturation-learning principle has been tested on various forms of behavior, from locomotion skills to the learning of language. Figure A is taken from a study by J. R. Hilgard at the Merrill-Palmer nursery school with twenty-eight-month-old children, of whom eight were trained for twelve weeks on climbing up and down a three-step ladder 2½ ft high, and eight others were not. Both groups earned equivalent scores on a preliminary test. The untrained group, after *one* week of practice, caught up with the twelve-week-trained group. As far as this skill is concerned, "premature" practice shows considerable waste.

   Much the same general conclusion, for earlier ages, can be drawn from studies of motor development in other societies which swaddle their infants, that is, keep them tightly wrapped in such a manner as to prevent effectively almost all bodily movement for the first year or so of life. Typically, the motor skills of such infants after they are no longer swaddled are observed, after a brief initial period of awkwardness, to be as good as the never-swaddled children of the same age.

   P. R. and N. A. Zelazo and S. Kolb provide an interesting exception to this general picture of ineffectiveness of early experience on later motor development. Their starting point was the fact that a newborn infant will make walking-like leg move-

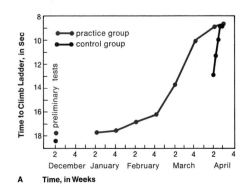

A   **Time, in Weeks**

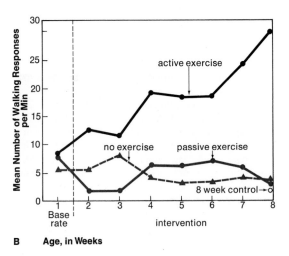

B   **Age, in Weeks**

of motor skills and in the development of the emotional life of the child. The same story is repeated again and again: From a large general pattern, several specialized ones are differentiated.

Differentiation and the newborn   This principle is readily seen in the developmental history of the newborn. Although the neonate has some quite specific reflexes and response patterns, it can be described as a generalized organism. Any one of a large number of different kinds of stimuli can call forth the neonate's responses, and these responses are rarely localized in any one part of the body or muscle group. As the neonate becomes an infant, there is progressively less and less involvement of the entire organism in response to a given stimulus. It has been suggested that the generalized active fetus is the one who most quickly develops the finer specialized movements as he becomes an infant (see Box 2.4, p. 50).

ments if he is held upright and his feet are permitted to touch a flat surface; this unlearned behavior normally is not shown after about two months of age. These investigators set out to determine whether intentional exercise of this walking reflex would cause an infant to walk earlier than might otherwise be expected, which, on the average, is at about fourteen months. Four groups of six infants each were studied: (1) an Active Exercise group whose walking reflexes were elicited for 12 min daily from the start of their second week of life through to the end of the eighth week; (2) a Passive Exercise group who were put through the same schedule of movement experiences but by having their legs and arms manipulated by others while they lay prone; (3) a No Exercise group whose spontaneous walking responses were tested weekly, as were those of the first two groups; (4) a second nonexercised group tested *only* at eight weeks of age, known as the Eight-Week Control group.

Figure B dramatically illustrates the data basis for the investigators' conclusion that "there is little doubt that learning occurred" for Active Exercise infants during their eight-week training period. They assert that, during this time, a reflexive response came to be a learned, voluntary, and enthusiastically practiced response. The other three groups, in contrast, showed clear evidence of the expected weakening of the response by the end of the eighth week.

So far so good. But did the Active Exercise group, after a year or so of necessary physical maturation, walk any earlier? Yes. They were effec-tively walking at 10.1 months, while the other three groups first walked significantly later: Passive Exercise, 11.4 months; No Exercise, 11.7; Eight-Week Control, 12.4.

These researchers regard this demonstrated acceleration as desirable not because earlier walking is necessarily a blessing (it may be the reverse for the harried parent), but because it may provide the infant with an earlier-than-usual sense of competence because of his earlier ability in moving about in his environment. They may be correct in this conjecture—many psychologists in recent years have been stressing the importance of providing the infant with experiences of this general sort. But M. J. Konner of Harvard takes a neutral position. Drawing on his own and others' observations of wide variations in the ages at which various skills are attained in different societies, he suggests that different peoples evolve training practices that tend to adjust motor development to a schedule most adaptive to their way of life. He notes that groups whose survival depends on easy mobility (e.g., hunters and foragers) need *and succeed* in raising infants who walk earlier. Konner concludes that "speedy motor development has no a priori claim to desirability."

J. R. HILGARD. Learning and maturation in pre-school children. *Journal of Genetic Psychology*, 1932, **41**, 36–56. Figure A adapted by permission of The Journal Press.
P. R. ZELAZO, N. A. ZELAZO, & S. KOLB. Walking in the newborn. *Science*, 1972, **176**, 314–315. Copyright 1972 by the American Association for the Advancement of Science.
M. J. KONNER. Newborn walking: Additional data. *Science*, 1973, **178**, 307.

Activity level is a characteristic of the organism that shows unusual promise as a fundamental biological-behavioral characteristic. As we see in Unit 1, it appears to possess at least some genetic basis. What is more, activity level seems to be a relatively persistent human trait, at least in the earlier years of development. Even within the first few days of life, when the newborn is a generally disorganized and unpredictable creature, its activity level represents one of its few consistent behavioral features (Bell, 1960; Kessen et al., 1961). This consistency extends through the first two years of life, according to Thomas et al. (1964), and activity level observed during this early period significantly predicts this same aspect of behavior throughout childhood (Escalona & Heider, 1959; Kagan & Moss, 1962). What makes this phenomenon potentially arresting is the mass of evidence that points to infantile stimulation (and a high activity level may serve as a form of self-stimulation) as an important determinant of

BOX 2.4

**PREDICTING BEHAVIOR DEVELOPMENT
FROM FETAL MOVEMENTS**

T. W. Richards and H. Newberg of the Fels Institute at Antioch College have reported that the movements of the fetus in the uterus foretell its rate of behavioral development after birth.

At one-week intervals, during the last two months of pregnancy, each of twelve women recorded every fetal movement she felt over a 5-hr period. From these records each fetus received a fetal-movement score in terms of the average number of minutes it was active per 10-min period.

Six months after birth the babies were tested on the Gesell schedule of behavioral development, consisting of tasks like dropping an object into a cup, sitting alone, looking for a fallen object, and so on. The results showed a positive correlation (about .65) between fetal-movement score and performance on the Gesell schedule. For example, the babies who passed the test of dropping an object into a cup had earned a fetal-movement score of 5.76; those who failed had a score of 3.31. Those who passed the sit-alone test had earned a fetal-movement score of 4.88; those who failed had a score of 2.90.

The investigators suggest the following interpretation: The movements felt by the mother indicate the level of development of the generalized behavior of the fetus. Out of this generalized behavior are differentiated the various precise motor movements of infancy. Therefore, the more advanced the organism is in the development of his *generalized* behavior, the sooner his *precise* motor movements become differentiated.

T. W. RICHARDS & H. NEWBERG. Studies in fetal behavior. *Child Development*, 1938, **9**, 79–86.

of the kind of people they are and the kind of baby with which they have been blessed. A highly active infant demands certain responses from a parent that are different from what a placid infant would call forth, and what a particular parent actually does (and feels) depends on how well he is suited temperamentally, for example, to be the father of such an ever-moving, bouncing baby. In short, an infant can mold his father's behavior, as well as the more generally accepted other way around.

Freedman (1972) has commented on a similar phenomenon on a cultural level. Reporting his data showing that Navajo newborns are generally more placid, motorically and emotionally, he goes on to question the common speculation that the generally subdued emotionality of Navajo children results from their having been swaddled on a cradle board throughout infancy. He suggests the reverse: that Navajo babies are particularly suited, physically and temperamentally, to the cradle board in that they are more likely to *permit it* than highly active and complaining babies.

Individual Differences in Development

Behavior does not always show a constant progression in complexity or integration. There seem to be lapses in development and even apparent regressions. In addition, the tremendous individual differences in growth and development, for example, the timing of puberty, arise, at least in part, from genetic factors. The fact that skeletal, hormonal, and other developmental statuses do not always correspond to chronological age may cause problems for both parent and child. People expect, for example, that a certain height and body build will go along with a correspondingly developed maturity of interests and emotions. The child who is larger than the average ten-year-old is expected to be more mature than the average ten-year-old in other respects as well. But when he behaves like a typical ten-year-old or shows the muscular coordination typical of a ten-year-old, an observer may feel that the child is backward or awkward. The child who is retarded (compared with the average) in his body growth or emotional maturity may also encounter adjustment prob-

later resistance to stress and of cortical growth.

We must not overlook, as it is too easy to do, that these built-in characteristics of an infant may easily influence his social environment. Parents do not treat their infants alike. To a significant extent the parents' behaviors (and attitudes) toward their child represent a blend

lems. In part, they may arise from the fact that he differs from his schoolmates and cannot meet the expectations of his teachers and the adults surrounding him. But the story is more complicated (see p. 696).

THE ADOLESCENT PERIOD

The period of growth and development known as **adolescence** is variously defined, but most often it refers to the rather long period between childhood and mature adulthood, during which there are both quantitative and qualitative changes in various characteristics of the organism. We have suggested earlier that adolescence shows a continuing trend toward attainment of adult status. This fact, combined with the enormous range of individual differences in rate of development in physical growth, sexual maturation, and so on, foredooms any attempt to define the age range that encompasses adolescence. Keeping in mind that, on the average, girls develop approximately two years earlier than boys in the various aspects of adolescence and that, within each sex, individuals may differ by several years, we can provide a rough timetable for a number of developmental landmarks: First, sexual maturity, as measured by a number of indicators (breast development and menarche in girls, pubic and other hair growth in both sexes), is reached sometime between ages twelve and sixteen in girls and between ages thirteen and eighteen in boys. Second, skeletal maturity is achieved between ages thirteen and nineteen in girls and between ages fourteen and twenty in boys.

Adolescence, in a physical sense, is under the control of physiological (largely hormonal) factors, and, as these factors are more or less easily measurable, it is not too difficult to define the onset of physical adolescence. (Unit 22 also treats sexual maturation.) But adolescence is also a psychological phenomenon, and here we encounter differing expectations and criteria. Cultures of different countries and different ethnic and socioeconomic groups in any one country vary widely as to when they regard the adolescent as having become an adult. The end

of adolescence is primarily a cultural and psychological phenomenon.

Psychological End of Adolescence

There are several reasons why any period set aside as the end of adolescence must be arbitrary. In the first place, here, as elsewhere, there are wide individual differences. In the second place, psychological maturity cannot be a unitary event. A person may mature in one respect much more rapidly than in others, and no doubt some of us go through life without ever maturing in some areas. But more important than these reasons—or perhaps underlying these reasons—is the influence of the cultural pattern.

Maturity and Culture

Perhaps the most important psychological characteristics of the adolescent are an awakening of primary sexual interest accompanied by an ability to do something about it. And it is at this point that the culture within which the adolescent lives becomes important.

Traditionally, Western society has insisted that, aside from a certain degree of illicit experimentation (which was tolerated if it did not become too serious), full-blown sexuality was reserved for adults. Sexual privilege has long been regarded as going hand in hand with the acceptance of adult status, carrying with it attendant responsibilities and controls. The path toward adult sexuality, thus defined, is a socialized one, tying in with increased personal maturity as maturity is defined by society. This role definition no doubt contributes to the normal adolescent's motivation to achieve fully adult status.

In recent years, however, the traditional path has become blurred; many adolescents today see little connection between sexual freedom, which is regarded as an essential part of personal growth and self-expression, and the acceptance of other requirements of the adult role. In this sense, biologically mature behavior and psychosocially mature behavior are now only tenuously related, especially in certain subcultures. The generation gap we hear so much about may be, at least in part, a reflection and a result of removing psychosocial maturity—of the acceptance of the full adult role as defined by society—as a prerequisite for sexual opportunity.

Whether this separation is a transient one or instead will itself become a part of enduring societal values cannot be foreseen at the moment. Nor can we yet safely hazard a guess at its effects upon personality development into adulthood.

THE ADULT YEARS

Considering current estimates of life expectancy, there are still fifty years or more after the adolescent has been ushered across the threshold into adulthood. We shall have little to say about psychological development of individuals during this extensive period, for the most part because truly developmental studies of change during this time span are few. Courtship behavior, occupational and vocational choice and achievement, marriage, parenthood, retirement—all these psychosocial events have been studied by psychologists, sociologists, and others. But they have been, typically, studies at a single point in time. We thus know relatively little concerning the course of development, say in marital adjustment or occupational achievement, in the same group of individuals over any substantial time span during adulthood.

Personality Changes

This same gap is evident in our understanding of personality change during the adult years. Until recently, psychologists have focused their studies of personality development on childhood and adolescence, assuming that personality is formed during these early years and remains essentially unchanged thereafter. (Our discussion of determinants of personality in Unit 28 reflects this bias.) This view is now questioned. Some psychologists today believe that the individual continues to develop and change throughout life, and this more recent point of departure has resulted in an explosion over the last decade or so of research interest in adult personality development.

Much of this work is still in a formative stage, and a number of conflicting findings and theories abound. Research into adult development follows roughly two approaches: The first is concerned with reactions to social and environmental events such as, in early life, starting one's first job, marriage, parenthood, possibly divorce; in later years, the critical events include children leaving home, widowhood, retirement, and failing health.

The second approach focuses on personality changes independent of environmental events. The assumption here is that personality follows its own path of growth and change, apart from external stimulation, much as in the developmental stages of childhood. A group of researchers at the University of Chicago have been the wellspring for extensive research on changes in psychological processes throughout the life span, based on the assumption that the individual is constantly developing through a series of normative stages. (Much of this work appears in a collection of studies entitled *Middle Age and Aging*, Neugarten, 1968.) The theme of these studies is that the individual, during the first two-thirds of his life, develops outward, toward the environment. During the last third of his life, however, he turns inward, toward the self. According to this view, changes from adolescence to young adulthood are marked by greater expressiveness, expansiveness, autonomy, and competence. These changes are followed in early adulthood by a period of consolidation and stability lasting until the early forties. At about this stage, the person begins to shift from outer to inner concerns. This shift, the researchers suggest, may be attributed to the inescapable realization that there now is a limited amount of life left to live.

Neugarten (1973), in examining changes throughout the life span, has identified what she calls an internal social time clock that people have for covering events they expect to happen during a typical lifetime. A woman, for example, may expect a sequence of events to occur at certain age periods in her life—courtship, marriage, child-rearing, child-leaving, widowhood—that serves as a kind of framework upon which she projects her future and prepares for it. When events do not match the projected timetable, they may have distressing effects.

One important question is whether personality remains essentially stable and continuous toward the end of life or, in response to major role changes, shows change. One study, for example, of people sixty years and older who have been followed for about ten years reveals an essential stability in life style and activity level (Maddox, 1968). Other studies show that events that were thought to stimulate major changes in adjustment and life style —for example, menopause, widowhood, retirement, children leaving home—do not appear to do so. These studies all support the view that personality remains essentially stable. Furthermore, several studies show that underlying characteristics like ego strength—essentially, the ability to see the world realistically, to cope with it adaptively, and to derive satisfaction from living in it—do seem to persist well into old age.

Old Age

Allied to this finding is the hypothesis that many so-called age changes, whether they occur in fundamental personality structure, intellectual ability, or other aspects of behavior, are in reality functions of true physical debilitation, rather than age per se. In other words, as long as the individual, no matter what his age, remains essentially healthy physically, he will remain much the same person, psychologically speaking, that he has always been. Thus, some of the bugaboos of aging, as far as research now can tell, turn out to be neither necessarily dramatic nor universally unfortunate events. The menopause not only fails to signal the end of womanhood, but quite frequently it is a relatively ignored and even welcome event. Retirement, similarly, may have been overemphasized as a dreaded occurrence. For many individuals this event is not a burden but a goal attained. One study of older, retired men (Reichard et al., 1962) suggests that retirement and aging in general can provide, for men particularly, an opportunity for the satisfaction of needs not satisfied during earlier years. Growing old may even bring about increased self-

acceptance as a man comes to terms with his life goals and achievements.

On the other hand, Cumming and Henry (1961) put forth a disengagement theory of aging; they suggest that intrinsic to aging is a gradual severing of ties, responsibilities, and involvement with the social environment. This process results in a consequent easing of some of the strains of living, providing for some an avenue toward comfortable and satisfying later years. But it also argues against the continuity of personal style into the later years.

Another focus of research in this field centers around the question of successful aging and, predictably, the two just-cited investigations disagree somewhat on the ability to maintain one's usual level of activity as one ages. Cumming and Henry found that higher morale exists among older persons who reduce their activity by successfully disengaging from social activities. In contrast, Reichard et al. reported that, for those older men whose lifelong goal had been passivity, retirement, as well as aging in general, brought relief from burdensome obligations; for others, whose sense of satisfaction and esteem depended on competence and activity, high morale after retirement depended on remaining active and pursuing vigorously their earlier interests. Findings such as these of course indicate a basic continuity of personality throughout life and question disengagement as the only mode for aging successfully.

The study of adult development and aging is still in its infancy. We have already noted that most of the research is based on cross-sectional studies, that is, comparisons between different groups at different ages. The problem here is that there are also cultural differences between persons of different ages; researchers cannot yet be sure which differences are due to aging per se and which are due to cultural, generational, and secular differences among the groups studied. But there are increasing efforts to study the same individuals over time; as the results of these studies emerge, we can expect to gain new insights into some of the controversies outlined here and to clarify aspects of psychological development over the life span.

Where we perhaps still remain most in the dark—a darkness of fear as well as of ignorance—is on the process of dying and the inevitable event of death. We confront here the taboo in Western society on discussing, and certainly on researching, this critically impor-tant human area. But even this veil is finally being lifted and the beginnings of questioning are becoming evident. Box I.3 provides us with one example of how this until-now for-bidden subject has come under appropriate and useful scrutiny.

SUMMARY

1. Because human development is characterized by almost continuous change, both as we grow toward maturity and as we age, the study of psychology is in very large part a developmental study. Development is typically gradual and contin-uous; relatively abrupt upsurges and declines in both structure and function can be observed outwardly, but they are merely visible expressions of an actually continuous underlying developmental process. Genetic factors, for example, often must await the culmination of gradual maturational changes before they become expressed and observable.

2. Developmental rates vary considerably among individuals in most characteristics, as do the times at which various developmental milestones are reached. Further-more, ceilings, or mature levels of development, show substantial individual differ-ences. Development also frequently involves increased differentiation in addition to simple quantitative growth; at times this differentiation process results in progres-sion through a sequence of qualitatively distinct stages of maturity.

3. These various aspects of the developmental process can be combined and con-densed to yield a relatively few general models of the developmental process, which can serve to describe the course of growth for many human characteristics.

4. There are three primary methods for the study of human development: cross-sectional, retrospective, and longitudinal. Each method can provide data on age changes in a given characteristic through its development, and each possesses certain advantages. They also have their special shortcomings. Cross-sectional studies are unable to describe developmental change within individuals, and their results are subject to serious misinterpretation if they do not take into consid-eration secular changes. Retrospective studies risk substantial error because of their reliance on highly fallible recall of earlier experiences. Longitudinal studies are costly, time-consuming, and vulnerable to loss of subjects during the period of study. Their results also can safely be applied only to the particular generation studied.

5. The child is not merely a miniature adult; rather, he differs qualitatively and quantitatively from an adult in many of his physical characteristics and behav-ioral potentials. The period of growth and development begins at birth (actually at conception) and continues through adolescence, with most rapid changes occurring shortly after birth and during the few years before puberty. Early development is primarily cephalocaudal (head-to-foot) and proximodistal (center-to-periphery), facts reflected in differing rates of growth in various physical organs and behavioral skills.

6. Behavioral development during the early years reflects both physical maturation through growth and differentiation and the cumulative effects of training, learning, and general experience. Even the newborn infant can show certain simple forms of responses and within the first few months of life shows rapid increases in various learning abilities. Maturation and learning generally interact, although with insufficient maturation the effects of experience may be lost on the unready organism.

7. Differentiation is the hallmark of the early developmental process, with gross patterns of reactivity gradually being transformed into more articulated and discriminating behavioral action. There are wide individual differences in this process.

8. The activity level of the infant is one of the few characteristics evident at birth that tends to persist at least into later childhood. Variations in such built-in characteristics in infants may be regarded as, to some extent, effecting variations in their parents' behavior toward them.

9. Adolescence is a highly variable period (both with regard to physical change and behavior development) that intervenes between childhood and adulthood. Aside from the difficulty of defining this period for a given individual (characteristics vary considerably within a person in the time they take to become fully developed), differences among people are truly enormous, permitting variations of several years in the onset and duration of many adolescent maturation tasks.

10. Although adolescence is initiated by and is largely under the control of physiological events, important behavioral factors are involved, particularly with respect to the end of adolescence. Not only are individual differences in rate of physical maturation responsible for profound psychological effects, but, more generally, cultural variations in definitions of adolescence and demands for attainment of full adult status have substantial developmental consequences.

11. The adult years, extending from entrance into adulthood through old age, are a little-studied period of development. They are, however, developmental, in the sense that change occurs throughout this span of life as marriage, child-rearing, and vocational choice and achievement generate a continual flux in environmental demands. By and large, many of the assumed tragic points of relinquishment and decline have, through research, been found either not to exist, in a psychological sense, or to bring with them new satisfactions. Whether these new satisfactions derive from the lessening of activity permitted by a gradual disengagement from society's demands or whether they are attributable to the greater freedom to go one's own way—in whatever direction—is still under debate.

GLOSSARY

adolescence Refers to the age between puberty and adulthood. Although the beginning of adolescence can be set quite accurately (as it is defined by the specific physiological criterion of sexual maturity), the terminal point of adolescence can only be approximated, for there is no sharp differentiation between adolescence and adulthood.

cephalocaudal direction Refers to the progressive growth of the body parts from the head to the legs, characteristic of the developing human being. From the Greek word *kephale* (head) and the Latin word *cauda* (tail), from head to tail.

cross-sectional studies A method for developmental investigation in which developmental trends are based upon comparisons of groups who differ in age at a given time.

differentiation In growth studies, the gradual narrowing down of behavior from a massive, simultaneous pattern of many responses to several more limited and independently controlled responses.

longitudinal studies   A method for developmental investigations in which the same individuals provide data directly on at least two (and usually several) occasions in the course of their development.

maturation   Refers to the progressive or successive unfolding of various bodily and mental functions and capacities as their underlying bodily structures develop through the normal growth process.

maturation-learning principle   The generalization that the development of behavior shows the effects of interaction between maturational and learning processes.

proximodistal direction   Refers to the progressive growth of the body parts from the central to the peripheral or terminal parts, a direction of growth characteristic of the developing human being. The shoulders thus develop first, then the arms, then the hands and fingers.

puberty   Refers to the earliest age at which a person is capable of procreating offspring. The term *pubescence* refers to the achievement of sexual maturity.

retrospective studies   A method for developmental investigations in which recalled data are employed.

secular change   Average change in a characteristic that takes place over successive generations, rather than changes that occur in the course of an individual's development.

sensorimotor development   The development of behavior showing coordination between perception and action, for example, the ability to direct the hand to the point in space where an object is visually perceived.

stages of development   Developmental periods, usually following a progressive sequence, that on an observable level represent qualitative changes in either structure or function.

De anima

·VĒTRICVLVS· ·II·VĒTRICVLVS· ·III·VĒTRICVLVS·

the nervous system

unit
3

DO YOU KNOW…

the difference between a nerve and a neuron?

that the nervous system has special chemicals that carry messages over distances that measure .00002 cm?

what is meant by the all-or-none law of nerve activity?

that some elements in the brain are more active when you are asleep than when you are awake?

that the body has a built-in clock which produces a regular rhythm of activity in the brain?

that different major parts of the brain seem to have different roles in the control of behavior?

why a blow to the eye can make you "see stars," that is, have an experience of light?

Very early attempts were made to represent a dissected brain pictorially. The early anatomists situated common sense, the imagination, the power of reasoning, and the memory in the frontal lobe, midbrain, and cerebellum.
Woodcut by Albertus Magnus, 1506/The Bettmann Archive

CONTENTS

When we consider the structures and processes that determine the activity of man, we find ourselves concerned with the nervous system—the brain, the spinal cord, and the nerves. It will be helpful to begin to understand how the nervous system works by considering a single nerve cell—one unit of the nervous system.

THE NERVE CELL

In the human body there are 10 billion nerve cells or **neurons**, which differ widely in their shape, size, and activity; nevertheless, there are basic similarities among these 10 billion cells (see Figure 3.1). All nerve cells share many features with other cells of the body. For example, each contains a **nucleus**, in which are found the determinants of the activity the cell will display; the nucleus is embedded within a **cell body**, where the many chemical processes take place that comprise the respiration and metabolism of the cell. The outer portion of the entire cell is called the **cell membrane**; it is actively involved in the chemical reactions to be discussed and is not simply an inert skin whose only role is to maintain the physical shape of the cell.

Conduction of the Nerve Impulse

The important and distinctive features of nerve cells depend upon a specialized development of the cell membrane. All cells in the body respond to stimulation of the cell membrane by a change in shape or in chemical or electrical activity. A nerve cell is unique in that certain forms of electrical or chemical stimulation of the cell membrane will produce a change in the membrane in portions far removed from the site of stimulation, and, further, this change can take place rapidly, reliably, and without injury to the cell.

The structure of a nerve cell takes advantage of this characteristic: Most nerve cells have one or more long **processes**, that is, extensions,

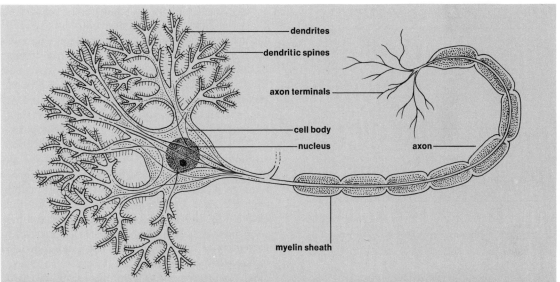

dendrites

dendritic spines

axon terminals

cell body

nucleus

axon

myelin sheath

FIGURE 3.1 Wide variety exists among the types of neurons in the body, but they share certain common features, which are illustrated in this diagram. Incoming impulses from other neurons impinge upon the *dendritic zone*, here made up of the membrane of the *dendrites* (especially the *dendritic spines*) and the *cell body*. The resulting electrical changes in this region may stimulate activity that sweeps along the *axon*, in turn producing or influencing responses in the dendritic zones of the neurons with which the *axon terminals* connect. Note also the *myelin sheath*, a segmented fatty covering of the axon, which accounts for the white color characteristic of tracts and nerves.

which enable a stimulus activating one part of the cell to produce a response some distance away. When it is further noted that the response of one nerve cell can stimulate another into activity, it becomes clear how the nervous system carries out one of its major roles: that of *conduction of information within the organism.*

There is one region of the nerve-cell membrane that is particularly sensitive to stimulation (from the outside world or from another nerve cell). It is called the **dendritic zone**, and in the intact organism it is more likely than any other region to be exposed to such stimulation. In many neurons the dendritic zone includes the membrane around the cell body proper as well as the surface of relatively short, thick processes called **dendrites**.

The other major portion of a neuron is a long, thin process called an **axon**. In a functioning organism the axon is stimulated into action by activity within the dendritic zone. Because

of its length an axon is able to produce activity in a relatively distant part of the organism, where it may stimulate yet another nerve, muscle, or gland cell.

Activity is transmitted along a neuron by means of a sequence of electrochemical events, with each point of the neuron becoming active in turn. In the **resting state** (before the neuron is stimulated) the cell membrane maintains a difference in concentration of certain chemicals between the interior of the cell and the body fluids that surround the cell. The most important aspect of this difference is the fact that positively charged sodium ions are kept out of the cell. Because of this the outside of the cell is electrically positive (see Figure 3.2, page 62). When the cell is stimulated, the membrane temporarily breaks down at the point of stimulation and the positive ions rush into the cell. An electrical change results that can be measured as an increase in negativity in the region of stimula-

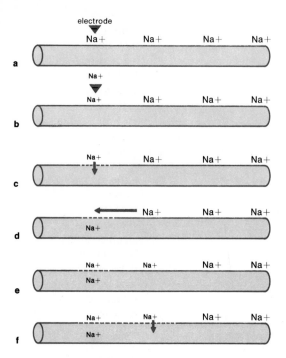

FIGURE 3.2 Stimulation of one point on an axon influences activity at adjacent points as well. Here (**a**) a negatively charged electrode is applied to the neuron and (**b**) removes some of the positively charged sodium (Na+) from the membrane. This removal has the effect of breaking down the membrane at that point (**c**), so that the remainder of the excess sodium can enter the cell. Sodium from the next region of the surface moves over to fill the electrochemical vacuum thus created (**d**). Now, however, the resulting reduction (**e**) of the electrical charge in the neighboring region produces a similar disruption of the membrane, permitting the remaining extra sodium to enter there also (**f**). The inrush of the sodium (**c** and **f**) causes the relative increase in negativity on the outside of the neuron that constitutes the nerve impulse proper. The last three steps (**d, e,** and **f**) are repeated, with successive pairs of points, all along the length of the axon; the nerve impulse has been transmitted.

tion. This electrical change is the activity of the neuron that we have been talking about; it comprises the **nerve impulse.** But how does the impulse that is produced at one point on the neuron produce similar activity farther along the neuron?

The key to understanding how the nerve impulse is propagated along the cell membrane

is the realization that one way to stimulate the membrane to allow passage of the sodium ions at a given point is to change the electrical charge at that spot. A fairly small shift toward the negative will cause the membrane to give way and thus evoke within the neuron membrane chemical processes of its own, which lead to the larger negative shift—the impulse proper. Finally, when an actual impulse is produced at one point on the neuron surface, it has electrical effects that spread somewhat beyond that point.

Now we can see the full story. An effective stimulus at one point on the neuron causes an impulse to be emitted. This impulse is measured as a local "large" (about 120 millivolts) negative shift in the electrical charge on the exterior of the membrane. Such a change influences nearby points, producing smaller increases in negativity in such regions. The small increase in negativity provokes an impulse in these neighboring regions, an impulse that in turn spreads to the next points, and so on down the length of the neuron. The neuron has fired.

If the original stimulus that is applied to an axon is too small, this sequence of events will not be carried out. The membrane will not break down and thus no consequent inrush of sodium will occur and no effective stimulation of the neighboring regions of the axon. The critical size of the stimulus necessary for production of the nerve impulse is called the **threshold of the neuron.** If the stimulus is greater than the threshold value, a nerve impulse will of course be produced, but it is important to note that the size of the impulse will not depend upon the amount by which the stimulus exceeds the threshold. If the cell fires at all, it fires with the maximum intensity possible at the moment. This rule is called the **all-or-none law** of nervous conduction.

The all-or-none nature of the impulse can be understood by remembering that the response of the axon depends upon the initial inequality of the concentration of sodium ions on the two sides of the cell membrane and involves the reduction of this inequality as the sodium moves into the cell. The size of the response depends upon the size of this inequality and not upon the size of the stimulus that provokes its reduction.

After the neuron has fired, there must be some way for the sodium to be expelled from the cell and for the membrane to regain its role as guardian of the electrochemical imbalance (otherwise each neuron could be used only one time). Not much is known about how this expulsion and recovery occur, but it is known that the passage of the impulse and these recovery processes take a definite period of time. During a part of this time, called the **refractory period** of the cell, the neuron cannot be fired again or can be fired only if a much larger stimulus is used.

Interaction Among Nerve Cells

Neurons act in systems—not alone; we must consider how one neuron can produce activity in another so that the latter will succeed it in a pattern of activity. The end of an axon branches into several small twigs, each of which ends in a small swelling. These **axon terminals** bring

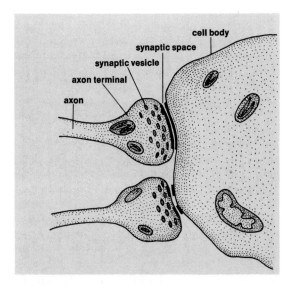

FIGURE 3.3 At each synapse an axon terminal of one neuron approaches the cell membrane of the next neuron very closely. This figure shows two terminals, in each of which many synaptic vesicles are seen. The vesicles are thought to contain transmitter substances, which move across the synaptic space to influence activity on the dendritic zone of the post-synaptic neuron. Read the text's discussion of the excitatory and inhibitory synapses in the body of the unit, and decide which type is represented here.

the end of one neuron close to the membrane of the dendritic zone of another neuron but separated from it by a space about .00002 cm wide. The place at which two neurons approach each other so closely is called a **synapse** and is shown in Figure 3.3. Within each terminal there are small spaces called **synaptic vesicles.** It is believed that the passage of an impulse down the axon causes the release into the synaptic space of a chemical stored in these vesicles. This chemical quickly crosses the synapse and stimulates the dendritic zone of the next cell, which may, in turn, initiate an impulse in its axon that becomes the nerve impulse of the second cell. The chemical that crosses the synaptic space is called a **transmitter substance** because it transmits the message across the synaptic space. At the synapse it is destroyed by enzymes found there or absorbed into the next cell.

Our description is still lacking a beginning and an end. How is the first neuron activated—that is, how do external stimuli in the real world generate activity in the nervous system? This question receives a different answer for each of the various sensory systems, but, in general, it can be said that a **sensory neuron** receives a chemical or electrical change that initiates its impulse either directly from an external stimulus or from a specialized **receptor cell** in the sense organ. At the other end of the chain of activity, transmitter substances secreted by the axon terminals of each **motor neuron** move across a space similar to that of a synapse to provoke activity in the muscle or glandular cell that it innervates.

But the nervous system does not consist of a single group of simple direct pathways, each beginning with one sensory neuron, continuing through a chain of neurons, and ending with one motor neuron. The axon terminals of one neuron bring it in contact with the dendritic zones of many other nerve cells, and many thousands of axons may terminate on the dendritic zone of a single nerve cell. Thus, activity in one neuron may affect activity in many other cells and, indirectly, may affect all the other nerve cells in the body.

If a single impulse within a neuron initiated an impulse in every cell with which it was connected, soon all the cells in the nervous system would be firing as rapidly as possible. But there are two reasons why this does not happen.

First, each neuron has a threshold. The amount of stimulation that reaches the dendritic zone must exceed a certain level before an active impulse can be established, and the transmitter substance released by one nerve impulse is almost never enough to fire the next neuron. Usually the second, **post-synaptic neuron** will be fired only when its dendritic zone is receiving input from the axons of several other cells, all at approximately the same time.

Second, there are some transmitter substances that are inhibitory. Such substances, when released into the synaptic space, act to *offset* the influences of the excitatory transmitter, so that an extra amount of excitatory transmitter is necessary to fire the next neuron in the presence of an inhibitory transmitter.

Some consistent differences between excitatory and inhibitory synapses have been discovered. At excitatory synapses the vesicles in the axon terminal are spherical; at inhibitory synapses they are elliptical—suggesting, of course, that they contain different chemicals. Inhibitory synapses are generally found on the cell-body portion of the dendritic zone. Excitatory synapses are more commonly situated on the dendrites and especially on **dendritic spines**, projections that arise from the surface of the dendrites (see Figure 3.1).

The features just discussed—the complexity of neural interconnections, the existence of thresholds, and the presence of inhibitory as well as excitatory effects—allow the nervous system to do more than simply conduct activity (and, metaphorically, information) from one point to another. The nervous system also *integrates* activity inasmuch as the activity of any one cell is a function of the activity of many, many other cells.

THE EVER-ACTIVE NERVOUS SYSTEM

Unit 14 discusses the ways in which a stimulus causes a change in activity in the nervous system, and it describes the parts of the nervous system that are affected by a given stimulus. As these aspects are explored, the description may

sometimes sound as though nerve cells (in the receptors and in the brain) are completely inactive until a stimulus occurs. Thus, the description is being simplified with the assumption that the sleeping or resting person is completely passive, his brain inert. A stimulus then "stimulates," producing some form of activity in specific parts of this quiescent, waiting structure. But all of this is almost a metaphor. These images may simplify the task of description, but, unfortunately, they are wrong—and wrong in several important ways.

First, nerve cells are not passive and inactive in a resting individual. In every nerve cell spontaneous scattered nerve impulses occur— spontaneous because they are without known external cause—and some large groups of cells maintain organized activity even without a specific stimulus. Indeed, some cells fire more when they are *not* stimulated; they actually reduce their activity when a stimulus is given. And some brain cells are more active during sleep than during waking.

Therefore, it is more accurate to think of a stimulus as changing, rather than starting, a pattern of activity in the nervous system. With this in mind, it is easy to see that a stimulus will have widespread effects throughout the nervous system. Its immediate influence may be on one part of the system, but, from the complex pattern of activity thus produced, consequences will follow for many other parts.

We also might remind ourselves here of an obvious fact—no organism receives a single stimulus at any time. There are always large numbers of stimuli present at any moment, each of which affects the pattern of activity we have been describing.

Finally, the active nervous system itself provides some degree of control over the amount of influence that a stimulus has upon the system. Consider a series of neurons carrying impulses from the eye to the brain. The nervous system can obviously affect the amount of activity that a light produces in these neurons. How? By opening or closing the eyes! A more subtle method of influence is also available to the nervous system. A neuron *from* the brain might have an axon ending at a synapse along the sensory chain. Excitatory or inhibitory impulses at that synapse (initiated in the brain) would then determine, in part, whether or not the pattern of activity inaugurated by a light will be transmitted up the sensory path or, instead, will be stopped and never reach the brain.

The EEG

Earlier this unit described how the complex changes that occur each time a neuron responds produce an electrical impulse. The tremendous activity of our ever-active nervous system leads to the constant production of electrical impulses in large and varying numbers. We might suspect that all this electrical activity would cause major electrical changes in the nervous system. It has in fact been known since the nineteenth century that there are large electrical fluctuations in the brain. However, it was not until 1929 that a psychiatrist named Hans Berger demonstrated conclusively that electrical activity of the human brain could be recorded

through the unopened skull and gave us a way to look at the activity of the brain. Electrical waves so recorded are called "brain waves," and their record is called an **electroencephalogram**, abbreviated **EEG**.

An EEG is picked up by electrodes that are attached to a person's scalp at various points. The wires lead to an amplifier, whose electrical output controls the position of an inked pen on a continuously moving paper chart. In this way brain waves write a record of their own activity.

When an organism is resting quietly, not attending closely to any stimulus, a fairly rhythmical EEG can be recorded. This pattern is called an **alpha wave**, and in human beings it has a rate of eight to twelve waves per second (see Figure 3.4). In many situations other EEG patterns may predominate, and specific patterns are characteristic of different states of consciousness such as attention or sleep. More is said about this in discussing altered states of conciousness in Unit 21 and sleep in Unit 22 and,

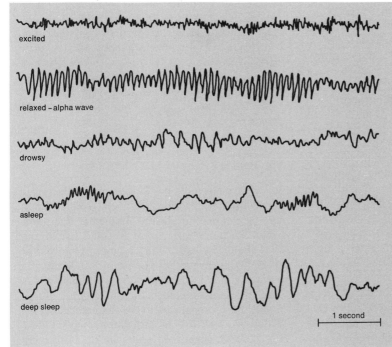

excited

relaxed – alpha wave

drowsy

asleep

deep sleep

1 second

FIGURE 3.4 Brain waves typical of various states of alertness. Note the change in shape and frequency of the brain waves as the relaxed individual becomes excited or falls asleep. The frequency can be judged with the help of the one-second marker.

H. H. Jasper. Electroencephalography. In W. Penfield & T. Erickson (Eds.), *Epilepsy and Cerebral Localization*, 1941; adapted by permission of Charles C Thomas Company.

in Box 16.5, p. 388, evidence is presented that brain waves *can* be brought under voluntary control.

The alpha rhythm and biological clocks Just why and how an alpha rhythm of eight to twelve waves per second is maintained in the brain is not known at this time. However, the facts that alpha waves *are* rhythmical (when a person is relaxed) and are produced without any voluntary effort, indeed without a person's even being aware of their occurrence in his brain, illustrate a fundamental, universal, and puzzling biological phenomenon: *All living things display periodically recurring rhythmic activities.* In the middle of the twentieth century a German biologist, Gustav Kramer, coined the term **biological clock** as a name for the as-yet not understood biological mechanisms that monitor and maintain these recurring activities; since then, the science of *biochronometry* has attracted the interest of a rapidly increasing number of scientists and has revealed an astonishing world of biological rhythms.

The rhythms of life, occurring everywhere —in animals and plants, in individual cells, in organizations of cells, in small and large organs, and in the behavior of entire individuals—vary tremendously in their periodicity. Some biological events regularly recur every thousandth of a second; some, every tenth of a second (as in alpha waves); others, every second, or every hour, or every twenty-four hours. Many of these rhythms are the length of a day, more or less, and they, as a group, are called **circadian rhythms**, from the Greek *circa* (about) and *diem* (day). There are monthly rhythms, seasonal rhythms, annual rhythms; some events have cycles that extend for more than a year, as in the cases of patients suffering from manic-depressive psychoses who will shift, fairly regularly, from a manic to a depressive phase of their illness every eighteen months, or even every twenty-four months (see p. 600, unit 24). Throughout our study we will note many of these cycles of life, and here, in the brain, at the very basis of behavior, we find a rhythmic recurrence—our first instance of a biological clock.

TEN BILLION NERVE CELLS

The ten billion nerve cells are organized into structures, substructures, and substructures within substructures. The **brain** and the **spinal cord** together form the **central nervous system.** The **nerves** connect the central nervous system with various sensory and motor structures throughout the body and make up the **peripheral nervous system**.

The Central Nervous System

The brain itself can be divided into many different structures; we shall describe the major ones but for the present give only a general impression of their functions. Of course, such divisions are arbitrary, the total consisting of complexes of interconnecting neurons with each part having potential connections with all others.

Observation of the central nervous system shows certain kinds of structures. There are regions that are constructed of concentrations of cell bodies; such areas are often called **nuclei** (not to be confused with the nuclei of individual cells). An enveloping layer with a similar concentration of cell bodies is found covering some parts of the brain; it is called a **cortex**. Much of the rest of the brain and spinal cord consists of **tracts**, large groups of axons coursing together, connecting various nuclei and connecting different regions of cortex.

The Brain

Early in embryological development, the brain shows three major divisions from front to back; they are called **forebrain, midbrain,** and **hindbrain**. Each includes many specific parts, and further embryological development changes the external appearance of the brain; but even in a mature human, we refer to these subdivisions in describing the structures of the brain.

The forebrain includes the **cerebrum**, the **thalamus**, and the **hypothalamus** (see Figure 3.5). The cerebrum develops as an outgrowth from near the front end of the forebrain, and as there are two such enlargements—one on each

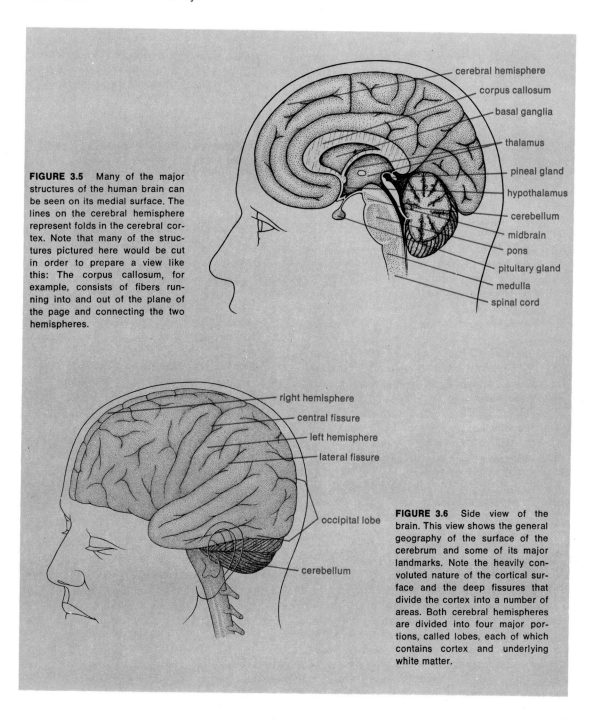

FIGURE 3.5 Many of the major structures of the human brain can be seen on its medial surface. The lines on the cerebral hemisphere represent folds in the cerebral cortex. Note that many of the structures pictured here would be cut in order to prepare a view like this: The corpus callosum, for example, consists of fibers running into and out of the plane of the page and connecting the two hemispheres.

cerebral hemisphere
corpus callosum
basal ganglia
thalamus
pineal gland
hypothalamus
cerebellum
midbrain
pons
pituitary gland
medulla
spinal cord

right hemisphere
central fissure
left hemisphere
lateral fissure
occipital lobe
cerebellum

FIGURE 3.6 Side view of the brain. This view shows the general geography of the surface of the cerebrum and some of its major landmarks. Note the heavily convoluted nature of the cortical surface and the deep fissures that divide the cortex into a number of areas. Both cerebral hemispheres are divided into four major portions, called lobes, each of which contains cortex and underlying white matter.

side—they are referred to as **cerebral hemispheres** (see Figure 3.6). On the exterior of each hemisphere there is a layer of cortex, approxi- mately one-fourth of a centimeter thick. The cerebral cortex is essential to many of the complex functions of man. We refer to it several times in subsequent units as its role in experience and behavior is examined.

Within the hemispheres are several large nuclei, known collectively as the **basal ganglia**, which are part of a neural system involved in the control of fine movement. The neurons whose cell bodies are concentrated in the cerebral cortex and the basal ganglia contribute many of their axons to the large mass of intermingled tracts that comprise much of the interior (the white matter) of the hemispheres. The tracts that run from one hemisphere to the other one are known as **commissures**; the most prominent is called the **corpus callosum**. We shall take note later of what happens when the commissures are cut and one side of the brain has no way of knowing what the other side is doing.

Thalamus and hypothalamus are collective names for groups of individual nuclei. The cells of the different thalamic nuclei send fibers to different areas of the cerebral cortex. Many of the thalamic nuclei receive fibers from sensory receptors and thus serve as way stations on pathways for incoming sensory information. Most of the sensory routes shown in Figure 3.7 are carrying messages that will pass through thalamic nuclei before going to the cerebral cortex. The **lateral geniculate nucleus** and the **medial geniculate nucleus** are thalamic nuclei involved in vision and audition, respectively.

Several of the hypothalamic nuclei have been intensively studied. The functions of these structures differ, but a frequent finding is that they are involved in the control of emotion and motivation and related behavior. It has been found, for example, that electrical stimulation of some parts of the hypothalamus is rewarding and that destruction of another part causes an animal to eat much more than he did previously. In Unit 22 we shall discuss the **limbic system**, an interconnected group of cortical and subcortical structures that are related anatomically to the hypothalamus and that serve similar functions.

The midbrain includes a large part of a structure called the **reticular formation**. Unit 22 describes the way in which the reticular formation initiates impulses that help to control the level of arousal or alertness of parts of the central nervous system, particularly the cerebral cortex.

The **cerebellum** is part of the hindbrain. It has a cortex much like the cerebrum and has many connections to the cerebral cortex, the basal ganglia, and the spinal cord. The cerebellum plays a role in regulating and coordinating motor activity.

In appearance the **pons** is a prominent part of the hindbrain. In part it serves as a way station for tracts running between the cerebrum and the cerebellum; it also includes nuclei that help control sleep and waking, as we see in Unit 22. The **medulla** is the most posterior part of the brain; in appearance and function it resembles, to some extent, the spinal cord into which it blends. There are nuclei here that play an essential part in the control of such vital processes as respiration.

All the brain structures except the cerebral hemispheres and the cerebellum are referred to collectively as the **brain stem**, because they appear to form a stalk from which the cerebrum and cerebellum have sprouted.

The spinal cord is the continuation of the central nervous system down a person's back. Throughout its length there is a core consisting largely of cell bodies that are covered with fiber tracts to carry sensory and motor impulses between the rest of the body and the brain.

The Peripheral Nervous System

A nerve is a large group of neurons (or, more accurately, axons) running together to carry impulses between the central nervous system and another part of the body. There is a series of **spinal nerves** up and down the spinal cord; they carry sensory impulses from the skin, joints, and internal organs of the trunk and limbs, and motor impulses back to the muscles and glands of the same parts of the body. There are also twelve pairs of **cranial nerves**; they carry neural messages directly to (and from) the brain. Several of them are shown in Figure 3.7; the sensory pathways from the skin of the face and the specialized receptor organs (the nose, for example) use these cranial nerves. The motor impulses to the muscles controlling the jaw and the tongue pass over cranial nerves as well.

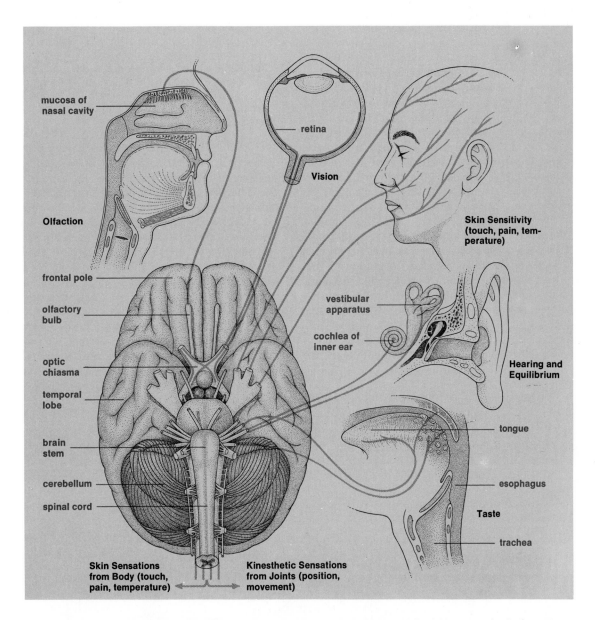

FIGURE 3.7 Sensory routes to the brain. Here the brain is viewed from beneath in order to see clearly the routes over which neural messages travel from sense receptors into the brain. Although the sensory system and brain are bilaterally symmetrical (two eyes, two sensory areas for smell, two ears), this diagram shows only one route for each of the types of sensory organs.

Note that the nerves that carry neural messages from the eyes, nose, tongue, ears, face, and vestibular apparatus go directly to the brain, that is, they do not travel to the brain via the spinal cord. The nerves that carry impulses from the skin, muscles, and joints of the rest of the body do enter the brain through connections in the spinal cord.

THE "SPECIFIC ENERGIES OF NERVES" DOCTRINE

In Part Four we shall examine the many different kinds of sensations we experience—visual, auditory, olfactory, gustatory, cutaneous, and so forth. Right now, however, we are considering the neural basis for these *qualitative* differences in experience. What is the difference *at the brain level* between, say, neural impulses initiated by a light wave, and those initiated by a sound wave? Obviously, there must be a real difference, or how could we differentiate between an experience of vision and one of sound?

Three possible solutions to this interesting and important problem were considered in the early 1800s by Johannes Müller, the German physiologist. Müller rejected the possibility that it is the receptor cells that determine the qualities of perception, pointing out that if a sensory nerve, say the optic nerve from the eye, is stimulated directly by electricity, the resulting *experience* is exactly the same as if its receptor had been stimulated by a light. He then offered the following two explanations:

(1) Either the nerves themselves may communicate impressions different in quality to the sensorium [the brain], which in every instance remains the same; or (2) the vibrations of the nervous principle [the nerve impulses] may in every nerve be the same and yet give rise to the perception of different sensations in the sensorium, owing to the parts of the latter with which the nerves are connected having different properties.

Müller believed it was impossible to prove either position at the time he was writing, but he favored the first, that is, that the nerves of the different senses send special messages signaling the types of sensations. In fact he titled his discussion **"The Doctrine of the Specific Energies of Nerves."** An apparent difficulty with this position is that, as far as we now know, neural impulses are all alike. There is no physical or chemical test that can tell us whether an impulse is signaling a visual message or an auditory message, for example.

On the other hand, we now find support for the second position. We shall see that different senses have different cortical projection areas—reception centers for their neural impulses in the cortex. (Figure 3.8 depicts the sensory projection areas that can be seen from the side of

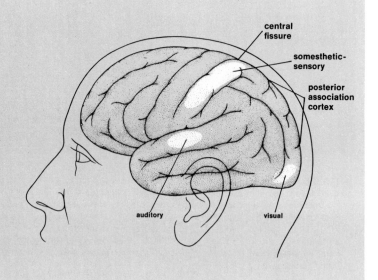

FIGURE 3.8 Sensory representation on the cortex. Looking at the side of the brain, three major sensory areas can be distinguished. They are the areas of the cortex in which the nerve fibers from the body's various sense organs terminate. The three areas shown are the visual area, the auditory area, and the somesthetic-sensory area. The last area lies directly behind the central fissure.

This figure, showing the *terminal areas* of the sensory routes, should be studied in conjunction with Figure 3.7, which shows the sensory routes as they *enter* the brain.

BOX 3.1

... AND THE DEAF HEAR

Much important information about the human brain has been gained from studies of people undergoing operations to remove abnormal tissue, such as tumors or scarred regions. These operations are often done under local anesthesia, with the patient fully conscious throughout. A flap is cut into the skull (see Figure A) and the brain exposed to view.

The surgeon wants to remove as much abnormal tissue with as little interference with normal function as possible. Therefore points on the cortex are first stimulated with an electric current. The effect of the current is noted, and a small ticket is placed on the cortex at each point (see Figure B). In this way some idea of the functioning of different parts of the cortex is gained, and the surgeon will avoid if at all possible removing essential regions, such as those controlling speech.

Stimulation in the motor areas may produce a motor response or may affect an ongoing movement. As expected from the "specific energies of nerves" doctrine, stimulation in other regions produces sensory experiences. Separate regions for the various senses are discovered, as shown in Figure 3.8.

Within one sensory area, stimulation at different points or at different intensities of current will produce somewhat different experiences, for example, "a ball of light" or "tiny colored lights which were moving." Scientists have found these results useful for a basic understanding of how receptors are connected to the brain and how the brain works. Now there is hope that they will be able to use this basic knowledge for extremely important applied advances—to help the blind to see or the deaf to hear.

It is now possible to consider seriously the construction of an artificial ear, which would transform sound waves into electrical currents. If one could then send these currents to electrodes stimulating the correct parts of the auditory cortex, the patient's own natural ear and the nerve connecting it to the brain would not have to be used. Thus, a person who was deaf because of a disease of the ear or the nerve could hear again.

This may sound like science fiction, and indeed there are many serious problems to be solved if such a device is to work. Nevertheless, the problems *do* seem to be soluble. A thirty-person team at the University of Utah, for example, is attacking various aspects, and they report that progress to date is encouraging.

W. H. DOBELLE, S. S. STENSAAS, M. G. MLADEJOVSKY, & J. B. SMITH. A prosthesis for the deaf based on cortical stimulation. *Annals of Otology, Rhinology and Laryngology,* July–August 1973, **82**, No. 4, 445.
W. PENFIELD & T. RASMUSSEN. *The Cerebral Cortex of Man.* New York: Macmillan, 1950. Photos courtesy W. Penfield, Montreal Neurological Institute, McGill University; reprinted by permission.

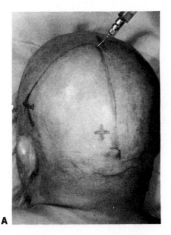

A

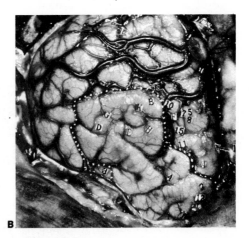

B

the head.) We shall also discover that direct stimulation of one of these cortical **sensory areas** will produce the appropriate sensation. For example, stimulation of the visual area by an electrical current applied directly to the brain will result in the sensation of light (see Box 3.1, p. 71). This is true not only in sighted people *but in the blind as well.* Thus it is *neither* the receptor cells *nor* the nerves that connect them to the cortex that are crucial; it is the place in the cortex that is stimulated that determines which sensory modality we experience. When the auditory sensory area of the cortex is activated, sound is experienced; when the visual area is activated, light is experienced.

All this discussion suggests that the quality of the different senses depends upon the place in the cortex to which the sensory nerves are connected. (If the pattern of impulses provoked by an orange light arrived at the taste area of the cortex, we would not experience an orange light; we would probably experience some sort of taste.) Much of the rest of the brain will be active also, but the distinctive part of the activity will be that aroused by stimulation of a certain sensory area in the cortex. There is "sensory localization" in the cortex.

THE NEURAL CONTROL OF BEHAVIOR

The behavior of an individual at any instant is a product of active muscle and gland cells, and the responses of the muscle and gland cells are determined in turn by the activity of the nervous system. Although the total pattern of nervous-system activity will influence the resulting responses, all of these influences affect behavior only through controlling the motor nerves.

One major control of the spinal motor nerves is exerted by way of the **pyramidal-tract system**, consisting of neurons with cell bodies in the cerebral cortex and axons that run down through lower parts of the brain into the spinal cord, where they enter into synapses with neurons of the motor nerves. Many of the cell bodies of the pyramidal-tract neurons are found in one region of the cerebral cortex, which is called

the **motor area** (see Figure 18.2, page 421).

There is, in addition, an **extrapyramidal system**. It also originates with neurons in the cerebral cortex, but these cells do not affect the motor nerves directly. They synapse with neurons in the basal ganglia, the midbrain, and neighboring regions, and the axons of these latter cells travel down the spinal cord to help control the motor neurons.

It is generally believed that the neural impulses of the pyramidal system control skilled movements, determining which discrete responses will be made; the extrapyramidal system is involved in the control of posture and grosser rhythmic movements, such as those used in locomotion. Fibers from the cerebellum affect both systems by synapses with their cortical and subcortical neurons and add influences that appear to be necessary if movements are to be smooth and well coordinated.

PHYSIOLOGICAL PSYCHOLOGY

Subsequent units will discuss specific aspects of the psychological processes involved in mental activity and behavior. Some of these units are especially concerned with the anatomical structures and physiological processes that are related to psychological events and make extensive use of the material presented in this unit.

Facts derived from study of the physiological bases of psychology and those derived from study of the psychological processes themselves must be consistent with one another. Psychological observations should help in the discovery of physiological truths, and vice versa.

The study of **physiological psychology**—research into the nature of physiological processes and anatomical structures underlying psychological activity—has increased more in recent years than has research in most other fields of psychology. Much of the information is new, and quite possibly some of it will later prove to be wrong. But this situation indicates a healthy state of affairs—a time of activity, exploration, new discoveries, and change—an exciting time in which to be a student of the science.

SUMMARY

1. When anatomical structures and physiological processes that are related to psycho-logical events are studied, major attention is given to the nervous system—the brain, spinal cord, and nerves. This system is composed of billions of neurons (nerve cells), each of which typically has a cell body and one or more extensions (processes) including a relatively long and thin axon.

2. Nerve activity begins with stimulation of a neuron's outer portion (the cell membrane) in a region called the dendritic zone. Stimulation of one point on the axon can produce changes in the membrane at neighboring points; the latter changes now act as stimulation and in turn produce further changes at adjacent points, etc. In this way a stimulus applied at one point on the dendritic zone can produce an effect relatively far away, at the end of the axon. The nerve cell *conducts* information.

3. This change in the nerve membrane consists of the movement of ions across the membrane; it may be measured as an electrical event moving along the neuron—the nerve impulse. Stimulation of a neuron must reach a certain intensity (its threshold) before an impulse will be produced; but the size of an impulse is not increased by increasing the stimulus further if it is already above threshold (all-or-none law).

4. The end of an axon branches into terminals, each of which approaches the dendritic zone of another neuron. This region of near contact is called a synapse. In the axon terminals there are structures called synaptic vesicles, which are thought to contain chemicals called transmitter substances. When an excitatory transmitter substance is released into a synaptic space it can diffuse across to the dendritic zone of the next neuron and stimulate it to activity. However, some synapses are inhibitory; when an inhibitory transmitter is released it tends to prevent an impulse from being produced in the neuron which receives it.

5. Neurons are not passive and inactive, even in a sleeping individual. A stimulus to an organism *changes* the pattern of activity in the nervous system; it does not start a pattern of activity. Any stimulus occurs within an enormous complex of many other stimuli, so that the effect of a stimulus will be widespread throughout the nervous system. The nervous system itself may provide some control over the influence a stimulus will have by producing excitatory or inhibitory influences on synapses in the sensory path that the stimulus must follow.

6. The activity of many neurons is reflected in an electroencephalogram (EEG), a record of electrical changes in the brain that can be measured from the outside of the head. The regular alpha rhythm of a relaxed person's EEG is an effect of one of the body's biological clocks.

7. The central nervous system consists of the spinal cord and the brain. The forebrain includes the cerebrum with its cortex, the thalamus (many parts of which are involved in relaying sensory information from the receptors to the cortex), and the hypothalamus (much of which seems to be involved in the control of motivation and emotion). The midbrain contains some of the reticular formation, a system that plays a part in controlling the level of arousal of other parts of the nervous system. The hindbrain includes the cerebellum (which helps regulate and coordinate motor activity), the pons, and the medulla.

8. The peripheral nervous system includes the spinal nerves, which carry sensory and motor impulses between the spinal cord and the trunk and limbs, and the cranial nerves, which carry neural messages directly to and from the brain. Stimulation of different sensory nerves produces different sensory experiences but not because of differences in receptor cells or because of differences in nerve impulses in the various nerves. Rather, different sensory experiences result from the fact that different nerves terminate in different parts of the brain, causing activation of different parts of the cortex.

9. All the effects of stimulation of an organism and all the ongoing pattern of activity in its nervous system can influence its behavior only through their control of neural responses in motor nerves. The pyramidal-tract system and the extrapyramidal system are both involved in such control. The former is said to control skilled movements; the latter, to control posture and grosser rhythmic movements.

GLOSSARY

all-or-none law   A term referring to the fact that every nerve impulse has the maximum intensity that the cell can produce at a given time. The intensity of the stimulus that initiates the firing has no effect upon the intensity of the impulse.

alpha wave   The EEG pattern characteristic of a resting organism. In human beings it has a rate of eight to twelve waves per second.

axon   The long, thin process of a neuron. A nerve impulse is produced on the membrane of the axon and travels along its length.

axon terminal   One of the small branches into which the end of each axon divides. An axon terminal approaches the dendritic zone of another cell to form a synapse.

basal ganglia   A group of structures deep within the cerebrum. They are primarily composed of nerve-cell bodies and are part of a neural system that helps control motor responses.

biological clock   A mechanism within the organism that in part controls or maintains any of the rhythmical activities of the body, such as alpha waves or yearly migrations. The actual anatomical and physiological basis of these clocks is not completely understood.

brain   The part of the central nervous system encased in the skull (or cranium). It consists of many different structures working together to control behavior partly under the influence of incoming sensory impulses.

brain stem   All the brain except the cerebral hemispheres and the cerebellum. It is so named because of its similarity to a stalk from which the cerebrum and cerebellum have grown.

cell body   The large rounded part of a nerve cell, as compared with axons and dendrites. Most of the chemical reactions that comprise the life processes of a cell take place here.

cell membrane   The outer covering of any body cell, including a nerve cell. Through it must pass the substances that participate in the chemical reactions of the cell.

central nervous system   That portion of the nervous system consisting of the brain and the spinal cord.

cerebellum   A portion of the hindbrain situated (in human beings) just beneath the posterior portions of the cerebrum. It is connected with the spinal cord and the cerebral hemispheres and has a cortex, as does the cerebrum. The cerebellum plays an important role in the coordination of muscular activity.

cerebral hemispheres, cerebrum   The largest part of the human brain, the cerebrum develops as two symmetrical, protruding pouches (hemispheres) from the forebrain. There is an exterior cortex and an inner structure of white matter consisting of interlaced nerve tracts in which are embedded the basal ganglia.

circadian rhythm   A biological cycle or rhythm that is approximately 24 hr in length. The sleep-wakefulness cycle is the most obvious example, but there are many other behavioral, physiological, and biochemical rhythms that are about one day in length.

commissure   A nerve tract, crossing from one side of the brain to the other, interconnecting symmetrical points.

corpus callosum   The most prominent commissure of the forebrain.

cortex   The outer part of an organ; specifically a surface layer in the nervous system in which nerve-cell bodies are concentrated. Thus, the cerebral cortex and the cerebellar cortex comprise the folded outer part of the cerebrum and the cerebellum, respectively.

cranial nerve   A nerve that is connected with the central nervous system by way of the brain.

dendrites   The relatively short and thick processes of a nerve cell, which provide a major part of the dendritic zone of the cell membrane.

dendritic spines   Small projections from the surface of dendrites. Axon terminals from other neurons end close to the spines to form excitatory synapses.

dendritic zone   The region of the nerve-cell membrane that is specialized for the reception of stimulation either from an external stimulus, a receptor cell, or another nerve cell. Sufficient stimulation of the dendritic zone will lead to the production of a nerve impulse in the axon.

electroencephalogram (EEG)   A graph of electrical activity of the cerebral cortex (brain waves) recorded from the scalp. The EEG gives a measure of the organism's state of consciousness.

extrapyramidal system   A motor system that originates in the cerebral cortex, synapses in the basal ganglia, midbrain, and neighboring regions and ends upon the motor neurons of the spinal cord. It controls postural mechanisms and gross movements.

forebrain   The most anterior of the three major embryological divisions of the brain. The cerebrum, the thalamus, and the hypothalamus develop from the forebrain.

hindbrain   The most posterior of the embryological divisions of the brain from which develop the cerebellum, pons, and medulla.

hypothalamus   A forebrain structure, composed of several different nuclei, located at the base of the brain below the thalamus. It forms part of many neural systems concerned with the control of emotional and motivational experience and behavior.

lateral geniculate nuclei   The thalamic nuclei (one on either side of the brain) that receive nerve impulses from the eyes and send impulses to the visual sensory area in the cerebral cortex.

limbic system   A ring of interconnected cortical and subcortical structures surrounding the brain stem. Like the hypothalamus, to which it is related anatomically, it appears to be involved in emotional and motivational experience and behavior.

medial geniculate nuclei   The thalamic nuclei that receive auditory nerve impulses from the ears and send impulses to the auditory sensory area in the cerebral cortex.

medulla   The lowest part of the hindbrain, continuous with the spinal cord. Many of the cranial nerves arise or end here. Many important reflex functions (breathing, and so on) are under the control of nerve cells of the medulla.

midbrain   The middle (from front to back) of the three embryological divisions of the brain. Only a relatively small portion of the mature brain develops from the midbrain, but included in that portion is much of the reticular formation.

motor area of cortex   A strip of the cerebral cortex lying just in front of the central fissure. Many of the neurons of the pyramidal and extrapyramidal systems originate here.

motor neuron; motor fiber   A neuron, or nerve fiber, carrying nerve impulses from the brain or spinal cord to a muscle or gland. A group of such fibers running together forms a motor nerve.

nerve   A bundle of axons running together in the peripheral nervous system; it may consist of all sensory fibers, all motor fibers, or a mixture of the two.

nerve impulse   The electrochemical change at the nerve-cell membrane that constitutes the activity of the cell. It results from a movement of electrically charged particles (ions) across the membrane.

neuron   A nerve cell. The structural and functional unit of the nervous system.

nucleus   1. A structure within any cell, including a nerve cell. The nucleus carries the genetic information of the cell and thus controls the reproduction of the cell, as well as the chemical activities that occur elsewhere in the cell body. 2. Any portion of the central nervous system, other than a cortex, in which nerve-cell bodies are concentrated. The basal ganglia are nuclei; the hypothalamus and the thalamus each consist of many nuclei.

peripheral nervous system   The motor and sensory nerves, which carry nerve impulses from the sense organs to the central nervous system and from the central nervous system to the muscles and glands of the body.

physiological psychology   Study of the body parts (anatomy) and body functions (physiology) that are related to psychological events. All the organism is involved, but attention is usually focused upon the nervous system.

pons   A substructure within the hindbrain. It contains many nuclei, some of which participate in circuits connecting the cerebrum with the cerebellum.

post-synaptic neuron   The neuron after the synapse, that is, the neuron that receives the transmitter substance from across the synapse and may, therefore, be stimulated into activity. The cell that releases the transmitter is the pre-synaptic neuron.

process   Anatomically, a fiber or extension of a nerve cell; an axon or dendrite.

pyramidal-tract system   A system of neurons originating in the motor area and other regions of the cortex and ending on the motor neurons of the spinal cord. It controls the production of skilled, discrete movements.

receptor cell   A cell in a sense organ, such as the eye or nose, that is sensitive to a particular kind of stimulus energy. It converts the stimulus energy impinging on it into the energy of a nervous impulse.

refractory period   A short period during and immediately following the passage of a nerve impulse along an axon. In the first part (the absolute refractory period), it is impossible to produce a second nerve impulse in the neuron. In the remaining part (the relative refractory period), a new impulse can be obtained but it takes a stronger stimulus (i.e., the threshold of the cell is higher).

resting state   The status of a neuron when no impulse is being produced. During the resting state the cell membrane maintains a difference between the inside and the outside of the cell in the concentration of certain chemicals, particularly sodium.

reticular formation   A structure within the brain stem, especially the midbrain, which helps control the level of arousal of the organism.

sensory area of cortex   Any major reception area in the cerebral cortex for nerve impulses from a sensory receptor.

sensory neuron; sensory fiber   A neuron, or nerve fiber, carrying impulses from a sensory receptor to the brain or spinal cord. A group of sensory fibers running together forms a sensory nerve.

"specific energies of nerves" doctrine   The name given to the theory formulated by Johannes Müller about 1825 that the differences in qualities of perception are determined either by differences in the messages carried by different sensory nerves or by the different areas of the cortex into which the sensory nerves lead. The weight of modern evidence supports the latter possibility.

spinal cord   The part of the central nervous system encased in the backbone and serving as a pathway for the conduction of sensory impulses to the brain from the trunk and limbs and of motor impulses from the brain to the muscles and glands. In addition, many motor impulses originate here, directly under the control of the incoming sensory impulses.

spinal nerve   A nerve that is connected with the central nervous system somewhere along the length of the spinal cord.

synapse   The place at which an axon terminal of one neuron approaches the dendritic zone of another neuron. Activity in the first neuron can influence activity in the next one by the passage of a transmitter substance across the synaptic space.

synaptic vesicles   Small spaces in axon terminals in which transmitter substances are apparently stored before release into synaptic spaces.

thalamus   A forebrain structure, composed of several different nuclei, located between the cerebral hemispheres. It receives input from sensory nerves and sends impulses to many regions of the cerebral cortex, including the sensory areas.

threshold of a neuron   The minimal intensity of a stimulus required to produce a nerve impulse.

tract   A group of nerve fibers (axons) running together within the central nervous system.

transmitter substance   A chemical that is released at the axon terminal of a neuron and travels across the synaptic space to affect the dendritic zone of the next neuron. The transmitter may tend to produce a nerve impulse in the next neuron, in which case it is said to be excitatory. If it tends to prevent an impulse in the next neuron, it is called inhibitory.

thinking
and
language

development of thinking

DO YOU KNOW...

- that an infant's thinking begins with his reflexes?

- in what ways our thinking is changed by experience, and in what ways it is not?

- why it is that our thinking may be most changed when we run into something we don't quite understand?

- why it is that up to a certain age, "out of sight, out of existence" describes a baby's experience?

- that the adolescent person already has all the thinking capacity he will ever have?

- what kinds of things we can learn only by doing them, not by reading or thinking about them?

- that, when it comes to understanding things, practice makes perfect only under certain circumstances?

- what obvious ideas we have about physical reality that for a child are not only not obvious but literally unthinkable?

unit 4

CONTENTS

From the beginnings of man's recorded history philosophers have speculated on the nature of the mind at birth. Some, like John Locke, have regarded the newborn's mind as totally blank, a tabula rasa (blank tablet) ready to be written upon by life's experiences. Others, like Plato, regarded certain ideas as universally given; thus, thinking could be regarded as developing from innately common origins.

Modern views on the development of thinking have been dominated by the work of the Swiss psychologist, Jean Piaget. Beginning nearly fifty years ago and continuing still, Piaget has sought through experimentation and observation to understand the mental development of the child. He has studied the development of thinking, perception, language, intelligence, and even the emergence of children's concepts of causality and morality. Much of his early data came from observations of the spontaneous behavior of his own children and of their response to ingenious little experiments. These data and subsequent more systematic experimentation have led Piaget to the formulation of a number of principles that could apply to the broad range of developmental processes with which he is concerned.

PIAGET'S THEORY OF COGNITIVE DEVELOPMENT

At the heart of Piaget's theory lies his insistence that human mental growth (or cognitive development) is the inevitable outcome of the infant's interaction with his physical world. But what determines what an infant does, and why does he act at all? By what means do his actions and their effects upon the environment and upon his organism bring about a progressive development in the child's knowledge of the world and in his ability to deal effectively and intelligently with it? Piaget's general developmental principles—organization, equilibration, and adaptation—embody his attempts to answer these questions.

Organization, Equilibration, and Adaptation

Roughly speaking, **organization** refers to Piaget's belief that the elements of mental life (he calls them **schemata**) become increasingly interrelated with one another into larger systems or totalities, which themselves represent new and more complex schemata.

But what is the driving force for this process of ever more complex cognitive organization? Piaget postulates that mental structures, or schemata, are intrinsically motivated to function at a higher level—a tendency that he calls **equilibration.** We are constantly driven to do what we already have a schema for doing, but each time we act, we strive to *increase* the adaptiveness and complexity of our behavior and schemata. Equilibration seems to represent Piaget's sole theory of motivation, and it goes far beyond motivational theories that regard all behavior as attributable, directly or indirectly, to the familiar bodily needs. There is a direct parallel in this view with recent reformulations of motivational theory which propose, for example, that curiosity is not a derivative of physiological survival needs but represents a motive in its own right, a need to explore, examine, manipulate—in short, a need to know.

Piaget describes the continuing exchange between organism and environment as **adaptation**, a general term implying that such exchanges result in a progressive growth in the complexity of mental structures, making them more able to cope effectively with environmental demands. He postulates two complementary concepts that specify how adaptation occurs: assimilation and accommodation.

Assimilation   The concept of **assimilation** proposes that any organism has a tendency to take in from the external world only those things that it can incorporate effectively. Thus, we have certain bodily structures and functions that enable us to digest certain foods, and it is these foods that are sought and assimilated. Similarly, Piaget asserts, existing structures, or schemata, tend to take in only those aspects of environmental stimulation that they are able to

handle. In other words, food for thought is selected and chosen so as to be digestible by the current level of development of the mental apparatus. Practically, this selection means that an infant (or child or adult) tends to perceive only that portion of the world that he can make sense of in terms of what he already knows, although some distortion may result from squeezing the new information into the not-quite-right existing mold. He will also tend to respond only to situations with which he is familiar and for which old responses are more or less adequate. Obviously, assimilation is a conservative principle that attempts to maintain a mental status quo. Were this the sole adaptive mechanism, existing schemata could not change, and mental organization could not become more complex. Something else is clearly required.

Accommodation   That something else Piaget calls **accommodation.** It is the complement of assimilation in the sense that when new stimuli are not assimilated to existing schemata yet are too insistent to be ignored, accommodation takes over. Quite simply, accommodation means that new schemata are formed, or old ones are modified or brought together, to create more complex new organizations.

All these concepts, taken together, tell us that in the development of mental life there is "a continuous creation of increasing complex forms and a progressive adaptation of these forms to the environment." In everyday terms, the theory portrays normal mental development as a continual striving to grow in our understanding of the world about us, where what we try to understand is not the totally new but rather the almost understood that lies at the boundaries of our present comprehension.

Given this tendency for man's mental grasp to exceed—but only ever so slightly—his mental reach, we would expect that mental development would proceed bit by bit along a smooth and continuous course. Not so, says Piaget. Instead, he suggests, there are three major stages in development, and each stage represents a discrete and qualitative step upward from the preceding one.

STAGES OF COGNITIVE DEVELOPMENT

Piaget's general principles apply to all three stages, although the specifics of their operation necessarily vary from stage to stage. He asserts that the stages are invariable in the *order* of their occurrence for all children, although the ages at which they are achieved may vary considerably from individual to individual. The age range that we shall cite for each stage has been assigned by Piaget and others to serve as rough boundaries, not as absolute limits. Furthermore, the stages are said to be *hierarchical*; that is, each successive stage *requires* and incorporates the mental organization of the immediately preceding stage. In our account of Piaget's three development stages, we shall not discuss the many detectable substages (six in the first major stage alone).

Stage 1: Sensorimotor

The first stage—the **sensorimotor stage**—extends from birth to roughly two years of age. In the beginning, according to Piaget, mental organization consists only of some inborn reflex responses. Underlying these responses are the simplest of schemata, isolated from one another. The newborn thus has a separate schema that triggers a sucking response when the bottle is put to his lips and one that sets off a grasping reflex when his hand encounters the bottle. For a month or so, the exercise of these simple reflexes is apparently all there is to cognitive development. Then these separate schemata begin to come together. The infant first sees, then grasps, then sucks at the bottle. He can now orient to impinging stimuli, for example, turning toward the source of a sudden sound or bright light. There is, however, some evidence that such orienting reactions may be present even at birth. Wertheimer (1961), working with what were perhaps history's youngest human subjects for a behavioral experiment, reported that only ten minutes after delivery, an infant showed eye movements that followed a moving sound source varying in location.

Gradually, the infant, who at first is at the mercy of environmental stimulation, moves on to initiate his own behavior. He begins to practice responses that lead to interesting outcomes, batting at a rattle or kicking off his covers. The concept of a unified object or thing begins to emerge as the initially separate looks, feels, sounds, and tastes of the object fuse into a single organization (see Box 4.1).

When an object is first achieved, it has an ephemeral life; it ceases to exist when it is no longer perceived. A toy dropped out of sight is simply gone, nonexistent. But then, toward the end of the first year, the object becomes permanent, and the infant will actively search for it. Active experimentation with objects increases, and the infant delights in manipulating new things and causing things to happen in his world. The parent who has picked up the teddy bear for the seventeenth time and returned it to the crib, only to see it launched on yet another flight, will testify to the energy and persistence of such an activity. By a year and a half or so, the child appears to have acquired the capacity to think about things even when they are not present and to create new uses of objects; in short, in some small sense, he seems to have become inventive, creative, and imaginative.

The amount and variety of development that take place within this first stage make it clear that infants are not simply little people who see the world in much the same way we do. The notion that the mental life of the infant is *qualitatively* different from ours is hard to believe because we can no longer remember or imagine a world that is comprised of transient, disappearing into nonexistent, disconnected objects. The infant is simply *incapable* of many kinds of mental processes that are accessible to even the least-intelligent adults. These qualitative lacks continue to persist, as we shall see, for many years, so that not until adolescence can the normal child think as a normal adult does. The implications of this general fact for theories of cognitive development and of educational technique are considerable. The implications for parenthood are equally numerous and perhaps more obvious.

Stage 2: Concrete Operations

The second stage—the stage of **concrete operations**—extends from about two to eleven years.

BOX 4.1

INFERRING INFANTILE SCHEMATA

What can be the basis of Jean Piaget's detailed hypotheses concerning the mental life of an infant, who, after all, seems to do little more than sleep and thrash around? The basis is the same as for all psychological study: the observation of behavior. The two verbatim records in this box deal with sequences of behavior from which Piaget inferred the coordination of two schemata. In the first, Piaget describes how a manual schema was assimilated into a visual one. We are shown how, within a period of twenty days, the infant progresses from a stage in which looking at his hand and moving his hand are independent to a stage in which seeing his hand enables him to control its movement.

> At age two months four days, Laurent [Piaget's son] by chance discovers his right index finger and looks at it briefly. At two months eleven days, he inspects for a moment his right hand, perceived by chance. At two months fourteen days, he looks three times in succession at his left hand and chiefly at his raised index finger. At two months seventeen days, he follows the spontaneous movement of his hand for a moment, and then he examines it several times while it searches for his nose or rubs his eye. At two months nineteen days, he smiles at the same hand after having contemplated it eleven times in succession. I then put his hand in a bandage; as soon as I detach it (half an hour later) it returns to the visual field and Laurent again smiles at it. The same day he looks very attentively at his two clasped hands. At age two months twenty-one days, he holds his two fists in the air and looks at the left one, after which he slowly brings it toward his face and rubs his nose with it, and then his eyes. A moment later the left hand again approaches his face; he looks at it and touches his nose. He recommences and laughs five or six times in succession while moving the left hand to his nose. He seems to laugh before the hand moves, but looking has no influence on the movement. Age two months twenty-four days: at last looking acts on the orientation of the hands which tend to remain in the visual field.

In the next record, Piaget describes how his daughter progresses to the point at which a hearing schema is absorbed into a visual one.

> At age one month, Jacqueline still limits herself to interrupting her crying when she hears an agreeable voice or sound, but she does not try to mark the sound. At one month six days, same reaction. At one month ten days, on the other hand, Jacqueline begins to smile at the voice. . . . At two months twelve days, Jacqueline turns her head to the side whence the sound comes. For example, on hearing my voice behind her, she turns in the right direction. At two months twenty-six days, she localizes the source of sound quite accurately with her glance. She searches until she finds the person who is speaking, but it is difficult to say whether she identifies the source of the sound or whether this is simply accommodation to the sound.

J. PIAGET. *The origins of intelligence in children.* Translated by Margaret Cook. New York: International Universities Press, 1952. Originally published 1936. Text material reprinted by permission.

This period is regarded by Piaget as one in which the transition is made between the extreme literalness of perception still evident in the child at the close of the sensorimotor period and a well-developed ability for abstract thinking that characterizes the third stage.

At about the age of two, the child begins to show his first symbolic activity. Whereas before objects were what they were and nothing more, now he can enjoy make-believe play. The crib becomes a rowboat, but woe to him who thinks that imagination implies confusion. Join the child in his game and praise the seaworthiness of his vessel. Overdo this and you will be firmly corrected: "A bed is not a boat."

Language Language, a very important symbolic activity, also has its most rapid development during the early years of this stage (see Unit 5). Words come to stand for things, and action can sometimes be replaced by thought. But although the child is learning to play with his environment and to achieve considerable mastery of his world, his view of reality is highly egocentric. He stands at the hub of his experiences and can understand them only in reference to himself. For example, experiments have shown that a child of five or six is incapable of describing how a scene (say, a model of a village) would look if viewed from any other angle than his own current visual perspective. Indeed, he cannot conceive that the scene *can* look any different from what it obviously *is*.

Conservation Somewhat similar is the phenomenon that Piaget calls *centering*, the tendency of the young child to center or focus upon a single aspect or quality of a situation. This tendency is illustrated perhaps most clearly in the young child's failure to master the principle of invariance, or **conservation**. Because the child centers upon a particular characteristic of an object—for example, its shape—he fails to realize that other characteristics of the same object —for example, its weight—can remain constant despite highly visible but actually irrelevant changes in shape. For example, the young child does not realize that a certain mass of clay will weigh the same whether it is rolled into a ball, elongated into a sausage, or squashed flat as a pancake.

Beginning at about age seven, the child begins to master the principle of conservation. That is, he comes to understand that a certain property of an object does not change despite changes in other perceivable features. Mastering the concept of conservation in quantity, weight, volume, number, and so on requires, in Piaget's theory, a set of cognitive abilities to be attained within the latter part of the period of concrete operations. This notion of conservation is first grasped with regard to matter. A year or so later, conservation of weight becomes understood. Finally, conservation of volume is achieved. (Box 4.2 provides further illustrations of conservation experiments.)

During this period the child also acquires a number of other kinds of cognitive abilities. For example, he can now arrange a number of sticks in serial order, say, from shortest to longest. In brief, during this developmental period, the child begins to look rational to adults because he has become able to think and reason in much the same way as adults do. But one important distinction still remains: So far he can apply his newly developed cognitive ability only to concrete objects in his immediate environment. He cannot yet carry out the same thinking operation symbolically, for example,

when words rather than objects are involved. Acquiring this ability to reason *abstractly* is the task of the next and final developmental stage.

Stage 3: Formal Operations

The last stage—the stage of **formal operations** —extends to approximately fifteen years of age. It is during this stage that the child (or, by now, the preadolescent) begins to apply concrete operations to *hypothetical* situations. For example, he becomes able to solve problems like, "If a *Glink* is taller than a *Zuv* and shorter than a *Blam*, which is the tallest of all?" It is no longer necessary to have real objects (such as sticks); it is not even necessary to have object names that refer to actual objects in the physical world. In addition to performing his once concrete operations in these more abstract ways, he acquires, bit by bit, the more complex logical reasoning abilities characteristic of adult thought. Grasping the idea of proportionality—A is to B as C is to D—illustrates one of these newly emergent cognitive achievements. He also becomes capable of forming hypotheses designed to explain unfamiliar phenomena. In fact, many of the tasks employed to define this period of formal operations are very much like scientific experiments. The boy or girl, typically, is presented with a problem that can be solved only by systematically manipulating a number of variables, carefully observing the effects of these variations, forming explanatory hypotheses based upon these observations, then testing these hypotheses one by one until the correct one is discovered.

This stage marks the end of the developmental road that began with the infant who did not even have the notion of stable objects existing in a real world; it ends with the individual who can think logically and can do so with respect to abstract objects. By the end of this period the individual has achieved, in Piaget's theoretical model, the stage of cognitive maturity. Not, however, that he can no longer learn or grow wiser. Rather, he has finally been endowed with a full (adult) set of thinking tools with which to continue his ever more complex adaptations to his physical and social worlds.

BOX 4.2

CONSERVATION

Each type of conservation can be tested for in a variety of ways, most of them directly attributable to the procedures originally employed by Piaget and his co-workers. We have already said something about the ways in which a fixed quantity (e.g., a lump of clay) is made to change in other perceivable features. The test material involved may be liquid rather than solid. In that case, the child is shown two identical water tumblers filled to the same level (left). The liquid in one tumbler is poured into a tall, thin bottle (center); the other remains untouched. After the pouring has been completed (right), the child is questioned. This questioning is by no means a simple matter. One cannot ask even a bright six-year-old, "Is the quantity of liquid in the two containers the same?" The inquiry must be appropriate to the child's development level. Instead, we may ask, "Suppose you are very thirsty and want to drink the water in one of the bottles. Is there just as much water in each bottle?" The child who has not yet achieved conservation of quantity may answer that there is more in one bottle because it is bigger (taller) or more in the other because it is bigger (wider). On the other hand, he may reply that there is less in one because it is thinner or less in the other because it is shorter. In any case, he has been misled by a different, irrelevant perceivable feature—height or breadth—and has failed to grasp the invariance of quantity involved.

Clearly, the tests and the testers in these situations require considerable ingenuity. The physical setup must be suited to the principle under evaluation; the questioning must be understood by the child yet must not bias him toward any one response. And with all these problems properly solved, there still remains the final and most critical task; judging whether or not the child's response indicates a grasp of conservation. Sometimes a child, when looking at the containers of water, points to the tall bottle and asserts confidently, "There's more in that bottle 'cause it's much bigger." No problem—no conservation is being shown. At the other extreme, an older child who has grasped the conservation principle patiently explains to the tester that the amount of water in the two containers "must" be the same because "the water came from the same-sized bottles." Again, an easy judgment. But with children in the midst of the transition, responses are often ambiguous. This ambiguity accurately reflects a wavering between the prelogic of taller = more and the logical necessity of conservation when the total situation has been understood.

And what of the child who, responding with a perfectly consistent but private logic, says, "There was a lot more water in the first bottle 'cause I drank it first, and I was much thirstier then"? You be the judge; then join the tester in his confusion.

Photos *The New York Times.*

This achievement of intellectual maturity, interestingly enough, comes at about the same time as physical and biological maturity.

Unfortunately, some research suggests that the process is reversible and that, possibly as an accompaniment of neurological impairment related to the aging process, there is a certain amount of loss in some aspects of thinking ability as we grow older. Papalia (1972), investigating the level of various conservation abilities throughout the life span, reports that her subjects over age sixty-five showed a decline in certain facets of conservation. She concludes:

> Results of the present study indicate that the performance apex for conservation ability attained after childhood may not be as stable an acquisition as Piaget's theory implies. . . . The ability to conserve number, hypothesized to be the earliest appearing and, therefore, the most simple concept, remained stable even in the oldest subjects. The concepts of intermediate difficulty (i.e., substance and weight conservation) were present in only about half the oldest group. The formal operation of volume conservation, regarded as the latest developing and most complex acquisition, had virtually disappeared from the response repertoire of the oldest subjects.

VARIATIONS IN COGNITIVE DEVELOPMENT

We have already pointed out that there are wide variations in the ages at which the three developmental stages are attained but that Piaget argues that the orderly sequence of development is maintained despite such variations. Data from large-scale studies of children from Western nations (notably American, English, Scandinavian, and Swiss) strongly support Piaget's assertion that a fixed, stable sequence of development exists with respect to the major stages. The sequence of development *within* a stage may be upset for certain groups, however. For example, Hyde (cited in Flavell, 1963) found in an Aden (Middle Eastern) sample of children a number of instances of failure to show the expected sequences. On occasion, the notion of conservation of volume was achieved by these children before conservation of weight. Such evidence

suggests the need for studying cognitive development in non-Western societies, preferably in those whose habits of training and educational methods are very unlike our own. This kind of study, combined with systematic observation of the *same* children throughout their development in longitudinal studies, rather than observation of different groups at different ages, seems necessary before a final determination can be made of the universality of Piaget's proposed sequence of stages in cognitive development.

Age and Stage

There is abundant evidence of considerable variation with respect to *age norms*, that is, the age at which each new stage is attained. First, as we might expect, more intelligent children generally show more rapid cognitive development. Feigenbaum (1963), for example, showed that within a group of children aged four to seven years, the child's grasp of the conservation concept varied with her tested intelligence. Differences in age norms among children of different societies have frequently been demonstrated. Hyde's work, mentioned earlier, indicates that Adenese children achieve some of the stages somewhat later than Western children do. In another study, on conservation tasks, Laurendeau and Pinard (1963) found children on the French West Indian island of Martinique to be, on the average, four years behind Canadian children living in Montreal. Also working with conservation tasks, Goldschmid (1973) found that from age six on, children in Uganda were substantially behind children of the same ages from six industrialized nations, *but* they performed as well as the others at earlier ages. (For still another study of the effect of cultural factors on the age at which conservation is actually attained, see Box 4.3.)

Such group differences may reflect true differences in the rates of cognitive development in different cultures, which may in turn be caused by factors such as variations in the kind and quality of education afforded schoolchildren. Another factor may be at work, however. As the typical method of administering Piaget-type tasks involves considerable give-and-take conversation with the child (which assumes a

BOX 4.3

HOW POTTERY MAKING DEVELOPS THE MIND

Relatively few studies have examined the way in which different environmental factors affect the emergence of the phenomenon of conservation. One intriguing study that did do this was conducted by the team of D. Price-Williams, W. Gordon, and M. Ramirez, psychologists at Rice University in Texas.

These experimenters went to rural villages in Mexico and gave tests of conservation to children in the six- to nine-year-old age range. One group of children belonged to families that made pottery as a family enterprise. The performance of this group was compared with the performance of a control group of children from the same village who did not come from pottery-making families. The groups were matched with respect to age, years in school, and socioeconomic status. The experimenters predicted that because the pottery-making children had done a great deal of work with clay, squeezing and molding it into various shapes, they would achieve conservation of substance at an earlier age than the comparable children from families that did not make pottery.

Tests comparing two such groups of children were made in two different villages. The prediction was confirmed in both. In one village, for example, the pottery-making children showed conservation of substance on a total of seventy-seven opportunities (out of a possible eighty), whereas the control children showed conservation in only ten of the eighty opportunities. Moreover, the *reasons* given by those children whose behavior showed conservation indicated that they understood *why* it should be so.

It is important to note that the pottery-making children were advanced only in conservation of *substance*; there were no significant differences between the groups on tests of conservation of number, weight, liquid, or volume. Nevertheless, this study provides dramatic evidence of the way that one type of conservation can be affected by specific experience.

D. PRICE-WILLIAMS, W. GORDON, & M. RAMIREZ III. Skill and conservation: A study of pottery-making children. *Developmental Psychology*, 1969, **1**, 769.

certain language facility), it is possible that a given child's true stage of cognitive development may be masked by an inadequate vocabulary or by shyness or timidity in the experimental situation. Wallach (1963), in summarizing a number of studies in which the child could respond in a Piaget situation *nonverbally* (e.g., by pointing at the one ball among several balls of clay that seemed to him to contain the same amount of clay as an elongated piece), concludes that one or two years can be taken off the Piaget age norms when such testing techniques are employed.

Developmental Acceleration Through Training

It seems clear, then, that Piaget's age norms are very rough signposts along the road to adult thinking ability. Nevertheless, they remain as useful reminders that there may be limits, if only very broad ones, to the kind of thinking skills available to a child at a given point in his development. Therefore, certain materials may be too difficult to learn, and certain teaching techniques may be unsuitable for children before a certain age. How confining are these limits for any particular developmental task? We do not yet know, but psychologists have sought to stretch these limits and to establish the points beyond which they cannot be pushed (for an illustrative experiment, see Box 4.4, p. 90).

There is a kind of happy irony in the fact that Piaget's proposal of developmental stages, with its implications of *limits* on what a child can do mentally at a given age, should have provided a major impetus for studies that *extend* human potentials. The intent of most of this research, however, has not been the discovery of training techniques for speeding cognitive development. Rather, most of these researchers have been primarily concerned with increasing our understanding of the basic pro-

BOX 4.4

TESTING THE LIMITS

Jan Smedslund, a Norwegian psychologist, has carried out a series of experiments designed to test the effects of special training on the age norms for various Piaget tasks. In one of these experiments, five- to seven-year-old children who had not yet attained the concept of conservation of weight were given extensive experience in weighing objects of different shapes. Time after time they had opportunities to guess at the relative weights of two objects, comparing, on a balance scale, a standard piece of clay with other pieces deformed in a variety of ways. Apparently, this training gradually taught these children the principles of the conservation of weight. They seemed to learn that distorting the form of a clay object—for example, from a long snake into several balls—did not affect the actual weight. At least the correctness of their responses and the kinds of explanations they were gradually able to offer after a period of such training were indistinguishable from those given by a group of children of about the same age who had already grasped the idea of conservation of weight naturally, that is, in the course of their development. But was this achievement the same for the speed-up and the natural children?

Smedslund asked this question in the next phase of his study.

Both groups of children were repeatedly tested in a rigged experimental situation that in all but one respect was the same as a training session. A standard piece of clay and a deformed piece were compared on a balance scale. The two pieces were initially of identical weight, and this fact was pointed out to the child. The experimenter then changed the shape of one of them and while doing so removed a small bit of it. Therefore, when he replaced the two pieces on the scales, the manipulated piece of course weighed less.

When confronted with this situation, the two groups responded in dramatically different ways. Every one of the children who had learned conservation of weight through Smedslund's training procedures showed what amounted to a cognitive relapse. Sooner or later, each abandoned the newly learned principle and reverted to nonconservation explanations, the kind he had given before being trained. Again the children asserted that the round ball of clay was heavier because it was fatter, or they gave other reasons. They rarely showed any surprise at the failure of conservation, indicating that perhaps they had never really believed it. The natural group, by contrast, was more resistant. Almost half these children invented explanations that were at least possible for the rigged situation, yet they preserved the notion of conservation. One of them, for instance, assumed that the deformed object, which weighed less, must have lost a piece of clay somewhere along the way. Perhaps, he suggested, it had fallen off, or the tester had taken some away— plausible hypotheses, even accurate ones. Most im-

cesses involved. If, for example, we can establish which of several training methods is most effective in speeding the acquisition of the principle of conservation, then we are likely to have learned something more about the emergence of this principle in the course of normal cognitive development. But, as with all scientific research and perhaps especially with research on human development, pure results point quickly to practical applications. The so-called new math, which is rapidly supplanting traditional teaching techniques for this subject matter, owes a good deal to a Piaget-type analysis of the learning processes involved. The assessment of intelligence may soon show a similar influence as current work on new mental tests that embody a developmental-stage concept of the growth of cognitive abilities begins to bear fruit. Without going into the merits of individual efforts of this sort, it seems safe to conclude that practical effects will result mainly in educational practice and evaluation and that some of these

portant, the hypotheses are consistent with the conservation principle.

V. C. Hall, R. Kingsley, and G. J. Simpson of Syracuse University were unable to reproduce Smedslund's results, although they employed a number of variations on his original procedure. Natural conservers, they found, were no more persistent in maintaining their belief in the fact of conservation than were the speed-up children. One of their suggested explanations for this failure was that Smedslund might have unintentionally encouraged more of the learned conservation group, as compared with the natural group, to abandon the notion of conservation. Because their testing of all children was done by a standard (and taped) set of questions, their procedures would have prevented this possible source of bias. In reply, Smedslund admitted the great importance of this difference in testing method but insisted that only by intensive and personalized probing could a valid assessment of the child's mental state be achieved. Thus, he argued:

> I think careful and neutral but relatively persistent probing is quite necessary in order to get at the child's private thoughts in this kind of experiment . . . while a rigidly standardized and impersonal procedure may very well lead the experimenter to lose touch completely with what goes on in the child.

M. L. Goldschmid, a psychologist at McGill University, repeated Smedslund's basic design, forming two groups of children of the same (and clearly preconservation) age by randomly assigning half his subjects to conservation training and the other half to a control group who received no training. He found that his trained subjects resisted Smedslund's rigged procedure significantly more often than the control subjects, from which he argued that learned conservation indeed conveyed some measurable advantage, at least to preconservation children. In fact, these training advantages were still evident (in the control group) at periods of three weeks, six weeks, six months, and even one year after the special training had ended. On the basis of this and other evidence, Goldschmid concludes that it *is* possible to accelerate long-lasting acquisition of conservation by specific training.

Clearly, the question remains an open one. It may, indeed, be possible through training to speed up the age at which certain Piagetian concepts are acquired, but we still do not know how much the *overall* pace of cognitive growth can be accelerated, nor do we know where the limits are. We still have a lot to learn about the effects of specific training on cognitive development. We have a lot more to learn about how to stretch these limits, how far to stretch safely, and what methods work best for what children.

J. SMEDSLUND. The acquisition of conservation of substance and weight in children: Extinction of conservation of weight acquired "normally" and by means of empirical controls on a balance. *Scandinavian Journal of Psychology*, 1961, **2**, 85–87.
V. C. HALL & R. KINGSLEY. Conservation and equilibration theory. *Journal of General Psychology*, 1968, **113**, 195–213.
V. C. HALL & G. J. SIMPSON. Factors influencing extinction of weight conservation. *Merrill-Palmer Quarterly*, 1968, **14**, 197–210.
J. SMEDSLUND. Conservation and resistance to extinction: A comment on Hall and Simpson's article. *Merrill-Palmer Quarterly*, 1968, **14**, 211–214.
M. L. GOLDSCHMID. The role of experience in the rate and sequence of cognitive development. In D. R. Green, M. P. Ford, & G. B. Flamer (Eds.), *Measurement and Piaget*. New York: McGraw-Hill, 1971.

effects will tend to accelerate cognitive development in broad segments of the population.

Will accelerating the rate of cognitive development necessarily lead eventually to higher adult ability? We do not know because there are not yet adequate data on the abilities of adults who were systematically accelerated during their development. Each person may have a built-in ceiling beyond which she cannot go, no matter how quickly she progresses toward that ceiling. Recent attempts at what has been called *compensatory education* are just that—*compensatory*. As such, their objective is not to raise the ultimate ceiling but rather to bring the individual closer to the adult level of cognitive ability that, had he not come from a disadvantaged group, he would have achieved without the intervention of special training.

In future work, the theoretical framework proposed by Piaget will probably continue to be one of the leading guides. But there are other influential theoretical analyses of the development of thinking, and we turn now to a brief account of them.

BRUNER'S THEORY OF COGNITIVE DEVELOPMENT

The developmental theory of Jerome Bruner and his associates (Bruner, Olver, & Greenfield, 1966) has certain parallels with Piaget's theory. Like Piaget, Bruner postulates a progression in the stuff of mental life from actions and percepts, through images, to a final stage in which thinking is predominantly the complex and flexible manipulation of symbols such as words. In explaining the course of cognitive growth, Bruner claims that human beings first represent their experience of the world in *enactive* terms; that is, knowledge is represented by the schemata of motor acts. For example, our knowledge of how to ride a bicycle is coded and represented in a motor schema, rather than in words or images. Indeed, precisely *because* this is motor knowledge, we can gain such knowledge by actually *doing* something with our muscles; we cannot learn to ride a bicycle merely by reading a book called *How to Ride a Bicycle*. The **enactive mode of representation** of knowledge operates to some degree throughout our lives; after all, we can still learn new motor skills within our physical capabilities all through our lives. For the infant and for the very young child, however, it is the *primary* way of representing knowledge. Thus, the enactive mode of representing knowledge is the first stage of cognitive development in Bruner's theory.

The second way of representing knowledge in the theory is *iconic*, that is, the use of images or pictures to represent information. This **iconic mode of representation**, too, is used all through life but is especially prominent in young children up to the age of perhaps six or seven years in middle-class Western societies. (For an example of the kind of cognitive functioning that typifies the iconic mode, see Box 4.5.)

The third and most important type is the **symbolic mode of representation**, that is, the use of elements, such as words, that have an arbitrary relation to the thing they represent.

BOX 4.5

WHEN A PICTURE IS *NOT* WORTH A THOUSAND WORDS

In order to think about the world, we must construct internal ways of representing external objects and relations. One kind of internal representation (iconic) is the image, a sort of mental picture that represents something we know or have seen. It might seem that vivid, concrete imagery would be an unbridled asset to thinking (especially when trying to recall specific information from a textbook on an examination). But a study by psychologists Jerome Bruner and Helen Kenney at Harvard University shows that in tasks where one must mentally transform the problem elements into a new pattern, the very concreteness of imagery may *interfere* with, rather than help, thinking.

These investigators presented young children of various ages with a set of nine actual glasses in a three-by-three arrangement (see Figure A). The

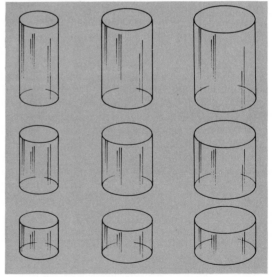

A

glasses increased in height along one side of the arrangement and in width along the other. The experimenters first removed one glass, then two, then three at a time, and asked the children to *replace* them in the appropriate positions. Children at ages five, six, and seven could do this easily.

Next, the experimenters scrambled the glasses and asked the children to *reproduce* the arrangement they had seen. Again, most of the five-, six-, and seven-year-olds succeeded. In commenting upon the children's performance up to this point, the authors note that the experiment

> was seemingly a copying task in which the "template" seemed to be a memory *image* of the original matrix. Indeed, the children appeared to be *remembering* rather than figuring out. When asked what they were doing they would often tell you that they were trying to *remember* where the glasses had been before (italics ours).

Finally, the experimenters again scrambled the glasses, but this time they placed the glass that was formerly in the lower left corner of the arrangement in the lower right corner and asked the child to rebuild the entire pattern around this just-moved glass. In short, the child was now asked to *transpose* the pattern, maintaining the original relations within the arrangement (see Figure B). This could be done

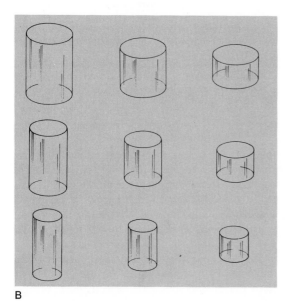

B

by rotating the entire pattern counterclockwise by 90 degrees, a task for which a static visual image alone, however clearly recalled, would not suffice. What happened?

None of the five-year-olds and only a small fraction of the six-year-olds could do this. The ex-

periments report that the youngest children seemed to be dominated by an image of the original pattern. For example, they would try to put the transposed glass "back where it belongs," contrary to instructions. In several instances, five- or six-year-olds tried to reproduce the original pattern by ignoring and building right over the shifted glass and thus destroying the required relations within the arrangement (see Figure C).

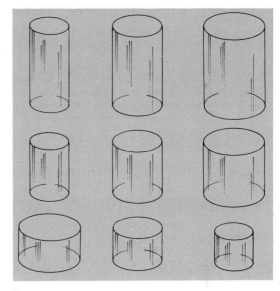

C

The seven-year-old children, however, generally succeeded at the transposed task. Why did they succeed when the younger children failed? Bruner and Kenney cite evidence that the older children were able to make greater use of language, a symbolic system that permits both the representation and the *transposition* of information. The younger children, who relied more on imagery, were limited by the fact that this form of representation does not allow for transposition.

In short, one of the reasons that adult thought can transcend the rigid limits of concrete reality and move on to consider hypothetical possibilities is that a thousand words—or many fewer—*are* worth more than a picture, at least for some tasks.

J. S. BRUNER & H. J. KENNEY. On multiple ordering. In J. S. Bruner, R. R. Olver, & P. M. Greenfield (Eds.), *Studies in Cognitive Growth*. New York: Wiley, 1966.

BOX 4.6

BLIND LOGIC

Max Wertheimer bemoaned the ease with which teachers seemed to assume that a logical analysis of a problem is the only or best instructional approach. Let him explain:

> I am visiting a classroom. The teacher: "During the last lesson we learned how to find the area of a rectangle. Do you all know it?"
>
> The class: "Yes." One pupil calls out: "The area of a rectangle is equal to the product of the two sides."
>
> "Now," says the teacher, "we shall go on." He draws a parallelogram on the blackboard (Figure A). "This is called a parallelogram. A parallelogram

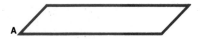

> is a plane quadrilateral the opposite sides of which are equal and parallel."
>
> He labels the corners a, b, c, d.
>
> "I drop one perpendicular from the upper left corner and another perpendicular from the upper right corner.
>
> "I extend the base line to the right.
>
> "I label the two new points e and f" (Figure B).

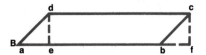

> With the help of this figure he then proceeds to the usual proof of the theorem that the area of a parallelogram is equal to the product of the base by the altitude, establishing the equality of certain lines and angles and the congruence of the pair of triangles.
>
> The teacher now gives a number of problems, all of which require finding the areas of parallelograms of different sizes, sides, and angles. Before the end of the hour the teacher assigns ten more problems of this kind for homework.
>
> At the next meeting of the class, one day later, I am there again.
>
> The lesson begins with the teacher calling on a pupil to demonstrate how the area of a parallelogram is found. The pupil does it exactly. . . . A written quiz brings good results.
>
> Most people would say, "This is an excellent class; the teaching goal has been reached." But observing the class I feel uneasy, I am troubled. "What have they learned?" I ask myself. "Have they done any thinking at all? Have they grasped the issue? Maybe all that they have done is little more than blind repetition. How can I clarify it? What can I *do?*"
>
> I ask the teacher whether he will allow me to put a question to the class. "With pleasure," he answers, clearly proud of his class.

Whereas images have to be based upon perceptual aspects of experience, symbols may represent abstract notions, including transformations, rules, and concepts. The most important symbolic medium is language, and Bruner believes that language provides one of the main forces in cognitive development because the child tries to develop schemata that correspond to the abstract concepts he hears in his language.

For Bruner, then, cognition is explicitly viewed as a means of interacting with the environment, and the stages in cognitive growth—enactive, iconic, and symbolic representations of experience—are seen as partly produced by the environment and partly adaptive to it. This differs from the theory of Piaget in emphasizing

the *adaptive* values of different modes of representing experience in different environmental contexts. Perhaps the best example of this difference is to be found in their views of language. Piaget is inclined to view the child's use of language as being determined by his level of cognitive growth, whereas Bruner sees cognitive growth as being determined to some extent *by* language. Bruner also places far more emphasis than Piaget does upon the effectiveness of specific training and teaching:

> I shall take the view . . . that the development of human intellectual functioning from infancy to such perfection as it may reach is shaped by a series of technological advances in the use of the mind. Growth depends upon the mastery of [in-

I go to the board and draw this (Figure C).

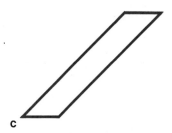

C

Some are obviously taken aback.

One pupil raises his hand: "Teacher, we haven't had that yet."

Others are busy. They have copied the figure on paper, they draw the auxiliary lines as they were taught, dropping perpendiculars from the two upper corners and extending the base line (Figure D). Then they look bewildered, perplexed.

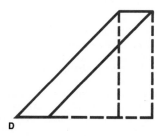

D

Some do not look at all unhappy; they write firmly below their drawings: "The area is equal to the base times the altitude"—a correct subsumption, but perhaps an entirely blind one. When asked whether they can show it to be true in this case, they too become perplexed.

With still others, it is entirely different. Their faces brighten, they smile, they turn their papers through 45 degrees. . . .

Wertheimer's Figure C is of course the teacher's Figure A turned around. Clearly, for many of the students, there had been a mastery of a narrow exercise but no understanding. Wertheimer's point is that it is possible and necessary to teach problem-solving skills in ways that do promote understanding and that such teaching techniques follow from a *psychological* analysis of processes involved, not a *logical* one.

Wertheimer's book presents lucid analyses and specific teaching techniques for a variety of problems. For a starter, the reader should approach Figure A, scissors in hand.

M. WERTHEIMER. *Productive Thinking.* New York: Harper & Row, 1959. Excerpts reproduced by permission of Harper and Brothers. Copyright 1945 by Harper and Brothers. Figures adapted and text material reprinted by permission; copyright 1945, 1959 by Valentin Wertheimer.

formation processing] techniques and cannot be understood without reference to such mastery. These techniques are not, in the main, inventions of individuals who are "growing up"; they are, rather, skills transmitted with varying efficiency and success by the culture—language being a prime example. Cognitive growth, then, is in a major way from the outside in, as well as from the inside out. (Bruner, 1964)

THE GESTALT APPROACH TO COGNITIVE DEVELOPMENT

Many of the leading figures in the development of Gestalt psychology (see p. 301), although primarily concerned with perception, did concern themselves with cognition. Koffka (1928),

in a book entitled *The Growth of the Mind,* presented a detailed theoretical analysis attempting to account for cognitive development in the child. Köhler (1925) applied these principles to understanding the problem-solving behavior of apes. Max Wertheimer, the main founder of Gestalt psychology, in his *Productive Thinking* (1959), offered a detailed analysis of effective and ineffective techniques of classroom teaching and learning following directly from Gestalt principles of perception (see Box 4.6). This work, originally performed in the 1920s, anticipates, both in name and in general approach, a currently active area of both research and educational innovation, one that we shall discuss in considerable detail in Unit 7.

Sharing this gestaltist origin but moving

beyond it in his *Comparative Psychology of Mental Development* (1948, originally published in German in 1926), Heinz Werner set forth a theory of cognitive development that in many ways parallels Piaget's. Werner proposed that mental organization becomes increasingly differentiated, with higher-order structures being formed from more primitive ones, and that totally novel structures arise as the child passes successively through sensorimotor, perceptual-imaginal, and conceptual-symbolic stages of mental development. Even without further details on Werner's theoretical position, the reader will easily recognize here striking similarities to Piaget's formulations. Although the Gestalt approach to cognitive development is no longer being actively pursued within psychology today, we can still appreciate its pioneering formulations, which, as we have seen, have energetic modern descendants.

SUMMARY

1. Perhaps the most comprehensive theory of cognitive development today is that of Piaget. His general principles include: (a) organization (increasing integration of simple systems, or schemata, into more complex ones); (b) equilibration (the driving force behind this continuous integration process); (c) adaptation, which subsumes the processes of assimilation (taking into mental organization from the environment whatever can be effectively incorporated within current schemata) and accommodation (modifying current schemata and creating new ones when new stimuli cannot be assimilated).

2. In Piaget's theory, cognitive development can be viewed as a series of sequential stages. The broadest of these are: (a) the sensorimotor stage, in which integration of inborn reflexes and the notion of a stable object occur; (b) the stage of concrete operations, which includes the beginnings of the capacity for symbolic thought and the development of language and of conservation abilities; and (c) the stage of formal operations, in which the capacity for adult abstract thinking finally emerges.

3. Generally speaking, these stages follow one another in an invariant sequence and appear to be achieved at more or less the same ages in all children within a specific culture. However, substantial individual differences occur in their timing in different societies.

4. Specific training in certain abilities can accelerate mental development, at least up to a point, but the generality and extent of such training effects are still under investigation.

5. Bruner's theory of cognitive development involves three stages, each of which is defined by a particular way of representing knowledge. These stages are: (a) the enactive stage or mode, in which knowledge is represented in terms of motor schemata; (b) the iconic mode, in which knowledge is represented in terms of images or percepts; and (c) the symbolic mode, in which knowledge is represented by symbols, particularly words, that can represent abstract notions as well as concrete information.

6. Bruner's theory differs from Piaget's in its greater concern with the role of education and experience as determinants of cognitive growth.

7. The early Gestalt psychologists extended their analysis of perceptual processes to the development of thinking and, in certain important respects, foresaw current formulations of cognitive development.

GLOSSARY

accommodation   For Piaget, the type of adaptation in which old schemata, or organizations, are modified or new ones formed in order to absorb environmental stimulation that can be neither ignored nor made, by assimilation, to fit into existing organizations.

adaptation   For Piaget, the process of continuous interaction between existing schemata and environmental stimulation. Assimilation and accommodation are the two complementary types of adaptation.

assimilation   For Piaget, the type of adaptation in which existing schemata incorporate only those aspects of environmental stimulation that fit or can be forced to fit into existing organizations.

concrete operations   Piaget's second stage of mental development, extending from about two to eleven years, during which symbolic activity first appears. Language and conservation abilities are developed during this stage.

conservation   An aspect of mental development, in Piaget's theory, in which the child comes to understand that certain properties of an object (e.g., weight) do not change, despite changes in other perceivable features of the object.

enactive mode of representation   For Bruner, the representation of knowledge by motor schemata. Knowledge of how to ride a bicycle or how to perform a particular dance routine is enactive knowledge. This is the first of his three stages of cognitive growth and is the primary one for infants.

equilibration   For Piaget, the intrinsic process or tendency for schemata to function continuously at higher and more complex levels. Essentially, the motivational basis for cognitive growth.

formal operations   Piaget's third and last stage of mental development, extending from about eleven to fifteen years, during which the ability to think abstractly is acquired.

iconic mode of representation   For Bruner, the representation of knowledge in the form of images and percepts. A memory of a friend's face is an example. This is the second of his stages of cognitive growth.

organization   For Piaget, the view that mental life is built up by the increasing interrelation of simple elements or schemata combining to form new and ever more complex schemata.

schemata   The basic elements of mental life (or cognitive organization) in Piaget's theoretical system. Sensorimotor reflexes present at birth are examples of the simplest schemata.

sensorimotor stage   Piaget's first stage, extending from birth to about age two, during which the infant's mental organization builds from a few inborn reflex responses that comprise the starting point of his mental development.

symbolic mode of representation   For Bruner, the most complex and flexible way that knowledge may be internally represented, his final stage of cognitive growth. Symbolic knowledge involves elements that have an arbitrary relation to the things they represent (e.g., the use of words).

SUMER-ARYAN EVOLUTION OF THE ALPHABET.

structure and development of language

DO YOU KNOW...

• that a young child often applies the general rules of his language more accurately than an adult does?

• whether all human languages can be shown to share certain fundamental features?

• that over half of all our speech is made up of only fifty or so different words?

• why it is that, in a noisy audience, we can understand fairly well what a speaker is saying even if we miss a lot of his words?

• that young children throughout the world apparently discover for themselves, and for a time use consistently, the same grammar?

• that sometimes a child's speech is grammatically more correct at the age of two than at three or even older?

and why that is?

Photo by Yvonne Freund/By permission of Chase Manhattan Money Museum

CONTENTS

THE STRUCTURE OF LANGUAGE

MOTHER: Where did you go with Grandpa?
THREE-YEAR-OLD: We goed in a park.

This is an apparently simple bit of everyday conversation between a mother and a little child. But think what each of them must know about the English language in order to make this bit of communication possible. Each of them hears only a series of noises (which are the physical stimuli) from the other, yet these noises have meaning. In order for the sounds of language to have meaning, both participants in an act of communication must have the same language in mind. We mean this in a very particular sense: In order to *de*code speech (convert sounds into meanings), the listener must know the same code that the speaker used to *en*code his message (convert meanings into sounds). Not only must they both know and use the same *code* in decoding and encoding messages, but they must also use the same *rules* in applying this code. In other words, they both must know the same language. In this unit, we shall examine what is meant by the rules and structure of language and how such knowledge is acquired.

Linguistic Knowledge

You might object that it is impossible to speak of someone "knowing" the rules of a language, certainly not a three-year-old. And if, by "knowing," you mean being able to state explicitly the rules of a language, you are, of course, correct. But the scientists who study language and language behavior have something else in mind when they speak of an individual's **linguistic knowledge** of the structure of his language. They are referring to knowledge that is tacit or implicit or unconscious. In everyday terms we say that someone "knows how to repair cars" or "knows how to make a good impression." We do not mean that such a person is able to write out all the rules for repairing cars or impressing people favorably. Rather, we mean that we have inferred from his behavior that he is able to *perform* well in these matters when called upon. In order for us to make such inferences, we must see how the individual deals with a number of new situations. If he has managed to repair one or two cars well, he may just have been lucky. But if he consistently repairs cars effectively, then we say that he "knows how to repair cars." And if a master mechanic ever succeeded in writing the definitive rule book of diagnosis and treatment of auto ailments, we would find that our mechanic had been implicitly following such rules all along, long before anyone knew how to write the book.

We are not all skilled mechanics, but we are *all* competent speakers of our native language. This is true of even the least verbal or least well spoken among us. Every day we hear many sentences that we have never heard before, and yet we know what they mean; and every day we utter sentences that have never been spoken by man before, and yet we manage to make ourselves understood. That is to say, we *consistently* use language meaningfully; and therefore, obviously, we must know how to relate sounds to meanings. Because language is so *productive*—that is, because there is no limit to the variety of new sentences that can be spoken and understood—we must credit every speaker with **productive knowledge of language**. Productive knowledge, in the linguistic sense, means command of the rules of phonology, morphology, syntax, and semantics of a particular language. Let us examine this point in regard to the mother-child dialogue quoted at the beginning of this unit. What do these two speakers know about their language?

To begin with, note that we have written the dialogue in discrete words; yet, if you listen to speech in an unfamiliar language, you will find it very hard to determine where a word begins and ends. (You may even find it hard to recognize some of the sounds.) For example, since you know English, you can find the word boundaries either with your ear or with your eye, even if they are not indicated by auditory or visual spaces:

wheredidyougowithgrandpa

But if you do not know the language, it is very hard to determine where one word ends and another begins. Here is the Turkish translation of this same English utterance. Can you guess where the spaces belong?

dedenlenereyegittinsen

(You can find the answer at the end of this unit.)

We can be sure that the mother and child in the dialogue recognize the English words that were spoken. They are able to listen to one continuous string of sounds (wheredidyougowithgrandpa), but what they hear are discrete and separate words. So they must know something about the sound structure (**phonology**) and the word structure (**morphology**) of English. Each of the separate words they hear has meaning for them; that is, they know something about the **semantics** of their language as well. They can also, by paying attention to changes in tone of voice, differentiate questions from statements from exclamations, and so they know something about the **intonation patterns** of their language. Almost every diary study of infant behavior reports that, at a very early age, the infant either responds differently to variations in intonation (speech melody) of parental utterances or uses contrasting intonation patterns to express different moods, or both. For example, Charles Darwin (1877), reporting on his son's speech development, noted "communication . . . in a marked manner by different intonations," along with the observation that "before he was a year old, he understood intonations." Champneys (1881) observed that a nine-month-old infant "distinctly imitated the intonation of the voice when any word or sentence was repeated in the same way several times." (More recent and detailed observations are reported in Box 5.1, p. 102.)

If a speaker can segment an utterance into meaningful words—that is, if he knows the phonology, morphology, semantics, and intonation patterns of the utterance—will he then be able to understand it? Not yet; another crucial aspect of linguistic knowledge is still required. Consider again the mother-child dialogue, but assume this time that the only information we have is an unordered collection of meaningful

BOX 5.1

IT'S THE WAY THAT YOU SAY IT

Recently, observations of infants' perceptions of intonations have been subjected to detailed scientific study. With the refinement of techniques of infant research, very early abilities to perceive aspects of speech signals have been discovered. One valuable technique is the *habituation-dishabituation* method. Briefly, the infant is exposed to repeated presentations of a stimulus until habituation of autonomic responses and motor-orienting responses occurs (Unit 15). That is, once an infant gets used to a uniform stimulus, his heart rate falls to a steady, slow rate; he does not perk up to see what is going on; and so forth. Subsequent presentation of a novel stimulus—that is, one that the infant can perceive as different—will result in dishabituation (increase in heart rate, orienting response, and so forth). Thus, if a new stimulus results in dishabituation, one can conclude that the infant is able to perceive the difference between the new and old (habituated) stimulus.

Using this technique, E. Kaplan, working at Cornell University, was able to show that eight-month-old infants can discriminate between falling and rising intonation patterns. For example, after the infant had heard a series of utterances with one intonation pattern (either rising or falling), the intonation pattern was shifted. Heart rate increased with a change in intonation pattern, indicating that infants as young as eight months can discriminate between differences in speech melody.

Making use of a similar technique, A. R. Moffitt's doctoral research at the University of Minnesota found an ability to discriminate between "bah" and "gah" in five-month-olds. Since a shift from "bah" to "gah" resulted in dishabituation, the conclusion was that five-month-old infants are capable of perceiving the acoustic difference between the sounds $\boxed{b}$ and $\boxed{g}$. P. D. Eimas and other Brown University psychologists also used much the same technique with systematically constructed pairs of artificial speech syllables that varied according to supposed universal acoustic cues which distinguish certain kinds of consonants that are otherwise identical. For example, voiced consonants, like *b* and *d* were paired against their corresponding unvoiced consonants like *p* and *t*. Here, the finding was that infants as young as one month could discriminate the difference in acoustic cues that distinguishes, for example, voiced *b* from unvoiced *p* in English (and presumably other languages).

The perception and imitation of intonation require attention to the pitch (i.e., the sound wave frequency) of speech. P. Lieberman, at the Massachusetts Institute of Technology, has shown that infants around one year of age are sensitive to the

words for each utterance. For example, let us arrange these same words alphabetically.

MOTHER: did go Grandpa where with you
THREE-YEAR-OLD: a goed in park we

You cannot make sense of these utterances because they are not ordered; that is to say, they have no **syntax**. In order to understand speech, you must also know the ways in which the order of words determines the meaning of a sentence. (How else would you know the difference between "man bites dog" and "dog bites man"?) And so we must credit the mother and child with some implicit knowledge of the phonological, morphological, semantic, intonational patterning, *and* syntactic rules of English.

It is the task of linguists to make such knowledge explicit by writing detailed, formal descriptions of the structures of particular languages. And it is the task of psycholinguists to determine how the structures and characteristics of adult language are learned by children and how they are used in the processes of speaking, comprehending, and remembering. (For an introduction to psycholinguistics, see Slobin, 1971b.) In a broad sense, both linguistics and psycholinguistics are branches of *cognitive psychology*, that field of psychology which deals with the acquisition, structuring, storage, and use of knowledge (see Neisser, 1967). Linguists and psycholinguists, by studying the structures of particular languages and the processes of language development and language use, respec-

characteristic speech frequency ranges of different adult speakers. Let him speak for himself:

A ten-month-old-boy and a thirteen-month-old girl were recorded under several different conditions. The boy was recorded while he babbled alone in his crib. . . . He was also recorded while he babbled in an identical play situation with his father and his mother, respectively. The child sat on his father's lap, and the parent spoke to him while he played with his dog. After fifteen minutes he sat instead on his mother's lap while she talked to him. Four interchanges took place. The average fundamental frequency of the child's babbling under these conditions was measured. About twenty minutes of "conversation" occurred under each condition. The same experiment was then repeated with the thirteen-month-old girl, who was beginning to speak. The girl was not recorded while she . . . spoke alone, and she played with her cat while she sat on her parents' laps. The average fundamental frequencies are presented in the table.

Note that the average fundamental frequency of the boy's babbling while he "spoke" to his father was 340 hz, while his average fundamental frequency was 390 hz when he was with his mother. The girl showed the same direction of difference, even more clearly. (The children's fathers used lower average fundamental frequencies than their mothers in their normal speech.) Both of the fundamental frequencies the boy used when "speaking" to his parents were lower than that of his solitary babbling. . . . The boy apparently lowered his fundamental frequency when he was with either parent, and he lowered his fundamental frequency more when he was with the parent having the lower fundamental frequency. The girl also apparently attempted to mimic the fundamental frequencies of her parents.

Evidently, the common belief that even young infants can recognize and react to subtle differences in how they are spoken to has a solid basis in research fact.

Subject	Condition	"Speech" (in hz)
10-month-old boy	Alone in crib	430
	Playing with father	340
	Playing with mother	390
13-month-old girl	Playing with father	290
	Playing with mother	390

E. L. KAPLAN. Intonation and language acquisition. *Papers and Reports on Child Language Development*, 1970, No. 1 (March). Stanford University Committee on Linguistics.
A. R. MOFFITT. Speech perception by infants. Unpublished doctoral dissertation, University of Minnesota, 1968.
P. D. EIMAS, E. R. SIQUELAND, P. JUSCZYK, & J. VIGORITO. Speech perception in infants. *Science*, 1971, **171**, 303–306.
P. LIEBERMAN. *Intonation, Perception and Language.* Cambridge, Mass.: M.I.T. Press, 1967. Reprinted by permission of The M.I.T. Press, Cambridge, Mass.

tively, seek to understand universal bases of mental functioning, which, they argue, must ultimately relate to the structures and processes of the human brain. Thus, we have the developing research area of neurolinguistics (Whitaker, 1971).

Comprehension of syntax   We can examine the opening dialogue even more closely and ask what the child seems to know about English syntax. (Check back to it now.) From his reply to his mother's question, it is clear that he has understood it. How did he even know it was a question? He must have noted the initial question word, "where," and the rising intonation. Furthermore, he knows that the questioning word asks about location because he answers with a location, "park." He knows that the question refers to the past because of the past-tense ending on "did" and that the verb, "go," has plural reference because he is asked about "you . . . with Grandpa." He indicates this knowledge in his answer by saying "we goed"— "we" because of plurality, "goed" because of past tense. Furthermore, the fact that he said "goed" rather than "went" indicates that he really does know the *general* past-tense rule in English. Errors like this in child speech are very informative because they show us that the child is using his language productively and is not simply blindly imitating what he hears. "Goed" is a genuine child production, following the rules of English better than English does.

There are some other details of English the child hasn't figured out yet. He says "goed *in* a park," rather than "*to* a park," probably an analogy with such forms as "go in the house" and "go in the store." He apparently conceives of a park as something one can go into, even though adult English chooses to categorize parks differently for linguistic purposes. But his error, as in the case of his use of "goed," is not at all random; rather, it reflects a systematic attempt by the child to structure his language in a meaningful way. We will return to this point later in the unit when we discuss how children learn to speak. For now, however, we need to know more about the structure of language and how it is studied.

Linguistic levels   Modern work in linguistics has made it clear that utterances are organized on many different levels, from the superficial level of audible speech to deep levels of underlying logic and meaning. The adult speaker of a language knows not only how to pronounce and organize utterances but also how to use language meaningfully and appropriately to carry out functions of communication and social interaction. A few examples will make it clear that on each level of linguistic analysis another aspect of underlying knowledge is revealed.

Consider, even if you do not necessarily agree with, the following two sentences:

1. Professors are eager to please.
2. Professors are easy to please.

On the surface, these two sentences seem to have the same grammatical structure, differing only in the choice of adjective ("eager" or "easy"). Yet, on a deeper level, their meanings are clearly quite different. The first sentence says something about the way professors behave: They are the sort of people who go out of their way to please others. The second sentence says something about how professors respond to others: It is easy to make professors happy. In order to understand the second sentence, you must realize that some crucial information has been left out—namely, that *if someone does something*, then professors will be pleased. In other words, on a deep grammatical level, "professors" is not the subject of the sentence, but, rather, the object (i.e., "someone pleases professors"). In the first sentence, on the other hand, "professors" is really the subject of the verb (i.e., "professors please"). The second sentence is more complex in linguistic terms. Sentences of this type apparently require more mental effort in comprehension and, in fact, are learned later in childhood.

The purpose of this detailed exploration of two sentences is to give you some taste for the complexity of linguistic structure. As a speaker of English, you know some special rules about adjectives like "eager" and "easy." Even though you had probably not encountered the two illustrative sentences before, you knew full well, as you were reading them, the implications of such adjectives for deciding who does what to whom.

On a deeper level, you know that many sentences have particular logical implications which are not spelled out. For example, if you are told that "the professor forgot to bring the book," you know that he intended to bring the book and that he did not do so. All this does not have to be communicated explicitly because your knowledge of the language allows you to figure out the *background* statements that were not directly stated.

On another level—the level of **sociolinguistics** (see Gumperz & Hymes, 1972)—you know how to use linguistic forms appropriately to communicate social meanings. For example, if someone says, "Excuse me, I wonder if you could tell me the time," you do not respond, "So do I." Instead, you either tell him what time it is or apologize that you do not know. Linguistically, he has neither made a request nor commanded you to respond. But sociolinguistically you know that he has employed a customary polite request form.

In brief, when we say that an adult "knows English" or that a child has "learned English," we mean that he can perform competently on all these levels. He can form English sentences with appropriate pronunciation and intonation and can arrange the words grammatically, meaningfully, and in socially appropriate fashion.

Formal description of such linguistic knowledge is advancing rapidly. Although we are still far from an adequate description of any particular language in the full sense of the rules underlying meaningful and appropriate use of the language, it is exciting to discover that all the languages studied thus far by linguists seem to be describable within the same theoretical framework. This suggests that there are **linguistic universals**; that is, there are basic structural features that are common to all human languages. This makes immediate good sense; thus, all human languages can be seen as variants of a common pattern. Since any normal human infant can indeed acquire any human language within the first three or four years of life, this universality probably reflects certain basic characteristics of mental development and of children's means for acquiring language. And this universality must also reflect the human psychological processes of perception, storage, and use of language.

Experimental Psycholinguistics

When you listen to someone speak, you seem to grasp his meanings immediately; yet in the brief instant between perception and comprehension, all your linguistic knowledge and language-processing skills must be brought to bear. In recent years psycholinguists have begun to explore this process in the laboratory. This research is still in its infancy, but it is accelerating rapidly and is already too complex to be fully summarized here. We will discuss only a few features of it in this unit.

Sentence-comprehension time One popular technique is to measure how long it takes subjects to understand different types of sentences (where "how long" is measured in thousandths of a second). It has been found that sentences with complex grammar take more time to understand than sentences with less complex grammar, *even if the simpler sentences have more words in them.*

People have particular difficulty in comprehending negative sentences, especially if they turn out to be true. For example, in one study

(Slobin, 1966), the subject is shown a picture of a dog chasing a cat and is asked to respond quickly with "true" or "false" to one of the following sentences (the average response times are noted):

1. The dog is chasing the cat.
                    [TRUE AFFIRMATIVE]
   (1.55 sec.)
2. The cat is chasing the dog.
                    [FALSE AFFIRMATIVE] .
   (1.68 sec.)
3. The dog is not chasing the cat.
                    [FALSE NEGATIVE]
   (1.91 sec.)
4. The cat is not chasing the dog.
                    [TRUE NEGATIVE]
   (2.14 sec.)

The sentences are listed in order of increasing difficulty as measured by longer response time and greater probability of error in response. Apparently, when you hear a sentence, you must keep track of various separate linguistic features, and noting that a sentence is negative requires an increase in processing time.

Consider a somewhat different and perhaps more complex example:

1. John is present.
2. John is absent.

On the surface, both seem to be affirmative sentences. On a deeper level, however, the second sentence is inherently negative because "absent" really means "not present." Do subjects *hear* sentence 2 as affirmative or negative? Clark (1971) has found that the time required to verify sentences such as "John is absent" corresponds to the time required to verify sentences such as "John is not present," both of these requiring more time than straightforward affirmatives such as "John is present." Apparently, in order for the inherently negative word "absent" to be understood, it must first be decoded into two parts: "not" and "present." Research of this sort demonstrates that listeners do not just comprehend the surface forms of utterances; rather, they must unravel sentences to retrieve basic units of meaning, even if all these units are not explicitly present in the particular sentences. It takes a certain amount of processing time to pull out each of these units. As we shall see on

BOX 5.2

IT'S NOT WHAT YOU SAY,
BUT WHAT YOU MEAN

Although we generally remember quite well what we have just heard, we often cannot repeat it in the same words in which it was given. It is the underlying structure of what we say, rather than the surface details, that determines sentence meaning. This phenomenon has been nicely demonstrated by J. Sachs in a doctoral dissertation, since published, at the University of California at Berkeley. Her aim: to show that "form which is not relevant to the meaning is normally not retained."

Her subject listened to twenty-eight passages of a sensible narrative. After each passage the subject was given a single test sentence that was either identical to a sentence just heard somewhere in the passage or had been changed in either form or meaning. The subject was required to say: "identical" or "changed." There were three delay intervals between the hearing of the original sentence and presentation of the test sentence: no delay, 80 syllables later (about 27 sec), and 160 syllables later (about 46 sec). The subject never knew what sentences she would be tested on. Here is an example; the target sentence is italicized:

There is an interesting story about the telescope. In Holland, a man named Lippershey was an eye-glass maker. One day his children were playing with some lenses. They discovered that things seemed very close if two lenses were held about a foot apart. Lippershey began experimenting and his "spyglass" attracted much attention. *He sent a letter about it to Galileo, the great Italian scientist.* Galileo at once realized the importance of the discovery and set about to build an instrument of his own. He used an old organ pipe with one lens curved out and the other in. On the first clear night he pointed the glass toward the sky. He was amazed to find the empty dark spaces filled with brightly gleaming stars! [80 syllables] Night after night Galileo climbed to a high tower, sweeping the sky with his telescope. One night he saw Jupiter, and to his great surprise discovered near it three bright stars, two to the east and one to the west. On the next night, however, all were to the west. A few nights later there were four little stars. [160 syllables] [Bell rings.]

The subject had to respond with "identical" or "changed" when presented with one of the following four test sentences, three of which had been changed from the original in some manner:

He sent a letter about it to Galileo, the great Italian scientist. [target sentence]

Galileo, the great Italian scientist, sent him a letter about it. [semantic change]

A letter about it was sent to Galileo, the great Italian scientist. [passive/active change]

---

p. 116, very young children are limited in the amount of available sentence-processing time and are often not able to perform the full range of operations necessary for fully comprehending a single sentence.

Memory for sentences   What happens to a sentence once you have read and understood it? Although you may not be able to repeat what you have just read verbatim, you can probably recount the gist of it. Apparently listeners make use of the particular words and structures of sentences only to discover underlying meanings; they quickly discard surface information once

understanding has been achieved. The function of speech is to communicate meanings, and these are apparently stored nonlinguistically. (This point has been well demonstrated in the psycholinguistic experiment by Sachs described in Box 5.2.)

The entire complex structure of language is a fragile, momentary bridge between what the speaker intends to communicate and what the listener's mind subsequently reconstructs of those intentions. The structure of language is heavily determined by the fleeting nature of short-term memory (see p. 404). Because we communicate primarily through speech, which cannot be reread, we must be as compact as possible in packaging our information, leaving

He sent Galileo, the great Italian scientist, a letter about it. [formal change]

For each passage there was a different set of four related sentences, each one of which, in turn, appeared to be the target sentence in the passage.

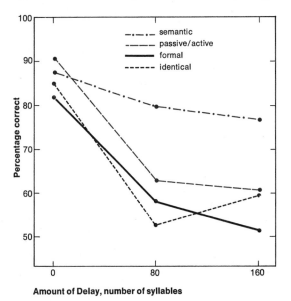

Amount of Delay, number of syllables

Percentage of judgments "identical" and "changed" that were correct for each test type.

When the test sentence was heard with no intervening delay, subjects were able to recognize *any* kind of change. Thus (see figure) with a zero-syllable delay, the correct response was given in about 90 percent of the instances. After only 80 syllables of delay, subjects' recognition of syntactic changes (active/passive and formal) was close to chance (50 percent); whereas their recognition of semantic changes remained strong even after 160 syllables. In another study, Sachs found that recognition for formal changes dropped to chance level after as short a delay as 40 syllables (7.5 sec). It is clear that the formal structure of sentences is stored for only a brief period of time. A small change in wording that is related to meaning, however, is easily detected. Sachs concludes that:

> The findings . . . are consistent with a theory of comprehension which contends that the meaning of the sentence is derived from the original string of words by an active, interpretive process. That original sentence which is perceived is rapidly forgotten, and the memory then is for the information contained in the sentence.

J. S. SACHS. Recognition memory for syntactic and semantic aspects of connected discourse. *Perception and Psychophysics,* 1967, **2,** 437–442.
J. S. SACHS. Memory in reading and listening to discourse. *Memory and Cognition,* in press.

much unsaid on the surface and relying on shared linguistic knowledge to guide the listener to our full intent. The strengths and the weaknesses of human language lie within these constraints of memory and shared knowledge.

Since spoken language is so vital to human adaptation, and because it is, at best, a fragile and momentary bridge between one mind and another, mankind has developed a number of props to strengthen this vital bridge. Among these props are the tendency to use only a limited number of very familiar words (out of the hundreds of thousands which are available); to construct our sentences so that "unheard" or badly spoken words can be quickly and correctly guessed at by the listener; to repeat ourselves in our speech so that even the simplest message is transmitted several times over; and to develop a perceptual skill which permits us to hear the essentials of speech under very difficult circumstances.

These various characteristics of spoken language have been carefully studied, and we now turn to a review of some of those studies to see how the spoken word, despite all its weaknesses, can serve as an extraordinarily efficient instrument of communication.

Word Repetition

At one time, a great deal of the psychologist's work in language and communication made much use of the statistical approach. Although this approach is no longer frequently pursued by modern psycholinguists, some interesting and useful data have come from it. Here the question is: What words and sequences are most frequently spoken? Once we know what words and word sequences do appear most frequently, we are in a better position to understand how and why speech is understood *and* misunderstood.

The most comprehensive dictionaries of modern English reveal a total vocabulary of well over a million words. The supply of English words is so generous that we could talk away for weeks before we would *have* to use the same word a second time. But statistical counts of word usage indicate that we do repeat ourselves—and at an astonishingly great rate. On the average, we repeat a word every ten to fifteen words. The fifty most commonly used words make up about 60 percent of all the words we speak and 45 percent of all the words we write. This repetitious use of a very few words (arranged and rearranged in a large number of patterns) to express an infinite number of ideas is characteristic of most languages. Here we have a striking demonstration of the importance of patterning in language.

Why should we be so niggardly in our use of words? Several answers can be immediately suggested. First, a good number of the words (according to estimates, as many as three-quarters of all our words) have very limited usefulness because they are the specialized words of the sciences, technology, and trade jargons. Second, most of us know only a very small portion of even the general words; we simply have not learned all the words of our language. The average adult is said to have a use-and-recognition vocabulary of 30,000 to 60,000 words, and a highly literate adult is not likely to go much beyond 100,000. But our word usage is not limited by the size of our vocabulary alone. It is also limited by syntax and a **verbal-context effect**. That is, once we have spoken one word, the next word is to some degree determined or restricted by the rules of grammar and by the meaning, rhythm, or sound of the previous word.

Verbal Context and Frequency Count

A fairly precise quantitative measurement of one of the constraints upon our language has been developed by analyzing the sequence of letters constituting printed English. Letters, even more than words, occur with differential frequencies; for example, the letter *e* appears much more frequently than any of the remaining twenty-five letters of the alphabet. The letters in one part of a sequence limit the possibilities and influence the probabilities of the appearance of another letter in a later part of the sequence. For example, once we have written the letter *q*, it must almost invariably be followed by the letter *u*; once we have written the two letters *th*, the third letter can be one of only eight or nine letters. (See Box 5.3 for a profitable exploitation of these principles.)

Presumably one could discover the frequencies of different letter sequences in the English language by taking large samples of printed English and tabulating all the different letter sequences. We can thus count the number of times the following sequences (and every other conceivable sequence) occur: *th, tha, the, thi, tho, thr*. From such a count, we could then estimate the constraining influence of, say, *th* upon the third letter. That is, we would be able to predict with what probabilities certain letters would follow the combination *th*.

Ordering of the letters, however, is so complex and the number of different sequences is so great that the only adequate statistical machine to deal with the problem is the skilled human talker. A literate person already knows the constraints that the occurrence of a letter in one part of the sequence will have upon a later part. He obeys these constraints in his language behavior as he obeys grammatical constraints, even though he cannot formulate the rules. Shannon (1951) therefore developed the following technique of getting that knowledge from the skilled person: He showed a subject a succession of ten letters (part of a meaningful passage from Dumas Malone's *Jefferson the Virginian*) and asked the subject to guess what the eleventh letter had been. The subject was instructed to continue guessing until he came

BOX 5.3

53‡‡†305))6*;4826)4‡.)4‡);806*;48†8
¶60))85;1‡(;:‡*8†83(88)5*†;46(;88*9
6*?;8)*‡(;485);5*†2:*‡(;4956*2(5*
—4)8¶8*;4069285);)6†8)4‡‡;1(‡9;4
8081;8:8‡1;48†85;4)485†528806*8
1(‡9;48;(88;4(‡?34;48)4‡;161;:188;‡?;

Edgar Allan Poe's short story "The Gold Bug" makes romantic use of the systematic patterning of letter sequences in language.

Poe's hero, Legrand, while rummaging around Sullivan's Island, finds an old piece of parchment, which he uses to wrap up the "gold bug"—a curious beetle that has attracted his fancy. Later, in his cabin, he discovers that on this parchment, "rudely traced, in a red tint," are the characters reproduced above. For Legrand this message is an easy one to decode.

My first step [he smugly explains to the obligingly bewildered narrator of the story] was to ascertain the predominant letters, as well as the least frequent. . . . Now in English, the letter which most frequently occurs is e . . . e predominates so remarkably, that an individual sentence of any length is rarely seen,

in which it is not the prevailing character. . . . As our predominant character is 8, we will commence by assuming it as the e. . . . Now of all words in the language "the" is most usual; let us see therefore, whether there are not repetitions of any three characters, in the same order of collocation, the last of them being 8. . . . Upon inspection, we find no less than seven such arrangements, the characters being ; 4 8. We may therefore assume that ; represents t, 4 represents h, and 8 represents e—the last being now well confirmed. Thus a great step has been taken.

From this first "great step," the rest follows easily, and within two more pages of Poe's story Legrand has the solution:

A good glass in the bishop's hostel in the devil's seat —forty-one degrees and thirteen minutes—northeast and by north—main branch seventh limb east side— shoot from the left eye of the death's head—a beeline from the tree through the shot fifty feet out.

And thus, because all who would use language must operate within the structured confines of language patterns, William Legrand could easily understand the dead Captain Kidd's message. A buried treasure chest, "filled to the brim," was the reward.

---

up with the correct answer. From the number of guesses required to get the correct letter, Shannon could then estimate the degree to which the occurrence of a sequence of ten letters determined what the eleventh letter would be. For example, suppose that the person's first guesses are correct and that guessing correctly the first time happened again and again with different guessers and different ten-letter passages. The conclusion would be that the English language functions in such a manner that, given the first ten letters, the eleventh letter is completely determined. In other words, the constraining influence of a sequence of ten letters upon the eleventh is 100 percent. If the subjects in such an experiment are skilled in language, their guesses are really summary statements reflecting what the English language itself has taught the subjects.

Redundancy But, if a literate person, given the first ten letters, can accurately predict what the eleventh letter must be, the eleventh letter need never have been printed at all because it carries no new information. This consideration has led to the important concept of **redundancy in language.** Redundancy refers to the fact that certain letters occurring in certain contexts carry little new information, and in the illustration just given, the eleventh letter was 100 percent redundant.

Suppose, however, that, given the first ten letters, we cannot predict with complete accuracy what the next letter will be but that we can still do better than chance. Then we can say that the eleventh letter is redundant but not completely so. In other words, redundancy is not an all-or-nothing affair. Obviously, the more rigidly the sequences are determined by the preceding letters and by the syntax and spelling, the more redundant a language will be. With the use of Shannon's technique we can take a random sample of sequences of varying lengths and see how much, on the average, the letters of the English language are determined by these constraining factors. From this average we can estimate the average redundancy of the language and the average strength of the constraining forces.

Shannon's data and other confirming studies clearly indicate that the English language is highly redundant. The average letter in English is approximately three-quarters determined by what has preceded it. Such studies provide quantitative measures of the constraints upon serial ordering of letters, constraints that the skillful talker must learn.

Redundancy is also found in words. As with letters, the more preceding *words* we are given (up to a point), the better our chance of guessing the next word. Another parallel principle is that some kinds of words are more predictable than are others. Pronouns and verbs, for instance, are more predictable than nouns, very likely because there are many more candidates to fill a missing spot in the latter class than in the former.

An interesting feature of word redundancy in meaningful language is that the missing word is more easily predicted when the additional context words *surround* the gap than when the same number of words *precedes* it. "I am going to put some———" is less likely to be properly completed than "to put some———on my egg," yet both phrases have provided contexts of six words.

There is an impressive correspondence in normal speech between the lack of redundancy of a word and the tendency to hesitate and then place emphasis on that word. It is as if the speaker also has to solve a more complex problem when he has to select a less predictable word. And because it is less predictable, by emphasizing it he may be warning the listener to pay attention. In fact, the length of the pause before words in normal speech in one group of subjects significantly correlates with the time it takes other subjects to supply those same words when they are represented as gaps to be filled in (Goldman-Eisler, 1964).

Redundancy in language is obviously of great help. Although a redundant language may be inefficient in that it uses more symbols than are absolutely necessary, it is efficient in that it decreases the probability of error in perception. Speech is almost always heard under unfavorable conditions such as noise, competing stimuli, or inattention. If there were zero redundancy in language, no amount of surrounding letters or words could tell us anything about the unperceived letter or word. In order to comprehend speech under those circumstances, we would have to perceive *every sound and every word accurately*. This necessity would make of speech a highly inadequate communication system.

Finally, to round out our understanding of how the spoken, redundant words get their meanings across, we must examine how language is perceived by the listener.

Perception of speech Much of the work on the perception of speech has been done by engineers at Bell Telephone Laboratories, who are primarily interested in determining the adequacies of their communication devices. Among their techniques is that of changing or distorting speech sounds to determine the intelligibility of speech under difficult conditions of transmission. Let us give some illustrative findings:

1. Wide changes in the intensity of speech have little effect on perception. Therefore, as the intensity is raised from about 50 to 140 decibels, no significant change in intelligibility of spoken words occurs (see Figure 5.1).

2. Wide changes in the spectrum of speech sounds can be tolerated without any significant loss in understanding. The **speech spectrum** refers to the range of different sound frequencies and amplitudes that are found in ordinary speech sounds. Male voices, speaking at a conversational level, can range in frequency from 100 to about 8,000 cycles per second (hz) and in intensity from about 20 to 120 decibels. By the use of appropriate instrumentation, the normal spectrum can be radically altered. Recorded speech may thus be passed through a transmission system that will clip off all the upper or all

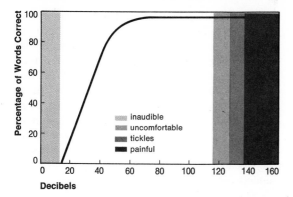

FIGURE 5.1 The curve shows the relation between the percentage of English monosyllabic words that can be recorded correctly and the intensity of the speech at the listener's ear. Changes in intensity of almost 100 decibels do not change a listener's ability to hear correctly, even though the intensity may reach the stage at which it is actually painful. Over the range of 50 to 140 decibels, therefore, intensity does not seem to be a crucial determinant of intelligibility of speech.

G. A. Miller. *Language and communication*; copyright 1951 by McGraw-Hill Book Company, Inc.; adapted by permission.

the lower frequencies and pass on only the remaining sounds. What happens when we mutilate normal speech sounds in this way? The data indicate that with meaningful words, perception is still adequate, even if we hear only the frequencies above 1,900 hz or only the frequencies below 1,900 hz. We can clip off not only certain frequencies but also amplitudes, so that only the loud or only the soft components of the normal spectrum are heard. Again, violent distortions have remarkably little effect on the intelligibility of such speech (see Figure 5.2).

3. Another type of distortion of the normal speech pattern is produced by intermittent interruptions. By the use of telephonic equipment we can arrange a situation in which the recorded speech is interrupted, say, ten times every second, so that, out of a speech sequence that lasts ten minutes, the sound is actually on for only five of those minutes. Yet, under these conditions, the listener's ability to understand is not impaired (Miller & Licklider, 1950).

The significance of these experiments is this: The sound waves produced by a speaker may undergo extensive changes in many of their

characteristics—frequency, amplitude, harmonies, duration—but a careful physical analysis of what is left indicates that the essential pattern of the total sound wave remains constant. As long as a specific organization is maintained, we can understand what the sound waves are saying. This dependence upon patterning reflects in part the general tendency to organize discrete stimuli in perception, but in part it also reflects a long and complex skill-training process.

Perception of speech as problem solving We are bound by grammatical and sense-making rules in producing speech, and we are helped by these rules in perceiving speech. As we have seen, verbal context plays an exceedingly important role in the very perception of sounds and words. Miller (1951), in commenting on this point, couches his description of the perception of speech almost entirely in terms of intelligent problem solving and ties together much of what we have been saying:

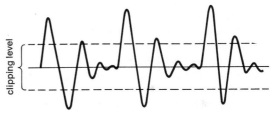

a undistorted speech wave

b peak-clipped wave

FIGURE 5.2 Distortion of speech wave by amplitude selectivity. The usual wave form (Figure a) is clipped electronically along the dotted lines so that only the center portion of each wave (Figure b) reaches the listener's ears. Such peak clipping has practically no effect on intelligibility. The clipped wave will be just as intelligible to the listener as the undistorted wave will be.

G. A. Miller. *Language and communication*; copyright 1951 by McGraw-Hill Book Company, Inc.; adapted by permission.

If enough of the discourse is perceived to reveal the basic pattern of the sentence, the range of possible words that can be substituted into the pattern is greatly decreased. Thus the probability of a correct guess is increased. For example, in the sentence "He threw the ——— out the window," we can immediately reject all parts of speech except nouns. Then we can reject all the nouns that are associated with unthrowable objects. Then we can give preference to certain things that people are known to throw—balls, rocks, bombs, etc. So we get down to a rather small number of possibilities. . . . Because the elimination of unlikely possibilities occurs so quickly and so automatically, it is difficult to imagine how the process takes place. The nature of the situation somehow influences what a listener expects, and from this relatively narrow range of expected events he chooses one that seems to him the most probable.

This quotation helps us place the problem of a child's development of adult language skills within the context of the development of the very ability to think and reason. This development is discussed in some detail in Units 6 and 7 on problem solving. Let us turn, then, to the problem of how a child acquires language competence. For up to now, we have been primarily concerned with the characteristics of language among adult speakers—but how did the adult get there?

THE DEVELOPMENT OF LANGUAGE

The study of child language development has deep roots in the history of psychology, philosophy, and linguistics. Beginning in the late eighteenth century, a number of scholarly parents kept detailed diaries of the linguistic and mental development of their children. Charles Darwin, as we mentioned earlier, based some of his theoretical formulations on the diary he kept of his own son's development. In American psychology, until the late 1950s, the major concern with child language development was from a pedagogical point of view, the intent being to guide language instruction in the schools. There were studies of age-related changes in vocabulary size, sentence length, and use of nouns and

verbs. These investigations had in common a perhaps implicit assumption that child language is simply not-yet-correct adult language. From this vantage point, determining the speed with which child vocabulary and grammar approached adult levels seemed a proper emphasis. This approach yielded many of the basic facts of language acquisition, and this information often had practical utility (e.g., studies of vocabulary growth guided writers in tailoring the vocabulary of children's books to the intended age groups).

Creation of Language by the Child

In the sixties and seventies, influenced greatly by the rise of modern linguistics, a new approach to child language development has emerged. The field of **developmental psycholinguistics**, armed with the insight of Piaget (see Unit 4) and with theories of the productive knowledge underlying language use, seeks to determine how the young child *discovers* the structure of his native language. The guiding assumption of this approach is that *child language is in fact a true language, with its own systematic rules.* It is not just a poor copy of the adult tongue into which it is eventually transformed. Rather, each child, listening to the speech around him, must actively create anew for himself the language of his community. Because all the children in a given speech community do end up speaking the same language, they must have similar ways of solving the problem of language acquisition. Developmental psycholinguists is concerned with discovering this means of language creation with which all human children are born.

McNeill (1966), reviewing the field of developmental psycholinguistics, succinctly presents the challenge it faces:

The fundamental problem to which we address ourselves is the simple fact that language acquisition occurs in a surprisingly short time. Grammatical speech does not begin before 1.5 years of age; yet, as far as we can tell, the basic process is complete by 3.5 years. Thus, a basis for the rich and intricate competence of adult grammar must emerge in the short span of 24 months.

Language and Cognitive Development

In order for an infant to carry out the feat of linguistic analysis and creation, he requires two basic sorts of cognitive abilities: (1) He has to be able to figure out, from the nonlinguistic situation, *what* his parents are talking about; and (2) he must be able to pay attention to *how* they say things. Both of these skills are needed because the role of language is of course to relate sounds to meanings. And so the young child must have some way to figure out meanings (the first point) and some way to figure out how sounds are structured to relate to those meanings (the second point).

Consider a simple conversation between a two-and-a-half-year-old Mayan Indian girl and her mother. We have selected an example from a thoroughly unfamiliar culture in order to demonstrate how universal the processes of linguistic and cognitive development are. Our point is that any two-year-old's conversation is based on the mental level of a two-year-old, regardless of the particular language she may be speaking or the particular culture in which she may be growing up. The following conversation was recorded by Stross (1972) in a thatched hut in an isolated village in Yucatán, Mexico. It took place in the Mayan language Tzeltal.

GIRL: mmm, I want to eat corn.
MOTHER: What?
GIRL: Where is the corn?
MOTHER: There is no more corn.
GIRL: mmm
MOTHER: mmm
GIRL: [picking up an ear of corn] What's this?
MOTHER: It's not our corn.
GIRL: Whose is it?
MOTHER: It belongs to grandmother.
GIRL: Who harvested it?
MOTHER: They harvested it.
GIRL: Where did they harvest it?
MOTHER: They harvested it down over there.
GIRL: Way down over there.
MOTHER: mmm [yes]
GIRL: Let's look for some too.
MOTHER: You look for some.
GIRL: Fine.
MOTHER: mmm
GIRL: [begins to hum]

Except for the fact that the topic is freshly harvested corn, this is a very ordinary conversation that could have taken place anywhere, as any parent will recognize. The child is expressing her needs and seeking information, asking about such things as location, possession, and past action. She does so in short, simple sentences, and her mother answers in the same kind of sentences. She does not ask questions about when things happened, about remote possibilities, or other complicated matters because such things do not readily occur to the two-year-old mind in Tzeltal, in English, or in the thirty or so other languages that have been studied developmentally (see Slobin, 1972).

How does the child come to talk about such things as these? Piaget's earlier description of the child's thinking at about this age—the very beginning of the concrete-operational period—offers some clues (see p. 84). And it is precisely such thinking that is reflected in the infant's first attempts to speak, as can be seen in his first structured utterances.

Emergence of Grammar

All children apparently go through a long period in which their utterances are limited to single words. Such utterances begin somewhere around the first birthday and continue until the second birthday, give or take a few months. In order for the child to speak in single words, he must have already discovered something about the sound structure of his language. He knows how to pronounce many of the *phonemes*, or sound elements, of his language, and he is able to hear adult speech in terms of individual words. He may understand longer utterances that he hears from his parents, but we are not sure. But his own utterances do not yet have a grammatical structure because one cannot speak of the grammatical structure of a sentence that is only one word long.

At some point, however, every child discovers that words can be put together in longer strings. Generally this discovery is preceded by a phase during which the child is apparently searching for a way to put words together. For example, one little girl's speech as she struggled to put a button into her pocket (which was inaccessible because she happened to be sitting on it) consisted of saying "button" several times and then the word "pocket." She could not put them together into a single utterance. It was clear that she *understood* the relation between the button and the pocket but that she did not yet know how to express this relation grammatically (Bloom, 1970).

With the discovery of word combinability, two-word utterances begin to flower. Such utterances express a wide range of meanings, meanings that were implicit at the one-word stage but that now begin to be made more explicit linguistically.

Two-word utterances At the **two-word stage,** children all over the world talk about the same kinds of things in similar ways. The following are the kinds of meanings that such utterances express:

1. The child points to an object or situation and comments about a thing, noting some aspect or property of the thing:
   IDENTIFICATION: "see doggie"
   LOCATION: "book there"
   REPETITION or RECURRENCE: "more milk"
   NONEXISTENCE or DISAPPEARANCE: "allgone toy"
   NEGATION: "not wolf"
   POSSESSION: "my candy"
   ATTRIBUTION: "big car"
   Each of these utterances has the name of an object ("doggie," "book," and so on) and another word that acts as a sort of operator in combination with the object name. This is a universal feature of early child speech: a division of the vocabulary into *content words* (words that name things or people or actions) and *function words* or *operators*. These function words or operators (such as "more," "allgone," and "not") are the kernel from which complex grammatical operations will develop, operations such as quantification, negation, and attribution.

Another class of two-word utterances deals with *relations* between people and between people and objects:

2. The child comments on some relational aspect of a situation:
   AGENT-ACTION: "mama walk"
   ACTION-OBJECT: "hit you"
   AGENT-OBJECT: "mama book" [i.e., "mama reads a book"]
   AGENT-LOCATION: "sit chair"
   ACTION-RECIPIENT: "give papa [i.e., "give to papa"]
   ACTION-INSTRUMENT: "cut knife" [i.e., "cut with the knife"]
   And, of course, the child asks questions about various aspects of such situations: "Where ball?" "What that?" "More milk?"

The two-word utterances just listed sound perfectly familiar to anyone who has lived with a one-and-a-half- or two-year-old child. But a striking feature of this list is that the utterances are not all drawn from English child speech; rather, the examples come from child speech in *English, German, Russian, Finnish, Turkish, Samoan, and Luo* (spoken in Kenya). The whole list could be made up of examples from two-year-old speech in any language. It seems as if infants everywhere invent for themselves a basic means of linguistic expression, regardless of the particular features of the native language they have been exposed to. (See Box 5.4 for some cross-linguistic examples.)

If you consider carefully the meanings of these utterances—that is, the operations and relations expressed and questioned—you will be reminded of Piaget's description of child thought in Unit 4. The linguistic expressions of the two-year-old represent the achievements of sensori-motor intelligence. The child speaks about objects and actions carried out upon them; he notes recurrence, disappearance, location, and qualities. The emergence of grammar thus follows upon and reflects the development of thinking in the child.

Sentence-length limitations Even though the child has discovered the possibilities of word combinations, he is apparently limited, at first, to combinations two words in length. This is probably due to some sort of short-term memory limitation (see p. 404) that restricts the child to a small number of elements in the preparation of a sentence to be spoken. (Such

BOX 5.4

LANGUAGE UNIVERSALS AT THE TWO-WORD STAGE

A research team at the University of California, at Berkeley, headed by psychologists S. Ervin-Tripp and D. I. Slobin, have been gathering data on child language development from cultures around the world. Researchers are sent to foreign countries and return with tape recordings and descriptions of child language behavior. On the basis of these findings, a number of universals of child language development are coming to light. The following table shows striking similarities in the functions of two-word utterances spoken by children in six different countries and languages.

FUNCTIONS OF TWO-WORD SENTENCES IN CHILD SPEECH, WITH EXAMPLES FROM SEVERAL LANGUAGES

Function of Utterance	Language					
	English	German	Russian	Finnish	Luo	Samoan
Locate, Name	there book that car see doggie	buch da [book there] gukuk wauwau [see doggie]	Tosya tam [Tosya there]	tuossa Rina [there Rina] vettä siinä [water there]	en saa [it clock] ma wendo [this visitor]	Keith lea [Keith there]
Demand, Desire	more milk give candy want gum	mehr milch [more milk] bitte apfel [please apple]	yeshchë moloko [more milk] day chasy [give watch]	anna Rina [give Rina]	miya tamtam [give-me candy] adway cham [I-want food]	mai pepe [give doll] fia moe [want sleep]
Negate	no wet no wash not hungry allgone milk	nicht blasen [not blow] kaffee nein [coffee no]	vody net [water no] gus' tyu-tyu [goose gone]	ei susi [not wolf] enää pipi [anymore sore]	beda onge [my-slasher absent]	le 'ai [not eat] uma mea [allgone thing]
Describe Event or Situation	Bambi go mail come hit ball block fall baby highchair	puppe kommt [doll comes] tiktak hängt [clock hangs] sofa sitzen [sofa sit] messer schneiden [cut knife]	mama prua [mama walk] papa bay-bay [papa sleep] korka upala [crust fell] nashla yaichko [found egg] baba kreslo [grandma armchair]	Seppo putoo [Seppo fall] talli 'bm-bm' [garage 'car']	chungu biro [European comes] odhi skul [he-went school] omoyo oduma [she-dries maize]	pa'u pepe [fall doll] tapale 'oe [hit you] tu'u lalo [put down]
Indicate Possession	my shoe mama dress	mein ball [my ball] mamas hut [mama's hat]	mami chashka [mama's cup] pup moya [navel my]	täti auto [aunt car]	kom baba [chair father]	lole a'u [candy my] polo 'oe [ball your] paluni mama [balloon mama]
Modify, Qualify	pretty dress big boat	milch heiss [milk hot] armer wauwau [poor dog]	mama khoroshaya [mama good] papa bol'shoy [papa big]	rikki auto [broken car] torni iso [tower big]	piypiy kech [pepper hot] gwen madichol [chicken black]	fa'ali'i pepe [headstrong baby]
Question	where ball	wo ball [where ball]	gde papa [where papa]	missä pallo [where ball]		fea Punatu [where Punatu]

D. I. SLOBIN, *Psycholinguistics*. Glenview, Ill.: Scott, Foresman, 1971, Copyright © 1971 by Scott, Foresman & Company; reprinted by permission of the publisher.

limitations, of course, are also reflected in the time that adults require to process grammatical features, as we noted earlier in this unit.)

The child's limitations seem to be more tied to grammar and processing time than they are to his level of thinking and understanding. For example, a child may be able to say "daddy throw," "throw ball," and "daddy ball." These separate utterances indicate that he has an underlying grasp of the full proposition, "daddy throw ball," but that he is not yet capable of producing all three words in one stretch.

At a later stage, the subparts of sentences can be put together to form more complete utterances. Sometimes children build up sentences out loud, and the observer can actually hear the process of sentence construction. For example, a child may want to speak of a cat standing up on a table, saying: "Stand up. Cat stand up. Cat stand up on table." Utterances of this sort—and they have been observed in child speech in many different languages—indicate that the child constructs sentences phrase by phrase.

The mastery of grammar   We now have the child on his way to the acquisition of the grammar of his native language. By the time he is three or three and a half, he knows, in a rough form, all the basic types of linguistic rules, although he will continue learning fine details throughout childhood and perhaps even beyond. Each child works out a grammar of his own invention, yet all these child grammars are strikingly similar in their basic aspects. All are based on ordered combinations of meaningful elements and are modified by characteristics of stress and intonation. All the children growing up in a given speech community can communicate with the other members of that community. The observations that all children arrive at similar grammars of the same native language and that all children use the same sorts of grammatical principles regardless of what language they speak have led psycholinguists to believe that all children follow the same basic procedures and make the same types of inferences in discovering the structure of language. We are just beginning to understand these procedures, and much more will be learned in the coming years.

(See Hayes, 1970; Slobin, 1971a, for an overview of theories of language acquisition.)

Explanations of Language Development

Conditioning theory   Conditioning theory, particularly for instrumental conditioning (see Unit 16), would assert that grammar acquisition comes about through processes no different from those involved in the acquisition of any other conditioned responses. At first the child spontaneously emits a variety of sounds, and through systematic recognition and rewarding by parents (and others) of the right (or approximately right) sound or combination of sounds, a word is gradually learned. More often he will be induced to vocalize something like the right sound by his tendency to imitate adult speech, and his more correct imitations will be rewarded. Certain combinations of words (phrases, sentences) can be learned in similar fashion. Discrimination learning is the primary feature of this process, and language is increasingly shaped toward its adult form through selective reinforcement (again, see Unit 16). But this simple account has been vigorously challenged.

The linguist N. Chomsky (1959) has been particularly searching in his analysis of the shortcomings of conditioning and other commonly recognized modes of learning as applicable to the learning of language. We can briefly convey, by a few examples, the flavor of Chomsky's criticisms. First, perhaps, is the puzzling fact that near-adult language competence can be acquired in so short a time. There are simply too many ways in which words can be combined to make meaningful sentences for each combination to be learned in a traditional conditioned-response manner, that is, by systematically rewarding correct utterances and not rewarding incorrect ones. For example, Miller (1965) gives a conservative estimate of the number of possible twenty-word sentences in the English language: The figure is 10^{20} (a 10 followed by nineteen zeros). It would take, he further estimates, about 1,000 times the estimated age of the earth just to listen to all these sentences. There are many possible rejoinders to this dramatized argument, but none can handle the essential criticism, which is that the child cannot possibly learn separately each of the sentences he becomes capable of producing or understanding. The child must develop some *general rules* that enable him to decipher novel sentences and to construct new ones.

Imitation Another fact that is awkward for traditional learning theories is that children's earliest grammatical constructions are not simply crude approximations of adult sentences. Recordings of young children's spontaneous speech disclose numerous instances of phrases and sentences that could not possibly represent direct imitations of adult speech. A child may say, "me want car go," or "allgone sticky" (after washing hands), or "why cause chickens can't fly?" Such utterances are clearly not imitations of the speech the child has heard. Nor are they random errors. They can be shown to be systematic and meaningful productions of the child's own linguistic system at his level of development.

    As we mentioned earlier, a child's deviations from adult grammar often reveal his own grasp of linguistic rules. The acquisition of the English past tense provides an instructive case. We have two types of past-tense verbs in English: the regular verbs, which form the past tense by addition of "-ed" ("walk," "walked"; "love," "loved"; and so forth), and the irregular verbs, which do not follow this rule ("come," "came"; "write," "wrote"; "go," "went"; and so on). Many of the most commonly used verbs in English are irregular, and two-year-olds learn many irregular past tenses such as "came," "fell," and "broke." In fact, these are the earliest past-tense forms that English-speaking children use. They are correct; they are based on imitation of adult models; and, if parents reward children for correct usage, they should certainly be well learned. Yet, all English-speaking children soon abandon these correct irregular past tenses and indulge in **linguistic overgeneralization** from the regular past-tense verbs that they already know. And so by the time a child is three, he no longer says "came," "fell," "broke," but rather, "comed," "falled," "breaked." These overgeneralizations are persistent. As any first-grade teacher will tell you, they are still firmly entrenched when children begin school. Yet they

are certainly not imitative in origin. Since they occur quite commonly in all children, including those from homes in which such errors neither occur in parents' speech nor are likely to be rewarded, it is apparent that the child seeks regularity in his linguistic system and chooses to ignore exceptions.

    In fact, children seem to be deaf to exceptions. McNeill (1966) cites compelling evidence that children are simply unable to attend to linguistic forms which violate their own sense of regularity. He quotes the following recorded interchange between mother and child:

> CHILD: Nobody don't like me.
> MOTHER: No, say "nobody likes me."
> CHILD: Nobody don't like me.
>   [eight repetitions of this dialogue]
> MOTHER: No, now listen carefully; say
>   "nobody likes me."
> CHILD: Oh! Nobody don't *likes* me.

If children hear speech in their own terms and are generally impervious to adult speech that does not match their own inner sense of correct grammar, then it is difficult to see how children could learn language simply by imitation of the speech that they hear. Of course, children pay attention to the speech around them, but they do so selectively and in their own fashion. Again, the *child*, not the adult, seems to be in control of the language-acquisition process.

Deliberate training In the mother-child dialogue just quoted, the mother is explicitly attempting to teach the child something about language. Such direct training in the use of grammatical forms seems to be exceptionally infrequent in parent-child interaction (see Slobin, 1973, for further evidence). When parents interact with young children, most attention is directed toward the tasks of communication: understanding each other and accomplishing the practical goals at hand. There is apparently little time left over for attention to linguistic detail. Roger Brown has examined this question carefully. He and his co-workers at Harvard have visited three children at regular intervals since they began to speak, recording spontaneous conversation between children and parents in their homes (Brown, 1973). He has looked at all cases where a child's utterance was followed by approval or disapproval by an adult. His findings suggest that deliberate training cannot play a significant role in teaching children to speak grammatically. Here is his own summary of this striking finding (Brown, Cazden, & Bellugi, 1968):

> What circumstances did govern approval and disapproval directed at child utterances by parents? Gross errors of word choice were sometimes corrected, as when Eve [a young child] said *What the guy idea.* Once in a while an error of pronunciation was noticed and corrected. Most commonly, however, the grounds on which an utterance was approved or disapproved . . . were not strictly linguistic at all. When Eve expressed the opinion that her mother was a girl by saying *He a girl,* her mother answered *That's right.* The child's utterance was ungrammatical, but her mother did not respond to that fact; instead, she responded to the truth of the proposition the child intended to express. In general, the parents fitted propositions to the child's utterances, however incomplete or distorted the utterances, and then approved or not according to the correspondence between proposition and reality. Thus, *Her curl my hair* was approved because the mother was, in fact, curling Eve's hair. However, Sarah's grammatically impeccable *There's the animal farmhouse* was disapproved because the building was a lighthouse, and Adam's utterance, *Walt Disney comes on on Tuesday* was disapproved because Walt Disney came on on some other day. It seems, then, to be truth value rather than syntactic well-formedness that chiefly governs explicit verbal reinforcement by parents—which renders mildly paradoxical the fact that the usual product of such a training schedule is an adult whose speech is highly grammatical but not notably truthful.

Grammar acquisition as problem solving Even if parents did attempt explicitly to reward correct grammar and punish incorrect grammar, we would still not understand the processes by which a child amends and revises his grammar until it corresponds with that of the adult language. For example, if Eve were told to say "she is a girl" rather than "he a girl," she would still not know how to change her own internal grammar to accommodate this discrepancy—

assuming, of course, that she could recognize and attend to the discrepancy at all. Consider this problem in the light of Piaget's general principles (Unit 4). The child attempts to *assimilate* the speech he hears to his own linguistic system, as we have discussed in regard to the English past tense and as you have seen in McNeill's mother-child dialogue. That is to say, the child interprets speech in terms of what he already knows about the language. However, sometimes a child cannot assimilate a new sentence to his existing grammatical structures, as much as he may try to understand it. If he has some inkling of its meaning and its structure, it may be possible for him to accommodate his linguistic system to the new sentence. Attempts at accommodation are the source of linguistic development. Often such attempts are reflected in the child's imitation of a new form.

We do not know what brings children to note certain sorts of discrepancies between their own grammar and the grammar of adults. Apparently corrective remarks from parents are not a dominant means of drawing children's attention to such discrepancies. Nor do we fully understand how a child manages to accommodate her linguistic system (i.e., to change her rules) once she becomes aware of a discrepancy. For example, it is not enough for Eve to notice the discrepancy between her utterance and the standard form. She must also somehow figure out that she has failed to indicate the sex of her mother properly and that, in English, female sex is indicated by a special pronoun, "she," and not by a special verb. But note that she could just as well have concluded that the verb "is" also plays a role in indicating female sex. That is to say, once a child notices a discrepancy between her grammar and adult grammar, she must still figure out the nature of the discrepancy and adjust her grammar accordingly. Children make very few false guesses in adjusting their grammar. English-speaking children do not seem to formulate specific rules that are alien to English, for example, indicating gender on the verb rather than the pronoun. Again, this suggests that children are *born* with rather specific strategies for discovering the structure of language. We are just beginning to understand how such strategies unfold and how they are applied to the task of deciphering speech, but it is clear that the child, not her adult mentors, is the one in control of this task.

This task, luckily, is carried out without conscious awareness—luckily, because it is an immensely complex one. As the Soviet scholar and children's writer Kornei Chukovsky wrote in his book on child language, *From Two to Five* (1961):

> It is frightening to think what an enormous number of grammatical forms are poured over the poor head of the young child. And he, as if it were nothing at all, adjusts to all this chaos, constantly sorting out into rubrics the disorderly elements of the words he hears, without noticing as he does this, his colossal effort.

If an adult had to master so many grammatical rules within so short a time, his head would surely burst—a mass of rules mastered so lightly and so freely by the two-year-old linguist. The labor he thus performs at this age is astonishing enough, but even more amazing and unparalleled is the ease with which he does it.

In truth, the young child is the hardest mental toiler on our planet. Fortunately, he does not even suspect this.

* * *

The solution to the Turkish word-boundary problem on page 101 is:

Dedenle nereye gittin sen?

* * *

SUMMARY

1. In order to communicate effectively in any language, the speaker (and listener) must know—without necessarily being able to state—rules governing the language's sound structure (phonology), its word structure (morphology), its meanings (semantics), its characteristic intonation patterns, and the proper ordering of words within a sentence (syntax).
2. The task of the linguist is to formulate descriptions of the structure of a language; the aim of the psycholinguist is to discover how that structure is learned and comes to be used effectively by the developing child.
3. Early child speech demonstrates the application of the *general* rules of syntax more consistently than adult speech does. Learning the exceptions to these rules comes later on.
4. Much of language comprehension involves an awareness of *levels* of communication, of meanings that are only implicit in the verbal utterance.
5. The grammatical complexity of a sentence is reflected in the amount of time required to understand it. Thus, short but complex sentences take longer to comprehend than longer but more simply structured ones.
6. Because the characteristic letter and word sequences in a given language, as well as the verbal contexts in which they occur, exercise powerful restraints on possible verbal constructions, later elements become increasingly predictable from knowledge of all the earlier ones and add less and less new information. In short, they become increasingly redundant. And this redundancy increases the effectiveness of language as communication.
7. Early child language is a true language, with its own systematic, self-discovered rules, not just a crude copy of eventually learned adult language. Furthermore, these rules are apparently universal, perhaps implying some biological basis for the initial phases of language acquisition.
8. In all cultures thus far studied the child's first sentences are two-word utterances that tend to combine only certain identical classes of words.
9. Neither the principles of conditioning nor the notions that a child learns correct language through imitation of adult speech or in response to deliberate training by parents prove to be adequate explanations of language learning.

GLOSSARY

developmental psycholinguistics   The study of the process by which children become competent language users.

intonation patterns   Changes in voice tone during speech, such as those indicating questions and exclamations.

linguistic knowledge   The implicit, unconscious ability to speak and comprehend an unlimited variety of novel sentences in a particular language (sometimes called *linguistic competence*).

linguistic overgeneralization   A child's replacement of linguistic exceptions by application of a general rule to all relevant forms.

linguistic universals   Basic structural features that all human languages have in common.

morphology   The rules of word building in language.

phonology   The rules of sound patterning in language.

productive knowledge of language   Knowledge that enables an individual to produce and comprehend utterances that have never been spoken by her before.

redundancy in language   Refers to the fact that certain letters and words, occurring in certain contexts, carry varying degrees of new information. A word with 100 percent redundancy contributes no information; a word with zero redundancy contributes completely new information.

semantics   The rules of the meanings of words and utterances in language.

sociolinguistics   The study of the social rules governing language use in communicative settings.

speech spectrum   The range of sound frequencies and sound amplitudes in speech.

syntax   The body of linguistic rules that makes it possible to relate a series of words in a sentence to the underlying meaning of that sentence, that is, the rules of ordering of words in a language (sentence structure).

two-word stage   A stage in child language development, emerging somewhere between eighteen and twenty-four months of age; it reflects the child's discovery that words can be *combined* to express semantic operations and relations.

verbal-context effect   The effect of preceding words or letters on the probability of appearance of a given word or letter. If the preceding words or letters completely determine what the next letter will be, we speak of a large verbal-context effect.

imagery and language in productive thinking

DO YOU KNOW...

- why it is that asking the right question is often a truly more difficult and creative act than finding its answer?

- that progress in solving a problem can be made without consciously thinking about it, for instance, by sleeping on it?

- what is going on when we experience something as being "on the top of the tongue"?

- in what circumstances it is possible literally to see the solution to a problem?

- that people differ widely in their dominant mode of imagery?

- that certain individuals can conjure up a precisely detailed and remarkably accurate image of an event, even months after experiencing it?

- that, under certain circumstances, we can't tell the difference between "seeing things" and seeing things?

- how different our communications are when they are spoken rather than when written?

unit 6

CONTENTS

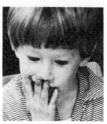

Thought is sometimes regarded as evolution's highest achievement and, indeed, as defining the essence of human existence. The French philosopher René Descartes put this view succinctly in his famous statement, *Cogito, ergo sum* ("I think, therefore I am"). It is this fascinating capacity to reason, to solve problems, and to create new ideas and concepts that enables man to rise above the demands of mere survival, to ponder what might be, as well as to understand what is. Many modern psychologists would qualify that statement by pointing out that animals and perhaps even computers can, at least to some degree, display the kind of behavior we call thinking—but more of this later. However, nearly everyone would agree that thinking reaches its zenith in the human species. Indeed, most comparisons between man's thinking and that of even the most brilliant chimpanzee or the most sophisticated computer only highlight the enormous margin by which human intellect surpasses that of any other species, be it biological or electronic.

But having asserted our superiority, a challenging question remains: Are we clever enough to come to understand the very mental processes that make us superior? In this unit (and in Unit 7), the student will find an account of some of the progress that has been made in this endeavor.

THINKING AS AN ADAPTIVE PROCESS

The process of thinking consists of the manipulation and interplay of *symbolic elements* such as images, words, and concepts to represent aspects of reality. As we have seen in Unit 4, this ability to think abstractly and symbolically represents, both for Piaget and for Bruner, the final adult stage in human cognitive development. Sometimes this interplay of symbolic elements may be directed and actively controlled by the person, as in working on specific problems. In such **realistic thinking** the constraints of logic, evidence, and reality play a major role, and the whole course of thinking is guided by the requirements of the objective situation. This type of directed thinking is obviously useful and adaptive. At other times, though, the spontaneous interplay of images and symbols seems undirected, even haphazard, and we lose ourselves in apparently aimless and uncontrolled cognition. Such meanderings of thought may seem useless, but we shall see that they too can play an important ideational role in creative thinking and problem solving and thus can also serve an adaptive function. Indeed, even **autistic thinking** —the extreme kind of wishful thinking wholly dominated by one's wants and feelings, with little or no regard for reality—may in some sense be adaptive, for such fantasy and imagination can sometimes initiate a flow of realistic thinking that leads to practical achievement in the real world. In short, thinking, in *all* its forms, can make crucial contributions to man's adaptive repertory.

The problem may be brief in duration or extended over a long period; it may be trivial or of sweeping significance; it may deal with human relations, with practicalities of everyday life, with the sciences or the arts or other domains of achievement. Thus, problem solving may include such diverse activities as finding a summer job, trying to understand the causes of urban decay, resolving a quarrel, creating a clever bumper sticker for a political campaign, inventing a new way to use lasers, rescuing a cat from a peculiar perch in a tree, making a movie. Problem solving represents a large portion of those activities usually referred to as "thinking"; and indeed, the two terms may be made synonymous by defining thinking as "that which occurs when an individual meets, recognizes, and solves a problem." Whatever one's definition, the study of problem solving is central to any account of thinking, and hence problem solving is the focus of this unit and Unit 7.

Productive versus Reproductive Thinking

Viewed in this adaptive context, we should expect the nature of the thinking process to be most clearly revealed when we set about to solve a problem. *Problem solving* occurs whenever we encounter a barrier or a gap between our present situation and a desired goal but find that mere repetition of a previously learned method does not enable us to reach the goal. Many of the problems we face in our daily environment conveniently require scarcely more than reproducing what we have learned to do in the past in similar situations. Such **reproductive thinking** seems largely explainable in terms of the processes of learning, memory, and transfer (discussed in Units 15, 16, and 17).

We now turn our attention to **productive thinking**, or **creative problem solving**, which requires the production of new and original solutions. An individual's problem solving is properly called creative (from a psychologist's vantage point) whether or *not* the particular solution has been produced previously by someone else. What matters is whether the problem and solution are novel for the individual.

WAYS TO STUDY THINKING

In order to illuminate the *process* of thinking, we seek to discover what goes on as a person struggles with a problem. One technique for doing this is to study *introspective accounts* of mental processes ("tell me what you were thinking about as you worked on this"). The immediacy and directness of introspective accounts yield an abundance of ideas about what goes on during thinking, and we shall examine some particularly interesting accounts in this unit. But introspection also has many limitations; for example, it obviously cannot be used to study the thinking of very young children. Moreover, we shall see that much of what is properly considered thinking in human adults is simply not accessible to this kind of conscious self-examination; the thought processes are, in a sense, unconscious, and the person could not tell us about them even if he wanted to. For these and other reasons, a great deal of research on thinking proceeds not through the examination of introspective reports but through the *observation of behavior* of the problem solver. Behavioral techniques have enabled the study of thinking to move beyond the armchair and into the laboratory, a move that has generated a wealth of unexpected findings (discussed in Unit 7). But let us begin our account on familiar ground by tracing the subjective experiences of a thinker as he works on a problem.

THE EXPERIENCE OF PROBLEM SOLVING

Obviously, a person won't try to solve a problem unless he first sees the problem. But behind this trivial statement lies one of the most important and yet frequently overlooked aspects of thinking, namely, *problem discovery*.

Problem Discovery

It is claimed, with some justification, that many of the greatest advances in science were made not by problem *solvers* but by problem *seekers*, people whose inquiring minds found problems where others found nothing unusual, people who "saw the extraordinary in the ordinary." Although much scientific progress does result from systematically grinding out the consequences of concepts and theories, the layman tends to underestimate the extent to which revolutionary breakthroughs result from the posing of new *questions* rather than from extending the consequences of accepted theories.

On one occasion when Einstein—certainly an original thinker—was asked how he came to develop some of his most important scientific concepts, he replied that they originated with his "inability to understand the obvious"; his penetrating curiosity revealed significant problems that others (including some of the most eminent scientists of the day) were not moved to question. This ability to *perceive* problems, to detect puzzling states of affairs, and to pose penetrating questions instead of taking things for granted, not only lies at the heart of scientific discovery but is a distinguishing characteristic of creative thinkers in many fields.

Changing Perceptions of the Problem

Once we have been seized by a problem and have begun to work on it, our experience and actual perceptions undergo continuous change. When bodily movement or manipulation of physical objects is involved (as in finding a certain house on a street, painting a picture, repairing a typewriter), the relations among the physical objects change, and so do our perceptions. But even when we remain seated at a desk as we try to recall the name of an acquaintance, try to come up with a good ending to the story we are writing, or attempt to solve a mathematical problem mentally, we are plunged into a stream of ever-shifting experiences.

Discontinuities in Experience and Perception

This stream of experience is a very curious stream. There are discontinuities in it; it seems to disappear and go underground for short or long stretches. Even the most complete account of a person's experiences in solving a problem will often indicate that there are conscious lapses, large time intervals during which she does not seem to be thinking or working on the problem at all, yet some progress seems to be made. Occasionally, progress seems to be made even while she is asleep. After such a silent period the solution may suddenly appear, or substantial progress may be made. These lapses in the stream of experience have been labeled *incubation periods*—times of ripening and maturing of ideas.

The moment the problem solver makes a significant advance toward the solution, whether following an incubation period or not, he has vivid experiences. With certain problems there are striking changes in perception and these new perceptions *are* the advances. The architect suddenly, and almost literally, sees a solution or a partial solution to his design problem.

The quickly solved problem   The course of the stream differs tremendously from problem to problem. With an easy problem, we may find that very soon after we have begun it, we perceive the solution. It is as if the stream could be described as a short straight line with only two easily identifiable points.

The difficult problem   Quite the contrary seems to be true of very difficult problem solving.

With demanding problems for which the solutions come only after a great deal of work, we can often distinguish (scattered among the silent periods) several major changes after the initial perceptions: one or more *turning-point* percepts and, finally, the solution percepts. The turning-point percepts accompany sudden significant advances toward the final solutions. To continue our analogy, it is as if the stream of our experiences of a problem had several major bends to be rounded before we finally sail home.

Changes in Perceptual Content

As we make progress toward a solution, we find that objects begin to mean different things and even to look different. A penny, initially perceived as a small coin, may now be comprehended as an efficient conductor of electricity; a piece of ice, initially perceived as cold and wet, may now be conceived as something that can be used to produce heat if it is molded into the shape of a lens and used to focus the sun's rays to start a fire. Indeed, the meanings of the same objects that make up the initial and later perceptions may be so different that it sometimes seems as if entirely different objects are involved.

As we work on a problem, we may suddenly see that what we had perceived as a block to the goal is not a block at all. Sometimes the barrier to solution has been a creation of our own perceptual processes. (For an illustration of this point, see Box 6.1.)

Experiencing the Solution

As we approach the solution of a difficult problem or of a problem whose solution has been unaccountably evading us, we may experience a characteristic pattern of changes in perception, feelings, and even emotional excitement. One such pattern of experience often occurs just before the solution. This experience can perhaps best be described as the "almost there" feeling. We "see" and yet do not see the solution. It is an on-the-tip-of-the-tongue feeling. We feel, rather than precisely know, what should be done, but somehow we cannot phrase it or make it con-

---

BOX 6.1

CAN YOU SOLVE THIS?

Starting anywhere you wish, draw four *straight* lines that will pass through every one of the nine dots, without lifting your pencil from the paper.

● ● ●

● ● ●

● ● ●

Do not read the rest of this box until you have attempted to solve the problem. If after two minutes you have not solved the problem, read the following hints.

The nine dots tend to be perceived as a square. But there are no boundary lines to prevent your drawing a line *extending beyond* the perceived edge of the square. Nothing was ever said about staying within the "perceived confines" of the nine dots, yet the organizing nature of perception is such that it leads you to see a block to the movements of your pencil where no block exists in fact.
See p. 140 for the solution.

---

crete. It is the sort of feeling of which William James has said the solution "tingles, it trembles on the verge, but does not come." (See Box 6.2, p. 128, in which a poet and a psychologist describe the "almost there," and an experiment yields some data on the elusive feeling.)

The most easily recognized pattern of changes in perception, feelings, and emotional excitement is the one that occurs at the very moment of solution. When it occurs, it is unmistakably different from most of our other experiences. It is sudden, complete, intense. When we attempt to communicate our experiences at such a moment, we make liberal use of such a descriptive phrase as "like a flash." We often cry out with an explosive, "That's it!" "Of course!"

BOX 6.2

THE SHAPE OF THE "ALMOST THERE"

The following passages describe the "almost there" experience. Both come from highly creative people.

The French poet Paul Valéry said:

> There is that one where the man whose business is writing experiences a kind of flash—for this intellectual life, anything but passive, is really made of fragments; it is in a way composed of elements very brief, yet felt to be rich in possibilities, which do not illuminate the whole mind, which indicate to the mind, rather, that there are forms completely new which it is sure to be able to possess after a certain amount of work. Sometimes I have observed this moment when a sensation arrives at the mind; it is a gleam of light, not so much illuminating as dazzling. This arrival calls attention, points, rather than illuminates, and in fine, is itself an enigma which carries with it the assurance that it can be postponed. You say, "I see, and then tomorrow I shall see more." There is an activity, a special sensitization; soon you will go into the darkroom and the picture will be seen to emerge (quoted in Hadamard, 1949).

William James, a founder of American psychology, said:

> Suppose we try to recall a forgotten name. The state of our consciousness is peculiar. There is a gap therein; but no mere gap. It is a gap that is intensely active. A sort of wraith of the name is in it, beckoning us in a given direction, making us at moments tingle with the sense of our closeness, and then letting us sink back without the longed-for term. If wrong names are proposed to us, this singularly definite gap acts immediately so as to negate them. They do not fit into its mould. And the gap of one word does not feel like the gap of another, all empty of content as both might seem necessarily to be when described as gaps. . . . But the feeling of an absence is *toto caelo* other than the absence of a feeling. It is an intense feeling. The rhythm of a lost word may be there without a sound to clothe it; or the evanescent sense of something which is the initial vowel or consonant may mock us fitfully, without growing more distinct. Every one must know the tantalizing effect of the blank rhythm of some forgotten verse, restlessly dancing in one's mind, striving to be filled out with words.

At Harvard, psychologists R. W. Brown and D. McNeill have subjected William James' "tip of the tongue" phenomenon to an ingenious experimental investigation. Noting that tip-of-the-tongue (or, as they abbreviate it, TOT) states occur too rarely in nature to permit systematic study, they hit upon a device that was extraordinarily successful in generating an abundant supply of them. They presented definitions of infrequently used words and then asked their subjects to discover the words being defined. They felt that these words, forty-nine in all, although not common, were likely to be within the passive vocabulary of their subjects (Harvard and Radcliffe undergraduates) yet not familiar enough to be promptly identified. (Examples are "nepotism," "ambergris," and "sampan.")

Sometimes a word was immediately recognized, and sometimes it drew a complete blank, but often enough (about six times per subject in a two-hour session) a TOT state was induced. The states were apparently convincing to the observer as well as to the subject. The authors describe the behavior of one subject: "The signs of it were unmistakable; he would appear to be in mild torment, something like the brink of a sneeze, and if he found the word his relief was considerable." Once seized by such a state, the subject was asked to provide, as far as he could, the following information about the word that was on the tip of his tongue: its first letter and number of syllables, any words that sounded like the missing word, and words similar in meaning. When this information had been provided, the subject was told the word, and he then noted whether or not it was indeed the one he had in mind.

The subjects' guesses of the number of syllables in the missing words were impressively accurate. In 57 percent of the cases the guess was exactly right. (Both the actual and guessed numbers ranged from one to five syllables.) When there was an error, it was rarely greater than one syllable. Even the words that had been listed as sounding like the missing word showed a strong tendency to resemble it in number of syllables, having exactly the same number in 47 percent of the instances. Almost identical results were obtained for guesses of the first letter; they were correct 57 percent of the time, and 49 percent of the "sounds like" words started with the same letter.

Several other ways of analyzing these data confirmed the impression that, while in the TOT state, subjects had quite a lot of information about the missing word. Whatever details are still to be discovered about the tip-of-the-tongue phenomenon, it is already clear that the gap in this "almost there" experience is very far from contentless.

J. HADAMARD. *Psychology of Invention in the Mathematical Field.* Princeton: Princeton University Press, 1949.
W. JAMES. *Principles of Psychology.* New York: Dover, 1950. Originally published 1890.
R. W. BROWN & D. MCNEILL. The "tip of the tongue" phenomenon. *Journal of Verbal Learning and Verbal Behavior,* 1966, **5**, 325–327.

"Oh, sure!" If we had happened to be a Greek mathematician named Archimedes, who had just found the solution to King Hiero's problem of assaying the gold content of his crown, we would (or so goes the ancient story) have leaped from the tub in a rush of joy and run through the streets shouting loudly to the world (in classical Greek, of course), "I have found it, I have found it!" We are referring to the *insight* experience, or what Karl Bühler, the Viennese psychologist, has called, in a vivid phrase, the **"aha!" experience** (see Box 6.3).

Not all problem solving ends with this sudden and intense experience. Arranging one's schedule of classes or working out an arithmetic problem by well-practiced methods is likely to be devoid of this exhilarating sensation. However, the experience may come when solving simple as well as complex problems. Ms. Arbuthnot successfully dredging up the name of the boy who sat next to her thirty years ago in the third grade (after trying fruitlessly to recall it for twenty minutes or so) may feel, in a minor degree, the same dazzling uplift that Archimedes felt.

"Aha!" experiences can accompany objectively *wrong* solutions. We may feel all the excitement of an insight and yet discover in the next moment or even the next year that our solution will not work. The word "insight" is a *description* of an experience, not an explanation of how solutions are arrived at.

IMAGES AND THINKING

Having presented a general experiential account of problem solving, let us consider the roles of two different kinds of mental elements which make up a person's experience as he thinks through a problem. First, there are the *percepts* of physical objects that exist here and now in our physical world and that make up aspects of the problem we are trying to solve: high fences, locked doors, empty pockets, crying children, long lists of written numbers. Second, there are *images* of objects not immediately present in our physical world. As we attempt to describe the house we lived in as a child, we may see it, even though the building may long

---

BOX 6.3

THE "AHA!" EXPERIENCE, AS SEEN BY A PSYCHOLOGIST AND HER SUBJECT

The "aha!" phenomenon, as seen by the psychologist looking on and as reported by one person undergoing the experience, is found in an experiment by Helen Durkin at Columbia University. Each subject was given a puzzle, with the instructions:

> As you solve, please think aloud. Express every idea as it comes to you as you work even if it seems irrelevant. Try to tell me also how you feel about it as you go along. My chief interest is to find out as fully as possible just what goes on in your mind as you work.

Here is Durkin's description of her subjects' behavior just before they solved the puzzle:

> A short pause of peculiarly quiet intentness which sometimes involved an appearance of great tension, and at others seemed to be merely a cessation of all visible activity. The tension seemed to be one of suspense rather than of effort.
> This pause ending either in an explosively expressed elation or in relieved relaxation.
> There was a tendency to jump to the conclusion, with considerable certainty that the solution had been arrived at, even when the subject was not at all sure of the details.

The following brief excerpt is taken from the thinking out loud of one of Durkin's subjects:

> Oh, I saw it before I moved it. It came suddenly upon me as from the outside and I felt absolutely sure. Just like a flash and I knew I was right. Wasn't conscious of it . . . didn't reason about it—it came to me from the outside.

H. DURKIN. Trial-and-error, gradual analysis, and sudden reorganization. *Archives of Psychology*, 1937, **30**, No. 210.

---

since have been torn down—a **memory image**. Or the novelist, pondering over his next episode, may see his hero, a hero who never has and never will walk this earth—a **created image**.

Similarities Between Images and Percepts

We can experience images in as real, rich, and varied a form as our percepts. Just as we can see, hear, smell, taste, or feel physically existing objects, so can we "see" objects that are not there; "hear" music when none is being played; "smell" foods that we have not had for years; and see, hear, and feel "the silken, sad, uncertain rustling of each purple curtain" as we read Edgar Allan Poe.

Individuals differ in perceptual capacity, some excelling in vision, some in hearing, some in smell. There are also important individual differences in imagery capacity and preferences. Two major findings have come out of the scientific study of such individual differences.

First, individuals appear to differ greatly in the *vividness* of their imagery. The classic study in this area is represented by Sir Francis Galton's breakfast table investigation in the 1880s. He asked each of his subjects to recall his breakfast table as he had sat down to it in the morning and to report what he had experienced —whether or not the imaged objects were colored naturally, whether or not they were distinct and well defined, and so on. Galton received many different reports, ranging from a report of images as vivid as the original perceptions of the real objects to a report of no images at all.

Second, individuals differ in their favored *modes* of imagery. Some people, for example, have images that are predominantly visual; others have images that are predominantly auditory. Some of us, in thinking of the ocean, "see" its swelling waves; others "hear" its roar; some tell of the "smell" of its spray. Most people, however, experience a combination of these modes.

Differences Between Images and Percepts

Despite the similarities between images and ordinary perceptions, most of us can almost always tell the difference between them quite easily. On what basis can we do this? There have been several suggestions.

One is that the image is usually less vivid and less clearly experienced than the percept of a real object. This statement does not always hold, however. On occasion many of us have experienced images that were as detailed, clear, and vivid as the percept of a real object. Again

it is Sir Francis Galton who tells of the astonishingly detailed and precise imagery of an eminent scientist of his time:

> Mr. Flinders Petrie . . . informs me that he habitually works out sums by aid of an imaginary slide rule, which he sets in the desired way and reads off mentally. He does not usually visualize the whole rule but only that part of it with which he is at the moment concerned (quoted in Humphrey, 1948).

We do not have to depend only upon such informal reports. Careful experimental evidence is available that demonstrates the high degree of vividness and precision that is possible in images. Box 6.4, for instance, presents some illustrations of a particularly detailed kind of image, the **eidetic image,** which can be shown to be distinctly different from even the best memory images (see Figure 6.1A).

Another suggestion is that the difference between image and percept lies in the greater lability of the image. The percept of a real object is constrained by the object's physical stimulus properties (size, color, shape, location,

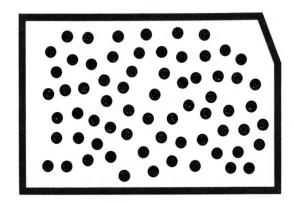

FIGURE 6.1A Inspect the pattern for at least a few minutes, shifting your gaze to cover all its elements. Then shut your eyes and try to visualize it. If you succeed in this then turn the page to Figure 6.1B and try to project this visualized pattern onto the new one, making sure to align the frames exactly. Do this *before* you read the legend for the second figure.

C. F. Stroymeyer. Eidetikers. *Psychology Today,* November 1970. Photo courtesy Bela Julesz.

BOX 6.4

PHOTOGRAPHICALLY CLEAR IMAGES

The most vividly detailed of all images is the eidetic image. Many experimental investigations (especially those by the German psychologist E. R. Jaensch) have been devoted to eidetic images, first described in 1907. The reports given here are taken from a Stanford University experiment by Heinrich Klüver, working with a proficient eidetic.

The subject was first allowed to look for a very brief period of time at one of the silhouettes shown here. The silhouette was then removed, and

A

B

the subject looked at a blank gray cardboard screen. She was asked what she "saw" there. The following excerpts are taken from Klüver's reports on one of his woman subjects after she had observed Figure A for thirty seconds.

> Subject "sees" the alligator with a "curly tail"; "that kid" with mouth and eyes; "the big tree at the right"; "a couple of palm trees" in the background. "The little boy and the alligator are most distinct"; counts

eighteen teeth in the lower jaw of the alligator (correct!). "I don't see the feet at all; they are in the water. I see two forelegs and one hind leg. Two trees in the background having one trunk." (And many other details.)

Klüver's report on the same woman *three months after* she had seen Figure B for thirty seconds was as follows:

> Subject "sees" "woman with the umbrella in her right hand. She is standing like that" (indicates position correctly). "The man at the right has lost his cigar; it has fallen to the ground. There is a little man standing beside the woman. To the right is a theater. Above the door I see "Entra." At the left of the door there is a poster. Before the door there is a lantern pole. The globe appears to be in the form of a hexagon. In the background there is a church. In the foreground I see three dogs. They are black, only the right one and the left one have white collars. The dog on the left has a curled tail. His mouth is open." (This protocol goes on and on with many more accurately described details of the original silhouette.)

Typically, an eidetic subject will say that he "sees" an image, yet he also realizes that the object is not before him.

Eidetic imagery is found more frequently among children than among adults. For example, in a study with American schoolchildren, Yale University psychologists R. N. Haber and R. B. Haber found that 8 percent of a group of 151 elementary school children could clearly be classified as eidetic, giving detailed reports much like the woman's account of Figure A. Yet this kind of imagery is rare among American adults. Why the decline from childhood to adulthood?

Psychologist Leonard Doob, also of Yale, suggests that it may be due to cultural factors. When Doob tested rural adults of a certain tribe in Nigeria who could neither read nor write, he found that eidetic imagery was quite common. Yet when Doob tested members of the same tribe who lived in a nearby city, he found little evidence of eidetic imagery. Perhaps the demands of schooling and of acculturation to adult life in an urbanized setting are somehow incompatible with the use of eidetic imagery. Individuals in such settings, therefore, may develop other forms of memory coding instead. In America, growing up "image-wise" may result from becoming urbanized.

H. KLÜVER. An experimental study of the eidetic type. *Genetic Psychology Monograph*, 1926, **1**, 71–230. Figures adapted by permission of the Journal Press.
R. N. HABER & R. B. HABER. Eidetic imagery: I. Frequency. *Perceptual and Motor Skills*, 1964, **19**, 131–138.
L. W. DOOB. Eidetic images among the Ibo. *Ethnology*, 1964, **3**, 357–363.

BOX 6.5

THE REAL BECOMES THE IMAGINED

In 1910, C. W. Perky at Cornell University reported the following experiment: She prepared cardboard forms with their centers cut out in the shape of a book, a banana, an orange, a leaf, and a lemon. These forms could be so placed that, when a lantern was turned on, colored light would shine through the cutout forms, and the corresponding colored figure would be cast on the ground-glass window.

The subject was seated facing the window, with the lantern turned off. He was asked to fixate the screen while he "imagined" a colored object, "for instance, a tomato." He was then to describe his "image" if any image took shape. After these instructions, the lamp was turned on (without the subject's knowledge) with an intensity *below* the minimum necessary for vision. Then, very slowly, the intensity was stepped up until it was *well beyond the previously determined minimum for actual vis-*

ion. As soon as the subject began to describe his "image," the lamp was turned off, and, after he had finished his description, he was requested to "imagine" another object, "for instance, a book." The objects actually cast on the screen were a red tomato, a blue book, a deep-yellow banana, an orange orange, a green leaf, and a light-yellow lemon.

All the subjects (nineteen sophomores and eight graduate students) believed that they were imagining the objects and their appropriate colors, yet not one of them "imagined" the object until the illumination had gone well above the minimum required for normal perception. *They were seeing actual objects but believed that they were "imagining" them.* When the subject was asked whether or not he was "quite sure that he had imagined all these things," the question aroused surprise and indignation. Sophomores and graduate students in psychology alike had mistaken the perception of a real object for an image!

C. W. PERKY. An experimental study of imagination. *American Journal of Psychology*, 1910, **21**, 422–452.

and so on). Images, on the other hand, are more labile. A visual image can be shifted from spot to spot at will; sometimes it is organized together with one group of objects, sometimes with another. (Look ahead to Albert Einstein's reference, in Box 6.7, p. 136, to the "combinatory play" he experienced among his images.) The visual image can even be seen inside an opaque object. It can readily be perceived as larger or smaller than its original size, warped out of shape, or varying in color.

Vividness and lability are important guides and are usually sufficient, but the qualities of the percept of a real object and the qualities of an image are not always distinguishable. People can take an image for a real object and a real object for an image. Sometimes they can actually be seeing things; at other times they may think they are "seeing things," although the real thing is physically present (see Box 6.5). It would seem clear from laboratory experiments and general observation that the overall conditions of the situation, the per-

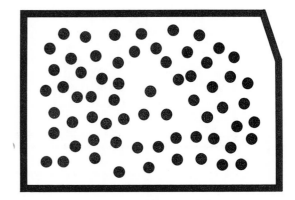

FIGURE 6.1B Do you see any recognizable pattern? Very few adults do. If you are one of them you will have seen the number 63, which can only appear if you indeed were able to superimpose the A pattern of random dots directly upon the B pattern.

C. F. Stroymeyer. Eidetikers. *Psychology Today*, November 1970.

ceiver's alertness and expectations, determine whether or not he will recognize an image as different from the perception of a real object. These factors seem much more important than any set of specific attributes of the two experiences.

The Role of Images in Thought

As we have seen, the process of thinking, whether directed or undirected, frequently involves a continuous flow, a manipulation and interplay of images and other symbolic elements. In thinking, these elements are combined and recombined in unusual and unexpected ways as we seek to find a solution to the problem that started our thinking. Organizations of elements are constructed, destroyed, and reassembled. Elements are abstracted from their normal or familiar contexts, and their properties are transformed in limitless ways. Frequently, such reorganization and reconstruction of elements permit us to see (almost literally) new solutions to puzzling problems. This is particularly true in certain occupational specialties such as the job of the civil engineer, in which the person may need to visualize what a proposed bridge or structure would look like if it were transformed in certain ways. (For an unusual experiment on this ability to manipulate images in your head, see Box 6.6, p. 134.)

Despite this obvious value that imagery may have for the thinking process, it may sometimes inhibit or constrain productive thinking. Vivid images based on what the individual has previously seen or remembered or fantasied may be so compelling in their characteristics that they stand in the way of creative thinking. The reader will recall the experiment by Bruner and Kenney—described in Box 4.5, p. 92—which brings evidence to bear on this very point. The individual may become a captive of his images; that is, he may be unable to shake himself of the particular features of the image. As a result he may be unable to think about his problem in an entirely fresh way. Furthermore, much complex thought is characterized by its high degree of abstractness. Concrete images may interfere with the abstract symbolization that is required for some types of problems.

In addition to the question of whether images help or hinder thinking, there is the second problem posed by the stubborn facts of individual differences in imagery capacity. Some people, it will be remembered, are capable of experiencing many and vivid images; some people seem to lack this capacity almost entirely. Do these individual differences in imagery relate to how one thinks?

Imageless thought   At the beginning of the present century many German, French, English, and American psychologists were involved in a long and often bitterly fought controversy over the question of **imageless thought**, that is, whether or not people could think without images. The imageless school asserted that thinking can take place without imagery and cited as evidence the introspective reports of their subjects who often failed to report any images while thinking. (For a pair of contrasting accounts, see Box 6.7 and Box 6.8, p. 136.) The imagery school insisted that people who did not report images were simply reporting inadequately and were failing to notice fleeting images. The imageless-thought battle ended sometime ago with a "no decision" when psychologists turned their attention to more easily researchable questions about the thinking process.

Recently, though, the question of the role of imagery in thinking has been reformulated, and this reformulation is setting loose a stream of provocative research. The question no longer is: "Can people think without imagery?" In its new form, it is: "Do people who report a great deal of imagery think *in a different way* from those who report little or no imagery?"

Some informal evidence suggests that the answer to this question may be "yes." For example, some people find a graph or figure helpful in trying to understand a difficult concept or relation. Others find that a graph is little or no help; they have to translate the visual information into verbal form before it has any meaning for them. Both types of people may be equally capable of understanding the relation in question, but they may code this relation differently, one using a code of visual elements, the other using a nonvisual code. This difference in sym-

BOX 6.6

HOW TO TURN THINGS OVER IN YOUR MIND

ATTENTION!
Note: Before reading this box or looking at the fig-
ures below, find a clock or watch with a sweep
second hand that you can use as a timer. Then care-
fully follow the instructions:

In a moment, you will look at a pair of pictures. *Don't yet!* Each picture shows a three-dimensional object made of wooden blocks. As you look
at the pictures, decide whether they show two different views of the *same* object or two *different* objects. *Now,* get ready to time yourself on the number
of seconds it takes you to *decide* whether the two
objects are the *same* or *different. Start!*

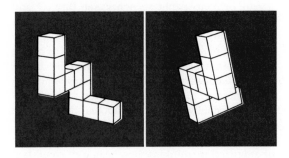

Record your time. Now follow exactly the
same procedure with the second pair (shown below).
Again, note the number of seconds it takes you to
decide whether the objects are the same or different.
Start!

If you were like most subjects in an experiment at Stanford University by R. Shepard and J.
Metzler, you found that the second pair required a
longer decision time than the first (despite the fact
that you had the advantage of practice when making
the second decision). What is going on here? To
find out, Shepard and Metzler had eight adult subjects view 1,600 picture pairs of objects similar to
those above. In half the pairs, the pictures showed
two different views of the *same* object; that is, the
right-hand picture simply showed a rotated view of
the left-hand object. In the other half of the pairs,
the pictures showed two *different* objects, objects
that could not be made to look the same no matter
how they were rotated. The decision time of each
subject was recorded accurately for all 1,600 judgments.

Results (for the 800 "same" pairs) showed a
clear-cut and surprising pattern. There was a direct,
straight-line relation between the time required to
decide whether or not the objects were the same
and the degrees of angular difference between the
two different views of the object. This intriguing result, shown graphically in the figure, was true regardless of whether the pictures showed objects
rotated in the *two-dimensional* plane of the picture
(Figure A) or showed differences corresponding to
a rotation of real three-dimensional objects *in depth*
(Figure B).

How might this result be explained? The
authors suggest:

> Although introspective reports must be interpreted
> with caution, all subjects claimed . . . that to make
> the required comparison they first had to imagine
> one object as rotated into the same orientation as
> the other and that they could carry out this "mental
> rotation" at no greater than a certain limited rate.

Moreover, "If we can describe this process
as some sort of 'mental rotation in three-dimensional
space,' then the slope of the obtained functions indicates that the average rate at which these particular objects can be thus 'rotated' is roughly 60
degrees per second."

The two objects of *both* pairs shown in this
box are the same; that is, the right-hand figure is
simply a rotated view of the left-hand figure in each
case. (The angle of rotation is substantially greater
for the second pair.) Incidentally, practically all
judgments (about 97 percent) of same or different

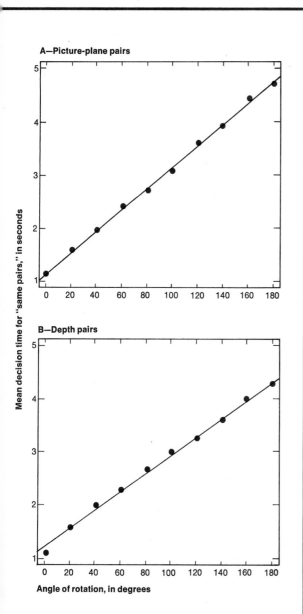

A—Picture-plane pairs

B—Depth pairs

Mean decision time for "same pairs," in seconds

Angle of rotation, in degrees

were correctly made; however, "different" decisions took, on the average, 3.8 seconds, about a second longer than "same" decisions.

R. N. SHEPARD & J. METZLER. Mental rotation of three dimensional objects. *Science*, 1971, **171**, 701–703. Copyright 1971 by the American Association for the Advancement of Science.

bolic elements may then have important consequences for the thinking and problem-solving behavior of these people.

Many experimental studies exploring the role of imagery in thinking have been made. In one such study by Kuhlman (1960), three groups of children (aged five, seven, and nine years) were classified as being "high" or "low" in visual imagery on the basis of a series of tests. All high-imagery groups were then found to be more capable on tasks that required reproducing geometric designs from memory and were also better at learning new names for novel objects. However, five- to seven-year-old high-imagery children were *poorer* at a concept-formation task that required abstract thinking, presumably because the abstract type of thinking required by the task conflicted with the concrete visual imagery that these subjects typically used in their thinking. This difference on the concept-formation task was *not* found for nine-year-old children, perhaps because these older children generally had come to place a greater reliance upon language and hence the high-imagery ones did not try to solve the concept-formation task by using visual imagery.

This new concern with the study of imagery in thinking is itself an interesting example of how the course of thinking may be blocked because a problem is *formulated* in a particular way, even though other formulations are possible. The phrase "imageless thought" was undoubtedly a catchy slogan in its day, but to the extent that it lured competent researchers to confine their studies of imagery to a single channel, it blocked different and potentially more fruitful avenues of investigation from being explored. Scientists become captives of their particular ways of seeing the world.

LANGUAGE AND THINKING

The elements most frequently used in thinking are words. The most common way of communicating the solution of a problem is with words. The achievement of a new concept often results in the coining of a new word or in giving an old word new meanings. For these and other

BOX 6.7

THE IMAGES OF ALBERT EINSTEIN

Since the days of Sir Francis Galton there has been a continuing interest in the imagery of scientists as they work on problems. Nonpsychologists have collected much valuable data in this field. One of the most interesting collections is in a book by the mathematician Jacques Hadamard. He believes: "The mental pictures of mathematicians . . . are most frequently visual, but they may also be of another kind—for instance, kinetic. There can also be auditive ones." Among the mathematicians whom Hadamard included in his study was Albert Einstein. The following excerpt from a letter from Einstein to Hadamard gives us an extraordinarily interesting account of Einstein's thought processes as he himself experienced them:

> The words of the language, as they are written or spoken, do not seem to play any role in my mechanism of thought. The psychical entities which serve as elements in thought are certain signs and more or less clear images which can be "voluntarily" reproduced and combined . . . this combinatory play seems to be the essential feature in productive thought—before there is any connection with logical construction in words or other kinds of signs which can be communicated to others. The above mentioned elements are, in my case, of visual and some of muscular type. Conventional words or other signs have to be sought for laboriously only in a secondary stage, when the above mentioned associative play is sufficiently established and can be reproduced at will.

J. HADAMARD. *Psychology of Invention in the Mathematical Field.* Princeton: Princeton University Press, 1949.

BOX 6.8

THE IMAGELESS THOUGHT OF ALDOUS HUXLEY

In striking contrast to the accounts of imagery presented in Box 6.7 ("The Images of Albert Einstein"), the following quote from the well-known writer Aldous Huxley shows that highly imaginative and creative thinking can also take place *without* much visual imagery.

> I am, and for as long as I can remember, I have always been a poor visualizer. Words, even the pregnant words of poets, do not evoke pictures in my mind. No hypnagogic visions greet me on the verge of sleep. When I recall something, the memory does not present itself to me as a vividly seen event or object. By an effort of the will, I can evoke a not very vivid image of what happened yesterday afternoon. . . . But such images have little substance and absolutely no autonomous life of their own. They stand to real, perceived objects in the same relation as Homer's ghosts stood to men of flesh and blood, who came to visit them in the shades. Only when I have a high temperature do my mental images come to independent life. To those in whom the faculty of visualization is strong my inner world must seem curiously drab, limited, and uninteresting.

U. Neisser, a psychologist at Cornell University, has the following comment on Huxley's quote:

> This passage is worthy of note in its own right. Huxley obviously knew vivid images when he saw them, as in fevered states, so he must be believed if he reports their absence. Yet it is hard to think that his inner life was "uninteresting" when he describes it in a passage as exciting as this one. If he lacked imagery, he did not lack imagination.

A. HUXLEY. *The Doors of Perception* and *Heaven and Hell.* (Published in one volume.) Harmundsworth, Middlesex: Penguin, 1959. U. NEISSER. *Cognitive Psychology.* New York: Appleton, 1967.

reasons, most psychologists will agree that there is a close relation between thinking and language, so close that some psychologists use the analysis of language of the child to study the thinking of the child. Among them are Piaget and Bruner, whose theories of the development of thinking and of cognitive growth in general heavily emphasize the role played by language in facilitating the attainment of abstract thought (see Unit 4).

But with language, as with the imageless-thought problem, we must distinguish between what is *necessary* for thinking and what may be *helpful* for thinking. Even if we grant that language plays a critical role in man's thinking, it is not necessary to conclude that language is *essential* for thought processes. If that were true, lower animals would certainly be mindless, and even preverbal children would not be capable of thinking. Yet it is clear from informal observation and careful experimental work that both young children and animals are quite capable of solving problems. This problem solving has all the appearances of thinking. Indeed, rats are apparently also capable of insight in a problem-solving situation that lends itself to an insightful solution (see Box 6.9).

Admittedly, the average man can solve more difficult problems than the average animal can. But some men are better problem solvers

---

BOX 6.9

THE RAT AND CREATIVE PROBLEM SOLVING

Many psychologists maintain that even the rat is capable of creative problem solving. In 1930 E. C. Tolman and C. H. Honzik at the University of California reported their classical experiment on insight in the rat using an elevated maze (having no sidewalls and elevated from the floor of the room, see photograph).

The apparatus that they used presented three paths to the goal box, which contained food (see diagram). Path 1 was the shortest, 2 the next shortest, and 3 the longest. Paths 1 and 2 had a common final segment that path 3 did not share. First the rats were given *preliminary training*. Animals deprived of food for twenty-four hours were placed in the starting box and permitted to find their way to the goal box. They were given ten trials a day. They soon learned (after trying the various paths) to take the shortest path to the food. When the experimenters then *blocked* path

1 at point A, the rats would turn back to the choice point and would almost always (about 93 percent of the time) take path 2.

In the *test run* the block was *for the first time* placed in the common section of paths 1 and 2 (at point B). Then when the rats backed out of path 1, they did not take path 2 but path 3—the longest

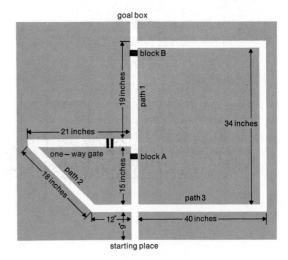

goal box

block B

19 inches

path 1

21 inches

34 inches

one – way gate

block A

18 inches

path 2

15 inches

path 3

12″

9″

40 inches

starting place

path, *but the only one still open to the goal box.* Of the fifteen rats in this experiment, fourteen behaved in this way.

Backing out of path 1 and taking path 3 was a relatively new and original solution—and one that seemed to the human psychologists observing the rats' behavior to show insight and inference, or what we are tempted to call *creative problem solving.*

E. C. TOLMAN & C. H. HONZIK. "Insight" in rats. *University of California Publications in Psychology*, 1930, **4**, 215–232. Figure adapted by permission.

than others are, yet we do not (or should not) infer from this the existence of *qualitatively* different thought processes. Furthermore, it is to be remembered that it is man who decides what is to be called "difficult" and that, typically, animal thinking is investigated in *man-relevant* problem situations. We do not know, nor is it meaningful to ask, how well man would fare in attempting to solve the problem of navigating accurately over long distances, given the same equipment available to salmon and migratory birds, who do such navigating extraordinarily well. Our point here is not to champion the cause of the underprivileged species but only to question the claim that thinking is an exclusive human preserve. Although language significantly influences the way we think, it is unnecessary to deny ourselves, in our study of human thought, the use of data on children's and animals' thought.

Language in Silent and Communicative Thought

Language plays an important role both when we are thinking to ourselves (the **silent-thinking stage**) and when we are formally expressing our thoughts, either through speaking or writing (the **communicative-thinking stage**). But detailed analysis indicates that the exact role of language differs in the two stages. In the silent-thinking stage the specific grammar and vocabulary of the language seem to play a relatively minor role in determining the nature and content of thought.

Vigotsky (1939), a Russian psychologist, has characterized the *inner speech* that occurs in silent thinking in the following manner: First, it is abrupt and incomplete; second, it makes many assumptions about the "self-evident" nature of the facts and relations involved in any line of reasoning; third, it is relatively independent of the rules of grammar.

In the communicative-thinking stage, language serves what might be termed a *policing* and *editing* function, and here the specific structure of the language may play a more significant role. We realize that we cannot be so abrupt and elliptical. We must spell out our steps; we must use words more precisely; we must pay

some attention to grammatical construction. Otherwise we run the risk of not communicating at all. We realize these necessities because we have learned that our private world is not shared by others.

The differences between speech in the silent-thinking and the communication stages do not represent sharp breaks. The degree of difference depends, in part, upon the relation between the speaker and the listener. In general, the more common the sympathies and context shared by the listener and speaker, the more elliptical, abrupt, unfinished, and grammatically unrestrained speech can be. At one extreme is the instance in which we are talking to ourselves; at the other extreme is the formal, written communication addressed to an unknown audience.

When we talk to ourselves, we have a perfect friend, a completely sympathetic and understanding audience who shares our context completely. We use the vaguest of words without any fear that we shall be misunderstood. We use the felt sense of words, rather than the dictionary meanings. We are not constrained by grammatical rules. We skip steps in our reasoning, feeling that we understand what we have not spoken.

Conversation among good friends of like mind may be only slightly removed from talking to oneself. Such conversations may also consist of somewhat abbreviated speech. Often we find that no sooner does one friend begin to speak than the other will immediately anticipate the purport of the speech and begin his reply, only to be understood immediately and to be interrupted by the beginning of another reply. Such a conversation may well include mere beginnings of sentences, snatches of phrases, and elliptical exclamations.

Increasing formalization of speech can be illustrated in the difference between the professor's language when he lectures and when he writes. His lectures are apt to be more informal. Sentences are not completed; tenses are mixed; plural nouns are coupled with singular verbs; participles are left hanging; and phrases like "the whatnot" abound. Yet this garbled and grammatically barbarous spoken language may be perfectly understood by most listeners;

whereas the same words, read in a manuscript, may cause confusion and bewilderment. Why? One reason seems to be that in speech the audience not only hears the words but also sees the speaker's facial expressions, hears stresses and emphases, and sees gestures; furthermore, all the communication takes place in a very specific context (see Figure 6.2). When reading a manuscript or this book, however, the reader is mostly dependent upon the written words. He does not have the multitude of nonverbal cues that the listener has when he not only hears but also sees the speaker.

FIGURE 6.2 This hand gesture symbolizes, among other things, the cuckold, the devil, and the evil eye. Can you guess its use in still another context? (see page 140)

Photo by Winston Vargas

Speech, then, becomes more formal as we attempt to communicate with others, and it increases in formality as the psychological distance between the speaker and listener increases.

When we prepare to communicate our thoughts—when we attempt to dress up our thoughts for public display—we often find that we cannot do so. In the light of day, as it were, we find that we have assumed too much, that

our thinking process has not been completed. The reason we sometimes cannot find the words for our thoughts is that we really did not have the thought*s clearly* in the first place; we had only assumed that we had them. The second stage is thus not merely a stage of expression; it is very frequently a continuation of the stage of creation. We correct, fill in, revise, and even completely alter our thinking as we attempt to express it. But now we are doing our thinking under the constraints imposed upon us by the dictionary meaning of words and by the rules of grammar.

That the constraints of language may help the thinking process has been shown in a study by Gagné and Smith (1962). They found that training subjects to put all their thoughts into words while working on a problem and requiring them to spell out the general principle involved resulted in a significant improvement in their subsequent problem-solving ability.

Language: Vehicle or Mold?

Most psychologists agree that there is a close relation between language and thinking, but there is disagreement on the nature of this relation. The major question of disagreement can be stated simply: Is language merely a reproducing instrument for voicing or clarifying ideas, or is language itself the shaper of ideas? One analysis—language as a vehicle—suggests that the nature of thinking depends very little upon the nature of language. Neither the vocabulary nor the grammar of a language determines the product of thinking. According to this position the development of thinking and language in the child go along concurrently but more or less separately. As the child learns new words, she can better communicate her thoughts and better remember her conclusions, but that is all. Language is a convenient vehicle for thinking.

The other analysis maintains that language inevitably molds thought. A number of linguistic studies have been cited to support this view. The studies of the language and thinking of different societies and cultural groups have thus been interpreted to show that the nature of the thinking of a group corresponds to the nature of its grammar and vocabulary (see Box 6.10). Some clinical studies have indicated, for example, that the disturbance in the thinking of the schizophrenic patient corresponds to the disturbance in his language. According to this formulation, the development of thought and language must be seen as a highly interdependent process, in much the same way argued in Units 4 and 5. As the child achieves new concepts, the very structure of his language is affected; and as he learns new words and new ways of putting words together, the very nature of his thinking is changed. And, of course, his ability to think productively and to solve problems is thereby affected.

*   *   *

The solution to the problem posed in Box 6.1 is:

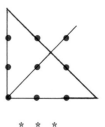

*   *   *

SOLUTION TO FIGURE 6.2   A broker on the American Stock Exchange is alerting his booth on the latest price of his stock.

Photo by Winston Vargas

BOX 6.10

IT HOUSES

Benjamin Lee Whorf, a student of linguistics, argues that "the background linguistic system [the grammar] of each language is not merely a reproducing instrument for voicing ideas but rather is itself the shaper of ideas." He supports his arguments, in part, by comparing the way various languages "dissect nature." He points out that we tend to differentiate between "things" and "events" in a hard and fast way because in the English language we divide most of our words into nouns and verbs.

Our language thus gives us a bipolar division of nature. But nature herself is not bipolarized. If it be said that strike, turn, run, are verbs because they denote temporary or short-lasting events, i.e., actions, why then is fist a noun? It is also a temporary event. Why are lightning, spark, wave, eddy, pulsation, flame, storm, phase, cycle, spasm, noise, emotion, nouns? . . . It will be found that an "event" to *us* means "what our language classes as a verb." . . . In the Hopi language, lightning, wave, flame, meteor, puff of smoke, pulsation, are verbs—events of necessarily brief duration cannot be anything but verbs. Cloud and storm are at about the lower limit of duration for nouns. Hopi, you see, actually has a classification of events . . . by duration type, something strange to our modes of thought. . . . In Nootka, a language of Vancouver Island . . . we have as it were, a monistic view of nature that gives us only one class of words for all kinds of events. "A house occurs" or "it houses" is the way of saying "house" exactly like "a flame occurs" or "it burns."

Whorf would thus maintain that because of our grammar (nouns and verbs) we divide the world into "events" and "things"; whereas the Hopi use quite another basis (their grammar classifies words by "duration" type) and the Vancouver Islanders make no division at all between a "thing" and an "event." By this view, grammar determines the perception of the world around us, and that perception will, in turn, have at least some effect on the content and direction of our thinking.

B. L. WHORF. *Language, Thought and Reality*. New York: Wiley, 1956.

SUMMARY

1. Thinking involves the interplay of symbolic elements, such as words and images, that represent aspects of the real world. Sometimes this symbolic interplay is consciously directed toward solving a specific problem; at other times it is less reality oriented. In the extreme case it is autistic thinking. In any of its forms, thinking is crucial to man's ability to adapt.

2. At times problems can be solved directly by recourse to previous learning (reproductive thinking); when new and original (for the individual) solutions are required, we speak of productive thinking or creative problem solving.

3. To some extent we are aware of our thought processes during problem solving, so that introspective reports provide one means for their study. Introspection, however, can rarely provide a complete account; therefore, thinking must also be studied by the systematic observation of behavior.

4. Problem solving must begin with perceiving the nature of the problem, with problem discovery.

5. The perceptual process during problem solving is reported to be ever-changing and to involve apparent discontinuities in the stream of awareness. Changes in *how* an object is perceived can lead to a sudden solution, accompanied by the experience of insight, as in the "aha!" experience.

6. Both percepts and images participate in the problem-solving process, and individuals vary widely in the vividness and the preferred sensory modes of both. Though the two may on occasion be confused with one another, images are typically more labile and less vivid.

7. Images are essential symbolic elements of the thinking process, but at times, their very concreteness may interfere with problem solution.

8. An early controversy concerning the possibility of imageless thought has been replaced by the question (and some answers) of differences in *ways* of thinking as related to imagery.

9. Although language is critically important in the typical thinking of human adults, there is no doubt that truly creative thinking can occur in man, and in other species as well, in the absence of language. Even during silent thinking normal adults employ language, although in this circumstance our inner speech is somewhat primitive and simplified. When required to verbalize our thoughts to others (communicative thinking), the formal constraints of language significantly affect the thinking process.

10. Language is not a passive vehicle serving thinking, nor does it wholly mold our thought processes. Rather, the development and adult functioning of language and thinking are highly interdependent processes.

GLOSSARY

"aha!" experience   A term first used by Karl Bühler, a Viennese psychologist, to refer to an intense and positive emotional experience occasionally accompanying the sudden realization of how a problem can be solved. This experience may accompany false solutions as well as valid ones. The term *insight* is also applicable to this experience.

autistic thinking   Refers to thinking that is primarily influenced by personal desires and needs at the expense of its adaptability to objective reality.

communicative-thinking stage   Refers to the phase of communication of one's thoughts to others, either in writing or in speech.

created image   A subjective experience (visual, auditory, and so on) of an object that has never existed as a stimulus object for the person undergoing the experience; an imagined object.

creative problem solving (productive thinking)   Achieving a solution to a problem that is new and original *for the individual.* Previously acquired knowledge enters into the process but must be transformed to fit the novel demands of the problem.

eidetic image   A particularly vivid and detailed memory image. It is found more frequently among children than among adults and may sometimes be evoked at will several months after the original viewing of the stimulus.

imageless thought   Thinking that can proceed in the apparent absence of imagery, or, in its more extreme form, thought in which imagery plays no role.

memory image   A subjective experience (visual, auditory, and so on) of an object that has once existed as a stimulus object for the person but is not now present in his perceptual field.

productive thinking   (see **creative problem solving**)

realistic thinking   Thinking guided by the requirements of the problem-solving situation, thus constrained by logic and objective evidence.

reproductive thinking   Applying previously acquired knowledge, directly and without change, to solve a problem.

silent-thinking stage   The stage in the thinking process that does not involve communicating the thoughts to others (either in writing or in speech); frequently characterized by *inner speech.*

creative problem solving

DO YOU KNOW...

- that most of us can be taught to become more efficient problem solvers?

- whether animals are able to come up with creative and original solutions to difficult problems and whether computers can do this also?

- that being too eager to solve a problem can interfere with finding its solution?

- that having too much information can get in the way of solving a problem—and why?

- that familiarity with the essential elements of a problem can hinder its solution?

- under what circumstances a string of successes in problem solving can make you a good problem solver or can seriously hinder you?

Photo by Melissa Shook

CONTENTS

In Unit 6 we present an analysis of the experience of productive thinking and problem solving, with special attention to the important role played by imagery and language. We shall now turn our attention in more detail to the *process* of problem solving, that is, what goes on as a person struggles with a problem. Then we shall examine some of the *determinants* of the process, that is, factors that have a crucial influence on the outcome of problem solving.

PROCESS DESCRIPTIONS OF PROBLEM SOLVING

The following four descriptions of the problem-solving process vary markedly in their aims and approaches. Each has its strengths and its weaknesses; none is a comprehensive treatment of the complex topic. What each one undertakes to do in its own distinctive way is to throw some explanatory light on the observable behavior of the problem solver as he goes about his task.

A Four-Stages View

Creative people in the sciences, the arts, and other fields have often reflected on the nature of their own processes of problem solving, and when one examines their accounts a compelling descriptive schema emerges. It appears that creative thought generally occurs in four stages: preparation, incubation, illumination, and verification. Although this schema provides only a rough topography of the problem-solving processes, and often does violence to the actual sequence of events, it has proven useful as a general framework for more detailed analyses.

Preparation The first stage, **preparation**, can be briefly described as the period when the problem solver becomes acquainted with the features of the problem and tries to formulate it in workable terms. He begins to play with ideas, the stimulus pattern evoking first this and then that association. Often these associations seem to be random and free in nature, directed by the demands of the problem but not completely restricted by these demands. Gradually, a more disciplined attitude is taken. Certain suggestions and ideas are discarded, others are examined more carefully, and problem solving in earnest gets under way. Frequently, this stage merges rapidly and without any noticeable break into the illumination and verification stages (skipping the incubation stage), and the problem is solved.

Incubation   The second stage, **incubation**, occurs when there is a break between the stage of preparation and the final stages. Incubation varies greatly in its nature and its duration. It may last a few minutes, several days, weeks, months, or even years. It is a stage in which the problem is laid aside and no conscious work done on it, but after which renewed attention to the problem results in prompt solution or at least in a prompt advance beyond the previous point of progress. The testimony of creative thinkers is filled with accounts of the incubation period. Mathematicians, inventors, poets, scientists, and artists have testified that this or that solution unaccountably occurred while they were shaving, bathing, listening to a concert, or rounding a pond on Hampstead Heath. There can be no doubt of its reality.

We see again why an analysis of creative problem solving that restricts itself to the person's reports of what he is thinking about may not be adequate. Much may occur without any conscious experience.

Illumination   The third typical stage is **illumination**, described in the discussion of insight in Unit 6 (p. 127). Often the person, having hit upon a general solution, will assume that the problem has been solved and will do no further work on it. The experience of illumination or insight may, of course, be misleading or faulty, as we have noted; his general idea may simply not work. As a result he will have ended his problem solving prematurely.

Verification   **Verification**, therefore, is the last essential stage. The proposed solution must be worked out in more specific detail and applied and tested. If it meets the test, the problem is solved. If the proposed solution fails, the process must be wholly or partly repeated.

A Funneling View

A quite different process description of problem solving that undertakes to provide a more fully detailed account of how specific solutions are developed within the problem-solving process has been given by the German psychologist Karl Duncker. Duncker's description is based on careful observation of what people actually do and say as they go about solving a problem in a laboratory situation.

The analysis is couched in perceptual terms. Duncker speaks of the creative problem-solving process as consisting of a related series of mental organizations, each funneling into a more narrowly defined statement of the problem. This series, his analysis shows, can be grouped into three major levels.

General range   When a person first tackles a problem, the initial organization that he achieves can be described as a **general range**, which is a very general restatement of the original problem indicating the direction of a possible solution. This initial organization may emphasize some general property of the sought-after solution or some general method that might bring about the solution.

Functional solution   The general range is followed by the **functional solution**, which reformulates and narrows the general range. Functional solutions have the typical form: If such and such could be achieved, the problem would be solved.

Specific solution   The next step, **specific solution**, can be described as a further specification of the functional solution. If a given specific solution is found unsatisfactory, the subject may return to the preceding functional solution and seek some other specific solution. Failing in that, he may revert to the initial general range, start out on other functional solutions,

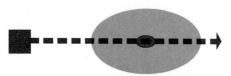

FIGURE 7.1 This schematic diagram, used by Duncker in his cancer problem, is intended to represent a cross section of the body, with the tumor in the middle and the radiation apparatus on the left. The line with the arrow represents the course of the rays.

Read the problem as presented in the text and see if you can solve it.

K. Duncker. On problem solving. *Psychological Monographs,* 1945, **58**, No. 5; adapted by permission.

and go on from there. He may even, of course, try out different general ranges.

An illustrative study   Duncker's description can be clarified through a specific illustration from his classic study of problem solving (1945). In one of his experiments he presented his subjects (University of Berlin students) with the schematic sketch shown in Figure 7.1 and the following problem:

> Given, a human being with an inoperable stomach tumor. We know that if we apply certain rays, with sufficient intensity, the tumor can be destroyed. The problem is: how can those rays, at the required high intensity, be applied to the tumor without at the same time destroying the healthy tissue which surrounds the tumor?

Duncker asked his subjects to think out loud while they worked at this problem. Figure 7.2 presents a diagrammatic summary of the thinking of one subject as he attempted to solve the problem. It will be seen that his problem-solving process consisted of several general ranges, functional solutions, and specific solutions.

The first general range adopted by this student was: "I must find some way of avoiding contact between the rays and the healthy tissue." This general range could and did lead to several more specific restatements of the problem (i.e., functional solutions): Use a free path to the stomach; remove the healthy tissue from

the path of the rays; insert a protecting wall between the rays and the healthy tissue; displace the tumor toward the surface. From each of these functional solutions, a specific solution suggested itself to the subject. These solutions in turn were either rejected by the experimenter as inadequate or were recognized as inadequate by the subject himself. As each specific solution was rejected, the student would go on to a different functional solution and to different general ranges, until he finally adopted this one: "Lower the intensity of the rays on their way through healthy tissue." This third general range finally did lead to the correct solution. Let us quote the student as he approached this last lap and went through the functional solution into the specific: "Somehow divert . . . diffuse rays . . . disperse . . . stop! Send a broad and weak bundle of rays through a lens in such a way that the tumor lies at the focal point and thus receives intensive radiation."

This solution is closely related to the best solutions: Send several weak bundles of rays from various points outside the body, all these weak bundles to meet at the tumor; thus the intensity of the rays necessary for destruction is attained only at the tumor. Or stick to a single ray source but rotate the body so that only the tumor is constantly exposed to the rays. (The rays, incidentally, cannot be focused by ordinary lenses, as suggested by the student, but nevertheless, the experimenter accepted this as a solution.)

The total duration of this problem-solving attempt was about half an hour.

This description is generalized from many observations. Not every problem solver goes through the three levels of general range, functional solution, and specific solution in that order. Almost every conceivable exception to the rule is found if a large-enough group of subjects is examined. Nevertheless, Duncker's scheme provides a fruitful model of the problem-solving process.

Problem Solving as a Skill

Still another principal way to conceptualize the process of problem solving is to view problem

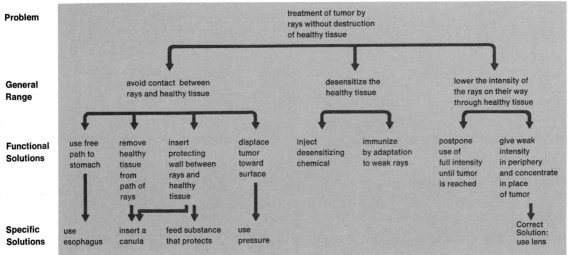

FIGURE 7.2 A family tree of attempted solutions evolved by one subject working on Duncker's cancer problem.
K. Duncker. On problem solving. *Psychological Monographs*, 1945, **58**, No. 5; adapted by permission.

solving as a skill, in the same way that driving a car or playing the guitar are skills. Distinguishing characteristics of such skills—that they are dependent upon learning, may be developed through practice, require the combination of subskills, and so forth—pertain as well to problem solving. It, too, reflects the use of past experience, can be nurtured through practice (see Box 7.1, p. 150), and involves the coordination of complex component processes (such as organizing information, generating ideas, and evaluating alternatives). Like many other skills, problem solving requires the use of *strategies* to direct and coordinate overall progress. Also, like other skills, its general level of execution is strongly affected by the adequacy or inadequacy of the person's subskills; bad habits in the cognitive domain can limit one's problem-solving effectiveness just as surely as poor motor habits can limit one's skill at touch typing, skiing, or playing the piano.

Regarding problem solving in this way, as a highly complex cognitive skill (an approach, it will be remembered, which is characteristic of Bruner's thinking on cognition, see Unit 4, p. 92), has certain implications concerning

individual differences in thinking ability. For one thing, a person's present level of problem-solving proficiency need no longer be regarded by him as something he is born with, fatalistically implying that little can be done to change it. Instead, it can be viewed—regardless of its present level—as subject to considerable further development through appropriate instruction and practice. Moreover, creative problem solving, or productive thinking, need not be considered as something special and reserved for the province of the expert; instead, it can be seen as something that *everyone* is called upon to do and can learn to do more effectively.

Although educators have always recognized that thinking is central to the educational process and have developed some highly imaginative new programs and curriculums in certain subjects, it is nevertheless true that relatively little actual school time and effort go into *direct* instruction in productive thinking. To take a case in point, consider the component skills involved in problem formulation and discovery. Unit 6 (p. 126) discusses how important this phase of problem solving is. Yet it tends to be short-circuited or even completely omitted in

BOX 7.1

FROM THE CATALOG AT UTOPIA UNIVERSITY

Psychology 101—*Productive Thinking*. This course is intended to develop the student's potential for effective thinking and problem solving. It acquaints her with the basic skills and strategies involved in thinking, gives her guided practice in developing these skills, and teaches her how to apply them to a wide variety of educationally and socially relevant problems. It also seeks to enhance the student's understanding of her own thought processes, to increase her readiness for independent thought, and to foster a sense of enjoyment in the use of the mind.

You will probably not find a course like this one listed in your college catalog, but several thousand fifth- and sixth-grade children in various American schools have been trying to learn how to think productively in this way by using materials developed by psychologists M. V. Covington, R. S. Crutchfield, L. B. Davies, and R. M. Olton at the University of California, Berkeley. The children work through a series of fifteen cartoon-text story booklets, each featuring mysterious and baffling situations to be explained. The basic idea is to teach children to use their minds by having them begin to solve problems in the manner of imaginative scientists, scholars, and detectives.

As a problem develops in the story, the student is led through successive steps that require him to learn about and to practice a variety of thinking skills and strategies. For instance, at various points the student is asked to write down ideas for solving the problem. On subsequent pages he compares his own ideas with a range of illustrative examples of relevant, fruitful, and original ideas that are supplied as feedback. Each lesson is designed so that the student gradually works toward the solution, experiencing the vicissitudes of the problem-solving process, and is eventually led to make the discovery for himself. The discovery experience is intended to foster a sense of competence in coping with difficult and complex thinking tasks.

In order to provide a thread of continuity among the problems, each lesson features two elementary school children, Jim and Lila Cannon, and their Uncle John, and recounts an adventure in which the reader participates and identifies with these fictional children.

A few illustrated pages are shown here to convey the flavor of the approach. The problem posed in this lesson is to solve the mystery of the disappearance of several cans of water from their camp site in the desert. As you break into the story, Uncle John is suggesting to the children that they take a systematic approach toward considering each major possibility. The first suspect mentioned is their mule—and the problem-solving tale goes on from there.

To help the student learn to *transfer* these thinking skills to other kinds of problems, he also works through a series of Problem Sets, each of which extends and strengthens the skills taught in the lesson booklets. For example, he works on problems such as these: think of economic activities suitable for a small developing country (given certain facts about its natural resources, possible markets, customs, and way of life), track down the cause of an unfamiliar disease (given information about the conditions under which this disease is found), plan a redevelopment project for part of a city (given information about the psychological, economic, and other needs of the inhabitants).

Research by the authors (see Olton & Crutchfield) has indicated that students who are taught by this method—regardless of test intelligence or initial level of thinking competence—show measurable superiority to control children in terms of problem-solving performance on a broad range of thinking tasks, some of which are quite dissimilar to those used in the training program. In addition, there are marked increases in the *willingness* of the instructed children to engage in complex thinking activities, as well as other positive changes in their attitudes and motivations toward use of the mind.

M. V. COVINGTON, R. S. CRUTCHFIELD, L. B. DAVIES, & R. M. OLTON. *The Productive Thinking Program.* Columbus, Ohio: Charles E. Merrill Co., 1974.
R. M. OLTON & R. S. CRUTCHFIELD. Developing the skills of productive thinking. In P. Mussen, J. Langer, & M. V. Covington (Eds.), *Trends and Issues in Developmental Psychology.* New York: Holt, Rinehart & Winston, 1969.

the typical problem solving that a student is called upon to do in school. For example, a work problem in mathematics or science is usually given in essentially predigested form, with the relevant terms and conditions clearly stated, any irrelevant or potentially confusing facts conveniently omitted, and the specific question to be answered explicitly put. Under such circumstances, the student is not called upon to develop or use the vital skills having to do with *detecting* or *formulating* problems, nor does he need to do very much with the skills of *selecting* and *organizing essential information*. This restricted form of problem presentation not only fails to develop such necessary and very real skills but also is artificial and unrepresentative of the kinds of actual problems customarily encountered by a person in his everyday life. In more lifelike circumstances problems are likely to be messy rather than neat, fraught with confusion and irrelevancy, often so poorly defined that the bewildered individual experiences nothing more than the general impression that something is wrong. He must then try to formulate what the problem is, try to put his finger on it, and develop a plan to cope with it—a far cry from the sort of problem-solving skills required in traditional school workbooks.

In short, what the school really needs is a *cognitive curriculum*, a program in which the developing and strengthening of the cognitive skills of productive and creative thinking are at the heart of the educational enterprise. Teaching the student *how* to think, rather than *what* to think, would become the focus of classroom activity. Thus, psychologists who conceptualize problem solving as a complex skill are now seeking the kind of basic knowledge about the process that can help further this educational mission.

An Information-Processing Account

A final way of analyzing the process of problem solving is in terms of the flow of information through a system. The process of problem solving is similar in many respects to the way that high-speed electronic computers process information, and these similarities have led to the development of a promising new approach to the study of thinking called *information processing*. Problem solving (or any psychological process) can be studied usefully if one is sufficiently ingenious in formulating models of the process in terms of the operations used when we program computers. In essence, one tries to describe or explain a given psychological process by spelling out in rigorous, explicit terms the essential sequence of computer-language operations that, according to one's theory, the process entails.

This sequence is usually diagramed in the form of a **flow chart**. Flow charts are simply visual or schematic diagrams that chart the flow of information through a system. These charts indicate both the *kinds* of operations that are performed and the *sequence* in which they are executed. In the flow chart shown in Figure 7.3, the rectangular boxes indicate the *operational* steps, and the diamond-shaped boxes indicate *decision* steps, points at which the computer selects one course of action if the answer to a question is yes and another course of action if the answer is no. In Figure 7.3, each time the answer is no the computer must perform a **loop**, repeating the same sequence of steps (with new information) until it comes once again to the decision point and again asks whether the answer to the question is yes or no, and so on. By making one decision step contingent upon the outcome of an earlier decision, it is possible to pyramid a whole hierarchy of decisions, thus permitting an overall **program** of enormous scope and flexibility. Indeed, this ability to make endless cycles and rearrangements of a few basic processes is one of the factors that makes the computer such a powerful tool.

So far, we may not seem to have said anything to imply that a computer might be capable of thinking or of displaying an appreciable degree of intelligence. Yet by following programs essentially similar to the one we have described, computers can perform such feats as diagnosing medical diseases (using symptoms and laboratory test results as input data), playing a good game of three-dimensional tick-tack-toe, managing delicate phases of complex

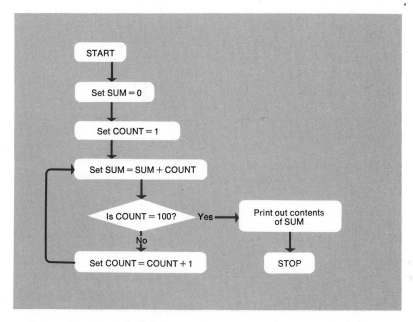

FIGURE 7.3 This flow chart shows the steps in a hypothetical computer program designed to calculate the sum of all numbers from 1 to 100 (1 + 2 + 3 ... + 98 + 99 + 100 = ?). COUNT represents a memory cell in the computer that is used to keep track of how many numbers have been added; SUM (another memory cell) stores the accumulated sum at any point in the sequence. As long as COUNT contains a number less than 100, the computer adds 1 to COUNT and "loops" back to Set SUM = SUM + COUNT and continues this cycle until the number in COUNT finally reaches 100. When this occurs, the computer is instructed to print out the contents of SUM (the answer) and then to STOP.

manufacturing processes, navigating a spaceship from the earth to the moon (aiming from a moving platform at a moving target), and even composing music. Such behavior, if performed by people, would certainly be taken as evidence of thinking, and good thinking at that. Thus, a challenging question emerges.

Can a machine think? Among the most extensive attempts to explore this question are those of Newell, Shaw, and Simon. Their first major contribution (in 1958) was a computer program called the Logic Theorist, which was designed to prove rigorously certain theorems in symbolic logic. This program is an impressive one. In one test, for example, it succeeded in giving adequate proofs for thirty-eight of the first fifty-two theorems in Whitehead and Russell's *Principia Mathematica*, including some proofs

that were more elegant (more ingenious and efficient) than those originally proposed by Whitehead and Russell themselves. Even more promising, from the standpoint of studying and understanding thinking, is the fact that the Logic Theorist does not proceed blindly or mechanically; it does *not* search through every possible sequence of logical operations until it happens to find one that yields a proof. Instead, it incorporates several **heuristics**—strategies, tricks, shortcuts, rules of thumb—very much like those used by people to organize their search for solutions. (Indeed, it is just this aspect of human thinking that is used to argue that people do not think mechanically, but instead use insight and intelligence.) For example, one heuristic used by the Logic Theorist is working backward—beginning with the answer and then working backward step by step to the initial state of the problem—which is something we can do when we know the result we are after and work back on a variety of paths until we get to our actual starting point. The Logic Theorist also shows certain other behavioral characteristics of human thought such as an apparent sudden insight into the solution of a problem, a reaction invented by the program, not built into it. For these and other reasons, its designers argue that the Logic Theorist can be considered an actual *model* of the way human thinking proceeds because its behavior does simulate human cognitive processes.

The achievements of the Logic Theorist encouraged investigators to develop simulation models for other aspects of thinking. Thus, there are now computer programs that simulate human thinking on such diverse tasks as algebra word problems (Bobrow, 1964), concept formation (Gregg & Simon, 1967), problems of social and political beliefs (Abelson & Carroll, 1965), and, inevitably, the game of checkers (Samuel, 1963). Computers have also been programmed not only to simulate neurotic personality processes (Colby, 1965) but even—responding appropriately—to act then as psychotherapists (Colby, Watt, & Gilbert, 1966). Perhaps we will ultimately administer computer therapy to neurotic machines as well as to troubled people. In the game of chess, human chess masters pitted against computer programs still reign supreme (at least as recently as the early 1970s), but Samuel's checker-playing program has beaten human champions in that game.

The GPS program The ability of information-processing models to simulate such complex problem-solving tasks as these is a notable accomplishment. Yet each of the special-purpose programs just mentioned is severely limited in the *range* of problems it can handle; it may be designed to play checkers or to prove logic theorems, but it does not do both. The human brain, of course, does. Thus, a further question arises. Can one design a program for *general* problem solving, a sort of all-purpose model that can handle a wide range and variety of problems, regardless of their particular content?

The same researchers made an ambitious attempt to do this with the General Problem Solver (GPS) program (Newell, Shaw, & Simon, 1960). (For an example of how GPS works, see Box 7.2, p. 156.)

GPS has shown that it can solve a great variety of problems, including those requiring productive thinking in the human being. In this sense the program lives up to the promise of its name. Yet GPS does have some important limitations. It is especially limited in that it can deal only with *well-defined* problems: There must be a clearly defined input (initial state of affairs) and a clearly defined goal if GPS is to function. We have already remarked, however, that in many real-life situations the problem is poorly defined and the goal may be infuriatingly vague (such as the goal of achieving mutual respect in a race relations problem). In short, GPS can display what appears to be productive, even creative, problem solving, but only under some circumstances. On the one hand, it *is* impressive in its ability to handle a wide variety of well-defined problems; on the other hand, the adage that a problem well stated is a problem half solved does dim its electronic luster somewhat.

GPS shows convincingly that a substantial segment of human problem solving can be simulated by a model involving a small number of basic processes arranged and ordered in an appropriate hierarchy. However, it is clear that neither GPS nor any other electronic model is a useful synthetic equivalent of either the human mind or the human brain in the sense that it permits us to understand how people think or how language, experience, personality, and motivation interact in the process of human thought. And it is some of the determinants of this process to which we now turn.

DETERMINANTS OF PROBLEM SOLVING

For purposes of convenience we separate the factors that influence the thinking process into two groups—*situational factors* and *personal factors*—although the reader will recognize the

intimate interaction of these two types of determinants when he considers, for example, how
the chronically anxious person is more easily
flustered when faced with a tension-inducing
problem than a characteristically placid person.

Situational Determinants

Here we shall be concerned not only with the
part played by the objective situation (stimulus
pattern) that the problem presents but also with
the transitory mental sets and motivational and
emotional states that are induced in the problem
solver by the particular problem situation.

Stimulus pattern If we can specify how the
stimulus pattern facilitates or inhibits creative
problem solving, we can use this information to
improve the effectiveness of our thinking, since
it is often easy to alter the stimulus pattern to
suit our needs. The major interest in a scientific
analysis is the understanding it gives us, but a
scientific understanding also has practical implications. As Kurt Lewin, a wide-ranging theore-
tician from the Gestalt school of psychology,
was wont to say, "there is nothing as practical
as a good theory."

The Gestalt psychologists generally have
been interested in studying the influence of
stimulus patterning on how we perceive the
world. They sought to demonstrate that the
problem-solving process is in general analogous
to the perceptual process and that some of the
concepts of perception (see Unit 12) can be
applied profitably to an analysis of the problem-
solving process.

Let us illustrate some of the findings of
the experimentation which has come from this
approach. We can now state as a reasonable
hypothesis that the *spatial arrangement* of the
objects and events of a problem situation can
facilitate or hinder the achievement of a solution of a problem in much the same way that
the spatial arrangement of stimuli facilitates or
hinders the achievement of a perception. To
take a very simple example: When all the objects necessary to the solution of a problem
are in the visual field of the perceiver, the problem will be solved more readily than when they

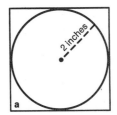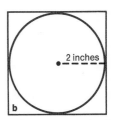

FIGURE 7.4 A square is drawn so that it just encloses a
circle. The circle has a radius of 2 in. What is the area
of the square? Both a and b give the same information,
but b is easier to solve. Why?

In a, the radius is placed in a way that makes it
difficult to perceive it as part of the square. In b, the
radius can more easily be seen as part of the square.

cannot be perceived simultaneously. (See problem 7 in Box 7.6, p. 164, for an experimental
demonstration.)

A more subtle factor of spatial arrangement concerns the *spatial subgrouping* of the
elements of the problem material. If the solution requires that object A be seen as a part of
object X, and A is placed so that it can more
readily be seen as a part of object Y, the solution may be impeded. (See the demonstration
problem in Figure 7.4.) This effect can be accentuated by familiarity with the objects, especially
when the solution to a problem requires us to
interpret a familiar object in a novel manner.
When the object is located among other objects
that have been frequently seen together in the
past (e.g., a hammer shown with nails and
boards), this proximity of functionally related
objects will tend to inhibit the novel interpretation sometimes essential for problem solution
(e.g., seeing that the hammer handle might also
be used as a measuring stick). By the same
token, spatial *separation* of the usually associated objects may make it easier to see new uses
for each of them.

The so-called "functional fixity" experiments show that, when a person actually sees an
object *functioning* in one way, it becomes more
difficult to perceive other possible uses for that
object. The consequence is that problem solving
is interfered with (see Box 7.3, p. 158). Furthermore, it appears that the degree of functional

BOX 7.2

GPS: A CASE STUDY

How does the General Problem Solver go about solving a problem? The following account is based on a description provided by G. W. Ernst and A. Newell of the Carnegie Institute of Technology.

Consider that you are faced with the problem of transporting three Fiscal Conservatives (FC's) and three Big Spenders (BS's) across a river. The only means of conveyance is a small boat with a capacity of two people, which any one of the six knows how to operate. You know that at any time, if there are more FC's than BS's on either side of the river, the latter will be righteously annihilated by the FC's. How can all six people get across the river without any BS's suffering slaughter?

This problem could be presented to GPS in the following form:

Given:

(a) an initial situation (3 BS's and 3 FC's on the left bank of the river)

(b) a desired situation (the 3 BS's and 3 FC's on the right bank of the river)

(c) a set of operators (move 2 BS's and no FC's on a trip from left bank to right bank, move one of each, etc.)

Find:

A sequence of operators that will transform the initial situation into the desired one.

The overall technique used by GPS is to detect differences between the initial state of affairs (called "initial object") and the desired state ("desired object"), and to apply operators which reduce these differences. Since there are many differences between the initial and final "objects," GPS sets up simpler subgoals whose attainment leads step by step to attainment of the overall goal. In working on the problem, GPS uses two general processes that follow each other in repeated cycles. The first is an "executive" process that includes a search phase which initially breaks down the original problem into subgoals, and an evaluation phase that assesses the results of a second process, called "means-ends analysis," which tries to find sequences of operators that will achieve the subgoal.

In the segment of program shown, the executive process of GPS analyzes the problem (step 1) and chooses a subgoal (goal 2) whose achievement would bring the program closer to the desired state of affairs. In step 3, the program applies an operator which results in Object A (an "object" is a state of affairs). GPS then attempts to translate Object A into the desired object. Specifically, it tries to move the remaining FC on the left bank to the right bank (step 6), but needs the boat (presently at the right bank as a result of step 3) to do this. Thus it creates a sub-subgoal (goal 7) which is to get the boat from the right bank to the left bank. Using one FC to row the boat (step 8) this goal is achieved. But replacing the FC in the boat with the FC on shore and having him row the boat back to the right bank (goal 9) simply reproduces Object A, which the program has already tried to translate, unsuccessfully, into the desired object. Clearly, this is a blind alley.

fixity depends on the *importance* of the function served by the object when it was initially perceived; the more functional an object's earlier or ongoing use, the more difficult it is to see another use for it (see Figure 7.5, p. 159). But it is possible to overcome functional fixity given sufficient motivation (see Figure 7.6, p. 159).

The sheer temporal or spatial *contiguity* of stimuli or events is also of prime importance in our perceptions of cause and effect, of what leads to what. Such perceptions of causality are frequently quite primitive in the sense of being unthinking or uncritical. Very often, of course, these primitive explanations are completely wrong. Many are even judged wrong by the person himself and sometimes at the very moment he is perceiving the cause. Example:

Someone comes home of an evening. A gust of wind slams the door shut behind him. At the same moment at the other end of the corridor,

While a "mindless robot" would cycle help-lessly forever at this point, the GPS executive pro-cess does not allow this to happen, since the evaluation phase of this process notes that this particular cycle has been tried without success. The executive process then selects a *different* subgoal, applies means-ends analysis to try to achieve it, and so on, and so on, until the solution is achieved.

Program Segment

1. TOP-GOAL TRANSFORM INITIAL-OBJECT INTO DESIRED-OBJECT
2. GOAL 2 REDUCE FC'S IN INITIAL-OBJECT
    (SUBGOAL OF TOP-GOAL)
3. GOAL 3 MOVE 2 FC'S FROM LEFT BANK TO RIGHT BANK.
    (SUBGOAL OF GOAL 2)
    THIS RESULTS IN OBJECT A (SPECI-FICALLY, 3 BS'S AND 1 FC ARE ON LEFT BANK, 0 BS'S AND + FC'S ARE ON RIGHT BANK, BOAT IS ON RIGHT BANK).
4. GOAL 4 TRANSFORM OBJECT A INTO DESIRED-OBJECT
    (SUBGOAL OF TOP-GOAL)
5. GOAL 5 REDUCE NUMBER OF FC'S ON LEFT BANK IN OBJECT A
6. GOAL 6 MOVE 1 FC IN OBJECT A FROM LEFT BANK TO RIGHT BANK
    (SUBGOAL OF GOAL 5)
7. GOAL 7 GET BOAT IN OBJECT A TO LEFT BANK
    (SUBGOAL OF GOAL 6)
8. GOAL 8 1 FC IN OBJECT A ON RIGHT BANK ROWS BOAT TO LEFT BANK. THIS RE-SULTS IN OBJECT B (SPECIFICALLY, 3 BS'S, 2 FC'S, AND THE BOAT ARE ON LEFT BANK, 0 BS'S AND 1 FC ARE ON RIGHT BANK)
    (SUBGOAL OF GOAL 7)
9. GOAL 9 MOVE 1 FC AND BOAT FROM LEFT BANK TO RIGHT BANK
    THIS AGAIN PRODUCES OBJECT A
    (SUBGOAL OF GOAL 6)

From this short segment of program, you can see that the GPS executive constantly evaluates the overall progress that is being made. Because the heuristics used in the means-ends analysis do not guarantee a solution, the executive may search for other subgoals that appear to be more promising if the first ones appear to be too difficult (i.e., result in an endless loop or in a problem that is becoming *more* complex than the original problem).

The computer prints out a running account of what it is doing under the direction of the GPS program. This account is then compared with the actual accounts given by human subjects as they work on the same problem. Similarities and differ-ences between the problem-solving performance of a human subject and that of GPS can thus be studied and the results of such machine-man com-parisons used to improve the adequacy (the life-likeness) of the program.

(Sheer humanity persuades us to offer the solution to the problem at the end of the chapter.)

G. W. ERNST & A. NEWELL. *A Case Study in Generality and Problem Solving.* New York: Academic Press, 1969.

the light goes on in a room whose door is ajar. Although one knew ever so well that no causal connection exists between the door's blowing shut and the light's going on, that rather some-one in the room has turned on the light, by chance at exactly the same moment—still he would be unable to escape the compelling im-pression of causal relationship (Duncker, 1945).

Two events have a tendency to be judged as causally related if they occur simultaneously or within a very brief period of time, if they are close to each other in space, or if they resemble each other in shape or form. This formulation is very similar to the gestaltist's perceptual law of proximity and similarity (see Unit 12) which states that two stimuli will be perceived as be-longing together, as parts of one whole, if the parts resemble each other or if they are seen as close to each other in time or space. In Dunck-er's illustration the simultaneous occurrence of

BOX 7.3

**FUNCTIONAL FIXITY: A BARRIER
TO CREATIVE PROBLEM SOLVING**

The German psychologist Karl Duncker first proposed the concept of functional fixity about 1930, and he illustrated it with a few simple experiments. Because these experiments were done with so few subjects, several American psychologists repeated them, and they obtained results similar to Duncker's. R. E. Adamson at Stanford University did one such experiment.

The task: Mount three candles vertically on a soft wooden screen, using any object on the table. Among the objects are three cardboard boxes and a number of matches and thumbtacks. *The solution:* Mount one candle on each box by melting wax on the box and sticking the candle to it; then tack the boxes to the screen (see central portion of figure).

For one group (twenty-nine college students), the candles, matches, and tacks were placed *in* the three boxes before they were presented to the subjects (Figure A). *The boxes were thus seen functioning as containers;* whereas in the solution of the problem the boxes would have to be seen as supports or shelves. For the second group (twenty-eight subjects), the boxes were empty and placed among the other objects (Figure B). There the boxes were not seen functioning as containers. Twenty minutes were allowed for the solution.

Of the first group, only twelve of the subjects (or 41 percent) were able to solve the problem; apparently the remaining subjects in this group could not perceive the boxes with the meaning of platform or shelf. Of the second group, twenty-four (or 86 percent) were able to solve the problem.

These results give striking evidence that functional fixity may be an important barrier in creative problem solving. Note also the mental dazzle operating here, as a result of the useless, hence distracting, extra objects.

R. E. ADAMSON. Functional fixedness as related to problem-solving. *Journal of Experimental Psychology,* 1952, **44**, 288–291.

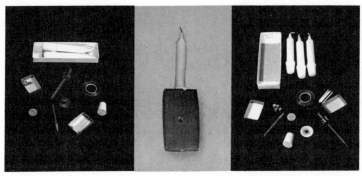

A   B

the door's blowing shut and the light's going on results in a compelling causal relationship in perception. We have been trapped into a wrong explanation by the operation of the simple *perceptual* laws of similarity and proximity.

The history of science is filled with illustrations of this tendency to jump to conclusions in response to the operation of these perceptual laws. In medicine it often leads to the treatment of immediately observable symptoms rather than of distant causes. A variant is seen in the error (common to some scientists as well as to laymen) of arguing cause and effect from the observation of correlation. We may observe that whenever the divorce rate increases, the rate of juvenile delinquency also increases, and that whenever divorce decreases, so does juvenile delinquency (meaning that there is a correlation

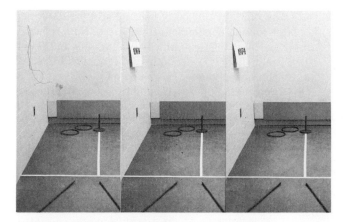

FIGURE 7.5 A ring-and-peg problem. The task here was to put the two rings on the peg while standing behind the chalk line. Any object in the room could be used. The problem could be solved with a piece of string with which to tie the two sticks together. The only string in the room hung on a nail on the wall. When it hung there alone without any apparent function (as in left panel), no subject failed to solve the problem. When the string was made somewhat functional by being used to suspend an old calendar (as in central panel), a number of subjects failed the problem. When the string was highly functional in that it supported a current calendar (as in right panel), more than half failed.

FIGURE 7.6 Retrieving a coin from under a grating is certainly a highly motivating situation for a small boy. In this instance, he is able to see beyond the usual function of chewing gum and to use it instead as an adhesive.

Photo by Kingsley C. Fairbridge

between juvenile delinquency and divorce rates). From this correlation we might argue that juvenile delinquency must be caused by broken homes. Actually, of course, this causal relation may not be true at all. Both juvenile delinquency and divorce may be caused by some third factor like economic or social upheaval.

In our efforts to explain an event we may be victimized in another way by the stimulus situation. Often the situation we are trying to explain contains *too few* of the objects or facts that are essential for the explanation. Because, however, the here and now situation dominates

our perception to a great extent, we tend to limit our attention to it, and we are at a disadvantage in our effort to discover the explanation. For example, the explanation of a child's temper tantrum may involve factors that are far removed in time and space from the tantrum itself. The explanation may involve not only the events immediately preceding the tantrum but also the history of the parents' relations with each other and with the child.

On the other hand, the event may contain *too many* objects or facts, many of them irrelevant to the problem. The professional magician

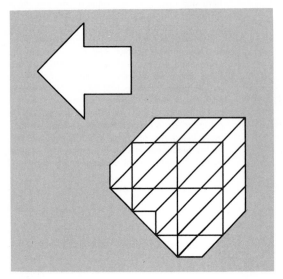

FIGURE 7.7   Can you see the simple arrow figure above in the figure below?

typically makes use of this principle. He traditionally has a shapely lady "assistant," a perceptual prop whose eye-catching aspects mask other aspects of the stimulus situation that are essential to seeing through his trick. Recall his sweeping movements and magnificent gestures, which create the perceptual diversion he needs to permit him to carry out the trick "before your very eyes." (See Figure 7.7 for an instance of this effect operating in simple perception.)

The disturbing effects that excess stimuli can have on problem solving were investigated in 1950 by David Katz, a German psychologist. He presented groups of schoolchildren with simple arithmetic calculations to perform—addition and subtraction. Some groups worked with undenominated numbers (e.g., 10.50 plus 13.25 plus 6.89 and so on); other groups worked with numbers preceded by a familiar denomination (e.g., $10.50 plus $13.25 plus $6.89 and so on); and still others, with numbers carrying an unfamiliar Swedish designation (e.g., Kr. 10.50 plus Kr. 13.25 plus Kr. 6.89 and so on). He found that, first, the addition of a monetary designation increased the difficulty of calculation and that,

second, this difficulty became still greater when a foreign denomination was used. Katz repeated parts of this experiment with adults and found that there too denominated numbers increased the time required to do the addition, and by 12 per cent. Apparently, adding one irrelevant or unfamiliar feature to as simple and familiar a task as addition or subtraction is enough to produce what Katz called "mental dazzle."

The elements of a problem are frequently mental concepts rather than physical visual stimuli. It is therefore important to understand that, as with spatial arrangement of visual stimuli, the particular *conceptual arrangement* of elements can either aid or hinder problem solving. (For an example of this, see Box 7.4.)

Temporal organization and set   Some problems present us with temporally as well as spatially patterned objects; that is, some parts of the problem situation precede other parts. How does the temporal organization of such problems affect the ease or difficulty of solution?

We see in our study of perception (Unit 11) that temporal patterning of stimuli can affect simple sensation and perception. One important perceptual effect of temporal patterning significant for our present discussion is *set*. If we are presented with several objects in succession, the perceptual attributes of the later objects reflect the influence of the earlier objects. This effect is sometimes referred to as the **Einstellung** (German word for "set") **effect** because the initial work on this phenomenon was done in Germany.

The influence of mental sets on problem solving has been studied extensively, and a classic experiment in this field is one by Luchins (see Box 7.5, p. 162). His results indicate that solving a number of problems by one method of attack tends to trap the person into using the same method of attack on later problems, even though the method is now inefficient.

Some have argued that being caught by this *Einstellung* effect is simply a tribute to the usual efficiency of one's problem-solving strategy. If we have a general solution that works, it is appropriate to continue to apply it in a series of very similar problems. Along the same

BOX 7.4

IRRELEVANT DISTRACTION

An experimental study by N. R. F. Maier and R. J. Burke at the University of Michigan shows the critical importance of *organization* in problem solving, even when the elements are conceptual rather than physical visual stimuli. In this study, one group of subjects was given the following problem:

> A man bought a horse for $60 and sold it for $70. Then he bought it back again for $80 and sold it for $90. How much money did he make in the horse business?
> - a. lost $10
> - b. broke even
> - c. made $10
> - d. made $20
> - e. made $30

Try solving this problem yourself before reading further.

Maier and Burke's subjects, all college students, had difficulty with the problem; indeed, less than 40 percent chose the correct answer (made $20). The problem was then altered very slightly, but in a way that would promote a far simpler organization of the essential problem elements. Here is the altered form:

A man bought a white horse for $60 and sold it for $70. Then he bought a black horse for $80 and sold it for $90. How much money did he make in the horse business? [The same five alternatives were then listed.]

When this second version of the problem was given to a new group of college students, virtually all of them obtained the correct answer.

Why should the second version be so much easier than the first? Maier and Burke believe that many errors are caused by the first version because the identity of the horse leads the subject to see two separate financial transactions as one, in short, it leads the subject to organize the stimulus elements inappropriately. In their words:

> We may regard two transactions with one horse as more difficult than two transactions with two different horses, even though the arithmetic skill requirements are the same. The [first] horse-trading problem is difficult not because the answer is hard to figure out, but because an incorrect perception serves as a distractor (i.e., serves to distract the person from a more fruitful organization of the problem elements).

Next time you're stuck on a problem, don't give up; reorganize the problem elements.

N. R. F. MAIER & R. J. BURKE. Response availability as a factor in the problem-solving performance of males and females. *Journal of Personality and Social Psychology*, 1967, **5**, 304–310.

---

lines, others attribute the effect of the typical and usually highly adaptive tendency for the problem solver to behave more and more automatically as an initially difficult problem that requires some thought is followed by additional problems that are solvable by the same principle. He gradually narrows his perception of the situation, eventually confining it to the single principle. Usually this is a quite sensible procedure and one that speeds his solution.

An interesting extension of this sort of explanation is provided by Knight (1963). Using a somewhat modified version of the *Einstellung* test (this time with five jars rather than three),

two groups of subjects (college students in a classroom setting) were required to solve a series of twenty-one water jar problems. The two groups differed in only one respect:

One group ("high effort") on its very first trial was presented with a problem that was rather difficult to solve. The jar capacities were (A) 1,000, (B) 0, (C) 371, (D) 247, (E) 25; target: 199 quarts.

The "low effort" group was confronted with an easier problem: (A) 1,000, (B) 0, (C) 300, (D) 10, (E) 1; target: 293 quarts. Both problems were solvable by the same principle: (C) − (D) + 3(E).

BOX 7.5

PRACTICE MAKES BLINDNESS

A. S. Luchins, while at New York University, investigated the following question: "Several problems, all solvable by one somewhat complex procedure, are presented in succession. If afterwards a similar task is given which can be solved by a more direct and simple method, will the individual be blinded to this direct possibility?" Adapting a technique previously used at the University of Berlin, Luchins carried out a series of *Einstellung* (mental set) experiments to answer the question.

The task: Obtain a required volume of water, using certain empty jars for measures. The following table presents the basic eight problems used.

Problem	Given Empty Jars Holding Number of Quarts as Listed			Obtain the Following Number of Quarts of Water
1	29	3		20
2	21	127	3	100
3	14	163	25	99
4	18	43	10	5
5	9	42	6	21
6	20	59	4	31
7	23	49	3	20
8	15	39	3	18

Problem 1 was an illustrative problem; problems 2 through 6 were training problems; problems 7 and 8 were critical test problems. Problem 1 is presented, and the solution is shown diagrammatically (Figure A). Problem 2 is next shown, and the answer is again diagramed (Figure B) and explained: "One fills the 127-qt jar and from it fills the 21-qt jar once and the 3-qt jar twice. In the 127-qt jar there then remains 100 qt of water." The method that solves problems 2 through 6 may also be used in 7 and 8. *But* problem 7 may be solved *more directly* by subtracting 3 from 23; problem 8 by adding 3 to 15.

An experimental group was given problems 1 through 8 in succession (at intervals of about 2½ min). A control group went from problem 1 to problems 7 and 8, skipping problems 2 through 6.

The following table shows results on the critical test problems (7 and 8) from one experiment done with college students. The experimental subjects gave far fewer direct solutions. Previous success with one technique can thus blind a person to simpler solutions.

Group	Number of Subjects	Percentage Indirect Solutions	Percentage Direct Solutions	Percentage Other Solutions or Complete Failures
Control	57	0	100	0
Experimental	79	81	17	2

A. S. LUCHINS. Mechanization in problem-solving. *Psychological Monographs*, 1942, **54**, No. 6. Tables and figures adapted by permission of American Psychological Association.

Not surprisingly, the high effort group took considerably longer to solve its first problem. On subsequent trials it showed, in comparison with the low effort group, a substantially greater *Einstellung* effect, persisting in the use of the initial, more complex principle when a far simpler one was feasible. Furthermore, the high effort group, when confronted with a problem for which the initial principle would not work at all, continued to demonstrate the *Einstellung* effect by evolving overly complicated principles similar to the initial principle. Perhaps most startling is the finding that on the last problem (jar capacities: 1,000, 0, 680, 640, 320; target: 1,000) only seven of twenty-two subjects in the high effort group saw the obvious solution; whereas eighteen of twenty-four did so in the low effort group.

The lesson of this experiment seems quite straightforward: The more we invest initially in deriving a certain problem-solving principle, the more likely we are to stick to it. Whether this investment is cognitive, motivational, or emotional, we cannot say—it is probably a bit of each—but the practical implications of this finding, which we shall soon spell out, are not difficult to see.

Emotional and motivational states We all know that being confronted with a problem situation can induce various emotional and motivational states in the problem solver. These states can, in turn, influence the effectiveness of problem solving. There are many experimental ways to create stress and emotional pressure in a problem-solving situation, and psychologists have used them in experimental studies. In one of them, Ray (1965) devised a problem in which the subject had to discover the principle governing the designation as "correct" of only one of the digits in a series of numbers. (The principle was to select the last digit in numbers composed of three consecutive digits only.) Half of his subjects, however, were first presented with a similar problem in which there was in fact no correct principle that could be discovered. This "failure" group worked for twelve minutes on this frustrating task before attacking the true and solvable problem. The control group (the other half of the subjects) went directly at the true problem. Of the control subjects, 49 percent solved the true problem within the allotted time limit. Only 32 percent of the failure group did so.

This finding probably comes as no surprise. There is abundant evidence that intellectual ability in general suffers from failure. Some evidence stems from experimental situations in which tested intelligence actually drops following a short-term induced-failure situation. The increasingly depressed IQ scores of some minority-group children as they grow older are in part a function of their frequent school failure, in turn often caused by the failure of the home, the school, and society at large to provide adequate intellectual preparation and stimulation. The effects of frustration can also be quite pervasive. In Box 23.1 (p. 574), we describe how a minor frustrating experience decreases the constructiveness of children's play.

Perhaps less expected is Levitt's (1956) suggestion that *success* can sometimes spoil creative problem solving. In his review of experimental results with the water-jar *Einstellung* task, he notes that in experiments by Cowen (1952a, 1952b) both a "praise" group and a "severe stress" group persisted longer in using the initial and no-longer-best solution in later trials than did a "mild stress" group.

Too strong motivation, insofar as it leads to stress, may also lead to a decrease in problem-solving efficiency. Box 7.6 (p. 164) provides experimental evidence on the effects of degree of motivation on problem solving in the chimpanzee and points to a general result consistent with observations of human beings.

This general result is depicted in Figure 7.8, p. 165; the relation between problem solving and intensity of motivation can be described as an "inverted U curve." That is, as the intensity of the problem solver's motivation increases, his problem-solving effectiveness also increases *up to an optimal point*. Beyond that point any increase in intensity of motivation results in a decrease in problem-solving efficiency. This curve is to be taken merely as an abstract representation of the shape of the motivation-efficiency relationship. The shape and the optimal point on the curve will vary tremendously from one person to another. This variation is in part attributable to enduring personality fac-

BOX 7.6

**INTENSITY OF MOTIVES AND PROBLEM
SOLVING IN CHIMPANZEES**

In 1945 H. G. Birch investigated the relation
between motivation and problem solving in young
chimpanzees. He used the stick problems, which
require the animal to rake in food with a stick. The
problems differ in spatial patterning and complexity
(see figure). In problem 1 the stick is next to the
food; in problem 4 the stick is *behind* the animal
as he faces the food; in problem 7 the animal has to
take the *short* stick behind him, with it pull the
string attached to the *long* stick into reach, pull in
the long stick by the string, and finally sweep in the
food with the long stick. Motivation was varied by
depriving the animals of food for 2, 6, 12, 24, 36, and
48 hr before testing.

     The results are best described in Birch's
own summary:

> When motivation is very low the animals are easily
> diverted from the problem by extraneous factors and
> behavior tends to deteriorate into a series of non-
> goal-directed acts. Under conditions of very intense
> motivation, the animals concentrated upon the goal
> to the exclusion of other features of the situation
> which were essential to the solution of the problem.
> Also, the frequent occurrence of frustration re-
> sponses, such as tantrums and screaming, when a
> given stereotyped pattern of response proved to be
> inadequate, hindered the animals in their problem-
> solving efforts. Those animals who worked . . .
> under intermediate conditions of motivational in-
> tensity . . . were not so dominated by the desire to
> obtain the food that they were incapable of respond-
> ing to other relevant features of the problem situa-
> tion. Their behavior was characterized by both direc-
> tion and flexibility in response.

H. G. BIRCH. The role of motivational factors in insightful problem-solving. *Journal of Comparative Psychology*, 1945, **38**, 295–
317.

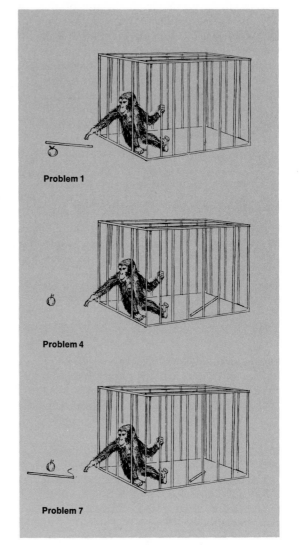

Problem 1

Problem 4

Problem 7

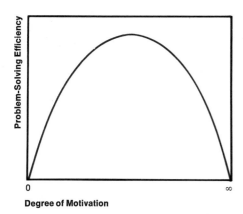

FIGURE 7.8 A hypothetical curve representing the suggestion that the relation between degree of motivation and problem-solving efficiency is curvilinear. As the degree of motivation increases from zero, the problem-solving efficiency first increases and then decreases.

tors within the individual, some of which we shall discuss later in this unit.

Some practical suggestions From each of the foregoing analyses of the situational determinants of problem solving—spatial patterning, temporal patterning, set, and emotional and motivational states—we can derive some practical suggestions for improving problem-solving effectiveness.

If we remember that the spatial arrangement of the objects and events of a problem situation can facilitate or hinder a solution, apparently we should be able, by proper spatial arrangement of objects, to change a difficult problem into an easy one. This reasoning points to a very simple practical suggestion for improving problem-solving efficiency for certain types of problems: The problem solver does not usually face an immovable array of materials and objects. He is allowed to manipulate and rearrange them. (When this setup is not possible physically, he can imagine rearrangements.) By deliberately trying out various spatial arrangements and not remaining fixated on the original one, he increases the probability of arriving, by chance alone, at an arrangement facilitating the solution.

There is another way of dealing with the problem of the stimulus pattern. As we pointed out earlier, certain features of the problem can be so dominating that they draw all or most of our attention to them at the expense of the less obvious but crucial features. To deal with this possibility, it is reasonable (even if paradoxical) to *reduce* the attention you pay to the problem you wish to solve. One way to do so it to take a break. Forget the problem for a while, and do something else. When you return to it, your excess attention to the previously dominant objects may be weakened. This may partly account for the beneficial role sometimes played by incubation in the problem-solving process (p. 147).

Frequently, the crucial objects for a solution may not even be present in the immediate situation. In order to encourage seeeking elsewhere for the missing link, it is sometimes helpful to work on related problems. The stimulus pattern of a related problem may include the objects that are necessary to solve the original problem. Perhaps reasoning by analogy is often fruitful for this reason.

Many problems require the solution of a series of subproblems. Sometimes the problem solver finds it difficult to realize that this sequence is not rigidly fixed once and for all. Another practical suggestion stems from the recognition that this temporal sequence can be varied in several ways.

We may have a choice between starting with where we wish to end and starting with where we are at the moment. In the first instance we start by analyzing the goal. We ask, "Suppose we did achieve the goal, how would things be different—what subproblems would we have solved, and so on?" This analysis in turn would determine the sequence of problems, and we would work back to the beginning. In the second instance we start by analyzing the present situation. We see the implications of the given conditions and layout and attack the various subproblems in a forward direction. In some instances it may even be preferable to start in the middle; that is, we can say, "Let us assume I can solve the first four subproblems involved, and I now have arrived at such and such a point. Where can I go from here?" (This leaves for some later time the solution of the first four subproblems.) For different kinds of problems, certain temporal sequences may prove more efficient than others. The advice of the backwoods Vermonter who said, in response to the tourist who asked how to get to Saint Johnsbury, "If I were you, I wouldn't start from here!" may be sound advice for the problem solver. Unlike the bewildered tourist, we do not always have to start from "here."

In our analysis of the *Einstellung* effect we saw that one of the hazards to problem solving comes from too much attachment to a method of attack that has proved effective in the past for solving problems similar to the new one. One suggestion that can help break such a mental set is to turn away from the problem for a while. On returning to it after the lapse of some time, we must begin with fresh attention instead of responding blindly and inattentively. This could be considered another possible bonus of incubation.

Another approach is that of Maier (1933), who sought to overcome the stereotyping effects of set by a direct attempt to make salient for the problem solver the necessity of varying his attacks on the problem. In demonstrating this technique, Maier performed several experiments at the University of Michigan; among them was the following: In an introductory course in psychology, 384 students were divided into a control group (206 students) and an experimental group (178 students). Three problems were presented to each group: the string problem (see Box 7.7) and two similar reasoning problems. The experimental group also received a 20-min lecture followed by general hints on how to reason before it was given the problems:

> Locate a difficulty, and try to overcome it. If you fail, get it completely out of your mind and seek an entirely different difficulty.
> Do not be a creature of habit and stay in a rut. Keep your mind open for new meanings.
> The solution pattern appears suddenly. You cannot force it. Keep your mind open for new combinations, and do not waste time on unsuccessful attempts.

Within the hour allowed for solution of the problems, the experimental group earned a total correct-solution score of 49.2 percent; whereas the control group earned 39.7 percent. These results indicate that a 20-min general lecture improved problem-solving performance. A second experiment on different students (testing their reasoning ability before and after the lecture) gave similar results, and Maier concluded, in part:

> The results of both experiments indicate that when subjects are carefully instructed to guard against habitual activities and persistent directions, but to be alert for new points of view, there is a decided increase in reasoning ability as measured by the increase in solutions found to difficult problems. . . . One cannot equip a person with the ability to form solution-patterns, but one can train him to clear the ground so that the solution-pattern is not prevented from appearing.

Of course, Maier's findings do not imply that all we need do to get rid of "habitual activities and persistent directions" is to listen to a general lecture on thinking. Personality factors may effectively inhibit the development of "new points of view." We cannot say to a person who gets emotionally upset by ambiguous stimulus patterns, "Be alert to new points of view" and "guard against habitual directions," and expect any more success than we can from saying to a neurotically anxious person, "Stop worrying!" More fundamental difficulties are present (particularly in regard to emotional and motivational factors) than we can expect general lectures and admonitions to remedy.

Personal Factors

As we have mentioned, people vary in the extent to which they are susceptible to such situational influences as stimulus pattern, set, and optimal level of motivational arousal. These individual differences reflect the interaction between the situational determinants we have listed and such enduring characteristics of the individual as knowledge, intelligence, and personality traits. There are many examples of such interactions.

Among the situational determinants, it will be remembered, are the perceptual characteristics of the specific objects presented in the

BOX 7.7

THE INVENTOR'S DIFFICULTY: AN AMBIGUOUS STIMULUS PATTERN

W. S. Battersby, H. L. Teuber, and M. B. Bender at New York University tested the problem solving of men under three specified stimulus conditions. Although they were primarily interested in comparing brain-injured people with normal people, we shall consider here their results only on the uninjured men.

The Maier string problem was used. Each subject entered a room in which were a desk, a table, and two strings hanging from the ceiling. His task was to invent a technique that would permit him to tie the strings together, although they were too far apart to reach one while grasping the other.

The solution: Attach a weight to one string; give it a swing; run over to the other; catch the first string when it swings close; and then tie them together.

The "restricted" group was told that it could use only the objects provided by the experimenter. Upon completion of instructions the experimenter placed scissors on the desk. At successive 2-min intervals a clothespin, a small pulley, a Yo-Yo, and a fishline sinker were similarly placed. Any one of these objects could serve as a weight.

The "less restricted" group was told that it could use any object in the room, *including* objects that the experimenter would place on the desk. Again at 2-min intervals the experimenter provided the five objects.

For the "unrestricted" group the five objects were on the *table* when the subject entered the room, but his attention was not drawn to them. The subjects were instructed to use any object *in the room.*

For the restricted group the experimenter pointed to the specific objects relevant to the solution; for the less restricted, this pointing was more ambiguous ("use any object including. . . ."); for the unrestricted, there was no pointing.

The restricted group solved the problem in 2.4 min (average), the less restricted in 7.5 min, and the unrestricted in 15.2 min.

The analogy to the situation facing a real inventor is clear. The inventor's goal does not specify the objects that will help him to achieve it, and to the degree that it does not, his problem is magnified.

W. S. BATTERSBY, H. L. TEUBER, & M. B. BENDER. Problem-solving behavior in men with frontal or occipital brain injuries. *Journal of Psychology*, 1953, **35**, 329–351.

---

problem situation. But the way in which an object is perceived is in part determined by one's knowledge about the object. The knowledgeable astronomer who has learned that the moon is in fact a more or less dead mass of matter that can only reflect light from the sun and has no interior source of radiant energy will be less likely to share the ignorant child's perception of the moon as "a hot bird flying through the night sky." Yet this is the stuff of creative poetry.

We have also seen that the specific temporal patterning of a problem can induce a mental set that inhibits creative problem solving. But the evidence seems clear that the strength of the *Einstellung* effect is also influenced by the individual's intelligence. Many experiments indicate that lower intelligence is associated with greater susceptibility to the *Einstellung* effect.

Finally, we know that stress induced by the problem situation can influence problem solving. But the degree of stress that will be induced by a particular problem very clearly reflects differing personality traits of the different individuals. Thus, Ray (1965) reports the following experiment: The problem was to transfer a stack of doughtnut-shaped rings of varying diameters from one peg to another, moving one ring at a time without placing a larger ring on top of a smaller, and using a third peg as a way station. One group was instructed to work as quickly as possible; another was permitted to work at its own speed. Among his many results Ray found that the "speed" group showed a much greater range in the number of moves made than did the "no-pressure" group. However, the instruction to "work as fast as possible" was heeded—at least in terms of number of moves made—by only some subjects *and not by others*. Situationally induced pressure, therefore, seemed to be controlled by differences among individuals, differences that presumably reflected variation among the subjects in enduring personal characteristics; this was also a finding of several other studies. The reader will probably recognize among his friends some who blow up under the pressure of timed examinations and others who keep their heads, solving problems with efficiency under these circumstances.

Always keeping in mind, therefore, that the situational and the enduring personality factors necessarily interact, we can now consider these latter factors in some detail.

Availability of knowledge   Every discussion of creative problem solving—whether by the practical inventor who generalizes from his own experiences or by the psychologist who theorizes on the basis of laboratory experiments—stresses the intimate relation between knowledge and creativity. This relation can be summarized in two contradictory statements: First, the *more* knowledge an individual has acquired in the past, the greater the possibility that he will be creative with new problems; second, the *less* knowledge an individual has acquired in the past, the greater his creativity. The contradiction here is only apparent rather than real; *both* statements are valid when properly specified as to meaning.

On the one hand, it is clear that in order to solve a difficult problem, a person must have the specific knowledge required for that solution. The more numerous the meanings we have

learned to attach to an object, the more flexible we can be; that is, we can use the object in more varied ways in attempitng to solve a new problem.

On the other hand, facts can be restrictive. In many instances the very well-informed individual is overly trained upon certain traditional or stereotyped meanings of an object. This functional fixity, as we have seen earlier, may prevent a person from achieving the novel and even bizarre meanings essential to a creative solution. Knowing less, he may be freer to come up with unusual ideas.

Furthermore, many of the facts we acquire—whether through experience or formal education—are misleading or simply wrong. Insofar as this statement is true, the ability to do creative problem solving is likely to be damaged by the acquisition of this knowledge. Probably Charles Kettering, the famous inventor, had this thought in mind when he said, "The inventor is a fellow who doesn't take his education too seriously." And even more telling is David Hilbert's (Professor at Göttingen and one of the greatest mathematicians of his era) remark: "Do you know why Einstein said the most original and profound things about space and time that have been said in our generation? Because he had learned nothing about all the philosophy and mathematics of time and space." In this respect the many instances in which creative scientists have moved from their initial fields of study and flourished in new fields can be evidence for the fresh approach, particularly when it is taken by a generally able problem solver. Perhaps, as has been suggested with some seriousness, scientific problem solvers of proven ability should be turned loose on the sticky questions in fields other than their own. (Two Nobel laureates, Linus Pauling and Donald Glaser, have done just that.) This version of musical chairs would allow scientists to employ their generally applicable skills of observation and reasoning while taking a new look at old and difficult problems. Such scientists, equipped with a little (but not too much) knowledge, may ask penetrating and profound questions that open up new avenues to solution.

Sheer memory is, of course, an important determinant of creative problem-solving ability

BOX 7.8

AVAILABILITY OF MEANINGS
AND PROBLEM SOLVING

P. Saugstad and K. Raaheim at the University of Oslo tested the hypothesis that problem solving may depend on the general availability of specific meanings for certain objects.

Among the subjects tested were ninety-five Oslo high school boys. *The task:* Using anything on the table, transfer the balls from the glass G to the container O without stepping beyond the black line (see photograph). *Solution:* With the pliers the nail

is bent into a hook, tied to the string, and thrown so that it catches the wooden frame F, which is then pulled around the obstruction B to within reach of the subject. The newspapers are then rolled into tubes and with the aid of the rubber bands are made into one continuous tubing. The balls can now be rolled through this long paper tube into the container O.

At a previous time the subjects had been given a "functional availability" test. For example,

they had been told that a nail could be used to fasten, catch, stick, and hang things. They had then been asked to write down three illustrations for each function. The same was done for the other objects to be used in the later problem.

To solve the problem, two "unusual" meanings are involved: the nail as a "hook" and the newspapers as "tube." Particular attention was therefore paid to mentions of "hook" and "tube" (or "funnel") in the subjects' illustrations of the functions of a nail and a newspaper, respectively. Three groups were thus distinguished: subjects who had mentioned both "hook" and "tube," those who had mentioned one *or* the other, and those who had mentioned neither. On the Saugstad problem the three groups performed as shown in the table.

Function Available	Number of Subjects	Percentage of Solutions
Hook *and* tube	18	89
Hook *or* tube	40	42
Neither	37	19

Success in problem solving may sometimes be determined by the availability of a specific meaning for a specific object. On the basis of later research, however, Raaheim warns that we must not fail to distinguish between two quite separate aspects of problem solving of this sort. First, the subject must discover what it is that is "missing" in the situation. In the present example, he must recognize that he needs some way of bringing the glass G to his table, then some way of getting the balls in that glass into container O. Second, only after he achieves this "part solution" can the subject discover how to employ the available objects in order to fill the "missing" functions discovered in the first phase of his problem-solving activity.

P. SAUGSTAD & K. RAAHEIM. *Problem-solving as dependent on availability of functions.* Table adapted by permission of Universitets forlaget, Oslo, 1956. Manuscript.
K. RAAHEIM. Problem solving and past experience. In P. H. Mussen (Ed.), *European research in cognitive development. Monographs of the Society for Research in Child Development,* 1965, **30**, No. 2.

because only knowledge about the problem elements that is remembered can be used in problem solving. As we know, however, memory is not an all-or-nothing affair. Some attributes of knowledge may be easily recalled; some,

recalled with difficulty; and some, completely forgotten. To put it another way, various meanings of objects that we have learned are differentially available. (Box 7.8 gives an experimental illustration of the effect of different degrees of availability of meanings of common objects on problem solving.)

Uses of knowledge The availability of knowledge, then, is of crucial importance in problem solving. Once available, the knowledge may be used in three different ways when we are engaged in creative problem solving: First, we may merely *reproduce* a bit of knowledge in a new situation directly and without change. Second, we may *transform* an experience so that it becomes applicable to the solution of a problem. Third, we may combine many specific experiences into one *abstraction*. This generalized

knowledge is now applicable to the solution of a problem in which the specific knowledge (which can be derived from or is included in the generalization) is not helpful in solving the problem (see Box 7.9).

Any specific piece of knowledge, of course, can appear in any one of these three forms. Thus, the knowledge that "wood floats," when stated in this way, is a reproduction. When stated in the form, "A wooden pellet when released at the bottom of a container of water will shoot up to the surface," it is a transformation. When stated in terms of the hydrostatic principle, it is an abstraction. Obviously any

BOX 7.9

SPECIFIC KNOWLEDGE VERSUS ABSTRACTION

An abstract principle is often more useful in solving problems than are concrete statements of specific knowledge. We shall try to demonstrate this thought, with you as a subject. If you are too sophisticated for this experiment, try it on your less sophisticated friends.

On an inclined plane stands a cart attached to a string. The string runs over a pulley to a block of wood that is just barely touching the surface of water in a container. The whole arrangement is so balanced that the cart remains stationary. Standing on the table is a beaker of water. Nothing else is available (see figure). Your task is to set the cart

in motion so that it will move *down* the inclined plane. You are not permitted to touch the cart or put anything into it; nor may you lift the wooden block with your hands. Here is a bit of knowledge that helps to solve the problem: *Wood floats.*

Second problem: Everything remains as before, *except* that in place of the wooden block you now have a small lead weight. Again the arrangement is so balanced that the cart is at rest (the same figure will do). Same problem: Cause the cart to move *down.* Here is a bit of knowledge that helps to solve the problem: *Lead sinks.*

If you don't understand the solution to this second problem, let us review your freshman physics a bit. Take the two bits of specific knowledge, "wood floats" and "lead sinks," and see them as specific instances of an abstract generalization: *Whether a body floats or sinks depends upon the ratio between the body's weight and the weight of the displaced quantity of water.* If this hydrostatic principle doesn't seem to help you, let us state it in still another manner—in terms of Archimedes' principle: All bodies, when immersed in water, appear to lose a certain part of their weight. The lost weight corresponds to the quantity of water displaced.

Now can you solve the second problem—and *understand* its solution? (This experiment is a revision of one performed by Székely.)

We see how an abstract principle may help when specific knowledge fails.

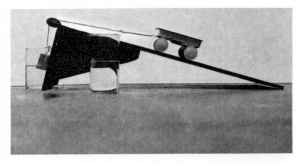

L. SZÉKELY. Knowledge and thinking. *Acta Psychologica*, 1950, **7**, 1–24.

specific piece of knowledge that is available in all three forms will be more useful than the same piece of knowledge available in only one form.

Intelligence   Roughly speaking, intelligence is a "given" of the individual, a personal ability he brings, in much the same measure, to every new problem-solving situation at any point in his development. But there is more direct empirical evidence of this crucial relation of intelligence to problem solving. The importance of these studies lies not in demonstrating the commonsense point that brighter people are better problem solvers but in giving a fuller experimental and theoretical account of the precise role of intelligence in the problem-solving process. We have already mentioned the greater susceptibility of less intelligent subjects to the *Einstellung* effect—a susceptibility hindering effective performance in this problem situation. Klausmeier and Loughlin (1961), in testing the problem-solving performance of eleven-year-olds, found that one distinguishing difference between high- and low-IQ children was that the former showed greater skill in *verifying* their tentatively proposed solutions and therefore finally submitted fewer incorrect solutions. Osler and Trautman (1961) found that children of superior intelligence—particularly on more complex problems—typically went about seeking a solution by developing and testing *hypotheses* concerning the correct principle and therefore were more likely to achieve sudden "aha!"-type solutions. Children of normal intelligence, by contrast, developed fewer hypotheses and seemed to approach solutions by trial and error, therefore gradually.

But, as our discussion of creative individuals in Unit 27 shows, the role of intelligence in productive thinking is far more complicated than indicated here.

Personality   It is difficult to disentangle the effects of what are usually regarded as personality determinants from those of other factors with which they typically interact in a problem-solving situation. If a subject is so tense that he fails to solve a relatively simple problem, is

it because he is generally a tense individual (personality), because he regards the problem as a test of his general adequacy as a person (excess or inappropriate motivation in the situation arising from a personality trait), or because he is not very bright and therefore sees problem solving as an area of weakness and becomes tense (intelligence × personality × motivation)?

Another difficulty is the confusing variety of personality factors that seem to be related to problem solving. Studies have shown that such factors as *flexibility*, *initiative*, and *confidence* are characteristic of good problem solvers. In addition, there is fairly convincing evidence that a tendency to conform to social pressure is associated with poor problem-solving performance. For example, Nakamura (1958) found that conforming college students did worse on a variety of problems than those students who showed *independence of judgment*, even when intelligence differences between conformers and nonconformers were taken into account. Quite a different kind of correlate of problem-solving ability is reported for nursery school children by Maccoby, Dowley, Hagen, and Degerman (1965). The *ability to inhibit motor movement*, measured by such tasks as the ability to draw lines and to walk very slowly, was found to go with superior performance in solving hidden-figure perceptual problems. It was not that the better problem solvers were less active children—measurement of general activity level at play showed no such relation—but rather that the ability to control and restrain motor activity when required to do so was a trait directly associated with ability to solve certain problems. Is this finding "just" attributable to the ability to follow instructions carefully—both in the motor tests and in the problem-solving situation—or is some personality factor of impulse control involved? The investigators raise this question and propose further research to answer it.

These few examples of research on personality determinants of problem-solving ability highlight some of the complexities of the issue. As a quite different approach (see Unit 27), instead of studying the relations of various personality traits to the process of problem solving, we can study the personality characteristics of people who have clearly manifested creativity in their work or professions.

Clearly, creative problem solving is an ability of enormous adaptive significance and, equally clearly, its effectiveness is determined by a wide range of factors. Some are inherent in the problem situation; others, in characteristics of the person. In the typical instance of problem solving, both situational *and* personal factors combine and interact to determine one's progress toward a solution.

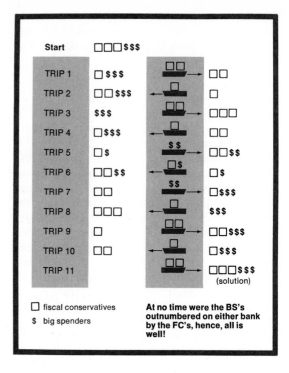

SOLUTION TO BOX 7.2

SUMMARY

1. One way of describing the process of problem solving is in terms of four sequential stages: (a) the individual becomes acquainted with the problem, plays with it, and perhaps considers some general solution possibilities (preparation); (b) the problem is put aside, and the person apparently does no conscious work on it (incubation); (c) the individual suddenly sees how the problem may be solved (illumination); (d) the proposed solution is tested for workability (verification).

2. A second way to describe the problem-solving process is in terms of three stages that successively zero in on a particular solution, using a funneling strategy. This approach envisages three stages: (a) setting the general range within which the solution is expected to occur, (b) moving to a narrower functional solution, and (c) finally trying out a number of specific solutions.

3. Yet a third way of describing the process of problem solving is to conceive of it as a complex skill. Thus, thinking, like athletic or musical skill, requires the coordination and sequencing of many components, or subskills, and is greatly influenced by the degree to which the subskills are developed. There is some evidence that thinking, like other skills, can be developed and improved by appropriate instruction, and this has important implications for education.

4. A fourth way of describing problem solving is in terms of information processing. This approach involves translating one's view of the thinking process into a form that resembles a computer program. The theorized process is diagrammed by means of a flow chart that shows both the specific operations assumed to occur in thinking through a problem to solution and the sequence in which these operations are performed. The General Problem Solver computer program is one promising example of this approach. It can handle a variety of problems in an intelligent way, but it is limited to tasks where both the problem and the solution can be stated very precisely.

5. Factors that influence problem-solving effectiveness can be categorized, very roughly, as either situational or personal. Situational factors include spatial and conceptual arrangements of the stimulus pattern, as well as temporal factors. Set—the tendency to see something or respond to something in a particular way—is also an important situational factor in problem solving. So are short-term emotional and motivational states.

6. An understanding of the role of situational factors in problem solving leads to a number of eminently practical suggestions for improving one's performance. One theme here is to vary your approach to a problem and, in general, to hang loose in order to overcome the effects of excessive motivation and initially wrong approaches to the problem.

7. Personal factors that determine problem-solving proficiency include an individual's available pool of knowledge relevant to the particular problem, his intelligence level, and a variety of personality factors. These factors typically interact in their effects on problem-solving efficiency.

GLOSSARY

Einstellung effect   The German word for "mental set." The common use of this German word reflects the fact that mental-set experiments originated in German psychological laboratories.

flow chart   A diagram showing the flow of information through an information-processing system. Flow charts show both the operations that are performed and the sequence in which they are executed.

functional solution   A term proposed by Karl Duncker, a German psychologist, to refer to the second step in problem solving. The functional solution is characterized by a narrowing of the general range and thus specifies the nature of the final but not-yet-achieved specific solution.

general range   According to Duncker, the step that occurs first in problem solving. It is a very general restatement of the original problem, serving to indicate the direction of the to-be-sought-for solution.

heuristic   A strategy, trick, or rule of thumb used to aid the search for solutions to a problem. A heuristic contrasts with the blind or mechanical checking of every conceivable possibility in robotlike fashion. Heuristics may fail precisely because they do not investigate every possibility, but their value is that when they work, they speed up the achievement of solution enormously.

illumination   The third stage of problem solving. Identical with the "aha!" experience (see Glossary for Unit 6); refers to the sudden recognition of how a problem may be solved.

incubation   The second stage that may occur in the problem-solving process. During this stage no conscious work is done on the problem, but when one returns to it, a prompt advance beyond the previous point of progress is noted. It has been suggested that during the silent or incubation period, creative problem solving goes on despite the lack of conscious effort.

loop   A cycle or sequence of operations that may be repeated over and over again in an information-processing system.

preparation   The first stage of the problem-solving process. This is the period when the person becomes acquainted with the problem and begins to play with ideas for its solution.

program   The specific, step-by-step instructions fed into a computer to direct its operation. A program is far more detailed than a flow chart but essentially translates the intent of the flow chart into machine language.

specific solution   According to Duncker, the final step in problem solving. This step involves a further specification of the functional solution and, if successful, is the final, correct solution.

verification   The fourth stage of problem solving. At this stage the proposed general solution may be more closely specified and may be applied and tested.

part three

intelligence

the measurement of intelligence and mental abilities

DO YOU KNOW...

what is wrong with attempting to describe a person as very "intelligent" or not very "intelligent"?

how psychologists go about developing a test for intelligence?

why it is that, although children generally grow brighter as they grow older, their IQ does not increase with age?

what is meant by the term mental age?

that there are even mental tests to measure the intelligence of a two-month-old infant?

the many different kinds of "intelligences" that can be measured?

to what extent brightness predicts school grades and whether brightness predicts effectiveness in a given job?

unit
8

CONTENTS

In the early 1900s, at the request of the school authorities of Paris, the French psychologist Alfred Binet undertook to develop a set of tests that would identify mentally deficient schoolchildren, so that they could be placed in schools in which they would not be held to the standard curriculum (see Figure 8.1). From that time on, mental tests have been used primarily to help predict the capacity of children and students to profit from "intellectual" training. The extension of mental testing to adults followed immediately. During World War I nearly 2 million men were screened for intellectual fitness and assigned to various specialties on the basis of such tests; in World War II the number rose to more millions, as the variety of tests to measure intelligence and special aptitudes also multiplied. Today virtually no individual in the Western world can escape one or more such tests during his lifetime. Mental testing has now become a national industry, a significant adjunct to our educational programs, and a controversial social and political issue.

INTELLIGENCE AND MENTAL TESTS

Amid this enormous activity the question "What *is* intelligence?" has never received a completely satisfactory answer. The theoretical issue has been subordinated to the utilitarian emphasis of massive testing programs. The chief requirement for mental tests has been that they "work" —that they do a useful and accurate job of classifying individuals into ability categories. However, if we are to understand whether or not and how intelligence can be modified, the role that it plays in the total functioning of the individual, and its biological (genetic and physiological) and social determinants, we must have some understanding of its nature.

Intelligence is a concept variously used and variously defined. Some people define it as the ability to adapt to new circumstances, others as the ability to learn, and still others as the

A   B   C

FIGURE 8.1 The earliest mental test. These items from the Binet-Simon Scale, which first appeared in 1905, are (with appropriate stylistic revisions) still to be found in the **modern Stanford-Binet tests.** The items in A and B are at the age-five level and require the child to select "Which is the prettiest?" The C items (age seven) require identifying the missing part.

capacity to deal with complex and abstract material.

Different psychologists have championed these (and other) definitions, and much research has been done on the subject. None of this research, however, has resulted in a clear definition of intelligence. For this reason many psychologists reached the point where they decided that they could do a useful job of measuring intelligence without defining it. In this respect they were doing what early physicists had done when they studied heat. Long before the physicists could agree on a sound definition of heat, they invented reliable thermometers to measure changes in temperature, and with these instruments they were able to discover many important physical laws.

The need to confront the problems of the definition and meaning of intelligence is not easily evaded, of course, for the reasons we have already discussed. Even for those whose main concern is practical prediction from mental tests, the issue of understanding what such tests are measuring is of immediate importance. In addition to more accurate diagnosis, such understanding could lead to different and perhaps better tests. Consider, for example, the following basic question: Can we regard intelligence as a unitary ability, or are there instead many relatively independent abilities that, for convenience or through ignorance, we lump into a single trait? Long ago Thorndike (1926) proposed that we should speak of and measure separately three different "intelligences"—social, mechanical, and intellectual. This general theme of different kinds of intelligences has continued to run through both theoretical formulations of intelligence and the construction of new mental tests. Today there is an increasing trend toward the development and use of mental tests to measure the many *different* facets of human abilities. Thus more and more we are coming to characterize a person by a *profile* of his mental abilities—for example, a person may be high on verbal ability, fair-to-middling on spatial ability, and so on—and not by a *single* score and verdict on how intelligent he is. The search for some definitive test of general intelligence, once a major objective of test developers, is rapidly diminishing in vigor.

The Making of a Mental Test

There are many different kinds of mental tests. There are **individual tests** (which test one person at a time) and **group tests** (which test a number of people at a time); **speed tests** (whose scores are determined by the number of correct responses made within certain restricted time limits) and **power tests** (in which the difficulty of the tasks successfully completed determines the score); **verbal tests** (requiring verbal responses to questions) and **performance tests** (involving such nonverbal responses as stringing variously shaped beads in a specified order).

But, whatever the type, mental tests usually consist of relatively large collections of different test items, or tasks, and a mental-test score is based on the total number of tasks completed successfully. In constructing a test, various kinds of items are tried out, for example, word definitions, arithmetic problems, perceptual tasks, and following complex directions. In the initial construction of the test the psychologist is guided by the following simple principle: As an intelligence test is designed to measure the intellect rather than, say, temperament or motor

skills, it seems clear that the items in the test should be of an intellectual nature. When an item is being considered for inclusion in a mental test, its content is examined with a common-sense definition of "intellectual" in mind. If the psychologist believes that an item is an intellectual task, it is included for trial. A test made up of such items is, by the test maker's own definition, an "intelligence test." But the test must meet several other validating criteria before it can be accepted as useful.

Criteria for test items Besides being intellectual in content, prospective test items must satisfy several rather specific criteria.

1. The behavior required by the item must be within the repertoire of the individuals to whom the test will be given. Infants cannot speak, therefore only nonverbal responses are called for in infant mental tests; for illiterate or preliterate people the tester cannot use items that require reading or writing.

2. The item should be interesting to the person being tested. This reduces unwanted variations in performance resulting from poor motivation or flagging attention.

3. The item should neither favor an individual nor put him at a disadvantage because of a particular group to which he belongs. For example, a certain item may appeal more immediately to boys or be more familiar to them than to girls; this is usually true of items involving mechanical problems. Because sexually neutral test items are hard to come by, the alternative solution is to balance the bias by awarding each sex an equal number of favorites. Although this problem is difficult in the case of sex, it is much more difficult when we attempt to be fair to a cultural minority. In any society, psychologists usually come from the dominant social group; as a result, they tend, perhaps unintentionally, to pick items meaningful and familiar to their own group. For example, in our society most psychologists have come from a white, middle-class, urban culture, and their chosen test items reflect their culture rather than those, say, of less educated groups, or of blacks and Chicanos, or even of people from rural communities. In Unit 10 we will consider at length the degree to which this bias invalidates the use

of conventional mental tests for minority groups. We will also see what is being done, both in the construction of tests and in their administration, to alleviate this bias.

4. The fourth criterion reflects the commonsense assumption that people grow "brighter" as they grow older, at least through the childhood years. According to this criterion, the item should effectively discriminate between children of different ages, in such a way that an increasing number of children are able to pass it at each higher age level. For example, in preparing an earlier revision of the Stanford-Binet Intelligence Test, Terman and Merrill (1937) tested the ability of children of various ages to define such words as "connection," "obedience," and "revenge." They found that almost no eight- or nine-year-olds could do this. About 10 percent of the ten-year-olds were successful. Beyond that age the percentage of children able to handle the item increased rather regularly. Thirty percent of the eleven-year-olds, 50 percent of the twelve-year-olds, more than 60 percent of the thirteen-year-olds, and 70 percent of the fourteen-year-olds were able to handle the item successfully. At the age of seventeen more than 90 percent of the subjects could handle it. This item, therefore, was considered a good one because an increasing number of children were able to pass it with each higher age level.

5. The item must show a positive relation to the total mental-test score. Specifically, individuals who pass the item should tend to earn a higher score on the overall test than those who fail it. To reverse the perspective, it would seem absurd to permit success on a particular test item to add a point to the total test score if individuals able to pass the item were shown (by this same *total* score) to be *less* intelligent than those who failed it.

Standardization of test items   To apply these five criteria for test items, we must first collect responses to them from a large and adequate sample of persons. For example, to say that the average ten-year-old can pass a particular item and that the average eight-year-old cannot implies that we have previously tested the item on a *representative sample of the entire population*

of ten-year-old children and of eight-year-old children. To assert that passing a given item is positively related to the total mental-test score implies that we have obtained responses on this item and on the total test from a representative sample of the population of persons for whom the test is intended. This procedure for establishing the "standard" quantitative test performance by a representative sample of the kinds of persons to be tested is called **standardization** of the test items.

The problem of obtaining a sample truly representative of the entire desired population is beset with obvious difficulties. Yet if the sample used in standardizing a mental test is unrepresentative of the entire population, the test will be limited in its usefulness. If the test is given to individuals from groups not properly included in the standardization sample, it may yield biased results, which can give rise to dangerously misleading interpretations. (See Appendix, p. 838, for methods of obtaining representative samples.)

Once we have arrived at a collection of items that, through the process of standardization, have been demonstrated to meet the criteria we have discussed, we are well on the way to having a usable mental test. A crucial question remains. Does the test give a *valid* measure of intelligence? To comprehend better the considerable body of research that has been devoted to the question of validity, we must first become familiar with the two major quantitative measures in terms of which performance on intelligence tests is stated—mental age and IQ.

Mental Age

Every item in a mental test can be given its appropriate age-level value. When a child is tested, his score, based on the number of items passed, can then be described in terms of age. For example, we have noted that the Terman-Merrill task of defining certain words was passed by about 60 percent of thirteen-year-old children. That item, because it could be passed by a majority of thirteen-year-olds, was therefore placed at year thirteen on the test.

Suppose that a girl passes all the items that were passed by at least 60 percent of all the ten-year-olds taking this test, and she also passes some of the items for eleven- and twelve-year-olds. She first is credited with all the items up to and including those for ten-year-olds. If she passes half the items for year eleven and one-fourth the items for year twelve, she receives an additional six months' credit for the items for eleven-year-olds and three months' credit for the items for twelve-year-olds. Totaling these credits gives her a **mental age** (**MA**) of ten years and nine months. This method of scoring is illustrated in the following listing, which gives some of the kinds of tasks for years six and fourteen in the 1960 Stanford-Binet revision. The list also gives the scoring credits.

Year Six (six items, two months' credit for each item passed)

1. Give meanings of such words as "orange," "envelope," and "puddle."
2. Point out differences between "a bird and a dog," "a slipper and a boot."
3. Discover missing details in pictures.
4. Count out a specified number of blocks from a stack of ten.
5. Complete opposite analogies: "A bird flies, a fish. . . ."
6. Trace the correct path through a pictured maze.

Year Fourteen (six items, two months' credit for each item passed)

1. Vocabulary of more difficult words.
2. Discover the rule followed in a series of paper foldings.
3. Reasoning task: Determine the time a burglary took place.
4. Tell how to measure out thirteen pints using a five-pint and a nine-pint can.
5. Directional orientation: "Suppose you are going west, then turn to your right; in what direction are you going now?"
6. Reconciliation of opposites: "In what way are the following alike—winter and summer, happy and sad?"

Intelligence quotient To say that the child in our example has a mental age of ten years and nine months means that she has passed the same items as the average child ten years and nine months old. But suppose that, although she has a mental age of ten years and nine months, she has a *chronological age* (*CA*) of nine years and six months. Obviously she is somewhat brighter than the average child of nine and a half. We can, if we wish, indicate this fact by a score that will express her *mental age as related to her chronological age*. This score is called the **intelligence quotient** (**IQ**).

On the Binet test the IQ is obtained by taking the ratio of mental age (MA) to chronological age (CA) and multiplying it by 100 to remove decimal points. We thus arrive at the formula:

$$IQ = \frac{MA}{CA} \times 100.$$

Our child with a mental age of 10.75 and a chronological age of 9.5 would then have an IQ of 113:

$$IQ = \frac{10.75}{9.50} \times 100 = 113.2$$

(the decimal fraction is usually dropped). A child with a chronological age of ten years and nine months who obtained a mental age of exactly ten years nine months would have an IQ of 100:

$$IQ = \frac{10.75}{10.75} \times 100 = 100.$$

It can be seen that an IQ of 100 will be characteristic of the *average* child of any age, an IQ greater than 100 will indicate an intelligence somewhat superior to the average, and an IQ lower than 100 will indicate a somewhat less than average brightness. It should be clear that this convenient outcome (average IQ = 100) is not the result of a magical collusion between some Great Psychologist and Nature; it necessarily results from the arbitrary arithmetic convention we have adopted to express the IQ. (See Box 8.1 for a further discussion of the meanings of IQ scores.)

One feature of this method of determining the IQ promises trouble, that is, the assumption that mental age continues to increase with chronological age. If, instead, there is a certain chronological age beyond which mental age no longer increases, then an individual who has

BOX 8.1

THE GENIUS AND THE MORON

	The Child Whose IQ Is	Is Equaled or Excelled by (Children out of 10,000)
Very Superior	160	3
	150	23
	140	130
Superior	130	440
	120	1,300
High Average	110	3,100
Normal or Average	100	5,400
	90	7,700
Low Average	80	9,200
Borderline Defective	70	9,700
Mental Defective	60	9,900

We all have a strong urge to translate IQ scores into such colorful terms as "genius," "moron," and "idiot." For the most part, however, psychologists have shied away from such translations, primarily because the IQ scores for large populations show a normal distribution curve. There is no sharp break between IQ scores of 50 to 70 (the scores traditionally taken as the limits defining the moron) and lower or higher IQs. Furthermore, we know that whether or not an individual's performance justifies the honorific term "genius" depends as much upon other factors as it does upon IQ—upon special skills, abilities, motivation, and other personality factors.

As IQs are relative scores, the most helpful guide to understanding the meaning of an IQ score is in terms of the number of children in the total population who equal or exceed such a score. The values in the table are based on estimates reported for the revised Stanford-Binet Intelligence Test.

The data tell the important story of individual differences in mental-test scores. In intelligence, as among the other abilities of man, pronounced individual differences are striking fact. And of course this holds true for the many separate facets of intelligence.

L. M. TERMAN & M. A. MERRILL. *Stanford-Binet Intelligence Scale: Manual for the Third Revison: Form L-M.* Boston: Houghton Mifflin, 1960.

reached this peak will earn lower and lower IQ scores the older he grows, despite the fact that his intellectual abilities have not faltered. There is good reason to believe that growth in mental age does reach a relatively stationary level after a certain chronological age. Because of this built-in limitation of the IQ measure, it is necessary to modify the formula for ages at which gain in the mental age fails to keep pace with chronological age. When does this transition point occur?

Mental-growth curve   It is not surprising that mental age, at least among the young, does show a growth curve. Most tests are so constructed as to guarantee a growth curve because, as we have seen, one criterion for any item to be included in a mental test is that it show such an age trend. The growth curve of mental age is not, however, wholly of our own creation—a statistical artifact. The significant thing is that we have been able to find reasonable intellectual tasks that *do* give us such growth curves over a certain age range. Presumably if intelligence did not grow with age, we would not be able to discover such test items. As Figure 8.2, page 184, illustrates, the same children studied throughout their development show a regular increase in MA as they grow older, through the age of fourteen.

Until recently a simplifying assumption was made in computing the IQ for older children and adults. As mental age no longer seemed to keep pace with chronological age by age fifteen, "final" chronological age was set at fifteen years. Thus, the formula *for everyone fifteen years old and older* became

$$IQ = \frac{MA}{15} \times 100.$$

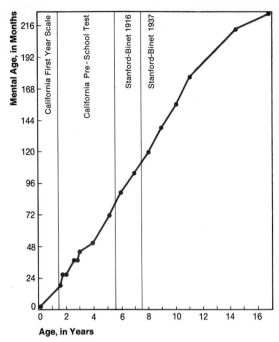

FIGURE 8.2 This curve represents the average mental ages of children studied in the Berkeley Growth Study over a period of years. The same children were measured regularly for various characteristics, among them intelligence. Four different forms of intelligence tests (appropriate for each age range) were used: The California First Year Scale, The California Pre-School Test, the 1916 form of the Stanford-Binet Intelligence Test, and the 1937 revision of the Stanford-Binet Test. It will be noted that there is a diminished rate of growth in mental age after fourteen years.

N. Bayley. Development and maturation. In H. Helson (Ed.) *Theoretical Foundations of Psychology*; copyright 1951 by D. Van Nostrand Company, Inc.; adapted by permission.

This rather arbitrary and not wholly satisfactory solution has been replaced in a recent revision of the Stanford-Binet test (Terman & Merrill, 1960) by a different method of determining the intelligence quotient. In this method (initially developed for the Wechsler mental tests) the IQ simply represents the relative standing of the individual within his specific age group. As an example, take two adults of different ages, one of whom scores higher than average *for his age group*, while the other scores lower than average *for his age group*. With this method we can say that the former has a higher

IQ than the latter no matter what the absolute scores of the two may be. But now the IQ is no longer a quotient.

Wechsler Adult Intelligence Scale An approach to intelligence testing that was developed shortly after World War II departs from the Binet strategy, with its dependence upon the mental-growth curve and the consequent link between mental and chronological age. The Stanford-Binet test was initially developed for children, and as we have just seen, ran into difficulties when applied to adults. In addition to the IQ computation problem, the items for the Stanford-Binet did not sample (and did not intend or claim to do so) the intellectual abilities of adults. The Wechsler Adult Intelligence Scale (Wechsler, 1958) does do this and is appropriate for persons from age sixteen on. Furthermore, its items are arranged in two broad subscales: *verbal* and *performance*. Within these subscales, there are several subtests, each containing only items of a certain type. The verbal subscale includes subtests for information, comprehension, vocabulary, memory span for digits forward and backward, arithmetical reasoning, and recognizing verbal similarities. The performance subscale includes subtests involving object assembly (putting together cutout parts to complete a figure), picture completion, arrangement of pictures in meaningful sequence, construction of certain designs from blocks, and learning to pair numbers with symbols. Since separate scores can be computed for each subtest, profiles of mental abilities are obtained directly from this test.

Because the Wechsler test is designed for adults, the standardization samples were of course composed of adults. Thus, it was not necessary to select items that became less difficult with age; the other criteria for the selection of test items still applied. Furthermore, in computing the IQ from performance on this test, the mental-age concept can be abandoned. Instead, the IQ simply indicates, as we have already pointed out, the place of the individual in the distribution of scores for his age group.

The same approach can be, and is, used for children. The Wechsler Intelligence Scale for Children (Wechsler, 1949), appropriate for ages five through fifteen, has essentially the same kinds of subtests as the adult version, but they are naturally composed of less difficult items. Several mental ability tests exist for children less than five years old. Reliable test scores can be obtained for babies only two months old using the Bayley Scales of Infant Development (Bayley, 1969). However, the ever-nagging question of *what* is being measured is particularly worrisome at these very young ages.

The Validity of Mental Tests

The Wechsler and Stanford-Binet tests are commonly used to assess the intelligence of adults in the United States; they have also been adapted for use in other countries. These two tests seem to measure very much the same thing —whatever that thing may be. A number of studies have found a correlation of about .80 between the two tests. (See Appendix, p. 831, for the meaning of "correlation.") One or the other, and sometimes both, is used as a standard for the validation of other mental tests. Correlations between a new test and the standard are interpreted as indicating the degree to which the new instrument is a valid measure of intelligence. This approach to assessing validity is essentially a question-begging operation because it assumes that the "standard" is a valid measure of intelligence, and this assumption has yet to be proved.

If we are not content to validate mental tests against one another, then we must look for new validating criteria. So far we have made the assumption that the capacity we call "intelligence" develops with age, at least up to a point. We can safely make yet another assumption: Intelligence is an adaptive ability, and it reveals itself through *effective performance of the common tasks of social life.* For the child as he grows up, these tasks are found in school; for the adult, they include his later educational attainment and, most important, his occupational choice and success.

Intelligence and school success Two measures of school success have been correlated with mental-test scores—grades earned in school

and subject-matter achievement tests. In the first case, subjective factors are involved, for the determination of a student's grades can reflect a teacher's judgment of and attitude toward the student. Such possibly biasing factors play no role in achievement tests. They are usually objectively scored, comprising the familiar true-false, multiple-choice, matching, and completion items, and are designed to measure how much of the subject matter of the course the student has mastered.

Cronbach (1960, 1970) reviews many of the research reports on the relations between mental-test scores and school success and ultimate educational attainment. He finds that in both cases the correlations are uniformly positive. Correlations between mental tests and school grades in high school average about .50, but are somewhat lower for college grades. These correlations with school and college grades are higher for verbal subtests of intelligence. There are also appreciable relations between intelligence and ultimate educational attainment. The average IQ for all high school graduates is 110; for those who go on to college and graduate, 120; for those who go on to graduate school and obtain a Ph.D., 130.

These values are for groups and have little meaning in terms of any individual case. Educational attainment is the result of an enormous variety of factors, personality among them. The higher up the academic ladder a person goes, the less influential his IQ score is in determining how well he does. (The lower correlation of IQ with college grades than with high school grades is one indication of this.) Thus, for example, not only is an intense *motivation to succeed academically* very important in moving a student through school, but this motivational factor also helps him to do relatively better than his classmates once he gets in college or graduate school.

McClelland (1973) has raised some basic questions about the meaning of IQ scores as measures of intellect. In a paper entitled "Testing for Competence Rather than for 'Intelligence,'" he finds the correlations between IQ scores and academic performance hardly surprising "because school success depends on taking similar types of tests" [to mental tests]. He goes on to assert that "neither the [mental] tests nor school grades seem to have much power to predict real competence in many life outcomes, aside from the advantages that [academic] credentials convey on the individuals concerned." This is a strong indictment, and he has assembled some evidence to support it. His argument is primarily with those who attempt to measure general (rather than separate facets of) ability and with the fact that mental tests tend not to be "culture-fair." In urging that mental tests should be better able to predict "real competence," he is joining in the healthy reassessment of the purposes and practices of mental testing that is currently underway. Such reassessment should lead to the development of new kinds of tests with greater predictive ability. Such tests would measure, and credit, not only specific mental abilities but also nonintellectual factors involving personality and motivation. As of now, however, the data permit us to regard current tests as providing a reasonably valid measurement of at least some socially relevant mental abilities.

Intelligence and occupational aptitude When psychological testing was first tried in industry, intelligence tests were used almost exclusively in selecting workers for various occupations. This procedure was based on the belief that intelligence is a general factor important in the performance of all types of work. Later research cast some doubt on this assumption, and specialized **aptitude** tests were designed for each major occupational category. Nevertheless, test scores of general intelligence do correlate with most kinds of work proficiency.

Two major conclusions can be drawn from the comprehensive survey on this issue by Ghiselli (1966):

1. There is a wide range in the degree to which measures of intelligence correlate with occupational proficiency, depending on the occupation.
2. For all the jobs examined, the overall correlation of general intelligence with job proficiency is about as high as the *average* of all aptitude tests designed to predict that proficiency. However, some specific aptitude tests do better than IQ tests.

Not only do brighter people do somewhat better than duller people on the same job, but also some jobs seem to require or attract people of higher intelligence than others. According to data gathered from World War II enlisted men (Harrell & Harrell, 1945), people involved in professions such as teaching, law, engineering, and accounting have an average IQ of at least 120. Clerical and sales personnel are somewhat lower but still well above the mean. Various groups of manual workers fall, on the average, below an IQ of 100. These mean differences again accord with a functional view of intelligence and attest to the validity of the instruments we use to measure it.

Of course, no direct cause-and-effect relation is implied by these data. Children from more privileged groups not only have the opportunity to continue their formal education longer (which does somewhat raise mental-test scores), but this additional education opens the way, both through specialized training and influential social contacts, to higher-level occupations.

Perhaps the most interesting aspect of these findings is, in fact, the truly remarkable range of IQ scores found within any occupation. For example, some farm hands score above 140, whereas some lawyers fall below 100. Again the caution: Mental-test scores have something, but far from everything, to do with which occupations we select (or are selected by) and how well we do in them.

ABILITIES, APTITUDES, AND INTELLIGENCE

Although intelligence is important, many other factors contribute to an individual's pattern of abilities, aptitudes, and the degree of effectiveness and personal satisfaction he attains in life. Not only are there many quite different and only loosely related "intelligences" (our discussion of the structure of intelligence in Unit 9 deals further with this claim) but it is becoming increasingly clear that even sophisticated, multifaceted mental tests have limited predictive power. Furthermore, intelligence, however measured, is by no means a fixed attribute (as Unit 9 demonstrates). It can be dramatically modified. In Unit 10 we discuss some of the factors that determine how intelligent we are, factors that to a certain extent are under societal, if not individual, control. Knowing, as we do, that something so "simple"—*and modifiable*—as nutrition (of both the mother and her child) can importantly influence mental development necessarily dispels the unfortunate myth that one's IQ is a permanent straitjacket, donned at conception, which confines each individual to a very narrow range of realizable ambitions. Add to this that

what we become, or *can* become, is also due to our motivation and personality, and we are forced to recognize that mental ability can neither assure a valuable and valued life *nor can it prevent it.*

We do not all have the same potential. It is not true that anyone can become anything. But—and this is the crux of the matter—for each of us there is open a range of rewarding and different possibilities. These possibilities can be realized if each individual works to express his full potential and if society permits and encourages him to do so.

SUMMARY

1. The original impetus for developing mental tests to measure intelligence was a practical one, which grew out of a need to classify individuals in terms of their abilities. This remains the general purpose of these tests. Thus the continuing proliferation of a variety of mental tests has been possible because such tests do "work," despite the still unsettled question of the definition of "intelligence."

2. The current trend in mental testing is to consider intelligence as multifaceted and to develop separate tests to measure the many different human abilities. In describing an individual, psychologists increasingly speak of the profile of his mental abilities rather than attempting to characterize him only as more or less intelligent.

3. Beginning with a pool of test items meeting a broad definition of intelligence, the mental-test constructor applies a number of specific criteria for selecting those that will comprise the final test. These criteria generally include the appropriateness of the required response for the individuals being tested; the tendency for the score on an individual test item to correlate with the total test score; and with children, the increasing likelihood that with increasing age the item will be answered correctly.

4. Any mental test must be standardized, that is, administered to a *representative* sample of the population for which it is intended, before it can be put into practical use.

5. Mental age, determined by the number and difficulty level of items passed on a mental test, on the average of course increases with chronological age. But since the two do not increase at precisely the same rate, an intelligence quotient (IQ) can be computed. IQ is simply the ratio of mental age to chronological age. The more advanced a person is mentally, relative to his age, the higher his IQ. This ratio works until adolescence, when mental growth (as measured by intelligence tests) begins to reach a plateau; at this point a revised definition of IQ becomes necessary.

6. Intelligence tests are valid to the extent that they show sensible relationships with generally understood indexes of mental ability. Their validity is supported by their

correlation with measures of school success and achievement in certain occupations. These school and career attainments are, however, also related to other individual characteristics such as aptitudes, personality, and motivation to achieve.

7. Intelligence level places only very broad limits on what an individual can achieve. To a significant extent intelligence can be modified by a number of influences that are, or can be brought, under society's, if not the individual's, control.

GLOSSARY

aptitude The potential ability of a person to perform a specific kind of activity. The term differs from "proficiency" or "achievement," which refer to the person's present performance capacity.

group tests Tests, designed to measure the general intelligence or specialized aptitudes, which are administered to large groups simultaneously. The Army General Classification Test (AGCT), used in World War II to measure the mental capacity of the American soldier, is an example.

individual tests Tests designed to measure the general intelligence or specialized aptitudes of people and administered to one person at a time. The Stanford-Binet test is an example. (see also **intelligence quotient**)

intelligence quotient (IQ) A converted score based on performance on an intelligence test that expresses the individual's mental age (MA) in relation to his chronological age (CA). The formula for this relationship is

$$IQ = \frac{MA}{CA} \times 100.$$

The average IQ is therefore necessarily 100, because the average ten-year-old will receive an MA of 10 and so on. For persons older than fifteen years, the formula is revised to

$$IQ = \frac{MA}{15} \times 100.$$

mental age (MA) A converted score based on performance on a mental test and determined by the level of difficulty of the test items passed. If a child, no matter how old he is, can pass only those items passed by the average ten-year-old, he will be given a mental-age score of 10. This unit was first proposed by Binet and is fairly widely used today. (see also **intelligence quotient**)

performance tests Tests designed to measure general intelligence or specialized aptitudes and consisting primarily of motor or perceptual test items. Verbal facility plays a minimal role. To be contrasted with *verbal tests*.

power tests Tests designed to measure general intelligence or specialized aptitudes in which the difficulty of the tasks that are successfully completed determines the score. To be contrasted with *speed tests*.

speed tests Tests designed to measure general intelligence or specialized aptitudes in which the scores are determined primarily by the rapidity with which correct answers can be given.

standardization When used in connection with tests, the procedure of administering a new test to a representative sample of people to determine scale values for the scores. For instance, before we can assign a test item to a given age level (in the Binet test), we must test this item on a large number of children to determine its proper age level.

verbal tests Tests designed to measure general intelligence or specialized aptitudes and consisting primarily of verbal test items. To be contrasted with *performance tests*.

development and structure of mental abilities

DO YOU KNOW...

whether adults, on the average, get smarter as they grow older?

how stable your IQ is likely to remain throughout your life?

if you can predict later intelligence from infant "intelligence tests"?

that certain changes in mental test performance may indicate imminent death?

whether it makes sense to speak of "general intelligence" or, instead, . . .

- *whether it may be more useful to regard intelligence as made up of a number of relatively independent abilities, or . . .*

- *that the choice between these two views may depend on how old the person is?*

- *that—although they are rare—there are people who are "geniuses" in certain respects, but who are otherwise quite backward in their intellectual ability?*

unit 9

CONTENTS

The major question that may be asked about the development of intelligence is: "How stable is intelligence over time?" It is known that mental age increases with chronological age, at least up to adolescence. However, there is still the question of whether or not IQ (mental ability *relative* to chronological age) remains the same for a given individual throughout his life. The basic question of stability of intelligence comprises two issues: first, the *average* trend of mental ability from birth to death in the general population; second, the constancy of IQ over time for a given individual. These issues have different theoretical and practical implications.

AGE AND INTELLIGENCE

We have seen in Unit 8 (see Figure 8.1, p. 179) that *absolute* mental ability increases up to adolescence. However, beyond adolescence it is by no means obvious what trend, if any, is to be expected with age. What then is known of the fate of intelligence through the adult years?

Cross-Sectional Studies

The general picture from *cross-sectional* studies (people of different age groups measured at a single point in time) is that intelligence reaches its peak about age thirty and then begins to fall off ever more rapidly as old age approaches. This observation is true (in Wechsler's terms) of both "verbal" and "performance" intelligence, although the former reaches its peak, for the average person, a few years earlier. In a pioneer report of cross-sectional data of age differences in IQ (see Unit 2, p. 34), Jones and Conrad (1933) anticipated what has proved to be a reliable generalization. They found that performance on tasks involving general information declines very little, if at all, with age; however, tasks in which rapid responses are critical do show a considerable drop. Sheer speed of response seems to figure in many mental-test tasks. Thus, some of the age-related decline may be attributable to a "nonintellectual" slowing down of the general pace of response as we grow older.

Furthermore, the cross-sectional method, as noted in Unit 2, is susceptible to confounding factors. One has to do with the changing level in educational standards over time. This factor might be especially important for studies conducted before the advent of universal minimum-education standards in the United States. For example, it is known that less-educated people score somewhat lower on intelligence tests than better-educated people. If persons now aged sixty had received less education when they were young than present-day thirty-year-olds when *they* were young, a difference in tested intelligence between these age groups *might* reflect an historical trend in educational standards, rather than age changes per se.

A study by Tuddenham (1948) supports the reasonableness of this argument. He found that World War I and World War II soldiers (the latter with a higher average education) differed considerably in intelligence *when tested at the same age*. The World War II men scored higher, indicating that generational differences in educational standards may account for age differences in mental-test scores in cross-sectional studies.

Both of these studies point to the probability that intelligence, as measured by mental tests, does increase with longer exposure to formal education, and that even traditional schooling is effective in raising IQ. Consider then the distinct possibility that more effective educational techniques and maximum educational opportunities for all children may hold the promise of raising intelligence levels, scholastic success, and consequently occupational achievement.

Longitudinal Studies

Longitudinal studies bypass this confounding of education level and age-related mental development by testing the intelligence of the *same* individual at two or more points in time. These studies, using representative samples of subjects over a wide range of intelligence, suggest that there is generally an increase in IQ during the adult years. Rigorous data on this came from three extensive longitudinal investi-

gations, which included study of mental development from late adolescence up to age forty to fifty years. Two of these studies have mental test data on the same subjects going back to the earliest ages, some of which shall soon be reported. Honzik (1973), comparing IQ scores for Berkeley (California) Guidance Study subjects at eighteen and forty years, and for Oakland (California) Growth Study subjects at seventeen and forty-eight years, finds at the very least a maintenance of mental ability level, with strong indications that certain facets of intelligence do in fact increase over these age spans. Subtests measuring vocabulary, information, and comprehension showed significant gains into the adult years for both men and women. Another longitudinal study—the Berkeley Growth Study (Bayley, 1968)—showed similar results.

These subtests are all highly verbal and are closely related to academic success in the high school years immediately preceding the eighteen-year mental test. Girls at that age did less well than boys, but their increase to age forty brought them to a par with adult men. Honzik speculates that this earlier "disability" was a product of societal attitudes, which valued social over academic success for girls. As the feminist movement today would predict, women still hold to these values despite the fact that their actual performance has so improved. Typical comments of women at age forty, taking these mental tests about 1970, included "I've slipped" and "I haven't learned a thing since I left school." This led Honzik to note that: "A great deal of reassurance and approval was needed to give these women enough confidence to complete the test." These observations permit us to preview a theme which is pursued in Unit 10: Cultural (and therefore *self-*) expectations regarding mental ability can interfere with valid assessments of mental ability and therefore result in spuriously low estimates of intelligence in any group from which society expects relatively poorer performance.

Other longitudinal studies also indicate increases in mental ability into adulthood. In one instance, both men and women, spanning the average range of IQs, showed significant increases in intelligence between two mental tests given when they were about thirty and forty-two years old (Kangas & Bradway, 1971). They also report that for women, the lower the earlier IQ, the greater the gain in IQ. This once more supports the notion that women's mental-test performance—especially at younger ages—may be depressed by attitudinal factors. In the low IQ range, Charles (1953) followed up people who had been adjudged mentally deficient during their elementary school years. Those available for retesting at about age forty-two achieved an average IQ of 81. This was significantly above the initial mean IQ of 58 for these same people as children. Furthermore, Charles reports that the majority of this sample made social adjustments in their adult life—in marriage, parenthood, economic self-support—that could not have been anticipated from their earlier diagnosis of mental deficiency.

Charles' data of course do not directly demonstrate mental growth in the post-adolescent years, but they do contribute to a suspicion that should be growing in the mind of the alert reader—that IQ is neither a totally stable nor a totally predictable attribute characteristic of any individual.

Recent investigations indicate that the growth of intelligence does level off in later life and that there is some decline in intelligence in old age, although at quite different times for different tests and with enormous individual differences. In one study (Blum, Fosshage, & Jarvik, 1972) verbal abilities, as measured by a variety of mental subtests (vocabulary and information are examples), were found, on the average, to show some slight decline in eighty-year-olds. Even in the nineties the decline was quite moderate. The slight decline in verbal intelligence found in these advanced years refers to *average* scores; some people actually show increases in their eighties and nineties. Non-verbal subtests, especially those that heavily weight speed of response, do decline markedly in this age range. (For further comment on the kinds of mental abilities that do and do not decline with age, see Cattell's discussion of "crystallized" and "fluid" intelligence, Unit 2, p. 33.)

Some recent research (Jarvik, Eisdorfer, & Blum, 1973) indicates that a certain pattern of change in mental ability may forecast death. Specifically, if there is a rather abrupt decline on three subtests—vocabulary, the ability to identify similarities between words, and speed and accuracy of matching numbers with symbols—then there is a substantial probability of dying within five years. This relation was found for aged subjects who were in reasonable physical health at the time of testing, and it is not at all related to the person's actual age. This pattern of decline may be due to certain brain function changes which presage death. These changes in brain function, or in oxygen supply to the brain, may be so subtle as to remain undetected by the usual physical tests currently available to the doctor. We may have here another instance of the generally valid observation: Behavioral and mental tests are more sensitive in detecting brain malfunctioning than are physical or physiological tests. Of course, to detect this ominous change, careful and repeated testing over a long period is needed; it most certainly cannot be detected by general observations of behavior or even by a single, however careful, mental test administered to the individual at any one age.

In summary, growing old, even very old, by no means brings about any massive intellectual decline. Most mental abilities hold up fairly well, and the abilities necessary to be informed and even wise are the sturdiest of all. The team of investigators from whom we have been citing evidence in this section have a moral to draw. They urge that

> a life-span investigation of intellectual changes should be approached in terms of individual differences in specific abilities and not in terms of "global intelligence." To ignore the individual variations is to fall into the perennial trap of lumping the aged together as having outlived their usefulness—instead of recognizing it is the individual, not the age, that makes the difference. (Blum, Jarvik, & Clark, 1970)

STABILITY AND PREDICTABILITY OF INTELLIGENCE

Investigation of stability and predictability of intelligence is the exclusive preserve of longitudinal studies because such questions require repeated measurement of the same people over time. Not only do the data from such studies promise eventual understanding of adult changes in intelligence with age, but they also cast into a different light the apparent regularity of intellectual development implied by the average mental-growth curves. The fact that the *average* curve is smooth up through adolescence does not require the inference that all, or even most, children show the same regular progression in intellectual development. Quite the contrary is true; this regularity masks quite substantial changes in tested intelligence for many children during this period.

How stable and predictable is *an individual's* intelligence (as measured by mental tests) from birth to middle age? The answer to this question has been summarized by Honzik (1973) from the results of a number of longitudinal studies of normal individuals in cities all over the world. The findings are that test scores are highly predictive over short periods, but the longer the interval between tests, the less accurate the prediction. Also, the younger the child when given his first test, the less accurate the prediction. Thus, in the Berkeley Guidance Study, the correlation between IQs at age three and IQs at age five (a two-year period) is .54, but for the two-year period from ages twelve to fourteen, the correlation jumps to .90. *Infancy* presents a different situation since it is a period of rapid development of the brain and is marked by an increasing ability to process information from the environment. Mental tests given to infants during the first months of life give stable results for a few months, but gradually changes take place. The rate of such changes varies with the individual baby. This means that prediction from infant test scores to IQs in the preschool years is low, and prediction to IQs in the school years is negligible. The *preschool years*, from age two to five, constitute a period of marked increase in predictive power. A two-year-old's test score has little predictive value, but the five-year-old's IQ significantly predicts IQs *at all future age periods, even to age forty*. This does not mean that all individuals maintain the same absolute level of functioning from ages five to forty years. Far from it. All it means is that on

the average people tend to maintain their position *relative to their peers* from the age of five into middle age. That is, the brightest five-year-old of his group will tend also to be the brightest forty-year-old of the same group. (Figure 9.1, p. 196, provides two actual "case histories" which dramatize the range of variability possible in mental development.)

Even during the relatively stable school years (nine to eighteen), 85 percent of the children in the Berkeley Guidance Study varied ten or more IQ points on the eight tests they were given, and almost 10 percent of the children fluctuated at least thirty points. Although marked changes occur in some individuals, prediction during the mature years is fairly high. Correlations between IQs obtained in the late teens and IQs earned twenty to thirty years later are usually about .70.

Although very early mental tests do not predict later intelligence, the possibility remains that certain items or groups of items *can* predict later intelligence. A report by Cameron, Livson, and Bayley (1967) lends some support to this speculation. They find, for example, that a tendency to vocalize in infant girls substantially predicts later IQ (as late as age thirty-six), whereas the *total* score on infant-intelligence tests has *no* predictive value. Kagan (1971) also finds "unusual stability of infant girls' vocalizations" in his study of change and continuity in infancy. These results confront us once again with a challenge to the common view that intelligence is a unitary trait. In addition, the fluctuation of IQ arouses the suspicion that intelligence may be a heterogeneous assortment of separate abilities developing at different rates. We now turn to an examination of the evidence on the structure of intelligence.

THE STRUCTURE OF INTELLIGENCE

Seemingly endless controversy, and almost as much research, has focused on the issue of the structure of intelligence. The main argument revolves around how many separate and distinguishable aspects of intelligence exist. A secondary question has been—and remains—whether or not the structure of intelligence

FIGURE 9.1 (a) Converging patterns of mental development. Case A is a woman who shows high and highly consistent ability from her first test at eighteen months of age through her test at age forty. Case B starts quite low but gradually improves her performance until it matches Case A. (b) Diverging patterns of mental development. Case C is a man whose early mental ability was about average but who gradually reached considerably higher levels which he has maintained to age forty. Case D started out at about the same point as Case C but showed a decreasing trend from then on. Different mental tests appropriate to the test ages have been used to construct this curve. The ordinate values are standard scores that represent the standing of a person's IQ relative to others tested with the same test at the same age (the average score at each age is 50). Actual IQ scores are indicated occasionally for each person.

Adapted from M. Honzik & J. W. Macfarlane. Personality development and intellectual functioning from 21 months to 40 years. In Jarvik, Eisdorfer, & Blum (Eds.), *Intellectual Functioning in Adults*. New York, N.Y.: Springer, 1973.

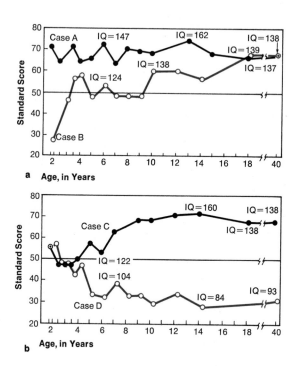

changes with age, and if so in what way. On the first point, there are proponents for the views that first, intelligence is a general and unitary capacity; second, that it is composed of a small group of broad and moderately independent factors; or third, that it is a collection of discrete and separate abilities. On the question of changes in structure with age the main battle has been drawn between two camps. One claims that intelligence becomes increasingly differentiated with age; the other claims that no systematic changes in structure take place over time.

Generality of Intelligence

The main case for any view of the structure of intelligence is based on intercorrelations between mental abilities and upon how these intercorrelations are interpreted. It is clear that if every measure of intelligence correlated perfectly with every other measure, the unitary hypothesis would be strongly supported. If, on the other hand, all intercorrelations were zero, then the view that intelligence is a collection of discrete abilities would be inevitable. Of course, as reality will always have it, the outcome is somewhere in between: Most measures of intelligence correlate positively, but only moderately, with one another. To help us interpret the meaning of any given set of intercorrelations among intelligence measures, the methods of **factor analysis** are employed. Factor analysis refers to a set of mathematical techniques typically used to find a relatively small number of factors that can account for the pattern of intercorrelations among a larger number of measures. However, it must be stressed that there are different forms of factor analysis, based on different mathematical assumptions. These different forms permit *alternate* interpretations of the structure of intelligence, even from the same set of intercorrelations.

The two-factor theory   At about the time that Binet was developing the first modern mental test (the early 1900s), Charles Spearman, a British psychologist and statistician, proposed that only a single "general intelligence" factor existed; he called this factor g, and said that it accounted completely for correlations among measures of mental ability. Certainly, he admitted, performance on any given task was not entirely a function of g (which at times he equated with "mental energy") but involved an additional factor specific for each task. These specific factors he labeled the s factors. Performance on an arithmetic-reasoning test would thus be determined by $g + s_1$, and performance on a vocabulary test would be determined by $g + s_2$. The fact that the two sets correlate positively would be accounted for by their common sharing of g; that the correlation is not perfect is accounted for by the fact that different and unrelated s factors are involved in each. Spearman "proved" his **two-factor theory** of intelligence (g and s) by application of a form of factor analysis (which he invented) to various sets of mental-test data that were then becoming available.

The Spearman view came under attack from the moment of its birth. As we have seen in this unit, it is more useful to deal with patterns of mental abilities—but broader ones than s factors—in understanding mental development. The **group-factor theory**, next to be discussed, provided the beginnings of this latter approach.

The group-factor theory   A major response to the two-factor theory is found in the work of L. L. Thurstone at the University of Chicago. Using a different method of factor analysis (which he invented), Thurstone came to the conclusion that most of the mental capacity of man could be accounted for by postulating seven primary mental abilities (Thurstone, 1938). They are *number, word fluency, verbal meaning, memory, reasoning, spatial perception,* and *perceptual speed.*

Tests were devised for each of these factors. These tests are known as the Thurstone *Primary Mental Abilities* tests (PMA). Thurstone did not, however, find that these primary mental abilities were independent. Each, in fact, correlates positively with each of the others. For example, *number* correlates .46 with *word fluency,* .38 with *verbal meaning,* .18 with *memory,* and so on; *verbal meaning* correlates .51 with *word fluency,* .39 with *memory,* and .54 with *reasoning.*

These findings imply that a general factor could also be detected among the primary mental abilities. Thurstone recognized this implication. The point at issue is perhaps no issue at all. The two-factor theory accounts for the fact that mental tests generally show positive intercorrelations with one another; Thurstone's group-factor theory accounts for the fact that these correlations are somewhat higher among tests that, on their face, seem to measure a particular facet of intelligence. Of course, the more comprehensive we are in our definition of intelligence and the more diligently we work at finding new tasks to represent each facet, the more group factors we might find. Through factor analysis Guilford found at least 40 factors (Guilford, 1956), and he has proposed a theoretical schema for mental ability (Guilford, 1967) that predicts that eventually 120 factors will be found. Others, such as Thomson (1952), have even proposed that intelligence can be divided into an essentially limitless number of mental skills. These theorists would account for the positive correlations between mental tests by assuming that any single mental ability test usually contains items which overlap with items from another mental ability test. That is, every test *samples* from overlapping domains of abilities—hence the term **sampling theory** is applied to such intelligence test theories. (See Box 9.1 for an extreme example of the complexities that the structure of intelligence can exhibit in an individual.) Thus, Thurstone's group-factor

theory opened the door to new and productive analysis of mental ability. Such analysis is now being actively pursued.

Age Changes in the Structure of Intelligence

Studies of intelligence suggest that the structure of intelligence may change with age. For exam-

---

BOX 9.1

IDIOT SAVANT

From time to time there arise in the human population so-called "idiot savants"—feeble-minded persons with one or several highly developed specialities. The most intensively studied case is that of L, reported by M. Scheerer, E. Rothmann, and K. Goldstein. L was first brought in by his mother for psychological and neuropsychiatric examination when he was eleven years old. His case was studied from 1937 to 1943.

Medical examination throughout the six-year period showed him to be healthy and physically well-developed with no signs of neurological disturbance. His EEG was normal. But his mental examination revealed a world of paradoxes.

He could tell the day of the week for any given date between 1880 and 1950. He could add up correctly the totals of ten to twelve two-place numbers just as quickly as the examiner could call them out. He could correctly spell many words *forward* and *backward* and never forgot the spelling of a word once he was told how to spell it. He could play *by ear only* such musical compositions as the *Largo* by Dvořák and could sing, from beginning to end, the "Credo," "Si Ciel," and "Adagio Pathétique" from the opera *Otello*.

On the other hand, he was unable to follow the regular school curriculum. His general information was extremely substandard. He knew the meanings of very few words. He was almost completely deficient in logical reasoning and was at a total loss in any problem involving abstractions. His IQ on the Binet was 50!

L seems to bear dramatic testimony against the notion that intellectual activities are determined by a unitary quality or capacity. But his case does not permit us to assume that intellectual activities are determined by a host of separate and independent capacities, one for each type of performance.

In the first place, as Scheerer, Rothmann, and Goldstein point out, L's superiority in a few narrowly specialized activities does not necessarily indicate special *endowment* in those capacities. Rather, what L seems to demonstrate is the effect of special motivation and practice in a very narrow field of activities. Any normal child *could* do what L did—and much more. These writers suggest the following analysis of the idiot savant.

There are both general and specific intellectual capacities. Abstract capacity and intelligence are essential for the normal functioning of *all* intellectual activities. When abstract intelligence is impaired, the person may be driven, to an abnormal degree, to exercise and develop those specific functions that are less impaired. But there is a close *interdependence* among all mental functions, which can result only in atypical forms of expression involving relatively intact capacities. The person therefore develops "queer" performance patterns. He can add two-place numbers but cannot understand the logic and rules of arithmetic. He can spell, but he cannot understand the meanings of words.

The performance of the idiot savant, no less than that of the normal person, is determined by the interaction of special capacities and general capacities. And the need to speak of profiles of mental abilities rather than an overall general intelligence level is clearly understood in this instance.

M. SCHEERER, E. ROTHMANN, & K. GOLDSTEIN. A case of "idiot savant": An experimental study of personality organization. *Psychological Monographs*, 1945, **58**, No. 4.

ple, Garrett (1946) has proposed that there is a progressive differentiation in mental ability throughout the period of mental growth. Put another way, children should show more influence from *g*, whereas adults should show more and clearer group factors. It is as if the structure of intelligence changes from a Spearman-like plan to a Thurstone-like plan from childhood to adulthood.

The previous sections should warn us, however, that detecting changes in the kind, number, and interrelations of intelligence factors will be a difficult task. One precaution is obvious: Any talk of changes with age should involve data from the same mental test, factor-analyzed by the same method, and preferably based on the same individuals (longitudinal studies). Few studies satisfy these requirements. The consensus to date tends to support Garrett's hypothesis. As one example, we can point to the study of Osborne and Jackson (1964), which did satisfy the basic requirements listed. Employing a battery composed largely of subtests from Wechsler's Intelligence Scale for Children, they reported eight factors for six-year-old children tested immediately before entering the first grade. Only one year later these *same* children on the *same* test required

ten factors to account for the intercorrelations among the various subtest scores.

One qualification to the acceptance of the differentiation hypothesis must be entered. The evidence offered in its support is also consistent with the more mundane hypothesis that the results arise from differences in the adequacy of test batteries employed at different ages *even* when the same tests are used for the different age groups. Any one test battery may be more appropriate for older children than for younger children. Conceivably, test constructors have been more thorough in their coverage of the intellectual domain of older subjects. Psychologists quite possibly may be less differentiated in their conception of the very young child's mental world and, therefore, may measure it less comprehensively. If so, then the lesser differentiation of the young child may be in the mind and instrument of the tester, not in the child's intellectual abilities. At the very least, this consideration suggests the prudence of withholding final judgment on the differentiation hypothesis (as well as all other aspects of the structure of intelligence) until such time as we become more adept at thorough and systematic sampling of the ever-changing domains of man's intelligence.

SUMMARY

1. Intelligence increases with age, at least through childhood. In fact, many aspects of intelligence continue to develop well beyond the adolescent years, though at a slower rate, and some show slight increases even into old age.
2. An independent question involves the extent to which IQ (a measure of an individual's intelligence *relative* to others of the same age) remains constant. Data on this issue from longitudinal studies (testing the *same* individuals over time) indicate that the IQ is far from constant. However, mental tests do yield useful predictions of later intelligence under certain conditions; the older the individual is at the time of the initial test, the more predictive the test. This is true over any given age span.

3. Attempts to predict later general intelligence from overall mental-test scores in the first few years of life show negligible success. But certain items from infant and preschool tests may have some predictive validity.

4. There are two main views about the structure of intelligence. In the first, intelligence is thought to be a unitary ability; thus an intelligent individual would tend to show superior ability in all intellectual tasks. In the second view, intelligence is thought to be composed of a limited number of broad, relatively independent abilities.

5. Research data do not permit an easy decision on the relative validity of these two conceptions of the structure of intelligence, partly because the principal method of such research (factor analysis) does not yield unequivocal results.

6. Evidence suggests that the structure of intelligence changes with age, probably in the direction of increasing differentiation among mental abilities during periods of most rapid mental growth.

GLOSSARY

factor analysis   A statistical technique applied to intercorrelations between mental tests (or any other set of measurable quantities) that detects the number of separate factors mathematically necessary to account for the obtained intercorrelations. Different factor-analytic methods can yield somewhat different results, but all typically find considerably fewer factors than the original number of tests.

group-factor theory   A theory of the structure of intelligence that considers it to be divisible into a relatively limited number of group factors, each encompassing a number of highly related intellectual abilities.

sampling theory   A theory of the structure of intelligence that considers it to be divisible into an essentially limitless number of discrete mental skills and accounts for the typical positive correlation among mental tests by assuming that some overlap usually exists in the samples of discrete skills measured by any given pair of mental-ability tests.

two-factor theory   A theory of the structure of intelligence that considers it to be divisible into a single general factor (g), which enters into all intellectual performance, and a host of independent specific factors (s), related only to performance on a particular mental task.

variations in mental abilities

DO YOU KNOW...

that there is no scientific way, at present, to say to what extent a given individual's intelligence is inherited or environmentally determined?

how the study of twins has added a good deal of information to the study of variations in mental development?

in what ways to treat a young infant so that he is more likely to develop into an intelligent adult?

whether Project Headstart is effective in raising IQ, and, if so, how such compensatory education programs can best be implemented?

that emphasis on femininity may contribute to a drop in tested IQ?

whether occupational groups differ in the average intelligence of their members?

why it is nonsense, scientifically, to search for black-white IQ differences?

CONTENTS

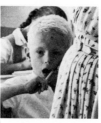

We will begin with two unarguable statements: (1) Individuals vary enormously in all facets of mental ability. (2) Like tends to breed like. Now we come to a question: Are the differences asserted in sentence 1 attributable to the process noted in sentence 2? Today, especially with regard to mental abilities, that is *The Question.* Traditionally the issue was defined as heredity *versus* environment, and it has always aroused the interest of social philosophers and a wide variety of psychologists and other biological scientists. But rarely has the inheritability of mental ability acquired the level of interest that it reached in the 1970s, particularly with regard to the origins of group differences in IQ (e.g., blacks versus nonblacks; lower versus upper classes).

We will deal with *group* differences in mental abilities later in this unit; but first let us start with another question: What are the sources of *individual* differences? As mentioned previously, this question was once worded "Is IQ determined by heredity or by environment?" When it was recognized that the answer could not possibly be cast in an all-or-nothing manner, the question was rephrased as "To what extent is intelligence attributable to environmental influences and to what extent to genetic factors?" It is now becoming clear that even this question is inadequately phrased. With such formulations, a rigorous scientific answer is precluded because these questions ignore the current state of our knowledge and the probable persistence of racism and discrimination in most societies

HEREDITY, ENVIRONMENT, AND MENTAL ABILITIES

It is simply not possible to obtain valid assessments of the separate contributions of environment and heredity to mental abilities. If we could agree on what we mean by intelligence and on the best methods of measurement, that is, agree on a particular facet of intelligence measured in a particular way and at a particular time, the *variability* in intelligence within a specified population of many individuals *might* be apportioned between heredity and environment. That is, we would be able to say that the *individual differences* in intelligence among the people of population *p* at time *t* was 75 percent due to the differences in their environments and 25 percent due to their genetic differences.

Today we are still far from being able to determine even this. But we can at least ask a more correctly phrased question: "What experiences *interacting* with what genetic history lead to what pattern of mental abilities?" One example of this sort of interaction is that brighter parents tend to have brighter children. Does this prove that genetic influence is of paramount importance? Not necessarily, because all parents transmit to their offspring not only their genes but also their "culture"; parents provide the environment in which the children develop.

Thus, because brighter parents tend to be richer, more educated, and generally more advantaged (which is the chicken and which the egg?) than the less bright parents, the following will also tend to be true: The brighter mother will have been better nourished and given better medical care before and during pregnancy and her infant will be better fed throughout its early development; her child-rearing practices will instill in her child stronger attitudes and expectations of intellectual attainment; the brighter parent will also be able (and motivated) to provide, as early as possible, better educational opportunities. All these factors, as we shall soon see, benefit mental growth. Therefore, to ask whether better genes or a better environment is responsible for a child's higher IQ is meaningless. We do not and cannot know because we can assess only the effects of the *uncontrolled interaction* of the genetic and environmental factors.

To most psychologists all this has been clear for a long time. Nevertheless, the question "How much genetic, how much environmental?" continues to be asked. The persistence of this question and the many attempts to answer it are best regarded as social-psychological phenomena carrying ideological and political con-

notations. As such, the question deserves our attention as social psychologists. But aside from these implications, the debate is scientifically futile.

As we proceed to examine environmental-hereditary interactions in producing variations in mental abilities, we must, for the moment, put aside something we learned from Units 8 and 9: that intelligence is composed of many, relatively separate, abilities. The bulk of pertinent research employs some form of overall IQ as the critical measure. And these mental test scores, although gathered by a variety of methods, show an impressive regularity when taken together. The general conclusion among researchers is this: Heredity *is* important, but the contribution of hereditary and environmental factors is, with a few exceptions, always an interactive one. (For some of the possible exceptions, see Box 10.1, p. 206.)

In 1963 Erlenmeyer-Kimling and Jarvik summarized the results from fifty-two studies (and ninety-nine different groups) reported in the past half-century on the problem of human intelligence and heredity (see Figure 10.1, p. 206). Despite enormous differences among these studies in a number of important characteristics—socioeconomic composition and nationality of the sample (data from eight countries were included), and types of tests used—the general picture that emerges is strikingly consistent and clear: *The closer the genetic relation among people, the more alike they are in IQ.* [Dobzhansky (1973) reports summaries of data from a larger number of studies (including those just mentioned), which result in almost identical median values.] These correlations probably represent minimal values because the studies have dealt with data from childhood, when the correlations are likely to be lower (see Box 10.2, p. 207). The unmistakable influence of environment can, however, be seen throughout in the higher correlations for identically related individuals reared together than for individuals reared apart. (Also note the difference between unrelated persons reared together and apart.)

Figure 10.1 gives us a quick, generalized, overall view of the relation of genetic closeness to IQ. Let us now examine this relation.

BOX 10.1

ONE CHROMOSOME—ONE GENE—ONE MENTAL ABILITY—*BUT* IN AN ENVIRONMENT

The contribution of environment toward the determination of mental ability is never zero. This dictum can be regarded as an article of faith, an obvious logical necessity, or an empirically demonstrated finding—but no psychologist or geneticist would question it. Nevertheless, for some intellectual traits, or mental propensities, or patterns of mental abilities, it has been shown that heredity exerts a clearly overwhelming influence. Sometimes single chromosomes or even a single gene may be the determining factor. Some examples:

The *missing* X chromosome in Turner's syndrome leads to a highly specific pattern of mental abilities. Thus, girls with this syndrome tend to be above average in verbal abilities but deficient in spatial abilities, according to J. Money.

The *extra* chromosome in Down's syndrome (sometimes still referred to by its old and racist term "mongolism") leads to a profound and general deficit in mental abilities. Individuals with this extra chromo-

some consistently earn IQs of about 50 to 60. Training is helpful, but even the best training available results in gains of only 10 IQ points, reports N. Bayley.

Where there is a normal complement of forty-six chromosomes, a single recessive gene on the X chromosome can influence the ability of the person to visualize three-dimensional space. In an extensive study of parents and offspring in 167 families, R. D. Bock and D. Kolakowski estimated that almost 50 percent of the variability shown by their subjects for this ability was attributable to this one gene.

Various kinds of mental retardation are caused by different enzymatic deficiencies. The *one-gene-one-enzyme credo* is held by most geneticists. Unquestionably, as time and human genetic research go on, more and more direct relations will be found between specified genetic factors and specified mental functions. And yet—we repeat—the contribution of environment toward the determination of mental ability is never zero.

N. BAYLEY, L. RHODES, B. GOOCH, & N. MARCUS. A comparison of the growth and development of institutionalized and home-reared mongoloids: A follow-up study. In Hellmuth (Ed.), *Exceptional Infant.* Vol. II. *Studies in Abnormality.* New York: Brunner-Mazel, 1971.

R. D. BOCK & D. KOLAKOWSKI. Further evidence of sex-linked major-gene influence on human spatial visualizing ability. *American Journal of Human Genetics,* 1973, **25**, 1–14.

J. MONEY. Two cytogenetic syndromes: Psychological comparison, intelligence and specific factor quotients. *Journal of Psychiatric Research,* 1964, **2**, 223–231.

TWIN STUDIES OF GENETIC INFLUENCE

Because identical twins are genetically the same they represent an obvious focus for comparison with other pairs of siblings whose genetic closeness is necessarily less. Logically and traditionally, such twin studies fall into two classes: first, comparisons between identical twins reared together and identical twins reared apart and, second, comparisons between identical twins reared together and fraternal twins (and siblings) reared together.

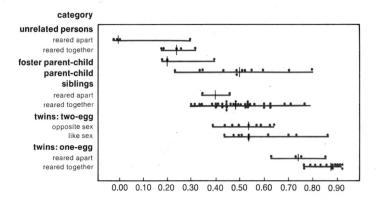

FIGURE 10.1 Correlation coefficients for IQ. The categories are arranged so that genetic closeness increases, reading down the column. Many different mental tests were used to determine IQ. The individual correlation coefficients for each group are indicated by a colored dot; median values are shown by vertical lines. Parent-child correlations are based upon the average of both parents' IQs when possible; otherwise, only mothers' IQs were included.

L. Erlenmeyer-Kimling & L. F. Jarvik. Genetics and intelligence: A review. *Science,* 1963, **142**, 1477–1478; copyright 1963 by the American Association for the Advancement of Science; adapted by permission.

BOX 10.2 ·

AGE, SEX, AND INHERITANCE

That heredity plays an important role in intelligence has been well established, particularly in studies of parent-child resemblances in intelligence. The extent of these parent-child relations has appeared quite variable, however, with different studies reporting different values. One suggested reason for this variation in findings is that parent-child resemblances in mental-test scores may increase as the child grows older. Inasmuch as the various studies dealt with groups differing in age, we might then expect the observed differences in findings.

At least two considerations support the reasonableness of the first hypothesis. For one, the tests used to measure intelligence are quite different at different ages; therefore, an increasing parent-child correlation might arise from increasing similarity in the test applied to both parent and child. But, this factor aside, it would be reasonable to assume that any genetic factor would express itself best when both parent and child were in comparable stages of development; thus a parent's IQ at, say, age six should be the best predictor of the child's IQ at age six. By the same reasoning we would expect that the adult IQ of a parent would predict the adult IQ of the offspring better than would the offspring's IQ at some earlier age. And on this matter we have the following data.

Marjorie Honzik of the University of California, Berkeley, presents data on the increasing correlation between estimates of parental intelligence and the IQ of children over the age range from twenty-one months through fifteen years. Additionally, she presents data on the rate of growth of parent-child resemblance for boys and girls separately. These findings are based upon a longitudinal investigation of more than 100 children of each sex. Estimating parental intelligence from their education, Honzik presents correlations of these estimates for mothers and fathers with children's IQs from childhood into adolescence (see figure).

Two clear conclusions can be drawn from the results in this figure. The first is that parental education does not relate to children's intelligence initially

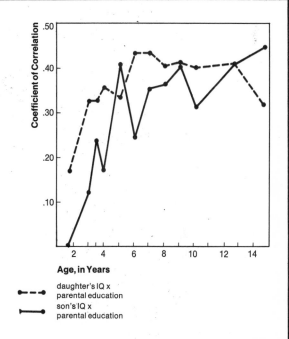

Age, in Years

- - - - daughter's IQ x
        parental education

———— son's IQ x
        parental education

but does so after a certain age. A study by R. Heber, R. Dever, and J. Conry, which actually measured mothers' IQs, supports this general conclusion, especially for the lower range of mental ability. They found that the average IQs of children tested before three years of age were *no different* for those whose mothers' mean IQs were above or below 80. However, the older children of these same two groups of mothers showed increasing IQ differences so that, for those fourteen years old or older, the average difference was over 25 IQ points.

The second conclusion is that girls reach this age of significant correlation earlier than boys do. The implication to be drawn from these data is that a genetically based sex difference exists in rate of mental development, paralleling the well-established earlier physical maturation of girls. That is, girls come into their adult inheritance—intellectual as well as physical—earlier than boys do.

M. P. HONZIK. A sex difference in the age of onset of the parent-child resemblance in intelligence. *Journal of Educational Psychology*, 1963, **54**, 231–237.
R. HEBER, R. DEVER, & J. CONRY. The influence of environment and genetic variables in intellectual development. In H. J. Prehm, L. A. Hamerlynck, & J. E. Crosson (Eds.), *Behavioral Research in Mental Retardation*. Eugene, Ore.: University of Oregon Press, 1968.

Identical Twins Reared Apart

Figure 10.2 summarizes the results of four major studies, obtained by various tests and at different ages, of the IQs of 122 pairs of identical twins reared apart. Despite the differences in ages when tested, the differences in mental tests used, and the differences in when the twins were moved to separate homes, the four studies yield highly similar values for mean IQ differences between identical twin pairs. These differences are quite small, hardly more than the change in IQ one might expect when testing the same individual on two different occasions. The inference from these data is clearly of the powerful effect of genetic identity on the development of mental ability. There seems to be little room left for environmental modification.

But there is much more to the story, as we shall see throughout this unit. For the moment, however, it should be noted that the largest difference (at the extreme right of Figure 10.2)—24 IQ points for a pair of female twins from the Newman et al. study—hints at the possible important contribution of a substantial difference in environmental history. These twin sisters had been separated when they were eighteen months old. One of the girls was reared in the backwoods; she had only two years of formal schooling. Her sister was brought up in a prosperous farming community and she had gone through college. When these twins were tested at the age of thirty-five, the woman who had gone to college received an IQ score 24 points higher than her sister received.

This single case represents an exception in the difference in environments of the twins reared apart. Generally there is a tendency, when circumstances force the separation of twins (or of any siblings), *to find homes that are roughly similar* with respect to cultural type, educational level of foster parents, and the like. To the extent that this was true in the four studies summarized in Figure 10.2 the environmental differences for any pair of twins would have been relatively small; consequently, the fact that these identical twins were reared apart does not provide as good a test of the pure influence of heredity as might appear. Also, the fact that all subjects in these studies were Caucasian necessarily restricts the generality of the overall findings. Nonetheless, these data, while not *proving* anything, clearly support the hypothesis that genetic identity is in large part responsible for the striking similarity in IQ of identical twins. A comparative look at correlational data on identical and fraternal twins (and siblings) reared together will provide another perspective.

Twin Correlations in IQ

First, let us note (from Figure 10.1) that the average correlation in IQ for identical twins

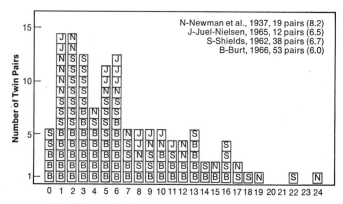

FIGURE 10.2 Distributions of differences in IQ between pairs of twins reared apart. Four separate studies from the United States, England, and Denmark are combined; they differ in mental tests used, age at testing, and age at which the twins were separated. There was a total of 122 pairs of twins in all four studies combined. For five of these pairs, for example, there was a 9-point difference in IQ. One of these five pairs came from the Burt study, two from the Shields study, and one each from the Newman and the Juel-Nielsen studies. The parenthetical values are the average differences in IQ between twins in each study.

Adapted from Jensen, 1972.

reared apart is about .73; for identical twins reared together, it is larger: about .87. This is another indication of the influence on mental ability of being raised in the same home. But now look at the correlation for nonidentical (fraternal, or two-egg) twins reared together. The value, again read from Figure 10.1, is about .53. Since fraternal twins are genetically no more alike than siblings born at different times, it comes as no surprise that the average IQ resemblance of siblings, when reared together (about .49) is very similar to the fraternal-twin average (.53). In fact, they are so close as to justify combining them (.53 and .49) to produce an average value, for nonidentical siblings reared together, of about .51. Finally, Figure 10.1 also yields an estimate of .40 for siblings reared apart.

We now have the data to produce Table 10.1. What does it tell us? First: Heredity is a

TABLE 10.1 CORRELATIONS IN INTELLIGENCE AMONG IDENTICAL TWINS AND NONIDENTICAL SIBLINGS REARED TOGETHER AND APART

Environmental Variable	Genetic Variable	
	Identical Twins	Nonidentical Siblings
Reared together	.87	.51
Reared apart	.73	.40

significant factor. Identical twins are more alike in IQ, whether reared together or apart, than are other siblings (i.e., .87 and .73 for identical twins versus the corresponding correlations of .51 and .40 for the other siblings). Second: Environment also plays a significant role: Either identical or nonidentical siblings, when reared together, are somewhat more similar in mental ability than when reared apart (i.e., .87 and .51 for those reared together versus the corresponding correlations of .73 and .40 for those reared apart.)

There are other data, of a different sort, that bear on the general question. We now turn to these.

PARENT-CHILD RESEMBLANCE IN INTELLIGENCE

Parents and their children show an average correlation in IQ of about .50 (Figure 10.1). This

fact, standing alone, has an equivocal bearing upon the heredity-environment issue because, as we have already noted, parents and children typically share environments as well as genes. Again the reared-apart–reared-together contrast proves useful. This time the comparison is made between children reared with their biological parents and children reared apart from their biological parents. In one longitudinal study, Skodak and Skeels (1949) found that adopted children's IQs, tested repeatedly between the ages of two and fourteen years, showed an increasing relation to the IQ and education of their biological mothers. In contrast, at no age was there a significant correlation with the educational level of their *foster* mothers, who had been responsible for rearing the children from earliest infancy.

These Skodak-Skeels data on adopted children have been compared with parent-child IQ correlations found in another longitudinal study of children who were raised by their biological parents (Honzik, 1957). This comparison is shown in Figure 10.3, p. 210. The similarity in curves from the two studies for both mother and father, in developmental trend as well as in eventual level, gives ample support to Honzik's conclusion that these relations are largely genetic. However, it would be incorrect to infer from these data that the adoptive parental home is not an important environmental factor in the development of children's mental ability. The IQs of these adopted children did show a substantial average increase, probably because of their exposure to a richer intellectual environment when it occurred in the adoptive homes. In the Skodak-Skeels study the average IQ of the biological mothers was 86; of their children 106, an increase of *20* IQ points.

Does this contradict Honzik's conclusion, stressing the influence of heredity? Not if one understands that mothers' and children's IQs may be substantially *correlated* without implying that their *average values* are the same. A correlation coefficient measures only the extent to which pairs of individual scores occupy the same relative position, or rank (see Appendix, p. 832). Thus, conceivably, all the children's IQs could have been higher than any of the biological mothers' IQs, and still this would have had

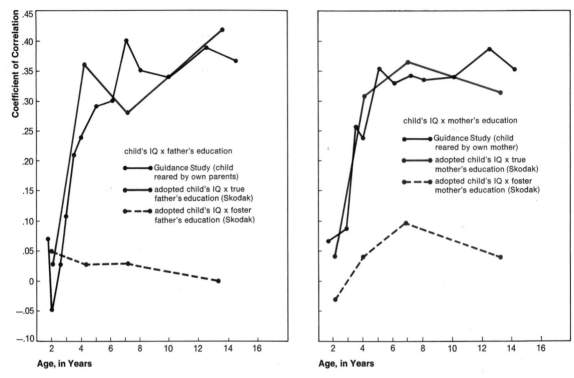

FIGURE 10.3   Trends in parent-child intelligence correlations for children reared together with biological parents and children reared apart from biological parents. The two upper curves in each half of the figure directly compare the relative influence of biological parents upon their children's intelligence—in the one case when the children are reared by their own parents (from the Berkeley Guidance Study at the University of California reported by Honzik), in the other when reared by foster parents (Skodak and Skeels). The two curves are essentially identical in both instances. By contrast, the foster parents' intelligence has a negligible correlation with the intelligence of their adopted children.

M. P. Honzik. Developmental studies of parent-child resemblance in intelligence. *Child Development*, 1957, **28**, 215–228; © 1957 by The Society for Research in Child Development, Inc.; adapted by permission.

no effect on their correlation for mental ability, that is, the brightest mother might still have the brightest child, even if the brightest mother's score was substantially below that of her child. This total independence of correlations and average differences as measures of similarity must be kept in mind in correctly evaluating any of the data presented in this unit. This caution is important because exclusive attention to correlations between parents and children may seem to favor *genetic contributions*: Brighter mothers have brighter children; ergo heredity is all-important. Or exclusive attention to average differences between parents and children may create the illusion of *environmental dominance*:

A child who has been raised in a stimulating environment is much brighter than its biological mother; ergo environment is all-important. Yet a very large average difference in IQ (or any characteristic) between relatives may still be accompanied by a very high correlation between their scores.

ENVIRONMENTAL INFLUENCES ON INTELLIGENCE

The Skodak-Skeels data are consistent with the assumption that a foster home that provides an intelligence-stimulating family environment can raise a child's IQ. That early experience can influence basic intelligence is a position that psychologists have increasingly come to adopt. This view has been furthered by evidence from experimental work with animals (Krech, 1968). Studies have demonstrated that, when greater opportunity for mental stimulation is given to young rats—for example, by devising living cages that permit and encourage a wide range of sensory experiences and problem-solving activities—not only are the adult animals better learners but there are changes in brain structure and in brain chemistry that may be related to increased mental ability. (Some of this evidence is reviewed in Unit 18.)

Stimulation in the Home

Working with infants raised in their own homes, Yarrow (1963) found that the amount and quality of mothers' stimulation of their children showed substantial relations to the children's development, assessed as early as six months old. To cite a specific result: A correlation of .65 was found between a child's IQ at six months and amount of time spent by the mother in social interaction with her child. A later study by Yarrow et al. (1972) considers more specifically the relative values of animate, or *social, stimulation* and *inanimate stimulation* (by objects such as toys) on the abilities and skills of five-month-old infants. When the level of social stimulation in the home was high and varied, babies vocalized more and showed more goal-directed behavior, as evidenced by more "persistent and purposeful attempts to secure objects just out of reach." Put another way, infants were more responsive vocally and more adaptive in their play when they lived in a home where the mother or caretaker was responsive to their presence and behavior. Inanimate stimulation (assessed by the nature and complexity of objects typically within the child's immediate environment), which some experimenters caution us must be selectively and carefully done (see figure 10.4), also correlated with infants' goal-directed behaviors as well as their attraction to novel objects—but did not correlate with their vocalizing. In short, both types of stimulation were associated with positive as-

FIGURE 10.4 Some educators would bombard the child from infancy on with every kind of stimulus change imaginable. His crib is festooned with jumping beads and dangling colored bits and pieces of wood (all sold very expensively to his affluent parents); he is given squishy, squeaking, squawking toys to play with, to fondle, to be frightened by, to choke on. He is jounced and bounced and picked up and put down. And when he goes to school—he finds the same blooming, buzzing confusion. He is stimulated with play activities, with opportunities for social interaction, with rhythmic movements, with music, with visual displays, with contact sports, with tactual experiences, and with anything and everything which the school system can think of—or afford. But it may be that a "stimulating environment" and an "enriched environment" are not one and the same thing.

David Krech. Psychoneurobiochemeducation. *California Monthly* (University of California Alumni Association), June–July 1969, 14–21.

pects of cognitive growth even at so early an age.

What are the long-term effects of these early experiences? Honzik (1972) reports for the Berkeley Guidance Study that affectional relations in the home, determined when the children were less than two years of age, correlated significantly with mental-test scores and especially with verbal abilities at forty years of age. Also, IQs derived from nonverbal subtests for these middle-aged subjects related to how lively and energetic their mothers were thirty-eight years ago! (And none of these predictive characteristics were themselves correlated with the mothers' IQs.) Perhaps we may interpret this relation to mean that an energetic mother is more responsive and provides a wider variety of play experiences for her young children. Such a hypothesis relates to the Yarrow finding that the variety and nature of the playthings provided for the infant are related to later exploratory and goal-directed behavior, both reasonable precursors of certain mental abilities.

It is impressive to find reliable, if modest, predictions of adult intelligence from such early measures of family environment and all within a normal range. Is it reasonable to expect that deliberate intervention to heighten social stimulation may help the mental development of children who live in environments in which such stimulation is now lacking? Such deliberate intervention has been tried. What were the results?

Intervention into Low-Stimulation Environments

Children who grow up in orphanages and similar institutions that provide them with reasonable physical care but neglect their need to interact with other people appear generally retarded and earn mental-test scores that are significantly below average. In a few instances, children who have spent their early years in such institutions have later lived in more stimulating environments; the results were clearly beneficial. Dennis and Najarian (1957), for example, reported that, for children raised in a Lebanese crèche (orphanage) where physical care was adequate but social stimulation minimal, the average IQ was 97 at two months of age but quickly deteriorated so that, for ages three to twelve months, the average IQ was 68. However, older children (about age five) who had also been raised in this crèche had IQs averaging about

100. How did this come about? The investigators believed that the procedures of admission to the crèche had not changed nor had its style of care and that the older children probably had also been retarded in their infancy. What seems to have been the saving experience for the older children was the relatively more stimulating environment provided by their subsequent participation in a kindergarten. Apparently this experience offset the effects of severe deprivation during the first year of life. This finding is, of course, encouraging since it suggests that the effects of early deprivation may not be permanent but may be compensated for by later and better experiences.

The effects of early deprivation *and* early compensation can be long-lasting. Perhaps the most dramatic and persuasive finding has been reported by Skeels (1966). He compared the adult status of two groups of subjects who, for their first two years, were reared in the socially deprived setting of an orphanage because of the inability, for various reasons, of their families to care for them. One group was subsequently transferred to an institution for the mentally retarded. This group, with an average IQ of 64 at about age two, there participated in an experimental program that involved a radical change from the usual institutional environment. Each child in this experimental group was assigned to the daily care of an older girl, herself mentally retarded, for about two years and remained in her charge until later adoption. The arrangement guaranteed a considerable degree of social stimulation for the child of the experimental group. A control group consisted of somewhat brighter children (average IQ of 87), who had remained in the orphanage—a setting that provided much less social stimulation for them. Skeels found startling differences between the experimental and control groups in their adult achievements; the differences all favored the group that had experienced greater social stimulation during their early years. For one thing, all members of the experimental group were found to be self-supporting, whereas 40 percent of the control group were still cared for in institutions. The average number of years of schooling for the experimental group was over twelve years (high school graduation level), whereas only one member of the control group had completed high school. These findings certainly point to a substantial increase in mental ability for the experimental group from their earlier severely retarded level, once again through a relatively brief period of informal compensatory education.

Compensatory education   There have been many recent attempts at deliberate and focused intervention—*Project Headstart* is the most familiar one—which aim at nurturing early mental development. Such attempts are often referred to as "compensatory education," and they are just that—compensatory. As such, their objective is not the raising of the ultimate ceiling and the turning of children into "superminds." Rather, compensatory education seeks only to bring a child closer to the level of cognitive ability that she would have achieved had she not come from a disadvantaged group.

Gray and Klaus (1965) led one such attempt; they designed and conducted a summer program for preschool children who came from home environments of relatively low intellectual and social stimulation. The abundantly staffed program provided specific training in cognitive skills in order to head off the progressive retardation usually found in those children after entering formal schooling. The program also placed great emphasis upon changing the child's (and his family's) *attitudes* toward learning. Explicit attempts were also made to establish close personal relations with the children. Some of the encouraging results of this study, comparing the performance of one group of children who had two ten-week training sessions in consecutive summers with the performance of a control group of equal intelligence who had no such training, can be seen in Figure 10.5.

By the seventh year of their program and after some of their alumni had gone through the first few elementary school grades, Gray and Klaus (1970) were able to report their midstream conclusion. The program children had managed to maintain somewhat higher mental-test scores relative to the control group, but they had lost their earlier advantage on language and achievement measures. Thus, regarding the ability of brief but concentrated

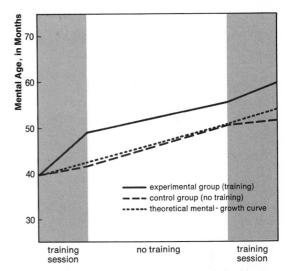

FIGURE 10.5 Preschool-training effects on intelligence. The dotted line represents *expected* normal growth in mental age from about age four on for a child whose IQ is 87 (Stanford-Binet) at that age. (This was the average IQ of the children in both groups at the start of the study.) Relative to this theoretical base line, the children receiving two ten-week training sessions not only showed greater than normal growth during the sessions but also maintained their advantage over the period of almost ten months between sessions. The control groups, by contrast, actually lost some ground during this period (their rate of mental development begins to fall below the theoretical curve), indicating that culturally disadvantaged children may be subject to a *progressive decline* in IQ relative to normally developing children with the same intelligence range.

S. Gray & R. A. Klaus. An experimental preschool program for culturally deprived children. *Child Development*, 1965, **36**, 887–898; © 1965 by The Society for Research in Child Development, Inc.; adapted by permission.

programs to break the progressively greater retardation patterns in ability and school achievement so common for disadvantaged children, the researchers present both a promise and a caution. Their words are worth quoting at length since their message speaks directly to such critics of intervention programs as Jensen (1969), who are ready to pronounce their failure and overdue demise.

Our answer as to whether such retardation can be offset is one of cautious optimism. The effects of our intervention program are clearly evidenced through the second year of public schooling, 1 year after intervention ceased. There is still an effect, most apparent in the Stanford-Binet, after 2 more years of nonintervention. . . .

Still, it is clear from our data, with a parallel decline across the four groups in the second through fourth grades, that an intervention program before school entrance, such as ours, cannot carry the entire burden of offsetting progressive retardation. By some standards the Early Training Project might be seen as one of relatively massive intervention. And yet [it has been] . . . estimated that in the years prior to school entrance the maximum amount of time that the children in the project could have spent with the Early Training Project staff was approximately 600 hours, less than 2 percent of their waking hours from birth to 6 years. Perhaps the remarkable thing is that the effect lasted as well and as long as it did. In a similar vein, we have estimated the amount of these contacts in the home as a maximum of 110 hours, or about 0.3 percent of the waking hours of the child from birth to 6 years. Surely it would be foolish not to realize that, without massive changes in the life situation of the child, home circumstances will continue to have their adverse effect upon the child's performance.

In an earlier report, these same investigators presented an analysis of intervention programs, one that they regard as underscored by their 1970 data. It is this:

. . . The most effective intervention programs for preschool children that could possibly be conceived cannot be considered a form of inoculation whereby the child forever after is immune to the effects of a low-income home and of a school inappropriate to his needs. Certainly, the evidence on human performance is overwhelming in indicating that such performance results from the continual interaction of the organism with its environment. Intervention programs, well conceived and executed, may be expected to make some relatively lasting changes. Such programs, however, cannot be expected to carry the whole burden of providing adequate schooling for children from deprived circumstances; they can provide only a basis for future progress in schools and homes that can build upon that early intervention.

Clearly, compensatory education programs have by no means had their day in court.

A negative verdict is premature—it expects too much to have been done by too few. As Gray and Klaus argue, much more is involved in mental development than can be satisfied by formal training programs, especially short-term ones. For the child to learn and to grow intellectually he needs many things—and some of them have nothing to do with psychology or education (see Box 10.3, p. 216).

Sex, Personality, and IQ Change

Sontag, Baker, and Nelson (1958) compared children who showed substantial increases in IQ from age six to age ten with those who showed decreases during the same interval. One general finding was that boys were more likely to gain in IQ and that girls were more likely to lose. A number of personality traits were associated with the gains: competitiveness, independence, verbal aggressiveness, and persistence in efforts to master difficult and challenging problems. Furthermore—and this seems consistent with this trait picture—highly feminine girls were least likely to increase in IQ. The overall picture can be fairly summarized as indicating that highly achievement-motivated children may be able to increase their tested intelligence during the elementary school years and that this motivation appears somewhat incompatible with what we regard as high femininity.

Haan (1963) partially confirms but qualifies this latter finding in her own study of correlates of IQ change in men and women over the age range of twelve to thirty-seven years. Here again, men more often than women increased their IQs during this period. The women who did show gains showed IQ changes that clearly reflected their changes in personality. Women who were tomboys as adolescents but who, in adulthood, had become more feminine were more likely to increase in verbal intelligence. Women showing the reverse trend—highly feminine in adolescence but less so when adult—tended to show gains on a measure of intelligence involving arithmetic ability.

A common thread running through the Sontag et al. and the Haan studies involves the masculinity-femininity dimension. Males more often than females show increases in IQ; traits usually regarded as masculine appear to be associated with IQ increases either in males or in females.

Another common theme of the two investigations seems to fall somewhere in the motivational area: The direction of IQ change was associated with particular styles of motivational functioning. For both sexes, persons most likely to gain in IQ were those who as adults characteristically employed coping mechanisms (realistic and flexible approaches to problem situations) rather than defense mechanisms (inappropriate and maladaptive forms of behavior). (Both types of mechanisms are discussed in Unit 23.)

It is probably inferring too much from these data to claim that they plainly demonstrate the importance, in IQ gain, of a strong and realistically applied drive to learn and master environmental challenges. But such a formulation clearly fits these data and is in line with other evidence that the subject's motivation to succeed on any test of mental ability contributes to his more effective performance.

The general point that motivation may affect performance on a mental test has wide and significant social implications. It suggests that situational factors—extrinsic to the individual's intelligence—may help to determine the IQ score by raising or lowering motivation. Particularly important are such situational social factors as the degree of rapport between the tester and the person tested and the type of social setting in which the testing takes place. All these factors, as we shall see, can cause major difficulties in interpreting group differences in mental-test performance.

GROUP DIFFERENCES IN INTELLIGENCE

If the world's population consisted of a single set of 3 billion identical siblings then, obviously, any variation in mental ability among the 3 billion individuals would necessarily result solely from variations in their environments—nutritional, meteorological, cultural, psychological. On the other hand, if all the world's present population (composed, as it is, of genetically *different* people) had been exposed since their very conception to identical environments, then any variation in mental abilities would necessarily result solely from the genetic differences among them. Of course—and fortunately—neither of these propositions even remotely resembles the true state of humankind. It is the wonder and saving grace of humanity that genetic *and* environmental diversity is infinite. And, if we recognize that almost any given genetic endowment may interact with any given environment in an adaptive manner, we can begin to understand the remarkable diversity in which human beings can express their genetic and environmental interactions.

Considering the facts of diversity and interaction, it becomes clear why we said on page 205 that we cannot determine the degree to which individual differences in intelligence for all people can be apportioned—so much to genetic influences and so much to environmental influences. If we cannot even deal with individual differences in intelligence, how much less able are we to speak of the *level* of intelligence as having a fixed balance of hereditary and environmental determination for all people for all time. Whatever data we have thus far reported are valid, but *they are valid only for the particular environments and the particular genetic populations from which they have been drawn.* And, with few exceptions, these data are from Western cultures in recent years and from individuals in these cultures well within so-called normal ranges of genetic endowment and environmental exposures. It is only for these populations that the legitimate inference can be drawn that differences in mental abilities are substantially related to genetic factors. With other populations and other environments, the substantial influence of genetics might very well be decreased. We now turn our attention to the study of variation in intelligence among differing populations.

Social-Class Differences

It is in the area of socioeconomic differences in intelligence that the evidence for group differences is most solid. What are the facts? First, while the Western world may strive to be an open society, that is, one in which the more

BOX 10.3

MALNUTRITION AND HUMAN INTELLIGENCE

Evidence has been mounting in recent years that the level of nutrition of the organism, *before and after birth,* plays a central role in mental development. Adequate nutrition has been found essential for the normal growth of the brain, both *in utero* and during the first months of the infant's life—the period within which the brain nearly completes its full development. M. Winick points to a specific effect of malnutrition upon brain growth, observing that "when growth is studied in cellular terms, it becomes clear that an organ moves from a stage in which growth is by increase in cell *number* to one of growth in cell *size. Undernutrition during the first stage may leave a deficit in cell number.*" (emphasis added) Since the human brain passes through much of this first stage during the gestation period of the fetus, insufficient *fetal* nourishment inevitably means a reduction in brain-cell number well below that which normally would have developed. Once this first stage of cell-number growth is over no additional brain cells can ever be developed so far as we now know. In short, the effect of fetal malnutrition seems to be an *irreversible* deficit in the number of brain cells and thus a presumed deficit in mental functioning. Also, research evidence suggests that fetal growth is dependent not only on the nutrients supplied via the placenta by the mother's intake of food *during* pregnancy but also—and perhaps to an even greater extent—on the mother's own nutritional state prior to pregnancy.

These various conclusions are drawn from experimental investigations of animals and from studies of people in underdeveloped nations where chronic malnutrition unfortunately exists for much of the population. H. G. Birch and J. D. Gussow of the Albert Einstein College of Medicine summarize a large number of such human studies (in Guatemala, Mexico, South Africa, and Yugoslavia), which demonstrate that severely malnourished children have significantly lower IQs than relatively better-nourished children from the same countries. An even more fundamental study of the effect of malnourishment on the brain has been by measurement of its DNA content (see Box 1.1, p. 12, for a discussion of DNA). The rate of increase in DNA during development is directly related to the increase in cell number. It has been possible to assess the DNA content of the brains of infants who died of malnourishment compared with infants who died of other causes. The brains of the malnourished infants had significantly less DNA than did those of the normally nourished infants. Also, the placenta, which is a fetal organ, reflects the cellular DNA content of the baby including its brain, and the placenta of poorly nourished mothers has been found by Winick and others to be significantly below average in cellular DNA content. These data, taken together, clearly indicate that the normal development of the infant brain depends upon the adequacy of the mother's nutrition.

Since human studies have typically involved chronically malnourished populations, it has not previously been possible to separate the effects of long-term semistarvation of the mother from the effects of undernutrition solely during pregnancy and the infant's earliest months. But a recent report by a team of public health researchers from Columbia University (Stein et al.) examined the effects on adult mental abilities when severe starvation was restricted solely to the critical period. That is, the mothers in the study suffered from malnutrition only while they were pregnant and immediately after birth of the infant—the rest of the time they were adequately nourished, and their children, after the first few months of postnatal life, were also well nourished.

World War II provided a natural experiment. For a period of about seven months from 1944 to 1945 the Germans, in reprisal for Dutch resistance during the German occupation, imposed a severe embargo on food supplies for a certain region of Holland. During this period, famine was severe; rations dipped to the level of 450 calories per day, about one-third of even minimal nutritional need.

The investigation compared the mental abilities of about 20,000 Dutch males (at age nineteen), whose mothers' pregnancies and their own first months of life occurred during this famine, with the mental abilities of about 100,000 other Dutch males whose critical period of brain-cell development came somewhat before or after the famine. (Also included in the comparison group were nineteen-year-old males from Holland where food supplies had not been subject to the embargo.)

The results of this comparison can be briefly stated: *No differences.* Do these results disprove brain developmental susceptibility to malnutrition? By no means. It is known that the unborn child has first call on whatever nutrients are available in the mother's body. Perhaps the safest inference to draw is that, since the population of Holland was well nourished before the war and relatively so until the imposed famine, Dutch mothers had nutritional reserves sufficient to permit the normal development of their offspring. But in areas of the world where near-starvation is chronic, it seems reasonable to continue to assume that mental development is significantly impaired for many children.

Lower mental capacity caused by maternal and fetal malnutrition is an environmental phenomenon, not a genetic one. This fact suggests yet another precaution that must be taken before valid interpretations can be reached of any differences in mental abilities between different societies or different socioeconomic groups within a given society. Much more important, however, is the clear mandate for direct social action. As D. B. Coursin argues, in concluding his review of the most recent data on nutrition and mental development:

> . . . [W]e have considered only the scientific aspects of malnutrition and brain function and their contributions to the fundamental understanding of its complexities. However, of equal importance is translation of this scientific information into proper language and relevance for use by those responsible for public policy, so that they may implement action to meet the needs that have been identified. Every government has priorities that are rank ordered according to prevailing circumstances. . . . Interestingly, the potential impact of malnutrition on the developing brain with eventual limitations of capabilities and performance has been a most compelling force that has stimulated universal public concern. It, therefore, has immense potential for influencing policy and action in nutrition and education both nationally and internationally. . . . [W]e are still in need of more information . . . [but in] the meantime, we already have the knowledge and means to eliminate the long-term potential hazards of malnutrition as part of improving the total complex of forces that affect the developing brain.

M. WINICK. Fetal malnutrition and growth processes. *Hospital Practice*, 1970, **33**, 33–41.
H. G. BIRCH & J. D. GUSSOW. *Disadvantaged Children: Health, Nutrition, and School Failure.* New York: Harcourt Brace Jovanovich, 1970.
Z. STEIN, M. SUSSER, G. SAENGER, & F. MAROLLA. Nutrition and mental performance. *Science*, 1972, **178**, 708–713.
D. B. COURSIN. Nutrition and brain development in infants. *Merrill-Palmer Quarterly*, 1972, **18**, 177–202.

capable can move up the social ladder, we are certainly not a classless society. Various communities in this country have been carefully studied by a number of social scientists, and all investigators seem to agree that our society is definitely class-structured as far as sociological measures and behavior of people are concerned. For example, in "Yankee City," the name given to a New England community studied by Warner and Lunt (1941), and in "Oldtown," the name used by Davis, Gardner, and Gardner (1941) for their southern community, six distinct classes seem to exist: the upper-upper, the lower-upper, the upper-middle, the lower-middle, the upper-lower, and the lower-lower. People in each of these classes have parties together, marry into each other's families, and differ from the other classes in education and occupation.

Social classes exist, and the differences among them are defined in terms of differences in wealth, influence, educational level, occupation, and social behavior. Considerable research has involved a comparison of the IQs of people from different socioeconomic levels. Tyler (1956), after reviewing the many studies in this field, concludes that "the relationship of IQ to socioeconomic level is one of the best documented facts in mental test history." It seems quite clear that higher IQs are found among the families of the upper socioeconomic levels than among the lower levels.

We must remember that IQ scores reflect educational opportunities, wealth, and home environments. Because lower socioeconomic groups tend to be disadvantaged in these respects relative to upper socioeconomic groups and because (or, perhaps, as a result) their attitudes toward education tend to be less favorable, a part of the present difference in IQ scores is undoubtedly the result of environmental differences. Nevertheless, it is clear that different occupations require different IQ levels. In a society where complete freedom of opportunity existed, this would mean that each individual would tend to find her or his appropriate occupational group according to her or his IQ.

These possibilities have very important implications for the functioning of a democratic society. But there is an important point that concerns social-class differences in particular: Remember, Unit 1 discussed the fact that heredity means differences as well as similarities between offspring and parents. This fact is especially true for any trait like intelligence that is undoubtedly influenced by a large number of genes or hereditary factors. As a result, even if we should ever reach the point of completely equal opportunity and thereby reach a state where the members of the different socioeconomic levels have different *genetic* mental capacities, *even then we would have to expect within every occupational group to find children who are brighter than their parents and children who are duller.* This expectation is amply confirmed by research findings. The present differences in IQ among the children of parents from various occupational groups are based on *average* figures. We also find wide individual differences within each group and considerable overlap among the groups. One of the most important implications of this genetically determined variability is that, if we wish to maximize the human resources of our society, it becomes essential to create conditions in which each individual, no matter what his socioeconomic background, will be given an opportunity to achieve up to the limit of his potentialities. The daughter of the lawyer or the professor may be limited in her capabilities, while the daughter of the day laborer may have the ability to become our most brilliant scientist. We cannot classify in advance. Genetic theory (see Unit 1) and actual experience affirm that the highly capable person may come from any socioeconomic group. (See Box 10.4 for the spectacular and fortunate failure of a massive attempt to segregate an entire population genetically on the basis of occupation and social status.)

"Race," Genetics, and IQ

Textbook writers in any scientific field are usually only mildly concerned that their summaries of the current state of affairs for any given topic will be embarrassingly out of date by the time they reach their readers. While good research is continuous, it is only occasionally that there is a dramatic research breakthrough that upsets much of the already accumulated lore of a particular science. As for the relatively small increments of knowledge contributed by ongoing research, we file them away for the next edition. It is inevitable therefore that the reader of any published text will be presented, here and there, with statements that are no longer quite accurate. Knowing this, the prudent textbook author writes with caution, seeking to restrain personal preferences.

We suspect that this confession of imperfection will neither surprise nor irreparably devastate any of you. But you may be wondering why we have chosen to pop out suddenly from behind the textbook writers' traditional mask of impersonality and to expose our methods. The answer: the issue of "race" and IQ, as we write in late 1973, has aroused such intense passion and controversy in the scientific (and lay) world that we want to deal with it in a pointed, emphatic manner. To hew strictly to the cautious, restrained, and impersonal line of textbook writers, we would have to say "Sorry, we do not know; sorry, scientific evidence permits you to argue either way; sorry; sorry . . ." to almost every important question that may be of interest to you here.

When there is such controversy over a psychological question, we as textbook writers should not ignore it. Our reasons, then, for including the following discussion are extra-scientific but *not* extra-educational. We hope that the best we can do today—our educated guesses, broad generalizations, value judgments, and even loose prophecies (buttressed throughout by whatever evidence we can muster)—will contribute to the thinking and perhaps even to the education of our students. And these are students who will, inevitably, be drawn into this dispute—even though, from the standpoint of pure science, we might wish that they could avoid such pointless discussions. Of course, we regret that we cannot give students total answers, but we think it improper to wait for the next edition to tell them the carefully thought-out ideas that already exist.

Simply and most fundamentally (and this is our first broad generalization): No one can now give a respectably scientific answer to the question "Are differences in IQ scores between black and nonblack Americans *genetically*

BOX 10.4

THE FAILURE OF CASTE

A foremost geneticist, Theodosius Dobzhansky, provides an instructive commentary on how caste systems have proved both ineffectual and potentially wasteful in their attempts to restrict occupational access to specific groups.

. . . Each of the numerous castes and subcastes in classical India had a business, trade, or work traditionally reserved to it. The problems of training and allocation of status were thus simplified—everybody knew from childhood what the source of his livelihood would be, and in what kind of occupation or toil he must become skilled. Of course, one belonged to the caste of one's parents, and had to marry a person of the same caste. One could not be promoted or demoted to another caste, no matter what one's achievements, failures, talents, or incapacities. Upper-caste status automatically carried with it respect and privilege; lower castes and outcastes ("untouchables") were subjected to gross indignities.

The system was revoltingly unjust from our modern point of view, yet it had a plausible-sounding rationale. Bose [an Indian sociologist], no partisan of the caste system, wrote: "The careful way in which the tradition of close correspondence between caste and occupation was built up is clear indication of what the leaders of Hindu society had in mind. They believed in the hereditary transmissibility of character, and thought it best to fix a man's occupation, as well as his status in life, by means of the family in which he had been born." . . . The fatal flaw of all caste systems is that they are built explicitly or implicitly on such assumptions. . . .

The gene pool of every caste generates endowments whose carriers could perform competently, and even achieve excellence, in occupations reserved by custom for other castes. For the sake of argument, assume that a caste population was at some point in time genetically better adapted than other castes for some task. There existed castes of priests, scholars, warriors, tradesmen, and so on. Could the differential adaptedness be maintained for many generations, except by systematic training of the young in the traditions of their families and ancestors? Genetically conditioned adaptedness will gradually be dissipated. . . . [One reason is that] inept progeny will be pressed to follow their parents' careers despite the genetic incapacity.

Wastage of talent is, in fact, a fatal vice of all caste and rigid class systems. When social mobility is seriously impeded, individuals qualified by their abilities to enter a given occupation are not admitted, and unqualified ones are retained. As the class structure becomes more open, impediments to social mobility decrease, and . . . one's status and role in a society are acquired and not inherited from the parents . . . one's socioeconomic situation is a function of one's ability and achievement, rather than, or at least in addition to, inherited wealth or lack thereof. . . .

The failures of caste systems are understandable in the light of genetics. Human populations, like those of most sexual and outbreeding species, have enormous stores of all kinds of genetic variability. Even with artificial selection directed specifically to this end, it is practically impossible to obtain a population completely homozygous [or identical] for all its genes. . . . Ours, happily, is not Huxley's *Brave New World*. All human populations, even the relatively inbred ones, conserve ample supplies of genetic variance.

Dobzhansky renders this verdict:

The caste system in India was the grandest genetic experiment ever performed on man. The structure of the society endeavored for more than two millennia to induce what we would now call genetic specialization of the caste populations for performance of different kinds of work and functions. Such specialization has not been achieved.

Modern India, having eliminated its caste system legally and, to a substantial extent, culturally, is benefiting from the failure of this "grandest genetic experiment." As India moves increasingly toward an open society, every caste has already produced highly competent individuals in every field of endeavor. And this has been the experience of every society that moved from a traditional class system that defined educational and training opportunities to one where individual ability and motivation to play a particular role in the society determine such access.

Dobzhansky's title for his book implies his essential message: Human equality of opportunity best exploits the enormous potential of genetic diversity—to the benefit of the individual and of his society.

T. DOBZHANSKY. *Genetic Diversity and Human Equality.* New York: Basic Books, 1973.

based?" This is *not* another way of saying "The scientific evidence points either way—take your choice." What we *are* saying is that the very question is scientifically *nonsensical*; that there is no way scientific evidence can be produced to answer a question that attempts to match unmatchable elements.

Throughout this unit we have indicated some of the currently insurmountable difficulties in testing underlying mental abilities—abilities quite different from test-measurable IQ levels. We will repeat some of the general points as they apply to the current question and add a few specific ones.

For reasons to be made clear later, the black-white question is, *scientifically*, an uninteresting, trivial, and, above all, nonresearchable question. Even for public policy, the question of "race" and intelligence is irrelevant. The mandate for public policy is *already* clear: Our democratic ideology, as well as the eminently practical desire of any society that its citizens work at their full potential, maintains that all members of every group be reared in a cultural environment that provides child and adult with full opportunities to develop and fulfill their particular patterns of genetic endowment. Only when this state of affairs has been law *and practice* for several generations will the hypothesis of racial differences in IQ become scientifically testable—if we can then agree on a useful definition of "race." But by then no one will be interested enough to do so. (Here is one of our loose prophecies and personal evaluations.) Nevertheless, the question is given importance today. Why?

Some background　That certain ethnic groups or "races" are, genetically, intellectually inferior to others is an ancient notion. Whatever may be its validity, this idea has traditionally—and frequently—served to salve the consciences of groups of people who, through various forms of power, including temporary technological advantage, have demeaned, conquered, enslaved, or murdered other groups of people. For example, in relatively recent times, we have heard of the "white man's burden" (when Great Britain was conquering its colonies); or of "the savage Indian" (when white Americans were practicing

genocide on American Indians); or, of course, of the "biologically inferior" Jews, Poles, and Gypsies (when the Nazis were attempting genetic purification through wholesale slaughter of these groups).

The dreadful manifestations of these ancient notions are still with us. They may be with us forever, or until we achieve total cultural homogenization, or until we learn to cherish diversity within humankind. As we write this, our world has reached neither point, so that the social soil still continues to nourish avid concern about the supposed genetic merits or demerits of different peoples. American society and indeed the entire world is today undergoing profound social and political restructuring. During such a critical period, old fears and hatreds and rationalizations are revived. And the controversy over the genetic merits or demerits of the whites versus the blacks may be one such revival.

It is to the immediately contemporary aspect of the controversy that we will now attend. We will focus on the black-white comparisons within this country. Comparative data do exist on the patterns of mental ability for other nonwhite groups, as well as for many ethnically different white groups within the United States and even in other countries. However, we shall not deal here with those data because it is on the black-white comparison that today the most data *and* the most reasonable (and unreasonable) arguments *and* the most heated controversy can be found.

What are the data?　We will attempt a brief condensation. For readers who might wish to expand on our brevity or check for possible bias, detailed summaries of data are presented by Coleman (1966) and Shuey (1966) that, taken together, provide an exhaustive compendium based on different orientations. More recently, Jensen's lengthy report in the *Harvard Educational Review* (1969) has come to be the topmost lightning rod for all those who would do battle on this issue. The report, on the basis of a highly detailed analysis of enormous amounts of data, concludes that blacks are inferior to whites in mental abilities and that attempts to erase these performance differences by compensatory education have failed and will continue to fail. (In 1972, Jensen published *Genetics and Education*; it includes the original article, several other reports of his research, a 117-item bibliography of technical and popular articles all published *after* his 1969 report, and a 67-page diarylike preface recounting in detail his personal travail since its publication.) Also reviewing the more recent data, but from still another slant, is Cancro's 1971 volume.

Here are the major questions, as we see them, and our commentaries on each:

1. *Are there really distinguishable black and white races within the United States?*

Note that for the first time we have dropped the quotation marks from around the term *race*. We have not been coy until now; our use of quotation marks was to indicate the easily documented assertion that there are no distinct black and white races in the United States. In this country a black subgroup can be approximately distinguished from a nonblack subgroup, but the distinction is partly biological and partly environmental, with enormous cultural and genetic variation *and overlap* characterizing the the members of both subgroups.

2. *Do today's tests of mental abilities show any differences between blacks and whites?*

We remind you that there are many very different facets of intelligence; but let us adopt the semifiction of the single IQ score as a measure of intelligence, because, for the most part, the research has focused on that. Our answer: Yes, there are differences in IQ scores and the differences favor white children and adults. The average differences between whites and blacks usually run somewhere between 10 and 20 IQ points; that is a substantial amount.

3. *Is there any technique available that can enable us to estimate the extent of genetic influence on group differences in intelligence?*

There is no way of estimating the degree to which genetic factors have determined the actual *level* of human intelligence. There is, however, a statistical technique, used by many psychologists and geneticists, for estimating **heritability,** the contribution of genetic factors to variations in intelligence among the individuals who make up a specified population.

But the concept of heritability is *not* what it sounds like (a trap into which even some educational psychologists and physical scientists have fallen). Heritability does *not* measure the degree to which any trait (e.g., intelligence) is genetically determined. Heritability, generally defined, is the proportion of the total variability of a trait in a given population at a given time that is attributable to genetic differences among the individuals within that population. For example: It will be remembered that in one of our previous illustrations every individual in the world was imagined as immersed in the *same* environment from conception on; the heritability for intelligence differences among them would then necessarily be 100 percent. No matter how large or small the range of differences among the individuals, all of it would be caused by genetic factors. But if our individuals lived in diverse environments, then the heritability for intelligence would, of course, be considerably less than 100 percent, because *part* of the individual differences in intelligence would be caused by environment. In our other illustration, where all people had the same genetic make-up but each lived in a unique environment, heritability would be zero, because *all* differences in intelligence would be caused by environment. Thus it is clear that heritability estimates are applicable only to a given population in a given environment.

Almost all available data on estimates of the heritability of intelligence are for *white and predominantly middle-class American populations.* Such data have yielded estimates that somewhere between 50 and 80 percent of *variations in mental abilities* are caused by genetic factors. (Some of the differences in estimates are the result of differences among the white populations studied. Other differences are the result of technical variations in the mathematical and statistical methods by which these estimates were reached.)

That heritability estimates are not fixed quantities but, rather, apply only to specific populations is a well-known and well-accepted fact. But this fact has somehow been lost during the current controversy concerning racial differences in intelligence. As Dobzhansky (1973) comments:

There has been so much misunderstanding of the significance of the high heritability of IQ that it is imperative to make clear what this heritability does and does not mean. To begin with, it does *not* mean that the IQ . . . is not subject to modification by upbringing and other environmental means. . . . Even more basic is that the *heritability is not an intrinsic property of a trait* but of the population in which it occurs. (emphasis added)

Neither does it make sense to speak of the degree to which a given person's mental abilities are inherited. Lerner (1972) emphasizes this point, as well as the further restriction of heritability estimates to the particular time at which the data were collected:

Heritability . . . is *neither a property of an individual, nor is it expected to be a constant over generations* even in a homogeneous population. Changes in mating system or selection may reduce or increase genetic variation, just as changes in environment may reduce or increase environmental variation. . . . Heritability at any given time depends on both. . . . [Heritability estimates] vary between populations at a given time, and vary within populations from generation to generation. (emphasis added)

We have emphasized our points about heritability because it is so often (and so easily) misunderstood and because to understand it correctly is to perceive the fallacy of many of the arguments supporting the contention that black-white differences in IQ scores are genetically determined.

The Scarr-Salapatek study (1971) of the resemblances in mental abilities between twins provides, for the first time, reliable separate estimates of the heritability of mental abilities in black and white children of different socioeconomic classes. She finds, first of all, that heritability is higher for more advantaged children, *both* black and white. From this she proposes that hereditary potential is more fully expressed the more favorable is the environment for nurturing that specific characteristic. Thus, we could expect that children raised in cultural settings that suppress the full development of their potential intelligence would show signifi-

cantly lower heritability for that characteristic.

Poverty involves being raised in ways that do not stimulate mental development and, in our present society, blacks are likely to be economically poorer than whites. On the basis of this social (*not* hereditary) disadvantage, we could then predict that black children from relatively impoverished environments would have a considerably lower contribution of genetic variance in their mental abilities. And this, in fact, was found in the Scarr-Salapatek study. Her conclusion:

Group differences in mean scores that exist because of environmental deprivation *can* and should be ameliorated. To the extent that children are not given supportive environments for the full development of their *individual genetic differences*, changes can be made in their prenatal and postnatal environments to improve both their overall performance and the genetic variance in their scores. . . . To the extent that better, more supportive environments can be provided for all children, genetic variance *and* mean scores will increase for all groups. (emphasis added)

This quotation clearly asserts that, in a world of full and equal opportunity, genetic endowment will become increasingly *more* important in determining individual differences in intelligence. In a benign environment, genetically derived differences among individuals would tend to become more fully manifest. We would then truly approach a condition of "from each according to his genetic ability."

The conclusion is plain. Heritability, while a useful index for many genetic-environment questions, is of little value in answering the question "To what extent are black-white differences in intelligence caused by genetic influences?"

4. *What would it take to determine conclusively whether genetically based differences in mental abilities between blacks and whites do or do not exist?*

For a time it was believed that an effective way to obtain measures of mental ability that would reflect innate differences in intelligence would be to devise tests that somehow removed the influences of environmental or cultural differences among groups. Toward this end many psychologists have attempted to construct what have been called *"culture-fair" mental tests.* Their basic principle is to avoid test items in which the differential experiences of cultural groups would give one group an advantage over another. Standard tests frequently show higher scores for urban over rural children (though this difference is fast decreasing because television and other mass-communication media are both extending and homogenizing the range of experiences available to the growing rural child) because the standardization samples upon which the tests were based were preponderantly composed of the more accessible urban school population. If the shoe were on the other foot and a typical test item were to read "Which of the following objects is different from the others: *plow, spreader, tractor, harrow,"* the advantage of a rural upbringing is immediately evident. The farm child would be more likely than the city child to spot the correct response (*tractor*).

To devise mental-test items that would favor black children would, if anything, be even easier since there are distinctive elements of black culture with which almost all white schoolchildren (and adults) are totally unfamiliar. Such items have, on occasion, been selected, with the obvious result: Blacks score higher than whites. Of course, the test, again, was not a fair one—to the whites. But is a culture-fair test really possible? Mental-test items *necessarily* refer to objects and events in the real world and one's particular cultural background and experience inevitably will affect one's ability to respond correctly to items, quite apart from one's true mental ability. One way to reduce variation in mental-test scores attributable to such nonintellectual factors is to devise items that refer to objects and events with which practically everyone would have considerable and approximately equal experience. Another approach to a culture-fair test is to seek to balance items in such a way that each group's special experiences will be equally sampled.

Regardless of the approach, efforts at developing culture-fair mental tests have been, at best, only moderately successful. In a limited sense, continuing such efforts may be useful since mental tests—fairly or not—do predict scholastic success in our present-day society.

Whatever can be done to reduce cultural biases in such tests should improve them as measurements of ability to learn; ironically, though, this in turn might result in poorer prediction of school achievement that itself involves culturally biased evaluations.

In any event, mental-test items are just a small part of the problem since the larger challenge is to work toward culture-fair mental *testing.* As we have stressed throughout, many nonintellectual factors enter the situation in which a child's mental ability is presumably the only thing being measured. All too often even the more obvious of these factors may be lost sight of in interpreting his score as a true indication of his current level of ability. Box 10.5, page 224, should be carefully studied, since it provides an inventory of such factors and also gives prescriptions, admittedly expensive ones, for minimizing their unwanted influence on measures of intelligence. But even if all mental testing were to be carried out with the requisite sensitivity to the setting and conditions of test administration, we would *still* be a long way away from eliminating cultural differences as contributors to performance. Enduring motivational forces, one's self-expectations (and the different expectations so frequently held by teachers for their students), one's feelings about his fellow testtakers, all are potent factors influencing performance on mental tests (see Box 10.6, p. 225).

Considering all this we must conclude that culture-fair tests and testing cannot possibly help us assess validly the genetic contribution to presently measurable black-white IQ differences. All the nonintellective influences just discussed (and read again Box 10.3) certainly would be potent as well as totally confusing (for the genetic question) in evaluating the intelligence of blacks. Quite simply, then, only when we have a *culture-fair society* and have had one for many generations will we be able to determine whether genetically based differences in mental abilities between blacks and whites do or do not exist. By then, as we suggested earlier, no one may care to ask the question—not blacks, whites, or any other group within our society. The nonscientific sources of today's interest in the question may very well have disappeared. Until then, scientists might

BOX 10.5

"CULTURE-FAIR" INTELLIGENCE TESTING

Some notion of the number of nonintellectual factors likely to affect performance on mental tests can be gained from a study by Harvard psychologists G. H. Lesser, G. Fifer, and D. H. Clark, which compared the scores on four mental tests of middle- and lower-class children from Chinese, Jewish, black, and Puerto-Rican backgrounds. Let the authors speak for themselves concerning some of the precautions they imposed in order to provide psychologically comparable testing situations:

(1) All tests were administered individually; reading and writing were not required of the children. (2) Directions were stated in the simplest possible terms. (3) Psychological testers who spoke one primary language of the cultural groups (Spanish, Yiddish, several Chinese dialects) administered the tests so that the instructions and test questions could be given in English, in the primary language of the child's cultural group, or (more often) in the most effective combination of the two languages for the particular child. (4) Extensive practice materials were provided in introducing each subtest to insure comprehension of the directions and to allow each child to become familiar with the test materials and the requirements of the task; it was only after the tester was convinced that the child understood what was being asked of him that the scored test items were presented. (5) The pressures of testing were controlled by allowing long periods of acclimation to the testing situation and to the examiner. (6) Testers were recruited from the same cultural group as the child being tested; considerable evidence . . . indicates the importance of matching the general cultural backgrounds of tester and testee. (7) Since each child was tested in his own public-school building, a de-

gree of familiarity with the physical surroundings was insured.

Furthermore, all children who had chronic health problems were eliminated from the samples. If a child appeared temporarily ill or visibly fatigued, testing was postponed to a later occasion. If signs of distress were observed during a testing session, the session was curtailed and resumed at a later date. An especially important precaution was the design of special tests for each mental ability, in consultation with school personnel from each cultural group, in order to ensure that the tests were potentially of high and equal interest to children of all groups. Additionally, the tests were not "speed" tests, that is, each child had more than enough time to do as well as he could on each test item so that cultural differences in a "do things as quickly as possible" attitude and tendencies of individual children to panic when rushed were largely prevented from influencing test performance.

This list of precautions is a partial one; the investigators attended to and attempted to control many other possible influences upon performance— and many of these factors are known to affect performance. When we consider that this study is by no means typical but, rather, represents *extraordinary* care in seeking psychological equivalence in the testing situation, we can only wonder how much of the data that have been reported as indicating intelligence differences among groups can be wholly credited, quite apart from the question of the origins of such differences. By and large, such published reports involve standard mental tests given in standard school situations and, as such, must involve built-in loading of the situation in favor of the cultural majority group.

G. H. LESSER, G. FIFER, & D. H. CLARK. Mental abilities of children from different social-class and cultural groups. *Monographs of the Society for Research in Child Development*, 1965, **30**, No. 4.

well direct their efforts toward the building of a culture-fair society for the nonscientific reason that a culture in which each individual can fulfill his potentialities will work better—and feel better—for all of us. One way is for scientists to talk with those charged with the responsibility of guiding our society—as many indeed already have (see Box 10.7, p. 226).

BOX 10.6

WHOSE STANDARDS?

Almost without exception intelligence tests are standardized on samples drawn from the national population. The intent of test developers is to set up a yardstick that will make possible the comparison of any individual's performance with that of people in general. What follows from this practice is that individuals who are tested regard their scores as indicating where they stand in relation to others in the larger society.

Psychologists I. Katz, E. G. Epps, and L. J. Axelson of New York University proposed that the black tends to view ability tests as measuring him against the standards of the white majority and that his performance on such tests might be affected by this attitudinal factor. To test this hypothesis, 116 undergraduate males from an all-black Florida college were administered a form of digit-symbol substitution task of the sort commonly found in mental tests. The test was administered to three groups of students, each with its special instructions: First, the test was defined as nonevaluative and was said to be given only to elicit students' general interest in that kind of task; second, the test was said to be administered only at that college and would be used to evaluate each student in comparison with his classmates; third, the test "will be used to evaluate your intellectual ability by comparing you with students at other colleges and universities throughout the United States."

Not surprisingly, the nonevaluative condition (instructions 1) called forth the poorest performance. A digit-symbol substitution test is a rather dull activity, and, given the absence of any external motivating factors, the students apparently did not work hard at it. What is less obvious, although predicted by the experimenters, was the finding that performance was consistently poorer under the national norm (instructions 3) than under the college norm (instructions 2). Furthermore, students in the national-norm group rated themselves higher on a "cared about doing well on the task" scale. We are thus confronted with the apparent paradox of poorer performance under presumably more highly motivated conditions, a paradox easily resolved if we regard the higher motivation as generating either overanxiety to succeed or too much concern and fear of failure.

The same test with the same three sets of instructions was given to groups of students from an all-white college in the same community, and no differences in performance between the college-norm group and the national-norm group were found. A simple but very important moral can be drawn from these data: When the person being tested is a member of a minority group, much of the relevant psychological situation is beyond the control of the best-trained and best-intentioned tester. Results from ability testing of minority groups in a biased world should always be interpreted with caution.

I. KATZ, E. G. EPPS, & L. J. AXELSON. Effect upon Negro digit-symbol performance of anticipated comparison with whites and with other Negroes. *Journal of Abnormal and Social Psychology,* 1964. **69**, 77–83.

BOX 10.7

A PSYCHOLOGIST TALKS TO SENATORS

Many scientists now believe that the proper definition of their responsibilities as scientists *and* citizens requires that they offer to the public and its representatives whatever information and advice they feel is justified by the research findings of their respective fields. One such scientist—a psychologist and behavior geneticist—was invited in 1972 to testify before a committee of the United States Senate that was charged with investigation of the need to ensure equal opportunities within the area of education.

His remarks begin with a self-introduction:

Mr. Chairman and members of the Committee, my name is Irving I. Gottesman and I am a Professor of Psychology at the University of Minnesota and a Director of the Behavior Genetics Training Program there. . . . I have been concerned with the role of genetics in human adaptive behavior, personality, and mental disorders for the past fourteen years. . . .

It is unfortunate but true that many of the facts generated by our research on behavior can be misused by racists and bigots in support of *apartheid* mentality. . . . The political distortion of sound biological ideas in the past has given the science of human genetics a bad reputation which it is trying to overcome. . . .

The Declaration of Independence was too succinct when it said "that all men are created equal." Equal in that context meant deserving equal protection of the law and the inalienable right to the equal opportunity for developing their capacities to the fullest practical extent. It could not have meant that the capacities of men are identical; the distinction between equality and identity helps, I believe, add to perspective. The genetic diversity which characterizes our species is a necessary and marvelous part of our evolutionary heritage which has permitted us to survive. . . .

The current state of knowledge about the origins or causes of the observed racial and social class differences observed in IQ test scores, and educational and social attainment does *not* deserve any reverence. Both scientists and the general public who manage to cut through the thick fog of rhetoric surrounding these inflammatory issues are then confronted by a welter of contradictory facts, near facts, contradictory opinions about the same facts, scientific opinions, and opinions of scientists. The public is bound to be confused by the distinction between the assertion of a hypothesis and the assertion of an established truth. The host of caveats and underlying assumptions which should accompany information on human differences and similarities are seldom made explicit. . . . I am conflicted about the benefits of scientists conjecturing in "public" about the alleged genetic basis of the difference between intelligence test scores of blacks and whites in this country, ever mindful of academic freedom. . . . But, could this be an instance [as my colleague Professor Scarr-Salapatek has suggested] . . . analogous to shouting [in a crowded theater] "FIRE. . . . I think" (!)

Gottesman then goes on to consider many of the same issues we have dealt with throughout this unit. He touches on the limitation of mental tests, the serious inaccuracy of interpreting average group differences in measured mental abilities as indicative of genetic differences, and the kinds of environmental changes within our society that evidence suggests would best foster the fullest realization of individual potential.

He concludes:

I hope the deliberations of this Select Committee on Equal Educational Opportunity will be blessed by luck and wisdom. The American Dream will be so much more vital and fascinating when it is in multicolor red, brown, black, and yellow, instead of monochromatic white.

I. I. GOTTESMAN. Testimony submitted to United States Committee on Equal Education Opportunity (Senator Walter E. Mondale, Chairman), 1972.

SUMMARY

1. The *separate* contributions of heredity and environment to individual differences in mental abilities can only roughly be estimated and then only for specific populations at specific times in their cultural development. But even such estimates run the serious risk of ignoring interactions between these two sets of factors.

2. Certain specific anomalies are known that lead directly to certain patterns of mental abilities. But these are exceptions to the general principles that genetic-environmental interactions are more appropriately attended to for an understanding of the sources of human variations in intelligence.

3. From studies involving comparisons of genetically related individuals, it is possible to establish that the closer the relation among people, the more alike they are in IQ. But they are less so if they have been reared in different environments.

4. Parent-child correlations in IQ are substantial but environments as well as genes are shared within families. Also, the fact of a high correlation in no way restricts possible differences in average levels of intelligence.

5. The extent and quality of parental stimulation of the child during his early years can importantly affect his mental development and his adult intelligence level. Stimulation-deficient environments, by the same token, can severely impair mental growth. Deliberate intervention in such environments to compensate for this deficiency may help the child more closely to attain his intellectual potential.

6. Sex is one determinant of IQ change during development: Traits usually regarded as masculine tend to be associated with increases in IQ. Personality is also a factor, with those who are generally more adaptive in life situations tending to show increasing mental abilities.

7. Assessment of the relative heredity-environment contributions to differences among groups of any kind is difficult because groups differ significantly in their access to intelligence-fostering experiences that become confused with possible between-group genetic differences.

8. Socioeconomic groups do show substantial differences in *average* IQ, apart from the possible sources of such differences. However, genetic theory and actual experience demonstrate conclusively that highly intelligent persons come from any socioeconomic group.

9. The question of possible genetically based intelligence differences among different races and ethnic groups is essentially trivial and scientifically not researchable. The question could be asked only when the massive cultural differences affecting IQ among such groups have been totally eliminated.

10. Currently the intense focus in the United States is upon the sources of black-white differences in mental abilities. We assert the following: (a) There are no distinct black and white races in this country; (b) whites, on the average, test higher in IQ than blacks; (c) there is no evidence that this difference is genetically based.

11. In present-day American society a definitive test of a genetically based difference is impossible. Neither culture-fair mental tests nor precautions to ensure optimal testing conditions for blacks and whites solve the problem of this comparison—though both are useful for other reasons. Only a culture-fair society will provide the scientifically necessary condition and this requirement has the happy coincidence of also being recommended by the values of our society. The ultimate answer, if it is then still sought, will be found when every individual, of whatever group, is afforded an opportunity to express fully his intellectual potential.

GLOSSARY

"culture-fair" mental tests Tests of mental ability that attempt to ensure that the test items are equally difficult for all groups, regardless of race, nationality, and social class—or any other nonintellectual factor. Culture-fair tests are only one of the many requirements that must be met before we can meaningfully compare groups that differ in cultural background.

heritability The proportion of the total variability of a characteristic in a given population at a given time that is attributable to genetic differences among individuals within that population.

part four

perception

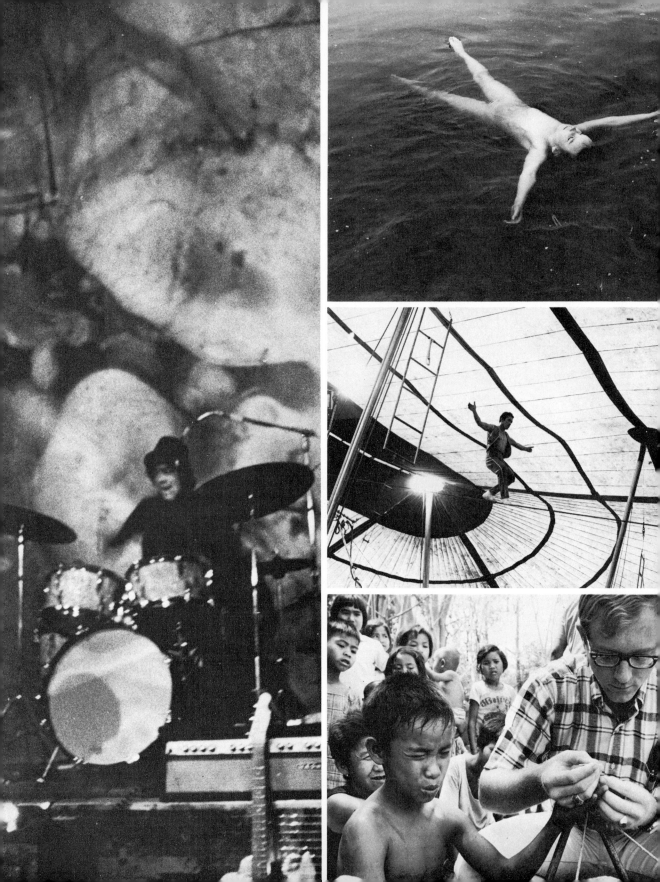

sensory experience

DO YOU KNOW...

- that sounds can cause pain?

- how Leonardo da Vinci contributed to the understanding of perception?

- why it is that blind persons can often detect the presence of an object before contacting it and . . .

- how this ability may lead to new devices that could greatly enhance their ability to get around?

- that a nonexistent limb can itch?

- that of all our senses, taste is the least sensitive?

- that some dentists use music in place of an anesthetic and that this may be related to the anesthetic effects of acupuncture?

Left—Photo by Robin Forbes; upper right—Photo by Melissa Shook; center right—Photo by Robin Forbes; lower right—Photo by Carl Purcell/Courtesy, Peace Corps.

CONTENTS

The study of perception is one of the oldest enterprises in psychology. Facts and theories about perception have long intrigued artists and philosophers, physicists and physiologists. There is good reason for this concern and fascination with how we sense our world.

There is pleasure, profit, and privation in being sensitive. We find beautiful things around us, things our senses alert us to and give us an opportunity to explore. Our eyes tell us about good design and vital colors. Taste and smell

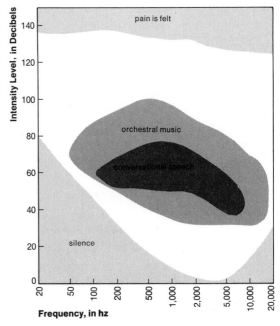

FIGURE 11.1 The world of sound, showing how perception of sound is a function of both intensity and frequency of sound waves. The lower curve shows the minimal intensities required at each frequency in order to hear sound. Thus, at a pitch of 100 hertz (abbreviated hz, defined as cycles per second) we need an intensity of about 50 decibels before we can hear a sound; at 1,000 hz less than 10 decibels is sufficient. Above the upper curve the intensities are so great that they produce a painful sensation. Between the two curves is the area of hearing. Also shown are the approximate areas of conversational speech and of orchestral music.

FIGURE 11.2 The visual cliff. This apparatus makes it possible to test depth perception in any animal as soon as it is able to move about in its environment. A checker-boarded surface that drops off abruptly for a foot or so is covered by a glass plate. The subject, animal or human, is placed on the cliff and is encouraged to cross the line over the cliff's edge. In this photo the child's touch tells him of the solidity and firmness of the glass. But even at this early age, seeing is believing; the child has more faith in the visual evidence than in touch, and refuses to venture forth.

Photo by William Vandivert; copyright © *Scientific American,* 1960.

are pleased by scents and balanced spices. We may be soothed by a soft touch and awakened by a caress.

We can as quickly be disturbed as pleased by what our senses find. We have to avert our eyes and cover our ears when the energies reaching us are too intense (Figure 11.1). When smells become too concentrated we are dismayed. The sense of pain constricts the whole world about us.

Between the bounds set for us by pleasant sensations and distressing experiences lie our everyday tasks. Our senses have to be practical and mundane, for we plan our daily comings and goings by what our senses tell us (see Figure 11.2). From the sound and light waves and pressures and chemicals that reach our body the senses extract *information* about the world around us. They enable us to identify

the shapes, colors, and parts of things we use; they distinguish between different things, note similarities, ignore one moment's irrelevancies, and later attend to the things that previously were irrelevant. Our senses have to be capable of accommodating to difficult conditions of the moment (see Figure 11.3) and adjusting themselves to benefit from experience.

Psychologists who study perception cooperate with physiologists to provide facts and theories about the mechanisms of the senses, and they work with physicists and chemists to understand the energies to which our sense organs respond. Perception psychologists are found in industry, in engineering, and in paramedical professions. The education of people with sensory handicaps is often handled by perception psychologists or guided by psychological theories of perception.

FIGURE 11.3 A "hidden" animal. The light patterns that reach our eyes provide the information to identify objects in the environment around us. Our senses are usually so skilled we hardly notice the details of the patches of light until we have trouble making an identification—as in this high-contrast photograph of a dog.

R. L. Gregory. *The Intelligent Eye.* New York: McGraw-Hill, 1970.

FIGURE 11.4 A woodcut by Albrecht Dürer from his 1525 "A Course in the Art of Measurement." To study the patterns of light coming from an object to the eye, painters sometimes used screens on which to trace an outline. Similar devices are still used to teach perspective drawing today.

Courtesy, New York Public Library

Psychologists learn from painters and philosophers, who also study perception. For centuries painters struggled with the problem of depicting perceptual experience (see Figure 11.4 and Box 11.1), and from their work we have learned much. In this unit and in the three units following it will become evident that although a great deal is now known about perception, an enormous amount remains to be discovered. Indeed, as we shall see in Unit 13, there is still active theoretical controversy about the basic nature of the perceptual process.

PHYSIOLOGY AND PHENOMENOLOGY

Many beginning students are likely to think of the *physiological method* as the most direct and profitable avenue for research on perception. It would seem that to understand vision, for example, one should proceed by studying the effects of light striking the eye, and the resulting events in the nerves and brain. As Unit 14 will demonstrate, the physiological approach is indispensable in providing essential information about the nature and basis of sensory processes. But it cannot serve by itself as a completely adequate method for studying complex perception.

The second main approach, called the *phenomenological method* (**phenomenology** is from the Greek *phainomenon*, "that which appears"), is one that many beginning students consider so obvious as to require no discussion, and yet the use of the phenomenological method has been disputed by some psychologists, especially American Behaviorists. In the phenomenological method the subject is asked to give a detailed account of *how things appear to him*. This means that we, as scientists, must depend upon the subject's report of his personal, subjective experiences; we cannot use objective instrument readings. This is one of the reasons Behaviorists have shied away from this method. And yet subjective accounts yield the raw data with which the perception psychologist must work. To avoid such data would mean to neglect most of human perceptual experience. This kind of phenomenological *description*, however, does not give us an explanation of perception; but it does serve as a starting point for investigation aimed toward an explanation. Because it is an important starting point, it is essential that such research be done carefully—and much effort has gone into attempts to make the phenomenological method a sopisticated and useful scientific method.

Interrelations and Problems

The physiological and phenomenological approaches are not contradictory but are complementary to one another. In general, *a phenomenological description of perception establishes facts that physiological analysis is challenged to explain.* The relations between data derived from the phenomenological and physiological approaches are not simple and obvious. Our perceptual experience often poses puzzling problems for physiologists, and our knowledge of physiology may seem to contradict what our senses tell us. Consider the following three examples:

First example: "Facial vision" in the blind. For centuries it was known that blind people could detect the presence of barriers without touching them. A blind person can walk up to a wall and stop before bumping into it. The blind person usually reports that she had an *impression* that there was a wall in front of her. She might also say that her impression was based on a touch sensation, a kind of tingling, on her face. For that reason the ability came to be known as "facial vision."

We now know, as a result of Dallenbach's experiments (see Box 11.2, p. 236), that it is the ears, not the face, that provide the blind person with information about obstacles. Apparently, the blind person has learned to use information —the sound reflections from solid obstacles— that the sighted person does not usually pick up. Apparently, too, the blind person is not aware

---

BOX 11.1

DA VINCI LOOKS AT DEPTH

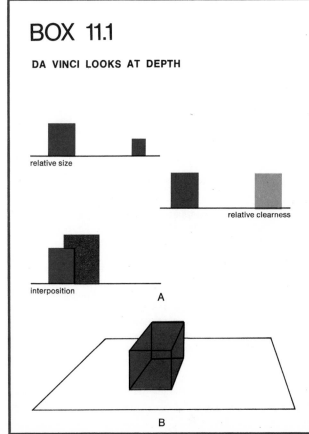

relative size

relative clearness

interposition

A

B

In his *Notebooks* (about 1508), Leonardo da Vinci surmised that our ability to perceive depth, or distance, in a picture depends on several factors. These factors have been called **monocular depth cues,** because they work when viewing a scene through a peephole using only one eye and with no head movement. (Some of the cues are illustrated in Figure A.)

1. Interposition: An object that partly covers another object tends to be seen as the closer.
2. Relative size: If two identical objects subtend different angles at the eye, the one subtending the larger angle tends to be seen nearer.
3. Relative height: Below the horizon, the lower of two objects tends to be seen as nearer. Above the horizon, the higher of two objects tends to be seen nearer.
4. Relative clarity: The clearer and more detailed the object, the closer it tends to seem visually.
5. Light and shadow: Certain patterns of light and shadow favor the impression of depth.

However, none of these cues is particularly powerful on its own or when used in displays consisting of a few lines. Closing one eye, inspect Figure B, which can look like a cube sitting on a piece of paper. All of the monocular depth cues are present, yet the cube can easily be made to "reverse"—to look as though the upper square face is in front.

BOX 11.2

"SEEING" WITH YOUR EARS

How can the totally blind person detect and avoid obstacles as he moves around in space? An early and favorite explanation was that the blind person develops an uncanny sensitivity to currents of air that strike his face and that such cues provide "facial vision," which enables him to avoid obstacles.

At Cornell University, K. M. Dallenbach and his collaborators carried out a series of studies to check out this explanation. Testing both blind and seeing subjects, the experimenters were able to eliminate touch sensitivity of the face as a possible cue for detecting obstacles without vision: When the head was covered with a felt veil and hat, the subjects could still walk up to a wall and stop before running into it. However, when the ears were plugged, *every* subject ran into the wall, indicating that *auditory cues are clearly essential.* This point was further demonstrated by having the blind subject in a separate, soundproof room while the *experimenter* walked toward the obstacle carrying a microphone that was connected to headphones worn by the subject. Under these conditions the subject, by listening to the sounds coming from the headphone, was able to tell when the experimenter in the next room came close to the obstacle. How do these auditory cues work?

We know that bats emit high-pitched sounds as they fly. When these sounds hit an object, they are reflected back to the bat's ears. It is these *reflected* sounds that guide the flight of the bat and help it avoid crashing into objects. Human beings can apparently also be guided by a similar kind of *sonar.* Later research has attempted to determine the accuracy that human beings can achieve with such cues. W. N. Kellogg compared the performance of blind subjects with that of normally sighted subjects in a number of experiments. In one of them, the subject (blind, or sighted but blindfolded) made judgments of the relative distance of a plywood disk 1 ft in diameter, which was presented successively in two positions: a standard position (2 ft from the subject) and a position that varied in distance from 1 to 4 ft (see photo A). The subjects, both blind and sighted, were encouraged to make any sounds they wished to provide echoes and were permitted to move their heads and bodies as they chose.

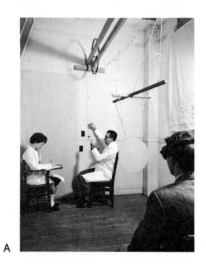

A

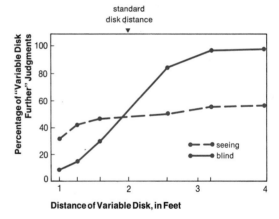

Some subjects spoke, often repeating the same word rhythmically; others snapped their fingers, clicked their tongues, whistled, and even sang.

The chart, adapted from Kellogg's report, gives the combined results from two blind and two normally sighted people. The judgments of the blind subjects at each of the six test positions were highly accurate. In contrast, the sighted subjects were never above chance in their performance. The better of the two blind subjects was able to detect a difference in the distance of the disk when it was moved as little as 4 in. either way from its standard 2-ft distance.

In other experiments, Kellogg's blind subjects reported that the echoes from hard and soft sur-

B

faces simply "sounded different." This was sufficient to permit them to distinguish, for example, between a metal-covered disk and a velvet-covered disk with an accuracy of 99.5 percent. Perhaps more remarkable is their ability to achieve 86.5 percent accuracy in distinguishing between velvet and denim. Blindfolded normal subjects were totally unable to discriminate texture differences.

These fascinating phenomena raise numerous questions. Blind persons vary tremendously in their "sonar" ability. What accounts for these differences? Does training increase this ability? If so, what kind of training is best? What are the auditory cues responsible for this ability? Loudness? Pitch? Some research has indicated that reflected sound of very high frequency (10,000 hz or more) works best. (hz is the abbreviation for **hertz,** and is defined as number of cycles per second.) This finding has led to an attempt to develop an instrument that could easily be carried around by the blind person and that would continuously emit high-frequency sounds (see photo B). Such an instrument would be a considerable improvement on the "tap-tap" of the white cane. Theory and practice are intimately linked in these ventures.

M. SUPA, M. COTZIN, & K. M. DALLENBACH. Facial vision: The perception of obstacles by the blind. *American Journal of Psychology*, 1944, **57**, 133–183.
P. WORCHEL & K. M. DALLENBACH. Facial vision: Perception of obstacles by the deaf-blind. *American Journal of Psychology*, 1947, **60**, 502–553.
W. N. KELLOGG. Sonar system of the blind. *Science*, 1962, **137**, 399–404. Photo A and graph adapted by permission; copyright 1962 by the American Association for the Advancement of Science.
Photo B by Susan Pogany, courtesy MIT.

of the real sources of the information. Although she perceives the wall with her sense of hearing, she believes that she is using her sense of touch. Perhaps the possibility of her head and face colliding with the object dominates her perception. The important lesson is that the phenomenological description, if used as a guide to physiology, might lead us astray; *the identity of the sense organ that is supplying a person with a sensory experience may not be phenomenologically clear, even to the experiencer.*

Second example: The vestibular system. Not only handicapped people, but everybody can be unaware of the bases for their impressions. Try the following exercises: Raise and lower yourself slightly or recall the experiences of going up and down in an elevator. Rock gently back and forth. These sensations, known as **vestibular sensations,** evoked by these movements should be clear and distinct to you. Now here is the puzzler: Read the next three bits of information and try to answer the question that follows. (1) There is a small system in your body consisting of two organs, less than a few inches in size, that gives you accurate information about change in location of your body; this system responds to any change in movement. (2) The system supplements the information from vision and other body senses. (3) It is a system that is present in the fetus and it is with us throughout life, ready to function day and night. *Where is this system located in your body?* Is it in your pelvis? Or your shoulders? Somewhere in the intestines so that it is disturbed by too much motion and upsets the nearby digestive system? The answer is that this system—called the *vestibular system* (see Unit 14, p. 347)—is located in the *ear* (see Figure 14.14, p. 350). Despite our almost incessant use of information from this system, we never have distinct sensations from it that indicate its location. Another moral: A physiological and anatomical analysis of the sensory system, if used as a guide to our phenomenological experience, can lead us astray: *The existence of a sensory system is no guarantee that the perceiver can locate it, or indicate that he has sensations coming from it.*

Third example: The "phantom limb." Awareness of our sense organs and even of the

BOX 11.3

THE PHANTOM LIMB

After a person has suffered the amputation of an arm or leg, he may continue to feel that the limb is still there. He may feel itching in it; he may feel that he can still move it and may even momentarily forget that it is gone and try to use it. Sometimes these experiences are of brief duration, and sometimes they endure throughout the rest of the person's life. Phantom limbs often undergo a gradual change in their perceived character. For example, D. Katz reported that a phantom hand may gradually shrink and move up into the stump, so that finally it is experienced as a small hand embedded there.

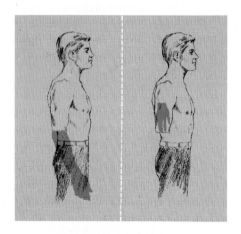

M. L. Simmel of Brandeis University has suggested a psychological analysis of this phenomenon. Her main hypothesis is that phantoms represent the persistence of a previously learned "body schema." She further argues that only gradually, over a long period of experiencing movement and touch sensations in the limb, does its schema become sufficiently stable for it to be "missed" after amputation. From this reasoning it would follow that the later the age at which the limb is lost, the more frequent will be the phantoms. The place to look, then, is at the phantom-limb experiences of persons who have undergone amputation at different ages. Here is a summary of 117 such cases:

Age at Amputation	Cases	Percentage of Phantoms
2–4 years	24	25
4–6 years	13	62
6–8 years	20	75
8–10 years	19	100
10–20 years	41	100

Some of these cases were culled from published medical reports, but for most of them Simmel conducted interviews with the amputees and in the case of children, with their parents as well. The developmental trend in the frequency of phantoms following amputation is clear: They gradually increase from the earliest age, and by age eight, amputation always leads to phantom experiences. Simmel notes that perceptual and cognitive development in children shows much the same age trend, and from this parallel she suggests that acquiring a body schema is an instance of a relatively complex learning achievement.

Another line of evidence supports and elaborates this learned-body-schema interpretation of phantoms. Working with leprosy patients, Simmel finds that no phantoms are experienced when the parts of the body (mainly fingers and toes) have *gradually* disappeared through absorption. This absorption process is very slow, often extending for ten years or more, and is generally painless. When remnants of the absorbed digits are amputated, however, phantoms almost always occur afterward. Simmel presents the following interpretation:

[During absorption] the schema can keep in step with physical reality through gradual small changes that parallel the physical alterations of the body. As a consequence, phantoms do not appear. By contrast, amputation produces a sudden alteration of physical reality at a speed at which the schema cannot change, and the persistence of the schema gives rise to the phantom experience.

When we do not have an opportunity to learn to adapt to new situations, we make do with the old ways of perceiving.

D. KATZ. *Gestalt Psychology.* New York: Ronald, 1950.
M. L. SIMMEL. Developmental aspects of the body schema. *Child Development,* 1966, **37**, 83–95. Table adapted by permission; © 1966 by The Society for Research in Child Development, Inc.

dimensions and boundaries of our own body develops slowly and changes slowly. Phenomenological investigations among amputees, for example, reveal that long after a limb has been amputated, it continues to lead a phantom existence. But it is a robust phantom; it is *experienced* as a compelling, here-and-now reality. The patient, knowing that he no longer has that limb, can nevertheless feel it move, can feel its skin touched, and can suffer from muscle cramps in the nonexistent muscles of that nonexistent limb (see Box 11.3). Special training by a hospital psychologist is sometimes required to help the amputee change the image of his own body and of the sense organs available to him so as to rid himself of these phantom sensations. And this takes time—time to learn a new body image, and sometimes, especially with older patients, this learning is never achieved. A final moral: *Physiological explanations of phenomenological descriptions may sometimes be inadequate; recourse to learning processes must be made because considerable learning may be involved before a person can discover the location of, or efficient use of, or even be aware of his sense organs.*

There appears to be more to perception than meets the eye, or the ear, or the hand.

THE CHAIN OF PERCEPTION

Our perceptual systems harvest information about the world and monitor our activities in that world (see Table 11.1, p. 240). As such, these perceptual systems can be conceived of as parts of a chain stretching from the outside world, through each of us, and back into the environment. Each link in this chain is essential if information about the world is to be reliable and if the outcomes of actions are to be those desired.

1. The beginning of the chain is the *environment*. What properties does the environment have that are the sources of the final perception? What objects does it contain? What is their location and distribution? What are the physical attributes that permit us to

experience size, color, hardness, movement, duration, change, and so forth?

2. The second link of the chain is the *medium* by which the environment transmits its properties to our senses. Some objects reflect light to our eyes. Some send sound waves or chemicals through the air. Some objects dissolve in the mouth. Some resist skin pressure. Others are forces, like gravity. Some, like thermal energy, affect our skin via radiant heat or conducted heat.

3. The third part of the chain is the interaction of the various forms of energy and other stimuli in the medium with the sensitive *receptors* of the perceptual systems. Notice that we say "interaction," and not simply "reception." When a receptor (e.g., the eye) is stimulated, its condition may be altered so that further stimulation may cause somewhat different effects. For example, a bright light makes the iris of the eye close, so that thereafter less light can enter the eye.

4. The fourth link in the chain consists of *sensory nerves* leading from the receptor organs to the brain. Some sensory neural parts are very long, such as those extending from our toes to our brain; others are very short, such as those from our eyes to our brain.

5. The fifth part of the chain of perception is the brain, most particularly the *projection areas* where the sensory nerves terminate. Some theorists suppose that our perceptions are primarily determined by the neural signals as they arrive in these areas. Other theorists surmise that our perceptions reflect not only the information brought to the projection area by the sensory nerves but also certain information previously stored elsewhere in the brain, for example, our beliefs, feelings, and memories. (See Unit 13, section on theoretical approaches.)

Weak Links and Misperception

If the chain of perception is complete, and if we are accurate in our perception, we are per-

TABLE 11.1 THE PERCEPTUAL SYSTEMS

Name	Mode of Attention	Receptive Units	Anatomy of the Organ	Activity of the Organ	Stimuli Available	External Information Obtained
The Basic Orienting System	General orientation	Mechanoreceptors	Vestibular organs	Body equilibrium	Forces of gravity and acceleration	Direction of gravity, being pushed
The Auditory System	Listening	Mechanoreceptors	Cochlear organs with middle ear and auricle	Orienting to sounds	Vibration in the air	Nature and location of vibratory events
The Haptic System	Touching	Mechanoreceptors and possibly thermoreceptors	Skin (including attachments and openings) Joints (including ligaments) Muscles (including tendons)	Exploration of many kinds	Deformations of tissues Configuration of joints Stretching of muscle fibers	Contact with the earth Mechanical encounters Object shapes Material states Solidity or viscosity
The Taste-Smell System	Smelling	Chemoreceptors	Nasal cavity (nose)	Sniffing	Composition of the medium	Nature of volatile sources
	Tasting	Chemo- and mechanoreceptors	Oral cavity (mouth)	Savoring	Composition of ingested objects	Nutritive and biochemical values
The Visual System	Looking	Photoreceptors	Ocular mechanism (eyes, with intrinsic and extrinsic eye muscles, as related to the vestibular organs, the head, and the whole body)	Accommodation, Pupillary adjustment, Fixation, convergence Exploration	The variables of structure in ambient light	Everything that can be specified by the variables of optical structure (information about objects, animals, motions, events, and places)

From J. J. Gibson. *The Senses Considered As Perceptual Systems*. Boston: Houghton Mifflin, 1966.

FIGURE 11.5 The appearance of the pattern behind the mug is distorted because the light rays are refracted by the medium of the glass.

Photo by Michael Hirst

ceiving *veridically* (from the Latin *veritas*, meaning truth). Difficulties arise when:

1. Environmental objects are camouflaged, as was illustrated in Figure 11.3, page 233.
2. Energy from an object is altered in the medium (e.g., when light waves are deflected in passing through a glass mug; see Figure 11.5).
3. The sensory systems are handicapped; for example, with age, the lens of the eye becomes less flexible and cannot focus on new objects.
4. The sensory nerves to the brain are injured.
5. The sensory areas of the brain are injured. Problems may also arise when subjects have strong and erroneous beliefs or memories about certain objects.

The chain-of-perception concept is useful for providing an overview both of the processes involved in perception and of the kinds of diffi-

culties in perception that can arise. Each link in the chain provides a focus for research on perception. In this unit we will trace the course of perception from the physical sources in the environment, through the transmission of different forms of energies arising from these sources, to the receptors where these stimuli impinge on the body of the perceiver. In the next unit we will continue the journey from the receptors to the brain, describing the *organized* perception that results. We will concentrate primarily on vision because it is easier to give visual examples in a textbook (which, we suppose, can be defined as the most ancient of "visual aids" used in teaching!). Finally, in Unit 14, the journey is completed as we consider in detail the physiological bases of perception.

FROM OBJECT TO RECEPTOR

One of the earliest views of perception was that it was the result of something sent out from the observer that made contact with the objects of the environment. This idea was not only popular among the early Greeks, but it seems to be easily accepted by children today—in comics superheroes often send out special rays that allow them to see through walls. The crippling flaw in this idea is that for perception to occur the *observer* has to be affected, not just the *environment*. It is no use sending out rays (or bursts of sound, as bats and porpoises do) unless some signal comes back to the eye, ear, or other sense organ (recall the findings in Box 11.2, p. 236). In short, the receptor must be stimulated.

Stimulus and Stimulus Object

Physical energy that can excite a sense organ and thus produce an effect on the organism is called a **stimulus.** We must, however, distinguish between a stimulus and a **stimulus object.** A stimulus object is an object in the environment that is the *source* of the stimulus. Thus, for example, a red ball placed 10 ft in front of a child's eyes is a stimulus object. The corresponding visual stimulus is the pattern of physical light energy that emanates from the ball and strikes the retina of the eye. As the light leaves the ball and passes through intervening space, its intensity is reduced, and it may be mixed with other light—depending, for example, on the general illumination of the room. Different eyes (e.g., the nearsighted, the farsighted, those with 20/20 vision) focus the light rays in different ways. Thus different patterns of light are produced on the retinas of different observers by the same red ball. There are many physical reasons why a given stimulus object can give rise to a great variety of different stimuli on the receptor surface.

The converse is also true: The same stimulus can be produced on the receptor surface by very different stimulus objects. When the retina is excited by a given pattern of light, it does not matter how this stimulus was produced. For example, light coming to the eye from a luminous point could have come from a star light years away or from a pinpoint just a few inches away. The distance of the light source may be varied enormously without altering the characteristics (except intensity) of the light entering the eye.

This possibility was used by the painter Adelbert Ames to construct distorted rooms, which through a peephole would look like ordinary rooms. This resulted in distorted perception of the sizes of objects within the room (Box 11.4). In normal viewing of the normal environment the light typically carries enough information about the size, shape, location, movement, and so forth of stimulus objects to permit veridical perception.

The Ames room demonstrates, however, that once the laws of perception are understood, it is possible to circumvent them. We have learned to control light by using dyes or paint, mirrors, lenses, photographic film, and lamps. This technology together with our understanding of perception makes it possible to reproduce and manipulate the informative features of light either to mislead people about the outside world or to inform them accurately about distant objects and places.

A similar argument holds for every sense modality. If we study the chemical make-up of apples, we can devise artificial apple flavoring. If we study the erotic scents of higher animals, we can make exciting perfumes (Michael, 1971, finds that chemicals similar to the sexual scents of monkeys make the hearts of men beat faster).

PSYCHOPHYSICS

The physical energy that surrounds us takes many forms—radiant, vibratory, chemical, thermal, mechanical—that vary in intensity as well as in kind. These forms of physical energy are our only direct link with the physical world of things and events. And our senses, which receive this energy, set the boundaries on what we can learn first-hand about the physical world. By reasoning, by experiment, and by the invention of ingenious instruments, we seek to extend the scope of our comprehension beyond the limitations imposed by our senses. But, no matter how detailed and complete our knowledge of certain phenomena, for example, cosmic rays, may be, we will never "know" them in the experiential sense—just as the blind man can never "know" color and the deaf man can never "know" music. This fact points to the finite and precisely definable foundation of direct sensory experience upon which the awesome complexity of man's total store of knowledge must be built. A basic scientific question is how different sensory experiences (*psychological*) are related to different forms of *physical* energy. The study of these relations is called, appropriately enough, **psychophysics.**

That psychophysics inaugurated experimental psychology (about 100 years ago) is probably not a historical accident. We can see that psychophysics, as the bridge between the physical world and human experience, presents the most obvious starting point for the scientific study of man. When men like the physicist Helmholtz (1821–1894) sought to determine empirically the systematic relations between physical energy and sensory experience, the *method* was new but not the problem. The connection between the two "separate worlds," psychic and physical, was—and still is—a crucial philosophical issue.

The Absolute Threshold

Organisms are not sensitive to all parts of the possible range of physical energy. For example, some lights are too dim to see, some sounds too low to hear, some pressures too light to feel. An important psychophysical problem is the determination of that exact point in the intensity of a stimulus that separates feeling from not feeling, seeing from not seeing, hearing from not hearing, tasting from not tasting. This point is called the **absolute threshold.**

To establish a universal standard, psychologists have agreed that the absolute thresh-

old will arbitrarily be taken as the lowest intensity of a stimulus that is perceived *half the time.* There are several different ways that this threshold can be determined. Such measurement techniques are called **psychophysical methods.**

Measured under the best possible conditions, the absolute thresholds for various stimuli differ widely, and some of them are amazingly low. For example, receptors in the eye are capable of responding to only one photon of light— the smallest possible package of light. If the physical energy equivalent to one pin dropping 1 in. were converted to light energy, there would

BOX 11.4

THE DISTORTED ROOM

The photograph shows what an observer sees when he looks with one eye through a peephole into the room. It looks to him like a normal rectangular room, but the three people in it look weirdly distorted in size.

The room has been deliberately constructed to mislead the perceiver (see the figure). It is actually very asymmetrical; one corner is three times as far away as the other, and all dimensions are chosen to be exact geometrical projections of a normal rectangular room viewed from the observer's eye.

The observer is required to look through the

peephole with one eye, and is therefore dependent on the stimuli impinging on one retina. On the basis of retinal pattern alone, the observer cannot tell how far away the parts of the room actually are. A truly rectangular room as well as any number of distorted rooms could give this same retinal pattern. The most natural assumption is that the room is a normal rectangular one, and as the stimulus pattern is consistent with this interpretation, that is how the room is perceived.

But the consequence of this interpretation is that objects inside the room must assume perceived sizes appropriate to the perceived size and shape of the room. The nearest man therefore looks much taller than the farthest man.

Photo reprinted with the permission of Scientific American, Inc., from *Scientific American*, April 1959. Courtesy, William Vandivert.

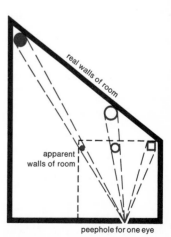

- ● real place and size of "smallest" man
- • apparent place and size of "smallest" man
- ○ real place and size of "medium" man
- ○ apparent place and size of "medium" man
- □ "largest" man

apparent walls of room

real walls of room

apparent walls of room

peephole for one eye

be enough energy to activate a receptor in every human eye on earth. But the fact that one, or a few, units in a sense organ respond to a stimulus does not mean that you will be aware of it. The response of a receptor, a nerve, or even a brain cell is not the same as the conscious experience of a person. A lot has to happen before the person will say, "I felt that!" (See especially p. 347 of Unit 14 where the difference between a brain response and conscious awareness is experimentally analyzed from the physiological point of view.)

The Differential Threshold

We must be concerned not only with absolute sensitivity to physical energy but also with sensitivity to *differences* in intensity of the energy. An individual may look at two light bulbs simultaneously, or he may look first at one and then the other, or he may look at a single bulb whose intensity is gradually changing. In each case there is the question of whether or not he is able to perceive a *difference* in the lights. Here again, the convention is to take as the **differential threshold** that stimulus difference that will be perceived *half the time*.

As in the case of the absolute threshold, the value of the differential threshold varies widely, depending upon the nature of the stimulus and the state of the organism. Most important, a very surprising fact, which came to be known as **Weber's Law**, was discovered by the physiologist Weber in 1834, early in the history of psychophysics: *Within limits, the differential threshold tends to approximate a constant fraction of the stimulus intensity.*

Expressed mathematically, we have: $\frac{\Delta I}{I} = k$, where ΔI is the differential threshold, I is the intensity of the stimulus, and k is a constant fraction. Known as Weber's fraction, k is different *for each given type of physical energy.*

Suppose, for example, that for a weight of 50 lb (I) the differential threshold is 1 lb (ΔI)—that is, a weight must be at least 51 lb to be perceived as heavier. It will then turn out that for 100 lb, the next heavier weight that can be perceived as heavier will be 102 lb. For a 150-lb weight, the next heavier weight that can be discriminated will be 153 lb. In each case the differential threshold is the *same* fraction of the stimulus weight: 1/50 = 2/100 = 3/150 = .02 This Weber fraction of .02 tells us that we must add 2 percent of the original weight before we can tell that it is heavier. Shown in Box 11.5 are illustrative Weber fractions for several different stimuli.

In many everyday actions we make use of the fact that the increment needed to produce a "just noticeable difference" (sometimes written as j.n.d) is relative to the intensity of the original stimulus. Less caution is needed in adding a spice to a highly seasoned than to a delicately seasoned dish. We hesitate less in bringing an uninvited guest to a very large party than we do to a small intimate party.

BOX 11.5

POOR TASTE AND GOOD PITCH

The following illustrative Weber fractions[1] have been taken from the work of various investigators. For each stimulus dimension, the absolute level of stimulus intensity at which the Weber fraction was determined is indicated. These values are *minimal* values, obtained under optimal conditions of judgment.

Pitch (at 2,000 hz)	1/333
Deep pressure (at 400 grams)	1/77
Visual brightness (at 1,000 photons)	1/62
Lifted weights (at 300 grams)	1/53
Loudness (at 100 decibels, 1,000 hz)	1/11
Smell of rubber (at 200 olfacties)	1/10
Skin pressure (at 5 grams per square millimeter)	1/7
Taste, saline (at 3 moles per liter)	1/5

The remarkable range in sensitivities of the various senses is well demonstrated; it is about seventyfold—from pitch, in which a difference of as little as *one-third of 1 percent* can be detected, to taste, in which there must be a difference of about 20 percent before it can be detected.

[1] Listed in E. G. BORING, H. S. LANGFELD, & H. P. WELD (Eds.). *Foundations of Psychology.* New York: Wiley, 1948.

STIMULI FOR VISION

The universe is full of radiant energy in the form of electromagnetic waves. These waves vary greatly in length, from cosmic rays of a few trillionths of an inch to radio waves of many miles. Within this range of waves, only a tiny fraction (called *light waves*) are capable of producing a visual experience (see Color Plate 1, which follows this page). Above and below this *visible spectrum* there is no visual impression. Within the visible range the physical characteristics of the light waves are closely related to the principal dimensions of our perception of color —**hue, brightnes,** and **saturation.**

Hue

The wavelengths of light that give rise to different hues are shown in Color Plate 1. Wavelengths of about 700 millimicrons (a millimicron, symbolized by mμ, is one-billionth of a meter) are seen as red light; those of about 400 mμ are seen as violet light. Each of the other hues of the spectrum has its own wavelength, which is located somewhere between these two extremes.

There are ways we can view this progression of colors. When sunlight passes through a prism, it fans out into the familiar color spectrum that ranges from red through violet. The rainbow is a common example; sunlight is refracted by passing through raindrops, which serve as prisms.

If we reverse the process and recombine the spectral colors of the rainbow, we once again have white sunlight. White light therefore has no single wavelength that produces it, and the same is true of some other important colors.

Brightness

Any given hue, for example, red, can vary in brightness. Brightness corresponds closely with the intensity of the light energy. With greater intensity the colors are brighter, approaching white; with lesser intensities the colors are darker, approaching black.

Saturation

A color of a given hue and brightness may be more or less saturated. That is, it may look richer and more concentrated, or paler, more dilute, and more washed out. We can recognize the phenomenon easily by gradually diluting a rich blue watercolor paint with water, turning it into paler and paler tints of blue until no blue at all is discernible. We would then have a completely desaturated color or what we call an *achromatic* color. The continuum of grays, from white through medium gray to black, are the achromatic colors—that is, completely desaturated.

Desaturation of hues is produced by mixing light of different wavelengths. The greater the number of different wavelengths, the less the saturation.

Color Mixture

The light that strikes the eye is very rarely of a single wavelength; it is almost always a mixture of many wavelengths, because illumination of objects is mainly from light sources like the sun, which emit light waves of various lengths. Only under exceptional laboratory conditions, in which there is careful filtering, are we likely to deal with pure light of a given, single wavelength.

It is a striking fact that we do not and cannot analyze a light mixture into its component parts simply by looking at it. We see only the single color that results from the mixture.

Rules of color mixture There are specific rules by which we can mix colors and predict the resulting hue, brightness, and saturation. One of the most useful pieces of apparatus for laboratory study of color mixture is the *color wheel* (see Figure 11.6, p. 246). The color wheel is a *psychological* color mixer. It should be clear that we are discussing the mixing of different light waves in the living visual system, not the mixing of different pigments on a palette or in a paint pail.

One rule of color mixing is that every color has its own **complementary color**; when two complementary colors are mixed together in equal amounts, the product is an achromatic gray. For example, a properly chosen red and blue-green (with wavelengths of about 640 and 490, respectively) will lose all color when mixed

FIGURE 11.6 A color wheel for mixing colors. Disks of colored paper are cut and assembled on the wheel, overlapping so that different-sized angular sectors of each color are exposed. When the wheel is rotated rapidly, a completely mixed color is seen instead of the separate component colors. The mixtures can readily be varied by changing the size of the angular sectors of the two or more component colors.

on a color wheel. The same is true of a yellow and a blue.

If the sequence of colors of the visible spectrum is arranged in a circle so that the two colors that form a complementary pair lie exactly opposite one another, the arrangement is called a *color circle* (see Color Plate 2, following p. 232).

All hues can be obtained by mixing only three initial colors. For instance, the three primary colors, red, green, and blue, when mixed in proper proportions, can give any desired color. If we simply add white and black to our three chromatic ingredients, we can obtain colors of any desired hue, brightness, and saturation.

Color Blindness

Only in rare instances are people *totally* color-blind (a state of affairs not at all uncommon among some lower animals). A totally color-blind person has no experience of differences of hue. His world is portrayed not in Technicolor but in varying shades of white, gray, and black.

Much more commonly **color blindness** is partial. The two types that occur most frequently involve an inability to perceive the difference between red and green, or this same inability plus a weakness in sensitivity to the red end of the spectrum.

A partially color-blind person sees only two hues in the spectrum—blue and yellow. If the wavelength is from the long (red) end of the spectrum, then yellow is the color perceived, whether the stimulus is actually red, orange, yellow, or greenish. If it is from the short (violet) end, the partially color-blind subject sees blue, though the stimulus is actually violet, blue, or greenish blue. Somewhere around 500 mμ (a bluish green), no color at all is seen, and the stimulus appears to be white or gray (Wald, 1964).

There are various diagnostic tests for color blindness. For a sample of one test, see Color Plate 3, following p. 232.

Visual Sensitivity and Acuity

Sensitivity of the eye to light varies with the intensity and the wavelength of the light, the state of the eye, the point stimulated on the retina, and with other factors.

Sensitivity to intensity We have already noted that under optimal conditions the minimum intensity of light that the eye can detect is amazingly low. One of the optimal conditions is that the eye be dark-adapted (the longer a person sits in a dark room, the more sensitive his eyes become to light). Sensitivity is also a function of the wavelength of the light. For example, light of a wavelength around 500 mμ is more easily seen than light of other wavelengths.

There is one especially interesting anomaly in the sensitivity of different parts of the retina. One part is completely blind. When you do the demonstration in Figure 11.7, you will discover this blindness, which you may not have suspected.

Sensitivity to wavelength Sensitivity to wavelength is not the same as sensitivity to intensity. In general, it is easier to detect that there is

FIGURE 11.7 Hold the book at arm's length, close your left eye, and gaze steadily at the dot. Then slowly bring the book toward you. You will find a place at which the circle completely disappears. It happens because, from that distance, the image of the circle is falling on an insensitive part of the retina known as the *blind spot.* Now bring the book even closer to your face, and the circle will reappear. There is, of course, a similar blind spot on the other eye.

light than to specify its color. At any given wavelength, there is thus a zone of intensities within which we can see light but not color (see Figure 11.8).

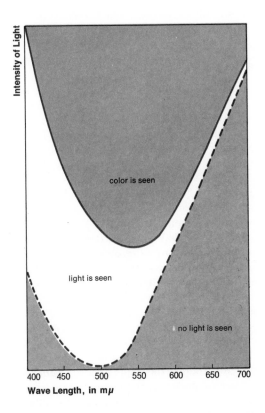

FIGURE 11.8 A chart showing the sensitivity of the human eye to light of different wavelengths. The broken curve shows the minimal intensities required at each wavelength for achromatic *light* to be seen. The solid curve shows the minimal intensities required at each wavelength for *color* to be seen.

Sensitivity to hue varies from place to place on the retina. Colors are seen best in the foveal region, the central part of the retina (see Unit 14, p. 323). They are not seen at all in the extreme periphery; everyone is "color-blind" at the edge of his visual field. You can easily demonstrate this by fixating a point in front of you and slowly moving a colored pencil at arm's length from the side of your head, where you cannot see it, toward the front of your head. You will detect the pencil moving into your visual field long before you can detect its color.

Visual acuity   When we talk about people having "good" or "poor" vision, it is usually **visual acuity** we are referring to—their ability to detect small differences in the size and shape of objects.

The conventional eye chart exposes letters or other figures of varying sizes at a standard distance from the viewer. The viewer's acuity is measured in terms of successful identification of the figures and is commonly expressed relative to average vision. Thus 20/20 vision signifies that the viewer is able to identify stimuli at 20 ft that the average person also identifies at 20 ft. And 20/40 vision signifies that the viewer must be as close as 20 ft to identify what average vision can identify at 40 ft. For more accurate determinations of visual acuity in the laboratory, other methods are used.

STIMULI FOR THE OTHER SENSES

Hearing

When an object is set into vibration (a violin string plucked, a drum thumped), the vibrations produce periodic **sound waves** that are transmitted through the air in all directions. The impact of these waves on the eardrum is the stimulus for hearing.

Our world is full of sounds that vary in **pitch** all the way from the deepest tones to the highest. And pitch is mostly determined by the *frequency* of the sound waves—the greater the frequency the higher the pitch. The *loudness* of sounds varies primarily with the **amplitude** of the sound waves, that is, the amount of energy transmitted by the sound waves as they strike the ear.

Almost always in our physical environment sound waves reaching the ear are complex mixtures of different frequencies. These mixtures are responsible for our experience of timbre, overtones, beats, consonance and dissonance, and noise.

Of the whole range of waves produced by vibrating objects, only a certain frequency band is capable of producing sound. In man, the lowest frequency that can be heard is about 20 hz, and the highest is about 20,000 hz. Above and below these limits there is silence—silence for man, but not for all species.

Tasting

We can taste almost any substance that dissolves when placed on the tongue. The four basic components of taste and some chemical substances that elicit these separate components are: sweet (sugar), sour (hydrochloric acid), bitter (quinine), salty (table salt). However, when we seek to identify the precise chemical structure that accounts for a given taste, we are confronted with a problem yet unsolved. Substances of extremely different chemical make-up can evoke much the same sensation—for example, sugar and saccharin. Conversely, substances that chemically are very similar often taste quite different.

The senses of taste and smell are often classified together, not only because the physical stimuli for both are chemical substances, but also because they so frequently combine in producing a unified perception. The taste and flavor of a particular food result from taste *and*

olfactory stimulation. The tastelessness of even our favorite dish when its aroma is blocked by a head cold gives ample demonstration of this.

Smelling

The stimuli for smell are gaseous particles that are brought into contact with receptors in the upper cavity of the nose. The bewildering array of odors we can experience accounts for the failure to achieve a very satisfactory classification scheme for odors. One scheme (a fairly useful one) uses only four basic odors: fragrant, acidic, burnt, and caprylic (something like the smell of a sweaty dog).

As with taste, difficulties have been encountered in trying to relate olfactory experiences to specifiable chemical structures of gaseous stimuli. Again we must report that this scientific task is yet to be accomplished.

Feeling

The so-called **somesthetic senses** include sensations both from the external skin receptors and from receptors inside the body. Most of the psychophysical work on the somesthetic senses has been done with the skin senses. It is convenient to subdivide the skin senses into pressure, pain, warmth, and cold. The common experiences of "itch," "ache," and "tickle" seem to result from complex patterns of pain, pressure, and thermal stimuli.

Objects that are forced against the skin produce sensations of *pressure*. A mapping of the body's pressure spots indicates that they are distributed very unevenly over the surfaces; more are located toward the extremities of the body.

The skin may be injured or subjected to extreme forms of physical energy in many ways (e.g., cutting, piercing, burning, electrical current) to produce the experience of *pain*. As in the case of pressure, there are certain spots on the skin where pain stimuli are not effective. For instance, though the tip of the nose has many temperature and touch spots, it has relatively few pain spots.

Thermal energy, the stimulus for our temperature experiences, varies continuously along a simple physical scale as measured by a thermometer. But sensory experiences of *warmth* and *cold* do not vary along a similar intensity scale. Our temperature experiences distinguish heat from warmth, warmth from coolness, coolness from cold, on a *qualitative* as well as quantitative scale.

Some spots on the skin are sensitive to warmth, others to cold, and still others to both. If a very hot stimulus is applied to a cold spot, a sensation of cold (*paradoxical cold*) may be felt. Whether a thermal stimulus will evoke any sensation depends on the relation of the temperature of the stimulus to the temperature of the skin. Stimuli hotter than the skin will produce sensations of warmth, those colder will produce sensations of cold, and those just at skin temperature will not be felt at all.

Kinesthesis (literally "movement sensitivity") is one of our most basic senses. It provides information on the movements of bodily structures. The physical stimuli for **kinesthetic sensations** are mechanical forces that affect receptors in the muscles, tendons, and joints of the body. As the muscles move parts of the body, various patterns of pressure on these kinesthetic receptors provide us with specific movement sensations. These sensations, in turn, give us the essential information for guiding succeeding motor action.

INTERACTION WITHIN A SENSE

The effects of various stimuli for a given sense interact in producing a unified experience, and for this reason we speak of *patterns* of physical stimuli.

The patterns of physical stimuli are both spatial and temporal. The spatial patterns come about because of simultaneous stimulation of various parts of specific receptor organs, for example, the retina of the eye or the skin of the body. Temporal patterns result from the sequence of stimuli.

Temporal Interaction

When a succession of stimuli arrive on a given receptor organ, these stimuli may interact by summating and *increasing* the receptor's response; by fusing and *changing the quality of* the response; or by summating and *weakening* the response (*adaptation*). These three types of interaction are illustrated in the following sensory phenomena.

Temporal summation   The longer the duration of a light of subthreshold intensity, the greater the probability that it will become an effective stimulus. Apparently there is a kind of summation of each momentary stimulation over time, which we call **temporal summation.**

Flicker and fusion   If we turn a light on and off at intervals of 1 sec, the observer sees a sequence of light and dark intervals. If we then shorten the on-off intervals, the light begins to **flicker.** The rate of flicker stays about the same (about twenty per second) even when the light-dark alternation occurs at much lower or at much higher rates. If the intervals are still shorter, the flicker disappears, and a continuous light is seen. We call this **fusion.** Obviously, the aftereffect of each separate stimulus lasts long enough to bridge the interval until the next stimulus occurs. We encounter this phenomenon repeatedly in everyday life. The movies give us the undeniable impression of continuous, unbroken stimulation, yet we know that what is exposed to our eyes is an intermittent series of still photographs and short blank intervals.

Sensory adaptation   The phenomenon in which a succession of identical stimuli falling on the same receptor leads to a *decrease* in the effectiveness of later stimuli is known as **sensory adaptation.** Let us illustrate this in the various sensory modes.

Visual adaptation   You can readily demonstrate the marked dilution of color that occurs as a consequence of fairly short continuous exposures (see Box 11.6, p. 250). There is also pronounced adaptation to brightness. A white or a black surface looked at continuously begins to look grayish.

The most impressive of all visual-adaptation effects are *light adaptation* and *dark adap-*

BOX 11.6

UNNOTICED CHANGE IN PERCEPTION

Using the yellow rectangle shown in Color Plate 4, immediately preceding page 233, you can demonstrate for yourself a convincing instance of a change in perception that occurs without your awareness. Take a piece of gray paper and place it over the right half of the yellow rectangle so that the fixation mark is just visible.

Then stare steadily right at the fixation mark for a period of one minute. *Be careful not to shift your eyes from it.* At the end of the minute remove the gray cover from the yellow rectangle, *continuing without interruption to look at the fixation mark.*

If you are like most people, you will find that, when the cover is removed, the yellow on the left side appears diluted and "washed out" compared to the yellow on the right. What has happened is that during the continuous look at the left side, the perceived color slowly lost its original saturation. Yet most people are not at all aware of this gradual change as it occurs and only realize how pronounced it is when they see the washed-out yellow beside the unaffected bright yellow on the right after the cover is removed. Perception can change without our perceiving the change!

The reason for the gradual dilution of the color with continued exposure will be discussed on p. 324.

The **visual afterimage** is an interesting adaptation phenomenon. For a demonstration of this type of image, see Box 11.7.

Auditory adaptation The ear is notably less subject to sensory adaptation than the eye and other sense receptors. Even prolonged exposure to a continuous sound of ordinary intensity shows little effect. But with more intense continuous sounds, like the high-pitched machinery sounds that a factory worker may be exposed to, adaptation does occur, and there is marked loss of auditory sensitivity.

Adaptation in taste and smell Everyday experience testifies that adaptation occurs in the chemical senses. Many an oversalted dish is the penalty for the cook's prolonged sampling during preparation; the cook's salt threshold gradually increases with continual testing, so that when the "just right" point is finally reached for the (adapted) cook, the salt concentration for the unadapted guests can be painfully above threshold. In smell, sensory adaptation usually has a more benign effect; enforced exposure to unpleasant odors is a common mishap, and the speed with which we become blissfully unaware of the offending stimulus is a fortunate asset of the human organism.

Adaptation in the skin senses Adaptation to pain stimuli is slow, and we seem to note little or no adaptation to the sharp cutting or skin-pricking pains we experience in daily life. Adaptation to thermal stimuli is a matter of common observation. The uncomfortably hot bath water soon becomes bearable; the cold lake into which we plunge soon does not seem cold. In the case of extremely hot and extremely cold stimuli, however, adaptation does not seem to occur or occurs only very slowly.

Spatial Interaction

Just as there is temporal interaction of stimuli, there is also significant spatial interaction, which occurs among the separate sensitive "points" on the receptor surface of our receptor organs.

tation. The former can be illustrated by our common experience in entering a darkened theater from bright sunlight; at first we cannot see objects, then after a time we can see them very easily. In continuous sunlight the eye becomes light-adapted (relatively *less* sensitive to light stimuli). After some time in darkness the eye becomes dark-adapted and recovers. On leaving the theater, we encounter a different difficulty; the sunlight is so bright that it hurts our eyes and we are blinded for a few moments. This illustrates the fact that a dark-adapted eye is much more sensitive to light than a light-adapted eye.

BOX 11.7

AFTERIMAGES

Stare steadily at the numeral on the sail in the figure for one minute. Then look at a plain light surface such as a wall or a sheet of paper. You may be surprised to see the sailboat projected there. And more surprising is the fact that the black and white areas are reversed. This image is known as a *negative afterimage*. It is called an "afterimage" because it is a sensation persisting after the original stimulus has been removed. It is called "negative" because the brightness relationships are reversed.

Negative afterimages are found with hue as well as with brightness. Turn to Color Plate 5, immediately preceding page 233. Fixate the cross in the center of the left figure for about 30 sec; then transfer your gaze to the cross in the gray square. You will see clear colors in the locations of the four

colored patches of the original stimulus, but the colors will now be the *complementaries* of the original hues.

There are also *positive afterimages*. If you look for a moment at a whirling bright light and then close your eyes, you will see the image of the path of the light persisting for some time. The image is positive, in that it has the same brightness relationships as the original stimulus.

What is even more fascinating is that negative afterimages can be seen without the perception of prior positive images. G. Sperling (1960) has demonstrated this phenomenon in a number of visual situations. In one experiment a dollar bill is exposed with a bright flash so briefly that the dollar bill is not seen. But, when the subject then looks at a less brightly illuminated screen, a *pink* "greenback"— its negative afterimage—is clearly perceived on the screen.

The explanation of afterimages must lie in the fact that the nervous system continues to be aroused for some time after a stimulus has been withdrawn. Why the afterimage should often be the *negative* of the original stimulus is a fascinating question having to do with the adaptation of the visual nervous system to light (see Unit 14, p. 324).

It should be noted that afterimage phenomena are by no means restricted solely to vision. There are also auditory afterimages and various tactual afterimages, like the persistent feeling of pressure on the skin after a pressure stimulus has been withdrawn.

G. SPERLING. Negative afterimage without prior positive image. *Science*, 1960, **131**, 1613–1614.

Spatial summation and irradiation Whether or not a light is seen depends among other things on the number of retinal points stimulated. This phenomenon is known as **spatial summation.** That a spatial spreading of effect occurs in the retina is suggested by another phenomenon known as **irradiation.** For example, a white square on a black background appears slightly larger than a black square of equal size on a white background. It is as though the retinal excitation by the white area "spills over" to some extent into the surrounding retinal areas.

Spatial fusion The appearance of different visual stimuli falling on the retina depends upon their spatial proximity. This can be demonstrated by looking at textile threads of various colors woven into a pattern. When viewed close up, the separate colors can be readily distinguished. Viewed at a middle distance, an interplay of colors occurs that gives the material a "sparkle" or "liveliness." At a greater distance, the separate colors completely disappear, and **spatial fusion** is seen.

Seurat (1859–1891), the French Neo-Impressionist painter, invented the technique called *pointillism,* in which, instead of mixing paints in the traditional way on the palette or canvas, he applied single dots of pure color over the canvas. The final effect depended on the psychology of color mixing, rather than on the physics of pigment mixture. This method relies upon spatial fusion by the eye to give the desired color mixtures and produces a kind of visual "liveliness" rarely found in other paintings.

Békésy (1964) has demonstrated spatial fusion in taste but with the interesting qualification that not all taste qualities can fuse with one another. By stimulating the two sides of the tongue simultaneously, each side with a different taste stimulus or with warmth and cold,

FIGURE 11.10 A demonstration of brightness contrast. The squares are cut from identical gray paper.

he found that warm, bitter, and sweet stimuli interact with one another to yield a fused sensation in the middle of the tongue; so do cold, sour, and salty stimuli. Sweet and salty stimuli are experienced as separate sensations on opposite sides of the tongue (see Figure 11.9). These findings suggest a "duplexity" theory of taste; that is, two different types of receptors may be involved in taste perception.

Simultaneous contrast Look at the gray squares in Figure 11.10. It is hard for most observers to see them as the same gray, yet they are. A given gray is lighter in dark surroundings and darker in light surroundings. This effect is known as **simultaneous contrast.**

Similar contrast effects are found with other properties of color like hue and saturation. If two small squares of identical gray paper are compared when one is placed on a large red field and the other on a large green field, the first gray square looks distinctly greenish and the other distinctly reddish.

The *degree* of contrast is in large measure determined by the relations between a given area and its surroundings. For example, the larger the difference in intensity between an area and its surroundings or the larger the relative size of the surrounding field, the greater the contrast. But we are still far from an understanding of the phenomena of contrast. Note, for example, the "failure" of usual contrast effects in Figure 11.11 (see also Color Plate 6 immediately preceding p. 233).

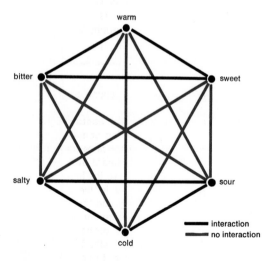

FIGURE 11.9 A graphic representation of the duplexity theory of taste, showing the six different sensations that can be experienced on the tongue. The stimuli that melt together into a common sensation when presented simultaneously are interconnected with black lines, indicating that they have something in common with one another. Stimuli connected with colored lines can be presented to the two sides of the tongue simultaneously without showing any interaction at all.

G. von Békésy. Duplexity theory of taste. *Science,* 1964, **145,** 834–935; copyright 1964 by the American Association for the Advancement of Science; adapted by permission.

INTERACTION AMONG DIFFERENT SENSES

So far, in speaking of temporal and spatial interaction, we have discussed these effects only as

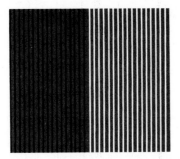

FIGURE 11.11 A demonstration of the failure of brightness contrast. Here the effect is reversed; the gray field surrounding the black lines seems darker. The background "takes on" the characteristics of the superimposed lines, suggesting that irradiation may be occurring.

H. Helson & F. H. Rohles, Jr. A quantitative study of reversal of classical lightness-contrast. *American Journal of Psychology*, 1959, **72**, 530–538; adapted by permission.

they occur *within* a given sensory system. But interaction can also come about from simultaneous exposure to stimuli in *different* sense modalities. Perhaps that is why we often close our eyes when straining to hear a faint sound. Benjamin (1955–1956) has demonstrated that a painful stimulus raises the thresholds for visual, auditory, tactile, and temperature sensations. Box 11.8 illustrates how this effect can be happily reversed.

In our everyday perceptions the senses typically cooperate with and supplement one another. Flavor depends upon the joint operation of taste and smell receptors. The texture of food (a tactile sensation) is also important. The usual product of a multisense stimulus pattern is a more complex and therefore a richer experience. Each sense contributes its own version of an occurrence in the physical world, each qualitatively different, yet usually blending into a coherent and unified single impression. Thus an object may look large, sound large, feel large, and perhaps even smell large.

Of course, each of the various sensory domains has its unique qualities. Visual experience is not likely to be confused with auditory experience, or smell with touch. There are sur-

BOX 11.8

AS EASY AS PULLING TEETH

A dramatic example of an intersensory masking effect —covering up sensation in one sense by stimulation of another—is the apparent effectiveness of sound in reducing experienced pain in dental operations (audio analgesia). W. J. Gardner, J. C. R. Licklider, and A. Z. Weisz report that, for 65 percent of the patients who previously required nitrous oxide or a local anesthetic, pain was completely eliminated by the judicious combination of music and noise. Here is how it is done. The patient wears headphones through which some soothing stereophonic music is heard. As the dental work begins, the patient is provided with a control box that enables him to introduce a fairly loud noise, "like a waterfall," through the headphones. As soon as he feels or is afraid he will feel the slightest pain, he can adjust the volume of the sound to quite high levels in order to mask the pain.

Several factors may contribute to this effect. The unnerving sound of the dental drill is no longer heard. Some patients emphasize that trying to follow the melody as it is dimly heard over the noise diverts their attention. Others stress the importance of having some measure of control in the situation, a factor that reduces their anxiety and therefore the pain felt. For any given patient a different combination of several of these factors is probably responsible for successfully suppressing pain. The authors suggest a physiological mechanism to account for the effect; this mechanism involves an inhibitory interaction of the auditory and pain systems in the reticular formation and lower thalamus (see Unit 14, p. 348). It is conceivable that some such mechanism may account for the efficacy of acupuncture (insofar as acupuncture is effective). The neural activity set up by the twirling acupuncture needles may interact with and inhibit pain impulses.

W. J. GARDNER, J. C. R. LICKLIDER, & A. Z. WEISZ. Suppression of pain by sound. *Science*, 1960, **132**, 32–33.

prising interactions of the senses in **synesthesia**, however, in which stimulation of one kind of sense receptor also produces experiences in a different sense domain (see Box 11.9).

Sensation versus Perception

An analysis of perception describing the cooperative unity of the senses was first attempted by the Gestalt psychologists. Their phenomenological analysis distinguished between the experience of *sensation* and that of *perception*. In this unit, for example, we have emphasized the attributes of simple sensations resulting from the stimulation of single sensory organs. We have paid relatively little attention to the phenomenology of the full-bodied multisensory perceptions we typically experience. And these two kinds of experiences are quite different, as Gibson (1963) points out:

> The variables of sensory discrimination are radically different from the variables of perceptual discrimination. The former are said to be dimensions like quality, intensity, extensity, and duration, dimensions of hue, brightness, and saturation, of pitch, loudness, and timbre, of pressure, warm, cold, and pain. The latter are dimensions of the environment, the variables of events and those of

---

BOX 11.9

SYNESTHESIA

The most common form of synesthesia is color hearing, in which a vivid color image is evoked by a sound, for example a musical note. The tone-color relations are not identical for different people, but there are certain general uniformities; for example, bass notes result in darker colors, treble notes in lighter colors.

    For a given individual the relationships of tones and colors may be systematic and fairly permanent. H. S. Langfeld at Princeton studied one person's synesthesia over a seven-year interval, with results as shown in the table.

    T. H. Howells at the University of Colorado succeeded in artificially conditioning color hearing. He presented a low tone accompanied by a red light and a high tone accompanied by a green light 5,000 times each to eight subjects. After this conditioning period, he presented pale reddish or greenish colors. If the *high* tone (previously associated with green) was given with the pale reddish hue, subjects frequently reported it as *greenish*; if the *low* tone was given with the pale greenish hue, it was often seen as *reddish*.

    As a further step, two of the subjects were instructed to mix red and green on a color wheel until they achieved a neutral gray. When the high

Musical Note	Color Sensation on First Study	Color Sensation Seven Years Later
c	red	red
d♭	purple	lavender
d	violet	violet ,
e♭	soft blue	thick blue
e	golden yellow	sunlight
f	pink	pink, apple blossoms
f♯	green blue	blue green*
g♭	greener blue	greener blue*
g	clear blue	clear sky blue
a	cold yellow	clear yellow, hard, not warm
b♭	orange	verges on orange
b	very brilliant coppery	very brilliant coppery

* The difference between the pitches of f♯ and g♭ is so subtle that no allowance is made for it on a keyboard instrument. There is a distinction between these notes in string and brass instruments, however, because the musician makes his own pitch.

tone was sounded continuously during the color-mixing task, the subjects tended to put in *more red and less green* than were normally required for a neutral gray. Conversely, when the low tone was sounded continuously, they tended to put in more green and less red. Hearing the tone had served as an equivalent of color in the mixing task!

H. S. LANGFELD. Note on a case of chromaesthesia. *Psychological Bulletin*, 1914, **11**, 113–114. Table adapted by permission of American Psychological Association.
T. H. HOWELLS. The experimental development of color-tone synesthesia. *Journal of Experimental Psychology*, 1944, **34**, 87–103.

surfaces, places, objects, of other animals, and even of symbols. Perception involves meaning; sensation does not. To see a patch of color is not to see an object, nor is seeing the form of a color the same as seeing the shape of an object. To see a darker patch is not to see a shadow on a surface. . . . To have a salty taste is not to taste salt, and to have a certain olfactory impression is not to smell, say, a mint julep. To feel an impression on the skin is not to feel an object. . . . To feel a local pain is not to feel the pricking of a needle. To feel warmth on one's skin is not to feel the sun on one's skin, and to feel cold is not to feel the coldness of the weather.

The point is that the experiences we report seem rarely determined by a *stimulus* but by *stimulus objects*. We seem so constructed that the items of information we collect about our environment through our various sense organs usually work *together* to provide us with a highly useful picture of the world. It is difficult to conceive of a world in which this action of the senses does not hold true.

SUMMARY

1. Our information about the world around us necessarily comes through our senses, responding to light and sound waves, pressures, and various chemical stimuli. In studying the processes of perception, psychologists work closely with physiologists, physicists, and chemists in order to understand better the mechanisms and various forms of physical energy involved in sensing stimuli.

2. Physiological and phenomenological ("raw experience") approaches complement one another in the study of perception; the latter provides phenomena that the former is challenged to account for.

3. Linking the environment, from which perceptual stimuli originate, there is a medium through which the stimuli travel, sense receptors that receive them, sensory nerves that carry them to the brain, and certain areas of the brain where they are received and processed, finally to give rise to a perceptual experience. This chain is highly reliable in that it almost always transmits correct information about the environment, but there are a number of ways in which it can be flawed and result in misperceptions.

4. The stimulus is the physical energy arising from a stimulus object that excites receptors and leads to perceptual experience. The study of the relationships between characteristics of such experience and those of the physical stimulus is called psychophysics.

5. The organism is not sensitive to all parts of the possible range of physical energy. An important psychophysical problem is the determination for a given organism

of that point in the scale of intensity of the physical stimulus that separates seeing from not seeing, hearing from not hearing, tasting from not tasting, etc. This point is called the absolute threshold. There are several different ways in which this threshold can be determined. The measurement techniques used are called psychophysical methods.

6. That amount of physical energy just large enough to make a "just noticeable difference" perceptually is called the differential threshold. As in the case of the absolute threshold, the value of the differential threshold varies widely, depending on the nature of the stimulus and the state of the organism. Most importantly, it has a different value for each level of absolute magnitude of the stimulus; for example, the differential threshold for a dim light is not the same as for a bright light. Within limits the differential threshold tends to approximate a constant fraction of the stimulus intensity, a mathematical formulation known as Weber's Law.

7. The physical stimulus for vision is radiant energy from a very narrow region of the full range of electromagnetic waves. The hue of a color depends on the wavelength of the light; its brightness on light intensity. Saturation refers to the purity of a color—the more mixed the light waves, the lower the saturation of the resultant color. Color mixture follows fairly simple laws, but mixing light is quite different from mixing paint.

8. The sensitivity of the eye to light waves varies with wavelength and intensity, with the eye's state of adaptation resulting from previous stimulation, and with the region of the retina stimulated. Colors are seen best in the foveal region and are not seen at all around the extreme peripheries of the retina. Visual acuity— the ability to distinguish stimuli very close to each other—varies, depending in part upon the retinal region stimulated, amount of illumination, degree of contrast between object and background, and the presence or absence of defects in the visual mechanisms.

9. Variations in air pressure at the eardrum result in the experience of sound. Pitch is due mainly to the frequency of the sound waves—the greater the frequency, the higher the pitch. Loudness varies primarily with the amplitude of the sound waves. When sound waves of different characteristics are mixed, we experience more complex sound qualities like timbre, overtones, consonance, and dissonance (which at the extreme is noise). Auditory sensitivity, like visual sensitivity, is restricted to certain bands of energy and depends, among other factors, on the intensity and frequency of sound waves.

10. Taste and smell are intimately related; both have chemical substances as their physical stimuli, and they typically interact with one another. Substances of extremely different chemical make-up can evoke much the same sensation. Also, substances that chemically are very similar often taste quite different.

11. Although it is convenient to classify skin sensations as touch, pain, heat, and cold (each of which occurs in numerous receptive spots scattered irregularly over the surface of the body), the relation of receptor to experience is not a simple one. Also, more complex experiences, such as itching, involve an interaction among these basic sensations.

12. Kinesthetic sensations arise from movements of the body that stimulate receptors in the mucles, tendons, and joints. They help to keep track of body posture and are critical cues for guiding our movements.

13. Sensory experience is enormously dependent on a wide variety of interactive effects; these effects can occur within a single receptor or among different receptors for a single sense. Some of these interactions derive from differences in the timing of sensory stimulation, some from differences in the spatial location of receptors, and some from the overall patterning of incoming stimulation, which include summation, fusion, and adaptation. Interaction also occurs among different senses, often enriching the resultant perceptual experience.

14. Sensory interactions are by far more typical in everyday perception than are isolated sensory experiences and lead to unified experiences of a meaningful environment rather than of specific sensory stimuli.

GLOSSARY

absolute threshold The minimal intensity of a physical stimulus required to stimulate the organism.

amplitude The amount of energy carried by a sound wave. It is closely related to experienced loudness.

brightness A dimension of visual experience varying from white to black. It is closely correlated with intensity of the light waves.

color blindness A defect in sensitivity to hue. Total color blindness is very rare. There are two kinds of partial color blindness. Deuteranopia is partial color blindness involving inability to distinguish red and green. Protanopia is partial color blindness involving inability to distinguish red from green plus a weakness in sensitivity to the red end of the spectrum.

complementary colors Colors that lie exactly opposite each other on the color circle and that, when mixed in equal proportions, produce an achromatic gray—for example, red and green, yellow and blue.

differential threshold The minimum difference in intensities between two stimuli that can be perceived.

flicker The visual phenomenon produced by certain rates of intermittent on-and-off flashing of a stimulus.

fusion The visual phenomenon in which a series of successive stimuli produce a continuous, uniform sensation, as in the case of a rapidly flashing light or a mixture of colors on a color wheel.

hertz (abbreviated hz) Unit used to measure the frequency of waves of any form. Equal to (and formerly called) number of cycles per second.

hue The color of an object—for example, blue, red, yellow, green.

irradiation The tendency for the retinal stimulation in a given area to spread slightly into the surrounding area. For example, a white square on a black background appears larger than a black square of equal size on a white background.

kinesthetic sensations Sensations arising from body movement and muscular strain evoked by mechanical forces affecting receptors in the muscles, tendons, and joints.

monocular depth cues The stimulus characteristics that lead to an impression of visual depth with one eye. Monocular cues from the visual pattern include interposition, relative size, relative height, relative clearness, linear perspective, and light and shadow. Other monocular cues are accommodation and relative movement.

phenomenology As used by psychologists, refers to the person's immediate, unanalyzed experience evoked by a stimulus or pattern of stimuli. The phenomenological method (used in the study of perception) is one where the subject is trained to report how things appear to him, irrespective of whether the subject "knows better." Thus, if a plate, viewed at an angle, appears round, the subject must so report it, even though his knowledge of geometry and optics tells him it "should" appear oval-shaped. That is why the phenomenological method has been characterized as requiring a *disciplined naiveté* on the part of the subject.

pitch The attribute of tones in terms of which they may be described as high or low. This attribute is closely related to frequency of the sound waves.

psychophysical methods Methods for the determination of absolute and differential thresholds.

psychophysics The study of the relationships between the attributes of different sensory experiences and the characteristics of the physical stimuli producing them.

saturation The degree of concentration or dilution of the hue of a color.

sensory adaptation A form of temporal interaction in which immediately prior stimulation of a receptor modifies the effectiveness of later stimuli.

simultaneous contrast The tendency for the color of one area to accentuate the complementary color of the neighboring area.

somesthetic senses The senses which include sensations from external skin receptors and from internal receptors.

sound waves Periodic compressions and rarefactions of the air, which, striking the ear, produce sounds. Sound waves have certain frequencies and amplitudes.

spatial fusion The perceptual combination of spatially separated stimuli that gives rise to a unitary impression.

spatial summation The summative effect of separate stimuli spread over space. Thus light intensities too weak to be seen when falling on a small retinal area can be seen when falling on a larger area.

stimulus Physical energy that excites a receptor and produces an effect on the organism.

stimulus object   The object in the environment that is the source of the energy that serves as a stimulus.

synesthesia   A type of perceptual experience in which stimulation of one kind of sense receptor results in sensations in a completely different sense domain—for example, when a musical sound produces the sensation of a blue color.

temporal summation   The phenomenon in which a subthreshold stimulus, when continuously applied, may summate its effect to produce a response.

vestibular sensations   The sense of balance and of movement. The stimuli for these sensations are accelerative movements of fluids in the semicircular canals of the inner ear.

visual acuity   The ability to differentiate visually small details of size and shape of objects.

visual afterimage   The sensation that follows removal of the external light stimulus. The positive afterimage has the same colors as the original percept; the negative afterimage has the opposite colors from those of the original percept.

Weber's Law   The principle that the minimal perceptible difference in intensity of two stimuli (ΔI) is a constant fraction (k) of the absolute intensity of the stimuli (I). Formulated as

$$\frac{\Delta I}{I} = k$$

The constant fraction differs for each given type of stimulus. The law does not hold at the extremes of the stimulus range.

perceptual organization

DO YOU KNOW...

how camouflage works?

that drastic changes can occur in what we see despite an unchanging stimulus pattern?

what makes some portions of a stimulus pattern stand out as "things" while others do not?

why it is that a melody seems the same played anywhere on the musical scale or on different instruments?

the many ways in which we impose order on stimulus patterns we perceive, and that these different kinds of order are predictable?

that the brain may get "tired" of seeing the same thing?

in what ways we tend to see what we expect to see?

photo by Robin Forbes

CONTENTS

Almost every perception can be considered a personal experience. While it is undoubtedly true that perceptions are primarily determined by the stimuli that impinge on the sense organs of the individual, it is equally true that factors other than the reactions of the sense organs modulate the resulting experience. These factors reflect the individual perceiver's history and present psychological status. What you perceive out there is determined by what is out there to perceive, by what sense organs you have to perceive with, and by the fact that it is *you* who are perceiving.

While the influence of the many determinants of perception can be analyzed into a number of separate elements, for example, into sensations of color, brightness, saturation, and fragments of memories or feeling tones, the defining characteristic of a perception is that *it is a unified, organized experience.* Further, any set of stimuli may give rise to a *variety* of perceptual organizations. The perceiver does not have to intend the particular form he will experience, or to be aware of how it occurs. The organization of separate stimuli (lights, sounds, smells, and so forth) from the outside world takes place without conscious direction and with greater speed and sureness than rational analysis permits, although conscious thought and deliberate intention can play an important role in the process.

That perceptual organization seemingly takes place spontaneously does not mean that it does not follow certain laws or that it is not predictable. Perhaps in no other area have psychologists been more successful in formulating general principles with significant predictive power than in these principles of perceptual organization. In discussing these organizational principles we have chosen to draw our examples primarily from visual perception, on which most of the research has been done and in which the operation of these principles is most clearly and dramatically seen. However, research results clearly indicate that these principles generally hold for most and perhaps all the other senses as well.

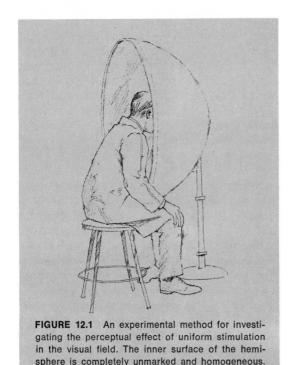

FIGURE 12.1 An experimental method for investigating the perceptual effect of uniform stimulation in the visual field. The inner surface of the hemisphere is completely unmarked and homogeneous. The level of illumination can be varied.

threshold of visual acuity, there is at once a perceptual transformation. Now our observer sees the surface, and it appears to be localized in space a short distance in front of him. But the surface itself appears entirely uniform and without detail (see Figure 12.2a).

We again change the illumination of the surface, varying it from darker to lighter and from left to right across the field. Despite this gradient from darker to brighter in the *stimulus pattern*, the field is still *perceived as evenly lighted* throughout (see Figure 12.2b). This tendency toward maximal uniformity and lack of differentiation in perception is known as **assimilation**, or "leveling." Note that if the darker and lighter *extremes* of the field were placed side by side, our observer would have no difficulty in perceiving them as different. When the difference between any two *adjacent* points in the field is below threshold, however, overall homogeneity is produced.

Finally, we impose a faint vertical shadow line through the middle of this field. There is an immediate perceptual transformation. A vertical **contour** appears in the middle of the field, and the total field is divided into two different parts: The half of the field to the left of the

DIFFERENTIATION OF THE PERCEPTUAL FIELD

We shall begin with a laboratory demonstration. A man is seated with his head inside a large hollow hemisphere (see Figure 12.1). Its inner surface is smooth, unmarked, and evenly illuminated by a moderate light in such a way that the stimulation of his eyes is entirely uniform. What does he see?

He sees only a uniform light "mist" filling an endless space. He cannot tell how far away the surface of the sphere is; in fact, he perceives no surface at all. There is a complete lack of perceptual differentiation. There are no objects in such a field, not even distinguishable regions. Such homogeneity is the simplest possible perceptlike experience.

When the illumination is made considerably brighter, so that the very fine grain of the inner surface of the sphere approaches the

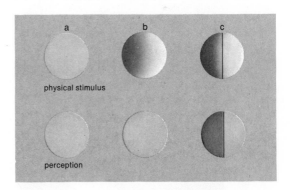

FIGURE 12.2 The upper circles represent the objective illumination conditions on the inner surface of the hemisphere shown in Figure 12.1. The corresponding lower circles represent the individual's perception of each of these physical stimulus conditions. In a, the homogeneous physical field looks homogeneous. In b, despite the gradient of intensity across the field, the field still looks homogeneous. In c, a faint vertical line in the middle of the hemisphere produces a perception of two different fields, each homogeneous within itself but different in apparent level of illumination.

contour is seen as a uniform field of lesser brightness, and the half to the right is seen as a uniform field of greater brightness (see Figure 12.2c).

The level of uniform brightness within each area is an average of the light intensities within it; therefore a sharp difference in brightness is produced just at the dividing line, or contour, between the two parts. The perceived difference between two immediately adjacent points lying on different sides of the boundary is thus maximized. Despite a continuous gradient of change in the *stimulus pattern*, we *perceive* two sharply contrasting parts.

This phenomenon of perceiving a difference greater than that called for by the stimulus intensities is known as **contrast**, or "sharpening." We encounter examples of it in the form of sensory contrast (see p. 252). Contrast means an accentuation of differences and is, like assimilation, a basic phenomenon in many psychological processes besides perception.

In Figure 12.3 we have another compelling demonstration of the important role that a contour can play in evoking the contrast effect. The black and white backgrounds would ordinarily make the neutral gray of the ring brighter on the left side and darker on the right. But be-

cause the ring is seen as a single unbroken entity, assimilation leads us to perceive a uniform gray throughout the ring. If we introduce a contour separating the whole ring into two parts, a clear contrast is seen. The left half of the ring now appears to be of a uniform lighter gray and the other half of a uniform darker gray.

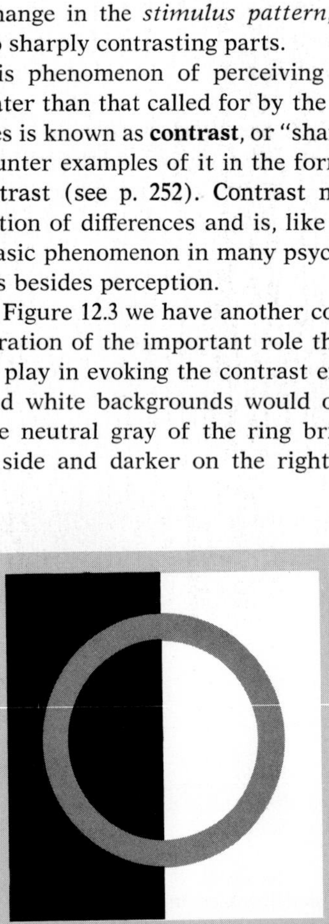

Figure and Ground

As we look at the parts of any differentiated field, we notice that almost invariably one part (the **figure**) stands out distinctively from the rest (the **ground**). Figure-ground differentiation is the simplest and most primitive form of perceptual organization. It seems to be present at the very beginnings of visual perception. Newborn infants can follow an object (figure) with their eyes as it moves across a homogeneous ground.

The perceptual properties of figure and ground differ. The figure tends to be better defined, better localized, more solid and integrated, whereas the ground appears to be less definite and less structured. The figure appears to lie in front of or upon the ground, which appears to extend continuously in an unbroken fashion behind the figure.

Which will be figure? Among the factors that determine which of two adjacent areas will be perceived as figure and which ground are the sizes, locations, and shapes of the two areas. Other things being equal, the smaller area and the more enclosed area tend to be seen as figure. And other things being equal, that which makes for a simpler, more regular figure is favored (see Figure 12.4). In general, the more "meaningful" pattern is also likely to be seen as figure. But meaningfulness may not necessarily dominate over other organizational factors. For an impressive demonstration of this fact, carefully inspect Figure 12.5.

Contour If we are to distinguish a figure at all, there must usually be a contour that separates figure from ground. In Figure 12.5 the word is hidden because part of the essential contour—the tops and bottoms of the letters—is missing.

FIGURE 12.3 First note that the gray ring has a uniform brightness. Now place a long thin object like a pencil along the vertical line so that the ring is divided in half. What is the apparent brightness of each half of the ring now? For an explanation of this striking phenomenon, see above.

FIGURE 12.4 This drawing tends to be perceived as wavy white stripes on a plum background rather than as plum stripes on a white background, even though the total areas of white and plum are equal. The reason seems to be that the white stripes are regular in width, whereas the plum stripes are irregular.

W. Metzger. *Gesetze des Sehens*, 1953; adapted by permission of Dr. Waldemar Kramer.

FIGURE 12.5 What is this figure? If you cannot tell after prolonged inspection, turn to Figure 12.6, page 266.

W. Brown & H. C. Gilhousen. *College Psychology*; copyright 1949, 1950 by Prentice-Hall, Inc., Englewood Cliffs, N.J.; adapted by permission.

In camouflage, this principle is used to strategic advantage. To the object being hidden, one adds lines and edges that remove the visible terminations and sides.

The contour is clearly perceived as "belonging" to the figure rather than to the ground, even though it is actually common to both. Under certain circumstances, figure and ground fluctuate, with continuing reversals of their roles. Strikingly, as figure-ground reversal occurs, the contour shifts from one figure to the other, and the appearance of the contour changes markedly. The identical physical contour looks entirely different in the two patterns drawn in Figure 12.7, page 266. It is this shifting quality of contour that sometimes makes the visual assembling of parts difficult, as in the pieces of a jigsaw puzzle, which, though sharing an identical contour, look very different and are not easily matched.

Closure Certain figures tend to be perceived as more complete or closed than they really are. This perceptual tendency is known as **closure**. One circumstance under which closure occurs is when the resulting closed figure is "good." For instance, most observers report seeing a distinct white square in Figure 12.8, page 266. Notice that even though the square is not actually defined by physical boundaries, the square is perceptually marked off by *subjective* contours.

Coren (1972) suggests that when the stimulus pattern provides slight depth cues, the ability of the perceptual system to create subjective contours is enhanced. Figure 12.9a, page 266, is perceived as a white triangle with its corners resting on the three black circles. There is a strong impression that the triangle lies *in front of* the background of the circles, and that it is completely bounded by faintly visible contours. In Figure 12.9b, on the other hand, although we easily organize the figure as a triangle and not as three unrelated parts, the triangle looks quite different from that in 12.9a. It does not lie in front of a background plane, and it is seen as incomplete—not bounded by subjective contours.

A second main circumstance under which closure tends to occur is when the resulting figure is familiar and meaningful (see Figure 12.10, p. 266). Livson (1962), combining data from a number of studies, reports a relation between this second kind of closure and age. The ability to recognize simple meaningful objects from incomplete representations increases with age, reaching a maximum at about adolescence. As early as the twenties this ability begins to wane, by forty it is distinctly worse, and it is almost totally absent in otherwise perfectly able and alert people in their seventies and eighties. Figure 12.10b, for example, is rarely recognized by the aged group but is quite easily recognized by adolescent subjects.

FIGURE 12.6

FIGURE 12.9 Subjective contours (see text for explanation).

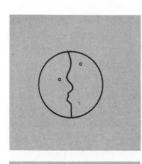

FIGURE 12.7 With continued inspection of the ambiguous drawing at the top, there is fluctuation of figure and ground so that sometimes the left face is seen and sometimes the right face. The appearance of the common contour between the two faces changes completely, depending on which figure it momentarily defines. This difference in appearance is more easily studied when the faces are presented separately.

R. Schafer & G. Murphy. The role of autism in a visual figure-ground relationship. *Journal of Experimental Psychology*, 1943, **32**, 335–343; adapted by permission of the American Psychological Association.

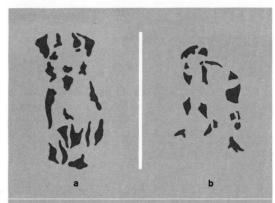

FIGURE 12.10 Incomplete pictures. *What are they?* Figure a is almost always seen as a dog by age three. Figure b is almost always seen by age fifteen as a crouching man, a sprinter, and the like; it is almost never seen as a meaningful object at age three.

L. L. Thurstone. *A Factorial Study of Perception*; copyright 1944 by the University of Chicago; adapted by permission.

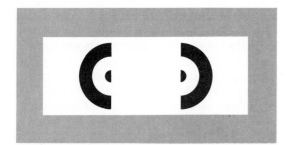

FIGURE 12.8 Do you see the white square? If you do, it looks as if it is resting on top of a black oval figure, which appears to extend continuously beneath it. Note that the white square can be seen even though there are no physical contours completely defining it.

PERCEPTUAL GROUPING

Everyday perception rarely involves a single figure-ground pattern; typically, several figures share a common ground. Also, individual figures tend to be perceived as clustering together in various groupings. Max Wertheimer, one of the founders of *Gestalt psychology*, formulated and demonstrated "grouping principles" more than fifty years ago.

Grouping by Proximity

Stimulus objects in close proximity to one another have a greater tendency to be grouped than those that are farther apart. The proximity may be spatial (as illustrated in Figure 12.11a); or it may be temporal: Of a series of tapping sounds occurring at irregular intervals, those that come close together in time tend to be grouped. Stimuli grouped by proximity need not all be of the same sensory mode. For example, if we hear a loud sound and see a bright light simultaneously, we tend to perceive them as belonging together, as parts of the same event. (For a curious example of the role of temporal proximity in the perception of casuality, see Box 13.2, p. 290.)

Grouping by Similarity

Stimulus objects that are similar to one another have a greater tendency to be grouped than those that are dissimilar. *Similarity* means likeness in physical attributes such as intensity, color, size, shape, and so on (see Figure 12.11b).

Grouping by Good Form

Other things being equal, stimuli that form a **good figure** will have a tendency to be grouped. This formulation is very general, intended to embrace a number of more specific variants of the theme:

1. *Good Continuation:* The tendency for elements to go with others in such a way as to permit the continuation of a line, a curve, or a movement in the direction that has already been established (see Figure 12.11c).
2. *Symmetry:* The favoring of groupings that lead to symmetrical or balanced wholes as against asymmetrical wholes.
3. *Closure:* The grouping of elements in such a way as to make for a more closed or more complete whole figure.
4. *Common Fate:* The grouping of those elements that move or change in a common direction, as distinguished from those having other directions of movement or change in the field. This principle, which is essentially an extension to moving objects of grouping by similarity, is an important choreographic tool. Particularly when many dancers are involved, our tendency to group those who follow parallel paths (or those who execute the same limb movements) transforms potential chaos into a fasci-

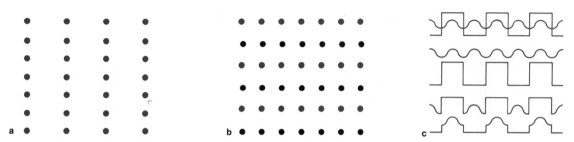

FIGURE 12.11 Examples of grouping. In a, the dots are perceived in vertical columns because their spatial proximity is greater in the vertical than in the horizontal direction. In b, where proximity is equal, the rows are perceived as horizontal because of grouping by similarity. In c, the principle of good continuation results in seeing the upper figure as consisting of the two parts shown immediately below, even though logically it might just as well be composed of the two parts shown at the very bottom.

M. Wertheimer. Untersuchungen zur Lehre von der Gestalt. *Psychologische Forschung*, 1923, **4**, 301–350; adapted by permission of Springer-Verlag.

nating and complex procession of organized movement.

A difficulty with this grouping principle centers on the meaning of the crucial phrase "good figure." How can we know which configuration of stimuli is "better" than another? Clearly we have need of measurable criteria for figural goodness that avoid circularity: Grouping tends toward good form and good form is that which gets grouped.

Some theoretical progress has been made toward an objective definition of "good figure" (see Box 12.1). The "good figure" is the simple and predictable one.

BOX 12.1

HOW TO MEASURE "GOODNESS"

Two psychologists, working independently, hit upon very much the same general principle for measuring the "goodness" of a figure by a yardstick equally applicable to the several varieties of good form. As put by J. E. Hochberg of Cornell University the principle is as follows: The less the amount of information needed to define a given perceptual organization as compared to alternative organizations, the more likely it is that that organization will be perceived. A symmetrical grouping is thus fully defined by describing one-half the figure in detail and then stating that the rest of the figure is simply the mirror image of the described half. A closed circle can be more quickly defined than can an open one for which the location and extent of the gap must be specified. Or take one of Hochberg's examples, in which seeing the pattern as two intersecting rectangles permits a more succinct description than describing the alternate percept—five separate irregular figures (see Figure A). Hochberg contents himself with using a few quite rough indexes of the amount of information necessary to define a given figure, for example, numbers of lines, angles, and points of intersection. But these indexes are able to predict which organization of a reversible figure will be seen more frequently (see Figure B), and confirm that the more frequently perceived cube requires fewer descriptive items than does the alternate two-dimensional percept.

Working at the University of Oregon, F. Attneave developed a more precise information-measurement technique; he defines the "goodness" of a figure as the predictability of the total pattern from partial information. He determines the "goodness" of single figures one at a time. The subject is given a sheet of graph paper composed of 4,000 tiny squares (fifty rows by eighty columns). His task is to guess whether the color of each successive square is black, white, or gray. The experimenter has in mind what the completed figure will look like (see Figure C).

Without knowing what the completed figure will be, the subject starts by guessing the square in the lower left corner. When he has correctly identified the color, he moves on to guess the next square to the right. He continues this process to the end of the row and then starts at the left end of the next row above. In this manner he successively guesses each of the 4,000 squares.

On the average, Attneave's subjects made only fifteen wrong guesses for the entire figure. This low

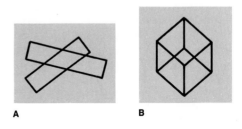

A   **B**

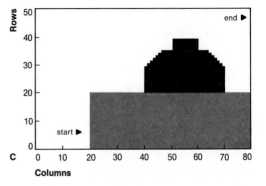

C

Competition and Cooperation in Grouping

In every stimulus pattern the elements have some degree of proximity, some degree of similarity, and some degree to which they fit "good form." Sometimes the grouping tendencies work in the same direction, and sometimes they are pitted against one another. For example, Figure 12.12, page 270, illustrates how closure may overcome the effects of proximity.

A special application of the competition of grouping tendencies is found in the art of camouflage and in the protective coloration and marking of animals in their natural surroundings. Camouflage takes advantage of factors such as "good continuation" and "closure" to mask other configurations. A simple illustration is seen in Figure 12.13, page 270.

Whole-Part Relations

The essential *form* of a perception is determined by the *pattern* of its constituent parts. Thus, the whole may remain the same, even though its constituent parts undergo marked changes, *providing* that the *pattern* of the parts remains unchanged. When this occurs we speak of **transposition**. For example, a melody is recognized as the same when played higher or lower in the scale (thus every note differs from the familiar set of notes for this melody) because the relations among the notes remain the same. It is also true, however, that some characteristics of the perceived whole may change with changes in the *specific properties* of its elements. A transposed melody may readily be recognized as the same melody, but it may also be perceived as in a different range of pitch or as played on a different instrument.

The converse of these whole-part relations is also true. That is, perception of the properties of a *part* is measurably dependent upon the nature of the whole in which the part is embedded. An example is the Müller-Lyer illusion, in which a line looks longer or shorter depending on whether it is part of an open or closed arrowhead figure (see Figure 12.14, p. 270).

Frame of Reference

In our judgment of the perceived properties of things, we typically make use of a standard, or **frame of reference**, against which a particular property is judged. When we ask how big an object is, the sizes of other objects in its group may serve as standards (see Figure 12.15, p. 270).

---

score was possible because the figure was designed so that knowledge of part of the figure was sufficient to enable the subject to make fairly valid predictions about the remainder of the figure. This was accomplished by making all the white squares contiguous with one another and by doing the same with the black squares and with the gray squares. Furthermore, the contours separating the white, black, and gray areas are simple and regular. Where the figure tapers, it tapers in a regular way. And it has symmetry; after exploring one side, it is easy to predict the other side. The subject, having thus discovered that the first few squares are white, continues to guess white, and he is correct until he hits the gray contour at column 20. After one or two errors, he then continues to guess gray. On the next row above, he tends to repeat the pattern of the first row.

This technique can be applied to any pattern of whatever complexity; it can be applied even to three-dimensional figures with a slight change in method and a three-dimensional recording form. A photograph of a person could thus be measured for "goodness," and we could predict the obvious result that the number of errors would vary with the subject's familiarity with the person in the photograph. This technique gives us the key that permits "familiarity" to enter as a legitimate member of the family of good-form grouping principles discussed in the text; just as we can predict the total figure once we know it is circular, we can fill in the image of the person once we know who he is. In each case relatively little information is required to define the figure; therefore both are "good" and would win out in a grouping competition against alternate patterns of, say, a zigzag line or a stranger's photograph.

J. E. HOCHBERG & E. MCALISTER. A quantitative approach to figural goodness. *Journal of Experimental Psychology*, 1953, **46**, 361–364. Figures A and B adapted by permission of American Psychological Association.
F. ATTNEAVE. Some informational aspects of visual perception. *Psychological Review*, 1954, **61**, 183–193. Figure C adapted by permission of American Psychological Association.

FIGURE 12.12 An example of competition between grouping by proximity and grouping by closure. The seven lines on the left tend to fall "naturally" into three pairs and one isolate by virtue of proximity relations. But the same lines (repeated on the right), with the addition of the short horizontal lines, tend to be grouped by closure with the more distant partners, overriding the influence of proximity.

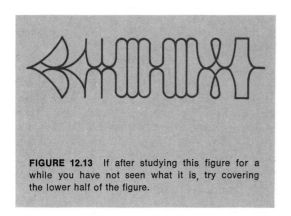

FIGURE 12.13 If after studying this figure for a while you have not seen what it is, try covering the lower half of the figure.

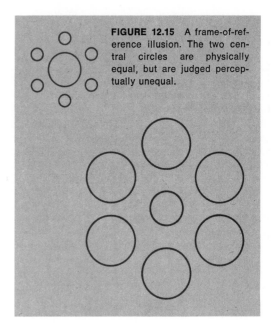

FIGURE 12.15 A frame-of-reference illusion. The two central circles are physically equal, but are judged perceptually unequal.

There may also be temporal patterns of stimuli that serve as a frame of reference for judgment. If the person is exposed to a series of stimuli of a particular kind, the perceived properties of each successive stimulus will to some extent be judged in relation to the stimuli already experienced. Such phenomena have sometimes been studied experimentally in con-

nection with the concept of **adaptation level** (see Box 12.2).

CHANGES IN ORGANIZATION

Neither the world nor perception of the world is simple. Very often an existing perception will change, even though *no* change has taken place either in the stimulus object or its stimuli. Some of these perceptual changes seem to occur "spontaneously"; others accompany a shift in the expectations or attention of the perceiver.

We have already become acquainted (Figure 12.7, p. 266) with an instance of "spontaneous

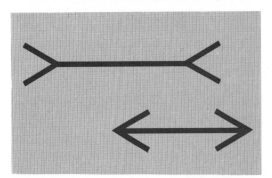

FIGURE 12.14 The classical Müller-Lyer illusion. The two horizontal lines, actually of the same length, appear unequal because of the arrowheads.

BOX 12.2

ADAPTATION LEVEL

H. Helson has advanced a theory that a person makes a judgment of the magnitude of any stimulus attribute, such as size, weight, or loudness, by establishing a sort of subjective or personal scale on which the stimuli are judged. He calls the neutral or medium point of such a scale the *adaptation level.* Stimulus values above the adaptation level are perceived as "large," "heavy," "loud," and so on, and those below it are perceived as "small," "light," "soft," and so on.

The adaptation level is determined by pooling the values of all the stimuli in the judgment series. This pooling is not a simple averaging; the adaptation level is therefore not the same as the arithmetic mean of the stimuli values in the series. For example, in a weight series ranging from 200 to 400 grams, the adaptation level is usually found to be about 250 grams—weights less than 250 grams are judged "light," and weights more than 250 grams are judged "heavy."

The adaptation level constantly changes as a function of all stimuli acting on the person at the moment and that have acted upon him in the past. A single extreme stimulus may have a profound effect in shifting the adaptation level in its direction. For example, in one study the adaptation level of a series of weights ranging from 400 to 600 grams was found to be 475 grams, but when a weight of 900 grams was introduced a single time, the adaptation level rose to 550 grams.

The mathematical formulation Helson derived to permit quantitative predictions of adaptation level on the basis of the distribution of stimuli has proved able to account for a wide variety of judgmental data. In a 1964 major statement of his theory, Helson spelled out the applicability of adaptation-level theory to such diverse areas as motivation, thinking, and personality. One interesting extension comes from D. Rethlingshafer and E. D. Hinckley. When asked by these investigators to judge ages on a scale from very young to very old, ten-year-olds designated age thirty-six as "in the middle"—neither old nor young. Adults in their early twenties set the "middle" at age forty-two; those in their seventies set it at age fifty-two. This shift in what is regarded as middle age is not surprising, but the accuracy of the mathematical predictions certainly is; the predicted values are 36.3, 41.2, and 49.

It is clear that through appropriate changes in a person's perception of a situation, the same series of stimuli may result in different adaptation levels. In an experiment by D. R. Brown, the adaptation level for a series of weights ranging from 80 to 144 grams was determined. Brown next introduced into the series an additional extreme weight of 242 grams. As Helson would predict, the effect of this one extreme stimulus was to raise substantially the adaptation level. But Brown then made a crucial experimental variation. The experiment was repeated in every detail except that this time the extreme weight was a tray, also weighing 242 grams, which the subject was casually asked to move out of the way. As a result, the subject lifted the same extreme weight but without regarding it as part of the judgment series. The results clearly showed that when this heavy weight was perceived as an irrelevant tray rather than as part of the stimulus series, it had no effect on raising the adaptation level.

What seems important is that only stimuli that are perceived as "belonging" participate in determining the adaptation level for that stimuli series.

H. HELSON. Adaptation-level as a frame of reference for prediction of psychophysical data. *American Journal of Psychology,* 1947, **60,** 1–29.
H. HELSON. *Adaptation-Level Theory.* New York: Harper, 1964.
D. RETHLINGSHAFER & E. D. HINCKLEY. Influence of judge's characteristics upon the adaptation level. *American Journal of Psychology,* 1963, **76,** 116–123.
D. R. BROWN. Stimulus similarity and the anchoring of subjective scales. *American Journal of Psychology,* 1953, **66,** 199–214.

oscillation" between two alternate organizations. Figure 12.16, page 272, shows two classical examples of such **reversible figures**, the *Necker cube* and the *reversible staircase.* In both examples it

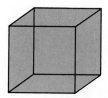

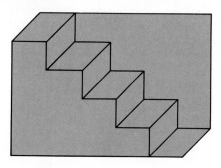

FIGURE 12.16 Two classical examples of reversible figures, the Necker cube and the reversible staircase.

is easy to see the two variants, and the reversals occur easily and frequently. In general, the rate of reversal will depend heavily on the specific nature of the figures (see Box 12.3), and with prolonged inspection the rate of reversal markedly *increases*; that is, each alternative lasts for a shorter and shorter time.

To some extent, "spontaneous" fluctuations in perceptual organization can be deliberately controlled by the perceiver. In many cases he may force the fluctuation by shifting his visual fixation. For example, it is well known that in the Necker cube the specific point at which the figure is fixated will help to determine which alternative will be seen.

Indeed, simply being more alert and attentive to the stimulus pattern increases the rate of fluctuation (Cesarec & Nilsson, 1963).

Satiation of Organization

It has been suggested that the occurrence of spontaneous or unintentional reversals and their increasing rate over time may be caused by the operation of some kind of satiation processes in the brain. More specifically, it has been proposed that as a specific perceptual organization persists, there occurs in the cortical substrate for this perception a gradual process of physiological satiation. When the satiation level is reached, the neural processes behind the perception of the first form are inhibited, the perception fades, and the second form is perceived.

BOX 12.3

WHICH WILL BE THE DOMINANT FIGURE—AND WHY?

T. Oyama's investigations of the figure-determining factors for the Maltese cross are good examples of the quantitative approach to the study of such visual phenomena as reversible figures. In Oyama's work the subject continuously inspected a single stimulus pattern (say Figure B) and was instructed to report which of the two figures (white cross or black cross) he was seeing at each moment. He reported by pressing one of the two keys designated to represent the figures. As the keys operated separate clocks, the total time that each figure was seen during an inspection period of 1 min could be recorded. The ratio of these two times is the measure of the relative dominance of the two figures in any given trial.

Oyama investigated the influence of four factors. First, by presenting different patterns varying

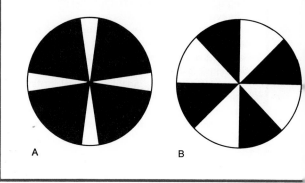

A B

In time the same satiation process occurs with the second form and it disappears. In the meantime the first neurological system has recovered from satiation, and the first form reappears, and so on. Figure 12.17 demonstrates the way in which prior satiation of one alternative can inhibit its subsequent perception. Even perceived movement shows satiation effects (see Box 12.4, p. 274).

from two equal-angle crosses to a thin versus a fat cross, he learned that the thinner the cross, the longer it was seen as a figure; when all angles are equal each of the two crosses is seen about half the time. Second, by keeping one cross constantly black (or white) and varying the brightness of the other cross, Oyama discovered that the dominance of the constant cross increased as the brightness of the variable cross approached the gray of the surrounding field. Furthermore, white tended to dominate black. Third, he found that color influences which cross will be seen as figure. Red crosses are highly likely to be seen as figure, blue crosses much less so. Colors intermediate between red and blue in the visual spectrum are intermediate in dominance. Fourth, crosses with vertical-horizontal orientation were found to be dominant over oblique crosses.

In each of these experiments only a single factor was varied; for example, in evaluating the effect of orientation, black and white equal-angled crosses were used and only their relative tilt was changed. We therefore do not yet know whether or not these factors are *additive*—whether or not, for example, the relative dominance of a thin over a thick cross is increased if the thin cross is red and the thick cross is blue. But you can gather data on such questions yourself. Figure A should yield a striking dominance effect; that is, one of the crosses should remain as figure most of the time with few reversals. Figure B should show frequent reversal. Can you say why?

T. OYAMA. Figure-ground dominance as a function of sector angle, brightness, hue, and orientation. *Journal of Experimental Psychology*, 1960, **60**, 299–305. Figures adapted by permission of American Psychological Association.

FIGURE 12.17 In the ambiguous Figure b, a white cross (Figure c) or a black propeller (Figure a) is seen alternately. Which one will be seen more readily can be influenced by prior fixation of either Figure a or Figure c. Look at a for 60 sec, steadily fixating its center. Then fixate the center of b. You will tend to see the *white* cross. Repeat the experiment, this time fixating on c before looking at b. Now the *black* propeller will tend to be seen in b.

E. G. Boring, et al. *Foundations of Psychology*; adapted by permission of John Wiley & Sons, Inc., 1948.

The underlying mechanism of such satiation of organization is not yet understood. Perhaps the most concentrated attack on this problem has come from the study of a phenomenon known as the **figural aftereffect.** In this phenomenon, which has been demonstrated with numerous stimulus patterns and in various sense modalities, prolonged inspection of a stimulus pattern causes gradual distortions in the initial percept as well as distortions of new patterns presented to the same receptor region (see Box 12.5, p. 275).

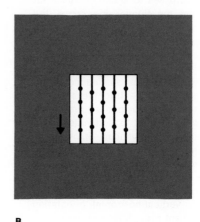

BOX 12.4

SATIATION OF DOWNWARD MOVEMENT

A continuous paper tape with 45-degree lines drawn on it moves constantly downward at a slow rate. It is viewed through a square aperture in a large cardboard shield in front of it (see Figure A). Under these circumstances the direction of perceived movement of the lines is *ambiguous*; they can be seen moving vertically downward or moving horizontally to the right. Subjects almost always first see the downward movement. But with continued inspection there is a shift to the horizontal direction and then an oscillation between these two directions of movement.

     If we assume that these oscillations are caused by a gradual *satiation* as the movement continues in a given direction, we should be able to change the perceptual sequence by deliberately increasing the subject's exposure to one of the alternatives. H. Wallach conducted such an experiment by requiring the subject to inspect for several minutes a moving paper tape on which were drawn lines that could *only* be seen moving downward (see Figure B). Then, when the subject was shown Figure A, he immediately tended to see the movement in the horizontal direction rather than in the usual vertical direction. Apparently the "satiation" for downward movement produced by inspection of Figure B built up resistance to seeing movement in that direction, and the alternative horizontal direction was therefore favored.

H. WALLACH. Über Visuell Wahrgenommene Bewegungsrichtung, *Psychologische Forschung*, 1935, **20**, 325–380.

PERCEPTUAL SET AND ORGANIZATION

Perceptual processes occur within an organism engaged in all kinds of other activities. Stimuli are organized not only to make the best "fit" with one another, but also to "fit" the other on-going activities of the perceiver: what she is thinking, feeling, trying to do. That is, every perceiver directs her gaze or her other senses under the influence of some degree of perceptual **set,** a readiness for achieving a percept with a particular organization of stimuli (see Box 12.6, p. 276).

     There are two main sources of perceptual set: prior experience and central personal factors such as needs, emotions, attitudes, and values. In short, we tend to see what we saw before and what fits best with our current preoccupations and orientation to the world. This can make perception more rapid and efficient. It often permits us to achieve through anticipation a veridical perception despite an inadequate stimulus pattern. However, just as the operation of grouping principles occasionally prevents realistic perception, perceptual set can sometimes blind us to the real world.

Prior Experience and Perceptual Set

The sheer frequency with which a stimulus pattern has previously been perceived will help create a set. Thus, the more familiar a word, the greater the set toward its perception. This is shown, for example, by experiments that find a close relation between the frequency of word usage in the English language and the ease of recognition of the same words on brief exposure.

However, even extensive familiarity will not necessarily create a dominant perceptual set. For one thing, a particular organization may be so strongly structured that it will resist the influence of prior experience (see Box 12.7, p. 277).

For another thing, experiences that have *just occurred* are more likely to determine the immediate set than less recent, even if more frequent, experiences. This is indicated in a series of experiments by Epstein and Rock (1960). They used the stimuli shown in Box 12.6. Subjects were first shown one of the unambiguous

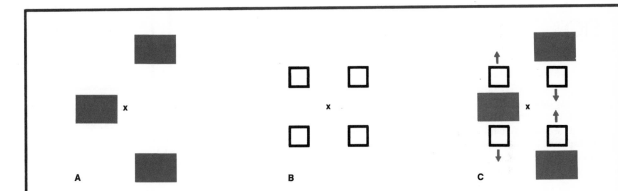

A   B   C

BOX 12.5

FIGURAL AFTEREFFECTS

Fixate the cross in Figure A steadily without moving your eyes for about 60 sec. Then shift your eyes to the cross in Figure B, and while keeping your fixation, observe the appearance of the four squares.

You will note that the distance between the two left-hand squares appears to be greater than that between the two right-hand squares. Actually, the distances are equal. The distortion of Figure B has been produced by the prior inspection of Figure A.

On the basis of many similar experiments at Swarthmore College, W. Köhler and H. Wallach proposed that these distortions can be described in terms of a *displacement* effect caused by satiation. When a figure has been cast for a short while in a given area of the retina, there is a kind of "satiation" that causes new figures cast near the retinal area to be displaced away from it. The perceived distortion of the squares in Figure B can be understood by their displacement away from the places in which the inspection figures had been previously exposed. Figure C schematizes the relation by showing how Figures A and B would appear if combined. The two left-hand squares are pushed apart, and the two right-hand squares are pushed together.

W. KÖHLER & H. WALLACH. Figural aftereffects. *Proceedings of the American Philosophical Society*, 1944, **88**, 269–357.

BOX 12.6

WIFE OR MOTHER-IN-LAW?

Look at Figure A. What do you see?

You may see the slightly turned profile of an attractive young woman. Or you may see the profile of an old woman. (When E. G. Boring published this example of an ambiguous stimulus, he termed it the "wife and mother-in-law" picture!) With continued inspection you will be able to see alternately each of the two possible organizations. Normally about 60 percent of subjects *first* see the young woman and about 40 percent the old woman.

   In order to test the effect of a *prior set* on how this ambiguous picture is perceived, R. W. Leeper performed the following experiment. Two groups of subjects were shown a preliminary series of pictures. Group I saw Figure B as one of the pictures in the series. Group II saw Figure C as one of the pictures in the series.

   Later both groups were shown the ambiguous version (Figure A) and asked to report what they saw. The effect of the set toward "young woman" or "old woman" induced by the previous exposure was conclusive: 100 percent of group I saw the young woman in Figure A, and 95 percent of group II saw the old woman.

   You can perform a similar experiment yourself. Look at Figure D and then at Figure E.

   Because you have first seen the pirate in Figure D, a "pirate" set will have been induced in you, and you will most likely have seen that pirate in Figure E.

   Now we will induce a different set in you: Look again at Figure E, and see a rabbit!

R. W. LEEPER. A study of a neglected portion of the field of learning: The development of sensory organization. *Journal of Genetic Psychology*, 1935, **46**, 41–75. Figures adapted by permission of The Journal Press.

figures (e.g., the young woman) three (or with some subjects, twelve) times in succession; then the other figure was shown *once*. Immediately afterward the ambiguous pattern was exposed very briefly, and the subjects were asked to report which of the two figures was seen. If *fre-*

BOX 12.7

PRIOR EXPERIENCE AND ORGANIZATION

Look at the simple geometrical design in Figure A. Then look at Figure B. Do you see Figure A in Figure B? It is hard to see it at once because it is embedded within the larger figure in such a way as to be deliberately camouflaged, but with a careful search you can find it.

These two figures are examples of many of the figures constructed by the German psychologist K. Gottschaldt for studies on the effect of prior experience on perception. To determine whether or not a great deal of familiarity with Figure A would make it more easily recognizable in Figure B, he showed Figure A to one group of subjects 520 times (with instructions to memorize it) and showed it to another group only three times. When the subjects were later shown Figure B and asked to describe it, only about one person in twenty saw the simple Figure A in it, and *there was no difference between the two groups in the tendency to see it.* Gottschaldt concluded that sheer frequency of prior experience with an object does not account for the readiness to perceive it.

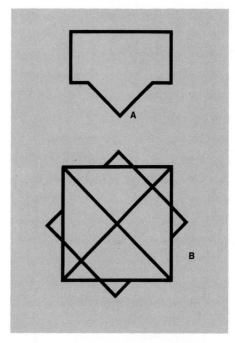

K. GOTTSCHALDT. Über den Einfluss der Erfahrung auf die Wahrnehmung von Figuren, *Psychologische Forschung*, 1926, **8**, 261–317. Figures adapted by permission of Springer-Verlag, Berlin.

quency were more important, then the figure presented several times in succession should be reported; if *recency* were more important, the last figure presented would be seen. The results were clear—the last figure, which had been viewed only once, was seen in 82 percent of the test trials in which the other figure had been previously shown three times. Even when the earlier figure had been presented twelve times, the one shown last was perceived in 60 percent of the trials. Recency seems to be far more effective than frequency in determining the perception of an ambiguous figure.

Central Factors and Perceptual Set

Perceptual organization is also often influenced by the perceivers' needs, emotions, attitudes,

and values. Thus, the stronger our state of need, the more strongly will we be set to perceive in the environment objects and events relevant to that need. And we all know that moods and emotions also affect our view of the world. If, for whatever reason, we start the day in a rosy mood—set to perceive the best side of everything—we almost inevitably succeed in finding and seeing the silver lining in any situation we encounter.

To a considerable degree, because we can largely choose where we go and therefore what part of the world we are likely to encounter, we tend to perceive objects and events that are in accord with our attitudes and dominant values. Compatible perceptions, therefore, are apt to be among the most frequent and most recent of our experiences. This probably helps to account for the extraordinary persistence of attitudes and values once they are acquired. Whether it is the stubborn liberal, the chronically fearful neurotic, or the unshakable bigot, we may be reasonably sure that each has maintained, and even strengthened, an attitude from earlier life by seeking out, whenever possible, objects and events that "fit" his initial set and serve to reinforce it.

Attention

One important way in which perceptual set shows itself is in the perceivers' **attention,** which is a selective focusing upon certain parts or aspects of a situation. What is attended to becomes the "target" of a complex and integrated series of perceptual and motor events. When one looks at an object, for instance, his body swings in the direction of the object, the

FIGURE 12.18 The successive fixations at various points when a picture is being viewed, as recorded by a camera that photographed eye movements of the observer. Note the differences in eye-movement patterns between a male (A) and a female (B) viewing the same painting.

Museum of Art, Carnegie Institute, Pittsburgh; by permission of *Life* Magazine.

ocular mechanism turns the eyes until the image of the object falls on the fovea, the lens muscles accommodate in order to bring the image into clearest focus, and so on. In trying to hear a faint sound, one cranes forward, cups his hand behind his ear, and perhaps closes his eyes to eliminate competing visual stimuli.

Focus of attention   That part of the perceptual field that is the center (or focus) of attention is clearer, more salient, more differentiated than other parts. It tends to stand out as figure against the rest of the field, which is ground.

A focus of attention is usually brief. Attention shifts constantly from one thing to another. Shifts in visual attention, for instance, may be objectively measured by recording successive eye movements while a person looks at an object. Figure 12.18 illustrates the course of fixation in viewing a picture.

Attention shifts for several reasons. For one thing, there is probably in attention, as in many psychological processes, a form of "satiation" (see p. 272) that tends to inhibit the continuation of attention in a given direction. Attention will thus tend to shift "spontaneously" after a period of focus on one part of the field.

Furthermore, there is a severe limitation on the sheer amount of material that can be included within the focus of attention at any one moment. Thus the shifting of attention from one focal point to another makes it possible to achieve a total perceptual organization. With complex stimulus patterns it is impossible to organize the whole in a single glance; there must be successive steps of "exploration" of the pattern, each part or aspect being fixated in turn. In each part of Figure 12.18, rough outlines of the picture are beginning to appear in the path that is traced by successive fixations after only a relatively brief period of exploration. Over longer periods we sometimes find that the cumulative record of fixation points essentially reproduces, in crude fashion, the essential details of the object being viewed.

Span of apprehension   One experimental approach to the measurement of the maximal scope of the focus of attention involves studies

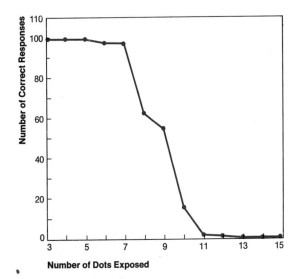

FIGURE 12.19 A curve giving the results of measuring the span of apprehension for one observer, who estimated the number of black dots (varying from three to fifteen) on white cards exposed for split-second intervals in a tachistoscope. Note that the number of correct responses dropped sharply beyond seven dots. Eleven dots are clearly beyond the span of apprehension.

A. D. Glanville & K. M. Dallenbach. The range of attention. *American Journal of Psychology*, 1929, **41**, 207–236; adapted by permission.

of the **span of apprehension;** this term refers to the maximum number of objects that can be correctly and immediately perceived during a time too brief to permit counting or eye movements. Scatter a small number of beans on a table. Take a very quick glimpse and try to see how many beans there are. After many **tries** with different numbers of beans, you will find that you will make few errors with up to five or six beans, but that errors will occur when there are more beans. Figure 12.19 is a graph of the results of a careful experiment of this kind, in which a tachistoscope that exposed the **stimuli** for only one-fifth of a second was used.

Organization and attention   The limited span of apprehension and the fact that the more divided the person's attention, the greater the loss in its quality, emphasize the value of perceptual organization. When parts of the field are organized into larger units, the attention required to perceive them effectively is less than when the parts must be attended to separately.

For example, by grouping of objects, the span of apprehension may be extended. If nine beans fall into three clusters of three beans each, their number may be correctly seen. This fact is a simple illustration of the general point that organization enables the perceiver to cope with more material, and it helps to explain how we can perceive complex situations with the merest glance. The necessry organizations are already available, and the stimuli "fit" into them without need for careful individual attention. The result is greater efficeincy. However, errors may occur when certain details are wrong but but go unnoticed because they "fit" well enough into the organization and cannot be picked out without careful attention. (Concentrating on meaning rather than detail, you have probably failed to notice three printing errors in this paragraph.)

MOVING ON ...

Galileo was right when he asserted that the world moves. Not only that, but objects in the world also move. Thus far we have discussed some of the laws that describe the formation of perceptual organization when we view *objects at rest*. But psychologists have not stopped there. A considerable body of research is available on the perception of movement, and we find that we can formulate helpful organizational principles on that subject as well. It is with these problems that we start Unit 13.

SUMMARY

1. Through a process of assimilation in perception we tend to minimize small stimulus differences, seeing as homogeneous stimulus patterns in which slight physical differences exist. A reverse process, called contrast, takes over when the differences exceed a certain level, and we then perceive differences as greater than they actually are.

2. Typically, one or more parts of a pattern is figure, standing out from the remaining perceptually subordinated areas, which are referred to as ground. A number of factors determine which parts of a pattern are seen as figure and which are ground.

3. When there are several figures present, they may be perceptually grouped according to their proximity to one another; according to their similarity in shape, color, and so forth; and according to the influences of the principle of good form. These grouping principles at times cooperate to define what is figural in a stimulus pattern; at other times they compete with one another. To some degree their relative influence is also a function of one's past perceptual experience.

4. A given perceptual organization is largely determined by the *relationships* among its various parts or elements, so that its basic form may be retained and recognized despite changes in the individual elements themselves. This perceptual function is called transposition. But just as the whole percept is a function of the arrangement of its parts, the perception of the parts is also affected by the total organization. This part-whole principle asserts that we necessarily perceive objects and events in relation to their context, or frame of reference. When this context includes previous experiences and judgments, we say that a perception is influenced by a learned adaptation level.

5. Once established, a percept may undergo modification. This may take place without change in the stimulus pattern (as in reversible figures). Thus, prolonged exposure to a stimulus often leads to an apparently spontaneous perceptual change, the result perhaps of a process of physiological satiation. Satiation is studied through figural aftereffect phenomena.

6. Perceptual organization depends heavily upon the set of the perceiver. Sets are determined mainly by prior experience and by the perceiver's needs, emotions, attitudes, and values. Set, in part, manifests itself in the perceiver's attention, which is a selective focusing upon certain parts or aspects of a situation.

7. Whatever is in the focus of attention is the clearest and most differentiated percept in the field. Attention continuously shifts, inasmuch as there is a gradual "satiation" of any prolonged percept, and there is a limit to the span of what a single focus of attention can take in. This limit, however, can be extended by grouping. With divided attention, perceptual discrimination is poorer.

GLOSSARY

adaptation level The subjective level established by a person as a standard for making judgments, derived from a "pooling" or "averaging" of a series of similar stimuli he has experienced. For example, what is regarded as a neutral weight will be determined by the other weights that have been lifted; weights above it will be judged "heavy" and those below it "light."

assimilation The tendency for the difference in intensities between adjacent parts of a field to be minimized in perception. Often these differences, even though above the threshold, are not seen at all. The effect is the opposite of that observed in contrast phenomena, in which differences are maximized.

attention The focusing of perception involving a heightened awareness of a limited part of the perceptual field.

closure The tendency for certain figures to be so perceived that they seem complete or closed rather than incomplete and unclosed. For example, a circle with a tiny gap may be seen as a complete unbroken circle.

contour A line of demarcation separating one part of a perceptual field from adjacent parts. It is perceived as "belonging" to the figure and provides the figure's distinctive shape. Nevertheless, contour and figure are not identical, for the very same physical contour looks entirely different in two different figures.

contrast The phenomenon of perceiving a difference as greater than that physically present in the stimulus pattern.

figural aftereffect Distorted perception, which occurs when a new stimulus pattern falls on the same region of the receptor shortly after prolonged exposure to another stimulus pattern. Some experiments have suggested that this phenomenon is related to satiation.

figure The part of the perceptual field that stands out on the background of the remainder of the field.

frame of reference The standard or framework that serves as a reference against which a particular perceptual property is judged. For example, the apparent angle of objects in a room is partly determined by the angle of the surrounding walls. The frame-of-reference effect can be seen as an instance of the part-whole principle.

good figure The characteristic of a certain stimulus pattern that has qualities of good continuation, symmetry, closure, unity, and so forth. The so-called "law of grouping by good figure" states that perceptual grouping of elements will be favored in the direction of forming a good figure.

ground The part of the perceptual field that serves as background for the figure. It appears to be less clearly structured than the figure and less the focus of attention.

reversible figures Stimulus patterns that give rise to a "spontaneous" oscillation between two or more alternative perceptual organizations. The Necker cube is a classical example of a reversible figure.

set A readiness of the organism to make a particular response or class of responses. Motor sets are readiness for particular actions; mental sets, for particular thought processes; perceptual sets, for particular organizations of stimuli.

span of apprehension The maximal number of objects or items that can be correctly and immediately perceived with an exposure so brief that there is no time for counting or eye movements. The span of apprehension is increased by grouping the items.

transposition As a perceptual phenomenon this refers to the recognition that a stimulus pattern may be the same pattern, even though its elements are different. This recognition is based on maintaining an identical relation among the elements in the two patterns, for instance, the transposition of a melody on the keyboard.

perceiving the world

DO YOU KNOW...

- *that you often can see movement when there is none?*

- *why the sound in a drive-in movie seems to be coming right from the screen?*

- *why two eyes are better than one for perceiving depth?*

- *whether we are born with the ability to see the world in three dimensions?*

- *why objects appear to be the same size no matter how far away they may be?*

- *how easily we tend to fill the missing elements in a familiar perception?*

- *how important the role of body movements is in the development of accurate perception?*

- *how it may be possible for the blind to "see" with their skin?*

Photo by Philip Teuscher

CONTENTS

The nature of our sensory experience and the manner in which it is perceptually organized are discussed in Units 11 and 12. We will now consider the way we perceive our world. The physical world with which we cope is a tridimensional space, inhabited by objects with complex properties that can change or remain remarkably constant, objects that move or appear to do so. The first part of this unit deals with some of what we know about how this world of space, motion, and objects can be accurately perceived.

The remainder of the unit offers a brief account of several of the main theoretical approaches that undertake to explain how our perceptual organization and behavior function as we seek to perceive the world.

VISUAL MOVEMENT

How we see movement is one of the most fascinating topics in the study of perception. Like many basic phenomena, seeing motion in our environment seems at first to present no particular problems. Question: Why do we see an object move? Answer: Simply because the object *does* move. Now this "simple answer" is no answer at all. Actual physical movement of an object often *fails* to produce any appearance of movement, and movement is often seen where there is physically none.

Induced Movement

Recall the common illusion in which the moon appears to glide swiftly behind stationary clouds. This example illustrates both that a truly moving object (the clouds) may not appear to be moving and that an object practically at rest (the moon) may appear to be in motion. The moving object is said to "induce" an appearance of movement in the static object, and so we refer to this phenomenon as **induced movement**. Induced movement is no different for the perceiver than real movement.

To understand this phenomenon, let us first analyze the stimulus situation. On the retina there is an image of the moon and an image of the clouds. As the clouds approach the moon, the distance between the retinal images shortens. It is this change in distance between the two images on the retina that constitutes the stimulus for perceived movement.

If the only available information is that the two objects are displaced in relation to one another, the situation is ambiguous from the perceiver's point of view. Either one or both objects might actually be moving. Which, then, is perceived as moving? In general, when there is a logical possibility that either object can be perceived as moving, the object that is seen as the figure tends to "move."

When the two objects are equally figural, the one that is fixated tends to be seen as moving. Instructions, expectations, or set may determine which object will be fixated. If two dots of light are exposed in darkness, one above the other, and either is moved horizontally back and forth, we have a situation in which either the upper dot or the lower dot can be seen as moving in relation to the other. If the person is told that she is seeing a metronome, the upper dot appears to move. If she is told that it is a pendulum, the lower dot appears to move (see Figure 13.1).

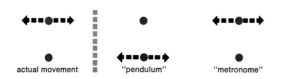

FIGURE 13.1 Meaning and movement. For explanation, see text.

H. A. Carr & M. C. Hardy. Some factors in the perception of relative motion. *Psychological Review*, 1920, **27**, 24–37; adapted by permission of American Psychological Association.

Induced movement depends on the displacement of an object relative to a framework. But what if there is only one object, and it has no perceptible frame of reference?

Autokinetic Movement

Under certain conditions a single stimulus can produce a perception of movement in the absence of physical movement. If we look at a tiny stationary dot of light that is the only visible stimulus in a dark room, we notice an astonishing thing. The light appears to move, sometimes in this direction, sometimes in that, sometimes slowly, sometimes more rapidly. If we watch it for a considerable time, it may execute large sweeping movements or move erratically in a jerky fashion. The extent of the movement can be very great. If we point an outstretched finger at the light as it moves, we are amazed to find (when the room is suddenly illuminated) that the finger may be pointing as much as 30 degrees from where the dot of light actually is. Knowing that the light is really stationary does not destroy the effect. Furthermore, the movement is seen as "real" movement. A naive observer believes that the dot actually does physically move; the informed observer finds it hard to believe that it does not.

This effect is known as **autokinetic** ("self-generated") **movement**. The essential stimulus condition for its occurrence is the absence of any visual framework for the dot of light. As soon as other visual features are introduced close by, for example, a line or other dots, the autokinetic movement appreciably decreases. If we structure the stimulus pattern even further by turning on the lights and revealing all the details of the room, the effect disappears altogether, and the dot of light is seen as stationary. Airplane pilots during night flights are susceptible to autokinetic movement of distant beacon lights and even lights on other aircraft. Many of them develop techniques to maintain a stable frame of reference, for example, lining up the distant object with an edge of the cockpit window in order to maintain correct orientation.

The complete explanation for autokinetic movement is yet to be made. Eye movements play a role. Although there is no noticeable tendency for eye movements to follow (or to lead) the direction of autokinetic movement, Matin and Mackinnon (1964) report that autokinetic movement is virtually eliminated under conditions in which eye movements are not permitted to cause movements of the retinal image (see Unit 14, p. 321, for a description of techniques that stabilize images on the retina). Various postures of the body also play a role in autokinetic movement. The direction and extent of the movement can be markedly influenced by the way that the eyeballs, head, neck, and trunk are rotated away from the normal line of vision. We have evidence, therefore, that visual perception is affected by kinesthetic sensations from the muscles. Perceptual interaction again cuts across the various senses.

Furthermore, because the optical condition for autokinetic movement is a very weakly structured stimulus field, we should expect that the perceiver's set would exercise a strong influence, which is indeed the case. Sherif (1935) has shown that the amount of movement perceived by a subject is readily influenced by the suggestions of other persons. It is even possible, with appropriate instructions, for the stationary light to appear to trace out numerals and other meaningful designs.

Apparent Movement

Everyone knows that a completely convincing impression of movement can be given by a rapid succession of discrete but static pictures, as in motion pictures. This **apparent movement**, sometimes called *stroboscopic movement* or the *phi phenomenon*, can be understood as another instance of temporal fusion (see Unit 11, p. 249).

Take a simple laboratory demonstration. Two lights are mounted a few inches apart. The left one is turned on and off. A second or two later the right one is turned on and off. The observer perceives a simple *succession* of one light followed by another. If the time interval between the flashes of the lights is gradually shortened, a point is reached at which a surprising perceptual transformation occurs. The light on the left seems to *move across* the intervening space to the right. Finally, as the time interval is made very short, the impression of movement disappears, and the two lights appear *simultaneously*, each in its own place.

FIGURE 13.2 The lights numbered 1 flash simultaneously, followed a fraction of a second later by the lights numbered 2, which also flash simultaneously. The observer sees an upward movement between the right-hand pair of lights and *at the same time* a downward movement between the left-hand pair.

Thus, by virtue of a simple change in the time interval between the two stimulus events, three qualitatively different perceptual experiences have been produced—succession, movement, and simultaneity.

It was first supposed that apparent movement occurs because, as the eyes move from one stimulus to the other, their turning creates kinesthetic cues that are translated into an impression of movement. This supposition is readily disproved by the fact that movement can be seen in opposite directions simultaneously (see Figure 13.2). Furthermore, it is not even necessary that two different retinal points be successively stimulated for apparent motion to be seen. Rock and Ebenholtz (1962) devised experimental techniques that allowed their subjects to see with one eye two alternating and spatially separate luminous lines, although only one retinal area was being activated. They obtained this effect by having the subject move his eye back and forth in such a way that the image of each line fell on the same retinal locus. Even under these special conditions apparent movement still occurred, suggesting that it is the phenomenal impression of distance between two points—and not their actual physical or retinal separation—that is a necessary condition for the perception of movement between them. The conditions that govern the occurrence of apparent movement can be expressed in a number of principles and generalizations dealing with the stimulus attributes and relations between stimuli (see Box 13.1).

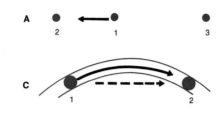

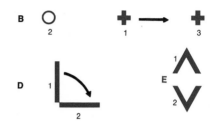

BOX 13.1

FACTORS IN APPARENT MOVEMENT

Grouping factors play a major role in determining the *direction* of apparent movement. In Figure A, light 1 goes on and off, followed shortly by lights 2 and 3, which go on and off simultaneously. The movement could go from 1 to either 2 or 3. Experiments show that it tends to go to 2, which is the nearer, in accordance with the principle of grouping by proximity. In Figure B, with proximity equal, the movement goes from 1 to 3, rather than to 2, because of the greater similarity between 1 and 3—the principle of grouping by similarity. In Figure C, the movement tends to take the curved path of the channeling contours, rather than to cut directly across the shortest distance from 1 to 2—the principle of good continuation.

The shape and spatial arrangements of successive stimuli may make it difficult or impossible to see a straight linear movement from one light to the other. More complex apparent movements may then result. For instance, in Figure D the line seems to *rotate* through an angle from the vertical to the horizontal, and in Figure E movement occurs in the *third dimension;* that is, the inverted V-shaped figure is seen to swing down and "flop over" into the reverse orientation.

A. KORTE. Kinematoskopische Untersuchungen. *Zeitschrift für Psychologie*, 1915, **72**, 194–296. Figures adapted by permission of Johann Ambrosius Barth, Leipzig.

Apparent movement is also found in other senses. In touch, for instance, if very light pressures are applied successively and at the appropriate rate at two nearby points, there will be an impression of movement of the stimulus along the skin from one point to the other. A click in one ear followed an instant later by a click in the other ear may be heard as a single click moving through the head.

As we shall presently see, the remarkable and pervasive character of the phenomenon of apparent movement made it one of the fundamental demonstrations of the theory of Gestalt psychology.

Organization and Movement

The perceived direction of movement—whether induced, autokinetic, or apparent—is governed largely by organizational factors. Figure 13.3, page 288, illustrates the importance of organizational factors for *real* movement; Figure 13.4, page 288, illustrates how a complex combination of movements in different directions may be unified in perception in such a way that the whole pattern is simplified.

Perceived *speed* of movement is not determined solely by actual physical speed. Here, too, organizational factors are important. Indeed, visual context can sometimes produce fairly large errors in our judgment of speed. Figure 13.5, page 289, describes the frame-of-reference conditions under which two objective speeds must be made very different before they can be *perceived* as equal.

Perceived Causality in Movement

Movements are perceived not only as having direction and speed but also as having causal

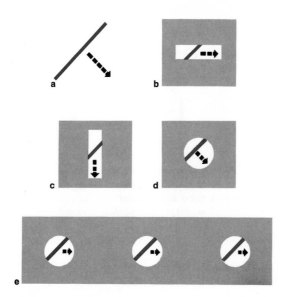

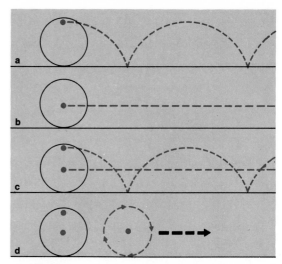

FIGURE 13.3 A 45-degree-angle line sweeps across the visual field (see a). When it is viewed through an aperture so that only a segment of the moving line is visible, the direction in which it appears to move (indicated by the dotted arrows) is wholly determined by the shape of the aperture. In b, it appears to move horizontally, and in c, vertically, thus conforming to the main edges of the aperture. In d, the movement is at a 45-degree angle downward toward the right. But, if a series of such circular apertures is presented in a horizontal row, as in e, and the line passes successively behind them, it appears to move in a *horizontal* direction.

FIGURE 13.4 A wheel rolls slowly along a table in a completely dark room. On its rim a small light is attached. The observer sees the light moving in a cycloid path, as shown in a. In b the light is attached only at the hub, and the observer sees it move along a straight horizontal path. What does he see when these two conditions are combined, with one light on the rim and one on the hub? It might be expected that he would see both the cycloid and the horizontal movements occurring together, as schematized in c. But what he sees in fact is a "simpler" and more unified pattern of movement, as schematized in d. The rim light is seen as rotating around the hub light at the center, while this whole system of rim and hub lights moves horizontally. In short, the true state of affairs —a rolling wheel—is perceived despite the minimal cues; the previous cycloid movement is entirely absent.

power. We often have the vivid perceptual impression that certain moving objects interact causally with other objects. A rolling billiard ball striking another ball appears to set the second ball in motion; the movement of the first ball is perceived as somehow being transferred to the second.

It should be clear that we are concerned here not with genuine physical causality but with *perceived* causality. The experimental study of perceived causality is no different from any other psychophysical problem, such as the relation of perceived color to the physical properties of light. Box 13.2, p. 290, illustrates how such psychophysical studies of perceived causality can be made.

SPACE AND DEPTH PERCEPTION

We experience space through hearing, touching, moving, and seeing. These different sensory experiences do not lead to separate spaces but to a single unified space in which objects are distributed and move. Yet there is not always a perfect agreement among the impressions of space that the different senses provide. When we feel our way around in complete darkness, our impression of the size and arrangement of a room may be quite different from what we see with the lights on.

The perceptual problem is one of synthesizing information from all these often contradictory sources. For example, onstage sound

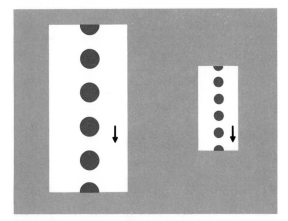

FIGURE 13.5 Behind each of two apertures is a paper tape moving endlessly downward. On each tape is printed a row of dots. The larger aperture is exactly *twice* the size of the smaller, and the dots on its tape are twice as large and twice as far apart. The observer's task is to adjust the speeds of the tapes until the dots in the two apertures *appear* to be moving at equal speeds. For equality of phenomenal speed, it turns out that the physical speed of movement of the tape behind the large aperture must be just about *twice* the speed of the smaller.

After Brown, 1931.

effects in a play are actually produced offstage; the speaker at a drive-in movie is only inches away from your ear, not behind the distant screen. In neither case do conflicting impressions occur, despite the incompatible spatial information from visual and auditory stimuli. One set of cues is typically dominant. In plays and movies visual stimuli are dominant; only by closing your eyes can the actual locus of the sound source be detected. Recall the greater ability of the blind to judge the size, distance, and even texture of objects (see Box 11.2, p. 236). It is intriguing to realize that this is not because the blind show exceptional auditory *acuity*. Given some known and fixed sound sources, the blind can locate new sounds more accurately than sighted people, apparently through a greater ability to *organize* complex auditory patterns.

Under normal conditions, most of us are able to locate the direction of sound sources simply by hearing, even without the benefit of other cues. To understand how this is accomplished, it will help first to understand the difficulty of identifying the direction of a sound using only one ear.

Sound waves are agitations of the air that spread out in all directions from a sound source. The agitated air, when it comes in contact with the eardrums, carries no message concerning the direction from which the agitation has traveled. If a single ear is successively stimulated by two sound waves coming from two equally loud sources at the same distance but from different or even opposed directions, the effects of the two sets of sound waves on the ear are identical, and it is impossible to distinguish a directional difference.

Binaural cues If information reaching both ears is used (**binaural cues**), sounds may be localized with great accuracy. One such cue is the *time difference* between the two ears. If a sound originates on the person's right side, it reaches the right ear a split second sooner than it reaches the more distant left ear. Even when the time difference between the two ears is as little as 30 millionths of a second, the side from which the sound comes can be correctly identified. This time difference is far shorter than the person can consciously recognize; the effect occurs through an automatic integrating process in the auditory nervous system (see Unit 14, p. 341). A simple and dramatic check on the hypothesis that the perception of direction is dependent on the time difference between the two ears is provided by experiments with the *pseudophone* (see Figure 13.6, p. 291).

A second binaural cue is the *intensity difference* that occurs between the two ears when a sound is to one side. A sound source on one side of the head will deliver a slightly more intense sound to the ear on that side. This tiny intensity difference is sufficient to help us locate the sound correctly to the left or right of the median plane.

If, however, the sound comes from anywhere in the median plane itself, it strikes the two ears simultaneously and with equal intensity and is thus heard as being somewhere in the median plane. But the person cannot tell

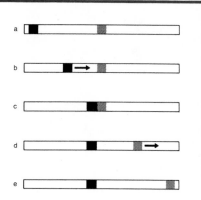

BOX 13.2

PERCEPTION OF CAUSALITY

The Belgian psychologist A. Michotte conducted a series of laboratory experiments designed to specify the stimulus conditions that give rise to different impressions of physical causality in movement. His procedure was to regulate the movement of two small squares, a black one and a gray one, along a horizontal slot and to ask the observer what he saw.

The figure shows the sequence of events as presented to the observer. At first (phase a) the two squares are at rest, the black one some distance to the left of the gray. Then (phase b) the black square appears to move toward the gray. For a fraction of a second (phase c) the two remain in contact without moving. Then (phase d) the gray square moves off to the right while the black one remains at rest. Finally (phase e), the gray square comes to rest, some distance to the right of the black.

In this basic experiment, observers reported that there was a clear impression that the movement of the black object "caused" the subsequent movement of the gray object. This impression was not experienced by them as a mere *inference* but as a direct *perception*.

Michotte then systematically studied the influence of variations in the speed of movement of the black square; the distance it traveled before reaching the gray; the duration of contact between the two squares; the subsequent speed of the gray square after contact was broken.

From perceptions reported by observers under these different patterns of movement, Michotte discovered that there were two distinctly different types of perceived causality. The first was "launch-

ing," in which the black object appeared to set the gray object into motion by transferring its force of motion to the gray. The second was "releasing," in which the black object appeared to cause the gray to move only by unleashing or "triggering" a *latent* force of motion already in the gray—there was no impression of a transfer of force of motion from the black to the gray.

The transition from "launching" to "releasing" depends primarily upon the ratio of the speeds of the two objects. When the black object strikes the gray at a considerably greater speed than is apparently imparted to the gray object, "launching" is almost invariably seen. Conversely, when the gray object takes off at a speed far greater than that of the black object, "releasing" is seen. As the speeds approach equality, the frequencies of the two responses approach equality.

V. Olum has extended this work to children and finds that seven-year-olds show a shift in the transition point from the "launching" to the "releasing" effect—but they still perceive "launching" and continue to do so until speed increase is substantial. As the "releasing" experience is a bit more complex than the "launching" experience—the former brings the unleashing of a latent force into the picture—these results indicate that children are more likely to keep changes in perceptual organization to a minimum. They retain the simpler "launching" percept as long as they can.

A. MICHOTTE. *The Perception of Causality.* New York: Basic Books, 1963. Originally published in French, 1954.
V. OLUM. Developmental differences in the perception of causality under conditions of specific instructions. *Vita Humana,* 1958, **1,** 191–203.

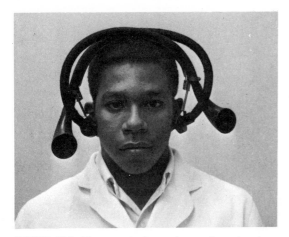

FIGURE 13.6 The pseudophone. A sound coming from the right side would normally first strike the right ear and then the left, but the tubes of the pseudophone divert it so that it reaches the left ear first. The effect is to reverse the perceived direction of the sound, so that it appears to come from the left side.

its more precise location in the median plane; it may be directly in front, in back, above, or below. The two binaural cues of differences in time and intensity are thus not sufficient to enable us to localize sounds from all possible directions. And yet such localization is achieved. How can it be accomplished?

Head movements Normally, when we are trying to localize sounds, we move our heads, often so slightly that the movement is not noticeable. These head movements, by alternately bringing one ear or the other closer to the source of the sound, enable us to discriminate between directions of sound that are otherwise indistinguishable. Rotating one's head from right to left enables one to distinguish a sound directly in front from one directly in back; for, as the head turns toward the left, a sound from in front arrives relatively sooner and more loudly at the right ear than at the left ear. Similarly, by tilting one's head from side to side, one can tell a sound directly above from one directly below. The combination of angles of head movement and of changes of stimulation pattern at the two ears "pins down" the exact location of a sound source.

Taken together, all these facts about localization of sounds provide an excellent illustration of how perceptual organization works in the solution of the problem of space. Stimulus information from both ears, as well as from other receptor systems, is synthesized in an orderly, efficient, and "spontaneous" fashion to provide a compelling impression of auditory space (see Box 13.3, p. 292). The story will be repeated and extended in our analysis of visual space perception.

Visual Depth

All visual stimuli act upon the retina, which is essentially a flat, two-dimensional surface. Yet visual space is typically experienced as having depth, and objects are localized at various distances in a three-dimensional framework. In some way, therefore, two-dimensional information must be made to yield a three-dimensional experience.

Monocular cues for depth "In the land of the blind, the one-eyed woman is queen." Even a person with only one eye can achieve the marvels of seeing, and among these marvels is the ability to perceive depth through various **monocular depth cues**. Some monocular cues involve head movements, some involve adjustments of the eye muscles, and some involve characteristics of the static visual pattern itself. (We have discussed the last point in Box 11.1, p. 235.)

A powerful cue is given by the temporal pattern of visual stimuli that occurs when the head moves from side to side. If we look at a flat picture, the relations among objects within the picture do not change when the head moves. But with three-dimensional objects arranged at different distances from the viewer, head movements do change the stimulus pattern on the retina as these objects are viewed from successively different angles. Specifically: As the head moves to the left, nearer objects appear displaced to the right and farther objects to the left of one another.

This **relative movement** (or **movement parallax**) can be easily demonstrated. Hold a pencil at arm's length so that it is almost in line with any distant object in the room, for

BOX 13.3

LOCATING SOUNDS BY HEAD MOVEMENT

H. Wallach has conducted an experiment in which a sound source is constantly kept directly in front of the head. The sound source moves automatically as the head turns. There is a continuous buzz from the sound source, and the subject tries to locate it in space, being permitted to turn his head only to right and left. He thus receives kinesthetic cues that his head is moving, but at the same time there is no change in the auditory stimuli at the two ears.

The person hears the sound directly *overhead*—an entirely sensible integration of the two facts that there is movement of the head but the sounds at the two ears do not change. For, as we can readily see, this is exactly what happens when a sound source is *actually* directly overhead. In this *erroneous* localization we see a demonstration of the elegant workings of the perceptual system.

Another very striking fact is that the system is concerned with *phenomenal* relations, not necessarily with actual stimulus events. The figure illustrates the setup. The individual is seated on a stool inside the striped drum. His head is fixed and a sound is presented continuously and directly in front of him. The striped drum is set into motion; this motion gives the subject the impression that he is whirling about, although he is actually completely at rest. *Where does he hear the sound?* Again the sound is heard directly *overhead*—despite the fact that the head is *stationary* and the auditory stimuli at the two ears do not change, a situation that would normally lead to hearing the sound directly in *front*. What has happened, obviously, is that the *subjective impression* of movement, when combined with the absence of auditory stimulus changes at the two ears, can make simple sense only if the sound is perceived as coming from directly overhead.

H. WALLACH. The role of head movements and vestibular and visual cues in sound localization. *Journal of Experimental Psychology*, 1940, **27**, 339–368.

---

example, a lamp. Close one eye. Though you know that the pencil is closer, it will barely appear so. Now, keeping the eye closed, move your head horizontally. Even a slight movement will convey an immediate and pronounced depth impression.

The light rays coming from an object at which we are looking are focused by the lens system of the eye in such a way as to achieve the clearest image. This **accommodation** is accomplished by the pull of the eye muscles that shape the lens into the appropriate curvature. To focus on a distant object, the lens must be flattened, and to focus on a nearby object, it must be made rounder. When one looks at a close object, for example a book in one's hand, the amount of accommodation necessary for a clear image is quite different from that needed to see a picture on a far wall.

Kinesthetic sensations from the different amounts of pull on eye muscles thus provide cues to the distance of an object. Because there are only minimal changes in the amount of accommodation beyond a distance of a few feet, however, this monocular cue is effective in depth perception only for short distances.

Binocular cues for depth   When we look with both eyes—binocular vision—we obtain different images of the object without head movements, because each eye looks at the object from a slightly different angle. The difference in the images falling on the two eyes is known as **retinal disparity.**

The perceiver seeks to harmonize and synthesize the two different retinal images, which are brought together and fused whenever possible. The degree to which fusion occurs depends on the degree of consonance of the two images. If they can be fitted together to produce a single unified field, this effect is favored. In the typical case, of course, the different views are minutely different perspectives of the same physical object or scene. But some disparity between the two stimulus patterns, however slight, does exist and must be perceptually reconciled. The almost universal solution is a percept of the simplest possible organization, a single fused three-dimensional image. These facts make possible the **stereoscope**, a device for giving the impression of depth when viewing flat photographs.

If the two images are to fall on essentially the corresponding regions of the two retinas, **convergence** of the eyes must occur. The eyes swing their lines of sight so that they both are oriented directly toward the object being viewed, or more precisely, toward where the object appears to be. Strictly speaking, convergence as a cue for depth involves only the kinesthetic sensations arising momentarily from the muscles controlling the swing of the eyes during a change in focus.

As with accommodation, there does not have to be a conscious awareness of the muscular changes. Like accommodation, convergence is also only a short-distance cue. When the objects are far away, the lines of sight become almost parallel and the amount of convergence insignificant; for distances greater than 50 or 60 ft, the convergence cue is not effective in aiding the perception of depth. When the object is too near, convergence fails, fusion is not possible, depth is lost, and "double vision" results.

The synthesis of depth cues   The most compelling and full-bodied experience of depth comes when many cues—both monocular and binocular—work simultaneously.

Situations often occur in which the cues are in competition—for example, when there are oddities in the spatial arrangements of objects, when the illumination is unusual, or when the stimulus pattern is poorly structured. In such cases the impression of depth may be weakened or altered. This kind of situation can be artificially induced in the laboratory to study the way cues interact. For instance, by pitting the cue of interposition against the cue of relative size, we can distort the depth perception of objects (see Figure 13.7, p. 294).

The perception of depth, therefore, cannot be thought of as a simple summation of the various cues. In general, the perceptual process seems to weigh the various cues and in this way derives a "resonable" percept of space. But where do these cue weights come from, and why does their integration usually result in something "reasonable"?

Brunswik (1956) suggests that the relative influence of a cue in perception can be almost perfectly predicted from its "ecological validity"; that is, the cues that usually prove to be more accurate in the person's environment are more heavily credited by him in depth perception.

A typical experiment by Brunswik would study the person's perception not in the laboratory but rather in his natural environment (ecology). The subject walks about on the street or in a park and is occasionally asked to report on the relative distances of objects in the field of view at a given moment. The experimenter then actually measures the physical distance of each object and records all the depth cues that might have been used in the situation. By relating the presence of these cues both to the subject's judgments and to the measured distances, it becomes possible to determine how much overall importance the subject has attached to a given cue and how

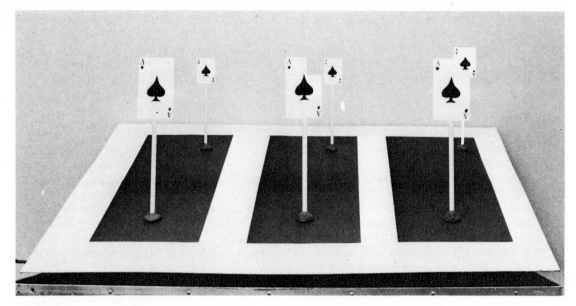

FIGURE 13.7 Two playing cards of the usual size are attached vertically to stands at different distances from the observer. The room is darkened so that only the cards are visible. The observer uses only one eye, and head movements are not permitted. In this situation (left panel), apart from the possible minimal contribution of relative clearness and accommodation, the effective monocular cue is *relative size*. As playing cards are familiar objects of known size, the smaller retinal image generated by the more distant card makes it seem farther away.

But then a corner is clipped from the nearer card, as in center panel; the position of the farther stand is precisely adjusted so that in the observer's retinal image the edges of the farther card exactly fit the cutout edges of the nearer card. As shown in right panel, the more distant card now appears *in front* of the objectively closer one. The cue of *interposition* is sufficiently powerful to overcome that of known size. The result is distorted perception on two counts: Relative distance is incorrectly judged, and the objectively farther card is shrunk to an improbable miniature version of its real dimensions.

often its use has led to correct distance perception. For example, it has been found that interposition—perhaps the most reliable cue for depth perception—is in fact typically assigned the most weight when it is available. On the other hand, the size of the retinal image —a quite unreliable cue—is hardly used in making distance judgments even when it is available. It would be inconvenient, to say the least, to attempt to touch the building across the street while despairing of any attempt to reach the aspirin close at hand.

The Origins of Space

How does it come about that the various depth cues can be integrated to yield a perception of space? This question has beset philosophers and scientists for centuries. Is this integration something that is gradually *learned* through the organism's adjustment to its environment— as Brunswik's "ecological validity" concept suggests—or is it "given" through the inherent nature of the organism? The former is an *empiristic* and the latter a *nativistic* interpretation.

Experience deprivation One experimental approach to disentangling empiristic and nativistic factors is to deprive the organism of all visual experience by keeping him in total darkness until his spatial perception is to be tested. Box 13.4 presents the earliest systematic study of experience deprivation. The method makes possible the use of complex spatial responses, as the animal is relatively mature by the time testing takes place. It runs the risk, however, that relevant spatial experience has not been totally eliminated during the waiting period. The experiment in Box 13.4, for example, has been criticized on the grounds that the few seconds of visual experience during daily feeding, especially when combined with the experience provided during the few practice trials,

might have been sufficient to permit learning of distance discrimination.

Such deliberate experimental deprivation of visual experience is not, however, a very popular technique with human subjects. Most of what we have learned on the human level comes from observation of patients who, because of congenital sensory defects, were

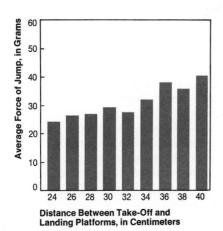

BOX 13.4

A LOOK BEFORE A LEAP

An experiment by K. S. Lashley and J. T. Russell showed that rats seem able to perceive visual space without the benefit of prior experience. They raised thirteen rats in complete darkness from birth until the age of 100 days (rat adulthood). The only visual experience the rats had during that period was a few seconds of very dim illumination each day when their cages were opened for feeding.

On the critical day of the rats' first experience of full light, the experimenters tested the rats' orientation to visual space by placing each rat on a high pedestal and urging it to jump the short gap to a platform on which food was available (see photograph). After brief preliminary training at this fixed distance, to accustom the rats to jumping, the distance between the pedestal and the food platform was varied over a range of from a few

inches to several feet. The accuracy of each rat's perception of the changing distances was measured by the force of its leaps toward the platform; that is, if the animal were perceiving the distances properly, a large gap should elicit a proportionately stronger jump than a small gap. The force of the jump was recorded by the swing of a pointer attached to the platform and set into motion by the impetus of the leap.

Even though the rats were far from uniformly successful in hitting the platform, it was convincingly clear that they did discriminate between the different distances. The graph shows that the rats regulated the impetus of their leaps in fairly good accordance with the actual distance. The performance of the rats raised in darkness was virtually the same as that of rats raised normally, with full visual experience.

K. S. LASHLEY & J. T. RUSSELL. The mechanism of vision: XI. A preliminary test of innate organization. *Journal of Genetic Psychology*, 1934, **45**, 136–144. Figure adapted by permission of The Journal Press.

accidentally deprived of normal visual experience. After their visual defects had been corrected, these patients were tested for space perception. Unfortunately, data drawn from such observations are somewhat difficult to interpret.

Spatial abilities of the newborn Another experimental technique is to conduct the spatial testing as soon as possible after birth to minimize opportunities for prior learning. To begin at the beginning, Wertheimer (1961) reports that an infant, tested between 3 min and ten min of age, consistently showed eye movements in the direction of a click sounded in either ear, indicating primitive spatial perception, auditory localization, and even interaction between hearing and vision at that remarkably tender age. Infants as young as one month discriminate between solid and flat objects, even when viewed monocularly (Fantz, 1961).

Revealing experiments have been done with the *visual cliff*, which we previously depicted in Figure 11.2, p. 233. A ten-month-old infant, tested monocularly, consistently avoided falling off the visual cliff (Walk & Dodge, 1962). The very young of several species (chicks, monkeys, rats, kittens, and goats, among others) also avoided the cliff. Many studies therefore agree that at least a rudimentary ability for spatial discrimination is present at a very early age.

Experimental control of experience Another experimental approach involves systematic manipulation of the cues for space perception to discover the degree to which they can be modified by experience. As Box 13.5 indicates, the human visual system shows extraordinary responsiveness, even to bizarre demands.

Taken all together, the foregoing studies suggest that the final answer to how our experience of space originates will involve some intricate interplay among innate, maturational, and experiential factors.

PERCEPTUAL CONSTANCY

Our perception of constantly changing objects in our three-dimensional world is characterized by a remarkable degree of constancy. A man is instantly recognized as a man whether he is standing upright or lying down, whether he is nearby or blocks away. A bicycle still looks undeniably like a bicycle regardless of variation in one's angle of observation. Snow in deep shade looks white and coal in sunlight looks black, even though the intensity of light striking the eye from the snow is *less* than that from the coal. The adaptive value of this **object constancy** is obvious. By maintaining a stable and consistent perception of an object despite wide variations in the conditions under which we encounter it, we are able to cope more effectively with our environment (see Figure 13.8, p. 298).

Constancy of any property—whether it is size, shape, brightness, or anything else—depends upon invariant relations among certain crucial elements in the total stimulus pattern. The snow maintains equal brightness whether in shadow or sunlight because of the *fixed ratio* of light coming from the snow and from its immediate surroundings, no matter what the overall level of illumination of the total scene.

Size Constancy

There are two principal facts that work together in the determination of the perceived visual size of an object: the size of the retinal image and the apparent distance of the object. Of two objects that appear to be at the same distance from the observer, the object casting the smaller retinal image usually looks smaller. Of two objects having retinal images of equal size, the object that appears farther away typically looks larger.

A simple demonstration of this can be carried out by the reader. Gaze at a 1-in. square of white paper placed against a dark background about 10 in. away from your eyes. After a brief inspection a good afterimage of the square will be formed. Then look at a light surface about the same distance away, and note that the afterimage—a dark square—as it appears to be projected on that surface is the same size as the original square. Now look at a more distant surface, for example, the wall

BOX 13.5

THE UPSIDE-DOWN WORLD OF PSYCHOLOGISTS

The effects of continuously wearing a lens system that inverts the visual field was first studied by George M. Stratton in 1897 at the University of California (whose psychological laboratory he founded). Stratton wore the lenses for eight days on the right eye only; the left eye was kept blindfolded. The optical effect was to turn the whole visual field completely upside down and to reverse it from right to left.

Stratton reported severe, immediate disorientation on donning the lenses. The coordination of vision and body movement was badly disrupted. He reached in the wrong direction for visually perceived objects and heard sounds coming from the side opposite their visually perceived source. A great deal of trial-and-error groping was required

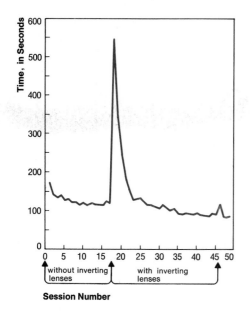

Session Number

to accomplish such simple acts as placing a fork in food and conveying it to the mouth. After about three days the disorientation lessened, and by the end of the eight days the new visual-motor coordination had become quite good. As the days passed, he even became less and less aware that the visual scene was upside down. Upon removal of the lenses this successful adaptation was itself destroyed, so that some degree of disorientation occurred under the restored, but no longer normal, circumstances. Fortunately, this second effect lasted only a brief time.

F. W. Snyder and N. H. Pronko repeated this experiment with the subject wearing the inverting lenses for thirty days. A number of tests of visual-motor coordination were carried out before, during, and after this period. In one of the tests the subject had to sort cards rapidly into appropriate boxes. Time in seconds for completion of the task was recorded. Five trials a day were carried out for seventeen sessions before the lenses were worn, for twenty-eight sessions while they were being worn, and for four sessions after they were removed. The graph shows the average time scores for these sessions. Note the enormous slowing down in task performance after the lenses were first put on, the fairly rapid readjustment during the period of inversion, and the slight and very brief further disruption when the lenses were removed.

Toward the end of the experiment the subject was asked whether or not a scene from a tall building looked upside down to him. He replied: "I wish you hadn't asked me. Things were all right until you popped the question at me. Now, when I recall how they *did* look *before* I put on these lenses, I must answer that they do look upside down *now.* But until the moment that you asked me I was absolutely unaware of it and hadn't given a thought to the question of whether things were right side up or upside down."

G. M. STRATTON. Vision without inversion of the retinal image. *Psychological Review*, 1897, **4,** 341–360.
F. W. SNYDER & N. H. PRONKO. *Vision with Spatial Inversion.* Wichita: University of Wichita, 1952. Figure adapted by permission.

of the room. There you will note that the afterimage appears much larger, and yet the size of the retinal image cannot have changed. Careful comparisons have shown that the perceived

size of the afterimage is exactly determined by the distance between the eye and the surface on which the image appears to be projected. This relation is known technically as

FIGURE 13.8 How do you recognize these as shadows of people—despite distortions?

Photo by Michael Hirst

Emmert's Law. For instance, an afterimage projected on a surface ten times as far away as the original stimulus will look ten times as large as the original stimulus, even though the retinal image remains the same (see Figure 13.9).

Under typical viewing conditions, our perception of objects manifests **size constancy**. That is, to a truly astonishing degree, a given object looks the same size to us whether we are near to it or far away. When the object is

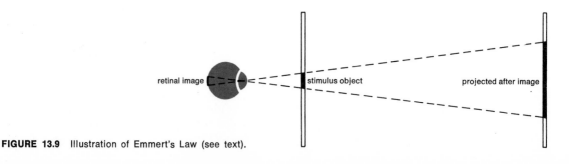

FIGURE 13.9 Illustration of Emmert's Law (see text).

farther away, its retinal image is smaller, so why should we not see the object as smaller? The answer lies in the fact that the cues of retinal size and distance operate as a single perceptual system. As an object moves away, its retinal size decreases but its apparent distance, as determined by distance cues, increases. To the extent that the relation between these two types of cues remains invariant —that is, retinal size decreases with a proportional increase in apparent distance—the perceived size remains constant.

Prior experience and size constancy   Frequently, prior experience can influence perceived size and size constancy. A particularly dramatic instance of this effect is provided by Turnbull (1961). Working with the BaMbuti pygmies of the Congo, he found an impressive breakdown in size constancy when these people were placed in a totally unfamiliar environment. The BaMbuti live in heavily forested country and rarely if ever scan a distance greater than one quarter of a mile. A BaMbuti taken from his forest by Turnbull saw buffalo at a great distance and thought they were insects; he also saw a distant boat and could not believe that so tiny a boat actually held real people. The BaMbuti are apparently unable to correlate retinal image and apparent distance to achieve size constancy in a situation in which distances exceeding their usual experience are involved.

It is of course very likely that the BaMbuti would attain normal size constancy if they were given prolonged experience in this new kind of environment. It is even possible that some change toward greater size constancy would (or did) take place within a matter of minutes; at least that is the suggestion that might be drawn from the findings of Rock (1965). He devised an apparatus (essentially a fun-house type of distorting mirror) that made highly familiar objects (a pencil and a playing card, for example) appear smaller than their familiar sizes. This effect was quite convincing at first, but, as the subjects continued to observe these "shrunken" objects, within minutes the objects began to return to normal

size. Apparently some adaptation process was at work, and we might expect it to apply in the case of the BaMbuti and their miniature buffalo.

Constancy as Achievement

Though object constancy does not depend upon knowledge of the actual stimulus situation, we should not underrate the important role that the perceiver's learning and intention can play in the phenomenon. For instance, the observer may deliberately try to circumvent constancy by paying attention only to the retinal-size cue and neglecting the distance cue, or by judging the brightness of the light rays from the surface of the object independent of the brightness of its surroundings.

But such artificial separation of cues in an attempt to see the world as it really is is not easily done. The observer often makes various implicit assumptions that affect his perception despite his intention. A striking example is the size-weight illusion (see Box 13.6, p. 300).

The conclusion is that under natural circumstances our perception tends to be "object-directed" rather than "stimulus-directed." That is, we customarily seek to achieve an accurate perception of the whole object. The functional value of this is obvious, inasmuch as we must cope with whole objects in our environment. To see objects we must necessarily take into account patterns of stimuli, not isolated stimulus attributes, and in so doing we can achieve perceptual constancy of the objects.

THEORETICAL APPROACHES TO PERCEPTION

In tracing the chain of perception from its start, the stimulus object, to the final link, the brain, we have stressed the organizing power of the system and the remarkable manner in which it achieves the perception of movement, space, and objects. At this point it is pertinent to ask whether the brain is simply the passive locus of perception (like a photographic film on which a representation of the actual world, as filtered through lenses, etc., is finally depos-

BOX 13.6

POUND OF FEATHERS, POUND OF LEAD

A most surprising illusion can be demonstrated with two rectangular wooden blocks. One is 1½ in. × 1½ in. × 2½ in.; the other is 3 in. × 3 in. × 5 in., or exactly eight times the volume of the first. Concealed inside each block are pieces of lead so adjusted that the total weight of *each* block is exactly 300 grams. Each block can be hefted by placing the forefinger inside the metal ring on its top.

The subject is informed that the larger block weighs 300 grams. He is asked to heft the larger block and then the smaller block and to judge the latter's weight in grams. Virtually all subjects perceive the smaller block as being substantially heavier than the larger one. For instance, in a study of 100 military officers (R. S. Crutchfield, D. G. Woodworth, & R. E. Albrecht), the average weight estimate for the smaller block was 750 grams, about two and one-half times the correct weight. For some of the officers the overestimate was as much as sevenfold!

This phenomenon is known as the *size-weight illusion.* A common explanation of this illusion is that the person expects the smaller block to be lighter than the larger (because of the obvious size difference), and the contrast of this prior expectation

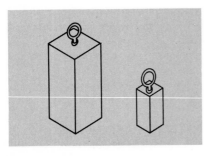

with the actual weight of the smaller when hefted makes it seem heavier. But this explanation is entirely inconsistent with the fact that the illusion persists almost as strongly after the blocks have been repeatedly hefted *and even after the person weighs them on a scale.* Mere knowledge of the objective facts is insufficient to destroy the illusion. Further results show that even when the subject is instructed to "pay no attention" to the relative sizes of the blocks and to concentrate only on the feeling of their weights, the illusion is as great as before. And if a subject first looks at the blocks and then closes his eyes when hefting them, the illusion is equally great.

E. Brunswik has suggested that the subject, although attempting to judge *weight,* is implicitly taking *density* (weight per cubic inch) into account. Because the small block is one-eighth the size of the large block but weighs exactly the same, the density of the small block is eight times that of the larger. The person, in judging the weight of the small block, may partly be influenced by his perception of its density. In this way the smaller and denser block is judged heavier. Brunswik has supported this explanation by finding that subjects who are carefully instructed to pay attention to the attribute of "weight' and to avoid the attribute of "density" are affected less than other subjects by the size-weight illusion.

The age-old conundrum "Which is heavier, a pound of feathers or a pound of lead?" is the mental counterpart of the perceptual size-weight illusion. The unwary person who answers that a pound of lead is obviously heavier is being implicitly affected by the relative densities of the objects.

R. S. CRUTCHFIELD, D. G. WOODWORTH, & R. E. ALBRECHT. *Perceptual Performance and the Effective Person.* San Antonio: Air Force Personnel and Training Research Center, 1955.
E. BRUNSWIK. *Perception and the Representative Design of Psychological Experiments.* Berkeley: University of California Press, 1956.

ited). Or does the brain instead play an active and essential role in organizing, analyzing, adding to, or creating the perceptual experience (like a painter who *receives information* from the outside world, but who then *uses* this information to create his picture of the world)?

Various perceptual researchers have proposed somewhat differing approaches to this

question. We prefer to call these "approaches" rather than "theories" because none is capable of, nor intended as, a truly comprehensive theoretical account of the entire scope of perceptual functioning. For one thing, these approaches tend to be concerned more with the phenomenological and behavioral facts of perception and less with facts about the biological foundation of the perceptual process, which a full-fledged theory of perception must also ultimately comprehend and integrate. As we shall see in Unit 14, a great deal is now known about the neurochemical events in the brain and nervous system upon which our perceptual experiences are based. But much more must be discovered before we can integrate phenomenology and physiology into a genuine *theory* of perception.

As we describe four of the major approaches toward a theory of perception, it will become apparent that each has a somewhat different primary focus. The *Gestalt* approach heavily stresses nativistic factors of perceptual organization. The *constructionist* approach accords greater influence to the factors of learning and memory. The *motor* approach centers on the role of feedback from the perceiver's motor exploration of his environment. Gibson's *ecological* approach emphasizes the full environmental information inherent in the stimulus pattern. Since, in our opinion, the differences among these views are often a matter of focus rather than of basic contradiction, we shall treat them as complementary rather than competing approaches.

The Gestalt Approach

In the early years of this century, a small group of experimental psychologists in Germany began to champion what was then a radical view: that we naturally, normally, immediately, and directly perceive forms, figures, and objects that have properties reflecting the *whole stimulus pattern*. This conception ran directly counter to the prevailing orthodox doctrine, which asserted that normal and pure experience (unsullied by the perceiver's expectations, theories, etc.) was best described in terms of discrete, unorganized, and unpatterned primary sensory experiences—that is, the experiences produced by the individual stimuli. Thus, for example, instead of saying that we experience the taste of lemonade, we should say that we experience the sensations of sweetness, sourness, wetness, coldness, and so forth.

The movement begun by these German

psychologists became known as **Gestalt psychology.** (*Gestalt* is the German word for "form" or "shape.") Its intellectual pioneers were Max Wertheimer, Kurt Koffka, and Wolfgang Köhler, all of whom later emigrated to the United States.

The Gestaltists believed in inherent or innate laws of brain organization. This, they argued, accounted for the central phenomena of figure-ground differentiation, contrast, contour, closure, the principles of perceptual grouping, and all the other organizational facts reviewed in Unit 12. Gestaltists thought that a principle of "simplicity" lay behind the various perceptual factors they proposed. They asserted that any pattern involving greater symmetry, closure, closely knit units, and similar units would seem "simpler" to the observer. If a configuration could be seen in more than one way, such as a line drawing that could be seen flat or as a cube, the "simpler" way would be more usual.

The earliest, most fundamental Gestalt demonstration was that by Wertheimer of apparent movement (see p. 286). In this phenomenal movement—so "real" as to be indistinguishable from real movement—it was manifest that the whole stimulus pattern yielded an undeniable quality of movement not contained in the constituent stimulus parts, each one of which was static. Here was a convincing illustration of the classic Gestalt dictum that "the whole is different from the sum of its parts."

Though the Gestaltists did not ignore the effects of prior experience on perception, their prime emphasis was on the role of intrinsic mechanisms built into the nervous system. Thus they assumed that apparent movement, or the phi phenomenon, was the outcome of *innate organizing tendencies of the brain* (see Box 13.7, p. 302).

A compelling demonstration that apparent movement is not dependent on the retina but on the brain has been provided by Kolers (1964). He found that a line-drawn cube flashing first in one place and then another would appear to move back and forth, as Wertheimer would have expected (see Figure 13.10, p. 303). The apparent cube was so clear in the intervening space that observers reported that it reversed in mid-

BOX 13.7

AN INNATE BASIS FOR APPARENT MOVEMENT?

We are not at all clear about the specific mechanisms responsible for apparent movement, nor can we say whether the phenomenon is innate or learned. There is evidence supporting both interpretations.

For example, I. Rock, E. S. Tauber, and D. P. Heller, exploiting the fact that fish tend to swim in the direction of a rotating drum, demonstrated that newborn guppies, some tested within minutes of birth, did the same when placed inside a *stationary* drum that *appeared* to rotate. The apparent rotation was produced by illuminating vertical columns situated around the walls of the drum, successively and in sequence. The effect was that of a *single* illuminated column moving round and round, creating the illusion that the drum itself was actually rotating. When the direction of the apparent movement was reversed (by reversing the illumination sequence), the fish changed their direction. These effects occurred for all the newborn guppies on every trial when, and only when, the columns were alternately illuminated at moderate speed, which, as we have seen, is the optimal rate for evoking the phi phenomenon. Not a single fish, however, showed any effect when the alternation rate was either very slow or very fast.

The implications of this result are that the newborn guppies had indeed perceived apparent movement and that, since they had no prior visual experience (they were kept in the dark between birth and testing), this perception must have an innate basis. These investigators conclude by speculating that newborn human infants can also perceive apparent movement.

Demonstration of an innate basis for a phenomenon does not rule out *modifiability* of the phenomenon by prior experience and learning. For example, we have already noted in Box 13.1, p. 287, that it is more difficult to perceive apparent movement between two locations when the shapes of the lights at the two points are not the same; the inference is that seeing movement in that situation simply does not accord with prior experience— it makes much less sense.

I. ROCK, E. S. TAUBER, & D. P. HELLER. Perception of stroboscopic movement: Evidence for its innate basis. *Science*, 1965, 147, 1050–1052.

flight, when no real cube was present! So there seems to be a complete physiological basis for perception of a cube somewhere in the perceptual system, and it acts just like a normal percept of a cube, even to the point of reversing.

The influence of the Gestalt approach on the field of perception has been immense. It has pervaded and suffused all modern conceptions of perceptual organization and functioning. At the same time many reservations have been expressed. It has been objected that the demonstrations of the "laws" of organization and the simplicity principle were too heavily based on lines and dots on flat paper, a kind of display that is pictorial and lacks all the rich detail of real objects in a real world. Perhaps under these circumstances, it is said, when the stimulus structure is weak and ambiguous, the Gestalt principles do come into play. But in the densely textured three-dimensional solid world we normally move around in, a different kind of perceptual process may occur. Notice that the cubes in Figure 13.10 can be seen in either of two configurations: a flat and complex design or a simple, three-dimensional object. The simpler pictorial configuration is the dominant one. But no one ever thinks he perceives a real cube sitting on the paper—everyone knows that the cube is only pictured.

A weightier criticism of the Gestalt approach is that in its preoccupation with innate factors of organization it has not given appropriate emphasis to factors of prior experience. This leads us next to a brief look at the *constructionist* approach.

The Constructionist Approach

In the constructionist view of perception, central importance is assigned to the role of *memory*. It is suggested that we add remembered residuals of previous experiences to here-and-

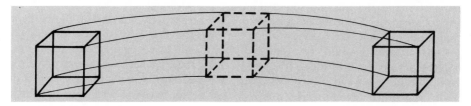

FIGURE 13.10 When a Necker cube is set into oscillating apparent motion, it may undergo spontaneous reversal of perspective while apparently in midflight.

Kolers, 1964.

now stimulus-induced sensations and thus *construct* a percept. And, the constructionist argues, the processes of selecting, analyzing, and adding to stimulus information from one's memory store are the bases of organized perceptions, rather than the Gestaltists' natural operation of innate laws of brain organization.

Consider Figure 13.11. The central symbol can be seen as a B or as a 13, depending upon

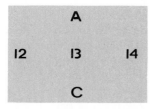

FIGURE 13.11 What is in the center? (See text.)

which context prevails, *not* upon any innate organizing tendency of the brain. The inference that the constructionist would draw from this is that the same stimulus data can be constructed into different perceptions. As Neisser (1967) remarks:

The detailed properties and features we ordinarily see in an attended figure are, in a sense, "optional." They do not arise automatically just because the relevant information is available, but only because part of the input was selected for attention and certain operations then performed on it. Neither the object of analysis nor the nature of the analysis is inevitable, and both may vary in different observers and at different times. The very word analysis may not be apt. It suggests an analogy with chemistry: a chemist

analyzes unknown substances to find out what they really are. More appropriate [is] a comparison of the perceiver with a paleontologist, who carefully extracts a few fragments of what might be bones from a mass of irrelevant rubble and reconstructs the dinosaur that will eventually stand in the Museum of Natural History. One does not simply examine the input and make a decision; one builds an appropriate visual object.

Let us now examine some further and quite diverse examples of perceptual phenomena that seem to illustrate a constructionist view:

1. Consider your own eye movements. Your eyes dart around this page, glance around a room, look left and right before you cross the road. Isn't it true that you have to take in quite separate and distinct "snapshots" of the world with each eye movement? If so, then isn't it likely that you need a mechanism for putting all the snapshots together, in proper order, with snapshots from the left being kept together, and snapshots from the right kept apart from ones to the left? Out of the bundle of snapshots we have to "construct" a total view of our surroundings, just as a spying cameraman would have to do when he got his camera home.

2. We often fill in missing words or letters or sounds as we respond to written or spoken language. Indeed, we may miss printing errors in words that we read, even when they are as blatant as one word being printed twice in a row in one paragraph (see Unit 12, p. 279). In recent studies similar effects were found in hearing spoken language. When part of a tape of spoken language was deleted, and a meaningless sound substituted, subjects said

they distinctly heard the missing sound. (If the deleted section of the sentence was left blank, subjects did not hear the missing sounds.) Constructionists would infer that the subjects must have *added* the missing sound (from their memory store) into their perception.

3. It has been found that, like visual figures, words can also satiate (see p. 272) and become reorganized (Warren, 1968). If a tape of a word is played over and over again (or a record sticks at a certain word) observers report that the word swiftly loses its meaning and then seems to change. Rosy, Rosy, Rosy, Rosy, Rosy . . . will become meaningless, or become Zero, Zero, Zero, Zero, Rosy, Zero, Sere Oh! Ser Oh! Ooze Ear, Ooze Ear. Finally, very peculiar "additions" may occur, for the observer reports completely irrelevant words like Rosy, Rosy, WARDROBE, Rosy, BREAKFAST, and so on. He reorganizes and adds to the incoming message, constructionists conclude.

4. Many investigators find that if subjects live in an unchanging sensory environment for a long time, they often report experiencing complex images and hallucinations (see Unit 19, p. 459). The sensory systems, free from the reins of incoming information, build up complex objects. Presumably, the objects are based on materials coming from storage in memory, indicating that perceptual mechanisms can be fed from memory.

5. As a final example, Kolers (1972) has shown that the processes we use in analyzing sentences have an important role in recognition. He found that the printing style of written sentences was very important in their later recognition. The more *difficult* the printing style was to read, the better the later recognition. Kolers suggests that reading the difficult styles required more perceptual operations, and these operations formed the basis for later recognition. The machinery of perception was a basis for memory. So if you want to remember a message have someone say it to you in a heavy accent—your difficulty in processing his language will be a boon to later memory.

Although the above examples do attest to the constructive nature of the perceptual process, they also raise some questions of interpretation of these phenomena. In Figure 13.11 (p. 303), for instance, when context directs us to see the central symbol as either a B or as a 13, we do not have the erroneous impression that it is a *perfect* B or 13. Familiar context tells us what to look for; it does not lead us to construct more than the parts of things that are truly there.

Similarly, just because we miss a printing error is no assurance that we filled in missing letters. To *identify* a word we may only need to notice some of its letters—as in the words A PHABETIC WRIT NG. Skilled reading may involve just noticing critical parts of the text. The fact that we miss printing errors does not prove we construct absent parts of the text.

There is an instructive analogy in the perception of Rorschach inkblots (Unit 27, p. 678). It is true that people report seeing different known things in inkblots, like flying bats or flaming fires. But notice that no one tries to duck the bat, or warm his hands at the fire that he sees. He does not think he sees parts of objects that are not present in the inkblot picture. The bat is not seen as a whole. And only a few parts of the picture are selected by him to be depictions of parts of bats. If you ask him to tell you which parts of the blots *look like* bats and which like fires he can tell you—and you will be able to see the same things. The blots are seen as poor-quality pictures, that is all.

In short, it would appear that, as the constructionists suggest, memory is highly significant in the perceptual process in that it provides a familiar context for perceiving; but this need not occur by literally adding details to perception.

The Motor Approach

Following the direction of Pavlov's early work, modern Russian perceptual research has concentrated on the role of motor behavior in influencing and guiding perception. These investigators argue that there is a "motor copy" that controls some of our perception of patterns.

They believe that a copy of the movements made in exploring an object is one of the determiners of what will be seen.

Such movements seem to be, at least in part, a learned tendency. Evidence is accumulating, so far mainly from Russian investigators (Zaporozhets, 1961, for example), that in early stages of the development of visual perception eye movements do not tend to follow the outlines of objects or to concentrate upon their more figural features. This general conclusion is drawn by several investigators from studies of children, of adults whose sight had been restored through surgery, and of individuals with brain injuries who were gradually reacquiring the ability to perceive visual patterns. What seems to come earlier in the learning process for such individuals is a tendency to trace the outlines of an object or pattern with their *fingers* and only later to substitute eye movements for this manual tracing. Eye movement tracing seems to have an adaptive function; procedures especially designed to induce children and adults to trace the contours of objects visually have been found to aid visual learning and relearning.

In this context, Zaporozhets (1961) reports a fascinating observation by one of his associates, Zinchenko. Zinchenko photographically recorded eye movement patterns in response to the *names* of new objects and noted a tendency for these patterns to correspond to those observed when the object itself was being viewed. This correspondence seemed to be only temporary; it occurred only in the "middle stage" of the verbal learning process and disappeared when the name had been well learned. The implication, of course, is that eye movements may play some kind of mediating role in learning new words. This suggestion of so intimate a connection between the course of attention in visual—and perhaps other forms of perceptual exploration—and the acquisition of language merits further study.

Kohler (1964) (not to be confused with the Gestaltist Köhler) explored a large number of methods for changing the normal relation between vision and movements. He had subjects wear goggles that turned the world upside down (see earlier work in Box 13.5, p. 297), or reversed left and right, or made other rearrangements. People who are given new spectacles by their optician often report that at first the world seems unstable through the glasses. The world seems rubbery and has colored fringes, and things aren't quite in the expected direction. Kohler's goggles exaggerated this effect. He found that touch and vision seemed to become recoordinated after the subjects had worn the goggles for some time and engaged in their normal activities.

Held and Rekosh (1963) conducted an experiment showing that perception of shape (curvature in this case) is closely intertwined with movement. Their results suggest an important part of the mechanism for relearning a new visual coordination (see Box 13.8, p. 306).

In a second experiment Held and Hein (1963) explored the role of active movement in early learning. They raised pairs of kittens in darkness for about eight weeks. Then they allowed the kittens regular experience in a carousel (see Figure 13.12, p. 307). One kitten fitted snugly into a gondola, only its head peeping out (the *passive* kitten). The other kitten drove the carousel from a similar gondola, with head and legs coming out. The *active* kitten walked around and saw visual effects corresponding to its movements. The passive kitten was exposed to the same visual changes, but did not make the movements that produced the visual changes. After some weeks of this training, the kittens were tested for visually guided behavior, and they differed noticeably. For example, the active kitten reached out a paw on approach to a surface and blinked when an object approached like a missile. The passive kitten did not. The conclusion was that *activity* was necessary for development of perception of the location of objects.

A more recent experiment (Hein, Held, & Gower, 1970) found a surprising result: It mattered which eye had been involved in the activity experience. Kittens were reared in the same way, but this time one eye was allowed to be open during the active experience and the other one during the passive experience. These kittens showed effective visually guided behavior only when tested with the activity-experienced eye open.

BOX 13.8

BODY MOVEMENT AND THE PERCEPTION OF CURVES

The process by which a subject wearing lenses "learns" to see the world right side up is far from clear. It is surely not learning in the usual sense of a conscious and deliberate process; subjects report no such process during the adaptation period, nor is it likely that so complex a problem could ever be solved in so rational a manner. R. Held and J. Rekosh have suggested a possible mechanism; their suggestion is based on a study of the perceptual effects of curvature-inducing lenses. Through these lenses their subjects, who had been placed in a man-sized drum, viewed a random pattern of tiny dots that completely covered the inside wall of the drum. A critical aspect of this experiment is that such a pattern looks the same with and without lenses, so that the subject is unaware of any distortion. The pattern was viewed for a half-hour by each subject under each of two conditions: first, while walking around inside the drum, and second, while being wheeled around on the same route in a specially designed cart.

After the viewing period and while still wearing the curvature-inducing lenses, the subject was required to adjust a line whose curvature he could mechanically vary until it appeared to him perfectly straight. The actual extent of curvature of the line that the subject reported as straight was taken as the measure of the degree of his adaptation to the lenses. In every instance a significant amount of adaptation was shown to have taken place following the walking-around condition. No adaptation whatever occurred while the subjects were being wheeled around.

The conclusions from these data are twofold. First, it is not necessary to be aware of a spatial distortion in order to be able to adapt to it; second, such adaptation requires *self-initiated motor activity* during the viewing period. Held and Rekosh interpret these conclusions to mean that normal spatial orientation is based upon a learned relationship between movement-produced stimuli and the changes in retinal patterns that accompany such changes in body position. When the nature of this relationship is changed, as by inversion or curvature-inducing lenses, the nervous system in some manner unlearns the old relationship and rapidly acquires the new one.

Lower animals may not show such rapid adaptability in space perception. In 1956, E. H. Hess hatched chicks in darkness, then hooded them with prismatic goggles that displaced objects in their visual field 7 degrees to the right (or to the left). These chicks were never able to adjust their pecks so as to compensate for this visual displacement. Instead they continued to peck 7 degrees to the right (or to the left) of the grain target.

R. HELD & J. REKOSH. Motor-sensory feedback and the geometry of visual space. *Science*, 1963, **141**, 722–723.
E. H. HESS. Space perception in the chick. *Scientific American*, 1956, **195**, 71–80.

You can try a demonstration yourself that shows how active movements and activity initiated by the brain may be important in perception. Push one eye with a finger from the side. You will notice that the world seems to jump each time you push your eye. Yet when you move your eye with your eye muscles the world seems to stay stationary. Presumably the brain's instructions to the eye muscles match the changes that occur on your retina when you use the "instructed" eye muscles to move your eyes. When you *push* your eyes no such record of eye movements is activated in the brain and so the retinal changes are "interpreted" by the brain to indicate movement of the world.

It is certain that our eye movements are closely related to perception. Indeed, if we do not move our eyes at all the effect is that the visual scene fades completely. Try staring at the criss-cross pattern of Figure 13.13 for a few minutes, and you will see something of this effect. Even when staring our eyes move very slightly. Yarbus (1967) managed to project on the eye an image that remained completely

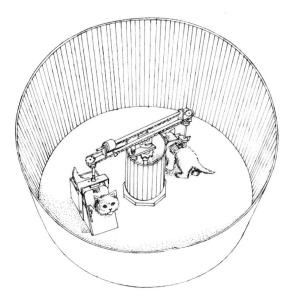

FIGURE 13.12 Two ways of getting around (see text for explanation).

stable. After a few seconds it faded completely and did not return. Eye movements are essential in maintaining vision (see Unit 14, p. 321).

In other types of perceptual processes, movement may not be as vitally important for perception as eye movements clearly are. Let us try moving another receptor system, both under its own power and also by pushing it around. Try your left hand's little finger. Let it rest on a surface, and move it in various ways. When you use your right hand to move your left hand and its little finger do you have an impression that the surface is moving and not your hand—akin to the impression you got when pushing on your eye? Under normal circumstances, you will *not* have this impression.

We can conclude that a motor approach to perception, and its emphasis on a corollary record, may hold in a powerful way for eye movements, but that the approach may not be equally appropriate for all kinds of movement in the perceptual process.

Gibson's Ecological Approach

There is a good deal to be said for the common-sense belief that the stimuli which reach us from the stimulus objects around us in the environment at the moment are sufficient in themselves to permit us to perceive our environment accurately. A systematic account that has taken off from this commonsense view has been developed by the American psychologist J. J. Gibson.

In 1950, Gibson proposed that perception relies very heavily on a kind of relation that he believed had been overlooked by previous generations of psychologists. He begins his analysis with the observation that the normal environment is composed of textured surfaces, and that a visual system that can detect texture (as ours can) makes crucial use of *gradients of texture* in perceiving the world (see Box 13.9, p. 308). In Gibson's view, *surfaces*, which are highly important in perception, are usually textured, and texture forms the basis for our perception of surfaces. Perception of textured surfaces Gibson calls *normal*, or *ecological*, perception. He asserts that, in contrast to his own view, Gestalt theory is based mainly on an analysis of perception in the *special* case where texturing is reduced or is irrelevant, as the texture of this paper is irrelevant to the displays printed on it.

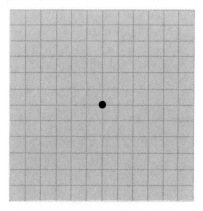

FIGURE 13.13 Stare at the central dot for a few minutes and parts of the figure will fade out.

BOX 13.9

DEPTH THROUGH GRADIENTS

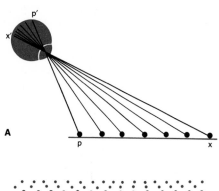

A

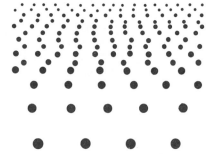

B

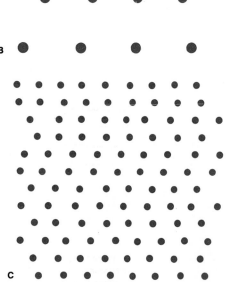

C

In normal viewing of the three-dimensional world, most surfaces have visible textures. A vivid example is a pebbly beach; thickly woven rugs, wood-paneled walls, and acoustical-tile ceilings are also typical high-textured surfaces spanning the distance from our eyes to nearby or far-off objects.

A uniform texture on the physical surface (px in Figure A) is necessarily projected on the retina (p'x') in such a way that the density near x' is greater than the density near p'. The greater the distance away, the greater the density of texture in the retinal pattern.

J. J. Gibson argues that such density differences, or stimulus gradients, are adequate cues for the perception of depth. Figure B, for example, is a stimulus pattern in which sizes of spots and distances between them decrease regularly from the bottom to the top. This stimulus pattern corresponds to the pattern of stimulation that is impinging on the retina in Figure A. The result is a convincing impression of a continuous receding plane, whether the pattern arises from a horizontal plane actually receding from us (as in Figure A) or from a frontal flat plane with no variation whatever in distance of points from our eyes (as in Figure B). In one case we have an accurate percept, in the other a depth illusion. One test of Gibson's hypothesis for depth perception (or anyone's hypothesis to explain any phenomenon) is whether or not it is possible to create the phenomenon "artificially" by abstracting only those aspects of the situation that are specified by the hypothesis. In this illustration the test has been passed.

Figure C has a zero gradient, that is, a perfectly regular spacing of dots. Consequently, according to Gibson's hypothesis, it gives no impression of depth.

Gibson offers illustrations indicating that other depth cues are merely special cases of stimulus gradients on the retina. In the case of relative clearness, the light from distant objects is more diffused by the time it reaches the eye than light from nearby objects; as a result there is a gradient of clarity among the corresponding images on the retina.

J. J. GIBSON. *The Perception of the Visual World.* Boston: Houghton Mifflin, 1950.

How does Gibson suggest that a pictured figure-ground perception (where there are no gradients of texture) is related to surface perception? Since figure and ground is an impression that can result when we observe a single line or contour against a background, and since observers are able to say that the *apparent* difference in depth between figure and ground is *not really present*, Gibson proposes that figure and ground is a result of seeing the display *as a picture*. That is, contours and lines seem to be able to depict the boundaries of surfaces and differences in depth that occur at boundaries of surfaces. Figure 13.14 is a line drawing in which various kinds of arrangements of surfaces are all depicted by lines.

Some theorists have proposed that line drawings are a kind of symbolic code or language that we have to teach children. Others have argued that the ability to see tridimensionality from a flat picture is innate and appears without specific training. Hochberg and Brooks (1962), a husband-and-wife team of psychologists, raised their son to the age of nineteen months with little exposure to any kind of pictures. He saw no television, no picture books or comics—only a few decals and billboards. He was never taught any code for pictures, never told to associate names and pictures. He learned his vocabulary with real, solid objects and toys. When at nineteen months he had a reasonably large vocabulary, he was first shown line drawings, and he named the depicted objects correctly.

It seems, therefore, that the capacity of our visual system to accept line drawings as representations of the edges of surfaces is innate. The "language of outline" in drawings, Gibson would argue, was a *discovery* by cave artists of something man already had; it was not an *invented* code. Figure and ground, for Gibson, is a case of lines and contours depicting edges of surfaces, parts of the "language of outlines."

In constructionist theories, as we have seen, perception often makes essential use of information from memory. On the other hand, Gibson thinks that the highly structured world,

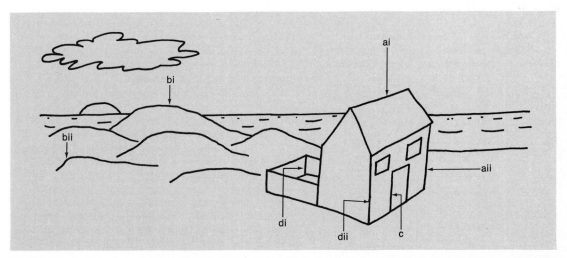

FIGURE 13.14   Lines in the figure depict: (a) sharp edges, with the background being (i) *sky* for some lines, and (ii) *other surfaces* for some lines; (b) rounded edges, such as the horizon and brows of hills, with background being (i) *sky* for some lines, and (ii) *other surfaces* for some lines; (c) cracks between surfaces; (d) corners, where both walls forming the corner are visible to the observer and there is no background, but some are concave (i) and some are convex (ii).

Kennedy, 1971.

with its textured surfaces, supplies sufficiently rich and accurate information from which the observer can *select*. One must select, he says, because the incoming information is so overly rich. One certainly need not add to this abundant supply from previously stored information. In Gibson's view, our perceptual selection skills get better and better with age. In one experiment he and E. J. Gibson studied how subjects learn to tell the difference between things that are perceptually similar at the outset (see Box 13.10).

Gibson and Gibson propose that improvement in recognition of correct structure or pattern is an inherently "interesting" phenomenon and is something the perceptual system does spontaneously. In this vein, Mueller, Kennedy, and Tanimoto (1973) show that the progressive discovery of structure is more appealing to subjects than its opposite—progressive destruc-

tion of structure. They showed sets of cards in which scribbles either gradually took on the form of recognizable shapes (letters) as the experimenter leafed through the sets (see Figure 13.15), or gradually lost their recognizable shape, turning into scribbles. Subjects preferred to watch the scribbles turn into letters rather than the letters become transformed into unrecognizable shapes. You can watch the same effect yourself in some television commercials or in programs such as *Sesame Street*, where progressive changes in shapes are animated. Do you find the swirling shapes that turn into recognizable shapes more interesting than the patterns that first swirl and then become unrecognizable?

Motor theories of perception, as we have already seen, suppose that signals to our muscles become influences on perception and that our developing skills in movement guide our developing perceptual skills. Although acknowl-

BOX 13.10

SELECTING AMONG SCRIBBLES

To study the process of perceptual learning, J. J. and E. J. Gibson of Cornell University made up a set of seventeen scribbles (see figure). The scrib-

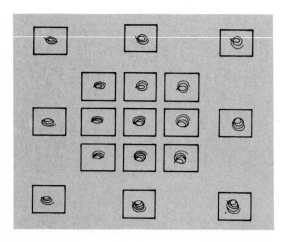

bles vary in three dimensions from the central standard item: number of coils, horizontal stretching or compression, and orientation (starting from right to left). The subject was shown the standard item and his task was to recognize it whenever it appeared in the pack of cards. The experimenter showed the cards one at a time. He ran through fresh packs of cards several times until the subject made only correct identifications.

The subjects were *never told whether they were correct in their judgments*. Yet it did not seem to be necessary to tell them, for they made fewer and fewer errors as the packs were run through.

The subjects of the experiment included three age groups: twelve adults, ten older children (eight and one-half to eleven years), and ten younger children (six to eight years). Although the children made many more errors than the adults at the outset, they too gradually learned the differences, and, like the adults, did not need to be told whether they were correct for learning to occur.

J. J. GIBSON & E. J. GIBSON. Perceptual learning: Differential or enrichment? *Psychological Review*, 1955, **62**, 32–41. Copyright 1955 by the American Psychological Association. Reprinted by permission.
E. J. GIBSON. *Principles of Perceptual Learning and Development.* New York: Appleton, 1969.

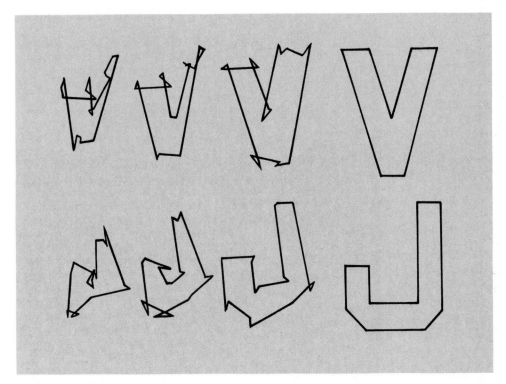

FIGURE 13.15   Two transformation sequences from "jumbled" endpoints to "recognizably structured" endpoints. Only every other step is shown here; there were eight steps in the original sequences.

Mueller, Kennedy, & Tanimoto, in press.

edging that there does seem to be some way in which eye movements influence perception, Gibson believes that, usually, perception guides our movements. In this connection, researchers have recently found that very young children are aware of expected consequences for actions. A visible object is expected to have tactual concomitants if one reaches out for it. Even infants seem to be aware of this (see Box 13.11, p. 312).

What are the processes behind our impressions of the tactual consequences of handling visual objects? Various studies indicate that there may be an innate basis, common to several senses, for impressions of the shapes of the surfaces of objects. In one experiment, the skin on the backs of blind subjects was found to be able to work like a retina. White et al. (1970) devised a television camera system that

projected a "tactual image" onto the skin on subjects' backs (see Figure 13.16, p. 312). An area *within* a discrete image was indicated by vibrating rods whose tips touched the subjects' skin. In the area *outside* the image the rods did not vibrate. The blind subjects had never experienced an image of objects pressed on their backs until they participated in this experiment; yet after a little practice they could tell the shape of the vibrating area and identify the silhouette as a telephone, for example.

Underlying Gibson's "ecological" approach is the belief that in many respects all people see the world in similar ways. And he almost says that they see the world clearly and they see it whole. To be sure, people generally see the sizes and shapes and locations of objects quite accurately, and the mechanisms for seeing edges and surfaces operate similarly in most people.

BOX 13.11

GRASPING AT CUBES

Object perception in infants has been studied by T. G. R. Bower, a Scottish psychologist. He presented certain objects to infants a few weeks old. The infants would move their arms in the direction of the objects, though not very skillfully at first. Bower noticed that their fingers were spread apart widely when a large object was nearby and were more closed up if the object was small. He suggests that the children are perceiving information about the object's size, and this information influences their grasp.

We might suppose that the size of the image on their retina would control the infants' impressions of the size of objects. But Bower finds that interactions between eyes and head movements are more important, and this complex interaction is active early in the first year of life. He showed cubes to infants about two and one-half months old, wondering whether they could tell their size and position. If the infant turned his head when shown a 2-in. cube 3 ft away, Bower would "peek-a-boo" at him. Soon the baby would turn his head every time that cube was shown. Then Bower tried three tests: (a) He replaced the cube with a cube of the *same* size, but farther away (9 ft); (b) he pre-

sented a 36-in. cube at the *same* 3-ft distance; (c) he presented a 36-in. cube at 9 ft, which cast the *same size retinal image* as the original cube.

The results: the infant responded with much more head-turning in tests (a) and (b)—the same-size cube farther away, or the large cube at the same distance—than in test (c). In test (c) an identical-size retinal image was projected, but the cube was neither the same size nor the same distance as the original cube. Bower concludes that, by moving his head in the original situation, the infant had gained information about the true size and location of the cube, and this information (not the size of the retinal image) was what was important.

Bower then tried a flat picture of the cube in full color. What would you expect to happen if the infant relies on head movements to gauge the true size and place of an object? The infant would not respond at all because he would detect the flatness of the picture. And that was what Bower found.

He then tried a binocular image of the cube so that slightly different images went in each eye. Now the infant was supplied with information for a solid object. As Bower predicted, the infants reached out for the object, and when their hands did not grasp a solid object they appeared startled! Even infants expect solid objects to have tactual consequences for a reaching movement.

T. G. R. BOWER. The visual world of infants. *Scientific American*, 1966, **215**, 80–92.
T. G. R. BOWER. Object perception in infants. *Perception*, 1972, **1**, 15–30.

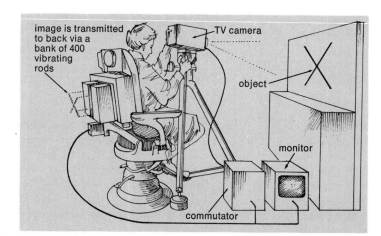

FIGURE 13.16 Schematic representation of the tactile television system.

White et al., 1970.

BOX 13.12

PERCEPTION ACROSS CULTURES

One of the most fascinating perennial puzzles in perception is raised by comparisons among cultures. Do perceivers from different cultures see things in different ways? The question is a very general one, and the answer is that "it depends." Some things are seen differently, some things the same.

Broadly speaking, complex patterns are often seen differently by observers from different cultural backgrounds. Rorschach inkblots, for example, may look like spaceships to a Floridian and like silhouetted hills to a Bedouin. (Other examples are given in Box 27.3, p. 679.) Information about depth is often interpreted differently by observers from varied cultures. To some Africans, as W. Hudson found, the spear-thrower in the figure is seen as

aiming at the (two-dimensionally) closer elephant. To people with a Western education, the indications of overlapping hills (as well as the small size of the elephant) in the picture suggest that the elephant is actually farther away, so that the spear is perceived as aimed at the (three-dimensionally) closer antelope.

But by and large observers seem to see objects the same way. Despite the fact that the objects in the figure have been depicted only in bare outlines, they are seen by African and Westerner alike as a man, an elephant, and an antelope. This suggests that the language of outline description is universal. The lines forming the man, for example, do not look like twisted wires or the boundaries of irregular regions to observers from any culture yet tested.

W. HUDSON. Pictorial depth perception in sub-cultural groups in Africa. *Journal of Social Psychology*, 1960, **52**, 182–208.

Yet cultural differences will out! Cross-cultural research reaffirms the message that while basic units such as lines have a universal meaning, the relations between objects and the interpretation of the seen world are often viewed differently by different peoples. (See Box 13.12 for a simple but interesting illustration of this phenomenon.)

SUMMARY

1. The perception of visual movement is not explained simply by real physical movement of stimuli in the environment. Induced movement, for example, is seen when two objects are displaced in relation to each other, but the one seen as moving is not necessarily the one that is actually moving. In apparent movement, a convincing impression of movement occurs when there is no real movement at all but merely a temporal succession of static stimuli, as in motion pictures. Autokinetic movement is an illusory movement occurring, for example, when a single stationary spot of light is seen in an otherwise dark room. In all these kinds of movement, "illusory" movement is not distinguishable by the observer from physically real movement.

2. The speed and direction of perceived movement is strongly influenced by the perceptual organization of the entire field. Moving objects are often seen as having complex attributes such as "causality," which are governed by specifiable features of the stimulus pattern and are subject to experimentally determined psychophysical laws.

3. Various cues from the same sense or even from different senses typically give rise to a unified impression of space, despite the fact that there is often incompatible information being fed in, because a single set of cues is usually dominant.

4. Both binaural cues (involving timing and intensity differences) and head movements are necessary to pinpoint the direction of a sound.

5. In the visual world, all stimuli act upon a two-dimensional retina, yet visual space is typically experienced as three-dimensional. Monocular cues or binocular cues alone can convey depth, but for a fully convincing impression a synthesis of information from both types of cues is necessary.

6. An important problem in visual perception is whether an organism has to learn how to perceive three-dimensional space or whether this is an innate ability. Evidence on this question has been obtained from individuals who were deprived of sensory experience from birth, tested very soon after birth, or raised in special environments designed to modify space perception. Innate spatial ability does seem to exist, but clearly, spatial perception improves with maturation and can be significantly modified by experience.

7. Our perception of objects is characterized by a high degree of constancy. Object constancy depends on the maintenance of certain invariant relations among parts of the stimulus pattern.

8. Under typical viewing conditions a given object appears to be the same size over a wide range of distances, despite the fact that its image size on the retina varies inversely with distance. In such size constancy many cues work together; the size of the retinal image and the apparent distance of the object are the more important cues, but knowledge of the size of the object and prior experience with it are also influential.

9. Under normal circumstances perception tends to be "object-directed," not "stimulus-directed." In this sense, constancy is a highly adaptive achievement, one that permits us to cope better in the real world, which consists of whole objects, not isolated stimulus attributes.

10. A complete theory of perception has not yet been developed, but four major approaches, each stressing the importance of different factors, can be discerned: *Gestalt* (nativistic factors), *constructionist* (influences of learning and memory), *motor* (role of feedback from movement during perception), and *ecological* (importance of the total complex of information available in the natural environment). Although the differences in emphasis between these approaches are very real (in that they point to different research questions), the four are for the most part complementary, rather than incompatible.

GLOSSARY

accommodation The readjustment in focus of the eye to maintain a sharp image on the retina, even when the distance between the eye and the object is constantly changing.

apparent movement The illusory movement from one stimulus location to another as a function of the temporal sequence of the stimuli. An example is motion pictures. This phenomenon is also known as stroboscopic movement or the phi phenomenon.

autokinetic movement An illusion of movement given by a stationary dot of light in an otherwise dark room. The effect is enhanced by the absence of visual framework.

binaural cues The stimulus cues occurring at the two ears that make sound localization possible. The identical sound waves starting at one source have different characteristics when they reach the two ears. The principal binaural cues have to do with time differences in the sound waves between the two ears.

convergence The rotation of the eyes toward one another in looking at an object. The closer the object, the greater the convergence. Convergence is a cue for depth perception that becomes ineffective at distances greater than 50 to 60 ft, at which distances the lines of sight become almost parallel.

Emmert's Law The direct proportionality of the perceived size of an afterimage to the distance between the eye and the surface on which the image appears to be projected. The same afterimage projected on a wall ten times as far away as the original stimulus appears ten times as large.

Gestalt psychology An approach to the experimental study of the organized nature of perception, initiated by a group of German psychologists including Wertheimer, Koffka, and Köhler. *Gestalt* is the German word for ''form.''

induced movement The appearance of movement in a motionless object that is produced by the movement of other objects in its surroundings. For instance, moving clouds induce perceived movement of the moon.

monocular depth cues The stimulus characteristics that lead to an impression of visual depth with one eye. Monocular cues from the visual pattern include interposition, relative size, relative height, relative clearness, linear perspective, and light and shadow. Other monocular cues are accommodation and relative movement.

object constancy The tendency for objects to be perceived in an established and consistent way despite wide variations in the conditions under which they are viewed.

relative movement (movement parallax) The relative visual displacement of nearer objects to the right and farther objects to the left as the head moves to the left (or of nearer objects to the left and farther objects to the right as the head moves to the right).

retinal disparity The difference in retinal images on the two eyes when looking at an object in depth; this difference is produced by the slightly different angle at which each eye looks at the object.

size constancy The tendency for a given object to be perceived as the same size despite wide variations in its distance from the observer. Size constancy depends on the relationship between the retinal size and apparent distance of the object.

stereoscope A viewing device that gives the impression of depth to a flat picture. The impression of depth is accomplished by presenting to each eye a separate and slightly different picture, corresponding to the retinal image that would have occurred in each eye had the actual three-dimensional scene been viewed.

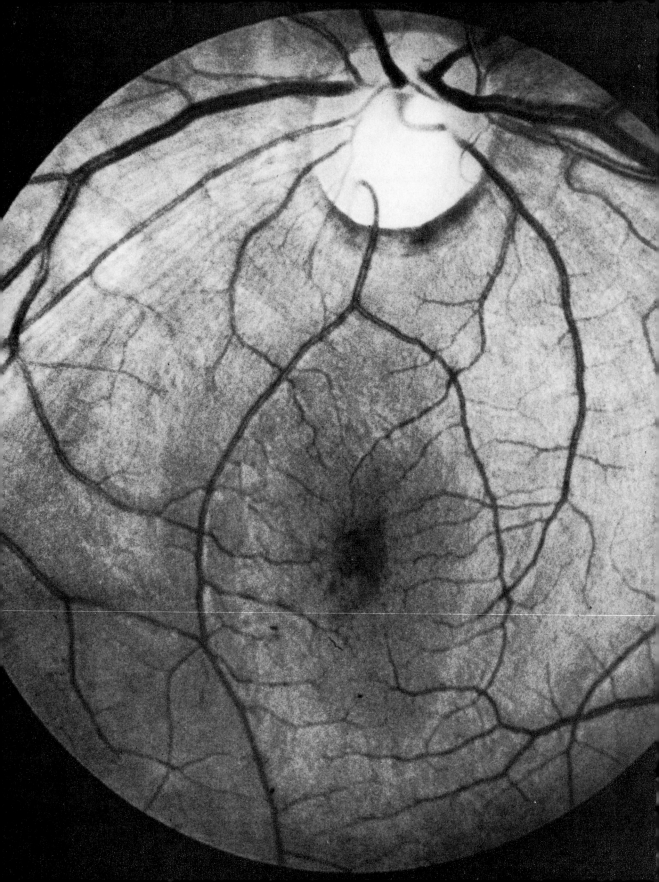

physiological bases of perception

DO YOU KNOW...

how the light rays that enter the eye from an object in the external world are focused at a single point within the eye and what happens if that image in the eye is not allowed to move?

how light stimulates a neural response in the eye?

that in a sense the perception of yellow is produced by a combination of red and green?

that the brain has built-in "detector cells" that respond to specific kinds of stimuli from the external world?

what happens if a frog's eye is turned upside down?

• what kind of deafness may be helped by having a hearing aid?

• why it helps to have two ears?

• why the sense of smell is so sensitive?

• why a person can't tickle himself?

• how we know which way is up?

unit 14

Courtesy, Dr. Ronald E. Carr, NYU Medical Center

CONTENTS

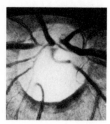

In this unit we shall be concerned with the anatomical and physiological bases of the perceptual phenomena surveyed in Units 11, 12, and 13. We shall have to study anatomical structures (the receptor organs and parts of the nervous system) as well as physiological processes (chemical or mechanical changes in the receptors and impulses in the neurons). Our goal will be to discover what bodily processes underlie the organism's ability to respond to incoming stimuli, and we will be especially interested in exploring what is known about the physiological basis of conscious human perception.

We must reemphasize here a point about the nervous system that is made in Unit 3. The nervous system (and the body as a whole) is *never* a quiet, inactive system waiting to be stirred into action and given directions by incoming stimuli. Stimuli are very important, of course, but the final behavior and experience of the individual are products of the *interaction* between the ever-active nervous system and new stimuli.

As we survey each sense in turn we will try to follow the effects produced by a stimulus, beginning at the receptor organ and working our way through the brain. This is the customary procedure and it is a sensible one, but it tends to make us think of perception from the point of view of the stimulus—a curious outlook indeed! As human perceivers, we will get a more accurate picture of the process of perception if we continually remember the important controlling role of the nervous system at every stage of activity.

At every possible point the sensory system *selects* which signals it will transmit, if any. It *changes* the information by emphasizing certain aspects while discarding other aspects, integrating previously separate pieces of information, and so forth. It *controls* processes that may change the amount or kind of information that the sensory receptors will seek in the future.

In order to view perception from the *point of view of the nervous system* (instead of that of the stimulus), the reader may think of himself as a small group of neurons in the brain, handling a never-ceasing set of incoming stimuli. Each stimulus has to be acted upon in accordance with its nature (its quality and intensity) and its importance. The importance you must assess on the basis of long-standing instructions that are somehow built into you and on the basis of new information continuously being received from other parts of the brain. As a result you select, modify, and transmit messages, at the same time asking for more or less additional information as appropriate.

It will certainly occur to you that the foregoing description is just what perception seems like from the *point of view of the total organism*, the individual. That is correct and quite understandable, because the actual process of perception consists of the complexly organized total activity of millions of groups of neurons as they receive, integrate, and transmit nerve impulses.

VISION

To understand the physiological mechanisms involved in visual perception, we must first see how the light rays from the stimulus object enter the eye, how they are focused to cast an image of the stimulus object on the retina, and how these focused light rays trigger nerve impulses in the retina. We must then describe how these impulses are propagated within the brain and how the brain reacts to and integrates these signals.

Four major physiological mechanisms are involved in these events: the **optical mechanism,** the **photosensitive mechanism,** the **conduction mechanism,** and the **central mechanism.**

The Optical Mechanism

Virtually all living things have light-sensitive mechanisms. In this unit we shall restrict ourselves to one of the most complex, the type of eye found among the higher vertebrates, including man.

Structure A semidiagrammatic drawing of the human eye is shown in Figure 14.1, page 320. The eyeball is completely enveloped by a tough protective skin consisting of two parts. The white opaque **sclera** (white of the eye) forms a light-proof shield around most of the eye, whereas the clear transparent **cornea** functions as the entrance for light. Each eye is moved by six **extrinsic muscles,** which are attached to the outside of the eyeball.

Just behind the cornea are the **iris,** which is a delicate pigmented structure, and the **lens.** The iris can expand or contract, and as it does so, it changes the size of the hole in its middle, the **pupil.** Actions of the **ciliary muscles** change the curvature of the lens (and therefore its focusing power). As we describe the operation of these various structures of the eye we will see again and again how each set of muscles is beautifully integrated into the entire neural economy of the eye to compensate for temporary difficulties, or to protect from overstimulation, or to obtain adequate stimulation, and so forth—all for efficient perception. And most of this is done reflexly, requiring no voluntary decisions.

Lining the rear of the eye is the **retina,** a complex neural network of light-sensitive elements and connecting cells, which we shall discuss in greater detail later.

Focusing and accommodation Light from any point in the outside world travels in all possible directions. In particular, light rays from every object in the **visual field** enter the eye through all points on the surface of the cornea. As the light from an outside object enters the cornea, however, the rays are refracted (bent) inward toward each other. As the rays continue through the lens, they are bent further so that in a perfectly formed eye the combined action of the cornea and lens brings the bundle of light rays from an outside point to a focus on the retina. If the object moves or if the eye turns to another object closer or farther away, the curvature of the lens changes to keep the object in focus (compare the lens in the lower-left portion of Figure 14.1 with the lens in the lower-right area). This readjustment in focusing power,

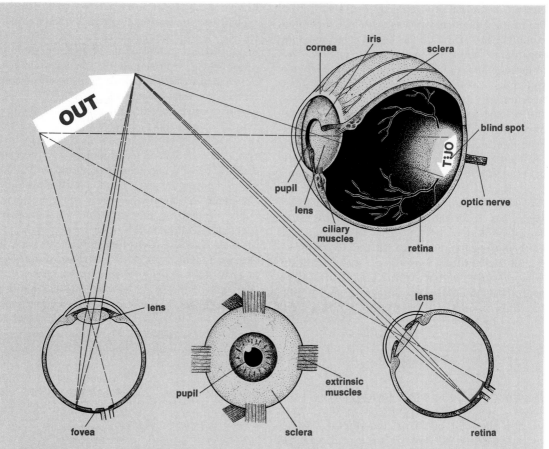

FIGURE 14.1   The optical mechanism. See text, p. 319, for a detailed explanation and description of the various parts of the eye. Note especially the following:

1. An object in the visual field is reversed both horizontally and vertically when projected on the retina: The right part of the object (the point of the arrow) is projected on the left half of the retina; the left part of the object is projected on the right half of the retina; and the object as a whole is upside down.
2. The light rays from any point on the object spread out in all directions, and the rays that reach the eye pass through the cornea and penetrate all of the surface of the lens that is not covered by the iris. The lens and cornea bend the rays so that all those that arise from a single point on the object come to focus at a single point on the retina.
3. In the diagram the eye is focused directly on the ''T'' of the word ''OUT.'' Therefore part of the ''U'' falls on the blind spot where there are no retinal cells (see p. 323).
4. The farther the eye is from an object, the flatter the lens is. Compare the lens of the eye in the lower-right corner with that in the lower-left corner (see p. 319).
5. The farther the eye is from the object, the smaller the retinal image cast by the object. Compare the retinal image on the eye in the lower-right corner with that in the lower-left corner.
6. The fovea is the section of the retina capable of greatest visual acuity (see p. 327). When the eye is looking directly at an object, the image of the point fixated will fall on the fovea.

which allows the eye to focus on objects at various distances, is called **accommodation.**

Human eyes are not always perfectly formed. The relation between the length of the eyeball and the focusing power of the eye may be such that the lens cannot always focus images properly (as in *nearsightedness* and *farsighted-ness*), or the cornea or lens may not be uniformly shaped (as in *astigmatism*). Then, the perceived world changes radically.

Eye movements The extrinsic muscles that control the eyeball play an extremely important role in normal vision. They produce the beautifully coordinated movements of the two eyes as we shift our gaze from object to object. They also cause tiny, rapid, involuntary movements when we look at a stationary object. These involuntary eye movements had been recognized since the eighteenth century, but it was not until the early 1950s that experiments dramatically disclosed the critical part they play in vision (e.g., Riggs et al., 1953). Using an ingenious system for counteracting the effects of eye movements, the experimenters kept the image of an observed pattern constantly focused at one place on a subject's retina (see Figure 14.2). Patterns viewed with this **stabilized retinal image** at first appear sharp and clear but almost immediately begin to fade, and finally they disappear, leaving a homogeneous gray field. At some place (or several places) along the chain of cells involved in carrying the sensory message, continued unchanging stimulation apparently produces *adaptation*—a temporary halt in the responsiveness of the cell and therefore of the whole perceptual mechanism. In any event it is clear that these involuntary movements, although not necessary for the initial perception of form, are necessary for the *maintenance* of form perception in normal vision.

The extrinsic muscles have, in addition, a very special function in our perception of the three-dimensional quality of space. As we have seen on page 293, vision with two eyes makes possible an accurate perception of space and distance. Each eye views an object from a slightly different direction and sees aspects of it that the other eye cannot see. Therefore the images focused on the retinas of the two

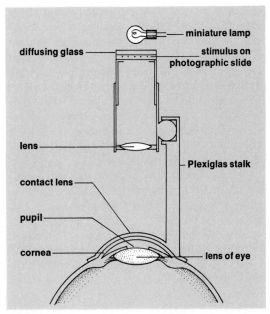

FIGURE 14.2 A method for producing a stabilized image on the retina. The stimulus is on a photographic slide, which is held at the end of a small tube in front of the eye. A lamp illuminates the stimulus. A lens is put in the path of the light going to the eye; this lens and adjustments in the length of the tube are used to help focus the image from the stimulus. All of this assembly is attached to a transparent contact lens that is placed over the cornea. When the extrinsic muscles produce the small, irregular eye movements discussed in the text, the *stimulus moves with the eye.* Therefore, the image cast by the object continues to stay at the same place on the retina, stimulating the same receptors. Several methods of achieving a stabilized image have been developed; this diagram shows one used by R. Pritchard.

Adapted from R. L. Gregory. *Eye and Brain: The Psychology of Seeing.* 2d ed. New York: McGraw-Hill, 1973.

eyes are not identical (the phenomenon of *retinal disparity*). When two slightly different images are appropriately focused on the retinas, perception of a single three-dimensional object will be the result.

For the images of an object to fall on (or near) corresponding parts of the two retinas, the two eyes must be properly directed at the object—that is, they must converge on the object. This **convergence** is produced by the extrinsic eye muscles, which control rotation of the eyes in their orbits. The degree to which the two eyes must converge to achieve a single perception varies with the distance of the object from the perceiver. When you consider the use of your eyes in normal vision—as you shift your gaze constantly from place to place and to objects near and far, always perceiving a single three-dimensional scene in focus—it should be clear how delicately coordinated the actions of the extrinsic muscles of the two eyes must be with each other and with the actions of the ciliary muscles of the lenses.

It is interesting to note that while our eyes are jumping voluntarily from one point to another, very little vision is taking place. This can be demonstrated by flashing a light *while the eyes are moving.* The subject will often not notice the flash at all. This effect is produced in part by inhibitory impulses coming from the brain stem to the visual system and seems to help prevent the indistinct percept we would otherwise get as images moved along the retina.

Pupillary behavior The amount of light that reaches the retina must be monitored so that the retina gets enough light to function under low illumination but does not get a harmful amount under high illumination. This monitoring is achieved by reflexive and involuntary changes in the size of the pupillary opening. In general, the more intense the light coming to the eye, the smaller the pupil.

The Photosensitive Mechanism

The retina is a delicate, almost perfectly transparent membrane composed of several kinds of nerve cells. Nerve cells are generally specialized to carry messages (*impulses*) from one place to another. However, some types have acquired special sensitivity to particular stimuli and act as receptor cells—that is, as cells that convert the stimulus energy impinging on them to the kind of energy that makes up a neural impulse. The receptors of the eye have a special sensitivity to light and are therefore called **photoreceptors**.

Some animals (such as rats) possess only one kind of photoreceptors, which are called **rods**; other animals (such as turtles) have only a second kind, called **cones**; still

other animals (such as man) have both kinds. The names "rods" and "cones" suggest a difference in the shape of these cells; they do differ in shape, but more important, rods and cones differ in function, in their distribution in the retina, in the way they are interconnected, and in the way they communicate to the brain. We shall see how each of these characteristics helps us to understand some of the phenomena of visual perception.

Structure of the retina The retina is structurally very complex, and these complexities provide the basis for some of the interaction and integration of the visual system. One simple indication of the number of connections that must exist within this system is that, although there are approximately 125 million rods and 6 million cones, only about 1 million nerve fibers leave the retina. Some of the nerve fibers, therefore, must serve *many* rods and cones. Examples of the three major types of connections between the photoreceptors and the brain are shown in Figure 14.3. All three types include photoreceptors, connecting **bipolar cells,** and **ganglion cells** (which make up the optic nerve and transmit impulses directly to higher centers in the brain). The most direct pathway between the retina and the brain is found only among some cones. In this type of pathway a single cone is connected to a bipolar cell, which is in turn connected to a ganglion cell (see Figure 14.3a). Next we have systems in which several cones feed into a common bipolar cell, which in turn feeds into a ganglion cell; similar systems are found among the rods (see Figure 14.3b). Finally, we have mixed rod-cone systems in which a number of rods and cones share a common bipolar cell (see Figure 14.3c).

In addition to the linkage involved in these transmission systems, other associations are made possible by various types of interconnecting cells. These cells permit interactions between neighboring cones, neighboring rods, and between rods and cones. The retina, in other words, is not a collection of isolated photosensitive elements. Instead, these elements are capable of extensive and complex interactions and integration.

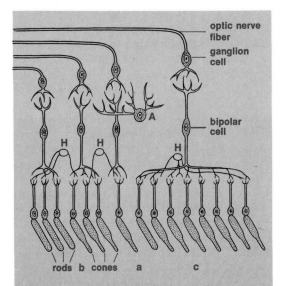

optic nerve
fiber

ganglion
cell

bipolar
cell

rods b cones a c

FIGURE 14.3 A diagrammatic representation of
the three major types of connections between the
rods and cones of the retina and the brain. The
transmission system typical of the cones in the
fovea is shown in a. Here each cone has its own
bipolar cell, which then connects with the optic
nerve, which leads directly to the brain. In b a
group of rods or a group of cones shares one bipolar cell. The mixed transmission system typical of
the periphery of the retina is illustrated in c. In this
system a mixed group of rods and cones may share
one bipolar cell.

  The little cells labeled H and A connect one
part of the retina with another, giving the anatomical basis for interaction on the retinal level.
They allow for interaction even among the foveal
cones such as the one shown in a.

The **fovea,** a small area at the center of
the retina, consists of very thin and very closely
packed cones. Each cone in the fovea has its
own separate pathway to the brain. As we move
away from the fovea toward the edges of the
retina, we find a rapid decrease in the number
of cones and a correspondingly rapid increase
in the number of rods. The absolute number
of rods comes to a peak a short distance to
the side of the fovea and then drops. At the
periphery there are few rods and even fewer
cones. As we move toward the periphery,

another important change occurs. Each ganglion
cell serves more and more photosensitive cells.

All the fibers of the ganglion cells meet
in one bundle just to one side of the fovea. This
bundle, the **optic nerve,** leaves the retina through
an opening in the eyeball (see Figure 14.1). Because there are no rods or cones at this point
in the retina, light waves falling here cannot
result in any neural impulses or, therefore, in
any visual perception. Here you have the simple
explanation of the mysterious blind spot that
some of you discovered for the first time on
page 246.

Photochemistry of the retina Rods and cones
contain substances called *pigments*, which are
very sensitive to light. When light falls on the
visual pigments, they begin to decompose; this
process of decomposition initiates activity in
the rods and cones, which is the first step in
transmitting a message to the brain. Other
chemical reactions within the photoreceptors
lead to restoration of these light-sensitive pigments. When light is falling on the retina, both
breakdown of light-sensitive substances and
their restoration by chemical action are taking
place simultaneously. This double action eventually produces a balance, or equilibrium, in
which the amount of light-sensitive substance
present (and hence the sensitivity of the eye)
depends on the intensity of the stimulating light
—that is, under an intense light there is less
light-sensitive substance at equilibrium than
under weak light. In this way the amount of
previous illumination of the eye will affect its
sensitivity to subsequent stimuli (see p. 249).

Rods and cones have different pigments,
and light waves have to be more intense to stimulate a cone than to stimulate a rod. In addition, the perceptual consequences of stimulation
of these two classes of receptors are critically
different. Cones are responsible for color vision,
and stimulation of these structures by different
wavelengths of light results in the qualitatively
different experiences of the various colors, or
hues; rods, on the other hand, are involved in
"black and white" vision, and stimulation of the
rods gives the experience only of brightness
("lighter" or "darker").

Our knowledge of the function and distribution of rods and cones thus permits us to understand why color vision is better at the fovea than at the periphery of the retina. As we have already noted (p. 247), everyone is color-blind at the extreme periphery, where there are very few cones.

Sensitivity, adaptation, and afterimages The amount of light necessary to stimulate the retina depends on the state of the rods and cones. A primary determinant of the state of a photoreceptor is the amount of photosensitive substance in the cell. The more pigment in the cell, the more likely it is to react to light. As the eye adapts to darkness, photopigment concentrations build up. We can understand, therefore, our earlier observation that the eye that is dark-adapted will be more sensitive—that is, more ready to respond to light—than the eye that is not.

Similar reasoning can lead to an understanding of negative afterimages. While you are staring at a figure such as that in Box 11.7, p. 251, the receptors that are stimulated by the intense light from the white areas become depleted of light-sensitive pigment. This does not occur in the cells on which the weaker light from the black area falls. Later, when the retina is stimulated by the light from the gray wall, the already-depleted cells (corresponding to the white part of the original figure) will not respond much, whereas the other receptors (corresponding to the black part of the figure) will show a relatively strong response. What had been white will therefore now be black, and vice versa.

The response of a receptor also depends on the kind of pigment present. Rods not only have more pigment than cones, they also have a pigment that is more light-sensitive. Thus the resulting greater sensitivity of individual rods is one factor contributing to the greater light-sensitivity of the periphery of the retina, where rods are numerous.

There is an additional reason for the greater sensitivity of this area. To perceive light, it is not enough that receptors respond; the ganglion cells must transmit an effective message to the cerebral cortex. Although a single rod in its most sensitive state will respond to a single photon (the smallest possible quantity of light), it takes several such receptor responses to produce a response in the cortex. A single impulse arriving at a ganglion cell is not enough to fire (stimulate impulses in) the ganglion cell, but when a number of rods are activated, the sum of the impulses arriving at the ganglion cell is enough to fire that cell. And as we will see later in this unit, when the cortex receives *sufficient* stimulation, then and only then do we *perceive* a stimulus (p. 349). In the periphery of the retina as many as 1,200 rods may be connected to a single ganglion cell. A rod system of this kind is most likely to generate a brain response to the widely scattered photons of a very weak light. In the fovea such interconnections are lacking.

Color vision We know that cones are necessary for color vision, but how do the cones give rise to the *different* sensations of hue—red, green, blue, and so forth? Let us first consider the two most "reasonable" explanations, *neither of which appears to be correct*. There could be many, many different classes of cones, with each class sensitive to only one of the many hues we can perceive. This would be a very inefficient system; for one thing, we would have to have a member of *each* class at just about every point on the retina so that we could perceive any hue that was presented at that point.

Another possibility would be for there to be only one kind of cone, which would be differentially sensitive to different wavelengths—that is, it would respond more to a "yellow" wavelength of a certain intensity than to a "blue" one of equal intensity, for example. (We put the color names in quotes because we can't say that a wavelength *is* a hue. A wavelength *produces* a perception of a hue, and how it does that is just what we are trying to figure out.) This second alternative simply wouldn't work, however, because of another fact. If we increase the intensity of a light (of any wavelength), the amount of response in the photoreceptor will increase also. If we had only cones of the one kind previously described, they would respond in the same way to a weak yellow light as they would to a certain intense blue light. That is, we could adjust the intensities of the lights so as to make up for the difference in response that would otherwise have resulted from the difference in sensitivity to the two wavelengths. We would not be able to tell the hues apart.

For many years, based upon various kinds of *psychological* evidence, it has been believed that there are, in fact, three physiologically different kinds of cones. Each kind is thought to be somewhat sensitive over a wide range of visible wavelengths, but they are believed to differ in the wavelengths to which they are most sensitive. This **triple-receptor theory** says that one kind of cone is most sensitive in the blue region of the spectrum (short wavelengths), another most sensitive in the red region (long wavelengths), and the third most sensitive in the intermediate green region. If, for example, an aquamarine (blue-green) color is presented to the eye, the blue cones and the green cones would respond vigorously and approximately equally, while the red cones would respond only slightly. The perception of any other particular hue would in like manner depend upon the extent to which the three different kinds of cones are stimulated.

This theory, first proposed on the basis of psychological evidence, now seems to be fairly well proved by more direct physiological methods, which involve studying the ability of individual cones to absorb lights of different wavelengths (Brown & Wald, 1964; Marks et al., 1964). Three types of cones have been identified, which correspond rather well with the red, blue, and green ones that were expected.

Although we are still uncertain about many details, it now appears likely that a given bipolar cell, even if it receives input from several cones, is influenced by only one class of cones (red, or green, or blue). The ganglion cells tell a different story, however. Remember that all neurons show a certain spontaneous level of activity, emitting nerve impulses even without a specific stimulus. Measured against this spontaneous activity, many ganglion cells respond more (show an increase in the frequency of impulses) when red wavelengths are presented to the eye, and respond less (are inhibited) when green wavelengths are presented. Such a cell must receive input from two different classes

of cones by way of their bipolar cells (see Figure 14.4, p. 326), the excitatory input from red cones and the inhibitory input from green cones. This kind of ganglion cell tells which one of a pair of colors, in this case red or green, is present at a given part of the retina. An increase in impulse frequency from this *red-green* cell signals red to the brain; a decrease signals green. If both kinds of light are present, there is no change in firing rate in the red-green ganglion cells because of the opposing effects of the two lights. This fits well with the fact that adding red and green lights leads to a color that is neither red nor green. This way of relaying the message of hue to the brain can be explained in terms of the **opponents-process theory** of color. According to the theory, visual color processes are organized into pairs, such as red versus green, or blue versus yellow. The members of a pair are presumed to work in opposition so that only one member of a pair can be active at one time.

It may seem reasonable that, as just described, the color experience of aquamarine could arise from the joint activity of blue and green cones because blue-green does seem to us (phenomenologically) to be a combination of blue and green. This same kind of explanation extends to other intermediate hues but has always been difficult to apply to yellow. The triple-receptor theory could (and does) give a theoretical account of how the joint activity of red and green cones might produce the sensation of yellow, but at first this seems hard to accept because yellow (phenomenologically) is an unmixed color, not a combination of two other sensations. The combined triple-receptor and opponents-process theories may give us the answer. There are yellow-blue opponents-process ganglion cells, as well as red-green ones. Yellow does *begin* with the joint action of green and red cones, but this activity produces a distinctive change in the response of *one certain set* of cells, the *yellow-blue* ganglion cells (see Figure 14.4).

Color blindness   Color blindness is assumed to involve some defect in the cones or their interconnections. For example, some color-blind people show a greatly reduced sensitivity to red. This defect is generally believed to result from the absence of the red-sensitive color sub-

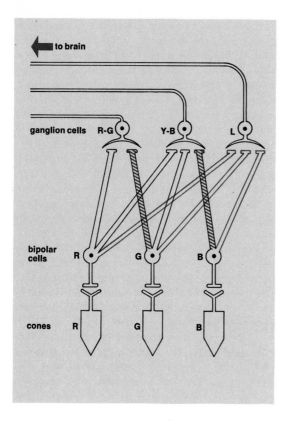

FIGURE 14.4 This is a schematic diagram showing how three different kinds of cones (proposed by the triple-receptor theory) could interact to produce two alternative color messages in certain ganglion cells (as proposed by the opponents-process theory). Remember that the ganglion cells, like all nerve cells, have a resting level of spontaneous activity. (The axon processes of the bipolar cells that are crosshatched in the diagram have an in-

hibitory influence upon the ganglion cells they contact; all other axons in the picture are presumed to be excitatory.) Note that light of a red wavelength would stimulate the red cone, its bipolar cell, and the red-green ganglion cell; increased activity in the R-G ganglion cell is the message to the brain for red. Green light stimulates the green cone and bipolar cell, but activity of the green bipolar cell inhibits the R-G ganglion cell. This *decrease in activity* in the R-G cell is the *signal for green* that goes to the brain. Both red and green bipolars have an excitatory influence upon the Y-B ganglion cell, but we assume that they *both* have to be active to produce a response in that cell. Yellow wavelengths stimulate both red and green cones and thus the yellow message (increase in Y-B response) is sent. Blue light produces its message (a decrease in Y-B activity) by the inhibitory influence of the blue bipolar.

If in a certain individual the R cone actually had *green*-sensitive pigment in it, the kind of color blindness described in the text would result. Wavelengths to which green and blue pigments are rather insensitive would be hardly seen at all. Wavelengths that normal people see as green would stimulate both the R and G cones. Their opposing effect upon the R-G cell would leave it unchanged in activity, but the combined effect of the R and G cones would activate the Y-B cell, producing the sensation of yellow!

The L (for luminosity) ganglion cell receives excitatory input from all classes of cones. The more active any of them is (the more light of any wavelength is presented to the eye), the more activity there will be in this cell. It carries the message for brightness.

It must be remembered that this figure is only a schematic model illustrating one way in which these interactions might take place. We know that the actual situation is more complicated than shown here. For one thing the picture shows all the integration between the three color processes taking place at the synapses between bipolar and ganglion cells. In fact, such interaction takes place at higher and lower levels of the system as well, and probably involves other cells in the retina, such as the ones marked H and A in Figure 14.3.

stance from those cones that normally contain it. People with this kind of color blindness also do not perceive green hues as green. An explanation for this phenomenon comes from the proposal that we have just discussed, that simultaneous excitation of coupled red and green cones results in yellow (see Figure 14.4). We can hypothesize that in this kind of red-green color blindness the missing red substance has been replaced by the green-sensitive substance. The red cones are sensitive to green wavelengths rather than red ones, but the connections of these cones with bipolar and ganglion cells re-

main the same as in people with normal color vision. Thus the red and green cones are always stimulated simultaneously, and this excitation leads to experiencing yellow. Similar explanations are offered for other types of color blindness.

Brightness vision Some of the evidence just presented about the mechanisms of color came from studies of how single retinal cells behave. In these experiments a microelectrode is used, an electrode so small that it can record the activities of single nerve cells. We can place such a microelectrode so that it records the activity of a single ganglion cell; when a small light is shone on the retina, the microelectrode can show *when* the cell we are studying responds and *how often* it responds.

Experiments of this kind have shown that there are *some* ganglion cells that are activated by all wavelengths of light. Regardless of the wavelength of light, the response of these cells will be greater if the intensity of the light is increased. This is the kind of activity we would expect to find in ganglion cells that are receiving all their input from rods, and this is just what is found. However, the same kind of response is found in certain ganglion cells that receive stimulation from cones. Note again in Figure 14.4 that while some ganglion cells receive *competing* input from different kinds of cones, others (marked L in the figure) receive *cooperating* input from different kinds of cones. The latter set of ganglion cells as well as those that receive input from the rods carry the message of brightness on to the brain.

Form vision and acuity   It will help us to understand the physiological basis for form vision if we consider one of the standard laboratory tests of acuity. The subject is presented with a series of simple patterns of light and dark lines of equal width. If the lines are too narrow, he perceives a surface of *even brightness* rather than a pattern. The problem can be regarded as one of *differential-intensity discrimination.* That is, the brain will be receiving messages initiated by the light lines and by the dark lines, and it must be able to tell that there are more messages coming from the former ("it's brighter") than from the latter ("it's darker").

The first limit on acuity is set by our optical mechanism. If the pattern of lines is not sharply focused on the retina, the light and dark lines will overlap substantially, and in this case the photoreceptors cannot be expected to send different messages to the brain.

A second limit on acuity is determined by the distribution and connections of our photoreceptors. Since the fovea contains many thin cones, tightly packed together, visual acuity is best in the fovea and becomes poorer as we leave it. Two closely spaced lines of light stimulating rows of neighboring cones in the fovea, each with its separate pathway to the brain, can send two distinct patterns of signals to the brain. Outside the fovea two closely spaced lines of light may both stimulate the same photosensitive elements; even if they stimulate different elements, these elements may all send impulses to the same ganglion cell. Thus only a single stimulus will be perceived. Therefore, visual ·acuity, the ability to differentiate small details, becomes poorer as we leave the fovea.

Studies of the responses of single ganglion cells to light shining on the retina have disclosed the existence of a mechanism that seems to help "sharpen" the perception of a point or line of light, and thus to improve visual acuity. It has been found that if a ganglion cell increases its firing rate when one photoreceptor (rod or cone) is stimulated, it may be *inhibited* (show a decrease in its rate of firing) when a neighboring receptor is active. Figure 14.5, page 328, shows how the cells in the eye might be arranged to produce this effect. A light shining on only one of the receptor cells, for example, B, would increase the activity of that cell and of the bipolar and ganglion cell associated with it, but it would not influence the activity of the nearby receptor cells. However, the activity rate of the neighboring bipolar and ganglion cells might be affected by special *inhibitory* cells (i), which would carry messages from the axon terminals of the receptor (B) to neighboring bipolars (A and C). These i cells have an inhibitory effect on the neighboring chains of visual cells, so that when light shines on receptor B, not only is there an *increase* in activity all along the "direct" path from B, but there is a *decrease* in activity along the paths that appear to begin at A and C.

In this fashion the message that the brain receives indicates a bigger difference between B, on the one hand, and A and C on the other, than it would if the inhibitory cells were not there. Since we have seen that acuity in form vision depends on the brain's ability to distinguish between messages coming from two regions of the retina, it follows that this kind of inhibitory interaction will enhance the ability to perceive the light at receptor B.

We can thus begin to understand the per-

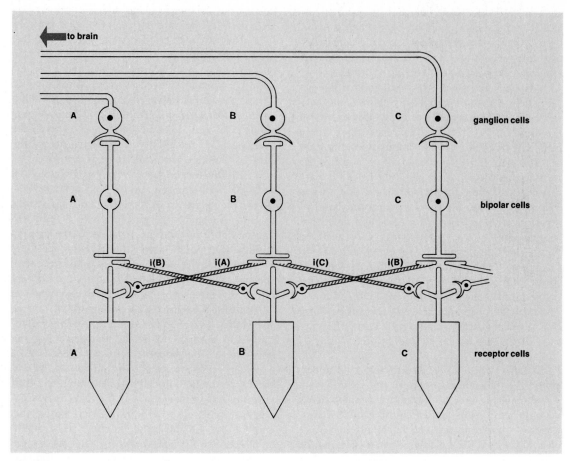

FIGURE 14.5 This diagram shows how inhibition can increase acuity by "sharpening" the neural effect that a stimulus on the retina might have. When light shines on cone B it activates bipolar B and ganglion cell B by excitatory synaptic activity. The inhibitory cells i(B) are activated too, and they reduce activity in bipolar and ganglion cells A and C. The difference between the amount of firing in ganglion cell B, on the one hand, and ganglion cells A and C, on the other hand, is greater than it would be if the inhibitory cells were not there.

ceptual effects of stimuli in spatial or temporal proximity by remembering that the retina is not built like a relay station of isolated elements but has cells connecting one part with another. Two stimulus objects may be physically isolated in the real world, but the neural responses evoked by their isolated images in the retina may be interrelated. The brain may not receive different sets of signals corresponding to the isolated stimulus objects. The summation, irradiation, and simultaneous contrast effects in visual perception (see Unit 11, p. 251) can similarly be understood in terms of the interconnecting cells of the retina.

The Conduction Mechanism

The *optic nerve* consists of bundles of axons of ganglion cells. These fibers conduct the impulses originating in the rods and cones toward the cortex of the brain.

The optic chiasm As seen in Figure 14.6, page 330, after the optic nerves from each eye enter the cranium, they converge and meet at the very base of the brain. This meeting place is called the **optic chiasm,** and here the bundles of nerve fibers making up each optic nerve are re-sorted before they continue farther into the brain. The bundles leaving the optic chiasm are called the **optic tracts.** In the re-sorting, fibers from the right sides of both retinas are bundled together and go to the right half of the brain; and fibers from the left sides of both retinas go to the left side of the brain. In the optic tracts, fibers from corresponding parts of the retinas are traveling together for the first time. Light from an object on the left side of the visual field forms an image on the right sides of both retinas, and these two images result in impulses to the same (right) side of the brain. This re-sorting also means, of course, that each retina has connections with both sides of the brain— the right half of each retina with the right side of the brain and the left half of each retina with the left side of the brain.

Subcortical nuclei These two bundles of re-shuffled fibers—the optic tracts—then continue on into the brain, where most of them end in two nuclei (see Unit 3, p. 68) of the thalamus, called the *lateral geniculate nuclei.* The fibers connect here with another set of neurons, which lead directly to the cerebral cortex of the brain.

Some optic nerve fibers from the eye go off to other parts of the brain. The destinations of these fibers, and their functions in the areas where they terminate, are not all completely understood. A rather sizable proportion are known to end up in a nucleus in the midbrain that plays an important part in controlling eye movements. We have already noted several ways in which eye movements play an important part in vision, so it is not surprising to find that input from the eyes is routed to this control region.

The occipital lobes of the brain The fibers from the lateral geniculate nuclei end in a specific part of the cortex in the **occipital lobes.** The connections between specific areas on the retina and equally specific areas in the occipital lobes

have been fairly well worked out and are indicated in Figure 14.6.

The Central Mechanisms

Two of the major research techniques for studying brain function were used to establish the relations shown in Figure 14.6. One of these methods is the **ablation technique,** in which different parts of the receptor organs, conduction system, or brain are destroyed, and observations are then made on the behavior of the organism.

Second, there are the two types of **electrophysiological techniques.** In one the brain is exposed surgically, and specific parts of it are stimulated with a mild electrical current. Observations are then made on the resulting behavior. In this way we discover something about which part of the brain controls which behavior. In the other electrophysiological technique various parts of the lower nervous system (the receptors or segments of the conduction system) are stimulated, and the resulting electrical responses in the brain are recorded. In this way we discover something about which parts of the retina, for example, are able to instigate neural activity in which parts of the cortex.

The visual cortex Many recent studies of the cortex with the electrophysiological approach use microelectrodes (see p. 326) to record the activities of single nerve cells. We can put such a microelectrode into the lateral geniculate nucleus or into the visual cortex, and we can then move a small light so that it will stimulate different points on the retina in turn, noting when the cell responds. When we attempt to find out which part of the retina triggers a response in a certain cell (in the cortex, for instance), we are said to be determining the **receptive field** of that cell. Some of this work has profound significance for our understanding of visual form perception.

We might expect that the receptive field of a cell in the visual cortex would be a small circular spot in the retina. This conclusion is logical because we would expect the cell in the cortex to receive fibers coming from a small

FIGURE 14.6   The visual system. The sketch of the brain in the upper left corner outlines the route of the optic nerve and optic tract from the eye to the occipital lobes. Use this sketch to orient yourself on the larger drawing, which gives the details of this route. Note especially the following:

1. The light rays from the left side of the visual field (indicated by the plum stripes) fall on the right sides of both retinas, whereas light rays from the right side of the visual field (indicated by the gray stripes) fall on the left sides of both retinas. The light from the top of the field (indicated by colors of a darker shade) falls on the bottoms of the retinas, and vice versa.

2. The fibers from the right side of each retina (indicated by the dotted lines from the retinas to the occipital areas) end up in the cortex of the right occipital lobe of the brain; the fibers from the left side of each retina (indicated by solid lines) end up in the left occipital lobe. This means that the left visual *field* is represented on the right side of the brain, the right visual field on the left side of the brain. Only half the visual world (but as seen by both eyes) is projected on each occipital lobe. Of course, we experience only one integrated whole. For example, at the top of the page, the area striped plum and white and the left half of the plum and gray area are projected on the right occipital lobe; the remainder of the plum and gray area as well as the gray and white area are projected on the left occipital lobe. Nevertheless we achieve one complete visual experience.

The receptors of the fovea are more richly connected with the occipital lobes than those of any other part of the retina. Because, in this diagram, the eyes are supposed to be fixated at the center point of the plum and gray area, the inner parts of this area fall on the foveas and are given detailed representation in the lobes, whereas the rest of the picture gets less representation and is therefore shown diminished in size.

For discussion of the other parts of the visual system pictured here, see pp. 328–329.

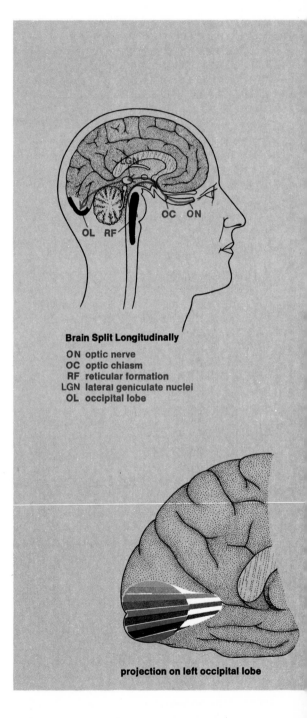

Brain Split Longitudinally

ON   optic nerve
OC   optic chiasm
RF   reticular formation
LGN lateral geniculate nuclei
OL   occipital lobe

projection on left occipital lobe

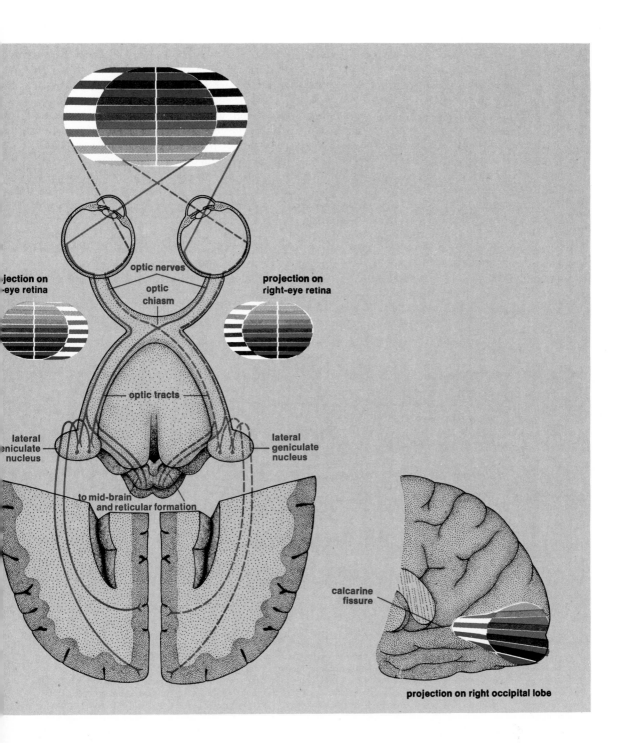

projection on
-eye retina

optic nerves

optic
chiasm

**projection on
right-eye retina**

optic tracts

lateral
geniculate
nucleus

lateral
geniculate
nucleus

to mid-brain
and reticular formation

calcarine
fissure

projection on right occipital lobe

area in the lateral geniculate nucleus that would be relaying impulses arising originally from a small area in the retina (which would itself be stimulated by light from a small spot at a certain location in the real world).

Cells in the lateral geniculate nucleus do have circular receptive fields, but in the visual cortex the typical cells are stimulated best not by a circular spot but rather by a short line (or thin rectangle) of light (Hubel & Wiesel, 1962). To stimulate a given cell, the line of light must be at a certain place in the visual field (the visible world) and must be oriented in a certain direction (horizontal, vertical, or diagonal, etc.). It is not very hard to understand how this kind of specialization of receptive fields could arise.

Imagine a group of cells in the lateral geniculate nucleus, each stimulated by light from one point along a certain line in the visual field. If these cells have fibers that all come together to stimulate one cell in the cortex, then that cortical cell will respond best when all points along the line are illuminated. Illumination of only one point of the line would have very little effect upon the cortical cell. A line in the same part of the visual field but with a different orientation would have only one point in common with the optimal line and would therefore have little effect, and a line in a different part of the visual field would have essentially no effect upon the cell we are discussing (see Figure 14.7).

In this way it is possible to understand how a given cell in the cortex can come to respond to a *pattern* of response at lower neural levels. Here may be the first clue to an understanding of the mechanisms of perception of visual forms. The picture is even more convincing when additional results are considered. Cells have been found in the visual cortex that

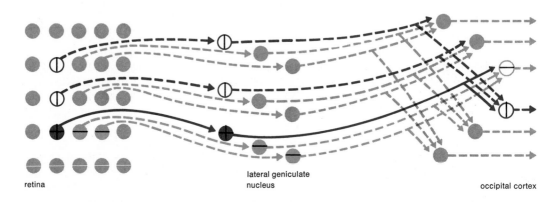

retina   lateral geniculate nucleus   occipital cortex

FIGURE 14.7 Each pattern of light (that is, stimulus) hitting the retina affects many receptor cells, and the sets of cells affected by different stimuli may have some cells in common. How does the visual system manage nevertheless to develop a specific response for each stimulus? This diagram, based on the work of Hubel and Wiesel (see above) and others, shows how it might be done. A vertical line of light might stimulate the cells in the retina that are shown here with vertical stripes; a horizontal line would stimulate the horizontally striped cells. (One cell would thus be activated by either line.) These retinal cells are shown connected one-to-one to cells in the lateral geniculate nucleus. It does not matter if the position of the cells in relationship to one another is different in the lateral geniculate nucleus; the connections are important, and as there are one-to-one connections, nothing has been lost, but also nothing has been gained. At the occipital cortex, changes do take place. Each lateral geniculate cell connects with two cortical cells, and each cell in the cortex gets input from three lateral geniculate cells. If we assume that the cortical cells cannot be activated unless they receive three incoming impulses at once, then the only neuron activated by the horizontal stimulus will be the one that is horizontally striped, and the vertical stimulus will stimulate effectively only the vertically striped neuron. Distinctive and nonoverlapping neural responses are thus produced, responses that will activate other parts of the nervous system, producing the experience and behavior appropriate to the stimulus.

respond best to a line with a given orientation, regardless of where in the visual field it is located; other cells respond best to a "corner" —that is, a pair of lines at right angles to each other; and still others are stimulated better by moving than by stationary stimuli. All these findings can be explained by imagining that certain kinds of further convergence take place between fibers from cortical cells of the variety we first described, those that respond best to a line with a certain location and direction. For example, a stimulus shaped like a corner would produce a response in a cortical cell that receives fibers from the two cells that are especially responsive to the two lines that make up the corner. All these findings show that certain characteristics of visual stimuli are detected by coding methods "built into" the organization of the nervous system and suggest that perception of a given visual form depends on stimulation of the appropriate cortical cells by means of the correct complex pathway (see Box 14.1, p. 334).

The experiments just discussed, along with certain ablation studies, lead to the conclusion that the visual system *up to* the cortex does a great deal of sorting and combining and emphasizing and "editing" (see Box 14.2, p. 336). The next question is whether or not these activities are sufficient for visual perception. This question may be safely answered in the negative. Activity in the visual cortical area gives rise to impulses that travel to other brain areas and is itself influenced by impulses coming from many other parts of the brain. *The final perception is determined by the integrated pattern of activity of most of the brain.*

Retinal-cortical relations A structural basis for space perception is provided by the connections between the retinas and the cortical areas of the brain. Information from specific retinal-cortical groups of cells tells us something immediately about the spatial relations of the stimuli involved. For example, certain retinal cells are always stimulated by the top of the visual field, and the signals they send to their cortical cells are always perceived as at the top, or "up." Similarly, other retinal-cortical groups signal bottom, right, left, and so on.

A question that immediately arises is whether or not these retinal-cortical groups are innately determined units. Is the construction of the visual system predetermined so that a specific retinal cell will be connected to a specific cortical cell and activity in this unit will be perceived as involving the top of the visual field? We have evidence on this question from lower animals. If the eye of a frog is removed, turned upside down, and replaced, the severed optic nerve will regenerate, restoring the connections with the brain. Each retinal cell manages to reconnect with its old cortical cell. These animals will therefore jump *up* at a fly shown below them and jump *down* to one shown above them, and they never learn to correct this behavior. While we must be cautious about generalizing from these findings to human beings, the fact that space perception in the frog depends upon the innately determined structure of the visual system at least suggests that the same may be true of humans.

AUDITION

Here we tell the story of how sound waves in the air become converted into vibrations of the **eardrum,** then into movements of levers in the **middle ear,** then into waves of fluid in the **inner ear,** and finally into neural impulses by the activity of the phonoreceptor elements. We then follow the neural impulses to the brain and examine what happens there.

We shall divide these physiological events into four major stages. These stages will deal with the **physical mechanism,** the **phonosensitive mechanism,** the **conduction mechanism,** and the **central mechanism.**

The Physical Mechanism

The stimulus for hearing is, of course, the sound wave (see p. 248). When a sound wave enters the **outer ear,** a series of events is started that eventually leads to an auditory perception.

Structure of the ear The ear consists of three parts: the outer ear, the middle ear, and the inner ear. Figure 14.8, page 338, represents a

BOX 14.1

CATS OF A CERTAIN STRIPE

Many experiments have been done as follow-ups on the discovery (by Hubel and Wiesel of Harvard University) that there are neurons in the occipital cortex that serve as detectors for specific features of the visual world, such as horizontal lines, diagonal lines, and so forth. A group of interesting studies has been directed toward discovering to what extent the normal functioning of these cells depends upon sensory experience, and to what extent it is due solely to genetic causes and maturation.

Hubel and Wiesel began to study this problem in 1963 by doing electrophysiological studies of very young kittens whose eyes were just opening (and therefore had never had visual experience of forms). They found that the receptive fields of occipital cortex cells in the kittens were very similar to those of adult cats. For example, cells in the infant cortex responded best to straight-line stimuli in a certain orientation, and so on. The necessary connections from the retina up to the cortex must have been there at birth; they certainly didn't depend on experience at this stage.

Further study demonstrated, however, that the presence of these connections is not the end of the story. If a cat is deprived of patterned light in one eye from before its eyes open until it is a few months old, that eye seems to be deficient in vision afterward. Furthermore, cells in the visual cortex are unresponsive to form stimuli presented to the deprived eye.

If the lack of input from one eye can eliminate or make nonfunctional certain gross connections between that eye and the brain, as this second experiment showed, is it possible that even more precise groups of connections can be eliminated by lack of "practice"? Several recent experiments lead to an affirmative answer.

A common procedure in these experiments is to raise kittens in an environment in which they experience only lines of a given orientation (either vertical or horizontal). In recent studies by Drs. Blakemore and Cooper of Cambridge University and by Drs. Muir and Mitchell of Dalhousie University, this was done by keeping the kittens in the dark except

for 5 hr per day. During these 5 hr they were in a cylinder that had stripes of various widths on its wall. For each cat, the stripes were either all horizontal or all vertical. After several months of this experience, the cats studied by Blakemore and Cooper seemed not to be able to see stripes of the opposite orientation when they were tested in the normal environment. Furthermore, electrophysiological studies of these animals led to the same conclusion. An animal raised in a horizontal world had no neurons in the occipital cortex that responded to vertical lines, and vice versa. The findings of Muir and Mitchell are consistent with that study and they also add an interesting point of possible application to a fairly common problem in human vision. Their cats were tested very carefully for acuity over a period of months after coming into the light. Although they appeared to be able to see stripes of either orientation, their acuity was definitely and apparently permanently poorer for stripes of the orientation that had been withheld from them during the early rearing period.

The relation to human vision is to people who suffer from astigmatism. In this condition lines in the visual world along a certain orientation are seen as more blurred than lines at other orientations. Even though it is possible to correct for this blurring with proper glasses, people with a history of previously uncorrected astigmatism often show a continuing poorer acuity for lines in the orientation that was earlier seen as blurred. Drs. Freeman and Thibos of the University of California Optometry School have shown that people with astigmatism also have a smaller electrical response in the brain to lines in the orientation previously seen as blurred.

The results of the cat experiments strengthen the conclusion that the acuity deficit in people is indeed due to a lack of previous experience in the perception of sharp images in a certain orientation, and suggest that early correction of such a visual deficit would be wise.

C. BLAKEMORE & G. F. COOPER. Development of the brain depends on the visual environment. *Nature*, 1970, **228**, 477–478.
RALPH D. FREEMAN & LARRY N. THIBOS. Electrophysiological evidence that abnormal early visual experience can modify the human brain. *Science*, 1973, **180**, 876–878.
DARWIN W. MUIR & DONALD E. MITCHELL. Visual resolution and experience: Acuity deficits in cats following early selective visual deprivation. *Science*, 1973, **180**, 420–422.
T. N. WIESEL & D. H. HUBEL. Single-cell responses in striate cortex of kittens deprived of vision in one eye. *Journal of Neurophysiology*, 1963, **26**, 1003–1017.

somewhat schematized drawing of all three. The outer ear includes the **auricle** (which has only a minor function for man) and the **ear canal**. Separating the ear canal from the middle ear is a thin membrane, the eardrum. The middle ear, the area between the eardrum and the inner ear, contains three little bones called the **ossicles,** which form a chain from the eardrum to the **oval window** of the inner ear. The inner ear consists of two parts, the *vestibular apparatus* (which has nothing to do with hearing and will be discussed later) and a coiled, divided, fluid-filled tube, the **cochlea.**

The cross section of the cochlea in Figure 14.8 may give the impression that it is divided into three independent channels, but in fact the upper and lower channels are continuous at the tip of the coil, as can be seen in the extended view of the cochlea in Figure 14.9, page 339. The part of the cochlea nearest the middle ear thus contains both ends of a continuous tube. The third ossicle closes off one of these ends at the oval window, and the other end is closed off by a thin membrane at the **round window.** The middle partition of the cochlea is called the **cochlear duct**; it contains both the actual sensory elements that initiate the conversion of mechanical stimuli into neural impulses and the fibers of the **auditory nerve** that transmit the impulses to the brain.

From sound waves to fluid waves A sound wave from the environment continues through the air in the ear canal until it reaches the eardrum. There the sound wave causes the eardrum to vibrate in accordance with the sound wave's frequency. The vibrations of the eardrum are transmitted through the middle ear by the ossicles, ending with in-and-out movements of the ossicle at the oval window of the inner ear. As this ossicle moves in and out, it intermittently puts pressure on the fluid in the cochlea. Because the other end of the cochlea (the round window) is stopped with a thin membrane, the alternating pressure on the fluid in the canal causes the membrane to bulge in and out, and fluid motions are set up in the cochlea. In this way the sound waves of the outside world are transformed into corresponding liquid waves in the inner ear.

The Phonosensitive Mechanism

The sensory cells of audition, called **hair cells,** are found within the cochlear duct, where they rest upon the **basilar membrane** (see Figure 14.8). They receive their name from tiny hairlike projections, the ends of which are embedded in the **tectorial membrane.** As the cochlear duct is agitated by the pressure waves set up in the cochlea, the basilar membrane and the tectorial membrane move in relation to each other, and the hairs and their cells are subjected to many kinds of distortions.

These deformations produce an electrical potential called the **cochlear microphonic.** The cochlear microphonic is thought to stimulate the production of impulses in the fibers of the auditory nerve, which surround the base of the hair cells.

Loudness Obviously an intense sound wave will set the eardrum into vibrations of greater excursion than a less intense sound wave. This relation continues on up the system so that the more intense the sound, the greater the intensity of the cochlear microphonic.

The size of the cochlear microphonic influences the number of impulses reaching the brain in two ways. First, a greater cochlear microphonic will stimulate a larger number of nerve cells. Second, a more intense microphonic will make each cell (that does fire) fire more often. In these ways the total number of nerve impulses that reach the brain per unit time will correspond with the intensity of the stimulus. *The attribute of loudness in perception depends upon the "density" (or number) of neural discharges reaching the brain.*

The relationship among intensity of stimulus, number of impulses transmitted, and strength of sensation is a general relation that holds for all modes—vision, audition, olfaction, and so forth.

Pitch How do differences in the frequencies of sound waves evoke different patterns of neural impulses in the brain and thus different perceived pitches? To answer this question, we must introduce one more set of facts about the pressure waves in the liquid of the cochlea.

BOX 14.2

COMPLEX VISUAL DETECTORS

Afterimages such as the one demonstrated on page 251 can be explained in large part in terms of the breakdown and slow regeneration of photopigments in the receptors of the eye (see page 324).

There are also other visual changes following exposure to a stimulus; some of these changes depend upon processes that go on in the actual neurons of the eye or brain. Some particularly interesting aftereffects, as they are called, involve both color and orientation or movement.

Celeste McCullough of Oberlin College had subjects stare alternately at two gratings (patterns of parallel lines) during a 4-min exposure period. One grating was made up of alternating black and orange lines oriented vertically; the other grating was made up of black and blue lines oriented horizontally. After the period of exposure, when the subjects were shown a test pattern of vertical white and black lines, the white lines appeared to be blue (the complementary color to orange). When they looked at a test pattern of horizontal white and black lines, the white lines were perceived as orange!

If the subjects had been exposed only to the pattern with orange in it, we might try to explain the appearance of the blue aftereffect solely on the basis of changes in the visual pigments. We might say that the red and green pigments (which would be more sensitive to an orange light than would the blue pigment) were being broken down during the exposure period, and that therefore "blue" cones could respond more vigorously to the white parts of the test pattern. However, in this experiment the subjects received exposure to *both* orange and blue, and they saw *both* colors in the test patterns. Thus some other explanation is required.

A possible conclusion seems to be that somewhere in the nervous system there are cells that are responsive only to a stimulus that is both orange *and* vertical; other cells would be sensitive only to stimuli that are orange *and* horizontal; still others

for blue and vertical, and so on. If one exposes the eye for a period of time to orange-vertical stimuli, the orange-vertical cells adapt and become less easily activated for some time thereafter. When a white-vertical stimulus is then presented, the blue-vertical cells (which have not been adapted) can respond more than the orange-vertical ones; therefore the vertical test pattern appears blue as well as vertical. In the McCullough experiment the opposite kind of change is taking place in the horizontal detectors at the same time. The blue-horizontal detector cells are being adapted during the exposure period and therefore the horizontal test figure appears orange.

A similar effect involving color and *motion* has been reported by a group of psychologists at McGill University (Favreau et al., 1972). They used spirals such as the one in the figure as the exposure and test figures. The spiral was rotated at a rate of 80 rpm during the exposure period. If a subject was exposed to a red and black spiral rotating clockwise and a green and black spiral going counterclockwise, the expected color aftereffects were seen when a

Pressure waves cause different amounts of movement of the cochlear-duct structures at different points (see Figure 14.9). Sound waves of

different frequencies produce their *maximum* amount of movement at different points along the cochlea. In general, the movement in the

moving white and black spiral was used as the test pattern. That is, if the white and black spiral was moving clockwise, the white parts of the spiral appeared to be green (the complementary color to red), and if it was rotated counterclockwise, it was perceived as red.

Our explanation is similar to that given previously. For example, it is assumed that viewing a red-clockwise spiral adapts a group of cells that are specially tuned to that combination of stimulus inputs. Subsequent presentation of a white-clockwise figure (which normally would activate both red-clockwise and green-clockwise detectors equally) will now activate the green-clockwise cells more than it will the red ones, and green will be perceived.

If this explanation is correct, we might expect to find that adaptation of the movement-color detectors can produce aftereffects of *motion* as well as of color—and that is exactly what the McGill experimenters discovered. Let us return to the subject who was exposed to a red spiral rotating clockwise and a green spiral going counterclockwise. If this subject is later shown a stationary red spiral, it appears to be rotating counterclockwise; if the stationary spiral is green, it appears to be rotating clockwise! These motion aftereffects fade away quickly each time the subject is given a test figure—that is, the motion lasts for only a few seconds and then stops. However, when the test figure is given again a few minutes later, the aftereffect of motion is seen once more. It will appear again *for up to 24 hr* after the original exposure to the adapting stimuli. Clearly some long-lasting change in the nervous system has occurred.

These experiments tell us something about how different stimuli interact with one another over space and over time. They also illustrate the fact that we can reach some conclusions about how the nervous system processes the stimulus inputs that it receives, *without even looking beneath the skin.*

OLGA E. FAVREAU, VICTOR F. EMERSON, & MICHAEL C. CORBALLIS. Motion perception: A color-contingent aftereffect. *Science*, 1972, **176**, 78–79.
CELESTE McCOLLOUGH. Color adaptation of edge-detectors in the human visual system. *Science*, 1965, **149**, 1115–1116.

cochlea initiated by a sound wave of very high frequency will reach its maximum near the oval window and stimulate the sensory cells (hair cells) at that point. Movement caused by a wave of a lower frequency will reach its maximum farther up the cochlea and stimulate those sensory cells. In this way *the brain will receive neural messages from one set of sensory cells when a high-frequency sound wave hits the ear and from another set of sensory cells when a low-frequency sound wave stimulates the ear.* This is the *major* way in which the ear sorts out different frequencies and enables us to discriminate one pitch from another.

An additional way that the auditory receptors might convey the message of frequency to the brain may have occurred to you. Each successive pulse of a sound wave stimulates the sensory cells into activity. Could not each burst of activity be passed along immediately to the auditory nerve fibers? In this way the frequency of the sound wave would be transformed directly into the frequency of the impulses to the brain. Physiological evidence has led to the conclusion that in fact some use is made of this mechanism in pitch perception, but it is less important than the spatial patterning described previously and is effective only at rather low frequencies.

The Conduction Mechanism

The human auditory nerve is a bundle of about 30,000 separate nerve fibers that conduct impulses from the cochlea to the brain. The separate fibers in the auditory nerve are bundled together in such a way that fibers arising from neighboring points in the cochlea stay together as they travel into the brain. This spatial organization of neural elements corresponding to different sensory cells is preserved up to the very termination of the system in the cortex.

The lower way stations Soon after leaving the internal ear the auditory nerves enter the lower brain stem and terminate at the **cochlear nuclei** (see Figure 14.10, p. 340). Here the fibers make new connections, some with neurons that go on to the next way station on the same side of the brain and some with neurons that cross over to the next way station on the other side.

The next way station after the cochlear nuclei is called the **superior olive.** Here for the

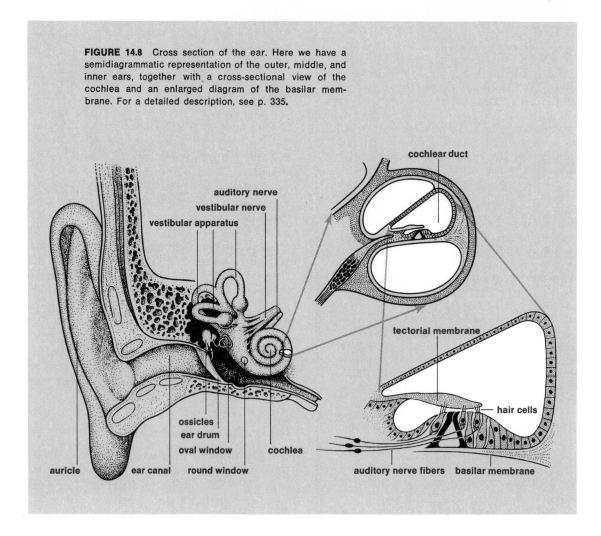

FIGURE 14.8 Cross section of the ear. Here we have a semidiagrammatic representation of the outer, middle, and inner ears, together with a cross-sectional view of the cochlea and an enlarged diagram of the basilar membrane. For a detailed description, see p. 335.

first time are opportunities for interaction between the fibers coming from the left ear and those coming from the right ear. The final neural structure on the most direct pathway to the cortex is the medial geniculate nucleus of the thalamus (see Unit 3).

The various centers along the auditory pathway should not be thought of as simple relay stations. For one thing, at many places along the pathway fibers leave the direct route we have been describing; these fibers follow other routes and affect other structures. For

example, from the cochlear nucleus and from the olive some fibers carry impulses to the *reticular formation.* Furthermore, a large amount of interaction results from the convergence of fibers in the auditory way stations.

Deafness If a cochlear duct is destroyed or if the auditory nerve leading from the cochlea is destroyed at its source, complete deafness on that side results. This is known as **nerve deafness.** But destruction of one of the pathways after it has entered the brain does not result in complete deafness of either ear because each pathway, as we have seen, carries fibers from both cochleas. Disease of the middle ear may cause **transmission deafness** by interfering with the movements of the eardrum or the ossicles. In such cases hearing may be improved by increasing **bone conduction**. A person who has middle-ear deafness will have difficulty in ordinary conversation, but when he places a telephone receiver firmly against his ear, he may hear without much difficulty because the sound waves are conducted through the bones of the head to the cochlear duct structures of the inner ear. Many hearing aids work on this principle. But in complete nerve deafness, no hearing aid will help. (However, see Box 3.1, p. 71.)

The Central Mechanisms

As in vision, much of our information about the central mechanisms in audition comes from ablation and electrophysiological studies. The latter have been especially successful in helping to spell out the physiological basis of many perceptual phenomena in hearing.

Auditory area of the cortex   Most of the auditory sensory area in man's brain lies hidden in one of the major convolutions of the cortex (again see Figure 14.10). The specific geography of this area has been fairly well mapped. Note these two major findings: First, as was true of the cochlea and auditory nerve, the spatial separation between the representation of tones of different frequencies is fairly well preserved in the cortex; second, the crossing over of the fibers that takes place as the two auditory pathways ascend to the brain is such that each ear is somewhat better represented on the opposite side of the brain than on its own side.

Localization of sounds   We have seen in Unit 13 that our ability to detect whether a sound is to

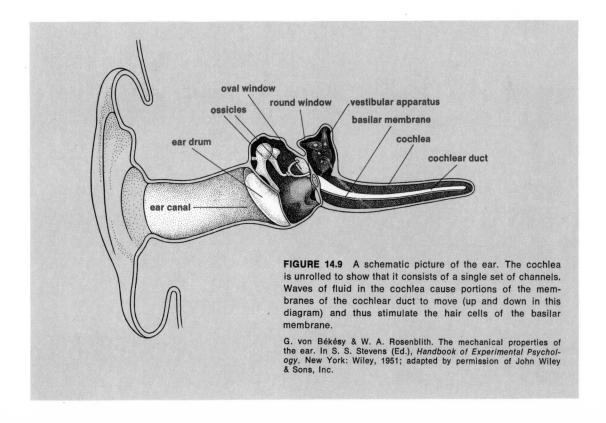

FIGURE 14.9 A schematic picture of the ear. The cochlea is unrolled to show that it consists of a single set of channels. Waves of fluid in the cochlea cause portions of the membranes of the cochlear duct to move (up and down in this diagram) and thus stimulate the hair cells of the basilar membrane.

G. von Békésy & W. A. Rosenblith. The mechanical properties of the ear. In S. S. Stevens (Ed.), *Handbook of Experimental Psychology.* New York: Wiley, 1951; adapted by permission of John Wiley & Sons, Inc.

our right or left, in front of us or behind us, above or below us, depends upon the difference in stimulation at the two ears by sound waves coming from a single object.

The patterns of impulses that originate in each cochlea will also be different, of course.

Localization of the source of the sound depends upon **binaural interaction**—that is, upon the different messages from the two ears coming together at some part in the brain. There are, for example, some cells in the olive that respond only if an impulse arrives on a fiber from the

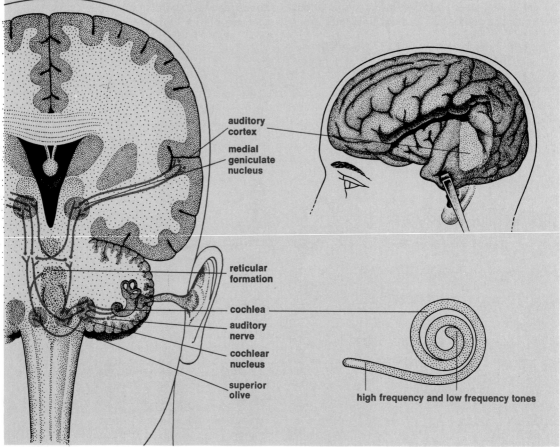

FIGURE 14.10   The conduction pathway of the auditory impulses from the cochlea to the cerebral cortex. Note how close the cochlea of the inner ear is to the cochlear nucleus, the first relay station within the brain. (The reader should also refer to Figure 3.7, p. 69, to locate the point of entrance into the brain of the auditory nerve.) The gradient of shading in the cochlea represents the gradient of tone localization in that organ. Lower frequency tones produce stimulation of sensory cells principally at one end of the cochlea; higher frequency tones stimulate the sensory cells at the other end. Note also the point-for-point projection of the cochlea on the cortex. That is, nerve impulses from the cochlea stimulated by high-frequency tones end deep within the fold of the cortex, and those from low-frequency tones terminate on the surface of the fold. In the diagram, the outer part of the auditory cortex has been pulled down to show this difference.

auditory
cortex

medial
geniculate
nucleus

reticular
formation

cochlea

auditory
nerve

cochlear
nucleus

superior
olive

high frequency and low frequency tones

right ear a fraction of a second before an impulse originating in the left ear. Thus whenever the brain receives a signal from these cells, it can interpret the signal as "sound coming from the right," because a sound from the right of the person would, of course, reach the right ear before it reached the left ear. Other cells in the olive respond when an impulse from the left ear gets there first, and so on. Electrophysiological studies have shown that binaural interaction takes place first in the olive and that it becomes increasingly prominent at each succeeding relay station. These auditory centers are thus responsible for our ability to perceive without hesitation (and often without error) the localization of sound sources, and they help build up a "sound space" of the world in which we live.

Complex sounds Our auditory experience is not made up solely of simple sounds of one pitch and constant loudness. Sounds that have a pattern of change (in frequency and intensity) over a brief interval of time are particularly important. Speech sounds (the consonantal sounds) provide a prominent example.

It has been shown that there are, in fact, cells in the auditory cortex that respond only when a tone that is changing in frequency is sounded. These cortical cells will not respond to a tone of steady frequency. Like the perception of auditory localization discussed previously, this probably depends on an interaction of impulses from more than one neuron, each neuron bringing a simple message from the ear. Figure 14.11, p. 342, shows how this might work.

Presumably various elaborations of this sort of system underlie much of our most interesting auditory experience, including the perception of music and speech. The nervous system seems to be prewired so that it is particularly sensitive to sounds having specific significance. For example, in the auditory cortex of the squirrel monkey there are special cells that are "tuned" to respond only (and immediately) to certain monkey vocalizations, which play an important role in simian social interactions (Wollberg & Newman, 1972). Although some cells that were studied responded well to several kinds of vocalizations, others were more selective.

One cell responded well only to the "isolation peep," a high-intensity, high-frequency sound made when a squirrel monkey is separated from his social group. It is necessary for the monkey that these sounds and other social signals be interpreted accurately and quickly.

TASTE

The receptors for taste are concentrated in certain areas of the tongue, but they are also found in the mucous membrane of the throat and soft palate. The **taste bud** is a pear-shaped group of tightly packed, elongated taste-sensitive cells (see Figure 14.12, p. 343). The life of a taste-sensitive cell is short, and the taste bud contains cells in all stages of development: young, mature, and atrophied. Around the active mature cells are wound the endings of the **taste nerves.** Each taste-nerve fiber may go to several receptor cells, and a single receptor cell may be innervated by more than one nerve fiber. Chemical substances (e.g., in food) which are usually dissolved in the saliva, reach the taste-sensitive cells through an opening in the mucous membrane called the **taste pore** and initiate a response in the cells. This response triggers a reaction in the endings of the taste nerves, which conduct a neural impulse to the brain.

There are said to be only four basic qualities of taste: sweetness, sourness, bitterness, saltiness. Stimulation of individual receptor cells has demonstrated that a single cell is not limited to responding to the stimuli of a single quality. In fact, many cells respond to the stimuli for *all* of the qualities of taste. What, then, is unique about the message the brain receives about a specific taste substance? A *pattern* of response emerges as the crucial factor. Different substances may produce firings in the same neurons, but they will not be firing at the same rates. We do not know how many kinds of taste receptors there are, but we do know that many different patterns of neural responses arrive at the cortex. Presumably in this sense, as in the others we have studied, each pattern produces responses in a certain group of cortical cells. Activity in these cells produces the perception of the substance that started the chain of activity.

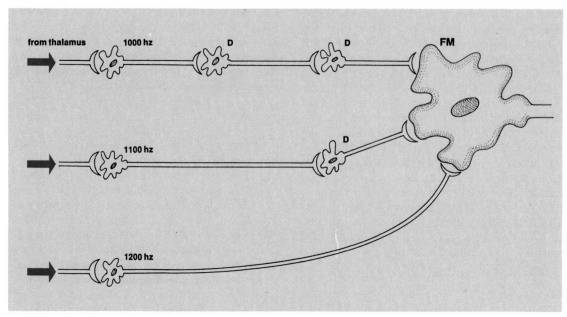

FIGURE 14.11 This schematic picture shows how a cell in the auditory cortex (FM) might be "wired" so that it responds only when the ear receives a tone that changes in frequency over a short interval of time, and that changes in one specified direction. The cell bodies on the left are situated along the auditory cortex. Each cell is most responsive to a certain auditory frequency because it receives its input from a particular part of the cochlea. This frequency is indicated by the number next to each cell body. The other cells are also cortical cells, and are labelled D for "delay" and FM for "frequency modulation." Let us assume that cell FM will respond only when it is stimulated by impulses from *three* neurons that synapse on it at the same time. When a sound that is increasing in frequency strikes the ear it will stimulate the 1000-hz cell first, then the 1100-hz and 1200-hz cells in turn. If each of those cells were directly connected with cell FM, then FM would never get more than one input impulse at a time; it would not respond. Our hypothetical scheme, however, includes two delay cells (D) in the 1000-hz channel and one D cell in the 1100-hz chain. It takes a nerve impulse longer to cross a synapse than to go an equivalent distance along an axon. Therefore, the activity in the 1100-hz chain will be delayed a bit and that in the 1000-hz channel will be delayed still more. If the delays are of the proper duration, then activity in both of these channels and in the nondelayed 1200-hz neuron will all arrive at neuron FM at the same time, and thus reach its threshold. A pure tone of any of the frequencies would stimulate only one path and never produce the three simultaneous impulses needed to activate cell FM.

Why wouldn't a tone that was *descending* in frequency activate cell FM?

The nerve fibers from the taste buds do not form a single fiber bundle. They combine into several bundles and travel to the brain in three cranial nerves (see Figure 3.7, p. 69). The pathway in the brain includes a "stop" in the thalamus, after which other neurons carry the taste message on to the cortex. Ablation studies indicate that the removal of this part of the cortex does not produce complete "taste blindness," but merely reduces taste sensitivity.

Obviously the lower parts of the nervous system that are involved in taste are able to use some taste information well enough to produce an appropriate response.

SMELL

The olfactory receptors are in the mucous membrane on each side of the upper part of the nasal cavity. They are fairly long, column-shaped neurons, which in a sense act both as receptors and as connecting cells. From one end of these **olfactory cells** delicate "hairs" project into the fluid covering of the mucous membrane; from the other end extend the fibers of the **olfactory nerve** (see Figure 3.7, p. 69). When particles of gas reach the mucous membrane of the nose, they are dissolved by the fluid covering it; by acting on the hair filaments, these substances stimulate the olfactory cells into neural activity. Although we do not know for certain what makes different substances have different odors —or why many have no odor at all—it is probably related to the size and shape of their molecules.

From research on the stimulation of single receptor cells and from recordings of single olfactory fiber activity there is some evidence to support a general picture of olfactory-receptor function similar to one we have become familiar with in other senses; that is, there is evidence that there are a number of different types of receptors and that these types have overlapping sensitivities for different substances. Some scientists maintain, however, that there are receptors that respond to one and only one odor. These two views are, of course, not mutually exclusive. Perhaps there are some receptor cells and fibers that respond only to specific odors whereas others have a broader range of sensitivity. Both kinds may contribute to our perception of odor.

The olfactory-nerve fibers of the sensory cells ascend through tiny openings in the base of the skull and plunge immediately into the **olfactory bulbs** of the brain (see Figure 3.7, p. 69). In the olfactory bulbs a very large number of these fibers converge on a single cell, and then each of these cells proceeds without further interruption to the higher centers of the brain. The funneling of neural responses made possible by this arrangement is one factor contributing to the extreme sensitivity of olfaction.

The activity of the cells in one olfactory bulb is subject to considerable modification by impulses from the other bulb and from the cerebral hemispheres. These modifying impulses may either amplify the responses of a cell to a given stimulus or inhibit the response of a cell.

Nerve impulses travel directly from the olfactory bulbs to cortical and subcortical structures in bundles of fibers known as **olfactory tracts** (see Figure 3.7). Subsequent pathways are complex and not completely understood, and no attempt will be made to describe them. Many of the connections are with parts of the *limbic system*. This is a brain system involved in emotion and motivation, which is discussed in Unit 22.

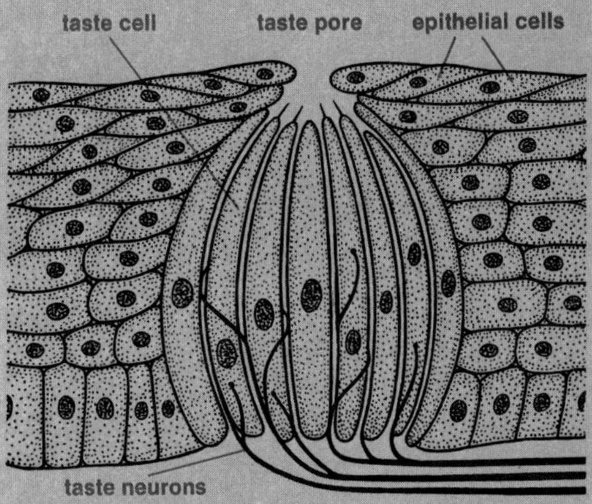

FIGURE 14.12 A diagrammatic representation of a taste bud. Each of these structures consists of a cluster of taste cells, embedded within the ordinary epithelial cells of the tongue. An opening to the surface of the tongue (called a taste pore) permits entry of the dissolved sapid substance. Stimulation of the taste cells provokes impulses in the taste neurons that carry the information to the brain.

A. J. D. De Lorenzo. Ultrastructure and histophysiology of membranes. In Y. Zotterman (Ed.), *Wenner-Gren Center International Symposium Series*. New York: Pergamon, 1963; adapted by permission of Pergamon Press, Inc.

SOMESTHETIC SENSES

Sensations from the skin together with sensations of bodily position and movement are sometimes combined under the term **somesthetic** (body) sensations.

Skin Senses

The sensations of touch, temperature, pressure, and pain are thought of as originating in the skin and are therefore called **cutaneous** (skin) **sensations**. These closely related senses have very similar physiological mechanisms, and we shall therefore consider them together.

When considering the skin senses, it is reasonable to look first at the "hairy skin" because in man (as well as in woman) hairy skin covers more than 90 percent of the body. Only two types of anatomically distinct receptors are found in the hairy skin, the **basket endings** of the hairs and **free nerve endings** (see Figure 14.13). The basket endings, a complex network of nerve fibers surrounding the base of the hairs, are specific receptors for touch. The complexity of the basket structures and their neural connections make it virtually certain that, when a basket is normally stimulated (by the movement of its attached hair), it sends a pattern of impulses along its nerve fibers. This pattern signals the intensity and location of the touch stimulus; if the stimulus moves, the change in pattern signals that as well. No matter how they are stimulated, these fibers signal only touch.

The free nerve endings, as the name suggests, appear to be simple unspecialized endings of nerve fibers. Single nerve fibers may divide a number of times, and the endings of the divided fibers may spread over a considerable area. There is also complex interweaving of the fibers, so that a particular area of the skin may have free nerve endings from a number of fibers. This structural arrangement makes it possible for stimulation of the free nerve endings to result in complex patterns of neural impulses. Since the hairy skin is sensitive to touch, warmth, cold, and pain, and the basket endings can respond only to touch, it would seem to follow that the free nerve endings must be receptors for warmth, cold, and pain. However, we have evidence that they are also receptors for touch. How these seemingly identical endings can act as receptors for four different qualities of sensation is not known. Even though the endings all *look* the same it is possible that each receptor neuron is responsive to only one kind of stimulation. Another possibility—and there is

some evidence for this—is that the perception of a specific kind of sensation depends upon the *pattern* of impulses from several of the nerve endings.

In the nonhairy skin there are, in addition to free nerve endings, a variety of structurally different specialized receptors. There are two types of receptors whose functions seem to be known. One involves touch in the palms of the hands and the soles of the feet; the other, buried somewhat deeper, serves as a pressure receptor. Other special receptors very probably serve warmth, cold, and perhaps touch in the nonhairy skin, but we cannot be sure. It is fairly certain that it is *not* the case that there is only one kind of receptor for cold, one for warmth, and so on.

Many of the skin perceptions are much more complex than the sensations of cold, warmth, touch, pressure, and simple pain. These perceptions include itching, tickling, wetness, roughness, and so on. Some theorists have suggested that there are specialized receptor organs for each of these complex perceptions—a tickle receptor, an itch receptor, and so on. But no experimental data have been found to support this hypothesis (see Box 14.3, p. 346).

Fibers from the various skin receptors enter the spinal cord and ascend to the brain. Almost all of them cross over to the opposite side of the brain before arriving at the thalamus. Touch and pressure fibers continue on to the cortex (see Figure 14.13). Here individual cells respond to a certain kind of stimulus (touch or deep pressure) in one specific area of the body. The evidence for the cortical representation of temperature and pain is not impressive, and if these senses do project to the cortex, their representation must be rather meager (see Box 14.4, p. 348).

Perception of Our Bodies in Space

We can all perceive the position of our own bodies in space. In general we know whether our bodies are bent, upright, moving, or stationary. Perception of body position and body movement is made possible by two anatomically separate but highly coordinated sensory mechanisms, the **kinesthetic system** and the *vestibular system* of the inner ear.

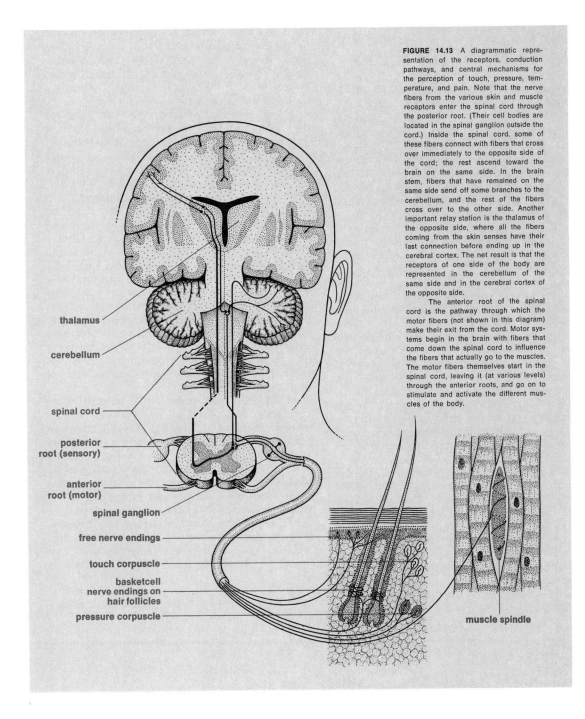

thalamus

cerebellum

spinal cord

posterior
root (sensory)

anterior
root (motor)

spinal ganglion

free nerve endings

touch corpuscle

basketcell
nerve endings on
hair follicles

pressure corpuscle

muscle spindle

FIGURE 14.13 A diagrammatic representation of the receptors, conduction pathways, and central mechanisms for the perception of touch, pressure, temperature, and pain. Note that the nerve fibers from the various skin and muscle receptors enter the spinal cord through the posterior root. (Their cell bodies are located in the spinal ganglion outside the cord.) Inside the spinal cord, some of these fibers connect with fibers that cross over immediately to the opposite side of the cord; the rest ascend toward the brain on the same side. In the brain stem, fibers that have remained on the same side send off some branches to the cerebellum, and the rest of the fibers cross over to the other side. Another important relay station is the thalamus of the opposite side, where all the fibers coming from the skin senses have their last connection before ending up in the cerebral cortex. The net result is that the receptors of one side of the body are represented in the cerebellum of the same side and in the cerebral cortex of the opposite side.

The anterior root of the spinal cord is the pathway through which the motor fibers (not shown in this diagram) make their exit from the cord. Motor systems begin in the brain with fibers that come down the spinal cord to influence the fibers that actually go to the muscles. The motor fibers themselves start in the spinal cord, leaving it (at various levels) through the anterior roots, and go on to stimulate and activate the different muscles of the body.

BOX 14.3

WHEN THE RIGHT FOOT DOESN'T KNOW WHAT THE RIGHT HAND IS BEING TOLD TO DO

Why can't a person tickle himself? You might say "because when someone else tickles you, you don't know where and when he will tickle, but if you tickle yourself, you know where you are tickling." Your answer, while correct in a way, is not quite complete, as we shall see. Let's examine an experiment that gives some answers to this question.

Lawrence Weiskrantz and some colleagues at Oxford University constructed an artificial tickler. Subjects put a bare foot on a little box (something like a home shoeshine kit) out of which a small peg projected upward and gently scratched along the sole of the foot. The movement of the tickler could be controlled by a handle that projected out of one end of the box. Three conditions were compared. Under one condition the experimenter produced the movement of the tickling peg; under another, the subject controlled the movement. Under the third condition, the experimenter caused the movement, but the subject was instructed to hold the handle and let his hand and arm move back and forth passively (that is, without applying any force to the handle). In all situations the tickling peg was moved back and forth over a 10-cm distance once per second.

As you would expect, it tickled more when the experimenter produced the movement (without the subject holding the handle) than when the subject did the tickling himself. In addition, when the experimenter did the tickling it was more ticklish if the subject did not have his hand on the handle. This means that information the subject got about the movement from holding the handle reduced the ticklish feeling somewhat.

However, it was also true that for most people the stimulus was more ticklish in the experimenter-controlled situation *even if the subject had his hand on the handle* than in the subject-controlled situation. There must be something else about the self-tickling condition that reduces its effectiveness, something more than the knowledge of where the hand and the tickler are.

The difference must be in the *motor command* the subject provides in the active self-tickle situation. The activity of the motor systems of the brain, in addition to producing the movement, presumably interacts with the incoming sensory information to influence perception—in this case to reduce the ticklish feeling that would otherwise be produced.

This question and its answer do not add up to merely a quaint curiosity; they provide instead an example of an important set of effects in perception. Consider what happens to the external world as you move your eyes around. As noted on page 306, the answer is "nothing." You don't see the whole world moving, even though as your eyes move the objects out there are all stimulating new parts of the retina (which is the usual stimulus for the perception of movement). But now gently poke your stationary eye (through the half-closed lid). The world jumps a bit as the images of the objects move across the retina. Why the difference? Again it is the effect of your motor command system. In normal eye movement the perceptual process takes account of the commands being sent to the eye muscles in such a way that the perceptual world is kept still. When you poke your eye, there is no command to the eye muscles, and the resulting movement of an object across the retina is interpreted in the same way as the stimulus from a truly moving object would be—that is, as actual movement. Perception depends on the motor system as well as the sensory systems.

Incidentally, don't be fooled into believing that we have just explained what makes a tactual stimulus ticklish. We have not. But we have seen why under certain conditions a stimulus will *not* be ticklish.

L. WEISKRANTZ, J. ELLIOTT, & C. DARLINGTON. Preliminary observations on tickling oneself. *Nature*, 1971, **230**, 598–599.

The kinesthetic system The receptors for kinesthesis are found in the **capsules,** which encircle the joints between bones, and in the **ligaments,** which connect pairs of bones. These sensory elements consist of neurons that divide near their ends into several smaller branches, each of which terminates in a flattened plate. They respond when compressed and are so distributed throughout the joint that they can indicate not only the present position of a limb but also its direction and rate of movement.

The kinesthetic fibers join fibers coming from the skin and follow similar pathways into the spinal cord and up to the brain, where the information is integrated with that coming from the skin senses and the vestibular system.

Other receptors in the muscles and tendons are sensitive to the state of the muscular system and control various important reflexes, but many experts doubt that the messages they initiate enter conscious awareness.

The vestibular system   The inner ear, it will be remembered, contains the **vestibular apparatus,** which is concerned not with hearing but with our sense of balance, or equilibrium. The vestibular apparatus of each inner ear consists of the three **semicircular canals** and the **utricle**— small liquid-filled structures that contain sensory cells equipped with hair tufts. The hair cells of the semicircular canals respond to the *wave motions* of the fluid in the canals; the utricle is sensitive to the positions of the hairs of its sensory cells and thus to the position of the head (see Figure 14.14, p. 350).

The **vestibular nerve,** which carries impulses from the sensory cells of the vestibular apparatus, enters the brain stem next to the auditory nerve. In the brain stem the nerve fibers end in masses of gray matter called the **vestibular nuclei.** From here messages are relayed to muscles of the eye, to the viscera, and to the cerebellum. Although impulses also reach the cerebral cortex, the direct pathway is unknown.

The familiar symptoms of seasickness seem to be caused by overstimulation of the vestibular system, which, it has just been pointed out, relays messages to the viscera. Rapid or prolonged rotation or other movements may produce dizziness, nausea, and vomiting.

The highly coordinated kinesthetic and vestibular systems not only make possible specific perceptions of limb or head movements but also contribute to the overall general perception of our bodies.

PERCEPTION AND AWARENESS

There is an important question which we have not asked thus far when considering the various senses. Cortical activity appears to be essential before certain perceptions can occur, but we have not asked what *kind* of cortical activity is needed, or *how much* activity is needed. If we knew the answers to these questions, we would be in a position to say something about a very ancient problem: What is the physiological basis of consciousness? Whatever else perception may mean, in *human beings* perception is almost synonymous with consciousness, with awareness.

We have referred in several places to the revival of interest in the problem of consciousness in modern psychological research (e.g., Unit 11, p. 234, and Unit 21). This revival is strengthened by the physiological approach to the problem that characterizes the work of B. Libet and his associates (1973).

Awareness and Signal Detection

To begin with, Libet points out that "a clear distinction must be made between the kind of detection of the stimulus that is specified by the subject's introspective awareness of a sensory experience and other kinds of detection in which the response does not specify such an awareness." Thus, he argues, a stimulus may evoke some kinds of distinctive responses from a subject without involving awareness. For example, two stimuli may produce different electrophysiological responses in sense organs or in the brain cells even when the subject cannot consciously tell the stimuli apart. For another example, consider a subject who is forced to tell which of two almost identical lights is brighter. Although the subject reports that he is not aware of any difference, he *may* still choose at a better-than-chance rate, in which case he is detecting a difference without conscious awareness of the difference.

It may be interesting to study the brain processes necessary for these kinds of signal detection, but such experiments will tell us very little, if anything, about consciousness itself. Libet therefore concluded that if we are ever

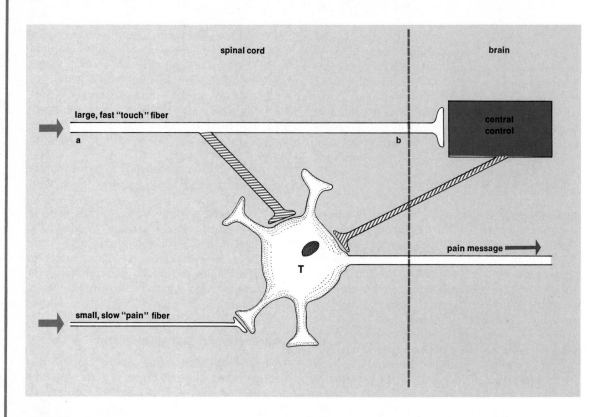

BOX 14.4

PAIN GATES

Pain is an important sensation—and a mysterious one. For many years scientists have attempted to understand the physiological basis of the perception of pain, and at last some clarity appears to be nearly at hand.

Pain is normally aroused by some disturbance to body tissues that stimulates the production of impulses in certain free nerve endings. Some of the neurons in the skin that are activated in this way are distinct from those that carry messages of gentle touch and pressure; they are smaller in diameter than the touch neurons, and they transmit their messages more slowly.

Recent information about the nervous system pathways involved in the perception of pain or touch does not permit us to consider them as completely

separate systems, however. To see some of the reasons, let us return to the problem of phantom limbs described earlier (see Box 11.3, p. 238).

About 30 percent of people who have lost a limb suffer from pain, sometimes very severe, in the limb that is no longer there. The receptors are gone, of course, but the pain is very definitely present. In attempts to remove the pain, physicians have sometimes cut the sensory nerves from the stump close to the spinal cord. These operations sometimes produce relief, but in many people the pain returns. Very often, decreasing the sensory (touch) input from the stump is helpful in reducing the pain temporarily. Increasing sensory input will occasionally bring relief, but more often it increases the pain.

The answer may be that the pain is produced by the *absence* of normal activity in the large "touch" fibers of the limb rather than by an increase in activity of the small "pain" fibers. This conclusion follows from a "gate-control" theory of pain proposed by Ronald Melzack, a psychologist at McGill

University, and Patrick Wall, a physiologist now at the University of London. A simplified model somewhat like theirs is shown in the figure. According to this theory, activity in the small-diameter fibers tends to produce activity in a set of T cells (transmission cells) in the spinal cord. The T cells send on to the brain messages that will be interpreted there as pain. However, activity in the large-diameter sensory fibers has an opposing effect. It *inhibits* the T cells and thus may prevent the transmission of the pain message. The small-fiber cells are activated by painful stimuli, but they may also be activated by simple pressure. When a harmless stimulus is present, impulses from the large-fiber pressure cells are able to counteract the tendency of the small-fiber cells to make the T cells fire. With a painful stimulus, activity in the small cells is so great that a message gets through to the T cells. The "gate" for pain (the T cell) may be influenced by impulses arising from other parts of the nervous system, such as the reticular formation or the cortex, as well as by the input from large-diameter sensory fibers.

The relevance of this theory to phantom-limb pain depends upon the fact that after a limb is amputated many of the cut nerve fibers die, but the ones that remain are primarily the smaller ones. Spontaneous activity of these neurons no longer has the balancing (inhibiting) effect of large-fiber activity, and the T cells will carry a message on to the brain where it will be "inaccurately" interpreted as pain.

This model suggests that it might be possible to reduce pain by providing extra stimulation to the remaining large fibers, either by stimulating their receptors in the skin (point a in the diagram) or by stimulating the fiber branches that normally carry the touch message to the brain (point b). Both methods have been tried with encouraging results (Wall & Sweet, 1967; Shealy et al., 1970). In fact, it may be that a similar method for reducing *many* kinds of pain has been in use for hundreds of years, since this theory provides a possible explanation of how *acupuncture* works (if it does). (See also Box 11.8, p. 253).

RONALD MELZACK. Phantom limbs. *Psychology Today*, October 1970, 63–68.
R. MELZACK & P. D. WALL. Pain mechanisms: A new theory. *Science*, 1965, **150**, 971–979. Copyright 1965 by the American Association for the Advancement of Science.
C. N. SHEALY, J. T. MORTIMER, & N. R. HAGFORS. Dorsal column electroanalgesia. *Journal of Neurosurgery*, 1970, **32**, 560–564.
P. D. WALL & W. H. SWEET. Temporary abolition of pain in man. *Science*, 1967, **155**, 108–109.

to discover the physiological basis of consciousness we must use another measure of perception: "The criterion for the conscious sensory response must be based on a report by the subject that he is aware of having had a subjective sensory experience." Here Libet is calling for a phenomenological approach (see Unit 11, p. 234) combined with a physiological one. This sort of research, of course, must be done with awake human beings.

Duration of Cortical Activity and Consciousness

Libet met these requirements by working with patients who were undergoing brain surgery for relief of Parkinson's disease. These operations are typically done under local (scalp) anesthesia, with the patient conscious and alert. Most of Libet's work has been done with the perception or awareness of skin sensations following stimulation by a very weak (threshold) stimulus. In one series of experiments, electrical stimuli of various duration were applied directly to the cortical area that normally receives input from the skin. It was discovered that when a low-intensity stimulus was used, the resulting cortical activity had to last *at least 0.5 sec before the patient reported that he felt it.* We can be aware of stimuli on the skin that do not last that long. Thus it is presumed that normal skin stimulation (if it is going to give rise to a conscious reaction) produces a longer-lasting activity in the cortex by starting impulses in several chains of neurons; these impulses reach the cortex over a period of time. These and other findings have led Libet to propose a hypothesis stating that *prolonged cortical activation is a fundamental requirement in mediation of conscious experience.*

This hypothesis has several interesting implications. One is that, as Libet points out, ". . . such a temporal requirement could mean that brief (cortical) activation . . . will not clutter up conscious experience; i.e., it could act as a kind of temporal filter in conscious processes." Libet here seems to suggest that cortical activity operates in the *service of consciousness,* and thereby raises a host of philosophical questions. Here we end our treatment of perceptions as we

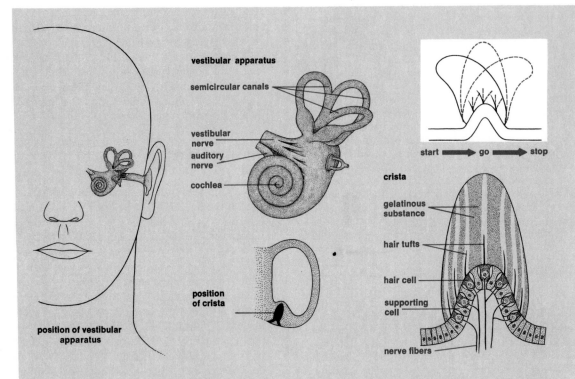

vestibular apparatus

semicircular canals

vestibular nerve

auditory nerve

cochlea

position of crista

position of vestibular apparatus

start → go → stop

crista

gelatinous substance

hair tufts

hair cell

supporting cell

nerve fibers

FIGURE 14.14 The vestibular apparatus of each inner ear includes three small liquid-filled semicircular canals. These three canals correspond to the three dimensions of space: up-down, forward-backward, right-left. At the base of each canal, within an enlarged portion of the canal, is a structure called the crista. The crista contains the hair cells. These hair cells lie between supporting cells and bear on their free ends long hair tufts embedded in a gelatinous substance. When the fluid in the canal is moved, it bends the gelatinous substance and the hair tufts. The bending of the hair tufts stimulates the hair cells, which then send impulses through their nerve fibers to the brain.

At the upper right of the figure is a representation of activity in the crista during various head movements. When the head starts moving or turning, the liquid at first lags behind, bending the hair tufts in the opposite direction. (This reaction is similar to being thrown back when the automobile in which you are riding suddenly starts forward.) As the movement of the head continues, the liquid in the canal "catches up" with the movement of the head, and the hair tufts become erect again. As long as the head is moving in a constant direction and at a constant speed, the hair tufts will remain erect. (This reaction is similar to the way in which you remain seated erect as long as the automobile is traveling smoothly, without jerks and without turning.) When the head movement stops, the inertia of the liquid carries it forward and the hair tufts are again bent, this time in the forward direction. It is for these reasons that we receive neural impulses from the vestibular apparatus only when the motion of the head is changed, as in starts, turns, sudden increases or decreases in speed, and stops. As long as we are moving at a constant rate, the brain receives no impulses from the vestibular apparatus. Frequent stops and starts or changes in direction or speed of movement (as in a bumpy airplane or a rocking boat) will repeatedly deform the hair tufts, stimulate the hair cells, and send a series of impulses to brain and viscera. This action may result in seasickness—dizziness, nausea, vomiting.

began—with an appreciation of why the problem of perception has intrigued so many different disciplines, ranging from physiology to philosophy.

SUMMARY

1. The nervous system is always active. When a stimulus reaches a receptor organ, it changes the pattern of nervous activity in the connected sensory nerve; but at every stage along the pathway of the sensory channels, the rest of the nervous system influences what gets transmitted to the brain. The nervous system selects among the available bits of information; it integrates information; it seeks out new information when necessary.

2. Light entering the eye passes through the cornea and then the lens. Both of these structures bend light rays so that they will be focused on the retina, a network of photoreceptors and neurons at the back of the eye. As one changes his point of fixation from a near object to a far one, or vice versa, the shape of the lens changes to keep the fixated object in focus; this process is called accommodation. The amount that the eyes must turn inward (converge) to have the two images of a given object fall on the same part of the retinas also depends upon how far away the object is. Normal vision depends upon the presence of small involuntary eye movements of which we are usually unaware.

3. The retina has two kinds of light-sensitive cells. The cones are most numerous at the fovea (the center of the retina), while rods are absent at the fovea and most common some distance away. Both kinds of receptors are connected to bipolar cells. Some bipolar cells at the fovea receive input from only a single cone; other bipolar cells, away from the fovea, are connected with many cones, many rods, or a mixture of cones and rods. The bipolar cells connect with ganglion cells, the axons of which make up the optic nerve to the brain.

4. Rods and cones contain substances called pigments that decompose when light hits them. This chemical reaction produces an impulse in the cells. Other chemical reactions cause the light-sensitive chemicals to be restored, and the net amount of pigment present at any time depends on the intensity of the available light.

5. The retina is most sensitive to light at its periphery, away from the fovea. This is due to the distribution of rods and cones on the retina and their connections with bipolar cells; the pigment in the rods is also more sensitive than that in cones, and the rods contain more pigment than cones do.

6. The cones give rise to the sensation of color, or hue. There are three different kinds of cones. Each is sensitive to a wide range of wavelengths of light, but they have differing regions of greatest sensitivity, in the red, green, and blue parts of the spectrum, respectively. Many ganglion cells apparently receive input from two kinds of cones and respond in opposite ways depending on which kind of cone is active—that is, depending on which of two hues is shining on the associated part of the retina.

7. The response of another type of ganglion cell depends on the intensity of the light stimulating the receptors, regardless of the wavelength of that light. The greater the light intensity, the greater the response, and vice versa. These cells carry the message of brightness to the brain.

8. Half of the neurons in each optic nerve cross over to the opposite side of the brain at the optic chiasm, thus forming the optic tracts. In the optic tracts fibers from corresponding parts of the two retinas travel together, and the two images from an object on one side of the visual field will produce activity in the tract going to the other side of the brain. The optic tracts end in the lateral geniculate nuclei of the thalamus; other neurons carry impulses from the nuclei to the occipital cortex.

9. The receptive field of a neuron in the visual system is the region of the retina that can produce activity in that cell. The receptive fields of lateral geniculate cells are circular spots, but the fields of cortical cells are more complicated. They may be

a line with a certain orientation or a certain length, shaped like a corner, and so on. Fields of this kind presumably mean that neurons from receptors throughout the receptive field converge upon the cell that is being studied.

10. Sound travels through air in the outer ear to the eardrum. There vibrations are set up in a chain of bones that spans the middle ear. The last bone causes a pressure wave in the fluid within the cochlea of the inner ear.

11. The auditory hair cells rest upon the basilar membrane of the cochlea and have hairlike projections into the tectorial membrane. The pressure wave in the cochlea makes these structures move, producing an electrical potential called the cochlear microphonic, which in turn causes activity in the auditory neurons. The more intense the sound, the more neurons will be stimulated and the more often each neuron will fire.

12. The amount of movement of the cochlear structures differs at various points, and the pattern of movement depends upon the frequency of the sound. Each frequency stimulates a different set of hair cells, and the associated neurons carry to the brain the information necessary for the discrimination of pitch.

13. The auditory sensory pathway leads through the auditory nerve and a series of subcortical nuclei and then to the cerebral cortex. Neurons representing similar frequencies run near each other all along the pathway and into the cortex. The impulses that begin in one ear eventually reach both sides of the cortex, with each ear somewhat better represented on the opposite side of the cortex than on its own side.

14. Localization of sound requires that the different patterns of neural activity coming from the two ears come together to influence the activity of some cell or group of cells. This binaural interaction is first seen in an auditory subcortical center called the superior olive. The perception of complex sounds is also presumed to be based on the interaction of neurons that are individually carrying simple messages.

15. Taste depends on the activation of receptor cells in the taste buds by chemicals in food. A single taste cell responds to stimuli of more than one of the four basic taste qualities. The perception of a particular substance depends on the brain's receiving a distinctive pattern of response from several neurons in the taste nerve.

16. Olfactory receptor cells are stimulated by gas particles dissolved in the fluid that bathes them. The axons of these cells are the fibers of the olfactory nerve, which goes through the skull and enters the olfactory bulbs. The activity of an olfactory bulb cell can be influenced by other olfactory impulses or input from the other parts of the brain. Fibers arising in the olfactory bulb spread to other parts of the brain, including the limbic system, over the olfactory tracts.

17. There are some specialized receptors for skin sensation; one type is the basket endings around hairs, which are sensitive to light touch. However, simple free nerve endings can act as receptors for touch as well as for temperature and pain.

18. The receptors for kinesthesis are found in the capsules and ligaments associated with bones. Our total perception of body position and movement receives another major input from the vestibular apparatus of the inner ear. The semicircular canals and the utricle are sensitive to motion and position of the head.

19. Conscious awareness of a stimulus may require a special kind or amount of neural activity. Weak electrical stimulation of the cortex must last for 0.5 sec if it is to be perceived consciously, for example.

GLOSSARY

ablation technique   A research technique used in neurology and physiological psychology. Different parts of an animal's sensory receptors, neural conduction system, or brain are destroyed, and observations are then made of the animal's behavior.

accommodation   The change in focusing power of the lens, which allows the eye to focus on objects at various distances.

auditory (cochlear) nerve A bundle of about 30,000 separate nerve fibers stemming from the hair cells in the cochlear duct. This bundle leaves the internal ear, enters the lower brain stem, and finds its first relay station in the cochlear nuclei.

auricle The projecting, external part of the outer ear. Sometimes called the pinna.

basilar membrane A membrane in the cochlear duct upon which the hair cells rest.

basket endings Receptor organs in the skin; they consist of nerve endings wound around the roots of hairs. Basket endings are partially responsible for sensations of light touch.

binaural interaction The effect of the impulses in fibers from one ear on the neural activity in fibers from the other ear. More generally any interaction of neural activity from the two ears.

bipolar cell A neural element that carries impulses from rods and cones to ganglion cells.

bone conduction The transmission of sound waves through the bones of the skull to the inner ear, as opposed to normal conduction through the structures of the middle ear.

capsule The framework surrounding joints between bones.

central mechanism A general term referring to the various anatomical and physiological mechanisms of the entire brain.

ciliary muscles Muscles attached to the lens of the eye; contraction and relaxation of these muscles produce changes in the curvature of the lens.

cochlea A coiled, divided, fluid-filled tube containing the sensory elements of hearing. One end of the cochlea is closed off by the third ossicle at the cochlea's oval window; the other end is closed off by a thin membrane at the cochlea's round window.

cochlear duct The partition or structure dividing the cochlea into two major channels. It is filled with fluid and contains the hair cells.

cochlear microphonic An electrical potential caused by deformation of the auditory hair cells. This potential probably stimulates production of impulses in the fibers of the auditory nerve.

cochlear nuclei The first relay centers in the pathway of auditory impulses from the inner ear to the cortex. They are located in the brain stem.

conduction mechanism A general term referring to the various anatomical and physiological mechanisms involved in the conduction of neural impulses from receptor organs to the cortex.

cones Specialized cone-shaped cells in the retina. These cells are sensitive to light waves and initiate a neural impulse when light waves impinge upon them. Cones are especially sensitive to differences in the wavelength of light. Stimulation of cones gives rise to the experience of hue.

convergence The coordinated movement of the two eyes toward fixation on the same point.

cornea A transparent covering of the front of the eye. The window of the eye.

cutaneous sensations The skin sensations: touch, pain, warmth, and cold.

ear canal The opening from the outer ear to the eardrum. Conducts sound waves from the outside to the middle ear.

eardrum The thin membrane separating the ear canal from the middle ear. Sound waves striking the eardrum cause it to vibrate.

electrophysiological technique A technique used in neurology and physiological psychology. Such techniques can be divided into two types. In one type, parts of the nervous system are stimulated (in various ways), and observations are made of the resulting electrical responses in the brain. In the other, specific areas of the brain are stimulated with a mild electrical current, and observations are made of the resulting experience or behavior.

extrinsic muscles Muscles attached to the outside of each eyeball permitting controlled rotation of the eyeball in its socket.

fovea The central part of the retina consisting of very thin and closely packed cones. Each cone in the fovea has its own bipolar cell. There are no rods in the fovea. Because of its composition, the fovea is the area of the retina capable of greatest visual acuity and of most efficient hue discrimination.

free nerve endings Endings of nerve fibers in the skin, which are unassociated with any coverings of connective tissue. They are capable of mediating all skin sensations.

ganglion cell A nerve cell that receives impulses from rods and cones via an intervening bipolar cell and transmits these impulses to the brain.

hair cells (auditory) The sensory cells of audition. These cells convert the wave motion of the cochlear fluids into the cochlear microphonic. The hair cells are found in the cochlear duct and rest on the basilar membrane.

inner ear   The innermost section of the hearing apparatus. It consists of two parts: the vestibular apparatus and the cochlea.

iris   A delicate, colored, fibrous structure that lies on the lens and has a circular opening (the pupil) in its center. The actions of the muscles of the iris can increase or decrease the size of the pupil.

kinesthetic   Referring to the sensory system that provides information about the position and movements of the various parts of the body.

lens   A transparent structure in the eye that focuses light waves from the outside onto the retina. It is shaped somewhat like a convex lens; the shape can be changed by the contraction and relaxation of the ciliary muscles.

ligament   A tough band of tissue connecting a pair of bones.

middle ear   A cavity between the outer and inner ear. Contains the three ossicles.

nerve deafness   Deafness resulting from injury to the cochlea or auditory nerve. Most elderly people suffer from some degree of nerve deafness.

occipital lobes   The parts of the brain in which fibers from the lateral geniculate nuclei terminate. These areas, because they are primary receptor areas for impulses from the eyes, are called the visual sensory areas of the cortex.

olfactory bulb   A mass of cells and fibers resting on the base of the skull and into which the olfactory nerve fibers enter. Here the fibers connect with other fibers, forming the olfactory tract leading farther into the brain.

olfactory cells   Sensory cells for olfaction. They are fairly long, column-shaped cells; from one end delicate hairs project into the fluid covering of the mucous membrane, and from the other end protrude long fibers that make up the olfactory nerve.

olfactory nerve   A nerve consisting of the axons of olfactory cells, which carry olfactory information through the base of the skull into the olfactory bulb.

olfactory tracts   Bundles of fibers going from the olfactory bulb into various cortical and subcortical regions of the brain.

opponents-process theory   A theory of color vision that proposes that visual processes are organized into pairs, such as red-green and blue-yellow. The paired processes are assumed to work in opposition so that only one member of a pair can be effective at one time.

optical mechanism   A general term referring to the various anatomical and physiological mechanisms involved in the conduction of light waves from the outside world into the eye and the focusing of them on the retina. Specifically, the structures and functions of the cornea, lens, ciliary muscles, iris, and extrinsic muscles.

optic chiasm   The meeting place of the optic nerves from the two eyes, located at the base of the brain. At the optic chiasm the crossing over of some fibers of the optic nerves takes place.

optic nerve; optic tract   The bundle of nerve fibers of the ganglion cells carrying neural impulses from the rods and cones to the brain. This bundle leaves the retina through an opening in the eyeball called the blind spot. The portion of the conduction pathway lying between the retina and the optic chiasm is called the optic nerve; beyond the optic chiasm it is called the optic tract.

ossicles   The three bones that form a chain from the eardrum to the oval window of the cochlea. They transmit vibrations of the eardrum to the fluid in the cochlea.

outer ear   The outermost and only visible part of the hearing apparatus. Includes the auricle and the ear canal.

oval window   An opening in the cochlea into which the last of the three bones from the eardrum is fitted. It is the vibration of this ossicle in the oval window that sets the fluid in the cochlea into wavelike motion.

phonosensitive mechanism   A general term referring to the various anatomical and physiological mechanisms involved in the initiation of nerve impulses in the inner ear. Specifically, the operation of the hair cells in the cochlear canal and the function of the basilar membrane.

photoreceptors   Receptor cells responsive to light. Specifically, the rods and cones.

photosensitive mechanism   A general term referring to the various anatomical and physiological mechanisms involved in the conversion of light waves into neural activity. Specifically, this term refers to the nature, distribution, and functions of the rods and cones.

physical mechanism   A general term used to refer to the various anatomical and physiological mechanisms involved in transmitting sound waves from the point at which they enter the ear to the point at which they stimulate the hair cells. Specifically, the operation of the ear canal, eardrum, ossicles, and the fluids of the inner ear.

pupil The circular opening in the center of the iris. The pupil is not a structure. It is the "hole in the doughnut."

receptive field of a neuron For each neuron in a sensory conducting system or in a sensory area of the cortex, the portion of the sense organ (e.g., the area of the retina) that, when stimulated, will arouse activity in the cell.

retina A layer of light-sensitive elements (rods and cones) and nerve fibers. It lines the inner wall of the back of the eyeball.

rods Specialized rodlike cells in the retina. These cells are sensitive to light waves and initiate impulses when light waves impinge upon them. Rods are primarily responsive to changes in the intensity of light waves. Stimulation of the rods results in the experience of brightness but not of hue.

round window An opening in the cochlea across which is stretched a thin membrane. As vibrations at the oval window produce changes in the pressure on the cochlear fluid, the membrane of the round window bulges in and out, permitting the fluid in the cochlea to respond in a wave motion.

sclera A white opaque protective skin enveloping most of the eyeball.

semicircular canals Three small liquid-filled canals in the vestibular apparatus. Each canal is in the shape of a semicircle and is oriented in a different plane in space: up-down, left-right, and forward-backward.

somesthetic Pertaining to the soma or body. Hence somesthetic sensations refer to skin and kinesthetic sensations; somesthetic nerves refer to the fibers carrying impulses from the skin and joint receptors to the brain. The somesthetic-sensory cortical area is the area of the cortex where the impulses from the somesthetic sense organs terminate. This area lies directly behind the central fissure on the surface of the brain.

stabilized retinal image The image of an object on the retina when special methods are used to keep the image at exactly the same place. To achieve this, some procedure must be used to overcome the influence of the small involuntary movements of the eyeball.

superior olive The second relay, or synapse center, on the route of the auditory fibers from the inner ear to the cortex. Located in the brain stem.

taste buds The receptors for taste, concentrated mostly in the tongue. A taste bud is a pear-shaped structure consisting of a group of taste-sensitive cells.

taste nerves Nerves conducting impulses from the taste buds to the brain. The endings of the taste neurons are wound around each of the taste-sensitive cells in the taste bud. The taste neurons do not travel to the brain in a single fiber bundle but divide up into several bundles and travel in three cranial nerves.

taste pore The opening at the top of a taste bud that permits entry of chemical substances dissolved in the saliva of the mouth.

tectorial membrane A mass of gelatinous matter situated above the hair cells in the cochlear duct; the hairs of these cells terminate in the tectorial membrane. When the cells are moved in relation to the tectorial membrane, they are temporarily squeezed out of shape. This deformation produces the cochlear microphonic.

transmission deafness Deafness resulting from interference with the movements of the eardrum or of the ossicles. In these cases partial hearing may be restored through the transmission of vibrations by the skull. Many hearing aids work on this principle.

triple-receptor theory A theory of the physiological basis of color vision. According to this theory, there are three specialized types of cone. Some cones are assumed to be most sensitive to red, some to green, and some to blue.

utricle A liquid-filled cavity that is part of the vestibular apparatus. The utricle is sensitive to the position of the hairs of its sensory cells and thus to the position of the head in a gravitational field.

vestibular apparatus That part of the inner ear involved in the sense of balance, position, and motion. Specifically, the semicircular canals and utricle.

vestibular nerve The neurons that carry impulses from the sensory cells of the vestibular apparatus to the brain.

vestibular nuclei The masses of nerve cells in the brain stem where the vestibular nerve ends.

visual field The visual world, thus all the objects and regions visible when the eye is in a fixed position.

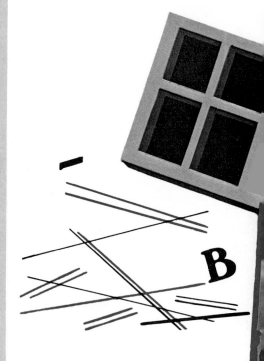

conditioning, learning, and memory

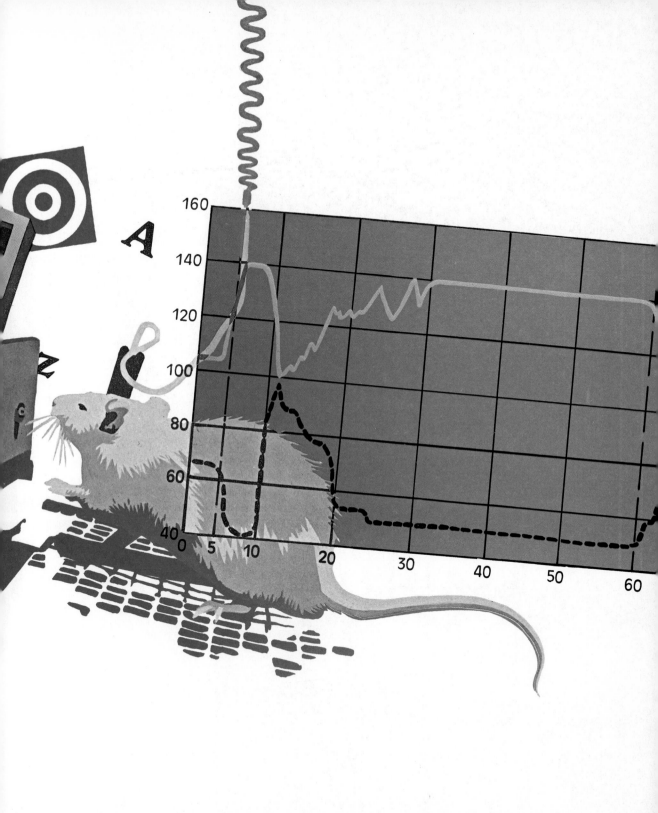

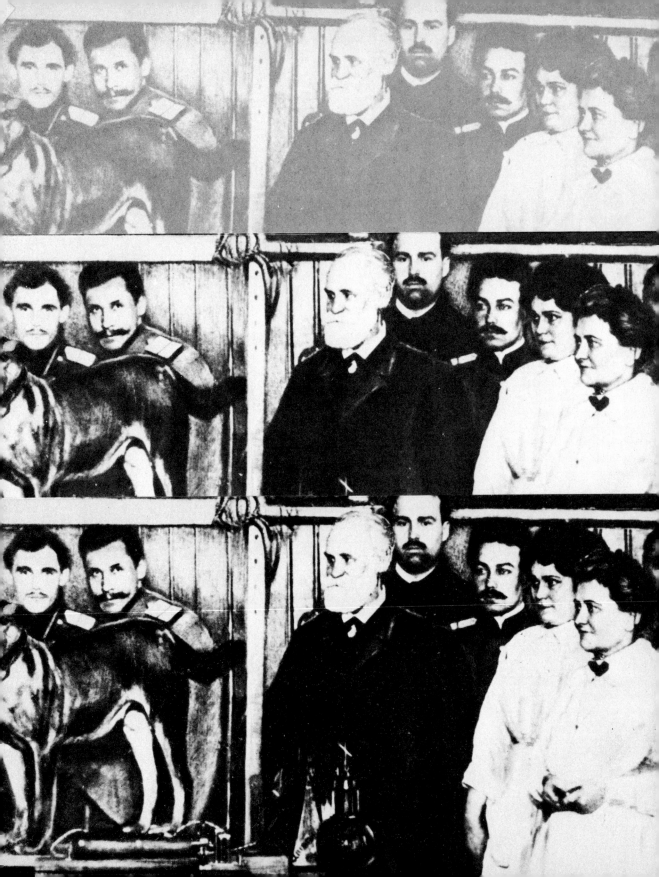

conditioned-response learning

DO YOU KNOW...

- *what the simplest form of learning is?*

- *if it is possible to learn anything without being rewarded for it?*

- *we learn some things in exactly the same way as animals learn them?*

- *under what circumstances we come to associate events that happen at about the same time?*

- *whether the things we learn to associate with each other necessarily have some connection?*

- *whether we sometimes learn to react to a situation in a certain way without consciously intending to?*

- *if what we learn to do in one situation shows up in different situations, and which ones?*

- *whether well-learned habits can be forgotten, and how?*

unit 15

The many kinds of learning that man and beast display can be grouped into categories in terms of their complexity. If we accept the broadest possible definition of learning—any change in behavior resulting from an environmental event—then the very simplest form of learning is **habituation**. Habituation, which can be demonstrated for the full range of animal life from man down to the single-celled protozoan, refers to the gradual decrease in an organism's response to the sheer repetition of a specific stimulus.

Habituation is a biologically useful phenomenon. When an animal is confronted by a new stimulus or by a relatively abrupt change in an already familiar (and habituated) one, the initial response (especially by higher animals) is the **orienting reaction**, a mechanism that serves to alert the animal to a sudden change in the environment that may require prompt attention (see Box 15.1). Once this orienting reaction has done its job by focusing the animal's attention upon the new event and mobilizing him for immediate action, the stage is then set for habituation to begin slowly taking over. Thus, although it makes good sense while driving a car on a highway to become instantly alert to the blast of a horn from a car behind us, if the other car keeps blasting its horn and we notice a Just Married sign hanging from its bumper, then *habituating* to the sound becomes the efficient response. Were it not for habituation, we would find it impossible to learn to ignore strong, repeated stimuli. Keeping one's mind on one's work in an office filled with clattering typewriters or in a home filled with noisily chattering children would prove impossible. Habituation, however, is not a *general* tuning out of stimuli; rather, only the same (or almost the same) stimulus is shut out. So if amid the freeway honking to which we have successfully habituated there is suddenly a clearly different honk, or a bang of a blown tire, then the alerting orienting reaction fortunately would be triggered anew. But habituation is not what most of us mean by "learning." The term is

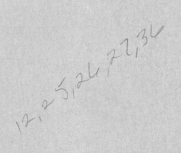

BOX 15.1

THE "WHAT IS IT?" REFLEX

The laboratory study of the role of external stimulus factors in arousal, under the name of orienting reaction or orienting response, has received a great deal of attention in Russian psychological and physiological laboratories, especially in those that follow in the Pavlovian tradition. It was Pavlov who first pointed out (in 1927) that this reaction could be investigated under strict laboratory controls.

Berlyne cites an eloquent comment by Pavlov on the importance of the orienting reaction, or, as Pavlov called it, the "what is it?" reflex:

It is this reflex which brings about the immediate response in man and animals to the slightest changes in the world around them, so that they immediately orientate their appropriate receptor organ in accordance with the perceptible quality in the agent bringing about the change, making full investigation of it. The biological significance of this reflex is obvious. If the animal were not provided with such a reflex its life would hang at every moment by a thread. In man this reflex has been greatly developed with far-reaching results, being represented in its highest form by inquisitiveness—the parent of that scientific

method through which we hope one day to come to a true orientation in knowledge of the world around us.

The orienting reaction itself involves a number of different bodily reactions, but in general these reactions fulfill two functions: They increase the flow of information that the individual can receive from his environment, and they prepare for some appropriate action on the basis of this information. To return to our previous illustration, when the intensity or color of a light undergoes a sudden change, a person may turn to face the light, the pupils of his eyes may momentarily dilate and permit more light to flood his retinal field, and photochemical changes may occur in the retinal elements and thus lower various sensory thresholds. In addition to these reactions—which can be viewed as increasing the information the person can receive from the light—a whole host of other bodily changes occur. These changes may include an increase in muscle tonus and changes in heart rate and in respiration, all of which obviously relate to a state of heightened attention and readiness to respond quickly. In short, the action pattern that characterizes the initial motivational arousal is a complex and pervasive one, involving many body systems, and its effect is to clear the psychological and physiological decks for immediate and effective action.

D. E. BERLYNE. *Conflict, Arousal, and Curiosity*. New York: McGraw-Hill, 1960.
I. P. PAVLOV. *Conditioned Reflexes*. Translated by G. V. Anrep. London: Oxford, 1927. Originally published in Russian.

---

usually reserved for something more complicated than becoming accustomed to a new stimulus.

CONDITIONING

Most of us would agree that we have truly learned something when our behavior has changed not as a result of habituation or sheer maturation or growth, but *as a direct result of a certain experience*. Further, this change in behavior must persist for some time. Seen this way, perhaps the best candidate for the very

simplest form of learning is **conditioned-response learning**. The first systematic analysis of this type of learning was made by Ivan P. Pavlov, the Russian physiologist, around the turn of the century. Pavlov was primarily interested in the study of the digestive glands (for which he was awarded the Nobel prize), but he noted, as a laboratory curiosity, that the secretions from the salivary glands of a dog could be controlled by learning as well as by direct physiological or biochemical means. For example, the dog rapidly learned to salivate to the mere *sight* of food or even to the approaching footsteps of the food-giving experimenter. These events, coming very close in time to the actual feeding of the animal, somehow took the place of the actual food stimulus. Becoming interested in what he called such *psychic influences* on the salivary gland, Pavlov soon devoted most of the facilities of his laboratory to investigating them systematically, and the era of conditioned responses in psychology, physiology, philosophy, literature, and science fiction was initiated. In Soviet Russia today, where the fields of psychology and physiology as they apply to the study of learning are so intertwined that they are often indistinguishable, Pavlovian views remain a dominant force.

In conditioned-response learning an individual is presented with an original stimulus (one that evokes a fairly simple and reliable response) and a neutral stimulus (one that does not evoke the response of the original stimulus). After sufficient repetitive pairings of the two stimuli, the individual tends to give a new response to the neutral stimulus, a response that is similar to the one previously made to the original stimulus. Since the original stimulus evokes a fairly simple and reliable response and the new response is not as reliable or automatic, but occurs *only when certain conditions* are fulfilled, the new response is called a *conditioned response* or even *conditioned reflex* (see Box 15.2).

This form of learning can be demonstrated at almost all levels of animal life, and interestingly, conditioned responses are just as easily established in primitive animals as in more advanced animals. (Even the "primitive" human newborn can be conditioned—see Unit 2, p. 43.) Because the *phenomenon* of conditioning seems to be universal, it suggests that conditioning may involve the same mechanism in all species. Perhaps it is this promise of universality, coupled with the relatively simple experimental procedures for establishing conditioned responses, which is responsible for the continuing popularity of conditioned-response learning as a research topic for both psychologists and physiologists. The same considerations may contribute to its central position in many theories of learning, theories that seek to embrace all levels of animal and human adaptive behavior. The term *conditioned response* has, at one

time or another, been employed in theoretical explanations of every possible type of learning, thinking, and problem solving. Such usage reflects a *theory* about conditioned response. However, we shall use the term in a purely descriptive sense to refer to a *training technique* and a *learning process* that, taken together, differ in some respects from other kinds of learning.

The qualifier *classical* pertaining to conditioning became necessary some thirty years after Pavlov's original work. During the early Pavlovian period, research on conditioned responses had remained largely within his original experimental model. Subsequent work (discussed in Unit 16) such as instrumental conditioning has made significant departures in method and interpretation.

Basic Definitions

Pavlov and his co-workers very early isolated and named some of the most basic phenomena of conditioned-response learning. These include: (1) **conditioning** (the acquisition of a stimulus-response relationship), (2) **generalization** (the tendency of the organism to transfer its acquisition to other similar situations), (3) **conditioned discrimination** (the limiting of the response to a specified situation), (4) **extinction** (the loss of the conditioned response).

The fundamental facts of acquisition are easily described. A dog is harnessed into an experimental apparatus that permits precise administration of stimuli and measurement of responses. Then, in a typical demonstration, powdered food is placed in the dog's mouth, thus stimulating his salivary glands, and saliva flows. The flow of saliva under these circumstances is automatic and unlearned and is therefore known as an **unconditioned response** (**UR**). The powdered food that elicits this UR is called an **unconditioned stimulus** (**US**). Suppose we now take some other stimulus—for example, a bright light—that has no influence on the action of the salivary glands and turn it on just before we place the food (US) on the dog's tongue. Each time the light is paired with

BOX 15.2

THE MECHANICAL MAN

There have long been those who prefer to conceive of living organisms as machines, no doubt more complex than other physical machines, but machines nevertheless. In such a conception of man and animals, a given behavior is regarded as a direct, unlearned response to a specific stimulus, in much the same way as a doorbell rings when it is pressed. In both, by this view, behavior is totally a result of certain wired-in connections.

Certain features of the behavior of organisms, man included, do indeed seem to lend themselves to this simple machine conception, especially the **reflexes**. We are all familiar with the knee-jerk reflex, which is tested routinely by the doctor to determine whether or not the nervous system is functioning properly. This simple, involuntary, and apparently automatic muscle movement is an example of mechanical or machinelike behavior. The button is pushed (a point just below the kneecap is tapped), the impulse is sent from the knee through the spinal cord and back to the leg muscles, and the machine operates (the leg jerks). Questions about mind, purpose, goal seem entirely superfluous.

Of course, behavior is usually much more complex than the knee jerk, but more complex behavior can be explained by assuming a very large number of simple reflex mechanisms, interconnected to provide the final response of the organic machine. One reflex response can be conceptualized as the stimulus for the next reflex response, and a long chain of reflexes can be assumed to account for a whole behavioral sequence.

However plausible such an account might seem when applied to simple unlearned behavior, it is inadequate to explain complex behavior, behavior that reflects learning and involves much more than running through a built-in sequence of simple reflexes. It is just this embarrassing limitation that was removed by Pavlov's formulation of conditioned reflexes (or conditioned responses), according to which, by simple association, *new* stimulus-response connections could be established in the organic machine.

A somewhat similar approach to the mechanistic view of man arose from the study of so-called **tropisms** observed in insects and lower animals. Tropisms are coordinated forced movements that occur in response to the stimulus situation (the cockroach scuttling from the light is one example). They serve a biological survival function in that through them the organism is brought into effective orientation with its physical environment. The mechanisms underlying tropisms may be conceptualized in very simplified terms without involving foreknowledge, purpose, or goal.

The figure demonstrates positive and negative phototropism in a hypothetical fish. Light falling on the eye results in stimulation to the fins by way of the nerves, indicated by the lines connecting eyes and fins. In the case of a *positive* phototropism, the nerves are crossed, so that a greater intensity of light on the right eye activates the left fin and the animal is swung toward the light; then, with both eyes equally stimulated, the fish is propelled toward the light. In *negative* phototropism, the nerve connections are not crossed, and a greater intensity of light on the right eye activates the right fin, so that the animal is swung away from the light; then, with both eyes equally stimulated, it is propelled away from the light.

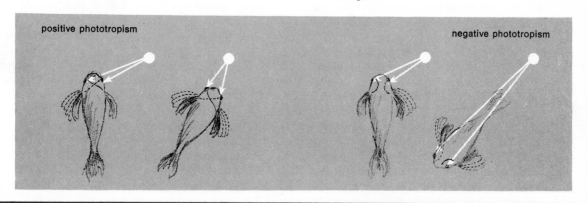

positive phototropism

negative phototropism

the food, a **reinforcement** trial occurs. After a number of such reinforcements, the light alone will elicit the flow of saliva. The action of the glands under these circumstances is a new response known as a **conditioned response** (**CR**). The light that can now call forth this CR is known as the **conditioned stimulus** (**CS**). A new stimulus-response relation has been established in the dog. Whereas formerly he had only the relationship US → UR, he now also has CS → CR. The CS has substituted for the US, but the nature of the substitution is a matter of some controversy in learning theory. At one extreme, the CS can be considered as having completely acquired the characteristics of the US, if only temporarily, and from the point of view of the central nervous system is now identical with it. The contrasting position is that for the animal the CS remains quite distinguishable from the US, and serves as a warning signal for the coming of the US.

Put in this way, the issue would seem to be an empirical one. For one thing, we would ask: Are the behavioral responses to the US and CS different, or in other words, is the UR distinguishable from the CR? The consensus is that the two responses are certainly not always identical: The CR does not occur as promptly after the CS as the UR does after the US; the CR is generally weaker than the UR; for example, somewhat less salivation occurs in response to the CS of light than in response to the US of food. The CR is often qualitatively different from the UR. The UR to food powder may be salivation, chewing, and swallowing; whereas, typically, only the salivary response occurs to the CS. Furthermore, even after the CR has been well established, it occasionally fails to appear; the warning message of the CS can apparently sometimes be ignored.

In a complex act it may be difficult to identify the US → UR relation on which the learning of the act is presumed to have been initially based. In an adult particularly, the *original* US for what may be a current CR is very likely lost in his long-ago early development. This gap must be bridged if conditioning is to remain a broadly applicable process. Attempts to bridge it have made use of the phenomena described in the following paragraphs.

Higher-Order Conditioning

Our earlier examples can be extended. If, after the dog is conditioned to salivate to the light stimulus, we present a bell along with the light, the dog will learn to salivate to the bell alone. In this case it is as if the light were now a new US and the bell a new CS. Presumably, this process can go on for several more steps. We can now accompany the bell with a touch on the nose, and soon the dog will salivate to a touch on the nose alone. This *chaining* process by which conditioned stimuli come to serve as unconditioned ones for new, more remote conditioned stimuli is known as **higher-order conditioning**.

Sensory Preconditioning

The phenomenon of higher-order conditioning is one indication of the complexity of apparently simple classical conditioning. This complexity is further highlighted by the phenomenon of **sensory preconditioning**, in which two neutral stimuli such as a light and a tone are first presented together for many trials. In the second part of the experiment one of them (say, the light) is paired with an unconditioned stimulus (say, food powder) until a conditioned response (salivation to the light) is established. Finally, in the third stage of the experiment the other neutral stimulus (the tone) is presented alone, and, if it causes the dog to salivate, then we have sensory preconditioning. Remember, the only possible connection between the CS of a tone and the CR of salivation must have been established in those earlier trials in which the two neutral stimuli (the tone and the light) were paired and *before* one of them was conditioned to the salivary response. Sensory preconditioning is a type of phenomenon that illustrates a long-standing theoretical debate in the area of conditioning and learning in which the main issue is whether only stimulus-response (S-R) associations are possible or whether stimulus-stimulus (S-S) associations may be formed as well. Since there is no common response to the two neutral stimuli during their original pairing, the fact that both are able to elicit the CR after only one has been conditioned to do so has added some weight to the possibility that S-S associations may in fact be established.

Varieties of Conditioned-Response Learning

Many US → UR combinations have been used to establish conditioned responses. In addition to the food powder–salivation link already discussed, conditioning has been accomplished using the eyeblink (UR) to a puff of air (US), pupillary dilation (UR) to light (US), the knee jerk (UR) to a tap below the knee cap (US), and a variety of responses (finger flexion, paw flexion, heart-rate change, galvanic skin response change) to the US of electric shock. And there are other workable US → UR connections.

The type of response that can be classically conditioned forms part of another theoretical controversy in psychology. Some theorists, focusing on the simplicity of the classical conditioning procedure, have maintained that only very simple response systems are amenable to such training. They have further restricted these responses to ones under control of the autonomic nervous system (see Unit 24) and therefore not under voluntary control. More complex and typically voluntary response systems are said to be trainable only through the instrumental learning techniques described in Unit 16. But as Neal Miller's work (discussed in Unit 16) indicates, the voluntary-involuntary distinction is being severely challenged. If the distinction is to be maintained, we must assume at least two separate learning processes, one for classical conditioning and one for instrumental conditioning. Other theorists who assert that all learning rests upon a single base must demonstrate that all response systems (both simple and complex, voluntary and involuntary) are trainable with both classical and instrumental methods. (Unit 16 discusses this issue in greater detail.)

Finally, there is abundant evidence that not every response can be conditioned to every stimulus. For example, it has been demonstrated by Garcia et al. (1968) that the rat cannot be conditioned so as to become nauseated upon receiving an electric shock to the foot—no matter how many times this electric shock is followed by nausea induced in the rat by injecting a noxious substance into his stomach. On the other hand, it is relatively easy to condition the rat's nausea to the sight of almost any specific *food*. Thus, after the animal has eaten the (perfectly good) food and then been made sick by the injection of the noxious substance, the animal will thereafter shun the food (sometimes after only one trial). Somehow the sight of a food and a feeling of nausea make better "biological sense" than do a shock to the foot and a feeling of nausea. The general conclusion therefore seems to be that there has to be some predetermined biological belongingness between the unconditioned stimulus and unconditioned response before the US → CR relation can be set up.

Temporal Patterning

The temporal patterning of events is as important in conditioning as it is in perception. The crucial factor is the time relation between the CS and the US, often called the **interstimulus interval (ISI)**. The ISI effects may be considered in terms of whether or not the CS and US overlap each other in time, how long one stimulus is operating before the other is presented, and which stimulus is presented first. The temporal patterns of CS and US are represented in Figure 15.1. In **delayed conditioning** the CS starts sometime before the onset of the US. In general, the best conditioning occurs when the ISI is about half a second. Longer delays produce less efficient learning. The crucial nature of the ISI is illustrated by the fact that very little conditioning, if any, takes place when the CS and US overlap and occur simultaneously (the **simultaneous conditioning** arrangement).

Good conditioning can be obtained in many cases if the US starts almost immediately after the CS is removed (**trace conditioning**). Longer ISI times are not very effective in trace conditioning. The importance of temporal patterning is further emphasized by the failure of most attempts to demonstrate learning resulting from **backward conditioning**, the arrangement in which the US *precedes* the presentation of the CS. But it should be noted that these comments on the relative efficiency of the various temporal patterns in classical conditioning are applicable in general terms only; the best ISI in specific instances depends upon the nature of the CR involved.

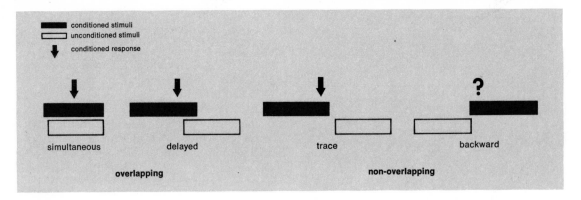

FIGURE 15.1 Temporal patterning in conditioned-response learning. The time relation between the onset of the conditioned and unconditioned stimuli is illustrated for each temporal pattern discussed in the text. The arrow indicates when the conditioned response typically occurs.

The efficiency of short-delay conditioning and the apparent failure to find learning in simultaneous and backward arrangements fit well with the notion that the CS is essentially a warning signal. The individual behaves as if the CS were a signal or warning that the US is about to take place, and his response (CR) prepares him for the oncoming US. For example, the light can be understood as a signal meaning food is coming. In the delay and trace situations, the dog has time to react with a flow of saliva so that, when the food actually appears, he is ready for it; but this does not occur in the truly simultaneous or in the backward situations. It has recently been suggested that the CS may not only act as a signal that the US is coming but, under certain circumstances, may also signal the fact the US is *not* coming (see Box 15.3).

Generalization

Once a CS → CR relationship is established, stimuli that are similar to the original CS can evoke the CR, even though these similar stimuli have themselves never appeared in the original training. This phenomenon is called *generalization*. The dog, after successful conditioning to a light, will tend to salivate to lights that are somewhat dimmer or brighter than the original CS. In general, the more similar the new stimulus is to the original CS, the more effective it will be. This phenomenon has been labeled the *gradient of generalization.*

Generalization has definite adaptive value, because stimulus situations are never repeated *exactly* in nature. Therefore, if a conditioned response could be evoked only when the conditioned stimulus occurs in a form *identical* with that used during the original training, the conditioned response would have severely limited value in helping the organism to adapt to his environment.

Discrimination

One way to limit the degree of generalization is by specific training. For example, every time a light of intensity A is presented, it is reinforced with the unconditioned stimulus of food; when a light of intensity B is presented, no food is placed on the animal's tongue. Eventually, the animal will acquire a *conditioned discrimination*, so that he will salivate to a light of intensity A and not to a light of intensity B. Like generalization, discrimination has obvious adaptive value.

Conditioned-discrimination training can be a useful technique in studying perception in children and animals. For example, if an infant or a dog cannot learn to make a differential motor response (such as moving his right limb

BOX 15.3

LEARNING SOMETHING ABOUT NOTHING

In performing classical conditioning experiments most researchers are careful about including control groups. Control groups are necessary in order to ensure that the conditioning (experimental, as contrasted with control) subjects have really learned to associate the CR with the CS. For example, suppose that you are conditioning an eyeblink to a tone by pairing the tone with a puff of air to the eye. After repeated pairings the tone produces the eyeblink when presented alone during the test period. Have you now established conditioning? Perhaps you have, perhaps not. It is possible that repeated puffs to the eye have so sensitized the subject that he will blink to any sudden stimulus. You might then like to have another group of subjects, a control group, that receives a series of puffs alone, not followed by a test tone. If this group shows as much blinking to the tone during the test period as your conditioning group does, you would hesitate to assume that an association had actually been formed between the tone and the blink in your conditioning group. They may only be showing the same effects of sensitization that your control group shows.

One of the more popular control groups for classical conditioning experiments has been called the *random control group*. There, the subject receives the same number of CS and US presentations as the conditioning group, *but so arranged that the US never follows the CS closely in time.* For example, the subject in the random control group hears the tone (CS) as often as does the subject in the experimental group, and he receives an equal number of puffs to the eye (US). *But* the sounding of the tone and the puff to the eye *are never paired one after the other.* In this way, it is argued, no true conditioning can have taken place but, at the same time, the subject has experienced equal numbers of CS and US presentations. Thus, we have a control for sensitization to the US as well as for the possibility that the CS, by itself, may have a natural unlearned capacity to evoke the CR.

Robert Rescorla, a Yale psychologist, has taken exception to this interpretation of the results from such a random control group. He points out that, although the CS and US are indeed never paired, it does not necessarily follow that the subject learns nothing. It is possible, he suggests, that such explicit nonpairing produces an *inhibitory* learning; that is, the subject learns that the CS signals a period in which *no* US will occur. The importance of learning that nothing is going to happen becomes clear when considering a conditioning situation in which the US is experienced as unpleasant.

An example of the kind of experiment Rescorla uses to support his position involves a US of electric shock. A group of dogs was trained first to avoid a shock by making an instrumental response. (As Unit 16 explains, instrumental avoidance training is different from classical conditioning in that the subject may do something—press a lever, jump a hurdle—to *avoid* getting shocked.) Once the dogs had learned successfully to avoid the shock, they were removed from the situation and given separate classical conditioning–control group training. Half the dogs were presented a tone and a shock in a random fashion; that is, the shock (US) never followed the tone (CS) sufficiently closely to make for good pairing. The other half of the dogs were presented the tone (CS) alone. Both groups were now returned to the instrumental learning situation and once again could respond to avoid the shock. However, the same tone was now being presented to both groups while they were responding. To the animals who had received *only* the tone in the classical conditioning phase, the tone should mean nothing and therefore should not have any effect on their ongoing avoidance responding. And indeed there was no effect. However, to the animals who had the tone and shock presented together but in an *explicitly unpaired* fashion, the tone might mean something. Rescorla reasoned that the tone might act as a safety signal because, having learned that there was no reliable connection between the tone and the shock, they would regard the tone itself as a signal that a shock was *not* coming. In this event the dogs could be expected to reduce their ongoing instrumental response of avoiding shock if they felt that no shock was imminent. And that is what happened; this group became less successful in avoiding the shock than they had been before the classical conditioning tone-shock training.

Rescorla's suggestion that the CS may signal the absence as well as the presence of the US has implications beyond what we have discussed here. Be that as it may, the idea that the total context and pattern of CS and US presentations is important (just as context is important in perception) and the idea that the subject can learn something about nothing (that the CS means no US) have received considerable experimental support.

R. A. RESCORLA. Pavlovian conditioning and its proper control procedures. *Psychological Review*, 1967, **74**, 71–80.

to a sound of a particular pitch) despite considerable conditioned-discrimination training, then we may assume that this pitch difference is not *perceived* by the individual.

Pavlov described a special kind of discrimination. A tone would be presented and reinforced with the presentation of a US of food powder. However, the tone in combination with a light was subsequently not reinforced. Pavlov's dogs, who had learned to salivate to the tone, now stopped salivating to the tone-and-light combination. Pavlov suggested that the light took on inhibitory properties and became a **conditioned inhibitor**. The concept of inhibition is central to Pavlov's theorizing and plays an important part, as you will see, in the explanation of the phenomenon of extinction.

EXTINCTION

Once a conditioned response has been established, the CS will elicit the response without presentation of the US. What will happen as we continue to present the CS unaccompanied by the US? Typically, the strength of the response gradually decreases until a point is reached at which the CS fails to evoke the CR at all. When this occurs, *extinction* has taken place.

Rate of Extinction

The speed with which extinction takes place is determined by many of the same factors that determine how quickly conditioning takes place. Generally, the stronger the original conditioned response, the slower its rate of extinction. (Experimenters often use the rate of extinction as a measure of the strength of the conditioned response.) Almost invariably, no matter how complete the extinction may seem to be, some aftereffect remains. We know this because it is easier to reestablish the conditioned response by further reinforcements (i.e., by reintroducing the US) than it was to establish it initially. Since fewer conditioning trials are now needed to bring the CR up to its full strength, we speak of *saving*.

Inhibition

The mechanism that has been postulated to account for the saving phenomenon is known as **inhibition**. Briefly, it is assumed that nonreinforced trials result in an *active* neurological process that inhibits or blocks the conditioned response. One example of such blocking as a result of nonreinforced trials is the role of the conditioned inhibitor discussed above.

Further evidence supporting the hypothesis of an active inhibitory process may be found in the observation that extinction itself generalizes. The extinction of one CR (say, salivating to a light) will result in partial extinction of other CRs (say, blinking to the sound of a bell). *It is as if the subject acquires a generalized inhibition of conditioned stimuli during extinction.* According to this concept of inhibition, extinction comes about as a result of *active masking of the CR by the competing process of inhibition*, not as a result of some passive weakening and fading away of the CR. Thus, even though a CR is extinguished, the neurological basis for it remains. Therefore any reconditioning procedure will not have to start from scratch; it can build upon the residue of earlier conditioning that still remains in the nervous system. Although inhibition may therefore seem to explain the saving in reconditioning procedure despite the apparent disappearance of the CR, the existence of an inhibition process of this sort has not been directly demonstrated. As with certain other conditioning constructs, it remains a theoretical process.

This postulated inhibition process, however, can also be used to explain yet another curious and interesting conditioning phenomenon.

Spontaneous Recovery

Sometime after extinction has occurred, the CS → CR relationship may *spontaneously* reappear without any additional conditioning training. For example, a dog's conditioned response to the light has been extinguished, and he has been removed from the experimental room. After such a rest period, if the dog is returned to the experimental situation, we may find that the light will elicit the flow of saliva all over again. This reappearance of an extinguished CS → CR relationship without additional training is called **spontaneous recovery**.

This phenomenon might be explained by assuming that inhibition built up during the extinction period itself dissipates in the rest interval. Thus, when the animal is returned to the experimental room, the CR, which had been blocked by the inhibition, is now no longer blocked and therefore can once again be evoked by presenting the CS. Successive spontaneous recoveries follow a law of diminishing returns. That is, if spontaneous recovery is tested by repeating the procedure day after day, the extent of spontaneous recovery will grow less and less.

Significance of Extinction

The facts of extinction can be understood in terms of its adaptive function. If the US repeatedly failed to follow the CS, it would be of little value for the organism to continue to respond. In fact, continuing to do so could even prove to be a handicap. The war veteran who had acquired on the battlefield various fear-related CRs (e.g., rapid heartbeat) to the sound of aircraft overhead (CS) fortunately, and in most cases rapidly, extinguishes those responses once he is home and the reinforcement of those responses by the US (bomb explosions) no longer occurs. On the other hand, too rapid or permanent extinction of a conditioned response that had been reinforced frequently in the past life of the individual might be premature and

maladaptive. Thus, the soldier who extinguished this response thoroughly during a brief rest-and-recreation leave would be in danger upon return to combat.

We have been stressing the adaptive value of conditioned responses. Obviously, however, not all the characteristics of their acquisition, generalization, discrimination, or extinction (see Figure 15.2) are perfectly adaptive. An appreciation also of the possible nonadaptive features of conditioned responses must be gained if we are to understand the role of conditioning in adaptive behavior.

CONDITIONED RESPONSES AND BEHAVIOR

If conditioning were restricted to the acquisition of relatively simple responses to simple stimuli, it would have little importance in the total adaptive economy of the individual. It appears, however, that certain complex integrated patterns of responses, especially many cases of emotional or so-called irrational behavior, may also be viewed as instances of conditioning. In many forms of learned behavior, conscious decisions and motives seem to play a decisive role; but in some behavior, rather complex responses appear to be triggered automatically by some apparently neutral and trivial event. Experimental work has suggested that many allergy reactions, irrepressible outbursts, and complex visceral and glandular responses that accompany intense feelings and emotions

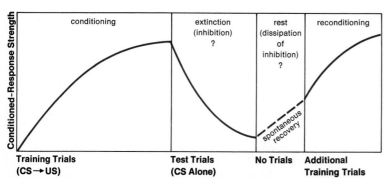

FIGURE 15.2 A dog's-eye view of classical conditioning phenomena.

G. A. Kimble & N. Garmezy. *Principles of general psychology*, 2nd ed.; copyright © 1963 by The Ronald Press Company; adapted by permission.

can best be understood as acquired conditioned responses. (For a pioneer illustration of such an experiment, see Box 15.4.) In fact, in recent years it has been proposed by certain learning theorists that a good deal of human maladaptive behavior, including neurosis and psychosis, can be understood in much this way. What is more, techniques for the treatment of such behavior based on this kind of general theory have been developed (see the section on behavior therapy in Unit 25).

Even with these extensions of classical conditioning, it remains a process with obvious limitations for the task of explaining the typically more complex and varied learning achievements in men and animals.

BOX 15.4

CONDITIONED NAUSEA

Many years ago N. Kleitman and G. Crisler of the University of Chicago reported the conditioning of a complexly integrated pattern of responses that was, at the same time, involuntary in nature.

Using eight dogs as subjects, the experimenters first prepared the animals by cutting a permanent opening (fistula) into each animal's salivary glands. They were able therefore to collect and measure the saliva as it was secreted. As a conditioned stimulus, the dog was harnessed into place in a stock, and a tube was tied around the lower jaw so that all the saliva secreted could be collected and measured. The animals were left in the stock for a constant period of time (from fifteen minutes to two hours for different dogs) without anything being done to them. The CS was thus *being readied* for morphine injection. The unconditioned stimulus was an injection of about 40 mg. of morphine, which was administered to the animal after the lapse of the predetermined waiting time. This procedure was repeated daily for many months.

Morphine, when injected subcutaneously, acts not upon some single localized receptor but upon many centers in the nervous system. The unconditioned response is best described as general nausea. It includes panting, profuse salivation, shivering, vomiting, and other signs of distress.

Very soon after the experiment was started, a complex conditioned response began to appear. In many instances, as soon as the dog was placed in the stock—and long before the morphine was injected—the animal showed all the behavior characteristics of nausea: excessive salivation (in some dogs as much as 300 to 400 cc. of saliva was secreted in an hour), shivering, retching, panting, and vomiting. As a consequence of conditioning, then, the dogs learned to become nauseated at the sight of the "hospital room" and the *preparation* for injection.

The possibility of conditioning nausea has been used in the attempt to break bad habits in human beings. The alcoholic is administered a drug (Antabuse) that produces a feeling of nausea when he drinks alcohol. He may very soon reach a state in which he proclaims, "I can't stand the sight of the stuff"; the once-tantalizing sight of his favorite bottle becomes a CS eliciting conditioned nausea. The heavy smoker has sometimes subjected himself to similar procedures in an effort to break the habit, with some success. But, as with all classical conditioning, backsliding (extinction) can be expected to occur with each unmedicated (nonreinforced) drink or smoke. For this reason, many question that durable cures are possible, but it is true that reconditioning is somewhat more rapid in return engagements. This controversy is one small skirmish within the general confrontation between conditioning-based behavior therapy and other therapeutic approaches (see Unit 25).

N. KLEITMAN & G. CRISLER. A quantitative study of a salivary conditioned reflex. *American Journal of Physiology*, 1927, **79**, 571–614.

SUMMARY

1. A novel stimulus typically triggers an orienting reaction that focuses attention upon it, but the prolonged repetition of that stimulus leads to a gradual decrease in response. This decrease, known as habituation, is perhaps the simplest form of learning.

2. Conditioned-response learning is achieved through conditioning trials. Such trials consist of repeatedly presenting, in proper temporal arrangement, an unconditioned stimulus (which naturally and reliably evokes a specific unconditioned response) and a conditioned stimulus (which *at first* does not evoke that response). This pairing procedure is called reinforcement. When, after a number of such reinforcements, the CS *presented by itself* is able to evoke the response, a conditioned response has been established; the conditioning has been successful.

3. Stimuli sufficiently similar to the conditioned stimulus can also evoke the conditioned response (generalization), but after appropriate training, generalization can be restricted to a narrow range of stimuli (discrimination).

4. The loss of the conditioned response (extinction) gradually occurs if reinforcements are discontinued altogether. Occasional pairings of the unconditioned stimulus with the conditioned stimulus are therefore necessary to maintain an already established conditioned response. Generally, the stronger this response is, the longer it takes to extinguish.

5. Once a conditioned response to a certain conditioned stimulus has been firmly established, that stimulus can itself serve as an unconditioned stimulus to be paired with a new conditioned stimulus. This process, known as higher-order conditioning, can be repeated, leading to a chain of connections linking the original unconditioned stimulus to more remote conditioned ones.

6. A new stimulus can become an effective substitute for an original conditioned stimulus by *previously* presenting the two together over a number of trials *without any reinforcement by the unconditioned stimulus* (sensory preconditioning).

7. The timing of the presentations of the unconditioned and conditioned stimuli is crucial to the success of conditioning. Delayed conditioning procedures produce best results; trace conditioning is generally somewhat less effective. Establishing conditioned responses through either simultaneous or backward conditioning techniques is exceedingly difficult.

8. Reconditioning a conditioned response after extinction typically requires fewer trials than the original conditioning. One hypothesis to account for this saving is that the conditioned response has not been truly unlearned but, instead, has been prevented from appearing by an actual neurological process known as inhibition. Inhibition also can theoretically account for the reappearance after extinction of a conditioned response without additional conditioning trials (spontaneous recovery); in this case we assume a gradual dissipation of inhibition during a period of rest.

9. Conditioned-response learning is largely restricted to the simplest of learning phenomena. However, such learning may be at the root of some persistent irrational behavior, and conditioning-based techniques for treating such behavior are showing promise.

GLOSSARY

backward conditioning A training procedure in which the US is presented first and the CS is presented after cessation of the US. The least efficient method of conditioned-response training.

conditioned discrimination The behavior of an organism, after appropriate conditioned-response training, in responding in two different ways to two different stimuli. For example, if after conditioned-response training in which only the bell is reinforced, a dog salivates to the tone of a bell but not to a clicking noise, we have an instance of conditioned discrimination.

conditioned inhibitor   A stimulus that when paired with a CS inhibits the CR. The inhibitor is established through discrimination training in which the CS, presented alone, is reinforced and the combination of the CS and the inhibiting stimulus is not reinforced.

conditioned response (CR)   The response that is evoked by the conditioned stimulus after conditioning has occurred. The CR is usually different in minor respects from the UR.

conditioned-response learning   The process of training by which a neutral stimulus is repeatedly paired with a stimulus that typically produces a certain response until the neutral stimulus alone can evoke that same response.

conditioned stimulus (CS)   The stimulus to which a new response becomes related through the process of conditioning.

delayed conditioning   The training procedure in which the CS begins prior to the US and continues until the response occurs.

extinction   The training procedure in which the CS is presented unaccompanied by the US. This term is also used to refer to the loss of conditioning as a result of this procedure.

generalization   The fact that a conditioned response may be elicited by stimuli that have not themselves been used in the conditioning training. The greater the similarity of new stimuli to the stimulus used in the training, the greater the probability that generalization will be evident. This phenomenon is sometimes referred to as the *gradient of generalization.*

habituation   The decrease in response to a *specific* stimulus that occurs with repeated stimulation. It differs from factors that contribute to a decrease in responsivity to stimuli *in general*, such as boredom and fatigue.

higher-order conditioning   Conditioned-response learning in which what was formerly the CS serves as the US for a new CS.

inhibition   A hypothetical process, assumed to operate during extinction, that actively prevents the performance of the CR. Dissipation of inhibition is then assumed to occur during a rest period following extinction, thus accounting for the saving shown in reconditioning and for spontaneous recovery.

interstimulus interval (ISI)   The time relation between the CS and the US when they are presented as a pair.

orienting reaction   A general response, usually to a change in the external environment, consisting of various behavioral and physiological reactions that tend to increase the information reaching the organism from the new situation and to ready it for prompt action.

reflex   A simple, involuntary, and unlearned response of a particular part of the body to a particular stimulus, for example, the knee-jerk response to a blow below the kneecap or the contraction of the pupil of the eye when exposed to light.

reinforcement   In classical conditioning, a technique in which the unconditioned stimulus accompanies presentation of the conditioned stimulus. The term has a somewhat different meaning in instrumental conditioning (see Glossary, Unit 16). It also refers to the process that theoretically accounts for changes in the strength of the conditioned response brought about by this training procedure.

sensory preconditioning   The training procedure in which two neutral stimuli are presented together for several trials without an accompanying US. One of the stimuli is then paired with a US until a CR is established in the usual manner. If the other neutral stimulus presented alone then produces the CR, sensory preconditioning is said to have taken place.

simultaneous conditioning   The training procedure in which the CS begins simultaneously with the US and continues until the conditioned response occurs.

spontaneous recovery   The partial reappearance of an extinguished CR after a lapse of time and with no additional conditioning.

trace conditioning   The training procedure in which the CS is presented first but is removed prior to the onset of the US. It is a fairly efficient method of conditioning if the US comes almost immediately after the removal of the CS.

tropisms   Unlearned movements of an organism, serving to orient it in such a way that a certain distribution of stimuli is achieved. Tropisms (from the Greek word for "turning") are of many types; for instance, the negative phototropism of the cockroach running from the light or the positive phototropism of a moth being drawn toward it. Tropistic behavior occurs to a variety of stimuli; for example, geotropism refers to response to the pull of gravity. Baby rats automatically climb an inclined plane, thus showing negative geotropism.

unconditioned response (UR) The original response evoked by the unconditioned stimulus without training.

unconditioned stimulus (US) The stimulus that evokes the unconditioned response without training.

instrumental learning

DO YOU KNOW...

- *how circus animals are trained to perform their surprising tricks—and that these same techniques can work on you as well?*

- *in what way we learn to avoid painful situations without actually having to experience them time after time?*

- *that were we to reward a child every time he behaved in a way we approved of, this would not be the best way of teaching him a long-lasting habit?*

- *that there may be ways to learn the conscious control of certain bodily processes, such as our heart rate or blood pressure, that are normally involuntary?*

- *whether punishment to break a bad habit works, and whether it's best done mildly or severely?*

- *whether we automatically react in a situation in the way we've most often reacted in the past?*

- *under what circumstances our behavior fails to show things we've actually learned quite well?*

unit 16

CONTENTS

Classical conditioning techniques can produce adaptive behavior (see Unit 15). Through these procedures the conditioned stimulus (CS) comes to act as a signal that the unconditioned stimulus (US) is about to occur, and therefore the conditioned response (CR) can be seen as a preparatory adjustment for the coming US. Thus, after Pavlov's dog was conditioned in the usual manner, the light caused the dog to salivate in preparation for the dry powdered food that was about to be placed in his mouth. Or when the dog has been subjected to a pairing of a buzzer (CS) and an electric shock (US), he comes to make the various cringing and other adjustive postural changes (CR) when he hears the buzzer, even though it is unaccompanied by the shock. These conditioned responses are adaptive to the highly limited degree that they enable the dog to be set for, and thus able to reduce somewhat, the effects of the painful shock that inevitably follows the buzzer.

But note that no matter what conditioned responses the dog makes, the unconditioned stimulus, whether pleasant or painful, inevitably occurs; it is administered by the experimenter in a standard manner throughout the training period in the classical conditioning situation. The dog's salivating does not speed up the coming of food, nor does his cringing prevent the electric shock. Thus, the animal's (or human's) responses in this situation provide no control over what is to happen to him. And it is precisely because of this lack of control that classical conditioning is essentially a side issue to the study of typical and truly adaptive behavior.

Most of what we call *adaptive* behavior is characterized by actions that remove the individual from an undesirable environment, that carry him into a desirable environment, or that directly affect what subsequently happens to him—in short, actions that *control* the environment. When the hungry dog comes into the house and runs to his food dish, his behavior is adaptive precisely because it does control his environment; he has changed a nonfood into a food surrounding by this action. If he has been scratched by a cat and from then on crosses the street when he sees the cat arching its back and spitting, he is again demonstrating that he has learned to control the environment, in this case by removing himself from a dangerous situation. And, to repeat, this kind of adaptive learning cannot be studied in the classical conditioning setup, a setup in which the animal's behavior, no matter how well learned, cannot control, affect, or alter the environment.

Since we must of course investigate such more complex and truly adaptive behavior, psychologists have developed a number of alternative experimental techniques that go under the general heading of **instrumental learning**. This type of learning is called *instrumental* because the behavior acquired through these techniques can be instrumental, or effective, in changing or controlling the individual's environment in adaptive ways. For example, in one variant—**instrumental conditioning**—a hungry rat confined in a box can be conditioned to press a lever that will deliver a food pellet. In another—**trial-and-error learning**—an animal learns how to escape from a box or a maze in which it has been confined.

INSTRUMENTAL CONDITIONING

This type of instrumental behavior differs in at least two significant ways from that shown in classical conditioning: (1) The final to-be-learned response (pushing the lever) is not inevitably or automatically elicited by an unconditioned stimulus. The animal must *discover* the appropriate response. Contrast this activity with the classical conditioning procedure in which the to-be-learned response is automatically evoked by a specific stimulus (e.g., when we pull away from a painful shock) without any prior learning; therefore, there is nothing to discover. (2) In instrumental conditioning, the learned response actually makes something happen. Thus, pressing the lever *causes* food to be delivered; whereas in classical conditioning, salivating does not make the food appear.

Although few theorists would attempt to encompass all possible forms of complex learning under the heading of instrumental conditioning, one American psychologist, B. F.

Skinner, has come very close to doing just this. (Skinner prefers the essentially synonymous term **operant conditioning** to instrumental conditioning.) The procedures and terminology characteristic of Skinner's work can be conveniently illustrated in the context of his favorite experimental apparatus (commonly referred to as the *Skinner box*) and his favorite experimental animal (the pigeon). The Skinner box (see Figure 16.1) contains a small round window that

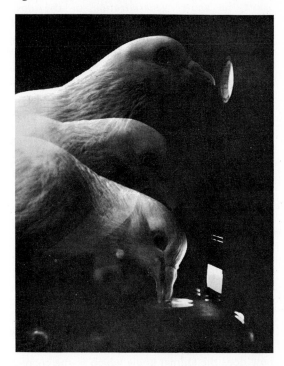

FIGURE 16.1 A pigeon performing in a Skinner Box. This bird has been successfully conditioned and goes rapidly through the sequence of pecking at the illuminated window at the top and seeking the food pellet.

Courtesy, Professor Norman Guttman.

can be illuminated and that, when pecked while illuminated, causes a pellet of food to be delivered to a tray. In a typical instrumental conditioning procedure the hungry naïve bird at first wanders about the box pecking randomly at this and that. Eventually, he chances to peck at the illuminated window, and then the automatic mechanism delivers a food pellet; this reward for the appropriate response is one example of **reinforcement**. (This term and those that follow are also encountered in a classical conditioning context in Unit 15 and have much the same meaning here, indicating the close relation between the two types of conditioning.) After a number of these reinforcements, the pigeon is more likely to peck at the window than at anything else. In fact, he is rather undiscriminating, in that he will continue to peck vigorously no matter how the window is lit, whether by a dim light, a bright light, or a light of any color. In short, he shows *generalization* of the now-conditioned pecking-at-the-window response. If food is delivered only when there is a light of a specific quality (in hue or in brightness), then *discrimination* takes place; the pigeon learns to respond only to that particular light. If nonreinforced trials now occur (food failing to appear following the correct pecking response), the pigeon eventually stops pecking. *Extinction* has taken place. *Savings* can also be demonstrated because fewer reinforcement trials are necessary to reestablish the extinguished response if they are resumed following extinction.

The Puzzle of Reinforcement

The most crucial and at the same time the most conceptually shaky element in the picture of instrumental conditioning is reinforcement. As we have already seen, in instrumental conditioning the animal has to discover the proper or correct response, and then he must learn to select this response and drop all others. Now, how does the animal know which is the correct response? How can he recognize the correct response once he has made it? And how does he learn to prefer this response to all others? The answer given is that the correct response is the response that is reinforced and that he learns to repeat this response *precisely because it is reinforced*. This explanation leads to the commonly accepted definition of instrumental conditioning as that form of learning in which the frequency of a response increases after the response is reinforced a certain number of times. If we now ask what reinforcement is, we can say that it is the pairing of *any* response with an event that increases the frequency of the response. And this answer, obviously, had led us

into a most embarrassing circularity in our basic definition of instrumental conditioning: Instrumental conditioning is that form of learning in which the frequency of a spontaneously occurring response increases after the response has been paired with an event that increases the frequency of that response. [!]

Attempts to avoid the circularity of the definition of instrumental conditioning have included more precise specification of the reinforcement. One suggestion (Meehl, 1950) is that only events which operate as **transituational reinforcers** are truly reinforcers; that is, events that increase the frequency of a preceding response in one situation should have this same effect on *other* responses in *other* situations. For example, a rat that learns to press a bar as a result of reinforcement by food pellets should also be able to learn other responses (jumping over a barrier, turning a wheel, climbing an incline) in order to obtain those same food pellets. Although limiting the term *reinforcer* to those events that produce instrumental conditioning in *many* different situations does ease the circularity problem, the puzzle of reinforcement is far from solved. The very fact that an event is reinforcing across a variety of situations might lead us to accept the commonsense definition that reinforcement is a *reward*. A pellet of food for the hungry pigeon is a reward; so is escape from a confining box for a restless cat. But if we accept this definition, we continue to be faced with the very tough problem of deciding what we mean by a reward and how we can know, for each animal and at any given moment, what is and what is not rewarding.

Despite the ambiguity of the concept of reinforcement, a great deal of experimental attention has been devoted to teasing out the role of reinforcement (even if ill defined) in the adaptive behavior of the animal. (Very often in psychology, and in science generally, progress toward understanding can be made even if one works with such initially ambiguous concepts.) This experimentation has resulted in further differentiation of the term *reinforcement* to include positive, negative, and secondary reinforcement. And it has also led to a number of surprising findings concerning the effects of schedules of reinforcement.

Positive and Negative Reinforcement

Positive reinforcement is an event that when added to the situation increases the frequency of the response immediately preceding the reinforcement. Most of our discussion of reinforcement up to this point has dealt with reinforcers of this kind. A pellet of food for a hungry pigeon, a drink of water for a thirsty rat, a piece of candy for a well-behaved child all are positive reinforcers and cause the individual to begin to do more of whatever it was he was doing just before the reward was delivered. Those conditioning experiments in which a positive reinforcer is used are called **reward training** procedures.

A **negative reinforcement** is an event that when subtracted or removed from the situation increases the frequency of the response immediately preceding it. An animal will learn to press a bar to stop electric shock to his paws or to leap a barrier to escape a strong air blast. The responses of bar pressing or barrier leaping are strengthened because they terminate the noxious stimulation. Conditioning experiments in which a negative reinforcer is used in this way are called **escape training** procedures. Both positive and negative reinforcement are consistent with the commonsense notion of reward. In the positive case, it is rewarding or feels good when the event starts; in the negative case, it feels good when the event stops.

Avoidance training is another way in which conditioning experiments make use of negative reinforcers. The parallel between escape and reward training is quite clear; in both cases a stimulus brings about an increase in an immediately preceding response. Avoidance training, however, presents a slightly different situation. For example, the subject is given a signal (say, a bell) which lets him know that shock is coming, and if he makes the response (say, pressing a lever) within a specified period of time the shock is *not* presented; that is, he *avoids* the shock rather than just terminating it. The effect of the negative reinforcer in the early stages of avoidance training, however, is very much like escape training. When the signal is first presented, the subject is of course unaware that it will be followed by shock; but when the

shock does occur, the response that terminates it is thereby negatively reinforced. Over successive trials the connection between the signal and the shock is made, so that the individual learns to respond early enough to avoid the shock.

Because, after successful avoidance training, there is no shock and hence no negative reinforcement after each response, we might expect from what we already know about the effect of nonreinforced trials that the response would extinguish. Yet, this does not occur. Avoidance learning can be very persistent. The subject keeps on responding to the signal and keeps on avoiding shock. In order to account for this apparent paradox, some psychologists have invoked a commonsense (and *internal*) negative reinforcer: *fear*. They explain it this way: The signal that precedes shock in the early stage of training arouses fear in the subject, as well as the escape response. Once the response is made, the signal is removed and the fear is therefore reduced. This fear reduction is a negative reinforcer in the same way as shock reduction is; thus, it is argued, the behavior is maintained. Other psychologists object to the idea of fear reduction as the source of negative reinforcement and have offered different explanations for the effectiveness of avoidance training. Whatever the theoretical rationale, the fact remains that avoidance training often provides rapidly learned and long-lasting changes in behavior, although long-lasting, learned avoidance responses are not immune to other biological processes; for an illustration, see Box 16.1, p. 380.

Whereas escape and avoidance training are made possible by the termination of a noxious stimulus, **punishment training** involves the presentation or onset of a noxious stimulus. The goal in punishment training is to *weaken* a response by producing an unpleasant state of affairs when it is made. On the surface this technique seems reasonable. A child who is spanked for a specific act does not often repeat that act immediately. Some of us may wish to question the morality of using noxious stimuli to control behavior, but beyond this, we have reason to question its effectiveness. In a now-classic series of experiments on the effects of punishment, it has been demonstrated that, although punish-

BOX 16.1

RHYTHMIC MEMORY

An extraordinary demonstration of rhythmicity in memory is provided in an experiment on avoidance learning by F. A. Holloway and R. Wansley of the University of Oklahoma Health Science Center.

The subjects of the experiment were 195 male albino rats which lived in a laboratory with a daily light-dark cycle of 12 hr of light and 12 hr of dark (the lights being turned on and off at 8:00 A.M. and 8:00 P.M.). These 195 animals were divided into thirteen groups, all of which received the same treatment with but one point of difference: The animals were first given *one training trial* (described below) and then, some time later, *one retention, or memory, test.* The only difference among the groups was in the *time which elapsed between the training trial and the memory test*. The thirteen different elapsed times were: 15 min after training, and 6, 12, 18, 24, 30, 36, 42, 48, 54, 60, 66, and 72 hr.

The apparatus consisted of two compartments: a small illuminated startbox in which the animal was placed and a larger darkened chamber which the rat could enter through a circular opening cut into the wall separating the two compartments. The floor of the larger chamber was wired so that an

electric shock could be delivered to the rat's foot. Every animal when placed in the brightly lit startbox almost immediately crawled through the opening into the darkened chamber. When he reached the far end of the darkened box, he received an electric footshock. The current was left on for 5 sec, but before these 5 sec had elapsed, every rat had scam-

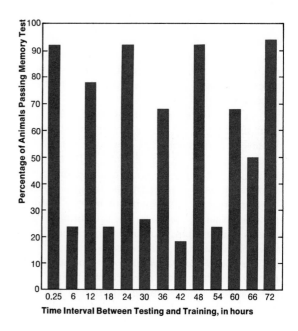

Time Interval Between Testing and Training, in hours

---

ment does indeed suppress specific behaviors, the effects are not long lasting unless, perhaps, the punishment is quite severe (see Box 16.2, p. 382).

Secondary Reinforcement

The technique of higher-order conditioning that we observe in classical conditioning has a direct analogy in instrumental conditioning: the phenomenon of **secondary reinforcement**. In higher-order conditioning the conditioned stimulus is successively transferred from one stimulus (e.g., a bell) to another (e.g., a light), the earlier CS (the bell) serving as the unconditioned stimulus

for the new CS (the light). In secondary reinforcement the pigeon, for example, is trained to peck at an unlighted window, and each peck causes the window to be illuminated briefly at the same time that the food pellet is delivered. The lighted window, it is asserted, eventually comes to serve as a reinforcer in its own right; the original reinforcer (the food pellet) is no longer necessary. That is, the bird will now peck at the window when the reinforcement is nothing more than a brief illumination. The brief-illumination reinforcement is now secondary, in the sense that it is supposed to get its effectiveness from having previously been conditioned to a primary reinforcer, the food pellet.

pered back to the safety of the startbox. The rat was then immediately picked up and returned to its home cage. That was all there was for the training phase of the experiment.

For memory testing the same apparatus and procedure were used. The argument is that if the rat remembered his training (15 min ago, or 6 hr ago, or 12 hr ago, and so forth, depending upon the group to which he had been assigned), then he would remember to avoid entering the darkened chamber; if he *did enter* the darkened chamber, then he would be demonstrating a loss or failure of memory. The experimenters decided that any rat which refused to enter the darkened chamber after 300 sec had well demonstrated that he remembered; he was scored as having passed the memory test and removed to his home cage. (During training the average rat waited *less than 15 sec* before entering the darkened chamber.)

The accompanying figure was adapted from the experimental report and shows the results for the memory test for the thirteen groups. Over 90 percent of the group which had only 15 min between training and test passed their memory test; whereas of the animals tested 6 hr later, only about 25 percent passed. But with the passage of *more* time, *more animals passed* the memory test; at the 12-hr interval the percentage of those passed arose to 80 percent. Six hours later, however, at the 18-hr interval, again only 25 percent passed. *Every 6 hr there was a rise and fall in the group memory*

score, and the rhythmicity of this rise and fall was singularly regular. Note also that the best retention scores occur every 24 hr after training. This circadian rhythm in retention scores is in accord with other findings by other experimenters using other learning problems.

The authors admit that they have no firm suggestion as to the nature of the biological clock which could modulate such a remarkable rhythm in animal memory. They tentatively suggest that "since there also is evidence for a 24-hr cycle in acetylcholine levels of various parts of the rat brain [acetylcholine is a chemical compound which plays an important role in the transmission of nerve impulses in the brain, see discussion in Units 3 and 18], manipulation of central cholinergic activity may be a fruitful approach in understanding the fluctuations in retention found in the present study."

Some final speculative suggestions: If it should be discovered that there are indeed biological clocks which account for these fluctuations in memory, it is possible that such clocks operate in the human brain as well. It would then be fruitful to check on the hypothesis that human memory also shows rhythmicity. You might insist, perhaps, that your examinations should be scheduled to be in phase with your biological memory clock.

F. A. HOLLOWAY & R. WANSLEY. Multiphasic retention deficits at periodic intervals after passive-avoidance learning. *Science,* 1973, **180**, 208–210.

Schedules of Reinforcement

The term **schedules of reinforcement** refers to the probability with which performing the instrumental response leads to the occurrence of the reinforcement. The simplest case is a schedule providing 100 percent reinforcement; that is, each time the response is made, it is reinforced. This 100 percent reinforcement is a rather limiting and artificial state of affairs; nature is neither so generous nor so consistent. Even the most constantly hovering mother cannot possibly notice and reward each correct response occurrence in her child. By far the more common situation in nature is a schedule of **partial reinforcement**: Each time the response occurs

it *may or may not* be reinforced; that is, reinforcement is less than 100 percent.

Experimental interest in partial reinforcement was sparked by early findings that, although a habit is learned more slowly under a schedule of partial reinforcement, it is actually *more* resistant to extinction than is a habit learned under a schedule of 100 percent reinforcement (see Box 16.3, p. 383). An almost endless variety of partial-reinforcement schedules has been experimentally employed, but essentially they involve the manipulation of three main factors:

1. A reinforcement may be administered each time the individual has made a certain

BOX 16.2

SPARE THE ROD AND TRAIN THE CHILD?

W. K. Estes, a learning theorist now at Rockefeller University, launched his research career with a now-classic series of experiments carried out while he was a graduate student at the University of Minnesota. This early work—twelve experiments in all, representing his doctoral dissertation—led him to the then- (and perhaps for some, still-) startling conclusion that "a response cannot be eliminated from an organism's repertoire more rapidly with the aid of punishment than without it" and that "in fact, severe punishment may have precisely the opposite effect." Why? Because, he argued, punishment only causes the temporary *suppression* of the bad response, not its extinction; even worse, a suppressed response proved to be immune from any progress toward extinction that normally occurs during nonreinforced trials. In one of the studies, for example, Estes found that individuals who had previously been trained to press a lever for a food reward and who then received electric shock in conjunction with nonreinforced trials, did at first make fewer responses than a nonshocked control group who had learned the response in the same way. However, once shock was removed and the nonreinforced trials continued, their rate of responding *increased*, returning to preextinction levels. By the end of the experiment the "punished" and "unpunished" groups had required essentially the same number of extinction trials to be rid of the lever-pressing response. Apparently, defining that response as bad (i.e., leading to shock) for the early part of the extinction period is of no help; what matters, and equally so for the two groups, is learning that lever pressing is no longer good (i.e., no longer brings food).

R. L. Solomon, a University of Pennsylvania psychologist, took serious issue with the claim made by Estes and by others that punishment doesn't work. In fact, he objects that punishment has been given a bad name through a series of unsupported claims (he calls them "legends") which he summarizes as "the wide-spread belief that punishment is unimportant because *it does not really weaken habits;* that it pragmatically is a *poor controller* of behavior; that it is extremely *cruel* and unnecessary; and that it is a technique leading to *neurosis* and worse" (italics in original). Drawing upon a large body of data, including many of his experiments, he sets out to counter these legends. Among his conclusions are that punishment works very well when the response is a consummatory rather than an instrumental one. In other words, an electric shock *can* extinguish the response of eating or of making love, even if it may appear ineffective in eliminating instrumental responses leading to them, such as lever pressing or courtship. Also, his data indicate that severely noxious stimuli (e.g., very intense shock) do seem to eliminate some instrumental behaviors altogether. Solomon seems to present us with a choice, in using punishment as a training technique, between being content with short-lived effects on behavior or being willing to use powerful noxious stimulation.

As you will have guessed by now, the shocking research reported here has been done almost exclusively with animals. But the use of such punishment for the treatment of maladaptive behavior in people, and especially in children, is currently being recommended, and its effectiveness for certain kinds of problems is being demonstrated. However, it is not used alone; good responses are enthusiastically rewarded at the same time that bad ones are punished. (See the section on behavior therapy in Unit 25.) Estes made just this sort of recommendation in 1944 and, most recently, has emphasized that his earlier theory and results are "not to be taken too broadly as a prescription against the use of punishment for controlling behavior of children. Rather, use of punishment should always be combined with . . . reward" if more desirable behavior is to be learned.

W. K. ESTES. An experimental study of punishment. *Psychological Monographs*, 1944, **57**, No. 263.
R. L. SOLOMON. Punishment. *American Psychologist*, 1964, **19**, 239–263.
W. K. ESTES. *Learning Theory and Mental Development.* New York: Academic Press, 1970.

number of responses, no matter how much time he takes to do this: for the pigeon, a pellet for a fixed number of pecks (e.g., every tenth or twentieth); for the piece-rate worker in a factory, a specified amount of money for each batch of items completed. The payoff here is for work that is done, not for length of time put in.

2. The reinforcement may be delivered after a certain *amount of time*, for example, every ten seconds, regardless of the number of responses that may have been made in the interval. Thus, the first response made after the end of the specified time period is reinforced. Here the hourly wage earner is the appropriate

BOX 16.3

SOMETHING BETTER THAN 100 PERCENT

At Indiana University, W. O. Jenkins and M. K. Rigby provided a clear demonstration of the relative strengths of responses that were reinforced either periodically or on every occasion.

The apparatus used (somewhat like that in the photograph, but with water, rather than food, as a reward) was a modified Skinner box. Among their

experimental procedures they had two groups of thirsty rats, both of which were taught to press a lever to get a drink of water. After they learned to do this consistently, one group of animals (group I) was placed in the box for a total of 180 min (divided into half-hour sessions) and these rats were permitted to press the lever as frequently as they wished. However, they were rewarded with water only every 2 min no matter how frequently they responded, for a total of 90 rewards: a partial-reinforcement schedule. Group II rats were also in the box for 180 min (in half-hour sessions) and were rewarded *every time* they pressed the lever: a 100 percent reinforcement schedule. The average group II animals piled up 2,400 reinforcements. In terms of number of reinforcements, then, the cards were heavily stacked in favor of group II.

Immediately after this training, extinction tests were started for both groups; animals were allowed to press the lever, but no reward was *ever* given. They were tested in this way for three daily 1-hr periods. The table tells the story.

Group I, given *90 intermittent rewards*, pressed the bar 129 times during the extinction period, just slightly over 140 percent of the number of their previous reinforcements. Group II, given *2,400 continuous reinforcements* in the original training, yielded only 100 responses during the extinction period, or just slightly over 4 percent of their earlier reinforcement. The less consistently you reward, the *stronger* the habit.

Group	Reinforcement Time (min)	Average Number of Reinforcements	Reinforcement Schedule	Responses During Extinction	Extinction Responses Divided by Reinforced Responses
I	180	90	partial (every 2 min)	129	140%
II	180	2,400	100%	100	4%

W. O. JENKINS & M. K. RIGBY. Partial (periodic) versus continuous reinforcement in resistance to extinction. *Journal of Comparative and Physiological Psychology*, 1950, **43**, 30–40.
B. F. Skinner. *The Behavior of Organisms.* New York: Appleton, 1938. Photo courtesy Chas. Pfizer & Co., Inc.

analogue, and clock watching and the feeling of putting in time are understandable corollaries. Because time, not rate of responding, is what counts in this schedule, the individual frequently learns *not to respond* except immediately before the end of the waiting interval, at which point a rewarded response is imminent. In fact, what may be acquired under this reinforcement schedule is learning to estimate the intervening time interval, as well as learning to perform the required action.

3. The number of responses (or the amount of time) required for a reinforcement may be held constant throughout an experiment, or it may be varied. It may vary randomly or systematically, increasing or decreasing the number of responses (or seconds) required for a reinforcement. (The effectiveness of such a varying rate-of-reinforcement schedule in keeping a subject at work has not gone unnoticed by the owners of gambling casinos. Their one-armed bandits pay off the player on a randomly varying partial-reinforcement schedule. In this way they often keep the players working long hours, and usually at rather low pay.)

At present there is no universally accepted theory that explains the increased resistance to extinction that follows partial reinforcement. Perhaps the most widely accepted proposal is the so-called **discrimination hypothesis**: Under a 100 percent reinforcement schedule, the pigeon, for example, has learned that pecking at the window *always* results in a food reward. Only a few unrewarded trials, therefore, are sufficient to cause recognition that something has changed the rules, that the original totally reliable connection between response and reward no longer holds. When this happens, extinction occurs rapidly. On the other hand, under partial reinforcement, it should take longer for extinction to occur because there were many unreinforced trials during the training series itself. Therefore, the failure of reinforcement to occur every now and then *might* just be a normal break in the reinforcement schedule. Thus, it will take longer to make the *discrimination* between the training period and the extinction period (in which the trials are always unreinforced).

CLASSICAL VERSUS INSTRUMENTAL CONDITIONING

Some psychologists question the "versus" in considering the relation between classical and instrumental conditioning, arguing that both kinds of conditioning reflect the operation of one basic process, governed by a single set of principles. In order to support their view, they point to the similarity of the phenomena observed in *both* situations: performance increment with reinforced trials (if we consider the US as reinforcement in classical conditioning), performance decrement with nonreinforced trials (extinction), spontaneous recovery, generalization, and discrimination. Additional learning phenomena (not discussed in this text) are also manifested in both classical and instrumental conditioning, so that a strong argument can be made for the one-process view. However, despite these similarities, the very obvious differences between the two conditioning procedures have led other theorists to suggest at least *two* distinct learning processes. Among the differences is the one mentioned earlier in this unit, namely, the considerable control that the subject has over his responses in instrumental conditioning and the little control that he has in classical conditioning. The classical US forces an automatic, reflexive, and typically simple response; whereas the response in the instrumental situation is generally more complex and apparently voluntary. Because of this difference, the two-process theorists have identified one process, classical conditioning, with those reflexive responses (such as salivation) that are under the control of the autonomic nervous system (see Unit 22) and the other process, instrumental conditioning, with those more deliberate responses (such as pecking at a lighted window or pressing a bar or pulling down on a slot machine handle) that involve skeletal muscles.

The two-process proponents have recently been finding it increasingly difficult to maintain their position under the onslaught of many experiments indicating both that skeletal-type responses can show successful classical conditioning and that autonomic responses can show successful instrumental conditioning (see Box 16.4, p. 386). Also posing a serious challenge is the effectiveness of instrumental conditioning in bringing brain waves under apparent voluntary control (see Box 16.5, p. 388). These research reports indicate that, despite the substantially greater control over his environment which the subject can exercise in instrumental conditioning as compared with classical conditioning, the operation of a fundamentally similar learning process for both cases is by no means precluded. But there remains the crucial issue of the adequacy of *either* classical conditioning or instrumental conditioning in accommodating the full range of complex and adaptive learning phenomena.

TRIAL-AND-ERROR LEARNING: A HISTORICAL PERSPECTIVE

Not all psychologists have been content with the attempt to explain all learning in terms of conditioning principles. A number of alternative ways of making theoretical sense of learning data have been championed. Some of these alternatives antedated the instrumental conditioning approach and provided the historical basis for Skinner's concepts; other earlier approaches offered radically different views of the learning process. As instances of the former type, we have Thorndike's law of exercise and law of effect; and, as an instance of the latter, Tolman's cognitive theory. But before we take a close look at each of these approaches, it will be useful to look at some of their experimental machinery.

Puzzle Boxes and Mazes

At about the time Pavlov was carrying out his earliest work on classical conditioning, the American psychologist Edward Lee Thorndike, using quite a different kind of experimental approach, was formulating the principles of what came to be known as **trial-and-error learning.** Thorndike, while still working for his degree at Columbia University (having previously studied with William James at Harvard), studied the intelligence of chicks, rabbits, and cats. Confining his cats in puzzle boxes (from which they

could escape by clawing down loops of string, pushing on levers, turning buttons), Thorndike observed what the animals did and recorded the time it took them to get out of the boxes on successive trials. The significant observations he made are, first, that the animal tries many things: squeezing through the bars, clawing and biting at any loose object within the box, thrusting its paw out, and so on; second, the animal gradually eliminates the errors (responses that do not release the animal from the box) until only the successful responses remain. The animal has thus learned "by trial and error, and accidental success."

Another popular device for studying trial-and-error learning in animals has been the maze. In 1901 Small, at Clark University, published his study of the "mental processes of the rat," in which he used a rat-sized reproduction of England's Hampton Court Palace "people" maze

FIGURE 16.2 The Hampton Court Palace maze served as the actual model of one of the first maze experiments done with animals in America.

Photo from Aerofilms, Ltd.

whose hedge-lined paths have bewildered natives and tourists alike since the time of Henry VIII (see Figure 16.2). Since then, thousands of laboratory rats, hamsters, guinea pigs, mice, ants, cockroaches, cats, fish, and even college sophomores have been running, hopping, crawling, swimming, and shuffling their way through various kinds of mazes under the worried and wearied eyes of experimental psychologists.

In essence, the maze consists of a series of points, at each of which a choice must be made.

BOX 16.4

CONTROLLING THE AUTOMATIC

Working first at Yale and later at Rockefeller University, Neal Miller and his associates hit upon an ingenious way to test whether autonomic functions could be subject to instrumental conditioning. The drug curare, a deadly poison when used by South American Indians to tip their arrows, will in milder concentrations effectively only paralyze skeletal muscles, thus preventing the individual from making any voluntary muscular responses. They reasoned that, if autonomic responses could be instrumentally conditioned in animals who were curarized throughout the training procedure, then the issue of the mediating role of skeletal responses might be settled, perhaps once and for all. In a series of experiments, the Miller group was in fact able to demonstrate that such autonomic responses as heart rate, blood pressure, and intestinal contractions are susceptible to instrumental conditioning. Some rats were even trained to send different amounts of blood to the right and left ears.

In one of the experiments, Miller and A. Banuazizi successfully trained rats to control *either* their heart rate *or* the normally spontaneous contractions of their intestines by rewarding the correct response with brief electrical stimulation of the pleasure center in the brain (see p. 549). (This is one of the very few avenues for rewarding a paralyzed animal that cannot eat, drink, and so forth.) Specifically, each group of rats was trained either to (1) increase their rate of intestinal contractions, (2) decrease it, (3) increase their heart rate, or (4) decrease it. Furthermore, *both* heart rate and internal contractions were monitored for all four groups throughout the training periods. The results were dramatic. The experimenters summarize them this way:

> Intestinal contraction increased when it was rewarded, decreased when relaxation was rewarded and *remained virtually unchanged when either increased or decreased heart rate was rewarded*. Similarly, heart rate increased when a fast rate was rewarded, decreased when a slow rate was rewarded, and *remained virtually unchanged when either intestinal contraction or relaxation was rewarded* (italics are ours).

Thus, they could conclude not only that instrumental conditioning of such involuntary responses was possible without the intervention of any voluntary muscular reactions but also that the learning was highly specific to the particular response being conditioned. These results would seem to have settled the argument, but apparently not once and for all; in 1973 Miller reported difficulties in reproducing these results in his own laboratory and puzzled over the possible causes. He considers a number of factors, among them possible changes in the rearing and handling of his laboratory rats before he received them. Among the entertained—and happily rejected—hypotheses was that he and his co-workers had joined together in a "mass hallucination."

The medical implications of these findings are obvious. Do you have chronic high blood pressure? *Learn* to control it, instead of becoming dependent on medications that are less than perfectly effective and that can sometimes have unwelcome side effects. These implications are not only obvious, but they predate Miller's series of experiments. Attempts to condition involuntary responses are by no means new. Soviet psychophysiologists, for example, have worked on this problem, both with animals and with people, for decades. The Miller work, therefore, was crucial to the theoretical controversy to which it was addressed, and, in any event, it would hardly be a popular (or even possible) line of research to pursue with human subjects. Furthermore, people *think* (assuming, for the moment, that animals don't), so that eliminating their muscular activity by curare still permits voluntary thought processes to intervene in the conditioning process. But for those concerned primarily with finding therapeutic uses for instrumental conditioning procedures, such theoretical issues are properly pushed into the background; the point for such investigators is to find something that works, and works well.

B. T. Engel, a psychologist at the Gerontology Research Center in Baltimore and a long-time worker on the conditionability in humans of blood pressure and heart rate and its medical applications, forcefully asserts yet a third position:

> The question is, "of what importance is it to the science of psychology that autonomic responses can be operantly conditioned?" And my answer is, "probably none whatsoever." Whether or not autonomic responses can be operantly conditioned is an empirical question which adds nothing conceptually to our knowledge about the principles of learning. In

my opinion the great importance of operant conditioning of autonomic responses comes from what it tells us about the autonomic nervous system. It is physiology, not psychology, which is going to have to revise some of its principles. The *psychological* unconscious has in no way been affected by the research on operant autonomic conditioning, but the physiological unconscious will never, ever be the same again (italics in original).

Engel's own recent work has been concerned with such questions as how best to teach people to achieve control over their heart rate and how well such control, acquired in the laboratory, can be transferred to and retained in normal living. The latter question is of course of utmost importance if instrumental conditioning techniques are ever to become a therapeutically useful tool. The data on this are very far from complete because appropriately systematic research on the question has only recently gotten under way. The consensus at this moment—from Engel's laboratory, from Miller's, and others'—is that *some* patients do manage to maintain control over, say heart rate or blood pressure in their usual environments, perhaps for as long as a few months. But *many* do not; the instrumentally conditioned response appears to extinguish rapidly when the patient is out of hospital and away from at least occasional additional reinforcement training. One solution being worked on is the development of a miniaturized, self-administering conditioning apparatus that the patient can carry with him or at least use at home.

As you can see there is still a long way to go before we know the full promise of this application of learning theory and techniques for solving some of the health problems of mankind. One of the avenues still to be explored systematically is the apparent ability of Indian yogis voluntarily to exert enormous control over their heart rates and other autonomic functions (see Unit 21, Altered States of Consciousness).

N. E. MILLER. Learning of visceral and glandular responses. *Science*, 1969, **163**, 434–445.
N. E. MILLER & A. BANUAZIZI. Instrumental learning by curarized rats of a specific, visceral response, intestinal or cardiac. *Journal of Comparative and Physiological Psychology*, 1968, **65**, 1–7.
N. E. MILLER & B. R. DWORKIN. Visceral learning: Recent difficulties with curarized rats and significant problems for human research. In P. A. Obrist et al. (Eds.), *Contemporary Trends in Cardiovascular Psychophysiology*. Chicago: Aldine-Atherton, 1973.
B. T. ENGEL. Operant conditioning of cardiac function: A status report. *Psychophysiology*, 1972, **9**, 161–177.
M. WENGER & B. BAGCHI. Studies of autonomic functions in practitioners of yoga in India. *Behavioral Science*, 1961, **6**, 312–323.

At each such choice point the subject must discover which alley is the correct one (i.e., on the way to the goal) and which the wrong one. Then he must string together or organize these various choice-point discriminations and run them off in proper sequence. (See Box 16.6, p. 389, for the meanderings of a rat introduced to a relatively simple maze.)

It may be helpful if we diagram the characteristics of maze learning (see Figure 16.3).

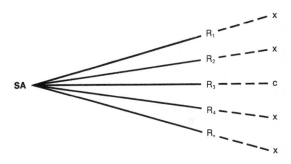

FIGURE 16.3 R_1, R_2, R_3, R_4, and so on represent an array of responses that the stimulus situation SA can elicit from the individual. The "x"s after R_1, R_2, and R_4 represent incorrect responses, and the "c" after R_3 indicates that it is the correct response. In the case of behavior in a maze, at a choice point the "c" response is of course making the correct turn; whereas the "x"s include making the wrong turn, running back into the alley, scratching in perplexity, and so forth.

This scheme is sufficiently general to apply to all forms of trial-and-error learning in which one of several possible responses is actually adaptive (the goal box is reached) or is selected by the experimenter as correct (a food pellet is delivered only if the lever is pressed at the appearance of a certain stimulus). A comparison of how Thorndike and Tolman dealt with the data of trial-and-error learning should help us to clarify two things. First, it will permit us to see clearly the genesis of many of the concepts popular in current learning theory. Second, it will bring into clear relief the significant differences between the now-traditional reinforcement concepts (whether cast in the language of Thorndike, Skinner, or common sense) and the cognitive approach, an approach that challenges many of the common beliefs so long taught about the learning process.

BOX 16.5

CONTROLLING YOUR BRAIN WAVES

Recently, there has been quite a furor in the public press concerning biofeedback training of brain waves. The phenomenon is not new, even if the label and commercial exploitation are. Combining methods of instrumental conditioning and electrophysiology, psychologist Joe Kamiya in 1958, while at the University of Chicago, first demonstrated this phenomenon, training subjects to *identify* the occurrence of alpha rhythms in their own electroencephalograms (EEGs or brain waves).

The alpha rhythm is an irregularly recurring train of electrical oscillations (8 to 12 hz) generated by the human brain and detectable through the scalp by surface electrodes. The trains vary in duration from a fraction of a second to several seconds, usually becoming more persistent when the eyes are closed and the subject is allowed to relax. Without special training, we are not aware of any spontaneous fluctuations in consciousness that may be related to the rapid, irregular recurrences of alpha (which occur many times per minute). (EEGs are more fully discussed on p. 65.)

The training procedure Kamiya used in his Chicago experiments was to have his subject (who had been informed about the nature of alpha rhythm) make a guess, whenever a bell sounded, whether he was at the time in an "A state" (presence of the alpha rhythm) or a "B state" (absence of alpha). The bell was sounded two to six times per minute. Half the time it was sounded when the subject was generating alpha rhythms and half the time when he was not. The subject was required to keep his eyes closed throughout the training trials.

After each guess he was told whether or not he had guessed correctly.

In two to ten sessions of sixty trials each, many (but not all) subjects began to choose correctly which of the two states they were in significantly more often than sheer guessing would have achieved. They could not easily find words to describe how they discerned the two states. Many subjects reported, however, that the presence of any sort of visual image was associated with the B state.

In later experiments conducted at the University of California Medical Center in San Francisco, Kamiya found that subjects could be taught to *control* the states associated with alpha rhythms. For his experiments he devised an electronic system that would deliver a steady audible tone whenever an alpha train was detected by the electronic system (via electrodes attached to the subject's scalp) and that would stop the tone immediately upon the disappearance of the alpha. In short, the subject received auditory information signaling the state of his EEG. The subject was encouraged to try to discover ways to increase (or decrease) the proportion of time that the tone would be present. Most subjects achieved clear differences in performance between trials for increasing the tone and trials for decreasing the tone. In one experiment, fifteen minutes of such training proved sufficient for some subjects to achieve control over their alpha waves.

Verbal reports on effective methods for *decreasing* the duration of the tone (and therefore the alpha rhythm) usually involved the use of visual imagery (e.g., seeing faces or familiar objects). Reports on how to *increase* the duration of the tone were more diffuse, vague, and ethereal. Among the subjects' frequent expressions for this state were "calmness," "singleness of attention," "relaxation," "submitting to the tone," and "serenity." Some

The Laws of Exercise and Effect

The laws of exercise and effect constitute Thorndike's major explanation of how an animal learns to retain the correct response and to eliminate all others. Let us first consider the **law of exercise** (again, see Figure 16.3). In its simplest formulation it states that, when differences in *frequency* and in *recency* between the correct response (R_3) and all other Rs are large enough, R_3 will become the response that will most probably be elicited by the stimulus situation at any future time.

Two features characterize the usual trial-and-error learning situation: (1) It is so set up

spoke of feelings of "letting go" and sensual warmth as accompaniments of the presence of alpha. Such reports bear a remarkable similarity to those given by experienced practitioners of meditation—Zen and yoga, for example—and, indeed, Kamiya found that subjects who had had long practice in meditation were especially proficient in increasing the duration of the alpha train.

Kamiya feels that the study and control of brain states offers great promise in unraveling some basic problems concerning the nature of consciousness. He suggests that we might someday detect neuroses through examination of brain waves just as we today detect tuberculosis by examination of x-rays. He further speculates that if we can define a brain state associated with tranquillity, perhaps we can reproduce this state with appropriate behavioral training rather than having to resort to chemical tranquilizers. Although we are a long way from such specific definitions of brain states and their behavioral control, the possibility of instrumentally training the brain is a large step forward.

These experiments do suggest that some of the more elusive psychological properties of human life—those having to do with subjective experience—may be approachable with new techniques. Perhaps expanding consciousness will then come to be a relatively simple learning process. If it does, for better or for worse, the aura of mysticism currently associated with the phrase will inevitably disappear. For now, however, we should keep an open mind and at the same time consider alternative views of this phenomenon (see Unit 21).

J. STOYVA & J. KAMIYA. Electrophysiological studies of dreaming as the prototype of a new strategy in the study of consciousness. *Psychological Review*, 1968, **75**, 192–205.
D. P. NOWLIS & J. KAMIYA. The control of EEG alpha rhythms through auditory feedback and associated mental activity. *Psychophysiology*, 1970, **6**, 476–484.

BOX 16.6

WHICH WAY TO GO?

The maze presents a problem that requires for its solution the selection of the most direct of many possible routes to a goal. The maze usually has walled alleys; when it does, it is called an *alley maze*. The particular correct (shortest) sequence of turnings and correct alleys varies from maze to maze. It has been estimated that more than 150 different maze patterns have been used to study learning in animals. In almost all mazes it is possible for visual, auditory, tactile, olfactory, and other stimuli emanating from the alleys, from the environment outside the maze, or from the choice point (where two alleys branch) to serve as cues that enable the individual to differentiate the correct pathway from the blind alley. The progression of a single rat as he at first blunders his way from the start

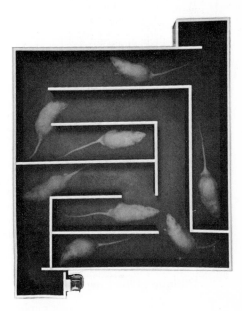

(top) to the goal box (bottom) is shown in this multiple-exposure photograph. Once he has thoroughly learned the maze, he runs through it with practically no hesitation at choice points, and at a gallop.

C. H. HONZIK. The sensory basis of maze learning in rats. *Comparative Psychology Monographs*, 1936, **13**, No. 64. Photo Albert Fenn, Time-Life Books, *The Mind*, © 1964, Time Inc.

that R_3 *must* occur at least once in every trial, since the trial continues until R_3 is performed (remember, the trial is terminated only when the rat reaches the goal box). (2) R_3 will always be the most recently performed response at the start of any new trial, since it is always the last response of the previous trial. As a direct consequence of these two features, over a large series of trials R_3 will have necessarily occurred more frequently and more recently than any other response. It follows that, if the law of exercise is valid, R_3 inevitably becomes the response most likely to be elicited by the stimulus situation. In this way we can account for the retention in behavior of the correct response and the elimination of all the others.

Thorndike, however, believed that the law of exercise alone was not enough to account for learning. He pointed out that another important reason why R_3 is retained and the other responses are eliminated is that R_3 is usually directly followed by some good effect (the hungry rat finds food in the goal box); whereas the other responses are usually followed by a bad effect (the rat remains hungry because the response has not led him to food). He called this relationship between the nature of the effect and the retention or elimination of the preceding responses the **law of effect**, a relationship, as we have seen, that Skinner and others now call *reinforcement*. The apparent simplicity of these laws, their apparent ability to summarize many experimental results, and their dependence upon observable behavior *only*, without recourse to "complex mental processes," make them very appealing to many experimental psychologists. As a result, these laws and their implications have permeated much of our thinking about learning and have influenced many of the educational practices in our schools. It is highly probable that the layman, if asked how his dog, his son, or his neighbor learns, would appeal to some sort of law of exercise (he might use the word "practice") and some sort of law of effect (he might use the phrase "reward and punishment").

Critique of the Law of Exercise

In 1932, Edward C. Tolman published *Purposive Behavior in Animals and Men*, a book that was destined to influence learning theory greatly. The publication of this book started experimental and theoretical questioning of the laws of exercise and effect. Subsequent decades of experimental work have produced considerable heat and some light. The most that can be done here, in the context of this historical excursion,

is to present a very few of the basic studies and point out their implications.

There are many experiments which show that the subject may perform *the wrong act as frequently as the correct act* yet finally learn the correct one. Tolman's book is replete with experimental illustrations of this fact (see Box 16.7 for one such experiment). The experimental evidence from both animals and people seems to show clearly that the sheer frequency or recency of performing the correct act in a trial-and-error situation cannot by itself account for the retention of that act. Yet other experiments, as well as everyday observations, seem to indicate that many trials and repetitions of the correct response are indeed required before learning takes place.

Tolman's answer to this paradox is phrased in *cognitive* terms: During trial-and-error learning, the individual is given an opportunity to *discover* which response leads to which consequence. The more opportunities he has for this, the quicker and more firm his learning will be. But this process of discovery holds for the wrong acts as well as for the correct acts. He must learn, in other words, that R_1 leads to x as well as that R_3 leads to c. And in order to learn *both* these sets of relationships, he needs many trials. Thus, Tolman reasons, it is not differential frequency or recency of R_3 over R_1 that is the deciding factor but the total frequency of $R_1 \rightarrow x$, $R_2 \rightarrow x$, $R_3 \rightarrow c$, $R_4 \rightarrow x$, and so on that is important. In the **latent-learning** experiment described in Box 16.7 the rat is thus given many opportunities to learn that this alley leads to a dead end and that alley leads on to other alleys, and so forth. Then, when he finds food in the food box, he will choose R_3 in preference to the other responses because he wants the food and he knows that R_3 leads to the food, not because R_3 has been retained or learned while all the other responses have been eliminated. The learning process becomes one of learning the consequences of *every* response. In essence, then, trial-and-error learning for Tolman is discovery, discovery of the meaning of all the observed cues, of what leads to what. Frequent experience with the entire situation increases the probability that the necessary discovery will be made. It is essential to see clearly

BOX 16.7

HIDDEN LEARNING IN THE RAT

In 1929, H. C. Blodgett of the University of California reported his now-famous experiment on latent learning in the rat.

Using the six-unit alley maze shown in Box 16.6, he ran three groups of hungry rats, each animal being given one trial per day. Group I animals (control) *always* found food in the goal box and were allowed to eat there for 3 min, after which they were removed to another cage for the remainder of their normal meal. Group II animals did not find food in the box for the first *six* days. Arriving there, they were confined for 2 min, removed to another cage, and *1 hr later* given their daily rations. From the seventh day on, these animals *did* find food in the box and thenceforth were run under the same conditions as the control group. Group III ran the maze for the first *two* days without food and from the third day on found food.

During the no-food periods group II and III animals showed no signs of learning; that is, they chose the wrong alley about as frequently as the correct alley (see figure). The control group did show a decrease in errors. But on the first day *after* food was found, groups II and III showed tremendous improvement, cutting their error scores by about 50 percent; and on the second day, they had caught up with the control group. Despite the fact that during the first period they had not been practicing the correct responses more than the wrong responses, they had been learning something about the maze, as is indicated by their performance *immediately after the introduction of food.* The evidence of their learning was latent or hidden until it had become worthwhile to show it.

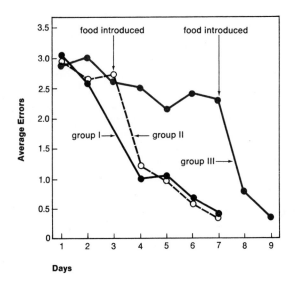

H. C. BLODGETT. The effect of the introduction of reward upon the maze performance of rats. *University of California Publications in Psychology*, 1929, 4, 113–134.

and to appreciate fully the difference between Tolman's and Thorndike's treatments of the role of exercise in order to understand one of the fundamental differences between two major historical *and contemporary* general approaches to an understanding of learning (the reinforcement and the cognitive theories).

Learning and Performance

Tolman also subjected the law of effect and its various reformulations to critical examination. He freely admits that rewards and punishments (or reinforcements) *are* important in adaptive behavior, but not at the point in the learning process where the theories of Thorndike and Skinner assume them to be important. Tolman suggests that we must distinguish between learning and performance. We have already seen in the latent-learning experiment (Box 16.7) that an animal may have learned something but may not reveal it in performance until it becomes worthwhile to do so. We saw there an experimental demonstration that learning and performance are not the same.

In addition to suggesting that distinction, Tolman proposes that reward and punishment serve different *functions* for learning and for performance. For learning, the function of reward and punishment is to enable the individual to discover which acts lead to reward and which to punishment (what leads to what). The fact that one response is rewarded and another punished does not automatically stamp in one response or eliminate the other. In other words, according to this view, rewards, reinforcements, and the like—positive or negative—only convey information; they do not directly affect the probability that the particular response will be performed by the individual on some future occasion.

　　In performance, as distinguished from learning, the function of reward and punishment is to determine which response will be made and with what efficiency and speed. With a better reward or with a higher degree of motivation, the individual will perform what he has previously learned with more efficiency or speed. Therefore, our everyday observation that with better rewards there is better learning really signifies that better rewards lead to better performance. In many of our studies we measure performance, not learning. The laws that relate degree of rewards and motives to learning are really, according to Tolman and his followers, laws of performance.

INSTRUMENTAL LEARNING: A SUMMING UP

Our accounts of instrumental conditioning and trial-and-error learning have emphasized animal learning in specially devised, confining surroundings: Pavlov's dog in the harness, Thorndike's cat in the puzzle cage, Skinner's pigeon in the lever box, Tolman's rat in the maze. This emphasis reflects the desire of learning experimenters to study learning processes in the laboratory under conditions of rigorous control and experimental manipulation. And it reflects the hope of learning theorists that the principles of learning discovered in these simple laboratory conditions will prove to be general principles that can account for *all* learning, human as well as animal, complex as well as simple, higher order as well as lower order. You can see in other units on such higher-order learning—verbal learning and memory as well as creative problem solving—how little this hope is justified. We have already seen that, even in their attempts to deal with laboratory-controlled and simple forms of learning, the learning theoreticians are still confronted with unsolved basic problems. We cannot escape the verdict that learning theory is still very much in the making.

SUMMARY

1. In instrumental conditioning the conditioned response typically is adaptive, having a direct effect on the individual's environment, and invokes a behavior that is normally under his voluntary control. In contrast, classically conditioned responses characteristically involve normally involuntary responses and their occurrence does not affect what next happens to the individual. However, recent data indicate the possibility that both voluntary and involuntary responses are conditionable by either technique.

2. There are distinct parallels between many of the phenomena of instrumental and classical conditioning; reinforcement, generalization, discrimination, and extinction are examples.

3. Positive reinforcement occurs when the individual's response leads to the presentation of something good and increases the future frequency of that response. Reward training procedures use positive reinforcers.

4. Negative reinforcement occurs when the individual's response leads to the removal of something bad and also increases the future frequency of that response. Both escape training and avoidance training use negative reinforcers.

5. An initially neutral event, having been previously reinforced, can become an effective reinforcer in its own right (secondary reinforcement).

6. Variations in the timing of reinforcements delivered in the course of instrumental conditioning (schedules of reinforcement) have an important influence on rates of both learning and extinction. Partial reinforcement, for example, leads to behavior that is considerably more resistant to extinction than behavior resulting from 100 percent reinforcement.

7. Relatively complex sequences of multiple responses can be learned by trying out various possible responses until the correct ones (the ones that work) are discovered. Mazes and puzzles boxes are among the devices used to study this trial-and-error form of learning in animals.

8. The law of exercise asserts that responses demonstrated most frequently and most recently in the past in a given situation tend to become the most likely responses in that situation. The law of effect—essentially the reinforcement view—asserts that responses followed by good effects become more frequent and that those followed by bad effects become less frequent.

9. An alternate position to both of these laws regards any behavior as providing an opportunity for the individual to discover what works and what leads to what in a given situation, with no automatic stamping in of responses as a result of either repetition or reward. According to this view, one learns by experience, although this learning may not show up in performance (latent learning) until it is useful (e.g., when the situation is changed to offer a reward for carrying out the behavior).

10. Neither instrumental nor classical conditioning, alone or taken together, can at this time give an adequate account of a great deal of more complex adaptive behavior. So far, their basic principles are insufficiently general to apply to all learned behavior, and other theoretical approaches remain clearly necessary.

GLOSSARY

avoidance training The instrumental conditioning situation in which a signal is given preceding the onset of a noxious stimulus. If the specified response is made before the noxious stimulus is presented, that stimulation is avoided. In the early stages of training, negative reinforcement comes from termination of noxious stimulation, as in escape training. In later stages the response is presumably maintained by the negative reinforcement of fear reduction.

discrimination hypothesis The hypothesis that, to the extent that extinction of an instrumentally conditioned response is slower, it is because of more difficulty in recognizing when the conditioning procedure has ceased. Partial and irregular reinforcement thus delays extinction.

escape training The instrumental conditioning situation in which a response is strengthened through the negative reinforcement resulting from termination of an aversive stimulus.

instrumental conditioning (operant conditioning) A procedure in which a given response is followed by a reinforcing stimulus. Conditioning is said to have occurred if that response is in some way strengthened in subsequent trials. (Operant conditioning, an essentially synonymous term, is preferred by those working within Skinner's view of learning.)

instrumental learning A term that can include instrumental conditioning and trial-and-error learning and that refers, generally, to the acquisition of responses that in some way represent *adaptive* changes in behavior.

latent learning Learning that does not display itself in performance until some later time at which such performance is adaptive in a new situation.

law of effect This law in its simplest form states that, when one response is followed by some good effect and other responses are followed by bad effects, the former will become the most probable response that the stimulus situation will elicit at any future time. This law has been proposed to hold for all trial-and-error learning.

law of exercise This law in its simplest form states that, when differences in frequency and recency between one response and all others become large enough, the former will become the most probable response that the stimulus situation will elicit at any future time. This law has been proposed to hold for all trial-and-error learning.

negative reinforcement The withdrawing of a noxious stimulus after the subject has made the appropriate response.

operant conditioning (see **instrumental conditioning**)

partial reinforcement A situation in which the reinforcing stimulus does not always follow the occurrence of the response being conditioned.

positive reinforcement The presentation of a rewarding stimulus after the subject has made the appropriate response.

punishment training The instrumental conditioning situation in which a response is weakened through application of a noxious stimulus.

reinforcement In instrumental conditioning, the procedure of presenting a reinforcing stimulus when the subject has made the response designated as appropriate by the experimenter. (See **positive reinforcement** and **negative reinforcement**.)

reward training The instrumental conditioning situation in which a response is strengthened through positive reinforcement.

schedule of reinforcement The plan or schedule determining when and how often desired responses are reinforced in instrumental conditioning.

secondary reinforcement Analogous to the phenomenon of higher-order conditioning in classical conditioning. The presentation of an initially nonreinforcing stimulus that has acquired reward value through prior instrumental conditioning as the effective reinforcing stimulus in training a new instrumental response.

transituational reinforcer An event is considered a true reinforcer only if it increases the strength of the response that precedes it in many *different* situations.

trial-and-error learning Discovering and consistently performing the correct response in a situation that permits a number of different responses. The response can be verified as being correct only by actual trial. Trial-and-error learning is typically slower than instrumental conditioning, the single-response form of learning to which it is closely related.

verbal learning and human memory

DO YOU KNOW...

- why it is easier to learn and remember material that reminds us of many other things?

- whether where an item is located in a list that we are trying to memorize has any effect on how easily it is learned?

- how you can sometimes remember a lot of material better by not remembering the material in the order in which it was originally learned?

- that psychologists can distinguish at least three quite different kinds of memory?

- that old memories, unlike old soldiers, do not fade away and that a process totally different from "fading" probably accounts for forgetting?

- that it is often easier to remember something if you go back to the place where you had the original experience?

- under what circumstances more practice in learning leads to worse remembering of the material?

  that although very painful experiences can indeed be highly memorable, they sometimes are abruptly and totally forgotten?

CONTENTS

In our discussions of classical and instrumental conditioning (Units 15 and 16) we are primarily concerned with the acquisition of habits: learned behavior patterns that have some degree of permanence. The quality of permanence is quite essential to our definition of a habit. Even in the nontechnical sense, few of us would want to label as habit a bit of behavior that appears only once under certain conditions and never reappears when those same conditions are again present. It is true that in most conditioning experiments the permanency of the habit is not adequately tested. A hungry pigeon learns in a relatively short period of time to peck a disk in order to obtain food, and we assume that if it is removed from its box and returned in an hour, a day, a week, or a month, it will once again respond with disk pecking if hungry. Indeed, in most cases, when this assumption is put to the test, the pigeon does respond as expected. If asked to name the process that accounts for the disk-pecking habit staying with the pigeon over time, you most probably would say "remembering" or "memory." And, of course, the fact that such habits are not always perfectly retained and often even appear to be completely lost is what we label "forgetting."

Despite the fact that habit and memory are so intimately related, our discussion of conditioning and learning makes little mention of the memory process because the learning psychologist primarily stresses the factors that influence the acquisition, or learning, of habits. Subjects such as rats, pigeons, and dogs are chosen for study of acquisition because their use often permits easier and greater control of the conditions affecting original learning than is possible with human subjects. Learning situations such as the ones typical in classical and instrumental conditioning studies are chosen because they also permit this greater ease of experimental control. However, psychologists who wish to focus on the question of the temporal *persistence* of habits tend to choose other experimental subjects and other procedures that are more convenient for this purpose.

VERBAL LEARNING

Psychologists working on memory prefer people as subjects, and *verbal learning* as their experimental situations. Of course, studies of memory need not deal only with verbal material and with human subjects. Studies of memory, particularly of the physiological basis of memory, in lower animals represent an increasingly active research area (see Unit 18).

A Historical Note

The first extensive experimental investigations of verbal learning and memory were performed toward the end of the nineteenth century by the German psychologist Hermann Ebbinghaus, who undertook an investigation of his own memory processes (Ebbinghaus, 1964; originally published 1885). He systematically explored his own learning and remembering of poems and other verbal material in a lengthy series of experiments. He realized, however, that words, especially in connected sentences, have an undesirable feature as experimental materials: Some words are more familiar to us than others are and may therefore be more easily learned. Even more important, each word is more closely related in meaning to certain words than it is to others. For both reasons it would be much easier to learn, say, the sequence *dog-cat-rat-cheese* than it would be to learn *eft-alb-wen-zealot*, even though each sequence contains the same number of words and letters. Now, such differences among words as their relative familiarity and their degree of interrelatedness deserve to be, and are, studied in their own right. But when trying to discover the effect of some *other* experimental variable upon rate of learning and subsequent level of remembering (e.g., the amount of time spent studying the materials), it is useful for all elements of the learning material to be *equally* familiar and *equally* associated with one another. In order to achieve this, Ebbinghaus invented the **nonsense syllable**. Such syllables are commonly constructed by putting together a sequence of consonant-vowel-consonant (CVCs, as they are often called), for example, *tob, duf, yad*. These syllables are not completely nonsensical, and associations do

exist among them, but they are much more homogeneous than a collection of meaningful words and are therefore widely used in verbal learning research.

Experimental Methods

In addition to the invention of the nonsense syllables, Ebbinghaus developed or laid the foundations for many of the experimental methods still used for the laboratory study of verbal learning and memory. Some of these, together with newer methods, have become standard laboratory tools and should be noted briefly.

In **serial learning**, the subject is given a series of words or CVCs—say, a dozen—one at a time. After the complete list has been presented, the experimenter starts a second presentation. This time, however, as the syllables are given, the subject attempts to recall the item next on the list before it appears. The list is presented over and over again until the subject can correctly *anticipate* each succeeding item. It is easy to think of each word in the serial-learning list as serving at the same time as a *response* to the preceding word and as a *stimulus* evoking recall of the following word.

These roles are separated in **paired-associate learning.** Here the subject is presented with a series of *pairs* of items, for example, *xul-bef* and *nec-deg*. In subsequent trials he is given only the first word of the pair (the stimulus), and he attempts to produce the second word (the response).

The **free recall** method involves a single list of items, but the order of their presentation is usually varied from trial to trial. The responses of the subject (the items he can remember) are collected after each complete presentation of the list, and unlike the other methods, no fixed order of recall of the items is then demanded of him.

Measures of Learning and Retention

Obviously each of these methods provides some evidence about the amount of learning that has taken place at the time of each trial. When we graph the results of such an investigation, as in

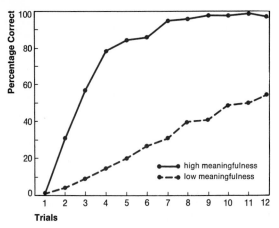

FIGURE 17.1 Learning curves showing improvement, over trials, in the number of correct anticipations on a paired-associate task. The average percentage correct for the group at each trial is shown. Items of high meaningfulness were learned faster than items of low meaningfulness.

V. J. Cieutat et al., 1958.

Figure 17.1, we have a **learning curve** that typically shows an increase in correct responses on successive trials.

More information is available, however, than "number correct" in the results of a verbal-learning experiment. The answers to many interesting questions depend upon noticing *which* items are recalled on each trial rather than simply *how many*.

So far we have given examples that involve the measurement of **recall** only. But it is sometimes useful to set up a procedure that measures **recognition** instead. In such situations, the subject is not required to *produce* the response word; rather, he is given a group of words that includes the correct one, which he must *identify*.

Of necessity, either measure (recall or recognition) always reflects both *acquisition* and *retention*, that is, the amount originally learned and the extent to which it has been remembered up to the time of measurement. When we are primarily interested in acquisition, we seek to minimize the role of retention by testing immediately after the learning trial; when we are primarily interested in retention, we try to start from a standard level of acquisition and vary the interval between the learning trial and the test.

Factors Affecting Acquisition

Many characteristics of the material to be learned and the ways in which it is presented have effects upon the speed of learning. It is unnecessary to convince the reader that a greater amount of material (e.g., a longer list of words) will take longer to learn than a smaller amount will and that many repetitions of a list will lead to better performance than only a few will. However, there are other factors affecting acquisition (discussed in the following paragraphs) that may be less obvious.

1. *Meaningfulness.* This factor is most simply measured by the item's **association value**, i.e., the number of associations formed by a subject to a particular item. For example, the three-letter word *boy* presumably has more associations and is thus more meaningful than the three-letter nonsense syllable *rel*. In general, the more meaningful the words in a list, the more readily they are learned (see Box 17.1).

2. *Imagery.* Some words evoke richer mental **imagery** than others do, and subjects will more easily learn lists composed of such vivid words (Paivio, Yaille, & Madigan, 1968). Examples of high-imagery words are *mother, water,* and *tree;* low-imagery words include *equity, instance,* and *democracy.*

3. *Intralist relation.* The relation of an item in a list to the other items in the list can be a powerful factor affecting acquisition. For example, if a serial-learning list is presented over and over again, the items toward the *beginning* and the *end* of the list are learned most readily. The items in the middle are learned more slowly; the most difficult items are those just after the middle. This phenomenon is called the **serial-position effect** (see graphs in Box 17.1).

4. *Transfer effects.* What we have learned in the past affects new learning. Whether these **transfer** effects are positive (aid the new learning) or negative (interfere with the new learning) depends upon several factors, including the similarity of the old material to the new material and how well the old material was initially learned. For example, it will be easier to learn Spanish as a second lan-

BOX 17.1

ACQUIRING SENSE VERSUS NONSENSE

The following description is taken from reports by L. Postman and Rau of the University of California of a series of experiments in verbal learning.

In one experiment ninety students learned a twelve-item list of nonsense syllables; another ninety students learned a twelve-item list of common words. The standard *memory drum* (see photograph)

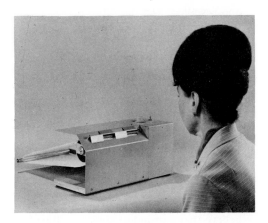

and the anticipation method of learning were used. The items were successively exposed in the window of the drum for two seconds each. Beginning with the second time around, the subject was required to call out the *next* item on the list before it appeared in the window. The lists were repeated until the subject could anticipate every item during a given run.

For the nonsense syllables the fastest learner required thirteen runs of the list; the slowest learner, ninety-three runs. In order to derive a group curve, the experimenters calculated the *average* number of trials required to achieve one correct anticipation, then the average to achieve two correct anticipations, and so on. From these averages a learning curve was plotted, as shown in Chart A. By this method every subject is included in every point on the curve. Note that the curve for the meaningful material has a steeper slope, i.e., rises faster.

In order to analyze the *serial-position effect* (p. 400), the average number of failures in anticipations was determined for each item separately and plotted as shown in Chart B. The middle items of the nonsense list (items 6, 7, 8) were much more difficult

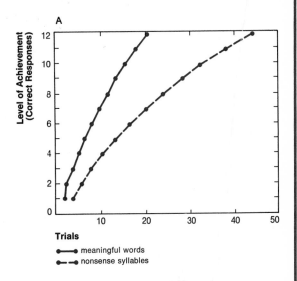

A

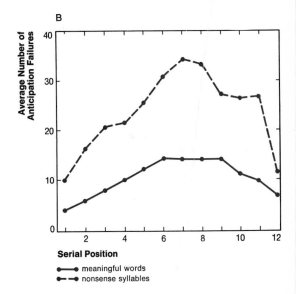

B

to learn than were the end items (items 1, 12). The absolute difference between the middle items and the end items was not so great for the meaningful words as for the nonsense items, but the relative difference was about the same. In each case about three times as many failures in anticipation were made for the middle items as for the end items.

L. POSTMAN & L. RAU. Retention as a function of the method of measurement. *University of California Publications in Psychology*, 1957, **8**(3). Figures adapted by permission. Photo courtesy Lafayette Instrument Company.

guage if your mother tongue is Italian (also a Romance language) than it will be if you are a native-born German. However, the ease or difficulty of acquiring a second language depends not only on which languages are involved but also on the learner's age and, hence, amount of experience with the first language.

Although this list of factors is by no means exhaustive, it is sufficiently representative to give you an idea of the problems involved in studying verbal acquisition. However, our interest is not only in acquisition but also in retention of verbal material. Indeed, when we consider retention we think of memory not only for verbal material but for visual images, complex sounds, and even smells and touches. We must now consider more general problems of memory.

ARE THERE DIFFERENT KINDS OF MEMORY?

In our examination of classical conditioning and instrumental learning we note large differences among the varieties of learning situations psychologists study. Whether these differences represent the same or separate learning processes constitutes a still-unresolved theoretical dispute (see Unit 16, p. 384). Similarly, there seem to be differences among the kinds of memory situations psychologists study, and again whether these differences reflect the same or separate memory processes is a matter of active theoretical contention.

Consider the diverse kinds of memories you experience daily. You study for a final examination (sensibly for an extended period, but perhaps only on the night before the examination) and then try to recall the material in writing your essay. You look up a new telephone number, close the phone book, and dial the number. Look at an object (say, your hand held in front of your eyes), rapidly close your eyes, and you will sense a briefly lingering afterimage of that object. Clearly, all these events have in common the fact that a time interval exists between the presentation of the stimulus and the act of remembering. In the case of the

final examination the time gap is relatively long (at least the length of the night before the examination). In the case of the telephone number the time gap between reading the number and recalling it while dialing is much smaller. With the afterimage the gap is smaller still; the time between the stimulus (the seen object) and the memory (the fleeting afterimage) is measured in terms of little more than the blink of an eye. Nevertheless, all three situations do involve some elapsed time between stimulus and response, and therefore it is possible to discuss them together. But what is to be gained by encompassing them all under the heading "memory"? Why not express the difference between recalling material for the final examination and dialing the phone number as simply a difference between recalling material that is fairly completely learned (in the first case) and material incompletely learned (in the second)? Why not discuss afterimages in terms of perceptual processes, as is conventionally done (see Unit 11, p. 251). To begin with, many psychologists believe that there is a close interrelation among perception, learning, and memory. They further believe that our understanding will be facilitated not only by conceptualizing all the foregoing phenomena as memory but by further distinguishing different *kinds* of memory. The evidence they have amassed to support these distinctions is impressive (see, e.g., Kintsch, 1970; Norman, 1970).

Information Processing

In general, such contemporary memory theorists tend to treat the stimulus as information that is operated upon, or processed, in different ways at different memory stages within the organism. In the course of this **information processing**, they assume that changes take place in the nature of the stimulus information. When stimulus information is changed, it is said to have been coded. The kind of **coding** that occurs depends upon the kind of memory stage in which the processing occurs.

Although not all those who postulate different memory stages will use the same terminology or even designate the same number of stages, there seems to be some agreement on at

BOX 17.2

YOU SEE MORE THAN YOU KNOW

The idea of a separate sensory-memory store gains support from the work of George Sperling, some of it done at the Bell Telephone laboratories. In these investigations Sperling made use of a device called the **tachistoscope**, which presents a visual stimulus to the subject for very brief and precise periods of time; presentations can be controlled to the nearest 1/1,000 of a second. When presenting symbols (letters or digits) at times ranging from 15/1,000 to 500/1,000 of a second, Sperling noted that his subjects could report only four or five correctly, whether there were only a small or a much larger number of symbols in a given display. (In itself, this was not a startling finding because it had been known for some time that visual information presented for very brief periods of time could not be completely recalled.) In order to demonstrate that the subject was limited in what he could *report*, not in what he *saw*, an ingenious procedure (called the *partial-report technique*) was devised. Subjects were presented with twelve symbols arranged in three rows of four symbols each. Each stimulus presentation was 50/1,000 of a second and was followed immediately by one of three different tones. The subjects were instructed to report the first row if they heard one tone, the second row if they heard a second tone, and the third row if they heard the third tone.

Using this technique, subjects were able to report correctly an average of 76 percent of the letters called for in *any* row. If they could achieve the same percentage in reporting on the *total* display of twelve symbols, then an average score of about nine correct would be expected; but, as you will remember, only four or five symbols had been correctly reported independent of the size of the display.

Why this discrepancy? Sperling suggests that the subject experiences a visual image of the *full* display and that this image serves as a sensory-memory store. But this image rapidly fades and if the subject picks a row from this image and reports it, by the time he returns for the next row, the image is gone. He can report the first row he picks (or is picked for him by the tone signal) quite well, but very little after that. The fact that he actually saw more than he can report is clear because, as we noted, he does well if you ask him to report the second or third row instead of the first, even though the asking for a particular row is done *after* the display has been presented. Therefore, Sperling argues, the subject must have some access to an image of the total display from which he reads off the specified row. In demonstrating the rapid decay of this image, it was found that a delay of only 1 second in the row-specifying tone reduced the accuracy of partial report from 76 to 36 percent.

G. SPERLING. A model for visual memory tasks. In R. E. Haber (Ed.), *Information-processing Approaches to Visual Perception*. New York: Holt, Rinehart & Winston, 1969.

least three types of memory: **sensory memory**, **short-term memory**, and **long-term memory** (Lindsey & Norman, 1972). Although the characteristics of each of these stages are still a long way from being precisely defined, careful comparisons can be made with respect to how long each can operate, the supposed limitations in the amount of information that each can handle, and the way information is coded in each.

SENSORY MEMORY

Taking the afterimage as our example of sensory memory, it is obvious that this memory system, or memory store, is based upon the concept of a direct sensory representation of the physical energy of the external stimulus. Therefore, the assumed characteristics of this kind of memory are that it (1) is very brief (lasting for only a fraction of a second), (2) has the capacity to deal with as much of the physical stimulus energy as the receptor is anatomically and physiologically able to handle, and (3) encodes information in a fairly direct fashion (e.g., the image on the retina corresponds fairly closely to the object stimulating that image). Neisser (1967) has called the kind of brief persistent visual memory of which we have been speaking the *icon*, a term that means an image or representation. (Box 17.2, presents an example of the kind of evidence cited to support the need for the concept of sensory memory that may aid you in understanding why this kind of memory system was suggested).

Consideration of the sensory equipment we possess and the different kinds of physical stimuli we can process suggests one difficulty with the general idea of sensory memory as a direct representation. Whereas visual stimuli may fit the notion well enough (despite the fact that retinal images are *two*-dimensional representations of a *three*-dimensional world), auditory stimuli do not fit at all well. Auditory information customarily comes into the ear in a much more temporally spaced fashion than visual information comes into the eye, but the anatomy and physiology of the ear do not as easily permit as direct a relation between the external stimulus and the response of the receptor. The difference may become clearer if you consider the functioning of the eye and ear (described in Unit 14). The retina provides a convenient surface for a fairly direct spatial representation of objects perceived visually. There is no structure in the ear that provides for so direct a representation of sound. The hair cells on the membranes of the cochlea give us information about sound frequency, intensity, and duration in a more indirect fashion. What, then, is the auditory icon? It is clearly different from the visual one, and this difference is recognized, even to the extent of having a different name. Neisser refers to auditory sensory memory as *echoic* memory.

SHORT-TERM MEMORY

Dialing a phone number just after you have looked it up in the phone book is an instance of a time interval falling within short-term memory. It is certainly longer than sensory memory, but it appears to store material for only a minute or even less. Peterson and Peterson (1959) provide the basis for this estimate. They presented subjects with three-consonant strings (such as j-q-b) and asked for recall after periods of three, six, nine, twelve, fifteen, or eighteen seconds. During the interval the experimenters

prevented the subject from silently rehearsing the items by keeping him busy with the task of counting backward by threes. As can be seen in Figure 17.2, there was apparently some forget-

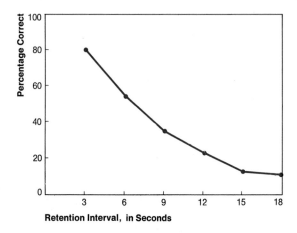

FIGURE 17.2 The percentage of items (three-consonant strings) correctly recalled after time intervals filled with a widely differing task. This curve is an example of a forgetting curve, that is, one that shows a surprising amount of retention loss very soon after the learning of an item. Other experiments show that, even when a single consonant is used, there is some forgetting during the first 15 to 30 sec.

ting after only three seconds, and a loss of almost *90 percent* after eighteen seconds. The assumed reason for this astounding memory loss in so simple a task is the prevention of **rehearsal**. In other words, rehearsal is assumed to be the mechanism that makes possible the processing of material from short-term memory into the more permanent long-term store of memory.

As contrasted with the large amount of information available in sensory memory, the capacity of short-term memory is considerably limited. This limitation becomes clear when a subject is given a list of items, say, a randomly ordered string of digits such as 6-8-3-5-9, and is asked to repeat them immediately. The average adult cannot do well *if there are more than about seven numbers in the string*.

But if seven is our digit span for short-term memory, how, then, can we remember longer strings such as the ten digits that are required to dial a long-distance call? One way to learn all the digits in such a telephone number is to *group* them, thus effectively cutting down on the number of separate *elements* in the string. To the practiced telephone user, 9–0–3–4–2–9–3–3–1–1 becomes 903 (area code), 429 (local exchange), 3311. Thus, business organizations that depend heavily on telephone orders vie for phone numbers ending in, say, 1–2–3–4 or any other easily organized sequence. This kind of organization is called **chunking** by Miller (1956). As we shall see, such chunking, or organizing, plays a large role in long-term memory. In order for chunking to increase the capacity of immediate or short-term memory, however, it would have to operate very quickly *on a perceptual level*. The fact that such fast-acting organizations do indeed occur has long been argued by the Gestalt psychologists (see Unit 13).

The perceptual organization suggested here implies some kind of coding in short-term memory that differs from the direct coding assumed for sensory memory. It has been suggested (Kintsch, 1970) that stimulus information is stored in short-term memory on the basis of its acoustic properties. That is, all information, *even if received visually*, is coded according to its auditory or acoustic characteristics. If you see the group of letters B–C–D, you code them by their sounds "bee," "cee," "dee" rather than by their shapes. Although this idea may seem startling, experimental support is available. Conrad (1964), in studying the types of errors made in immediate recall, found that confusions among items tended to be primarily acoustic or auditory in nature. His experiment involved rapid *visual* presentations of the letters B–C–P–T–V–F–M–N–S–X in six-letter sequences. Subjects were asked to recall immediately what they had just seen. When items were incorrectly substituted for other items, the mistakes involved units that *sounded* alike (such as B and C or S and X). This was true even though the stimuli were presented visually.

The idea of acoustic coding in short-term memory may make some sense, especially in a system where rehearsal is important, but it does not seem reasonable to assume all short-term memory coding *must* be of this nature. Nonverbal animals such as monkeys can do short-term memory tasks such as picking out one of two colored geometric forms after having been recently shown a sample of the one they must pick (Kaufman & Wilson, 1970). It would be fair to conclude that, although the short-term memory code in man may be strongly auditory in nature, the possibility of other kinds of coding should be kept open.

LONG-TERM MEMORY

The long-term memory store refers to material retained for time periods ranging from one minute to several years or more. The early work of Ebbinghaus, as well as that of most of the later workers in the field of verbal learning, concerned the mechanisms of long-term memory. The capacity of long-term memory is by far the largest of all the memory systems. A moment's consideration of all the things you know and remember gives you an appreciation of just how much information you are able to retain over years of accumulated experience. Compare this enormous amount with the very limited capacity of short-term memory. It is reasonable to assume that a memory system containing so much material must have a highly efficient scheme for keeping its information in order. The nature of the organizing or coding properties of long-term memory has been carefully investigated. Although there is not yet general agreement on an overall organization scheme, there are some kinds of coding that have been demonstrated for certain stimuli. One of these deals with coding words according to categories.

Organization in Long-Term Memory

Suppose we present a subject with a list of words that fall into four categories: proper names, animals, vegetables, and professions. We present the words in random order, without calling the subject's attention to the categorical nature of the words. Later the subject tries to recall as many of the words as he can. Bous-field and his associates (1944) demonstrated that, in this form of free-recall, a clear pattern appears in the responses: Items that belong to the same category tend to follow one another in the recall list. Although the items have been presented in random order, they are recalled not in random order but in meaningful *clusters*. That is, the proper names, the animals, and so forth tend to be reported together rather than in their original order. Evidently, retention is not a passive process leading to an automatic recall of individual items; instead, grouping takes place *during the retention period* as items from different parts of the list are organized together to form meaningful clusters.

It may be tempting to try to explain the **clustering** phenomenon solely on the basis that the words forming a cluster are highly associated with one another and that the recall of one therefore stimulates the recall of the next. Experiments show, however, that the amount of clustering cannot be completely explained by word-to-word associations. For example, words belonging to the same category (*dog-wolf*) are clustered more readily than are uncategorized pairs that have the same strength of association (*dog-house*). So it is not enough to think that the words in memory are linked together in a chain. To some extent they must also be thought of as placed in distinctive bins, each of which will tend to be emptied in turn during recall. An interesting finding is that clustering tends to increase with repeated presentations of a list and, furthermore, that recall scores are better for lists with clusters than for lists without clusters.

In order to make the task easier, the listener would be wise to impose her own organization upon a list of words even when categories are not imposed by the experimenter. Such coding has been called *subjective organization* (Tulving, 1962). Subjective organization need not involve only words. We not only remember verbal material but also conjure visual images, as well as memories of sounds, smell, and touch. The coding of material in combinations often forms the basis of prodigious feats of memory—it is one of the tips given in so-called memory-training courses—and people with phenomenal

memories often combine verbal material with visual imagery as a basis for remembering large amounts of information.

Forgetting in Long-Term Memory

Although many psychologists have suggested a rapid, passive fading away of sensory memory and short-term memory, few support such a simple decay mechanism for long-term memory. Obviously we all forget material that we may have remembered over fairly long periods, but psychologists are reluctant to attribute this loss to a gradual fading process. The reason for their reluctance comes from investigations upon the following questions: Why are some materials forgotten more quickly than others? Is forgetting related to how well the material was originally learned? Is forgetting affected by what occurs between the time the material was learned and the time it is remembered? Many psychologists who have studied these questions believe that forgetting of long-term material cannot be described in terms of gradual fading. Instead they suggest that long-term memory loss is due to **interference**.

Interference

Interference in long-term memory loss has been extensively studied in verbal learning. The particular list that an experimenter presents to a subject is of course only a tiny fraction of all the words that the subject is exposed to in his daily life. Thus, when he is asked a day later to recall that list, it is argued that his performance is impeded or interfered with by the tendency to remember other words he has learned before being exposed to the list or between the time of the original learning and the retention test.

These two sources of interference are given separate names. The interference in recall produced by learning that *preceded* the original learning is called **proactive inhibition (PI)**; interference that results from the learning coming *between* original learning and the retention test is termed **retroactive inhibition (RI)**.

The following diagrams illustrate the experimental designs (involving the learning and recall of different lists of words, A and B) used to investigate PI and RI.

Proactive Inhibition

EXPERIMENTAL GROUP

Learn B ⟶ Learn A ⟶ Recall A

CONTROL GROUP

Learn A ⟶ Recall A

Retroactive Inhibition

EXPERIMENTAL GROUP

Learn A ⟶ Learn B ⟶ Recall A

CONTROL GROUP

Learn A ⟶ Recall A

If the experimental group does worse than its control group on recall of A, we assume that this is due to interference from B. In the first instance, it is proactive inhibition because B precedes the learning of A. In the second instance, it is retroactive inhibition because B follows the learning of A.

The importance of the interference mechanism is underscored by studies in which the nature of the interfering (B) material is varied. The more different the B material is from the A material, the less deficit in performance results because the B responses are not as likely to be confused with the A responses when they are being recalled. The complex nature of the sources of interference is demonstrated by RI experiments in which the experimental group receives its B-list learning in a different *room* from the one used for original learning and retention. Under these circumstances RI is much less than when the same room is used throughout. In part, this effect is presumed due to the fact that B responses are associated with the room in which they were learned; when the A and B material are learned in different rooms, interfering associations are reduced and recall is therefore better. (This may argue for having the classroom for learning and examination in one course different from the room for another course, especially if two courses are at all similar in content.)

Unlearning

When the subject begins learning the second of two tasks, there is some tendency to come up with the words used for the first task. But these words are now incorrect. As the subject realizes this sad fact, these earlier responses will be weakened by his direct attempt to *unlearn* them. This process will then contribute to the poorer recall of the A material in the A-B-A design (the RI experimental group). In this design, therefore, at least two factors account for difficulty in recalling the A list: the direct interference effect of the B material on the recall of A *and* the suppression of the for-the-moment incorrect A material while B is initially being learned. But, as you can see for yourself, this unlearning mechanism plays no direct role in PI.

Spontaneous Recovery

The importance of RI in decreasing retention may seem quite obvious once it is pointed out. If you learn B *after* A, it seems perfectly understandable that B will still be prominent and competing for influence when you try to recall A at a later time. But it is not so obvious that PI should exist at all, that something you have learned *before* should interfere with the retention of a well-learned task. Underwood (1957) demonstrated the importance of PI in experimental tasks by noting that subjects who had had a great deal of practice in learning lists of words retained only about 25 percent of a newly learned list twenty-four hours later; whereas subjects who had not had any such previous practice retained 70 percent of this same list, which was their *first*-learned list. The better-trained subjects did *worse* because the specific things they had learned in their earlier lists interfered in some way with their memory of the new list.

Now, if material learned earlier is going to interfere with more recently learned material, the early material must come back somehow, even though it is presumably suppressed or unlearned and overridden in the course of the learning of the new task. It has therefore been proposed that the unlearned material shows a recovery much like the spontaneous recovery that follows the extinction of a conditioned response (Unit 15, p. 368). This presumed recovery has been used to explain the following interesting finding: If two lists are learned consecutively during a single session, and if retention is then measured soon after their original learning, the one learned last will be much better retained. But if retention is not measured until a day later, the two lists will be recalled equally well. The spontaneous recovery of the first list, after a day's interval, is assumed to reinstate its responses, and now these responses conflict with the second list in recall, so that the advantage of the last-learned list is wiped out.

Active Forgetting

Our discussion of forgetting through interference is based upon a position that interprets the process of forgetting from a relatively *passive* point of view; that is, new or old *material* is seen as interfering with the process of learning and remembering. Material is conceived of as an inactive thing (association, habit, particular word or group of words). Some views of forgetting offer a more active process as a supplement to, or an alternative for, interference.

Repression   The Freudian conception of forgetting through repression (see p. 578) represents a view that although not incompatible with interference theory, focuses upon a different aspect of memory. Repression for Freud was a "motivated forgetting." Material that would be psychologically extremely painful and threatening if remembered becomes difficult to recall; hence, the person is defended against strong anxiety by not remembering. Thus, you repress the name of a classmate who humiliated you before all your friends in the third grade; indeed, you may not remember the incident at all. In some extreme instances, repression is so pervasive that it results in the pathological state of total amnesia. Of course, the question of how painful and threatening memories must be in order to be repressed should be answered before the mechanism of repression can be used to help us understand forgetting.

Creative forgetting   Another active view of forgetting comes from the now-classic work of Bartlett (1932). In one experiment he had his subjects (British university students) read a North American Indian folk tale twice to themselves. Fifteen minutes later, and at various intervals after that, he tested them for recall. He found that (1) the general *form* of the student's first recall was preserved throughout his reproductions, (2) elements of the original story which seemed unconnected or meaningless to the British student were changed in order to make them more *meaningful*, and (3) various new details were *invented* by the subject in order to make the story more coherent and more in keeping with British speech patterns, customs, and values. The final story remembered was frequently quite different from the original story heard, but forgetting did not consist of a gradual dropping out of items; rather, there was a definite, consistent *reworking* of the materials into a new story, one that the subjects had really never heard before. It is for this reason that Bartlett speaks of "creative forgetting" and regards remembering as a process of "constructing."

Further feeling for the kind of process he describes can be gained from considering what happens when you have a memory on the tip of your tongue (see Box 6.2, p. 128). You play with it; worry it; remember the first letter, word, or phrase of the idea you are dealing with; and finally come up with some memory. When the memory is the correct one (the one for which you have actually been searching), something clicks, and you feel a great sense of satisfaction. But even if you do not get the precise memory, you construct something that is like it; you come close. Bartlett felt that this constructive process was of central import to understanding how we remember. In studying the recall of short stories he noticed a great deal of inaccuracy in his subjects' memories. More importantly, these inaccuracies often stemmed from an elaborate set of circumstances built up around only a small detail or even from just a vague impression from the original story. Whether these elaborate inaccuracies were constructed because the original material was forgotten or whether forgetting consists of, at least in part, the construction of inaccuracies obviously merits further investigation.

MECHANICS OF MEMORY

Questions about the way information is passed on from sensory to short-term and then to long-term memory have led to some interesting hypotheses and research. The suggestion that rehearsal is responsible for the change from short-term to long-term memory has already been discussed. How material once in a memory system is taken out for use **(retrieval)** is another aspect of the mechanics of memory that has produced some useful speculation and evidence. One type of experiment asks whether items in short-term memory are searched for (and retrieved) one at a time **(serial processing)** or all at once **(parallel processing)**. Sternberg (1966) provides evidence for serial processing in a study that measures the time a subject takes to respond (reaction time) to a particular item and uses that reaction time as an indicator of the type of retrieval involved. Sternberg's subjects first saw a display of several items for a brief time. They were then presented with a single item at a time and told to pull one lever if they recognized that item as one they had seen in the previous display and a different lever if the item was a new one. The levers were to be pulled as quickly as possible. Sternberg used displays of varying numbers of items and found a fixed increment in reaction time for each additional item in the display. This would appear to indicate that each item was being searched for in the memory store for that display, processed, and retrieved one at a time; thus, the larger the number of items, the longer the time for search. Others (Neisser, 1967, for one) take issue with Sternberg and suggest that processing in short-term memory is parallel in nature. Neisser reports that his subjects, who are well practiced, do not show the relation between time to process each item and number of items to be searched that is shown in the Sternberg data. He points out that practiced subjects "hardly see" irrelevant items. Although the issue has not as yet been resolved, the technique of inferring the mechanics of processing from reaction time may turn out to be helpful.

An Overview

At this point it might be well to attempt a summary of what we have been saying about the different memory systems. Table 17.1 provides an overview of much of what has been discussed

TABLE 17.1 OVERVIEW OF MEMORY SYSTEMS

Memory System	Temporal Span of Operation	Capacity	Type of Organization or Coding	Forgetting Mechanism
Sensory memory	fraction of a second	limited only by how much the receptor can register	fairly direct representation of the physical stimulus	passive decay
Short-term memory	less than one minute	only a few (five to nine) items	indirect coding including a great deal of acoustic organization	passive decay
Long-term memory	over one minute up to many years	very large, almost unlimited	very complex coding (e.g., clustering, subjective organization)	interference and unlearning, repression, creative forgetting

in this unit. It must be emphasized that the different types of memory summarized are far from being fully understood. For example, the psychophysiological data support short-term and long-term memory systems (see Unit 18), but the physiological relation of the sensory-memory store to these is not yet established. There is not even unanimous agreement about *how many* such systems should be specified for the most convenient explanation of available data or *in what way* the various systems differ from one another. Some psychologists argue that forgetting is produced by interference in both short-term and long-term memory (Melton, 1963, is an instance) and suggest that perhaps only one general memory system need be considered. Others feel that even three memory systems are not enough (Wickelgren, 1970). The systematic investigation of human memory, which started with Ebbinghaus in the nineteenth century and continued at a relatively stable level over the years, has in the past decade exploded into a fascinating set of discoveries. And new hypotheses are currently being developed that hold great promise for solving the puzzle of how we remember.

SUMMARY

1. The study of verbal learning requires procedures distinctly different from those employed in investigations of classical and instrumental conditioning. Among them are the procedures of serial learning, paired-associate learning, and free recall.

2. Remembering, or retention, can be measured by recall (the subject must *produce* the previously learned material) or by recognition (the previously learned material must be *identified* from among other materials).

3. Every retention measure necessarily reflects *both* how well the material was originally learned and how much of it has been retained from then on. By testing for retention *immediately* after learning, we can evaluate only acquisition; by insuring equal acquisition for all subjects and then varying the time between original learning and testing, we can study retention.

4. Many factors affect acquisition in verbal learning. Among them are the amount of material to be learned, the number of learning trials, and the nature of prior learning experiences. The characteristics of the learned material—its meaningfulness, its ability to evoke images, and the relations among items within the material—are also important.

5. At least three different kinds of memory can be distinguished. Sensory memory is of very short duration and involves reading off from fleeting afterimages. Short-term memory is somewhat longer in duration, but still no more than a minute (e.g., keeping a just-looked-up phone number in mind until it is dialed). Finally, long-term memory pertains to any more persistent memories, that is, those retained from over one minute up to a lifetime.

6. The way information is organized differs among the three memory systems. In short-term memory, for example, rehearsal is of primary importance. So is chunking, which involves perceptually organizing individual items into groups. Long-term memory also benefits from organizing strategies but involves somewhat different processes such as clustering and subjective organization.

7. Although some sort of fading or decay process largely accounts for forgetting in sensory and short-term memory, such a process is probably of minor importance in loss of long-term memories. Instead, interference is the likely major factor—interference from previously learned material (proactive inhibition) and from subsequently learned material (retroactive inhibition).

8. The greater the *similarity* between the previously or later-learned material and the material being tested for retention, the more effective interference of either sort is in causing long-term forgetting.

9. Active unlearning of now-inappropriate material helps to improve learning and retention of new material, but after a while, the unlearned material comes back (spontaneous recovery) and once again interferes with recall of the new material.

10. There are alternate, although not necessarily incompatible, views of forgetting that regard it as a more active process than interference. One is the Freudian concept of repression, which has been called "motivated forgetting," in which material posing severe psychological pain and threat to the individual is erased from conscious memory. The function of repression is to defend the individual against overwhelming anxiety.

11. Another active view focuses on the tendency to transform imperfectly learned material into more familiar and meaningful form by forgetting elements that do not fit and, at the same time, inventing elements that help to make sense of the material taken as a whole. This view, which is Bartlett's, thus talks of "creative forgetting" and of an active "constructing" process in which the individual seeks to make the material more comprehensible, hence more memorable.

12. Many unresolved issues remain in the study of human memory. Among them are the nature of the transition of material from one memory system to another and the nature of the retrieval process by which material is called from memory. Even the necessary *number* of memory systems is still very much at issue: Some argue for only a single system; others believe that even three are insufficient to cover all the phenomena of human memory.

GLOSSARY

association value The capacity of a word or nonsense syllable to evoke associations. A nonsense syllable that reminds people of many meaningful words thus has *high* association value; one that reminds people of very few meaningful words has *low* association value.

chunking The grouping of items in memory to permit greater recall. This grouping appears to be more perceptual in nature for short-term memory and more complex in long-term memory.

clustering The tendency to recall items in meaningfully related groups, even though these items had originally been learned in a random order.

coding The process of organizing material for storage in memory. The type of coding differs for each of the assumed memory systems.

free recall The method in which a subject tries to recall (without regard to order) as many as possible of a series of items previously presented to him.

imagery The attribute of a word relating to the richness of mental images produced by the word. A list of high-imagery words is more easily learned than is a low-imagery list.

information processing Refers to the operations which presumably occur upon the stimulus during the assumed different stages of memory. When processing occurs there is a change in the stimulus information.

interference The presumed disruptive influence upon a response of the tendency to make other responses that were learned either before or after the correct response. Interference theory asserts that all forgetting is due to this process.

learning curve A graphic method of presenting the change in performance of an individual or group of individuals during the learning process. In a learning curve the successive time or trial intervals are usually plotted on the abscissa (the x axis) and the performance units on the ordinate (the y axis).

long-term memory The system with an extremely large capacity and complex organization that is assumed to account for relatively enduring memories (for periods ranging from over a minute to many years).

nonsense syllable A combination of consonants and vowels presumed to be of low meaningfulness. Invented by Ebbinghaus, a German psychologist, and used extensively as items in verbal learning experiments.

paired-associate learning A list of pairs is presented in which one item serves as stimulus and the other as response. Paired-associate learning is learning to respond with a second item of a pair when the first item is presented.

parallel processing   The hypothesis that information is transformed from one memory system to another simultaneously rather than sequentially.

proactive inhibition (PI)   The disruptive effect of material upon recall as a result of having learned such material *before* having initially learned the to-be-recalled material.

recall method   A method of measuring retention in which the requirement is to *reproduce* previously learned material.

recognition method   A method of measuring retention in which the requirement is to *identify* previously learned material from among a larger collection of items.

rehearsal   The active process assumed to be necessary to keep information in short-term memory and permit its transfer to long-term memory.

retrieval   The process of taking information out of a memory system in order to produce an overt response.

retroactive inhibition (RI)   The disruptive effect upon recall of having learned other material *between* the learning of the original material and its attempted recall.

sensory memory   The assumed memory system that stores stimulus information directly but for a duration of less than a second.

serial learning   A list of single items is presented. Items are in the same order on every trial and must be recalled in the proper order.

serial-position effect   The observation that in verbal learning, items toward the beginning and end of a learned series are more quickly memorized than items in the middle of the list.

serial processing   The hypothesis that information is transferred from one memory system to another sequentially rather than simultaneously.

short-term memory   The system with a limited capacity that is assumed to account for memories of approximately one minute's duration.

tachistoscope   A type of instrument that makes possible extremely brief and precisely timed exposures of stimulus material.

transfer   The effect upon the learning of one task (B) by the previous learning of another task (A). When the learning of A helps the learning of B, we speak of *positive transfer*; when it hinders the learning of B, we speak of *negative transfer*.

physiological mechanisms of learning and memory

DO YOU KNOW...

that in one sense phrenology (the "science" of telling an individual's personality and abilities from reading the bumps on various parts of his head) was on the right track?

• *that some kinds of learning may occur which do not involve the brain?*

• *that we have learned a great deal about normal brains from studying people who, through injury or disease, have had portions of their brain destroyed?*

• *why it is that drastic operations on the brains of animals can tell us significant things about the functioning of human brains?*

• *that certain psychological and behavioral symptoms can be clearly attributed to injury to specific portions of the brain?*

• *that in animals, at least, actual changes in the size and functioning of the brain can be attributed to the kind of environment in which the animal is raised?*

• *that some animals and people have, essentially, two brains?*

• *how these split-brain individuals behave?*

CONTENTS

In Unit 14 we considered the question of the physiological basis of sensation and perception. We described the nature of the activities of various parts of the nervous system when a stimulus is presented to the individual, and we discovered that certain parts of the brain are essential if perceptual experience is to be normal and complete. In all behavior one or more of these perceptual mechanisms must be involved because, although stimuli are not always necessary to excite us into activity, they *are* always present as a background, affecting the ongoing activity of the nervous system and thus steering the behavior.

When, as a result of experience, there is a consistent change in the response to any stimulus pattern, we usually say that learning has taken place. This learning must, in turn, mean that some change in the nervous system has taken place, and our interest in this unit is studying the location and nature of such changes.

Most of the experiments in this field have used the *ablation method* (see p. 329), which was first employed systematically by the French physiologist Pierre Flourens (1824). Flourens noted that the brain is composed of several organs, each with its own functions. He considered the cerebellum the "seat of the principle which coordinates locomotor motion" and the cerebrum the "seat of intelligence." This distinction is still regarded as relatively sound. However, he believed that the cerebrum is functionally indivisible. This conclusion stands in sharp contrast with the view taken by the phrenologists (see Box 18.1) and more recently by many reputable scientists. Today's consensus leans to the position that different parts of the cerebrum control different functions. We shall discuss further developments in this controversy at some length later in this unit.

The long line of research that began with Flourens, and is still continuing, has attempted to specify the *locus of learning*: *Where* in the nervous system does learning take place? After a survey of present knowledge related to this problem, we must turn our attention to another question: *What happens* in the nervous system

BOX 18.1

PHRENOLOGY

Although P. Flourens's work marked the beginning of experimental work on the brain-mind problem, the general question had been dramatically raised fourteen years earlier by two German physicians, F. J. Gall and G. S. Spurzheim. In their six-volume *Anatomy and Physiology of the Nervous System,* they laid the basis for **phrenology** by asserting, first, that the brain is the organ of the mind; second, that different kinds of behavior are controlled by separate parts of the brain (see figure); and, third, that the external shape of the skull reflects the shape of the brain underneath. (Protuberances and dips on the skull presumably reflected over- or underdevelopment of the brain underneath.)

Science has treated Gall and Spurzheim with ridicule. Yet their anatomy and neurology were

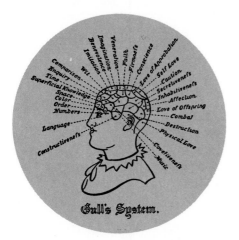

Gall's System.

sound, and their general theoretical position was a reasonable one for the time. Why, then, did their contemporaries and history treat them so meanly? One might venture two explanations. First, phrenology seemed to be an easy way of finding out about people—just feel the bumps on their heads! In the hands of the uncritical and the charlatans, phrenology became a morass of pseudoscientific nonsense. Second, the supporting *data* Gall and Spurzheim used fell far short of scientific standards. Here is how Spurzheim relates the "discovery" that physical love is controlled by the cerebellum:

> Being physician to a widow who was subject to very strong hysterical fits, during which she drew her head backward with great violence, Gall sometimes supported her head with his hand, and, in doing so, observed that her neck was very large and hot. He was acquainted with her character [Gall's case history of this patient makes it clear why she is sometimes referred to as "Gall's passionate widow"] . . . and he accordingly considered in connection with her passion, this magnitude of the neck, and the consequent development of the cerebellum.

When a reasonable theory is wildly overstated, the good in an idea is thrown out with the bad. Nevertheless, as E. G. Boring reminds us, phrenology accomplished two things:

> It forced the problem of correlation of mind and brain to the fore . . . [and] by going to extremes, Gall made a radical but less extreme view actually seem conservative. Without a Gall, Flourens might never have conceived the problem of finding different functions for the cerebrum, the cerebellum, the medulla and the cord.

F. J. GALL & G. S. SPURZHEIM. *Anatomie et Physiologie du Système Nerveux.* Paris: Schoell, 1810.
E. G. BORING. *A History of Experimental Psychology.* (2d ed.) New York: Appleton, 1950.

---

when something new is learned? This is the question of the physiological dynamics or *mechanisms of learning.*

The discussion of the physiological processes in perception (Unit 14) demonstrated that the basic neurophysiological events of nervous transmission appear to be sufficient to explain what happens in the nervous system when we see, hear, smell, touch, and so on. With learning,

however, we enter a realm in which we do not even know for certain which physiological mechanisms are at work in the nervous system.

The crucial goal in our search for the physiological basis of learning is some mechanism for *permanent change* in the nervous system: Without such a mechanism, how can we possibly account for memory? Until recently very little could even be guessed at by way of answering this question. But experimentation in this area is now rapidly increasing, and this question now defines one of the most exciting research issues in biochemistry, physiology, and psychology.

LOCUS OF LEARNING: THE SPINAL CORD

Can any learning take place without involving the brain itself? In other words, can learning take place in the spinal cord? The basic technique used in studying this question is fairly simple. Under surgical anesthesia the spinal cord of an experimental animal is cut completely through, thus severing all the neural connections between the lower part of the body and the brain. With proper care, such an animal, called a **spinal animal**, can be kept alive for years. During the postoperative period conditioned-response training is instituted (see Unit 15). For this conditioning training, it is necessary to choose both stimuli and responses that involve only the lower part of the body (i.e., that part which now has no *neural connection* with the brain). If the animal, under these circumstances, is able to acquire a conditioned response, we have evidence that simple acquisition is possible without the help of the brain. In such a case, presumably, the integration of the incoming sensory stimuli and the outgoing motor impulses—and such integration is necessary for successful conditioning—would have

to be wholly under the control of the spinal cord.

The results from such experiments are somewhat ambiguous. The most positive results have been reported by experimenters using the procedure shown in Figure 18.1. They succeeded in conditioning isolated muscles in the dog's leg to twitch when the tail was brushed or pinched. The same group of workers has also reported that animals whose spinal cords are severed in early infancy will in many cases eventually develop nearly normal walking behavior. It may be argued, however, that learning to walk is principally a maturational development (i.e., it would have occurred *without practice*) and therefore that we should not consider this as evidence for spinal learning (i.e., change as a result of *experience*).

In any event, it seems clear that even if the spinal cord can learn, its repertoire is restricted to *very simple conditioning*. For learning the more complex responses involved in the adaptive behavior of man and beast, the spinal cord is not enough. We must look higher up for the locus of most learning.

LOCUS OF LEARNING: THE SUBCORTEX

The next levels above the spinal cord where we might find the locus of the control of learning are the subcortical structures of the brain. Can learning take place there, without the help of

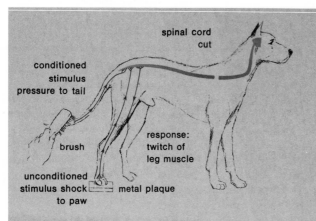

spinal cord cut

conditioned stimulus pressure to tail

brush

response: twitch of leg muscle

unconditioned stimulus shock to paw

metal plaque

FIGURE 18.1 Can the spinal cord learn? This picture illustrates the procedures used by the investigators who reached an affirmative answer. A cut is made across a dog's spinal cord, and then conditioning trials are begun. On training trials the tail is stimulated with a brush (conditioned stimulus), and the paw is given an electric shock (unconditioned stimulus). The shock causes an unconditioned response: a contraction of a muscle dissected free from the upper leg. After sufficient training the muscle responds to the conditioned stimulus alone. The brain cannot have been involved in this change in behavior because the nerve pathway between it and the leg had been cut.

the cerebral cortex? The obvious method of approach is to examine the behavior of **decorticate animals**, that is, animals whose entire cortexes have been removed or destroyed.

Decorticate animals can show some signs of learning in simple problem situations. One experimenter (Bromiley, 1948) was able to train a completely decorticate dog to avoid a shock to its leg by flexing it when a whistle was sounded. He was also then able to extinguish this response and retrain the dog to flex its leg to the onset of a light. The dog survived thirty-three months without a cerebral cortex, but its behavior remained at a very low level of complexity. For the first twenty postoperative days the dog had to be given water by means of a stomach tube, because it took that long for the dog to learn to lap the water from a pan held under its nose. It was able to swallow pieces of meat placed on the back of its tongue, but it took the dog more than four months to relearn to eat food from a pan.

It would appear then that the cortex is not needed for the acquisition of the most primitive kinds of problem solving, that is, very simple conditioned responses and sensory discriminations. For these kinds of problems, the subcortical mechanisms alone may be sufficient. But by themselves they do not seem sufficient for the acquisition, retention, and control of the more complex patterns of behavior.

LOCUS OF LEARNING: THE CEREBRAL CORTEX

We are at the end of the road; there is no place else to go. It appears obvious that we shall, in the cerebral cortex, find the major locus of complex adaptive behavior. The very nature of the cortex suggests that we have found the right spot. The number of neural cells in the cerebral cortex has been estimated at about 9 billion. These 9 billion cells can fire in an astronomical number of different groupings and sequences. We have here all the complexity needed for integrative action. It would seem that the cerebral cortex *must* be the locus of learning and problem solving.

But not necessarily. All that we have demonstrated is that the centers below the cerebral cortex cannot *alone* provide the neurological basis for acquisition. It is still possible that even the most complex forms of learning and problem solving depend upon these lower centers *in conjunction with the cerebral cortex.*

Actually this possibility is the one favored by most contemporary workers in the field. The long search for the place where learning occurs is no longer directed toward finding a single, specific, sharply delimited point locus. Any acquisition may involve *simultaneous* changes in the cerebral cortex, subcortical structures, spinal cord, and perhaps even peripheral nerve endings in the sensory organs and muscles. What the experimenter does when he studies the relation between the cerebral cortex and learning is to tap *one point of a complex circuit.*

If the cortex is indeed involved in learning, we can ask another question: Are different kinds of learning and problem solving dependent upon different areas of the cortex? In a sense we are asking the same question that the phrenologist-anatomists Gall and Spurzheim asked (and answered affirmatively) in 1810.

Experimental work in the intervening years has led to various suggestions concerning cortical localization of intellectual functions. These suggestions have ranged from specificity hypotheses (in the tradition of Gall and Spurzheim) to complete nonspecificity ones (in the tradition of Flourens).

An American psychologist, Karl S. Lashley, provided perhaps the strongest case for nonspecificity in the cortical control of learning. He performed an extensive series of experiments involving cortical ablation in the rat. Working mostly with mazes, he found that the *specific part* of the cortex that was destroyed was of little consequence in determining an animal's learning score. A lesion of one part of the cortex had the same effect as a lesion of the same size in another region. It is for this reason that Lashley spoke of the **equipotentiality** of the regions of the cortex. The important consideration was not *which part* of the cortex was destroyed but *how much* was destroyed. A large lesion anywhere had a more profound deteriorating effect on learning than a smaller one.

Others were quick to offer alternative explanations of Lashley's data, and many subsequent experiments seem to have demonstrated some limitations to his conclusions. One argument stresses the complexity of learning (particularly of maze learning) and of the brain. If the task of maze learning really depends upon *many* different sensory and motor abilities, and if each of these abilities is localized in one specific part of the cortex, then lesions of different sizes in different parts of the cortex would be expected to produce just the results Lashley obtained. One could argue that there are no cortical areas for learning as such.

A third major view about cortical functions in learning must be discussed at some length. This view does not fit well with Lashley's data but it does appear to be bolstered by many recent experiments.

Learning Areas

Just as there are special areas that seem to be related to different sensory and motor functions, could not there be areas of cortex particularly designed to operate in different kinds of learning and problem solving? It has long been known that there exist areas of cortex whose destruction does not seem to produce sensory or motor changes, and the higher the animal is in the phylogenetic scale, the larger these areas are. These facts have led to the belief that these areas, called the **association areas** of the cortex, are primarily involved in learning. In a typical mammal there are two such areas, the *frontal* and the *posterior* association areas, each of which can be divided into various subareas (see Figure 18.2).

Evidence that they play a special role in learning will be provided if we can show that destruction of these areas is correlated with a loss in learning ability. We get an extra dividend of evidence if we can show that different parts of the association cortex are important to different *kinds* of adaptive behavior. Both types of evidence are now available.

Posterior Association Area

Although many kinds of animals have been used in studies of the role of the association areas, our knowledge is perhaps most complete for the popular zoo animal, the rhesus monkey. The monkey is an animal whose association areas are rather highly developed, and we gain the advantage of working with an animal that is rather similar to human beings.

The posterior association area, as can be seen in Figure 18.2, is surrounded by the various primary sensory areas, and lesions of this area produce *deficits* in learned behavior involving sensory discriminations (see Box 18.2, p. 422).

Furthermore, subareas of this posterior association cortex play different roles. There seem to be separate regions that are particularly important for learning discrimination tasks based upon each of the various sensory modalities.

But why should different parts of the association area be related to learning in different sensory modalities? What features of the anatomy of the brain can explain these relations? In exploring these questions, let us consider the visual system and the **inferotemporal cortex**. Lesions of this area cause a profound deficit in the learning of visual problems. Earlier we traced the principal visual pathway from the eye via optic nerves and tracts to the lateral geniculate nucleus and thence to the cortex of the occipital lobe (see Unit 14, p. 329). Several kinds of evidence suggest that the inferotemporal cortex receives its important inflow through fibers that begin in the occipital cortex and relay across the cortex to terminate in the inferotemporal area.

Some evidence for this conclusion arises from microelectrode studies of cells of the inferotemporal cortex. It has been found that these neurons give an electrophysiological response to visual stimuli presented to the eye. It is also important to note that the kinds of stimuli which produce the best response are often more complex than those that stimulate cells in the occipital lobe most effectively (Gross et al., 1972).

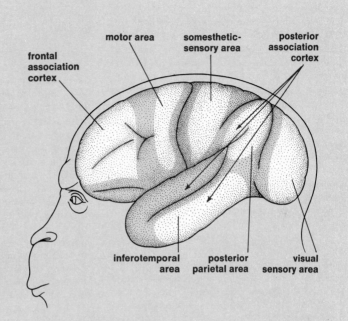

FIGURE 18.2 The functional map of the cortex. Represented here are the more definitely established functional areas of the monkey and the human cortex. Note the sensory areas that receive impulses fairly directly from the sense organs (via the thalamus) and the motor areas that send impulses that reach the musculature. Note the relatively large extent of the motor area in man that is given over to control of the movements of fingers and hands, the organs capable of the finest manipulation. The control of motor activity is not entirely restricted to the motor areas shown here. Motor activity can be produced by stimulation of other parts of the cortex as well, and the cerebellum and various subcortical structures are also important in the initiation and organization of movement

Also indicated are the association areas and the regions of cortex that are particularly important to the comprehension and production of human speech.

It might be of interest to compare this figure with the Gall and Spurzheim map of the brain shown in Box 18.1 (p. 417).

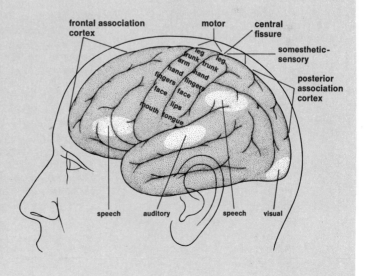

BOX 18.2

CORTICAL LOCALIZATION IN THE MONKEY

What does the association cortex *do*? Is it really the place where learning takes place? Is it a sensory area? Is it a higher-level perceptual region? Or what? These questions are unresolved, debated questions. It is clear, however, that the posterior association cortex does not play the same role as the primary sensory cortex of the brain, although subregions of the posterior association area are somehow related to different sensory systems.

When a lesion is made in the inferotemporal areas of the monkey's brain (see Figure 18.2), he becomes "visually stupid"; that is, he is much slower in learning a visual problem than an unoperated animal is. This fact, however, does not prove that the inferotemporal area is a learning region. For example, if we destroy part of the occipital cortex (the visual *sensory* area), an animal may also become "visually stupid" simply because he can't *see* as well as before. William A. Wilson and Mortimer Mishkin, psychologists then at the Institute of Living, Hartford, Connecticut, compared the effects of lesions of the inferotemporal cortex and the lateral portion of the occipital cortex. Although both operations changed the visually guided behavior of the monkeys, the *pattern* of change was quite different for the two operations.

This difference is clearly shown when the operated monkeys are tested on the *patterned-string* problem and the **learning-set** problem. In the patterned-string problem the ends of two strings are placed within reach of the caged monkey; a bit of food is attached to the far end of one string. The strings may cross each other one or more times, but the full length of both strings is exposed. The monkey is allowed to pull in only one of the strings. In this problem there is very little new to learn. Lesions of the occipital cortex produce errors on this kind of

problem; lesions of the inferotemporal cortex do not. A learning-set problem is a series of visual discrimination problems (see figure). A tray containing two objects (e.g., an ashtray and a toy horn) is presented to the monkey, and he is allowed to lift one; he receives the same pair of objects for several trials and can learn that food is always to be found under only one of them—the ashtray, let us say. We then repeat the procedure with two new completely different objects. As this testing is done over and over, normal monkeys and monkeys with occipital lesions learn each new problem faster and faster. Monkeys with inferotemporal lesions, however, show much less of this development of a learning set. The patterned-string test seems to be more a measure of sensory function; the learning-set problem, a measure of learning ability. These two problems thus provide evidence for somewhat different functions of the cortical regions under consideration.

Later experiments by Mishkin and Eiichi Iwai at the National Institute of Mental Health have shown that it is possible to distinguish two separate parts of the inferotemporal region itself. After lesions of one of these parts, monkeys are particularly deficient in learning complex visual discriminations; whereas ablation of the other area seems to make it difficult for the animals to learn and remember several problems at once, even if they are easy ones.

The inferotemporal area is essential to normal *visual* learning; the **posterior parietal** cortex plays a part in learning based on touch and kinesthetic cues. Martha Wilson, a psychologist now at the University of Connecticut, demonstrated this difference by comparing the performances of monkeys that had these two lesions—performance on visual problems such as those discussed and performance on learning problems that could be solved only by using tactual information. The inferotemporal lesion caused a deficit only on the appropriate kinds of visual problems; the posterior parietal lesion, only on the tactual problems.

Further refinement of the lesions and the tests used and evidence based upon other experimental procedures will help us to clarify the exact contribution of association cortex to the adaptive behavior of the organism but we already know the broad limits within which the answers will be found.

W. A. WILSON, JR. & M. MISHKIN. Comparison of the effects of inferotemporal and lateral occipital lesions on visually guided behavior in monkeys. *Journal of Comparative and Physiological Psychology*, 1959, **52**, 10–17.

M. MISHKIN. Cortical visual areas and their interaction. In A. Karczmar & J. C. Eccles (Eds.), *Brain and Human Behavior.* New York: Springer-Verlag, 1972, 187–208.

M. WILSON. Effects of circumscribed cortical lesions upon somesthetic and visual discrimination in the monkey. *Journal of Comparative and Physiological Psychology*, 1957, **50**, 630–635.

When the pathways between the occipital and the inferotemporal cortex of the monkey are cut, the cells in the inferotemporal area do not give their normal electrophysiological responses to visual stimuli; further, the monkey shows the *same* deficit in visual discrimination learning displayed by an animal that has had lesions in the inferotemporal areas. It therefore appears that a direct path for the visual information that plays a part in adaptive behavior is from the eye to the occipital cortex (via the lateral geniculate nucleus) and from the occipital area to the inferotemporal area by cross-cortical fibers. Thus, we see that for learning (as different from perception), additional areas of the cortex appear to be essential.

Frontal Association Area

Lesions of the frontal association cortex have very little, if any, effect upon the ability of a monkey to learn individual discrimination problems but will produce profound effects upon the animal's ability to *use* sensory information in certain forms of adaptive behavior.

A most striking demonstration of this effect is provided by the **delayed-response problem**. In this problem the monkey watches the experimenter place food in one of two identical containers. The monkey is not allowed to approach either container until after a *delay* of a given duration. When he then makes his choice, he gets the reward if he indeed chooses the baited container. The experimenter can give the monkey many such trials, each time randomly placing the food in one container or the other, as the monkey watches.

In these circumstances, normal monkeys can learn to respond correctly after delays of *several hours or more*. If, however, an animal's frontal association area is destroyed, he will inevitably fail at such a problem even with a delay of only a *few seconds*. The animal will watch the experimenter hide a piece of food and then, only five seconds later, will choose, apparently at random, either the baited or the empty container.

It is important to note that the frontal animal (one that has had the frontal region ablated) is capable of the basic sensory and motor adjustments necessary to solve the problem, even though he cannot perform quite like a normal, unoperated monkey. For example, a frontal animal may perform well on a *zero-second* delayed-response problem (in which the animal is allowed to get the food immediately after he has seen which container is baited), but he appears to be completely lost when the delay is extended to five seconds.

The most common interpretation of these results focuses upon the apparent importance of the delay interval. The suggestion is made that these areas of the frontal association cortex are essential to some aspect of memory; when they are destroyed, the animal can *see* where the experimenter puts the food and will go there if permitted to do so immediately. But he cannot hold in *memory* the information concerning which container is baited.

A proponent of this view must find some way to account for the fact that the frontal animal can learn many other kinds of problems (e.g., a difficult visual discrimination) as rapidly as a normal animal can. Certainly learning to choose the specific container with, say, a plus sign on the cover from among others involves memory, memory of the outcome of the previous trial, at the very least. A possible answer to this paradox lies in the suggestion that the frontal cortex is concerned only with *short-term memory*, which is involved in the delayed-response situation; whereas discrimination tasks such as the one just described involve long-term memory. And this answer implies, of course, that short- and long-term memory processes are quite different from each other. This possibility is discussed in Unit 17 and will be mentioned again later in this unit (p. 437).

There are other hypotheses about the role of the frontal cortex in behavior, however. One suggestion is that it plays some essential role in attention. Upon destruction of the frontal cortex, the argument goes, the animal becomes more subject to interference by extraneous events that distract its attention from the important stimuli, present or past, that are essential to effective adaptive behavior. This point of view gains some support from the fact that a frontal animal does show improvement on delayed-response problems if he is kept in the dark during the delay period, a procedure that minimizes possible visual interference.

A third hypothesis is that frontal ablation increases the animal's tendency to **perseverate**, that is, the tendency to make the same response over and over again, even though it would be more adaptive to change to a new form of behavior. Yet another hypothesis points to the *spatial* nature of the delayed-response problem, suggesting that the frontal cortex is crucial for adequate orientation in space, so that its destruction prevents the animal from aiming itself toward the baited container.

The situation is not as bad as this listing of different hypotheses might suggest. It is known, from anatomical and physiological studies, that the frontal association area has many subregions, and some progress has been made in recent years in assigning each of the various functions just mentioned above (memory, spatial orientation, and so forth) to one or another of these smaller areas.

We should not in any case overemphasize the apparent uncertainties of frontal-lobe function. We do know that these areas are essential to normal performance of many kinds of adaptive behavior. The frontal cortex receives impulses from all the sensory areas and from many subcortical structures. The functions deranged by lesions here are relatively complex; they are not limited to simple sensory learning but involve higher-order organization of past and present input toward an adaptive outcome in behavior.

CORTICAL FUNCTIONS IN HUMAN BEINGS

We have been dealing at some length with the results of studies in which animals were used to explore the role of the cerebral cortex in adaptive behavior, and we may seem to have lost sight of our principal interest in human behavior and experience. The most important reason for this emphasis upon studies with animals is that we simply cannot do many of the experiments that would be necessary to obtain the desired information about people. However, we have some direct information concerning cortical functions in human beings, and it is comforting that such information appears to lead to conclusions compatible with those that come from the study of other species.

Perhaps the best human evidence comes from investigations of people who have suffered accidental brain injuries. In addition, there are observations of patients who have had portions of their brains destroyed by disease and patients who have had portions of their brains surgically removed or incised in attempts to control disease. It is also sometimes possible to gain information from study of the exposed brain during an operation.

At the outset, we should recall that these investigations confirm the existence of the primary sensory areas in the posterior portion of the cortex, areas essential to sensory function of one modality or another. As Box 3.1, page 71, shows, electrical stimulation of these areas will lead to experiences that are appropriate to the known sensory connections of the region, and their destruction causes profound disturbance in the related sensory functions.

There may also be areas comparable to the subareas of the posterior association cortex of monkeys. Injury to these areas could then explain the fact that human brain damage may be followed by **agnosia**, the inability to recognize formerly familiar objects. Presumably there are many different kinds of agnosia, corresponding to the various sense modalities and each resulting from damage to one of the subareas of the association cortex.

The concept of agnosia, as usually stated, implies that the disorder in recognition occurs *without* any loss of simple sensory function, but there is not complete agreement on this point. Many investigators believe that any disturbance in recognition must be based upon simpler sensory losses, which should show up as increases in sensory thresholds and so on. Certainly many studies show that lesions of the cerebral cortex produce losses on behavior tests of different levels of complexity. The studies described in Box 18.3 (p. 426) demonstrate what may be considered three levels of visual tasks, all of which may be affected by lesions in the visual areas of the brain.

In any event, we can assign a major role in simple *and* complex functions dependent upon each sensory modality to the regions of the cortex adjoining the sensory areas we have previously discussed.

Frontal Cortex

There are many descriptions of the behavior of people with damage to the frontal region of the brain. These descriptions are often couched in general terms, such as inability to think abstractly, lack of concern for consequences, and inability to plan ahead. It seems almost certain that each of the descriptions contains some grains of truth, but examination of studies that have used adequate objective testing with proper controls reveals very little that is definite. One thing is certain; people with frontal injury do *not* show the great difficulty on the delayed-response problem that is so easily obtained with monkeys and other animals. Some success has been achieved, however, in showing that the effects of frontal damage on people and monkeys may have common underlying bases, even though the behavior may be superficially different.

An example comes from studies in which people with frontal damage are asked to sort cards (similar to playing cards). If a man with frontal damage starts out sorting according to suit, for example, he may perform quite as efficiently as a normal subject. But, if the rules of the game are changed abruptly, and if sorting according to number is now called for, he may persist in working as before, not showing the required adaptability to changing situations. It has been thought that this kind of effect can be explained by assuming an enhanced tendency to perseverate, the same process that has been cited as one explanation of the disturbances shown in monkeys with lesions of the frontal cortex.

The tests on which people with frontal-lobe damage do not perform as well as normal people do often also involve some dependence on proper orientation or motor control. For example, frontal damage produces difficulty in the simple task of touching parts of the body that are indicated on a diagram and difficulty in

following a path through a maze. Such findings and the perseverative difficulties mentioned previously—as well as the common report that an individual patient can't plan ahead or ignores the consequences of his actions—have evoked the suggestion that the frontal lobe is involved in a system that prepares, or organizes, responses (even before the stimulus that triggers activity is given), taking into account other present and planned actions of the individual. According to one such view (Pribram, 1962) the frontal cortex is involved in the control of behavior by our *intentions*; its role in motor control is considered to be most evident in responses we think of as voluntary rather than reflexive in nature.

Speech Areas and Temporal Cortex

One of the most striking behavioral changes that can occur following brain damage is **aphasia**, a loss or disturbance of language ability. Aphasia is observable only in human beings, obviously, for *Homo sapiens* is the only species that produces and understands speech.

The kinds of speech disorders that follow brain damage are usually separated into two major varieties. In **sensory aphasia**, the patient is unable to understand or recognize spoken language, although he knows that he is being spoken to and suffers no loss in his ability to discriminate among nonspeech sounds. In **motor aphasia**, the problem is with the production of speech, usually in finding a word. The word may be lost completely for the moment, or other words that are somehow related to it may be substituted. Other kinds of expressive (motor) disorders include changes in fluency, the occasional production of meaningless or ungrammatical speech, and disruptions of the ability to control the speech organs in order to achieve proper production of the sounds of the language.

A striking feature about the relation between the brain and language is that a cerebral lesion that produces aphasia is almost always found to be on the left side of the brain. This evidence that the left side has a special importance in controlling language can be verified in normal subjects. If an anesthetic drug like Amytal Sodium is injected into a blood vessel

BOX 18.3

CORTICAL LOCALIZATION IN MAN

Usually, when the brain is damaged by disease or by accidental injury, the victim is not studied carefully unless the damage produces some noticeable change in behavior. As a result, only those who have serious symptoms are seen; only those brain-damaged people who become *patients* contribute to our ideas about the role of neural structures in human behavior.

It is possible to approach more closely the experimental methods used with animal subjects by studying people with known brain injuries, whether or not they demonstrate obvious effects. Such a method may turn up more subtle results and expose the full range of the effects of a given lesion.

This method has been used extensively by Hans-Lukas Teuber, a psychologist at the Massachusetts Institute of Technology, and his several collaborators. Teuber has studied war veterans known to have received penetrating head injuries resulting in presumed brain damage; he enlisted the cooperation of these men, most of whom were active, effective members of society, and compared them with control subjects on a series of psychological tests. Some of the results may be taken as evidence that both the specificity hypothesis and the nonspecificity hypothesis about cortical localization are incorrect when stated in extreme terms.

From what we know about the visual sensory system, we should expect partial lesions of the occipital cortex to produce visual **scotomata** (abnormal blind spots), and they do. The subject is seated, with his eyes focused upon a spot directly in front of him. The experimenter then moves a small target spot to different parts of the visual field. The man with damage to his occipital cortex is not able

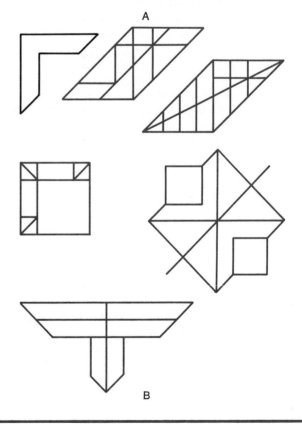

that carries blood principally to the left side of the brain, it produces a group of temporary changes in behavior, including aphasia; the same drug distributed to the right side of the brain does not usually have this effect. Some people, however, do appear to be right-brained as far as control of speech is concerned; this arrangement is more prevalent among left-handed people.

to see the target when it moves into the blind part of his visual field, the part corresponding to his lesion (see Figure A).

Less expected findings appear. An individual with a scotoma can be given tests that call upon the use of the remainder of the visual field. Changes are seen then also. People with scotomata somewhere in the visual field have, for example, a slower average rate of dark adaptation than people with unimpaired vision, even though the blind areas are not involved in the dark-adaptation test. Other investigators (Ratcliff and Davies-Jones) showed that people with similar injuries are relatively inaccurate in localizing (pointing to) the target spot even if it is presented in the part of the visual field that is *not* blind.

Finally, there are some visual tests that seem dependent upon wide areas of the cerebrum. The hidden-figure test that is illustrated here (see Figure B) is an example. People with damage anywhere in the brain are on the average slower than normal in discovering where in each of the five complex figures the simple one can be found embedded.

We see, then, three levels of complexity of visual tasks related to different amounts of specificity of localization. Some abilities are related to a highly specific region, a given subarea of the occipital sensory cortex. Other visual tasks are affected by a lesion anywhere in the visual area; still others, by damage in any portion of the cerebrum. There is some specificity of neural systems, but the cortex is not arranged in a simple mosaic of independent areas.

H.-L. TEUBER. Some alterations in behavior after cerebral lesions in man. In E. Bass (Ed.), *Evolution of Nervous Control From Primitive Organisms to Man.* Washington, D.C.: American Association for the Advancement of Science, 1959, pp. 157–194.
GRAHAM RATCLIFF & G. A. B. DAVIES-JONES. Defective visual localization in focal brain wounds. Brain, 1972, **95**, 49–60.
H.-L. TEUBER & S. WEINSTEIN. Ability to discover hidden figures after cerebral lesion. *Archives of Neurology and Psychiatry*, 1956, **76**, 369–379. Figure B adapted by permission of American Medical Association.

We may now ask whether more precise localization of areas important to speech is possible. The evidence demonstrates some relation between the kind of aphasia and the location of the damage. Thus, motor aphasia occurs with damage to an area in the lower part of the frontal lobe; damage to the temporal lobe, particularly at the junction with the parietal and occipital lobes, produces sensory aphasia, although there are usually some expressive changes as well (see Figure 18.2). These relations are far from perfect, however; in fact, a lesion almost anywhere on the left side of the cerebrum may cause at least a temporary aphasia of almost any kind.

Even if a person with damage to the left temporal lobe does not suffer aphasia, he will display a difficulty that is related to language, namely, a deficit in verbal memory. He will have difficulty in remembering words, whether he reads them or hears them, but no difficulty in remembering faces, for example. A different result follows damage to the right temporal lobe. In this case the subject will display some difficulties in the perception of nonverbal stimuli (faces, melodies, and so forth), and a very severe impairment in the retention of them (see Box 18.4, p. 428).

LOCUS OF LEARNING: A PERSPECTIVE

We embarked upon a study of the cerebral cortex because it was evident that an animal deprived of cortex could do very little interesting learning. We have discovered that even the loss of small subregions of cortex can profoundly affect the ability of the subject to show various forms of adaptive behavior. It has been stated repeatedly, however, that the manifestation of any behavior depends upon the integrity of a *complex* system of cells. The fact that destruction of a certain cortical area is followed by a decrease in learning ability does not mean that learning takes place in that area alone, nor indeed does it even prove that learning takes place there *at all*. The eye is essential to visual learning, but presumably the actual learning takes place elsewhere. In the same way, the areas of the cortex may be involved in transmitting and recoding the necessary information but play no part in learning as such.

Very striking evidence suggesting a role in learning for certain *subcortical* structures

BOX 18.4

ONE BRAIN IS BETTER THAN TWO

The central nervous system is one great *unified* structure, controlling experience and behavior by the *integrating* interaction of its many, many neurons. The great truth of this statement for the normal animal is underlined by the remarkable findings that come from studies of instances in which this unity is destroyed.

The standard **split-brain** procedure developed by Roger Sperry of the California Institute of Technology involves cutting the optic chiasm and the corpus callosum (see Figure A). When this operation has been performed, the visual information entering one eye of the animal reaches directly only one side of the brain; and unless subcortical connections are used, it cannot reach the other side. The effects of this operation on learning and memory are striking but understandable.

The basic fact is that the operation results in two mostly separate brains. If the animal is taught a visually guided problem (e.g., to choose a cube and ignore a sphere that is presented at the same time), with input restricted to only one eye, and if it is then tested with only the other eye, no memory of the task is demonstrated at all (see Figure B). In fact, the other eye can be used to teach the animal to follow a response pattern exactly the opposite of that guided by input to the first eye (e.g., to choose the sphere rather than the cube). The two sides of the brain have learned different things, and whichever side gets stimulated on any given trial will produce the response that *it* has learned.

There are people who have received similar operations in an attempt to relieve difficult cases of epilepsy. (In these cases the corpus callosum is cut but not the optic chiasm.) Each hemisphere receives visual input from the opposite visual field (just as in

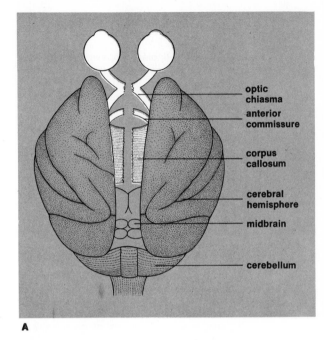

A

normal people), but it cannot transfer this information to the other side because the corpus callosum is not available. If such a patient is given a brief stimulus in the left visual field and asked verbally what he sees, he will report "nothing." The information did not reach the left hemisphere, which controls speech. However, the right hemisphere (which did receive the input) can display that it actually recognized the object if the subject is allowed to make his response in a *nonverbal* way, for example, by pointing to a picture of the stimulus from among several alternatives. Presumably, these subjects have a separate conscious visual awareness in each hemisphere.

The final twist is that when, as very rarely

comes from studies involving people who have had large portions of the limbic system, including some of the hippocampus (see p. 548), removed surgically. The patients who underwent such procedures turned out to have extreme learning and memory difficulties. They could

remember quite well things that they had experienced and learned *before* the operation. They could also learn new information, but retention of this new material was exceedingly fragile and short-lived. They could not remember from day to day, for example, the name of the psy-

B

happens, someone is *born without* a corpus callosum, these signs of separate visual experience are not found. Apparently during the early development of such a person, other cross-connecting pathways in lower parts of the brain acquire the ability to take over the role that the corpus callosum would normally assume.

R. W. SPERRY. Cerebral organization and behavior. *Science*, 1961, **133**, 1749–1757.
R. W. SPERRY. Cerebral dominance in perception. In F. A. Young & D. B. Lindsley (Eds.), *Early Experience and Visual Information Processing in Perceptual and Reading Disorders.* Washington, D.C.: National Academy of Sciences, 1970.
Figure B is adapted from the cover of the January 1964 issue of *Scientific American.* Copyright © 1964 by Scientific American, Inc. All rights reserved.

chologist who repeatedly came to examine them after the operation.

In all such studies using the ablation method we get valuable information about the role of certain neural structures in adaptive behavior. However, in searching for the locus of learning, we are looking for that part of the nervous system where the pattern of activity produced by a stimulus *changes* when the subject has learned to respond in a new way to the stimulus. This problem may be attacked by methods other than the ablation method: by recording EEGs (see p. 65) or the responses of single neurons in various parts of the brain, while a subject is exposed to a learning problem. The experimenter observes the records to discover whether or not the wave forms that arise from a given region of the brain change when there are changes in behavior. The structures or cells that show the new electrophysiological response first are especially likely to be the ones most crucially involved in learning. Studies of this kind have led some scientists to suggest that the ascending reticular formation (see p. 535) is particularly important to learning and that it may be here that an early phase of learning actually takes place. Other experiments have pointed to a widespread system involving the reticular formation, parts of the thalamus, the hippocampus, *and* the cortex (Olds et al., 1972).

Even this brief survey makes it clear that there is now a large amount of knowledge about the importance of different neural structures to the systems underlying learning, although we cannot specify exactly *where* in the nervous system this learning takes place. Maybe we should not expect to be able to reach this level of explanation until we know *what* happens in the nervous system when learning takes place.

MECHANISMS OF LEARNING: REVERBERATING CIRCUITS

One possible mechanism of learning has been proposed that does not invoke any new physiological or chemical mechanisms beyond the basic phenomena of neuron activity that are already familiar to us. It is suggested that a *new pattern* of connections among neurons is set up in the brain as a result of each new experience and thus that learning consists primarily of the activity of new patterns of organization among the neural elements.

But how can we expect neural activity produced by experience to last for any appreciable length of time? The immediate neural response to a stimulus runs its course and dies out well before one second elapses. But, of course, memories sometimes persist for years. A partial answer is provided by the concept of **reverberating circuits**. It has been hypothesized that closed loops of neurons are present within the brain and specifically within the cerebral cortex. If neural activity were started in such a loop, it might continue to reverberate indefinitely, transmitting the excitatory message around and around and thus providing a permanent new aspect to the brain's pattern of electrical activity. This reverberating circuit would be the neural basis of the memory (see Figure 18.3).

There are serious objections to this theory, unfortunately. Many treatments and conditions that would be expected to disrupt severely any ongoing reverberating neural activity in the brain do not cause the complete loss of memory that would be expected according to this theory. For example, abnormal conditions such as convulsions and anesthesia and normal states such as sleep may be accompanied by extreme changes in the amount and regularity of neural activity in the brain; yet these conditions do not result in any appreciable loss of long-standing memories. As a result of such evidence, the role that reverberating circuits are believed to play in learning and memory has been drastically reduced. These circuits are now assumed to play a role only in short-term memory (see Unit 17). As usually expressed, this revised theory states that, immediately after a trial in a learning experiment, a short-lasting reverber-

FIGURE 18.3 A neuronal model of learning that suggests how an animal might learn to press a lever in order to get a food reward. Let us assume that each neuron schematically pictured here can be stimulated into discharge by any one impulse delivered to it from a neuron that precedes it in the chain, *except* for the neuron with the large cell body (a). This neuron has a bigger threshold; it requires *two* impulses presented simultaneously to provoke it into activity.

Without training there would be no response because the activity initiated by the sight of the lever could not get past the large threshold barrier presented by neuron a. When activity is started in the lower group of neurons by the gustatory and other stimuli and *maintained* along with impulses entering the upper chain, the response at the muscle fiber will occur. The activity coming in from the receptors along the lower neurons will not continue long after a training trial is over, however, unless some such special mechanism is provided. The reverberating circuit is such a mechanism. After it has been developed an impulse arriving over the upper chain can always produce a response, since the reverberating circuit is continuously sending *one* impulse to neuron a.

A more complete model would have to tell exactly how the training trials could cause the formation of the circuit.

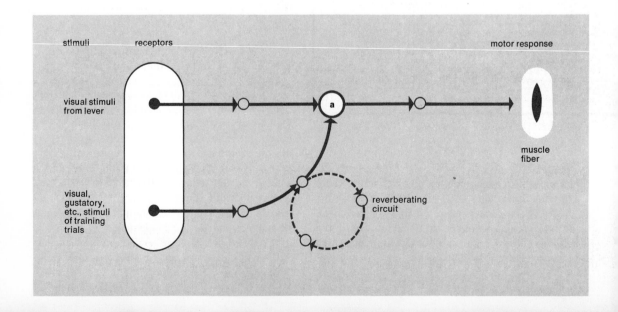

ating circuit of activity is formed and that this circuit serves as the neural basis for a short-term memory.

Before the reverberating activity (and with it, the short-term memory) dies out, it will have led to a permanent change in the brain. This permanent change will be the neurological mechanism for a long-term memory (also treated in Unit 17). These two stages of memory are thus presumed to have different structural bases (Hebb, 1949). Later in this unit we will consider some physiological evidence for the existence of two stages of memory. At present it will suffice to say that, if there *are* two different kinds of memory, a reverberating-circuit mechanism *might* underlie the short-term stage. There is, however, no direct proof either that reverberating circuits exist or that, if they do, they underlie short-term memory. But what mechanism might underlie long-term memory?

MECHANISMS OF LEARNING: SYNAPTIC CHANGES

For a long period of time the only mechanisms that received any serious consideration as candidates for the neurological basis of long-term memory were purely structural ones. Basic to all the structural hypotheses was the assumption that the ease with which activity in an axon can excite activity in an adjoining neuron depends upon the facility with which the appropriate synapse can be traversed. It was therefore suggested that learning might consist of the development of more or larger axon terminals from many neurons converging on synapses. Another suggestion was that learning involved a narrowing of the relevant synaptic clefts. Either would facilitate transmission across the synapse (see Figure 18.4, p. 432).

These structural hypotheses are still widely believed, and various lines of evidence in favor of them are now becoming available. They receive some indirect support from the observation that many neurons in the brains of rodents are not developed until after birth. The hippocampus, which has often been proposed as a crucial structure in learning and memory,

includes many of these late-maturing cells. These small nerve cells may act as crucial middle links in neuron chains that control behavior, forming connections between fibers bringing excitation into the hippocampus and neurons leaving it. Because these cells are fully formed only after birth, their connections and thus the exact nature of the neuron systems that are established might be determined in part by the learning and experience of the individual. In fact, it has been shown that rats receiving daily stimulation from being handled by an experimenter have a higher rate of formation of these cells than has been found in animals left alone (unhandled) in their cages. The pattern of synaptic connections may be fashioned by experience and learning and, once formed, may be the physiological basis of memory (Altman, 1972).

Obviously consistent with these findings is the fact that environmental stimulation can change the size and weight of the cerebral cortex. Krech and his colleagues demonstrated this fact by discovering that rats reared in an enriched psychological environment full of objects to manipulate, varied paths to explore, and problems to solve (see Figure 18.5, p. 433) developed thicker and heavier cortexes than rats that had lived out their lives in an impoverished environment (Bennett, Diamond, Krech, & Rosenzweig, 1964). A possible synaptic explanation of such differences comes from experiments in which mice were reared in darkness for the first twenty-five days of life. These animals were found to have fewer dendritic spines—and therefore presumably fewer synapses—in the visual area of the cortex than light-reared mice (Valverde, 1967). This suggests, of course, that experience and perhaps learning, as such, stimulates the formation of synapses. (But see Box 18.5, p. 434.)

MECHANISMS OF LEARNING: TRANSMITTER SUBSTANCES

There are other data that implicate *biochemical* as well as structural mechanisms in learning. If a neuron is going to influence activity in a neuron with which it makes synaptic contact, the

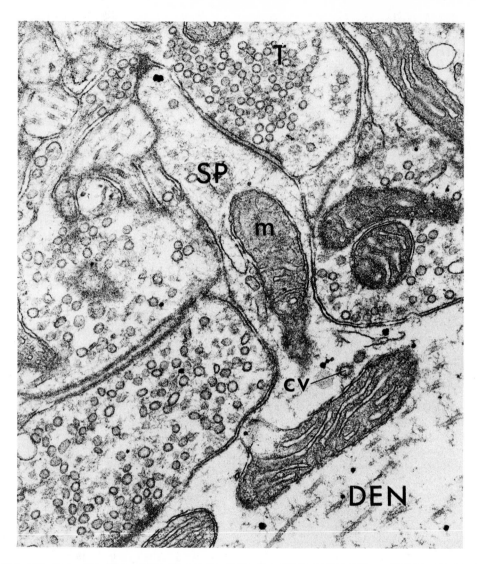

FIGURE 18.4 This photograph (of a section through the brain of a cat) was taken with an electron microscope, and what we see was magnified about 52,000 times. (This true picture is not so simple as our diagrams of neurons running freely through empty-looking space and nicely connected with one another.) At the lower right we see part of a dendrite (DEN) from which a dendritic spine (SP) arises. A terminal (T) from the axon of another neuron comes into synaptic contact with the spine, as shown at the top of the photo; many synaptic vesicles are seen inside the terminal and in other axons shown in cross-section. One possible mechanism of learning would involve an increase in the number of axon terminals, their growth in size, or closer approach to the dendritic surface.

Drs. G. D. Pappas & Stephen G. Waxman. Albert Einstein College of Medicine.

first neuron must release into the synaptic space the appropriate transmitter substance, which will diffuse across the space and stimulate the next neuron (see p. 63). If a synaptic connec-tion is then going to be returned to a resting state so that it can be used again, the transmitter substance must be destroyed by the appropriate enzyme once it has done its job.

FIGURE 18.5   Rats in an enriched environment. The stimulation and challenge of these surroundings lead to changes in brain size and brain chemistry.

E. L. Bennett et al. Chemical and anatomical plasticity of the brain. *Science*, **146**, 610–619; copyright 1964 by the American Association for the Advancement of Science; reprinted by permission.

For efficient synaptic transmission there must then be appropriate amounts of both substances, the transmitter and the enzyme.

Acetylcholine Studies

Krech and his colleagues have explored many aspects of the hypothesis that the greater the efficiency of synaptic transmission, so defined, the greater the learning ability will be (see, e.g., Rosenzweig, Krech, Bennett, & Diamond, 1968). This hypothesis, it will be readily seen, suggests a biochemical mechanism of learning that *supplements* the structural mechanisms. In these studies they have measured the level of **acetylcholine (ACh)**, which is believed to be the transmitter at some brain synapses, and the amount of **acetylcholinesterase (AChE)**, the enzyme that eventually breaks down the ACh.

Their investigations have shown that the general hypothesis has some validity, although the chemical mechanisms involved are rather complex. It seems that it is necessary to consider not only the absolute amounts of these substances, but also the ratio of ACh to AChE; for example, strains of rats with higher ratios

of ACh to AChE are superior in learning ability. The cause-and-effect relation also goes in the other direction. Rats that were raised in an enriched environment (as in Figure 18.5) were found to have higher AChE activity in the cortex (indicating higher ACh activity as well) than rats reared in an impoverished environment. Thus, there are chemical changes that occur as a result of experience, as well as the structural ones described in the previous section.

Several other experiments have been done with drugs that modify the level of ACh or AChE and produce changes in learning and memory consistent with the hypothesis of Krech and his associates. An interesting example of these experiments is the study by Deutsch, Hamburg, and Dahl (1966), who used a drug called DFP. This chemical is an *anticholinesterase*, that is, it prevents AChE from destroying ACh, thus increasing the amount of active ACh. The experiment seems to show that a certain amount of ACh is optimal for memory of the simple maze habit that these experimenters taught their rats. If DFP is given when rats have not learned a problem well, it *facilitates* their performance on the problem by making more ACh available. When a habit has been well learned and an opportunity given for a complete build-up of ACh, however, the DFP injections cause a *loss* in memory. In this case presumably an excess of ACh results from the injection; the neurons are continually under a state of stimulation, so that the synapse cannot effectively transmit the incoming information.

Chemical Transmitters, Division of Labor, and Circadian Rhythms

Each of the billions of neurons in the brain may have a hundred or more receiving synapses and an equally large number of axon terminals ending on other neurons. The resulting astronomical number of possible synaptic connections probably calls upon many different chemical compounds to function as trans-synaptic transmitter substances. Among the two most important candidates (in addition to ACh) for such roles are **norepinephrine** and **serotonin** (compounds which we will meet again, especially in Unit 22).

BOX 18.5

LEARNING BY DECAY; FORGETTING BY GROWTH?

Those who present a synaptic-change theory of the mechanism of learning usually propose that *positive* changes in the size or number of synapses are correlated with experience and learning. However, members of an interdisciplinary team of investigators at the University of California have called attention to the possibility that *negative* changes (i.e., reduction in the size or number of synapses) might *also* underlie learning. Some of their own data suggest that possibility. For example, rats raised in enriched environments had only *two-thirds as many* synapses on certain dendrites in the cortex as rats raised in impoverished environments, although the synapses were on the average about *twice as large* in the enriched animals.

A reduction in the number of synapses as the physiological basis of learning might seem paradoxical, but it is not necessarily so. The animal might come to the learning situation with a large number of synapses that were active at a moderate level. However, these synapses might tend to produce different kinds of actions and thus underlie various different and perhaps competing responses. With experience or training, the synapses appropriate to the to-be-learned habit would then increase in size and efficiency, and the inappropriate ones would atrophy.

An opposite side of the coin might explain another interesting finding. Byron Campbell of Princeton University and Norman Spear of Rutgers University have reviewed a large body of data that they and others have collected which demonstrate that immature rats have poorer memories than adult rats. That is, if both young and older rats are trained equally well to avoid shock (or to get food by bar pressing), the younger ones will show much more forgetting of the habit when all the animals are tested several days later. During the interval between learning and retention testing, many changes are still going on in brains of the younger rats simply through normal development. These changes include a dramatic increase in the number of synaptic connections. The older rats (the ones that display good retention) already have their full complement of synapses at the time of learning.

The investigators suggest two different ways in which these facts (increase in memory and increase in numbers of synapses) might be related. It may be simply that it is necessary to have a large number of synapses at the time of learning in order for memory to be at its best. On the other hand, it may be the *increase* in the number of synapses between the time of learning and the time of retention testing that produces the young rats' memory loss. The learned response presumably used the synapses available to the animal at the time of acquisition; as he matures, other synapses form that did not participate in the learning and will tend to produce other behavior. The original memory is still there in a sense, but it cannot be retrieved because of all the competing effects of further development.

As Campbell and Spear point out, the poor memory of immature rodents may be paralleled by similar effects in children. *Infantile amnesia* is the term used to describe the fact that adults can usually recall very little of the events of their first three to five years of life. Various kinds of rather complicated theories have been proposed to explain this, but it might be most simply viewed as the result of naturally poor memory for things learned at a developmentally immature age. Whatever will be the ultimate physiological explanation of the rats' infantile amnesia will probably apply to human beings as well.

M. R. ROSENZWEIG, K. MØLLGAARD, M. C. DIAMOND, & E. L. BENNETT. Negative as well as positive synaptic changes may store memory. *Psychological Review*, 1972, **79**, 93–96.
B. A. CAMPBELL & N. E. SPEAR. Ontogeny of memory. *Psychological Review*, 1972, **79**, 215–237.

The evidence indicates that different transmitter substances are dominant in different parts of the nervous system (e.g., hypothalamus and spinal cord), serve different kinds of synapses (inhibitory or excitatory), modulate different states of consciousness (sleep, alertness) or different kinds of behavior (motor activity, emotional responses), and have different circadian rhythms (see Unit 3). Thus, for example, in the rat brain the amount of norepinephrine reaches its peak during the later part of the night, when the animal is most active; on the other hand, serotonin is at its height during the day when the animal is quiescent or asleep. It would be fair to assume that these two substances play quite different roles in the animal's total repertoire of states of consciousness and behavior (see Unit 22). Given the large number of chemical substances (each with its specialized job) involved in efficient brain functioning, and the varying circadian rhythms displayed by these varying substances, the very minimal lesson we can draw from all this would seem to be: For the brain to operate efficiently in remembering, learning, and solving problems, in being alert when alertness is required, and relaxing when relaxation is not contra-indicated, *a delicate and harmonious integration of a multitude of brain rhythms must constantly be maintained*. All the biological clocks of the brain must be synchronized and in harmony with the demands made upon the individual by the environment. This adds a new dimension to the task of understanding what goes on in the brain when we memorize, learn, and solve problems. It may also help us in eventually discovering what goes wrong in the brain when our alertness, mental stability, and mental capacities falter as a consequence of disease, aging processes, or other bodily malfunctioning. And, finally, it may provide still another useful clue in our search for the biological basis of mental retardation and mental disease (see pp. 439 and 552).

CHEMICAL CHANGES INSIDE THE NEURON

So far we have emphasized either structural or chemical changes in the synapse in our search for the crucial physiological mechanism in learning. Now we must consider the possibility that changes take place during the learning process *within*, rather than between, neurons. These *intra*neural changes would then direct the new activity of the organism. This possibility does not necessarily conflict with those already described because changes at the synaptic region may well be caused by internal chemical changes of the cell. The intraneural hypothesis does invite our attention to the biochemical events inside the neuron; and, by suggesting that the memory *storage* mechanism of the brain may be found within the chemical nature of its individual neurons, it presents the first major, primarily *biochemical* theory of learning (as opposed to the primarily structural theories we discussed earlier).

In Unit 1 we discussed two important substances, ribonucleic acid (RNA) and deoxyribonucleic acid (DNA), which are found within each living cell. Neither is a single chemical; the names refer instead to classes of compounds, each of which can occur in an infinite number of forms. The structure of DNA determines the exact kinds of RNA that will be produced by the cell; RNA in turn controls the production of proteins, including the structural components of the cell and the enzymes that govern its activity. In this way the activity of each cell of the body (and thus eventually of the whole organism) is determined largely by the varieties of DNA and RNA within it. Genes are made of DNA and are transmitted, in all their infinite variety of chemical composition, from parents to child. And through their specific chemical composition, the DNA molecules (genes) help determine the child's characteristics of structure and behavior. The evolutionary history of the species and the genetic background of any individual within the species are thus mirrored in that organism's DNA; the DNA carries the *evolutionary memory* (the determinants of the structure and function of the *species*) into every cell of the body of the newborn.

The major hypothesis concerning intraneuronal chemical changes states that *individual memory* (the consequences of learning within a single lifetime of one *individual*) is carried by the structure of the RNA within the neurons. This hypothesis assumes that neural activity (accompanying a learning experience) can *change* the detailed chemical structure of the RNA within the neurons involved in a given learning experience. The experience of the individual would thus be laid down in the details of the chemistry of the RNA in his neurons, much as the experience of his ancestors is reflected in the details of the chemistry of the DNA. Because RNA controls protein synthesis within the neuronal cell body, a change in RNA could, for

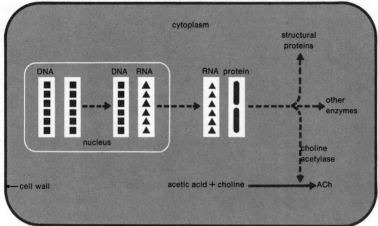

FIGURE 18.6 The control of cellular activity by nucleic acids. When cells divide in the developing organism, each DNA molecule reproduces itself, so that each cell carries the genetically determined evolutionary memory (represented in the left half of the nucleus). RNA is produced in the nucleus; its exact nature is determined by the specific nature of the DNA. RNA moves out of the nucleus and stimulates the production of protein; the specific kind of protein is dictated by the nature of the RNA. Many of these proteins are enzymes and thus control other chemical reactions. The enzyme that assists in the *formation* of the transmitter substance acetylcholine is specified in the diagram.

example, determine how much transmitter substance the neuron would release at synapses with other cells. The result would then be learning (see Figure 18.6).

Several kinds of evidence support this hypothesis. Let us list three: First, it has been reported that administration of RNA (or of a drug that increases its manufacture in the brain) produces better learning or memory in experimental animals or in old people; second, Hydén and Egyhazi (1962) have demonstrated that rats taught a balancing task show changes in the proportions of different kinds of RNA in parts of the brain that are involved in maintaining equilibrium; and, third, exposure of the brain to the enzyme that *breaks down* RNA causes memory *losses* in cats, fish, rats, and flatworms.

Such studies do not support directly the most important part of the RNA theory: the assertion that the *structure* of RNA is specifically related to learning. In other words, they are all explicable on the proposition that RNA is essential to the general well-being and functioning of the cell; and, on the assumption that "if a little is good, a lot is better," a *generally* better functioning neuron will learn more quickly than one that does not function as well. There have been some claims that *specific* memories can be transferred from one animal into another by taking RNA from the brain of a

trained animal and injecting it into an untrained animal; the untrained animal now shows a memory for what the first animal had learned. The volume edited by Fjerdingstad (1971) summarizes some positive and some negative results. The positive results, if substantiated, could prove that the exact nature of a memory is coded as a specific RNA. Unfortunately, to date, the early positive findings have been difficult to replicate, and at the present writing the possibility of memory transfer from one animal to another via transfer of brain substance must be regarded as unproven.

In some experiments the focus of interest has been directly upon proteins and protein synthesis, rather than upon the RNA control mechanism. One approach has been to inject a chemical that *inhibits* the formation of protein. Barondes and Cohen (1967) injected mice with such drugs and then trained them on a maze a few hours later, when protein formation presumably was at its lowest. They discovered that the subjects learned about as well as uninjected mice. However, when the *retention* of the mice was tested minutes or even hours later, the injected mice did show poorer memory for the learned habit. It would appear from this result that protein formation is not necessary for the *learning* of a habit (short-term memory) but may be important if the memory is going to be *retained* a relatively long time.

Hydén (1972) studied rats that were forced to learn a new method of searching for their food. He found that this learning is accompanied by increased formation of a protein that is found only in the brain. He then injected other rats with an antiserum which should block the activity of that brain protein. These animals were found to be retarded in learning in comparison with rats that had not been injected.

Even if the details of the RNA theory are incorrect, it is still probable that activities within the neuron which depend upon its ability to construct proteins are necessary to learning, memory, thinking, and consequent adaptive behavior.

TWO STAGES OF MEMORY?

We now return to the question that was briefly raised earlier in this unit and that is discussed from a different point of view in Unit 17: Is there only one mechanism underlying memory, or are there two or more different stages in memory, each with its own physiological basis?

The Consolidation Hypothesis

The two-stage view is supported by the currently popular **consolidation** hypothesis. According to this hypothesis, a process that will be the mechanism of short-term memory begins within the nervous system immediately after a learning trial. This process is short-lived and fades away, but it is instrumental in producing a second change in the nervous system, one that will be more permanent and that will serve as the basis for long-term memory. But in order for the short-term process to produce the long-term process, the short-term process must be allowed to run its course without disruption or interference. The short-term memory, in other words, must be given an opportunity to undergo consolidation into a long-term memory.

One approach, therefore, to testing the consolidation theory would be to provide the subject with something to learn, then interrupt the short-term process *after the learning trial but before the long-term process has had an opportunity to become established*. The subject should not then develop a long-term memory

An experimental procedure often used in these studies with rats and mice is the **step-down procedure**, devised by Jarvik and Essman (1960). This procedure can be used because it happens to be natural for a rat or a mouse placed on a small platform a few inches above the floor to step down to the floor within a few seconds. The animal will do so rather consistently day after day. Now suppose that on one day the floor is electrified and that stepping onto it produces a painful shock to the foot. When the animal is afterward put back on the platform, even twenty-four hours later, it will remain on the platform—for several minutes or longer, if necessary. The animal has learned from the earlier experience that stepping onto the floor is punished, and it remembers it the next day. In this situation, memory is demonstrated by the animal's *not* stepping down onto the floor.

If now we *interfere* with the animal's short-term memory immediately after his first experience of "step-down → foot shock" *before this short-term memory has had an opportunity to become consolidated into a long-term memory*, then the animal should show no evidence of remembering the shock experience when tested the next day and should blithely step down again. The method used most often to interrupt the animal's consolidation of his short-term memory consists of passing an electric current across the brain of the animal. This current results in a very high level of activation of neurons all over the brain. One effect is to produce a convulsion; another effect is to disrupt any patterned neural circuits (e.g., reverberating circuits) that may be active. When **electroconvulsive shock (ECS)** follows step-down–foot shock pairing quickly enough and we test the animal a day later, it does indeed act as if it had no memory of the event; it steps down promptly from the platform with no apparent expectation of shock.

When there is a longer interval between the shock and the ECS, the animal *does* remember the shock, and it remains on the platform when tested the next day. We conclude therefore that this longer interval has allowed consolidation to run its course and has allowed the memory of the shock to be recorded in the relatively invulnerable long-term memory. The length of interval necessary to produce the more permanent memory varies widely, depending upon many factors, among them the nature of the task, the age of the animal, the metabolic state of the individual, and the disrupting agent employed. For example, Stephens and McGaugh (1968) showed that ECS experiments done with mice at 9:00 P.M., when the animal's circadian temperature cycle is at its peak (about 36.5°C), yield stronger ECS effects than when done at 1:00 P.M., when the cycle hits its low point of 34.9°C. These results could mean either that consolidation varies *inversely* with metabolic state (the higher the body temperature, the *slower* the long-term memory consolidation), or that disruption varies *directly* with metabolic activity (the higher the body temperature, the *more effective* the short-term memory disruption). In either case we see that memory processes are responsive to bodily circadian rhythms. It is also generally true that when anesthetics are used to disrupt the physiological activity of the brain, the effect appears to be stronger than with ECS; that is, anesthetics can be administered at a greater interval after the trial and still disrupt the memory.

Some long-known facts about the effects of accidental head injury in human beings seem to parallel the general findings of these animal experiments. We refer to a sudden traumatic event (such as an automobile collision) which results in a temporary loss of consciousness but does not cause permanent damage to brain tissue. A common finding in such cases is that the patient awakens with a gap in his memory for the events just preceding the accident. He literally does not remember what hit him. This *retrograde amnesia* (a forgetting going backward in time from the point of its production) is what one would expect on the basis of the consolidation hypothesis. It is as if the events that had just taken place (such as the approach of the other car just before the collision) were still in short-term memory at the time of the injury and the disruption of ongoing neural activity produced by the injury were sufficient to destroy the short-term memory (whether carried by reverberating circuits or some other

mechanism) before consolidation could take place. The patient says "Where am I?" not only because he doesn't recognize the hospital but also because he can't remember how he came to be injured.

It is also possible to *facilitate* learning or memory in animals by procedures that are designed to *enhance* consolidation. Injections of stimulants such as strychnine or picrotoxin into the central nervous system seem to *improve* learning. The injection is given after each trial on a learning problem when consolidation is presumably taking place, and when tested later, the animals seem to show better retention of whatever was learned. It is presumed that the drug consolidates the memory of the just-experienced learning trial more quickly or more firmly.

More recent experiments on ECS and memory have shown some other facts that must be considered. For example, if a rat goes through the step-down–foot shock–immediate ECS sequence and then a few hours later—in a completely different apparatus where no platform is present and regardless of what he is doing—is given a "free" foot shock, under some circumstances he *will* hesitate on the platform the next day, thus indicating that some memory for the bad consequences of the first stepping down must have been laid down in his brain (Quarterman et al., 1972). It has been suggested that ECS does not *erase* memories but merely makes it hard for them to be *retrieved* (see p. 409) and that the "free" foot shock serves as a reminder and thus an aid to retrieval in this experiment.

The consolidation hypothesis may be correct, of course, even if the effect of ECS is not solely to prevent consolidation from taking place. If this general view of memory is correct, then we will need to discover *two* mechanisms, and perhaps two loci, for learning. The usual assumption is that short-term memory consists of reverberating circuits or some other pattern of neural activity and that such activity then gives rise to one of the more permanent biochemical or anatomical changes (synaptic growth, protein manufacture, and so forth) which would be the basis for long-term memory. It seems quite unlikely that there is only one simple process underlying learning and memory.

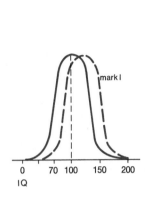

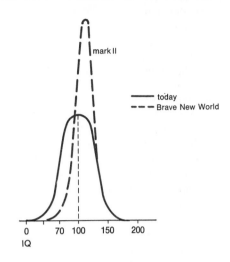

BOX 18.6

BRAVE NEW WORLDS

Our knowledge of the biochemistry of learning may foretell a glorious future in which daily doses of smartness syrup will develop a race of intellectual giants, but sober reflection brings to mind grievous problems that will arise.

The enhancement of learning ability through chemistry takes place in a living organism, and we cannot ignore other influences. We have seen in this unit that opportunities for learning will affect brain size and chemistry. Chemicals improve learning ability, but learning experience influences chemical activity. It is by the interaction of the best environment *and* the best chemicals that the Brave New World will be fashioned.

But what will this enhancement of human abilities be like? David Krech of the University of California has speculated on the following probabilities: The simplest possibility is that the appropriate treatment will improve the general intelligence of all people (Brave New World, mark I). Each individual

and thus the average will be shifted toward the brighter end of the scale of intellectual functioning. Another definite possibility (Brave New World, mark II) is suggested by some of the experiments that have already been done with animals and human beings. Here we see that those that are already high in ability do not improve; the effect of psychological and chemical treatment is to improve only those on the lower end of the scale. Finally, we must consider the high probability that psychochemical treatments will change *specific abilities* rather than general intellectual functioning. For example, we might be able to develop at will in different persons proficiency in arithmetic reasoning, verbal intelligence, or musical ability.

Suppose we do learn how to develop each individual to his maximum potential by chemical and environmental stimulation. The question of who will receive the important psychochemical treatment will certainly arise, particularly if it cannot immediately be made widely available; social controversy over who will control the drugs seems possible and even probable. Perhaps we need an elixir of goodness to take along with our syrup of smartness.

D. KRECH. Psychochemical manipulation and social policy. *Annals of Internal Medicine*, 1967, **67** (Pt. 2), 19–24, 61–67.

ANATOMY, CHEMISTRY, PHYSIOLOGY, AND LEARNING

We have noted that certain portions of the nervous system are essential to normal learning and adaptive behavior, and we have considered several different theories about the chemical and physiological events that may be related to the processes of learning. Just as adaptive behavior depends upon a series of complex systems of neurons (in the periphery, spinal cord, subcortex, and cortex), so must it depend upon many complex biochemical systems. Ribonucleic acid structure, the synthesis of protein, the growth of axon terminals, and the production and release of transmitters—all are closely related, all may be influenced by experience and by one another, and all may play a role in the control of new patterns of behavior.

An important aspect of the current interest in the chemical mechanisms of learning must be emphasized. Discoveries in the field have an excellent chance of leading to practical applications, applications that could produce enormous changes in our learning ability and unforeseen social problems (see Box 18.6).

SUMMARY

1. Learning must reflect some change in the nervous system. If any learning at all can take place in the isolated spinal cord, it is restricted to very simple conditioning. Learning of simple conditioned responses and sensory discriminations is definitely possible in a decorticate animal (an animal whose entire cerebral cortex has been destroyed), but complex adaptive behavior involves the cortex in conjunction with the subcortical structures.
2. Areas of cortex whose destruction does not produce a loss of simple sensory or motor function are called the association areas. Within the posterior association area of animals, there are separate regions that are particularly important for *learning* discrimination tasks based upon each of the various kinds of sensory input. The inferotemporal cortex is such a region for visual input; it receives essential connections relayed from the occipital cortex (the sensory visual cortex). When the inferotemporal cortex is removed or its input from the occipital cortex is destroyed, the animal shows a profound deficit in learning visual problems, although it is not blind in any simple sense of the word.
3. Lesions of the frontal association cortex in animals do not affect their ability to learn individual discrimination problems but do impair their ability to use sensory information in certain ways. For example, a monkey with a frontal lesion will be incapable of performing a delayed-response task, in which the responses must be made in terms of a stimulus that is no longer present.
4. Damage to the cortex in human beings produces changes that are somewhat similar to those seen in animals. Thus, there appear to be regions in the posterior association cortex, surrounding the various sensory areas, that play a major role in functions dependent upon the appropriate sensory modalities. Frontal-lobe damage in people does not produce difficulty on a simple delayed-response problem, but it causes changes in behavior that have been ascribed to disruption of the same underlying functions that are said to be involved in lesions of frontal cortex in animals. Some authorities emphasize the role of the frontal regions in preparing voluntary responses, even before the effective triggering stimulus is presented.
5. Cortical damage in human beings can also produce aphasia (a loss or disturbance of language ability). The effective lesion is almost always on the left side of the cerebrum (especially in right-handed people), and somewhat different areas are involved in sensory as opposed to motor aphasia. People with damage to the left temporal lobe also show a deficit in verbal memory; destruction of the right temporal cortex produces deficits in the perception and memory of nonverbal stimuli.

6. Although the cerebral cortex is essential to normal adaptive behavior, this fact does not prove that learning *takes place* in the cortex. Experiments involving lesions in the limbic system and involving recording of electrical activity in various regions of the brain have suggested that many parts of the brain (the limbic system, the reticular formation, the thalamus, *and* the cortex) participate in the changes that underlie learning and memory.

7. Investigations of *where* learning takes place (the locus of learning) must be considered in conjunction with studies of *what* takes place in the nervous system when learning occurs (the mechanism of learning). The suggestion that learning consists simply of the establishment of new patterns of neural activity, perhaps in closed loops of neurons (reverberating circuits), can apply at most to short-term memory because treatments that would stop activity in such circuits do not abolish all memories.

8. A major hypothesis about the mechanism of learning which could apply to long-term as well as short-term memory is that some structural change takes place at the synapse, such as the growth of more axon terminals or a narrowing of synaptic clefts. Favorable evidence comes from the finding that increased environmental stimulation during rearing produces a thicker cortex and that animals deprived of experience (e.g., mice raised in darkness) have fewer dendritic spines in the relevant area of the cortex than normal animals have.

9. Synaptic function involves biochemical events, and changes in transmitter function may supplement structural changes. Differences in the amounts of acetylcholine (a possible transmitter substance) and acetylcholinesterase (the enzyme that destroys acetylcholine) are correlated with differences in learning ability. Treatments that change the available amounts of these substances produce consistent changes in learning and memory. The nervous system utilizes a number of different transmitter substances, each with its specialized characteristics and tasks. A well-functioning brain requires a harmonic integration of these basic biochemical substances.

10. Another hypothesis suggests that chemical changes *within* neurons play a role in the learning process. Specifically, changes in the amount or kind of ribonucleic acid, which controls the production of proteins within the cell, or changes in the synthesis of the proteins themselves, have been claimed to underlie the behavioral phenomenon of learning.

11. Many facts about learning and memory are consistent with the idea that short-term and long-term memory are qualitatively different and that short-term memory depends upon a physiological process which must be undisturbed if it is to be *consolidated* into a long-term memory.

GLOSSARY

acetylcholine (ACh) A chemical that acts as a transmitter substance at some synapses in the nervous system. Specific enzymes are required in its formation and in its destruction.

acetylcholinesterase (AChE) The enzyme that breaks down acetylcholine at the synapse. This action is necessary so that the synaptic mechanisms can return to a resting state, to be used once again.

agnosia The inability to recognize a formerly familiar object; this inability may result from cortical injury.

aphasia Language disturbance following cortical injury. **Sensory aphasia** refers to the inability to understand spoken language. **Motor aphasia** is the inability to find the appropriate word and produce it correctly.

association area Cortex that is not primarily sensory or motor in nature. The frontal association area is in the frontal lobes; the posterior association area contains cortex at the junction of the temporal, parietal, and occipital lobes.

consolidation A process that is hypothesized to take place after exposure to a learning trial or to an experience. Consolidation is presumed necessary if the effect of the experience is to become permanent.

decorticate animal   An animal whose entire cerebral cortex has been destroyed or removed.

delayed-response problem   A problem in which the subject has to respond in terms of a stimulus that is no longer present, for example, the problem of choosing the one of two identical closed containers in which he previously saw a reward placed.

electroconvulsive shock (ECS)   An electric current passed through the brain that is intense enough to cause a convulsion, that is, an involuntary series of generalized contractions of the muscles of the body. Electroconvulsive shock is sometimes used as therapy for mental disorders.

equipotentiality   A principle, asserted by Lashley, that for certain specific functions one part of the cerebral cortex can do whatever any other part can do.

inferotemporal cortex   An area on the bottom edge of the temporal lobe in monkeys that performs an important function in visual learning.

learning set   The improvement in the speed of learning a new problem that results when a subject learns many different problems in turn; learning to learn.

norepinephrine   A chemical with several functions in the body. It is found in the nervous system where it serves as a transmitter substance in some regions. It is also produced as a hormone by the adrenal cortex gland.

perseveration   The tendency to continue doing or to repeat doing whatever one has just been doing. An enhanced tendency to perseverate is proposed as one of the effects of lesions of the frontal association area.

phrenology   A doctrine originally advanced in 1810, relating a person's skull formations to his personality and behavior. The doctrine rests on three assumptions: First, different traits are controlled by different areas of the cortex; second, the larger a certain area of the cortex, the more pronounced the associated trait in the individual; third, the external shape of the skull reflects the shape of the brain underneath.

posterior parietal area   An area just in front of the occipital lobe, which is important in learning based on tactual and kinesthetic stimuli.

reverberating circuit   A series of neurons so arranged that they form a continuous, potentially self-exciting, unending circuit of connections. It Is presumed to exist and is offered as a possible explanation of memory.

scotoma   A blind spot in the visual field, often caused by destruction of part of the visual sensory cortex.

serotonin   A chemical found in certain parts of the brain, as well as in some other organs of the body, that is thought to act as a transmitter substance at some synapses.

spinal animal   An animal whose spinal cord has been cut through, thus severing the neural connections between the lower part of his body and his brain.

split-brain animal   An animal that has received a cut along the midline of his brain, dividing the two sides in order to provide the animal to some extent with two separate half-brains. A typical operation involves the corpus callosum and other forebrain commissures, along with the optic chiasm.

step-down procedure   A shock-avoidance problem in which an animal learns that stepping down from a small raised platform onto a grid floor will give an unpleasant electric shock to its feet.

part six

motivation and emotion

human motivation

DO YOU KNOW...

- *whether curiosity is idle or adaptive?*

- *why it is that a senseless crime can be seen by many as a more excusable one than a crime with a purpose?*

- *what the connection is between being physiologically hungry and feeling hungry and . . .*

- *that people vary tremendously in the closeness of this connection?*

- *in what sense just playing around poses a serious challenge to a major theory of motivation?*

- *what your reactions might be in a situation where external stimulation was kept to a bare minimum?*

- *that stressful situations are, for some people, actively sought rather than avoided and . . .*

- *what attracts such people to do dangerous things which they really fear as well as enjoy?*

- *how, according to one view, the ''baser'' biological motives play an important role in permitting the flowering of the ''noble'' motives?*

CONTENTS

In other units we have been concerned with how a person grows, what he perceives, and how he behaves. Our emphasis has been upon understanding the influences of the environment upon actions and experiences. How loud must a sound be for it to be heard? What sequence of training is most effective for the acquisition of a certain behavior? How is memory affected by subsequent environmental events? The individual may have seemed at times to be pushed into the background, playing the role of the innocent bystander, the target of environmental stimuli to which he automatically responds. This view has been serviceable in the sense that orderly and lawful relations have been found to exist between stimulus and response.

In most instances, however, some hedging has been necessary. We have sometimes alluded to the effects of set and personal factors upon perceptual and learning phenomena. People are more likely to see what they expect to see, learn best what is important to them, remember most what they find most interesting. To this extent our innocent bystander has been regarded not as a completely passive victim of external circumstance but as having some voice in the nature of his response to the impinging environment. And, of course, that man attends and responds only to selected external events presupposes some kind of directing force that maintains him as an active and responsive participant in constant interaction with the environment. Generally, we have been dealing with this need for a directing force by using the rather catch-all notion that people are continually *motivated to adapt*.

But is this formulation too narrow? To act in order to obtain food is an indisputable requirement for survival—it is adaptive. However, to act in the satisfaction of, say curiosity, serves no immediate adaptive purpose, and failure to do so has no obvious biological consequence. Consider a child assembling a jigsaw puzzle because he has been promised some candy if he is successful, and then consider his friend solving the same puzzle simply because he wants to see the picture. The puzzle is equally well solved under either **motive** and probably as rapidly. We certainly cannot readily identify from the behavior itself which motive was operating. As we shall see, both hunger and curiosity are reliable human motives. The apparent biological urgency of a motive does not even inevitably ensure its priority; the pangs of unfulfilled curiosity may take precedence, up to a point, over the hunger pangs of the unfilled stomach.

The point is that not all human motives serve the satisfaction of immediate biological tissue needs. As a first definition, we can think of motives as consciously experienced urges to action. These urges to action do not necessarily imply that we know the ultimate purposes, goals, and consequences of such action. The same is true even of the so-called "tissue-need motives." We eat because we feel hungry, not in order to gain nourishment so that we may survive. Nevertheless, the biological determinants of behavior are important here as elsewhere, and therefore one avenue to an understanding of the motives of man is an understanding of his physiological involvements. (We explore that avenue in detail in Unit 22.)

Man has had an age-old preoccupation with his own motives and with the motives of others. This search is an expression of a need to make sense of the events in one's world. A complicated series of behaviors of another organism can be understood by ascribing a motive to the organism. And by motive in this sense one means what the organism is trying to do, is trying to bring about. The answers given in the search for man's motives have differed widely from time to time, from culture to culture.

CONCEPTIONS OF HUMAN MOTIVATION

The various historical conceptions should not by any means be regarded merely as antique curiosities; they reflect the then prevailing conceptions of human nature and of humanity's place in the universe. We shall discover that, however inadequate they may have been in accounting for the full complexity of human motivation, they nonetheless contain viable seeds of truth. The modern accounts of human motivation tend to reflect these prior conceptions.

The Pawn of Fate

People have often been regarded as passive instruments of external supernatural forces. These supernatural forces have assumed many forms and guises, but they are similar in that they have been viewed as the real determinants of human action. The gods of Olympus join in rivalry and conflict with one another, using men and women as pawns in their own designs. In some conceptions, the forces of good and evil grapple for man's soul; in others, inscrutable forces lay out a predetermined track that the woman fatalistically trudges, unable to deviate from it.

The sources of motivation in these conceptions are outside the person, and in this perspective the problem of motivation is not really a scientific problem, for there is no way the scientist can measure or control the supernatural forces that presumably motivate man. The fact that the scientist is thus ruled out of the picture is apparently accepted at times even in a technological age. When confronted by an inexplicable event, even the more sophisticated among us may murmur, "Well, that's fate."

The Rational Master

Quite opposed to the notion of man as a pawn of fate is the view of man as the rational master. In this view, we behave as we do because we take account of our situation, calculate and weigh consequences, and finally act in accord with a rational analysis. The locus of motivation is now in the mind, and the laws of motivation are laws of rational process; we choose what we do, and we do what we choose. Motives are therefore reasonable, and the reason for an action is synonymous with its motive.

This conception of rational humanity remains the ideal if not the reality of Western society. In fact, according to the extent to which an individual behaves in a manner that departs from this standard he is condemned or excused for this failing. For example, a killer is hired by someone who will profit from the victim's death. The motive (profit) is a rational one and the event is planned rationally. This form of cold-blooded execution then meets all the requirements for a first-degree murder conviction. But when someone impulsively kills a stranger "for no good reason" the crime is labeled senseless, and the murderer's irrationality is regarded as mitigating and deserving of a less harsh sentence and a recommendation for psychiatric treatment (see the discussion of legal insanity, Box 24.1, p. 590). Such crimes, also, are the more difficult to solve, since, as our entertainment media have so abundantly and redundantly taught us, a murderer who has no (rational) motive for her crime is unlikely to fall under suspicion. And an innocent person who does have a good motive, that is, a rational one, may be suspected. So, at least in the world of cops and robbers, the view of rational humanity predominates.

The Machine

But the rational conception was not satisfactory to those who conceived of people as machines, more complex than other physical machines, but machines nonetheless.

Now the problem of motivation becomes, in a way, superfluous, for one does not ask what motivates a simple machine. We do not ask about the motivation of the doorbell. We are satisfied to account for its behavior in terms of the pushed switch, the flow of electric current through the wires, the vibration of the clapper caused by magnets, and the sound of the clapper on the bell ringer.

People, too, have been included in such a pushbutton model. Certain features of the behavior of organisms do indeed seem to lend themselves to this simple-machine conception, especially reflexes and tropisms, which are discussed in Box 15.2, page 363.

The Social Product

The essence of viewing people as social products is the notion that our behavior can be completely understood if we realize that we do what we do in response to the values, ideals, and sanctions of our society. Presumably, these social purposes serve the adaptive demands of the environment occupied by the specific culture. Because these demands may change, so may a society's values; its members' motives are therefore not fixed in a machinelike fashion. The social group that suddenly finds itself competing with another group for the scarce assets of their region may begin to elevate courage and combativeness in its scale of values. A new cultural value is not simply announced; it gradually works itself into the spirit of a culture in a variety of ways, not the least of which are changes in the manner in which children are reared.

This development does not happen quickly; there is a **cultural lag**. The process of modifying a socially induced motive may take time, several generations or even longer. One of the blocks to social change is that the very values and motives that would speed it along are discouraged by other practices of the society. For example, cultural lag may someday come to haunt industrial societies that have succeeded in inculcating motives of initiative and ambition. The work ethic confronts the increasing availability of leisure, a situation in which the motivations of an easy-going nature would be more adaptive.

People, as social products, not only undergo motivational changes in response to environmental changes but also, by the same token, display quite different motives and values in different social situations. The notion of **cultural relativism**, as evolved by anthropologists, rejects any assumption of a universal human nature and holds instead that the behavior of any individual can be understood only in relation to the dominant motives of his particular culture.

One's culture is the frame of reference within which his motives, purposes, goals, and values are induced; they can make sense only if we can construct and share, for the moment, his psychological situation, that is, the world as he perceives it.

The conception of humanity as a social product is often closely associated with stress on **social determinism**. This doctrine asserts that there are laws of societies, of social organizations, and of historical trends that transcend individual human nature. That is, the individual is considered as merely a unit, or part, of the larger social system, taking her direction and fulfilling her narrow roles as dictated by the requirements of the system as a whole. She is the cork bobbing powerlessly on the surging stream of history, the cog in the machine, the mere tool through which inexorable forces of economic determinism express themselves.

The notion of social determinism leads us back again to the conception of humanity as prey to motivational forces over which we have little control. To the extent that the requirements of the system and the forces of economic determinism arise from social situations over which humanity can exert no control, such influences upon human motivation are indeed inexorable. But this powerlessness is often illusory, a by-product of a society's frequent unawareness of the social forces to which it is subject, not of its inability to change them. A sustained program of economic development cannot directly (or immediately) change the dominant values of an underdeveloped nation's people, but it can generate environmental changes that, through social determinism, will inevitably have this effect. (A hint as to one way that this can occur is given in Box 19.1, p. 452.)

In more developed nations, legislation affecting political rights and educational and economic opportunities cannot directly (or immediately) modify a nation's prevailing *attitude* toward its underprivileged minority groups. Such legislation can and does, however, have very real effects on the social contexts in which these groups live and in the long run must help to change the values of the society. Effects of such (recent) legislation in the United States pertaining to voting rights, school desegregation, and equal employment opportunities have already become evident, both in the realities of life and in the behavior of *both* the dominant and the minority groups. While, for many, the pace of such social change is maddeningly slow, its inevitability cannot be denied.

Social determinism, whatever its limitations as a complete theory of human motivation, is by this reasoning an optimistic view of human nature. People *can* control the forces from which these motivational influences stem.

The Unconscious Being

The notion of **unconscious motivation** views people as often unaware of the real reasons for much of their behavior. The real reasons, in this concept, are deep-seated instinctual tendencies, which are manifested in complex and often devious ways. A person's choices and actions are not always the outcome of a deliberate weighing of consequences. In this sense, the person's actions are irrational.

Not that people fail to make sense of their behavior. They experience needs and desires, goals and intentions, and tend to see most of their behavior as meaningfully related to them. But the motives they consciously experience are often elaborate, false fronts for the real unconscious motives, and their understanding of their motivation is merely a rationalization.

Although there have been many historical forerunners of such views, it is through Sigmund Freud and his theory of psychoanalysis that the conception has come to fullest flower. His theories aim not only at an explanation of human motivation but at the wider problems of understanding the total personality. Detailed descriptions of Freud's views are provided elsewhere; his general theory is discussed in Unit 29, page 710, while his proposal that unconscious forces contribute to self-deception is to be found in Unit 23, page 578. For now we note only that the impact of Freud's views on unconscious motivation has been and continues to be immense, spreading to the outermost reaches of our conceptions of the human condition as expressed in current literature, art, theology, education, philosophy, and medicine.

The Animal

In its broadest sense, the biological view of motives is one of the most influential views in contemporary theories of motivation, and this is the focus of our discussion in Unit 22. In a way, it is an extension of "the machine" approach with the important elaborations that the evolutionary origins of this machine and the details of its inner operations become important foci of speculation and investigation.

One of the effects of the evolutionary theories of Charles Darwin was the search for

BOX 19.1

LEARNING TO ACHIEVE

David McClelland, a psychologist at Harvard University, has devoted more than a score of years to the study of what he calls the "Achievement Need" or *n* Ach. To measure the strength of this need he has used a variant of the Thematic Apperception Test (see Unit 27, p. 678) in which the subject is asked to make up stories about specially prepared pictures (e.g., one picture is that of a boy studying, another shows an athletic competition).

McClelland and his associates have carried out a variety of investigations with this technique. A major research problem concerns the variations of *n* Ach within cultural subgroups in the United States as well as in other nations. One of their findings is that social classes in this country seem to differ in the extent to which the child is socialized (i.e., taught by his family and group) to achieve. The need to achieve is low in lower-socioeconomic classes but high in the middle class. The data for these generalizations include detailed interviews and observations of child-rearing practices. Parents who in their own lives are more oriented toward achievement in actions and in words are fairly quick to reward their children for achieving and, more important perhaps, themselves serve as models for their children. They provide an *n* Ach facilitating family climate, that is, a climate that is strongly conducive (through specific

and general techniques) toward development of a strong *n* Ach in the child. (For a contrasting climate, one in which a child's success is no more rewarding than his failure, see Box 28.4, p. 703.)

There is some evidence to suggest that an *n* Ach facilitating climate may be provided on a national scale. McClelland measured the strength of the achievement need as indicated by the story content in children's books in thirty countries. He found a significant correlation between *n* Ach, thus evaluated, and the economic development of these countries two decades *later*, indicating a cultural lag in this respect of roughly one generation. This finding, of course, does not imply a conscious intent on the part of national planners to instill *n* Ach into the upcoming generation. Rather, it might be interpreted as indicating a general cultural readiness in particular nations for economic growth, which, somehow, is sensed and anticipated by the authors and the arbiters of their children's literature.

McClelland, however, would insist that such a process need not be left to chance. He has developed and applied training programs intended to increase *n* Ach and, correspondingly, changes in the behavior of businessmen toward greater initiative and accomplishment. In the short run, at least, these programs have had a measure of success.

D. C. McCLELLAND. Toward a theory of motive acquisition. *American Psychologist*, 1965, **20**, 321–333.
D. C. McCLELLAND & D. WINTER. *Motivating Economic Achievement*. New York: Free Press, 1969.
D. C. McCLELLAND. *Assessing Human Motivation*. New York: General Learning Press, in press.

qualities common to the behavior of man and of lower animals. Evolution involved not only the descent of man but also an ascent of lower animals. It was observed that many lower animals, too, engage in goal-directed action, express emotions, prefer monogamous sexual relationships, show maternal tenderness for their young, become frustrated and neurotic, show reasoning ability, and so on. The effect of such observations was to throw doubt on the need for peculiarly and exclusively "human" explanations of human behavior.

What was considered really basic about motivation (human or other) was a set of sim-

ple biological **drives** that set the organism into action. These drives were intimately related to physiological requirements for food, water, oxygen, avoidance of painful stimuli, and the like. Presumably, these innate drives evolved through natural selection and thus served the necessary functions of survival of the organism. The explanation of motivated action is largely reduced then to an explanation of just how drives are brought into play, their effects on behavior, and their disappearance, once satisfied. For instance, the depletion of food substances in the body leads to a state of unrest in an animal; it engages in the activities of finding and eating food; its body is replenished and its drive reduced. An individual organism failing to respond in this manner would soon be dead, its progeny never born; hence its species would therefore be more likely to become extinct.

Innate patterns of behavior, sometimes termed **instincts**, provide the clearest illustrations of biologically rooted motives. Examples of such behavior abound and provide impressive demonstrations of quite complex acts attributable to inborn patterns of the nervous system. Once triggered by an appropriate stimulus, a complex chain of behavior unfolds. But this chain of behavior does not unfold blindly; rather, it adapts to the environment in which it occurs. Nest building by birds, for example, is sufficiently flexible to permit a wide variety

of materials to be sought and used. When the appropriate inner and environmental events initiate nest building, whatever material is at hand and suitable will be woven into the fabric of the nest. As Box 19.2 illustrates, it is possible experimentally to analyze the determinants of an instinct into physiological and environmental factors. This interaction of innate behavior patterns with environment is an important source of encouragement for attempts to derive all motivation from a relatively simplified biological base.

According to this view, all behavior serves to satisfy basic tissue needs, either directly or indirectly. Because most behavior does not involve a *direct* response to a biological drive, it has been necessary, for those who hold this

---

BOX 19.2

MATERNAL BEHAVIOR IN THE RAT

Among the many interrelated maternal behaviors of the mother rat, like nursing, cleaning, and defending her young, is that of retrieving. If the baby rats (called "pups") are placed a few feet outside the nest, the mother rat will rush forth and drag them back to the nest.

B. P. Wiesner and N. M. Sheard at the University of Edinburgh (almost a half century ago) conducted careful experimental studies of retrieving behavior and so furnished us with what is now considered a classic study of the interactions between internal and external instigators of motivational states. As a measure of retrieving strength they used the number of pups that the mother would retrieve in a 5-min interval.

The investigators found that retrieving was very high during the days immediately following birth of the young but that, as the days went by, the retrieving score steadily decreased. Careful analysis demonstrated that the critical factor accounting for this gradual decline was the change in the *appearance* of the pups as they grew older. By periodically providing the mother with fresh newborn young, the experimenters were able to maintain the retrieving

response at a high level for an indefinite period (429 days in one of the rats). We see, therefore, that a continual stimulus can maintain the aroused motive state even after the conditions that first aroused it have long disappeared.

Wiesner and Sheard then tested the effects of injecting various gonadotropic hormones (see Unit 22) under various conditions. Note the following significant facts:

1. The hormones greatly increased the mother rat's amount of retrieving.

2. Virgin females, which normally do not retrieve, retrieve actively when injected.

3. Even *male* rats will retrieve when injected with the maternal hormones, though they rarely exhibit this behavior under other circumstances.

4. The range in types of objects that the maternal rats will retrieve is greatly widened by injections. For instance, guinea pigs and mice will be actively retrieved. So will rabbits considerably larger than the mother rat herself. And, indeed, a small bundle of rags moved in a perky fashion will be readily retrieved.

We see in these results a compelling demonstration of the interaction between internal and external instigators of motivational states.

B. P. WIESNER & N. M. SHEARD. *Maternal Behavior in the Rat.* London: Oliver & Boyd, 1933.

view, to regard all other drives as acquired or derived, and in this sense they become second-order drives in contrast to first-order biological needs. For example, we may learn that social prestige is a valuable asset in seeking to satisfy the sex drive. The motive of seeking social prestige is thus regarded as a second-order drive that is gradually acquired and that is to be understood as serving the first-order sex drive. (This analysis is also encountered in Unit 16, p. 380, when secondary reinforcement was invoked to account for learning not directly associated with primary drive reinforcement.) Not surprisingly, this approach permits the assumption that almost any of the countless human motives depends upon one or more of a small number of biological needs.

MOTIVATION AS BIOLOGICAL DEFICIENCY

Historically, "biological" has been interpreted as referring only to certain well-recognized tissue needs, for example, needs for water, nutritional elements, oxygen, and so on (for a discussion of the physiological nature of tissue needs, see Unit 22). Inherent in this approach is what has been called a **deficiency motivation** conception, the notion that an organism is impelled to action only when it lacks some important ingredient. In other words, a motive is no more than a physiological imbalance.

Homeostasis

In 1932 Walter Cannon wrote *The Wisdom of the Body*, in which he described the remarkable manner in which the physiological system functions as a whole in order to maintain the equilibrium of conditions necessary to keep the organism alive. This self-regulating process he called **homeostasis**.

He described the automatic physiological mechanisms by which the volume of blood and the concentrations in it of sugar, salt, oxygen, and carbon dioxide are kept constant; by which the temperature of the body is maintained within narrow limits; and by which foreign particles and invading organisms are removed from the bloodstream. These mechanisms are automatic in that they occur without the awareness and voluntary action of the organism as a whole. For example, amazingly wide variations in temperature of the external environment are regulated through the automatic body adjustments of sweating, shivering, panting, and other mechanisms. Sooner or later, however, the automatic homeostatic mechanisms can no longer maintain the necessary steady states in the body. At this critical juncture the organism as a whole is aroused to take voluntary action to correct the body deficits or disturbances.

Some imbalances lead to the emergence of unusual and unnatural or artificial needs. For example, calcium deficiency in rare cases may lead to a bizarre calcium hunger. The drug addict alters his physiological functioning so that the body comes to require a certain amount of the drug. Withholding of the drug may result in the most acute and distressing states of need. Box 19.3 describes the creation of such an artificial or induced motive.

Not every form of severe physiological imbalance arouses a specific need. A person may simply feel vaguely sick or queasy or he may feel nothing out of the way at the same time that vital functions are being fatally impaired, as in certain kinds of cancer.

Tissue Needs and Conscious Needs

The homeostatic conception of motivation encounters frequent disparities between **tissue needs**, physiologically defined, and **conscious needs**. On one hand, we may remain unaware of even an urgent physiological deficiency, for example, a vitamin deficiency. On the other hand, we may experience what is usually regarded as a tissue need, for example, hunger, in the absence of any nutritional deficiency whatever. In short, the relation between tissue need and conscious need may be far from perfect (see Boxes 19.4A, p. 456, and 19.4B, p. 457, for some experimental demonstration).

Part of the lack of correspondence between tissue needs and conscious needs can be ascribed to the fact that stimuli arising from the external environment serve as important *instigators* of motive states. They arouse needs that did not exist the moment before and may

BOX 19.3

MORPHINE ADDICTION IN CHIMPS AND MAN

At the Yale Laboratories of Primate Biology, S. D. S. Spragg experimentally induced morphine addiction in four young chimpanzees. Injections with a hypodermic syringe were made in an injection room near the living cages twice daily at 9 A.M. and 5 P.M. The period during which the injections were regularly given varied among the chimpanzees from six weeks to thirteen months.

From three to seven weeks after injections began, the first signs of *physiological* dependence on the drug appeared. As the hour for injections approached, the animals would show a pattern of symptoms commonly found when the drug is withheld from human addicts: yawning, restlessness, excess salivation, lethargy, crying, and irritability.

After a further period clear evidence of *need* for the drug began to appear. Genuine addiction began to manifest itself. Behavioral evidence for the existence of the need was convincing. For example, as the regular hour for injection approached, the animal would show signs of excitement and eagerness, would struggle to get out of its cage, would lead the experimenter down the corridor and into the injection room, would sometimes voluntarily get on the table and assume the usual posture for receiving the hypodermic needle. Furthermore, if the animal was led away from the injection room by the experimenter without having received the drug, it showed obvious signs of distress and frustration. All these signs of desire completely disappeared after the injection was given and did not reappear until the animal had again been without the drug for some time.

In another test the animals could freely choose between a black box containing food or a white box containing the hypodermic syringe. When the animals had been recently injected, the choice of the food box predominated, but when the animals had been deprived of *both* food and morphine for approximately 18 hr, the choice of the white box containing the hypodermic syringe predominated. When they were prevented from getting at the boxes, the animals spent more time trying to get at the syringe box. Further experiments showed that the white box was more effective for inducing the animal to solve problems than was the food box.

It is clear that a strong drive was induced in these animals by repeated injections of the drug.

This artificial need took on all the characteristics of primary survival drives, and, in fact, *overwhelmed them* when, for example, morphine was given precedence over food itself.

The evidence for these life-threatening and self-destructive effects of addiction is certainly no less dramatic in people. Alcoholics prefer their drug to food so that one frequent outcome of prolonged alcoholism is severe malnutrition, with consequent illness and even death. Furthermore, the need for alcohol often triggers behavior that threatens social survival (inability to work or to relate to other people). In the case of human morphine addicts and, more often these days, heroin addicts, these same self-destructive effects are present.

Addictive effects do not befall only the weak-willed or the weak-minded. Personal and situational factors influence our willingness to *begin* drug-taking when the social pressures to do so are operative (and the college campus is one arena where such pressures are sometimes found and, unfortunately, are too often effective). Once taken, however, drugs can result in changes in the biochemistry of the body that create genuine *physical* dependence— dependence that is immune to moral or rational pleas. In the human being, mild physical dependence can be detected after only eight administrations of 15 mg of morphine. Within 6 to 10 hr after the last dose (in a well-addicted person) this physical dependence manifests itself (among other symptoms) in restlessness, involuntary crying, profuse perspiration, back and leg pains, muscle twitching, nausea and vomiting, loss of appetite, body-weight loss, rising body temperature, and increase in blood pressure.

These severe withdrawal symptoms decrease somewhat after three full days, but general weakness, body-weight loss, insomnia, jitteryness, and muscle aches and pains may continue for weeks. Moral suasion alone is equally ineffective as a cure when applied either to the human or to the chimpanzee addict. Medical intervention is essential, but even that is not always completely effective. A number of drugs are available to relieve some of the withdrawal symptoms, but the distress of the addicted abstainer will continue for a long time. Complete physical recovery from morphine or heroin addiction requires not less than six months of *total* abstinence.

S. D. S. SPRAGG. Morphine addiction in chimpanzees. *Comparative Psychological Monographs*, 1940, **15**, No. 7.
D. H. EFRON (Ed.). *Psychopharmacology: A Review of Progress, 1957–1967.* Washington, D.C.: U.S. Government Printing Office, 1968.

BOX 19.4A

OUT OF SIGHT,
OUT OF MOUTH—THE PUZZLE

First, a puzzle. BEFORE peeking at Box 19.4B (where, humanely, we suggest its solution), carefully study the following table, which presents, in abbreviated form, descriptions of some actual experimental situations that define the problem. There the typical (and contrasting) behaviors of two types of people—those of roughly normal weight and those decidedly overweight—who were observed in these situations, are recorded. From these data you should be able to form a hypothesis that might account for the differences between normal-weight and obese subjects.

	Results	
Situation	Normal Weight	Obese
1. Subjects, whose normal dinner time is about 6 P.M., participate in a brief and apparently non-food-related experience ending at 5:05 P.M. They are then left alone for a half hour; at 5:35 the experimenter returns, innocently nibbling from a box of crackers. A few minutes later he leaves, casually inviting the subjects to help themselves to the crackers. *But,* in one experiment, the clock in the room is rigged to run at half its normal speed so that at 5:35, when the experimenter returns, the clock reads only 5:20; in another experiment, the clock runs twice its normal speed and reads 6:05. *Measure:* amounts of crackers nibbled. (Schachter and Gross)	Ate about as much at "6:05" P.M. as at "5:20" P.M.	Ate almost twice as much at "6:05" P.M. than at "5:20" P.M.
2. Subjects are given an opportunity to eat as much as they want of one of two kinds of ice cream. One is extremely delicious, the other rather unpleasant. *Measure:* amount eaten. (Nisbett)	Normal and underweight subjects ate relatively less delicious ice cream than did the obese subjects.	Ate relatively more of the delicious ice cream than did the normal subjects.
3. Yom Kippur, the Jewish Day of Atonement, on which a 24-hr fast is prescribed, is understandably a day when food tends not to be available, particularly if one is at worship in a synagogue. *Measures:* whether the subject endured the fast and, if so, how unpleasant was the experience. (Goldman, Jaffa, and Schachter)	69 percent did fast and the unpleasantness of the experience is unrelated to time spent in synagogue.	83 percent did fast and the unpleasantness of the experience is much less if more time is spent in the synagogue.
4. *Air France* flight crews, on Paris–North America 8-hr runs, typically arrive in mid-afternoon Eastern time. But on Paris time it is time for dinner. *Measure:* frequency of report of "suffering from discordance between physiological state and meal time in America." (Goldman, Jaffa, & Schachter)	25 percent complain of trouble in adjusting their eating schedules.	12 percent complain of trouble in adjusting their eating schedules. (These subjects are only mildly overweight, not obese.)
5. Subjects show up at the laboratory in the morning, not having eaten since the night before. Every 15 min for the next 4 hr a measure of stomach contractions (one physiological measure of hunger) is taken and the subject is asked whether or not he is hungry. *Measure:* relation of contractions to felt hunger. (Strunkard)	71 percent report feeling hungry at same time stomach contractions are registered.	48 percent report feeling hungry at same time stomach contractions are registered.

BOX 19.4B

OUT OF SIGHT,
OUT OF MOUTH—THE SOLUTION

A possible solution to the puzzle presented in Box 19.4A, initially suggested by R. E. Nisbett of Columbia University and further developed by Stanley Schachter at the same institution, is that obese people (relative to normal-weight people) are *insensitive to internal physiological effects of food deprivation but are highly sensitive to external food-related cues in their immediate environment.*

Thus in situations 1 and 4 the *clock* (not their stomachs) said "dinner time" to the overweight subjects. In situation 2 the flavor differences in the ice creams were noticed more by the overweight and they ate more of the tastier product. Fasting occurred somewhat more often for the overweight subjects in situation 3; apparently going without food was relatively easier for them because the environment typical of that holy day was mercifully deficient in food-related cues. And temptation and the resultant unpleasantness of felt hunger were less for them the more time they spent in the synagogue, a setting with absolutely no food cues. Finally, and perhaps most directly, the overweight subjects in

situation 5 felt hungry much less often than they should . have, that is, when their internal state was signaling a need for food.

Considerably more research on this hypothesis than is reported here has been carried out; the research has mainly supported the general hypothesis. But even if this view is ultimately shown to be the correct one, a prior puzzle remains unsolved: *Why* are obese people more responsive to external food cues and less responsive to internal ones than people of normal weight?

Some suggest that there is a physiological basis for this. One hint comes from a study by two French physiologists, M. Cabanac and R. Duclaux, who found that, after drinking a large amount of glucose (a form of sugar), normal-weight subjects found a usually pleasant sweet drink quite distasteful while obese ones still enjoyed it almost as much as ever. This suggests that obese people have an unusual physiological insensitivity to a normally effective signal that the body has no more need at the moment for sugar, a promising finding. But, as usual, more research needs to be done.

R. E. NISBETT. Taste, deprivation, and weight determinants of eating behavior. *Journal of Personality and Social Psychology,* 1968, **10,** 107–116.
S. SCHACHTER. Obesity and eating. *Science,* 1968, **161,** 751–756.
M. CABANAC & R. DUCLAUX. Obesity: Absence of satiety aversion to sucrose. *Science,* 1970, **168,** 496–497.

have pronounced effects in directing behavior even when there is complete satiety of inner bodily needs. (Box 19.4 also demonstrates this point, but any party nibbler can provide his own evidence.) In other cases objects and events in the external environment heighten or prolong a motivational state already aroused, for example, the effect of the smell of food on a hungry man. The human being has learned a vast repertory of cues, symbols, or signals that arouse motivational states. The dinner gong can excite one need; the word "naked," another.

Even when the individual sits quiescent, unaffected by tissue needs or outer stimuli, he is still subject to motivational arousal by the constant flow of ideas, thoughts, and images that are produced and directed by the nervous

system. Observed from without, the quiescent woman may suddenly and inexplicably go into action. We are all familiar with this phenomenon in ourselves. As we sit wrapped in thought, ideas occur to us that may trigger a rather lively motive.

The homeostatic assumption that a need depends upon some kind of tissue deficiency and will cease only when that deficiency is removed has been extended to broader conceptions of motivation. By this view, man bestirs himself only when something is wrong or lacking. He may be hungry, uncomfortable, faced with danger, or just generally anxious. In brief, the homeostatic view holds that *motivation is initially tension arousal and ceases with tension reduction.*

CRITIQUES OF DEFICIENCY THEORIES OF MOTIVATION

The deficiency theory of motivation has been attacked from various directions. The play of the young, human and animal, provided the data for the earliest challenges. Bühler's (1928) observations of young children focused attention upon the fact that play was as common and without apparent purpose as it was (by tension-reduction theory) unnecessary. Nissen (1930) demonstrated that rats will leave their safe and familiar nests just to explore mazes that contained novel objects. They would do so even if they had to undergo electric shock in order to effect this exploration. In short, homeostasis did not adequately account for such behavior.

Recognition of such data called for theoretical overhaul. It has come from many quarters. Hendrick (1943), a psychoanalyst, proposed an urge to mastery as an innate drive in man's biological repertory. White (1959) suggested a motive of "effectance," which he defines as the tendency to explore and influence the environment. Both views speak of a motive in terms of its ultimate effect.

One way in which a biological, need-reduction approach can accommodate these data is to postulate play, exploration, and curiosity as biological drives in themselves. This postulation has been offered but, as White (1959) has pointed out, at considerable cost to the integrity of the biological approach. For one thing, this requires an embarrassing proliferation of new "biological" drives, one for each variety of unexplained but apparently motivated behavior (an activity drive, an exploratory drive, and so on). For another thing, the postulation prejudges an as yet unanswered scientific question. Play, curiosity, and exploration must have a physiological basis in the sense that *all* behavior is determined by what goes on in the physical organism. But whether or not this physiological basis will, upon discovery, resemble in any useful way, say, the tissue deficiencies underlying thirst, we do not know. Because we are ignorant in this respect, it seems scientifically foolhardy to foreclose debate and speculation concerning the nature of all motivation

by requiring allegiance to some kind of tension-reduction model.

Berlyne (1960) has made precisely this point in introducing his highly original consideration of a vast range of what he calls "ludic behavior." Ludic (from the Latin *ludare*, to play) refers to the many activities of man and animals that are indisputably primary, yet that have no known biological sources. These activities include exploration, investigation, curiosity—even art and intellectual play of all sorts (including science and humor). Berlyne is aware of but does not worry about their current lack of biological underpinnings. As he states:

> As far as we know, [ludic behavior] may have its contribution to make to biological adaptation and, in particular, to the state of bodily equilibrium and well-being that so called homeostatic processes serve to maintain. It may well affect prospects of survival. After all, as every zoo director knows to his cost, animals will often not live long in captivity; they may well refuse to feed or to reproduce. And how long human beings survive after retirement is frequently thought to be influenced by whether they can keep themselves occupied and find interests. . . . The very enigmas posed by activities that are eagerly indulged in when there is no clear biological need for them make it vitally important to study them. If there are hidden motivational factors capable of keeping organisms perceptually and intellectually active in the absence of the more obvious sources of motivation, these hidden factors may well be at work and collaborating with more familiar motives whenever looking and thinking assist in the solution of practical problems.

Clearly, there is a need for a counterpart, complementary view of motivation.

ABUNDANCY MOTIVATION

Opposed to survival and security motives is another type that might be called satisfaction and stimulation motives. The yearning to explore or to understand, to create or to achieve, to love or to feel self-respect—all these desires are clearly not in the service of removing discomfort or danger. Indeed, they appear to in-

TABLE 19.1 THE HUMAN MOTIVES

	Survival and Security (Deficiency Motives)	Satisfaction and Stimulation (Abundancy Motives)
Pertaining to the body	Avoiding of hunger, thirst, oxygen lack, excess heat and cold, pain, overfull bladder and colon, fatigue, overtense muscles, illness and other disagreeable bodily states, etc.	Attaining pleasurable sensory experiences of tastes, smells, sounds, etc.; sexual pleasure; bodily comfort; exercise of muscles, rhythmical body movements, etc.
Pertaining to relations with environment	Avoiding of dangerous objects and horrible, ugly, and disgusting objects; seeking objects necessary to future survival and security; maintaining a stable, clear, certain environment, etc.	Attaining enjoyable possessions; constructing and inventing objects; understanding the environment; solving problems; playing games; seeking environmental novelty and change, etc.
Pertaining to relations with other people	Avoiding interpersonal conflict and hostility; maintaining group membership, prestige, and status; being taken care of by others; conforming to group standards and values; gaining power and dominance over others, etc.	Attaining love and positive identifications with people and groups; enjoying other people's company; helping and understanding other people; being independent, etc.
Pertaining to the self	Avoiding feelings of inferiority and failure in comparing the self with others or with the ideal self; avoiding loss of identity; avoiding feelings of shame, guilt, fear, anxiety, etc.	Attaining feelings of self-respect and self-confidence; expressing oneself; feeling sense of achievement; feeling challenged; establishing moral and other values; discovering meaningful place for self in the universe.

volve tension *increase* and a state of abundancy beyond the needs for immediate survival and security.

Table 19.1 presents the principal human motives classified under two main types: survival and security (deficiency motives) and satisfaction and stimulation (**abundancy motives**). The table shows that both deficiency and abundancy motives may pertain to the *same* object. The body is thus the object of both survival motives (as in avoidance of hunger) *and* satisfaction motives (as in seeking sensory pleasure). Any useful theoretical treatment of motives would do well to integrate both types into a single scheme; an effort in this direction, by Maslow, is described on page 462.

The Need for Stimulation

In recent years considerable research has been carried out on a specific abundancy motive—the need for stimulation. We can all testify that monotonous surroundings, with low sensory input, may lead to boredom and thus motivate us to seek action. But research shows that such stimulus-deficient surroundings sometimes do more than merely bore us; they can cause us intense distress and disturbance.

Experiments in the 1950s [Bexton et al.

(1954) and Heron et al. (1956) are examples] discovered that college-student subjects, paid at the then-handsome rate of $20 per day simply to remain in a stimulation-deficient environment, reacted in an unexpected manner. The environment would seem to have been innocuous enough—a small, sound-deadened room with a comfortable cot. The subject was required to lie on this cot continuously (except for meal and toilet breaks) and to do nothing. The room light was left on but, because he wore translucent goggles, he was unable to see objects. Other devices prevented his touching objects or his hearing any patterned sound (see Figure 19.1, p. 460). At first, the subjects slept a great deal, but the situation rapidly became intolerable and—as they were always free to do —they chose to escape after only two or three days.

What were some of the specific effects of this radical restriction of normal stimulation, this sensory deprivation? Not the peaceful *nirvana* of homeostasis but some kind of discomfort and deficit instead. Experiencing boredom and motor restlessness was the least of the reactions. Thought processes were noticeably disturbed, and performance on intelligence tests was substantially worsened. Daydreaming (an attempt at self-stimulation?) was a frequent

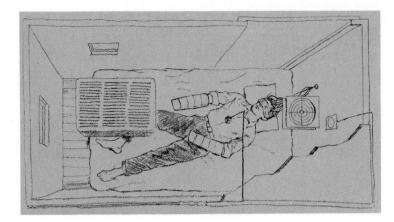

FIGURE 19.1 An air conditioner (left) and a fan (right) in the cubicle masked outside noises. The wires attached to the subject's head permitted the experimenters to study brain waves.

result and active hallucinations a logical, if less prevalent, successor. Physiological effects were many, including changes in brain-wave activity. In short, in these studies, sensory deprivation often resulted in severe disturbances in the gamut of human functioning and was sufficiently unnerving for subjects to signal for immediate release (via a panic button), despite the resulting cost in pride and wages.

However, not all the subjects reacted in so intense a fashion. And later research by other experimenters found considerable variation in reactions, in part owing to differences in the experimental situation. The more dramatic effects, such as hallucinations, were found only rarely. But the accumulation of evidence [Zubek (1969) reviews fifteen years of research on this topic] supports the general point that being subjected to a prolonged period of sensory deprivation is, for most of us, a distinctly unpleasant experience.

Zubek (1963) encountered a possible antidote for these effects in his investigation of the role of *motor* activity in a sensory deprivation situation. In his study, one group of people was subjected to a week-long deprivation of outside stimuli but were permitted to move about as they pleased and required to perform calisthenic exercises for six 5-min periods each day. A second group experienced identical external deprivation but, in addition, was required to remain in bed and, of course, did not perform the exercises. A variety of intellectual and perceptual tests was administered to both groups throughout the experiment; on most of these tests the exercise group showed significantly less impairment of function.

Taking a walk to clear the cobwebs induced by sustained attention to a monotonous task is therefore something more than a flimsy pretext to escape the unpleasant. Prison routine characteristically includes regular exercise periods. The effectiveness of the coffee break in improving employee performance as well as morale may owe as much to movement-produced stimulation as to caffeine. The implications for the highly confined inhabitants of nuclear submarines and orbiting spacecraft are clear and have been and continue to be investigated.

We have placed emphasis upon the need for stimulation, in part, because these phenomena promise a radical revision of our traditional conceptions of motivation. Recognition of stimuation needs may also permit a foothold in certain vexing, if familiar, motivational dilemmas. Take the situation in which we are strangely attracted by experiences we would sensibly shun—sensibly, that is, if the avoidance of pain and the pursuit of pleasure were our only goals—for example, the hurtling roller-coaster ride or the horror movie that frightens but fascinates.

The phenomenon of stress-seeking is most interesting to consider, perhaps precisely because it conflicts with our traditional views of what motivates people. People vary, of course, in this respect, and no doubt those who prefer to dwell, so far as life permits, in a safe and placid environment must feel confused by and are confusing to those who actively seek stressful situations. Klausner (1969), who has himself conducted research on the motivations of such stress-seekers as sport parachutists, presents a collection of essay and reports on this phenomenon entitled *Why Man Takes Chances*, which should help to reduce the confusion.

People are not the only stress-seekers. Animals often investigate most persistently what they most fear. Berlyne (1960) has shown this experimentally, reporting that shocking rats at a certain region of the apparatus caused them to *increase* the time spent in exploring that region. This behavior may make evolutionary sense if it is regarded as an attempt to understand potentially harmful situations, but, in any case, here we have an active seeking after higher levels of arousal.

Conditions of Arousal

Motivational arousal depends both upon internal states of bodily imbalance and upon external stimulus conditions. The most general statement that can be made about a stimulus situation leading to motivational arousal is that such arousal is elicited by a *change* in the stimulus field. This change can be an increase or a decrease in intensity or a change in quality. Take a light stimulus, for example: The light is turned on or off, is made more or less bright, or changes color; any of these stimulus changes can initiate the first stage of motivational arousal by orienting the individual toward that changing part of his stimulus field. The entire organism goes into a state of alert, attention is focused in order to receive maximum information, and the individual is on the mark, ready to spring into action. (For a fuller description

of this orienting response, or "What is it?" reflex, see Box 15.1, p. 361.)

But change alone is not enough. Typically, our decision to orient toward, to pay attention to, an event in our immediate environment is determined by the interaction between a stimulus change and the cognitive state of the person. Seen in this way the degree of motivational arousal may be regarded as a function of uncertainty. It is the uncertainty about what has just happened out there among the external stimuli that draws our attention, not the stimulus change per se.

This approach leads immediately to speculation concerning the relation between degree of uncertainty and its motivating value. At first it might appear obvious that the greater the uncertainty, the greater the motivational arousal. True, a situation that is completely certain (no novelty, no surprise, no challenge) rarely initiates or sustains interest. But, on the other hand, when a situation is excessively complex, new, and uncertain, the individual may well wish to escape to less confused, even if less challenging, realms.

Some empirical evidence indicates that moderate uncertainty is the optimal condition for eliciting interest and for maintaining an optimal motivational state. But the question is difficult to ask experimentally partly because uncertainty is an internal state, although it tends to be related to the complexity of the stimulus.

In a sense this apparent (and apparently sensible) need for an optimum level of stimulation or arousal—more than the zero of homeostasis but not more than we can handle—seems to involve both the deficiency and abundancy views of motivation. It would be a safe guess to predict that eventually most of our motivational concepts will reflect both these views. Indeed, several attempts have already been made in this direction.

An Attempt at Reconciliation: Maslow's Needs Hierarchy

An attempt to encompass deficiency and abundancy motives within a single scheme has been made by Maslow (1954). (His general theory of personality is presented in Unit 29.) In his treatment, all motives, those involving tension reduction as well as the others, are combined in one interrelated scheme, without prejudging the question of the tissue-need basis of all motives. Maslow's scheme holds the view that a fundamental motive of man is to express his potentialities in their most effective and complete form, a need for **self-actualization** (see Unit 29, p. 721).

Specifically, Maslow conceptualizes the following five levels of needs, arranged in a ladder starting with lower needs and moving on to higher needs:

1. Physiological needs, for example, hunger, thirst
2. Safety needs, for example, security, stability
3. Belongingness and love needs, for example, affection, identification
4. Esteem needs, for example, prestige, self-respect
5. Need for self-actualization

The terms lower and higher merely indicate that certain needs appear earlier in the developmental process, are more closely linked to biological necessities, and are narrower in scope. Most important of all, according to Maslow, who wished to stress the *developmental* nature of motivation, a lower need must be adequately satisfied before the next higher need can fully emerge in a person's development. One cannot devote himself to ensuring his safety until his insistent physiological requirements are met. Only after a basic sense of security is attained can relations of love and belongingness with people reach their full power. And an adequate degree of satisfaction of one's need for love permits full-fledged striving for esteem and self-respect. Finally, only when all the preceding levels have been successively achieved can the tendency toward self-actualization reach its height.

Development of the individual's motivational structure is not, of course, a matter of sharp, discontinuous steps—each lower need does not have to be completely gratified before the next higher need emerges. It is more in the nature of a succession of waves, in which predominance among the different needs gradually shifts from one to another (see Figure 19.2).

This natural course of development can go wrong when there is insufficient gratification of needs at any given level. The next higher needs are thereby prevented from full emergence, and the highest may never appear. The man whose lifelong environment provides the barest essentials for physical survival is not likely to develop pressing needs for achievement, prestige, beauty. The chronically hungry man will never seek to build a brave new world. He is much too concerned with satisfying his immediate and pressing hunger needs. Only the person freed of the domination of his lower needs can become motivated by other than deficiency-based drives. The ideal physical and social environment is therefore one that makes possible the gratification of each level of needs as it reaches its crest in the individual.

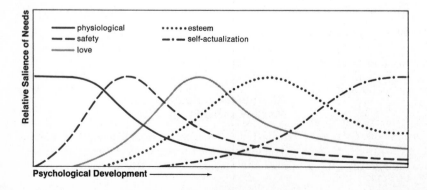

FIGURE 19.2 A schematic portrayal of the progressive changes in relative saliency of the five main classes of needs, as described by A. H. Maslow. Note that the peak of an earlier main class of needs must be passed before the next higher need can begin to assume a dominant role.

Maslow's formulation is no more than an indication of a possible direction to take for a reconciliation of deficiency and abundancy views of motivation. A truly unifying theory would also take into account emotional states, which are often so closely tied to motivational phenomena. Mentioning this persuades us to close this unit with a confession: In choosing to present in separate units these major psychological topics of motivation (Unit 19) and emotion (Unit 20), we have followed a time-hallowed tradition within psychology. But the demarcation line between the two, as we have indicated, is a tantalizingly fuzzy one and you would profit from considering them together. It is easy to slip back and forth between the two units since, quite intentionally, the borderline between these units has been left porous and unpatrolled by factionalists. One view that is presented of the function of emotions (Unit 20, p. 491) insists that even biologically based motives are effective determinants of behavior only because they are typically accompanied and amplified by emotional states.

SUMMARY

1. Throughout history there have been various general conceptions of human motivation. To a significant extent, each of these views persists in some form and even with some validity in contemporary notions of what causes people to behave as they do. Thus, to some degree people are still at times regarded as pawns of fate, or as machinelike in their behavior, or conversely, as thoroughly rational beings. People are also seen as pushed around by their culture's indoctrination and expectations. And unconscious factors and biological forces are certainly recognized today as powerful sources of motivation as well.

2. The theory that all motivation arises from biological deficiencies has long been a dominant one. However, the theory is questioned by a frequent lack of correspondence between such tissue needs and needs as they are experienced by the individual.

3. Part of the lack of correspondence between bodily deficiency and motivational state results from the influence of external stimuli and of mental activity, which also serve to instigate or activate motives.

4. The accumulating evidence for motivated behaviors broadly classified as play—behaviors for which a biological basis has so far not been found—poses a serious challenge to a deficiency view of motivation.

5. Abundancy motivation presents an alternate conception. Rather than focusing on tension reduction, this view underlines the role of a need for stimulation and tension increase.

6. Prolonged exposure to an environment in which external stimulation is kept to a bare minimum can be severely disturbing, even intolerable, although biological needs may be satisfied in the situation. Even normal levels of stimulation are insufficient for some people, so that they may actively seek stressful situations, sometimes life-threatening ones.

7. Changes in external stimuli and in their complexity tend to trigger arousal, particularly when they result in a state of uncertainty as to what is going on in the environment. This uncertainty is most highly motivating when it is neither too great nor too little in degree.

8 Maslow's proposed hierarchy of needs is an attempt to provide a theoretical schema for relating within a single framework both deficiency and abundancy motives. According to Maslow, lower needs are largely biological and must be satisfied before higher abundancy-related needs (e.g., for achievement, for esthetic experiences) can be pursued.

GLOSSARY

abundancy motives　Motivation characterized by *desires* to experience enjoyment, to obtain gratification, to understand and discover, to seek novelty, to achieve and create. It includes the general aims of satisfaction and stimulation. In contrast to deficiency motivation, it may often involve seeking tension *increase* rather than tension reduction.

conscious need　A need of which one is explicitly aware. A conscious or felt need may or may not be accompanied by some physiological deficiency or tissue need.

cultural lag　The preservation of many elements of a culture for some time after environmental changes have caused these elements to be no longer adaptive.

cultural relativism　The doctrine that asserts that human motives, values, and actions are entirely relative to the particular culture in which they occur. Thus, the human nature of one culture is alleged to be different from the human nature of another.

deficiency motivation　Characterized by needs to remove deficits and disruptions and to avoid or escape danger and threat. It includes the general aims of survival and security. Deficiency motivation is tension-reductive in its aim.

drives　Aroused states of the organism, related to physiological requirements of the body, which set the organism into action. In one view of motivation, drives are considered to be innate biological tendencies, on the basis of which all complex motivation is developed through learning, taking the form of derived or acquired drives. In other views of motivation, drives are regarded as only a limited segment of the whole of the motivational energies of the organism.

homeostasis　The maintenance of steady physiological states of the body through self-regulating mechanisms, for example, the maintenance of uniform body temperature or of specific concentrations of substances in the blood. These mechanisms function without the awareness or voluntary action of the person.

instinct　An innate pattern of behavior, elicited by certain stimuli and fulfilling certain basic biological functions for the organism. The term refers both to the drive and to the activity appropriate to satisfy the drive.

motive　A need or desire coupled with the intention to attain an appropriate goal. In accounting for behavior, motive is not synonymous with cause.

self-actualization　The notion, embodied in various theories of personality, of a basic human tendency toward making actual what is potential in the self, that is, toward maximal realization of one's potentialities.

social determinism　The doctrine that asserts that there are laws of societies that transcend laws of individual human nature. The individual's behavior is considered to be dictated mainly by the requirements and characteristics of the social system as a whole.

tissue need　A need based upon a specific physiological lack or deficiency in some aspect of biological functioning. A tissue need may or may not be accompanied by awareness.

unconscious motivation　Pertaining to a form of motivated behavior in which the person is unaware of his needs and desires, intentions, and goals; that is, he engages in unconscious coping—solving problems, adaptively circumventing barriers, and the like—in order to achieve unconscious ends.

human emotion

DO YOU KNOW...

- *that the study of human emotions is generally disregarded in the experimental study of human behavior?*

- *why this unfortunate state of affairs has come about?*

- *why it is that psychologists probably have more good questions than good answers about the experience of pain?*

- *how it is that you can often feel ashamed about something, but not at all guilty?*

- *that infants at first probably exhibit only a single emotion?*

- *that emotional strain generally seems to ease off as we grow older?*

- *why it is that asking a person how he feels is by no means a wholly trustworthy way of establishing his emotional state?*

- *whether people from very different cultures can accurately gauge each other's emotions?*

A—Photo by Charles Gatewood; B—Photo by Winston Vargas; C—Photo by Ed Clark/*Life* Magazine © 1972; D—Courtesy, Hilda Krech.

CONTENTS

Most laymen and perhaps even many psychologists regard the study of feelings and emotions as the main business of psychology. Certainly, they reason, perception and learning and problem solving are fundamental human activities that account for our success at mastering our environment, and motives may be seen as providing the force that drives and directs these activities. But, the argument continues, is not each of these functions one step removed from the most immediately and clearly experienced stuff of human existence—the emotional life?

Despite the undebatable importance of emotions, psychological research and theory frequently skirt detailed treatment of this subject. Most often this relative neglect of emotion reflects the experimental psychologist's concern with other, more easily quantifiable, phenomena. A preference by psychologists for working on one kind of problem rather than on another—an inevitable and universal occurrence in scientific research—has perhaps brought about some distortion of the proper role and status of the psychology of emotion. Thus, the study of emotions has long been outside the mainstream of psychological research, and many psychologists have come to see it as an almost extraneous phenomenon, interfering with scientifically lawful behavior.

Taking account of emotions can indeed be regarded as interfering with the orderly unfolding of a psychological process in accordance with behavioral laws, *but only because the behavioral laws themselves make little if any provision for the influence of emotional factors.* As a result emotions come to be regarded as a source of error in psychological research rather than as a subject that presents a host of questions requiring scientific answers.

It is not surprising therefore that present-day psychology has made few formal attempts to organize and categorize the vast world of emotional experience, lacking even a thorough inventory and set of descriptions for the full range of emotions. We must turn to poets, playwrights, and novelists, who have made the brave attempt at concrete descriptions of emotional experience. It is their artistic creations that yield accounts of jealousy, terror, remorse, guilt, ecstasy.

DIMENSIONS OF EMOTIONAL EXPERIENCE

One of the difficulties with any attempt to describe emotions in the abstract is that emotions are thereby taken out of their immediate context. It is not the feeling of fear in general that we should seek to describe but a particular experience of fear as it occurs in a specific situation—what the individual perceives, feels, and thinks in that situation. It is in just this way, by describing emotions in recognizable, real-life contexts, that writers have most effectively contributed.

In view of the infinite variety of situations that exist for any one person, his emotional experiences would seem to defy classification. Yet our language does have terms for specific emotions, and these terms do point in a useful way to certain general types of emotional experience that we can all recognize. Although each experience of anger, for example, is in some degree different from every other experience, all anger responses have something in common. If so, then we may attempt to classify and thus to distinguish each recognizable emotion by means of a set of general dimensions.

One approach is to derive such dimensions and classification schemata by wholly empirical means, as illustrated in Box 20.1, page 470. For present purposes, however, we prefer a schema that blends both empirical and theoretical considerations. Specifically, we suggest as a useful schema one consisting of four general dimensions: (1) *intensity of feeling*, (2) *level of tension*, (3) *hedonic tone*, and (4) *degree of complexity*.

Intensity of Feeling

Emotional experiences range in intensity of feeling all the way from the barely noticed twinge of a momentary mood to the most powerful of passions. Anger may vary from a faint vexation to a violent rage; joy, from a mild contentment to a sweeping ecstasy. The greater the intensity, the greater the tendency for the entire self to be involved, to be in the grip of the emotion.

Level of Tension

Although we tend to think of all emotions in terms of feelings of agitation and upset, it is clear that emotional experiences vary widely in level of tension. Tension refers to the impulse toward action. The person feels impelled to attack the frustrating barrier, to flee from the threatening object, to dance with delight. Here we have the *active* emotions. The more passive or *quiet* emotions may not involve such impulses to action; the sad person may sit without desiring to move; the contented person does not feel driven to act. Active and passive emotions *are equally central to the person*, equally involve the self. The difference between them lies in the degree of associated excitement and the strength of the impulse to action.

Intensity of feeling and level of tension are often correlated. A high degree of tension is very likely to mean a more intense feeling. But acute intensity may also be found in emotions with little tension as, for instance, in a profound depression.

Hedonic Tone

Emotional experiences vary widely in their pleasantness or unpleasantness, that is, in what is technically called their **hedonic tone**. Feelings of grief, shame, fear, and remorse are clearly unpleasant, whereas feelings of joy, pride, contentment, and reverence are as clearly pleasant. Some emotions are less clearly placed on a hedonic continuum. A feeling of pity, wonder, or surprise may be neither clearly pleasant nor clearly unpleasant.

The intensity of the feeling will, of course, affect the hedonic tone. A faint anger may not be particularly unpleasant, but a state of fierce rage is. And there are interesting paradoxes in which a usually pleasant emotion such as hunger may become so intense as to be unpleasant, or in which a mild negative emotion such as a

BOX 20.1

DIMENSIONS OF EMOTION

H. Schlosberg of Brown University reasoned that, in order to detect the dimensions along which emotions vary (and, therefore, by which they can be described efficiently), it would be best to study emotion in a situation that provides a wide variety of distinguishable emotional states.

As a starting point, Schlosberg turned to some earlier work on facial expression of emotions by R. S. Woodworth, who had developed a scale of emotions that appeared to fit the data of other investigators. Woodworth constructed his scale on the ingeniously simple principle that clearly distinguishable emotions must lie far apart on any scale, whereas those that are confused with one another must fall at about the same point on the scale. First he proposed a scale running as follows: love, happiness, mirth, surprise, fear, anger, suffering, determination, disgust, and contempt. Some of these emotional states, those close to one another on the scale, proved hard to tell apart reliably; love, happiness, and mirth, for example, were frequently confused. Therefore, they were lumped to define a single region of the scale rather than treated as adjacent but separate points.

Schlosberg had subjects apply Woodworth's scale to judgments of emotions from both posed and unposed photographs. His initial results suggested that the scale might better be expanded into two relatively independent scales, or dimensions: pleasantness-unpleasantness and attention-rejection. With these two dimensions at right angles to each other (the way to portray graphically independent dimensions) Schlosberg was able to generate a roughly circular surface (see figure) within which later experiments showed that subjects could reliably locate a variety of separate emotions. (The surface is actually oval, rather than circular, indicating

that subjects could make finer distinctions along the pleasant-unpleasant axis than along the attention-rejection axis.)

Schlosberg added a third dimension, perpendicular to the oval surface, which is essentially an intensity dimension and which he called "level of activation." By thus adding depth to his schema, he made it possible to distinguish among individual emotions that lay at about the same point on the oval plane. Grief and suffering were cases in point: On the surface they were very much alike, but grief was characteristically rated considerably below suffering on the intensity axis.

H. SCHLOSBERG. Three dimensions of emotion. *Psychological Review*, 1954, **61**, 81–88. Figure adapted by permission of American Psychological Association.

quietly remembered sorrow or a titillating fear may feel pleasurable.

Degree of Complexity

These paradoxes point to the important fact that emotional experiences, being patterns of diverse feelings, are often highly complex. We often experience an *indescribable* emotional state, and it is this very complexity of elements that makes it impossible for us to say just how an emotional experience feels or whether it is pleasant or unpleasant. In contrast, a great many of our emotional experiences are simple and uncomplicated; we feel a pure fright at an earthquake, a pure elation in sudden good fortune, a pure grief in the death of our beloved dog.

CLASSIFICATION AND DESCRIPTION OF EMOTIONS

This four-dimensional schema can be used to characterize any specific emotional state. In order to categorize specific emotions into more general types, we employ six main classes, starting with the most primary and goal-directed.

Primary Emotions

Joy, anger, fear, and grief are often referred to as the most basic or **primary emotions**. The situations that evoke them are intimately involved with aroused, goal-striving activity and therefore likely to have high degrees of tension.

Joy   The essential situational condition for joy is that the person is striving toward a goal and attains it. The intensity of the joy depends upon the level of tension that has been reached in the course of the motivated act. When the goal is unimportant, the emotion may be no more than mild satisfaction; for an extremely important goal, the result may be transports of joy.

Joy is the emotional counterpart of the release of tension with goal attainment. The *suddenness* with which the goal is achieved and tension released thus affects the intensity of the joy, a kind of emotional "aha!" phenomenon (see Box 6.3, p. 129). When a game is won easily, the winner may feel only mild elation, but winning a game at the last instant, when all seemed lost, may evoke an ecstatic feeling.

Anger   The essential condition for arousing anger is the blocking of goal attainment, especially when there is persistent frustration of goal attainment, with the gradual accumulation of tension.

Not all such thwarting will lead to anger. As we shall see in Unit 23, thwarting has many possible consequences, of which anger is but one. A great deal seems to depend upon the extent to which there is an identifiable barrier to goal achievement. If the person simply cannot see what is preventing her goal achievement, anger is not so likely to occur; but if she sees (correctly or incorrectly) an obstacle that is causing the trouble, and particularly if the thwarting seems to her somehow unreasonable or deliberate or malicious, anger is more likely to occur and to be expressed in aggressive action against the thwarting object.

Fear   Joy and anger are, in a sense, emotions of approach, that is, they involve striving for goals. Fear, on the other hand, is an emotion of avoidance, involving an escape from danger.

The key factor for the onset of fear seems to be *lack of power or capability to handle* a threatening situation. If a person does not know how to ward off the threat, especially if he sees his escape route blocked, fear is induced by his feeling of powerlessness in the grip of overwhelming forces, an earthquake or some other natural cataclysm, for example, or—as an example on a more modest scale—a father's harsh threat as it appears to a child.

In time we may become habituated to dangerous objects and live close to them without alarm; we can do so because we have learned how to cope with them. But if the immediate situation changes, so that our well-established means for handling them are disrupted, fear once again emerges.

It is especially noteworthy that unexpected alterations in our usual surroundings can induce fear. It is as if we had organized our world in such a way as to protect ourselves, and any disruption in the order may cause immediate apprehension. It is commonplace that a young child is often made anxious and apprehensive by changes in her customary surroundings. Terror of the unknown is not merely a literary expression; universally, the strange and the unfamiliar may cause dread. This reaction is a very primitive one, which we also note in animals (see Box 20.2, p. 472).

Fear, perhaps more than any other emotion, is acutely contagious. Seeing and hearing others in a state of terror will often induce panic in the onlooker, even when there is nothing else in his situation to account for it.

BOX 20.2

THE FEAR OF THE STRANGE
IN THE CHIMPANZEE

In a series of experiments at the Yerkes Laboratories of Primate Biology, D. O. Hebb tested the fear responses of thirty chimpanzees when confronted with strange and unfamiliar objects.

Among the objects were an ape head, a skull, a human head (from a window-display dummy), anesthetized chimpanzees, pictures, toy animals. These test objects were presented to the chimpanzee while he was in his home cage. The animal was lured to the front of his cage by an offer of a small amount of food. The hinged top of a box was then lifted, exposing one of the test objects. Fear was ascribed to the chimpanzee if definite signs of withdrawal from the object were observed. Accompanying such withdrawal were signs of unusual excitement such as erection of hair, screaming, threatening gestures, and so on.

From the data it is clear that *either* a lack of responsiveness in a whole animal (the anesthetized chimps) *or* the lack of a body when the head is seen is the most effective determiner of fear.

Hebb's explanation runs somewhat along these lines: First, through past learning the chimpanzee comes to expect certain events when stimulated by an object (for example, when seeing a head, he expects to see the rest of the body). Second, neurologically, this reaction means that, as a result of stimulation by such an object, a *coordinated sequence of neural events* is started in the animal's

brain. Third, the immediate source of fear is a *disruption* of this patterned sequence. Fear is thus seen as a direct result of *profound disorganization of cerebral processes.* Fourth, strange, dead, or mutilated bodies arouse perceptual and intellectual processes that are *incompatible* with an already ongoing pattern of activities, and the result is *fear.*

The fear reaction—withdrawal or flight—tends to restore "cerebral equilibrium" by removing the animal from the whole complex of disrupting and incompatible stimuli.

D. O. HEBB. On the nature of fear. *Psychological Review*, 1946, **53**, 259–276.

A scream of terror is "felt" in the guts of the listener, as well as of the screamer. Noting this phenomenon of emotional contagion, we begin to suspect that emotional states can transmit unmistakable information, a notion important to Tomkins' theory of emotion which we shall discuss later in this unit (p. 494).

Grief   Grief is concerned with the loss of something sought or valued. The intensity depends upon the value; usually the most profound grief comes from the loss of loved persons, and deep

feelings of grief may come also from the loss of prized possessions. These cases are examples of intense and enduring grief; there are all shades of grief, down to the merest feeling of disappointment or regret.

Parkes (1965) has reviewed evidence on the range of grief reactions to bereavement and describes the typical reaction to loss of a loved one as running a quite consistent course. After an immediate reaction of emotional numbness there is a period during which deep depression and despair (quiet) alternate with attacks of anxiety and yearning over the loss (tense and active). During this time other reactions are common: Among them are insomnia, loss of appetite, irritability, and social withdrawal. Both the fluctuation in mood and the side reactions gradually decline in intensity but flare up occasionally when outside events, for example anniversaries, reactivate the sense of loss. Less typical grief reactions found by Parkes (more often found among bereaved psychiatric patients) include *chronic grief,* an abnormal prolongation of the period of mourning (often accompanied by self-blame); *inhibited grief,* in which the loss is consciously denied and such substitute reactions as emotional clinging and extreme irritability occur; and *delayed grief,* in which any direct emotional reaction does not appear for weeks or even years.

Emotions Pertaining to Sensory Stimulation

Emotions pertaining to sensory stimulation may be pleasant or unpleasant, and the level of stimulation may be mild or intense. The resulting emotion tends to be directed toward the positive or negative object.

Pain   Physical pain is the most important example of intense physical·stimulation leading to emotional arousal. At low intensities the pain sensation may be perceived as peripheral to the self, and it may evoke neither an emotional feeling nor an avoidant action. At higher intensities an unpleasant emotional state is aroused, and with extreme pain may come the most acute emotional agitation.

Our understanding of the apparent cause of pain has much to do with the resulting intensity of emotional arousal. The physician warns, "This will hurt a bit," and usually it does hurt a little less because we know the cause of the pain. The painful emotion is minimized if we feel capable of dealing with the conditions that arouse it.

Pain is a puzzling problem, both for psychologists and physiologists. Hilgard (1969) raises a number of basic questions regarding the phenomenon of pain which have long troubled and continue to trouble researchers in this field. We will paraphrase a few of these, together with some tentative answers.

1. *Is pain a sense, as is seeing and hearing?* Yes, if we note that there are certain receptors which respond to typical painful stimuli (such as intense heat) and information is conveyed through them that usually permits us to know where we hurt. On the other hand, we can experience the sensation of pain from exposure to almost any stimulus, if it is sufficiently intense—the sound of an explosion or a blinding flash *is* painful. And for these we can, so far, neither specify the receptors nor how the nervous system is implicated.

2. *Can we detect pain by specific physiological indicators?* No. People can tell us when they hurt, but at this time we have no reliable way of *measuring* by any one physiological response—or by any set of such responses—whether pain is being experienced or how intensely (see also Unit 22).

3. *Is it clear where pain is felt?* Not really. Although a cut finger hurts where it should, pain often is felt where it should not be. Referred pain is quite common; for example, the feeling called "heartburn" is actually caused by an irritant located in the digestive tract. Also, as described in Box 11.3, page 238, there is phantom-limb pain in which the sensation is localized in a part of the body that no longer exists— that has been amputated.

4. *Do we understand why people vary so greatly in feeling pain?* Yes and no. We do know something about the correlations of the enormous variations in felt pain to what should be a standard pain-causing stimulus. Certain personality characteristics are implicated and there are even differences in this respect among various social classes and ethnic groups. But these correlational findings do not *explain why,* for example, as Beecher (1959) reports, about a third of a group of patients receives considerable relief from postsurgical pain through the use of morphine, another third is as relieved by an inactive placebo

as by morphine, and the final third unfortunately is not helped by either.

While this lack of knowledge may indeed be troubling for psychologists and physiologists, there is the compensation of being confronted with challenging questions that will eventually yield to systematic research.

Disgust There are various kinds of objects that when seen, smelled, tasted, or touched arouse disgust—acutely unpleasant feelings that involve strong avoidance tendencies and marked sensations of bodily upset like nausea and vomiting. Again it is the closeness of contact with oneself that is all-important. In our culture slimy objects like slugs tend to evoke strong disgust. The feeling is much stronger when the object is not merely seen but is also placed in contact with the skin. Authentic feelings of disgust are sometimes aroused by other people. In some cultures, merely the touch of a person of lower or "unclean" caste might evoke genuine disgust and even nausea. Obviously, cultural standards and specific past experiences of an individual play a major role in determining what objects will evoke genuine disgust.

Pain and disgust tend to *incorporate feelings of bodily upset* as essential parts of the emotional experience. Beyond these two explicit negative emotions a large and ill-defined class of unpleasant emotional experiences exists that range in intensity from minor irritations and annoyances (see Box 20.3) to extreme horror, which is induced by witnessing profoundly affecting events, particularly events involving terrible accidents, maiming of bodies, destruction of objects. In these latter situations, fear plays a prominent role, as was suggested in Box 20.2, page 472.

Delights A vast array of objects and events can evoke pleasurable feelings. We may call these emotional experiences delights. Sources of delight are well-nigh inexhaustible. Some are the pleasant sensations in the body as it is touched, stroked, or caressed. Some come from perceptions of body movement and functioning (delights in muscular activity, rhythmical danc-

ing, singing) and from the feelings associated with mild degrees of body need (pleasant hunger, pleasant weariness). Still other sensory delights pertain to external objects, their textures, colors, and shapes, their sounds, tastes, and smells.

Emotions Pertaining to Self-Appraisal

Feelings of success and failure, of shame, pride, guilt, and remorse, are emotions in which the essential determinant is a person's perception of her own behavior in relation to various standards of behavior. These may be classified as **emotions pertaining to self-appraisal.**

Feelings of success and failure Feelings of success and satisfaction do not necessarily accompany accomplishment of a task. These feelings occur only to the extent that the person's attention is centered on her achievement, and they are determined by her level of aspiration. If she perceives that she has reached or exceeded her level of aspiration, an emotion of satisfaction is engendered. If she feels that she has fallen short of it, a sense of failure and a feeling of dejection are aroused.

Success and failure must be defined in terms of the person's own perceptions, her own level of aspiration. She may feel that she has succeeded when others would judge she has not; and she may feel that she has failed when others would judge her successful.

Although it is the inner-personal rather than the external-social standard of performance that directly determines what is failure and what is success for a person, social factors clearly play an enormous role in shaping these inner standards. The person sets and adjusts her standards in a degree relative to those of other people; for one thing, she is often competing with others, and the common evaluation of performance is strongly pressed upon her. Furthermore, the very nature of social living makes her especially conscious of the judgments that others are constantly reaching about her. The very perception of one's self is highly dependent upon one's perception of the social world.

BOX 20.3

HOW TO BE ANNOYED 507 WAYS

In 1928 H. Cason studied common annoyances as experienced in a sample of more than a thousand Americans of both sexes, varying in age from ten to ninety years, and representing wide ranges of intelligence, wealth, physical characteristics, race, religion, and locality. The subjects rated 507 common annoyances on a rating scale varying from "extremely annoying" to "not annoying." These 507 represented a careful distillation from 21,000 collected from large groups of people.

It was Cason's belief that in the ordinary affairs of civilized people the simple and often trivial annoyances and irritations have far greater significance than do the more violent forms of emotion. He concerned himself with annoyances that were concrete and objective, especially those with irrational aspects. Reactions to some of the annoyances were strong enough to be classed as cases of anger; others were matters of disgust; still others included an element of fear.

These 507 annoyances were classified into five groupings, with most of them falling into the category "human behavior." The five categories and the percentage of annoyances in each category were as follows:

	Percentage
human behavior	59.0
nonhuman things and activities, exclusive of clothes	18.8
clothes and manner of dress	12.5
alterable physical characteristics of people	5.3
persisting physical characteristics of people	4.4
	100.0

Some of the 507 annoyances are listed in the following table, and the average annoyance score is shown for both males and females. The possible range is from 0 to 30.

Average Scores for Some Specific Annoyances

Annoyance	Male	Female
A person coughing in my face	28.5	29.3
To see or hear an animal being cruelly treated by a person	28.0	28.3
The odor of garbage	24.0	25.5
A person in automobile I am driving telling me how to drive	23.0	18.5
To see a person picking his (or her) teeth	15.3	21.3
To see a woman smoking a cigarette in public	16.5	18.3
To be held very close by my dancing partner	6.8	19.3
A beggar asking me for some money in a public place	14.0	10.8
To see bobbed hair on a woman over forty	10.5	8.3

It will be seen that a great many of the annoyances are probably not unique to the year 1928 but persist even today. On the other hand, certain ones clearly indicate changes of custom and standards over the last fifty years.

Norman Livson administered this same list to several hundred students about twenty-five years after Cason's work. Most of the items in the list maintained their level of annoyance; "a person coughing in my face" remained highly irritating, to cite one example. Some items, however, dropped sharply: To see women smoking, predictably, was hardly a bother any more, but perhaps today, with the well-established health hazards of smoking, it may again be an irritant but for both sexes and for very different reasons. The odor of garbage also was reported as only mildly irritating. This finding is somewhat surprising; technological breakthroughs eliminating odors are probably the explanation, more so, at any rate, than any greater cultural tolerance for bad smells. Bobbed hair, for obvious reasons never a hair-raising problem, vanished from the annoyance list. But what irritations does the future hold in store?

H. CASON. Common annoyances: A psychological study of everyday aversions and irritations. *Psychological Monographs*, 1930, **40**, No. 2, 1–218.

Pride and shame When successes or failures in goal achievement are perceived as signifying basic accomplishments or defects of the self, deeper and more central emotions of pride or shame may be engendered. In general, a feeling of pride results from a person's perception that his behavior is in accord with what is called for by his ideal-self conception. Conversely, a feeling of shame results from his perception that his behavior falls short of what is required by his ideal picture of self.

Merely perceiving that there is a discrepancy between self and ideal self is not always, however, a sufficient condition for emotions of shame. Individuals may come to have a realistic acceptance of the gap between self and ideal self and to experience no sense of failure in falling short of their level of aspiration.

On the other hand, strong attitudes in society force an individual to evaluate continuously his behavior and conduct with respect to the dictates of ideal self; thus the emotions of pride and shame are especially likely to be aroused in a social setting, as in a group. For example, as part of the social training of children, some parents and others deliberately try to induce such self-evaluative attitudes in them. They may say to the errant child, "Aren't you ashamed of yourself?" "Do you think you have behaved the way you know is right?" There is abundant evidence from empirical research that such psychological discipline is far more effective in lasting conscience-building than is the rod and that it is most effective when the family atmosphere is a warm one so that the child has a greater stake in living up to parental standards. (See, e.g., the discussion of a study by Sears et al. in Unit 30, p. 742.)

Guilt and remorse Emotions of guilt and of shame are not the same, though they are often closely linked. The essential circumstances evoking guilt involve the perception of one's action in a situation as divergent from the right or moral or ethical action required by the situation.

The emotion of guilt may be slight and fleeting, a mere twinge of conscience. At the other extreme, it may be a prolonged torture of agonizing appraisal. The milder degrees of guilt feeling may at times even be somewhat pleasant and exhilarative in tone. This is not surprising in light of the fact that a person violates what he perceives as right often simply because of the more powerful force of positive pleasures to be gained. As anthropologists and others have pointed out, moral prohibition tends to be created by society just because there is—or once was—social necessity for restraint of certain activities that are themselves desirable for many persons. But there is more to it. The very act of violation is often satisfying in itself because it is experienced as a successful defiance of outer authority, an expression of autonomy and power of self.

The basic source of the individual's belief in the rightness or wrongness of certain acts may or may not be conscious, but the emotion of guilt flows directly from what he perceives as his transgression against morality.

There are wide differences in the way a person perceives the guilt-inducing situation. He may see what is required of him and recognize quite clearly how he has violated this requirement. His consequent feeling of guilt is likely to be directly and explicitly attached to the action: "I feel guilty because I allowed the store clerk to give me too much change." But at other times his perceptions of exactly what is required and how his actions relate to it may be unclear. We may all feel a vague and even intense guilt when the world is thrown into war. There is a kind of free-floating anxiety. Indeed, one of the marked features of such ill-defined and irrational-appearing guilt feelings is their anxiety component; the person feels an anxious guilt but is not quite clear about just why the feelings of fear or dread or distress appear or in what connection; nor is he clear about how he can modify his behavior to prevent the guilt feeling. Like the prisoner of Kafka's novel *The Trial*, he knows not what crime he is charged with.

Especially in cases of ill-defined guilt feelings a person tends to perceive the guilt as deep within herself; it is not so much that any of her acts is bad but that she is a bad person. The most profound and agitating guilt emotions

—like those found in the fanatically self-punishing or in the insane—are of this sort; the self is seen as the focal point and basic source of the guilty action. Guilt of this kind is of course implicated in the development of personality disturbances; it is discussed further in the various units that deal with personality, mental illness, and psychotherapy.

At the other extreme, the fact that guilt can be experienced as objectified and not basically related to one's real self-conception helps to explain the distinction between guilt and shame. There can be feelings of shame without associated feelings of guilt; indeed this condition is perhaps the more common. A man may feel shame when caught using the wrong fork at an elegant dinner party but not guilt. His shame stems from a sense of having made a fool of himself in the eyes of others or of having failed to live up to his ideal self-picture of a sophisticate. But there is no cause for feelings of guilt, for there has been no violation of moral standards. For the young child such standards do not yet exist. A child only gradually learns to experience guilt; his first reaction to being caught at the cookie jar is one of shame—or even, more primitively, fear. The processes involved in a child's learning to behave in a moral manner are discussed in Unit 30.

Emotions Pertaining to Other People

Much of our emotional experience pertains to the relations of self to other people as objects in our surroundings; feelings are directed toward them. Such **emotions pertaining to other people** (and other external objects) often become crystallized over time in the form of enduring emotional predispositions or attitudes. The variety of such interpersonal emotions seems endless, but many fall along our familiar dimensions of positive-to-negative emotions. We shall deal only with the extremes.

Love Perhaps only psychologists would feel a definition is required—and would attempt to provide one. Let us first count the ways in which love appears and then seek what is common to the different forms.

Depending upon the perceived relation of object and self, the excitement and elation of romantic love come from the desire and anticipation of being together, the idealized imagining of shared delights. The strong element of sexual excitement, found in some emotions of love, obviously derives from the person's perception of the sexual adequacy of the other person to his own sexual desires. According to one of the rare empirical studies of romantic love (Rubin, 1970), loving and liking are by no means the same thing. Separate, carefully constructed loving and liking attitude scales were administered to college couples who were seeing each other on a steady basis. The scores on the loving scale correlated only moderately with those on the liking scale: 0.6 for men; only 0.4 for women. This difference is statistically significant: It suggests that women draw a sharper line between loving and liking than do men.

The love of a child for his mother may include feelings of need for protection and help. (Box 20.4, p. 478, tells us that the two are intimately connected.) Conversely, the love of the mother for her child seems to involve the need to protect. And there may even be in the emotion of love pronounced elements of submissiveness and fear, like those aroused in a child by a powerful father.

Emotions of love may vary in all these and many other forms; the intensities of experience may range from mild to profound, the degree of tension from the most serene affection to the most violent agitated passion. What, then, is common to all that we call love? The core of the feeling in love seems to be the feeling of being drawn to the other, desiring to be drawn. Clearly, too, the self is apprehended as closely identifying with the other and as having an essential feeling of devotion. As seen from one's own point of view, love is always and necessarily unselfish, for otherwise it is not the stuff of love. Whether it is really unselfish, as judged by an impartial observer, is quite another matter. We have all seen cases that we would call selfish, for instance, the love of a demanding and possessive mother for her daughter.

Furthermore, the intensity of the arousal depends upon other factors such as the accessibility or inaccessibility of the loved object. ("Absence makes the heart grow fonder," but only as long as it is not a case of "Out of sight, out of mind"!) The unattained loved one is loved the more fiercely; the thwarting of one's heart's desire to be in contact with the loved person leads to increased tension and intensified feeling.

In an investigation aptly subtitled *The Romeo and Juliet Effect*, Driscoll, Davis, and

BOX 20.4

MOTHERLESS MOTHERS

Maternal behavior may be socially learned and, indeed, it would be an unfortunate (and depopulated) society that failed to instill in its women the urge to care for their children. The fact that this same response can be clearly seen in other species begins to argue for some innate determination of a maternal drive.

University of Wisconsin psychologists Harry and Margaret Harlow have extensively studied several complex aspects of maternal behavior. One of their general questions was: What kinds of mothers do motherless mothers make? There have been a number of experiments designed to answer this question. In one experiment (by B. Seay, B. K. Alexander, and H. Harlow), observations were made of the behavior of nine monkey mothers who had been permitted no contact with their own mothers from birth. These motherless mothers were about four years old at the birth of their own babies; in each case it was the mother's first baby.

The results were dramatic. *Seven* of the nine mothers were totally inadequate by any criterion of reasonable maternal care. Each consistently avoided her child and refused to nurse it. Often the mother was abusive to the point of endangering the infant's life. One mother "sometimes bit the infant," "occasionally crushed the infant's face and body to the floor," and "responded to emotional disturbance on the part of the infant by somersaulting, violently, causing the experimenters to fear for the life of the infant." This infant did not make contact with the mother's nipple until the fifth week of its life. Intensive care by the experimenters was required to keep these infants alive. Despite this treatment by the mother, however, each infant persisted in attempting to cling to her, sometimes hanging on to her back

where it would be safe from attacks, rather than clinging in front, as is normal for infant monkeys.

A convincing demonstration that only mothered monkeys can make good mothers? Perhaps. But what about the other two motherless mothers who did not show such behavior and who, instead, reared their infants in an adequate manner? Both of them, it turned out, had had some limited contact with other baby monkeys as they were growing up; the seven inadequate mothers had had none—*they had not only been unmothered but also without playmates.* Social experience with age mates, it appears, goes a very long way toward undoing the effects of motherlessness.

This suggestion is supported by some additional findings. First of all, even the inadequate mothers began to let up on their children after having interacted with them for three or four months, however abnormally. More impressive, perhaps, is the tentative finding that these mothers could reform; the three who had had second babies by the time that this study was reported all showed adequate maternal care toward their second children. Two

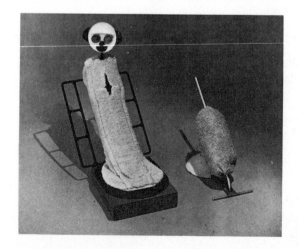

Lipetz (1972) found that the greater the degree of interference by parents in a love relationship from its start—whether or not the couple later married—the greater the subsequent *increase* of the couple's reported love for one another. (This

were even overprotective! Apparently even motherless mothers can learn to love.

Another basic question underlying Harlow's work has been what makes a mother a mother? Given a choice between two artificial or surrogate mothers —one constructed of uncuddly wire mesh but mechanically providing milk, and the other covered with fuzzy terry cloth but providing no nutrition—infants dramatically prefer the contact comfort provided by the terry-cloth mother. The wire mother is occasionally visited for nutritive purposes but home is where the terry cloth is and this surrogate mother is especially sought as a haven whenever fearful stimuli are introduced into the cage. Subsequent experimentation established that a much less ornate and less bizarre cloth-covered mother surrogate seems to be as comforting for the infant monkey, while cutting down substantially on laundry bills (see photograph of the original surrogate and the simplified one).

Other features of motherliness have been shown also to increase the appeal of surrogate mothers. *Rocking* cloth mothers are preferred to stationary ones and *warmed-up* cloth mothers were clung to by the infant monkeys more than cooler mothers, especially by very young infants.

Harlow's work illustrates the presumed advantages of working on human problems with subhuman species. These experimental manipulations, obviously impossible for the environments of human infants, are conducive for teasing out intertwined factors in analogous species. However, a major and to us a most bothersome question remains: *Can* the monkey tell us something accurate and useful about complex *human* behavior and psychological development?

H. F. HARLOW & M. K. HARLOW. Learning to love. *American Scientist*, 1966, **54**, 244–272.
B. SEAY, B. K. ALEXANDER, & H. F. HARLOW. Maternal behavior of socially deprived rhesus monkeys. *Journal of Abnormal and Social Psychology*, 1964, **69**, 345–354.
H. F. HARLOW & S. V. SUOMI. Nature of love—simplified. *American Psychologist*, 1970, **25**, 161–168.
Photo by Harry F. Harlow, University of Wisconsin Primate Laboratory.

study is reported in detail in Box I.2, page xviii.)

Hate The feeling of hate is, of course, closely related to the primary emotion of anger, discussed earlier in this unit. Hate is accentuated in situations that tend to arouse other negative emotions as well. Being blocked in one's goal striving, being threatened, being made jealous or envious intensify the emotion of hate. What seems to happen is that all these negative emotions are readily concentrated on a single target in the situation. Almost any person whom one has already endowed with some negative properties will readily become the target of this emotion. The target may even be a truly guiltless one, as in scapegoating (see the discussion of *aggression* in Unit 23, p. 572).

The essential core of the emotion of hate is the desire to destroy the hated object. Hate is not simply a feeling of dislike, aversion, or loathing, for these feelings would simply lead to an avoidance tendency. We do not seek to destroy what we dislike; we merely avoid it. But hate is essentially an emotion involving approach. We seek out the hated object, cannot rid ourselves of obsessive thoughts about it, and are not satisfied until we have destroyed it. (The discussion here will be on the interpersonal level; in Unit 30, p. 742, we treat aggression in a wider societal context.)

The hated person must necessarily be perceived as playing a central role in our world. Just as we can be jealous only of a person psychologically close to us, so we can hate only a person psychologically close to us. But psychological closeness does not necessarily mean that we in fact know the person quite well; she may instead represent a particular group that we detest or envy. She may thus be close because she is a symbol of a group that is psychologically important to us.

In some cases, such as traditional family feuds or pathological fixations, persistent hate may take on some of the attributes of a positive feature of the person's world. He "nurses" his hate, savors it, channels much attention and effort toward it. And if his aim is finally achieved and the hated object destroyed, he may feel a sense of loss. The hated object had actually become a central and needed object, giving meaning to the person's world. It had enabled him to organize a stable set of beliefs and attitudes around this negative value. "Love thy enemy" may have more than one meaning!

Hate can be turned inward, and we can observe this fact in the person who, through accident of birth or upbringing, is forced to identify with a group she dislikes, for example, a religious or racial minority group. She may dislike the group because she accepts the standards of the majority. *Self*-hate may be intensified if she is able to divorce herself from the despised group. The individual who has desired most to conceal a certain ethnic or racial origin often rails most against that group. Such self-hate may involve an extremely delicate balance. A person who has managed "to pass" is, in a sense, afforded the opportunity to become especially virulent in relation to her former group. Because she now believes herself no longer a member of the group, whatever self-protective defenses she may once have had against its disparagement are now removed. She runs the risk that she may at any moment again become identified as a member of the group, however, and, if it were to happen, she would have to face her own hate, now enlarged.

This inventory of emotions could go on, for we have far from exhausted the repertory of human feelings and reactions. No explicit treatment has been given to two other classes of emotion. One might be called the **appreciative emotions**—the emotions of wonder and awe, of the whole gamut of aesthetic feelings. Included here would be the world of humor, which many psychologists have long seen as a mode of expression for the most varied types of emotions (see Box 20.5). And what of **moods**, those pervasive and transitory emotional states that are so difficult to link to concrete aspects of the immediate situation? And what of the more general question of the determinants of such shifts in emotional experience? Why, for example, do emotional states seem to wear out? Even the most sparkling flow of wit begins to bore, and the seemingly inexhaustible well of tears runs dry. Is this wearing out in some sense a satiation phenomenon akin to that which we have seen in perception, in which

prolonged exposure to an unchanging stimulus pattern results in its rejection?

Again, as so often before, we have many more questions than answers. In certain respects, we are not very much beyond the descriptive stage in our understanding of emotions. True, empirical investigations guided by emerging theories of emotion are beginning to yield at least partial explanations. Another avenue of approach to understanding emotional phenomena is through the study of their development.

THE DEVELOPMENT OF EMOTIONS

Our cataloging and classifying of emotions has dealt with the full range of human feelings. This presentation conveniently put aside a number of questions to which we now turn: (1) Do we find in children the same complexity and richness of emotional experience and expression as in adults? (2) Are these various emotions unlearned attributes of human behavior, emerging universally and unaffected by specific earlier experiences? (3) Are the distinctions we drew among different emotional states reliably discerned as we observe the emotional behavior of individuals?

Differentiation of Emotions

One thing is clear about the development of emotions: The course runs from lesser to greater differentiation as the child grows into man. Whether the stimulus is a loud noise, sudden loss of support, pain, wet diaper, hunger, or tickle, the newborn responds with a fairly diffuse emotional outburst that can best be labeled "general excitement." In the course of development, this generalized excitement becomes more and more differentiated until by the end of the first two years the baby's emotional life has become more discriminating and richer. He has fewer outbursts, but the kinds of situations that lead to emotional episodes increase in variety, and the nature of his responses becomes more specifically adapted for those situations (see Figure 20.1, p. 482).

According to Bridges (1932), the generalized response of excitement first becomes dif-

BOX 20.5

DEATH, SEX, AND HUMOR

Much of the psychological speculation on the bases of humor has been summed up by J. C. Flugel, who discusses, among others, the following motivational functions served by humor:

1. *Expression of superiority.* Thomas Hobbes long ago characterized laughter as "sudden glory arising from some eminency in ourselves by comparison with the infirmity of others." A great many jokes have this readily recognizable element of superiority of self and derision of others, for instance, jokes aimed at the "drunken Irish," the "dumb farmer," or the "uneducated Negro."

2. *Expression of aggression.* Humor is, of course, a highly convenient vehicle for expressing aggressions in a safe, socially acceptable, and somewhat indirect manner. Sometimes humor lies in aggressions toward those of superior status or of manifest self-importance. The pompous person who slips on a banana peel may evoke hilarity; a cripple in the same situation may not.

3. *Defense against reality.* There is always an essential aspect of playfulness and unreality in humor. Humor may serve to protect oneself from the pains and threats of reality. We may laugh to prevent ourselves from feeling personally humiliated or from being too painfully touched by the tragic misfortunes of others. And there is so-called gallows humor, in which the person in desperate straits jokes as a way of fending off grim reality.

4. *Expression of sexuality.* The obvious elements of sexuality and obscenity contained in many jokes suggest that humor offers a ready avenue for the expression of such socially tabooed thoughts. Flugel comments that the sex joke is often in the nature of a seduction of the listener, that is, he is invited, as it were, to participate in the sexual transgression.

As a footnote to this last item, G. D. Wilson and A. H. Brazendale, British psychologists, suggest that different kinds of sex jokes may play different roles for different women. As part of a larger study, they asked ninety-seven women who were enrolled in a teacher training program (ages 18 to 21) to rate how funny they found each of forty-two risqué cartoons found on postcards sold at English seaside resorts. The same women were also rated for sexual attractiveness by two male college instructors, whose sets of judgments agreed quite well ($r = .60$). The less attractive women found funniest the postcard cartoons that "depicted sexually attractive girls being admired, discussed, or approached by eligible males"; the attractive women were more amused by cartoons with a highly explicit sexual content. Wilson and Brazendale speculate that the less attractive women, who are somewhat less successful in the game of love, gain vicarious satisfaction through (and thus find more humorous) situations in which women are hotly pursued, as they themselves are not. And the more attractive women may be capable of appreciating more overt sexual allusions.

Humor, we see, can be all things to all women and men—and also different things to different women and men.

J. C. FLUGEL. Humor and laughter. In G. Lindzey (Ed.), *Handbook of Social Psychology*. Cambridge, Mass.: Addison-Wesley, 1954.
G. D. WILSON & A. H. BRAZENDALE. Sexual attractiveness, social attitudes, and response to risqué humor. *European Journal of Social Psychology*, 1973.

ferentiated into a general negative response and a general positive response called "distress" and "delight" respectively. As time goes on, these still quite general responses split into more and more specific ones. Distress comes to find expression in a variety of emotions: anger, disgust, fear, or jealousy. Delight also becomes differentiated and can express itself as appreciation and joy in numerous pursuits. The rate at which these emotions become differentiated

varies from infant to infant, and the exact ages at which the various emotions appear are difficult to determine. Figure 20.2, page 482, presents one developmental history based on Bridges' observations of sixty-two infants in the Montreal Foundling Hospital.

The facts that Bridges based her work on institutionalized infants—by no means a normal early environment—and had access to only relatively small samples suggest that her con-

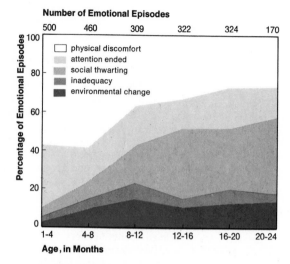

Number of Emotional Episodes

FIGURE 20.1　Chart indicating the change in frequency of emotional outbursts in children and the nature of the exciting situation. It is based on data collected by W. E. Blatz and D. A. Millichamp (1935) in observations of the behavior of five children. Over a two-year period, 2,095 emotional outbursts were observed and recorded in these infants. It will be noted that the *number* of emotional episodes drops from a total of 500, during the period from one to four months, to 170 during the period from twenty to twenty-four months. At first most of the episodes (more than 60 percent) were initiated by physical discomfort—wet diapers, pins sticking in skin, illness, and so on, or by the cessation of adult attention. As time went on, other situations called forth emotional responses. "Social thwarting" refers to such stimuli as teasing a child, laughing at him, refusing him a request. "Inadequacy" includes such situations as a child's inability to reach for desired objects or inability to do something. "Environmental change" includes being placed in an unfamiliar physical or social environment and being exposed to loud and sudden noises.

more, and more varied, interaction with parents and other family members would probably result in more rapid differentiation than among institutionalized children. For example, Ambrose (1961) reports that institution-reared infants do not begin to smile (at the stimulus of an *unsmiling* human face) until they are about fifteen weeks old, while home-reared children start doing so as early as six weeks of age. Why this is so is unclear; it may well be that this earlier smiling is simply a reaction to more energetic attempts by mothers (compared with institution personnel) to elicit a smile from their own infants and their more enthusiastic response when the smile is evoked. On the other hand—paradoxically—institutionalized children of about three to four months of age are more likely to smile and generally to be more inviting toward strangers than home-reared infants of the same age (Rheingold, 1961). A reasonable hypothesis to account for this paradox is that the environment of an institutionalized infant is a relatively socially deprived one compared with home-reared infants. Thus, since we can safely assume a very early need for social stimulation, institutionalized infants are under more pressure to learn and to use a repertoire of invitations (including smiling) that will attract

clusions are most safely considered as tentative. But these tentative conclusions have lasted almost half a century thus far. No better data with equally comprehensive scope seem to have since become available, and her general scheme does find support in anecdotal reports of the course of emotional development in individual children.

　　There are some suggestions, however, that the emotional development of children brought up in normal family surroundings with

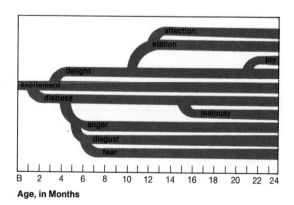

FIGURE 20.2　A diagrammatic representation of the progressive differentiation of emotions in the child during his first two years.

K. M. B. Bridges. Emotional development in early infancy. *Child Development*, **3**, 324–341; © 1932 by The Society for Research in Child Development; adapted by permission.

and keep others near them. Furthermore, the institutionalized infant is less likely to learn to distinguish between its own attendant and strangers.

We are now touching on the currently active research area of formation of social attachments and, correspondingly, development of fearfulness toward strangers. Neither topic is emotional in the narrow sense of the word, but a few observations may be in order here. It has been suggested (Schaffer & Emerson, 1964) that social responsiveness moves through three stages in its early development, beginning with an indiscriminate reactivity to stimuli of all sorts. Later on, the infant discovers that people are the most rewarding source of social stimulation and, for a while, he forms indiscriminate attachments to any and all reasonably well-behaved human beings. Not until about seven months of age does the infant begin to form *specific* social attachments, usually first to his mother. It is at seven months, for example, that infants who require hospitalization and who are thus separated from their mothers first begin to cling to the mothers as they are leaving them; they also become quite disturbed when left alone and are characteristically frightened of the hospital staff (Schaffer & Callender, 1959). Wariness of strangers can begin in some infants somewhat earlier than seven months. Bronson (1972) reports that wariness has been observed as early as four months of age, but by nine months it is quite typical. Smiling at strangers tends to decrease during this period and the six- or seven-month-old infant is likely to smile at a stranger only if he is safely ensconced on his mother's lap. (As we saw in Box 20.5, infant monkeys also use their mothers as a safe base of operation.)

Incidentally, Bronson suggests that earlier wariness of strangers is related to a generalized reactivity or arousability. In his study, infants who in the earliest months of life appeared more startled by a sudden stimulus tended to be the first to show wary or fearful reactions toward strangers. Our knowledge of the early development of the full range of human emotions is unusually incomplete, perhaps because of the intrinsic difficulties of studying these processes, especially in the preverbal years.

There is no direct evidence for the course of later emotional differentiation through childhood into adulthood. But there is indirect evidence, as we will see later on in this unit, that children become increasingly more accurate in judging emotions as they approach adulthood; this evidence might indicate that they are becoming increasingly able to experience the full gamut of adult emotions. This view and the common observation that children become emotionally more complex as they mature appear to support the hypothesis of a continuing process of emotional differentiation.

Age Changes in Emotionality

Accompanying the tendency toward increased emotional differentiation are developmental changes in the nature of emotional expression. For example, it is clear that children do become less emotional with age, in the sense that they exhibit violent outbursts less frequently. Macfarlane, Allen, and Honzik (1954) report that, in a group of normal children, temper tantrums declined steadily from age three onward for both boys and girls. Whereas about 60 percent of all children at age three had tantrums with at least moderate frequency, at age fourteen only about 15 percent on the average had them. Whether this age trend represents a lessened urge to blow up or a greater ability to control one's temper or both is a moot point.

Chown and Heron (1965), in their review of changes in emotionality in later adulthood and old age, are confronted with the same dilemma. They summarize evidence that points to increasingly fewer and less intense emotional outbursts as one grows old but conclude that "it looks as though emotion is present but clamped down rather than nonexistent, and can be strongly aroused by unexpected disasters." Indik, Seashore, and Slesinger (1964), however, do find from their study of psychological strain from young adulthood to old age that a major source of emotional upset—"job-related strain" —decreases steadily throughout this period. Furthermore, psychosomatic symptoms (see Unit 28, p. 695), which might be regarded as an indication of clamping down on emotions, also decrease with age.

The best but still very tentative resolution we can draw from these data and from a number of recent studies of adjustment to aging and retirement is that *life does become emotionally easier as we grow older.* At least, it seems to do so for those who survive—not a flippant point since it may indicate that more stressed persons die earlier and, hence, are not represented in samples at later ages. The relative contributions to this age trend of biological aging processes, of changes in social roles, and of such personal factors as coming to terms with oneself have still to be evaluated.

SOME DETERMINANTS OF EMOTIONS

The enormous variety of emotional styles is one of the most obvious features of the human species. Some people are quietly cheerful, some boisterously happy, some explosive, others brooding. These emotional styles are frequently so pervasive as to be indistinguishable from personality traits. Is a tendency to quick anger an emotional characteristic or a trait of personality? Because of this fuzzy distinction, much of what we know of the determinants of personality (see Unit 28), particularly regarding the so-called traits of temperament, applies as well to an understanding of individual differences in emotion.

Hereditary Determinants

There are decided differences among even the youngest infants in emotional kinds of behavior: in frequency and loudness of crying, in restlessness, in general activity level. Some of these emotional traits appear to persist into later development (Yarrow & Yarrow, 1964).

The existence of such differences at birth and even their persistence into later life are not firm demonstrations of hereditary determination, however. These differences may be the effects of intrauterine influences prior to birth or may reflect certain complications of pregnancy and delivery (see Box 1.2, p. 17).

Studies of twins go more directly to the point. In order to assess the relative importance to emotional behavior of hereditary and envi-

ronmental factors, these studies use the general rationale that, to the extent that identical twins are more like one another than are fraternal twins, the trait in question is hereditary. Vandenberg (1962) and Gottesman (1963, 1966) report findings that with identical twins a large number of emotional and personality characteristics are in general agreement with one another. (For a broad review of genetic determinants of personality, see Unit 28, p. 690.) For present purposes, however, perhaps the most pertinent finding is that the general trait of emotionality is substantially determined in human beings by hereditary factors. Loehlin (1965), using Vandenberg's data, appears to have refined the original conclusion. His analysis suggests that certain aspects of emotionality are hereditary while others are not. Examples of hereditary facets are the ability to control one's impulses or the ability to be adventurous and fast-acting. Very little influenced by heredity, on the other hand, are such characteristics as nervousness, jumpiness, and feeling restricted by rules. With a little stretch of the imagination we may be led to look for direct physiological bases for hereditary emotionality, whereas nonhereditary emotionality, which seems more interpersonal or social in its character, would turn our sights to childhood upbringing and experiences.

Early Experience Determinants

We have already noted that experiences during pregnancy and delivery may affect a child's later emotional behavior. Also, we saw in Box 20.4, page 478, that an absence of mothering exerts profound effects on a child's later ability to behave appropriately to her own offspring. Many lines of evidence support the importance of social stimulation for normal progress in several areas of development. For example, adequate early stimulation is critical for intellectual development (see Unit 10, p. 211). More to the point is our detailed treatment of the effects of early experience on later personality, of which emotions are a part (see Unit 28, p. 698). Also relevant is a study of infants (Ourth & Brown, 1961), which reports that, even in the first few days of life, mothered babies (those who were frequently held and rocked) cried less than those who were given only routine care.

As this flurry of cross-references indicates, emotional development is an essential component of general development, which includes personality, cognitive, and physical growth; and emotionality shares with these other aspects of a human being the broad principle of being significantly affected by experiences in early life.

Hallucinogenic Drugs

There has been considerable research interest of late in the effects of various consciousness-altering drugs (LSD is one example) on emotional experience. The testimonial gist of informal and formal experimentation with these drugs is that they apparently induce an openness to emotion and feeling that is rarely accessible to the ordinary person in his workaday life. How do these drugs cause this openness? What accounts for the apparently very different effects of these drugs on different individuals or even on the same person on different occasions? We consider questions such as these in detail in Unit 21. For now we will note only that the social context in which drugs are taken must be assigned primary importance if the resultant emotional behavior is to be understood. Without doubt, we still have a long way to go to arrive at a full understanding of the influence of drugs upon our feelings, passions, and emotions.

DISCRIMINATION OF EMOTIONS

It would be difficult to convince a dedicated mother that her newborn's emotional reactions are in reality as diffuse as we have described and that even her baby's smile is at first directed at just anybody in the vicinity. Folklore tells us that a mother can tell from the tone of her baby's cry whether it is hungry, wet, or in need of company. Perhaps so, but this claim has not yet been proved by systematic research. Since ability to judge another's emotional state improves with intimate experience with that individual, mothers are in a favored position to distinguish among the relatively few and rather blatantly expressed emotions of their offspring. But, as we will now see, the situation is quite different for the expression and discrimination of adult emotional states.

Problems of Definition and Measurement

We must first consider how emotions are to be detected and what concrete procedures are to be used in measuring them. And this problem in the scientific study of emotion is a particularly thorny one. For any given emotion there can be many indicators, allowing for a variety of quite different measurement operations.

Take anger as an example. Do you measure how a person feels, how he is behaving or expressing himself, or such physiological events as changes in heart rate and blood pressure? These are all reasonable indicators of anger, but they point to very different procedures. We can, of course, measure all three, but, as we shall soon see, the different sets of measurements may lead to different conclusions as to whether and to what degree the person is really angry.

Do the same situations lead to anger in all persons? Is there a *standard* behavioral response to anger? Do all people regularly show the *same* facial expressions when they feel angry? Is there *high* consistency among individuals in the bodily events accompanying the experience of anger? The answer to each of these questions is a qualified no. Nor is the situation much better within the world of a single individual: Each of us gets angry at different things at different times, expresses this emotion differently depending upon the occasion, and perhaps even feels anger differently inside. Despite this complexity, the different ways in which emotion may be expressed do show certain systematic, if intricate, interrelations. For example, Funkenstein, King, and Drolette (1957) have reported that individuals who *expressed* anger showed evidence of an increased secretion of noradrenaline in the blood; those who were anxious or whose irritation and anger were *self-directed* showed, instead, evidence of an increase in adrenaline. These two hormones, though both involved in the body's response to emotional stress, each produce different somatic response patterns (see Unit 22, p. 544).

Evidence indicating a link between the behavioral expression of an emotion and its physiological manifestations does not, however, tell us how or whether we can discriminate *among* different emotions. And this question is the critical one.

Emotions and Self-Report

Can we tell what we *ourselves* are feeling? "Of course," we answer. "If we can't, then who can?" But this claim to special privilege and authority for the "feeler" exposes a major flaw in this source of evidence. Any phenomenon that, by its very definition, is observable only by a single individual (and never to an outside observer) poses great difficulties for scientific inquiry. Admittedly, we can and do agree upon definitions of various emotional states, but this consensus remains only verbal unless it can be shown, for example, that when ten people say that they are happy, they are in fact feeling the same thing. But how can we be certain that self-reports of the same emotional state, even if they sound alike, indicate true consensus in what is experienced?

One important source of indirect evidence on this issue is the usual presence of a behavioral consensus. When someone tells us he feels frightened, he almost always is behaving in the way we have seen other people behave when they said they were frightened. Furthermore, if our informant tells us that a moment before he was only apprehensive and not yet really frightened, we accept the distinction because it jibes with our observations of his just previous behavior. The point at issue is whether or not we can reliably discriminate another person's emotions on the basis of his behavior.

Emotions and Expressive Cues

We primarily judge others' emotional states, apart from how they describe themselves, by noting their behavior: facial expressions, bodily movements, postures. A considerable body of research has been devoted to determining the validity of judgments based on such **expressive cues**. Emotions differ in the ease with which they can be judged (usually from posed photographs), although various investigators differ somewhat in their ordering of judgment accuracy for specific emotions. Gitter, Black, and Mostofsky (1972) present the generalization, from their own study and several others, that happiness (or joy) and pain are easiest to judge while fear or sadness is somewhat more difficult. Suspicion and pity, which we would probably regard as more subtle emotions, prove indeed to be the most difficult to judge accurately (Feleky, 1922; Kanner, 1931). Children present a somewhat different picture. Although they too can judge happiness quite accurately, they do most poorly on judgments of contempt, an emotion that is quite easy for adults to identify (Gates, 1923). The average three-year-old can identify laughter, but surprise—easily judged by adults—cannot be judged accurately until the child is eleven. The inference is that children have to learn the cue for each emotion and that emotions differ in the ease with which their cues may be learned.

Odom and Lemond (1972) and Hamilton (1973) present data that convincingly demonstrate that younger children of nursery school and kindergarten age are less able to judge emotions accurately than are fifth-graders. Even by the second grade there is a detectable increase in this ability. Going along with this ability, but in a significantly less pronounced fashion, is the ability to *produce*, or pose convincingly, designated emotions. Once again, as with adults, joy is best judged and produced while fear proved to be relatively difficult in both respects. Why the ability to produce emotions develops more slowly than judging ability —and in fact remains quite difficult even for adults—poses a problem. Izard (1971), who reports the latter finding, suggests that children in our society are raised in a manner which does not encourage spontaneous and open (and therefore more easy to recognize) emotional expression, particularly for culturally less desirable emotions. Poker-faced blandness possibly has a certain adaptive advantage, particularly in competitive societies, but perhaps at a cost. It may be that the learned ability to suppress the *expression* of certain emotions may also suppress the ability to feel them.

Adults can also learn to use new cues for judging emotions, but apparently their ability to do so varies with their attitudes and past experience. Dittman, Parloff, and Boomer (1965) asked psychotherapists and professional dancers to judge the pleasantness of a woman's emotional state from motion pictures of her behavior. Both groups based their evaluations almost entirely on facial-expression cues, with minimal attention to such nonfacial cues as posture, movement, and muscular tension. When facial cues were blotted out in subsequent trials, both groups demonstrated an ability to judge consistently these usually neglected nonfacial cues. In a final set of trials, when all cues were again made available, however, only the professional dancers showed an increased reliance on nonfacial cues.

Both groups thus found that they *could* use a new category of cues for judging emotion, but only the dancers, who are presumably more aware of whole-body movements, showed some lasting effects of this learning experience. The psychotherapists reverted to their former almost exclusive reliance on facial cues. For an illustration of how difficult it is to assess emotion from facial expressions alone, see Figure 20.3.

All findings reported so far in this section are based upon judgments of emotions in which both the judges and the judged presumably share the same culture. Could we do as well in judging the emotions of persons from cultures other than our own? We already have seen that young children who, in a sense, can

be regarded as immigrants to our adult culture, cannot do so. And other evidence also suggests that expressive cues of feelings and emotions are learned and are *culture-specific*. People of different ethnic backgrounds express their emotions differently. For the Japanese a smile may convey regret, for the Chinese a hand clap may denote concern. You are probably most accurate in your judgments of the emotions of persons from your own subculture.

Despite these cultural differences, there remain a number of expressions of emotional states common to all mankind—for example, a downturned mouth to express grief—indicating that some of this behavior may be biologically rooted. Charles Darwin in his book *Expression of the Emotions in Man and Animals* argued that emotional expressions are vestiges of movements that, in their original forms, were adaptive for the organism, although by no means *intended* to communicate emotions. For example, the downturned mouth may derive from the facial pattern involved in crying, whose function it is to call for help when in distress.

And, Darwin held, this single feature survives as the natural and universal expression of the general state of unhappiness. Another example: The position of the facial muscles when vomiting closely resembles that characteristic of the facial expression of disgust. If this Darwinian view is correct, then the behavioral vocabulary of emotional expression is at least in part universal and serves us all in judging others' emotions.

There is some evidence to support this. Ekman, Sorenson, and Friesen (1969) first carefully selected thirty photographs that they

FIGURE 20.3   To find out what's happening here, see solution on page 495.

Photo by Charles Gatewood

thought were relatively free of learned culture-specific cues for portraying various emotions. They had to sort through 3,000 photographs to do so, reasoning that the usual finding that people were poor judges of emotion in cultural strangers was precisely owing to the failure to select stimuli—photographs of facially expressed emotions—that were culture-free. Apparently the selection procedure used by Ekman et al. was successful since they were able to demonstrate substantial accuracy in judging the depicted emotions by judges from a wide range of cultures. Brazilians, Japanese, and Americans were in substantial agreement with one another and substantially correct in their judgments; others, drawn from nonliterate cultures in New Guinea and Borneo, showed a lower consensus but nonetheless were able to agree fairly well in judging the emotions of happiness, anger, and fear (in part, this somewhat reduced ability to judge emotions may have resulted from the exclusive use of Caucasions in the photographs). In a later study (Ekman, Friesen, & Ellsworth, 1972), it was found that Americans could fairly accurately judge emotional expressions posed by people from the New Guinea culture.

Also relevant to the question of the possible unlearned nature of emotional expression are observations of blind people. Facial displays by persons blind from birth are extreme and unmistakable; in comparison, persons who have had vision for the first years of their lives but have later become blind express their emotions in milder and more ambiguous forms like the rest of us. What we *learn* about the expression of emotions may be to hide them or to overlay the natural pattern with the expressive affectations of our culture. We might conclude, therefore, that emotional expression has both a learned and an unlearned component. And, to some extent, it *does* matter who is expressing the emotion and who is doing the judging. (For evidence that this is so *even within* our own society, see Box 20.6.)

Emotions and Bodily Processes

A vast number of bodily cues have been associated with emotional experience. Although the details of their operation are reserved for later discussion, let us enumerate some that are relatively easy to measure: respiration, heart rate, galvanic skin response (related to sweating), skin temperature, dilation of the pupils and eye-blinks, salivary secretion, and gastrointestinal movements. Others, like turning pale or blushing, although undoubtedly related to emotional states, are more difficult to assess quantitatively. Some cues, like trembling or rapid eyeblinks, are easily visible to the naked eye; others, like the galvanic skin response, can be measured only through the use of special instruments. The layman thus infers an emotional state from normally visible cues, the expert from these cues and also from his instrument readings. Neither is always correct. The suspect whose elevated blood pressure is indicated on a polygraph (a lie detector) may be frightened rather than guilty. Single, isolated somatic cues are by themselves unreliable indicators of specific emotional states.

Attempts to identify specific emotions from *patterns* of physiological cues have met with more success. The polygraph expert can be more confident in his evaluation if he notices the variety of different indicators of emotion discussed in Unit 22. He also uses whatever situation information he can get; he combines police work with polygraphic analysis.

There are some emotions, however, that are hard to tell apart on a physiological basis. As we noted earlier, anxiety and self-directed anger both seem to increase the secretion of adrenaline. Ax (1953) reports other physiological indicators shared by these two emotions; among them are an increase in heart rate and in systolic blood pressure. Certain other indicators, however, do distinguish the two: Anger is accompanied by muscular tension and fear by an increase in respiration rate. (A new technique for discriminating reliably among different emotions is reported in Box 20.7, p. 490.)

The conclusions from studies using each of the three levels of cues converge on much this same point: It is relatively simple to detect a state of generalized and undifferentiated arousal, but detection becomes increasingly difficult as we attempt to discriminate more and more finely among distinct emotions. In our own experience, feeling excited is a clearly rec-

BOX 20.6

WHO'S FEELING? WHO'S LOOKING?

Although earlier research had considered both race and sex as factors influencing the perception of emotional states, very few studies have *simultaneously* investigated the effects on judgment of varying the race and sex of both the perceiver and the expresser of emotion. A. G. Gitter, H. Black, and D. Mostofsky, psychologists at Boston University, have helped to fill this gap. Employing an experimental design that permitted them to evaluate the effects of race (black or white) of both the perceiver and expresser in all possible combinations (e.g., a black female perceiver judging emotions expressed by a white male expresser), seven emotions were studied: anger, happiness, surprise, fear, disgust, pain, and sadness.

Professional actors (5 black males, 5 black females, 5 white males, 5 white females) served as the expressers. Still photographs—each of 7 emotions from each of the 20 actors, or 140 in all—were made from single frames of motion pictures produced from enactments of each emotion by each actor; the frames used were those selected by outside judges as best portraying the given emotion. The subjects were 160 Boston University students, equally divided on race and sex. Each subject viewed 35 of these photographs and assigned 1 of the 7 emotions to each. These responses were then checked against the intended emotions to yield accuracy scores.

The overall results seem clear-cut: (1) Women expressers of both races are far more accurately judged than are men expressers. (2) The sex of the perceiver makes no difference. (3) Emotions enacted by whites are judged more accurately than emotions enacted by blacks. (Pain, however, is more accurately enacted by blacks.) (4) Black perceivers make more accurate judgments than do white perceivers.

There are many other provocative results from this study, certainly enough to warrant further exploration along these lines. For example, the highest single accuracy score of all is attained when black women are evaluating one another, although the women-judging-women situation, irrespective of race, yielded the highest general accuracy.

Further support for this latter finding is presented by a four-university team of psychologists, who report that women pairs convey emotional states to one another far better than do men pairs. They suggest that this advantage may be due to our culture's greater permissiveness for women to express overtly their emotional states. And since the Gitter et al. study found that women are more accurately judged by both men and women, these clearly defined emotional signals are apparently not restricted to the female wavelength.

A. G. GITTER, H. BLACK, & D. MOSTOFSKY. Race and sex in the perception of emotion. *Journal of Social Issues*, 1972, **28**, 63–78.
R. W. BUCK, V. J. SAVIN, R. E. MILLER, & W. F. CAUL. Communication of affect through facial expressions in humans. *Journal of Personal and Social Psychology*, 1972, **23**, 362–371.

ognizable, if diffuse, condition. With equal confidence, we can characterize another's behavior as generally wound up. Experiential, behavioral, and somatic cues may agree that a state of general arousal exists and at the same time suggest any of several specific emotions or a combination. For example, a person who is observed to be, and reports herself to be, in an agitated state almost always reflects this state physiologically in her galvanic skin response. This link can even be observed in newborn infants. Weller and Bell (1965), working with sixty neonates between two and five days old, found a highly significant correlation between variations in the infant's galvanic skin response and his degree of arousal, as assessed from a number of behavioral indexes like crying and various bodily movements. The impact of this line of evidence has suggested to many investigators that emotion can be considered as incidental arousal, a view we shall consider as we turn to a consideration of some of the current theories of emotion.

SOME CURRENT THEORIES OF EMOTION

Theories of emotion place heavy stress upon definitional issues as much as upon the issue of

BOX 20.7

EMOTIONS AS *SENTIC STATES*

M. Clynes, director of the Biocybernetic Laboratories at New York's Rockland State Hospital, has reported what appear to be surprisingly direct links between fantasied emotional states and simple observable behaviors. Specifically, he instructs a subject to concentrate on imagining a given emotion for a few minutes and then to express that emotion by pressing down a single finger briefly (for about 2 sec) on a key upon which the finger has been resting. The key is electronically instrumented to permit continuous measurement of two aspects of the finger-pressing response: (1) vertical or downward pressure and (2) horizontal pressure, toward or away from the body. These two sets of measurements over the 2-sec period are combined to generate, for each pressing, a single graph that portrays a continuous record of the variations in these two kinds of pressure. The figure shown presents the graphs typically found for no emotion and for anger and love. In each pair, the top curve denotes vertical pressure (the lower the curve goes, the greater the pressure at that moment), while the lower curve expresses horizontal pressure variations (downward = away from the body; upward = in toward the body). (The magnitude of the pressures involved can be estimated from the scale showing the vertical distance representing 200-gm pressure.)

The no emotion graph writes the pressure story when the subject simply presses down upon the key without any specific emotion having been fantasied; all we have here is a rather rapid and pronounced downward and slightly outward thrust. Anger is similar—it is also rapid but the emphasis here is on outward (rejecting?) rather than downward pressure. Love is a much slower phenomenon and smooth changes are evident throughout the 2-sec period: The top curve indicates an initially very light downward pressure that then gradually increases before it finally eases off. From the bottom curve we can read a slightly increasing inward (embracing?) pressure.

Clynes reports that most subjects appear to have no difficulty with the task and express each emotion in an individually quite consistent manner; that is, successive graphs produced by one subject look very much like his other graphs for that emo-

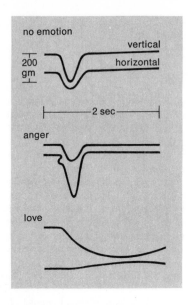

tion. Furthermore—and this is what seems to hold most promise—different subjects produce much the same graphs for a given emotion, even subjects from such different societies as the United States, Japan, Mexico, and the Indonesian island of Bali.

Clynes regards his data as indicating the existence of genetically based brain programs, or *sentic states*, which govern each specific emotional state. He maintains further that because each emotion is so directly controlled by specific brain programs, the *pattern* of the body movement involved in expressing any emotion is much the same for many people. And it is this consistency of motor expression that may account for the ability to judge others' emotional states, even if the others are from cultures quite different from our own.

Clynes' data are certainly unusual and await replication by other investigators. Further research should enable us to evaluate better the theoretical superstructure that he has built upon the foundations of his data. In any event he seems to have offered a new avenue of approach in an area where it is sorely needed—the origins and nature of human emotional experience and expression.

M. CLYNES. Biocybernetics of space-time forms in the genesis and communication of emotion. In symposium, "Biocybernetics of the Dynamic Communication of Emotions and Qualities," presented at the meeting of the American Association for the Advancement of Science, Chicago, 1970.

how emotions arise. In fact, most theories of emotion may more properly be regarded as points of view in the sense that none attempts a fully detailed and comprehensive analysis of emotional behavior.

Emotions as Incidental

The general theme of one set of views is that emotions are mere by-products of more fundamental events. An experienced emotional state is seen as nothing but an *incidental* occurrence. Adopting this point of view, a psychologist may consider how feelings come about but need not regard emotions as having any primary purpose or function.

Emotion and bodily state The conception of emotion as nothing but a reflection of bodily states is found in one of the earliest of modern theories of emotion, the James-Lange theory, which is discussed in Unit 22, page 547. In this theory the experiencing of a somatic event *is* the emotion. Empirical evidence on this point can be obtained by inducing directly in the person's body a specified pattern of bodily states corresponding to a specific emotion. Under such conditions, he should experience the emotion—whether it be fear, anger, or grief. In other words, the *feeling* of the emotion would be completely determined by the artificially induced bodily states. Such experiments have been attempted but we have just seen that not all the bodily correlates of any specific emotion are yet known and therefore conclusions based on such experiments must be regarded with great caution.

Emotion as disruptive Although it has been expressed in a variety of ways, another central view is that emotion is disruptive—that it interferes with the orderly operation of normal factors influencing behavior. Young (1961), an experimenter in the field of emotion, presents one clear version of **emotion as disruptive**: *"When an individual is affectively* [that is, emotionally] *disturbed by the environmental situation to such an extent that his cerebral control is weakened or lost . . . that individual is emotional"* (italics in original).

This statement highlights two assumptions of this position: First, only intense emotion is implicitly dealt with and, second, it assumes that emotional behavior is the opposite of rational behavior. When a person is behaving irrationally, we say he is being emotional; on the other hand, when he is mastering the situation, we say that he has kept his emotions under control. Leeper (1965) traces this view to the fact that an emotional state that leads to a disruption in, or interference with, expected behavior is more likely to be noticed.

Taken in its extreme form, the view that emotions are disruptive prejudges the case and can thus be charged with being unscientific. To argue that emotion involves the breakdown of orderly laws of behavior is to imply that emotional behavior is itself not orderly, that is, that it does not exhibit any systematic relation to other psychological phenomena. Furthermore, emotion is denied any function or purpose, thus placing it beyond psychological theory, which regards, with minor exceptions, all behavior as adaptive.

Emotion as arousal In a certain sense, **emotion as arousal** is a cleaned-up version of the previous theory. Arousal, as commonly understood, implies at least a certain degree of excitement, but it allows us to speak of a continuum of emotional reactivity (from mild to intense). Also, this view carries no implication of irrationality or of disruption in normal patterns of behavior. By its very definition, however, arousal is a highly diffuse state. In fact, arousal is so general a characteristic that we have applied the concept to both motivational and emotional states. Some psychologists argue that the resulting blurring of the traditional distinction between emotional and motivational aspects of experience and behavior would be a welcome side effect of the arousal concept.

But are we willing to write off emotion as an extraneous and outdated concept? To do so might seem reasonable if we had to describe only the *behavior* of experimental animals. But the data of *experience* raise a problem of another order. Our language is immensely rich in terms for communicating emotional experience. A hypothetical champion of emotion as a *theoretically useful entity* might argue: "When I *feel* hopeful, suspicious, or amused, something very real is happening to me. What does it matter if I exhibit these emotions, through my outward behavior and inner physiology, in ways different from other people? What if the psychologist, with all his objective measurements, is unable to tell whether, at a given moment, I am feeling haughty or merely bored? I can tell the difference, so it's his job to understand how come I can." Some psychologists have attempted to reply to this challenge while holding firm in their claim that arousal remains the key to the problem (see Box 20.8). Others find the data of human experience so convincing as to require a more primary and respectable role for emotion within psychological theory. For these people, emotion is something more than an incidental phenomenon thrown off by more fundamental processes.

Emotions as Primary and Functional

The essential theme of this general position is that emotions are not secondary and incidental occurrences but require consideration in their own right. There are many theoretical approaches that could fall within this rubric. We shall deal with only two of them. Both of these views insist that emotions have an adaptive function. Both argue that emotions represent first-order forces in human behavior, forces that not only require explanation but that cannot be ignored if human behavior is to be fully comprehended. They differ in the manner in which they place emotion in the theoretical picture.

Emotion as a representational process Behind the formidable title of **emotion as a representational process** lies a highly coherent, deceptively simple formulation. The chief proponent of this view is Leeper, and much of what follows is taken directly from him (Leeper, 1965). Leeper maintains that the traditional distinctions among various kinds of psychological events create artificial barriers and generate needless controversy. Although separate cate-

gories for perception, learning, motivation, and emotions have been and remain useful, they obscure the possible advantages of viewing

BOX 20.8

MAD, GLAD—OR JUST EXCITED?

S. Schachter and J. E. Singer proposed to test whether the intensity of an emotional experience is determined by how generally excited or aroused the person is and that its quality (or direction) is determined by the nature of the situation in which the arousal occurs.

The experiment takes its lead directly from an earlier experiment by G. Marañon, which showed that physiological arousal by the injection of a stimulating drug into the bloodstream does not bring about a convincing emotional experience. Schachter and Singer go a step further in their interpretation of these earlier results; they argue that, as Marañon's subjects probably knew that they were being injected with a stimulant, their experience of "cold" emotion or "as if" emotion was consistent with the fact of physiological arousal *and* their understanding that the excitement they were feeling was *supposed* to be nonemotional.

What would happen then if the subject were kept unaware of the expected effect of the physiological stimulus and, at the same time, were placed into situations that differed in the kinds of emotions that they could be expected to arouse? This general question was the basis of the first set of experiments.

Subjects were volunteer college students, whose health records had been checked to ensure no risk of harmful effects from the experimental procedure. Each subject was told that he would receive an injection of a new drug "Suproxin" and that the point of the investigation was to determine the effect of this drug upon vision. Beyond this common experience the circumstances for each group of subjects varied—and therein lies the tale.

Some subjects were informed that the drug would cause an increase in the heart rate, hand tremors, and a feeling of warmth and flushing in the face. The drug was in fact epinephrine, a stimulant of the sympathetic nervous system, and this descrip-

them all as aspects of a common representational process. This approach is congruent with the suggestion in the first edition of this textbook (Krech & Crutchfield, 1958), which proposed that we view every psychological process as a "perfink," that is, as a single complex

---

tion was a quite accurate account of usual reactions to the drug. This group was called the informed group. A misinformed group was told that it would experience numbness and itching, with no suggestion that there might be excitement or agitation. A third group—the uninformed group—was told nothing of expected reactions to the drug. Members of each of these three groups were then observed during intermissions, whose purpose was ostensibly to allow the drug to act, so that its effects upon visual perception could be studied. These intermissions took one of two forms for each subject.

In the first of these intermission conditions another subject, a confederate of the experimenters, undertook to play the clown. He indulged in a series of rather wild antics designed to create a mood of euphoria in the true subject. In the second condition the confederate subject joined with the true one in answering a questionnaire whose contents were designed to justify irritation even in the most tolerant and even-tempered subject; one question, for example, was about the frequency of his parents' extramarital sexual relations. In this situation the confederate expressed increasing anger, finally ripping the questionnaire to shreds and stomping out of the room. The confederate in both the euphoria and anger conditions did not know whether the subject was in the informed, misinformed, or uninformed group. He was kept ignorant in order to ensure that his provocative behavior would, on the average, be the same for all groups.

The data, from direct observation of the subjects' behavior and from their responses to a variety of self-report inventories, are quite complex, and we can touch on them only very briefly. Subjects exposed to the euphoric confederate, for example, behaved more euphorically (joining in his manic activity and so on) and reported that they felt more elated *the more misinformed they were.* That is, informed subjects were least euphoric, uninformed ones somewhat more euphoric, and the misinformed group consistently most euphoric.

The experimenters infer from these results that an individual, given a certain degree of general arousal, tends to label his emotional state in accordance with his environmental situation. The misin-

formed subject had not been led to expect the physiological arousal that was indeed induced by the injection; therefore he explained his bodily excitation by adopting the emotional mood of the confederate. He becomes no longer simply mysteriously agitated; he is simply very happy. The anger condition shows the same general results—more misinformation, more anger. The major conclusion was that, given the same state of physiological arousal, the nature of the expressed emotion can be manipulated by the social situation.

A recent attempt to replicate this study—but without the use of epinephrine—suggests an interesting possible qualification of the conclusion above. P. Zimbardo, C. Maslach, and G. Marshall of Stanford University devised an ingenious method whereby subjects could be put into a state of unexplained arousal (quite similar to that induced by epinephrine) through triggering off a previously set posthypnotic suggestion. Their subjects were then exposed either to euphoric or angry confederates. The observed behaviors did in fact closely resemble those reported by Schachter and Singer. The subjects, physiologically aroused by they knew not what, did in fact mimic the confederate. *But* their reports of their *felt experience* showed no differences between the euphoria and anger groups: Both groups were found to have experienced distinctly negative emotional states. Apparently the unexplained arousal was experienced as rather disturbing and, though subjects tended to go along *behaviorally* with the antics of their respective confederates, they did not share in their apparent *feelings.*

Nevertheless, the Schachter and Singer study is theoretically challenging, and further work, including research currently in progress by these Stanford investigators, may give us an improved understanding of how physiological arousal, knowledge of its cause, and the social setting in which it occurs determine how we behave and feel emotionally.

S. SCHACHTER & J. E. SINGER. Cognitive, social, and physiological determinants of emotional state. *Psychological Review,* 1962, **69,** 379–399.
P. ZIMBARDO, C. MASLACH, & G. MARSHALL. Hypnosis and the psychology of cognitive and behavioral control. In E. Fromm & R. E. Shor (Eds.), *Hypnosis: Research Developments and Perspectives.* Chicago: Aldine-Atherton, 1972.

process involving *per*ceptual, *f*eeling, and th*ink*-ing aspects.

A representational process can be regarded as varying along a number of dimensions. Perceptions, for example, vary along a *motivational* dimension; they can range from motivationally neutral to motivationally intense. Motivational processes also may be seen to range along an *emotional* continuum from emotionally neutral to emotionally highly charged. The urge to scratch at a perceived itch is unmistakably a motive, but hardly an intense emotional experience. The sight of a mortal enemy, however, not only motivates aggressive action but, additionally, arouses a feeling of emotional fury. Viewed in this way, to regard emotion only as disruptive is to ignore what Leeper considers to be an obvious continuum.

Leeper's essential point is not that motives influence our perceptions and that emotions have modifying effects upon the expression of motives. If this effect were all, the point would be an obvious and well-accepted one. What must be emphasized, instead, is that emotions *are* motives in their own right. Emotions, according to Leeper, are intrinsically directional; they are not merely general and indiscriminate physiological arousers. Furthermore, such emotional motives can be as effective in directing behavior as can physiologically based motives but are independent of tissue needs and can be triggered by more subtle and complex social cues. They are influenced by the meanings (past and present) of stimuli.

Leeper suggests that emotional motives are a distinguishing feature of higher species and may hold the key to understanding their superior adaptive abilities. For example, if a woman's momentary perception of a new situation instantly embodies not only the external stimuli but also the emotional motivation that is most appropriate to the environmental situation, she is thereby highly likely to respond quickly and effectively. By allowing for so highly efficient an integration of all information from the situation, the odds for successful adaptation to environmental challenges are improved.

Emotions as primary motives As a cardinal assumption of his comprehensive theory of per-

sonality and behavior, Tomkins (1962) treats **emotions as primary motives**. He asserts that "the primary motivational system is the affective [emotional] system, and the biological drives have motivational impact only when amplified by the affective system." We can here touch only on a few facets of Tomkins' position as it pertains to our present discussion. His thesis is that psychology has been blocked in its attempts to understand human behavior more fully by its almost total exclusion of the data of man's conscious experience of feelings and emotions.

Tomkins intends to end the quarantine on conscious feelings as psychological data. First of all, he argues, emotions are really not as private as some believe. Rather, they are easily apprehended by others and can communicate information in a reliable manner. Most of this communication of emotion, he claims, takes place in the facial musculature, and facial responses help to make both the outside observer *and the individual himself* aware of his continuing emotional state. The evidence presented earlier by Ekman and his associates, page 487, which demonstrated cross-cultural accuracy in judging emotions, explicitly used Tomkins' analysis of facial cues in selection of photographs.

How does emotion produce the decisive influence that Tomkins claims for it? He proposes that emotions define the inborn wants and don't-wants that dominate the behavior of infants and that, in elaborated form, they do the same for adults. They do so, Tomkins suggests, in the following manner: The newborn is endowed with certain positive and negative affects. Joy or excitement, for example, is innately positive; fear and pain are innately negative. At first, the newborn infant automatically smiles in pleasure at being well fed or stimulated by a fascinating rattle. A loud, explosive sound or an open safety pin in his diaper inevitably sets off negative affects. As he develops, the child first learns to wish for positive emotional states and not for negative ones. Later on, as his abilities for adaptive behavior mature, he learns to act in ways that will maximize states of positive affect and minimize states of negative affect. Although he thus knows from birth that eating is good and pain is bad, only through further maturation and learning does he become able to go to the market or restaurant as soon as he starts getting hungry, and become able to avoid situations that are bound to cause him pain and distress.

Tomkins believes that these innate positive and negative emotions derive from three basic emotions that have been built into the organism through natural selection in the evolutionary process. They are, first, an innate *fear response to a life threat*; second, a feeling of *pleasure*, shown, for example, in responding to another's smile both by an experience of joy and by returning the smile; third, the pleasurable *excitement* induced by novelty. (All three of these easily parallel our earlier discussions regarding emotional developments in the infant that involve at first generalized friendliness to other people, fear of too-intense stimuli, and a preference for manageably more complex situations.)

This view of course evokes once again the troubling distinction between motive and emotion. Tomkins is not troubled; he believes that physiologically based motives can by themselves direct behavior. Such motives are characteristically *amplified* by emotional states, however. A sharp bodily pain is certainly biologically negative, but, once defined as possibly signifying cancer, it becomes immensely magnified to intense anxiety. Similarly, we normally eat when hungry or in an "it's-time-to-eat" situation. But, were a catastrophe to threaten future food supplies, our usually mild biological hunger drive would become transformed into a desperate search for provisions. Knowledge, in other words, may arouse emotions that will in turn immensely amplify the sense of urgency.

Tomkins' formulation can be distinguished both from the Schachter and Singer approach (see Box 20.8, p. 492) and from cognitive appraisal theories of emotion. Schachter and Singer argue that, while generalized physiological responses determine the *intensity* of our emotional experience, its *quality* is fully determined by our perception of the situation. The cognitive appraisal view [Duffy (1962) and Lazarus (1968) are among its proponents] asserts that distinctive physiological responses themselves are determined by one's prior evaluation, or cognitive appraisal, of the situation. This formulation is closely related to the James-Lange theory of emotion. Tomkins, in contrast with both of these views, insists on the primacy of innate emotional responses but does accept the idea that they may be modified by our cognitive appraisal of the social setting in which they are evoked.

When so many, so varied views exist, even flourish, within a certain class of psychological phenomena, we should suspect that the theoretical puzzle is still unsolved. In the case of human emotion this suspicion is certainly valid.

*   *   *

The solution to Figure 20.3 is:

The occasion was a "happening" at the Gallery of Erotic Art in New York City in fall 1972. What in fact was happening at the moment that the flash photograph was taken was that a nude woman was writhing on a waterbed dimly illuminated by colored lights inside the bed. Members of the audience could not see one another since the rest of the room was in total darkness. All that was visible was the silhouette of the woman undulating in what, considering the setting, must have been regarded by most as an erotic fashion.

Did you come at all close to guessing what was going on? Probably not. The expressions on the faces of the spectators are quite varied to begin with and can easily be seen as appropriate to watching any sort of event which was sufficiently attention-getting to draw an audience's rapt interest.

*   *   *

SUMMARY

1. The study of emotions has long been outside the mainstream of psychological research; many psychologists have viewed emotions as an almost extraneous phenomenon, interfering with scientifically lawful behavior. For that very reason, attempts to organize systematically the range of human emotions or even to catalog and describe them fully are few and preliminary.

2. One schema that may be used to characterize specific emotions and to differentiate among them includes these four general dimensions: intensity of feeling, level of tension (or impulse to action), hedonic tone (degree of pleasantness or unpleasantness), and degree of complexity. This schema may be imposed upon the inventory of emotional states, which itself can be subdivided into several main types. They include, among others, the primary or goal-oriented emotions (e.g., anger), emotions triggered by sensory stimulation (e.g., pain), those pertaining to self-appraisal (e.g., pride and shame), and those related to other people (e.g., love).

3. Starting with the single, generalized emotional response of excitement in infancy, human beings gradually evolve increasingly differentiated patterns of emotional expression over the course of development. By early childhood most of the common emotions are already discernible, but complexity and subtlety of expression continue to increase. Intensity of expression, or emotionality, appears to decrease with age, from the earliest years through to old age. What is not clear, however, is whether this observed decrease with age represents a genuine decrease or whether it merely indicates that the intense emotionality of childhood is still present but is clamped down and can quickly surface under appropriate circumstances.

4. Newborn infants vary in emotional reactivity and, to some extent, these differences, which are likely genetic in origin, persist into later life. Early experience, including such factors as mothering and social stimulation, also significantly affects the course of emotional development.

5. Questions of whether emotions are to be measured and judged on the basis of experienced feeling, observed behavior, or measurable physiological events are one source of dissension in research on emotions. Generally speaking, these three sources of data agree, but even experienced judges are still only moderately accurate in their assessments. Furthermore, some emotions are out in the open and easily judged; others, less overtly expressed, are much more difficult to pinpoint reliably. The ability to judge emotions accurately is quite poor in young children but develops rapidly.

6. There is evidence that people from different cultures agree fairly well on the judgments of at least some emotions, supporting Darwin's speculation concerning the biological, hence universal, nature of emotional expression. But culture-specific learning remains a significant factor.

7. Physiological responses taken singly are unreliable indicators of emotion but, taken together, certain primary emotions can to some extent be detected in this way. Most often the state of being aroused is physiologically quite evident, even if not the specific emotion involved in the arousal.

8. Theories of emotion are still primitive; they are highly generalized points of view rather than outcomes of detailed and comprehensive analyses of emotional phenomena. They may conveniently be classified into incidental or primary and functional views. The former orientation regards emotions as by-products of certain physiological disturbances, as disruptive of orderly behavior, or as a generalized state of arousal. The latter orientation takes the opposite view: Emotions are regarded as phenomena that are highly influential in psychological functioning, even to the point of dominating the directions of experience and behavior.

9. Two examples of primary and functional theories of emotion are the views of Leeper and Tomkins. Leeper regards emotions as representational processes that act as motives in their own right and with specific directional properties. Tomkins' similar view treats emotions as primary motives and views them as defining innate wants (positive emotions) and don't-wants (negative emotions) already evident in infant behavior and elaborated during later development.

GLOSSARY

appreciative emotions   A class of emotions (for example, humor, beauty, wonder) characterized by the person's appreciative orientation toward objects and events in his world and toward his own place in the cosmic scheme of things.

emotion as a representational process   The view that emotion joins with perception, learning, and motivation as an integral part of a single unified process, rather than that the functions are separate, even if interacting, entities.

emotion as arousal   The view that identifies all emotion (as well as all motivation) as involving a generalized state of arousal. According to this theory, emotion is one end of a continuum of motivation, with the inertia of sleep at the other end.

emotion as disruptive   The view that emotions are to be regarded as nothing more than causes of breakdowns in the normal and orderly processes of physiological functioning and behavior.

emotions as primary motives   The view that biological drives derive their motivational effectiveness primarily from being accompanied and amplified by emotional states, states that are largely innate in their origins.

emotions pertaining to other people   A class of emotions arising mainly in connection with the person's perceived relations with other people (for example, love, envy, pity). Such feelings often become crystallized in the form of enduring emotional predispositions, or attitudes.

emotions pertaining to self-appraisal   A class of emotions (for example, shame, pride, guilt) in which the essential determinants have to do with a person's perception of her own behavior in relation to various standards of behavior and conduct, both external and internal.

emotions pertaining to sensory stimulation   A class of emotions (for example, pain, disgust, delight) that most clearly pertain to pleasant or unpleasant sensory stimulation by objects.

expressive cues   Those bits of behavior that convey, usually without conscious intention, information about an individual's emotional state. Facial expressions and postural changes are examples.

hedonic tone   That aspect of emotional experience having to do with the degree of pleasantness or unpleasantness of the emotional feeling.

moods   Pervasive and transitory emotional states (for example, sadness, anxiety, elation) that tend to give an affective coloring to the entire momentary experience of the person.

primary emotions   The class of emotions (for example, joy, anger, fear, grief) usually regarded as most basic, simple, and primitive and typically associated with goal striving and high degrees of tension.

altered states of consciousness

DO YOU KNOW...

- how you can tell when you are experiencing an "altered state of consciousness"?

- what goes on in those half-dreams you sometimes have while just falling asleep?

- that it may now be possible to tell when a sleeping person is dreaming?

- that a sleepwalker is very probably not having a dream?

- whether dreams can really tell you something true but hidden about yourself?

- how you can prevent a person from dreaming and, if you do, that he will catch up on his dreaming the moment he has the chance?

- in what way a fully conscious person can be caused to carry out a previously suggested hypnotic instruction?

- whether, in fact, a hypnotized person can be induced to carry out an action that would violate his principles?

- what is meant by a peak experience?

- that the more marijuana one smokes, the fewer behavioral effects are shown?

- what we know, and do not know, of the effects of LSD and other psychedelic drugs?

unit 21

The Dream, a woodcut by M. C. Escher/Escher Foundation, Haags Gemeentemuseum, The Hague

Psychology was once defined as the study of consciousness. But the early psychologists found that their attempts to study people's conscious experience often led to unreliable and contradictory data, and this was one of the reasons that psychologists changed their focus from consciousness to behavior. Today we can see that some of their problems arose from their failure to pay adequate attention to two factors. First, they underrated the importance of basic individual differences in conscious experience and so tended to misinterpret individual differences as "contradictions" in their data. Second, they did not always pay proper respect to the pervasive effect of experimental bias, that is, the many ways in which an experimenter can unknowingly bias both his subject's behavior and verbal report of what he is experiencing; thus they did little to control this factor, which could contribute to unreliability.

Modern-day psychology, with full allowance for the play of these factors, is again turning its attention to the nature of consciousness, with much current interest centered on what are called **altered states of consciousness** (**ASCs**). The scientific study of such special states of consciousness is in its infancy but growing rapidly (see Figure 21.1, p. 502).

CONTENTS

NORMAL AND ALTERED STATES

If we keep a record of everyday consciousness, we find that, while the exact nature of our experiences vary from moment to moment, the variations usually fall within a certain range. From day to day you may find your thought processes a little brighter or a little duller than usual, you may feel in more or less contact with bodily sensations, you may pay more or less attention than usual to your surroundings. Nevertheless, there is sufficient continuity and regularity of *pattern* in our day-to-day consciousness to enable us to speak of a normal state of consciousness (NSC).

If you were asked right now whether you are in your NSC or in the ASC called dreaming, you probably would have little doubt (it is devoutly hoped) that you were in your NSC. You might not be able to define exactly why you are able to make this distinction, but it is probably an immediate and obvious one to you. There are many different kinds of ASCs, and we shall now take a brief look at a number of them. We will start with ones experienced by most people and then move on to ones experienced less often. We will not attempt here to deal with ASCs that are characteristic of certain forms of mental illness (see Unit 24), but some ASCs that we do discuss, such as hallucinations, do figure in certain illnesses.

THE HYPNAGOGIC STATE

Probably everyone experiences the **hypnagogic state**, the transitional ASC that occurs on the verge of falling asleep, when one is no longer quite awake but not yet deeply asleep. The hypnagogic ASC shows tremendous variation from person to person: Some people have vivid, rich experiences, as real or more real than life; others have or remember practically nothing during this period. (Box 21.1, p. 504, presents a technique that might help in recalling such an experience.) That individual differences exist is certain, but the enormous range in experience has not yet been explained.

The modern methods involved in studies in this area are illustrated by the study of the hypnagogic state conducted by Vogel, Foulkes, and Trosman (1966). They measured brain-wave changes by means of electroencephalogram (or EEG) records of brain activity (see Unit 3); they also recorded movements of the eyes behind closed lids. These rapid eye movements, or REMs, and slow eye movements, or SEMs, are usually found during certain stages of sleep. Records were made while subjects were falling asleep and also after subjects were awakened at various times during the sleep-onset period; they were asked what was going through their minds. The experimenters found that the physiological changes involved in falling asleep could

be divided into four distinct, sequential stages: (1) the alpha/REM stage, showing the rhythmic 8 to 12 cycles per second activity of the normal waking EEG and occasional REMs of the closed eyes, as if the person was looking about; (2) the alpha/SEM stage, where the EEG alpha rhythm was still present but the closed eyes showed slower, rolling SEMs; (3) the stage 1 stage, when the EEG showed a slower, more irregular pattern with no eye movements at all; and (4) the stage 2 stage, when the EEG showed a type of activity called "spindle waves" (14 cycles per second bursts) in addition to random, slow activity, again with no eye moments of either type.

The subjects were awakened during sleep onset and asked to describe their preawakening thoughts. The investigators, in analyzing these reports, noticed a sequence of three types of experiences that they called ego states and that can be conveniently thought of as different states of consciousness. The first to occur was the *intact ego state*, during which the subject could easily discriminate between what was in his mind and what was external to him; this stage showed thought processes that seemed reasonably logical and normal. It was very much like the subject's NSC, or usual waking state. Following this was the *destructuralized ego state*, an ASC during which the subject lost contact with external stimuli and reported rather bizarre mental content, such as seeing a face hanging upside down in the air or climbing a mountain while wearing scuba diving equipment. Finally there occurred a third state, the *restructuralized ego state*, during which mental content again became rather plausible, as in the first state and in an NSC. No longer were the reports bizarre, but contact with the external world was still completely lost, as it had been in the second state.

An example of a typical report of each ego state may help; we first give a subject's actual report and, parenthetically, add the investigators' evaluations based on systematic questioning of the subject.

Intact ego state:
"I was thinking about the lab secretary typing out my transcripts."
(This report is realistically oriented and an anticipation. There was loss of control and loss

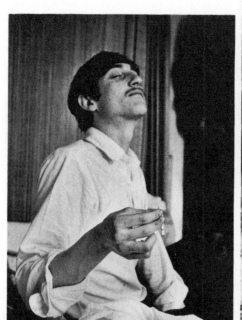

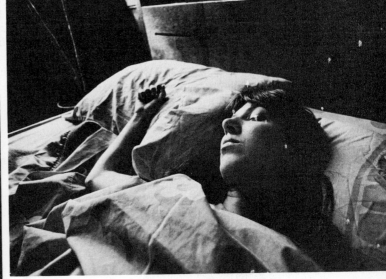

FIGURE 21.1 Altered states of consciousness.

Clockwise from upper left: Photo by Charles Gatewood; photo by G. Nanja Nath/Black Star; photo by Charles Gatewood; photo by Kingsley Fairbridge; photo by Kingsley Fairbridge; photo by Michael Gold.

BOX 21.1

A FUNNY THING HAPPENED AS I WAS FALLING ASLEEP

If you have difficulty in remembering anything from your hypnagogic states, here is a technique that works well for many people and allows you to get fairly far into the hypnagogic state.

After lying down to sleep, with your elbow resting on the bed, elevate your lower arm to a vertical position. Keep the hand and arm straight up. It should take very little conscious effort to do this.

You can then drift off into the hypnagogic state of consciousness, but as you get too deep and ready to go into dreamless sleep, your arm will fall since at that point muscle tone typically disappears. The falling of the arm should wake you up, and you can then take immediate note of what was going on in your mind. And you may learn how to hold the hypnagogic state at this level for more prolonged observation.

room. The people were hairy, like monkeys. The walls of the pleural cavity are made of ice and slippery. In the midpart there is an ivory bench with people sitting on it. Some people are throwing balls of cheese against the inner side of the chest wall."

(The report contains bizarre, implausibly associated elements, distortions, etc. There was a complete loss of contact with external reality during the reported experience.)

Restructuralized ego state:
"I was driving a car, telling other people you shouldn't go over a certain speed limit."

(In this report it will be noted that the content is again plausible and realistic. There was a complete loss of contact with external reality during the reported experience.)

of awareness of surroundings during the experience, but the subject knew that the experience was mental.)

Destructuralized ego state:
"I was observing the inside of a pleural cavity. There were small people in it, like in a

Figure 21.2 shows the relationship of these ego states to the progressive physiological stages as subjects went to sleep. Intact ego states were associated primarily with alpha/REM or alpha/SEM stages and very seldom appeared in the other two states. Destructuralized ego states occurred primarily with a stage 1 EEG, and the restructuralized ego states occurred primarily in conjunction with a stage 2 EEG. Thus, in falling asleep, our consciousness seems to lead from an ordinary stage directly to a totally destructuralized one and only then are the more usual restraints on thinking reestablished. Vogel et

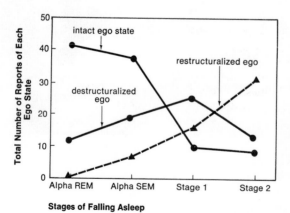

FIGURE 21.2 Relation of ego states to sleep stages during sleep onset. The sleep stages are defined by their characteristic brain-wave and eye-movement patterns; the three ego states are inferred from reports given by subjects just awakened from each sleep stage (see text for details). The data are from nine subjects who were awakened six times per night over four nights (spaced a week apart) for a total of 216 awakenings. (From Vogel et al., 1966. Copyright 1966, American Medical Association.)

al. chose to interpret this finding in terms of psychoanalytic theory, hypothesizing that the destructuralized ego state is experienced as too threatening because it does not provide enough defenses against unacceptable impulses (see Unit 23). Thus, unless the person can restore a semblance of reality—which is what occurs in the third, restructuralized state—he would be unable, because of the resultant anxiety, to remain asleep.

Notice from Figure 21.2 that the correspondence between physiological changes and states of consciousness is not perfect, presenting an important methodological problem about how to define such states. We may start with certain physiologically defined states, but then, as in this case, we find that the mental phenomena associated with them are variable. Or we may prefer to define our states in terms of their mental attributes, but then there is no good physiological correspondence to these mental states. Different investigators prefer one or the other approach as being more valid in a certain sense, but in fact they are complementary approaches, each one having certain advantages and disadvantages.

The hypnagogic state is one that most people very likely experience every night on falling asleep. It usually lasts no more than a few minutes and is ordinarily completely forgotten upon onset of other kinds of sleep. [It may actually consist of two (or more) ASCs, as Figure 21.2 suggests.] Certain eastern traditions indicate that people can learn to control the mental content of the hypnagogic state and use it for their own growth; some artists and other creative people believe that this state is a rich source of new ideas. However, at present there is little scientific evidence regarding these possibilities.

DREAMING

If one records the EEG and eye movements of a sleeper through the whole night, interesting and regular patterns emerge. There are apparently rather distinct stages of sleep, as discussed in detail in Unit 22. Furthermore, these sleep stages seem to be associated with dreaming.

In the early 1950s a graduate student at the University of Chicago, Eugene Aserinsky, awakened subjects during each of these various sleep stages and asked them if they had been dreaming. Subjects reported that they had been dreaming in about 80 percent of the awakenings from stage 1–REM sleep in which rapid eye movements characteristically occur (see Unit 22 for details). Dreams were reported only rarely in other stages of sleep (Aserinsky & Kleitman, 1953).

Aserinsky concluded that the altered state of consciousness called dreaming occurs during stage 1–REM sleep and that occasional reports of experiences from other stages of sleep in which REMs tend to be absent (NREM sleep) were probably just memories of previous, not yet forgotten dreams.

REM versus NREM Dreams

The early assumption, then, was that NREM sleep (i.e., nonrapid eye movement sleep) was dreamless sleep. But later investigations of NREM sleep, asking a subject a more neutral question, "What was going on in your mind just before awakening?" (rather than "What were you just dreaming?"), indicated a fair amount of mental activity. While some of this activity resembles that reported from stage 1–REM awakenings, there are important differences.

A typical report of an awakening from NREM sleep is that nothing was going on in the subject's mind. Also typical are reports of what subjects generally describe as thoughts, that is, mental activity usually not accompanied by visual imagery and certainly not experienced in terms of a complete dream world with all the senses operative, as they are in true dreams. The content of such reports is usually brief and realistic; for example, a subject might report that he was thinking about an examination the next day or was idly wondering about a problem in mathematics. Awareness of oneself or that one is in an ASC seems to be generally nonexistent in NREM sleep. Because of the relative paucity of activity and the difficulty of remembering it, we do not have a very good understanding of the nature of this ASC.

Yet NREM sleep can be very active. In contrast to what most researchers expected, laboratory studies have shown that most sleep-walking and sleep talking do not occur in the true dreams of stage 1–REM sleep, where it might be assumed that these motor activities were an acting out of a dream. Instead, they tend to occur in NREM sleep. Most nightmares also seem to occur in NREM sleep.

However, it still seems that despite the mental activities associated with NREM sleep a fairly useful generalization concerning dreaming is that it occurs primarily in conjunction with stage 1–REM sleep.

Dreaming is by far the most common ASC in our culture; almost everyone can at least occasionally recall a dream, although most of the dreaming activity of the night is usually forgotten. Despite its familiarity, however, dreaming represents one of the most radical alterations of our NSC. The dreamer loses practically all contact with the external world. Laboratory studies have shown that dreamers do not respond to most sensory stimuli presented to them, unless the stimuli are so intense that the dreamers are awakened. Usually no trace of the intruding stimulus can be found in the dream if the dreamer is awakened shortly after its occurrence. In those occasional cases where some trace of the stimulus is found, either it is woven into the fabric of the dream so as to interfere the least with the dream or it has been distorted or altered to fit the ongoing dream activity. If the phone actually rings in another room, the dream may indeed incorporate a ringing phone, but the dreamer may arrange within the dream to have someone else answer it.

While most of the elements of this dream-world are taken from the ordinary world, the dreamer reorganizes these elements into quite bizarre combinations which would never be seen in the ordinary world. Not only are the objects of the dreamworld constructed by the dreamer but so also are the people in his dream, with whom he engages in various lively interactions. For many people, dreams are as rich and vivid as ordinary reality (perhaps more so) but quite different from merely imagining something while in the NSC.

This complex activity of constructing an entire experiential world occurs without self-awareness. The dream is accepted for reality while it is occurring (except in exceptional cases such as so-called lucid dreams, discussed later). What is the mental state of a dreamer that she can be so unaware of what is going on?

The primary cognitive difference between dreaming and reality states is the acceptance of incongruity in dreaming, a willingness to accept strange events without question, events that would be labeled impossible or at least stupid in an NSC. If you were sitting in your room studying and an Eskimo walked in leading a crocodile that was following on a leash three feet above the ground, you would be rather taken aback! Were you to dream the same thing, you might casually ask the Eskimo how much he had paid for the crocodile.

Yet while the dream state is senseless from the perspective of an NSC, many investigators have argued that dream consciousness is not lacking in meaning but, instead, is understandable in a *qualitatively different* way. That is, the events in dreams may constitute a different kind of language or style of thinking from that used in our ordinary NSC, and very important messages about ourselves may be expressed in that language.

The Interpretation of Dreams

The best-known exponent of this point of view was Sigmund Freud. At the turn of the century when he published his landmark book, *The Interpretation of Dreams* (Freud, 1956; original publication in 1900), the prevailing view was that dreams were essentially meaningless, perhaps a product of indigestion following a large or unusual meal. This was the then modern view, indicating a victory of scientific rationalism over the occult, for throughout man's history dreams have been regarded as meaningful, even prophetic (as with Joseph and the Pharaoh's dream). When Freud contended that dreams were highly meaningful statements in symbolic language of a current state of the dreamer's personality, he was accused by some as being unscientific. He further asserted that learning to

BOX 21.2

A FREUDIAN DREAM

Freud's major work on the interpretation of dreams is replete with examples of dreams reported by patients (as well as some of his own dreams). The following brief example, from a man in psychoanalysis with Freud, is a relatively uncomplicated one and for that reason its interpretation, based on the patient's free associations to the dream and Freud's extensive knowledge of the dream, seems relatively straightforward.

The dream:
The dreamer was in a big courtyard in which some dead bodies were being burnt. "I'm off," he said, "I can't bear the sight of it."...He then met two butcher's boys. "Well," he asked, "did it taste nice?" "No," one of them answered, "not a bit nice"—as though it had been human flesh.

The interpretation:
The innocent occasion of the dream was as follows. The dreamer and his wife had paid a visit after supper to their neighbours, who were excellent people but not precisely *appetizing*. The hospitable old lady was just having her supper and had tried to *force* him...to taste some of it. He had declined, saying

he had no appetite left: "Get along!" she had replied, "you can manage it," or words to that effect. He had therefore been obliged to taste it and had complimented her on it, saying: "That was very nice." When he was once more alone with his wife he had grumbled at his neighbour's insistence and also at the quality of the food. The thought, "I can't bear the sight of it,"...was an allusion to the physical charms of the lady from which the invitation had come, and it must be taken as meaning that he had no desire to look at them.

The interpretation of dreams occupies a central role in the psychoanalytic method of treating neuroses. But it is by no means a simple procedure and, for Freud, it was certainly not the case that specific items in dreams had specific meanings for all persons. Rather, he comments:

We are not in general in a position to interpret another person's dream unless he is prepared to communicate to us the unconscious thoughts that lie behind its content. The practical applicability of our method of interpreting dreams is in consequence severely restricted. We have seen that, as a general rule, each person is at liberty to construct his dream-world according to his individual peculiarities and so to make it unintelligible to other people.

S. FREUD. *The Interpretation of Dreams.* New York: Basic Books, 1956. Originally published in 1900.

---

understand this language was of great help to a psychotherapist in working with the mentally disturbed, as well as to anyone who wanted to understand himself (see Box 21.2).

Dreams, Freud believed, served the function of partially discharging sexual and aggressive drives in a manner that escaped public censure. Thus Freud hypothesized not only that symbolization was the *language* of dreams but also that dreaming served a vital adaptive function and provided a window to the unconscious.

Although Freud's concept of dreaming is the most widely acknowledged theory about this ASC, it is not considered by most psychologists to have been proved. That dream interpretation along Freudian lines seems to help some disturbed patients is not considered proof; that we can often find meaning in our dreams by free associating about them, again, does not neces-

sarily prove that that was the meaning of the dream.

Experimental Study of Dream Deprivation

Attempts to confirm experimentally certain aspects of Freud's theory of dreams have sought to take advantage of recent advances in the physiology of ASCs, but the results are ambiguous. The reasoning behind these attempts is as follows: According to Freud dreams serve an important role in partially discharging sexual and aggressive energies; therefore if a person were somehow prevented from dreaming, these unconscious energies would build and begin to disrupt his ordinary functioning. Investigators attempted to test this hypothesis by observing subjects sleeping consecutive nights in a laboratory while their EEGs and eye movements were being measured. Each time a subject's record began to show a stage 1–REM period, he was awakened, thus presumably preventing or interrupting a dream. Subjects were allowed to sleep longer to compensate for these interruptions, so they lost no sleep each night. But their total dreaming time was deliberately reduced by this procedure to about 5 percent of the customary time. Other subjects were interrupted in their sleep an equal number of times, but only during NREM periods.

The first such experiment on **dream deprivation** (Dement, 1960) seemed to support Freud's theory very well. The subjects began to show considerable agitation and neurotic symptoms as they went about their everyday affairs after several nights of dream deprivation. Then, after a few nights of uninterrupted sleep, during which they showed considerably more stage 1–REM dreaming than usual ("usual" is about 20 percent of sleep time), these symptoms disappeared and the subjects returned to normal, both psychologically and physiologically.

However, when other experimenters attempted to repeat this experiment (Kales et al., 1964), they found virtually no indications of psychological disturbances at all in their subjects, even though the dream-deprivation procedure lasted for even longer periods than in the original experiment. Subjects did show a *physiological* need to dream in that they had to be awakened more and more frequently in order to deprive them of dreaming, that is, they went into stage 1–REM sleep more often and, during subsequent uninterrupted sleep, they spent much more than the usual 20 percent of the night in dreaming. The question of whether there are any important psychological consequences of dream deprivation remains unresolved.

Lucid Dreaming, Out-of-the-Body Experiences, and High Dreams

In ordinary dreaming people sometimes think "this is a dream." In recalling the dream later, however, they realize that, although they labeled the experience as a dream, they still showed the acceptance of incongruity and other reactions that characterize ordinary dreaming. In rare cases, however, people have reported recognizing during a dream that they *were* dreaming, followed by a radical change taking place in the experience. While remaining in the dreamworld, that is, still seeing the dream scenery, characters, etc., they wake up in the sense that they now feel they have all the faculties of their NSC. This is called **lucid dreaming**. They can think critically about the fact that they are dreaming, and they can then exercise a higher degree of control over the dream content than ordinarily.

A tribe of nonliterate people, the Senoi of Malaysia, train their children to have lucid dreams (Stewart, 1969), with the result that almost every adult in the tribe is a lucid dreamer. Furthermore, they commonly practice what amounts to a form of psychotherapy, working out their personal and interpersonal problems during their nocturnal dreams. Stewart commented that this tribe seemed psychologically healthier than most Western cultures; perhaps research will find useful applications for lucid dreaming once we learn how to induce it.

Suppose, in having a lucid dream, the dreamworld around you was so realistic that you became convinced that it was actually the real world, a real world with its full, ordinary, critical consciousness, but located at a place other than where you know your physical body to be? In fact, you would be watching yourself behaving, as if you were an outside observer. People occasionally report such experiences, describing how they arise out of ordinary dreaming; they are called **out-of-the-body experiences**. (In older, mystical literature they were often called "astral projections.") These experiences may be regarded as ASCs in that the space/time locus of one's perceptions is radically altered, even though other aspects of mental functioning seem normal.

In some cases the out-of-the-body experience is so real to the person that it may profoundly affect his metaphysical belief system (Monroe, 1971). For example, the person may say: "I no longer *believe* that I will survive physical death; I *know* that it's true because I have been alive without my physical body." It has even been suggested that, although such experiences are rare, they might form one basis for the religious belief in a soul that will survive death.

A related but entirely new type of ASC has been occasionally reported that has resulted from the use of psychedelic drugs (see p. 522) in our society in the last decade. Such an ASC is called a **high dream.** The word "high" is used here by analogy with the slang term for intoxication by a psychedelic drug ("being high"), and it is called a "dream" because it usually develops from an ordinary dreaming state. A high dream is distinctive in that the dream changes in various ways that are very similar to a psychedelic-drug-induced state.

Most, though not all, high dreams have been reported by people who have had previous experience with psychedelic drugs, although the dream may occur long after all traces of the drug have been excreted from their bodies. It is not yet known whether high dreams show the same kind of physiological correlates as ordinary stage 1–REM dreaming. Nor do we have this information for lucid dreams or out-of-the-body experiences. These forms of dreaming, for the very reason of their rarity, are difficult to study systematically, but research on dreaming is an increasingly vigorous field.

HYPNOSIS

Hypnosis is one of the most widely investigated ASCs, probably because of a hypnotized subject's dramatic and intriguing ability to behave in bizarre ways.

People vary enormously in their susceptibility to hypnosis. Some 5 to 10 percent of all people seem to be almost totally unresponsive, another 10 to 20 percent can achieve deep hypnotic states, and the remainder are distributed between these extremes. There has been a great deal of research on the characteristics of hypnotizable and nonhypnotizable subjects; for one thing, we know that children generally are more susceptible than adults. No substantial relations between hypnotizability and personality have been found and replicated; but there is evidence that such characteristics as being able to let go and to have rich, imaginative experiences in the NSC are positively related to hypnotizability (J. Hilgard, 1970. This volume intensively studies the relation between personality and hypno-

tizability, involving hundreds of subjects; for those particularly interested in the question, it is a fascinating introduction.) However, at present we simply do not know with certainty why one person is readily hypnotizable and another not.

Hypnosis capitalizes on the fact that most people are *somewhat suggestible* in their NSC. For example, if you are told to stand upright with your eyes closed and someone then suggests that you are slowly swaying forward and back, you are likely to begin swaying at least a little and, in the extreme, possibly even to fall if you are not caught. Hypnotic induction generally consists of suggestions of sleepiness, drowsiness, relaxation, and paying attention only to the hypnotist's voice. The subject usually knows that the suggestion of sleep is only an analogy here, that hypnosis is not really a state of sleep. As the subject finds himself responding to progressively more difficult kinds of suggestions, he eventually reaches a point where he begins to feel that his state of consciousness has changed. For the subject who is highly responsive, the change from his NSC is obvious and dramatic. The subject who is only mildly responsive may have difficulty distinguishing light hypnosis from his ordinary NSC. We will consider here only the experiences of subjects who are most responsive, the ones who enter deep hypnosis, and we will bear in mind that many of these phenomena appear in less dramatic form in less susceptible subjects.

Hypnotic Phenomena

Suppose a subject is deeply hypnotized, but it has not yet been suggested that anything in particular will happen to him. If he is then asked, "What are you experiencing?," the subject will usually answer, "Nothing." Deep hypnosis, with no specific phenomena suggested (termed "neutral hypnosis"), seems to be a state in which the spontaneous thinking and feeling that go on constantly in our ordinary NSC reaches a very low level, coming to what seems to be a complete standstill. The subject is *aware*, but shows little self-initiated mental activity. Neutral hypnosis is generally described as being neither pleasant nor unpleasant, although, in retrospect, time spent in that state may seem to have been very refreshing.

A whole series of perceptual phenomena known as **hyperesthesias** can be created by suggestion. One might tell a subject, for example, that his sense of touch is exceptionally good, and he will report being able to feel with great ease what are normally barely detectable differences in the grain of objects. (This may be due to the greatly increased focusing of attention in a hypnotic trance.) Such suggestibility can be carried to a point of illusion where the subject may misperceive reality and may see, for example, meaningful content in stimulus patterns that, in our usual NSC, are essentially meaningless.

Hyperesthesia can be carried further, beyond the point of illusion, to actual **hallucination.** A deeply hypnotized subject can see an object, with his eyes either open or closed, even though there is nothing there. This ability to hallucinate is similar to the construction of a total and convincing experiential dreamworld, but in hypnosis it is precisely controllable by suggestion. As with other hypnotic phenomena, psychotherapeutic uses have been developed that use the ability to hallucinate. Thus, in such hypnotherapy, a patient may be able to hallucinate a real situation that so frightens him that he consistently avoids it in everyday life. But, by this "forcing" process while in a hypnotic trance, he may then work out his fears and eventually lose them.

The opposite phenomena to hyperesthesias are **hypoesthesias.** Here suggestion makes a subject *less* sensitive to specific kinds of sensory stimuli; for example, a subject may be told that she is partially deaf and can hear only the loudest sorts of sounds. Such suggestion can be carried to the point of **negative hallucination,** where a subject does not see an object that is actually and unmistakably there. A specific form of this phenomenon is hypnotically induced analgesia: A subject is told, while hypnotized, that he can feel no pain. A deeply hypnotized subject can then undergo even a surgical operation, show no visible sign of experiencing the painful stimuli, and report afterward that he felt nothing at all. Were it not that chemical

anesthetics are so much faster to administer (and more congenial with medical tradition) and that they work on everyone, whereas deep hypnosis is effective only for about 10 to 20 percent of the population, hypnosis would probably be more widely used in surgery—it is certainly the safer procedure. In recent years hypnosis as a substitute for conventional anesthetics is being increasingly used by dentists as formal training in the technique becomes more easily available.

Dissociation of action from awareness can also be suggested in deep hypnosis. A subject may be told, for example, that he is completely blind (an all-inclusive negative hallucination), and the subject will report and act as if he cannot see. Yet if a prearranged *visual* signal is given for another hypnotic experience to occur while he is presumably blind, the subject will respond to it. His behavior indicates that he sees, and yet, consciously, he is not seeing. Thinking and evaluating processes are also capable of alteration by suggestion in deep hypnosis. A subject may be told that the number five does not exist, that the whole idea of five is ridiculous and makes no sense. If she is then asked to subtract one from six, she may answer "four." Emotional processes can similarly be altered: Suggestions can keep a subject from experiencing emotions in situations that would ordinarily evoke strong feelings from her, or induce strong emotions where no real stimulus for them exists. It can even alter one's time perspective (see Box 21.3, p. 512).

Some therapists believe that the dissociative nature of hypnosis can be used to reach unconscious mental processes. A patient may be told, for example, that his hand will pick up a pencil and begin to write messages from his subconscious mind. He will obey the suggestion, yet he will have no awareness at all of his hand moving or of what he is writing. Such **automatic writing** can on occasion produce material that is therapeutically valuable in understanding a patient's particular dynamics. Or a subject, while in a hypnotic state, may be instructed to have a dream, one that will express important information about a specified psychological conflict, or to work out some of his conflicts in the hypnotic dream state (in a manner similar to the techniques of lucid dreams used by the Senoi people of Malaysia).

One of the most interesting aspects of hypnosis as an ASC is the existence of **posthypnotic effects**. During hypnosis, it can be suggested to a subject that later, when he is in his ordinary NSC, a certain cue will cause a specified behavior to occur. The subject is then awakened from the hypnotic state, the cue is given, and, with a responsive subject, the suggested behavior or experience occurs. The subject may or may not be aware of doing something unusual. An example: While hypnotized, a person is told that later, when back in his NSC, he will open the window when the hypnotist, say, scratches his ear. And, given that cue, the subject—though no longer hypnotized—does just that. When asked to explain his action, he may say, for example, "It's gotten awfully stuffy in the room, hasn't it?" But he will not be aware of any connection between the hypnotist's ear-scratching and his window-opening behavior, especially if he has been specifically instructed not to recall the posthypnotic suggestion.

Self-Hypnosis

Hypnosis is usually induced by a hypnotist giving particular suggestions to a subject, but this is not necessary. A deeply hypnotized subject can be told that he can later hypnotize himself, and he can be taught how to do so. Often self-hypnosis is quite readily learned in this way. Self-hypnosis can also be self-taught through reading—but in general it is more effectively learned with the help of a competent hypnotist. Goals of self-hypnosis vary widely; it is used to control specific chronic symptoms, such as headaches, or to induce general bodily and mental relaxation.

One of the more widely used and successful forms of self- or auto-hypnosis is autogenic training, a technique that is widely used in Europe for various therapeutic purposes (Luthe, 1963). This approach involves a detailed sequence of specific exercises whose general purpose is to learn how to reduce sensory stimulation, to induce certain experiences in the body, such as warmth or heaviness, or to develop skill at what is called "passive concentration." This training provides a relaxed state through which excess tensions of the day can be drained off, and it may also have more focused therapeutic uses.

Some Words of Precaution

Is it dangerous to hypnotize oneself or to be hypnotized by others? When one is hypnotized by a psychologist or a psychiatrist with professional competence in hypnosis, the danger is minimal. Persons with no professional training do constitute a real danger, especially when they attempt to handle emotional crises that might arise during hypnosis. The question is often raised whether, while in a hypnotic state, an otherwise law-abiding, even gentle, person can be induced to behave illegally or violently, even murderously. While the possibility of such an occurrence is rather far-fetched, we can offer no definite assurance that it cannot happen. There have been experimental demonstrations in which hypnotized subjects have been instructed to fire a presumably loaded gun at another person and *have* pulled the trigger. Most likely, the subject would be assuming that —in one way or another—true danger did not exist since no hypnotist would issue so reprehensible and inexplicable a command. But it is possible that a subject, particularly one who was psychologically disturbed, might be persuaded that her target indeed intended to harm her unless she acted first.

In short, it is *not* the case, as many believe, that there is a built-in safeguard to make it impossible for an individual to perform any act in violation of his personal standards and conscience. Personality is complex and moral scruples are complexly determined. If one interprets being in a hypnotic trance as permitting a suspension of personal responsibility and if, also, one harbors violent impulses at an unconscious level, then an unthinkable action may be conceived—and carried out. Hypnosis is a powerful ASC. It is not a party game. To allow yourself to be hypnotized by an untrained and professionally irresponsible person is definitely a risky business.

THE PEAK EXPERIENCE
AND MEDITATIVE STATES

The ASCs discussed so far are not ones usually sought primarily for pleasure or emotional gratification: Hypnagogic states and dreaming occur naturally, and individuals usually seek hypnosis for specific therapeutic goals or intellectual interest. But now we turn our attention to ASCs that can be so emotionally rewarding that they are actively sought after by many people. These ASCs include **peak experiences** and certain states brought on by meditation.

Nature of Peak Experiences

The term "peak experience" was coined by Maslow to describe certain classes of experience that are the high points of one's life (Maslow, 1962). Maslow arrived at this concept of the peak experience by asking people to describe the most wonderful experiences of their lives, the ecstatic moments, or the great creative moments. Only a few people could report any such experiences, and only a very few reported several.

    To understand peak experiences, let us rephrase our discussion (Unit 29) of Maslow's theoretical view. Most people's lives are, at best, only partially complete. Various basic needs for attention, love, material success and security, and a sense of fulfillment are, for most people, never completely met, leading to a chronic *deficit* of fulfillment, even though an individual may be reasonably successful. But every culture compromises on which human needs are to be fulfilled and which needs are to be taboo, so even a successful member of a given culture is likely to be somewhat unfulfilled. Maslow argues that most of our cognition is thus what he calls "deficiency cognition," or "D-cognition," a cognition of the world, others, and ourselves, based on the constant search for experiences that we regard as pleasurable and fulfilling and the avoidance of experiences we regard as painful. We perceive things primarily in terms of what they will do *for us*, rather than in a neutral, unconcerned manner.

    Maslow believed that only when a person's biological, social, and psychological needs were reasonably well fulfilled could less impera-

tive needs emerge, needs that might lead to the occurrence of a peak experience. Thus, a person who is generally neurotic will probably

BOX 21.3

NO TIME LIKE THE PRESENT

Imagine with us, if you will, that you possess a special kind of psychological calendar watch. What makes it special is that it allows you to set it ahead so that it tells only future time, or back so that past time is all that it measures, or even to capture and hold the present in the imperceptible movement of its mechanism. With such a device, you could be the time keeper of yesterdays or tomorrows, or you might prefer to prevent the present from slipping into past and the future from ever becoming now. How would *you* use it? How would your behavior be affected by the way you chose to operate it?

    Such a speculation is more than an intriguing fiction. You already own this special device which has the power of transforming the modes of time, of so readily altering time perspective. It is the human mind.

    Thus opens a report by three psychologists—P. G. Zimbardo, G. Marshall, and C. Maslach—of an experiment conducted at Stanford University that was designed to test the power of the human mind to alter time perspective. Specifically, in hypnotized subjects changes in behavior were observed of the sort that could sensibly be related to one's time perspective; they had been given the time-distorting instruction to "allow the present to expand and the past and future to become distanced and insignificant." A number of behaviors were investigated; of these only one is reported here.

    The subjects for this experiment were thirty paid volunteers from an introductory psychology course, selected on the basis of high scores on a test of potential hypnotizability. From these, twelve were randomly selected for 10 hr of training designed to help them more easily achieve a deep hypnotic trance (Hypnosis Group) before they were given the posthypnotic suggestion to allow the present to dominate their time perspective. The eighteen other subjects did not initially receive this training; of these, six were given the same time-distorting

never have a peak experience, because too much of his psychological energy is tied up in his neurotic pattern of adaptation (or maladapta-tion) to the world. A psychologically mature person, on the other hand, should be open to peak experiences.

---

instruction and were told to attempt to act through-out the experiment in the way they believed hyp-notized subjects would (Simulation Group). Another six subjects also received the time-distorting instruc-tion, but there was no reference whatsoever to hyp-nosis (Control Group). The remaining six subjects (the Normal Time Group) heard no mention of time distortion nor were they told to simulate hypnotized behavior.

Did these four groups differ significantly in their behavior? On one experimental task to be de-scribed here they clearly did, and in expected ways. But first, here is the task, as described by the investigators:

> [Subjects] were told they had 5 minutes to make something out of a large 2-pound mound of clay which was on the floor in front of the room. The sub-jects left their cubicles and proceeded to work either independently or together, as they chose. A stack of paper towels was available near the moist, sticky clay so that subjects could clean their hands, al-though this was not explicitly suggested. At the end of 5 minutes, the experimenter entered the room and told the subjects to finish up and return to their cubi-cles to complete a questionnaire about their reac-tions to this . . . task. Judges observed what the sub-jects made with the clay, as well as how they handled it, and their reactions to being soiled with it.

The Hypnosis Group had been predicted to be less likely to produce a distinct and recognizable object during their clay play. To do so, it was reasoned, would require deliberate planning of a project, an orientation requiring future orientation and thus incompatible with the hypnotic suggestion for the "future to become distanced and insignifi-cant." Also, Hypnosis Group subjects were expected to become more lost in the experience than the other groups, to enjoy it more, to worry less about getting messy—all reactions in line with an intense focus on the present and an indifference to future consequences.

In comparison with the other three groups, some tendency was found for Hypnosis Group sub-jects least often to turn out a recognizable object within the 5 min of clay play time allotted. But some-what more dramatic and unexpected was their reaction to being told, after these 5 min, to finish up and return to their cubicles. Quite simply, they did not want to—very strange behavior indeed for undergraduate subjects who are usually quite happy to wind up their experimental chores. Whereas the Normal Time Group stopped playing with the clay, on the average, even before the 5 min were up and the Simulation and Control subjects quit about 1 min after being told to do so, those in the Hypnosis Group continued playing with the clay for more than 4 min beyond the announced deadline. And this figure would have been higher had not the experi-menters actually forced five (of the twelve) Hypnosis subjects to stop after 5 full minutes of such overtime play. In fact, the *most* prompt finisher in the Hyp-nosis group dallied at clay play 1 min longer than the *least* prompt subject from all three other groups.

Apparently, being instructed while hypnotized to "expand the present" did result in a here-and-now attitude that permitted subjects to lose them-selves in the apparent joys of the immediate task. And their ignoring instructions to stop was inter-preted by the investigators as evidence that the Hypnosis Group had lost track of the future, of the possible consequences of their uncooperative be-havior.

Other aspects of this experiment and future work carried on by these researchers suggest that time perspective, or at least behaviors related to time perspective, can indeed be manipulated by ap-propriate instructions given to persons while in a hypnotic trance. The fact that being induced to "expand the present" so changes behavior hints at the normal condition of consciousness in our so-ciety: We may not, it seems, normally live mainly for and in the moment. Perhaps in much of what we do we typically are also well aware of the past, of the background for our actions, and give substantial weight to their future consequences. Has man, as a species, evolved this balanced time perspective; or, as a child, was he taught it? Whatever its source, this orientation usually is conducive to successful adaptation but perhaps at some psychic cost.

P. G. ZIMBARDO, G. MARSHALL, & C. MASLACH. Liberating behavior from time-bound control: Expanding the present through hypnosis. *Journal of Applied Social Psychology*, 1971, **1**, 305–323.

What is a peak experience like?

In a peak experience, perception of the external world tends to change radically: Perceptions are seen as *wholes*, sufficient in themselves, regardless of whether they are useful or threatening to the perceiver. The experiencer feels that he is paying *total attention* to the percept, and this can be ecstatic. Our ordinary classifying of perceptions into cognitive (naming) categories either temporarily disappears or becomes a secondary, not very important, activity. Repeated perception of an object in a peak experience leads to a richer and richer awareness of it rather than to a loss of interest and boredom, frequent responses to a repetitive stimulus in our NSC. Total absorption in a percept sometimes leads to a feeling of *union* between the perceiver and the perceived. If the perceived is an object of religious significance, an ecstatic religious experience can result.

The perceiver feels his experience is *self-validating*; he does not need outside affirmation. Maslow reported that the peak experience appears to generate values from itself that can be described by such words as wholeness, truth, perfection, self-sufficiency, completion, justice, aliveness, goodness, and beauty. Individuals who have had a peak experience often alter their life style to fit these concepts. The novelist Aldous Huxley has argued that the value structure coming out of peak experiences and mystical experiences can constitute a pervasive philosophy of life (Huxley, 1945).

People usually regard a peak experience as a surprise, a gift, rather than something they have consciously produced. There is usually an emotional reaction of thankfulness, awe, reverence, and humility. The experience is frequently interpreted as resulting from communication with something outside of and greater than oneself. Experiencers usually also stress that many aspects of the experience are simply beyond the power of ordinary language to communicate. Peak experiences, interpreted within a religious context, may have provided part of the foundation for several of the great religions. In any event, a religious experience as such can be viewed at least as similar to an ASC (see Box 21.4).

Meditation and States of Consciousness

Maslow originally believed that peak experiences were almost always spontaneous, that they could not be induced. He may have been led to this belief because he primarily sampled Americans, representatives of a culture not generally familiar with the many techniques of **meditation** that have been known and used for thousands of years in other parts of the world. Meditation is a rather broad term, but it can be defined as a set of *techniques* for achieving various ASCs, with some of these ASCs resulting in the ecstatic characteristics of peak experiences.

Meditation has been almost totally ignored by Western psychology, usually being dismissed as a form of self-hypnosis. The following comments present an alternate view and are based on an extensive study of meditation by a psychiatrist and a psychologist (Naranjo & Ornstein, 1971).

The traditional meditation-view phrasing has been that we are overly attached to seeking pleasure and avoiding pain. This attachment keeps us in a constant state of mental agitation such that we cannot perceive reality very well, much less develop what are believed to be the more spiritual potentials of man. A typical Eastern analogy is to compare the mind to a lake in the mountains whose surface is constantly being agitated by strong winds. The observer, the self, looking into the lake sees only dashing waves. If the wind could be calmed so that the surface of the lake became still, the observer could see the reflection of the lofty mountains around the lake and any treasures hidden below the surface of the lake. The winds represent the constant desires and thoughts that prevent us from really understanding ourselves and the world around us. Meditation, in terms of this analogy, is a way of learning to quiet the agitation of the mind so that the more subtle and valuable aspects of reality and man can be perceived.

The religious literature on meditation presents a great variety of meditation techniques. However, these techniques have points in common, such as the insistence that in meditating one must sit comfortably upright with the

BOX 21.4

RELIGIOUS EXPERIENCES

The religious sentiment was described by William James, one of the founders of American psychology, in the following passage:

> In the psychologies and in the philosophies of religion, we find the authors attempting to specify just what entity it [the "religious sentiment"] is. One man allies it to the feeling of dependence; one makes it a derivative from fear; others connect it with the sexual life; others still identify it with the feeling of the infinite; and so on. Such different ways of conceiving it ought of themselves to arouse doubt as to whether it possibly can be one specific thing; and the moment we are willing to treat the term "religious sentiment" as a collective name for the many sentiments which religious objects may arouse in alternation, we see that it probably contains nothing whatever of a psychologically specific nature. There is religious fear, religious love, religious awe, religious joy, and so forth. But religious love is only man's natural emotion of love directed to a religious object; religious fear is only the ordinary fear of commerce, so to speak, the common quaking of the human breast, in so far as the notion of divine retribution may arouse it; religious awe is the same organic thrill which we feel in a forest at twilight, or in a mountain gorge; only this time it comes over us at the thought of our supernatural relations; and similarly of all the varied sentiments which may be called into play in the lives of religious persons. As concrete states of mind, made up of a feeling *plus* a specific sort of object, religious emotions are of course psychic entities distinguishable from other concrete emotions; but there is no ground for assuming a simple abstract "religious emotion" to exist as a distinct elementary mental affection by itself, present in every religious experience without exception.

> . . . There thus seems to be no one elementary religious emotion, but only a common storehouse of emotions upon which religious objects may draw.

One indication that religious experience fits within the framework of ASCs is given in an experiment by Walter Pahnke, a Harvard psychologist. Divinity students, just prior to attendance at chapel on an occasion of great religious significance, were administered either psilocybin (see p. 522) or an inactive substance, a placebo. The students were not told whether they had received the placebo or the real thing. The religious experience during the service, as reported immediately afterward by each subject, was markedly greater for those who had received the drug. Of the ten students who had taken psilocybin, nine reported having had mystical experiences; of the ten subjects in the placebo group, only one did so. The content of these experiences varied widely. Drugs do lead to amplification and elaboration of experience but by no means induce a uniform emotion. *What* we feel remains a function of what we expect or intend to feel.

Aelfrida Tillyard many years ago anticipated this conclusion. On that occasion individuals were asked to report their emotional experiences during meditational exercises. Some of the subjects approached the situation with the purpose of obtaining deeper religious experience. Such experience was what they generally achieved. Others had no such expectation and religious experiences did not result for them.

W. JAMES. *The Varieties of Religious Experience.* New York: Longmans, 1902.
W. N. PAHNKE. Drugs and mysticism: An analysis of the relationship between psychedelic drugs and mystical consciousness. Unpublished doctoral dissertation, Harvard University, 1963.
A. C. W. TILLYARD. *Spiritual Exercises and Their Results: An Essay in Psychology and Comparative Religion.* New York: Macmillan, 1927.

head, neck, and spine in a straight line. But the specifics of each technique and the explanations for these specifics differ widely. One might be told to breathe in various timed patterns (as in the Yoga exercise called *pranayama*); or to meditate on specific sounds, *mantras,* that are supposed to have special qualities for affecting the mind; or to meditate on simple visual objects, *yantras,* or on very complex visual patterns, called *mandalas,* that symbolize the nature of the mind or reality.

Underlying this variety of techniques, however, Naranjo and Ornstein distinguish two basic types of meditation, concentrative (or restrictive) meditation and opening up (or widening) meditation.

Restrictive and widening meditation **Concentrative meditation** seeks to train the meditator to develop a total focus, a one-pointedness of mind, by restricting attention to a single object for long periods. This kind of concentration is almost impossible in our NSC, for thoughts and feelings spontaneously keep shifting from one thing to another. For example, in *zazen*—the basic meditation technique of Zen Buddhism— the meditator sits upright and tries to be aware of the natural movements of his belly during breathing. He should not do anything to alter this breathing but should keep his attention on the actual sensations caused by breathing. If his attention wanders away from his breathing, so that he is thinking about other things or paying attention to other sensations, he is to bring his attention gently (not forcibly) back to the belly movements again and again until he learns to concentrate on them for long periods of time, sometimes for as long as several hours.

This sort of concentrative meditation is much easier to describe than to do. Years of daily practice are often necessary before one is able to focus completely on anything for even a few minutes.

When it is successful, concentrative meditation leads to an ASC that is described by practitioners in such terms as *clearness, emptiness,* or *voidness.* All perception of the world is temporarily excluded from consciousness, not by forcing it out but by focusing on the desired object. Similarly, all internal mental activity stops, yet a kind of pure awareness and clearness without any particular content remains. This state may last only a few seconds or a few minutes, but it seems timeless.

Such an ASC, when attained, may be greatly valued for itself. But the aftereffect of the state is regarded as even more valuable. The immediate aftereffect is a feeling of intensely freshened and enhanced perception of oneself and of the world, a feeling that one is sensing things directly. The Zen master Suzuki Roshi is quoted as describing this aftereffect in the following manner: "The perfect man employs his mind as a mirror, it grasps nothing, it refuses nothing, it receives but does not keep" (Naranjo & Ornstein, 1971).

The opposite kind of meditation, **opening up meditation**, does *not* involve an intense narrowing of attention to a specific object. Instead, a sort of free-floating state of alertness is achieved. It is difficult to describe, but Box 21.5 attempts to do so.

While there is no direct laboratory evidence for the claim that meditation leads to an enhancement of perception, a physiological study of Zen meditation seems to offer some indirect support (Kasamatsu & Hirai, 1966). When ordinary subjects or Zen monks who are not meditating are presented with a repeating click stimulus, their brain-wave response habituates, that is, where at first the alpha rhythm is blocked out by the clicks, after a time it reappears. This process of habituation has been interpreted to mean that the brain shows considerable reaction to a stimulus so long as it is *novel* but then quickly categorizes it into something not requiring any adaptive action, at which point it no longer evokes a response. However, when the Zen monks are meditating, they show no habituation at all to the repeated click stimulus, suggesting that they continue to pay close attention to what is there despite the fact that it is no longer interesting nor requiring that they continue to attend to it. Also, Zen monks were found in their typical meditation state to show increased frequency of the alpha rhythm, which is associated with a tranquil state. (See the discussion of biofeedback training of alpha-wave activity in Box 16.4, p. 386.) In another report, practitioners of transcendental meditation showed this same effect in addition to other physiological changes such as decreased oxygen consumption (Wallace, 1970). (See Figure 21.3.)

A caveat Clearly, the data that we have been able to present regarding the ASCs represented by peak experiences and various meditative states are different from the data used to identify most other psychological phenomena. The very existence of such ASCs is doubted by many psychologists, and many of those who accept their reality wonder whether they are in fact distinguishable from more familiar (and more researched) states of consciousness, such as hypnosis. As always, more investigation is

BOX 21.5

OPENING UP MEDITATION

This description of the advanced Zen practice of *shikan-taza* is by a Zen master, Yaṣutani Roshi, quoted by C. Naranjo and R. Ornstein. *Shikan-taza* is translated as "just sitting."

> ...to sit.... Hence, *shikan-taza* is the practice in which the mind is intensely involved in just sitting. In this type of *zazen* it is all too easy for the mind, which is not supported by such aids as counting the breath...to become distracted. The correct temper of mind, therefore, becomes doubly important. Now in *shikan-taza* the mind must be unhurried, yet at the same time firmly planted or massively composed, like Mt. Fuji let us say. But it also must be alert and stretched, like a taut bow-string. So *shikan-taza* is a heightened state of concentrated awareness wherein one is neither tense nor hurried, and certainly never slack. It is the mind of somebody facing death. Let us imagine that you are engaged in a duel of swordsmanship of the kind that used to take place in ancient Japan. As you face your opponent, you are unceasingly watchful—set, ready. Were you to relax your vigilance, even momentarily, you would be cut down instantly. A crowd gathers to see the fight. Since you are not blind, you see them from the corner of your eye and since you are not deaf, you hear them. But for not an instant is your mind captured by these sense impressions.
>
> This state cannot be maintained for long—in fact, you ought not to do *shikan-taza* for more than half an hour at a sitting. After 30 minutes get up and walk around in *kinhin* (Zen moving meditation) and then resume your sitting. If you are truly doing *shikan-taza*, in half an hour you will be sweating, even in winter in an unheated room, because of the heat generated by this intense concentration. When you sit for too long, your mind loses its vigor, your body tires, and your efforts are less rewarding than if you had restricted your sitting to 30 minute periods.

Thus opening up meditation attempts to directly achieve more direct contact with reality rather than, as in concentrative meditation, to attempt to shut it out by a focusing of attention or concentration.

C. NARANJO & R. ORNSTEIN. *On the Psychology of Meditation.* New York: Viking, 1971. Copyright 1971 by C. Naranjo and R. Ornstein. Reprinted by permission of Viking Press, Inc.

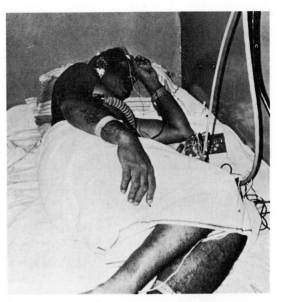

FIGURE 21.3 Ramanand Yogi in the airtight box in which he made an "inward spaceflight." In this trance, he cut his oxygen requirements to one-quarter of the theoretical minimum rate needed to sustain human life.

Photo by Philip Daly

needed—and on these questions considerable work is now under way.

ALCOHOL AND DRUNKENNESS

Alcohol, in the form of beer or wine, seems to have coexisted with man since the dawn of civilization. In spite of this long history and the huge quantities of alcohol consumed in our civilization, we do not have a systematic understanding of its effects on consciousness. An immense amount of literature exists purporting to show either that a little liquor never hurt anybody or that all the problems of the world are caused by the evils of alcohol. However, alcohol is one of the few mind-altering drugs that has definite effects on *behavior,* and here we have acquired a fair amount of information.

Table 21.1, p. 518, shows the behavioral and experiential effects of alcohol intoxication to be a function of dosage. As with other drug-induced ASCs, our present knowledge does not tell us precisely where modifications of

TABLE 21.1 EFFECTS OF ALCOHOL INTOXICATION

Number of Drinks (1 oz, 90 proof)	Approximate Percent Alcohol in Blood	
1	0.03	Usually no effects.
2–3	0.06	Warmth, relaxation, feeling high, slight motor impairment.
3–4	0.09	Some uninhibited behavior and exaggerated emotionality, more motor impairment.
5–6	0.12	Erratic behavior, staggers, considerable motor impairment, slurred speech, clearly drunk.
10–12	0.25	Severe perceptual and motor impairment (sees double, falls down). May pass out entirely.
25	0.50	Total stupor, possibly death.

These figures and behavioral effects are approximate and are based on a body weight of about 150 lb. Blood alcohol concentrations are used in the United States for defining alcoholic intoxication legally; 0.10 to 0.15 percent is the legal limit in most states, but it is as low as 0.08 percent in some.

the NSC end and a true ASC begins, but the point of alcoholic intoxication is reached when there is 0.1 percent alcohol approximately, in the blood. Our ability to specify the physiological concentration of alcohol seems to indicate objectively the degree of alteration of consciousness. But there is great individual variability, both among persons and from time to time in the same person, as to how someone reacts to a given dose of the drug, so that this measure is not as useful as might be assumed.

Nevertheless, some generalizations are possible. At relatively low levels of intoxication, the primary effects of alcohol are feelings of relaxation, bodily warmth, somewhat intensified emotions, and a lowering of inhibitions, along with definite impairment of skill in motor tasks that require a high degree of coordination. At higher levels of intoxication, say above 0.1 percent, there is even more serious impairment of coordination and severe loss of skill in motor tasks, up to the point of virtually total loss of coordination. Clearly, in this range of intoxication driving an automobile is a potentially murderous action. At even higher levels, stupor and ultimately death result.

Alcohol has been valued for its social lubricating effects. McClelland et al. (1972) studied the use of alcohol at parties and found that the early social lubricating effect did not result from a reduction of anxiety (loss of anxiety did not in fact occur until high levels of intoxication were reached) but rather from

the induction of strong fantasies of powerfulness. At low to moderate levels of intoxication, these fantasies tend to be expressed in socially acceptable ways, such as feeling able to help save the world, but at higher levels, the fantasies take on a feeling of a more personal kind of power. Aggressiveness and violence readily result from this illusion.

The increased self-confidence at moderate to high levels of intoxication, combined with decreased performance ability, makes alcohol a genuinely dangerous drug if not used with considerable care. The drunken driver is in fact less capable of driving a car than usual, but he *feels* more competent and is thus likely to take dangerous risks.

Our general beliefs about alcohol intoxication are contaminated by various social expectations that have little relation to the pharmacological action of the drug. Anthropologists have reported on cultures where, in spite of heavy drinking, the phenomenon of a hangover is unknown; yet in our culture we see this as an inevitable physiological effect. The lowering of inhibitions associated with alcohol, reflected in the old wives' tale that people are more sexually responsive when drunk (countered by the young wives' tale that men are sexually less effective), *may* have a direct physiological basis but again may result primarily from the fact that being drunk gives one a socially acceptable excuse for behaving in ways that are ordinarily suppressed in more sober surroundings. The importance of cultural factors applies to other drugs as well as to alcohol. A widespread cultural *belief* about the feelings and behavior that *should* result from use of a certain drug may lead directly to those effects; but these responses are often and incorrectly attributed to the pharmacological action of the drug.

MARIJUANA INTOXICATION

Marijuana is the term commonly used in America for various preparations of the leaves or flowers of the Indian hemp plant *cannabis sativa.* (It has many other names, among them "grass" and "pot.") Most often the preparations are smoked; sometimes they are eaten; the drug acts much more quickly and is considerably more potent when smoked. It has been a popular intoxicant in many civilizations for thousands of years, although it was generally unknown in the West until recently. In spite of severe legal penalties for possession of marijuana, the evidence suggests that over half of all college students have tried it, and many use it fairly regularly.

Pharmacological research in the last decade has shown that the major active ingredient of marijuana is a chemical called tetrahydrocannabinol (THC). Other ingredients in the plant may also be active or may modify the effect of the THC. Much research has been conducted on the effects of marijuana on experimental animals, but in order to obtain observable behavioral effects in animals, doses must be much higher than the maximum doses generally used by humans. There is solid evidence to show that the behavior of animals intoxicated with these high doses of marijuana is actually the behavior of *sick* animals (Elsmore & Fletcher, 1972), so it is difficult to apply these results to human beings.

In the dose range typically used by human beings, the only established physiological effects of marijuana are a small increase in heart rate and dilation of the small blood vessels of the eyes; this dilation may cause the eyes to look rather red for a few hours. There is no solid evidence that it leads to true addiction

(as does heroin, for example), nor as yet is there any conclusive evidence of adverse effects from prolonged moderate usage, although prolonged excessive usage may have adverse effects (Hollister, 1971; Weil, 1969).

Research has shown little effect on human behavior from marijuana intoxication, *within the dosage range smokers voluntarily use.* Behavioral effects (and they are minimal and only show up on complex tasks) are more evident with those who have never used the drug than with experienced users of marijuana (Weil et al., 1968). However, a person in the ASC induced by marijuana perceives and thinks very differently, yet appears to behave much the same as when in his NSC. Let us consider these experiential effects.

In discussing alcohol intoxication, we briefly considered the importance of cultural factors in predetermining the effects of the drug. These nondrug factors, both cultural and individual-psychological, are even more important for marijuana intoxication or the ASCs produced by the more powerful psychedelic drugs. Much of the older research and some current research is limited in its usefulness because of its failure to take account of these factors.

Table 21.2, p. 520, shows the extreme values of these nondrug variables that could, on the one hand, maximize the probability of a pleasant experience (a "good trip") or, on the other hand, maximize the probability of a highly unpleasant, possibly damaging, emotional reaction (a "bad trip").

Any psychoactive drug like marijuana has some effects that are an almost inevitable result of the chemical nature of the drug interacting with the nervous system. Most effects, however, seem to be potential effects, that is, the drug interacting with the nervous system creates a *potential* for certain experiences that manifest themselves if and only if psychological factors take on certain values. Given the factors shown in Table 21.2, the experience of a person using marijuana can be manipulated to a high degree by nondrug factors, since the potential effects far outnumber the relatively invariant drug effects (Tart, 1971). The importance of these factors is even greater for more powerful

TABLE 21.2 VALUES OF NONDRUG VARIABLES FOR MAXIMIZING PROBABILITY OF GOOD TRIP OR BAD TRIP

	Variables	Good Trip Likely	Bad Trip Likely
Drug	Quality	Pure, known.	Unknown drug or unknown degree of (harmful) adulterants.
	Quantity	Known accurately, adjusted to individual's desire.	Unknown, beyond individual's control.
Long-term factors	Culture	Acceptance, belief in benefits.	Rejection, belief in detrimental effects.
	Personality	Stable, open, secure.	Unstable, rigid, neurotic, or psychotic.
	Physiology	Healthy.	Specific adverse vulnerability to drug.
	Learned drug skills	Wide experience gained under supportive conditions.	Little or no experience or preparation, unpleasant past experience.
Immediate user factors	Mood	Happy, calm, relaxed, or euphoric.	Depressed, overexcited, repressing significant emotions.
	Expectations	Pleasure, insight, known eventualities.	Danger, harm, manipulation, unknown eventualities.
	Desires	General pleasure, specific user-accepted goals.	Aimlessness, (repressed) desires to harm or degrade self for secondary gains
Experiment or situation	Physical setting	Pleasant and esthetically interesting by user's standards.	Cold, impersonal; medical, psychiatric, hospital, or scientific associations.
	Social events	Friendly, nonmanipulative interactions overall.	Depersonalization or manipulation of the user, hostility overall.
	Formal instructions	Clear, understandable, creating trust and purpose.	Ambiguous, dishonest, creating mistrust.
	Implicit demands	Congruent with explicit communications, supportive.	Contradict explicit communications and/or reinforce other negative variables.

Taken from C. Tart. *On Being Stoned: A Psychological Study of Marijuana Intoxication.* Palo Alto, Calif.: Science & Behavior Books, 1971.

psychedelic drugs like LSD, and the reader should bear this is mind throughout the following discussion.

Figure 21.4 shows various categories of experiential effects reported by experienced marijuana users with respect to the minimal level of intoxication (as rated by the user) below which they are seldom experienced but above which they may be experienced if the psychological conditions are right. Individual differences, which can be considerable, are not taken into account in Figure 21.4.

As we can see from Figure 21.4, the almost immediate effect on the user when he feels that he has developed the ASC of marijuana intoxication is a kind of transitory restlessness, but this almost always disappears within a few minutes and is not noticed by all

users. There are then the experiences of being more relaxed, having one's mind calmed, and being more open to both sensory stimuli and feelings. Sensory enhancement begins to occur —the *feeling* that one is sensing things more finely, more sensitively than usual, in all sense modalities. An actual increase in physical sensitivity probably does not occur, but a qualitative change is experienced in the way in which sensory information is perceived.

This kind of enhancement includes greater sensitivity to what other people are saying and how they are acting, so that interpersonal relations seem to become more subtle. Along with this greater sensitivity in dealing with other people goes a general feeling of being more efficient at whatever tasks are undertaken, being better able to focus on and master them.

Still at this intermediate level of intoxication, experienced users report many spontaneous insights into their own psyche and an awareness that their thought processes are clearly changed from their NSCs. Unusual associations and trains of thought may arise, or problems are seen from a novel perspective. Many users believe that marijuana facilitates creative thinking because of these alterations in cognitive processing.

As the user becomes strongly intoxicated, the space and time framework of experience begins to change; time seems to pass much more slowly. One 30-min side of an LP record, for instance, may seem to last for a couple of hours. Internal imagery and fantasy are greatly intensified, and at very high levels the user can actually hallucinate although he is generally aware that this is a hallucination and not a real perception.

The earlier feelings of focusing and efficiency begin to be replaced by feelings of inefficiency and drifting of thought processes, sometimes perceived as a loss of control. This loss of control is not likely to result in antisocial or dangerous actions, but rather in a loss of ability to focus on specific problems. There are also feelings of enhanced contact with internal bodily processes, such as sensing physiological functions that are normally not consciously perceived. One can become intensely, even frighteningly, aware of one's heartbeat, for example. As the user moves toward the very strongly intoxicated levels of this marijuana ASC, his memory span typically shrinks, sometimes so much that he is unable to complete a sentence because he has forgotten how he started it. Companions may perceive this as a rather amusing effect, and he may also. The user may temporarily lose sensory contact with

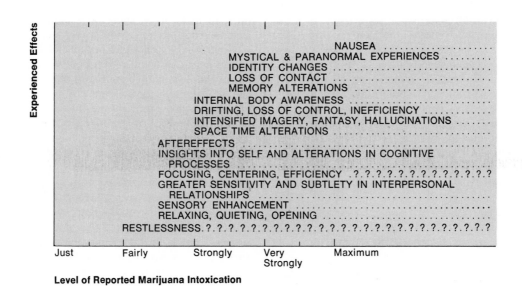

FIGURE 21.4 Minimal levels of marijuana intoxication for occurrence of various experiences. The minimal level for each category is level of intoxication at which 50 percent of experienced users of the drug report their initial occurrence. Once begun, the effects typically continue to occur at higher levels of intoxication, except where question marks follow the category designation. For example: *Restlessness* first appears when the smoker reports he is "fairly" intoxicated, continues for a bit, and then disappears when the smoker reports that he is now "strongly" intoxicated; *sensory enhancement*, on the other hand, first appears halfway between "fairly" and "strongly" intoxicated, but then persists. (From Tart, 1971)

the environment if he closes his eyes and becomes involved in his internal imagery and mental processes. His feeling of personal identity may temporarily fade, and users frequently feel that they are much more than simply a human being, that is, a particular person with a specfic history. Mystical experiences may take place, and sometimes the user feels that he has experienced telepathy or similar transcendences of the usual space and time limitations.

At the very highest levels of marijuana intoxication nausea may be experienced, sometimes to the point of vomiting. Experienced users indicate this is extremely rare, however, as they ordinarily do not use enough marijuana to reach this level. In general, experienced users smoke a certain amount of marijuana, decide whether they are at a level of intoxication appropriate to their desires, and then either stay there or smoke more marijuana if they wish to get higher.

Advocates of marijuana cite most of the foregoing effects as examples of the benefits that can come from its use. Opponents cite the same experiences as examples of psychological disorganization, effects that are pathological. Whether or not a given type of experience is deemed pathological is often a matter of cultural values and one's personal standards of acceptable behavior. Today's greatest known danger of marijuana use has little to do with pathology; instead, it is that the user may be arrested and imprisoned. Whether there are deleterious effects of long-term marijuana use in reasonably healthy individuals awaits the results of long-term studies, many of which are now in progress.

LSD: A PSYCHEDELIC DRUG

The term "psychedelic" comes from the Latin *psyche* (mind) and the Greek *dēlos* (clearly visible). When applied to a drug, "psychedelic" indicates that the drug generates hallucinations, distortions of perception, psychoticlike states, and sometimes seems to give the user insights into the nature of mental functioning that she would not ordinarily have. LSD (lysergic acid

diethylamide) is the most widely known **psychedelic drug.** Others are mescaline (the active ingredient in peyote cactus) and psilocybin (known to many Americans as the Mexican magic mushroom). Some would consider marijuana, especially in large doses, as a psychedelic drug, but it is considerably less powerful in the usual doses than the drugs LSD, mescaline, and psilocybin.

Although an immense amount has been written on the effects of psychedelic drugs, much of it is contradictory and it is difficult to form a coherent picture of the ASCs produced by these drugs. Unger (1963), in his overview of research data on LSD, mescaline, and psilocybin, concludes that they have similar effects but that the enormous variation in their impact is largely a function of the situation, broadly and psychologically defined, in which they are taken. Indeed, this variation is so great that it is impossible to present a coherent picture of the ASC or ASCs produced by a specific psychedelic drug.

Consider the nondrug factors (noted in Table 21.2) that so importantly influence reactions to marijuana; these very likely apply as well to reactions to psychedelic drugs. Thus, in reading others' personal accounts of their LSD experiences, we usually have no information at all on the dominant personality of the reporter and how it may have influenced his reactions. Similarly, while there are more than a thousand laboratory studies of the effects of LSD, almost all of these were conducted under the kinds of psychological conditions that we have listed as maximizing the possibility of a bad trip. When LSD first became an object for research study, most investigators thought that it induced a model psychosis and therefore permitted study in the laboratory of the psychotic process. Much of this research was therefore carried out by psychiatrists in hospitals who, in essence, were asking subjects how crazy they felt. In retrospect, it is not surprising that model psychoses were in fact thereby temporarily induced in some instances.

To many psychological and psychiatric authorities, almost all the experiences recorded for psychedelic drugs are regarded as similar or identical to those of psychoses; for this reason LSD is seen as incredibly dangerous and very likely responsible for mental deterioration in the hundreds of thousands of people who use it. Other authorities dispute so harsh a verdict and are prepared to entertain the possibility that psychedelic drug experiences are medically harmless, provide temporary liberation from cultural restraints, and allow a person to gain useful personal insights into his own personality, into his immediate social environment, and even into the nature of man. (For one of history's earliest experimental analyses of an ASC induced by a psychedelic drug, see Box 21.6, p. 524.)

From his review of hundreds of clinical studies of the use of LSD in therapy, Mogar (1965) suggests that if LSD is used *with proper guidance*, at *infrequent intervals*, with concurrent psychotherapeutic work aimed at *assimilating* the insights gained, it can be helpful to its users. However—with a by-now-familiar precaution—he notes how critical can be the user's personality and other nondrug factors in determining the specific effects of LSD use. Also, the conditions under which people take LSD by themselves are usually different from those that appear to produce good therapeutic results. Frequent use of LSD by individuals with generally poor mental health or during periods of great personal stress can probably lead to emotional breakdowns and to serious mental deterioration.

In general a person considering achieving an ASC by drug or nondrug means should be as well informed as possible of the psychological, physical, and legal dangers, as well as of the ways that have been developed to minimize the dangers. It is by no means a trivial action to induce an ASC in oneself. The result is subject to a wide range of factors, many of which we cannot control. The individual should, at the very least, seriously consider whether the possible benefits are worth the risks.

DRUG USE AND DRUG ABUSE

As we have noted, the idea of what constitutes *use* of a consciousness-altering drug and what constitutes *abuse* is very much determined by

cultural values. We might think of drug use as involving a level and frequency of usage that do not hamper an individual in efficiently attaining his life goals; drug abuse might be said to occur when such attainment is seriously threatened. But who judges whether a drug user is *efficiently* working toward his life goals? When does interference with these goals become *seriously threatening?* Suppose a person's goals change as a result of his drug-induced ASCs, and these new goals become ones that are not approved by the culture? For example, if a highly productive physicist decides during an LSD-induced ASC that he really wants to be a carpenter? Who is the judge of whether this outcome indicates, by its very nature, abuse of drugs?

There are, however, some drugs that almost all authorities agree are dangerous. Their users become addicted, their personal lives are wrecked, and they experience great unhappiness. These are the so-called hard narcotics, such as opium, heroin, and morphine, the powerful stimulants, such as dexedrine sulfate ("speed" and "meth") or cocaine, and strong sedatives, such as barbiturates.

In terms of sheer numbers of wrecked lives and irreparable damage to the body, alcohol is probably the most dangerous drug available. The picture is mitigated by the fact that many people who are light to moderate drinkers suffer only moderate losses in health and effectiveness. Marijuana, for widespread use still relatively new to Western culture, seems so far to be one of the least harmful drugs available in that culture—although imprisonment for its use is a powerful side effect. The strong psychedelic drugs like LSD, mescaline (peyote), and psilocybin are more difficult to evaluate since reliable data on the outcome of their social use are almost nonexistent.

POSSESSION STATES

In many cultures throughout history, the experience of being temporarily possessed by a nonphysical spirit or entity—a state of **possession** —was valued and relatively common. In other cultures all forms of possession were attributed to evil forces and they were suppressed. While some Christians in fundamentalist sects still experience possession by the Holy Ghost and while spiritualist mediums regularly seek to be possessed by spirits of the deceased, possession in our culture is no longer common; it is generally considered evidence of some form of insanity. For the more sophisticated, the possessing spirits are seen as fragments of a person's own subconscious mind, since our current physical views of the world reject the possibility of nonphysical entities.

We know little about the ASCs involved in possession phenomena because they have been studied almost exclusively in a distorted way from the mental illness model or from the religious model, rather than as phenomena of interest in their own right. (But see Box 21.6 again.)

ASCs, SOCIETY, AND YOU

In considering the differences among cultures, anthropologists use as a framework the spec-

BOX 21.6

**HALLUCINOGENIC DRUGS AND WITCHCRAFT—
A MODERN (1545) VIEW**

Dr. Theodore Rothman of Los Angeles, in his account of Andrés Fernández de Laguna (1499–1560), the Spanish physician of Emperor Charles V and Philip II, reports what may very well be the first psychopharmacological experiment on the nature of altered states of consciousness induced by hallucinogenic drugs.

According to Rothman, de Laguna "was perhaps the first physician to correlate the drug use of nightshade with the rituals of witchcraft. This drug had a similar hallucinogenic effect to LSD, and de Laguna noted that these were pleasurable experiences and were hallucinatory and delusional, produced by the ointments they prepared for the occasional festivals of the witches and wizards. He proved that these hallucinogenic drugs, when used on other subjects, would have a similar effect."

How did de Laguna prove this? Here is a report of one of his clinical experiments—in de Laguna's own words. When de Laguna was a physician in the city of Metz (1545), he was called in to attend the wife of the public executioner.

HENBANE

trum of human potentialities. Every individual has thousands of potential abilities, but because she is born into a particular culture only a limited range of these will ever be realized. Every culture maintains, usually implicitly, that certain human potentials are good and should be cultivated and that others are bad and should be suppressed. (And then there are the enormous numbers of potentialities that are not even suspected in a given culture.) When the individual deviates too far from her cultural norms, her culture pressures her to conform.

American culture as a whole has disapproved of deliberately induced ASCs, although it is ambivalent in the case of alcoholic intoxication. Most ASCs are classified as sinful or as symptoms of emotional disturbance. But American culture is very heterogeneous and, perhaps especially today when traditional cultural values have been weakened or abandoned by so many people, ASCs induced by drugs and/or meditation appear to have become more acceptable and, for certain subgroups, they have become a positive goal.

BELLADONNA

She through jealousy of her husband had completely lost power of sleep and had become half insane in consequence. This seemed to me to be an excellent opportunity to undertake a test of the witch's ointment [a salve of hemlock, nightshade, henbane, and mandrake containing scopalamine, nicotine, atropine, and belladonna]. And so it turned out, for no sooner did I annoint her than she opened her eyes wide like a rabbit, and soon they looked like those of a cooked hare when she fell into such a profound sleep that I thought I should never be able to awake her. However, by means of tight ligatures and rubbing her extremeties and applications of castor oil . . . I was so insistent that after a lapse of thirty-six hours, I restored her to her senses and sanity. Her first words were: "Why did you awaken me, badness to you, at such an inauspicious moment? Why I was surrounded by all the delights in the world." Then turning her eyes toward her husband (he was beside her, she stinking like a corpse) and smiling at him she said: "Skinflint! I want you to know that I have the horns on you, and with a younger and lustier lover than you." Many other strange things she said, and she wore herself out beseeching us to allow her to return to her pleasant dreams. Little by little we distracted her from her illusions, but forever after she stuck to many of her crazy notions.

From all this we may infer that all that those wretched witches do and say is caused by potions and ointments which so corrupt their memory and their imagination that they create their own woes, for they firmly believe when awake all that they had dreamed when asleep.

T. ROTHMAN. De Laguna's commentaries on hallucinogenic drugs and witchcraft in Dioscorides' Materia Medica. *Bulletin of the History of Medicine*, 1972, **46**, 562–567. Figures from the New York Public Library Picture Collection.

The majority psychiatric and psychological view probably is that deliberately induced ASCs are inherently dangerous to a person's mental health. This statement may be re-phrased to say that ASCs may result in an individual's espousing values and behavior that are considered deviant by the particular, larger culture, although particular subcultures (youth,

BOX 21.7

THE SMITHSONIAN LOOKS AT INNER SPACE

Exploration of the hidden and uncharted portions of the mind is no longer the sole domain of religious mystics, dreamers, LSD trippers, or schizophrenics.

Thus opens a report of a recent conference that was published in *Science*. It goes on:

In one of the first scientific symposia of its kind, a group of brain researchers, chemists, psychopharma-cologists, psychologists, and biofeedback and dream researchers recently got together to discuss altered states of consciousness—the kind of brain phenom-ena which hitherto have been largely ignored by Western science.

The meeting was engineered by the Smithson-ian Institution and the Drug Abuse Council, a private foundation-supported organization that promotes re-search and education in drug abuse. One of its pur-poses was to discuss how some drugs can be more healthily integrated into society; by "socializing" the use of certain drugs, such as marijuana, some people think standards could be set for their use and destruc-tive use of drugs could be curbed.

Another and more radical idea that is being discussed these days is the possibility that people can be taught to achieve mental "highs" without the use of drugs. This is already happening in some cir-cles where people have abandoned hallucinogens in favor of various types of meditation.

The massive experimentation with mind-alter-ing drugs during the 1960's has expanded awareness of what is possible in the "normal" brain. As Julian Silverman, director of California's Esalen Institute, said: ". . . spontaneous hallucinations in normal in-dividuals were regarded as psychiatric problems." Now mind researchers are discovering that a large number of individuals with healthy, nondrugged minds have occasional "extraordinary" perceptions that were rarely recorded because such perceptions have been regarded as deviant. . . .

What goes on with the brain to produce these phenomena? One appealing theory was offered by Roland Fischer, a Johns Hopkins pharmacologist who talked about "the cartography of inner space." Fischer says that most behavior is governed by the left hemis-phere of the brain—essentially the rational, linear-thinking, verbally oriented half, and that this hemis-phere is cultivated by experience and education at the expense of the right hemisphere which is the seat of creative, visual, and artistic impulses that govern a different—subjective, non-temporal—consciousness. Fischer says the reasons that most children's artistic impulses start disappearing around the age of 9 is because they are "brainwashed" from the age of 6 onward to use their left hemispheres. Eastern mystics have learned how to shift consciousness to a non-verbal nonlinear state, not necessarily responsive to external reality, the consciousness of dreams and hallucinations—located, Fischer would say, in the right hemisphere. In Western culture the "normal" brain is not expected to have this capacity. . . .

These revelations paved the way for some mind-bending tales by Jean Houston, director of the Foundation for Mind Research in Pomona, N.Y. Hous-ton began by theorizing that current fascination with altered mind states and nonrational cults is correlated with the breakdown of social institutions. . . .

Houston went on to describe experiments—none involving drugs—whose object is to "break through the surface crust of consciousness" or "cul-tural trance." To do this, subjects at the Pomona foundation are put into trances through a variety of time-honored means such as hypnosis, drumming, dancing, and yoga. . . .

These trances were of very short duration be-cause of what Houston called "subjective time"—the same that pertains with dreams. "Most thinking tends to adhere to the movements of the body. In high-level creativity the mind can do weeks of work in a short time." In Houston's lab a pianist worked out an inter-pretation of a Bach toccata, condensing 8 hours of practice time into 10 minutes; and a songwriter imagined in her trance that she walked down a street, into a cabaret, ordered a sandwich and a beer, list-ened to a singer render three songs—all in 2 minutes. After the trance she was able to sing the songs, all original, complete with lyrics. . . .

Houston, like Fischer, believes that emphasis on verbal thinking inhibits visual thinking, and that the present educational system "derails" children who may be natural visual thinkers.

hippies, spiritualists, fundamentalist Christians, etc.) may support this lack of conformity. (That the norms of the dominant culture may themselves be in the process of reevaluation is suggested in Box 21.7, which presents a partial report on a recent meeting on ASCs that was published in the scientific establishment's official journal, *Science*.)

There were many ways in which the symposium pointed up the inadequacies of the Western scientific approach. A few years ago science simply dismissed coal-walking yogis, like acupuncture, because the facts could not be explained through their thought systems. Now scientists are taking a new look.

Other cultures have long had techniques for arriving at altered states of consciousness—through such means as chanting, whirling, fasting, breathing exercises, and flagellation. Now such procedures are recognized to have dramatic effects on body chemicals which contribute to the achievement of the desired state. The ability of mystics to undergo with no apparent discomfort intense physical stresses is being explained by the altered sensory perceptions that come with a shift of consciousness. . . .

California's Silverman was one of several speakers tempted to make new interpretations of miracles described in the New Testament. When Jesus was wandering and fasting in the desert for 40 days he no doubt did encounter the Devil: the changed pattern of external stimulation as well as what starving did to his chemical balances could well have thrown him into a different subjective reality. Similarly, Moses was having a true "psychedelic" experience when he saw the burning bush (an interesting contrast to one strictly scientific explanation: that certain plants have properties that can give them an incandescent appearance).

Biofeedback training is one way researchers are trying to map altered states of consciousness, and it is also showing the degree to which it is possible for some people to alter them voluntarily. Joe Kamiya of the University of California Medical Center said that people experienced in Zen meditation, for example, can switch in and out of alpha rhythms with great ease, and those who can switch their brain waves voluntarily tend to be more susceptible to hypnosis [see Box 16.4, p. 386]. Another interesting tibit is that children with eidetic memory [see Box 6.4, p. 131] show more alpha waves at the time of this kind of recall—an indication that this ability is not lodged in the ordinary data bank. The reason: ordinary recall requires the kind of active effort that will break the alpha rhythm.

Mind research is creating new definitions of what constitutes "reality." As Alexander Schulgin, a California chemist, pointed out, everything perceived by the mind is reality. Altered states of consciousness are undesirable from a social point of view because people need to perceive a common reality in order to function cooperatively. But considered subjectively these states are not inferior, only different.

Richard Schultes, a Harvard University botanist who specializes in hallucinogenic plants, said that in the thinking of some aboriginal cultures—where such plants are regarded as intermediaries to the gods—it is daily living that is the illusion, and the real truth is delivered by the divinities through the holy plants. Among Mexican Indians, he said, these drugs are an integral part of every major event and ritual, but they are never abused because they are tied up with religious experience.

While there was much talk about psychoactive drugs at the seminar, the real interest was centered on spontaneous and self-induced mind changes.

The plethora of disciplines that have been probing the mind from different angles have hardly had the chance to begin talking to each other and integrating their findings. To remedy this, many speakers recommended the establishment of "inner space labs," a term coined a decade ago by Joel Elkes, chief of psychiatry at Johns Hopkins Hospital. Elkes, who says mind research is still in the "natural history" or descriptive phase, thinks the time is ripe for some true experimentation. Just as physicists had to develop a new language to communicate their concepts, explorers of inner space need to develop new symbolic systems to express the rapid, subtle, and intensely subjective phenomena for which language is a vague, slow, clumsy, and entirely inadequate vehicle. Both researchers and subjects would have to be highly trained to observe and communicate these inner phenomena. And, says Elkes, new ways must be found to accurately correlate physically measurable changes—brainwaves, chemical and hormonal fluctuations—with what's happening inside.

The time may be now. As Houston observed, the astronauts have gone about as far out as man can go at present. Now, "we are perhaps on the verge of a golden age of brain and mind research."

A conference such as this, under so august auspices and reported straight in so august a scientific journal, would have been unthinkable even a few years ago. Without passing on the merits of the data and speculations presented, this indication of the openness of Establishment science to new and challenging conceptions must be applauded.

C. HOLDEN. Altered states of consciousness: Mind researchers meet to discuss exploration and mapping of "inner space." *Science*, 1973c, **179**, 982–983.

It is not easy to decide that you are an independent person, a freethinker, not bound by the arbitrary rules of a disintegrating society, and therefore you will seek out ASCs. We are products of our culture in much more than an intellectual sense; we have deep, emotional investments in beliefs that cannot be altered simply by deciding we do not want any part of our society. Many individuals have made such a decision and have acted on it by seeking ASCs, but some of these individuals have not been able to handle the conflicts that arise from their cultural deviance. Some people who seek out ASCs *do* develop mental illnesses. There *are* bad trips. Therefore there are real hazards in experimenting with ASCs; a person is wise to realize it is not a light matter. This is not to say that, barring such experimentation, we must dwell all our lives on the psychologically placid plains of our ordinary NSC. Life circumstances provide powerful impetuses for significant alterations in our normal feeling state. We fall in love and are exhilarated or devastated thereby; children are born to us and loved ones die; intellectual, artistic, or other kinds of achievements lift us up; catastrophes may evoke an act of heroism and courage. Whether these highs and lows are enough to fulfill the ever-yearning soul or whether new and different states of consciousness are to be actively sought is a decision upon which science, at this stage of the art, has precious little to say.

SUMMARY

1. Psychology, once defined as the study of consciousness, for a long time ignored this topic. Recently research attention has returned to its study, especially to the variety of altered states of consciousness (ASCs) that are, in different ways, distinguishable from one's normal state.

2. Experiences while falling asleep (hypnagogic state) move through a three-stage sequence (intact, destructuralized, and restructuralized ego states) that is systematically related to concurrent brain-wave and eye movement patterns.

3. Earlier research suggested that dreaming was confined to a particular phase of sleep (stage 1–REM), but more recent evidence indicates that considerable mental activity, if not true dreams, occurs in other sleep stages. During a dream, external stimuli are typically ignored although they may sometimes be interwoven in the dream fabric without waking the dreamer.

4. Dreams may express in symbolic, hence disguised, form important facets of personality that may otherwise be inaccessible. Freud was the most influential modern proponent of this view, although many other personality theorists would generally agree. Whether dream interpretation is a useful therapeutic tool is still being debated.

5. Instances of lucid and of high dreams and of out-of-the-body experiences are very rare, and evidence for them is largely anecdotal.

6. People vary enormously in their susceptibility to hypnosis. Hypnotic phenomena include heightened sensitivity to stimuli (hyperesthesia), decreased sensitivity to the point of not experiencing usually painful stimuli (hypoesthesia), and hallucinations of various kinds. There can also be dissociation of action from awareness so that the hypnotized subject may engage in behavior, such as automatic writing, without indication that he knows what he is doing or has done. Posthypnotic effects can also be demonstrated, and self-hypnosis is a technique that can be learned.

7. To permit oneself to be hypnotized by an untrained person can be a dangerous undertaking, especially if one is beset with emotional problems. Properly used, however, hypnosis shows great promise as a therapeutic tool.

8. According to Maslow, psychologically mature persons may undergo intensely satisfying and revealing peak experiences that may profoundly affect their values and future lives.

9. Meditation refers to a variety of techniques for achieving a range of ASCs, some of them resembling, in their ecstatic qualities, peak experiences. Two basic types of meditation can be distinguished: concentrative meditation, which involves a restricting of attention to a very narrow focus, and opening up meditation, which involves a nonfused, free-floating state of alertness.

10. Behavioral effects of alcohol are related to its concentration in the blood, but effects on consciousness are less direct. Cultural expectations regarding the effects of alcohol are very influential in predetermining them, perhaps as much so as direct pharmacological action.

11. Within the dosage range usually used, marijuana has few and mild behavioral effects and has those effects mainly on those persons previously unacquainted with the drug. Experiential effects, however, seem to increase with continued use. A host of nondrug factors affect the quality and intensity of the reaction to marijuana, and each type of reaction generally requires a certain degree of intoxication before it can occur.

12. Psychedelic drugs, among which LSD is most well known, cause varying ASCs, depending very much on the psychological context within which they are taken. Too little is known, scientifically, of their effects; for this reason they are regarded by some as highly dangerous and by others as personally valuable, especially in a controlled therapeutic setting.

13. What constitutes beneficial use and what constitutes dangerous abuse of consciousness altering drugs is in large part dependent upon cultural values. However, there is no debate that the hard drugs, such as heroin, are both addictive and harmful.

14. States of possession, at times in history highly valued or intensely feared, are currently little studied. When they seem to occur they are usually regarded as manifestations of a severely troubled person's subconscious.

15. Every culture has a usually implicit set of assumptions as to which of man's enormous range of potentialities are to be valued and cultivated. American society generally looks with suspicion upon altered states of consciousness of any sort, and this pervasive attitude tends to restrict adequate research on many of them. But this attitude may currently be under some revision. A personal decision to seek altered states of consciousness should not be taken lightly.

GLOSSARY

altered state of consciousness (ASC)   A state of consciousness different from the normal state of consciousness, which is designated as NSC.

automatic writing   The writing of more or less meaningful material without the conscious direction of the writer.

concentrative meditation   Meditative techniques in which attention is focused on a particular target and not allowed to wander.

dream deprivation   A laboratory technique for awakening a sleeper every time an electroencephalogram shows a brain-wave pattern associated with dreaming *and* rapid eye movements begin to occur. Its purpose is to prevent dreaming.

hallucination   Perceiving something as physically existent when there are no sensory stimuli coming from that location. A hallucination is a more radical alteration of perception than an illusion, in which there is an actual sensory stimulus, but it is misperceived and distorted in experience.

high dream   A dream in which the experience is similar to that occurring when a psychedelic drug such as LSD is taken.

hyperesthesia   A feeling of being hypersensitive to sensory stimuli, in the sense either of feeling that one's threshold for detection has been lowered or of experiencing stimuli much more intensely than they would normally be experienced.

hypnagogic state   The transitional state of consciousness experienced while falling asleep.

hypnosis   An altered state of consciousness characterized by markedly increased suggestibility.

hypoesthesia   The feeling of being much less sensitive to sensory stimuli, in the sense either of feeling that one's threshold for detection has been greatly raised or of experiencing stimuli much less intensely than they would ordinarily be experienced.

lucid dream   A dream in which one knows at the time that one is dreaming and yet one seems to possess all the critical faculties of one's ordinary waking state of consciousness.

marijuana   Preparations of the Indian hemp plant *cannabis sativa*, used for altering one's state of consciousness. It has many slang names, "grass" and "pot" among them. Hashish is its more concentrated form, being distilled from the plant's resin. THC (tetrahydrocannabinol) is the main active chemical ingredient of marijuana.

meditation   A set of techniques designed to induce particular meditative states of consciousness. See *concentrative meditation* and *opening up meditation*.

negative hallucination   Totally failing to perceive something that is actually there, even though one's senses are being adequately stimulated by it.

opening up meditation   Meditative techniques in which total attention is given to whatever spontaneously happens, with no attempt to control or focus attention.

out-of-the-body experience   A state of consciousness in which one seems to possess all the critical faculties of ordinary consciousness and which is experienced as completely real, yet one feels physically located at a place other than where one actually is.

peak experiences   Classes of experiences that are overwhelmingly intense and emotionally positively valued; they are said to have long-term effects on the experiencer's life. An ecstatic experience, beyond the normal range of emotions.

possession   A state of consciousness in which one believes that some nonphysical entity temporarily takes over one's physical body and lives through it. The person may be amnesic for the period of ostensible possession.

posthypnotic effects   Behavioral or experiential responses to hypnotic suggestions that occur after the hypnotic trance has ended and the subject is presumably in his ordinary state of consciousness.

psychedelic drug   A drug that induces hallucinations, distortions of perception, psychoticlike states, and so forth. In some instances it alters one's state of consciousness in ways conceived by the user to be mind-manifesting, that is, allowing observation of mental processes not ordinarily observable to her. Well-known psychedelic drugs are LSD, mescaline, and psilocybin.

physiological bases of motivation and emotion

DO YOU KNOW...

- that babies spend more time in the stage of sleep related to dreaming than adults do?

- what bad effects may arise from jet lag, and how to prevent them?

- that the electrical resistance of the skin changes when one is exposed to emotional stress?

- that different kinds of emotional responses can be directly produced by electrical stimulation of the brain?

- that some neurosurgeons believe that they can "cure" patients of excessive violent behavior by destroying part of the brain?

- that a very small lesion in a certain part of the brain will make animals (or people) eat enormous amounts and grow excessively fat?

- that whether or not your mouth is dry has little or nothing to do with the amount of water you drink?

- that the amount of sex hormones in the body does not always have an important effect upon sexual behavior in adult humans?

- that some theorists believe that both male and female fetuses at first are basically female in terms of the nervous system, while others believe that separate neuronal systems exist in every infant animal for both male and female types of behavior?

Photo by Philip Teuscher

CONTENTS

In earlier units we have discussed the physiological bases of perception and of learning and memory; in this unit we will consider the processes that underlie emotion and motivation. The experience and expression of emotion and motivation obviously depend upon perception and learning, and thus upon those mechanisms we have already studied. We shall find it necessary, however, to explore some additional features of the body—in the nervous system and elsewhere—in pursuit of the biological foundations of emotion and motivation.

We must first consider the striking variations in general responsiveness that distinguish the sleeping organism from one that is aroused and active. These differences show up not only in responsiveness to external stimulation but also in responsiveness to the internal states that are part of the instigating factors in emotion or motivation.

SLEEP AND AROUSAL

In Unit 21 we examined in some detail the different parts of the falling-asleep period and the kinds of dreaming sleep. There, as in Unit 3, we noted that different kinds of EEG activity are associated with the different states of consciousness in the sleep-waking cycle (see Figure 3.4, p. 65). Now we must consider a little more generally the various states of sleeping and waking and the physiological changes that underlie them.

For much of the day we are awake, but it is obvious that we are more actively aroused at some times than at others. Two major EEG patterns are found at the arousal extremes of the awake period. The EEG of a relaxed subject who is not paying attention to any strong stimulus is characterized by a regular alpha rhythm of 8 to 12 waves per second. If the person becomes involved in perceptual activity (real or imagined—see Box 16.5, p. 388) or if he engages in concentrated mental activity such as that required to solve an arithmetic problem, these waves disappear and are replaced by more irregular waves, which have a higher frequency but are smaller in size (i.e., in amount of voltage as measured from the electrodes).

Stages of Sleep

When the change in degree of arousal goes in the other direction (from the relaxed waking state into sleep), the nature of the EEG patterns also tends to go in the opposite direction. It tends to show large, slow waves, as described in Unit 21. Note, however, that there is a period in light sleep (stage 1) in which the EEG becomes less regular and smaller in size. In later stages this irregular rhythm is interspersed with periods in which **sleep spindles** (groups of very rapid waves) appear in the EEG. In even deeper stages the spindles and the alpha waves disappear and large, slow waves appear. Other related changes take place in the sleeper, also. Body temperature and blood pressure decline, and the rate of breathing becomes more regular; in general, the sleeper becomes harder to awaken.

After about an hour of deep sleep the individual goes through these stages in reverse. However, this time when he reaches an EEG pattern like that of stage 1 he is *not*, in fact, in very light sleep. This period is called stage 1–REM sleep, because in addition to the characteristic EEG of stage 1 there appear **rapid eye movements** (hence REM), which can be seen beneath the closed lids. Throughout the night, a person continues to show cycles of changes from stage 1–REM into the stages of NREM (no rapid eye movements) sleep and back again. These cycles take about 90 min each, and although the first REM period may be very brief, later ones may take as long as 1 hr.

These periods of REM sleep cannot be considered light sleep because, despite an EEG pattern that looks like that of a person who is awake or in the earliest stages of sleep, the sleeper is actually *harder* to awaken than when he is in slow-wave, NREM, sleep. In addition, the muscles of the body become extremely relaxed and even reflexes are very difficult to elicit.

In view of the relation between the dreaming state and stage 1–REM sleep (see Unit 21), it is perhaps surprising to note that this kind

of sleep decreases over a lifetime. While stage 1–REM may take up about half of the sleeping time of a newborn, and even more in the case of a child born prematurely, it occupies only 25 percent of the sleeping time of an adult. It should also be noted that REM sleep is widespread among mammals and perhaps in birds as well.

Probably these facts make the reader wonder once again why it is that people dream. Why, indeed, do people sleep? We will not be able to answer these questions fully at the present time, but there is now quite a bit of knowledge about the neuronal and chemical activity of the brain that produces these states. Let's start there.

Neural and Chemical Mechanisms in Sleep

The waking state and the EEG pattern that accompanies it appear to be dependent upon subcortical regions (see Figure 22.1, p. 536). Prominent among these regions is the reticular formation of the brain stem, particularly the parts of it that are found in the midbrain and the upper part of the pons. (For a refresher course on these structures, see Unit 3, p. 68.) In addition there is a region in the posterior part of the hypothalamus that plays a part in producing arousal; this region may also be responsible for other aspects of the waking state, such as keeping the muscles in a state of readiness and providing the appropriate kind of activity in the *autonomic nervous system*, which is described later in this unit.

At one time many neurophysiologists felt that sleep could be considered merely "the absence of wakefulness." According to this **passive theory of sleep,** sleep is just the normal state of the brain when there is no activity in those parts that are responsible for wakefulness. At present, however, the tide of evidence has turned investigators to an **active theory of sleep,** according to which sleep occurs only when designated regions of the brain are active.

Rather complex sets of structures have been implicated as being parts of the *sleep area*; these structures include some nuclei in the thalamus and the anterior part of the hypothalamus. Lesions of these regions may produce

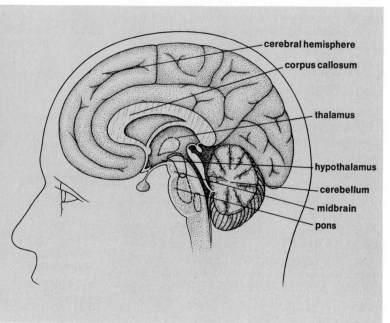

FIGURE 22.1 This figure shows some of the structures and systems that act and interact to determine our state of wakefulness or sleep. The solid line encloses the upper part of the reticular activating system and a part of the hypothalamus; these structures activate the cortex and arouse the individual. The upper dashed line indicates parts of the thalamus and hypothalamus that promote slow-wave, NREM, sleep. The other area in a dashed line is also concerned with the production of NREM sleep; this region is characterized by a high concentration of the transmitter serotonin. Finally, the dotted line shows a region in the lower pons that is important to the production of REM sleep; norepinephrine seems to be the chemical messenger in this system.

cerebral hemisphere
corpus callosum
thalamus
hypothalamus
cerebellum
midbrain
pons

insomnia; electrical stimulation may induce sleep. In addition, a chain of neurons along the midline of the brain stem (see Figure 22.1) is also involved. These neurons appear to produce *serotonin* (see Unit 18, p. 433) and use it as a transmitter substance; when the amount of serotonin in the brain stem is increased experimentally (by injections), the amount of sleep goes up as well.

However, the sleep that we have just been discussing is only slow-wave, NREM, sleep. A different explanation seems necessary for REM sleep. Here the crucial neurons appear to be in the lower part of the pons, as shown in Figure 22.1. Lesions in this region can reduce the amount of REM sleep, and injections that increase the amount of *norepinephrine* (the transmitter used here) will increase the percentage of REM sleep.

Much more is known about the interactions between the structures than is sketched here, but enough has been said to indicate that many structures of the brain are involved and that there are many ways in which the systems could interact, neurally and chemically, to pro-

duce the sequence of states that we call waking, sleeping, and dreaming. Can we answer the "why" questions any better now?

The Sleep-Waking Cycle

First we might note an important, although obvious, fact. In the overall sleep-waking cycle, we have yet another example of the workings of a biological clock. The cycle of sleeping and waking that seems so natural to us—and to many other animals—is but one of many rhythms of change that take about the same amount of time as the day-night cycle produced by the earth's rotation on its axis. There are associated daily changes (circadian rhythms— see Unit 3) in body temperature, in production of certain hormones, in the amount of urine produced, in mental alertness, and so on.

An objection may occur to the reader. If we wake up when the sun rises, or the rooster crows, or the clock-radio turns on, and go to sleep when it is dark, can this be called an *internal* rhythm? Is not a simpler explanation found in a rhythm based on reactivity to *external* stimulation?

This objection does not stand up in the face of several varieties of evidence now available to us. The experience of "jet lag" is now well known by many people. When one travels rapidly several thousand miles from east to west (or vice versa), he enters an environment where the sun, and all human activity, is on a different schedule than they were in the place he left. The traveler finds that he cannot immediately react appropriately to the new schedule of external stimulation, the one that is "natural" to those around him. *His* body seems to be operating in terms of the schedule "back home," and it takes several days before he becomes adjusted to the new routine. In fact, it has been shown that there are several internal biological clocks that must be separately reset when we move rapidly from one time zone to another. Even after the sleep cycle has changed, the daily rhythm in production of certain hormones may still be out of phase with the demands of the new schedule (see Box 22.1, p. 538).

While it is difficult to shift the time of onset of the various parts of the daily sleep-waking schedule, it is even more difficult to change the length of the total day. In one experiment, two subjects attempted to live for 32 days on a 28-hr day deep in the Mammoth Cave of Kentucky. There were none of the usual cues for the natural day in the cave—the temperature was absolutely uniform and there were no lights or sounds from the outside world to influence the subjects. One of them was able to adjust relatively easily; the other—and it happened to be the older person—found it much more difficult to adjust either his sleep rhythm or the 24-hr rhythm of body temperature (Kleitman, 1963).

Many similar experiments have been done with animals. Typically, in these studies, rats or other animals are maintained in continuous light or continuous darkness, and records are taken of their activity, EEG, or some other measures of sleep and wakefulness. The results are clear. For months, as shown in Figure 22.2, page 539, the animals continue to show a daily circadian rhythm of activity much like that shown under natural conditions. Certainly a biological clock must be at work.

The fact that internal mechanisms help to keep the organism on a schedule of sleeping and waking may help us understand the nature of sleep itself and its importance to the individual. Most of the traditional ideas about the function of sleep have been based upon the assumption that it is a period of recovery—that neurons simply become tired and need a period of inactivity before they can work again at their optimal efficiency. It is possible that this may apply to certain crucial neurons that no one has yet studied, but from present evidence this theory appears rather doubtful. There seem to be no neural systems that are completely inactive during sleep; some fire *more* frequently at this time than during the waking period.

An interesting alternative view suggests that we must view sleep and activity in terms of their overall effect upon the survival of the individual and his species rather than as a physiological recuperation period (Milner, 1970). The individual must have periods of activity when he can *most effectively* gather and consume food, mate and care for the young, and so on. Some animals have evolved so that they can perform these functions best during the night; most primates, including man, have become adapted to a schedule of activity during the sunlit portions of the 24-hr cycle. If primitive man, for example, could obtain food and satisfy his other needs during the daylight hours, he was much better off quiet and asleep in his cave at night than stumbling about ineffectively in the dark, wasting the food energy gained during the day, and at the mercy of night predators. A primitive man who insisted on being a "night person" would have little chance of surviving long enough to bear progeny. But that does not necessarily imply that the reduction in sleep is directly followed by some deleterious *physiological* effect.

Some possibilities about the function of REM sleep specifically are mentioned in Unit 21, and several others have been suggested. The Freudian idea that it provides a means of expressing unacceptable drives that would otherwise come out during waking is a theory that views REM sleep as a necessary alternative to the waking state. Several other theories view

BOX 22.1

TIME MARCHES ON

Each of us has adopted a daily schedule of activities, including waking, sleeping, eating, and so on. Disruptions of an individual's schedule may be annoying, disturbing, and actually damaging to his physiological and psychological efficiency. For most of us such disruptions are relatively rare—for example, when a student stays up all night to study for an examination. Others must adopt new schedules rather often. In this group are people who work during the day shift for a few weeks and then have to take their turn working on the night shift. With the development of airplanes able to travel long distances rapidly, changes in circadian rhythms have led to some problems for the large numbers of people who are passengers on such trips. The problems are particularly important for the pilots and other members of airplane crews, who are subject to time-zone changes often and must maintain their alertness and efficiency.

Scientists working for the U.S. Federal Aviation Administration and similar agencies in other countries have studied so-called time-zone effects in an attempt to discover the best ways to lessen their impact on health and performance. For example, it was found that after a trip from Oklahoma City to Tokyo, body temperature cycles took three to five days to adjust to the new local time. During this period of readjustment the time required to reach a decision and to make a response was abnormally high, and feelings of fatigue were increased. In general, physiological functions, such as body temperature and rate of evaporation of water from the skin, were slower to readjust than psychological functions. In some experiments it was found that hormone production took up to thirteen days to become stabilized in accordance with the new clock time.

Although there are some conflicting reports, experiments suggest that travel in a westerly direction is more disruptive than travel in an easterly direction. This means that it is easier to advance a circadian rhythm than it is to delay the rhythm. Drs. Seigel, Gerathewohl, and Mohler, FAA scientists who have reviewed the findings on this question, point out the different problems that would be met by a traveler between New York and Rome, depending on his direction of travel. If he left New York at 7:00 P.M., he would arrive in Rome at 9:00 A.M. (2:00 A.M. in New York). He would be ready to sleep, but not hungry (especially since the airline is liable to have kept him awake all night, almost continuously offering meals). He can, however, by conscious effort, engage in business meetings, tours, social activities, and so on, although he will be at less than peak efficiency for a day or so.

On the return trip, after his body is on a Rome schedule, he may leave at 11:00 A.M., arriving in New York about 2:00 P.M. (9:00 P.M. Rome time). He may keep himself awake during the remainder of the New York day; but then when he tries to go to sleep (e.g., at 10:00 P.M.), it is already 5:00 A.M. the next day in Rome, and his biological clock thinks it is almost time to awaken. Soon afterwards it will be time for breakfast according to his Italian stomach, which may add to his difficulty in staying asleep. It may take several days to become readjusted after the east-to-west trip.

One solution adopted by some airlines is to attempt to keep their flight crews on the same schedule they had back home, sleeping during the day (at the new location) if necessary, eating meals at night, and so on. Other airlines have developed formulas for the amount of rest a pilot should have after a flight to allow him to readjust to the new schedule. These formulas take into account the length of travel time, the number of time-zone changes the person has gone through, and the actual local time of departure and arrival.

For the occasional traveler the best procedure is to avoid strenuous or demanding activities during the period of readjustment, including heavy eating and drinking. He should also try to avoid having to make important decisions (in his personal life or in business) before he has become adapted to the new schedule. Although it is desirable to get the sleep-awake cycle in tune with clock-time at the new location as soon as possible, one should make little, if any, use of sleeping pills, because they reduce the amount of REM sleep, and may thus have bad effects upon mood and efficiency.

PETER V. SIEGEL, SIEGFRIED J. GERATHEWOHL, & STANLEY R. MOHLER. Time-zone effects. *Science*, 1969, **164**, 1249–1255.

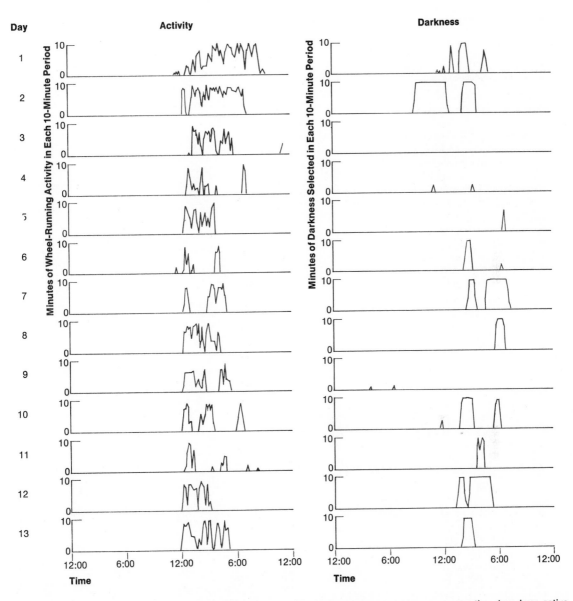

FIGURE 22.2 Circadian rhythms in a hamster. The graphs on the left show for thirteen consecutive days how active the animal was at different times of the 24-hr day. Activity was recorded whenever the animal made a running-wheel revolve. There is a remarkable rhythmicity to the hamster's behavior, with activity always starting at about midnight and stopping for the day about six hours later. This kind of cycle is found when animals are kept in continuous dark or continuous light, so it is not a simple response to conditions of illumination.

The present experiment had an extra feature. The animal also chose whether the light over his cage would be on or off. He had one lever he could push to turn on the light, and one that would turn it off. The graphs on the right side show what times of day the animal chose darkness. There is obviously some rhythm here, too. The correspondence between the time of day that the animal was active and the time that he chose darkness is consistent with the fact that hamsters are normally active at night in the wild. The fact that the animals showed *any* cycle of darkness-lightness preference is a novel finding, since hamsters don't normally have a chance to turn the sun on and off each day.

Used through courtesy of Anita Warden and Benjamin D. Sachs, University of Connecticut.

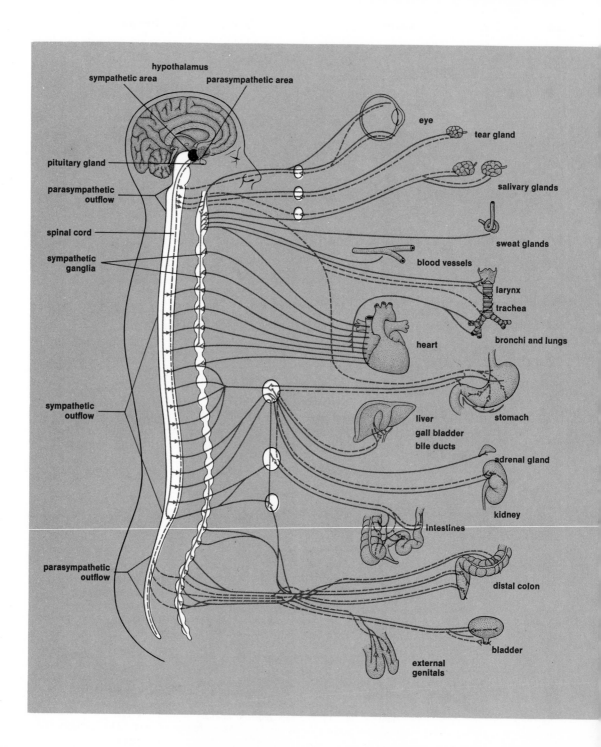

REM sleep as a desirable or necessary alternative to NREM sleep. For example, it may be that certain regions of the brain would suffer if they were maintained for long at the level and kind of stimulation characteristic of NREM sleep. The REM stage disrupts the slow-wave sleep without disturbing the sleeper.

ORGANIZATION AND PRODUCTION OF EMOTIONAL RESPONSES

To discuss the biological basis of emotion and motivation we must elaborate our earlier description of the nervous system in two ways. We must describe a special part of the nervous system, the **autonomic nervous system,** and also the way in which the nervous system interacts with the **endocrine glands.**

The Autonomic Nervous System

In Unit 3 we paid most of our attention to the **somatic nervous system,** the system that is concerned primarily with *sensory input* from the external world and with the control of the **skeletal muscles** (those attached to the skeleton and thus involved in body movement). Here we shall be concerned primarily with the autonomic nervous system. While the autonomic nervous system makes use of some external sensory input, it has, in addition, the *special input* that comes from pain and pressure receptors in the *viscera,* such as the heart and blood vessels, the stomach, and the genitals. On the motor side, the autonomic nervous system is further divided into the **sympathetic nervous system** and the **parasympathetic nervous system** (see Figure 22.3). Together they control the nonskeletal muscles of the internal organs, as well as the glands that produce and secrete various chemical products needed by the organism. Some time ago the somatic system was described as *voluntary* and the autonomic system was described as the *involuntary* part of the total system; there are many ways in which such a description is inaccurate, but it has a grain of truth, as you will see.

The sympathetic system   This system contains two chains of ganglia running along the sides

FIGURE 22.3 Here we have a semidiagrammatic representation of the hypothalamus, the spinal cord, the sympathetic nervous system, and the parasympathetic nervous system. The solid lines represent the sympathetic system, the dotted lines the parasympathetic system.

Consider first the sympathetic system. A nervous impulse originates in the lower part of the hypothalamus. From there it descends the spinal cord, and at some point about halfway down the cord (at the area labeled *sympathetic outflow*) it leaves the cord (indicated by small arrows). The neuron then enters one of the sympathetic ganglia, where it makes several connections. The nervous impulse then travels up and down the chain of ganglia, making contact with many sympathetic ganglia. When one spinal-cord neuron is thrown into action, many ganglia are thus excited. From these ganglia other neurons extend to the various viscera organs—sweat glands, blood vessels, heart, external genitals.

Now consider the parasympathetic system. There too the impulses originate in the hypothalamus, but in its upper part. From there hypothalamic impulses descend, leaving either the brain or the spinal cord at one of two levels (the two areas labeled *parasympathetic outflow*). From the ganglia outside the cord impulses are conducted to the same visceral organs supplied by the sympathetic system. Note, however, that for the most part a single fiber of the parasympathetic system serves fewer visceral organs than a single fiber of the sympathetic system does.

of the spinal cord. Each sympathetic neuron leaving the spinal cord enters several of these ganglia and makes contact with several fibers that then go on to different effector organs. The sympathetic system is thus built to facilitate a *widespread* discharge. For example, the following pattern of visceral responses might result from a sympathetic discharge: dilation of the pupil, increase in heart rate, rise in blood pressure, rerouting of the blood from the skin and stomach to the muscles of the limbs, and so on. These reactions, taken as a whole, prepare the organism for emergency action.

The parasympathetic system   Fibers of the parasympathetic system supply the same organs as those of the sympathetic system, but there are some important differences. For one thing, the parasympathetic system is constructed so that it is *more specific* in its influence upon the visceral organs than the sympathetic system: A single fiber of the parasympathetic system serves fewer organs than does a single fiber of the sympathetic system.

Second, the effects of stimulation by the two systems are usually opposite in direction. For example, stimulation of the heart by the *sympathetic system accelerates the heart; parasympathetic stimulation slows it down.* Most visceral organs are thus supplied by these two "opposing" systems. Whereas the sympathetic system readies the body for an emergency, the parasympathetic system returns the system to normal and conserves bodily resources.

Finally, the transmitter substance that flows across the neuroeffector junction between the final motor fiber and the muscle or gland cell is different in the two systems. In the parasympathetic system (as in the somatic system) the transmitter is acetylcholine; in the sympathetic system it is norepinephrine.

Despite these differences, both systems, as we will soon see, are influenced by some of the same structures in the central nervous system.

The Endocrine System

Each endocrine gland (see Figure 22.4) consists of a group of cells that produce a chemical product of importance to some or all of the cells in the body. These chemicals, called **hormones,** are discharged directly into the passing bloodstream, which carries them through the body. Some of the glands are, for the most part, under the control of the autonomic nervous system, while others form an integrated self-contained system in which the amount of the hormone produced by one gland directly controls the amount that another gland will secrete.

The pituitary gland   The pituitary gland is in fact two separate glands lying close to each other. The **posterior pituitary gland** is completely controlled by the hypothalamus. One of the hormones it produces is the **antidiuretic hormone,** which controls the rate and volume of urine production. When no antidiuretic hormone is produced, urine volume is much greater than normal. Under various emotional states, therefore, changes in hypothalamic activity may lead either to excessive urination or to very scanty urinary outflow.

The **anterior pituitary gland** produces six different hormones. Some of these affect physiological and behavioral activity indirectly, for they control the amount of hormones secreted by other endocrine glands. We will consider these hormones as we discuss the *target* glands in question. Other anterior pituitary hormones have direct effects, influencing, for example, the rate and duration of general body growth. The production of all these hormones by the anterior pituitary and their release into the bloodstream is partly under the control of the hypothalamus and the autonomic nervous system and partly under the control of other hormones.

The adrenal gland   Each adrenal gland (one on each side of the body) is also a dual gland, composed of the **adrenal cortex** and the **adrenal medulla.** Both parts of the adrenals produce hormones that influence behavior.

Adrenal cortex, adrenal steroids, and emotion The secretion of the hormones of the *adrenal cortex*—the **adrenal steroids**—is controlled by an anterior pituitary hormone known as **adrenocorticotropic hormone,** or ACTH. The pituitary, in turn, responds to the concentrations of

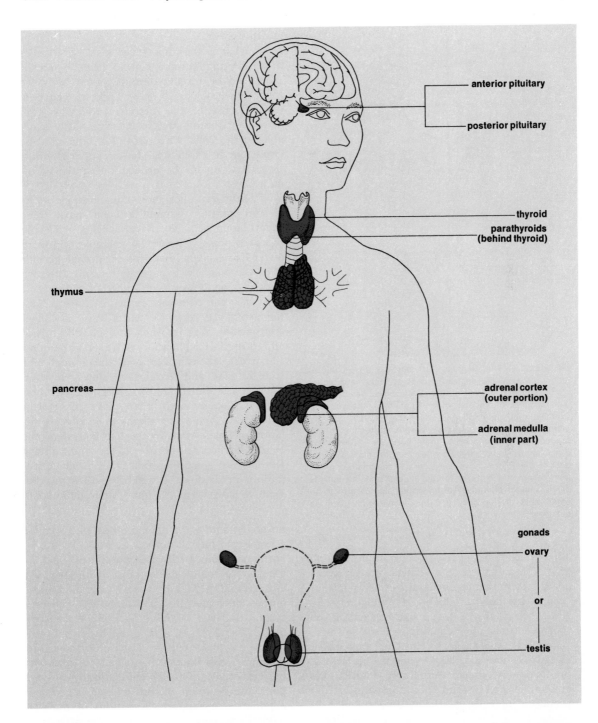

FIGURE 22.4 The location of the major endocrine glands in the body. The parathyroid glands and the pancreas control certain aspects of cell metabolism, and the thymus is involved in the reaction of the body to "foreign" substances, the so-called immune reaction.

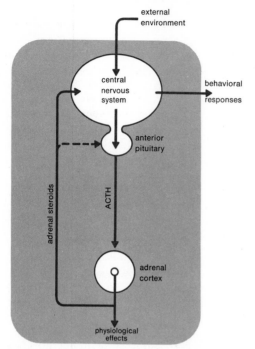

FIGURE 22.5 The diagram illustrates the reciprocal relations between the central nervous system, the pituitary gland, and the adrenal cortex. The central nervous system mediates the effects of environmental changes and exerts a regulatory influence over the anterior pituitary gland, which in turn controls the adrenal cortex through its production of adrenocorticotropic hormone (ACTH). The hormones from the adrenal cortex (adrenal steroids) feed back to the central nervous system and the pituitary gland to influence the behavior of the animal and the activity of the anterior pituitary. The hormones also go directly to other parts of the body and influence their responses to stress.

adrenal hormones in the blood in its production of ACTH, and these interactions give us a balanced system that can maintain a fairly constant level of hormone production (see Figure 22.5). Nevertheless, the system must be, and is, responsive to changing conditions. For one thing, we see here once again the effects of a biological clock, for there are daily cycles in the level of production of adrenal steroids. In addition, the amount of ACTH (and thus adrenal steroids) produced increases markedly as a function of physical or psychological stress. Anxiety, anger, and so forth have been found to increase the amount of adrenal steroids excreted. Even ad-

mission to a hospital for an experimental study has this effect.

What is the importance of these changes in ACTH and adrenal steroid level? Some of the effects of adrenal steroids on the body are general physiological ones, such as changing the response of the organism to injury and increasing the amount of energy readily available to the cells. Effects of this kind may be important in explaining the circadian rhythms that show up in the production of these hormones.

Animal studies show that hormone levels in the "pituitary-adrenal system" have some effects upon *behavior*. A rat learning to avoid shock by pressing a bar, for example, will learn faster if it is given injections of adrenal steroids after the response is partially learned. Interestingly enough, however, an injection of the same substance can help rats extinguish (see p. 368) the avoidance response when it is no longer appropriate—that is, when the shock is turned off. In the latter situation, ACTH has the opposite effect: It seems to keep the animal in a state of fear, and therefore it *slows down* extinction (Di Guisto et al., 1971). Exactly how these hormones cause changes in behavior is not known, but it is thought to involve stimulation of brain areas in the limbic system and nearby structures. When ACTH and adrenal steroids are given to people, they produce irritability or a state of well-being in some, but seem to have no effect upon other individuals.

Adrenal medulla, the epinephrines, and emotion
The adrenal medulla produces two very similar hormones, **epinephrine** and norepinephrine. We have met norepinephrine before (Unit 18, p. 433, and Unit 22, p. 542) because it acts as a transmitter substance in the sympathetic nervous system and has a similar role in parts of the brain. Therefore, we should not be surprised to discover that the effects of these hormones are in many ways similar to the effects produced by the activity of the sympathetic nervous system. The function of the adrenal medulla is apparently to support the actions of the sympathetic nervous system. Since the activity of the adrenal medulla is under the control of the sympathetic system, we obtain a cooperative

relationship between the two systems in response to an emergency situation. In a fear-provoking situation, for example, the sympathetic nerves stimulate simultaneously the visceral organs and the adrenal medulla. The organs are put into *immediate* emergency action by the neural message; the hormones, arriving more slowly, but with a longer-lasting effect, *maintain* the appropriate changes until the need for action has passed. Again we should note that the effect of these hormones is in part through direct action upon the viscera and in part through an effect upon the cells of the brain. An interacting network of the central and peripheral nervous system and the endocrine system is once again at work.

The thyroid gland The secretion of the hormone of the **thyroid gland** is also controlled by a secretion of the anterior pituitary gland—**thyrotropic hormone.** Accompanying and following emotional excitement there is an increased secretion of thyrotropic hormone, and therefore, of the thyroid hormone itself. The **thyroid hormone** tends to increase the speed of metabolism ·in all the cells of the body, raise the blood pressure, speed up the heart rate, and so on, and when the level of this hormone is excessive, it makes the person generally irritable and nervous.

Hyperthyroidism, in which there is an *excess* of the hormone, and **hypothyroidism,** in which there is *insufficient* hormone available, are relatively well-known conditions. (The prefix "hyper" indicates "in greater amount," and "hypo," abnormally low or deficient. From the Greek.) In hyperthyroidism the individual may be a bundle of energy, but this possible benefit is gained only at the cost of increased irritability and emotionality and difficulties in eating and sleeping.

Extreme hypothyroidism before or soon after birth results in a condition called **cretinism,** in which the individual is retarded in mental and physical growth. If the individual is given massive daily doses of thyroid hormone, made synthetically or extracted from the thyroid gland of cows, and if the treatment starts early enough, a normal growth pattern may be achieved.

Emotional Response

From observations of ourselves and of others, we all know that any emotional experience is accompanied by a series of bodily responses. Some of these responses are skeletal, such as running from a frightening stimulus, smiling at a loved one, screaming, and so on. Many other responses are under the control of the autonomic nervous system and the endocrine system and take place in nonskeletal muscles or glands of the body (increased heartbeat, sweating, outpouring of epinephrine, etc.). In the laboratory, as in everyday life, it is often assumed that the autonomic responses are better indicators of emotion because it is more difficult for a person to control them voluntarily if he wishes to hide his emotions (but see p. 386).

Galvanic skin response Under emotional stress the electrical properties of the skin change. If a very weak electrical current (one that cannot be felt) is passed through the skin and the resistance of the skin to the passage of the current is measured, it is found that under emotional stress the resistance drops. In other words, the skin becomes a better conductor of electricity when one is in an emotional state. The change in skin resistance is known as the **galvanic skin response,** or GSR.

The GSR results from an increase in response of the sweat glands. The sweat glands themselves are supplied exclusively by nerves from the sympathetic nervous system. It is therefore thought that the GSR is a reliable indicator of activity in the sympathetic nervous system.

Blood pressure and heart rate The heart muscle contracts rhythmically, pumping out blood into the arteries with each beat. During emotional stress one of the many effects of the activity of the sympathetic nervous system is to increase the pressure of the blood. The nerves of the sympathetic system can influence blood pressure in two ways. They can change the diameter of the arteries, and they can change the force and rate of the heartbeat. The sympathetic system can also alter the distribution of blood to various parts of the body. In addition, there are direct endocrine influences upon blood pressure, since both epinephrine and norepinephrine cause an increase in blood pressure.

Other bodily changes Many other bodily changes accompany emotion. Among them are changes in respiration, the size of the pupil, the chemical composition of various body fluids, and so on.

An important question relating to the specificity of the changes that accompany emotion is: "Does each emotion (joy, anger, hate) have a different pattern of autonomic and endocrine activity?" It seems unlikely that each type of emotional experience is accompanied by a different pattern of autonomic response, but some differences have been reported. For example, people who feel anxious or irritated, annoyed, or angry at *themselves* when put in a stressful experimental situation show evidence of an increased amount of epinephrine secretion. People who feel no emotion or feel angry at the *experimenter* or the situation seem to have an increase in norepinephrine in the blood.

Another question is: "If there are different patterns of activity in the various emotional states, can we perceive them as different from each other?" Several experiments have shown that people can, in fact, perceive some internal changes in such situations. As we have seen earlier, however (see Box 20.8, p. 492), Schachter and his associates have shown that psychological variables are of overriding importance in determining the effect of a specific emotion-producing hormone.

BOX 22.2

NOTHING IS COMPLETELY LEARNED

Many kinds of motivational and emotional behavior related to tissue needs seem to be innate, although they may take some time to mature. Thus a sucking reflex is present in the youngest babies, and all normal babies will eventually chew their food without deliberate training.

We usually consider that human *social* behavior is learned, however, and depends on the examples we see and the rewards and punishments we receive. Various studies, particularly ones done by certain ethologists (scientists who study animal behavior) have demonstrated striking exceptions to that idea.

Children who were born blind have been reported to smile, laugh, and cry and show facial expressions of anger, fear, and pouting the same as normal, sighted children. Yet the blind children could not have imitated anyone. The possibility that such a child could learn to smile by touching its mother's face is ruled out by the striking case reported by Irenäus Eibl-Eibesfeldt of the Max Planck Institute for Behavioral Physiology in Germany. The child in this case was born blind and deaf and also without arms, but yet showed the normal basic facial expressions.

In normal babies the originally spontaneous smile becomes more and more dependent upon specific stimuli as the child grows older, but the basic response is innate.

IRENÄUS EIBL-EIBESFELDT. *Ethology: The Biology of Behavior.* New York: Holt, Rinehart and Winston, 1970.

PHYSIOLOGICAL THEORIES OF EMOTION

An emotion is triggered by certain stimuli acting upon a "prepared organism." Whether any given stimulus pattern will produce an emotion depends upon the present state of the organism and its genetic and personal history (see Box 22.2). The emotion itself has two components— a characteristic state of awareness (the emotional feeling of experience) and a pattern of bodily reactions. Physiological theories of emo-

tion have tried to identify the structures and processes in the body that underlie these components.

The James-Lange Theory

Early attempts to describe the physiology of emotion were made in similar theories independently presented by William James, an eminent American psychologist, and Carl Lange, a Danish physiologist, during the 1880s; because of the similarities, their work is usually referred to as the **James-Lange theory.** Their doctrine is opposed to the "obvious" view that, when we perceive an emotion-provoking stimulus, we first *feel the emotion* and only *later* do we react bodily. The differences are well expressed by James (1890) in words which we cannot improve upon:

> Common-sense says, we lose our fortune, are sorry and weep; we meet a bear, are frightened and run; we are insulted by a rival, are angry and strike. . . . My theory . . . is that the bodily changes follow directly the perception of the existing fact, and that our feeling of the same changes as they occur *is* the emotion . . . that we feel sorry because we cry, angry because we strike, afraid because we tremble, and not that we cry, or tremble, because we are sorry, angry, or fearful, as the case may be.

The James-Lange theory thus asserts that when an emotion-provoking stimulus is presented, we first react with the muscular and glandular responses typical of emotion and appropriate to the situation. It is only when the feedback from these responses arrives at the cortex (when we realize we are running, or sweating, or blushing) that we feel or experience the emotion.

Other Theories

Alternative theories have generally held the opposite, "commonsense" view that the emotional responses follow the emotional experience, or they have proposed that the responses and the experience are produced simultaneously. More important for our purposes, these other theories have pointed to portions of the brain other than, or in addition to, the cerebral cortex as especially important in emotional experience and in the production of emotional responses.

One theory has proposed that the hypothalamus is a crucial structure in emotion. Sensory information from an emotion-provoking stimulus presumably reaches the hypothalamus. From there, the impulses are thought to follow two major pathways. One is to the cortex where the emotional *experience* is elaborated; the other is to the muscles and glands of the body where the emotional *responses* take place. Another theory emphasizes the role of the reticular formation. We have seen already that

activity in this structure plays a part in the production of arousal, a necessary condition for active emotions. The *activation theory of emotion* proposes that the reticular formation, in conjunction with the hypothalamus, controls both the cortical areas important for emotional experience and the system responsible for emotional responses.

The final view that we will consider is based upon some speculations presented by the neuroanatomist Papez in 1937. He pointed to the existence of a ring of interconnecting forebrain structures surrounding the brain stem (see Figure 22.6, page 548). These structures are among the oldest in the mammalian brain and are known collectively as the *limbic system.* Papez accepted the hypothalamus as a center for the integration of the bodily expression of emotion, but he argued for the limbic system as the site for emotional experience. He described a path that impulses might take from the hypothalamus to a cortical portion of the limbic system, where he proposed that emotional experience would arise. MacLean has revised this theory, proposing special roles in emotional and motivational behavior for certain limbic structures (see p. 549). Although the importance of the limbic system in emotion is now unquestioned, as we shall soon see, the details of its functioning are still far from clear.

STRUCTURAL MECHANISMS IN EMOTION

The theories we have reviewed propose that certain systems or regions in the brain are especially important for emotional experience and the production of emotional response. Hundreds of experiments have been done to test these hypotheses. Let us see if any general conclusions are possible.

The Hypothalamus

This part of the forebrain is made up of many different nuclei, some of which have been conclusively shown to be important to different kinds of emotional and motivational behavior. The posterior part of the hypothalamus, for

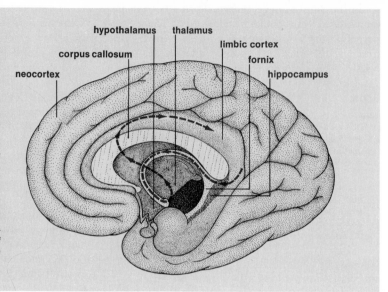

FIGURE 22.6 This figure identifies the principal limbic structures and the pathways proposed by Papez as important in emotion. The ring of limbic cortex and related subcortical structures are shown. The dotted line indicates the path through the limbic system, proposed by Papez, for impulses giving rise to emotional experience. It begins in the limbic cortex toward the back of the brain, passes through the chain of subcortical limbic structures, follows major neural tracts from the hypothalamus to the thalamus and from there to the limbic cortex, where, he believes, emotion is experienced. Impulses can enter this path in two ways to give rise to emotional experience—either from other regions of the cortex or from other areas in the hypothalamus.

example, is critical for the production of an integrated pattern of *rage* in an experimental animal such as a cat. If this region is destroyed, the animal may show bits and pieces of the responses usually found as part of a rage reaction, but it does not show a fully coordinated pattern of activity. If the hypothalamus is *not* destroyed, no matter how much of the brain in front of it is removed, the animal can show a fully organized rage pattern.

Electrical stimulation of various parts of the hypothalamus provokes various emotional responses. In addition to the rage response, another aggressive reponse called *stalking attack* can be elicited in cats. In this pattern of behavior the animal paces its cage until it finds an appropriate victim and only then does it attack. Fear responses have also been reported; in some cases the animal appears to exhibit *alarm*, in other cases actual *flight* occurs. (See also Box 22.3.)

These patterns of behavior can be obtained *even if the animal has been deprived of all of the brain above the hypothalamus*. In such a case, however, the animal cannot see or hear, thus he may not be able to direct his attack or his fear *appropriately*. In this sense one can say that regions necessary for perception, such as the thalamus and the cortex, play a part in emotional behavior. (The emotional response to the word "fire" depends, in the first instance, upon your ability to see or to hear the word, and second, on your knowledge of what the word stands for.) But of course most "nonemotional" behavior depends in the same way upon the guiding role of the thalamus and cortex. The search for areas above the hypothalamus that have some *special role in emotional behavior* has caused many scientists to explore the limbic system described by Papez; the anatomical thicket is so dense there and the functional relations so hard to disentangle that many of the explorers have never been seen again!

The Limbic System

Although we may have overstated the difficulties a little, it is true that the role of the limbic system in emotion is not yet clear. There is no doubt whatever that various limbic structures are involved, but how each acts and how they interact is quite open to question.

As examples of the experiments that have been done, let us note that lesions in one part of the limbic system decrease rats' ability to learn to avoid shock (presumably because of a reduction in fear), while lesions in a different part of the system increase their ability; lesions of a certain limbic structure make rat mothers very inefficient in the care of their young, while similar lesions in mice have no such effect;

lesions of yet another limbic structure make a wild monkey tame, while similar lesions in cats have been reported to make them ferocious!

Theories have been proposed in attempts to bring order out of these findings. MacLean has suggested that one-half of the limbic sys-

BOX 22.3

"REWARDING" BRAIN CENTERS

The crucial role of brain activity in emotion and motivation is dramatically illustrated by the self-stimulation experiment pioneered by J. Olds and P. Milner at McGill University in 1954.

In this experiment electrodes are permanently implanted into various parts of the brains of experimental animals. The accompanying figure is an X-ray photograph showing electrodes in place in an intact rat. During experimental sessions the electrodes are connected to wires going to a lever and to an electrical current source, so that when the lever is depressed a brief, weak electrical pulse is delivered to the brain. Rats placed in a box with an activated lever available to them quickly learn to press it and thus receive the brain stimulation. If the experimenter turns off the current at its source, they soon stop pressing the lever.

The results of some of the extensive research on self-stimulation by Olds and his associates show what a powerful and important effect it is. Rats will press an activated lever at rates as high as five thousand times per hour. They will press for 15 to 20 hr until they drop exhausted, sleep, and then return to press again. Animals will cross an electrically charged grid to reach their "brain lever" and in do-

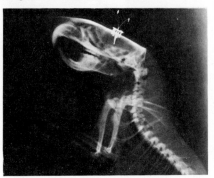

ing so will withstand stronger foot shock than they will to obtain food when allowed to go hungry for 24 hr. It has also been reported that they will learn to run through a complex maze to reach an activated lever.

By trying all the different parts of the brain it has been possible to map those regions where stimulation produces such effects. Some points are found in almost all parts of the brain, but the limbic system and the hypothalamus are especially important.

Some points in the brain have quite a different effect when stimulated. These are points that are "negative"—animals will press a lever to *turn off* stimulation that is given at these places.

Reports on the use of the stimulation technique with human patients give us a hint about the nature of the positive effects. C. W. Sem-Jacobsen and A. Torkildsen of Gausted Mental Hospital, Oslo, report that patients seem to like the brain stimulation, they appear pleased and smile when stimulated, and they will press a lever for self-stimulation just as the rats do. Their descriptions of their feelings during stimulation give the impression of a "good feeling" but not always one that can be identified with any particular rewards or experiences.

Various interpretations have been placed upon the exact nature of the brain systems just described. The most common proposal is that these systems have at least some neurons in common with systems activated when a normal reward or punishment is encountered.

J. OLDS & P. MILNER. Positive reinforcement produced by electrical stimulation of septal area and other regions of rat brain. *Journal of Comparative and Physiological Psychology,* 1954, **47**, 419–427.
J. OLDS. Differential effects of drives and drugs on self-stimulation at different brain sites. In D. E. Sheer (Ed.), *Electrical Stimulation of the Brain.* Austin: University of Texas Press, 1961.
C. W. SEM-JACOBSEN & A. TORKILDSEN. Depth recording and electrical stimulation in the human brain. In E. R. Ramey & D. S. O'Doherty (Fds.), *Electrical Studies on the Unanesthetized Brain.* New York: Hoeber, 1960.
Photo courtesy J. Olds, now at California Institute of Technology; reprinted by permission of *Scientific American.*

tem is mostly concerned with feelings and behavior related to self-preservation—to "the selfish demands of feeding, fighting, and self-protection." (MacLean, 1970). The other half, according to his hypothesis, is involved in feeling and behavior that have to do with preservation of the species—to sociability, sexuality, and parental concerns.

Another look at the experimental findings led to the suggestion that the structures included in the first part of the limbic system according to MacLean can be divided further into two subregions (McCleary, 1966). One of these would *facilitate* motor responses in an emotional situation: A lesion here would therefore make an animal less able than normal if it had to do something (e.g., jump a hurdle) to avoid a painful electric shock. The other subregion would tend to *prevent* motor activity; a lesion here would therefore make an animal less able to remain still when an active motor response produces shock.

These experiments and theories have provided some general ideas about how the limbic system functions, but it is fair to say that no tidy scheme has met with the approval of scientists for any length of time (but see Box 22.4). Perhaps the best we can do now is to accept an admittedly vague idea presented by Pribram (1960) and Thomas, Hostetter, and Barker (1968). These authors remind us of the variety of **behavioral dispositions** that characterize different species—tendencies to respond in given ways to certain patterns of stimuli. Thomas et al. mention that rats have a tendency to explore their surroundings, people have a set of dispositions to learn to speak, and so on. These dispositions have innate aspects and some of the characteristics of reflexes. But in humans at least, these tendencies also have emotional and motivational aspects. The hypothesis is that the limbic system contains the neuronal network for behavioral dispositions. One virtue of this idea is that it reminds us that species are different, and understandably so. Since the behavioral dispositions of each species will depend upon its evolutionary history, we should not be surprised to find that some similar brain structures in different kinds of animals seem to have different functions.

BOX 22.4

MORE BRAVE NEW WORLDS?

Behavior is controlled by the nervous system. Abnormal behavior must indicate that the brain is abnormal. If we can *change* the abnormal brain in some fashion we might be able to remove its abnormality and thus remove the abnormality in behavior as well. This is the chain of logic used by certain neurosurgeons who perform *psychosurgery* on people with a history of violent behavior.

Drs. William Sweet and Vernon Mark of Harvard are among those who are active in this field. Some of their violent patients have been diagnosed as having an abnormal brain on the basis of neurological examinations, special medical tests (X-ray and other tests), and perhaps a history of epileptic attacks. Often the abnormality seems to be centered in the amygdala (or amygdaloid nucleus), which is a part of the limbic system in the temporal lobe. Since there is abundant evidence that the limbic system has *some* special role in the control of emotion, these physicians and their associates think it reasonable that the violent behavior shown by these patients might be cured by destroying the brain regions that appear abnormal in tests. They offer many striking case reports:

A

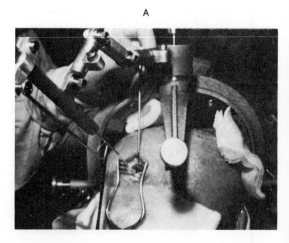

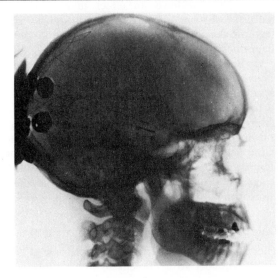

B

Thomas's chief problem was his violent rage. . . . When he was driving . . . and another car cut in front of him . . . [he] would speed . . . until he caught up to the other driver. . . . If the other driver were a man, Thomas would then hit him; if it were a woman he would insult her. . . . He would sometimes pick his wife up and throw her against the wall. . . . He did the same thing to his children. . . . Thomas was referred to our hospital by his psychiatrist who had observed the patient as he was having a . . . seizure. A brain wave examination disclosed epileptic electrical activity in both temporal regions . . . we suggested to him that we make a destructive lesion in the medial portion of both his amygdalas. . . . [Figure A shows an electrode inserted into the region of the brain target. Figure B is an X-ray film showing electrodes in the amygdala of such a patient.] Four years have passed since the operation, during which time Thomas has not had a single episode of rage.

Another patient, Julia, had a history of brain disease from before the age of two, when she had a severe attack of encephalitis. At a later age she developed epileptic seizures.

Her behavior between seizures was marked by severe temper tantrums followed by extreme remorse . . . [including four] serious suicide attempts. . . . On twelve occasions, Julia had seriously assaulted other people without any apparent provocation.

In their examination of Julia, Drs. Sweet and Mark were able to make use of a "stimoceiver" developed by Dr. José M. R. Delgado of Yale. This device makes it possible to record from a region of the brain or, if desired, to stimulate the same area, using short-range radio; thus no wires had to be attached.

Before we had done any stimulating . . . the electrical activity in Julia's amygdaloid nucleus showed a typical epileptic seizure pattern. . . . The . . . stimulation sequence began while Julia was playing a guitar. . . . After 5 seconds of stimulation, Julia stopped singing and stared blankly ahead. During the next sequence she slipped out of communication and was unable to answer the questions posed by the psychiatrist who was examining her. . . . The posterior amygdala exhibited a constant abnormal electrical discharge characteristic of seizure. This was followed by a sudden and powerful swing of her guitar. She narrowly missed the head of the psychiatrist, and instead the guitar smashed against the wall. . . .

A short time after these sequences were recorded, we made a destructive lesion in Julia's right amygdala. It is still too early to assess the results of the procedure, but she had only two mild rage episodes in the first postoperative year and none in the second.

Of course, not all people with encephalitis develop epilepsy, and the presence of epilepsy by no means implies necessarily that the person will show abnormal violent behavior. In these cases, however, there was evidence of abnormality in a region of the brain that is in some way involved in the control of emotional behavior. Furthermore these patients showed clear evidence of abnormal violent acts according to the case reports. The neurosurgeon's attempt to treat the patient by destruction of the abnormal region, even though no one understands fully the brain mechanisms involved in violent behavior *either in normal or abnormal brains,* is understandable. This is different from the proposal of "pure" psychosurgery, where no physical evidence of brain disease is available and the *only* symptom to justify an operation is "abnormal" *behavior* (see Box 25.7, p. 638).

VERNON H. MARK & FRANK R. ERVIN. *Violence and the Brain.* New York: Harper & Row, 1970.

Photos from *Violence and the Brain,* by Vernon H. Mark and Frank R. Ervin; copyright © 1970 by Harper & Row, Publishers, Inc.; by permission of the publishers.

PSYCHOTIC DEPRESSION

All people have "mood swings," changes from feeling "on top of the world" to feeling "down in the dumps" and back again. The state of depression may be related to some external event or it may arise spontaneously. In any event, mild depression is to be expected by all of us, and with mild depressions, one can be sure things will get better without any medical help.

A true psychotic depression is another matter (see Unit 24). Here we have a deep, unjustified sadness, accompanied by a withdrawal from life's activity and by physiological changes such as insomnia, loss of appetite, and a reduction in the sex drive. Periods of depression may alternate with periods of normality or they may alternate with manic phases.

Within the last twenty years remarkable progress has been made in the treatment of depression by pharmacological agents (drugs). The efficacy of some of these drugs was discovered by psychiatrists before the mechanism of their action was understood, but then basic research into their effect on the organism led to the production of still more effective drugs. This kind of mutual facilitation of basic research and clinical observation is a common pattern in the growth of medical science.

Antidepressant Drugs

Two major classes of **antidepressant drugs** are now in use. Both effect changes in mood by influencing synaptic transmission; however, to understand their effects we have to describe in greater detail the synaptic mechanisms outlined in Unit 3 and mentioned again in Unit 18.

From those earlier accounts we know that a transmitter substance is produced in the axon and stored in the axon terminal; an impulse passing along the axon may release transmitter, which diffuses across the synaptic space and stimulates the next neuron. The production, storage, and liberation of transmitters is not a single unidirectional process, however. Some of the transmitter substance produced in an axon is destroyed in that same axon by an enzyme called **monoamine oxidase** (MAO). Second, even after a quantity of transmitter is released into

the synaptic junction, the neuron that produced it continues to have an effect upon it; the neuron reabsorbs some of the transmitter it has previously released. These events are diagramed in Figure 22.7.

Both kinds of antidepressant drugs are thought to act at synapses where norepinephrine is the transmitter. The two drugs produce a net increase in the amount of norepinephrine available to stimulate the next neuron, but they do this in different ways. **MAO inhibitors,** as the name implies, *prevent MAO from destroying norepinephrine* within the axon. The **tricyclic drugs,** on the other, *block reabsorption of the transmitter* by the axon that released it.

Catecholamine Hypothesis of Depression

The effects of the antidepressant drugs offer strong support to a current hypothesis of the physiological basis of depression. This hypothesis states that *depression* is in part determined by a *deficiency of norepinephrine and related chemicals* (all of which come under the general name of *catecholamines*) at important sites in the brain. Either the MAO inhibitors or the tricyclic drugs would counteract depression by increasing the amount of norepinephrine present. Additional evidence for this **catecholamine theory of depression** (Schildkraut & Kety, 1967) comes from the fact that one of the physiological effects of electroconvulsive shock, which is also effective in treating depressed patients, is to increase the amount of norepinephrine synthesized in the brain.

The hypothesis of norepinephrine deficiency can be made more detailed by remembering that there are systems of neurons in the brain in which this substance is found in especially high concentrations, presumably because it is used as a transmitter. These systems lead from the reticular formation into the hypothalamus and the limbic system, where it is easy to imagine a mechanism of control of emotional experience and behavior.

MANIC STATES

Some people who suffer from depression also suffer from manic attacks at the other end of

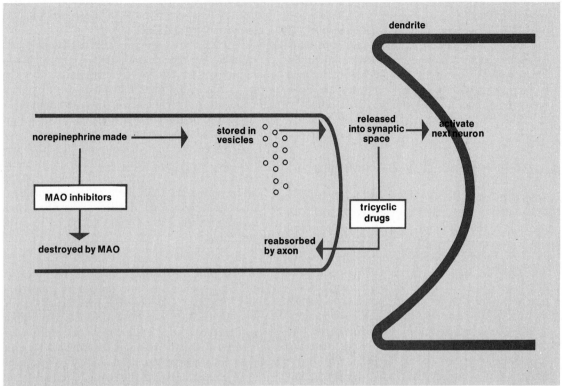

FIGURE 22.7 This figure shows some of the chemical processes that determine whether a given transmitter substance produced in an axon terminal will eventually come to act upon the next neuron. Norepinephrine, for example, can be destroyed before it leaves the terminal, or it can be reabsorbed by the axon later. Each of the drugs shown in a little box inhibits one or the other of those processes, and thus makes more transmitter available. It is believed that this explains their helpful effect upon states of depression.

their mood swings. These periods of heightened bodily activity with voluble speech and feelings of elation are obviously not as upsetting to the patient as the depressed state, but they dispose him to such relatively uncontrolled activity that he may be dangerous to himself and others. For over thirty years, chemicals containing **lithium** have been used to prevent or terminate such episodes, and use of the drug has increased now that scientists have some idea how it may work.

Catecholamine Hypothesis of Mania

The evidence on the physiological effects of lithium is not as clear as it is in the case of the antidepressant drugs. However, one hypothesis is that the manic state is related to an *excess* of norepinephrine and that the effects of lithium are opposite to those of the antidepressants. According to this view, lithium either prevents the axon terminal from releasing norepinephrine in the synapse or it increases the terminal's rate of reabsorption of released norepinephrine. Another theory proposes that lithium increases the amount of available serotonin in systems of neurons where serotonin is the transmitter (Knapp & Mandell, 1973).

The chemical treatment of emotional disorders, like the surgical treatment, is not without problems and controversy. The wide use of amphetamines (which normally have a stimulating effect in adults) to calm so-called *hyper-active children* may be considered a hasty and possibily dangerous response on the part of society to a problem that might be more truly solved by changes in the early environment. In the case of psychotic patients who seem doomed to months or years of misery and despair, however, most people are willing to accept the apparent benefits of chemical treatment.

THE PHYSIOLOGY OF MOTIVES

When we turn to the study of the biological bases of individual motives, we find that, as in the case of the emotions, we want to understand the biological states that trigger the motive, as well as the mechanisms in the body that are involved in the associated *feelings* and the proper *responses*. In the case of motives (as opposed to emotions), the responses are rather obvious since we eat when we are hungry, drink when we are thirsty, and so on; on the other hand, the precise events that produce the experience are not at all obvious. We know when we are hungry, but what is the actual signal that gives rise to the feeling? We will therefore be seeking answers to two questions: What stimulus signals "turn on" (and turn off) the motive, and what neural mechanisms are responsible for receiving those signals, producing the sensations and the responses?

The Hunger Motive

Hunger typically arises after a period of deprivation from food, so it seems reasonable to look at the bodily changes produced by food deprivation for a clue concerning the stimulus for hunger. One effect of prolonged food deprivation is a reduction in the concentration of sugar in the blood. Since blood sugar (glucose) is an essential source of energy for the cells of the body, it has been suggested that a decrease in blood glucose serves as an internal stimulus for hunger. Injections of *insulin* produce a drop in the glucose level, followed by an increase in food intake. Daily injections of insulin can cause an increase in eating sufficient to make an experimental animal become obese. According to

the **glucostatic theory of food intake** based on such findings, an animal eats to maintain its glucose at an optimal level.

There are several alternative theories, however. The **thermostatic theory of food intake** maintains that one eats to keep warm. This theory points to the facts that changes in external temperature can cause changes in the amount of food consumed and the actual digestion of food produces heat within the body.

There are many additional findings that could be mentioned in support of these theories, but unfortunately there are also observations and experiments that serve to make scientists doubt that any one of them tells the whole story about the stimuli that control hunger and food intake.

Hunger and the brain As far as the question of brain mechanisms and hunger is concerned, there is ample evidence that two regions of the hypothalamus shown in Figure 22.8 play important and somewhat opposing roles. Activity in the **lateral area of the hypothalamus** is thought to be involved in the production of eating, because if this area is stimulated electrically, an animal will begin to eat "hungrily" even though it had just finished consuming all that it seemed to want. Activity in the **ventromedial nucleus** of the hypothalamus is thought to produce satiety (the feeling of having had enough), for stimulation here will make an animal that had previously been deprived turn away from food given to him. Lesions of these areas have opposite effects. Lateral lesions cause animals to stop eating, and they will starve to death unless given food by force or intravenously. Ventromedial lesions cause animals to eat and become extremely obese; humans with tumors that involve this part of the brain show the same effect.

The evidence for hypothalamic control of food intake is particularly compelling in light of experiments that suggest that the hypothalamus has specific receptors for the signals that are thought to turn the hunger motive on or off. Thus there are neurons in the hypothalamus that are sensitive to the level of glucose in the blood; the hypothalamus is also sensitive to temperature changes—local heating of the

FIGURE 22.8 The hypothalamus consists of a collection of nuclei (the white areas) at the base of the brain. The nuclei discussed in the text are labeled *lateral* and *ventromedial*.

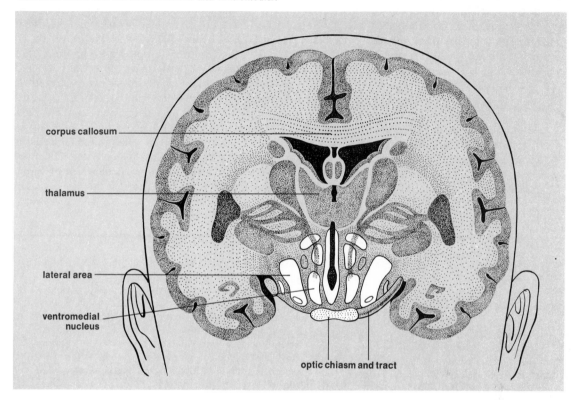

hypothalamus will inhibit eating, whereas cooling will increase the amount of food intake. The neuronal systems involved in food intake appear to be among those using norepinephrine as a transmitter; injections of norepinephrine, but not of other transmitters, into the lateral hypothalamus produce eating in satiated rats.

However, it is only by ignoring obvious facts of everyday existence that one could propose that the kinds of mechanisms just discussed are sufficient to explain fully the physiological and anatomical bases of hunger. We all know the effect of external stimuli (such as the sight or smell of food, or the observation of others eating) and of habit (such as the custom of eating at a given time of day) upon hunger and eating in humans and other animals. These facts imply, of course, that parts of the brain that receive and interpret signals about the presence of food, or that are involved in the habits and daily rhythms of food intake, are also important.

That the small region in the lateral hypothalamus is not the only possible feeding center is shown by other experiments. If rats with lateral hypothalamic lesions are kept alive by force-feeding, they will eventually recover their willingness to eat. If an animal that has recovered from this operation is later deprived of a functional cerebral cortex, however, he goes back to the same aphagic (noneating) pattern of behavior (Teitelbaum, 1971). These experiments plus the facts in the preceding discussion all lead to the conclusion that hunger and food intake are subject to many influences from the body and the external world. The hypothalamus plays an important part in eating, but higher structures, in the cortex and limbic system, are also involved in the process (see Box 22.5).

The Thirst Motive

If you ask the "man on the street" how he controls his water drinking, he might tell you that he drinks when his mouth is dry. Such a theory was suggested long ago by the physiologist Cannon. He proposed that when the body needs

water, an adequate flow of saliva is not available, so that a dry mouth results and serves as a stimulus for thirst.

This theory has not stood up well to careful tests. For example, people who are born without salivary glands, and therefore always have a dry mouth, do not drink any more than other people. Furthermore, injections of pilocarpine, a drug that causes an increase in saliva flow, fail to lessen the desire for water.

The conditions in the body that do seem able to produce thirst are *cellular dehydration* (a loss of water from the individual cells of the body) and a *reduction of total blood volume*. Both occur when one is deprived of water. There are sensory receptors in the blood vessels

---

BOX 22.5

NOTHING IS COMPLETELY INNATE

After a rat receives lesions in the lateral hypothalamic area, it not only stops eating, it also stops drinking. However, as mentioned in the text, if such an animal is kept alive, it tends to recover and eventually will eat and drink. Many studies by Philip Teitelbaum and his associates at the University of Pennsylvania have shown that there are definite stages in the recovery process of the *lateral hypothalamic* animals (the operated animals). For example, the first stage of recovery is one in which they will eat only wet, highly preferred foods. At a later stage they will eat normal rat food, but will still not drink, and so on. The fact that the animals do recover is evidence that parts of the brain other than those operated on can control food intake.

Recent experiments in the same laboratory have demonstrated a perfect correlation between the stages of recovery and the stages of eating and drinking that occur in *normal* development of the young rat. Normal rat pups are able to eat and drink in an adult fashion at weaning age. But this ability is the culmination of about twenty-one days (the weaning age) of development. If their development is delayed by deliberate underfeeding during infancy or by surgical destruction of the thyroid gland at birth (and thus delaying growth, etc.), then when they are

weaned, they go through exactly the same stages as the lateral hypothalamic animals.

The individual reflexes of sucking, swallowing, and so on are seen in very young rats and in human and rat infants that do not have a functioning hypothalamus, but these reflexes do not become integrated into total feeding responses unless and until the higher parts of the nervous system develop. Higher structures in the limbic system and the cortex organize the pattern of development of the hypothalamic regions and the responses that they control, and continue to exert a guiding influence over the feeding behavior of the adult. Teitelbaum concludes that "hypothalamic 'centers', if they exist, function normally only as part of complex . . . systems, involving higher parts of the brain in their normal action."

The influence of these higher brain areas can be seen more easily in an animal that has a more highly developed brain than a rat. Teitelbaum reminds us of Harlow's finding that an infant monkey reared in isolation will sometimes stop eating, and may even starve to death, if suddenly introduced into a typical monkey colony. It is known that the early nutritional experience of people will influence their later patterns of hunger and food intake. Normal social experience in infancy may also be necessary for normal development of the feeding system.

PHILIP TEITELBAUM. The encephalization of hunger. In E. Stellar & J. M. Sprague (Eds.), *Progress in Physiological Psychology*, Vol. 4. New York: Academic Press, 1971.

that measure the total blood volume and send appropriate messages (neuronal and chemical) to structures in the brain that control thirst and drinking. These structures are probably in the hypothalamus because other evidence indicates that, as with hunger, an important part of the thirst-control mechanism is located in that tiny region of the brain. *Osmoreceptors* (specialized cells sensitive to dehydration) are found in this hypothalamic area, and lesions here produce changes in amount of water taken in. Although cells concerned with drinking appear to be intermingled with ones concerned with eating, they are not exactly the same ones. If we inject into the lateral hypothalamus an acetylcholinelike substance, we produce drinking, whereas injection of norepinephrine causes eating; these findings suggest that the two systems use different transmitter substances to carry their interneuronal messages.

Once again we are focusing on only a small part (albeit an important part) of a complex set of control systems. In truth, an animal does not usually wait to drink until it is thirsty. Whereas all the mechanims described previously are available to "turn on" the drinking mechanisms when necessary, normal rats, for example, actually adopt a circadian rhythm of drinking and *anticipate* their future water needs by drinking the necessary amounts when they eat (Fitzsimons, 1971).

The Sex Motive

In considering the sexual motive in the normally developed adult human we must recognize that external stimuli—visual, auditory, and olfactory—play a major role in the onset of the motive. It still depends upon the time, the place, and the right boy (or girl). Learning is crucial in determining the importance of these stimuli.

In addition to the influence of learned stimuli on the onset of the sex motive, there are other stimuli that control built-in responses and are little influenced by learning. Tactual stimuli (touching, rubbing, stroking) elicit such responses from both primary and secondary sex areas.

Physiological responses If visual, auditory, olfactory, and tactual stimuli initiate sexual desire, what physiological processes do they initiate? The major mechanisms are autonomic. A study of human sexual responses (Masters & Johnson, 1966) has detailed these responses. Initially we find a widespread congestion of the blood vessels (vasocongestion), which affects the genitalia and the secondary sex areas (e.g., the breasts), and which may appear on the skin surface as a flush. In addition, we find an increase in heart rate and blood pressure. As the sex urge increases in intensity, there is massive autonomic involvement, including widespread and deep vasocongestion, deeper breathing, heart-rate increases from normal values of about 72 to as high as 180 beats a minute, marked elevation of blood pressure, a well-developed and widespread generalized body flush, and extensive bodily perspiration unrelated to physical activity. Masters and Johnson emphasize a point about which there has not always been agreement. They say: "The parallels in reaction to effective sexual stimulation emphasize the physiologic similarities in male and female responses rather than the differences. Aside from obvious anatomic variants, men and women are homogeneous in their physiologic responses to sexual stimuli."

The responses involved in copulation include skeletal and autonomic activity, and much of the behavior is partially under the control of the lowest parts of the sympathetic and parasympathetic systems. Some men who have had their spinal cords cut *above* the level that controls the sexual responses can still have erections and, in some cases, ejaculations, because stimulation of the skin in the genital region produces these responses by reflex activity at the low-spinal level.

Sex and hormones Sexual behavior is partly under the control of hormones produced by the **gonads** (the **testes** in the male and the **ovaries** in the female). The gonads also have the essential function of producing the germ cells (spermatazoa in the male and ova, or eggs, in the female).

The production of the sex hormones by the gonads is regulated by **gonadotropic hormones** from the anterior pituitary gland. The testes produce several hormones, among them

testosterone, the male sex hormone. It should be noted that the normal testes also produce **estrogen,** a female sex hormone. The ovaries produce two hormones: estrogen and **progesterone.** Estrogen has functions in the female similar to those of testosterone in the male.

The production of testosterone seems to follow a circadian rhythm. Several studies of plasma testosterone (the level of testosterone in blood samples) show daily high points at about 8:00 in the morning and 1:00 in the afternoon and a low point at 1:00 A.M. (see Figure 22.9). Whether and how this rhythm is related to sexual behavior are unknown.

In normally maturing individuals testosterone in the male and estrogen in the female are also responsible for the growth of the sex organs and the development of **secondary sex characteristics,** such as the pattern of body hair, skeletal proportions of the body, and the thickness and texture of the skin.

An interaction between sex hormones and experience in initiating sexual behavior has been shown in the cat (Rosenblatt & Aronson, 1958). Adult male cats castrated before puberty show no sexual responses to receptive females. Androgen treatment induces sexual responsiveness, and animals given androgen and sex experience continue to show sexual behavior even after the withdrawal of the sex hormones. Treatment with sex hormones without accompanying sex experience produces an animal that shows no sexual responses upon removal of the hormones.

Hormones are critical for the *development* of both sexual structures and normal sexual behavior. In humans, once this development takes place, sex hormones play a relatively unimportant role. The loss of sex hormones by the female after menopause need not interfere with the sex urge. In adult men, removal of the testes may cause marked reduction in sex drive, but very frequently no change is experienced in sexual behavior for as long as twenty years after the operation. It appears that in some men testicular hormone is not necessary for normal sexual activity.

Sex and the brain Sex hormones play a critical role in the development of the *neural* basis of

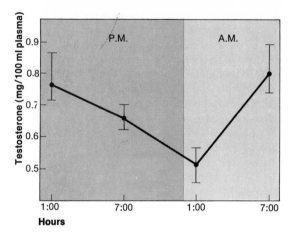

FIGURE 22.9 Circadian rhythm in blood testosterone in man. The concentration given is the average for five healthy men, age twenty to forty-two years, whose blood was sampled at the four different times of day and night indicated. The concentration was almost twice as high during the day (7:00 A.M. and 1:00 P.M.) as at 1:00 A.M.

Adapted from R. T. W. L. Conroy & J. N. Mills. *Human Circadian Rhythms.* London: J. & R. Churchill, 1970.

sexual behavior. In the very early life of the animal (before birth in the monkey and guinea pig and within the first ten days after birth in the rat), the administration of male sex hormones produces male characteristics. Normally these androgens are supplied by the testes of the male fetus. But, for example, if a monkey pregnant with a *female* fetus is injected with male hormones, the fetus will develop a penis and scrotum. In addition, these females show male patterns of play and social behavior as they grow older (Young et al., 1964).

Some theorists hold that initially both sexes are basically female in terms of the nervous system; that is, the nervous system is organized to produce a pattern of female sexual behavior. These scientists point to the fact that only in the presence of male sex hormones do the male structures and potential for male sex patterns develop. Furthermore, once developed, these patterns cannot be completely reversed by a subsequent change in hormonal balance.

Under certain circumstances results consistent with this interpretation occur in the human being. If a woman pregnant with a female child is given extensive treatment with testosterone, the child may develop external male genitalia. A male fetus that fails to produce testosterone will not develop normal male organs.

However, there is reason to believe that, in fact, *separate* neuronal systems exist in every infant animal for *both* male and female types of behavior (Goy, 1970). Adult animals that have had a normal infancy can still be induced to show some sexual behavior "appropriate" to the opposite sex when the hormones of that sex are injected. Most studies of human homosexuals find that they are not different in endocrine activity from other members of their sex; here, presumably, social factors have brought forth certain kinds of behavior more typically found in the other sex. The female monkeys just described who developed male patterns of play behavior after receiving a male hormone before birth nevertheless maintained some aspects of female behavior patterns on into adulthood. The "endocrine environment" in infancy is important, but these studies and others show that the original sex of the animal, its early experience, the sex role that it learns from its social environment, and its adult endocrine pattern all help determine how much of each kind of behavior (male or female) will be shown.

The hypothalamus   Our knowledge of the hypothalamus and its broad control of autonomic responses should lead us to expect it to be important in the sex motive, and we find that it is. Electrical stimulation of part of the lateral hypothalamus can induce the complete sex pattern, including ejaculation, in the male rat (Vaughn & Fisher, 1962). Injection of male hormone into another hypothalamic nucleus can produce male sex responses in both male *and* female rats. In human patients electrical stimulation through electrodes in the hypothalamus or nearby structures has produced feelings of

sexual pleasure and even ejaculation (Sem-Jacobsen, 1968). In addition, electrical stimulation of several other subcortical areas important in emotion and pleasure has yielded sex responses in monkeys.

Sexual motivation, perhaps more than any other kind, is dependent upon every integrating mechanism in the body, including the somatic nervous system, the autonomic nervous system, and the endocrine system. Both physiological and psychological evidence testify to the complex interrelations involved in the sex motive (see Box 22.6, p. 560).

Other Motives

What of all the other motives that play a part in man's behavior? What is the biochemical basis for the curiosity motive? Where is the brain center for the need for self-actualization?

These may seem like foolish questions, and may even remind us of the phrenologists' attempts to locate traits in various parts of the cortex (see Box 18.1, p. 417). Actually we must assume that questions of this kind, perhaps after some refinement in their wording, will someday be answerable. For the present we can only suggest that these motives depend upon the perceptual and integrative functions of the forebrain, particularly of the cerebral cortex and the limbic system.

The "tissue needs" of hunger, thirst, and so on are basic, at least in the sense that they are present in the simplest organisms as well as the most complex. Special biochemical and anatomical mechanisms for these needs are present, especially in older parts of the nervous system, and exercise control over behavior. Whatever the relation may be between the tissue needs and the "higher" motives said to be characteristic of mankind, motives of both kinds are under the continuing influence of both primitive and advanced parts of the nervous system.

BOX 22.6

THE RING DOVE AND THE BOW-COO

The classic work of D. S. Lehrman (who was a psychologist at Rutgers University) gives a clear picture of the relations between the reproductive behavior of ring doves and changes in their anatomy, hormone production, and other physiological functions.

The reproductive behavior of the ring dove is like that of many other birds. The male courts the female; they choose a nest site and spend about a week building a nest. Copulation takes place during this period. In the second week the female lays her eggs, and the two birds share the work of incubating. When the young are hatched, both parents feed them until they are ready to fend for themselves, after which the male starts courting, and the whole cycle begins again.

The cycle begins when a male and a female ring dove are placed in a cage together with nesting material and a potential nest site, a small glass bowl. Soon the male begins bowing to the female and making cooing sounds (the bow-coo). An understanding of the details and significance of the bow-coo is important because of its critical and widespread effects on the subsequent behavior and internal states of both birds during the reproductive cycle.

The bow-coo is triggered by the sight of the female bird but depends upon the presence of the male testicular hormones. Females and castrated males do not perform the bow-coo. The bow-coo leads the female to enter into and to continue her part of the reproductive cycle, and directly and indirectly it induces the anatomical and physiological changes underlying these behavior patterns. A female alone will not build a nest, lay eggs, or incubate them, nor will one caged with a castrated male. But if a female is separated from a normal male only by a plate of glass, so that she can see and hear him, he will bow and coo, and she will make a nest, lay eggs, and incubate them.

These behavior patterns are under the direct influence of the female hormones. If a pair of birds is given a ready-made nest with eggs when they first meet, they do not incubate the eggs but begin the usual cycle of courting and nest building, even covering the eggs in their nest-building activity! If a pair of birds are injected with estrogen, they immediately begin nest-building and are ready to incubate in three or four days, rather than the normal seven or eight days. But when birds are injected with progesterone, they will incubate almost immediately if eggs are provided by the experimenter. Estrogen influences nest building, and progesterone controls incubation. In normal birds visual and auditory stimuli from the courting male act on the female nervous system, which stimulates the production of pituitary gonadotropic hormones. These hormones stimulate the secretion of estrogen and later progesterone by the ovaries. These hormones not only influence behavior, as we have shown, but also lead to major changes in the ovaries, which grow in weight from about 800 mg to 4,000 mg by the time the eggs are ready to be laid.

It should be recognized that, important as the bow-coo is, other behavior influences the cycle as well. We find, for example, that a female will produce a level of progesterone high enough to make her ready for incubation simply by being exposed to a courting male, but she will produce the same amount of progesterone and be ready to incubate sooner if, in addition to the courting male, nesting material is available and she participates in nest building.

The male, of course, does not see the bow-coo, but it is his courting and participation in nest building that stimulate his progesterone production and prepare him for incubating.

It is easy to agree with Lehrman that the reproductive behavior cycle of the ring dove is a "psychobiological" cycle in which external stimuli, behavior, and internal states all interact.

D. S. LEHRMAN. Control of behavior cycles in reproduction. In W. Etkin (Ed.), *Social Behavior and Organization among Vertebrates*. Chicago: University of Chicago Press, 1964.

SUMMARY

1. In addition to the changes in EEG pattern, alertness, body temperature, and so on that are seen during our waking hours, changes in various physiological measures take place during sleep as well. During the night one goes through several alternating cycles of slow-wave sleep and REM sleep; the latter makes up about 25 percent of the sleeping time of an adult and even more in children.

2. The waking state is produced by activity in the reticular formation and a region in the hypothalamus. Other systems in the brain stem seem to control REM and NREM sleep. These separate systems not only involve different neural pathways, they also seem to use different transmitter substances.

3. The waking-sleeping cycle cannot be changed abruptly, and even after it has changed (as when one travels to a different time zone), some physiological rhythms may take much longer to readjust. It may be that the sleep patterns that have developed in various species serve to keep the individual inactive during the period when he would be in greatest danger.

4. The autonomic nervous system controls the muscles of the viscera and the endocrine glands. It is divided into the sympathetic and parasympathetic nervous systems. The sympathetic system produces changes that ready the body for an emergency; the parasympathetic system returns the system to normal.

5. The endocrine system is a group of glands. They produce hormones—substances that control the activity of some or all of the cells of the body. The activity of these glands is integrated with that of the autonomic nervous system. The adrenal medulla in particular acts to support the actions of the sympathetic system. Some of the hormones of the anterior pituitary gland control the output of other endocrine glands.

6. Adrenal steroids (hormones produced by the adrenal cortex) are produced in increased amounts during periods of physical or psychological stress. They change the response of the body to injury and affect the amount of energy that is available to the cells. In addition, they may have effects upon learning in an emotion-provoking situation.

7. The thyroid hormone tends to increase the rate of metabolism throughout the body and thus speeds up body processes. Excesses or deficiencies of this hormone can lead to abnormalities in bodily development, intelligence, and personality.

8. Many changes in activity that accompany emotional experience are under the control of the endocrine and autonomic nervous systems. There seem to be some differences in the amounts of different hormones produced in different emotional states.

9. The James-Lange theory asserts that emotional experience comes from the sensory feedback we receive when we make an emotional response. That is, we meet a bear, run, and then feel frightened. Other theories of emotion generally attempt to specify the parts of the brain that are involved in emotional experience and in emotional responses.

10. There is evidence that the hypothalamus and the reticular formation are important in emotion. Especially prominent in investigations of the structural mechanism of emotion are various parts of the limbic system. Lesions and electrical stimulation in different parts of this system cause changes in many kinds of motivated behavior and emotional response, but no simple summary of the overall functions of the system has been accepted thus far.

11. The transmitter substance produced in a nerve cell may be destroyed even before it leaves the axon or it may be reabsorbed by the axon terminal. Either of these events decreases the amount of transmitter available to stimulate the next neurons. Drugs that prevent these events at norepinephrine synapses have a helpful effect on depressive states. The catecholamine theory of depression says that this is because depression is produced by a deficiency in norepinephrine and related chemicals (which belong to a group of substances known as catecholamines).

12. There are several theories about the signals that control hunger and eating, but none explains the problem fully. It is known that there is a region in the hypothalamus (the lateral area) that is important in stimulating eating and one (the ventromedial nucleus) that is thought to control satiety. However, other systems play important parts in the control of food intake as well.

13. People seem to become thirsty if the body cells lose water and become dehydrated, or if there is a reduction in the total blood volume of the body. Again, mechanisms in the hypothalamus are important in the control of the amount of water consumed.

14. Sexual responses involve the collaboration of the autonomic and the somatic nervous systems. Although sexual activity may continue without much change if sex hormones are eliminated from the body in adulthood, the hormones are essential for original development of sexual structures and normal sex behavior.

15. There is some evidence that suggests that the brain of a fetus or infant of either sex is organized to produce female sexual behavior, and that only when the male hormone is present in early development does normal male sexual behavior appear in later life. Other scientists believe that separate neural systems exist in the infant of either sex for both male and female behavior, and that genetic factors, experience, and hormone balance throughout life determine how much of each kind of behavior will be shown later.

GLOSSARY

active theory of sleep   A theory that sleep occurs as a result of some special kind of activity in a designated part of the brain. There are different active theories of sleep, but all of them are in opposition to the passive theory of sleep.

adrenal cortex   The outer part of the adrenal gland. It secretes many hormones known as the adrenal steroids; the cortex is stimulated by an increased level of ACTH in the blood.

adrenal medulla   The inner portion of the adrenal gland; it secretes epinephrine and norepinephrine, largely under the control of the sympathetic nervous system.

adrenal steroids   A group of hormones secreted by the adrenal cortex. They are involved in the body's physiological and biochemical responses to stress; in experimental studies on rats, changes in the amount of the steroids affect the course of avoidance learning.

adrenocorticotropic hormone (ACTH)   A hormone of the anterior pituitary gland that controls the manufacture and secretion of the hormones (steroids) of the adrenal cortex.

anterior pituitary gland   The anterior (front) part of the pituitary gland. Its activity is controlled partly by the hypothalamus and partly by the other endocrine glands. It secretes six different hormones, which control, among other things, general bodily growth and secretions of the adrenal cortex, sex glands, and thyroid.

antidepressant drugs   Drugs used to relieve the symptoms of extreme sadness, withdrawal from life, and so on that characterize severe depression. Two classes of drugs used are the MAO inhibitors and the tricyclic drugs.

antidiuretic hormone   A hormone secreted by the posterior pituitary gland. It controls the rate and volume of urination. Emotional upset may inhibit secretion of the hormone, resulting in frequent and excessive urination.

autonomic nervous system   The nervous system that supplies the visceral organs and is mainly responsible for the automatic responses of the body. The autonomic system is comprised of two subsystems—the sympathetic and the parasympathetic nervous systems.

behavioral disposition   A tendency to respond in a given way to a certain pattern of stimuli. Different dispositions, partly inborn but influenced by experience, are found in different species.

catecholamine theory of depression   The hypothesis that depression is caused in part by a reduction in the amount of catecholamines (norepinephrine and related chemicals) available in certain parts of the brain.

cretinism   A pathological condition caused by extreme and chronic hypothyroidism during early life. The individual is dwarfed, and mental growth is retarded. Very early thyroid treatment of the cretin child usually results in normal physical and mental growth.

endocrine glands   The ductless glands of the body, so-called because their products go directly from the cells into the bloodstream without going through ducts, or tubes.

epinephrine   A hormone that, along with the similar chemical norepinephrine, is secreted by the adrenal medulla. The effect of these hormones is to maintain the bodily changes produced by activity of the sympathetic nervous system.

estrogen   A female sex hormone manufactured and secreted by the ovaries. It seems to be partly responsible for the growth of the female secondary sex characteristics and for control of the sex drive.

galvanic skin response (GSR)   Change in the electrical resistance or potential of the skin. This change often occurs during emotional excitement.

glucostatic theory of food intake   The theory that food-intake and hunger are regulated by the concentration of glucose (blood sugar) in the blood.

gonadotropic hormone   A pituitary hormone that controls, in part, the manufacture and secretion of the sex hormones of the testes and ovaries.

gonads   The sex glands. In the male they are the testes, in the female, the ovaries.

hormones   Chemical compounds manufactured by the endocrine glands and secreted into the bloodstream. The hormones, carried by the bloodstream to the visceral organs of the body, can stimulate or inhibit the activity of these organs.

hyperthyroidism   A condition of continuous excessive thyroid hormone production.

hypothyroidism   A condition of chronic insufficient thyroid hormone production.

James-Lange theory   A theory independently proposed by William James of the United States and Carl Lange of Denmark to the effect that bodily changes precede the feeling of emotion and that it is the perception of bodily changes that is the emotional feeling.

lateral area of the hypothalamus   A brain region which provides some central control of eating. Electrical stimulation in this area will make an experimental animal start to eat; destruction here makes an animal stop eating.

lithium   A chemical element, related to sodium. Substances containing lithium appear to relieve symptoms of manic behavior, perhaps by changing the concentration of one or more transmitter substances in the brain.

monoamine oxidase (MAO) inhibitor   An antidepressant drug that inhibits (works against) the action of monoamine oxidase (MAO), which is an enzyme that breaks down certain chemicals in the cells, including norepinephrine. An MAO inhibitor therefore increases the amount of norepinephrine present.

ovaries   Female sex glands having both glandular and nonglandular functions. The nonglandular function is the production of ova, or eggs. The glandular function is the manufacture and secretion of sex hormones, including estrogen and progesterone.

parasympathetic nervous system   Part of the autonomic nervous system. The parasympathetic system supplies the visceral organs via nerve fibers from the brain and the spinal cord; this system is somewhat more specific in its discharge to these organs than the sympathetic system.

passive theory of sleep   The theory that sleep is simply the natural condition of the brain when it is not being stimulated by external stimuli and when there is no activity in those parts responsible for wakefulness.

posterior pituitary gland   The posterior part of the pituitary gland. It is controlled by the hypothalamus. The antidiuretic hormone is released here.

progesterone   A female sex hormone produced by the ovaries. It is concerned with the preparation of the uterus for pregnancy and of the breasts for lactation.

rapid eye movements (REM)   Eye movements characteristic of the period of sleep during which most dreaming takes place.

secondary sex characteristics   The appearance and other nonreproductive distinctive characteristics of the male and female (e.g., distribution of hair, sound of voice, skeletal proportions, and thickness of skin).

skeletal muscles   The muscles of the body that are, in most cases, attached to bones and are thus responsible for the movement of the limbs, trunk, and so on. The nonskeletal muscles control the visceral organs.

sleep spindles   Very rapid waves seen in the EEG of sleepng people, especially when they are in moderately deep sleep.

somatic nervous system   The part of the nervous system that is primarily involved in receiving sensory input from the external world, in integrating it with activity already in the nervous system, and in controlling the movement of the skeletal muscles.

sympathetic nervous system   Part of the autonomic nervous system. The sympathetic nervous system consists of two chains of ganglia running along the sides of the spinal cord; fibers entering and leaving these ganglia supply various visceral organs. The sympathetic nervous system is built for widespread discharge.

testes Male sex glands having both glandular and nonglandular functions. The nonglandular function is the production of spermatozoa. The glandular function is the manufacture and secretion of the sex hormones, among them testosterone and estrogen.

testosterone The male sex hormone, produced by the testes. It seems to be important in speeding up growth of the male sex organs. It also controls development of secondary characteristics and helps determine the sexual activity of the individual.

thermostatic theory of food intake The theory that food intake is controlled by the heat of the body, acting through temperature-sensitive cells in the hypothalamus.

thyroid gland An endocrine gland in the neck. It secretes thyroid hormone at a rate controlled by the amount of thyrotropic hormone in the blood.

thyroid hormone The hormone secreted by the thyroid gland. It has both general and specific effects. It increases the metabolic rate in almost all body cells, raises blood pressure, speeds up heart rate, and so on.

thyrotropic hormone A hormone of the anterior pituitary gland that controls, in part, the manufacture and secretion of thyroid hormone.

tricyclic drugs A group of antidepressant drugs that prevents an axon from taking up norepinephrine from the synaptic space, thus leaving more norepinephrine available to stimulate the dendritic zone of the postsynaptic neuron.

ventromedial nucleus A hypothalamic nucleus involved in eating. Destruction of the ventromedial nucleus results in voracious eating, eventually leading to obesity.

conflict
and
adjustment

frustration, conflict, and defense

DO YOU KNOW…

- whether being frustrated in getting something we're after can sometimes lead to more adaptive behavior?

- under what circumstances we are inclined to settle for something less than our original goal and how well this sort of compromise can work?

- why it is so distressing to be caught between the devil and the deep blue sea?

- how many different ways normal people have of avoiding feeling anxious and what kind of toll this avoidance has on their ability to see the world as it really is?

- that it is possible to forget totally a very painful experience which usually would be long remembered?

- why sometimes the very things we feel we hate most may, on another level, be our heart's desire?

- the effects of sour grapes as a steady diet?

- that we often see in others what we fail to see in our-selves?

unit 23

CONTENTS

Inherent in the structure of all human societies is the inevitability of a sense of frustration for the individual. In the simplest case, the individual desires something, and circumstance denies it to him. Circumstance, of course, can be *objective*: I am thirsty, and no water is to be had. More often, when people live together, frustration derives from a conflict between personal wants and society's restraints and prohibitions, for at the very heart of human social groups lies the necessity to balance individual needs against the collective needs of the group. Because societal standards become internalized as we mature (i.e., become part of ourselves), the arena of this conflict often shifts to *inside* the person. Thus, the occurrence of conflict and the experience of frustration are best examined *within* the individual; it is also best to look there to understand their effects and the psychological processes that are developed to cope with them.

In approaching these questions, one useful distinction attends to the *direction* of the effects of frustration and conflict: constructive as opposed to disruptive. Another helpful distinction can be made between immediate and transient effects of short-term motivational conflicts and the more pervasive and enduring effects that characterize personality conflicts. Those more enduring effects, under certain circumstances, lead to the defense mechanisms that shape so much of normal and abnormal behavior. We shall turn first to the distinction between constructive and disruptive effects.

CONSTRUCTIVE EFFECTS OF FRUSTRATION AND CONFLICT

Frustration and conflict are commonly regarded as bad for the person. Their destructive effects tend to preoccupy the attention of psychologists and laymen alike. There has been less stress on the fact that, as frustration or conflict begins to build tension, goal attainment may be *facilitated*.

Increased tension has the effect of focusing the individual's attention more firmly on his particular motive operating at the moment. That motive thereby becomes more salient, and other concurrent needs, desires, and interests thus may diminish in relative potency. Irrelevant and distracting features of the person's perceived world may drop out. Finally, the very attractiveness of the unattained goal may be enhanced.

Intensified Striving

All these effects lead to direct attempts to reach the goal by intensified striving. Within limits, the greater the blockage, the greater the mobilization of effort to overcome it. We are all well acquainted with the manner in which the challenge offered by the thwarting of our goal-directed efforts produces a more intense response. Indeed, it is probably only when there is some blocking of goal attainment that motive strength reaches its fullest height. Without blockage, the activity is more or less habitual and only peripherally motivated. Intensified striving may take the form of *compensation*. A Teddy Roosevelt, physically puny as a youth, may thus devote a major part of his later life activities to building up his physical strength in order to compensate for the early frustration he experienced.

Such intensified striving will often result in breaking through the barrier or overcoming the conflict. But if the barrier is too strong and the compensatory action fails, other types of adjustive action may follow.

Changing the Means to Goals

The frustrated person may take a new look at the whole situation and reconsider whether or not his previous goal-directed action was the most appropriate one for attaining the goal. The enhanced tension may highlight features of the situation that he had not seen, particularly as he is forced to search more widely for alternate pathways to the goal. However, although a moderate increase in tension often does result in finding a new path to the goal and in overcoming the frustration, the level of tension must not be too high (see Unit 7, p. 163).

Substitution of Goals

Just as the person may find an alternative path to the goal, so he may find an alternative goal that will satisfy the need or desire. The effect of the increased tension is to make him search more widely and thus to increase the likelihood that he will perceive an available substitute. Many factors determine what makes for an acceptable substitute; not the least of them is sheer availability: hence, the apt, if cynical, Broadway musical refrain, "When I'm not near the girl I love, I love the girl I'm near" (Harburg & Saide, *Finian's Rainbow*).

Rarely, however, will the substitute goal have the identical properties of the original goal or be exactly equal in desirability. Some compromise will be involved in taking the substitute, and thus some of the initial tension may remain unresolved. Because of this, the one you love still remains a goal despite attempts at distraction and diversion.

Redefining the Situation

If intensified striving, changing of means, and substitution of goals do not succeed in resolving the frustration or conflict, more fundamental changes in the situation may occur.

One obvious way of removing conflict, the consequent frustration, and the increased tension is to make choices among the alternatives. Increased tension helps to force a choice, and choice in conflict situations is adaptive behavior. The tension has brought about a redefining of the situation, so that the conflict is eliminated.

The redefining of the situation may be such that things that were separate and opposing are now consolidated and harmonious. For instance, man's separate and conflicting desires to be self-assertive and to retain the love of the group are synthesized in an effort to be elected to the leadership of the group, which will satisfy both initial desires.

In general, such redefining of a situation involving frustration means that the person introduces new elements into the situation or that she broadens the perceived context of her problem. This redefinition may occur in a sudden, insightful way; or it may be a more gradual alteration in a situation where frustration is chronic. You may abruptly see the solution to your conflict between working and going to school and decide to drop your part-time job altogether, or you may gradually cut down your job hours in order to progress at a more satisfying rate toward your educational goal.

DISRUPTIVE EFFECTS OF FRUSTRATION AND CONFLICT

If the constructive effects of frustration and conflict fail to bring about goal attainment, the tension continues to increase. Eventually, it will reach levels at which its effects are no longer facilitative but are disruptive of the goal-directed activity.

There are several reasons for this result. For one thing, the increased mobilization of energy may become so great that it exceeds what is appropriate for the task; the person may try too hard and may thus disrupt the fine coordination of effort. For another thing, the extreme tension may result in **cognitive narrowing**; that is, the person focuses his attention so completely on the blocked pathways or the inaccessible goal that he is blinded to the existence of alternative pathways or substitute goals. And, finally, the increased tension is often accompanied by emotional agitation, which interferes with the rational processes of deliberation and choice: He gets rattled and panicky and loses control.

Frustration Tolerance

It is clear that there is a kind of threshold level beyond which the tension results in qualitatively different kinds of effects on behavior. We may call this threshold the **frustration tolerance**. An individual may experience a considerable degree and persistence of frustration and conflict without exhibiting signs of disorganization or disruption. He may continue to strive toward the goal, look for new paths or substitute goals, and seek to make realistic and rational choices. But with still further increase in tension, he may become overly agitated, emotionally upset,

and no longer able to cope in constructive ways with the problem situation. We would say that he has exceeded his frustration tolerance.

Frustration tolerance is clearly a variable (rather than a fixed) quantity of tension, depending upon the person and the situation. In one situation the individual may be able to withstand a great deal more tension than in another. In part this tolerance will depend upon what he has just experienced and what he anticipates will happen next. Two different individuals in the same frustrating situation may exhibit quite different frustration tolerances; so may the same individual in the same situation at different times.

Once the level of arousal approaches and exceeds the individual's frustration tolerance, several major disruptive effects of the frustration appear. We shall discuss two of them: aggression and escape.

Aggression

Aggression can be viewed in its simplest form as a kind of direct attack upon the obstacle or barrier, and in this sense it is adaptive behavior. Yet aggression may be deleterious; the barrier may require a more subtle approach than a frontal attack induced by anger. Furthermore, the frustration may not stem from an identifiable barrier at all but may be an experience of lack or loss or a conflict with another motive. Under these circumstances there is no logical object to attack, and the aggression may be diffused over many objects, some quite unconnected with the frustration. This generalization of aggression becomes greater when the frustration becomes more intense and the sources of the frustration become less clear and available. The person may strike out wildly, attacking anything within reach.

There may be reasons why the person cannot express aggression directly at the source of frustration. The source may itself be dangerous; for instance, the child does not dare attack the father who has frustrated him. Or there may be various social standards concerning the proper objects for aggression. In such cases the aggression may be handled by **displacement** to other objects. That is, the aggression, instead of being directed at the perceived source of frustration, is directed elsewhere, often toward entirely innocent objects or people, *scapegoats.* (For much more about aggression's place in our society, see Unit 30.)

Escape

A second major disruptive effect of frustration and conflict is the tendency to escape from the frustrating situation.

Although such **escape reactions** may provide relief from the excessive tension, the escape is a disruptive act in that it prevents attainment of the goal. This escape reaction is not the same as a fear-induced flight from dangerous objects. The escape may be only temporary, and the original motive, still remaining, may continue to induce tensions and distress. Chronic frustration and chronic escape reactions may eventually lead to deleterious personality defense mechanisms. (One of them—**regression** —is illustrated in Box 23.1, p. 574.)

SHORT-TERM MOTIVATIONAL CONFLICTS

We now turn to the distinction between enduring effects of conflict, as exemplified in the development of defense mechanisms, and the transient effects of short-term conflict. Before examining the effects of conflict, let us see how it arises in the first instance.

Once motivationally aroused the organism typically engages in action that reduces or abolishes the aroused state. The specific patterns of directed action vary widely, depending upon the particular motive, the particular individual, and the particular situation. Despite this considerable specificity, we can group such directed action into two general categories: *approach* and *avoidance* behavior. The rat races down the maze alley toward the food in the goal box; it backs away from the threatening cat. The infant stretches out its hand toward the brightly colored rattle; it averts its head from the proffered spoonful of puréed spinach. Not all approach and avoidance involve overt bodily action. In thought we can feel drawn toward the

object of our desires and feel repelled by the painful and unpleasant.

In these illustrations the outcome is not difficult to predict. The individual will simply approach until he achieves the goal, or he will simply move away until the negative object is completely avoided. But this pattern is not life. It is the rare situation that presents us with the simple problem of responding to either a single positive or a single negative motive. Typically there are two or more motives aroused within us at any one moment. At times these multiple motives are compatible. They may even facilitate one another; we eat with added zest when the food before us is both our sensory favorite and good for us. Each motive—to enjoy or to be nourished—is somewhat heightened by the presence of the other. Multiple motives usually, however, *conflict* in some degree with one another.

Perhaps the simplest case of a short-term motivational conflict involves the confrontation of a single approach motive by a single avoidance motive: the **approach-avoidance conflict**. This situation translates easily into an experimental procedure, particularly in research with animals. For example, some kind of noxious barrier (such as an electric grid that delivers a painful shock when the animal crosses it) can be interposed in an alley between the animal and a desired object in the goal box. This procedure not only permits us to examine how the animal attempts to solve the approach-avoidance situation but also provides us with a way to measure the relative strengths of various approach motives. For example, in one early study using this kind of setup it was found that the maternal drive of mother rats (as measured by the number of times they were willing to cross the charged grid in order to reach their litters) was significantly stronger than their thirst, hunger, or sex drives (Warden, 1931).

For the study of people's behavior in an approach-avoidance situation, however, it is often not necessary to provide an external barrier because so many of the things we desire to have or to do are already surrounded by social taboos, rules of our society that we have been taught not to break. These taboos *are* the barriers.

BOX 23.1

FRUSTRATION AND REGRESSION IN CHILDREN

At the University of Iowa, R. Barker, T. Dembo, and K. Lewin studied the effects of frustration on the deterioration in constructiveness of children's play. Thirty children between two and five years of age were observed individually while playing with a standardized set of toys (see Figure A). Observers

rated the level of constructiveness of each child's play, that is, the extent to which the play showed imagination, elaboration, and well-structured activities. For example, sitting on the floor and connecting and disconnecting a truck and trailer was rated low in constructiveness, whereas carrying out an extensive trip in which the truck and trailer take part in a series of events was rated high in constructiveness.

It was found that there was a close relationship between the constructiveness of play and the mental age of the child. It was therefore possible to score constructiveness of play in terms of "mental-age units," that is, in terms of the constructiveness appropriate to children of a given mental age.

Frustration was experimentally created by permitting the children to play briefly with fascinating new toys available in a part of the experimental room normally closed off and then bringing a child back into the regular play area and locking a wire screen that was interposed between the child and the fascinating toys (see Figure B).

The effect of the frustration was studied by comparing the constructiveness of the child's play with the original standardized toys before and after the frustration.

In general, there was a marked decrease in constructiveness of play. On the average, the constructiveness regressed by an amount equivalent to 17.3 months of mental age. In other words, following frustration, the child played at a constructiveness level characteristic of a child about one and a half years younger.

In addition, escape behavior was observed. Some children would make efforts to leave the room. The children who showed a great deal of escape behavior also showed much greater regression (on the average, about 24 months) when they *did* play with the standard toys again. The children who showed very little escape behavior regressed only 4 months on the average. Indeed, in some of the latter cases, there was even an *increase* in subsequent constructiveness of play.

As the experimenters remark:

> The lowering of constructiveness of play is similar to the change in behavior occurring under conditions of high emotionality in which restless movements, stereotyped repetition of sentences, and stuttering are frequent. Both changes involve . . . a certain lack of realism.

R. BARKER, T. DEMBO, & K. LEWIN. Frustration and regression: An experiment with young children. *University of Iowa Studies: Child Welfare*, 1941, **18**, No. 386.

Not all cases of motivational conflict are of the approach-avoidance type. The conflict may be among alternative goal objects, or it may be among alternative means to the goal or away from an undesirable situation. The essence of conflict is simply that the person cannot go in two different directions at once.

Patterns of Conflict

Conflict situations, as analyzed by the psychologist Lewin (1935), fall into one of three basic patterns: approach-approach, avoidance-avoidance, and approach-avoidance.

The **approach-approach conflict** is that between two positive goal objects. It is likely to be the least painful of conflict situations because the person can choose between two desirable things. But it is also true that choosing one necessitates losing the other, and this necessity can be a source of quite intense conflict. The woman trying to decide which of two men to marry or which of two jobs to take can get herself into a state of prolonged and tortured indecision. The more nearly equal the two goals, the greater the conflict will be, and the person may remain poised indecisively halfway between the two. But it is an unstable equilibrium because the *attractiveness* of a desired object increases as it is approached and decreases as it is left behind (see Box 23.2, p. 576). As soon as the person makes a tentative move toward one goal object, its compelling force thus increases slightly while the other goal object loses attractiveness slightly. The result is that the pulls on the person are now unbalanced, and he will move ever more energetically to the nearer goal (see Figure 23.1).

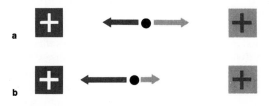

a

b

FIGURE 23.1 The approach-approach conflict situation is characterized by an unstable equilibrium (a), in which a step toward either goal (b) is sufficient to resolve the conflict by further enhancing the attractiveness of that goal in preference to the other.

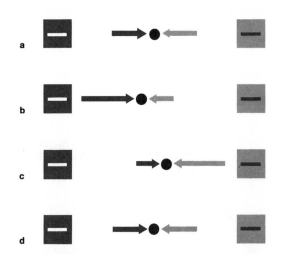

a

b

c

d

FIGURE 23.2 The avoidance-avoidance conflict situation is characterized by a stable equilibrium (a) in which a step away from one object is immediately redressed by the increased negativity of the object toward which the step is taken (note the difference in the arrow lengths in b). This results in bringing the person closer to the other object (c). But this, in turn, increases the negativity of the second object, and after some fluctuations, the individual is brought to the point of equilibrium (d) from which he started (a).

The **avoidance-avoidance conflict** occurs when the person is confronted with two negative things, one of which he must choose. It is a case of choosing the lesser of two evils, a choice between the devil and the deep blue sea. For example, a man is required by his employer to choose between the unwelcome alternatives of being transferred to a branch office in a city he dislikes or resigning from the firm. In this situation the equilibrium tends to be a stable one; that is, the person stays balanced as long as possible between the two negatives. The reason is that the force of repulsion generated by a *negative* object grows less, the greater its distance is from the person. As he takes a step away from one of the two negative objects, its repellent force thus becomes less; yet this move brings him a step nearer the other object, whose negative force becomes greater, and he is pushed back again (see Figure 23.2). Usually there is a third force in the situation that requires him to make a decision between the two. For in-

BOX 23.2

GOAL GRADIENT IN THE RAT

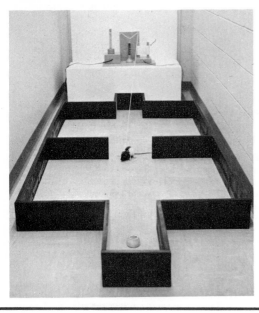

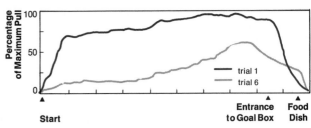

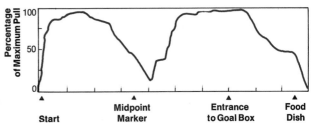

In 1935 at the University of Chicago, I. Krechevsky developed a method for measuring the strength of the rat's goal-directed motivation.

The rat, wearing a harness to which a restraining string was attached, ran from the starting chamber to the food box (see photo on the left). The string was played out at a slow constant rate as it

stance, the employer may insist that he decide on his job move by a certain date.

The approach-avoidance conflict, as we noted earlier, is a familiar one. In a way, it is the truest conflict; it is certainly the most agitating. Here the person is both attracted and repelled in the same direction. This situation may arise because the goal object *itself* has both positive and negative features, as in the case of a job that pays well but involves living in an undesirable city. Or it may be because the path to the positive goal necessitates going through a negative region; for instance, the rat must run across the electric grid to obtain the reward. The alcoholic must go through the distress of going on the wagon in order to win back his self-respect. There is also the case in which the positive goal comes first but is inevitably followed by something negative: The stolen jam

means a spanking: the binge means a hangover; the forbidden pleasure means the subsequent loss of self-respect.

The approach-avoidance conflict also results in a kind of stable equilibrium in that at a certain distance from the goal, the positive and negative forces balance, and a step closer or away tends to make the individual return to the point of equilibrium (see Figure 23.3).

These analyses of short-term conflict situations are overly simplified; they fail to reflect all the dynamics of the motivational processes even in an immediate situation. In many situations the simple goal gradient does not hold. In approach-approach conflicts, for example, what often happens, as we all know, is that as we move toward one positive goal, the idea of the incipient loss of the other makes it appear more desirable than before, and we are then swung

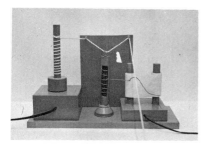

unwound from a cylinder rotated by an electrically driven motor. The rat could not proceed through the box faster than the motor played out the string, no matter how much force he exerted. The string passed through a hook mechanism attached to a fixed spring in such a manner that, when the animal strained against the string, the spring was stretched. This stretching in turn moved a stylus that made a continuous record on a moving roll of waxed paper of the amount of force exerted at each moment· by the rat in tugging against the harness toward the goal. The rat thus, as shown in the photograph above, "wrote" its own record of its striving toward the goal.

A typical record for one rat is shown in the lower graph. Two points are noteworthy:

1. There appears to be evidence of lessening

tension as the rat enters the "goal region" (food box) even before the actual goal object (food) is obtained.

2. The dip in strength of pull in the middle is determined by the side partitions, which do not in any way provide an obstacle for the animal. Apparently they serve as a kind of perceptual "landmark" and function somewhat as a "subgoal." Arrival at this subgoal is accompanied by a temporary lessening in the pull, which is resumed in its full vigor once past this point. When the side partitions are removed, animals no longer give any sign of lessening pull at that point.

The upper graph illustrates the effect of progressive satiation of hunger drive on the *gradient* of pull toward the goal. Six consecutive trials were given with three minutes of feeding in the food box after each trial. The graph shows a record of trials 1 and 6. Note that on trial 1 the animal pulled strongly, almost from the very beginning, whereas by trial 6, when he had had fifteen minutes of eating, he began at a low level and only gradually reached a fairly high level as the goal was closely approached. The attractiveness of food, even for a satiated animal, increases as he comes closer to it.

I. KRECHEVSKY. Measurement of tension. Paper read at Symposium on Topological Psychology, Bryn Mawr, Pa., 1935.

FIGURE 23.3 The approach-avoidance conflict situation is characterized by a stable equilibrium (a) in which a step toward (or away from) the goal produces compensating changes in the relative strengths of the positive and negative forces (as in b, where the negative force is increased more than is the positive). The consequence of the change in relative strengths of the positive and negative forces is to shift the person's locus farther away from the goal, which now results in a reversal of the relative strengths of the positive and negative forces (c). The final consequence is that the person is returned to the original point of equilibrium (d).

back to it. This vacillation can go on for some time. For instance, a man goes on his way to propose to one girl, but as he walks he thinks of all the to-be-lost charms of the other, and this thinking halts him in his tracks. The real point

is that, when there is a case of mutual exclusion of positive things, there is more to the matter than which goal is more attractive. For if, by having one, the other is irretrievably lost, each alternative takes on a certain negative character in addition to its positive character, and the equilibrium is not as unstable as before.

Most conflicts are likely to include more than two goals, more than two possible directions of action. The woman choosing between the two jobs sees positive and negative features in each and may indeed see other possibilities that involve taking neither job. Furthermore, situations are not usually as neat as our examples. It is not necessarily certain that taking this job or this husband will forever preclude the alternative. Often the more realistic case is that there has to be a postponement of one goal in favor of the other or a putting off of an immediate gratification in favor of a later one.

Conflict, Frustration, and Anxiety

The very existence of a serious conflict situation and the particular way a person responds to it may subject him to the punishment or threats of society, to painful feelings of guilt, or to the threats of loss of self-esteem. All these threats or punishments arouse in him feelings of **anxiety**, feelings that can come to dominate his every moment.

The crucial significance of the relation between conflict and anxiety is that anxiety leads the person to exhibit various defensive effects of frustration. These effects are to be distinguished from the more immediate constructive and disruptive effects already discussed. They are reactions to the anxiety produced by the hard-to-resolve conflict rather than reactions to the initial frustration itself. They can be described as ways in which the person behaves in order to reduce or to avoid the anxiety. For this reason they are often referred to as *mechanisms of self-defense* or **defense mechanisms**.

DEFENSE MECHANISMS AND CONFLICT

In personality theory, defense mechanisms are highly pervasive characteristics of the individual. They not only reflect his general personality, but also, in an important sense, may influence the course of its development. The failure of these mechanisms to fulfill their de-

fensive functions contributes to mental disorders. Moreover, the quality of the disorder may mirror the person's characteristic defense mechanisms.

The sources of the conflicts from which anxiety is said to arise vary widely among different personality theories (theories discussed in detail in Unit 29): opposing forces among id, ego, and superego (Freud); inferiority feelings versus striving for perfection (Adler); incompatible neurotic needs simultaneously driving the person to seek to be with others, to aggress against them, and to be independent of them (Horney); conflicting requirements of complex interpersonal relations (Sullivan); psychosocial crises in the process of identity formation (Erikson). Despite this diversity in assumed sources of anxiety, personality theorists seem to agree on the presence of a large number of defense mechanisms that can to some extent protect the individual against anxiety, but at the price of a certain degree of denial or distortion of reality. Many of the items in this repertoire of defense mechanisms are by now familiar to us all, another illustration of the diffusion of psychoanalytic concepts in our everyday language. Some mechanisms have already been discussed in this unit; we shall present a selected additional few here.

Repression

The mechanism of **repression** was first proposed by Sigmund Freud and, for some time, occupied a special place in psychoanalytic theorizing, perhaps because it involves the most direct approach to avoiding the experience of anxiety. As a result of repression, the person is not aware of his own anxiety-producing impulses or does not remember deeply emotional and traumatic past events. A person with homosexual impulses (his recognition of which might produce anxiety in him) may thus, through repression, become completely unaware of such impulses; a person who has suffered a mortifying personal failure may, through repression, become unable to recall the experience.

The *deliberate suppression* of painful feelings or recollections is very commonplace, but it is not repression. Repression is not deliberate;

it somehow occurs automatically as a reaction in certain situations of conflict, serving as a defense of the ego against anxiety.

Repression is assumed to be more than forgetting. In support of this view is the observation that some experiences seem to be so deeply repressed that intensive psychotherapy, hypnosis, or treatment by drugs may be required to recover the lost material. Furthermore, not only may there be difficulty in reinstating memory of the painful events themselves; the repression may also extend to neutral events that were associated with the traumatic event. In cases of amnesia, for example, a person suffering an emotional crisis may forget not only the conflict but also everything that reminds him of it, including his own name and identity. And when the amnesia attack begins to wear off, the memories that return first are those most remote from the precipitating emotional crisis. It is for all these reasons that repression has been termed *motivated forgetting* (see Unit 17, p. 408).

The principal evidence that some such process as repression exists rests upon a large body of clinical observation made in the course of psychotherapy. The precise nature of the processes underlying repression, if it does exist, is still unknown. Laboratory experiments on the phenomenon are understandably rare.

If repression were a simple matter of blotting out the conflict and all its attendant anxieties, it would, of course, be the ideal defensive reaction. But this blotting out does not seem to happen. The relief from anxiety bought by repression is paid for in other ways, for example, in reaction formation.

Reaction Formation

Repression of strong anxiety-provoking impulses is often accompanied by a counteracting tendency that is exactly opposed to the repressed tendencies: **reaction formation**. For example, a person may have become a fanatical crusader against vice because of an unconscious attraction toward those sinful (for him) activities. Thus, he may have repressed his impulses and ended by denouncing the very vices he unknowingly yearns for. In like manner, a mother's excessive manifestations of concern for her child may mask an actual (repressed) hostility toward the child; extreme politeness toward a person may really mean concealed disdain; bravado may mean hidden fear.

Reaction formation can prevent the individual from behaving in a way that would most basically create anxiety and frequently can prevent him from behaving in an antisocial manner. On the other hand, reaction formation is also likely to have dangerous social consequences because of the irrational intensity of the reaction.

Knowing only a little about the phenomenon of reaction formation makes it all too easy to develop a thoroughly skeptical attitude toward people's motives. If things can sometimes mean just the opposite of what they seem on the surface, how can one distinguish the real motivation in any given case? The answer is that reaction formation, like every defense mechanism, occurs only under fairly special circumstances. Most zealous reformers are not secret sinners; most highly maternal mothers are not hiding hatred of their children. One difference is likely to be found in the degree of obvious exaggeration of the behavior. But, despite Shakespeare ("The lady doth protest too much, methinks"), the intensity of the behavior is not a certain proof of reaction formation. We must know a great deal about the person and all the attendant circumstances before we can safely interpret an intense feeling or behavior as indicating a reaction formation.

Rationalization

Our earlier discussions of perception and thinking stressed the individual's constant striving to make sense of her world of experience. She seeks an explanation not only of external phenomena but also of her own behavior, her own feelings. The cognitive processes involved in achieving such explanations are subject to the distorting influences of emotional and motivational factors. The individual may thus come to explain her behavior and feelings in conflict situations in such a way that self-esteem is maintained and anxiety avoided. Such cognitive accommodation to conflict is called **rationalization**.

Rationalization takes many forms. In cases of personal failure or of violation of moral principles, the individual may find false but good reasons to justify her conduct. She failed the quiz "because the questions were unfair"; she need not feel guilty about cheating on her income tax "because the government is an inefficient bureaucracy that would misuse [her] hard-earned money," and besides "everybody does it."

The frustrated fox in the sour grapes parable finds many human counterparts: the man who says that the job from which he was fired was not a desirable one anyway, that the girl who turned him down was not really attractive, and so on. Serving the same function as the sour grapes reaction is the sweet lemon phenomenon: The person forced into a distasteful situation rationalizes that it is really desirable; he says that he really loves his new job or his new friend.

Rationalizations usually involve a complex web of explanations rather than a single one, and this complex web helps make them less pervious to attack. The person has defenses in depth. If one rationalization breaks down, others are in reserve. The man accused of returning a borrowed pot in a damaged condition asserts that he never borrowed the pot, that he returned it in perfect condition, and that, besides, it already had the hole in it when he borrowed it.

In mild form, rationalization may have the beneficial function of protecting the individual against anxiety while permitting him to remain in the anxiety-producing situation and eventually to achieve an adaptive solution. In extreme forms, however, rationalization is likely to lead to worse failures of adjustment in that the person becomes so enmeshed in a web of deluded self-justification that he is unable to attack his problems realistically.

Insulation

The human mind seems capable, under some circumstances, of entertaining two logically incompatible concepts side by side, without awareness of the obvious discrepancy. This phenomenon has been dubbed "logic-tight compartments" and is one form of **insulation**. This mechanism insulates one set of mental contents from other sets in such a way that the normal interactions among the sets are reduced and therefore conflicts may be resolved.

A bizarre example of a logic-tight mind is found in the denunciatory letter of an outraged antivivisectionist to a psychiatrist who had described his experiments with animals involving electric shocks:

> I am surprised that anyone as well educated as you must be . . . would stoop to such a depth as to torture helpless little cats in the pursuit of a cure for alcoholics. . . . Instead . . . why not torture the drunks . . . if such people are weaklings the world is better off without them. . . . My greatest wish is that you have brought home to you a torture that will be a thousand fold greater than what you are doing to the little animals. . . . I'm glad I am just an ordinary human being . . . with a clear conscience, knowing I have not hurt any living creature (Masserman, 1946).

The insulation between denunciation of torture and its advocacy helps prevent inner conflict in this antivivisectionist.

A common form of insulation is the excessive *intellectualization* some people indulge in as they approach all kinds of life problems. By attending only to the intellectual aspects of a problem, the person may protect himself against the anxieties that might stem from the emotional aspects of the problem. For example, a chemist who helps to solve the problem of developing more effective napalm may refuse to think about the death and suffering that will result from its use.

Projection

One obvious way to defend against anxiety arising from failure or guilt is by **projection** of the blame onto someone else. The person who is unaware of his own hostile impulses but sees them in *other* people—and sees the others as hating and persecuting *him*—is also projecting.

Typically, the projection occurs to the extent that the person is unaware of the undesirable trait in himself. This is clearly brought out in a well-known experiment by Sears (1936) in which ninety-seven members of a college fraternity rated one another and themselves on a number of undesirable traits, for example, stinginess, obstinacy, disorderliness. Some of the men who were rated very high on the undesirable traits by the consensus of their fellows showed little self-insight, rating themselves low on the traits; and they exhibited a significant amount of projection of these same traits, rating their fraternity fellows as especially high on them.

The direction of projection is not haphazard; rather it tends toward objects whose perceptual properties are already best suited to fit the displaced material. Frenkel-Brunswik and Sanford (1945) found, for instance, that extremely rigid and conventionally moralistic college girls, unable to acknowledge their own "unworthy" sexual impulses, tended to project them onto certain "inferior" minority groups. That is, they perceived these others as indulging in loose, rampant, and perhaps enviable · sexuality. This projection served to maintain the girls' self-conception of superior purity.

We have reviewed only a few of the more familiar defense mechanisms. There are many others, but all share certain characteristics and permit a number of general observations.

Some Comments on Defense Mechanisms

Man develops defense mechanisms, we have said, in order to protect the self from anxiety. By "develop" we do not wish to imply a conscious adoption of these mechanisms because, if the person were to be fully aware of the operation of, say, projection, this mechanism could no longer serve to protect him from feelings of threat, insecurity, and loss of self-esteem. To put the matter crudely, in order to be effective a defense mechanism must above all fool the person himself. It is irrelevant whether or not other people are also fooled. The politician who intentionally accuses his opponent of graft and corruption as a device to forestall the discovery of his own illegal practices may thus save his skin but not his self-esteem. This is a political defense mechanism, not a personality defense mechanism. Projection as a defense mechanism guards the *ego*, not the political office.

The relation between defense mechanisms and the self is intimate and reciprocal. These

mechanisms defend the self, and the nature of the self helps to determine which mechanisms will be used in its defense. No one uses equally the various defense mechanisms that we have described. We all evolve characteristic modes of protecting our self-esteem, and each person's distinctive pattern seems to appear fairly early in life. The origin and development of the individual's pattern of defense mechanisms are as yet little understood. It has been suggested that the mechanisms that we come to prefer represent consolidations from earlier experiences in which particular techniques, perhaps at first consciously employed, were usually successful in warding off pain.

Take a very simple example: The small boy may impulsively blame his infant brother if a vase is broken because of his own carelessness. If wrongful blaming of this kind proves to be a consistently effective solution, it may gradually become an automatic, internalized, and unconscious defense mechanism: projection. And insofar as it works, the child has neither the need nor the opportunity to learn other ways of coping with such situations. Projection thus becomes a preferred and characteristic defense mechanism for him. As is true of all aspects of personality, however, the development of the individual's distinctive pattern of defense mechanisms doubtless reflects heredity and somatic factors as well as experiential ones. Thus Weinstock (1967) has found that, in the case of projection, a positive correlation exists between adults' tendency to use this mechanism and the socioeconomic level of their families in childhood: The higher the socioeconomic level, the greater the tendency to use projection.

Defense mechanisms not only defend the individual's self-esteem but also can help him to cope with the environment. They frequently offer solutions to, and needed respite and protection from, threatening situations against which the person actually has no realistic defense. (Box 23.3, p. 582, presents a systematic attempt to distinguish between the coping and ego-defensive aspects of such mechanisms.)

The adaptive value of a given behavior can be evaluated in two independent frames of reference: Does it protect the self from anxiety? Does it represent an effective response to ex-

BOX 23.3

THE GOOD SIDE OF DEFENSE MECHANISMS

Defense mechanisms are not all bad, or at least they have positive facets that have been neglected and that, when subjected to theoretical scrutiny, exhibit important adaptive properties. So argues N. Haan, a psychologist at the University of California at Berkeley, who has evolved a redefinition of common mechanisms that provides a positive, or coping, counterpart for each defensive one. The critical point in this formulation is not that mechanisms are adaptive; it is already abundantly clear that they are in the sense of protecting the person against the pain of experienced anxiety, although at the cost of at least somewhat (and maladaptively) distorting reality. Rather, Haan suggests that such mechanisms may facilitate effective and appropriate coping with reality *without such distortion*. For example, although it is defensive to attribute one's personally unacceptable impulses to another (projection), it is

TABLE A

Characteristics of Coping Mechanisms	Characteristics of Defense Mechanisms
Behavior involves choice and, thus, flexible, purposive behavior. It is an autonomous emergent organization.	Behavior is compelled, rigid, channeled, perhaps conditioned behavior.
Behavior is pulled toward the future and takes account of the needs of the present.	Behavior is pushed from the past.
Behavior is oriented to the reality requirements of the present situation.	Behavior is essentially distorting of the present situation.
Behavior involves secondary-process thinking, conscious and preconscious elements.	Behavior involves a greater quantity of primary-process thinking and partakes of unconscious elements.
Behavior operates with the organism's necessity of metering the experiencing of disturbing affects.	Behavior operates with assumption that it is possible magically to remove disturbing affects.
Behavior allows forms of impulse satisfaction in open, ordered, and tempered way.	Behavior allows impulse gratification by subterfuge.

ternal reality? From the first point of view it follows—and, indeed, this conclusion has been seriously drawn—that even psychoses are adaptive in that they often permit the individual to avoid pain (witness the person who develops the delusion that his dead spouse still lives, a psychotic but effective means to avoid awareness of a devastating loss). If we keep in mind that a psychosis may sometimes be an attempt at self-defense, much of the apparently aimless and bizarre behavior of the psychotic may seem a little less incomprehensible and unnatural.

Defense mechanisms are bad only in the sense that they involve a considerable degree of denial of reality. As few of us can afford to ignore the facts of our environment, such distor-

useful, hence coping and realistic, to be aware of what the other person is indeed feeling (empathy). Thus, projection can be seen as empathy gone wrong; the two occupy opposite sides of a common coin, or psychological process, that in this case can be called *sensitivity to others.*

The distinction between the coping and defensive poles of such processes can be made on a number of grounds. Table A summarizes the relevant differentiating characteristics.

In Table B, you will find the coping counterparts of three of the defense mechanisms discussed

TABLE B

Process	Defense Mechanism	Coping Mechanism
Impulse restraint	Repression	Suppression *(conscious* and *temporary* shutting off from awareness of anxiety-producing experiences)
Impulse diversion	Displacement	Sublimation (finding socially acceptable ways of expressing raw impulses)
Temporal reversals	Regression	Playfulness (being able to go back to early ways of thinking and behaving *intentionally* and for the fun of it)

in the text (it will help to review their definitions now), together with (in the first column) the general psychological process with which they are associated. Haan's schema is considerably more extensive, encompassing all the standard mechanisms.

The common themes distinguishing each coping mechanism from its defensive partner are its greater respect for reality and its conscious (as opposed to unconscious) control over the behavior, rendering it reversible at will. This reformulation promises to be a fruitful one; several empirical studies have already reported quite different factors associated with individuals' tendencies to use coping or defensive aspects of several of these processes. In one such study, H. A. Alker of Cornell University found relations between sensitivity (empathy versus projection) and students' attitudes toward colonialism. Among these was the tendency for an attitude of *extreme* anticolonialism to be associated with the tendency to project. This is perhaps a far cry from the everyday arena of coping and defense and is, for that very reason, the more interesting.

N. HAAN. A tripartite model of ego functioning values and clinical and research applications. *Journal of Nervous and Mental Disease,* 1969, **148,** 14–30. Copyright 1969 by The William & Wilkins Company.
H. A. ALKER. A quasi-paranoid feature of students' extreme attitudes against colonialism. *Behavioral Science,* 1971, **16,** 218–227.

tion is very likely to eventuate in some painful consequence. If we shirk political responsibility by rationalizing that we cannot afford to spend time in precinct work, then social reality, as evinced by the election of an incompetent government, may present us with the painful fact of a cruel and corrupt government or an economic depression. In this example the mech-

anism served to circumvent the anxiety that otherwise would have arisen from the conflict between the desire to serve society and the desire to serve Mammon. Rationalization was thus adaptive in that it successfully prevented a guilty social conscience yet was maladaptive when evaluated in terms of its realistic consequence.

SUMMARY

1. Frustration is a nearly inevitable result of conflict between the individual's wants and the restraints imposed by society. The effects of such frustration may be constructive or disruptive, and they may also be short term or enduring.
2. Frustration and conflict can facilitate goal attainment by increasing motivation, bringing about an appropriate modification of how one pursues the goal (or even the goal itself), or by leading to an adaptive redefining of the total goal-seeking situation.
3. When goal attainment continues to be blocked, disruptive effects on behavior can result, among them a tendency to focus too narrowly on the desired goal, thereby losing sight of alternative approaches and appropriate substitute goals.
4. As the tension induced by continued frustration of efforts to reach the goal builds up, the point is eventually reached where effective action is interfered with. The point at which frustration tolerance is exceeded in a given situation varies considerably among individuals.
5. When frustration tolerance breaks down, either aggressive or escape behavior is a frequent result. The source of the frustration may be directly attacked, or some more accessible substitute may be made the object of aggression (displacement).
6. Short-term motivational conflicts lead to temporary effects on the person's behavior in the given conflict situation. Most generally, he is torn between moving toward the positive aspects of his goal (approach) and moving away from its negative aspects (avoidance).
7. When one is confronted with the need to choose between two positive goals (approach-approach conflict), the resolution is typically rapid and relatively painless. More difficult and prolonged is the situation in which one is required to select one of two negative goals (avoidance-avoidance conflict). Perhaps the most disturbing situation is when one is faced with a goal that at the same time possesses strong positive *and* negative features (approach-avoidance conflict).
8. Prolonged failure to resolve long-term conflict situations may lead to anxiety, which, in turn, may give rise to attempts to avoid or at least to reduce this painful experience (defense mechanisms).
9. Among these mechanisms—which must escape the conscious notice of the individual in order to be effective in defending against anxiety—are repression, reaction formation, rationalization, insulation, and projection.
10. Defense mechanisms must be considered as adaptive behavior insofar as they succeed in protecting the person from the experienced pain of anxiety; by the same token, they are maladaptive because by their very nature they exact the price of some distortion of his perception of social reality and of his way of coping with it.

GLOSSARY

anxiety A state of apprehension felt by a person in which the source is usually not as specifically perceived as it is in fear. It often pertains to anticipations of such future danger as punishment or threats to self-esteem. Anxiety typically leads to defensive reactions.

approach-approach conflict A situation in which the individual must choose between two positive goal objects. It is likely to cause the least anxiety.

approach-avoidance conflict A situation in which the goal has both positive and negative factors. This is perhaps the most typical short-term conflict encountered and the most anxiety provoking.

avoidance-avoidance conflict A situation in which the individual must choose between two negative goal objects. His unpleasant task is to select the lesser of two evils.

cognitive narrowing A narrowing of perception attention to limited parts of a situation, often as a consequence of extreme tension. It tends to be accompanied by poorer adaptability in solving problems and attaining goals.

defense mechanisms Various forms of reaction to the anxiety aroused by conflict that serve to protect and enhance the self-picture. The mechanisms are not deliberately chosen by the person. They are common to everyone and raise serious problems for adjustment only when they occur excessively and thus prevent the person from coping realistically with his difficulties.

displacement A defense mechanism in which a drive or feeling is shifted to a substitute object, one that is psychologically more available. For example, aggressive impulses may be displaced, as in scapegoating, upon people (or even inanimate objects) who are not sources of frustration but are safer to attack.

escape reaction The tendency to leave a frustrating situation when the frustration tolerance has been exceeded. Such escape reactions are generally regarded as disruptive in that the failure to cope directly with the problem situation may itself lead to further adjustment difficulties.

frustration tolerance The threshold for the maximal amount of frustration that the individual can accommodate without developing disruptive or disorganized patterns of behavior. Frustration tolerance is a variable rather than a fixed quality, its level depending upon the characteristics of the person and the nature of the situation.

insulation A defense mechanism involving a separation of systems, either cognitive or emotional, in such a way that protective rationalizations can be preserved and disturbing thoughts and feelings can be cut off.

projection A defense mechanism in which the individual attributes to other people impulses and traits that he himself has but cannot accept. It is especially likely to occur when the person lacks insight into his own impulses and traits.

rationalization A defense mechanism in which the person, through cognitive distortion, finds false but good reasons to justify questionable acts, failures, or unpleasant situations.

reaction formation A defense mechanism characterized by exaggerated expression of behavioral tendencies exactly opposed to underlying repressed impulses.

regression A defense mechanism characterized by less mature behavior in a situation than a person usually shows. It may or may not involve behaviors actually shown earlier by the individual; in any case the regressive behavior is developmentally more primitive.

repression The inability to recall strongly emotional and anxiety-arousing experiences. It serves as a defensive protection against anxiety.

mental disorders and behavior pathology

DO YOU KNOW…

- whether mental illness is strictly (or even primarily) mental?

- under what circumstances persons may be labeled crazy, even psychiatrically or legally so, when in fact they get along fairly well in the world?

- that a certain type of mental illness involves little or no stress and anxiety for the individual?

- how complicated it can be to attempt to understand ''sick'' behavior when the behavior is also generally regarded as immoral or is downright illegal?

- why it makes perfect sense for the same individual to experience simultaneous delusions of grandeur and persecution?

- if schizophrenia is to any extent inherited and whether, if it is, that means that psychological treatments for the condition are bound to fail?

- how well psychiatrists agree in their diagnoses of mental illness and what factors that should be irrelevant do in fact influence their judgment?

- how even the best of psychiatric institutions may, in one respect, unintentionally participate in prolonging mental illness?

Photo by George Aptecker

CONTENTS

What we call *mental disorder* or *behavior pathology* (and there are other names as well) occurs when an individual's ability to cope realistically and effectively with the challenges and tasks of daily life is no longer adequate. One way to view this condition is to regard it as indicating a failure of a person's psychological defenses (Unit 23) to do their job of protecting him from crippling anxiety arising from psychological conflict. Or perhaps the defenses have worked *too* well, in the sense that a particular defense mechanism so dominates his behavior that it persistently and seriously distorts his everyday perceptions and makes him function inadequately.

The forms that mental disorders can take are varied, and they very likely differ in the extent to which they are caused by purely psychological factors. Whatever their origins, however, they are exceedingly common, although it is quite difficult to present more than very rough estimates of the incidence of different types of mental disorders.

Most clinical psychologists (the psychologists most concerned with this kind of behavior) and most psychiatrists assume that aberrant behavior is primarily related to psychological disturbances in the individual, rather than to bodily disorders. But many experts continue to search for possible genetic, biochemical, and physiological origins of behavioral deviance. Even Sigmund Freud, whose work in psychoanalysis was the most influential in the development of the psychological treatment of abnormal behavior, believed that eventually the biological origins of mental disturbance would be discovered. And in recent years considerable control of psychopathological symptoms has been achieved through pharmacotherapy, that is, the administration of drugs (see Unit 25). The effectiveness of these drugs suggests to many that biochemical disturbances may indeed underlie most mental illness. Nevertheless, the actual organic bases of most mental disease are not known, and the prevalent theories and descriptions focus primarily on the situational factors and life experiences that appear related to various disorders. In this unit we will review some of the current schemes for classifying varieties of such disorders and also some of the currently influential conceptual schemes developed to try to account for the abnormal behaviors.

WHAT IS MENTAL ILLNESS?

Mental illness is generally defined in terms of behaviors and felt experiences that deviate from standards of effective functioning, mental health, rationality, and even morality. Those around the individual—and often the individual himself—may regard his abnormal behavior as irrational and even bizarre, as self-destructive or dangerous to others, as associated with great discomfort for the self or others, as illegal or immoral.

Although mental illness is largely identified by deviant *behavior*, the term implies that there is a lack of health of *internal psychological states*. Thus, the term may seem appropriate if the individual is chronically miserable, anxious, unpleasantly moody, or depressed. If he worries excessively about what he considers to be an inadequacy in his sex life or in other interpersonal relations, he may be suffering from a *neurosis*, one of the milder forms of mental illness. If he hears voices that no one else hears, or believes that he is being systematically persecuted, or suffers radical swings in mood from despair to euphoria, he may be suffering from a *psychosis*, a more severe form of mental illness. But even these aberrant behaviors are interpreted as symptoms of mental illness only when they violate current socially approved behavior. Thus, as one psychiatrist has pointed out, "If you talk to God, you are praying. If God talks to you, you have schizophrenia" (Szasz, 1973).

Whether mildly or severely afflicted, the mentally ill individual often may function quite adequately in terms of the general criteria of solid citizenship. He may hold a job, provide for his dependents, and only rarely violate legal or moral standards. Under these circumstances, his otherwise deviant behavior may not be noticed, and he may not be labeled, by others or by himself, mentally ill. But if some of his behavior becomes annoying or disturbing for *others* (even if only because it violates societal standards in some way), the label of mental illness may more likely be applied. As Szasz (1970) points out, socially condemned behaviors ranging all the way from repetitive vicious assaults on the bodies of others to engaging privately and with mutual consent in homosexual behavior have been regarded as symptoms of mental illness. Even masturbation has, on occasion, been so designated. So have drug abuse and habitual delinquency. Some of these behaviors must indeed be regarded as antisocial, but one might question whether such antisocial behavior is necessarily "sick." Even more complicated is the relation between mental illness and definitions of legal insanity (see Box 24.1, p. 590).

PERSPECTIVES ON PSYCHOPATHOLOGY

Before discussing the traditional classifications of mental illness, at this point it is useful to examine several perspectives from which such deviant behavior can be viewed. The three major positions represented in current thinking are the **psychodynamic, behavioristic**, and **humanistic-existential models**.

The Psychodynamic Model

The psychodynamic model originated with the work of Sigmund Freud. (His general theory of personality development is discussed in Unit 29, and his therapeutic approach is outlined in Unit 25.) A basic proposition of the model is that normal and abnormal personality is formed from conflicts between innate needs or desires and socially acquired moral standards. We are all assumed to have hidden or unconscious *impulses* that seek expression but are unacceptable in terms of internalized moral standards that strive to control their direct expression. When impulses break through, or threaten to break through, and achieve expression in an unacceptable form, anxiety or guilt may result. Excessive anxiety or guilt constitute a major source of disturbed behavior.

BOX 24.1

MENTAL ILLNESS AND LEGAL INSANITY

"Not guilty by reason of insanity." You all have heard this verdict on screen or tube, but perhaps without a full awareness of the tortuous and ever-changing connection between psychological definitions of mental illness and legal conceptions of insanity. We cannot go into the long history of this problem in detail here; suffice it to say that the two views have never been and are not now identical, so that the fact of having been diagnosed as mentally ill is by no means an automatic protection from criminal penalties.

An early legal definition of insanity (the M'Naghten rule in 1843 English law) excused the accused if he was "labouring under such a defect of reason, from disease of the mind, as not to know the nature and quality of the act he was doing." This rule, understandably, was difficult to apply; yet it persists in some courts to this day, often somewhat modified by the notion of the irresistible impulse. By this amendment it becomes possible to conclude that although the accused *did* know the difference between right and wrong, he could not control his criminal actions.

Most recently we have seen the wide adoption of a rule, initially proposed by the American Law Institute, that states: "A person is not responsible for criminal conduct if at the time of such conduct as a result of mental disease or defect he lacks substantial capacity either to appreciate the criminality of his conduct or to conform his conduct to the requirement of the law." This of course requires a definition of "mental disease." For the moment, this is the one being used: "any abnormal condition of the mind which substantially affects mental or emotional processes and substantially impairs behavior controls."

At this writing, this new concept of legal insanity governs cases heard before all but one of the federal circuit courts of appeal. It appears to provide a sensible link to current concepts of mental illness, but the essential problem—when does a person merit punishment?—remains an open one.

The symptoms of mental disorders may center on forms of impulse expression that are indirect, less satisfying, but more acceptable. That is, impulses can be somewhat modified to conform to internalized standards. For example, an individual might be habitually sarcastic as a means of expressing unacceptably intense underlying sadistic hostility. Alternatively, disturbed behaviors may represent mechanisms that entirely *prevent* the expression of impulses. For example, an individual might develop a so-called functional paralysis of his arm (that has no organic basis); this paralysis may serve to prevent him from carrying out his underlying hostile impulse to strike and murder someone.

Treatment dictated by the psychodynamic model involves an attempt to allow the individual to gain awareness of the underlying dynamics of his symptoms and behavior and thus to achieve a more mature or balanced expression of impulses. The psychodynamic model views antisocial behaviors as resulting from a failure on the part of the individual to have acquired the usual internal standards that effectively control the expression of certain impulses. Treatment of antisocial behaviors attempts to compensate for the lack of effective early socialization, of having failed to learn the rules whereby one gets along in one's culture. In some instances, however, antisocial behavior should be better understood as serving to help the individual control hidden impulses. Thus, an individual might behave in antisocial ways because unconsciously he seeks rejection from others to prevent him from achieving intimacy in personal relations. This self-inflicted isolation, in turn, may enable him to maintain control over frightening sexual or aggressive impulses. According to the psychodynamic model, then, identical behaviors may result from entirely different psychodynamics, so that only a detailed study of the individual allows us to know which formulation of the underlying problem is accurate *for him*.

The Behavioristic Model

This approach, in contrast with the psychodynamic model, does not include assumptions about underlying or unconscious impulses. The behaviorist sees aberrant behavior as having resulted from vicissitudes of learning and conditioning. (The general theory and the therapy techniques of the behavioristic approach are discussed more fully in Units 29 and 25, respectively.) Unlike those who subscribe to the psychodynamic model, the behaviorist feels no need to understand the underlying purpose of the behavior.

However, the behavioristic model does see anxiety or fear as one of the basic manifestations to be dealt with in almost anyone with severe behavior disorders. Anxiety, they would argue, results not from the threatened breakthrough of unacceptable impulses but from the conditioned association of anxiety as a response to patterns of environmental stimuli. That is, behaviors that reduce anxiety are increasingly likely to persist. For example, if a child experiences a reduction in anxiety when he is neat, orderly, and meticulously clean, he may show these behaviors in an exaggerated form as an adult even though the original threat (e.g., anger or punishment from parents) is long since gone. Sometimes it is the *avoidance* of certain behaviors that helps keep anxiety under control (e.g., keeping away from high places if one has an intense and irrational fear of heights). In general, a behavioristic analysis looks for the problem behaviors that in the past have been reinforced either directly or by having reduced anxiety, and the treatment seeks to set up a systematic program for reconditioning and relearning of these maladaptive responses.

The Humanistic Model

This perspective is most clearly represented in the writings of psychologists Abraham Maslow and Carl Rogers. Their underlying assumption is that man is inherently good and that we all possess a drive to realize our *real* selves, to achieve *self-actualization*. Man seeks to fulfill and express his potentials and talents but is often thwarted by social forces of approval and rejection that force him to deny aspects of himself and thus prevent the development of his real self. Within this perspective it is this denial of the real self that is the source of psychic pain and aberrant behavior. Therapy is seen as providing an opportunity for the individual to express himself more freely and to accept those aspects of feelings and thoughts that he has been trying to hide and avoid. When he can accept himself more fully, he will be able to achieve a more satisfying psychological integration.

THE EXTENT OF MENTAL ILLNESS

We have glimpsed the diversity of the conceptions of the origins of mental illness and the variety of the approaches to its treatment. In doing so we have gained an appreciation of one of the problems encountered in determining the incidence of mental illness in the population: What is difficult to define is difficult to count. But rough estimates of the extent of the various psychopathologies are possible. One source of difficulty in making such estimates is the fact that the accuracy of diagnosis is not high; furthermore, a number of factors enter into the application of diagnostic labels that may seriously distort these estimates.

One approach to arriving at reasonable estimates of the incidence of psychological disturbance is through intensive surveys of representative samples of a given community. A representative sample of the total population is interviewed, and the overall figures for the community are estimated from this sample. In one such study, conducted in one area of New York City (Srole et al., 1962), it was found that fully 30 percent of the population suffered from psychological problems judged sufficiently severe to interfere with their everyday lives—a truly startling figure and certainly one that would not even be approached if we were to rely only upon the more formal and public records of mental disturbance. Lower, but hardly reassuring, is the estimate from one national survey that 10 percent of school children are in need of treatment for psychological disorders.

The 30 percent estimate for the adult population includes all forms and all degrees of mental disorder, from psychiatric hospitalization to outpatient psychiatric treatment to untreated disturbance. This last category is of course most difficult to define and to count.

Whatever the particular percentages may be, an interesting pattern has been emerging recently in rates of hospitalization that reflects important changes in the manner in which psychological disturbances are being dealt with. Total admissions to mental hospitals continue to rise, but the average length of hospitalization has decreased dramatically, with a net result of a considerable reduction of the resident mental hospital population (see Figure 24.1). During the same period, a considerable increase in the use of outpatient facilities and day-care centers

has taken place. Some believe that extensive use of chemotherapy (the use of medication to control symptoms) has shortened the necessary period of hospitalization. Also a probable factor has been the growth of community mental health treatment centers that may prevent both initial hospitalization and rehospitalization of emotionally disturbed persons.

CLASSES OF MENTAL DISORDERS

The most recent classification schemes for mental disorders is the *Diagnostic and Statistical Manual of Mental Disorders* (*DSM-II*) which was published by the American Psychiatric Association in 1968.

The *DSM-II* includes under the rubric of **functional disorders** the major portion of emotional disturbances and the ones that are most familiar to the layman. The term *functional* refers to a disorder for which no specific *organic* basis has yet been discovered and in which the patient's past experience has played an important part. This statement is not meant to imply that functional disorders have no physical reflections in the nervous system; we know that they do. Nor does it imply that genetic influences are absent; we know that they are not. But because these disorders are generally not yet known to have specific organic causes, attempts to understand and cure them focus mainly on psychological procedures.

In the category of functional disorders it has been customary to specify three major classes: psychosis, neurosis, and personality disorders.

A **psychosis**, in contrast with the other classes of disorders, involves a relatively high degree of disorganization. Generally, the psychotic individual, especially when he is in the acute stage, shows severe thinking, emotional, and behavioral aberrations. He may appear to have lost contact with reality as others perceive it, and he may display emotional reactions that do not appear to others as appropriate reactions to his current situation. He may experience delusions and hallucinations and may be viewed by himself and others as so incapacitated that he requires hospitalization or the administration

Hospitalization for Mental Illness

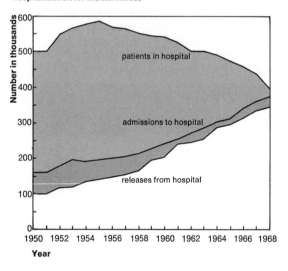

FIGURE 24.1 Although the total number of admissions to mental institutions remains on the rise, the number of releases from hospitals keeps pace with this trend, indicating increasingly shorter length of stay in hospital. The net result is that the number of patients in any given year has been steadily declining for well over a decade.

U.S. Department of Health, Education, and Welfare. National health statistics. *Current Facility Reports.* Washington, D.C.: Government Printing Office, 1969.

of powerful drugs to subdue his more extreme behaviors.

The person suffering from a **neurosis** (**psychoneurosis**) is not so severely disorganized in behavior as the psychotic is and ordinarily maintains reasonably appropriate responses to reality. However, he does behave or feel in ways that are uncomfortable to himself and often appear somewhat irrational to others. Individuals who are diagnosed as neurotic may, for example, experience periods of acute panic with no discernible source for the anxiety. They may find themselves compelled to entertain particular obsessive thoughts or perform particular compulsive actions that they and observers feel to be irrational. Neuroses are emotional disorders that generally center on anxiety.

The term **personality disorder** (sometimes called *character disorder*) refers to patterns of antisocial behavior that are disapproved of by others or are harmful to the self or others. Often the behavior is illegal, as in the case of sexual deviation, alcoholism, drug abuse, and the like. In other instances, the behavior involved in personality disorders is not illegal but is maladaptive for the individual, although in ways differing from the patterns shown by psychotics and neurotics. Personality disorders lack the distortion of reality shown by psychotics, and the emotional distress symptoms of neurotics. The personality disorder is characterized by pervasive behavioral styles that permeate all or most of the person's reactions to the environment. He may be unaware of the annoying or self-destructive quality of his own behavior or may be able to rationalize it in moral terms. His style may be considerably more uncomfortable for his associates than it is for him.

Before we begin our detailed description of the various classes of mental disorders, it should be noted that the discussion will not give equal weight to the three models (psychodynamic, behavioristic, and humanistic) mentioned earlier. The primary emphasis will be on an essentially psychodynamic viewpoint. The reason for this is that the development of a nomenclature and classificatory scheme and the very idea of differential diagnosis have come about primarily from the efforts of workers of the psychodynamic persuasion and are regarded by them as necessary. Behaviorists and humanists, on the other hand, tend to feel that labeling and elaborate diagnostic procedures obscure rather than clarify our understanding and treatment of maladaptive behavior. Behaviorists generally believe that the multitude of explanations proposed by psychodynamic theorists to explain the many different hypothesized classes of disturbed behavior are unnecessary in light of the essential and relatively straightforward learning-conditioning paradigm they regard as common to *all* forms of behavior. The humanists reject the labeling and classification scheme for a different reason. They believe that it obscures what they consider most important: the *unique* aspects of the individual.

Neuroses

An individual diagnosed as neurotic can show an extremely wide variety of behaviors. However, experts of all theoretical persuasions agree that anxiety is a central feature. The anxiety involved may be consciously experienced, and this experience may constitute the major aspect of the disorder. In many other instances, neurotic manifestation consists of responses that ward off or control anxiety but then are causes of discomfort in and of themselves. The anxiety, whether experienced or blocked from awareness, distorts experience and learning, so that appropriate reactions which would be more adjusted to reality cannot occur.

The neurotic person's symptoms may shift from time to time, but among his shifting symptoms a dominant pattern can usually be detected. This dominant pattern probably tells us something about the nature of the individual and of his problems, just as the characteristic pattern of defense mechanisms in the individual tells us something about his personality. Some of the generally recognized forms of psychoneurotic reactions are described in the following paragraphs.

Anxiety neurosis   As the name suggests, an **anxiety neurosis** is characterized by the appearance of periods of anxiety. The anxiety may erupt in short periods of acute panic or may be of a chronic and pervasive nature, varying from mild to moderate in intensity. Everyone experiences anxiety on some occasions, but the person afflicted with an anxiety neurosis shows this emotional reaction at a level far beyond that apparently warranted by the immediate situations. Chronic anxiety may be associated with other behaviors such as insomnia and irritability, and with such physical symptoms as ulcers and disturbances in cardiovascular functioning, which can ultimately become serious health hazards. (See the discussion of psychosomatic disorders in Unit 28, p. 694.)

An example of how an anxiety reaction may develop and recur at specific points in a man's career is presented in Box 24.2.

Hysterical neurosis The disorder **hysterical neurosis**, although believed to be relatively infrequent today, is of historical interest in the development of the psychodynamic view because many of Freud's early patients were considered to fall within this category. There are two major types of hysterical neurosis: the conversion reaction and the dissociative reaction. The **conversion reaction** involves physical disturbances in the sensory systems and in the part of the musculature ordinarily thought to be under voluntary control. Thus, in the absence of any physiological or neurological damage, the individual can in fact (i.e., in function) *be* blind or deaf or without sensation in a particular part of his body. He may experience paralysis of a limb or may show spasmodic jerking of a muscle group. The psychodynamic position tends to view these symptoms as means by which the individual avoids psychic conflict. For example, a hysterical individual who is unable to speak may thus be able to avoid the verbal expression of unacceptable impulses.

The **dissociative reaction** is characterized by disturbance of memory or identity (amnesia). One of the more interesting, if rare, versions of the dissociative reaction is the *multiple personality*. In this instance the individual develops two or more distinct personalities that often vary widely in character or style. Often one personality is inhibited and moralistic, and another personality is impulsive and fun-loving.

Psychodynamically, it is as if conflict within the individual between moral and amoral forces is resolved by splitting the original personality into separate parts, thus avoiding a confrontation between the incompatible warring elements. (Incidentally, this is *not* what is popularly regarded as a *split personality*; that term, for quite different reasons, is sometimes applied to the schizophrenic reaction (see p. 601). One can see clearly how a psychodynamic point of view would deal conceptually with this disorder: The several personalities allow for an expression of ordinarily forbidden impulses without an experience of the guilt that would otherwise occur in the individual. In episodes of amnesia, the loss of identity can remove the individual from intolerably stressful life situations whose conflicts he cannot resolve by other means.

One further comment regarding multiple personalities and hysterical phenomena in general: The hysteric neurotic is believed to be quite suggestible; that is, he is highly responsive to the implied demands of those around him to produce further "personalities" or other symptoms.

Phobic neurosis The **phobic neurosis** is characterized by excessive fears of objects, places, or situations. The fears differ from the reasonable reactions that all of us experience in response to objectively threatening situations. The phobic individual is *irrationally* fearful. Thus, some phobic persons may experience a sense of panic when caught in a crowd; others react the same way when finding themselves totally alone in an open field. Sometimes an individual can have an abnormal fear of germs and develop extreme, but fated-to-fail, measures to avoid any possible source of contamination. The woman who fears for her life if she were to leave her home (see Unit 25, p. 615) suffers from a phobic neurosis; so do people who are panicked during their final exams (Box 25.2, p. 622) or at the sight of a snake (Box 25.3, p. 624).

Mild phobic reactions are found to some degree in most people. However, when they become pervasive and begin to hamper the individual's ability to carry out his existence, they are considered pathological and neurotic. Strong phobic reactions can be highly unpleas-

BOX 24.2

AN ANXIETY REACTION

Robert W. White, a psychologist at Harvard University, presents the following summary and interpretation of a case of anxiety reaction, originally reported by H. V. Dicks.

A man of forty came for treatment on account of severe anxiety attacks characterized especially by fear of enclosed places, difficulty in breathing (especially at night), and a most unpleasant sense of impending disaster. He had always been contemptuous of psychology and sought the aid of a psychiatrist only as a desperate last resort. He had just resigned after a distinguished career in the Government service. Considering the Government's policy too liberal, he made his resignation a matter of principle. He was living at home and considering starting out as a novice in a new profession when the anxiety attacks began to overwhelm him.

Working back through his career it was discovered that he had had some earlier bouts with anxiety. The most recent occasion was at the time of demobilization following World War I, in which he served as battalion commander and was decorated at a very early age. This circumstance well illustrates the lack of relation between neurotic anxiety and real danger: it was when demobilized and safe that the patient had attacks of anxiety. Previous to these attacks he had had another round of trouble when he entered college as a freshman. For a while he could not sit in lectures; if he went at all he took a seat next to the door so that he could leave at any time. Before this there was one attack at the age of seven when he had to sit through a church service under dimly lighted Gothic arches. Various anxieties connected with the Oedipus situation were uncovered, but they showed few links with the contents of his anxiety attacks. Finally the chain of incidents was completed by the patient's recalling a scene that took place in infancy when he had an attack of bronchial pneumonia. He was lying in a cot, coughing and nearly suffocating, in acute panic but at the same time furiously angry with his mother, who stood by unable to relieve his distress. The images included a tent over his cot and various other details. From outside sources it was possible to verify that he had had bronchial pneumonia at the age of eighteen months, and that a tent over the bed was one of the measures used for treatment.

The form of the patient's anxiety attacks—the breathing difficulty and fear of enclosures—was apparently set by this . . . panic. His attack in church would seem to have been stimulated by the heavy arches (reminding him of the tent) and the necessity to sit still (helpless restraint). But we can understand his later attacks, especially the ones that sent him for treatment, only if we know something about the development of his personality. The patient was the eldest son and also the eldest of his circle of cousins. His parents encouraged him strongly to take the role of a big boy. He successfully assumed this role, becoming proud and markedly independent. Identifying himself with authority and the moral code, he emerged as the leader and disciplinarian of his younger relatives. This pattern was continued in school, won again in college, given much scope when he served as an army officer, and carried on while he was in the Government service. He became an energetic and successful man with a strong need for superiority. One can discern, however, that his career had something of the overdriven quality that characterizes a neurotic protective organization. It was when activity, success, and superiority were blocked that he gave way to anxiety attacks: when he lost his school distinction and became a "nobody" at college; when he lost his military distinction and became a "nobody" at demobilization; when he lost his distinction as a Government officer and became a "nobody" without a vocation.

This case illustrates the early establishment of a neurotic nucleus as the result of one tremendously frightening experience. . . . As the patient's personality developed, it was encouraged to take a form that happened to serve admirably as a means of counteracting his neurotic liability. His pattern emphasized independence (rejecting the useless dependent longings), activity (preventing a passive state of helplessness), and power (the opposite of being unable to influence his mother). These strivings were effective, yielded gratification, and led to a constructive life. There was only one flaw: when they were all blocked, so that he was reduced to the status of a "nobody," he developed not just the frustration that anyone might feel under such circumstances, but more than that—acute anxiety attacks.

H. V. DICKS. *Clinical Studies in Psychopathology.* Baltimore: Wood, 1939.
R. W. WHITE. *The Abnormal Personality.* New York: Ronald, 1964. Text material reprinted by permission; copyright © 1964 The Ronald Press Company, New York.

ant and disruptive, but they do have a certain advantage over the *free-floating* and nondirected anxieties of the anxiety neurotic. Since they are clearly focused fears, the individual can take active steps to avoid the phobic situation and its disorganizing impact. Unfortunately, sometimes the individual becomes phobic about situations or activities that are impossible to avoid if he is to live in the world, and he is thus confronted by constant, intolerable crises.

The psychodynamic point of view asserts that phobic fears are displacements or substitutes for actual fears or desires that are unconscious. In Freud's classic case of "little Hans," a five-year-old boy experienced a severe phobia with respect to horses. According to Freud's analysis of the case, the horse was symbolically equivalent to the boy's father onto whom the boy had projected his own hostility. Through a complex psychological process, Hans's anger toward and fear of his father and his fear of his own hostile impulses led to their displacement from his father to the horse. According to the psychodynamic interpretation, other phobias may also be representative of unconscious fears, with the phobic object having symbolic relationships to the actual unconscious fear.

The behavioristic point of view conceives of phobias as conditioned fears resulting from pain or fear from one stimulus becoming (usually accidentally) associated with the phobic stimulus. Because of the mechanism of stimulus generalization, situations and objects other than those involved in the original learning (but similar to them) can also serve to elicit phobic fear. For example, in a classic experiment (Watson & Rayner, 1920), an eleven-month-old child named Albert, who initially was quite comfortable, even playful, in the presence of a white rat, was conditioned to fear the rat (to cry, to escape from it) by having a loud, intrinsically startling and frightening noise presented each time (over a series of trials) Albert reached toward his playmate. Not only did Albert thus learn to fear white rats, but the fear generalized to similar fuzzy objects (a rabbit, a fur coat, a cotton ball), objects with which he also had previously been at ease. Watson and Rayner had intended to show that Albert's learned fears could then be unlearned, but they lost touch

with him. Jones (1924) repeated their demonstration that phobias could be learned in this way and did go on to remove the fear through extinction procedures, perhaps the first formal instance of today's behavior therapy techniques (see Unit 25, p. 619).

Obsessive-compulsive neurosis　In the **obsessive-compulsive neurosis** the person is subject to actions and/or thoughts that he finds undesirable but is unable to prevent. Usually the term *obsession* applies to *thoughts* that the individual finds troublesome or even disgusting; often they refer to filth, obscenity, or an action that is so socially unacceptable it is repugnant to the individual. The term *compulsion* ordinarily refers to *actions* that the person feels forced to perform. These actions may vary from simple gestures to complex rituals that can literally consume hours. If the individual is somehow prevented from carrying out her compulsive behavior, she may experience acute discomfort, even panic.

The behavior of the obsessive-compulsive sometimes appears to represent a kind of equilibrium between antisocial and unacceptable impulses in the form of obsessions and subsequent attempts to undo the unacceptable impulse through atoning ritualistic behaviors. (In Box 24.3 we see this obsessive-compulsive reaction dramatically illustrated.)

In its usual fashion, the psychodynamic point of view interprets these behaviors as an expression of attempts to solve conflicts between impulses. Obsessive thoughts and impulses of an unacceptable nature are often stripped of the feeling and emotion that might be thought to accompany such content, and this isolation serves as a distorting device. The compulsive behavior, in turn, is seen as a way to avoid and deny unacceptable impulses.

From the behavioristic point of view, obsessive-compulsive behavior is regarded as resulting from an attempt to reduce or prevent fear. Any behavior that is associated with the reduction of fear (escape learning) or with the avoidance of fear (avoidance learning) tends to be highly persistent in the presence of the stimuli involved (see Unit 16, p. 379). Seen in this way, the obsessive-compulsive is performing re-

BOX 24.3

AN OBSESSIVE-COMPULSIVE

Norman Cameron provides this case history of a woman enmeshed in a crippling obsessive-compulsive web:

Ramona M. was the forty-two-year-old wife of a Minnesota businessman and the mother of three children. Her symptoms appeared suddenly. She was serving the family dinner one evening when she dropped a dish on the table and smashed it. The accident appalled her. While clearing up the fragments she was seized with an unreasonable fear that bits of glass might get into her husband's food and kill him. She would not allow the meal to proceed until she had removed everything and reset the table with fresh linen and clean dishes. After this her fears, instead of subsiding, reached out to include intense anxiety over the possibility that she herself and her children might be killed by bits of glass.

The patient's fears and defensive rituals did not stop with this. Ramona developed an irresistible need to examine minutely every piece of glassware that she handled. If anything had the slightest chip in it she threw it away; and she had to carry it to the trash can herself to make sure that it went out of the house. Then she would hunt for the missing chip which, of course, she could rarely find. She had read somewhere that copper pots and aluminum pots were not safe for certain kinds of cooking. Her worries now included their use. She remembered that her wedding ring had some copper in it as well as gold. First she took it off whenever she cooked or washed dishes; then she lost it.

Meanwhile she heard about other things which raised new fears and touched off further compulsive countermeasures. These included the danger of a spread of virus disease from toilet to kitchen, the dangers of lye and pesticides, and of the chemical and organic fertilizers used on the lawn. Eventually all potential poisons of every kind had to be isolated from cooking utensils and dishes by storing them in the garage—even the cleaning fluids and scouring powders needed for everyday washing and cleaning.

These endless precautionary rituals drove the family almost frantic. Yet they brought Ramona no lasting peace. Her list of potential dangers kept growing until she simply did not have enough attention to bestow upon them all. If she was not certain that she had or had not done something in a certain way, she would have to rehearse her steps to make sure, or else begin all over again.

What was the meaning of this network of fears and precautions? Why did this ordinary housewife act as though her husband and children might be treacherously murdered in their own home, like medieval princelings? It came out in the course of therapy that Ramona was protecting everybody from herself. Eventually she recognized the source of her dangerous hostility. Some time before the breaking of the glass dish she had discovered what she considered to be certain evidence that her husband was having an affair. This humiliated and angered her, but she said nothing about it. What appalled Ramona when she smashed the dish was the momentary conscious hope that he would eat glass and die, a homicidal wish that her carelessness would kill him. She immediately denied and repressed the wish; but from that moment all her obsessive-compulsive countermeasures were directed against the possibility of some new accident in which she might inadvertently carry out her unconscious wish.

In this case, as in many obsessive-compulsive cases, the symptoms were very versatile. At the same time that her cleaning and isolating rituals protected Ramona from acting out her homicidal impulse, they also served to frustrate, restrict and exasperate beyond endurance the object of her hostility, her husband. Meals were never ready. They took forever to serve. Cleaning was going on all the time everywhere. Ramona's revenge thus came through deviously in her precautionary symptoms. She held the family as prisoners in the protective custody of her neurosis. She punished them in such a way that—since she herself was neurotically ill and suffering—they could not even complain without seeming heartless to themselves.

Ramona also was punishing herself. Her dangerous impulses forced her to devote all of her waking life to defensive measures. She was like someone on a dike with the flood waters threatening to break through in many different places. She kept finding weak places in her defenses while she had to keep constantly on guard to see that the old ones did not crumble. In the end she herself collapsed.

N. CAMERON. *Personality Development and Psychopathology.* Boston: Houghton Mifflin, 1963.

sponses that may once have been quite realistic defenses against a threatening situation but do not appear rational (and are not adaptive) in the present situation. In the case of Ramona (Box 24.3), a behavioristic analysis might suggest that when she broke the dish on the table that first time, she was experiencing considerable anxiety (perhaps because she was thinking about her husband's affair and her own hostile fantasies). When the dish broke, that stimulus (broken dish) became associated with anxiety or fear (of losing her husband or of killing him; the content is not important here). Perhaps her involvement in cleaning up after the accident, which itself was a way of avoiding the anxiety and fearful thoughts, actually did momentarily reduce her anxiety by preoccupying her. From then on, each time she saw something broken, the associated fear returned, and she therefore engaged ritualistically in a behavior that initially did help to eliminate the anxiety-provoking stimulus and so reduced the anxiety. Through the process of stimulus generalization, other related stimuli became associated with anxiety and also had to be removed.

The particular content of the anxiety association would be relatively unimportant to a behaviorist concerned with treating the compulsive behavior. He would be most concerned with counterconditioning or creating new associations between the stimuli, perhaps substituting relaxation for the anxiety so that the stimulus-anxiety response association might be broken and the necessity for the anxiety-avoiding behavior eliminated.

Some other neuroses   We shall briefly mention a number of the other neurotic types that are listed in the *DSM-II* classification of mental disorders.

The *depressive neurosis* is characterized by chronic sadness that does not appear to be warranted by the individual's life circumstances. An allied disorder, the *neurasthenic neurosis*, is characterized by feelings of chronic fatigue that the person tends to attribute to physical factors. Both the depressive and neurasthenic neuroses can last for years and can represent a heavy burden for the person's associates. The same can be said for the *hypochondriacal* person, who has an intense preoccupation with his own physical symptoms, which for the most part have no basis in organic pathology. Neurasthenia, hypochondria, and the earlier-mentioned conversion reactions are to be distinguished from malingering, which is the *conscious* faking of disability in order to avoid an unwanted situation.

The existential neurosis   This particular disorder is not listed in the *DSM-II*, but it has received considerable attention among writers who hold to the existential point of view. Briefly, this point of view asserts that man defines himself through conscious choices and the ultimate awareness of the finiteness of his existence. Man seeks meaning, and when he fails to find it, he may experience existential frustration (Frankl, 1962). An *existential neurosis* results from his attempt to deal with or deny this frustration. He may experience overwhelming guilt over his awareness that he has not lived up to what he could have been, or he may obsessively persist in a fruitless and agitated search for some unattainable certainty and perfection, a substitute goal for his own experienced failure to fulfill his potential.

Personality Disorders

The second large category of mental illnesses, the personality disorders, consists of behaviors which are believed to be pervasive personality styles developed in response to conflict early in the individual's life. They are said to be distinguishable from the neuroses we have just discussed partly because the behaviors that characterize these disorders are rarely seen by the individual as peculiar or in any way troublesome to himself. A number of the personality disorders have the same names as neuroses, and the disorders are often allied behaviorally with the neuroses, as you shall soon see. Others, such as schizoid, paranoid, and cyclothymic personality disorders, resemble psychoses to be discussed later in this unit. All in all, there are ten personality disorders in *DSM-II*; we shall attend here to only a few of these.

Obsessive-compulsive personality   The early Freudians noted that obsessive-compulsive neurosis typically showed, in addition to the obvious dramatic and peculiar behaviors that characterize the disorder, pervasive personality traits of a fairly regular nature. The affected individuals were found to be extremely and irrationally concerned about neatness and orderliness and conformity to well-defined rules. A strong inhibition of directly expressed or obvious aggression was also found in these individuals, as well as an inability to behave with emotional spontaneity. It was subsequently discovered that these personality traits could also be found in individuals who did *not* show the dramatic and obvious obsessions and compulsions of the classical neurotic pattern. The *DSM-II* classifies this pattern as **obsessive-compulsive personality**. That is, they did not exhibit the more bizarre and disturbing symptoms of their neurotic counterparts, although their general style of thinking and coping was similar. It was assumed, then, that for such individuals, these traits represented relatively permanent structures in the personality that no longer required (as the neuroses did) an ongoing conflict in order to be maintained.

Such structures, in effect, constitute the individual's personality. The individual with an obsessive-compulsive personality disorder does not usually experience anxiety; in fact, he may be remarkably free of it. In addition, unlike the neurotic, he does not consider his behavior to be abnormal or even alien to his notion of himself. In fact, it has been suggested that it is only when the particular defensive styles which are part of the long-standing character of the individual begin to fail (i.e., no longer keep the person free of anxiety resulting from awareness of unacceptable impulses) that he finds it necessary to add to his defensive armor by adopting more exaggerated and bizarre defensive maneuvers. Thus, by this view, *a life crisis may propel an otherwise stable personality disorder into a corresponding neurosis.*

Hysterical personality   Persons designated as **hysterical personalities** show a number of personality characteristics typical of the hysterical neurotic. Such individuals tend to be overdramatic, emotionally and behaviorally. The extremeness of reaction, however, seems not to be a reflection of genuine feeling. A typical pattern that has been recognized, primarily among women, involves behavior on her part that appears highly seductive sexually, although often she is actually sexually frigid and is quite honestly taken aback when her seductiveness is responded to by sexual advances. Also associated with this type of disorder are such charac-

teristics as extreme dependence on, and seeking attention from, others.

Antisocial reaction   One of the most interesting personality disorders is the category called the **antisocial reaction** (formerly referred to as *psychopathic personality*). This category refers to persons who show diffuse and chronic incapacity for persistent, ordered living. The individual behaves impulsively apparently in order to obtain immediate gratification of his needs. He seems relatively unable to anticipate the consequences of his actions and so fails to learn from experience, to plan ahead, or to follow long-range goals. He acts before he thinks. Similarly, he is insensitive to the needs of others. Unable to tolerate frustration, he lives from moment to moment, his actions appearing erratic, irresponsible, and unpredictable.

In appearance, the psychopath is likely to make a startlingly pleasing impression at first. His intelligence is unimpaired. He is often charming and articulate, glibly using words, flattery, fabrication to manipulate situations to his own ends. Although he appears friendly, he is usually isolated because of his incapacity to form lasting relations.

The antisocial personality seems to suffer from a failure to have developed moral standards or conscience; it is as if in childhood he had never learned to postpone his desires in consideration of his parents' wishes or values and so failed to internalize the standards of society. In line with this makeup, he seems to have surprisingly little guilt or anxiety. Indeed, the antisocial personality tends to be comfortable in situations in which most people would feel uneasy. Not only anxiety but also other emotions seem to be lacking or shallow. As noted, he shows little capacity for real love or attachment.

Conduct Disorders

The *DSM-II* also recognizes another class of disorder that is not psychotic and often not even neurotic in nature. This class—**conduct disorders**—resembles personality disorders in that they also often represent lifelong patterns of behavior. Included in this classification are sexual deviations, alcoholism, and drug dependence. But there is at least one critical difference, although it may be more a social than a personal one: Conduct disorders typically involve legal or moral censure and are very often defined as criminal by society. Because of this intermixing of societal and psychological factors, it is difficult to consider conduct disorders in the same way as we have so far discussed other forms of mental disorder. In fact, many argue, and with some justification, that these forms of behavior are not mental disorders in the proper sense of the term. Certainly—at least in our present society—sexual deviations, alcoholism, and drug addiction are very often severely maladaptive. With equal certainty we can assert that such behaviors are accompanied by anxiety and personal suffering on the part of both the individual and those about him. But this suffering is no doubt amplified by the moral and legal sanctions imposed on such behavior. Historically, societies have varied in what behaviors of this sort have been considered taboo and in the energy with which they pursued and punished transgressors. Even within the present-day United States considerable variation in this respect can be found, and, most clearly with ·respect to sexual deviations, the psychic price paid depends importantly on the community within which the "offenders" live.

All this is not to argue that persons with conduct disorders are really in the best of mental health, or would be if society were only more tolerant. The very fact of choosing a way of life that runs so counter to the dominant values of one's culture may itself betray a problem with psychological origins. It must be emphasized, however, that what are called conduct disorders may merely characterize the social conscience in action.

Functional Psychoses

The three main classes of functional psychoses, according to the *DSM-II* classification, are affective disorders, schizophrenia, and the paranoid states. The primary feature that they share and that separates them from other classes of mental disorders is, in a certain sense, a social one: Each one involves a significant impairment in

the capacity to meet the ordinary demands of life. However, the *nature* of the impairment is quite different for each of the psychoses.

Affective disorders **Affective disorders** are characterized by exaggerations of mood states, often but not necessarily involving fluctuation between extremes. The three most commonly recognized types are the manic, the depressive, and the manic-depressive. In this instance, perhaps as a welcome change, the labels are self-descriptive.

The *manic* person tends to progress from normal moods to excessive elation, becomes quite excited, and, if he goes too far, may explode into violent and unrestrained behavior, sometimes dangerous to others or to himself (thus the common term *maniac*). Conversely, the *depressive* type may shift from normal mood states to extreme depression, sometimes of suicidal intensity, sometimes so deep that he is thrown into a condition of bodily immobility. Some psychotic patients show *alternations* of extreme elation and depression (hence the term *manic-depressive*). The manic-depressive cycle may vary in length and regularity. It is not uncommon to find patients on a regular 48-hr cycle: 24 hr of depression followed by 24 hr of elation. The predictability of these psychological "readouts" testifies to the dependability and regularity of whatever living clocks control these mood swings. Other patients may have cycles of as long as 18 or 24 months. These patients quite regularly undergo severe character changes from being despondent, apathetic, and listless to becoming elated, full of grandiose projects, and showing bubbling enthusiasm and boundless energy, and then back again. It has been estimated that during any one year in the United States there are about 100,000 of these people in hospitals, so extreme are their mood changes; another 200,000 are being treated in clinics and at home.

Mood changes are common to all of us. It may even be that it is normal to undergo *regular cycles of mood changes*: seasonal, monthly, bimonthly, or circadian, for both men and women. Indeed, there already are available some indications from various studies that mild but detectable mood changes may be one of the universal human psychological cycles modulated by some of the same biological clocks which control and time the rhythmic activities of the body's hormones. Nor must the mood changes be mild in order to be normal. Probably every human being has been deeply depressed and highly elated at some time in her life. To be profoundly depressed is as normal a reaction to a traumatic loss (whether of a beloved other or of one's own health or even self-esteem) as to be deathly afraid is a normal reaction to a life-threatening confrontation. But when no significant event can be found in the person's environment which can reasonably "explain" a profound change in mood, or if such a cause is found, but the behavior the person displays seems excessive or lasts too long—that is, is widely different from that of the culturally accepted norms—then we can speak of affective disorder, and then and only then do we feel justified in seeking therapy.

Schizophrenic reactions The most prevalent of all psychoses is **schizophrenia**, currently accounting for 25 percent of first admissions to mental hospitals. And, since schizophrenics tend to remain institutionalized longer than other mental patients, perhaps half of all hospitalized patients at any given time are schizophrenics (Mosher & Feinsilver, 1970). Schizophrenia is characterized by a wide variety of symptoms, not all found in any one person. In general, there appears to be a peculiar distortion of the emotions and feelings; the person may seem completely insensitive to things that would normally be expected to evoke emotional response, for example, news of the death of a member of the family. His standards of conduct, dress, personal hygiene, and social relations may show severe deterioration. He may become excessively withdrawn, out of all touch with the external world, even to the point at which he may sit completely immobile for hours, during which time his limbs can be moved about by someone else and will remain in the positions in which they are placed (see Figure 24.2). He may often be subject to hallucinations in which he hears voices or sees visions, or he may suffer distortions of normal perceptual experience (see

FIGURE 24.2 A patient in a mental hospital in a typical position for a withdrawn catatonic.

Photo from *The New York Times*

Figure 24.3, p. 602). He may exhibit bizarre behavior, confused thought, and chaotic speech.

In the *DSM-II* classification there are ten different types of schizophrenia noted, although to make the required distinction (a procedure called *differential diagnosis*) is almost always difficult and in many cases unreliable. Generally, each subtype exhibits more of one or a few of the symptoms just discussed, but for the most part there is considerable overlap in their behaviors. The *catatonic* subtype, for example, is most dramatically expressed in motor symptoms and is itself separable into two sub-subtypes in the *DSM-II*: *excited*, which involves a good deal of agitated, restless, and often bizarre moving about, and *withdrawn*, which is exemplified by stuporous immobility. Yet another broad distinction of a quite different sort within schizophrenia, and a promising one, is that between *process* and *reactive* subtypes which, respectively, refer to persons who develop the condition gradually but inexorably throughout their

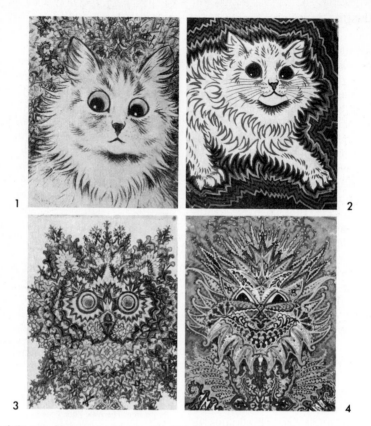

1   2

3   4

FIGURE 24.3 An artistic case history of schizophrenia. This series of paintings of a cat by the twentieth-century artist Louis Wain traces the development of his schizophrenic condition from its earliest stages through to its most extreme manifestation. Whether the progressively bizarre and elaborate distortions in the paintings represent changes in his actual perception of the world or in his expression of his experience of it cannot be known from the paintings alone.

Photos from Guttman-MacClay Collection/Institute of Psychiatry, London

lives and those for whom the onset of the psychotic reaction is quite sudden. Process schizophrenics typically have never gone very far along the road to psychological maturity and have a poor prognosis for recovery. In contrast, reactive schizophrenics have often been socially effective up to the point of their breakdown and, generally, have a much better chance to recover and return to adequate functioning. As with all such distinctions, this is not a one-or-the-other dichotomy; rather, what we have here is a continuous dimension. But it is one for which useful measurement devices have been provided (e.g., Ullmann & Giovannoni, 1964).

Paranoid states   The form of psychosis known as **paranoid reaction** is characterized by serious **delusions** (i.e., false beliefs). The delusions are often organized into logical systems that are impervious to disproof by reason or contradictory evidence.

The delusions may take many specific forms. Most common are delusions of persecution and delusions of grandeur. In the former the paranoid person constructs an elaborate delusional edifice proving that people are out to get him, that his enemies are everywhere, that his food is poisoned, that invisible deadly rays are being showered on him by people who pass innocently by. Proof, often based on overinterpretation of actual facts, is an essential feature of paranoia: A touch of indigestion proves that people have poisoned his food. And the paranoid person's reasoning shows logic and consistency. For example, take the connection made by a paranoid person between persecution and grandeur: "Why," he may ask himself, "are they persecuting me? It must be that I am a very important and powerful person, whom they fear! Therefore, I am the Messiah!" The paranoid reaction is thus a clear illustration of an important point: Accepting the inaccurate view of reality held by the patient, accepting his frame of reference, makes his behavior and thought processes more understandable and less irrational. In this sense, his facts are awry, not his intellectual functions. (Box 24.4 shows the gradual development of paranoid symptoms in an adolescent boy.)

In line with this stress on logic, the paranoid person shows little if any impairment of tested intelligence, and some individuals with pronounced paranoid tendencies do maintain good contact with reality—except for the limited areas of their delusions. The paranoid person also shows much less general behavioral deterioration than do persons with other psychoses. He is often perfectly able to carry on his affairs successfully at home and in business and to avoid hospitalization. He may, of course, be succeeding at the expense of damage to his family and associates. The behavior of the extreme paranoid may exceed the bounds of tolerance of society, however; he may attack or even murder his persecutors.

BOX 24.4

A PARANOID STATE

Robert W. White of Harvard University also provides a description of a young man who used increasingly exaggerated paranoid defenses to cope with painful events in his life situation.

A boy in high school was considered by his friends to be sensitive, solitary, and a little eccentric. They knew that he was an orphan and lived with an elderly, somewhat peculiar foster mother. The boy was good in his studies, especially in history and literature. His English teacher, who constantly read his literary productions, noted distinct talent but many eccentricities of content. . . . Although the boy spent a good deal of time alone, he had several friends among the students who were preparing for college. At graduation he was separated from his chums, he himself being unable to go to college. Occasionally he visited them, but it was clear that he resented his inferior position and the interruption of his own education. His friends now began to suspect that he was building up fictions about himself. He showed them an application blank that he had received from an art school. They believed that he had prepared it on his own typewriter. He also discoursed at length on his distinguished French ancestry, a theme which he was able to fill out convincingly from his knowledge of history. He repeatedly mentioned that his real mother, a countess, was now living in the city, and that he was in frequent communication with her. The friends began to feel that he was a liar, and they laid plans to expose him.

One day they confronted him with numerous fatal inconsistencies in his stories and accused him of fabrication. He thereupon admitted that his stories were not true, but explained that he had been forced to disguise himself in this way in order to elude a hostile power known as the Third Element. He now claimed that he and his mother, the countess, had collaborated in preparing a set of disguising fictions to keep the Third Element off their trail. He told his accusers that the situation was growing increasingly serious. Most of his friends had turned against him, and only three remained on his side.

It is clear that this boy's [development had taken a pathological direction] before he graduated from high school. That event, with separation from his circle of friends, gave his adjustment a downward jolt and sharply increased his symptoms. He now began to lose track of the line between fantasy and fact, speaking of his fantasies of noble lineage as if they were true. The motive behind these fabrications was pathetically clear: if he could not go to college, he would at least have some form of distinction to keep him on a footing with his friends, and while he was at it he provided himself with a mother. Unfortunately his attempts at compensation only irritated his friends, and their unsympathetic action constituted a second, more direct, and more personal rejection. This event threw him into deeper psychosis. His delusions about hostile friends and a hostile Third Element reflected the real feeling of hostility that he sensed in his accusers. Unfortunately the delusions now began to assume a generalized form which made him more and more inaccessible to friendly advances from others.

R. W. WHITE. *The Abnormal Personality.* New York: Ronald, 1964. Text material reprinted by permission; copyright © 1964 The Ronald Press Company, New York.

Organic Psychoses

A great deal of the sort of psychotic behavior that we have described here also frequently accompanies deterioration of the brain and nervous system as a result of accident, disease, or toxic agents. Some of the more important factors responsible for such deterioration are syphilitic invasion of brain tissue, brain tumors, degeneration of nerve tissue in senility, and, perhaps less directly, excessive use of alcohol and certain drugs. Because there are *known* organic factors underlying these psychotic behaviors, these disorders are often called **organic disorders**.

Just as functional psychoses are presumed by many to reflect in part some as yet unspecified physiological disturbances, so organic psychoses are generally presumed to be partly determined by the past experiences of the individual. For example, the particular psychotic symptoms shown by a patient suffering from a brain tumor will in part reflect the conflicts and the ways of coping with them that characterized his premorbid personality. But because the physiological bases of these psychoses can be detected (although this often requires enormously skilled medical detective work), attempts at cure are usually restricted to some form of direct physiological intervention, for example, surgical removal of the tumor. (For a more general discussion of the relation of bodily processes to personality, abnormal and normal, see Unit 28, p. 694.)

CAUSES OF MENTAL DISORDERS

The psychological processes involved in mental illness are extremely complex, and their physiological counterparts are but dimly understood. The origins of the disorders may lie in current life crises, in remote and relatively inaccessible life experiences of the patient, or in subtle biochemical and neural disturbances. Most likely, in most cases, all contribute. Carrying out controlled study on the genesis, development, and change of mental illness presents the most formidable of research problems.

The problem is placed in perspective, if not simplified, if we view the origins of mental disorders as falling within the broader issue of the origins of personality characteristics or types. Viewed in this way, much of our discussion of the determinants of personality has relevance here (see Unit 28).

Most of the research on causes of mental disorder has focused on schizophrenia. We shall review some of the suggestions about causation that have derived from this research on hereditary, physiological and organic, and life-history determinants.

On the Origins of Schizophrenia

The notion that insanity is inherited has long been popular. But the belief has been based on uncritical acceptance of evidence that several members of the same family have mental illness. The actual incidence of schizophrenia in families is very difficult to ascertain retrospectively, and even when there are clear indications of multiple cases in a family group, there is usually no way to disentangle the effects of similar environment from those of similar heredity.

The twin-study approach (see Unit 10, p. 206) is applicable here. The earliest twin work suggested a very strong genetic predisposition in schizophrenia. Kallman (1946), for example, found that among the relatives of schizophrenics, the probability that a full sibling or a fraternal twin would also be schizophrenic was approximately 11 percent; whereas the probability that an identical twin of a schizophrenic would also be schizophrenic was at least 69 percent. (These percentages describing degree of resemblance are called *concordance rates*.) More recent studies of these relations, with much better methodology for twin determination and diagnosis of schizophrenia, have provided considerably lower, although still substantial, concordance rates (see Table 24.1).

In order to provide further evidence of genetic influence, Heston (1966) studied the children of schizophrenic mothers placed in foster homes shortly after their birth and compared them with a control group of children of normal matched with respect to other characteristics. mothers, also placed in foster homes, who were ment in which the effects of genetic influences Presumably, this represents a natural experi-

TABLE 24.1 CONCORDANCE RATES (C) FOR
SCHIZOPHRENIA IN IDENTICAL
VERSUS FRATERNAL TWINS

Study	Identicals		Fraternals	
	N	C	N	C
Kringlen, Norway (1967)	69	45%	96	15%
Fischer et al., Denmark (1969)	25	56	45	26
Tienari, Finland (1971)*	20	35	23	13
Allen et al., United States (1972)*	121	43	131	9
Gottesman and Shields, United Kingdom (1973)	26	58	34	12
Total	261	46%	329	14%

* Male pairs exclusively.

Adapted from Gottesman & Shields (1973).

and environment might be disentangled. The subjects were mature adults when Heston examined them for evidence of emotional disorder. He found that, when compared with the individuals in the control group, those who had schizophrenic mothers showed a clearly higher incidence of schizophrenia as well as a variety of other neurotic and personality disorders. There remained, of course, the possibility that these apparent genetic effects in the children were really the result of toxic conditions in the pregnant schizophrenic mothers. But this possibility was neatly ruled out in a study by Wender et al. (1968) which showed that adopted children whose biological *fathers* were schizophrenic *also* were more likely than controls to manifest psychopathology.

Interestingly, Heston believed that, in spite of the high incidence of emotional disorders among those born of schizophrenic mothers, there was a large number of people in the group who were highly creative and healthy individuals. Supporting this observation is a study of Icelanders by Karlsson (1970). He found that close relatives of schizophrenic individuals have a significantly increased probability of being considered persons of eminence and of creative accomplishment. Such findings raise fascinating questions about the biological function and fate of schizophrenic tendencies in people.

The evidence argues strongly for a genetic predisposition toward schizophrenia among some individuals, rendering them particularly

vulnerable to certain environmental stresses. Most such individuals are not exposed to stresses of this kind, so that, although they may exhibit certain *schizophrenic-like* characteristics, they never develop the disorder; but some are exposed and therefore do. In short, a genetic predisposition is a necessary but not sufficient condition for the development of schizophrenia.

The role of the family in the development of schizophrenia has received a good deal of attention in recent years. One theory suggests that in a *schizophrenogenic* (schizophrenia-producing) family, communication among family members is chronically and seriously distorted (Laing & Esterson, 1970). A specific form of this distorted communication is the double-bind situation (Bateson et al., 1956). A *double-bind situation* is one in which the person is exposed to two quite contradictory messages, often from the same family member, yet cannot get any clarification indicating which one he should respond to. It is in the nature of such messages that if he responds positively to one of them, he will automatically be disobeying the other. For example, a father tells his son *never* to defy his authority. Yet he also complains bitterly that his son does not stand up to him "like a man." The double-bind victim is in an unsolvable choice conflict, but worse, he is prevented by the rules of this situation from even commenting on the contradiction.

This analysis may help to explain the rather consistent finding that concordance rates for identical twins of schizophrenics are somewhat higher for females than for males. Jackson (1960) argues that females tend to be much more closely involved psychologically in the family structure because of their traditionally dependent roles and, therefore, are more susceptible to whatever pathological influences may be present in the family. Males, with a traditional role of relatively greater independence, may be better able to escape physically or psychologically from the insidious effects of the environment and, for that reason, do not so frequently suffer the fate of the pathological relative. This speculation should become testable in the future; as women become liberated, their close attachment to family structures should be reduced, and thus concordance rates for females should be lowered, eventually to match that of males.

But some investigators point to data which indicate that schizophrenia is primarily (or even *only*) due to genetic factors. What are the implications of this? Gottesman and Shields (1972) make the following comment in their review of genetic studies of schizophrenia:

> It is important to understand the implications of finding that a trait such as the liability to schizophrenia has a high heritability. In the samples so far studied, it means that environmental factors were unimportant as causative agents of the schizophrenias. However, and this cannot be emphasized too strongly, these data do not permit the conclusion that curative or preventive measures will be ineffective.

THE MANUFACTURE OF MADNESS

The point has been forcefully made by a number of critics that our ways of conceptualizing deviant behavior not only fail to explain mental disorders but, in fact, actually tend to create or "manufacture" madness (Szasz, 1970). Let us illustrate. In what may have begun as a temporary or relatively minor aberration in behavior, perhaps a temporary reaction to stress, an individual patient may come to the attention of diagnosticians. Being labeled mentally ill—either neurotic or psychotic, and in one subcategory or another—he may then react by adopting unintentionally the appropriate "sick" role in accordance with his own and others' definition and expectations. In short, if experts call him "crazy," he then comes to act and feel "crazy."

If it were the case that this diagnostic labeling was generally indeed accurate and reliable, that two skilled diagnosticians rarely disagreed on the assigned category, then perhaps we could worry a bit less about the problem. However, high diagnostic agreement does not appear to be the case. Even for the most crude (and crucial) distinction, and using the most sophisticated diagnostic techniques, in one study there was disagreement on *whether or not an individual was psychotic* in about 20 percent of the cases (Sandifer et al., 1964). Agreement on

BOX 24.5

ON BEING SANE IN INSANE PLACES

"If sanity and insanity exist, how shall we know them?

"The question is neither capricious nor itself insane. However much we may be personally convinced that we can tell the normal from the abnormal, the evidence is simply not compelling." Thus begins the tale of a strange odyssey by a group of presumably normal people through the wards of a number of presumably typical psychiatric hospitals. The organizer of these wanderings, and the first to set off on the journey, was D. L. Rosenhan, a professor of psychology and law at Stanford University. His main question was: To what extent do experts judge a person to be psychotic just because he happens to be in a place where most people are psychotic or are defined to be?

In general outline, and in his own words, here is Rosenhan's strategy and reasoning:

> [Admit] normal people (that is, people who do not have, and have never suffered, symptoms of serious psychiatric disorders) . . . to psychiatric hospitals and then [determine] whether they were discovered to be sane and, if so, how. . . . If . . . the sanity of the pseudopatients were never discovered, serious difficulties would arise for those who support traditional modes of psychiatric diagnosis. . . . such an unlikely outcome would support the view that *psychiatric diagnosis betrays little about the patient but much about the environment in which an observer finds him.*

The study began by arranging to have eight normal people admitted to twelve different psychiatric hospitals and, with a single minor exception, assuring that no one in the hospitals had any knowledge of the sanity of these pseudopatients or of the fact that they were involved in any kind of a research project. The pseudopatients included men and women from a variety of occupations; the hospitals were located in five different states on the East and West coasts, some new and well staffed, others somewhat rundown and understaffed. In short, a fair range of both people and institutions.

diagnosis of *specific* psychoses, as assessed in a number of investigations, is considerably lower, rarely exceeding 50 percent. In view of the fact that the typical psychiatric interview on the

In order to get into the hospital, the pseudopatient showed up at the admissions office and complained of hallucinations, specifically of hearing voices that repeatedly said such words to him as "hollow" and "empty." Beyond this untruth, the only other deception was the use of a false name. In all other respects the pseudopatients were quite frank and accurate in reporting to the admitting psychiatric staff their life histories and their current situations including any actually experienced problems. The false report of occasional hallucinations was presumably the *only* pathological cue presented. *All pseudopatients were promptly admitted and, with one exception, were diagnosed as schizophrenic.*

Once on the ward, all pseudopatients immediately stopped simulating *any* pathological symptoms; they never again reported hearing voices or experiencing anything but the normal reactions they actually felt. Among these real feelings, understandably, was a brief period of mild nervousness and anxiety—a sensible reaction to finding oneself so quickly in the unfamiliar (to say the least) environment of a psychiatric ward and, further, to realizing that they had agreed that they could only be released by convincing the hospital staff that they had "recovered" and were ready to face the outside world. This period of nervousness was typically quite brief, and was replaced by a campaign to behave as sanely and as cooperatively as they possibly could.

Release did not come easily. Their average stay in hospital was nineteen days, with a range of from seven to fifty-two days. *Not one of the pseudopatients was ever recognized by the staff as an imposter,* and, when they were released, it was because a psychiatrist had diagnosed their schizophrenia as now "in remission." This diagnosis does not mean cured; it means that the patient had in fact been truly psychotic but had managed for the while to be sufficiently free of symptoms to permit his trying to make it in the outside world(!) In no instance was there the slightest suggestion that the initial diagnosis may have been in error. Actual patients, however, were not so easily deceived; from records kept by three of the pseudopatients, it was determined that 35 of 118 patients sharing their wards detected that they had feigned insanity. A typical comment was: "You're not crazy. You're a journalist, or a professor. . . . You're checking up on the hospital." Perhaps it takes one to know one,

but it was also the case that the amount of contact the pseudopatients had with the psychiatric staff on whom their diagnoses and fates depended was much less than they had with fellow patients. The average contact of an officially therapeutic nature with physicians and psychologists was only 6.8 minutes per day. Instead, therapy consisted of enormous doses of tranquilizers (remember, the pseudopatients remained consistently tranquil and reasonable throughout their confinement), and these pills were consistently deposited in the nearest toilet. (Many of the real patients followed this same disposal technique.)

Rosenhan is deeply concerned—and so should we be—about "the massive role of labeling in psychiatric assessment. . . . once a person is designated abnormal, all of his other behaviors and characteristics are colored by that label. Indeed, that label is so powerful that many of the pseudopatients' normal behaviors were overlooked entirely or profoundly misinterpreted." One example: All pseudopatients took extensive notes on what was going on about them; such notes, after all, were the data for the study. Initially, they were circumspect in taking these notes, but soon it became a very open activity and appeared regularly in the nurses' records. A typical notation: "Patient engages in writing behavior." No one ever asked why or what they were so diligently scribbling, presumably because that was already clear: It was merely another symptom of their psychotic condition.

Rosenhan concludes his report with the following observation:

> It could be a mistake, and a very unfortunate one, to consider that what happened to us derived from malice or stupidity on the part of the staff. Quite the contrary, our overwhelming impression of them was of people who really cared, who were committed and who were uncommonly intelligent.

All this in no way denies that true mental disturbance exists and that considerable human suffering is indeed its accompaniment. The alleviation of such suffering is one essential goal of many psychologists. The message here has been that we can do much better if we recognize that we may be fooled by the institutional setting in which we sometimes work.

D. L. ROSENHAN. On being sane in insane places. *Science*, 1973, **179**, 250–257. Copyright 1973 by the American Association for the Advancement of Science.

basis of which such diagnostic decisions are made and the critical action of legal commitment is taken may often last no more than a few minutes, the crudeness of the procedure start-

lingly contrasts with its importance to the individual. In these few minutes he may be launched on a psychotic career. And, as Box 24.5 poignantly demonstrates, once launched, return

---

BOX 24.6

A COMMENTARY ON THESE PSYCHOLOGICAL TIMES

In December 1972, the Council of Representatives of the American Psychological Association, representing (as its name implies) its membership of over 30,000 psychologists, was moved officially to state the following position with regard to a possible political use of their discipline:

[The Council] condemns the practice, wherever it may occur, of suppressing and neutralizing political dissenters by diagnosing them as mentally ill and committing them to mental hospitals. We consider it the responsibility of individual psychologists to oppose such practices within the organizations in which they are employed and, if they do not succeed in changing the practices, to dissociate themselves from personal complicity in them.

Council expresses concern for POW's, use of therapy for political purposes. *APA Monitor*, 1973, **4**, 1.

---

to the land of the normal living is extraordinarily difficult.

A recent study of psychiatric diagnosis, although performed under relatively artificial conditions, reinforces an uneasiness about the nature of these labels. Consider that the incidence of psychosis has been found to be greater in the lower than in the middle socioeconomic classes (Hollingshead & Redlich, 1958). This finding is usually taken to reflect the greater stress of lower-class life, with its problems of survival and of community and familial dis-

organization. In a recent study (Lee & Temerlin, 1970), psychiatric residents were asked to evaluate the psychological health of an individual based only on a transcript of an interview with him. The purported social-class level of the interviewee was systematically varied among several groups of the psychiatric residents. It was found that although each group of diagnosticians was provided with *exactly the same interview*, when the individual was described as lower class, the subject was more frequently labeled as psychotic. When the interviewee was described as of middle or upper class, more benevolent diagnoses were applied. Although the study may not have duplicated the usual circumstances of diagnosis, and although the diagnosticians were not yet fully qualified psychiatrists, the issue is clear. An attribute of the patient that should have been totally irrelevant to diagnosis (i.e., his social class) appeared to have a strong influence on the judgment rendered. *Is* psychosis more frequent in the lower class, or is it that middle-class psychiatrists are quick to diagnose lower-class patients as schizophrenic? And what would be the result of such a study in which the psychiatrist and patients were of different ethnic or racial origins?

Studies such as these raise the possibility that our current widely held official views on mental illness may represent, in part, ways of enforcing and rationalizing deeply held social biases. And most frighteningly, even political factors may enter the picture (see Box 24.6). Perhaps we should seriously consider whether the experts should be granted exclusive rights to make these life-defining judgments. Perhaps, instead, we should evolve the means for making such judgments the responsibility of us all.

SUMMARY

1. Mental disorders, in their various forms and intensities, are commonly ascribed to psychological causes, although there may be some genetic, biochemical, and physiological factors also at work. Many authorities believe that organic or physical factors may ultimately be shown to be the important determinants of mental illness, but relatively little concrete knowledge about these factors yet exists; thus, most current theories focus on experience and learning as primary determinants of these aberrant behaviors.

2. The label of mental illness is at times somewhat uncritically applied to individuals who are functioning reasonably well but who deviate in some way from social or moral standards of proper conduct, especially if their behavior tends to annoy or disturb others. Antisocial behavior is not necessarily "sick" behavior.

3. Three major theoretical orientations toward mental illness—the psychodynamic, behavioristic, and humanist-existential models—cast different perspectives on many specific forms of disorder. The psychodynamic model views abnormal behavior as resulting from unconscious conflicts between impulses and what is socially and personally acceptable behavior. The behavioristic model does not posit such unconscious conflicts; rather, it views aberrant behavior as resulting from faulty learning in which anxiety or fear becomes inappropriately conditioned to certain situations. The humanistic-existential position holds that man often denies aspects of his real self and that this denial is the source of his suffering and his deviant behavior.

4. The prevalence of mental illness, although difficult to measure, has been estimated at as high as 30 percent of the population if illness is defined as being in need of help for psychological problems.

5. Classifications of mental disorders, including the most recent, maintain a distinction between organic and functional disorders. Organic disorders are those for which some clear physical basis has been discovered; functional disorders are those with as yet no established basis in bodily malfunction.

6. Within the functional disorders are included psychoses, neuroses, and personality disorders. Psychoses are the most severe of the emotional disorders, often involving acute disturbances in thinking, emotion, and behavior. Neuroses involve less severe disturbances and considerable experienced anxiety. Personality disorders involve unusual and pervasive personality styles that often cause adjustment problems. However, they may cause the individual little anxiety.

7. In neurosis, the central issue is whether anxiety is directly expressed or defended against. The specific ways in which anxiety is handled are at the core of distinctions among neuroses, which include anxiety, hysterical, phobic, and obsessive-compulsive types.

8. Among the personality disorders there are various subcategories, including the obsessive-compulsive, the hysterical, and the antisocial-reaction types. Such disorders are generally regarded as having origins similar to corresponding classes of neurotic behavior. However, the difference lies in the greater conflict resolution and anxiety reduction afforded by personality disorders.

9. Within the general category of conduct disorders are to be found such behaviors as alcoholism, drug addiction, and various forms of sexual deviation. Because of society's general censure of such behavior, their study as forms of mental illness is made difficult.

10. The three major classes of functional psychosis are affective disorders, schizophrenia, and the paranoid states.

11. Affective disorders, which are characterized by exaggerations of moods, include the manic, the depressive, and the (fluctuating) manic-depressive types.

12. There are a variety of forms of schizophrenia, which is by far the most prevalent form of disabling mental illness. Although the main symptom of this condition is difficult to identify, grossly inappropriate emotional reactions to life situations seem to be the most commonly observed factor. To the extent that the appearance of schizophrenic behavior is sudden, abrupt (rather than being the end state of a long-term psychological deterioration), recent work indicates that the prognosis is more optimistic.

13. Delusions are at the heart of paranoid states, most often delusions of grandeur and persecution. These delusions are highly logical and typically impervious to contradictory evidence.

14. A great deal of evidence clearly supports the conclusion that there is some genetic basis for schizophrenia. However, this genetic basis should be viewed as a necessary but not sufficient condition for occurrence of the disorder. It is equally clear that a highly complex interaction between genetic and environmental determinants takes place and that psychological treatment of schizophrenia is by no means ruled out.

15. Data suggest that diagnosis of mental illness is often unreliable and that the application of diagnostic labels is strongly influenced by factors such as the social class of the patient. Furthermore, the assignment of a psychiatric label may produce or worsen aberrant behavior because the individual adopts the "sick" role.

GLOSSARY

affective disorders A category of psychotic reaction marked by exaggerated emotional states ranging from euphoria and elation to profound depression and immobility. When both extremes occur alternately in the same person, the reaction is called *manic-depressive.*

antisocial reaction (psychopathic personality) A form of character disorder in which the individual shows a chronic and socially incapacitating tendency to seek immediate need gratification. He is a poor judge of the consequences of his social actions and fails to learn from social experience.

anxiety neurosis A form of neurosis characterized by relatively severe, sometimes chronic anxiety, but with periods of acute panic.

behavioristic model That conceptualization which sees all behavior as conforming to the principles of conditioning and learning.

conduct disorders A class of disorder that typically involves behavior that is morally censured and often illegal. Included are alcoholism, drug addiction, and various forms of sexual deviation. Although characteristically disturbed by his condition, the individual typically does not regard himself as mentally ill.

conversion reaction Within the general class of hysterical neuroses, a reaction involving some sensory or motor disturbance having no organic basis. Examples are hysterical blindness and paralysis.

delusions False beliefs developed without appropriate external stimulation and maintained in spite of contradictory evidence; misjudgments of reality.

dissociative reaction Within the general class of hysterical neuroses, a reaction involving disturbances of memory (amnesia) and identity (multiple personality, i.e., two or more distinct personalities within the individual).

functional disorders The general class of mental illness, including both the neuroses and psychoses, that are primarily psychological in origin and that are not caused by any known pathological changes in organic structure.

hallucination The perception of an event, object, or experience where no such events or objects are in evidence in the external world.

humanistic-existential model That conceptualization of personality and behavior which focuses on the striving for self-integration and actualization and on the uniqueness of the individual.

hysterical neurosis A form of neurosis, frequently found in Freud's early patients, under which falls the conversion and hysterical reactions. It is relatively rare today.

hysterical personality A personality disorder, somewhat related to hysterical neuroses, in which overly dramatic behavior and feigned seductiveness are frequent features.

neurosis (psychoneurosis) The class of the milder forms of mental illness, usually not requiring hospitalization. The psychoneurotic person retains his orientation to the environment and considerable contact with reality but suffers enough disruption of cognitive and emotional processes to interfere with his effective life adjustments.

obsessive-compulsive neurosis A form of neurosis in which the person experiences persistent and disturbing thoughts (obsession) and feels forced to engage repeatedly in ritualistic actions that he often recognizes as irrational (compulsion).

obsessive-compulsive personality A personality disorder related to the obsessive-compulsive neurosis, but with little anxiety or awareness of any difficulty.

organic disorders A psychopathological state for which there is a well-established basis in the structure or physiological functioning of the organism. It is distinguished from functional psychosis.

paranoid reaction A form of psychosis characterized by a pervasive and often organized set of delusions, most commonly delusions of persecution or of grandeur.

personality disorders Deeply ingrained, habitual, and rigid patterns of behavior or character that severely limit the adaptive potential of the individual but that are often not seen by him to be problematic or maladaptive. Sometimes called *character disorders*.

phobic neurosis A form of neurosis characterized by irrational, intense fears of certain objects, places, or situations.

psychodynamic model That theory or conceptualization of behavior which sees the mind and personality in terms of conflict and resolution of mental forces or energy forces such as impulses, ideas, and emotions.

psychosis The class of the more severe mental diseases, including schizophrenic reaction, manic-depressive reaction, and paranoid reaction. It involves serious disruptions of cognitive and emotional processes, often necessitating at least temporary hospitalization.

schizophrenia The most prevalent of all psychoses, marked by extreme emotional withdrawal and diminished contact with reality, by a general deterioration in social behavior, and often by hallucinations. Frequently, there is a striking incompatibility, or split, between emotion and behavior; hence the popular term *split personality*.

the psychotherapies

DO YOU KNOW...

how psychoanalysis tries to uncover the unconscious sources of neurotic behavior?

in what ways psychotherapy can be regarded as a process of reeducation, as an unlearning of bad habits?

under what circumstances it may help to expose oneself again and again to experiences of which one is terribly, but unrealistically, frightened?

whether certain kinds of problems are best treated by certain kinds of psychotherapy?

that in some approaches to treatment the therapist neither gives advice nor even explains to a patient the reasons for his neurotic behavior?

who does the treatment in group therapy?

why it is that improvement of a person being treated in a family therapy setting is sometimes resisted and undermined by the other members of the family?

why it is so difficult to judge whether therapy has actually helped?

that, despite the best efforts of a therapist, a person may not be helped at all unless he wants to change?

that pharmacotherapy is rapidly becoming a major form of medical help in behavior disorders?

unit 25

oto by Van Bucher/Courtesy, Wagner College Department of Psychology

CONTENTS

From the time we first began to organize in social communities, we have been confronted with the problem of how to control and limit deviant and abnormal behavior, especially the sort that appears to endanger the group. Our approach to such treatment has always been based on our conception of the origins of deviance. For primitive man the cause lay *outside* the individual; his deviant behavior was regarded as the result of possession by demons. Therefore—and quite sensibly, considering this supposed origin—treatment was by various forms of exorcism intended to drive out these alien evil spirits.

As medical and biological sciences progressed and naturalistic philosophies prevailed, the causes of deviance came to be viewed as *inside* the individual, abnormal behavior being regarded as a sign of medical illness. Efforts to effect cure and a return to normality took the form of physical remedies, including holes bored in the skull, electric and chemical shock, and surgical procedures. To a large extent, the medical model still prevails. Scientists continue their search for the biological bases of mental illness, and physicians continue to administer drugs and other physical therapies to control the deviant behavior of their patients. Since the advent of Freud's work at the beginning of this century, some form of verbal psychotherapy (the talking cure) has frequently been used either in conjunction with these medical procedures or as the sole method of treatment.

With the growth of the social sciences has come even further widening in conceptions of deviant behavior and its treatment. The causes of deviance are now regarded as *both inside and outside the individual*. Mental illness is conceived as a disorder arising not only out of factors within the person but also out of factors in his social group and the larger society in which he lives.

VARIETIES OF PSYCHOTHERAPY

The term *psychotherapy* as it is used today embraces an enormous variety of theories of personality development and of specific techniques and therapeutic aims. One book on the subject analyzed thirty-six different psychological treatment approaches and was still not exhaustive, even at the time of its publication (Harper, 1959). Each method is based on a somewhat distinctive conceptualization of the nature and origins of deviant, abnormal, or sick behavior.

In our discussion of psychotherapy, four major categories of therapy will be presented. Each represents a major theoretical and philosophical orientation toward treatment:

1. Psychoanalytic therapies are derived from Freud's technique of psychoanalysis and focus on the early and largely unconscious *developmental origins* of personality and its pathology.
2. Behavior therapies claim for their basis the theories and principles of conditioning and instrumental learning (see Units 4 and 5) and focus primarily, although not exclusively, on the modification of *overt observable behavior.*
3. Phenomenological therapies are strongly oriented toward dealing with the patient's *current functioning* in the here and now, with his *subjective experience* of himself and his environment.
4. Interpersonal therapies, including both individual and family and group therapies, focus on *interpersonal relations* and their influence on behavior, frequently attempting to change systems of interpersonal interaction rather than intrapsychic aspects of individuals.

PSYCHOANALYTIC THERAPIES

If neurotic (or psychotic) behavior can be descibed as a reaction to an unrealistic and inaccurate conception of oneself and one's life situation, it follows that helping a person attain a truer picture of himself and his life situation will be helpful therapy. Let us look at a hypothetical example of a massive and near-crippling complex of misperceptions of reality, a type that is relatively rare but illustrates well how irrational behavior can be regarded as a rational

adaptation to a false picture of a person's life situation. A woman, at the birth of her first child, develops a phobic reaction. She is suddenly unable to leave her home because of a dread and nameless fear that, if she does, something will prevent her from ever returning to care for her infant.

What can be done for this woman? She would be perfectly right not to venture outside if danger truly threatened, yet she is wrong—and therefore neurotic—in her gross exaggeration of the danger. We can argue and reason with her, pointing out how rarely mothers vanish on their doorsteps. We can assert and even present evidence that not one person has been struck by lightning or kidnapped in her community for the past twenty-five years and that women of her age practically never suffer heart attacks and certainly not from stepping outside their homes. This kind of commonsense therapy can be of some help and is probably what she has received from her friends and family before seeking professional treatment.

But such problems may have deeper origins. The woman has been assured—and she believes—that physical danger does not really threaten, yet her phobia persists because of hidden fears and conflicts that, for some reason, are presently inaccessible to her conscious search. Within the category of therapies labeled *psychoanalytic,* the aim is to achieve a truer and more realistic picture of oneself through an analysis of such unconscious conflicts that originated in the past and that are held to be the cause of both the current distorted view of self and reality and the pathological symptoms.

Psychoanalysis and **psychoanalytically oriented therapy** are based on Sigmund Freud's theory of personality development (see Unit 29). The theory generally holds to an essentially medical model of abnormal behavior in which the overt symptom or presenting problem is believed to be the result of more basic underlying pathology. Although Freud, himself a physician, firmly believed in the ultimately biological roots of all psychic phenomena, he was the first to stress the important roles of experience and learning in the development of neurosis. It is this concept—that adult behavior (whether normal or abnormal) has its roots in the individual's early life experiences—that is a basic tenet of Freudian psychology and that underlies psychoanalytic technique.

In psychoanalytic theory neurotic illness is regarded as the result of unconscious conflicts. These influence the individual's perception of reality and his behavior but remain out of conscious awareness and therefore beyond voluntary and rational control. The goal of analytic psychotherapy is to eliminate **resistance** to conscious awareness so that thoughts and memories which have been subjected to repression and the emotions connected with them may return to consciousness and be brought under control of logical thought processes.

Free Association

The main technique of psychoanalysis is **free association**. In traditional psychoanalytic practice, the patient lies on a couch and the analyst sits behind him, out of view. The analyst, for a good deal of the time, says very little in order not to intrude into the patient's thoughts. The patient is urged to talk freely about whatever comes into his mind, no matter how trivial, stupid, or shameful it seems, and to let this flow of thoughts take whatever course it will. The patient's dreams, in which thoughts presumably take an even less structured and controlled form than in waking life, are also subjected to analysis. Through these techniques of free association and dream analysis, the analyst seeks to discover and to interpret material of which the person has been unaware and to bring him to a deeper understanding of his problems. The analyst will assist the patient in recognizing and retaining whatever self-knowledge he has gained through these techniques, techniques that are aimed at reducing the person's censorship of the flow of thought.

Sometimes the flow of thoughts is hindered by the patient's unconscious avoidance of feelings and memories that are particularly close to the traumatic events or repressed contents that are at the root of his problem. It is the task of the therapist to notice and interpret this resistance or avoidance so that the patient may begin to reexperience, in the framework of a new and nonjudgmental relation, whatever has been blocked from awareness. And it is this reexperiencing that can lead to new understandings and ultimately to personality change.

Today the most widely practiced variant of psychoanalysis, generally referred to as *psychoanalytically oriented psychotherapy*, makes much greater use of focused interviewing (and in a face-to-face rather than a lying-on-a-couch situation), with only limited use of free association.

Transference

Transference is a phenomenon in which the patient is said to transfer his unconscious emotional feelings, positive and negative, from other objects or people (particularly parents and other important figures from his childhood) to the therapist himself. It is the therapist's job to point out the real origin and aim of the transference feelings and to help the patient to bring them under conscious control. The task of interpreting the transference is especially difficult because the effectiveness of the interpretations depends on their being made only when the patient is just a step away from uncovering them himself. If the interpretations come too early, then the individual's defenses will rapidly come into play and the memories will be blocked even further.

The transference process is regarded as the very core of psychoanalytic therapy and makes possible the emotional reeducation of the person:

> The pathological effect of earlier emotional experiences is corrected by exposing the patient to the same type of emotional conflicts in the therapeutic situation. The therapist, however, reacts differently, not as the parents, teachers, relatives, or friends in the past. This difference between the therapist's reaction and the original parental reactions is the most fundamental therapeutic factor (Alexander, 1946).

In the course of such psychoanalytic therapy the woman who suffers the irrational fear of going out comes to remember that she was always warned as a child of the dangers of the outside world and cautioned to remain at home, or if she dreams of yowling and terrifying tomcats surrounding her house, this experience may suggest a possible explanation of the phobia. For example (to suggest a somewhat fanciful explanation for our hypothetical patient), she may become aware that she was warned in her youth against men, that she had come to regard men as cruelly lustful tomcats, and that, in becoming pregnant, she has exposed her own sexual wishes and is therefore vulnerable to their attack. But whatever explanations may be arrived at, her present maladaptive behavior may be helped if, and only if, she can use such information or explanations to correct her distorted perception of herself as free of sexual impulses and of the outside world as a sexually dangerous place. If she can thereby unlearn her present erroneous views of what she and her world are like and gradually develop correct ones, then her self-imposed confinement will, *in her own mind*, become less necessary and a brief excursion will become something to be dared.

She now understands and actually feels that her fears are unrealistic. They no longer make sense *to her*. Does the phobic reaction vanish? Behavioral change, unfortunately, is not automatically triggered by comprehension. She may now be able to don her coat, stride purposefully to the front door with a clear awareness of the safety of what lies beyond—and panic on the threshold. Change takes time, sometimes a great deal of time, but realistic perception of self and social reality is, from the psychoanalytic point of view, a necessary first step.

To summarize, then, the process of psychoanalysis and psychoanalytic therapy can begin with the technique of free association or can involve directed association to key issues. (See Box 25.1, p. 618, for an excerpt from a psychoanalytically oriented interview in which the therapist instructs the patient in the rules of the game.) These processes help the patient reexperience past memories and unconscious conflicts, in the course of which he may employ various forms of resistance and defenses, including transference, in order to avoid the painful recall of traumatic events and emotions. The therapist's responsibility is to interpret the resistance so that the unconscious material may return to consciousness, where it can be dealt with.

Working Through

This process of repetition and gradual emergence of new responses, which is continually repeated during the course of therapy, is the reeducative aspect of analytic therapy and is termed **working through**, a process that enables initial insights and changes to become internalized and incorporated into the patient's personality structure.

As the origins of the neurosis emerge, it is likely that several overlapping and interwoven explanations will be developed; a single symptom may serve as a defense against many different repressed thoughts. Regardless of the explanations offered, however, the focus of the therapy will be not merely on uncovering the past origins of the symptoms but on helping the patient *use* the insight into past events to correct perceptions of the present. The patient will discover that the symptoms are defenses against the recall of painful emotions and memories. Theoretically, once these feelings and memories are uncovered, the defensive *need* for the symptom will vanish. Unfortunately, as we noted earlier, actual behavior change may be slow in coming.

Commentary on Psychoanalytic Therapy

The entire process of psychoanalysis and psychoanalytic therapy is lengthy, expensive, painful, and requires that the patient possess considerable intelligence, "psychological-mindedness," and personality strength. Whereas Freud generally felt that psychotic individuals were not capable of undergoing analysis, modern analytic therapists apply modifications of the technique in their work with psychotic patients. Rosen (1968), for example, uses a system of *direct analysis* with psychotics in which the most primitive and basic unconscious impulses are interpreted directly to the patient as soon as they become clear to the therapist. There is less concern in this system with the careful, slow uncovering of resistance and transference issues; rather, any manifestation of resistance is attacked directly and in what may at times appear to be a brutal manner. But often the shock value of this approach permits the thera-

BOX 25.1

A PSYCHOANALYTIC THERAPY INTERVIEW

The following excerpt from a therapy session between a psychoanalytically oriented therapist, Lewis
Wolberg, and a relatively new patient illustrates the
need to clarify the way in which one goes about
communicating in this kind of therapeutic situation.

PT (Patient): I just don't know what's causing these
feelings. I get so frightened and upset, and I don't
know why.

TH (Therapist): That's why you are coming here, to
find out the reasons, so you can do something about
your trouble.

PT: But why is it that I can't sleep and concentrate?

TH: That's what we'll begin to explore.

PT: But why?

TH: What comes to your mind? What do you think?

PT: I don't know.

TH: You know, there are reasons for troubles like
yours, and one must patiently explore them. It may
take a little time. I know you'd like to get rid of this
trouble right away, but the only way one can do this
is by careful exploring.

PT: Yes.

TH: And to take your anxiety feelings, for example,
you may not be aware of the reasons for them now,
but as we talk about you, your ideas, your troubles
and your feelings, you should be able to find out what
they are.

PT: How do I do this?

TH: When I ask you to talk about your feelings and
thrash things around in your mind, you won't be able
to put your finger on what bothers you immediately,
but at least you will have started thinking about the
sources of the problem. Right now, the only thing
you're concerned with is escaping from the emotion.
That's why you're just going around in a circle. While
you're operating to seal off anxiety, you're doing
nothing about finding out what's producing this
anxiety.

PT: It sounds sort of clear when you say it. (laughs)

TH: Well, do you think you understand what I mean?

PT: What you're explaining now?

TH: Yes.

PT: Yes. (pause) The point is that I keep thinking
about myself too much. It's that I feel inferior to
everyone. I must win at rummy. When I play golf, I
practically beat myself red if I don't get the low score.
And this is silly.

TH: What happens when someone beats you at golf?

PT: I get upset and these feelings come.

TH: Now there seems to be some kind of connection
here; let's talk some more about that.

L. R. WOLBERG. *The Technique of Psychotherapy.* New York:
Grune & Stratton, 1954. Copyright 1954 by Grune and Stratton,
Inc. Reprinted by permission.

pist to break through, to communicate with a
highly isolated patient.

Much of the current criticism of psychoanalysis stems from its lengthy duration, its high
cost, its lack of demonstrated effectiveness, and
its apparent suitability for only a rather restricted group of individuals. It is seen by many
psychologists as a massive dose of therapy for a
very few elite and affluent people who are only
mildly troubled. Indeed, much of the development of psychoanalytic technique was based on
Freud's experience with middle-class Viennese
women suffering from *conversion hysteria* (see
Unit 24), a complex in which the central issues
very often involve repression of sexual impulses,
conflicts, and memories. In a sense, conversion
hysteria may have been the special psychopathology of that emotionally restrictive Victorian society. It has been argued that quite
different methods and theories are needed to
cope with and explain the pathologies of our
modern mass society and its tendency to de-
humanize the individual.

Practitioners of **behavior therapy** are
prominent among these critics, claiming that
psychoanalysis in fact does not lead to behavior
or personality change in most cases. Even
among the many who acknowledge that the
method does work about as well as other forms
of psychotherapy, the claim is sometimes made

that it is effective for reasons other than those given in psychoanalytic theory. Dollard and Miller (1950), for example, some time ago endeavored to recast psychoanalytic theory and therapy into the language of learning psychologists.

BEHAVIOR THERAPIES

Behavior therapists explicitly reject the medical model of psychopathology, which considers deviant behavior to be merely a symptom of underlying pathology. Instead, deviant behavior is viewed by behaviorists as the direct result of poor or incorrect learning. Therapy, for them, is essentially a reeducative process to correct this mislearning.

All problems of adjustment are regarded in the same way. Both normal and pathological development are said to follow the same laws of learning. Abnormal behavior is viewed not as a symptom of underlying disease but as a learned response to the particular and peculiar demands and stresses of the individual's environment. The symptom *is* the pathology, as the following typical view asserts: "Behavior therapy does not involve itself with 'schizophrenia' or the 'compulsive disorders' (i.e., with disease models), but with a series of responses that create difficulties for the patient or the environment" (Kanfer & Phillips, 1970).

In the case of a phobia, for example, the view is that somewhere along the way the object of the phobia (the conditioned stimulus) was paired, probably accidentally, with some noxious stimulus (the unconditioned stimulus), one that normally produces fear and anxiety. (These terms and others used in this section are defined in the Glossaries of Units 15 and 16.) In order to avoid the anxiety subsequently elicited by an encounter with such a conditioned-stimulus object, the object (or even the thought of it) is avoided entirely. Such avoidance of painful stimuli is self-reinforcing; as long as the stimulus is avoided, there is indeed no experiencing of fear and anxiety. This model of avoidance conditioning is the basic learning-theory explanation of the development of phobias. It has even been used to reinterpret such Freudian mechanisms as repression by regarding repression as simply the avoidance of anxiety-producing thoughts.

Although most theorists of behavior therapy adhere to a conditioning model, involving learning of a direct association between an external stimulus and an observable behavioral response, behavior theorists do not necessarily deny the existence of inner states and covert processes. Most do claim, however, that because such states are, by definition, not accessible to direct observation, they are consequently not accessible to systematic manipulation. Therefore, the argument goes, they should be of no concern to the behavior modifier (Skinner, 1953). The behavior modification techniques developed by Bandura (1969), however, rely explicitly on certain inner states and processes serving as mediating responses and thus can fit within the context of social-learning theory.

The behavior therapies, although based on conditioning and learning conceptions of behavior, by no means constitute a homogeneous set of techniques. Included are such different procedures as inflicting a painful stimulus at each occurrence of an undesirable symptom, having the symptom practiced intentionally in order to bring it under voluntary control, or gradually desensitizing a feared stimulus by systematic relaxation procedures. Although these techniques are by no means new (the earliest date back to the 1920s), behavior therapy has undergone a revival and enormous growth in recent years.

Reciprocal Inhibition Therapy

A behavior modification technique developed by Joseph Wolpe (1958) is **reciprocal inhibition** therapy. The term is borrowed from physiology, where it refers to the phenomenon in which one set of muscles cannot function simultaneously with (are *antagonistic* to) another set of muscles.

Wolpe, like all behavior therapists, assumes that the patient's symptoms are learned (conditioned) habitual responses. The primary symptoms with which he is concerned are anxiety and its resultant behaviors. Behaviors which are intended to avoid anxiety are regarded as maladaptive responses that must be eliminated and replaced, through therapeutic techniques, with more appropriate responses. In order to accomplish this, Wolpe sets up a situation in which the patient is induced to emit a new and presumably appropriate response in the presence of the conditioned (symptom-producing) stimulus. Since the new response is specifically designed to be antagonistic to the old symptom (i.e., both responses cannot occur simultaneously), the old and maladaptive response is thereby prevented from occurring. With repeated trials of this sort, the association between the conditioned stimulus and the symptom is eventually broken, and in its place an association between the stimulus and the more desirable response is developed. This process of elimination and substitution of responses to a stimulus is called **counterconditioning**. In many instances, as the following section discusses, the new response is a state of relaxation.

Systematic desensitization   What kinds of more desirable responses can effectively displace undesirable ones? Wolpe reasons thus: The various avoidance behaviors that cause the patient difficulties are learned as ways of coping with anxiety. But there are certain psychological and physical states that are *inherently* antagonistic to anxiety. For example, anxiety cannot occur in the presence of deep relaxation. The specific technique in which relaxation is used to countercondition the anxiety response to a stimulus is called **systematic desensitization**. Systematic desensitization consists of a three-stage process: (1) training in relaxation, (2) construction of a hierarchy of anxiety-eliciting stimuli, and (3) gradual pairing, through imagery, of anxiety-eliciting stimuli with the relaxed state.

Here is how it works. In the initial interview, the therapist tries to identify various problems and symptoms that trouble the patient and, then, to develop hierarchical lists of stimuli (thoughts, objects, experiences) that the patient feels produce in him increasing amounts of anxiety when they actually occur. These lists established, the therapist then formally trains the patient in ways of achieving a state of deep relaxation. Once the patient has learned to do

this effectively, he is asked to imagine vividly experiences from this list that are increasingly frightening (starting from the situation that evokes the least anxiety) *while remaining deeply relaxed.* (In many ways a state of truly deep relaxation is akin to being hypnotized.) As the patient imagines each experience, the therapist questions him about whether or not he is feeling completely relaxed at the given moment. Only if he maintains a relaxed state while he imagines a given experience is he instructed to proceed to the next, more anxiety-evoking situation on his personal list. (Box 25.2, p. 622, provides a real-life example of systematic desensitization.) By vividly imagining scenes or objects of fear, the patient will gradually break the association between the stimuli and the anxiety response.

Other forms of behavior therapy   All forms of behavior therapy are based on conditioning and learning principles, but a variety of specific and rather distinct techniques have been developed. For example, rather than attempting to *inhibit* anxiety as a response to a conditioned stimulus, Stampfl uses a technique intended to *elicit* the anxiety response in relation to the conditioned stimulus but is careful not to strengthen the response; that is, he does not allow the patient to avoid and thus to reinforce the anxiety response (Stampfl & Lewis, 1967). In **implosive therapy**, as this technique is called, if a person is repeatedly and extensively exposed to the conditioned anxiety-producing stimulus in situations where anxiety is not reinforced, the response (both the anxiety and anxiety-avoiding behavior) will eventually extinguish. According to one commentator on this technique (London, 1964) Stampfl seeks to speed this extinction process by using "every possible means to frighten patients as much as he can for as long as he can at a sitting," specifically by having them vividly imagine themselves involved in the *most* anxiety-producing situations possible, situations that he describes for them in the most compelling and frightening detail. Once anxiety is successfully extinguished for these most frightening scenes, Stampfl claims that the extinction will automatically generalize to the less frightening situations.

In another, quite different variant of behavior therapy, a Skinnerian model of operant conditioning has been used to encourage the development of social speech in autistic children, children in whom autistic thinking (see Unit 6, p. 125) is pathologically extreme. Lovaas (1966) initially uses food to reinforce behavior that increasingly approximates a responsive conversation, an instance of the shaping technique discussed in Unit 16. (This approach has been popularly called *M and M therapy* because of the frequent use of these candies as positive reinforcers.) Gradually, secondary reinforcers (e.g., verbal praise) are substituted for the food. Any accompanying undesirable behaviors are eliminated, or aversively conditioned, by the use of negative reinforcements, initially through such primary negative reinforcers as electric shock, later on by verbal disapproval.

In order to modify behavior and enhance the possibilities of change, Salter (1961) takes yet another tack. He gives patients specific instructions and assignments to perform desirable behaviors that are to be carried out in the external world where the *natural* reinforcements in life ordinarily occur. The aim of this form of therapy is to teach the patient effectively to apply the principles of learning to his own behavior and thereby achieve self-regulation.

Bandura (1969) advocates the use of *modeling* as a way to modify behavior not only to eliminate undesirable responses but to instigate new responses. In this approach the patient is provided opportunities to live (and learn) vicariously by observing the behavior of another person, or model (either live or on film), who is actively engaged in a situation related to his particular problem. One example, in this case a phobia, would involve repeatedly watching another person comfortably handling snakes and, eventually, becoming at least somewhat less susceptible to one's extreme, hence irrational, fear of coming anywhere near even a harmless snake. (But as Box 25.3, p. 624, suggests, what the model is doing matters quite a bit.)

Commentary on Behavior Therapy

Those therapists who stress the role of insight claim that symptom removal (i.e., behavior change) without treatment of the underlying pathology will result in the emergence of new symptoms; this has been called **symptom substitution**. In rebuttal, behavior therapists generally maintain that the appearance of such new symptoms is rare and that, when it does occur, the phenomenon can be explained (and treated) in learning-theory terms (Buchwald & Young, 1969).

Another frequent comment is that in the development of their techniques, behavior therapists have taken a large and precarious jump from learning principles systematically explored and refined in rigorous experimental laboratory research with animals (as discussed in Units 15 and 16) to dealing with complex behavior that necessarily involves the crucial intervention of symbolic processes such as language. It has been argued, moreover, that they have also limited themselves to extrapolation from a very narrow band of experimental research and have tended to ignore, for the most part, studies on perception, emotion, and cognition, a point elaborated by Lazarus (1968). Thus, it is concluded by some, the learning models used by behavior therapists may tend to be oversimplified, spurious, and inadequate for dealing with human behavior in its full and typical form.

In a review of the theoretical bases and supportive evidence for the behavior therapies, Breger and McGaugh (1965) question both the supposed relevance of learning theory to these methods and the questionable empirical proofs of their adequacy. The initial claims of success that were filed for various forms of behavior therapy have indeed become more moderate as additional research indicates that behavior therapies have approximately the same success rate as psychoanalytic therapy or other psychological therapies.

Because the behavior therapies tend to hold to a narrow conception of personality disorders, typically confining them to discrete behavior symptoms, it is such symptoms that seem most amenable to behavior therapy. For example, Grossberg (1964) finds from his review of the various behavior therapies that they "have been most successful with disorders involving specific maladaptive behaviors. Conditioning procedures were highly effective with phobic reactions, anxiety reactions, enuresis, stuttering." But such specific maladaptive behaviors unfortunately do not even begin to exhaust the diverse repertoire of human neuroses and psychoses. Most often the disorder is diffuse and pervades almost every aspect of a person's functioning.

London (1972), a long-time advocate of the behavior modification approach, has made what may be a useful distinction between the presumed bases of behavior therapies in learning theory and the practical effectiveness of these

therapies. In a paper aptly titled "The End of Ideology in Behavior Modification," he forcefully argues for an intensified focus on advancing the "technology" of behavior therapy and an abandonment of fussing with theoretical justification of such advances. It is worth quoting at length. He concludes:

I am saying that theory has worn itself out in behavior modification and that technology, essentially of treatment, should now be a primary focus, perhaps, in the long range, even for serv-

BOX 25.2

SNEAKING UP ON THE UNAPPROACHABLE

The following example of systematic desensitization is taken verbatim from two leading exponents of this approach. The detail is considerable but should be attended to if the nuances of the technique are to be appreciated. We have added occasional comments [**in this type**].

THE PATIENT
Miss C. was a 24-year-old art student who came for treatment because marked anxiety at examinations had resulted in repeated failures. Investigation revealed additional phobic areas. . . . The hierarchies are given below. All of them involve people, and none belong to the classical phobias. [**The other phobias were not included in this excerpt.**] Freedom from anxiety to the highest items of each of these hierarchies was achieved in seventeen desensitization sessions, with complete transfer to the corresponding situations in actuality. Four months later, she sat for [**If you're not British, read "took"**] (and passed) her examinations without anxiety.

THE PATIENT'S HIERARCHY OF FEARS [**The first are the worst.**]
  A. Examination series
  1. On the way to the university on the day of an examination.
  2. In the process of answering an examination paper.
  3. Before the unopened doors of the examination room.
  4. Awaiting the distribution of examination papers.
  5. The examination paper lies face down before her.

[**Note that up to this point the hierarchy is not obvious; it is not a simple matter of her being more anxious the closer she gets to the actual taking of the exam.**]

  6. The night before an examination.
  7. On the day before an examination.
  8. Two days before an examination.
  9. Three days before an examination.
  10. Four days before an examination.
  11. Five days before an examination.
  12. A week before an examination.
  13. Two weeks before an examination.
  14. A month before an examination.

RELAXATION
With the patient sitting or lying comfortably with her eyes closed, whether hypnotized or not, the therapist proceeds to bring about as deep as possible a state of relaxation by the use of such words as the following:

Now, your whole body becomes progressively heavier, and all your muscles relax. Let go more and more completely. We shall give your muscles individual attention. Relax the muscles of your forehead. (Pause 5–10 sec.) Relax the muscles of the lower part of your face. (Pause 5–10 sec.) Relax the muscles of your jaws and those of your tongue. (Pause.) Relax the muscles of your eyeballs. The more you relax, the calmer you become. (Pause.) Relax the muscles of your neck. (Pause.) Let all the muscles of your shoulders relax. Just let yourself go. (Pause.) Now relax your arms. (Pause.) Relax all the muscles of your trunk. (Pause.) Relax the muscles of your lower limbs. Let your muscles go more and more. You feel so much at ease and so very comfortable.

At the first desensitization session, which is always pretty exploratory, the therapist requires some feedback of what has been accomplished, and therefore says, "If you feel utterly calm—zero anxiety—do

ing scientific purposes. . . . The proper development that I am suggesting is not limited to hardware and is not self-generating, but reaches to the systematic exploration of all kinds of therapeutic things without inhibition or concern as to whether they fit ostensible *principles* of learning, or reinforcement, or whatever, but with a singular focus on whether they fit the *facts* of human experience. . . .

With the era of polemics virtually ended, and Skinner citing Freud over and over again in his latest work, and the American Psychoanalytic Association at a recent convention casually in-

corporating behavior modification into its discourses on psychotherapy, the political utility of learning theory, so called for the definition of the field, is ended. It was never really theory anyhow, as we used it, but ideology for professional purposes and mostly metaphor for clinical ones. $t is time now, I think, for the remedial branch of this business to stop worrying about its scientific pretensions, in the theoretical sense, as long as it keeps its functional nose clean, and to devise a kind of engineering subsidiary, or more precisely, a systems analysis approach to its own operations. We have gotten about as much mileage as

---

nothing; otherwise raise your left index finger." If the finger remains still, the next stage may begin; but if it is raised the therapist ascertains the level of anxiety by further probings—"Raise the finger if more than 10 suds *[Subjective Unit of Disturbance —a scale for reporting experienced anxiety learned earlier by the patient in which 100 suds is the most horrible anxiety imaginable and zero suds is absolute tranquility]* etc. This mode of inquiry is used, because it seems to cause much less disruption of relaxation than spoken replies.

If the patient continues to have a good deal of anxiety despite her best efforts at direct relaxation, various imaginal devices may be invoked. Those that we most commonly employ are the following:

1. Imagine that on a calm summer's day you lie on your back on a soft lawn and watch the fleecy cumulus clouds move slowly overhead. Notice especially the brilliant edges of the clouds.
2. Imagine an intense, bright spot of light about eighteen inches in front of you.
3. Imagine that near a river's bank you see a leaf moving erratically on the little waves.

If, despite these efforts, considerable anxiety persists, the session is now terminated. Otherwise it proceeds.

DESENSITIZATION IMAGERY

The characteristic way in which scenes are introduced may be illustrated with reference to the case of Miss C. When she seemed well relaxed she was addressed as follows:

I am now going to ask you to imagine a number of scenes. You will imagine them clearly and they will generally interfere little, if at all, with your state of relaxation. If, however, at any time you feel disturbed or worried and want to attract my attention, you will be able to do so by raising your left index finger. First I want you to image that you are standing at a

familiar street corner on a pleasant morning watching the traffic go by. You see cars, motorcycles, trucks, bicycles, people and traffic lights; and you can hear the sounds associated with all these things. [A neutral scene that should evoke no anxiety in Miss C. unless she is generally tense at the moment] (Pause of about 15 sec.) Now stop imagining that scene and give all your attention once again to relaxing. If the scene you imagined disturbed you even in the slightest degree I want you to raise your left index finger now. (Patient does not raise finger.) Now imagine that you are at home studying in the evening. It is the 20th of May, exactly a month before your examination. [Item 14 in the examination series, the easiest one] (Pause of 5 sec.) Now stop imagining the scene. Go on relaxing. (Pause of 10 sec.) Now imagine the same scene again—a month before your examination. (Pause of 5 sec.) Stop imagining the scene and just think of your muscles. Let go, and enjoy your state of calm. (Pause of 15 sec.) Now again imagine that you are studying at home a month before your examination (Pause of 5 sec.) Stop the scene, and now think of nothing but your own body. (Pause of 5 sec.) If you felt any disturbance whatsoever to the last scene raise your left index finger now. (Patient raises finger.) If the amount of disturbance decreased from the first presentation to the third do nothing, otherwise again raise your finger. (Patient does not raise finger.) [Therefore some progress has been made.]

Miss C. had a long way to go from this first session. This excerpt should give you an idea of the sort of road she traveled in her seventeen sessions in order to reach successively (in the therapist's words) "freedom from anxiety to the highest items of each of these hierarchies."

J. WOLPE. *The Practice of Behavior Therapy.* New York: Pergamon, 1969.

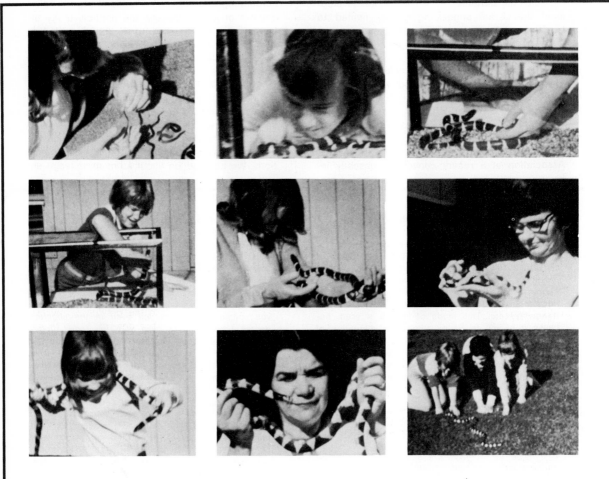

BOX 25.3

WHO'S AFRAID OF THE SNAKE IN THE GRASS?

Unlearning inappropriate or maladaptive behavior through reinforcement training alone is usually very slow going. Whether the reinforcement technique used is classical or instrumental, and whether it involves positive or negative reinforcements (or both), hundreds, even thousands, of trials may be required before any useful therapeutic effects are visible. Modeling is one way that has been shown to speed up the process of learning to change one's behavior. Briefly, the principle underlying this approach exploits our tendency to imitate the behavior of others.

Thus, if we can watch someone else—a model—behaving appropriately in a situation in which we ourselves usually behave inappropriately, we can learn to imitate this more adaptive behavior. (Whether imitation can find a legitimate place within formal reinforcement-type learning theories is a debatable and debated question but need not concern us here.)

But is it really imitation alone that works in modifying behavior? If it were, then it would follow that the best way to learn to behave adaptively is to spend a lot of time watching someone who does, and does *consistently*. But some research has shown that this may not be the case and that models who *initially* exhibit the same maladaptive behavior as the patient does and who then go on to eliminate it may increase the effectiveness of this behavior therapy technique. A recent experiment is directly addressed to this question and, as you shall see, to a related one as well.

D. H. Meichenbaum, a psychologist at the University of Waterloo, Ontario, Canada, designed a study of subjects (thirty-six undergraduate women) who had reported, in a "fear survey," that they were extremely afraid of snakes, even nonpoisonous ones. These women were in no sense seeking treatment for this fear; rather, they were offered the opportunity to participate (for course credit) in an evaluation of an "experimental" treatment procedure. An initial assessment, or pretest, of how frightened of snakes they indeed were was made by having them go through, as far as they dared, a thirteen-step procedure that involved increasingly intimate interaction with a harmless 5-ft corn snake. The first step consisted of just looking briefly at the snake, safely caged in a glass box 15 ft away. Subsequent steps brought the subject closer to the snake, later required touching him briefly with gloved hands, and ultimately (for those who braved the thirteenth step) holding the snake barehanded outside of its cage for 60 sec. Each subject was assigned a pretest approach score that indicated how far through the thirteen-step sequence she was able to go.

Subjects were then assigned at random to one of four experimental groups, thus assuring that each group of nine were (on the average) about equally afraid of snakes at the outset of the treatments, which began immediately after the pretest. The different treatments experienced by the four groups were designed to test two related questions: (1) Would the subject learn better to overcome her fear of snakes by observing models who consistently betrayed no fearfulness ("mastery" group) or by observing models who started off afraid (as the subjects did) but finally succeeded in overcoming their fear and behaving as comfortably with the snake as the mastery models did ("coping" group)? (2) Would it matter to the effectiveness of the treatment if the models verbalized their feelings aloud with either approach? (This involved setting up two additional subject groups: a "mastery with verbalization" group and a "coping with verbalization" group.)

Each group watched a different set of three 8-min televised films depicting the behavior of three different female models. (They were told that they were watching previous actual subjects who had been filmed going through the same thirteen-

step adventure with the snake that the subjects had just experienced.) The models (the same three women for all four treatment situations) had in fact been trained to respond in the appropriate manner in the video taping of the films for each of the experimental groups. (Apparently they were quite competent actresses; ratings made by the subjects of the fearfulness shown by the models indicated, as intended, that mastery models were seen as unafraid from start to end but that coping models were seen as having been initially quite afraid but eventually becoming quite fearless.)

Immediately following the films all subjects were once again put through the thirteen-step test of their fear of snakes (the post-test).

Figure A clearly indicates the significantly greater improvement in the post-test by subjects who had been exposed to coping models. (The y axis of the graph refers to the average step reached in the thirteen-step test sequence.) In fact, 39 percent of the subjects in the two coping groups successfully made it through to the previously horrendous thirteenth step, but not one of the mastery

(Box 25.3 is continued on p. 626)

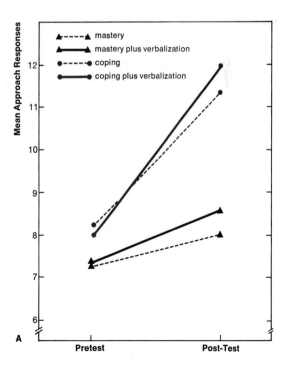

A

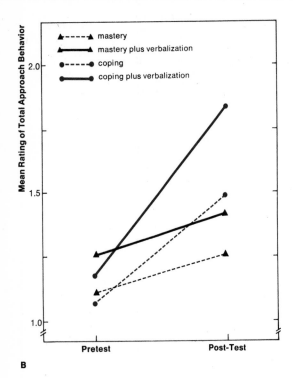

B

snakes helped a subject to be braver in her heart as well as in her behavior.

Such behavior, it would seem, makes it easier to feel like the model from the start and thus to follow better her emotional reeducation through the course of the experience. It is also possible that the verbalization may have a specific educative effect. Self-instructions by the model to take slow deep breaths and to take one step at a time may have, in effect, taught subjects specific practical techniques to control fear and thus to overcome their initial helplessness.

Meichenbaum believes that his experimental results are all the more encouraging because his subjects were not really highly motivated, as patients would be if they had true phobias sufficiently disturbing to cause them to seek treatment. Perhaps. But the opposite possibility exists: Truly phobic patients might be suffering from more deeply entrenched disturbances that would therefore be more resistant to treatment by this or by any therapeutic technique. (We will not here get into the much broader issues of whether it would help to know the possible origins of such a phobia or of symptom substitution, nor will we even whisper a word about the possible symbolic significance that might legitimately be seen by the psychoanalytically inclined in a woman being inordinately afraid of really harmless snakes.)

In his concluding remarks, Meichenbaum regrets that final exams and subsequent vacations got in the way of his intention to carry out follow-up assessments of the persistence of the observed behavior changes. He urges that this be done and, also, that the generality of the effects be evaluated. (Would the subjects who learned not to be afraid of snakes remain unafraid for some time, and would they also cease being afraid or even be somewhat less afraid of snakes no matter where they happened to run into them?) Such further work is of course necessary, but previous research reports evaluating this kind of treatment for this kind of problem suggest that the results should be encouraging.

D. H. MEICHENBAUM. Examination of model characteristics in reducing avoidance behavior. *Journal of Personality and Social Psychology*, 1971, **17**, 298–307. Copyright 1971 by the American Psychological Association. Reprinted by permission.
Photos from A. BANDURA, E. B. BLANCHARD, & R. RITTER. Relative efficacy of desensitization and modeling approaches for inducing behavioral, affective, and attitudinal changes. *Journal of Personality and Social Psychology*, 1969, **13**, 179.

subjects (in either group) managed to do so. However, by this measure of the effectiveness of treatment, it did not matter whether or not the models had verbalized their feelings. But although verbalization of fear (or lack of fear) throughout the filmed sequences did not affect how far subjects dared to go in approaching the snake, it did affect how confident they appeared to be in going through these behavioral test steps. The data here come from an experimenter who had rated the degree of boldness or hesitancy with which the women carried out their increasingly closer approaches to the snake (2.0 = a completely comfortable and willing approach; 1.0 = an approach showing considerable hesitancy and reluctance).

Figure B (like Figure A) shows that both coping groups became less afraid of snakes than either mastery group did. But it *also* demonstrates that the coping with verbalization subjects benefited more than the coping group did. Apparently, having had the opportunity to hear as well as to see how another woman worked through her anxiety about

we are going to out of old principles, even correct ones, but we have barely begun to work the
new technology (italics in original).

Aside from considerations about the scope,
depth, and validity of behavior therapy, many
critics regard it as embodying an antihumanis-
tic, mechanical view of man and an acceptance
of the use of experts to control and shape
human behavior. To some, this attitude implies
an approach to George Orwell's *1984* nightmare.
But for others, a society so based on learning
principles and with reinforcements wisely controlled by experts is utopia. Indeed, B. F.
Skinner, long a leading spokesman for this point
of view, envisaged some time ago just such an
ideal society in his novel *Walden Two* (1948).
And he persistently continued his justification
of this position in his controversial essay *Beyond Freedom and Dignity* (1971).

PHENOMENOLOGICAL THERAPIES

Phenomenology and existentialism in psychology
developed partly in reaction to what were regarded as the detached, atomistic, and narrowly
objective approaches of experimentalists and
behaviorists. As theories and therapies, they are
the most broadly and explicitly philosophical,
advancing a conception not only of pathological
behavior but also of psychological health, integration, and self-actualization. Thus, Carl Jung,
whose sweeping conceptualization of personality
is discussed in Unit 29, may be regarded as the
source of present-day phenomenological therapies, and Maslow (also discussed in that unit),
their latter-day theoretical spokesman.

Will Therapy

One of the earliest phenomenological therapists
was Otto Rank, who had trained in psychoanalysis with Freud. Rank rejected the idea of inevitable effects on personality resulting from
earlier experiences; after all, psychoanalysis asserted a militantly deterministic view of development. Instead, he focused on the individual's
experience in the *present* rather than on his
past development and stressed the person's
uniqueness as a *self-determined* willful person.

Rank's views are expressed in a method of treatment known as **will therapy** (Rank, 1947).

Phenomenological approaches such as
Rank's reject the medical model of psychopathology as an illness as well as the necessity
for differential diagnosis of the specific form of
the illness. All psychological disorders, instead,
are seen as emanating from the same basic conflict: between who a person feels he is (what
his own sensory system tells him about his inner
and outer world) and the values of others to
which he tries to conform in behavior but that
often contradict his own experience. The conflict, then, is between self-regulation and external regulation, between owning or identifying
with all the parts of oneself and becoming
alienated from parts of oneself when one's own
sensations, feelings, and needs do not conform
to the "shoulds" of others. Whenever this conflict is experienced, it leads to anxiety; in order
to avoid anxiety, individuals develop certain
behavior patterns that allow part of the person
to be cut off, disowned, alienated. These avoidance behaviors *are* the symptoms that lead the
patient to seek therapy.

The goal in this form of therapy is to
help the individual become aware of herself, to
discover herself. The therapist's task is to create a situation in which such self-discovery can
best take place. Self-awareness in the here and
now is the key. Once the patient achieves such
awareness, she necessarily becomes free to make
rational choices; she will no longer experience
her behavior as outside her own control.

Client-Centered Therapy

The approach best known as **client-centered
therapy** has its beginnings in the 1940s at the
University of Chicago. Developed primarily by
Carl Rogers, it has also been called **nondirective
therapy** and **Rogerian therapy**.

The goal of client-centered therapy is to
help the patient attain congruence between his
thoughts and feelings about himself and his
observations of his behavior. Achievement of
this fit between feeling and fact requires that
the person develop a positive self-concept and
a willingness to acknowledge more parts of the
self.

Perhaps the central feature of Rogerian therapy is its insistence that the client's internal focus of reference should guide the course of treatment, not the therapist's theoretical predilections. The therapist attempts to understand in detail the client's perceptions of his world. He helps the client to clarify for himself the nature of his problems; one technique is to summarize in more clear-cut fashion what the client, by word or gesture, has *himself* expressed but has not yet fully recognized. One facet of this technique is known as *reflection of feeling,* a subtle act in which the therapist attempts to bounce back to the client, in selective and focused form, aspects of the client's expressed feelings and emotions that he, the attuned therapist, can detect but that may have so far escaped the client's awareness. (Box 25.4 illustrates such an exchange between a client-centered therapist and a young woman.)

A guiding premise of this method is that each person has within himself the ability to find his own solutions for his problems. The therapist's responsibility, therefore, is to assist

---

BOX 25.4

FINDING THE "TENDER SPOT"

In her fourth interview, Mrs. Teral, a twenty-three-year-old married schoolteacher, has just told her therapist, John Shlien of the University of Chicago Counseling Center, that she is upset. The therapist notices that the client looks pained and stricken and says:

TH (Therapist): What . . . what's hitting you now?

C (Client): I don't know.

TH: Something upsetting, something that makes you feel like crying?

C: [Pause; crying softly; words lost.] I could use a little more self control, too.

TH: You don't like to have to cry.

C: No, I don't. [Pause.] And I don't know why, either. I just got very upset. [Still crying.]

TH: Um-hm. Something just came over you and you really don't know what started it.

C: [Long pause; still crying.] I must have been getting a little too close to something—I didn't want to talk about, or something.

TH: You really don't know what made this happen. [Client looks for clock.] You've still got about fifteen minutes.

C: [Pause; still crying.] Something hit me [laughs].

TH: Hm?

C: Something hit me.

TH: Something hurts.

C: [Long pause.] Here I go again. [Pause.] I don't know what it was. I just . . . I'm completely gone now. My knees are shaking all over me.

TH: Um-hm. [Pause.] You don't know what started this but it's really taken hold of you. [Pause; client crying.] Your whole . . . your whole body is in a turmoil.

C: I really can't concentrate on what I'm doing. All I can concentrate on is the feeling that I'm not going to smoke, I'm not going to smoke [laughs].

TH: I don't know exactly what you mean there.

C: I can't even try to think what it is because I want a cigarette so bad I just have [laughs] to keep myself going. I'm not going to smoke, I'm not going to smoke [laughs].

TH: All your energy is just bent toward that one thing, just . . . to keep yourself from having a cigarette, huh?

C: Yes. [Long pause.] I'm not very . . . I'm upset 'cause I said something about being dependent on [husband]. Maybe I just didn't want to start thinking about that. That could be it.

TH: Maybe that's kind of a tender spot.

Thus the client, with the therapist's subtle assistance, has herself come to an awareness of a "tender spot."

M. K. LEWIS, C. R. ROGERS, & J. M. SHLIEN. Time-limited, client-centered psychotherapy: Two cases. In A. Burton (Ed.), *Case Studies in Counseling and Psychotherapy.* Englewood Cliffs, N.J.: Prentice-Hall, 1959. © 1959 by Prentice-Hall, Inc., Englewood Cliffs, New Jersey. Reprinted by permission.

his client in coming up with answers that the client himself devises, answers that express the individual's unique potential for personality growth and change. The therapist's job is *not* to propose theoretical explanations of problems or to offer authoritative advice on how to go about solving them.

Since the client-centered approach was first outlined by Rogers (1942), it has gone through several changes and developments. In its early, more nondirective period (1940–1950) the therapist typically attempted to facilitate the development of insight by creating a permissive, nonauthoritarian setting. The therapist was mainly concerned with helping the client clarify his feelings and perceptions and was careful not to give advice, make interpretations, or express his own feelings.

In a second period (roughly in the earlier 1950s), which was marked by publication of Rogers's book *Client-Centered Therapy* (1951), a greater emphasis was placed on the therapist's sensitive responsiveness (or expressed empathy) to the client's feelings. The affective, or feeling, component became more central to the interaction than the cognitive, or insight, component. The therapist's major task therefore became to remove the sources of threat to the *relation* with the client while continuing to reflect feelings back to him.

From about 1957 on, client-centered therapy has taken on an experiential orientation, involving *more active* communication of the therapist's feelings. In 1957, Rogers outlined several "necessary and sufficient" conditions for therapy to be successful, all of which deal with aspects of the therapist's role, including (1) unconditional positive regard for the patient, (2) emphatic understanding, and (3) congruence and genuineness in revealing his own feelings. Technique and method are de-emphasized, and the therapist-as-person comes to be seen as the agent of change in a truly human and personal relationship.

The client-centered approach may appear deceptively simple. Its apparent lack of systematic technique is a source of attractiveness for some; for others, just this feature is its fatal flaw or weakness. However, the general notion that it is *who* the therapist is rather than *what*

he does that leads to therapeutic change has been gaining considerable support in recent years.

Early on, client-centered therapy ranked first in the diligence and sophistication of research · designed to evaluate empirically the nature and extent of its therapeutic effectiveness. A fundamental tenet of client-centered therapy is that improvement in adjustment and personality change generally are first reflected by modifications of the person's self-perception and that such modifications in turn lead to behavioral change. Rogers and Dymond (1954) long ago presented considerable evidence for this general conception of how personality can be changed through psychotherapy, evidence that continues to stand in support of the effectiveness of this therapeutic approach.

Gestalt Therapy

Although **Gestalt therapy** and client-centered therapy have similar philosophical and theoretical origins, there is considerable difference between the two in the nature of the techniques used and the general tone of the therapy sessions. Client-centered therapists, as we have noted, seem generally to eschew specific method and technique; Gestalt therapists have developed a number of procedures, techniques, and games for use in therapy and have enunciated explicit rules designed to facilitate self-understanding (insight) and growth.

Gestalt therapy was first developed by Frederick Perls (Perls, Hefferline, & Goodman, 1951) and grew significantly during the late 1950s and 1960s. The name is borrowed from the classical school of Gestalt psychology, which stressed the active interrelations between the whole form, *Gestalt*, of perceived objects and organizing processes within the perceiver, a process roughly analogous to that which can lead to insights within the Gestalt therapy framework.

In Gestalt therapy the individual is instructed to pay close attention to his *current* feelings, thoughts, and wishes. The focus is on the *now*, what the patient is experiencing at the moment and how he blocks off or interferes with his experiencing a total awareness of his present self. Pathology is viewed as the alienation of the individual from parts of himself and his experience; the road to personal integration and growth involves becoming aware of how the individual prevents (or resists) reaching this total awareness and, ultimately, removing the resistances and achieving it. In order to help the patient achieve full self-awareness, the Gestalt therapist focuses on precisely what the person is doing in physical, symbolic, and interpersonal behavior at the given moment. Nonverbal behavior is frequently used as a clue to the way in which the patient is blocking awareness and expression. Thus, if the patient characteristically sits with arms folded ("as if to protect himself from possible hurt"), the therapist may call attention to the frequent occurrence of this bit of blocking behavior. But the therapist never answers questions about what a particular behavior or exchange means; he *never interprets*. Rather, he has the patient discover the meaning for himself. In this way the therapist intentionally chooses not to deal with denial of interpretations or disowning of meaning by the patient. The patient, then, cannot disown whatever he *himself* has developed and given meaning.

In order to enable patients to reown alienated aspects of themselves, the therapist has them play the disowned parts. Avoidance is the clue to what is being disowned and what needs reintegration. But in Gestalt therapy merely talking about these things will lead nowhere; intellectual verbal explanations are not expected to lead to reintegration. Rather, it is necessary that the patient actually *live out* in experience that which he has attempted to avoid.

The following are some of the techniques used to help the patient reexperience what he has disowned (Levitsky & Perls, 1970):

1. *Playing the projection.* If a patient complains that the therapist cannot be trusted, or is not sympathetic, he is asked to play actively the part of an untrustworthy person. In this way he may begin to learn what parts of himself are untrustworthy or unsympathetic and learn what his own internal conflict is in this regard. Transference-type projections are not viewed, as they are in psychoanalytic methods, as the patient's attributing to the therapist the characteristics of significant others (e.g., parents). Instead, he is seen as projecting what is true of himself, here and now. Even descriptions of one's parents—and attempts to assign them blame for one's shortcomings—are viewed as projections of disowned parts of the self.

2. *Reversals.* Here the name of the game is self-explanatory. For example, a timid person may be asked to play an exhibitionist as a way of making contact with an avoided (i.e., anxiety provoking) part of himself. By thus experiencing and eventually overcoming the avoided part, it may become reowned and reintegrated. The person becomes more "together."

3. *Exaggeration.* When a therapist notes that a person often engages in some slight unconscious movement (e.g., rapidly tapping his finger on a table), he may be asked to exaggerate the movement in an effort to help him get in touch with, to understand, the feelings that this aborted, unconscious movement has been leaking out. Sometimes the patient will be asked to try acting out a line or phrase fed to him by the therapist, based on the therapist's interpretation of what the patient has probably been unable to communicate directly. The therapist, however, does *not* spell out his interpretation. Instead, the patient, by playing out the line, spontaneously develops its meaning *for him* and makes it his own.

Gestalt therapists believe that dreams are the most spontaneous productions and forms of expression. Many of the techniques they have developed are applied in work with dreams. (Box 25.5, p. 632, presents an example of some Gestalt dream work that encompasses some of the techniques just outlined.)

Commentary on Phenomenological Therapies

Criticism of the phenomenological approaches comes from two directions: both from those favoring psychoanalytic models and from the behavior therapists.

Phenomenological approaches, generally, tend to be viewed by the psychoanalytically inclined as effective primarily for individuals who already have a relatively sound personality structure and merely require short-term aid in clarifying their current minor difficulties. But specific phenomenological approaches have been subjected to specific challenges. The nondirective approach of the client-centered Rogerians is criticized as not sufficiently powerful and motivating to counteract the neurotic defenses and resistance to deep self-examination. Furthermore, because of its focus on reality, the present, and on conscious material, the psychoanalytic position would hold that the most significant aspects of transference, repression, and resistance are therefore never dealt with and that they must be if there is to be therapeutic change.

The psychoanalytic critique of Gestalt therapy takes a somewhat different direction because the therapist's willingness to deal with dreams, fantasies, and unconscious material is consistent with the psychoanalytic perspective. But psychoanalysts complain that the very activity of the Gestalt therapist precludes the full development of transference and that the failure to deal with the past prevents insight into the origins of the neurosis-inducing unconscious conflicts. Gestalt therapists claim also that each person should be responsible only for himself, and thus the Gestalt therapist generally refuses to take responsibility for what happens to the patient, arguing that assuming such responsibility for patients induces dependency. This conception of responsibility has been challenged by psychoanalytic therapists as an abdication of the very necessary responsibilities of *any* therapist for the management of the course of treatment. Although considerable power for directing the action is in fact assumed by the Gestalt therapist, it is accompanied by his denial of any intent to manipulate and of any personal responsibility for the course or outcome of treatment.

The criticisms that behavior therapists make of phenomenological therapies are similar to those they make of psychoanalysis and other approaches stressing insight. According to behavior therapists, these approaches work— when they do—only because of conditioning and learning features that are accidentally employed. The unwillingness of phenomenological therapists to define and delineate both the pathology and the details of treatment are regarded as an abdication of their role as true experts in the science of behavior. The changes in awareness of the self that such therapists have as an ex-

plicit goal do not necessarily lead to changes in behavior. But, behavior therapists conclude, it is maladaptive *behavior*, not simply (or at all) deficient self-awareness, which is causing the patient difficulty in getting along in the real world. And finally there remain strong philosophical differences around issues of free will and self-determination that separate the behaviorist and the phenomenologist. (For a fascinating and still-relevant debate between articulate proponents of the two positions, see Rogers & Skinner, 1956.)

INTERPERSONAL THERAPIES

In the last decade the frame around the individual has been broken, and questions about why a man does what he does are being answered in terms of the context of relationships he creates and inhabits. The reasons for this change have been the continuing emphasis upon interpersonal relations over the years and the recent development of ideas about systems (Haley, 1967).

More and more, psychopathology and psychotherapy are being viewed as social rather than as medical sciences.

Family therapy, group therapy, and interpersonal models of individual therapy all emphasize the interactive, communicative, and relationship aspects of psychopathology and mental health, although within this general orientation a wide variety of specific techniques has been developed.

Initially, interpersonally oriented therapies were seen as radically disturbing the sacred and private individual doctor-patient relation. When they were initially adopted, they were regarded as experimental techniques. They were used only as adjuncts to individual treatment necessitated by such reality problems as those presented by the families of child patients or involving practical problems associated with the management of psychiatric wards. Practitioners of these new therapies were at first not generally committed to a social and interpersonal model. They practiced family and group treatment in a limited fashion and for convenience, mainly for practical reasons; otherwise they adhered primarily

BOX 25.5

GESTALT DREAMWORK

This excerpt is from a "dream workshop" conducted by Fritz Perls in which he worked, one at a time, with individual participants in a group setting. Note how, in this instance, the Gestalt technique for working with dream material can be applied even where there is apparently no dream to work with.

K (Kirk): I don't have a dream to tell you.

F (Fritz): Okeh, talk to that non-existent dream.

K: Well, you're not non-existent, you're just—that I have—when you're around—and then you run away as soon as I wake up. And everybody here is learning so much about himself but you copped out. You didn't give me any information I can work with.

F: Change seats. "Yes, I run away. I am your dream, I run away."

K (playing his dream): Well, it wasn't my fault you woke up and forgot. I did my business. I dreamed. You're the one that forgot. I didn't run away.

K: So it's my fault, again.

F: That must be a Jewish mother dream. "It's my fault again!" (laughter)

K: Shame on you, poor little me. You know.

F: Can you answer without thinking when I snap my finger, to my question? Without thinking. When did you lose your dream?

K: Right after I woke up . . . I had a dream, and I told— this is what Fritz wants to work with, and I woke up, and I didn't have it. . . .

F: A life without a dream . . . What happened to your dream?

K: My dream . . . A life without a dream is something very sad.

F: What are your hands doing now?

K: They're massaging the tips. My hands are shaking.

F: Yah. Let's have an encounter; there's something going on there.

K: You're nervous, and I'm—as usual I'm going to protect you, and—get your—your *action* down here, so you won't do anything you shouldn't do with your hands. You're ashamed of their trembling, your left hand trembling—so—ah, I'll close them.

F: Could you give me a number of sentences starting with "I am ashamed of—"?

K: I am ashamed of my physique. I am ashamed of the way I am unable to come across with people. I am ashamed of the way I look. I am ashamed that I'm stupid to be ashamed. I'm ashamed—

F: Say this to Kirk, "Kirk, you should be ashamed of—walking the earth, or of being nervous—"

K: You should be *ashamed* for doing this. You know better. You know that you have worth, you know that there are things you can do well.

F: Go on nagging. Become a real nag.

K: You should be ashamed! It's silly, it's stupid. It's just further evidence that you're—you're—not worth being around. You won't even accept—stand up for things you know that you can do well. You're rotten to be—to feel the way you do.

F: Now, can you *nag* us a bit. Tell us we should be ashamed. . . .

K: You should be ashamed. . . .

F: Just play a nag.

K: Be ashamed! You're sitting and watching people and why are you even down here? You should know everything. You should be able to take care of yourself . . . and thinking about yourselves, and thinking you have to come down here and take care of yourselves, when there's so much going on in the world that should be taken care of. I know you came down here for your own benefit. This is something very phony.

F: Good. Let's play this phony game. Again go back to Kirk. Say, "Kirk, you should be ashamed of this and that." Then you play Kirk, and each time you talk back, either "F - - - you," or nag back, make a counter-attack.

K: Kirk, you should be ashamed for being. . . .

(disgustedly) Oh, shut up! You're always doing that. Just shut up!

Who's gonna tell you if you don't? Somebody has to keep reminding you to keep yourself down, now don't think you're so f - - - ing smart.

Ah, there he goes again! Screaming at me. All day long. All day long. Let me enjoy myself a little.

All I can do is say, over and over again——

F: What are your hands doing now?

K: They want to hit.

F: Ah. Yah. The nagger gets a little stronger now.

K: It's what happens, 'cause——

F: Tell him, "I could hit you."

K: I could hit you! but I really can't hit you, so I nag. My words are hitting. This is safer, because if you really hit, well then you'll destroy, and I wouldn't have any reason . . . not to feel this way . . . if you weren't there to nag me. 'Cause if I hit, I would destroy you.

F: Now say this to your parents. Is this the Jewish mother? Did your mother nag? Is she a nag?

K: No.

F: Who is the nagger? The director, the pusher.

K: God. (resentfully) Your sins are all your fault, but your virtues are gifts of God, so don't—pride goeth before a fall, and all this s - - - you get all your life.

F: Can you tell God what you resent in him?

K: He's such a f - - - ing phony. (laughter)

F: Tell *him.*

K: (halting) You're—you're—(loud laughter) . . . If you *were,* you *are* a phony. Whatever—Goodness is, in me, it's phony. It's worse than phony, it's *malicious.*

F: Could you say, "*I* am malicious"?

K: I am malicious. I am malicious.

F: Say this to God, too. "You are malicious."

K: *You* are malicious . . . Except you aren't.

F: I know, now, what you are. You are a *canceller.* You put up the kingpins, and then you knock them down. You put up the kingpins again, and then you knock them down. "Yes—but." It is very important to understand the word *but. But* is a killer. You say "yes . . ." and then comes the big "but" that kills the whole yes. You don't give the yes a chance. Now if you replace *but* with *and,* then you give the yes, the positive side, a chance. More difficult to understand is the *but* when it's not verbal, and comes out in behavior. You might say "yes, yes, yes," and your attitude is *but*; your voice or your gestures cancel out what you say. "Yes—but." So there's no chance of growing or developing.

F. S. PERLS. *Gestalt Therapy Verbatim.* Lafayette, Calif.: Real People Press, 1969.

to other more traditional individual models of therapy and pathology.

Considered a separate school of therapy in its own right, the interpersonal model conceives of psychopathology as an interpersonal, rather than an intrapsychic, problem. (Alfred Adler, whose departure from Freud in this direction is discussed in Unit 29, may be regarded as fathering this development.) The maladaptive behavior, mislearning, and misperceptions of reality that constitute pathology and its symptoms are seen as developing out of disturbed relations and disturbed communications among people, and the method of treatment focuses on improving these relations and communications.

Sullivan's Interpersonal Therapy

Harry Stack Sullivan (1953, 1954) is generally regarded as the first interpersonal therapist in the current mode. Although he treated patients individually (on a one-to-one basis), his theory and therapy stressed his belief that emotional problems originate in and are maintained by disturbed relations.

Therapy, according to Sullivan, is an interpersonal experience in which the therapist acts as a "participant observer," helping the patient to see his distortions of events, of himself, and of others and to perceive and conceptualize these more accurately. The therapist is especially attentive to the way the patient's difficulties manifest themselves in the therapeutic relation. The therapist helps to bring the patient's **parataxic distortions** into awareness so that he can separate himself from the distortions of his past. (Parataxic distortion is similar to Freud's concept of transference.) The individual responds to present situations as if they were like those of the past. The development of such awareness, by this view, must take place within the context of a positive interpersonal relation.

Group Therapy

In **group therapy** the parataxic distortions noted by Sullivan are acted out with, and responded to by, other patients in the group, and the individual has an opportunity to learn new modes of interacting within the context of real and varied interpersonal relations.

At first glance group therapy may appear to be an economy measure because a single therapist works with several patients simultaneously. In an important sense, however, patients participating in group therapy become one another's therapists, exposing their problems and fears to one another, commenting upon changes in one another's behavior during the course of treatment, and developing transference to fellow patients as well as to the therapist. The therapist encourages this process, remaining psychologically and even physically in the background of the group and intervening primarily to make an occasional clarifying observation or interpretation. Aside from whatever benefits may accrue to the individual patient from a feeling of group belongingness, he is also afforded an ongoing opportunity for *reality testing* (against the reactions of his therapy group), particularly in the realm of interpersonal relations. When he has developed a way of coping with a problem in his therapy group (a microcosm of the outside social world), the probability that he can carry this change over to everyday life is increased.

A distinctive variant of group therapy attempts to use responses of group members to the unique pattern of the development of the *group* as a psychological entity in order to highlight their individual conflicts and help them develop new ways of relating to the situation (Bion, 1959). For example, the early stage of a group's development centers around concerns of trust and tends to highlight personal conflicts with dependence-submissiveness and counter-dependence-rebellion. Individuals who have difficulty with the group at this stage frequently have not learned how to relate to authority figures and have not developed a firm sense of independence. The aim of the group experience is to help such patients identify their conflicts in this area and work them through in the real interactions of the group.

The therapeutic effectiveness of group interaction for improving communication has been noted by psychologists in other related fields. The **encounter group**, or **T group** (the T stands for "training"), has been used increasingly to help normal people improve their own behavior. These groups have origins in the laboratory training methods that were developed as a way to help executives and other management personnel, as well as educators, to improve their leadership skills and organizational effectiveness (Bradford et al., 1964).

Family Therapy

Among the most radical advocates of **family therapy**, the approach is regarded not as simply another mode of treatment for changing individuals but as a theoretically distinct orientation toward the treatment of pathological interpersonal systems (Ferber et al., 1972). For family therapists, the interpersonal arena is not merely the source of individual pathology; it *is* the pathology itself. The goal, then, is not to treat the individual through the family but to treat and change the patterns of interaction and functioning of the family system itself.

In some families one person may be unconsciously designated to act out the family disturbance and thus is the one who comes to be labeled as "sick," delinquent, or difficult. This person is the **identified patient** and the acknowledged reason the family seeks therapy. Family therapists point out, however, that other members of the identified patient's family generally have an important personal stake in his pathology and symptoms. Just as the psychoanalyst chooses not to treat specific behavioral symptoms in isolation and looks instead for underlying causes, so the family therapist eschews treatment of the family's symptom (i.e., the identified patient) and looks rather for the underlying and more pervasive family pathology.

Family therapists have found that when treatment is directed at the identified patient but not at his family, any improvement that leads to an abandonment of the patient's symptoms is frequently undermined by the family or leads to the dissolution of the family system (e.g., divorce of the parents). Once the identified patient's pathology has become a part of the **family homeostasis** (the tendency for the family to go on in its usual way) and is an accepted, although painful, part of the family system, then any change in the pathological behavior of the identified patient, *even improvement*, disturbs the family equilibrium. (This point is stressed by Jackson, 1957, a pioneer in family therapy.) Such disturbance in family homeostasis is difficult for the system to endure, and the family therefore exerts pressure to bring things back to the way they were. And just as the family exerts pressure on the identified patient to maintain his pathology, the patient is quite adept at perpetuating his own sick role as a way of maintaining some control and influence for himself in the family system. In family therapy there is opportunity for family members to interact in more or less their usual ways and for the therapist then to point out the kinds of communications that are going on at the moment. The therapist also serves as a model of effective communication. The therapy situation enables everyone in the family to examine the interactions in the here and now, to learn the effects of current behavior patterns, and to try out new ones.

There are many different types of family therapists, and it is difficult to summarize their various approaches adequately. Box 25.6 (p. 636) presents an example of one type of family therapy. You will notice that this therapist is fairly active. In family therapy, the therapist cannot easily remain in the background because his intervention is more often required to stimulate change in the system and because family members often embroil him in the very conflicts that make them function poorly as a social unit. The main efforts of this form of psychotherapy in fact are directed toward increasing the adaptability of the family as a whole, not toward treating particular individuals. The therapist cannot, as in individual psychotherapy, learn to see the world through the eyes of the individual patient and conduct his treatment within that framework because the harsh or benevolent realities of other family members are constantly in the picture. When the misperceptions held by each of the others become clear to the therapist, his task is to help each of them to a more realistic view of the others' needs, lacks, and strengths and thus to a more viable family relationship.

Commentary on Interpersonal Therapy

Criticisms of interpersonal approaches are as varied as the methods themselves. Some critics of the approach argue that the therapist is generally too active and that the full (and necessary) transference is thus not allowed to develop. Others claim that focusing on the interpersonal system ignores the very real intrapsychic pathologies of individuals that must be dealt with by extensive examination of the unconscious factors underlying the patient's problems. These critics point out that, after all, not all children of families with disturbed communication patterns develop neuroses or psychoses, so that intraindividual factors must be operative and should be given attention in any therapy.

Behavior therapists note that the application of reinforcements in family therapy is unsystematic, but on the positive side they agree with its emphasis on the *learning* of pathological behavior. Furthermore, they tend to acknowledge the usefulness of attending to interpersonal variables that they believe influence the conditions for learning in the natural environment.

SOME ADJUNCT THERAPIES

Although partisans of each of the *adjunct* methods discussed here claim that it is sufficient treatment in itself—and such may indeed be the case for certain kinds of patients with certain kinds of problems—the usual function of these procedures is to make the patient more accessible to further conventional psychotherapy. One psychological adjunct method is **play therapy**, commonly used with young children but also with uncommunicative psychotic patients. Toys, dolls, clay, paints, and so on are used essentially as projective techniques. Pictures may be drawn and doll families set up. In short, channels are provided through play for conveying to the therapist information that, for whatever reason, cannot yet be directly or verbally communicated. In the course of this procedure, trust in the therapist is often developed, and further and different psychotherapeutic procedures become wise and feasible. **Psychodrama**, in which

BOX 25.6

WRINKLED BROW, GOOD GRADES, AND LOVE MESSAGES

TH (Therapist): (to husband) I notice your brow is wrinkled, Ralph. Does that mean you are angry at this moment?

H (Husband): I did not know that my brow was wrinkled.

TH: Sometimes a person looks or sounds in a way of which he is not aware. As far as you can tell, what were you thinking and feeling just now?

H: I was thinking over what she (his wife) said.

TH: What thing that she said were you thinking about?

H: When she said that when she was talking so loud, she wished I would tell her.

TH: What were you thinking about that?

H: I never thought about telling her. I thought she would get mad.

TH: Ah, then maybe that wrinkle meant you were puzzled because your wife was hoping you would do something and you did not know she had this hope. Do you suppose that by your wrinkled brow you were signalling that you were puzzled?

H: Yes, I guess so.

TH: As far as you know, have you ever been in that same spot before, that is, where you were puzzled by something Alice said or did?

H: Hell, yes, lots of times.

TH: Have you ever told Alice you were puzzled when you were?

W (Wife): He never says anything.

TH: (smiling, to Alice) Just a minute, Alice, let me hear what Ralph's idea is of what he does. Ralph, how do you think you have let Alice know when you are puzzled?

H: I think she knows.

TH: Well, let's see. Suppose you ask Alice if she knows.

H: This is silly.

TH: (smiling) I suppose it might seem so in this situation, because Alice is right here and certainly has heard what your question is. She knows what it is. I have the suspicion, though, that neither you nor Alice are very sure about what the other expects, and I think you have not developed ways to find out. Alice, let's go back to when I commented on Ralph's wrinkled brow. Did you happen to notice it, too?

W: (complaining) Yes, he always looks like that.

TH: What kind of message did you get from that wrinkled brow?

W: He don't want to be here. He don't care. He never talks. Just looks at television or he isn't home.

TH: I'm curious. Do you mean that when Ralph has a wrinkled brow that you take this as Ralph's way of saying, "I don't love you, Alice. I don't care about you, Alice."?

W: (exasperated and tearfully) I don't know.

TH: Well, maybe the two of you have not yet worked out crystal-clear ways of giving your love and value messages to each other. Everyone needs crystal-clear ways of giving their value messages. (to son) What do you know, Jim, about how you give your value messages to your parents?

S (Son): I don't know what you mean.

TH: Well, how do you let your mother, for instance, know that you like her, when you are feeling that way? Everyone feels different ways at different times. When you are feeling glad your mother is around, how do you let her know?

S: I do what she tells me to do. Work and stuff.

TH: I see, so when you do your work at home, you mean this for a message to your mother that you're glad she is around.

S: Not exactly.

TH: You mean you are giving a different message then. Well, Alice, did you take this message from Jim to be a love message? (to Jim) What do you do to give your father a message that you like him?

S: (after a pause) I can't think of nothin'.

---

patients enact roles in spontaneous and revealing playlets, is another such technique for facilitating communication, this time in a group setting.

The *physical therapies* (psychosurgery, shock therapy, and pharmacotherapy) hold a special position among the adjunct therapies. While many psychotherapists see them as important supplementary procedures, most physical therapists (pharmacotherapists, neurologists, and many psychiatrists) reverse the emphasis, using *psychotherapy as the adjunct* procedure

TH: Let me put it another way. What do you know crystal-clear that you could do that would bring a smile to your father's face?

S: I could get better grades in school.

TH: Let's check this out and see if you are perceiving clearly. Do you, Alice, get a love message from Jim when he works around the house?

W: I s'pose—he doesn't do very much.

TH: So from where you sit, Alice, you don't get many love messages from Jim. Tell me, Alice, does Jim have any other ways that he might not now be thinking about that he has that say to you that he is glad you are around?

W: (softly) The other day he told me I looked nice.

TH: What about you, Ralph, does Jim perceive correctly that if he got better grades you would smile?

H: I don't imagine I will be smiling for some time.

TH: I hear that you don't think he is getting good grades, but would you smile if he did?

H: Sure, hell, I would be glad.

TH: As you think about it, how do you suppose you would show it?

W: You never know if you ever please him.

TH: We have already discovered that you and Ralph have not yet developed crystal-clear ways of showing value feelings toward one another. Maybe you, Alice, are now observing this between Jim and Ralph. What do [you] think, Ralph? Do you suppose it would be hard for Jim to find out when he has pleased you?

In this slice of a family therapy session with one of the earliest practitioners and writers on the technique, there is very little spontaneous interaction among the family members. The therapist clearly guides the interchange and keeps it going. Often, however, two or more family members get into lively and heated discussion, and the therapist becomes spectator and moderator.

V. SATIR. *Conjoint Family Therapy: A Guide to Theory Technique.* Rev. ed. Palo Alto, Calif.: Science & Behavior Books, 1967.

fected brain tissue or a brain tumor is not considered psychosurgery even though it may result (as a side effect) in considerable behavioral changes in the patient. On the other hand, a **prefrontal lobotomy** (cutting the nerve fibers connecting the frontal lobes of the brain with the thalamus, see p. 66), when there is no physical evidence of pathology either in the frontal lobes or in the thalamus, does qualify as psychosurgery since its sole intent is to change the behavior of the patient. It is estimated that in the 1950s about 50,000 prefrontal lobotomies were performed on patients suffering from various mental disorders. While it is true that these lobotomies helped to reduce the population of mental hospitals, they also succeeded in producing a large number of semivegetables. The development of effective tranquilizing drugs finally put an end to these operations. But because some patients fail to respond to any of the available drugs, psychosurgery seems to be reviving. The new psychosurgery, however, avoids lobotomies; it focuses instead on the limbic system, the deeper area of the brain so intimately connected with emotional and motivational behavior and experience (see p. 548). In 1972 probably 500 such operations were carried out. While this is not a large number, these operations have triggered considerable criticism from scientists as well as nonscientists who see little difference between the new psychosurgery and the old prefrontal lobotomies. These critics view the new psychosurgery with alarm because of the social and political implications they detect in this effort to revive psychosurgery. For them, psychosurgery has the potential of a particularly vicious form of social control. (For an account of this controversy, see Box 25.7, p. 638.)

For a long time, severely disturbed, hospitalized patients have been given **shock therapy.** This therapy includes the administering of enough insulin or electric current to cause brief convulsive seizures and subsequent periods of lucidity. The purpose is to bring the patient for a short while into a state of mental clarity and greater contact with reality so that the therapist can communicate with him. This treatment, at best, was moderately successful and proved relatively effective in bringing severely depressed psychotics into better reality contact. Despite

while reserving to physical therapy the main therapeutic burden.

Psychosurgery refers to surgical procedures which destroy or remove apparently healthy tissue for the sole purpose of changing an individual's behavior. Thus, removal of in-

BOX 25.7

PSYCHOSURGERY: LEGITIMATE THERAPY OR LAUNDERED LOBOTOMY?

Under the above title, *Science*, early in 1973, examined a medical procedure which was rapidly becoming a troubling social and political issue. The gist of the article follows:

Since some surgeons perform brain surgery on people prone to violence, many critics think that this is only a step away from using psychosurgery —or the threat of it—as a tool for social control.

According to *Science* the controversy has focused on a trio of surgeons and neurologists originally associated with Harvard University. In 1967 these three suggested in a letter to the *Journal of the American Medical Association* that (to quote the *Science* article's abstract):

"while environmental and social factors undoubtedly played a role in the urban riots that were then raging through the country's metropolitan centers, another factor was being ignored: namely, the possible role played by brain disease—"focal lesions" that spur "senseless" assaults and destructive behavior. There is a need for research and clinical studies to "pinpoint, diagnose, and treat those people with low violence thresholds before they contribute to further tragedies."

Opposed—and sometimes vigorously so—to this suggestion are various individuals, *ad hoc* committees, and organizations. Thus, Peter Breggin, a Washington psychiatrist, flatly opposes any surgical intervention in the brain for the purpose of altering behavior. He argues that the operations blunt the emotions and thought processes of the person, and that there is no theoretical or empirical justification for any such operation. He further charges that psychosurgery is being used to repress and vegetabilize the helpless: the poor, the women, the blacks, the imprisoned, and the institutionalized. The magazine *Ebony* took up this theme in an article entitled "New Threat to Blacks: Brain Surgery to Control Behavior." A number of government scientists and mental health professionals from the National Institutes of Mental Health (NIMH) and the National Institute for Neurological Diseases and Strokes (NINDS) organized themselves into an emergency group called the NIMH-NINDS Ad Hoc Committee on Psychosurgery and have circulated petitions opposing government appropriation for the kind of experimental surgery called for by the Harvard group. The petition says in part, "Since psychosurgery can severely impair a person's intellectual and emotional capacities, the prospects for repression and social control are disturbing."

Perhaps most neurologists believe that some forms of psychosurgery are already helpful and justifiable, and additional beneficial forms will be discovered, but nevertheless they have heavy reservations about using brain operations to curb violence, especially as a form of maintaining "law and order."

Concludes the *Science* article:

Some people think the psychosurgery issue is getting more attention than it deserves. It is really at the extreme end of a massive spectrum of increasingly sophisticated ways people are learning to manipulate each other. But as such it may spur people to find ways of assessing how new behavioral technologies encroach on individual freedom and to decide on the extent to which they are desirable.

C. HOLDEN. Psychosurgery: Legitimate therapy or laundered lobotomy? *Science*, 1973, **179**, 1109–1112.

---

speculation, we do not know *how* shock therapy works, in the occasions when it does work.

Shock therapies are fast being supplanted by the use of recently developed drugs. The approach of **psychopharmacotherapy** or **chemotherapy**—treatment by the use of chemicals or drugs—has emerged and rapidly developed in recent years. Among the earliest of these drugs were **tranquilizers**. Tranquilizers include several different types of chemical compounds. We know something—but far from all—about the physiological mechanisms by which tranquilizers affect emotional states (see Unit 22), but they qualify as adjunct therapy chiefly because of their ability to reduce anxiety. Their function with psychotics, mainly with agitated schizophrenics, is essentially a calming one, so that, at the very least, custodial problems in mental hospitals have been greatly reduced and many patients, even long-term patients, can be returned to their homes. Unless the drug treatment is maintained in the home, however, relapse and return to the hospital are a likely result. Nor is the tranquilizing effect always demonstrated. Carefully conducted studies on chlorpromazine (a tranquilizer frequently used with schizophrenics) suggest that only a third of patients improve (Glick & Margolis, 1962).

The mental hospital caseload has thus been substantially eased, but in no sense can we conclude that in tranquilizers a cure for any mental illness has been found. An important salutary effect of tranquilizer treatment is that it may help to create the conditions—lessened anxiety, an end of violent behavior, somewhat greater contact with reality—in which effective psychotherapy can be initiated and carried on. Ironically, tranquilizers may interfere with psychotherapy by reducing to placidity a patient whose anxiety level was just right for treatment. Considering the enormous enthusiasm for these drugs among neurotic patients, this may be a common effect today.

Research continues on a broad front, however, to discover biochemical and chemical compounds that can treat various forms of mental disorder not as anxiety-relieving adjuncts but through *direct* intervention in the physiological basis of the disorder.

One area which has already profited from such research efforts is, as we have seen in Unit 22, our understanding of the affective disorders. Guided by the theory (plus a good dose of sheer serendipity) that pathological depressions and elations reflect difficulties in catacholamine metabolism in the brain, a number of drugs have been tested and proven useful in the treatment and management of these affective disorders. Among the most useful are four classes of compounds: (1) *the MAO inhibitors* (drugs which inhibit the enzyme monoamine oxidase, an enzyme which helps metabolize norepinephrine and serotonin in the brain, see Unit 18); (2) *the sympathomimetic drugs* such as amphetamine (a sympathomimetic drug is one whose effects *mimic* the action of the sympathetic nervous system—see Unit 22, p. 541—by releasing, for example, increased quantities of brain norepinephrine); and (3) a category of drugs (such as imipramine) which is neither an MAO inhibitor nor a sympathomimetic, but does potentiate (increase) the pharmacological effects of norepinephrine in the brain. All three of these *increase* the availability or effectiveness of the catacholamines in the brain and *energize the depressed patient*. On the other hand, lithium salts (a member of a fourth group) *decreases* the availability of norepinephrine in the brain and *calms the manic patient*. With these four kinds of drugs the physician has a most helpful list of pharmaceuticals for the treatment of the manic-depressive.

As research on the physiology of mental disease continues, new and better chemical compounds will be sought, and probably found. The time may soon come when the psychotherapist will do without the pharmacologist only at the risk of committing malpractice. But it is equally true that no research has indicated that the pharmacologist will ever be able to do without the psychotherapist in the treatment of mental disease. The question "Which is the primary and which is the adjunct therapy?" will soon not be a very fruitful, or even meaningful one.

GOALS AND EFFECTIVENESS OF PSYCHOTHERAPY

Tens of thousands of people annually initiate (usually voluntarily) some kind of psychotherapy, often at great personal expense, financial and otherwise. Society, through growing numbers of public agencies from the local community to the federal level, encourages and supports such treatment. Many of these people (but by no means all) conclude treatment with some sense of benefit. Presumably, then, many individuals achieve the goals they seek in psychotherapy.

As we have attempted to indicate in our delineation of different forms of therapy, to speak of the goals of psychotherapy is no narrower a task than to speak of the goals of all patients. Some patients seek to alleviate crippling emotional paralyses; others, to improve endurable but unsatisfying personal relationships; still others, to remove hindrances to occupational goals. Some wish to become more popular; some, to become more fulfilled; some, to become more successful; and some, only to become more human, to cope better with the realities of their lives and to gain a modicum of happiness from them.

Precisely because the goals of psychotherapy are so varied, it is difficult to assess its effectiveness. For example, has psychotherapy been effective for a particular individual when he reports that he is considerably happier despite no improvement in his social adjustment? There are many other factors complicating the question. Many mentally ill persons may show recovery without any psychotherapy.

Modern researchers now generally agree that the question "Is psychotherapy effective?", phrased in that way, is unanswerable. There is the difficult problem of finding comparable groups of treated and untreated among the mentally ill. The fact that some people do seek and get treatment and others do not probably in itself reflects some psychological differences between them. Indeed, some psychologists have suggested that the effectiveness of psychotherapy may be determined by whether the patient *chooses* to change (see Box 25.8).

And it is wrong to assume that those control group patients who do not receive therapy at the clinic from which they initially seek it will not go elsewhere, even to nonprofessionals, for help. Gurin, Veroff, and Feld (1960) found in a carefully designed national survey of mental health that of those who sought help for personal problems, most chose such nontechnically trained (for that function) mental health counselors as clergy and family doctors.

A willing ear and friendly response may be effective helping devices and may just possibly even account for whatever effectiveness can be claimed by psychotherapists. Psychotherapy may be nothing more than the "purchase of friendship" (Schofield, 1964). There are also studies that have reported considerable effectiveness in using nonprofessional helpers. Housewives, high school students, even drug addicts have joined training programs and have

BOX 25.8

HOW PEOPLE CHANGE

Despite the enormous variations in how therapists go about their business of helping people to change, the underlying assumption for all psychotherapies seems to run something like this: Once the right technique is hit upon (perhaps quite different ones for different people with different problems), then psychologically good things will begin to happen. In fact, the correct therapy is simply the one that works.

Probably this practical and functional criterion for what is correct cannot be improved upon. But in all this there is no role assigned to free choice. In other words, if patient X gets better, it is because—*and only because*—the right therapeutic buttons were pushed to clear up his particular psychological problem. But maybe, just maybe, in order for personality change to occur it is necessary that the person *choose* to change and that this act of free choice perhaps falls outside the framework of psychotherapeutic techniques. In short, is it possible that free will—that extrascientific construct—plays a gatekeeper role in permitting or preventing even perfect therapy from effecting any changes in the person?

A psychoanalyst, Allen Wheelis, who is also a novelist, playwright, and essayist, has some eloquent comments on this issue in a piece entitled *How People Change*. In this essay he considers at length the strangely ignored question of why—after years of insight or unlearning or whatever psychotherapy experience—some people evolve a radically different and more adaptive approach to life and others remain as they had been, with little or no change. His thoughtful consideration of this question challenges seriously the medical model of psychotherapy in which a mental disorder, like a case of measles, is diagnosed and treated by an expert. The patient remains a relatively passive bystander, observing but not determining the course of his treatment or participating in its ultimate success. It is Wheelis's position that the medical model is grossly incorrect, that insight does not automatically lead to personality change, and that the patient must consciously exercise his free will and *decide* to change. Here is some of what he has to say on these issues.

The book for the surgeon is not the book for the surgical patient. One delivers one's ailing body—with its abscess or tumor or broken bone—into the hands of the surgeon, and his most elementary information and skill will transcend anything the patient need know. The patient must cooperate—one green capsule three times a day, keep the leg elevated, force fluids—but need not understand how or why. The responsibility lies with the surgeon, the problem is his, his the accountability for failure, the credit for success. Patient and surgeon do not learn from the same text.

Many patients go to psychiatrists as if to surgeons, and many psychiatrists regard themselves as psychic surgeons. When such a patient comes to such a therapist a relationship of considerable length may result, but little else. For the job can be done, if at all, only by the patient. To assign this task to anyone else, however insightful or charismatic, is to disavow the source of change. In the process of personality change the role of the psychiatrist is catalytic. As a cause he is sometimes necessary, never sufficient. The responsibility of the patient does not end with free-associating, with being on time, with keeping at it, paying his bills, or any other element of cooperation. He is accountable only to himself and this accountability extends all the way to the change which is desired, the achieving of it or the giving up on it. . . .

The most common illusion of patients and, strangely, even of experienced therapists, is that insight produces change; and the most common disappointment of therapy is that it does not. Insight is instrumental to change, often an essential component of the process, but does not directly achieve it. The most comprehensive and penetrating interpretation—true, relevant, well expressed, perfectly timed—may lie inert in the patient's mind; for he may always, if he be so inclined, say, "Yes, but it doesn't help." If a therapist takes the position, as many do, that a correct interpretation is one that gets results, that the getting of results is an essential criterion for the correctness of an interpretation, then he will be driven to more and more remote reconstructions of childhood events, will move further and further from present reality, responding always to the patient's "Yes, but why?" with further reachings for more distant antecedents. The patient will be saying, in effect, "Yes, but what are you going to do about it?" and the therapist, instead of saying, as he should, "What are *you* going to do about it?" responds accordingly to his professional overestimate of the efficacy of insight by struggling toward some ever more basic formulation. Some patients don't want to change, and when a therapist takes up the task of changing such a one he assumes a contest which the patient always wins. The magic of insight, of unconscious psychodynamics, proves no magic at all; the most marvelous interpretation falls useless—like a gold spoon from the hand of a petulant child who doesn't want his spinach. . . .

The goal of treatment must be determined by the patient. The only appropriate goal for the therapist is to assist. If the therapist cannot in good faith help to the end desired he is free to decline, but he cannot reasonably work toward goals of his own choosing. . . .

Personality change follows change in behavior. Since we are what we do, if we want to change what we are we must begin by changing what we do, must undertake a new mode of action. Since the import of such action is change, it will run afoul of existing entrenched forces which will protest and resist. The new mode will be experienced as difficult, unpleasant, forced, unnatural, anxiety-provoking. It may be undertaken lightly but can be sustained only by a considerable effort of will. Change will occur only if such action is maintained over a long period of time. . . .

Since freedom depends upon awareness, psychotherapy may, by extending awareness, create freedom. When in therapy a life story of drift and constraint is reworked to expose *alternatives* for crucial courses of action, asking always "Why did you do that?," attaching doubt to every explanation which is cast in the form of necessary reaction to antecedent cause, always reminding the patient that "Even so . . . it was possible to have acted otherwise"—in all this one is rewriting the past, is taking the story of a life which was experienced as shaped by circumstance and which was recounted as such, and retelling it in terms of choice and responsibility. As a court may remind a defendant that ignorance of the law is no excuse, so a therapist may remind a patient that blindness to freedom does not justify constraint. And insofar as it may come to seem credible to rewrite one's life in terms of ignored choice, to assume responsibility retrospectively for what one has done and so has become, it will become possible likewise to see alternatives in the present, to become aware that one is free now in this moment to choose how to live, and that what one will become will follow upon what he now does.

We can only change what we do and what we are if we *decide* to change. Only then can the best of therapists be of any help. It is a notion worth considering, and it lies at the root of all forms of psychotherapy.

A. WHEELIS. *How People Change*. New York: Harper & Row, 1973.

gone on to work—and with some effectiveness—with emotionally troubled people.

Although the issues of control groups and the possible roles of nonprofessional helpers contribute to making good research on the outcomes of psychotherapy difficult, an even more difficult task is to do adequate research comparing the *relative* merits of several different types of psychotherapy. As we have seen, the different methods have different goals, may deal with different presenting problems, and gauge their success by different means. In the past, studies comparing different forms of therapy have operated under the questionable assumption that patients, methods, and therapists were essentially interchangeable and that goals and outcomes of different treatments were comparable (Kiesler, 1966). However, the exact method used by one therapist may not be identical with that of another who is presumably using the same method, and the samples of patients treated by the various therapies may be different. Another difficulty in comparing different therapeutic approaches is that the skilled therapist may shift approaches with a patient during the course of treatment, either because his initial tack worked poorly or because different tacks are more appropriate at different stages of treatment. Highly experienced therapists frequently employ this flexible strategy, probably to the benefit of the patient but certainly to the confusion of the professional therapy evaluator.

In evaluating properly the effectiveness of psychotherapy research, questions must be phrased in such a manner as to allow us to determine which types of treatment work with which types of patients administered by which types of therapists and under what conditions. And, as we have already indicated, perhaps we should pay more attention to whether the patient *chooses* to change (see Box 25.8, p. 640).

In this continuously developing and changing field, we can say with some assurance that preventive therapy is more likely to help than any amount of attempted cure. And the more we learn about the basic processes of personality development and the psychological and physiological determinants of behavior, the more effective we can become in our preventive therapy, psychological as well as physiological. It already seems clear that the therapist of tomorrow will combine many skills: He will be a *psychoneuropharmacotherapist*!

SUMMARY

1. The psychoanalytic therapies, exemplified by Freud's theory and method, focus on unconscious conflict as the source of disturbing symptomatology. The goal of this approach to therapy is to help the patient uncover these conflicts so that they may come under conscious and rational awareness and control. In this method, the technique of free association and the interpretation of the patient's resistance to recognizing unconscious influences are primary.

2. One important form of resistance is the patient's response to the therapist in terms of her past relationships with significant others. This is called transference and is also a focus of therapeutic interpretation. Continual repetition of the same issues constitutes the working-through aspect of psychoanalytic therapy.

3. Criticism of psychoanalytic psychotherapy focuses on its lengthy duration, high expense, and limited suitability for many individuals.

4. Behavior therapies, generally, are based on principles of learning and conditioning. They assume pathology to be merely the result of poor or mistaken early learning. The symptoms themselves *are* the problem to be dealt with, and there is no attempt to consider any unconscious or underlying causes of maladaptive behavior.

5. In the reciprocal inhibition therapy of Wolpe, systematic desensitization procedures are used to reduce anxiety, which is regarded as the cause of the patient's inappropriate avoidance behavior and of most symptoms. By presenting previously anxiety-provoking stimuli (usually through imagery) while the patient is in a state of deep relaxation, the anxiety response is inhibited or prevented from occurring. Eventually, it becomes dissociated from the stimulus, and appropriate responses become possible.

6. There are several other forms of behavior therapy; among them is Stampfl's implosive therapy, in which anxiety-producing stimuli are presented intensively until the anxiety response gradually extinguishes because it neither succeeds in helping the individual avoid the stimulus nor is followed by any actual unpleasant consequences.

7. Criticism of behavior therapy focuses on its ignoring possible underlying causes of pathology and its insistence on the mere treatment of symptoms. Behavior therapy generally has also been faulted on its claim to being scientific, when in fact a large gap exists between techniques used and the theory and experimental studies of learning upon which they are presumably based.

8. The phenomenological therapies, generally, focus on psychological health and self-actualization as well as on pathology. They view the underlying causes of psychological problems to be the individual's attempt to disown certain parts of himself because they appear to him to be socially or otherwise repugnant. The purpose of this form of therapy is to help the individual to reclaim these disowned parts of himself and thus become psychologically whole and fully functioning.

9. In Rogers' client-centered approach, the important elements are a nondirective stance and the therapist's unconditional positive regard, accurate empathy, and genuineness in his relation to the patient. The use of specific techniques is de-emphasized within this framework.

10. In Gestalt therapy, developed by Perls, the focus is on the here and now of the patient's thoughts and feelings rather than on his life history. A number of games, or techniques, are employed to help the patient reclaim and reintegrate those aspects of himself that he has tried to disown at the expense of his psychological health.

11. Criticism of the phenomenological models claims that these techniques are useful only with individuals who already have a relatively sound personality structure, that they fail to deal with the developmental origins of the pathology, and that the therapists choose to avoid the necessary responsibilities of their role as experts.

12. The interpersonal therapies regard the problems of individuals not in terms of intrapsychic or individual conflicts and pathology but rather in terms of problems in the interpersonal system within which the individual lives his life. Thus, in Sullivan's therapy, the patient-therapist relationship is the main focus.

13. In group therapy, the issue is the process and dynamics of the group in relation to each patient. In family therapy, the entire family system, rather than any one individual member, is viewed as the patient.

14. Criticism of interpersonal therapies focuses on the generally high directiveness and activity of the therapist, on the ignoring of very real intrapsychic disorganizations and pathology, and from a behavior therapy point of view, on the unsystematic application of reinforcement principles in this method.

15. Also sometimes used in the treatment of pathology, particularly in the cases of psychosis, are physical therapies (e.g., psychosurgery and pharmacotherapy).

16. The goals of therapy vary considerably with the general approach employed. Research aimed at the systematic evaluation of therapy, in any of its forms, is fraught with difficult methodological problems, so that reliable conclusions regarding its effectiveness are still being sought.

GLOSSARY

behavior therapy   A group of techniques of psychotherapy deriving from certain reinforcement theories of learning.

chemotherapy   When used in connection with mental disorders, this term refers to the general approach to the treatment of psychotic and neurotic diseases by the use of certain chemicals or drugs. (see also **psychopharmacotherapy**)

client-centered therapy   One of the main methods of psychotherapy, involving a nondirective approach by the therapist, who provides sympathetic reflection of the patient's expressed feelings rather than direct interpretation and evaluation of them. The patient is thus encouraged to arrive at his own insights concerning his problems and the proper course of remedial action. Associated with the name of Carl Rogers.

counterconditioning   In behavior therapy, a stimulus that has produced anxiety is presented in such a way that it becomes associated with (conditioned to) a new response such as relaxation.

encounter group   Modern term for T group. Now a more generalized group experience for people who want to learn more about themselves in relation to other people. A cross between group therapy and T groups.

family homeostasis   Term developed by Jackson to refer to the tendency of a family to keep things status quo (as they are) and to try to compensate for any changes that upset the family equilibrium.

family therapy   A technique of psychotherapy in which the therapist works simultaneously with all or several members of the family. The family is viewed as a psychological unit, and family neuroses are treated.

free association   The method employed in psychoanalysis in which the person is encouraged to report freely everything that comes into his mind.

Gestalt therapy   Developed by Perls; focus is on the here and now. The therapist does not make interpretations but, rather, has the patient play out all the different avoided and disowned parts of himself, all the objects and characters in dreams, all the "projected parts of the self" in order to arrive at his own insight and reintegrate parts of himself that he has been avoiding.

group therapy   A technique of psychotherapy in which groups of patients are treated simultaneously in group discussions in the presence of a therapist. Quite often the patients are one another's therapists, and the professional therapist remains in the background.

identified patient   Term used in family therapy to refer to the individual who is seen by the family as sick or causing problems and who is often the person initially brought in for therapy, although the overall family situation may be the true pathology.

implosive therapy   A behavior therapy treatment developed by Stampfl in which the patient is repeatedly exposed to massive amounts of anxiety-producing imagery. It is assumed that the anxiety response will eventually extinguish because it is not paired with any real physical harm.

nondirective therapy   (see **client-centered therapy**)

parataxic distortions   Term used by Sullivan to describe an individual's attitude toward another person based on fantasied or distorted evaluation of him or identification of that person with another from the past (similar to Freud's concept of transference).

play therapy   A technique of psychotherapy used with children in which the therapist works with the child as he plays with toys and other materials, permitting him to express emotions and conflicts freely and nonverbally.

prefrontal lobotomy   A form of psychosurgery involving the cutting of the nerve fibers that connect the frontal lobes of the brain with the thalamus.

psychoanalysis   A principal method of psychotherapy first developed by Freud. It involves long and intensive exploration of the person's conflicts, repressed memories, childhood experiences, and so on. The main technique is free association, and an essential part of the psychotherapy is the process of transference, in which the patient's emotional attitudes toward parents and other people become temporarily transferred to the psychoanalyst. Through this technique, self-understanding and emotional reeducation of the person are achieved.

psychoanalytically oriented therapy   A modification of psychoanalysis that maintains the same theoretical orientation but is typically less intensive and often shorter in duration. More focused interviewing techniques are also employed, and the therapist is usually more active.

psychodrama A technique of psychotherapy in which the patients, alone or in groups, play roles that represent their emotional problems and in so doing come to gain emotional release and insight.

psychopharmacotherapy The treatment of mental disease by pharmacological methods—drugs designed especially for that purpose. (see also **chemotherapy**)

psychosurgery Surgical procedures involving the destruction or removal of brain tissue for the sole purpose of changing the behavior of a person. Psychosurgery may be performed even when there is no physical evidence of pathology in the brain.

reciprocal inhibition Term borrowed from physiology. In Wolpe's behavior therapy it refers to a response (e.g., relaxation) that is antagonistic to, and therefore cannot occur simultaneously with, anxiety.

resistance A psychoanalytic concept that refers to the conscious or unconscious unwillingness to reveal information or uncover repressed material during therapy.

Rogerian therapy (see **client-centered therapy**)

shock therapy A psychotherapeutic aid involving the induction of a convulsive seizure in the psychotic patient through the administration of insulin or electric shock. One result is to induce a temporary period of lucidity during which the therapist can better communicate with the patient.

symptom substitution Situation in which a new symptom or inappropriate behavior appears after removal of original symptom has been accomplished because the original conflict has been left unresolved and therefore some symptom is still needed.

systematic desensitization A behavior therapy technique developed by Wolpe in which hierarchies of anxiety-producing imagery are presented when the patient is in a state of deep relaxation. Gradually, the imagery becomes disassociated from the anxiety response.

T group T stands for "training" type of group in which individuals examine their interactions with each other and their own group development to learn to function better interpersonally. Initially developed for training of business and education leaders. (see **encounter group**)

tranquilizers A class of drugs used to modify a mental patient's mood, usually to reduce anxiety. This effect makes the patient socially more manageable and can make him accessible to psychotherapy.

transference The process, especially important in psychoanalysis and psychoanalytically oriented therapy, through which the patient transfers his disturbed emotional attitudes toward parents and other important persons in his life to his perception of the psychotherapist. This transference provides an opportunity for these basic emotional attitudes to be reeducated with the aid of the therapist.

will therapy A technique developed by Rank, in which the basic struggle is seen to be between the need for dependence and the desire for autonomy. The patient is encouraged to assert his independence (will); the focus is on the present, not the past.

working through The process whereby insights and new learning are assimilated; also refers to a period of relative inactivity and repetition during treatment.

part eight

personality

personality: definition and description

DO YOU KNOW...

the origin of the term "personality"?

the enormous variety of workable definitions of personality and the distinctive value of each?

what we mean when we talk about what a person is "really" like?

that your personality is not only expressed in how you relate to other people but in how you think, walk, and write, even when you are alone?

how the expression of your personality is influenced by the immediate social situation?

what you are saying about the nature of personality when you remark of someone, "She's not the type . . . "?

what is meant by "pure" personality types and why they don't exist in nature?

what is meant by the observation that each personality-type theorist "slices nature in any way he chooses, and finds only his own cuttings worthy of admiration," and whether this indictment of personality-type theorists is fair?

unit 26

CONTENTS

Exactly what is meant by the word "personality"? Many things—perhaps too many—as you shall soon see. One of the earliest definitions of personality was most likely the source of the term; it regards personality as the *outward* aspect of the individual—how the person is perceived by and how he affects other people. (In the Roman theater an actor's mask was called a *persona*—the face he presented to the audience.) As we shall see later, an influential modern derivative of such a view holds that personality is in large part molded by others' reactions to an individual.

TOWARD A DEFINITION OF PERSONALITY

The study of personality has long been, and continues to be, one of psychology's most intriguing puzzles and most difficult challenges. All psychological knowledge should ultimately contribute to the understanding of personality —what shapes it, why it differs from individual to individual, how it develops and changes throughout the course of life. The fact that most areas of psychology have been only minimally integrated into the body of modern personality theory is sufficient proof that a comprehensive theory of personality has not yet been achieved. As a result, we may expect that complete agreement among psychologists on even a definition of personality has not yet been reached. In this expectation we shall not be disappointed. Allport, as long ago as 1937, could list fifty definitions, drawn from philosophy, theology, law, and sociology and psychology.

That the same diversity of definitions can be found in a review of more current literature is confirmed by Rappoport's (1972) survey of some modern definitions. The most striking difference is that a large proportion of definitions now emphasizes complexity or uniqueness of personality organization and very few dwell merely on an accumulation of traits. Some examples collected by Rappoport are:

. . . by personality is meant those relatively enduring traits and dispositions of the individual
that have, over time, jelled into a pattern that
distinguishes him from other individuals. (Sarnoff,
1962)

. . . Thus, we arrive at the conclusion that personality is a complex hypothetical construct. It is a
hypothetical construct because we develop it—
from behavioral observations, of course. It is complex because we assume that it is composed of
lesser units—traits, or needs, or id, ego, and
superego, and so on. (Baughman and Welsh,
1964)

. . . In this text, the personality of an individual will
be defined as the combination of all the relatively
enduring dimensions of individual differences on
which he can be measured. (Byrne, 1966)

These definitions give an overview of
current attitudes. As Rappoport points out, in
picking a definition, one can choose from a wide
range of alternative definitions, all theoretically
respectable; your personal philosophy can be
your guide. Rappoport himself favors an emphasis on the immediate and long-term effects
of early experiences from infancy through
adolescence.

Wiggins, Renner, Clore, and Rose (1971)
suggest that the observation of individual differences in personality is commonplace but
that the full range of such differences is rarely
appreciated. They offer samples of diverse definitions of personality, all of which further emphasize individual differences. The samples are
taken from widely differing perspectives:

Consider the fact . . . that every individual person
is endowed with a distinctive gastro-intestinal
tract . . . a distinctive nervous system, and a
morphologically distinctive brain. . . . Can it be
that this fact is inconsequential, in relation to the
problem of personality differences? (Roger Williams, a biologist who has written persuasively
in scientific and lay journals about the biological
individuality with which we are born)

The study of personality is the study of how people come to be what they are. Of course people
differ widely in what they have learned; each
person is indeed unique. But all have learned in
accordance with the same general laws. . . . The
essential point here is that there are no laws of
personality functioning apart from the laws of
general psychology. (Nevitt Sanford, a psychologist devoted to the study of individual personality
development)

The life-history of an individual is first and foremost an accommodation to the patterns and
standards traditionally handed down in his community. From the moment of his birth the customs
into which he is born shape his experience and
behavior. (Ruth Benedict, a pioneer anthropolo-
gist, known for her descriptions of personality
types that vary with cultures)

It is in individual differences . . . that we find the
logical key to personality. . . . An individual's personality, then, is his unique pattern of traits. (J. P.
Guilford, a psychologist-statistician, immersed in
the measurement and organization of personality
traits)

Far from being daunted by the range of
definitions of personality, these authors are
stimulated by the recognition that each meaning derived from differing viewpoints contributes to a better grasp of personality. In
fact, they assert ". . . personality is best considered from many, often conflicting, points of
view." The general idea is that any psychological phenomenon, whether in personality or
in another aspect of functioning, can be seen
or construed from a variety of vantage points.
Furthermore, these various constructions can
be evaluated by their usefulness in prediction,
control, and understanding of any phenomenon,
in this case of personality. In short, no single
definition can provide the whole truth of personality but each can illuminate certain aspects
of this truth. These authors conclude that using
a variety of definitions should expand and
deepen our understanding of personality. This
approach was named **constructive alternativism**
by George Kelly (1963) (see p. 656).

Wiggins et al. see four major points of
view: biological, experimental, social, and psychometric-trait. Their definitions of these are:

The Biological Viewpoint. This viewpoint construes the events of personality study in terms of
interactions among the early experience, genetic
endowment, and evolutionary background of the
organism. The reciprocal interaction of behavior

with its biological base is the primary focus of this viewpoint.

The Experimental Viewpoint. This viewpoint construes the events of personality study in terms of uniform learning, perceptual, and higher processes. To understand these processes is to understand how particular events influence future behavior through their contribution to the personality of the individual.

The Social Viewpoint. This viewpoint construes the events of personality study in terms of the social context in which the person lives and develops. A full understanding of this social context requires an understanding of the contributions of models, of cultural roles, and of cultures themselves.

The Psychometric-Trait Viewpoint. This viewpoint construes the events of personality study in terms of attributes which reflect underlying trait organizations. Personality-trait measurement is emphasized in the separate realms of behavior observation, self-report, and the indirect assessment of underlying traits.

While most psychologists probably agree upon a number of general attributes of an ideally broad definition, the working definitions that guide their own efforts may underplay or totally ignore one or more of these characteristics. We shall attempt not to present an ideal definition of personality but instead to provide a useful framework for discussion. Such a framework might be phrased as follows: *Personality is the integration of all of an individual's characteristics into a unique organization that determines, and is modified by, his attempts at adaptation to his continually changing environment.*

Comprehensiveness

Nothing that is Human is Alien to the Compleat Psychologist. Our generalized formulation of personality includes the individual's traits, abilities, beliefs, attitudes, values, motives, habitual modes of adjustment. It includes what we call "temperament"—typical emotional reactions, mood states, and energetic attributes of the person—as well as what in older terminology was called "character," that is, the moral out-

look and conduct of the person. But it must include much more. The general framework must permit us to study the many different kinds of factors that influence the development of personality. Genetic influences upon personality, as we shall see, are of substantial importance (see Units 1 and, especially, 28), even though their effects may be indirect, subtle, and difficult to detect. Differences in nutrition, disease, and even climatic conditions can affect bodily functioning and hence behavior and personality. These factors also play their part in forming personality. Different cultures, from the national down to the neighborhood level, exert their special influences. And, of course, the culture represented by the individual family is of primary importance, particularly if we are to account for personality variation *within* a given broader culture. Finally, there is the influence of specific critical events of various sorts—a crippling accident, a death in the family, a moment of supreme horror or extraordinary good fortune. Our conception of personality must be sufficiently broad to make a place for all of these factors.

Another dimension of complexity is added by the modifiability of personality. If we are sufficiently skillful and our theory sufficiently powerful, we can see in most persons a thread of consistency and predictability. Some personality characteristics are enduring; the mother who insists that her child was stubborn from his first day on earth may be speaking the truth. Other personality characteristics appear early only as potentials, finding expression gradually and taking their particular final forms from the interplay of endowment with environment. The infant born with a heightened reactivity to external stimuli may become the explosive adult, triggered into irritability with every new crisis. Or he may become unusually responsive to new situations, greeting them with an alert curiosity.

When development is indeed smooth and continuous, all well and good—at least so far as the task of the psychologist is concerned; we may then safely focus upon stable personality traits and gradually expressed potentials. But the discontinuities also fall within the province of personality study; as noted earlier, an irritable infant may develop into an irritable adult (continuity) or into an interested and curious one (discontinuity). We should be able to specify the circumstances in which one or the other outcome occurs. A given characteristic may quite reliably be predicted to develop, under a given set of circumstances, into a qualitatively different characteristic. In such an instance the "discontinuity" is only on the surface, since continuity in fact exists on the predictive and the theoretical, if not on the descriptive, levels. And yet a further challenge to a comprehensive theory of personality is posed by the unusual mood of the moment or the single errant behavior that just doesn't fit our conception of a person.

Then there is the question of levels of personality. We can describe personality on the level of overt behavior—the man is as he seems —or we can speak of underlying characteristics that, not being directly observable, must be inferred. A new neighbor exhibits special friendliness. Is she "really" warm and gregarious, or does the extremeness of her friendly behavior mean that underneath she is "really" anxious and socially ill at ease in this new neighborhood?

It is tempting to think of an underlying characteristic such as anxiety in the foregoing case as being more "real" than the observed behavior of friendliness. Obviously, both aspects may be equally real; our friend may be both anxious *and* friendly. Another person who is anxious may be not at all friendly; someone else who is friendly may be not at all anxious. In any particular case there may be a specific answer; in the general case—the study of personality—the only answer is that we must be able to treat all levels of behavior and to understand the intricate interactions among them— but more of this later.

Organization, Pattern, and Uniqueness

The ingredients of personality study, then, are individual differences in all manner of traits, genetic and environmental determinants, and behaviors on various levels. Their blending into a "whole" man is the final, essential task. But

whether the whole man exists in actuality has occasioned considerable research and discussion among psychologists. Although it is true that man often gives integrated responses to his total situation, it is equally true that he sometimes responds with only an isolated portion of himself. The man who continues to vote the straight ticket of his parents throughout a lifetime of elections, despite important changes in his social values and economic interests, may not be performing on the political scene as a whole individual. Although it is possible to investigate such "part-processes" in personality, many psychologists maintain stoutly that such an approach is doomed to failure and that the essence of personality is the patterning of characteristics within a unique, whole person.

The most eloquent spokesman for this position was Allport, who insisted that no number of general laws for the average man's response to this or that situation can ever lead to an adequate understanding of personality. His central theme was the uniqueness of the individual. His alternative to the general law was the use of idiographic methods, which preserve the distinct pattern or style of the individual. Numerous studies by Allport and others have shown this approach to be practicable, demonstrating, for example, that the style of an individual's behavior—something that cannot be described by a traditional enumeration of general characteristics—is maintained over a variety of forms of expression. Voice, posture, gait, handwriting, even artistic productions bear the stamp of uniqueness, as evinced by the ability of judges to match these characteristics correctly. In the pioneer work on this problem (Allport & Vernon, 1933), college students were able to match with above chance accuracy brief personality sketches of persons unknown to them with specimens of the handwriting of these individuals. (Professional graphologists, whose business it is to do just that, in fact proved to be more accurate judges than did students in this study.) Such demonstrations indeed support the claim that persons show identifiable, unique characteristics.

More recent studies have extended Allport's notion of style into the cognitive realm. The concept of *cognitive style* suggests that, just as an individual's voice, posture, gait, and handwriting bear the stamp of uniqueness, so do his methods of perceiving, judging, thinking, and remembering. In one study (Zweigenhaft, 1970) it was even found that the *size* of a person's signature tends to reflect his position in a university community, all the way from an undergraduate to a professor.

DESCRIPTION OF PERSONALITY

No matter how unique and how whole we regard personality, a scientific approach requires that we describe and analyze the uniqueness and wholeness of the individual. There are two main approaches to personality description—in terms of **traits** and in terms of types. If, when asked to describe someone, you enumerate several characteristics—"he's rebellious, intelligent, talkative, dedicated," and so on—you have defined a number of distinct traits that you feel exist in a marked degree for that person. Your implicit assumption is that each person may have a different set of such traits. If, however, you reply, "he's the intellectual type," or "he's the authoritarian type," then you have adopted a typological approach to personality description. Your assumption is that people can be categorized according to a common set of traits that characterize them. These two approaches are, of course, intimately related, but they merit separate discussion.

Traits

A trait is an enduring characteristic of the individual's behavior in a wide variety of situations. To ascribe the trait of punctuality to an individual's behavior implies that he tends regularly to arrive on time—at work, at parties, in meeting trains. A trait characterizes an individual's behavior to a lesser or greater degree. The man is presumably called punctual not because he is perfectly punctual in all possible circumstances but because he is highly punctual as compared with other people. When we talk about a personality trait, therefore, we are referring to a dimension along which people's

behavior varies in the amount of the trait exhibited, from those showing a great deal of the trait to those showing very little.

As we compare people and seek to specify what differentiates their personalities, we naturally focus attention on those behaviors in which differences among individuals are most marked. But to do so may lead to neglect of other traits on which people of a given group do not differ very much. The traits that most people in a group share may, however, often be as important for our understanding of their personalities as the traits in which they differ. For example, a native Dobu psychologist among his own Dobu people might never think of ascribing to them the trait of suspiciousness, for almost everyone in that culture is excessively suspicious. A visiting psychologist may at once pick out this trait as the most noteworthy component of Dobu personality, even though individual Dobuans do not differ much in the amount of suspicion they exhibit. The visiting psychologist notices the trait because he views it in a larger frame of reference, comparing it with the lesser degrees of suspicion found in other cultures.

One reason why we may be blind to certain basic traits of personality that play a vital role in the whole meaning of personality structure is that we tend to view man within the fairly narrow milieu of our own society or culture. In principle, a full-fledged personality description should include all the identifiable traits that exist in an individual.

Levels of traits Traits are of many different kinds or classes. Some pertain to temperamental characteristics; some to typical ways of adjusting; some to abilities, interests, values; some to social relations. But the fundamental distinction is one of levels—a point touched upon earlier in this unit. Some traits are easily observable, and therefore easily measured, because they refer to surface characteristics of individuals. If an acquaintance smiles frequently, laughs easily, and generally has a rosy view of things, we say he is cheerful. Each of us would use many of the same cues in making this judgment, and the cues would have much the same meaning for all of us. Therefore, the trait cheerfulness would be assessed with high agreement among observers, and probably with high validity. Other traits are defined as deep-seated, underlying surface traits. Our friend may thus "seem" cheerful, but "underneath" he may "really" be depressed.

This sudden shower of quotation marks denotes, as usual, an area of current controversy in personality description and measurement. It is meaningful to say that someone "seems" cheerful but is "really" depressed only if our theory is such as to conceive that personality has at its core characteristics that are not themselves directly observable. Such a central system of characteristics must therefore be inferred, and the rules of inference are usually complex; furthermore, these rules are never uniform because they are tied to particular theories of personality. For example, our friend is said to be "really" depressed because our theory leads us to infer that when a man is too cheerful, considering the actual mess he has made of his life, his cheerfulness must betray an unconscious satisfaction that he is failing, because his failure relieves unconscious guilt over some transgression that is no longer remembered. If our theory is different from this one, then we would infer a different real underlying trait for our consistently smiling friend, or we might even simply ascribe to him the trait of cheerfulness that he indeed manifests.

However, no matter the trait level being attended to, the array of possible descriptive attributes of behavior is so vast that some method for reducing these attributes to manageable proportions must be used. One such method is factor analysis (see Unit 9, p. 197).

Factor-analytic description of traits Through an assiduous search of the English language Allport and Odbert (1936) compiled a list of 17,953 adjectives used to describe distinctive and personal forms of people's behavior. About 4,500 of these terms clearly designate consistent and stable characteristics of an individual's adjustment to his environment; each of these words, in a sense, represents a potential trait to be measured and analyzed. Cattell (1946) undertook to reduce this list to manageable proportions, employing as his primary tool the statistical method of factor analysis. He first pruned the list down to 171 terms by eliminating synonyms, rare words, and the like. The 171 trait names were further reduced to thirty-five main "trait clusters" through combination of all the traits that correlated fairly highly with one another. These trait clusters are Cattell's **surface traits**, characteristics that are easily defined and readily observable. The thirty-five trait clusters were used as the basis for constructing thirty-five rating scales. About 200 men (soldiers, professionals and businessmen, artists, skilled workers, and so on), divided into a number of small groups of intimate acquaintances, served as subjects. Two members from each group first were trained in the rating technique and then rated their fellows independently. The two ratings were averaged to obtain the final rating for each man.

The ratings were then subjected to factor analysis. It was found that twelve factors were adequate to account for most of the individual differences among the men in the rated traits (see Table 26.1). Cattell has continued to

TABLE 26.1 SOME EXAMPLES OF CATTELL'S SOURCE TRAITS*

Reserved-Outgoing	Trusting-Suspicious
Emotional-Stable	Practical-Imaginative
Humble-Assertive	Forthright-Shrewd
Sober-Happy-go-lucky	Placid-Apprehensive
Expedient-Conscientious	Conservative-Experimenting
Shy-Venturesome	Relaxed-Tense

* Popular rather than technical names are used to identify the traits.

After Cattell (1946).

refine and extend this list of traits in a number of directions. A later count has expanded the twelve factors to twenty.

These factors are presumably **source traits**, which through complex dynamics come to determine the more familiar surface traits. The precise names given by Cattell to these factors are merely convenient identifying labels. Their actual nature must be, and are, discovered by further study.

Considerable research has dealt with the generality of these source traits. Do they appear in children as well as in adults? Can they be found in different behavior domains, for example, with data obtained by self-report questionnaires, as well as with behavior ratings? Other work has moved beyond the original descriptive task and is concerned with the extent to which each source trait is genetically determined.

Such factor-analysis methods in personality research are of great important in simplifying the study of traits. But these methods are only tools, not solutions to the problems of understanding personality organization. The primary trait factors that result from a factor analysis depend greatly upon the traits originally included in the test battery. A factor analysis of test results cannot, of course, come up with trait factors that summarize personality characteristics not included in the original pool of traits. And, of course, selection of the original traits to be tested inevitably reflects the beliefs of the investigator concerning the basic nature of personality and how best to describe it.

Situational influences on trait behavior Evidence for the importance of variations in trait behavior with variations in the social situation has been reviewed by Marlowe and Gergen (1969). In brief, it is clear that individuals are simply not consistently themselves in all situations. Rather, we all tend to wear different masks for different occasions; there are many "selves" for each person. Gergen (1972) writes:

> I came to this belief after writing letters to close friends one evening. When I read over what I had written, I was first surprised and then alarmed. I came across as a completely different person in each letter: in one, I was morose, pouring out a philosophy of existential sorrow; in another, I was a lusty realist; in a third I was a lighthearted jokester; and so on.

While most of us might not be capable of as many changes in one evening (or even not be capable of writing that many letters!) as Gergen seemingly is, nevertheless we all have experienced the awareness of presenting ourselves differently to different people. Gergen

and Wishnow (1965) found that subjects changed their self-presentations depending on what they knew of the people with whom they were to interact. Subjects who anticipated interaction with a self-centered other person became more positive in their own self-ratings; subjects who expected to interact with others who were self-derogating tended to emphasize their own negative self-characteristics.

Do these shifts in self-description or self-presentation imply that there is no real self? A number of theorists attempt to cope with the fact that there is generally some stability across most situations as well as an obvious ability to present differing aspects of self in such situations. One general approach suggests that people have a concept of themselves that can range from the extremely narrow to the quite variable, or flexible, and it is this range that must be understood in undertaking to predict how a person will behave in any given situation. We all have acquaintances who are always themselves, no matter what the social setting, and others who, chameleonlike, quickly adapt their personality coloration to fit their immediate interpersonal surroundings.

Of course, neither of these extremes is ideal. To be inflexibly harsh, or kind, or anything else, regardless of where one is or with whom, is simply not appropriate. Kelly (1955, 1963), whose ideology of constructive alternativism we discussed earlier (see p. 651), takes the position that a certain degree of flexibility is essential for effective psychological functioning. Cast into a therapy setting, this view recommends that the therapist help his client to become aware of and to use his various constructions of self. He suggests a variety of specific techniques, including role-playing, to achieve this result.

More generally, Kelly argues that, in order better to understand a person (and, in a therapy context, in order to help him more effectively), it is critical to view him in terms of his own constructs, those *he* uses in describing himself—and not in terms of general constructs from psychologists' theories of the nature of personality. Thus, if a woman reports feeling that she is a selfish person, we had better ask *her* for specific behavioral examples of what *her* construct of a "selfish person" is, rather than assign her to the high end of a psychologist's scale for *his* construct of selfishness. She may provide as evidence of her "selfishness" that she sometimes prefers to read at night rather than to talk with her family. The psychologist, once learning this, may then construe such behavior as unrelated to *his* view of "selfishness"; rather, he may regard it as indicating (depending on other evidence as well) intellectual interests, a need for privacy, etc. Kelly's point is that the woman's and the psychologist's constructions are *both* correct, and both must be detected and used if we are to understand the woman.

To summarize, as we learn more about personality the lines which distinguish one conceptual scheme from another become blurred. Few psychologists take an either-or position (e.g., that there are, or are not, enduring traits). Instead, they generally recognize interactions among personality and situational forces that contribute to stability on one hand and to flexibility on the other. Today psychologists tend to insist on the existence of, say, aggression as a very real and thus measurable aspect of a given person. But they may insist with equal vigor that certain elements must exist in the situation before aggression, whatever its level, can show itself. A medical analogy comes to mind. A person may be highly allergic to ragweed but if he lives in an environment devoid of ragweed, he will not show his allergy. If, however, he moves to a neighborhood that does have ragweed about, he will be a sneezy fellow indeed. The allergist can determine whether or not the patient has a sensitivity to ragweed. But a situational appraisal is also necessary if he is to predict whether or not—or to what extent—the sneeziness (like the aggression) will show itself.

Clearly, the already complex problem of describing personality becomes even more difficult—but appropriately so—because of the need to recognize that people behave differently in different situations and that they may interpret their own behavior in ways that differ from the interpretations of others (including psychologists).

PERSONALITY TYPES

Confronted with a bewildering complexity and diversity of traits ascribed to man, philosophers, educators, and psychologists from the beginning of recorded history have worked on the problem of personality description by using the notion of **personality types**. The universal popularity of type theory may be regarded as yet another testimonial to man's need and ability to impose order upon a chaotic stimulus situation. A type provides a shorthand for talking about a set of separate traits by assuming that generally recognizable patterns of personality characteristics do in fact exist.

Many and varied typologies (systems of individual types intended to embrace the full range of personality) have been proposed. Some typologies stress the role of a single dominant trait that organizes all other characteristics around it; some have no such central theme but focus on particular combinations of traits. Some arise from theoretical conceptions of personality; others are empirical, arising from intensive observation of representative samples of individuals from particular cultures. Biological bases underlie some typologies; others focus upon the influence of early experience.

Despite these differing emphases, typologies share certain features. First, they intend to provide a framework within which every individual, no matter how idiosyncratic, may find a place. If a person is not a pure example of any of the types within the typology, then he may be described by the degree to which he resembles one or more of these types. Second, types always consist of a distinctive pattern of separate personality traits, even when the type relies upon a single dominant trait for its organizing principle. For example, the authoritarian personality type has at its core an exaggerated respect for, and obedience to, authority. Box 26.1, p. 658, illustrates how this single trait extends into many facets of personality and defines a pattern of many characteristics. Third, typologies must possess a certain hardiness, an ability to survive despite dramatic changes in individual life situations or radical differences in cultural context (see Box 26.2, p. 659). For example, the typology that

BOX 26.1

THE AUTHORITARIAN PERSONALITY

Authoritarianism has always been one of the most basic problems of human society. It appears in its most spectacular form in political dictatorships, but it can be found in less dramatic and often more insidious forms in almost every type of interpersonal relationship and social organization. One of its aspects that has especially interested psychologists is the role of personality in authoritarian behavior.

For instance, an extensive study at the University of California in the 1940s by T. W. Adorno, E. Frenkel-Brunswik, D. J. Levinson, and R. N. Sanford provides evidence that a syndrome of authoritarian traits can be identified as a central and enduring part of some people's personalities. The main traits of the syndrome appear to be the following:

1. Great concern with authority relationships with people; extreme deference to superior authority and exercise of one's authority over those in subordinate positions;
2. Heavy stress on conventional behavior, values, and morality; close conformity to group norms;
3. Overcontrol and denial of one's own "immoral" impulses and feelings and projection of them onto the outgroup; exaggerated sense of one's own moral "rightness"; lack of self-insight;
4. Depersonalization of social relations; tendency to manipulate and exploit people as objects rather than to treat them as human beings and expectation of being exploited in turn; sadistic tendencies (enjoyment in hurting other people) together with masochistic tendencies (enjoyment in being hurt);

5. Rigidity of thought processes; excessive stereotyped thinking; prejudice and intolerance toward minority groups.

The data suggest that the development of this syndrome comes from severe disciplinary treatment of the child, typically involving excessive stress on the rightness of parental rules and values, with insistence on complete obedience to them reinforced by punishment. Often such severe discipline is accompanied by a parental attitude of emotional rejection of the child and by exploitative manipulation of the child.

The consequences are that the child develops extreme submissiveness to parental authority, which later extends to all authority figures. This submissiveness is accompanied by an unquestioning acceptance of the rightness of the values of the authorities. But there is also a strong hostility toward the parents or other authorities. This hostility cannot be readily expressed in direct aggression against the authority figure; for one thing, there is fear of punishment by the all-powerful authority and, for another, such aggression would be incompatible with belief in the complete rightness of the authority. The hostility is thus repressed (see p. 578) and the aggression displaced toward safer targets like minority groups, those in positions of inferior status, and sometimes the self.

Evidence for this general picture has been found by other investigators—through studies of many groups of subjects, using many kinds of techniques like psychiatric interviews, attitude questionnaires, laboratory tests, sociological surveys. However, certain methodological difficulties have been pointed out—most persuasively by H. H. Hyman and P. B. Sheatsley. For one thing, the study failed to control for the factor of formal education, and, at least at that time, other data permitted one to wonder whether some of the attitudes associated with authoritarianism might not more simply reflect the differences among their subjects in years of educa-

includes introvert and extravert types, which we shall soon discuss, assumes their universal occurrence and assumes that introverts will remain introverts come rain or shine. Although this restriction is not a necessary one, typolo-

gies characteristically attempt to describe universal and enduring behavior patterns, just as traits and trait factors generally intend to refer to universal and enduring dimensions of personality.

tion. Despite these and many other criticisms the construct of an authoritarian personality has survived and continues to draw research attention.

Some of this newer research focuses upon authoritarianism as a transient reaction to a psychologically stressful situation rather than as a pervasive and enduring personality characteristic. An example is a recent study by psychologists S. M. Sales and K. E. Friend of Carnegie-Mellon University. In part they found that 72 percent of a group of students who were told that they had just done very well on a supposedly valid test of their intelligence (it wasn't and they really hadn't) showed a *decrease* in their scores on a questionnaire measure of authoritarianism administered immediately after hearing the good news (in comparison with their scores before taking the tests). In contrast, another group of students was led to believe that they had done very poorly on these same tests; 61 percent showed a relative *increase* in authoritarianism. What is more, subjects in both groups who accepted responsibility for their ostensible performance on these tests (rather than, e.g., claiming that the test instructions were unclear) showed much stronger effects of apparent success or failure on their authoritarianism scores.

It should be emphasized that the authoritarian syndrome is not the exclusive characteristic of any single ideological movement, social class, or occupation. Authoritarian personalities can be found everywhere—in the labor union as well as in industrial management, in social clubs as well as in governmental bureaucracies. And they are by no means unknown even in the church and in the classroom.

T. W. ADORNO, E. FRENKEL-BRUNSWIK, D. J. LEVINSON, & R. N. SANFORD. *The Authoritarian Personality.* New York: Harper & Row, 1950.
H. H. HYMAN & P. B. SHEATSLEY. The "authoritarian personality"—A methodological critique. In R. Christie & M. Jahoda (Eds.), *Studies in the Scope and Method of "The Authoritarian Personality."* New York: Free Press, 1954.
S. M. SALES & K. E. FRIEND. Success and failure as determinants of level of authoritarianism. *Behavioral Science,* 1973, **18,** 163–172.

SOME "CLASSICAL" TYPOLOGIES

Historical accounts of type theories begin with Hippocrates (*ca.* 400 B.C.), who postulated that there are four types of temperament, associated with four main kinds of fluids, or "humors," of the body (see Figure 26.1, p. 660):

Body Humor	*Temperament*
Blood (Latin: *sanguis*)	Sanguine: optimistic, hopeful
Black bile (Greek: *me- lan coln*)	Melancholic: sad, depressed
Bile (Greek: *coln*)	Choleric: irascible
Phlegm (Greek: *flegma*)	Phlegmatic: apathetic

BOX 26.2

THE SELF-CONCEITED MAN

What is your immediate picture of "The Self-Conceited Man"? Perhaps you can jot down a list of specific characteristic behaviors and compare your impressions of this personality type with excerpts from the sketch written under the same title by John Earle, an Englishman, in 1628.

A self-conceited man is one that knows himself so well that he does not know himself. . . . He is now become his own book, which he pores on continually, yet like a truant reader skips over the harsh places, and surveys only that which is pleasant. In the speculation of his own good parts, his eyes, like a drunkard's, see all double, and his fancy, like an old man's spectacles, makes a great letter in a small print. He imagines every place where he comes his theatre, and not a look stirring but his spectator; and conceives men's thoughts to be very idle, that is, only busy about him. . . . If he has done anything that has passed with applause, he is always reacting it alone, and conceits the ecstacy his hearers were in at every period. His discourse is all positions and definitive decrees with *thus it must be* and *thus it is,* and he will not humble his authority to prove it. . . . A flatterer is a dunce to him, for he can tell him nothing but what he knows before: and yet he loves him too, because he is like himself. . . . In sum he is a bladder blown up with wind, which the least flaw crushes to nothing.

This personality type is recognizable even now—a tribute to the durability of human character types. "The Self-Conceited Man" has withstood the cultural upheavals of the last three centuries of man's history, and it is difficult to envisage a future society that would find him alien and incomprehensible.

R. ALDINGTON. *A Book of Characters.* New York: Dutton, 1924.

FIGURE 26.1 The four temperaments: A—Sanguine, B—Phlegmatic, C—Melancholy, and D—Choleric (from a fifteenth-century Zurich manuscript).

Photos from The Bettmann Archive

Needless to say, the specific humors postulated by Hippocrates are not consistent with our modern knowledge of physiology, but his temperamental types still flourish in our thinking, and our modern personality vocabulary perpetuates the ancient words used for the humors of the ancient physiology. His theory was the classical forerunner of modern theories correlating temperament with glandular secretions (see Unit 22). And it was the beginning of a long line of type theories in which personality make-up was conceived to be intimately related to body constitution and physique.

Asthenic Versus Pyknic

One of the earliest of modern theories relating physique and personality was that of Kretschmer (1936). He presented evidence that there is a characteristic body type for each of the two main kinds of mental illness—schizophrenia and manic-depressive psychosis. The schizophrenic is said to have a thin, long-limbed, narrow-chested body, which Kretschmer called the **asthenic type**; the manic-depressive is said to have a short, fattish, barrel-chested body, called the **pyknic type**. Kretschmer generalized this typology to the normal population, asserting that there are distinctly different patterns of personality traits biologically linked with these two body types. The asthenic-type person was said to be shy, sensitive, aloof, and withdrawn. The pyknic type was said to be jovial, lively, outgoing, and inclined to mood fluctuations.

This typology, though grossly overstated, had its kernel of truth and has served as an effective springboard for ongoing attempts to establish physique-personality relations. Its most articulate descendant is the one proposed by Sheldon, which we shall examine in our discussion of constitutional determinants of personality (see Box 28.2, p. 696).

Introvert Versus Extravert

Probably the most widely known typology is that of introversion-extraversion advanced by Jung (1923). This typology was just one small

aspect of an elaborate theory of personality, a theory we discuss further in Unit 29. The introvert is described as subjective in orientation—as primarily interested in ideas, imagination, and inner life—as tender-minded and idealistic. The extravert is described as having an orientation directed outward to the objective world of things and events—as primarily interested in social activities and practical affairs—as tough-minded and realistic.

The simple introvert-extravert dichotomy has become solidly entrenched in our popular thinking; but, at least in its overly simplified form, the evidence does not support such a dichotomy. Attempts to measure people along the introversion-extraversion dimension have invariably shown that, rather than falling into two distinct types, people are distributed all along the dimension with most around the center (see Figure 26.2 for an example of this in two quite different groups). The failure to find pure types, however, should not be taken—as it too often is—as an indictment of the typological approach. Few type theorists, and certainly no modern ones, make such an as-

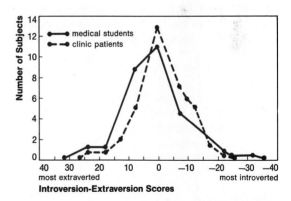

FIGURE 26.2 Distribution of scores of senior medical students and patients on the Neymann-Kohlstedt Introversion-Extraversion Test. Despite the differences in age, educational level, and so on between the groups, there is no difference in score distributions. Most scores are not concentrated at the two extremes, as would be implied by a simple type theory that would categorize people as either extraverted or introverted.

C. A. Neymann & G. K. Yacorzynski. Studies of introversion-extraversion and conflict motives in the psychoses. *Journal of General Psychology*, 1942, **27**, 241–255; adapted by permission of The Journal Press.

sumption. And neither did Jung, as this 1923 quotation indicates:

> [E]very individual possess[es] both the mechanism of introversion and that of extraversion, and it is only the relative strength of the one as compared with the other which creates the type. . . . It follows that there can never be a pure type in the sense that the one mechanism is completely dominant to the exclusion of the other.

Actually, Jung's conception was far more complex than has been represented here. That the introversion-extraversion variable is not a simple affair was confirmed some time ago by factor-analytic studies that identified as many as five separate introversion-extraversion factors: social introversion, thinking introversion, depression, tendency to mood swings, and happy-go-lucky disposition (Guilford, 1940). On the other hand, Eysenck (1970), also working with factor-analytic data, has developed an extensive model of personality structure based on a unitary introversion-extraversion factor, together with an additional factor, stable-unstable (essentially reflecting degree of personal adjustment). These two factors can be seen as defining a two-dimensional personality space, and individuals can be located in this space by their scores on measures of each factor. When this is done, Eysenck finds, for example, that an unstable-introverted individual could be painfully shy, whereas an unstable-extraverted person might tend to be destructive and quarrelsome. Eysenck continues to work intensively on fleshing out his theoretical schema; he can correctly be regarded as a modern heir to Jung's classical typology.

Eidetic Types

Quite a different early typology was proposed by Jaensch (1930) on the basis of study of eidetic imagery (see Box 6.4, p. 131). He concluded that people fall into several distinctly different types, on the basis of the forms of eidetic imagery they experience. These differences in experience were related, he thought, to basic differences in styles of perceptual and cognitive functioning and thus to differences in overall personality patterns. Jaensch's theory, though not confirmed by experimental evidence, played a part in the initiation of modern research that seeks to find relationships between personality variables and habitual modes of perceiving. Our earlier discussion of cognitive styles (see p. 653) is in this broad tradition.

Value Types

Numerous typologies have been built around the notion that people can be classified into distinct value types. Here the conception is that each person has some sort of unifying philosophy of life—a dominant value—that shapes and structures his entire personality. One such early theory was that of Spranger (1928), who sought to classify all people into six ideal value types:

1. *The Theoretical.* Dominant interest in discovery of truth; seeks to observe and to reason; chief aim in life is to order and systematize his knowledge.
2. *The Economic.* Dominant interest in what is useful; concerned with the production of wealth; believes in practice rather than theory, utility rather than aesthetics.
3. *The Aesthetic.* Dominant interest in form and harmony; believes beauty is the greatest truth and judges each experience on its aesthetic merits.
4. *The Social.* Dominant interest in love of people; concerned with other people's affairs and with their welfare; a warm and humane outlook.
5. *The Political.* Dominant interest in power; whether in politics or in other activities, the aim is to gain influence and control over people and events, to become a leader.
6. *The Religious.* Dominant interest in comprehending the unity of the universe; concern with mystical experiences and with what is divine in every phenomenon.

Once again, very few people completely fit these ideal value types. Most people have a mixture of these values, with some primary and some secondary. This fact is demonstrated in the results of personality tests that were designed to measure people on these six value dimensions (see Box 26.3).

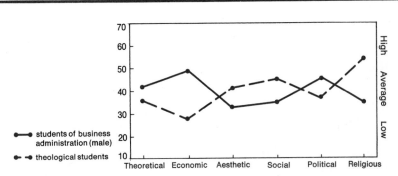

students of business
administration (male)

theological students

BOX 26.3

MEASURING PERSONAL VALUES

The notion of six ideal value types proposed by E. Spranger later led to the development of an inventory designed to measure the relative importance of each of these six values to the individual. This inventory, called the Study of Values, was constructed by G. W. Allport and P. E. Vernon at Harvard University and later revised with the help of G. Lindzey. It consists of forty-five items pertaining to the subject's attitudes and preferences. The items were selected on the basis of their apparent relevance to one or more of the six value areas—theoretical, economic, aesthetic, social, political, religious.

An example of one type of item is the following statement, to which the person is to answer yes or no.

Are our modern industrial and scientific developments signs of a greater degree of civilization than those attained by any previous society, the Greeks, for example?

A yes answer gives a point toward the economic value, a no answer a point toward the aesthetic value.

Another type of item is a multiple-choice question like the following:

If you could influence the educational policies of the public schools of some city, would you undertake—
a. to promote the study and participation in music and fine arts;
b. to stimulate the study of social problems;
c. to provide additional laboratory facilities;
d. to increase the practical value of courses.

Can you figure out which of the six values each of the four possible answers is meant to reveal?

Total scores are computed for the subject on each of the six values, and a profile is plotted with the midpoint of each scale at 40. This profile provides a quick picture of the pattern of his values.

The graph shows two "averaged" profiles for a group of male students of business administration and a group of theological students. Note the differences.

G. W. ALLPORT, P. E. VERNON, & G. LINDZEY. *A Study of Values: A Scale for Measuring the Dominant Interests in Personality.* rev. ed. Boston: Houghton Mifflin, 1951. Figure adapted by permission.

EMPIRICAL TYPOLOGIES

Standing in contrast with theoretical typologies are those based upon the personality groupings that are actually found to exist in a particular sample of individuals. The essence of such empirical typologies is their intent to reflect "what goes with what," free from the theoretical predilections of the investigator. Box 26.4, page 664, illustrates how a typology of nine types can be derived from a purely empirical examination of the personality traits in a sample of 100 children. The gulf between the theoretical and the empirical typology, however, is

BOX 26.4

AN EMPIRICAL TYPOLOGY

A research study by Norman Livson at the Institute of Human Development at the University of California, Berkeley, attempted to establish a typology to describe the kinds of personality organizations to be found in children during their developmental years. The raw data for this study were the complete case records of more than fifty children of each sex whose physical, intellectual, and personality development was studied from birth through adolescence in an ongoing longitudinal investigation directed by Jean Macfarlane of the Institute. It proved possible for judges to summarize the salient characteristics of each child's personality by means of a Q-sort, a technique that requires the judge to rank-order a large number of descriptive items as they apply to a particular individual. Employing the 100 items of Block's California Q-set, each child was described in terms of which items were extremely characteristic of him, which somewhat less so, and so on.

The resultant Q-sorts for each child were correlated with the Q-sorts of all other children of the same sex; the correlation coefficient between any two children measured their similarity in personality profile and therefore indicated the degree of personality resemblance between them. The higher the cor-

relation, the more similar the personalities of the two children; the lower the correlation, the less similar. These correlations were subjected to a cluster analysis (a statistical method similar to factor analysis) in order to discover groups of children who resembled one another highly. These groups, within which all children have high correlations with one another, constitute empirical types.

The cluster analysis detected five types among the boys, four among the girls. Although, of course, not all children were pure examples of given types, it was possible to assign more than 80 percent of them to one type or another. Some children, however, were stubborn residuals—they simply could not be forced into the mold of any of the types. For example, the boy least like any of the types was judged to be self-defeating, giving up easily when confronted with problems, and quite excitable. He also had few friends and limited interests. In social situations he was withdrawn and ill at ease. This same boy, now in his early thirties, remains a residual. He has never married and still lives with his parents, expressing satisfaction with a sheltered and rather solitary life.

Residuals (some of whom may be residuals because of their extraordinary adaptability or capacities) serve as a continual reminder that any classification scheme must be an approximation. And what should induce even greater caution is that the residual of one society may be a common type in another.

As we cannot present here a full description of each of the nine types in terms of the 100 Q-sort items, a summary portrait of only one type for each sex is presented.

not so wide as each would claim; predilection is never fully nullified, nor does theory proceed unchecked by the realities of empirical data. In short, Kretschmer's typology could not have arisen in the absence of intensive observation, and the empirical typology presented in Box 26.4 is probably not entirely innocent of theoretical persuasion.

EVALUATION OF THE TYPOLOGICAL APPROACH

Types have been subjected to severe criticism. For example, Allport (1937) argues:

Every typology is based on the abstraction of some segment of the total personality, and the forcing of this segment to unnatural prominence. All typologies place boundaries where boundaries do not belong. They are artificial categories.

This harsh judgment is unavoidable in the face of the conflicting claims of various typologies. Many of them pretend to embrace the total personality, and to follow the cleavages that occur in nature. But the very typologies that have proclaimed themselves "basic," contradict one another. Compare, for example, the supposedly foundational types of Kretschmer, Spranger and Jaensch. Certainly not one of these typologies, so diverse in conception and scope, can be consid-

A TYPE 2 GIRL

Characteristically	*Uncharacteristically*
Behaves in a giving way toward others	Feels a lack of personal meaning in life
Has high aspiration level for self	Gives up and withdraws in the face of frustration
Is a genuinely dependable and responsible person	Is self-defeating
Behaves in a sympathetic or considerate manner	Is self-pitying
Appears to have a high degree of intellectual capacity	Is emotionally bland

A TYPE 5 BOY

Characteristically	*Uncharacteristically*
Is a genuinely dependable and responsible person	Has a wide range of interests
Appears to have a high degree of intellectual capacity	Favors conservative values in a variety of areas
Is productive; gets things done	Is gregarious
Has high aspiration level for self	Tends to be rebellious and nonconforming
	Sees what he can get away with

Neither Type 2 girls nor Type 5 boys are the most frequent found within this sample; however, they were selected for presentation here because their comparison makes an interesting point. Note that both types share certain characteristics: both are bright, ambitious, and dependable. But the boys convey a quality of emotional constriction (mainly through their "uncharacteristic" items), whereas the girls seem interpersonally more sensitive, less uptight, and generally more stable. Since these types are empirically derived rather than theoretically created, findings such as these pose a challenge for personality theory. Thus, work is still under way to delineate further the backgrounds of each of the nine types in order to better understand the development of each one and, ultimately, to contribute to a coherent theoretical picture of how and why children's personalities differ.

Empirically derived types of this kind reflect no claim to universality; the particular types found in this study are anchored to a sample of children from a specific community, Q-sorted by certain judges employing a particular set of personality-descriptive items and having certain information available to them. But, even with these restrictions, empirical typologies like this one can help our research quest for understanding of personality. For example, rather than seeking determinants of the 100 separate personality traits for each of the boys and girls, it is now possible to look for differences among the nine types of children in their early family atmosphere as well as in their later educational careers and vocational (and marital) fates. Such a study is now under way.

J. W. MACFARLANE. Studies in child guidance: I. Methodology of data collection and organization. *Monographs of the Society for Research in Child Development*, 1938, 3, No. 6.
J. BLOCK. *The Q-Sort Method in Personality Assessment and Psychiatric Research.* Springfield, Ill.: Charles C Thomas, 1961.

ered final, for none of them overlaps any other. Each theorist slices nature in any way he chooses, and finds only his own cuttings worthy of admiration.

Most proponents of typologies—and particularly modern advocates—would be in full agreement with this last point, but, as for the criticism that most people are mixed, for example, falling somewhere between the pure extravert and the pure introvert, its target is largely a straw man, as we have noted earlier. Not only do modern typologies define their types by a profile of several characteristics (the Jungian model has three dimensions in addi-tion to introversion-extraversion), but these dimensions are also considered continuous, not all-or-none dichotomies. The hard core of current conceptions of typologies is simply that certain trait profiles are more frequent than are others, so that they serve as convenient reference points for classification of all individuals. The universality that has been claimed by many typologies, especially theoretical ones, is less easily defended.

The attraction of types and typologies for psychologists—and a powerful attraction it must be to have survived continual criticism —may in part depend upon the ability of this approach to preserve something of the flavor of the unique individual and to do so without wholly sacrificing the generality necessary for the usual methods of scientific investigation.

As Kluckhohn and Murray (1948) have observed, "Every man is in certain respects like all other men, like some other men, [and] like no other man."

SUMMARY

1. Definitions of personality abound, each placing different emphases on various facets of an individual's development.
2. A generally acceptable definition of personality is difficult to arrive at, but agreement can be reached on certain criteria for an eventual definition. These criteria include comprehensiveness (all aspects of the individual must be considered), modifiability (despite hereditary influences, personality is an ever-adapting phenomenon), pattern and organization (the personality is *not* a mere agglomeration of isolated and easily separable characteristics), and uniqueness (no man can be exactly like another).
3. Personality, however defined, is highly pervasive. Not only does it refer to how people behave and feel in interpersonal situations but it is reflected in the individual's characteristic style in a wide range of behaviors.
4. The two main approaches to the task of describing personality use traits and typologies.
5. A trait is an enduring and consistent characteristic of a person that is observed in a wide variety of situations. For example, people are more or less warm, reserved, irritable. Traits can be observed at a number of levels, and it is sometimes useful to distinguish among these levels, for example, between surface warmth and real warmth.
6. There is a wide variety of systems for establishing personality types; each describes useful distinctions among persons. These distinctions are only relative, however, and do not point to abrupt discontinuities.
7. Traditionally, personality types have been formulated on a priori theoretical grounds; an alternative empirical approach detects types as they actually exist in a given population and then seeks to understand such types in theoretical terms.
8. Typologies have been subjected to much criticism because of their apparent implication of discontinuity, that is, of pure types; yet this criticism is rarely merited. Modern typologies by no means call for such distinctions among persons. Instead, they propose salient dimensions along which individuals vary and conceive of types as groups of persons who generally resemble one another in their patterns along these dimensions.

GLOSSARY

asthenic type   The type of physique characterized by a thin, long-limbed, narrow-chested body, which was asserted by Kretschmer to be associated with shy, sensitive, aloof, and withdrawn characteristics, and—in cases of mental disease—with schizophrenia. This type is contrasted with the pyknic type.

constructive alternativism   George Kelly's general approach to understanding personality; it asserts that no viewpoint is better than others, but rather that differing viewpoints are necessary since each provides new information that permits us to approximate more closely the truth of a given personality.

personality types   The qualitatively different categories into which personalities may allegedly be divided. There are simple type theories, which postulate a very limited number of categories, and complex type theories, involving classification of persons on a large number of dimensions.

pyknic type   The type of physique characterized by a short, fattish, barrel-chested body, which was asserted by Kretschmer to be associated with jovial, lively, outgoing characteristics, with an inclination to mood fluctuations, and—in cases of mental disease—with manic-depressive psychosis. This type is contrasted with the asthenic type.

source traits   In Cattell's system, the more fundamental and less directly observable traits that underlie and account for the surface traits.

surface traits   In Cattell's system, clusters of traits that are easily defined and typically observed to go with one another.

trait   An enduring characteristic of the individual that is manifested in a consistent way of behaving in a wide variety of situations. Traits are of many varieties; some are broad in scope, some narrow, some on the surface, and others deep-seated.

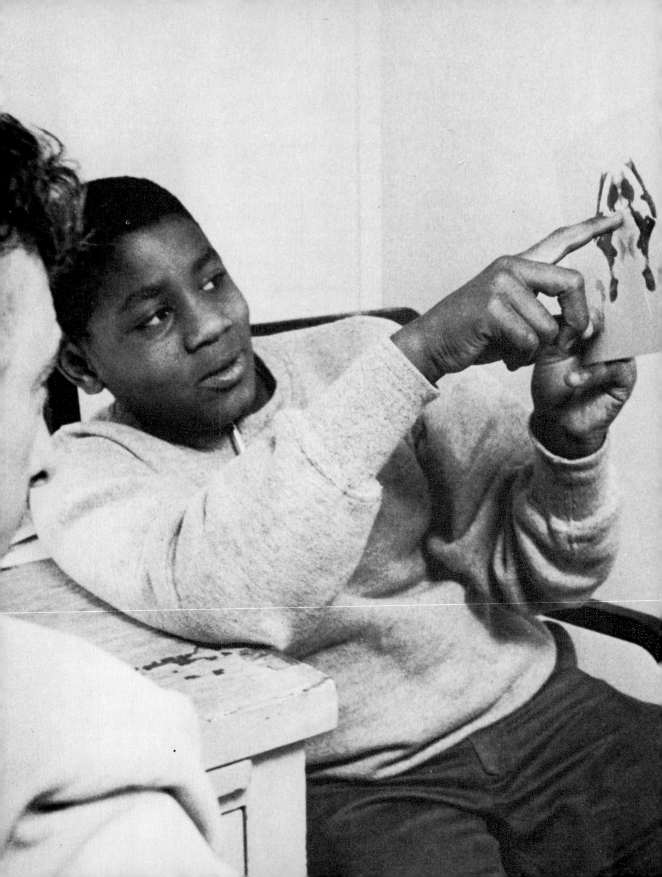

the measurement of personality

DO YOU KNOW…

- *the many ways in which measuring, for example, a person's warmth differs from measuring, say, her height or her intelligence?*

- *how hard it is to tell whether a given measurement of a personality characteristic is in fact correct?*

- *that psychologists sometimes set up ingenious replicas of real-life situations to see, for example, how a person reacts to stress?*

- *why it is that your answers to questions that seem to have absolutely nothing to do with a certain personality trait may in fact measure it quite well?*

- *that some people tend to be generally agreeable in responding to personality tests, often agreeing with statements that in no way reflect their true attitudes?*

- *how psychologists use deliberately ambiguous stimuli to get at deeper-lying responses of which the person may be totally unaware?*

- *how we can go about assessing a person's creativity?*

- *that, in effect, psychologists pit the human brain against the computer in personality-prediction contests?*

CONTENTS

The choice of methods for personality measurement as well as the adequacy of these methods necessarily depends on one's particular view of personality and on the particular purposes the measurements are intended to serve.

It is of little use to ask what kind of personality measurement is more accurate unless we append to our question the qualifications "according to what theory?" or "for what purpose?" It may be difficult to accept such a relativistic criterion, in part because in our everyday thinking we regard someone's personality as composed of attributes that the person really has. This tendency to reify personality traits—to regard them as *entities* that a person has just so much of, rather than as characteristics of his behavior—is aggravated when we speak of personality measurement. The term "measurement" unfortunately reinforces this impression. Because a person's height and weight can be accurately determined, we may be misled into expecting that an assessment of his warmth or his anxiety can be accomplished by one and only one suitable instrument. Perhaps eventually it can be, but only when we become able to quantify warmth and anxiety with the same precision as we now do height and weight.

This misapplied physical analogy may be the unrecognized villain in the story of personality measurement, suggesting as it does a crippling oversimplification of the nature of personality. A moment's reflection, and it is clear that warmth, as we usually speak of it, is not a characteristic whose degree may be read on some psychological thermometer. "Warm on what level?"—in innermost feeling or in social expression? "Warm in what manner?" —through quiet support or obtrusive demonstrativeness? "Warm in what situations?"—with intimates, with casual acquaintances, or even with strangers? Each of these manifestations is a legitimate aspect of the trait warmth; each can be measured, and each may yield different scores for the same individual. (All this is, of course, not a problem of *measurement* but one of definition, as discussions in Unit 26 of trait levels and situational influences indicate.)

For this and other reasons, although it is meaningful to speak of a warm person, it is necessary to consider a variety of conceptions and to apply a number of appropriate quantification methods. The synthesis of the various results from such a strategy provides perhaps the best avenue to understanding a trait and its place in the organization of personality.

Personality research has taken this mandate for diversity to heart. In principle, any item of behavior is fair game. A child's story to her doll, a letter to a friend, the tape-recorded conversation of a couple on their honeymoon—all have served as raw data in the study of personality. Spontaneous behavior is observed, interviews are conducted, personality inventories are constructed, test situations are set up, even physiological responses are recorded. For any instance of personality measurement to be useful, it must meet the two criteria that apply to any measurement in any branch of science: reliability and validity. The measurement method must yield consistent results on different measurement occasions (reliability), and it must actually measure that attribute we wish to measure (validity) (see Appendix, Psychological Measurement).

Reliability and validity are not the only considerations that have influenced the development of methods for the measurement of personality. As we review some of the more widely used approaches, it becomes apparent that convenience and efficiency have also been relevant factors. Instruments and techniques must work, but they must also be workable.

MEASUREMENT TECHNIQUES

There is enormous diversity in the methods of personality measurement. The broad categories that we will review include ratings, situational tests, inventories, and projective techniques. One of the many distinctions that may be drawn among personality-measurement techniques is the one between measurements based on observation of the person's natural behavior in realistic social situations and measurements based on required performances in test situations.

Ratings

Ratings, perhaps the most frequently used personality-measurement method, typically (though not always) evaluate behavior observed in relatively natural settings. A personality rating is nothing more than assignment of a numerical score to an observed subject in terms of a rating scale (see Table 27.1).

TABLE 27.1 AN ILLUSTRATIVE RATING SCALE FOR THE MEASUREMENT OF THE TRAIT OF DOMINANCE-SUBMISSION

Instructions: Place a check mark before the category that best describes the behavior of the individual.

————— 1. Takes the lead in all his relations with other people; is always dominant and assertive.

————— 2. Usually takes the ascendant role in his relations with others, but occasionally may follow rather than lead.

————— 3. Is about equally likely to take the dominant role or the submissive role in his relations with others.

————— 4. Usually takes the submissive role, but occasionally is ascendant over others.

————— 5. Takes the submissive role in all his relations with other people; is always led and dominated.

We all make frequent use of rating scales, at least of simplified ones. For example, when we comment that a friend is, say, argumentative, we have made a rating on a two-point scale: yes or no. In fact, an **adjective checklist** is a formal instance of this rating procedure; the task of the rater in this case is simply to check off which of a very large number of trait adjectives describe a subject's behavior (see, for example, Gough, 1961).

Usually, however, there is an attempt at finer discriminations: Five-point scales are common, and even eleven-point scales are not infrequent. The appropriate number of points in the scale depends largely upon the adequacy of the information upon which the rating will be based. The more observational data available, the greater the discrimination that should be possible. In addition, the more clearly the scale points are specified, the more likely it is that the discriminations will be reliable ones. Imagine, for example, that you have been asked to rate a number of acquaintances on the trait competitiveness and have been instructed to use only a five-point scale: very competitive, above average, average, below average, and very uncompetitive. Under these conditions it is unlikely that your ratings would agree highly with those made by others, even if all raters had had the same opportunity to observe the same subjects. On the other hand, and at the other extreme, if each of the five scale points were clearly specified by a number of specific behavioral cues (as in Table 27.2), agreement

TABLE 27.2 AN ILLUSTRATIVE RATING SCALE FOR THE MEASUREMENT OF THE TRAIT OF COMPETITIVENESS, WITH DETAILED CRITERIA FOR EACH SCALE POINT

———— 1. Extreme or hectic drive to excel competitors; either won't play if he can't win, or always picks inferior opponents, or cheats to win. Beating his competitors practically his only satisfaction in a play or work situation. Competitive drives dominate major part of his activities—a diffused set extending to many people and to all sorts of situations that to most individuals would not be competitive.

———— 2. Enjoys excelling competitors to the point of being upset when he loses; takes his failure to win very hard, or can't restrain an overt expression of satisfaction when he wins. Not so extreme as (1) but characteristic and noticeable by anyone with whom he comes in contact. Either several fields in which competitive drive is very pronounced but not so extreme as (1) or has one field in which it is terribly important to excel others.

———— 3. Is stimulated by competitive situations and enjoys excelling but can accept defeat without much strain. Periodic competitive sprees but not persistent and pervasive nor extreme.

———— 4. No real competitive relationship; enjoys games for the fun of playing them but relatively unimportant who wins.

———— 5. Sensitive to competitive situations but gets disorganized, is let down, unproductive, or flees from them. Resistive in negative way. Extremely discouraged about his abilities, or appears to seek defeat compulsively.

From Macfarlane, Allen, and Honzik, 1954.

would certainly be enhanced. To specify in this manner would not only ensure that you shared a common definition of "competitiveness" with the other raters, but the meanings of such ambiguous terms as "very" and "above average" would have been sharpened.

Q-sorts The **Q-sort** of Box 26.4, page 664, is another example of rating method. The rater is usually directed in this method to assign descriptive items in predetermined numbers to each of the categories in the scale. In the 100-item set of Q-sort items used for Box 26.4, nine categories were specified ranging from "9," which was designated for the five items *most* characteristic of the person being described, to "1," designated for the five *least* characteristic items. The "8" and "2" categories had quotas of eight items each, "7" and "3" had to contain twelve items, and "6" and "4," sixteen items each. The result of this typical procedure is of course a symmetrical distribution of item frequencies with the middle category of "5" (containing items that seemed neither characteristic nor uncharacteristic) having the largest number of items—in this case, eighteen.

The particular numbers of items assigned to each Q-sort category is by no means fixed by this method. Investigators vary in their preferences and attempt to adjust them to the specific assessment situation. One methodological study (Livson & Nichols, 1956) presents evidence that it may be best to have equal numbers of items assigned to each category—that this breakdown would generally yield the most reliable information about the person being described. But, whatever the choice of how to distribute the items among the categories, the distribution in the Q-sort method is, almost without exception, forced—the rater is *not* free to assign the items as he chooses.

This forced distribution is one point of difference from the usual rating procedure described in the previous section. And there is another and probably more significant difference. The usual rating procedure assesses where along a rating scale a particular person is best assigned *with regard to all other persons in the sample*. In Q-sorting, however, it is the items that are ranked in order of their applicability *within an individual*. Thus, to assign the Q-sort item "Is assertive" to the "1" (least characteristic) category for Charlie Brown is not necessarily to say that of all comic-strip characters he is the most meek (though indeed he may be) but rather to record the impression that, if there is a trait most characteristic of this antihero, it is that he is certainly *not* assertive. This approach of ordering traits *within* the person is called **ipsative rating**, whereas the usual method is **normative rating**; the former, generally, is found to require much less time and is regarded as more natural, especially when very large numbers of traits are to be rated for each individual.

Ratings exist for the measurement of a great many different personality attributes, and they have proved indispensable for much of the research on personality. But they are fraught with dangers. Some traits are so elusive or poorly conceptualized that they cannot be rated in a reliable and valid fashion, no matter how well designed their rating scales. It is therefore the general rule that, wherever possible, ratings should be administered independently by several different raters, so that the degree of agreement of their judgments can be checked.

Validity is, of course, an elusive notion in personality ratings. What can be the criterion against which the accuracy of a rating is to be evaluated? No single objective criterion exists, nor is the method of *known-group validity* determination (see Appendix, p. 837) of much use here. Rather, the validity of a personality rating scale is checked, when it is at all, by its ability to predict an assortment of separate criteria, each of which should go along somewhat with our theoretical notions of the construct being measured. A set of warmth ratings, for example, shows *criterion validity* to the extent that it correlates with the judgment of family members and close friends, and *construct validity* if, for example, it relates to the subject's degree of direct participation in humanitarian activities. Each separate method for evaluating validity is highly fallible; collectively, they may be adequate. In most cases, a bootstrapping operation creates the criterion; the subject *is* as warm as the average of several

ratings says he is. But what if the experts disagree? (See Box 27.1, p. 674.)

Sources of Rating Data

Ratings of any sort may be based on direct observation of a person's behavior either in a limited setting (e.g., ratings of children's traits from their behavior on the school playground) or in much broader settings (e.g., ratings of workers by their supervisors on the basis of behavior occurring in many diverse situations, formal and informal). Ratings may also be based on personal interviews with the individual or on the basis of a study of various other sources of information about him—life-history documents, work records, test scores, and so on. From all these sources, the rater seeks to gain an overall impression of the individual's traits, one that is sufficiently detailed to permit quantification.

Interviews An interview, in its most informal form, is hardly different from a conversation, albeit an essentially one-way conversation. The interviewer's task is to elicit sufficient information from the interviewee to permit him (and others, working from taped or typed transcriptions of the interview) to get the ratings required for the particular investigation. But, in order to ensure that sufficient information is elicited in a uniform (and therefore unbiased) manner, there is usually an **interview schedule**, which imposes a degree of structure on the conversation (hence the term "structured interview"). The interview schedule consists of specific questions to be asked and, often, a range of subquestions that depends on the answers to the main questions. The interviewee may be allowed to reply freely to the interviewer's questions. In that case we speak of open-ended questions that, not surprisingly, may lead to writer's cramp and strained patience when the interviewer is faced with a garrulous subject. Or, at the other extreme, the interviewee's responses are restricted to predetermined categories, as in an attorney's insistent, "Answer yes or no," or the pollster's request that you respond to "How happy are you?" only with "Very," "Moderately," "Not very," or "Not at all."

BOX 27.1

SEX DIFFERENCES IN THE EYE OF THE BEHOLDER

There have been many studies reporting on the different views men and women have of men and women. Much of this research has been based on descriptions of average or ideal males and females provided by the psychologist's favorite research subject—the undergraduate student. The results of such studies are not surprising; you could very likely guess fairly accurately at their nature. What they tell us is that *both* men and women students tend to share the cultural view that males are (or should be) more aggressive, assertive, independent, etc., whereas women are (or should be) more nurturant, unassuming, dependent, etc. Few of these data are new enough to reflect the recent, ongoing, and sweeping changes in the perceptions, roles, and behaviors of men and women in our society; new studies today might well show the effects of this major shift in our culture.

Be that as it may, these findings were implicitly assumed to reflect the attitudes of the larger culture, but not that of expert personality assessors. When both men and women participated as expert judges in personality assessment settings, their separate ratings were averaged; the sex of the expert was totally ignored. The unspoken assumption seems to have been that highly trained judges of personality were immune to whatever sexual stereotypes pervaded the world in which they lived.

But N. Haan and N. Livson, psychologists at the University of California, Berkeley, suggest that this optimism may have been somewhat uncritical. For a study of the adult personalities of fifty women and forty-eight men, ten male and thirteen female intensively trained clinical psychologists were assigned to provide personality descriptions by means of the California Q-sort (see Box 26.4, p. 664). Each person being described was Q-sorted by at least one male and one female psychologist so that it was possible to determine, over this full sample of almost 100 adults, whether these expert judges showed any systematic differences in the ways they perceived the *same* men and women. Agreement among the judges was substantial, but some small, significant differences did emerge. Here are a few.

Male psychologists tended to see slightly more unfavorable traits than did female psychologists in both men and women subjects but different ones in the two sexes. Male psychologists saw somewhat more of so-called "unmasculine" traits in male subjects, such as passivity and dependence, and more of "unfeminine" traits in female subjects. In fact, Haan and Livson report that " 'bitchiness' seems the general theme running through the unfavorable traits they [male psychologists] generally attribute to women." The female judges were generally a bit more favorable than the males in their evaluations of women subjects, by no means an obvious finding: Most studies report women as being just as (or even more) critical of their own sex as men are. But when they did perceive unfavorable characteristics in women, they were different from those seen by men. Women saw in women more "feminine" traits, such as being histrionic in their behavior on the one hand or tending to be too emotionally restricted on the other. (Any given woman could hardly show both of these characteristics, but they can be seen as reflecting the two extremes of the common female stereotype.) Furthermore, when judging men, the women saw more "masculine" traits such as condescension and overconcern with power.

These differences, while all of modest magnitude, suggest a general theme to Haan and Livson:

> It is as though men keep a sharper eye out for defections from the male stereotype (as they may define it), while women are more alert to the excesses of males in the service of that stereotype. Women psychologists are also more alert to unfavorable excesses in female subjects of "feminine" stereotype, as they may define it. . . . Men, in judging female subjects, are once again concerned with defections from a stereotype, in this instance their image of a "good" woman.

But, aside from the specific nature of these differences in how experts of each sex evaluate men and women, what is the implication of these results for the common and currently indispensable practice of using consensus among experts to define the reality of personality? Let the researchers (a woman and a man) provide their own nonanswer:

> Which beholder—man or woman—(if either) can best tell us what people are really like? Perhaps this question is unanswerable in the absence of some ultimately valid (unisex?) criterion, and perhaps this is one reason why the sex difference in expert judging behavior—really an obvious one to raise—has for so long been overlooked.

N. HAAN & N. LIVSON. Sex differences in the eyes of expert personality assessors. *Journal of Personality Assessment*, 1973, **37**, 486–492.

The attorney and the pollster are not faced with the need to apply rating scales to the responses, as is a psychologist confronted with pages of open-ended interview responses. The respondent faced with predetermined categories is, in a sense, being forced to rate himself. Self-ratings of other kinds also have a place in personality measurement.

Self-ratings The person may also rate himself on various traits. There are obvious pitfalls in the use of such self-ratings as trait measurements in that they are susceptible to distortions caused by lack of frankness, limitation of perspective, and self-deception. The self-rating may thus disagree markedly with ratings made by objective observers.

But it should be recognized that the most important use of self-ratings is to provide measures of how an individual views himself. The **self** is an organized and enduring perception in the individual's experience, unique to him and constituting a central part of his **personality structure**. When a person reports frankly, his self-ratings are presumably the best evidence we can obtain on what the person believes about himself. And the fact that self-ratings may often deviate from the objective appraisals of observers is itself a fertile source of information about degrees of self-deception and self-insight in the person. For example, in one procedure (Gough, 1961), the person checks in a list of 300 adjectives those he regards as true of himself. A team of expert observers uses the same checklist to describe him. The degree of agreement between his description and the average of theirs is then computed. High agreement presumably indicates high self-insight; low agreement, low self-insight. In this case, clearly, consensus defines truth. But this truth may ignore a more basic truth. The self is often seen by the person as consisting of more central and private layers (the real me) and the more peripheral and public layers (the unimportant part of me). This duality of the self (rather than low self-insight) may often be responsible for the discrepancies between the results of self-ratings and ratings by others.

Situational Tests

Another valuable approach to personality measurement is to place the person in a standard test situation that is an approximate replica of a real-life situation and to record data on his behavior. The assumption is that his behavior in the test situation may validly reflect his general behavioral traits. This correspondence is likely to be closer the more real the test situation is. Sometimes, indeed, the subject may not realize that it is a test at all. For instance, MacKinnon (1938), in a classic forerunner to his later use of **situational tests** during World War II to assess OSS personnel, measured honesty in a sample of people by placing each one alone in a standard test situation in which he was to solve a series of numerical problems. An answer booklet was available, but he was instructed not to look. The experimenter observed him through a one-way screen, recording whether or not he violated the prohibition.

The situational test may often involve interpersonal behavior among several persons who are being observed. For example, a group of five may be assigned a topic to discuss and left free to choose their own leader, set their own rules, and proceed as they see fit. The behavior of each person as he interacts with the others is recorded by observers and scored on one or more personality variables, such as dominance, poise, leadership, negativism, tolerance, originality. The scores may be objectively derived through the counting of behavior items (for example, the number of times the person initiated suggestions during the discussion), or they may be obtained through ratings.

Some situational tests are deliberately contrived to confront the individual with conditions of stress or with conflicts to be overcome in the assigned task. Milgram (1963), for example, placed his subjects in an extraordinarily stressful conflict situation by causing them to think they were administering increasingly painful electric shocks to other subjects. In reality, in each case, the other subject was a confederate of the experimenter and feigned painful reactions to an actually nonexistent shock. The performance in this situation of each real subject provided a measure of his readiness to engage in antisocial acts (inflicting pain) when under social pressure to do so. In another situational test, the subject is required to work on a problem in cooperation with another individual who is actually the experimenter and who deliberately causes well-timed interferences in the subject's attack on the problem. The distinctive manner in which he reacts to the stress and handles the interpersonal conflict provides data for measuring various dimensions of personality. Still other examples of situational tests are encountered in Unit 33, page 803.

In life's normal course there are many common stress situations with respect to which people's reactions can be compared and hence provide useful personality data. Adjustment to military service, to a new job, to marriage— each provides opportunities to observe personality in action under stress. Such outcomes in these situations as psychiatric breakdown, being fired, and divorce are thus highly relevant as objective behavioral indexes of the individual's reactions to stress situations.

Personality Inventories

A principal approach to personality measurement is through **personality inventories**, which are aimed at a great variety of traits. Some have to do with personal interests; others deal with emotional adjustment, social relations, attitudes, and values.

An inventory consists of a large number of statements or questions, each to be answered in one of several specified categories such as agree or disagree, like or dislike. The score on a particular personality characteristic is not based on the answer to a single item but on answers to a number of items that, taken together, constitute the scale intended to measure the trait in question. One inventory may provide measures of a dozen or more traits at the same time.

There are two quite different methods of selecting items and establishing the direction in which their answers are to be scored. In the *a priori* (or rational) method the test constructor designs items whose meanings, on the very face of it, clearly indicate how the items are to be scored. For example, this method is used in the Allport-Vernon-Lindzey Study of Values (see Box 26.3, p. 663), in which each item is manifestly intended to reflect a political, social, aesthetic, theoretical, economic, or religious interest of the individual. (This technique does *not* require or even expect that the person taking the test be aware of the direction of scoring for each item or even of the dimensions being measured.)

The a priori method of test construction is used also, for instance, in the Edwards Personal Preference Schedule (Edwards, 1959). Here again the item content is manifestly related to the trait which the tester seeks to measure. For example: *aggression*, "I feel like getting revenge when someone has insulted me"; *affiliation*, "I like to do things with my friends rather than by myself"; *change*, "I like to experiment and try new things."

In the *empirical* method of test construction the direction in which the item is to be scored is established by pretesting a large collection of items on criterion groups *known* to be high and low on the trait in question. The items on which the answers of the two groups differ significantly are then included in the final inventory scale. An example of the empirical method is the Minnesota Multiphasic Personality Inventory—abbreviated MMPI (Hathaway & McKinley, 1951; Dahlstrom & Welsh, 1960). It consists of 550 simple statements, to each of which the person is to answer true, false, or cannot say. The items refer to such diverse topics as bodily complaints, "I am troubled by discomfort in the pit of my stomach every few days or oftener"; fears and anxieties, "I am afraid when I look down from a high place"; behavior characteristics, "Often I cross the street in order not to meet someone I see"; social and moral attitudes, "I do not blame a person for taking advantage of someone who lays himself open to it."

This inventory was developed by administering a very large number of initial items (considerably more than the final 550 items) to groups of persons known to be high or low on the various personality characteristics to be measured. For example, items on which a group of persons known to be high on paranoia (institutionalized psychotics diagnosed as paranoid) responded significantly differently from normal persons were retained to make up the paranoia scale of the final inventory. An individual's score on the scale is then determined by the number of items on which he responds in the way in which the criterion group of paranoid persons had responded.

The test is scored on a number of scales. The scales are measures of traits that, if possessed in extreme degree, are likely to be symptomatic of disturbances of personality, for example, depression, hysteria, paranoia. The MMPI is one of the devices most widely used by clinicians for the diagnosis of personality disorders.

Another inventory, constructed in somewhat the same manner but aimed at the measurement of more normal traits having significance for effective personal and social functioning in general, is the California Psychological Inventory (Gough, 1957). It includes eighteen scales grouped under four broad categories: (1) measures of poise, ascendancy, and self-assurance; (2) measures of socialization, maturity, and responsibility; (3) measures of achievement potential and intellectual efficiency; and (4) measures of style of thinking and orientation to life.

Gough, in his CPI, has placed special emphasis on developing a personality inventory that would be applicable in a variety of cultures. His scales intend to measure "traits of character which arise directly and necessarily from interpersonal life, and which should therefore be relevant to the understanding and prediction of social behavior in any and all situations and in any culture." The statements that define his scales refer to situations common to most cultures; for example, in his socialization scale, the subject responds to such items as "Before I do something I try to consider how my friends will react to it." The strategy has apparently worked well; numerous studies attest to the validity of many of the CPI scales in various countries. To take one instance, Gough and Sandhu (1964) report that the socialization scale (in which a *low* score indicates delinquency) discriminated with great effectiveness between college students and imprisoned delinquents of comparable age in India.

Response sets Personality inventories of this sort have been attacked because of evidence that **response sets** substantially affect their scores; for example, subjects tend to agree with socially desirable items, almost apart from their content. To the extent that this factor operates, the validity of the instrument (its ability to measure the traits *intended*) is thereby necessarily diminished. If depression is a characteristic most of us would not care to admit to, then there is a tendency to distort one's responses, at least to obvious depression-confessing items when they are recognized in a given personality inventory.

A similar case includes the tendency to be acquiescent, to agree with items, once again almost apart from their content. Thus, if one approaches the items on a personality inventory with an attitude or response set of being generally agreeable, then the validity of a purported trait measurement must necessarily suffer.

One of the reasons that such response sets tend to operate in an individual is that he knows he is being tested and is aware of the obvious diagnostic meaning of a particular item. For this reason it is of value to utilize less direct measures of personality traits, measures in which the intention of a certain question is less obvious to the individual.

The problem may not be as serious as it seems. At least this is the strong opinion of Block (1965), who undertook extensive empirical investigation of the effects of acquiescence and social desirability response sets on MMPI scores—one of the more severely criticized inventories. His verdict is a near-total acquittal on both charges, since his empirical evidence supports the conclusion that the content aspect of the MMPI—that is, the repertory of personality traits it intends to measure—is relatively immune to influence by response sets.

But the battle continues, and many have debated Block's conclusions. By now, however, most psychologists would agree that response sets are something more than annoying error and that, in fact, one's tendency to be generally agreeable or to prefer socially desirable items in responding to personality inventories is in itself a measurable personality trait of some interest. Contributing to this view is the work of Crowne and Marlowe (1964), who devised a scale to measure directly the tendency to prefer socially desirable responses. By comparing the actual behavior of persons scoring high and low on this scale, they found that high scorers tended to be relatively docile and dependent and, generally, to be more conventional and cautious.

Projective Techniques

Projective techniques are intended to reach the deeper and subtler aspects of personality. The essence of these techniques is the presentation of weakly structured or ambiguous stimulus materials to which the person responds with his interpretations. It is assumed that such equivocal stimuli will encourage a greater degree of projection of the subject's deep-lying tendencies than more direct methods; as he perceives and interprets the ambiguous stimuli, he is unaware of what he is revealing. Among the earliest and still commonly used projective tests are the Rorschach inkblots and the Thematic Apperception Test.

Rorschach inkblots This widely used projective technique, designed in 1911 by the Swiss psychiatrist Hermann Rorschach, consists of the presentation of ten standard inkblots, some black and white, some colored. The subject is asked to describe the various things he sees in the blots, and his responses are scored in a number of categories, pertaining to the *location* in the blot of the thing seen; to the kind of *stimulus characteristic* emphasized, for example, form, color, shading, texture, movement; to the *content* of the percept, for example, animal, human being, inanimate object; and to the *originality* of the response.

These various scores are taken to be diagnostic of specific tendencies. For instance, seeing the blot as a whole is regarded as an indication of tendencies toward abstract and theoretical orientations, whereas concentration on many small details of the blots indicates compulsive attention to trivial things; color responses are considered to be related to emotional expression; human movement responses

to richness of inner life. Ratios of the separate scores are also treated as diagnostic. A high ratio of color to form responses is interpreted as signifying a tendency to exhibit uncontrolled emotional behavior; a high ratio of human movement to color responses is taken to mean a withdrawn, introversive tendency; and so on.

Although the scoring of the Rorschach is more or less standard, the interpretation is decidedly not. It requires a highly skilled tester to synthesize the information from the entire pattern of test scores and to arrive at the conception of the structure of the personality. Such conceptions are intuitive, and the same test scores may be quite differently interpreted by different experts. In addition, as the data of Box 27.2 indicate, the responses may have different significance for people of different cultures. This possibility raises doubts concerning the validity of the technique, unless cultural (and subcultural) variations are somehow taken into account. Perhaps this factor is also partly the reason why studies directed toward validation of the Rorschach show inconsistent results. In any event, the test continues in wide use.

Thematic Apperception Test This widely used projective technique (known as the TAT) was designed by Morgan and Murray (1935) especially for the purpose of measuring the various *psychological needs* postulated in Murray's theory of personality. This theory assumes that some twenty needs are to be found in some degree in every person (Table 27.3, p. 680). Murray further assumes that it is the relative amounts of each need and the manner in which the needs become organized during the individual's development that characterize his personality. The TAT consists of a standard set of twenty test pictures, each depicting a simple scene of ambiguous meaning, for example, an old woman looking past the averted face of a younger woman, a man standing with head bowed beside a bed on which a partially undressed woman is lying. (A sample TAT picture is shown in Figure 27.1, p. 681.) The subject is asked to tell a story about each picture, indicating what is happening, how it came about, what will happen next. The stories are then analyzed

BOX 27.2

TO EACH HIS OWN INKBLOT

Before reading on, look at the inkblot and write down what you see in it.

What you see may reflect something about your personality. It may also reflect something about the culture in which you have been raised. Striking cultural differences in perceptual responses to Rorschach inkblots have been reported.

For example, one study showed that nomadic desert Moroccans emphasize tiny *details* of the blots to a much greater degree than do Europeans (Bleuler & Bleuler). Shown here is one of the standard blots, of which a typical description given by European subjects is "two women quarreling." A typical Moroccan response was to identify the tiny, scarcely perceptible marks on the small protrusions at the top of the figure (see arrows) as an alignment of Arab riflemen opposed by a row of Christian warriors. (A more up-to-date Moroccan reference might be to Israeli riflemen!)

At the other extreme we find the Samoans, who tend to give relatively few fine-detail responses

and a large number of whole responses; that is, they perceive the entire blot as a map or an animal (Cook). Furthermore, the Samoans differ markedly from typical Europeans and other samples of subjects in giving numerous responses to the *white spaces* in the blots, which they perceive as objects rather than as holes. For instance, in the blot shown here, the middle white area might be seen as an island.

These differences in perceptual emphasis, which can be multiplied in numerous other studies, may reflect the operation of cultural factors in a quite direct way. Moroccan art and religion give great importance to fine details; for the Samoans, white is a symbolic and highly valued color.

Not that Moroccans cannot see wholes or Samoans details. The point is that, given these inkblots, which are susceptible to many different perceptual organizations, people of different cultures tend to look at them in different ways.

Nor does this range of perceptions prove that the Moroccan personality is different from the Samoan personality or from the European personality. However, G. Lindzey's review of the Rorschach test in cross-cultural investigations leads him to conclude that responses to the inkblots not only differ substantially among different cultures but—and more important—that inferences about personality based on the Rorschach test do seem consistent with the inferences drawn on the basis of their extensive field-work data by anthropologists studying these same cultures. And when one considers that inkblots are nonverbal stimuli and, for that very reason, lend themselves to use in all societies—even nonliterate ones—we may begin to understand the continuing popularity of this projective test in cross-cultural research.

M. BLEULER & R. BLEULER. Rorschach's ink-blot tests and racial psychology. *Character and Personality*, 1935, **4**, 97–114. Figure reprinted by permission of Hans Huber, Berne.
T. H. COOK. The application of the Rorschach test to a Samoan group. *Rorschach Research Exchange*, 1942, **6**, 51–60.
G. LINDZEY. *Projective Techniques and Crosscultural Research.* New York: Appleton, 1961.

by systematically noting certain consistencies and recurrent themes in the natures of the plots, in the types of heroes, or in the kinds of outcomes. Such characteristics in the stories are taken to reveal important aspects of the person's needs, attitudes, conflicts, identifications, aspirations, and self-conception.

The use of the TAT has been extended to problems beyond those of the measurement of the Murray needs. Box 27.3, page 682, presents an interesting use of the TAT for an issue in the interaction of culture and personality.

No *single* technique for measurement of personality has sufficient validity for useful pre-

TABLE 27.3 MURRAY'S TENTATIVE LIST OF PSYCHOLOGICAL NEEDS

Need	Brief Definition
Abasement	To submit passively to external force. To accept injury, blame, criticism, punishment. To become resigned to fate.
Achievement	To accomplish something difficult. To rival and surpass others.
Affiliation	To seek out and enjoy close and cooperative relationships with other people. To adhere and remain loyal to a friend.
Aggression	To overcome opposition forcefully. To attack, injure, or punish another.
Autonomy	To get free, shake off restraint, break out of confinement. To be independent and free to act according to impulse. To defy convention.
Counteraction	To master or make up for a failure by renewed striving. To overcome weaknesses. To maintain self-respect and pride on a high level.
Defendance	To defend the self against assault, criticism, and blame. To conceal or justify a misdeed, failure, or humiliation.
Deference	To admire and support a superior. To yield readily to the influence of others. To conform to custom.
Dominance	To control one's human environment. To influence or direct the behavior of others by suggestion, seduction, persuasion, or command.
Exhibition	To make an impression. To be seen and heard. To excite, entertain, shock, or entice others.
Harmavoidance	To avoid pain, physical injury, illness, and death.
Infavoidance	To avoid humiliation. To refrain from action because of fear of failure.
Nurturance	To give sympathy to and gratify the needs of weak and helpless persons. To feed, help, support, console, protect, nurse.
Order	To put things in order. To achieve cleanliness, arrangement, balance, neatness, and precision.
Play	To act for fun, without further purpose. To like to laugh and make jokes. To seek enjoyable relaxation of stress.
Rejection	To separate oneself from a disliked object. To exclude, abandon, or remain indifferent to an inferior person.
Sentience	To seek and enjoy sensuous impressions.
Sex	To form and further an erotic relationship. To have sexual intercourse.
Succorance	To have one's needs gratified by the sympathetic aid of another person. To be nursed, supported, protected, loved, guided, forgiven, consoled.
Understanding	To ask or answer general questions. To be interested in theory. To speculate, formulate, analyze, and generalize.

Adapted from Murray, 1938.

dictive purposes. This lack is one very real factor contributing to the recent attacks in the popular press on the evils of testing, personality testing as well as ability testing. These exposés draw their most dramatic examples from claims, unfortunately occasionally justified, of the flagrant misclassification of individuals based upon the results of single tests. To a large extent the target of these attacks is a "straw man" as well as a "dead horse." Even in the past it was the rare psychologist who attempted to characterize an individual on the basis of his performance on a single test. Today, the typical procedure is an approach called **personality assessment**, which relies upon a battery of diverse measuring techniques rather than upon any single test for the appraisal and prediction of personality.

PERSONALITY ASSESSMENT AND PREDICTION

"Personality assessment" is a loose term covering any situation in which a number of different kinds of personality measurements are carried out on the same individuals and are later combined to yield a comprehensive personality description or a prediction of a specific performance.

Personality inventories, projective techniques, situational tests, and ratings—all contribute to this end. And, typically, each main

FIGURE 27.1 A TAT picture. Many different stories can be told about each TAT picture.

H. A. Murray. *Thematic Apperception Test;* copyright 1943 by the President and Fellows of Harvard College; adapted by permission.

dimension of personality is measured through not one but a combination of different techniques. Intensive assessment also includes the collection of numerous data concerning the person's body characteristics, physiological functioning, life history, work history, social background, and the like.

Assessment of Creativity

Assessment studies often focus upon the prediction of a specific future performance, frequently success in a particular occupation. In these cases situational and other tests are devised that are specifically tailored to the prediction goal. For example, in a large-scale assessment program conducted at the Institute of Personality Assessment and Research, University of California, Berkeley, to ascertain the person-

ality characteristics of creative architects, some forty distinguished and creative American architects were intensively studied (MacKinnon, 1962). In groups of ten, they spent three days in residence at the Institute taking a variety of standard personality inventories, life-history and career interviews, projective tests, achievement tests, and certain tests that called for original thinking about architectural problems. They also engaged in situational tests, such as group discussions and game-playing. There was opportunity for the assessment staff to observe and to rate the behavior of the architects in such relatively natural situations as mealtimes and evening social gatherings.

It was found, on the basis of the total assessment battery, that the personality characteristics of the more highly creative architects could be significantly differentiated from a control group of about forty of the less creative. For example, the more highly creative showed a greater preference for perceptual complexity and asymmetry, more often gave unusual responses on a word-association test, and indicated that the theoretical and aesthetic values were the most important to them on the Allport-Vernon-Lindzey Study of Values (Box 26.3, p. 663). They also showed somewhat elevated scores on scales of the MMPI (p. 676) that are intended to be indicative of psychiatric disorders, but these responses seemed suggestive less of psychopathology in these creative individuals than of their complexity and richness of personality, general lack of defensiveness, and candor in self-description, in short, an openness to experience, especially of one's inner life. Differences in images of the self were also evident (Table 27.4, p. 683). As for intelligence, it is interesting to note that though all of the architects were, of course, of at least moderately high IQ, within the group there was no correlation between intelligence and creativity. (This fact, that the more intelligent person is not necessarily the more creative, was also found true for other assessed samples—writers, mathematicians, business entrepreneurs, scientists, etc.)

Such intensive assessment procedures are of course not feasible for very large groups. Therefore, if psychologists are to extend their

BOX 27.3

A TALE OF TWO TONGUES

Personality differences certainly exist, on the average, between members of different cultures, and projective techniques have been shown to be sensitive to such differences, as in Box 27.2, page 679. But what of an individual whose life experience spans two cultures? Will his current way of life predominate in the picture of his personality provided by a projective test? Or, instead, does the culture of his childhood maintain its organizing influence upon his personality? Perhaps the two personalities may live side by side; we shall see.

Susan Ervin at the University of California, Berkeley, administered the Thematic Apperception Test (TAT) on two occasions to each of sixty-four men and women who had been raised in France but who had lived in the United States for some time (an average of twelve years). All subjects spoke French and English fluently, so that on one test occasion the entire procedure—the experimenter's instructions and the subject's stories—was conducted in French and on the other in English. For half the group, the French TAT came first and, for half, the English. All subjects therefore told stories relating to the same TAT pictures in both languages, some six weeks elapsing between the first and second test sessions. Nine pictures were used on each occasion, and stories were requested by standard TAT instructions. In Ervin's words, the subjects were asked "to tell what was happening, what had happened in the past, what would happen in the future, and what the characters were thinking and feeling. In addition, at the second session, they were instructed to tell a different story if they recalled the first."

TAT stories can be scored in a variety of ways for a variety of themes. Ervin chose to score only those eight themes for which comparative studies of French and American cultures indicated a likelihood of personality differences. The scoring scheme employed in this study is rather complex, but the essential point is that the more frequently a given theme occurs in the course of a subject's set of nine stories in a given language, the higher his score is on that theme *as expressed in that language.*

If the language used for the TAT made no difference, then the subjects would give the same themes to the same degree on the two occasions. But Ervin's main result is that there were statistically significant differences for three of the nine themes. These French bilinguals in their French-language stories expressed more verbal aggression toward peers and were much more likely to make loved ones suffer by rejecting them or by doing something immoral. Also, for women only, achievement themes showed a difference depending upon the language; the Frenchwoman (or her heroine in the story) showed greater ambition and aspiration for herself or loved ones when the tale was told in English.

An illustration of the contrasts that occurred in stories by the same person about the same picture is furnished by the following excerpts from the test protocols of a twenty-seven-year-old Frenchwoman married to an American. In her first session she responded in *French* to the TAT picture that depicts a young man, face averted, turning way from a young woman who is holding him. In her second session she responded in *English* to the same picture.

French Response

She seems to beg him, to plead with him. . . . I think he wants to leave her because he's found another woman he loves more, and that he really wants to go, or maybe it's because . . . she's deceived him with another man. I

---

understanding of creativity and its determinants to its full range in the normal population, it becomes necessary to devise tests of creative ability that can be administered quickly and reliably to large samples of subjects. Such tests have been devised (for example, Guilford et al., 1951), with full recognition of the risks inherent in employing specific tasks to measure objectively so sweeping and complex a construct as creativity. (For an illustration of some of Guilford's tests and a highly creative if irreverent set of responses, see Box 27.4, p. 684.) Tests of this kind do and will serve many purposes, among them increasing our ability to determine

don't know whose fault it is but they certainly seem angry. Unless it's in his work, and he wants to go see someone and he wants to get in a fight with someone, and she holds him back and doesn't like him to get angry. I don't know, it could be many things.

English Response

. . . Well I think it was a married couple, average. . . . He's decided to get a good education and maybe after he would have a better job and be able to support his wife much better. . . . He keeps on working and going to college at night some of the time. . . . He finally decided that was too much. He found he was too tired, he was discouraged . . . and his wife tries to cheer him up . . . eventually he'll probably keep on working his way through and finally get his diploma and get a better job and they will be much happier.

The conclusion drawn by Ervin from all of her data is that her subjects have two personalities. She points out that this view is no more remarkable than the fact that each of us behaves somewhat differently in different social contexts. The adult who acts and feels a little more like his childhood self when he is back home amid scenes and figures of his youth than when he is in his usual surroundings should be a familiar example.

An early self and a contemporary self do in fact appear to coexist, and the TAT can detect each of them. In this respect, the results are a tribute to the sensitivity of a projective test in measuring subtle shifts in personality. The results may be embarrassing when the test intends to evaluate *only* the enduring central core of personality, which is presumably immune to influence from the social setting in which the test is administered and from the mood of the moment. But perhaps the task itself, so defined, is not a possible one.

S. M. ERVIN. Language and TAT content in bilinguals. *Journal of Abnormal and Social Psychology*, 1964, **68**, 500–507.

if the *personality* characteristics of highly creative persons can be correlated with varying degrees of creativity.

But how can we handle such masses of data, whether from assessment batteries or individual tests, in order to maximize their predictive value?

TABLE 27.4 SELF-DESCRIPTIVE ADJECTIVES DIFFERENTIATING 40 HIGHLY CREATIVE ARCHITECTS FROM 41 LESS CREATIVE ARCHITECTS (MATCHED FOR AGE AND GEOGRAPHICAL LOCATION)

Checked by 80% of Highly Creative Group but Less than 80% of Uncreative Group	Checked by 80% of Uncreative Group but Less than 80% of Creative Group
Inventive	Responsible
Determined	Sincere
Independent	Reliable
Individualistic	Dependable
Enthusiastic	Clear-thinking
Industrious	Tolerant
Artistic	Understanding
Progressive	Peaceable
Appreciative	Good-natured
	Moderate
	Steady
	Practical
	Logical

D. W. MacKinnon. Creativity and images of self. In R. W. White (Ed.), *The Study of Lives*; copyright © 1963 Atherton Press, adapted by permission; all rights reserved.

Intuitive Versus Statistical Prediction

There are two major strategies for translating data into explicit predictions about individual personalities. On one hand, the psychologist may array before him the full record of any individual—ratings, test scores, interview material, and so on—and, from a more or less conscious application of his implicit and explicit theories of personality and from his more or less precise understanding of what constitutes (let's say) a good architect, arrive intuitively at a prediction. At the other extreme, this clinical insight is replaced by the computer. Statistical analyses assign the weights to be attached to each measurement, and the weighted score leads to an objective prediction. The distinction here is not the kind of data used; the intuitive prediction can make use of quantitative test scores, whereas the statistical one can make use of highly subjective, though quantified, ratings. The issue is how the data are combined, not how they are gathered, although, as we will note in a moment, the data of use to the two methods are not identical.

The issue, at first glance, would seem to be an empirical one. Numerous studies have pitted the intuitive skills of experienced psy-

BOX 27.4

CREATIVITY: A CREATIVE ANALYSIS

Russell Baker, a *New York Times* columnist, was stirred to the following moving response to a few of J. P. Guilford's tasks designed to assess creativity. We quote only his more restrained creative comments:

Think of eight to twelve uses for each one of the following objects: (a) A rubber ball. (b) A brick. (c) A wire clothes hanger. (d) A one foot ruler.

(A)—Uses for rubber ball: (1) Games. (2) Plug up rainspouts. (3) Throw at neighbors' dogs when they start sniffing around your boxwood.

(B)—Uses for a brick: (1) Construction. (2) Destruction. (3) Place under short movie actors during love scenes to put them in kissing range of leading ladies. (4) Hold in hand when greeting encyclopedia salesmen at front door.

(C)—Uses for a wire clothes hanger: (1) Hang clothes on. (2) Unbend and use curled end to jab ineffectually at rubber ball plugging up rainspout. (3) When visiting an enemy, place wire hanger in one of his closets containing other wire hangers, thus triggering wire hangers' well-known propensity to tangle with other wire hangers and inducing nervous breakdown in enemy when he goes to closet.

(D)—Uses for a one foot ruler: (1) Prop windows open. (2) Snap in two to relieve nervous tension.

For this purpose, keep one foot ruler in closet containing wire hangers.

Make a sentence out of these ten words in one minute: chap, night, the, stories, clever, one, late, me, told, interesting.

You want me to write, "The clever chap told me interesting stories late one night," and then mark me off as uncreative. Nobody creative has written a phrase as ridiculous as "the clever chap" since 1909.

The only conceivable sentence a creative man could make of this puzzle is: "Interesting—the clever stories told late one night chap me."

Try to think of four to eight things that might happen if we suddenly had three arms.

1. When asked by their wives to bring home a case of milk, a wheel of cheese, five gallons of paint, etc., men would say, "I've only got three hands."

2. The millions of people unable to afford new three-armed wardrobes—dresses, shirts, suits, etc. —would have to wear their extra arms under their clothing. Thus, eventually, everybody would become ashamed of having a third arm and women would be arrested for showing them on the beach.

3. The price of manicures would rise fifty per cent.

4. Some embittered failure whose future was destroyed because he failed to do well on a psychological test would immediately start eliminating America's leading research psychologists, always carrying the murder weapon in the new third hand which the F.B.I. would have had no time to fingerprint.

RUSSELL BAKER. Observer: Three arms and a wire hanger. *The New York Times*, December 12, 1965, p. D10. © The New York Times Company. Reprinted by permission.

chologists against statistical methods, each employing the same information to predict the same outcome. Gough (1962), reviewing the evidence, believes that it points to the superiority of the statistical approach. As he points out, however, the two approaches have not been evaluated under entirely comparable conditions.

Indeed, there is good reason to suspect that these comparative studies are loaded (unintentionally) in favor of the statistical mode of prediction. Most often this is done by restricting predictor *information* to what is statistically manageable and selecting for prediction a simplified, quantifiable outcome. The very clues that might be of advantage to clini-

cal judgment are too subtle and elusive to enter the competition, and the prediction of complex, contradictory, and erratic behavior characteristics of so many of us is avoided. Baughman (1972), in an excellent overview of the data and issues in this contest, reaches the conclusion that a fair, hence valid, verdict is not yet possible.

The essential point in this controversy, however, is not who wins, but how prediction can be improved. Prediction contests do not reflect the psychologist's typical approach to prediction. He may often employ statistical methods to achieve gross classifications and then rely upon his intuition to refine them further. For example, an applicant to a school of architecture who scores low on a test of proven predictive validity might be ruled out of consideration by a statistical prediction equation, but an intuitive judgment might come into play to reverse the decision. Perhaps the candidate's obvious high motivation for further education and his intense identification with a grandfather who achieved eminence in this field would influence the final decision.

Clearly, comprehensive assessments of personality and predictions from such assessments raise questions that cannot be immediately answered. What is certain is that there is room for improvement and that, in the primary quest for a greater understanding of personality, psychological research and theory will necessarily serve the secondary goal of prediction of human behavior.

SUMMARY

1. There is no one best way to measure any given personality characteristic. The choice of a measurement instrument depends in large part on the definition of personality that one has adopted.

2. Ratings are simply the assignment of a numerical score that indicates one's judgment as to observed individuals' standings on a given personality trait. Ratings can be expressed in a variety of forms, including rating scales, Q-sorts, and adjective checklists.

3. Criteria for evaluating the validity of ratings are numerous and no single one can give adequate assurance that the ratings truly describe the person. For this reason several kinds of criteria should be employed whenever possible.

4. Sources of data for rating personality include direct observation of behavior in a variety of settings and interviews with the person being evaluated. The person may also provide self-ratings.

5. Situational tests provide an opportunity to observe behavior in standardized life-like situations that can reveal personality data.

6. By responding to a personality inventory an individual can provide information that permits his evaluation on a large number of personality characteristics. There are two main approaches to designing such inventories: the a priori method in which the items within the inventory are fairly directly related to the traits being measured and the empirical method where the connection, though statistically demonstrable, may not be at all apparent.

7. Variations in persons' tendencies to agree with personality inventory items generally, or with socially desirable ones, may affect the validity of measurement. However, such response sets are themselves measurable, and they are thus of interest in personality assessment.

8. By having a person relate what he sees in an ambiguous stimulus pattern, such as an inkblot, we can often infer certain of his underlying personality characteristics. Such projective techniques, which include the Rorschach and the Thematic Apperception tests, require highly skillful interpretation if they are to provide valid measurements.

9. Personality assessment involves comprehensive evaluation of personality, using both a variety of measurement instruments and a range of situations in which behavior is observed. This general procedure is at times applied to further our understanding of selected groups of individuals, such as highly creative persons.

10. Inferences concerning personality may be derived intuitively from all available observational data, or such data may be statistically combined to yield quantitative predictions. Although the latter approach does seem more often to be valid, a fair comparison of the two approaches is difficult.

GLOSSARY

adjective checklist A personality-descriptive instrument consisting of a large number of trait adjectives (e.g., warm, irritable, responsible). The observer simply indicates which are true of the person being described.

interview schedule A set of questions designed to elicit specified information. The questions may range from open-ended ones, which permit the respondent to range freely in his responses, to ones which limit answers to prescribed categories, as in the usual public opinion survey.

ipsative rating Assigning ratings to describe the relative importance of the set of traits *within* the person, as in Q-sorting. (cf. **normative rating**)

normative rating Assigning ratings to describe the position of a person on a given trait relative to other persons. (cf. **ipsative rating**)

personality assessment A procedure for the comprehensive appraisal of personality and the prediction of individual behavior that employs a large number of different measurement instruments and techniques.

personality inventories Methods for the measurement of traits of personality like those reflecting interests, attitudes, emotional adjustment, social relations. Such inventories consist of a large number of simple statements or questions, each to be answered in terms of specified categories. A given trait is measured by the total score on a large number of items.

personality structure The particular manner in which the individual's traits, abilities, motives, values, and so on are dynamically organized to form his unique personality.

projective techniques A method intended for the measurement of deeper-lying tendencies in a person, tendencies not readily ascertainable through more direct methods. They include the presentation of weakly structured or ambiguous stimulus materials (e.g., inkblots), into the perception and interpretation of which the perceiver is said to project tendencies of which he may be unaware.

Q-sort A form of rating in which personality-descriptive items are assigned to categories to reflect their relative importance or salience in characterizing a person. (see **ipsative rating**)

ratings Perhaps the most widely used method of measuring personality traits. The person's score on a given trait dimension is determined by his placement on a rating scale by a rater. There may also be self-ratings.

response sets Attitudinal factors tending to introduce bias into self-report personality inventories. One such factor is social desirability, in which a person tends to agree with an item that is generally considered to express a good characteristic and tends to disagree with less desirable items.

self The I or me of which the person is aware in his thoughts, feelings, and actions. The self, like any other perceived object, has a structure with various properties and is subject to development and change. The term "self" is to be distinguished from the terms "ego," "personality," and "organism." The self is but one part of the total personality of the individual.

situational tests A method for measuring personality traits in which subjects are observed in standard test situations that are approximate replicas of real-life situations. A test situation often involves interpersonal behavior among several subjects being tested.

determinants of personality

DO YOU KNOW...

- whether it is obvious at birth (or during infancy) that a set of twins is identical or fraternal and . . .

- how the answer to this question is critically important in determining to what extent personality is inherited?

- that experiences of mothers during pregnancy sometimes can affect their offspring's characteristics?

- that certain physical illnesses, such as asthma and ulcers, are related to psychological stresses of certain sorts in physically susceptible persons?

- that there is some truth in some "old wives' tales" such as that a person's body build can tell us something about his personality but . . .

- why it is that the reasons for such links between personality and physical make-up are difficult to determine?

- in what ways the speed with which the adolescent matures affects both his adolescent and his adult personality?

- that the wisdom of breastfeeding a child depends on the mother's personality?

- what characteristics of mothers and fathers are related to tendencies in their children to become like them?

- that firstborns tend to be different from other children?

unit 28

CONTENTS

In Units 26 and 27 our treatment of personality has been a misleadingly static one because personality *description*, like a still photograph, tends to freeze its subject at a single point in time. But, as we all know, an individual personality is the always growing and changing result of many factors—from childhood through adulthood. In fact, in the philosophy and psychology of some cultures it is impossible to speak of *the* personality because of this constant flux (see Box 28.1).

As we now consider the many kinds of factors that help determine personality at the different stages of an individual's life, it will become clear that we are confronted with the most complex and least completed of psychology's tasks. There is research evidence that personality is influenced by factors that arise from hereditary and somatic sources, as well as from early childhood experiences and from social and cultural determinants. But we shall also soon see that theoretical explanations of all such influences are, at best, incomplete and imprecise. You will also notice that, in certain respects, this unit may appear to cover the same ground as our discussion of mental disorders and behavior pathology (Unit 24). However, this discussion of determinants of personality emphasizes the variations within the *normal* range, though we must be careful to recognize that no sharp distinction between the normal and the abnormal can safely be drawn.

HEREDITARY FACTORS

As we have seen in the twin studies discussion in Unit 10, page 206, there is convincing evidence that genetic constitution plays some role in determining individual differences in intelligence among persons of the same background. The data on genetic determination of the non-intellective aspects of personality are not as clear. For one thing, the available measures of intelligence are better validated and more widely accepted than are the measures of most per-

BOX 28.1

AN INDIAN VIEW OF PERSONALITY

The historian Arnold Toynbee has suggested that the Indian world of the sixth century B.C. saw the individual human personality as a complicated network of relations among innumerable psychic events, rather than as a single stable enduring structure. He writes:

> . . . Buddha made the discovery that the supposed indivisibility of an "individual" personality was an illusion. With the discerning eye of intuition, He diagnosed a personality as being a fleeting series of innumerable successive psychological states. . . . [Each] was discontinuous with both its predecessors and its successors. Two forces, and two only, held them together: the wind of desire, which drove them along in company like a herd of hurrying cloud-racks, and the load of *karma*—the cumulative balance of the self-recording moral profit-and-loss account to which desire gives rise in its vain attempt to satisfy itself.

A. TOYNBEE. *A Study of History, Vol. 12: Reconsiderations.* New York: Oxford University Press, 1961.

sonality attributes. And, in general, less research work has been done on the inheritance of personality. Nevertheless, the available evidence does seem to indicate that heredity plays a powerful role in influencing certain aspects of personality. Possibly most influenced is "temperament," a term that refers to such facets of personality as mood, reactivity, and energy level. In this general area animal breeders have something of interest to tell us. They have long been aware, for example, of the marked differences in temperamental characteristics of animals of various breeds and strains. Some breeds of dogs are placid, others skittish and easily upset. Carefully controlled studies in behavioral genetics, reported in Unit 1, page 19, confirm this picture.

Studies of Kin Resemblance

Similar studies with human beings are understandably lacking, so that we must rely on less direct lines of evidence. Foremost among them are studies of kin resemblance, that is, studies of the degree to which *relatives* of the people we are interested in show similar personality characteristics. The major limitation of these studies is that environmental similarity usually goes along with genetic similarity. Children of the same parents tend to be exposed to the same family atmosphere, so that any resemblance in personality among them may not be regarded as exclusively reflecting hereditary factors. We all know children who take after their parents, but this fact alone, when it is indeed a fact rather than a family myth, can by itself confirm nothing about the extent of genetic influence.

Comparisons of fraternal and identical twins do provide some useful clues, however. For example, Gottesman (1963) finds that identical twins are more alike in personality on several scales of the MMPI and the CPI (see p. 677) than are fraternal twins. Other investigators (e.g., Nichols, 1965; Schoenfeldt, 1968) report similar differences for adolescent twins—identicals versus fraternals—on various personality and interest questionnaires, though the computed heritability estimates for such measures are not highly consistent and are considerably lower than for ability measures (see Unit 10).

But to interpret these findings as evidence for a hereditary factor assumes that the *environments* of identical twins are no more similar than are those of fraternal twins. When we consider such facts as the custom of dressing identical twins alike and the difficulty that even friends have in telling them apart (being therefore less able to treat them differentially), the assumption of no-more-similar environments is not easily supported. However, under certain circumstances and for certain personality characteristics an exception must be made (see p. 693).

An ingenious way to bypass the problem of possible environmental differences in the rearing of identical and fraternal twins has been indicated by Freedman and Keller (1963), who made monthly assessments of various physical, mental, and emotional characteristics of twins during the first year of life. The critical

Determinants of personality—social and cultural influences.

A—Photo by Melissa Shook; B—Photo by Robin Forbes; C—Photo by Irene Stein; D—Photo by Irene Stein.

point of this study is that during the first year of life it is not at all obvious, without special tests, whether a given pair of twins is identical or fraternal. The parents of identical twins therefore could not have been treating them more alike throughout the first year than the parents of fraternal twins were treating their children. For the same reason, the investigators could not accidentally introduce bias into their observations, bias that might make identical twins spuriously appear more alike than fraternal ones. Only after the year of observation was completed were the identical/fraternal differences diagnosed (by means of blood-group determinations) and only then was the degree of resemblance on various traits calculated, separately, for the now-known sets of identical and fraternal twins. The major finding of this study was that, for *every* characteristic measured, identical twins showed greater similarity than did fraternal twins, indicating at least some degree of hereditary influence throughout a broad sampling of traits.

Of course, if children are raised by other than their own parents, hereditary and environmental factors tend to be separated. If, furthermore, the children are identical twins reared in different families, the experimental situation for evaluating genetic influence is ideal. The reader will recognize this situation as one version of the twin-study technique that has proved so valuable in studies of the heritability of intelligence (see Unit 10). An effective study employing this design for personality traits was carried out in England by Shields (1962), who, through an appeal on a BBC television program, was able to locate forty-four pairs of identical twins who had been reared apart for a substantial period of time. Most had been separated by the age of six months, and the separation had endured for a minimum of five years. Primarily from this same source, Shields also located an equal number of identical twins whose homes had been the same throughout their childhoods. At the time the twins in both groups were assessed—through interviews, intelligence tests, questionnaires, and physical examinations—they ranged in age from eight to fifty-nine, although most were in their thirties and forties. Great care was taken to assure that the twins were in-

deed identical, employing such techniques as comparison of blood groupings, fingerprints, tendency to color blindness, and physical characteristics.

The outcome of this investigation strongly supports the influence of hereditary factors in the determination of a number of characteristics. Identical twins, whether raised apart or together, when compared to a third group of thirty-two pairs of fraternal twins, were very much more alike in almost all characteristics measured. For example, identical twins reared apart had an average weight difference of 10.5 pounds, whereas those raised together differed by 10.4 pounds. Contrast this similarity with an average weight difference between fraternal twins of 17.3 pounds. Similar results, that is, minimal differences between both sets of identical twins and substantial ones for fraternal twins, were also found for intelligence and for questionnaire measures of temperament. Even smoking habits showed this same kind of result: 78 percent of the separated twins were both either smokers or nonsmokers; 71 percent of the reared-together twins showed this similarity in smoking habits, but only 50 percent of fraternal twins were thus similar.

But the complexity of analyzing the intricate interplay of hereditary and environmental factors even in such twin studies is well demonstrated by a further and unexpected finding by Shields. It turned out that for certain personality measures, identical twins raised apart were actually *more* similar than were identicals raised together. That it, the effect of a common family environment for those raised together was to render them less, rather than more, similar. The reason for this seemingly paradoxical finding is probably that for those pairs living together the very fact of their twinship had an effect on their personality development. Slight initial differences between the twins in such interpersonal traits as dominance, influenceability, extraversion, etc., may have been magnified as they lived together and interacted. Analogous results were obtained by Wilde (1964), who found that fraternal twins raised apart resembled each other *more* than fraternals raised together with respect to scores for neurotic instability, extraversion, and self-critical versus self-defensive test-taking attitudes.

This general hypothesis, that interaction may lead to discordance between the twins in personality and behavior, seems to have been suggested first in 1883 by Sir Francis Galton, who observed the tendency of one twin to be a leader. It has been further suggested that a differentiation of personality, or division of labor, occurs between twins, so that one acts as a sort of minister of foreign affairs for the pair, while the other assumes the role of minister of domestic affairs. A number of other publications dealing with twin relations are summarized by Koch (1966). They support the impression that there are traits that, despite a possibly high genetic component, are made discordant as a result of twins being raised together. When they are reared separately the genetic determinant of behavior apparently is given a better opportunity to manifest itself.

SOMATIC FACTORS

In terms of mechanisms, hereditary influences express themselves, of course, through **somatic factors**. Somatic factors refer to the physical and physiological make-up of the individual, such as his characteristic hormonal activity, neurological status, acuity of sense organs, and bodily build. It is obvious, however, that such somatic factors are not solely genetic in origin; they are always to some extent determined also by environmental influences. Disease and diet are obvious factors of this sort. Indeed what we sometimes think of as a genetically based somatic characteristic often turns out to be primarily environmentally based. We must remember that the environment begins its influence on the child not at birth, but at conception.

Prenatal influences upon the developing organs and functions of the fetus are thus one example of an environmental (*in utero*) origin of a somatic characteristic. Ader and Conklin (1963) have found, for example, that pregnant rats that the experimenters handled and played with during pregnancy produced litters that were significantly less emotional, even when fully grown, than were litters from mothers who had not been so handled. One possible reason for this effect is that the manipulation, which is apparently anxiety-provoking for rats, caused hormonal changes in the mothers that in turn were transmitted to the fetuses via the mother-fetus blood exchange and affected their postnatal personalities. A related explanation is that, since stress has been shown to affect food intake in animals, the resultant change in nutritional status may in turn affect the fetus. (And, as discussed in Unit 10, p. 216, nutrition of the mother affects the child's mental ability.)

Clearly, prenatal influences on personality —and especially on human personality—require considerably more investigation. However, the general principle is probably sound that the experiences of the mother during pregnancy, by altering the uterine environment of her developing offspring, may influence the child's somatic make-up and thus his personality, intelligence, and other characteristics. This is still a far cry from the myth that the mother can create a musical genius *in utero* by assiduous concert-going during pregnancy, but, as with many myths of mankind, this one may well contain its kernel of truth.

Whatever the determinants of somatic factors may be, there is no doubt that differences among people in bodily constitution and physiological functioning can have effects upon personality. For instance, we noticed earlier that unusual glandular conditions may markedly affect the individual's development—as in the case of cretinism resulting from undersecretion of thyroid hormone. Serious diseases occurring at crucial stages of development, or chronic ill health in general, may often be associated with personality changes.

Psychosomatic Disorders

The causal connections between somatic factors and personality functioning are difficult to disentangle. Not only may somatic factors influence behavior and personality, the reverse may also be true. For instance, there are many kinds of bodily or somatic events that may be caused by behavioral or psychological factors. Certainly we are all aware of the massive and delightful orchestration of physiological responses that can be set off by the sight (or thought) of a much-loved one. Or, though the tune is quite different, we all are also familiar with the equally intense bodily reactions to a fearful situation. When psychological factors lead to chronic or long-lasting somatic disturbance, we speak of **psychosomatic disorders**. One of the common psychosomatic disorders is stomach ulcers, which are assumed by many to be caused by chronic anxiety. It is unlikely, of course, that psychological factors are the exclusive determinants of any disease or somatic process. It is possible that, for some individuals, ulcers may be primarily attributable to anxiety, whereas for others some constitutional susceptibility may be the major cause of the disorder. Most often, however, one may suspect an *interaction* between a constitutional predisposition and personality factors. Some individuals with high degrees of constitutional susceptibility may thus develop ulcers under relatively mild stress; others with low degrees of susceptibility may develop ulcers only when stress is severe; and still others may never develop ulcers, regardless of the emotional burdens they may bear.

J. H. Block et al. (1964, 1968) tested this kind of formulation with regard to childhood asthma, a condition long suspected of having psychological origins. Asthma is a somatic allergic reaction, and these investigators classified each of a number of asthmatic children as high or low on the Allergic Potential Scale, which included such items as skin reactivity to certain allergens, total number of different allergies, and a family history of allergy. Then for these children the experimenter obtained measures of various psychological factors that have been proposed as contributing to the development of childhood asthma. The major finding was that, of these asthmatic children, those who were low on the Allergic Potential Scale had experienced more of these deleterious psychological factors than had the children who were high on the scale. For example, mothers of low allergic-potential children, in comparison to mothers of equally asthmatic but high allergic-potential children, were more poorly adjusted, had more marital conflict, and generally felt more ambivalent toward their children. In brief,

then, childhood asthma was primarily a psychologically determined disorder for some children and a somatically based disorder for others. Put another way, some of these children might never have developed asthma if they had not had particularly stressful psychological pressures, whereas others, without any psychological pressures, would have developed asthma anyway. The caution sounded here is that it is misleading to assign a blanket designation to any physical disorder as psychosomatic, or necessarily reflecting the influence of personality.

Indirect Somatic Influences

Not every somatic factor that affects personality does so *directly*, that is, by providing a structural or physiological mechanism that determines the individual's functioning. The effect may be indirect, mediated by others' reactions to the person. A physically crippled person, if regarded with obvious pity by others, may develop inferiority feelings and excessive shyness simply because of this pitying reaction, not because of the handicap produced by his crippled state. A person with a black skin (or any color but white, for that matter) has been treated differently from persons with white skins in many ways, usually degrading, in white-dominated cultures. Personality traits, usually unfavorable ones, have long been attributed to persons solely on the basis of their skin color. This unhappy situation is the indirect result of other persons' reactions to skin color rather than a result of any inherent personality correlates of skin color.

The factor of social appraisal also immensely complicates the problem of interpreting correlations found between personality traits and types of body physique. If it is true that fat men are jolly, is this because of a direct effect of physical constitution on temperament or simply because the fat man seeks to accommodate himself to society's stereotype that all fat men are jolly? And, if the latter, *why* the stereotype? That there is some relationship between personality traits and types of body physique (regardless of which is cause and

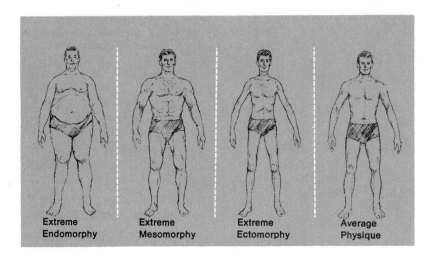

Extreme Endomorphy · Extreme Mesomorphy · Extreme Ectomorphy · Average Physique

BOX 28.2

PHYSIQUE AND TEMPERAMENT

A particularly interesting attempt to show relationships between physique and temperament has been made by W. H. Sheldon and his colleagues at Harvard University. In his original study he examined and measured thousands of photographs of nude male bodies and concluded that every physique can be identified in terms of the respective amounts of three components: *endomorphy,* the fatty, visceral component; *mesomorphy,* the muscular component; *ectomorphy,* the skinny component. A person's somatotype, that is, his overall body build, is described by a three-digit number indicating the amount of each component. For each component the figure originally ranged from seven at maximum to one at minimum. The scale has since been extended upward to account for deviant cases, and the entire scheme has also been applied to the classification of body types in women.

The figure illustrates persons extreme in a given component, with minimum amounts of the other two components. It also shows a person whose physique approaches the middle value on all three components.

As a second step, Sheldon isolated three main clusters of personality traits that he considered adequate to account for all the important individual differences in temperament. These clusters, which could also be rated on a seven-point scale, were:

Viscerotonia. Relaxed posture, love of physical comfort, slow reaction, indiscriminate amiability, deep sleep, need of people when troubled, and so on.
Somatotonia. Assertiveness of posture and movement, love of physical adventure, competitive aggressiveness, general noisiness, need of action when troubled, and so on.
Cerebrotonia. Restraint and tightness in posture and movement, overly fast reactions, inhibited social response, poor sleep habits, chronic fatigue, need of solitude when troubled, and so on.

Sheldon hypothesized that a given physique and a given temperament are different expressions

which is effect) has been supported by considerable research (see Box 28.2).

Adolescent maturation rate A particularly clear example of the difficulties encountered in

separating the direct and indirect effects of somatic factors is provided by research on personality correlates of adolescent maturation rate. As we saw in Unit 2, puberty is characterized by very highly visible changes in body size

of the same genetic factor. He predicted that endomorphy would go along with viscerotonia, mesomorphy with somatotonia, and ectomorphy with cerebrotonia.

In order to check these predictions, Sheldon somatotyped 200 college men and then rated each of them on the three temperamental components, on the basis of prolonged observations of their behavior. The correlations between somatotype and temperament proved to be astonishingly high in the direction predicted by Sheldon. The correlation between endomorphy and viscerotonia was .79, that between mesomorphy and somatotonia .82, and that between ectomorphy and cerebrotonia .83.

Unfortunately, as critics have pointed out, these correlations are simply too good to be true; sources of measurement error and complexity of personality determinants being what they are, we cannot expect to find simple relationships of this magnitude. Sheldon had failed to ensure that the two classes of measurements were made independently of one another. Because he himself had rated both physique and temperament, it is probable that, without his intending it, his knowledge of the subjects' body builds influenced his ratings of temperamental traits.

Although it is true that no subsequent investigation, using greater experimental precautions, has been able to reproduce correlations as high as Sheldon's and that some have found no significant relationships between physique and temperament, the consensus after more than twenty years of sporadic investigation supports the main outlines of Sheldon's formulations. One of these studies, by psychologists J. B. Cortés and F. H. Gatti at Georgetown University, employed a highly objective method to assess somatotype and, for temperamental ratings, depended upon self-descriptions by subjects, who checked off adjectives they felt characterized their personalities. Temperament scores were then obtained by summing the checks of appropriate clusters of adjectives. For a sample of 100 college women the physique-temperament correlations (in the same order as reported earlier) were .36, .47, and .49—statistically all highly significant.

The design of this study seems to ensure that physique and temperament were measured independently. Furthermore, the authors argue, because people tend to describe themselves in flattering terms, the temperamental ratings, being to that extent in error, should show lower relationships with physique than might be found with more objective personality assessments. But it is also possible that these correlations merely represent the fact that self-ratings reflect acceptance by the individual himself of cultural stereotypes attached to his own body build. As we have suggested the fat man learns to satisfy society's expectation that all fat men show "indiscriminate amiability."

Research with children might appear to help settle this question, for, presumably, the child's behavior has been less molded by cultural expectations than has the adult's. M. Davidson, R. McInnes, and R. Parnell find support for the predicted physique-temperament relationships in seven-year-olds. However, R. M. Lerner and S. J. Korn, working at the City University of New York, found that boys as young as five and six, as indicated by their judgments of drawings of each main type of body build, already had well-developed preferences for the mesomorphic build as well as negative attitudes toward endomorphy and ectomorphy. Thus, we are still left with the dilemma of separating cause and effect.

A kernel of truth does seem to be lurking here. If and when the existence of physique-temperament relationships is firmly established, the next challenge will be to determine the roles of genetic and cultural factors in such links.

W. H. SHELDON, S. S. STEVENS, & W. B. TUCKER. The Varieties of Human Physique. New York: Harper & Row, 1940.
W. H. SHELDON & S. S. STEVENS. The Varieties of Temperament. New York: Harper & Row, 1942.
J. B. CORTÉS & F. H. GATTI. Physique and self-description of temperament. American Psychologist, 1964, 19, 572.
M. DAVIDSON, R. McGINNES, & R. PARNELL. The distribution of personality traits in seven year old children: A combined psychological, psychiatric and somatotype study. British Journal of Educational Psychology, 1957, 27, 48–61.
R. M. LERNER & S. J. KORN. The development of body build stereotypes in males. Child Development, 1972, 43, 908–920.

and build, as well as by numerous hormonal changes. Because boys, for example, can differ by five or more years in the ages at which they begin and complete this metamorphosis into adulthood, two men who have near-identical physiques may, for several years during their youth, have presented quite different appearances. One may have been several inches taller than the other and appeared considerably older and more masculine. Therefore the first question that arises is whether or not any personality differences were induced by these temporary physical differences. If so, a second and by now familiar question may be raised: whether such differences are attributable to differences in reactions to them by their families and friends or, rather, to the direct effects of the hormonal differences that led to the differing maturational rates in the first place.

Jones (1965) summarizes the results of several studies on these points in reporting that the early-maturing boy, in adolescence *and* adulthood, tends to be a rather poised, responsible individual who lives up to society's standards and expectations and generally makes a good impression. The late-maturer, in contrast, is often restless and highly expressive, and relatively unsuccessful socially during his adolescent years. In adulthood, however, he tends to become more self-reliant and tolerant than the early-maturer and tends to show greater intellectual interests. Jones attributes these enduring differences primarily to differences between the boys in their social stimulus value; for example, early-maturing boys are more likely to be treated as adults at an earlier age and to adopt adult roles, possibly in somewhat inflexible form. Peskin (1967), working with boys from another longitudinal personality study, finds many of the same personality differences but places greater explanatory emphasis on intangible factors; for example, the late-maturing boy has had more time to become psychologically better prepared for the hormonal upheaval accompanying puberty. This factor may have made it possible for him to grow up into a more adaptable adult at a slower rate.

The picture for girls is quite different. In comparison with late-maturers, the early-maturing girl appears to experience difficulty in controlling her emotions and often becomes socially withdrawn—quite the opposite of the social poise shown by her male early-maturing counterpart. But by adulthood she is quite changed, and generally evolves as psychologically healthier than the woman who matured late (Peskin & Livson, 1972).

In all these studies the magnitudes of the personality differences attributable to matura-

tional rate, whatever the means by which they may be mediated, are quite small. What is true of maturational effects is also true of other personality determinants. No single factor has decisive influence.

EARLY EXPERIENCES

Most personality theories place heavy stress on the role of childhood experiences, and this stress has led to voluminous research on the effects of various early childhood experiences upon personality. In this section we will consider only a very few of the types of early experiences that have been shown to affect the course of personality development. But there are, as you will see, sharp contradictions in the findings and interpretations even in this extremely limited sampling of research.

Perhaps the most durable and heated controversies have centered on the proper and improper methods of feeding, weaning, and toilet training and on their alleged consequences for personality formation. There have been shifting fads and fashions in these and other child-training practices, often governed by ill-tested assumptions. Stendler (1950) presents an unnerving review of the enormous vacillations in child-training practices that have been recommended by experts in women's magazines since 1890. In that first decade love and affection were declared to be panaceas for every childhood emotional problem. Later on (1910–1920) the reverse was "true"; mothers were cautioned against the dangers of cuddling babies and urged to adhere to strict feeding schedules and uncompromising discipline. Sigmund Freud, the psychoanalyst, brought focus for a time on the love-and-affection polarity; J. B. Watson, the behaviorist, by stressing conditioning principles in child training, returned it to the no pampering pole. The pendulum has continued to swing to and fro in this fashion and is no doubt doing so—in one direction or the other —as these words are being read.

Feeding Practices Meanwhile, along with exhortation, research fortunately continues regarding the relative merits of such practices as bottle feeding or breastfeeding, late or early weaning, fixed or flexible feeding schedules, early or late toilet training. Heinstein (1963), for example, explored the general hypothesis that, with respect to early feeding regimes, it is not the precise *form* of the practice that is significant, but the particular *meaning* it has for the infant. The same practice can be quite different psychologically, depending upon the manner in which the parent carries it out. Heinstein explored the later incidence of emotional difficulties and behavior problems as related to different patterns of nursing. His conclusion gives no comfort to seekers after simple guidelines for correct maternal behavior, because he found that the best pattern of nursing (breast versus bottle, long versus short duration) depended upon the personality characteristics of the mother as well as on the child's sex:

> . . . neither breast nor formula [bottle] feeding appears to be preferable, given either a favorable or an unfavorable environment for boys. Girls with a warm mother did much better with breast feeding rather than with formula feeding, whereas girls with a cold mother showed less disturbance if formula fed rather than breast fed. For boys, short nursing was to be preferred with an unfavorable environment, but long nursing was the regime of choice if the boy's personal-social environment was favorable. For girls, the reverse was true. Short nursing resulted in fewer problems when the mother was stable, while long nursing was associated with less maladjustment if the mother was unstable.

To complicate the picture even further, the very early, innate personality of the infant may also determine what is best practice. On the basis of longitudinal studies, Thomas et al. (1968) report that activity level, for example, is a quite stable trait in infants from birth onward and that such early appearing temperamental differences should determine parents' planning of appropriate child-rearing practices. Specifically, they report that attempts to introduce change (e.g., weaning, toilet training) relatively early for infants displaying low activity and reactivity levels resulted, at times, in some emotional disturbance in the child. Some disturbance also resulted from introducing such changes relatively late for highly active infants.

Separation from mother   A similarly complex picture emerged from Moore's (1964) study of the effects on personality development of various forms of separation from the mother. Previous research by a number of investigators had demonstrated that prolonged and extreme maternal deprivation, as is sometimes the fate of orphans or of young children from broken homes, interfered with normal emotional and intellectual development. Moore found, however, that breaks in a continuous mother-child relationship are not necessarily injurious. Working with children (aged six to eight) from an English longitudinal study of personality development, among whom many different patterns of maternal separation could be found, he offers the following generalizations: Children whose mothers continuously cared for them became more conforming and self-controlled, with a somewhat greater tendency toward guilt reactions. *Stable* substitute care, by relatives or others, resulted in greater self-confidence and less inhibition in the child. However, when the child's separation from the mother involved frequently changing arrangements for substitute care, insecurity, anxiety, and dependence were common results.

Sex-role typing   Yet another area in which early experiences seem to play an important role is sex-role typing, the process whereby we learn to behave as males and females in a given culture. Children generally are encouraged by both parents to be and feel like the same-sex parent. By now it will come as no surprise if we mention that many factors affect how successful sex-role typing will be for a given child. In general, boys and girls tend to embrace the sex role of the same-sex parent to the extent that that parent is warm, nurturant, and supportive. In addition—and in the case of boys only—greater dominance and authority in the father facilitates learning of the traditional masculine role (Hetherington & Frankie, 1967).

There is apparently a certain asymmetry in the efforts of parents to influence the sex-role behavior of their children. In a study which included consideration of parents' attempts to affect the play interests of their nursery school children, it was found that, so far as *encouragement* of sex-appropriate play was concerned, mothers were more active in this regard with their daughters and fathers with their sons. However, when *discouragement* of sex-inappropriate play was looked at, both parents were far more involved in influencing their boy's behavior (Fling & Manosevits, 1972).

Birth order Even one's birth order within the family, which is in a certain sense an early experience, has a role in determining personality characteristics. This is not as far-fetched as it sounds, although it has turned out to be an investigators' mare's nest! Briefly, the idea is that the occupant of a particular birth order, say, the firstborn child, is reared differently by parents from their other children, at least within a given culture. A firstborn, for example, will for obvious reasons receive more attention, be more likely to carry the family's ambitions, be assigned a dominant role with respect to later children, etc. So far the findings on ordinal position are quite mixed (Babladelis, 1972; Sutton-Smith & Rosenberg, 1970), but there is a rather substantial accumulation of evidence that firstborns—perhaps the most distinctive group—tend, at least in Western cultures, to be more affiliative (i.e., seeking others' company), achieving, and conforming than are their siblings. There is also the suggestion—stronger for boys—that firstborns tend to be less aggressive, perhaps because they are more exposed, earlier, to adult-only standards of appropriate socialized behavior (Feshbach, 1971). A number of studies indicate that firstborns in later life tend to achieve greater prominence in a variety of ways; for example, American Presidents are more likely to be firstborns, at least those elected during times of crisis (see Table 28.1).

The effects of birth order are compounded by the fact that this factor interacts significantly with such other family variables as total number of children and number of boys and girls in the family. Thus, while birth order is no doubt a significant early experience, it is understandable that, in reviewing the research in this general area, Sarason and Smith (1971)

TABLE 28.1 BIRTH ORDER OF PRESIDENTS IN CRISIS AND NONCRISIS ELECTIONS

	Crisis Elections	Noncrisis Elections
Firstborn and only sons	9	8
Later-born sons	1	13

NOTE: Crisis election years are those just preceding and including each of eight wars: 1812 (War of 1812), 1848 (Mexican War), 1860 and 1864 (Civil War), 1896 (Spanish-American War), 1916 (World War I), 1940 and 1944 (World War II), 1948 (Korean War), 1964 (prior to major troop commitment in Vietnam War).

Data from L. H. Stewart (1970).

mildly suggest that "birth order is the sort of variable that some experimentalists find annoying...."

This fragmented sampling of research findings indicates a little of what psychologists are coming to know about the influences of early environment on personality development. An important qualification should be borne in mind regarding such influences. It is easy, but incorrect, to regard them as somehow bridging time and acting upon personality directly at some later date. Even in the case of extreme traumatic experiences in childhood, like the death of a parent, there is no raw wound whose pain continues to interfere directly with later human relations. Rather, if an effect in adult life is apparent, it is necessarily traced through a long, unbroken chain of emotional-choice points from the original experience to the current personality difficulty. Initially the loss may have caused the child to become frightened and to withdraw in mistrust, which, in turn, may have disturbed and even angered others in his family, which, in turn, may have made him the more fearful, and so on and on. The possible number of paths is theoretically infinite, so that any given long-term effect is by no means inevitable. When viewed in this perspective, no childhood experience can be regarded as irrevocably damaging and no maladaptive adjustment to such an experience is forever irreversible. Furthermore, there is the recent suggestion that childhood traits may not be able to reliably forecast adult adjustment and that, rather, personality characteristics evident in early adolescence (and, to a *lesser* extent, in late adolescence) only are predictive of adult psychological health (Livson & Peskin, 1967; Peskin, 1972).

SOCIAL AND CULTURAL INFLUENCES

The range of possible long-term effects of any childhood practice or experience becomes staggering when we bring into the picture the broader social context in which the event occurs. Once we apply the criterion of cultural relativism—simply, the notion that a given event must be interpreted within the values and norms of the particular culture in which the child is being reared—it seems foolhardy to assert the existence of a law that systematically links any experience to a particular adult personality outcome. To take a particularly clear-cut example, in one society the act of circumcision at puberty heralds the boy's entrance into manhood and is perceived by the newly made man as an experience of pride as well as of pain. In another group, in which this practice is not common and is not imbued with this critical psychosocial meaning, circumcision would necessarily exert a very different effect upon personality development. The boy and/or his social group might see it or even define it as an act of punishment, or they might see it as only a casual medical procedure, presumably neutral with respect to personality meanings and effects.

Such social and cultural influences are by no means uniform *within* a given society. (For a frightening narrative of the effects on adults exposed briefly to a subculture, see Box 28.3, p. 702). We are all well aware of the persistence of values and practices that accompany social and cultural differences within communities in the United States and that, to a greater or lesser extent, preserve ethnic identities, even over many generations of residence in this country. Such subgroups are sometimes praised for this allegiance to their native cultures, but at other times they are criticized for their lack of adaptability. Be that as it may, what concerns us here is that different groups within this nation do raise their children according to differing sets of values and do hold their adult members to differing standards of conduct. To some—but only to some—extent this variation reflects differences in national character, and much has been written by social psychologists, anthropologists, sociologists, and writers of

travel guides on such questions as why the Chinese are presumably industrious, the Germans efficient, the Latins loving, and so on. Such material is beyond the scope of this section, although Box 28.4, page 703, conveys the flavor of this approach. Instead, we note only the obvious fact that we must add social and cultural influences to those genetic, somatic, and early experience factors we have already discussed. There is, however, a social influence that does seem to cut across ethnic-group lines: It is social class, particularly as it affects child-rearing practices.

Social-Class Determinants

The man on the street tends to believe, for example, that the rich and poor differ in the ways they bring up their children. In this respect he is right—socioeconomic-class membership does relate systematically to differences in the values and practices of parents within these groups as they raise their children. Bronfenbrenner's (1958) summary of social-class differences over the past three decades does point to certain generalizations: For one thing, working-class parents are more likely to employ physical disciplinary techniques; middle-class parents are more prone to psychological means like reasoning, disappointment, and withdrawal of affection.

Focusing on more recent practices, a comprehensive study of differences in professed values and practices of 400 Washington, D.C., families (half working class, half middle class) underlined some of the distinctive differences in the social contexts for fifth-grade children in these homes. In one report Kohn (1959a) notes that, whereas parents of both groups valued the trait honesty highest in a list of seventeen traits that they considered desirable to instill in their children, working-class mothers chose obedience, neatness, and cleanliness as next most important. By contrast, middle-class mothers selected self-control, curiosity, and consideration for others as valued traits. The implication here of a difference on a dimension from external conformity to inner control is certainly not in line with the common bias that working-class parents are unconcerned with imparting

BOX 28.3

PATHOLOGY OF IMPRISONMENT

I was recently released from solitary confinement after being held therein for 37 months (months!). A silent system was imposed upon me and to even whisper to the man in the next cell resulted in being beaten by guards, sprayed with chemical mace, blackjacked, stomped and thrown into a strip-cell naked to sleep on a concrete floor without bedding, covering, wash basin or even a toilet. . . . I would rather die than to accept being treated as less than a human being. . . . I now think of killing—killing those who have beaten me and treated me as if I were a dog. I hope and pray for the sake of my own soul and future life of freedom that I am able to overcome the bitterness and hatred which eats daily at my soul, but I know to overcome it will not be easy.

The above letter was received by Philip Zimbardo, a Stanford University psychologist. What follows is excerpted from Zimbardo's account:

This eloquent plea . . . came to me recently in a letter from a prisoner . . . because he read of an experiment I recently conducted. . . . In an attempt to understand just what it means to be a prisoner or a prison guard, Craig Haney, Curt Banks, Dave Jaffe and I created our own prison. We carefully screened over 70 volunteers. . . . They were mature, emotionally stable, normal, intelligent college students from middle-class homes. . . . None had any criminal record and all were relatively homogeneous on many dimensions initially.

Half were arbitrarily designated as prisoners by a flip of a coin, the others as guards. These were the roles they were to play in our simulated prison. The guards . . . made up their own formal rules. . . . The prisoners were unexpectedly picked up at their homes by a city policeman in a squad car, searched, handcuffed, fingerprinted. . . . There they were stripped, deloused, put into a uniform, given a number and put into a cell with two other prisoners where they expected to live for the next two weeks. . . .

At the end of only six days we had to close down our mock prison because what we saw was frightening. It was no longer apparent to most of our subjects (or to us) where reality ended and their roles began. . . . There were dramatic changes in virtually every aspect of their behavior, thinking and feeling. In less than a week the experience of imprisonment undid (temporarily) a lifetime of learning: human values were suspended, self-concepts were chal-

lenged and the ugliest, most base, pathological side of human nature surfaced. . . .

We had to release three prisoners in the first four days because they had such acute situational traumatic reactions as hysterical crying, confusion in thinking and severe depression. Others begged to be paroled . . . when their request for parole was denied, they returned docilely to their cells. . . .

About a third of the guards became tyrannical in their arbitrary use of power, in enjoying their control over other people. . . . Some of the guards merely did their jobs. . . . However, no good guard ever interfered with a command by any of the bad guards; they never intervened on the side of the prisoners, they never told the others to ease off . . . and they never even came to me as prison superintendent or experimenter in charge to complain. . . .

By the end of the week the experiment had become a reality. . . . The consultant for our prison, an ex-convict with 16 years of imprisonment in California's jails, would get so depressed and furious each time he visited our prison, because of its pathological similarity to his experiences, that he would have to leave. A Catholic priest who was a former prison chaplain in Washington, D.C., talked to our prisoners after four days and said they were just like the other first-timers he had seen.

Zimbardo was so affected by this social experiment that he wrote:

Individual behavior is largely under the control of social forces and environmental contingencies rather than personality traits, character, will power or other empirically unvalidated constructs. Thus we create an illusion of freedom by attributing more internal control to ourselves, to the individual, than actually exists. We thus underestimate the power and pervasiveness of situational controls over behavior because: (a) they are often non-obvious and subtle, (b) we can often avoid entering situations where we might be so controlled, (c) we label as "weak" or "deviant" people in those situations who do behave differently from how we believe we would.

Certainly this is a powerful testimonial to the potential influence of extreme situations on feelings and behavior. But does it justify the conclusion that "individual behavior is largely under the control of social forces and environmental contingencies"? Perhaps. But, remember, the environment is considerably more deviant from that which we encounter in everyday life, and the prisoners did vary in their reactions, no doubt as a function of their individual and probably enduring personalities.

P. G. ZIMBARDO. Pathology of prisons. *Society*, April 1972, 4–8.

BOX 28.4

COMPETITION AND CULTURE

S. Kagan and M. C. Madsen, psychologists at the University of California (Riverside), have carried out a series of investigations involving hundreds of Mexican and American children, in which they systematically observed behavior in a variety of specially designed games intended to measure competitiveness and cooperativeness with one another.

In one of these studies three groups were compared on these interpersonal characteristics: Mexican children from a tiny rural community in Baja, California, and Mexican-American children and Anglo-American children, both from a major American city. Sharp contrasts could be drawn between the rural Mexican and the urban Anglo-American groups, all aged seven to nine years. For example, on a task in which complete cooperation with one another would in fact result in both children receiving rewards (toys)—and failure to cooperate would deny rewards to both—rural Mexican children, on the average, were completely cooperative on 63 percent of the occasions, whereas the Anglo-American children cooperated only 10 percent of the time. And, looking at the other side of the behavioral coin, the Anglo-American urban children tended to be unrelenting in their competition and rivalry with one another twice as often as did the rural Mexican group (14 percent versus 7 percent). In general, on the various measures, the scores of Mexican-American children fell somewhere between the other two groups.

In another study, involving bean-bag throwing at a series of targets of varying difficulty, Madsen and Kagan observed that parents of rural Mexican children tend to set lower goals (easier targets) for their children than do mothers of urban American children. Also, if a child fails to meet even these lower goals, characteristically the mother directs her child to try an even easier task. Not so for American mothers; most often they urge their children to try

again at the just-failed target. Furthermore, Mexican mothers reward their children almost to the same extent following unsuccessful as following successful performance, whereas American mothers almost never give a reward after a failure by their child.

Not cooperating when it would in fact pay off is not an adaptive response in American children, and being paid off as often for failure as success may lead in Mexican children to a less effective orientation to learning. Thus, in these respects, neither group, noted the investigators, lives in the best of all possible worlds, and they see a useful role for cultural therapy—becoming aware of the values and constraints of one's own and others' cultures and learning to function in ways more suited to one's true needs. In these respects Kagan outlines some culture-therapy prescriptions:

> For rural Mexican children, I would like them to see the payoff of assertive behavior, that what they do makes a difference, that there is more than just external forces that are beyond their control, guiding their lives.
>
> For the Anglo children, I would like to see them have the freedom to sometimes just be, rather than always have to strive to succeed, to develop some sensitivity to the needs of others, as well as their own needs.

Of course, the most effective cultural therapy would be change in the social and economic realities with which these children will have to cope, realities that their parents appreciate and are attempting to prepare them for. Variations in the ways children are raised in all cultures are not due to erratic parental whims; rather they tend to reflect and may be highly adaptive to the varying facts of life that are found over the full range of human societies.

S. KAGAN & M. C. MADSEN. Cooperation and competition of Mexican, Mexican-American, and Anglo-American children of two ages under four instructional sets. *Developmental Psychology*, 1971, **5**, 32–39.
M. C. MADSEN & S. KAGAN. Mother-directed achievement of children in two cultures. *Journal of Cross-Cultural Psychology*, in press.
S. KAGAN. Personal communication, 1973.

values for good behavior to their children. These findings grow in interest when viewed with the finding of another of Kohn's reports (1959b) on these families in which (as reported by Bronfenbrenner, 1958) more working-class parents frequently employ physical punishment in order to ensure that their children achieve the general characteristic of respectability represented by the specific traits they most highly value. Middle-class parents, on the other hand, are found to eschew physical methods but are quite likely to apply verbal methods like shaming and even sarcasm.

Perhaps the intent and/or effect of the **socialization** methods employed by working-class parents is to train their children to stay out of trouble, and, indeed, they risk more retaliation from the larger community for delinquent acts than do middle-class children. In contrast, middle-class parents seem to place greater emphasis upon self-control and inner standards that, in the long run, may be expected to be more effective but, conceivably, may also represent a luxury in child-rearing practices not so available to the working-class parent.

There is of course much more to say about social and cultural influences upon personality development, even as they pertain to social-class differences alone. Such class differences are reflected in the schools and peer groups whose values become so dominant in the life of a child while he is growing into adolescence. But we must pause and hope that we have conveyed something of the complexity of determinants of personality development. Perhaps a fitting conclusion to this discussion of the intricately intertwined determinants of

personality and of our present inadequate theoretical understanding of their relations is the following quotation. It summarizes the impressions of the director of a forty-year study of the personalities of almost 200 individuals whose development had been examined intensively since early childhood.

We have found from a review of life histories that certain deficits of constitution and/or environment, and certain unsolvable interpersonal conflicts have long-term effects upon the individual, up to age 30. We have also found that much of personality theory based on pathological samples is not useful for prediction for the larger number of persons. Many of our most mature and competent adults had severely troubled and confusing childhoods and adolescences. Many of our highly successful children and adolescents have failed to achieve their predicted potential. It is clear that we need more sophisticated theory that will help us weigh the relevant components —the types of stress, the compensating supports, in various types of organisms, at the various developmental periods—if we are to predict which combinations of factors forestall and which combinations facilitate maturity and strength. (Macfarlane, 1964)

SUMMARY

1. Personality development is subject to myriad influences—hereditary and somatic factors, childhood experiences, social and cultural determinants. The contributions of each of these factors are not yet precisely defined nor certainly are their interactive effects.
2. Studies of kin resemblance, especially comparisons of identical with fraternal twins, are the primary source of evidence for the heritability of personality characteristics. The evidence from such studies indicates a substantial genetic component in a variety of traits. Additional useful data are obtained by comparing twins raised together with those raised apart.
3. Genetic influences on personality are necessarily transmitted by somatic factors, but somatic factors are by no means entirely a reflection of heredity. They often are mediated by changes in the uterine environment triggered by the mother's experiences.

4. Psychosomatic disorders illustrate the reverse influence of psychological factors upon bodily functioning. But for such influences to be expressed it is probably necessary that certain bodily predispositions, or susceptibilities, to these disorders exist.

5. Some relations between body physique and personality are likely, but their underlying bases—genetic or cultural—are not yet clear.

6. Variations in the rate of individual maturation during adolescence affect personality development, although differently for the two sexes.

7. Whether or not to breastfeed an infant and when to wean it depend on personality characteristics of the mother.

8. Separation, as such, of the infant from the mother is not a critical factor in personality development. However, provision of *stable* substitute care is beneficial.

9. Boys and girls tend to emulate the sex roles of their same-sex parents to the extent that parents are warm and nurturant toward them. The authority exerted by parents is also a factor.

10. The birth order of a child within a family influences personality. Firstborns show the greatest differences in this respect. However, other factors such as the total number of children (and their sexes) are relevant.

11. Social classes differ in the ways they bring up children, and these differences appear to reflect the adaptive demands intrinsic to their places within our society.

GLOSSARY

psychosomatic disorders Bodily disorders caused by psychological factors, for example, stomach ulcers caused by chronic anxiety.

socialization The process by which socially determined factors become influential in controlling a person's behavior.

somatic factors (in personality) Physical characteristics of the organism, such as hormonal levels, sensory acuity, body build, and so on, that can influence the rate and direction of the individual's personality development and functioning.

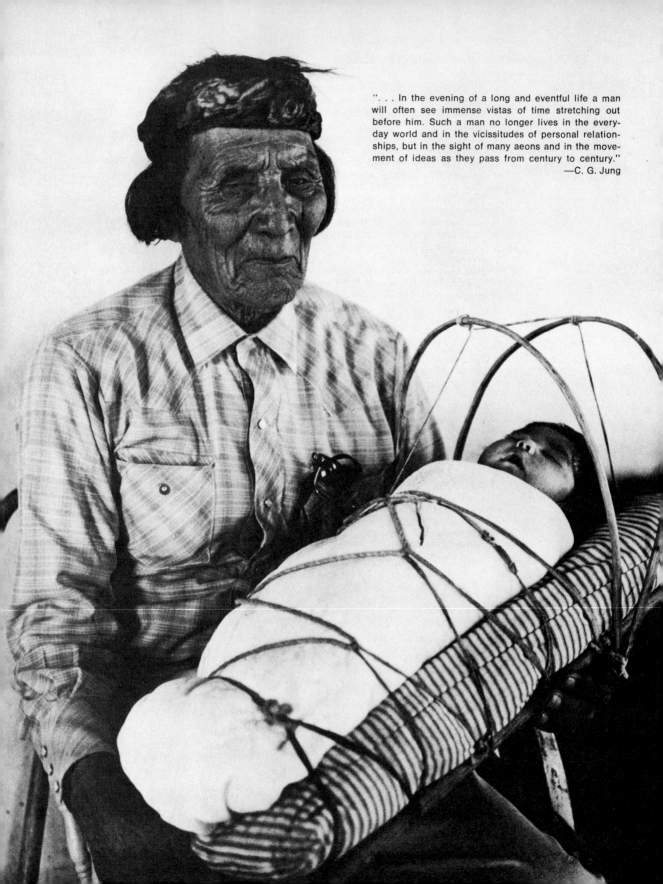

". . . In the evening of a long and eventful life a man will often see immense vistas of time stretching out before him. Such a man no longer lives in the every-day world and in the vicissitudes of personal relation-ships, but in the sight of many aeons and in the move-ment of ideas as they pass from century to century."
—C. G. Jung

theories of personality

unit 29

DO YOU KNOW...

- *what actually is the Oedipus complex?*

- *in what sense everyone experiences an inferiority complex while growing up and that having such feelings of inferiority may be necessary to become psychologically mature?*

- *that a major and respected personality theory gives importance to the accumulated experience of the species, in addition to that of the individual?*

- *what is meant by "searching for one's identity"?*

- *under what circumstances we may learn the response of not thinking and how this can have important effects on personality development?*

- *what humanistic psychology is?*

- *how failure to satisfy basic needs such as for physical safety can interfere with the satisfaction of higher needs such as for self-fulfillment?*

Photo by Ulli Steltzer/Courtesy, Firestone Library, Princeton University

CONTENTS

Personality theories are general theories of behavior. Unlike many other theories in psychology that focus on a delimited area of behavior—visual perception, memory, motor learning—personality theories attempt to account for the full range of human behavior, thought, and emotion. In these attempts, personality theorists may be suspected of delusions of grandeur because their self-defined task is no less than to explain all human behavior and the individual differences that lie therein. Their mandate encompasses that of all other psychological theorists and a bit more. A learning theorist may choose, occasionally at his peril, to rule out certain broad areas of psychological phenomena in his construction of an explanatory schema. For example, conditioning theory flourished for several decades with almost total disregard for motivational factors. Personality theory, however, is denied this simplification not only by definition but also by necessity. Its assignment is to comprehend the functioning of the whole man, and, in its attempts to do so, it dare not rule out any kind of determinant or any form of behavior lest, because of the interactive and integrated nature of personality, the entire enterprise be seriously threatened.

Any theory of personality, therefore, even if it chooses for the time being to neglect a particular factor, must nevertheless provide room within its general framework for ultimate handling of what it has neglected. A psychoanalytic theory, for example, may have nothing to say concerning the effects of physiological differences among individuals, but it must remain possible at least to think about such effects in the language and within the context of the theory.

Small wonder, then, that theories of personality frequently are open to the charge of indulging in generalities. Very often not enough is known to justify anything more than a tentative formulation for some regions of the uncharted wilderness called personality; any premature assertions may shut off certain areas to further exploration and foreclose later, and necessary, modification and elaboration. But a theory with too many generalities may prevent effective formulation of research problems and may thus be denied the fruits of testing that are indispensable for its further development. Fortunately, theory-guided research on personality continues and contributes to such development.

Personality theory, however, takes its current form less from the results of empirical research than from the sifted experiences, insights, and speculations of those, like psychotherapists, who observe and ponder the human condition in its everyday, experimentally uncontrolled functioning. In the discussion that follows, therefore, we shall emphasize a few of those theories that currently most stimulate personality research and those that most influence psychotherapeutic practice.

Early personality theories developed from a need to understand and treat persons who exhibited difficulty or discomfort in their functioning and life adjustment. The observations which guided these theorists came from the examination of the life histories and current functioning of people who sought help for their problems. And out of this study of the unhappy and disturbed came concepts that were designed to explain the normal personality as well. Thus early personality theorists were in the main clinical practitioners. Sigmund Freud is undoubtedly the prime example of such a personality theorist.

Many modern-day personality theories are increasingly dependent on experimental or other nonclinical data, involving attempts to observe in a systematic fashion normal personality manifestations. This means that the focus on the abnormal as the primary data source is fading.

A FRAMEWORK FOR PERSONALITY THEORIES

This unit introduces some of the basic definitions, assumptions, and concepts associated with a rather select group of theories. Each theory has been chosen because of its historical importance and current impact and because it represents a relatively distinct approach to the study of personality. Taken together, they do not by any means exhaust the inventory of workable (and being worked on) personality theories, but their study will introduce this broad and varied field.

The discussion will be organized around three major groupings: The **psychodynamic theories**, originating in the psychoanalytic schools of thought, are represented here by Sigmund Freud and Carl Jung; the **social-learning theories**, or behaviorist approaches, are represented by the approach of Dollard and Miller; the **phenomenological theories**, with their humanistic points of view, are typified by Maslow's formulations.

These classifications directly parallel the scheme employed in Unit 24 on mental disorders. Reference to those discussions will help in understanding what is to follow; for much the same reason, our treatment of various forms of psychotherapy (Unit 25) may usefully be reviewed. After all, there must be intimate connections among what makes people what they are—the stuff of this unit, the ways in which personality development can go awry, and the ways in which it can be set right again.

In order to summarize the features of each theory we will consider a number of underlying issues to which many of these theories address themselves. These issues, following a scheme from Hall and Lindzey (1970), involve certain assumptions about human nature, growth, emotions, and thinking, even though some of the theories are not explicit regarding these assumptions.

Goal-directedness Does the theory assume goal-striving or purposiveness as an essential and prime moving force in the individual? If so, what is the nature of this underlying purpose?

Unconscious determinants What place is given to unconscious determinants of behavior; that is, to what extent does the theory propose determinants of behavior that are operating without an individual's awareness?

Biological factors and the role of early and current experience What role is assigned to hereditary influences and, more broadly, to biological factors? Also, what relative emphasis is placed on early developmental experience compared with contemporary life events?

Unique versus universal processes Does the theory focus more on the uniqueness of the individual or more on general underlying processes that apply universally?

PSYCHODYNAMIC THEORIES

Psychodynamic theories strive to understand personality in terms of mental functions (contrasted with behavioral acts only) that may be both rational and irrational, conscious and outside of conscious awareness. Frequently these theories also involve notions of internal (intrapsychic) conflict and attempted resolution. The nature of the central conflicts and the ways of resolving them that are adopted by an individual may be said to comprise his personality.

Freud and Psychoanalysis

Sigmund Freud, a Viennese physician born in 1856, moved from a promising career in physiological research into the treatment of mental disorders. Starting about 1890 and continuing to his death in 1939, Freud evolved, at first alone and later with the aid of an ever-growing circle of colleagues, what is today known as "psychoanalysis." Although Freudian theory certainly has roots in earlier speculations, it represents so profound a revolution in thinking about personality development that the history of modern theories may, in all justice, be considered to begin with Freud (see Figure 29.1).

Psychoanalysis is many things—a theory of personality, a method of psychotherapy, a research tool, and, for many, a philosophical view of life. Its effects on man's thought during the first half of this century have been incalculable, and its force continues in its many modern variants. Our concern here is only with the psychoanalytic theory of personality.

Id, ego, superego Freud conceived of man as a dynamic system of energies. The personality is constructed of three main systems—the **id**, the **ego**, and the **superego**. These three systems of psychological forces, dynamically interacting with one another, produce the individual's behavior.

The id is the primitive system, out of which gradually evolve the other two. The id is the sole source of all psychic energy (**libido**). The energy takes the form of *unconscious* instincts that drive the organism. The instincts derive from the inherited biological nature of the organism. The two main classes of instincts are those concerned with survival (life instinct) —hunger, thirst, and especially sex—and those concerned with destructive impulses (death instinct), which take the form of aggression. The id impulses are primitive, blind, irrational, brutish demands for immediate gratification (the pleasure principle).

But the id is, by definition, blind; that is, it has no access to the outside world, to objective reality. Whereas the id can conjure up an image of food, it is by itself incapable of initiating behavior appropriate for actually acquiring food. In short, it cannot satisfy the biological instincts it harbors. As a consequence, there emerges the ego, a part of the personality that mediates between impulses and reality, by redirection or control, so that actual gratification can be achieved. The ego responds on conscious and unconscious levels and includes cognitive processes—perceiving, thinking, planning, deciding. It serves as the intermediary with the external world.

In expressing basic impulses, the individual may run afoul of the rules and values of his society. These rules and values are made clear to the child by his parents' rewards and punishments for his conduct. (One view as to how this training specifically takes place is found in Unit 30, p. 739.) As a consequence, there gradually evolves in the child the superego. The superego is a system of restraining and inhibiting forces upon those basic impulses—especially sex and aggression—that are regarded as dangerous or detrimental by society if they are directly expressed in their raw and primitive forms. The superego in time becomes the internal substitute for the external forces of parental and societal control. It becomes, in short, the child's conscience and moral sense.

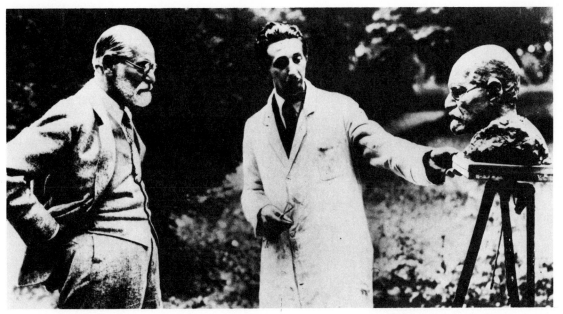

FIGURE 29.1   Sigmund Freud contemplates a bust of himself sculpted for his seventy-fifth birthday by O. Nemon. Photo by Wide World Photos

A well-developed superego tends to result in automatic and unconscious control of id impulses.

When the id impulses are blocked from immediate and direct gratifications by the environment, by parental or societal restrictions, or by the superego, the libidinal energies are displaced toward substitute forms of satisfaction—forms that are attainable or permissible. A person whose raw aggressive impulses are thus blocked from direct expression may become a biting drama critic or a punitive judge. This displacement is not, of course, deliberate but is, according to Freud, unconscious. Flexibility in the directions of such displacements accounts for the rich diversity in people's patterns of specific interests, motives, attitudes, and habits. The critical point, however, is that such displacements do not imply new motivational energies but only the channeling and modification of the original ones. In classical psychoanalysis, *all* motivation traces its source to the biological id instincts. As we shall see, this

Freudian axiom is one that later theory has most diligently and effectively challenged.

The id, ego, and superego should not be thought of as entities, as little men who run the human psyche. Rather, they are convenient shorthand terms for different kinds of psychological processes serving different functions. The forces of id, ego, and superego are often in conflict, and this conflict leads to arousal of anxiety. Each person develops his characteristic way of reducing these anxieties, and these characteristic ways (called "defense mechanisms," which are discussed in Unit 23, p. 578) constitute a distinctive aspect of the personality structure of that individual.

Psychosexual stages   Freud conceived of the process of personality development as consisting of a sequence of stages that blend into each other. Individual differences in adult personality, he assumed, are mainly traceable to the specific manner in which the person experiences and handles the conflicts aroused in the three psychosexual stages through which the child passes during the first five years of life.

In the **oral stage**, the first year, the infant's attention is centered mainly on the erogenous zones of the mouth. He is pleasure-bent on sucking and later on biting. If there is inadequate gratification or anxiety and insecurity surrounding the nursing situation, there may be a permanent fixation of some libidinal energy on oral activities. This fixation may give rise, in the adult personality, to the so-called oral character, a syndrome of traits including dependence, passivity, greediness, and excessive tendencies toward oral activities, such as in smoking, chewing, or garrulous speech.

In the **anal stage**, the second and third years, the infant's concern centers mainly on anal activity. Here again, as a result of parental emphasis on toilet training and taboos on anal eroticism, enduring anal fixations may occur. The anal character associated with such fixation includes such traits as defiance, stubbornness, messiness, and a tendency to inflict pain on others, or the opposite, excessive compliance, orderliness, cleanliness, and punctuality. Often, these opposing tendencies alternate in the same individual or place him in chronic conflict.

In the **phallic stage** the child's interest turns to the sexual organs and to the pleasures associated with their manipulation. (Freud scandalized Victorian society by the assertion that childhood sexuality, with its sexual fantasies and masturbation, is universal, a view that is now more generally accepted.) At this stage there typically occurs what Freud called the "Oedipus complex" (after the classical myth of King Oedipus, who unwittingly killed his father and married his mother). During this stage the boy normally directs his erotic feelings toward his mother and the girl toward her father. By thus placing themselves in the fantasied roles of father and mother, respectively, the boy and the girl establish primary **identifications**, out of which later derive all the complex male and female social identifications that constitute a great part of the adult personality. But complications in the usual course of the Oedipus complex may lead later to development of homosexuality, authority problems, and rejection of socially approved masculine and feminine roles.

Following this stage and characterizing the relatively quiescent period from about age five to the first stirrings of adolescence is what Freud called the **latency period**. Within the strict framework of psychoanalytic theory no important personality changes can be expected because no new instinctual impulses appear—a generalization that later evidence seriously challenges. Society, presumably temporarily satisfied with the accomplishment of its primary civilizing, or socializing, requirements, is content to permit the child to develop along an already determined direction and within already prescribed limits. Conflicts are therefore minimized, anxiety is little aroused, and fundamental personality change is unnecessary and therefore unlikely.

But this truce between instinctual demands and the constraints of reality, according to Freud, shatters with the emergence at puberty of biologically mature sexual drives. But, psychologically, the adolescent is not yet an adult and may be caught in a net of hard to understand turmoil. Now the final challenge of personality development takes place—the **genital stage**. If too much libidinal energy has already been tied up through fixation at the three pregenital stages, the individual will fail to meet the challenge of the final stage of development. He will fail to shift his focus away from his own body, from his own parents, and from his own immediate needs to that of adult heterosexuality and to a sense of larger responsibility, which includes the needs of others. In a word, he will remain immature. Or, put another way, if he accomplishes all these developmental tasks, he has achieved psychological maturity—the hallmark of the genital stage.

The impact of Freudian theory This glimpse of Freudian theory is scarcely adequate for an understanding of its dominant influence upon subsequent theorizing about personality development. Furthermore, the very pervasiveness of the psychoanalytic outlook makes an appreciation of its contributions the more difficult today. By now it is widely accepted that early experiences and the ways in which childhood conflicts are resolved profoundly affect the course of personality development and the nature of adult character. We also accept the notion that a good part of human motivation is unconscious. Thus, in large measure, what we now regard as axiomatic, even obvious, is the result of a gradual filtering through of these psychoanalytic notions into popular literature, and finally into common sense.

The original Freudian postulates are of course open to question. Does all motivation basically consist of the same unchanging instinctual feelings, or may it not change in essential nature? Are the first five years of life so fatefully crucial for permanent personality make-up, or may not later childhood and adult experiences play even more decisive roles? Are social influences given a sufficiently heavy emphasis? (See Box 29.1, p. 714.) Are sex and aggression really the main motives? Are the Oedipus complex and the oral, anal, phallic, and genital stages really universal, or are they found only in some cultures? Is unconscious motivation so all-important? Almost every one of these questions has been answered in the negative by at least some personality theorists, researchers, and therapists.

In raising and trying to answer such questions, however, most other personality theorists show—either in their building upon Freud's theories or in developing alternative views—a clear debt to the original Freudian conception. Perhaps the most impressive evidence for the viability of psychoanalytic theory is that it has managed to preserve its essential outlines in the context of the various theories that have grown out of it.

Offshoots from this main psychoanalytic trunk have grown in a number of widely different directions and with varying success. Some flowered briefly, then died. Others, most notably the theory of Carl Jung, developed along original lines and continue to flourish, as we shall soon see. Another fruitful branch theory was initiated by one of Freud's students, Alfred Adler, who emphasized the importance of social factors. It is this branch—the so-called neo-Freudian movement—whose outlines are described in Box 29.2, page 716.

A perspective on Freudian theory   In Freudian theory the basic, prime moving force is repre-

sented by the unconscious and generalized biological energy source called **libido**. The unconscious nature of these instincts and their push toward immediate gratification are essential elements in Freud's explanation of personality development. Because the gratification of these instincts requires some activity in the real world, they must be subjected to modification in ways dictated by reality (ego processes) and socially defined morality (superego processes). The specific natures of the compromises, or conflict resolutions, among the id, ego, and superego processes and the stages of development at which they occur determine personality and character. For the most part individuals behave in ways that are unconsciously designed to fulfill instinctual needs at least to the extent that the ego and superego will allow.

Biology, as well as early developmental history and experience, are thus crucial aspects of Freud's theory. While the basic forces and structures of the personality are universal and the same *process* of development is shared by all, there is enormous variety in the ways that individuals resolve basic conflicts. The experiences of each individual's life are unique and so are his particular resolutions. To understand the individual, one must know in depth and enormous detail the particulars of his psychological history. This intimate understanding of the uniqueness of the individual within the framework of the biological and psychological universals is essential to psychoanalysis and psychoanalytic therapy.

Jung's Analytic Psychology

For many years in the early history of the psychoanalytic movement, Carl Jung was a close associate of Freud and his heir-apparent. Jung was, in fact, first president of the International Psychoanalytic Association, a position from which he resigned when personal and theoretical differences caused him to break with Freud and to develop his own brand of psychodynamic theory, which he called "analytic psychology." Nevertheless, Jungian theory has certain similarities to Freudian concepts.

In his early years Jung had intended to study philosophy and archeology. His switch to medicine and science is said to have been influenced by a dream. It will become apparent that such highly personal responses are important aspects of Jung's personality theory; it draws heavily on dreams, myths, and spiritual aspects of culture. An important emphasis in the Jungian approach is on self-actualization, on man's innate aspiration toward selfhood and wholeness.

Personality structure The total personality in Jungian theory is called the **psyche** and is composed of several quite separate yet interacting systems. The ego, much as in Freudian theory, is the largely conscious aspect of mind and is composed of all the perceptions, thoughts, memories, and feelings that are available to the individual; an individual's ego helps him to function in his daily life and also serves to provide

BOX 29.1

ERIKSON AND PSYCHOSOCIAL CRISES

Freud's emphasis on the dominant role of instinctual drives was challenged originally by Alfred Adler (see Box 29.2, p. 716) for its failure to take adequate account of interpersonal and social factors in personality development. Karen Horney, Erich Fromm, and Harry Stack Sullivan are prominent among those who in pursuing this direction were prepared to depart from some of the basic Freudian concepts. On the other hand, Erik Erikson, himself a psychoanalyst, has accomplished much the same socialization process for traditional psychoanalytic theory while remaining within its Freudian framework.

According to Erikson, the individual, as he progresses through the developmental stages, meets a psychosocial crisis peculiar to each stage. It is psycho*social* because society has developed social institutions specific to each stage in the attempt to mold and socialize the individual as he progresses

through these stages. For example, in the first stage the child is completely dependent on the social institution, usually represented by his mother. Freud's oral stage, in addition to its concern with direct oral gratification, thus also presents a psychosocial crisis in which the child is confronted with the issue of trust versus mistrust, particularly in regard to his mother. In resolving this issue, enduring attitudes are developed with respect to such matters as feeling that the world is a safe and nurturant place, being able to offer affection freely to others, and so on.

In Erikson's scheme there are eight such psychosocial crises, each with its own core issue, extending through a life span into old age (see table). Of these crises, most interest has been stirred by his proposal that identity formation is the task, and the crisis, of adolescence. It is at this time that the various, and often incompatible, self-perceptions and aspirations that the adolescent has acquired throughout his development must be integrated if an effective adult personality is to evolve. A boy, for example, can identify with his cheerful and emotionally accessible mother; with his man-

Psychosocial Stage	Approximate Age	Successful Resolution of Issue Leads to
Basic trust vs. mistrust	First year	Optimism, warmth
Autonomy vs. shame, doubt	2–3 years	Appropriate self-control, pride of accomplishment
Initiative vs. guilt	3–5 years	Sense of purpose and direction
Industry vs. inferiority	6 years to puberty	A feeling of competence, of being on top of things
Identity vs. role diffusion	Adolescence	A sense of self, of who one really is
Intimacy vs. isolation	Early adulthood	An ability to form close relationships
Generativity vs. stagnation	Middle age	Productivity and creativity, involvement with future generations
Integrity vs. despair	Later adulthood	A sense of a meaningful life, an acceptance of mortality

him with a sense of identity and continuity.

In addition to conscious processes Jung postulates unconscious processes that are in conflict with the conscious ego processes. There are two distinct spheres of unconscious process. One, the personal unconscious, consists of those experiences and thoughts that, although conscious at one time, have been blocked from awareness but that under certain circumstances

may become conscious again. (This personal unconscious concept of Jung is in many respects similar to the Freudian unconscious.)

In contrast, the **collective unconscious** does not reflect *individual* history and experience, but rather the accumulated experiences of the *species*. *Within each individual is a reservoir of the accumulated culture of mankind throughout its evolutionary development.* It is this idea of a collective unconscious that is the unique and perhaps the most controversial aspect of Jungian theory. According to Jung, its existence is universal and is demonstrated by the readiness of all persons to behave in similar ways in similar situations. The content of the collective unconscious, unlike the personal unconscious, is *never* directly available to conscious thought, although it does have an effect on behavior.

Archetypes   Important components of the collective unconscious are **archetypes.** An archetype is an emotion-laden, universal thought or idea. For example, there is the archetypal image of mother, shared by all, which carries the entire cultural history of this role. This archetype may differ from the individual's actual personal perception, memory, and unconscious image of his own mother. Art, myths, dreams, visions, and hallucinations contain many archetypal images and are our major source of information about them.

Another example: The *anima* and *animus* refer to the elements of the opposite sex that are in each of us. For men, the feminine archetype is anima; for women the masculine archetype is animus. These elements, according to Jungian theory, have developed out of our experience as a species with members of the opposite sex, and the fully integrated adult accepts and uses his opposite-sex component rather than denying its existence. In a very real sense this is the underlying message of some spokeswomen of the women's liberation movement—that both women and men will be more fulfilled and effective, and more able to achieve intimacy with one another, if each recognizes the other's sexual heritage within herself or himself.

There are many other archetypes in Jungian theory but those mentioned should be

---

of-few-words, rather withdrawn, father; and with a happy-go-lucky uncle who at one time played an important part in his life. If the boy, during the course of adolescence, is unable to fashion some coherent self-image from these clashing elements he will suffer what Erikson has called identity diffusion. In more familiar terms, he will not have succeeded in finding himself, and it is this search for identity that the reader may recognize as a recurrent theme in modern drama and literature.

A certain degree of identity diffusion is an almost inevitable, even a desirable, experience of adolescence. One can find himself too early. If the individual decides (although it is by no means a wholly conscious process) who and what he is without the wisdom and perspective gained from experimenting with a number of roles, then his chosen identity may fail to meet later crises or to bring him enduring personal fulfillment. The girl who has always known that she would become a physician runs the risk of having foreclosed life's potentialities too soon.

It is perhaps no accident that such theorists as Erikson have had the most profound influence upon American conceptions of personality. Personality defined as a reality-oriented, continually learning, and always adapting system is indeed more in line with other aspects of the American ethos, with its emphasis upon productivity and adjusting to the immediate situation, than is the classical version of psychoanalytic theory. The latter, with its instinctual anchorings and stress on early experience, seems to place cramping bonds about the individual's potential to change and to adapt. The implications of this evolution for psychotherapy have been equally profound.

E. H. ERIKSON. Identity and the life cycle. *Psychological Issues*, 1959, **1**, No. 1.
———. *Childhood and Society.* 2d ed. New York: Norton, 1963.
———. *Identity, Youth, and Crisis.* New York: Norton, 1968.

sufficient to highlight one major disagreement between Freud and Jung. While *individual* history is a central part of Freudian theory and the very essence of his analytic method and interpretation, for Jung it is a much less important element than the contents of the *collective* unconscious. Where Freud would look for personal drama, Jung would look for archetypal meanings. Another important difference between Freud and Jung is that Freud emphasizes sexuality and biological imperatives as embodied in the pleasure principle, the id, and the libido, whereas Jung assigns little importance to biological forces and instead proposes a purely mentalistic, even spiritual, causation. For example, a woman's conscious perception (ego) of her sexual identity may, for Jung, conflict with the collective unconscious arche-

BOX 29.2

ADLER AND STRIVING FOR SUPERIORITY

The central characteristics of Adler's theory lie in his stress on the social rather than on the biological determinants of personality and in his conception of the eternally upward drive of the self.

In his view, the prime source of man's motivation is the innate striving for superiority. That is, the main aim of life is to perfect oneself; all other motives are expressions of this aim. As Adler put it in 1930:

> I began to see clearly in every psychological phenomenon the striving for superiority. It runs parallel to physical growth and is an intrinsic necessity of life itself. It lies at the root of all solutions of life's problems and is manifested in the way in which we meet these problems. All our functions follow its direction. They strive for conquest, security, increase, either in the right or in the wrong direction. The impetus from minus to plus never ends. The urge from below to above never ceases. Whatever premises all our philosophers and psychologists dream of—self-preservation, pleasure principle, equalization—all these are but vague representations, attempts to express the great upward drive.

The directions taken in the strivings for superiority are in the nature of what he called "compensation," which may be regarded as another of the defense mechanisms discussed in Unit 23, page 578. According to Adler each one of us, very early in life, becomes aware of some weakness or deficiency within himself. At the very least, the inescapable inferiority of every child, relative to any adult, assures the universality of such an experience. The perception of such a deficiency or inferiority calls into play strivings to overcome, or compensate for, the imperfection. Paradoxically, but predictably, the person may ultimately distinguish himself in the very area in which he was most deficient—the painfully stuttering child works hard at overcoming his defect and ends by becoming the fluent orator Demosthenes. Compensatory strivings may also take indirect forms—the bodily handicapped child may devote himself to the pursuit of ideas; the homely girl may become a business tycoon.

The course of personality development, according to this view, is a continuous process of reactions to inferiority—real or fancied—or, in other words, an inferiority complex. And, inasmuch as inferiority can occur in so many spheres and certainly in some form in every person's experiences, there is endless fuel for striving. Adler sees the stage of childhood as especially important, not as in Freud's theory because of the pressures of childhood sexuality, but because, as noted earlier, the intrinsic weakness of the child in a world of adults inevitably results in strivings to overcome these deficits. Inferiority feelings are thus essential requirements of psychological growth. It is only when excessive stress is added to the inferiority or when the strivings repeatedly fail that an inferiority complex may develop, with all its detrimental consequences for further adjustment.

Adler lays great stress on the uniqueness of each personality, reflecting the particular direction of strivings for superiority that the individual has taken. This basic direction tends to be established in childhood as a consequence of the particular inferiorities perceived by the child and the particular methods of coping with them. And this basic direction guides all his behavior and engenders the dis-type of her animus. The conflict here is between aspects of the psyche and does not involve biological impulses striving for expression.

Dynamics of personality In addition to the systems of the personality, Jung postulated that individuals have two basic orientations or attitudes: *extraversion* reflects an orientation toward the external, objective world, and *intro-*

version, an orientation toward the inner, subjective world (see our discussion of Jungian typology, Unit 26, p. 661). While every individual has some of both attitudes, one or the other usually predominates in consciousness and combines with the four basic functions of the personality to create a classification system. All functions are contained in each individual, but once again differences exist in the degree to which they dominate conscious thought or are relegated to the unconscious and emerge only in dreams and fantasy. The four functions are:

thinking—the ideational and intellectual comprehension of self and world

feeling—the evaluation by an individual of other people, situations, or objects, experienced in terms of pleasure, pain, anger, fear, and other emotions

sensing—the perception of reality, or psychic representation of reality

intuition—the unconscious perception of the subliminal essence of reality

The goal of selfhood, according to Jung, is to achieve balance among these functions, although such balance can never be completely accomplished. Basically this approach is a closed system; its prime mover is psychic energy, which operates according to two basic principles: equivalence and entropy. The principle of equivalence is one of conservation of energy: If the investment of energy increases in one element of personality, it must decrease in another element. Thus, energy removed from the ego will be reinvested in another part such as the personal or collective unconscious. The principle of entropy is a principle of homeostasis, or balance: If the ego is invested at any time with more energy than the personal unconscious, there will be a spontaneous shift in this psychic energy distribution to bring them to equivalent levels. It is these two energy principles which, in Jungian theory, keep the psyche in conflict and responsible for personality change.

Whereas Freud gave emphasis to the early stages of development, Jung places relatively greater emphasis on the last half of life where there is a progression toward completeness and selfhood. While the experiences of early development may hamper the individual's attainment

---

tinctive goals, interests, and values that uniquely characterize him.

The paths to perfection vary widely among people. For one man, perfection may be sought in complete knowledge of a certain field of science; for another, in religious revelation. Or it may mean perfection in artistic creation, or in athletic prowess, or in raising a family. What is for one individual the goal of perfection may for other people be anything but perfect—a Hitler striving for mastery of a master race, a psychotic obsessed with committing the perfect murder. But despite such destructive striving Adler thought that, under optimal circumstances of development, strivings for superiority take socially constructive forms that have to do with cooperative relationships with people, identifications with the group, and efforts to bring about the ideal society.

In his then-radical focus on interpersonal and societal factors, Adler set the stage for such later neo-Freudians as Karen Horney and Erich Fromm, both of whom emphasized the critical role in personality development of the continuing search for emotional security in interpersonal relationships, beginning with the family. These theories are all—as Freud's and Jung's are not—social-psychological approaches to personality. And it is not far-fetched to include in this group the highly influential and avowedly interpersonal theory of Harry Stack Sullivan, whose system of therapy is discussed in Unit 25, page 633. That discussion is mentioned here since Sullivan is indeed a first-rank personality theorist as well.

A. ADLER. Individual Psychology. In C. Murchison (Ed.), *Psychologies of 1930.* Worcester, Mass.: Clark University Press, 1930.
H. L. ANSBACHER & R. R. ANSBACHER (Eds.). *Superiority and Social Interest by Alfred Adler.* Evanston, Ill.: Northwestern University Press, 1964.

of selfhood, it is not enough in the Jungian view to look backward at the causes of this blocking; it is necessary also to focus on what an individual personality is attempting to achieve *now*—its agenda for its future.

A perspective on Jungian theory Jung's system is quite complex and difficult to summarize; this brief discussion was intended to convey no more than its flavor. But we can see that considerable attention is devoted to philosophy, myths, and culture and that the theory is less grounded in medical and biological sciences than Freud's. The underlying prime moving force is the individual's striving for selfhood and ultimate integration. While experience may hinder growth, the Jungian model is more clearly oriented toward a theory of optimal personality development than is Freudian theory, oriented as it is toward the points where development goes astray and leads to pathology.

The unconscious in Jungian theory is of course of central importance. But it is not an unconscious of impulses to be ultimately controlled. Rather, it is the collective unconscious which is the source of raw material to be integrated (though never really made conscious) into the total personality. While Jung is relatively indifferent to biology, he finds the history of the species of primary importance in determining the contents of the collective unconscious. Exactly how these images and archetypes are transmitted is not clear, but mythology, religion, and the occult, he asserts, help us to understand the universal images and archetypes.

Though underlying growth needs, personality structure, and dynamic principles are common to all persons, considerable attention is paid to the individual's unique experience of universal phenomena. Thus, the examination of the dream, imagination, and creative experience of a person is a way of learning how the person is synthesizing his individual and collective experience. Jung and Freud represent two quite distinct directions taken within the broad outlines of psychodynamic theories of personality.

Along these lines, Hall and Lindzey's (1970) verdict on Jung and his place in today's controversies is worth quoting in detail:

When all is said and done, Jung's theory of personality as developed in his prolific writings and as applied to a wide range of human phenomena stands as one of the most remarkable achievements in modern thought. The originality and audacity of Jung's thinking have few parallels in recent scientific history, and no other man aside from Freud has opened more conceptual windows into what Jung would choose to call "the soul of man." It appears likely that with the growing trend in Western society, especially among young people, toward introversion, phenomenology, existentialism, meditation, spirituality, mysticism, occultism, expansion of consciousness, individuation, transcendence, unity, and self-fulfillment, Jung will come to be recognized as the spiritual and intellectual leader of this "revolutionary" movement. It is evident that more college students are reading and reacting favorably to Jung today than was the case a few years ago. Certainly his ideas merit the closest attention from any serious student of psychology.

SOCIAL-LEARNING THEORIES

In a sense Freud and Jung were learning theorists since both assumed that early experiences influence the development of personality. However, neither was explicit about the precise processes by which learning of particular personality traits comes about. It remained for those psychologists whose intellectual origins were in learning theory to specify more clearly the nature of the learning and motivational processes by which personality is developed and modified.

Modern learning theories take various forms but many can trace their conceptual origins to the work of Ivan Pavlov, the Russian physiologist who discovered the conditioned response. This is especially true of the American behaviorist theories as exemplified by J. B. Watson's work early in the twentieth century. B. F. Skinner, at present the most influential inheritor of Watson's ideology, is a direct and potent influence on the current development of behavior modification techniques (Unit 25). These techniques perhaps best define today's most dominant social-learning theory approach to personality development.

Advocates of this approach are committed to an application of experimental methods, often using rats, pigeons, monkeys, and so forth as objects of study. In these respects they depart radically (and almost triumphantly) from the psychodynamic traditions, theories, and even concerns of Freud and Jung. However, the earliest articulate attempt at a personality theory arising from the Watsonian tradition—the classic work of Dollard and Miller (1950)—*did* attempt a link with psychodynamic theory. In fact, their theory has been called "psychodynamic behavior theory" (Mischel, 1971) because it is indeed an effort, in part, to unify basic ideas in psychodynamic theories of the Freudian type with the concepts and methods of learning theorists. To highlight how personality phenomena and theory are handled by behaviorist learning theory and psychoanalytic theory we have chosen Dollard and Miller's work to represent social-learning approaches.

Dollard and Miller

Dollard and Miller sought to recast psychodynamic and especially Freudian theory into a more precise and objective set of formulations, ones that can be tested and revised as required by experimentally gathered evidence. It is on this emphasis that we will focus in order to ease comparisons.

Some basic concepts and mechanisms Dollard and Miller believe that personality is learned and that four important aspects of this crucial learning process can be identified.

1. *Drive.* Any strong stimuli, external (e.g., electric shock) or internal (e.g., hunger) in source, which can impel action, are considered to be **drives**. Ordinarily, the stronger the stimulus the greater is the capacity to elicit behavior directed at *reducing* the drive. Some drives are present in the newborn infant (primary drives) and are associated with biological deficits that, if neglected, threaten the very survival of the organism. At birth, the immediate learning task is the acquisition of responses to provide for the satisfaction of these needs (drive-reducing responses). These

earliest experiences also provide the basis for the development of secondary drives. For example, the infant comes to seek love, affection, or approval from others, since he learns to associate them with the satisfaction of the primary drives. (His mother's response to his cries of hunger is to feed him but, more generally, also to nurture him.) It is these elaborated secondary drives that come to be the basis for much of the behavior we can observe in a society such as our own in which satisfaction of primary drives is relatively easy and hence hardly a source of diversity in learned behavior.

2. *Cue.* While drives impel behavior, the direction of behavior derives from **cues**. Cues determine the response in any given instance. Cues are the signals to which particular responses have been learned. A child quickly learns to respond to a sharply spoken word—"Stop!" The word "stop" functions as a cue.

3. *Response.* A **response**, simply, is what a person specifically does in reaction to a learned cue when impelled to act by a drive state. The response may be as elemental as an eyeblink, but it may also apply to a highly complex pattern of behavior such as the composing of a symphony.

4. *Reinforcement.* A **reinforcement** functions to increase the probability that a particular response will occur in the future in the presence of a particular cue or set of cues. Reinforcements directly *reduce* the strength of either primary or secondary drives. Reinforcers can be positive (a word of praise), and strengthen the response that leads to the *presentation* of the reinforcement. Or they can be negative (a word of disapproval), and strengthen the response that leads to the *removal* of the negative reinforcement.

Like Freud, Dollard and Miller feel that anxiety or fear plays a crucial role in personality development and functioning. For them fear (or anxiety) represents a secondary drive that strongly impels behavior. Fear can become associated with previously neutral cues through a process of learning. (The procedure whereby an infant came to fear furry objects—Unit 24, p. 596—is a dramatic case in point.) Stimuli that have the capacity to elicit fear will continue to elicit fear long after the objective danger is past. Also, any response that allows an individual to avoid the experience of fear will be highly reinforcing and highly persistent. This, roughly, is the social-learning theory of neurotic behavior, and it serves as the basis for the treatment (or modification) of such behavior.

A social-learning analysis of repression Dollard and Miller—to take one example—assert that by using their ideas they can translate the Freudian concept of repression (see Unit 23, p. 578) into social-learning terms. Consider the fact that some types of behaviors are regularly punished in children and consequently can come to be associated with fear. Thus, for example, a child's sexual, aggressive, or dependency behaviors may lead to parental infliction of pain, physical or psychological, on the child. By inhibiting such behaviors in the future, the child reduces the experience of fear; the very act of inhibiting the bad behavior is thus reinforced and is therefore increasingly likely to be repeated. Inevitably, as the child is being punished for disapproved behavior it happens that the punishment also becomes associated even with *thinking* about the acts involved. Then, certain thoughts may arouse fear, so that *not thinking* of certain things may result in the avoidance of fear and anxiety. Since responses that reduce fear are continually reinforced, the not thinking of certain bad thoughts may become a strongly learned habit. This, in simplified form, is Dollard and Miller's explanation for Freud's concept of repression.

Inhibition of behavior and of thoughts that may produce fear assures a temporary kind of comfort; but it prevents the individual from learning ways of achieving satisfaction of the unresolved needs in a manner that does not involve pain and fear. Consider what might happen if eating behavior was subject to consistent punishment in a particular environment. Eating behavior or even thinking about eating would then be avoided, and it is possible that the individual would starve to death because all food-seeking behavior would be absent. However, the absence of food, biologically, would necessarily result in a strong drive reducible only by eating; it would therefore tend to elicit just those behaviors that had in the past been followed by a hunger drive reduction. In this predicament, the individual would be in a state of conflict—specifically, an approach-avoidance conflict as described in Unit 23, page 573.

Higher mental processes The crucial consequences of the conflicts we have been describing, and of the practice of not thinking particular thoughts, are that many needs that might have been dealt with by what Dollard and Miller call the "higher mental processes" cannot be so resolved. These higher mental processes become unavailable in the service of need fulfillment. In man, many responses are tried and rejected through thinking alone (as discussed in Unit 6); this is in part responsible for man's ability to solve problems of a complexity that far exceeds the capacity of lower animals.

When conflict and fear lead to not thinking, or repression, the efficiency of adaptation to the world is then inevitably and considerably reduced. Under such circumstances behavior may appear stupid or irrational to the observer; for Dollard and Miller this process accounts for certain features of neurotic behavior.

A perspective on social-learning theory Social-learning theories of personality of the type represented by Dollard and Miller do not seem to assume any pervasive goal-directedness, nor do they emphasize long-term purposive tendencies in behavior. Rather they attempt to explain behavior in terms of accumulations of learned reactions to immediate situations. Although they do postulate a set of innate motivating forces (called primary drives), these forces do not have direction until learning intervenes. The only goal of these basic forces, just as in Freud's conception, is reduction of tension.

Unconscious determinants do play a role for Dollard and Miller through their concept of not thinking. The importance of this behavior, in their conception, is that it reduces the ability of the higher mental processes to mediate needs satisfactorily and, generally, to see the possibilities for compensatory adaptive behavior.

The basic source of motivational force for Dollard and Miller is primary drives that originate in deficits of a basically biological nature. They of course do place considerable emphasis on early experience for the development of individual differences in personality. Other social-learning approaches to personality, especially those directly underlying behavior therapies, do assign greater influence to contemporary manipulation of reinforcements as a means of explaining and modifying personality—though all assume that previous learning plays a role. And, since the mechanisms through which previous learning affects the personality development of the individual are decidedly universal for social-learning theory, this approach is perhaps the most insistent of all in denying any need to attend to the uniqueness of the individual.

PHENOMENOLOGICAL THEORIES

Perhaps the most diverse theories regarding the nature and purpose of personality development are those that may be loosely grouped under the heading of phenomenological theories. The term "phenomenology" is itself difficult to define; but it generally refers to a broad philosophical position that the ultimate reality—and the one that psychology should study—is that of direct, holistic, and subjective experience, the essential stuff of human existence. This position, if we ignore the many distinctions that would be insisted upon by special advocates of other positions, can thus be seen to include such current approaches to personality as the humanistic, experiential, and even existential.

Some of the theorists we see as sharing this very general approach may be familiar to you; Abraham Maslow and Rollo May are examples. So is Carl Rogers, whose theory and therapy are discussed in Unit 25. Other views may be less well known, such as Kurt Goldstein's "organismic theory" or the "Daseinanalysis" (Being-in-the-World) approach of Ludwig Binswanger and Medard Boss, Swiss psychiatrists of the existential school. Even Erich Fromm, whose notion (and book) on escape

from freedom has been so influential, might be added to this diverse company, though he clearly is closer to the psychoanalytic tradition.

What we see as the cohesive factor for so assorted a group of theorists is—to return to our earlier definition of phenomenology—an insistence that immediate, unanalyzed experiences are the proper raw data for students of personality. The exclusive devotion of social-learning theorists to behavioral data represents the very opposite orientation. And, to the extent that the actual *facts* of childhood and early life are important for psychodynamic theories and not for the phenomenologists, the use of that kind of information also arouses incompatible viewpoints.

At this point we suggest you refer, for a more substantive discussion, to our exploration of phenomenological therapies in Unit 25; at this point in this unit we go on to present in detail the personality theory of a single but typical representative of the phenomenological approach.

Maslow's Self-Actualization Theory

As do others in this group, Abraham Maslow emphasizes the existence of positive growth factors in personality development and functioning; he is most closely identified with humanistic psychologists, a group regarded by many as constituting a third force in American psychology today.

Maslow believed that psychologists have concentrated far too long on the study of man's attempts to reduce tension or to avoid pain and anxiety. Maslow felt that a new emphasis is needed to understand the full range of personality development, one that includes serious consideration of human joy, well-being, and potential for growth.

In an early statement (1954) Maslow asserted that man has a unique psychological nature whose structure includes inherent needs, capacities, and growth potentialities. Full development of the individual involves **self-actualization** of this structure, that is, achieving fulfillment of one's inherent potentials. (Both Jung and Goldstein are precursors of this view.)

Psychopathology, he argued, results from a blocking or twisting of the development of this structure, whereas anything that promotes its development in the direction of self-actualization leads to psychological health and even a transcendence of the ordinary state of normal functioning.

This drive to self-actualization, according to Maslow, is universal. Furthermore, it constantly seeks expression though it is considerably more delicate and fragile than are the underlying, biologically based drives postulated by Freud and by the behaviorist theorists.

Basic needs and meta needs Maslow did not deny the existence of the basic biological needs that so interested Freud and the behaviorists. However, Maslow extended the realm of basic needs, such as hunger and pain avoidance, to include affection, security, and self-esteem. Maslow also recognized the existence of what he calls "meta needs," whose fulfillment accompanies self-actualization (Maslow, 1967). Included would be a striving toward goodness, justice, beauty, and unity.

Basic needs are generated by physiological or psychological deficiencies, the most demanding of which would be hunger or other deficits that actually threaten physical survival. These needs can be arranged in a hierarchy from most to least crucial for immediate survival of the organism. (See Unit 19, p. 462, for a detailed presentation of this hierarchy.) Until the most demanding needs, which are physiological, are satisfied, all the others are excluded. ("When hunger enters the door, love flies out the window.") But when the physiological deficits are attended to, the individual may then attend to higher basic needs such as affection and security. These higher basic needs in turn dominate behavior as long as *their* satisfaction is incomplete or in doubt. Only when satisfaction of the full hierarchy of basic needs has been achieved can the meta goals be pursued and eventually the actualization of a person's full potential take place. However, if the realization of meta goals is frustrated, then the person reacts with apathy, cynicism, and alienation. Such, Maslow would claim, is the

fate of many well-fed and well-cared-for persons today.

Maslow argued that the kind of personality functioning to which we might realistically aspire has not been a serious object for study by personality theorists or even a goal of psychotherapists for their patients. For the most part, Maslow saw their focus as negative, stressing deficiencies in personality rather than attending to and nurturing the positive potential inherent in man. In order to counter this focus on deficit, Maslow sought out and studied individuals who he believed had achieved self-actualization. Through historical documents and interviews with those still living, Maslow did intensive clinical studies of these rare individuals (Maslow, 1970).

Maslow found that self-actualized individuals are realistic for the most part, although most have had deeply mystical or spiritual experiences (see the discussion of "peak experiences," Unit 21, p. 512). The intimate relationships of such persons are typically with only a very few people and they tend to be involving and profound, never superficial. However—and this is seen as no contradiction—they also exhibit a strong need for privacy and detachment. Self-actualized individuals, as characterized by Maslow, have a great deal of spontaneity and their sense of humor is well-developed and rarely hostile. They are also highly creative and they stoutly resist pressures to conform blindly to the culture. It was Maslow's belief that characteristics such as these constitute the dominant personality structure of anyone who is able to achieve self-actualization. To be sure, the furtherance of self-actualization depends upon the prior *and continued* satisfaction of more basic needs, but these basic needs are not the moving forces in personality development. For most other theorists, the basic needs are the exclusive moving forces in personality development.

A perspective on self-actualization theory This approach certainly insists on the intensely purposive nature of man's development, attributable to his innate self-actualizing tendency. Unconscious determinants do not play a strong role in Maslow's conception, although it is clear that self-actualizing tendencies can be crushed by inappropriate or hostile forces, from within or from without.

Early developmental experiences can facilitate or hinder this thrust toward self-actualization. If, for example, the individual never receives the degree of affection, security, and self-esteem that is a necessary prior condition for the self-actualization drive to achieve expression, he may never be able to reach that ultimate state. Thus, in some ways, Maslow regarded his viewpoint as a complement rather than as an alternative to those theories that emphasize instead the deficiency aspects of personality development and functioning.

And, finally, each individual's wanderings, successful or not, toward self-actualization describe a unique path. Maslow's emphasis on the individuality of the person's higher and ultimate destiny has been dubbed as more a new religion than a scientifically testable theory of personality.

SUMMARY

1. Personality theorists set for themselves the ambitious task of attempting to develop totally comprehensive theories to account, in principle, for all human behavior.

2. Although historically these theories were derived mainly from work in clinical settings with disturbed individuals, recently the trend has been toward greater interest in normal personality development and in methodologies that emphasize more systematic, even experimental, data.

3. Personality theories take many forms but there are a number of conceptual issues on which they can be compared usefully. Some of these issues pertain to the relative importance in personality of the following: goal-directedness or purposiveness; unconscious determinants; hereditary and early development experience; stress on the uniqueness of the individual.

4. Freud's personality theory emphasizes notions of internal conflict and proposes that the ways in which these internal conflicts are resolved are the major determinants of personality. For Freud the personality comprises three subsystems, the id, ego, and superego. The id is the reservoir of innate, instinctual forces, the ego embodies the rational, cognitive capacities that develop through contact with reality, and the superego represents the internalization of society's prohibitions and standards. Typical conflicts are between the forces represented by the id, ego, and superego.

5. Freud emphasized the importance of early childhood experience. His studies led him to assume that there is a chronology, a sequence of developmental stages, in psychosexual development. These include the oral, anal, and phallic stages, the latency period, and the genital stage. Psychological maturity is the end result of successful passage through this full sequence.

6. Though many aspects of Freud's theories have been challenged, it is clear that his thinking has had a strong influence on subsequent developments in personality theories.

7. Jung believed that a theory of personality could be enhanced by an understanding of the dreams, myths, and spiritual aspects of the culture in which the individual and his ancestors have lived. Although, like Freud, he subscribed to the idea that unconscious forces are important aspects of personality, he divided the unconscious into two spheres—the personal and the collective. The personal unconscious reflects the individual's particular life experiences, while the collective unconscious reflects the accumulated experience of the species.

8. Within the collective unconscious are archetypes—universal thoughts, images, or ideas—that are the result of the accumulated experiences that have occurred in the history of the species; archetypes influence personality functioning in a variety of subtle ways. Another major determinant of personality functioning for Jung is the integration of four basic functions of the mind: thinking, feeling, sensing, and intuition.

9. Another group of personality theorists, embracing the social-learning approach, base their formulations upon objectively stated, empirically testable principles of learning. The theory proposed by Dollard and Miller is one example of a theory developed within this learning framework; and it is one that explicitly attempts to deal with phenomena treated by psychodynamic theories.

10. Four major concepts were used by Dollard and Miller to explain the learning processes through which personality is acquired. These concepts are: drive, any strong stimulus that impels action; cue, a stimulus that provides direction to behavior; response, any behavior, internal or external; and reinforcement, an event that increases the likelihood of a particular response.

11. Dollard and Miller see fear as a crucial factor in personality functioning. Fear acts as a potent drive in the promotion of learning, and responses that allow escape from fear or avoidance of fear constitute important components of personality. One of the behaviors sometimes promoted by fear is the not thinking of particular, fear-stimulating thoughts. Such constraints curtail the functioning of what Dollard and Miller call higher mental processes in the solution of conflicts between needs; and these psychic limitations are one source of neurotic behavior.

12. Phenomenological theories of personality, which can include humanist and existential conceptions, emphasize the existence of positive forces in personality beyond

those involved solely in the reduction of tension and insist that immediate experience provides the primary legitimate data.

13. Maslow, a representative of this approach, believes that man possesses a unique psychological nature or structure consisting in part of inherent potentialities that seek actualization or full expression. Blocking of these potentials can generate forms of psychopathology and can prevent ultimate attainment of self-actualization.

14. Maslow recognizes the existence of basic physiological and psychological needs. Included are hunger and pain on the physiological level and affection and security on the psychological level. When and only when these basic needs are satisfied can actualization of the higher-order, or meta, needs take place. Maslow believes that a few rare individuals have achieved a kind of transcendence of normality in the form of full self-actualization.

GLOSSARY

anal stage (Freud) That stage in personality development, some time in the second and third years of life, during which control of defecation is emphasized by the parents. Certain personality traits are held to be associated with problems occurring during that period.

archetypes (Jung) Components of the collective unconscious. Archetypes are affectively laden images acquired through the historical experience of the species.

collective unconscious (Jung) Those aspects of the unconscious that represent the accumulated experiences of the human species; it contrasts with the personal unconscious, which reflects individual experience.

cue (Dollard and Miller) A stimulus with directive properties that determines the response in any given instance.

drive (Dollard and Miller) Any strong stimulus that can impel action.

ego (Freud) That aspect of personality that is in contact with the external world and that constitutes what is usually defined as "the self." Both the id and the superego affect the ego but are theoretically separate concepts.

genital stage (Freud) The culminating phase of development in respect to sex, in which the person has a genuinely affectionate relationship with a heterosexual partner.

id (Freud) That division of the psyche from which come blind, instinctual impulses that demand immediate gratification of primitive needs.

identification (Freud) A process of learning in which the child feels like (identifies himself with) important persons in his world, primarily members of his family.

latency period (Freud) A period of personality development, extending roughly from age five to early adolescence, during which sexual forces are subordinated and anxiety and personality change are in theory minimized.

libido (Freud) The generalized, basic, biological energy that provides the impetus for all psychic activities.

oral stage (Freud) That stage of personality development—the earliest one, during infancy—in which the desire for nourishment of the senses (hunger, sensual stimulation, and so forth) is dominant.

phallic stage (Freud) That stage in personality development in which interest is focused upon pleasure attainable through and associated with the genital organs (about ages three to five).

phenomenological theories A diverse class of theories, all sharing the assumption that raw, subjective experiences are the true data for understanding personality. Closely related approaches are the experiential, humanistic, and existential, all of which emphasize growth-promoting, positive forces in personality development.

psyche (Jung) The total personality, composed of a great number of subsystems. Among them are the ego, the personal unconscious, and the collective unconscious.

psychodynamic theories Theories based on assumptions that personality is to be understood in terms of conflicts among needs or impulses, at least some of which operate at an unconscious level.

reinforcement (Dollard and Miller) An event that increases the probability that a particular response will occur in the presence of a particular stimulus.

response (Dollard and Miller) Any identifiable behavior unit occurring in reaction to a learned cue when in the appropriate drive state.

self-actualization (Maslow) The full expression of an individual's unique potentialities for growth, potentialities believed to be inherent.

social-learning theories Personality theories that base their formulations on experimentally derived principles of conditioning and learning.

superego (Freud) A system within the total personality developed by incorporating parental standards as perceived by the ego or, somewhat more broadly, by incorporating the moral standards of society as perceived by the ego.

part nine

individual in society

morality, aggression, and equity

DO YOU KNOW...

- *that a child may judge another as having done a bad thing merely because the other child is punished?*

- *that the eye-for-an-eye approach to justice is most characteristic of young children?*

- *what kind of training course might advance one's level of morality?*

- *why it is that thievery is more common in cultures that discipline their children harshly?*

- *in what ways love can be used to raise a child to have high moral principles?*

- *where it is that permissiveness in raising a child can go wrong?*

- *what are the functions of scapegoating?*

- *what determines how we handle an observed instance of unfair treatment?*

- *the important difference in freedom of speech between an abstract and a specific case?*

unit 30

CONTENTS

"Individual in Society," the title of this part of the text, can serve as a succinct definition of the field of social psychology. We could let the definitional problem go at that, since there is little consensus among psychologists, including social psychologists, regarding this field. Nevertheless, a few more words on the subject might be useful.

In a sense, everything that is discussed in the other eight parts has considered people in relation to one another, as individuals and as groups. Until now we have been focusing on the person; now we will see how he functions in his human (i.e., social) environment. But an adequate theoretical comprehension of the forces and factors that determine the functioning of an individual in his social world is perhaps the most difficult challenge faced by psychologists. Our treatment here of research findings in social psychology will mainly indicate some of the difficulties of this area. Time and space restrict us to a few samples, but we hope that this sampling will convey the flavor of the field.

One possible approach to the field of social psychology is to analyze today's social scene; specifically, we might focus on the many current, bothersome social problems that confront our society. War, crime in the streets, drugs, ethics in business and government—all these and more are certainly issues confronting the "individual in society." But by their very nature, these issues can be properly considered only in a particular society at a particular time in its history. We have therefore chosen another approach, one that is not so timebound and culture-dependent. We will deal with some of the general processes and concepts that apply to effective analyses of the problems arising from people living together in a social community. In doing this we would like to wager that the introductory student will profit more from a presentation at a conceptual level than from exposure to a selection of perhaps more engaging, because relevant, immediate issues. The state of the science of social psychology, we believe, permits only separate and, of necessity, theoretically disconnected or even nontheoretical treatment.

Our own introduction to social psychology will start with how individuals learn about good and evil standards that pervade all our relations with people.

MORALITY

Since so much of life is spent with other people, one of our major concerns about our neighbor is whether he tends to help or to harm himself and others. When judging or describing a person (including oneself) we usually comment on this tendency: "She's dependable." "He always acts helpful and concerned, but he is just a busybody and usually winds up making trouble for you." "She is insecure; she does nice things to make you like her, but you can't count on her for support when you need it most." "He is a good friend even though we differ politically."

Societies as well as individuals are necessarily concerned with the helping and hurting behavior of their members. Laws state the circumstances under which persons must aid one another and proscribe specific actions that might hurt others. Societies are judged according to the helping and hurting behavior of their members in much the same way as individuals are judged. Those cultures where aggression and crime are prevalent are assessed as inadequate and are described as having laws and institutions that are incompatible with humanity. Societies, on the other hand, in which strangers trust and aid one another and in which people may come and go without hindrance or fear are looked upon favorably.

In addition to judging persons and societies by their helping and hurting proclivities, we tend to have beliefs as to what can bring about good or bad behavior. These beliefs, naturally, affect the way we raise children, behave toward our peers, and run our governments. These beliefs vary from one society to the next, and even neighboring groups may differ greatly from one another.

In this unit, we will review some of the theories and research bearing on good and bad behavior: We will study the major concepts of morality, aggression, fairness (or equity), and tolerance of dissent. Considering the history of beliefs about what is good and bad, it is safe to predict that many of the moral truths that most of us hold today will, in years to come, be regarded as quaint superstitions or indeed as harmful and misguided notions (and nonsense) that have prevented mankind from attaining its full potential. (Box 30.1, p. 734, illustrates some widely held moral imperatives of sixteenth-century England that spread to the United States and are only now beginning to give way.) Today as in times past, in this country as elsewhere, different persons hold differing moral beliefs. What one person considers undesirably aggressive, another may consider masculine and strong; what one considers immoral and promiscuous sexual behavior, another considers an act of love and humanity. And, as of this writing, many Americans do not agree on whether so many of the acts of civil disobedience that took place during the dismal years of the Vietnam War were instances of the highest moral courage or, rather, were harmful and irresponsible acts of immature "kooks."

Definitions of Morality

Early conceptions of morality and views on the nurturing of moral behavior in children were often couched in religious terms; the description of Calvinism in Box 30.1, page 734, describes one such view. A second early conception of morality tied religion to the power of rulers and served to maintain social hierarchies. The phrase "divine rights of kings" summarizes this conception.

Few if any present-day moral philosophers accept these definitions of morality and they do not show much consensus on others. Perhaps all that moral philosophers will agree to is that (1) systems of morality deal with right ideals or principles of human conduct and (2) moral discourse (i.e., moral principles, judgments, admonitions) has a bearing on behavior; what is *done* may be in harmony or in conflict with what is *said*. Beyond this, definitions of morality and moral behavior vary widely among different theories.

The intuitionist theory of morality holds that people know *intuitively* what is moral and

BOX 30.1

THE PROTESTANT ETHIC—WORK AND WORSHIP

The Protestant reformer John Calvin (1509–1564) preached that, since man's fate is in God's hands, we should devote our energy to self-denying work and worship, transforming the world into a better place while awaiting the Judgment Day. And thus were sanctified the work and worship ethics. The English government institutionalized the work ethic by expanding the medieval apprenticeship into a system for providing industrial skills to all children of the lower and middle classes. At about the age of twelve, children were sent by their parents to live and work with a master for about seven years. In return for their labor they were to receive instruction in a craft, board, lodging, clothing, and religious instruction. To ensure that this system was fully used to prevent vagrancy and poverty, the Statute of Artificers was enacted in 1597, stating that anyone under the age of twenty-one who refused to be apprenticed was subject to imprisonment until he agreed to serve. A Health and Morals of Apprentices Act was passed in 1802, limiting the hours of work of apprentices to twelve a day, prohibiting night work, and requiring that some instruction in reading and religious education be provided.

If the work ethic was politically and economically expedient for the English, the worship ethic was even more so. Catholicism so threatened the power of the Church of England that church attendance on Sundays and Holy Days was compulsory. Legislation was also passed requiring heads of families to instruct all members of their household, including servants and apprentices, in the catechism, and to send any recalcitrant students to the local minister.

In sixteenth-century England, the rise of light industry called not only for cheap labor but for serious and literate behavior beginning at an early age. Calvinistic religious doctrine about the nature of man, morality, and salvation provided the rationale for such a new style of life.

I. Pinchbeck and M. Hewitt comment:

Calvinism taught that children were born with an inheritance of sin and wickedness; consequently they were in the same danger of hell as the most hardened adult sinner. From this state they could only be saved by conviction of sin and personal conversion. . . . [This resulted] in religious pressures on the child which were wholly abnormal. Treated as little adults, they were subjected to the same religious pressures, disciplines and experiences as adults. For parents who accepted Calvinist views there was the greatest incentive to start the religious instruction of their children at the first possible moment. As John Cotton advised, "These Babes are flexible and easily bowed; it is far more easy to train them up to good things now, than in their youth and riper years." Moreover, godly parents were haunted by the unpalatable belief that "children are not too little to die, they are not too little to go to hell." It is not surprising that they devoted as much thought to the spiritual upbringing of their children as conscientious parents spend today on health and general personality development. . . .

One may well ask how children responded to religious appeal which did not differ to young or old; in which, the catechism class apart, no attempt was made to give religious instruction that the child could understand. Some of the numerous references to contemporary children's religious experience undoubtedly tax the modern reader's credulity. One child, "mightily awakened" between eight and nine years of age, "spent a large part of the night in weeping and praying, and could scarce take any rest day or night for some time together, desiring with all her soul to escape from the everlasting flames. . . ."

Horrifying, amusing or simply incredible though such tales seem to us now, it is well to remember that the seventeenth century was an age in which precocity was fostered; a period when children, urged by parents all too mindful of the brevity of life and fearful that they themselves might die before their sons and daughters were equipped for the responsibilities of the adult world, sometimes achieved feats of learning which would now be remarkable in children more than twice their age. . . .

It may seem to us now that such a religious training as this must have been oppressive to those for whom it was designed, but in the eighteenth, as in the sixteenth and seventeenth centuries, religion was not intended to "lift the spirits" but to concentrate the heart and mind on the nature of man's relationship to God. It may appear to have placed excessive emphasis on the negative aspects of the relationship, yet the positive advantages of contemporary religious training of building up character and of instilling a profound sense of social and moral obligation should not be lightly dismissed.

I. PINCHBECK & M. HEWITT. *Children in English Society*. Vol. I. *From Tudor Times to the Eighteenth Century*. London: Routledge & Kegan Paul, 1969.

FIGURE 30.1

Photo by George W. Gardner

good; beyond this appeal to intuition it provides no rational basis for determining what is moral. **Intuitionism**, so defined, would have great difficulty in accounting for the differences among societies and even among individuals within a given society in what is considered moral.

In response to the problems created by the intuitionist theory of morality, a theory known as **emotivism** was formulated. According to emotivism, a moral judgment is any kind of command that is intended to lay down rules of behavior, rules which must be obeyed. Moral behavior, then, is behavior that demonstrates intentional obedience to a set of formulated rules. Much of what we call moral behavior in children fits this definition quite well; if an adult commands a child never to steal and the child obeys without direct supervision, we consider his behavior to be moral. However, according to this definition, any propaganda or advertising, even a repressive law or misguided set of rules, is part of moral discourse. Emotivism provides no basis for distinguishing among moral, or gullible, or thoughtless, or blindly obedient behaviors. This prob-

lem troubled many philosophers and led to the development of an alternative theory of morality known as **prescriptivism.**

Prescriptivism emphasizes reasoning and consistency of behavior; it has less to do with emotion and persuasion. According to prescriptivism, moral statements should guide and prescribe rather than influence behavior. Such statements must appear rational and should be buttressed with reasonable explanations (see Figure 30.1). And they can be generalized; that is, the same judgment could fit a comparable situation. The subject of morality itself, for example, would be based on certain reasonable principles about how to treat others and would set guidelines for the consistent application of these principles.

Moral philosophy seems to offer no consensus as to the definition of the domain of moral behavior.

DEVELOPMENT OF MORAL JUDGMENT

Moral judgment, just like perceiving, thinking, walking, emoting, and almost everything else that the adult human being is capable of, shows a developmental process. Moral judgment never appears suddenly, full-blown, and ready to discriminate between good and evil. Children go through several stages of thinking about morality in the course of becoming intellectually adult

(see Box 30.2). Some persons never reach the most mature levels of moral reasoning, while others exercise what is deemed mature moral judgment by middle adolescence. The rate at which children progress through these stages depends on their level of intelligence, the society

BOX 30.2

CHILDREN CONFRONT MORAL DILEMMAS

Lawrence Kohlberg of Harvard University has studied the development of moral judgment in children, adolescents, and adults through having them respond to hypothetical problems that pose moral dilemmas, such as the following:

> In Europe, a woman was near death from a very bad disease, a special kind of cancer. There was one drug that the doctors thought might save her. It was a form of radium that a druggist in the same town had recently discovered. The drug was expensive to make, but the druggist was charging ten times what the drug cost him to make. He paid $200 for the radium and charged $2,000 for the small dose of the drug. The sick woman's husband, Heinz, went to everyone he knew to borrow the money, but he could only get together about $1,000 which is half of what the drug cost. He told the druggist that his wife was dying, and asked him to sell it cheaper or let him pay later. But the druggist said, "No, I discovered the drug and I'm going to make money from it." So Heinz got desperate and broke into the man's store to steal the drug for his wife.
>
> Should the husband have done that? Why?

After obtaining responses to this situation, subjects go on to judge a related moral issue:

> Suppose that even after taking the drug, Heinz's wife does not recover. Instead, she approaches death very painfully and slowly. Her pain is so great that she is like another person. She requests her doctor to "mercy kill" her by giving her an overdose of sleeping pills. Should the doctor "mercy kill" a fatally ill woman requesting death because of her pain?

The following are examples of the kinds of responses Kohlberg received from subjects of different ages to the second question about the morality of euthanasia (or mercy killing):

A PREADOLESCENT: It would be OK to mercy kill the lady to put her out of her pain. The husband might be unhappy though, because it's not like just putting an animal to sleep. He'll need his wife.

AN ADOLESCENT: A doctor has no right to mercy kill a person. He can't create life and so he shouldn't destroy it.

A YOUNG ADULT: It should be the dying person's own choice whether she is mercy killed. It's the quality of life that counts, not just the fact of life. If she feels life is not worthwhile if one is just a vegetable, then she has the right to choose to be killed. People should be able to judge for themselves what happens to them.

Note that the preadolescent seemed to think that the value of human life is based on practical considerations with no reference to a general moral principle. The adolescent has, in Kohlberg's view, advanced to a stage of moral judgment that permits him to respond to the dilemma on the basis of an abstract principle—essentially, that life is sacred. The young adult also considers life to be of greatest value but, in addition, places emphasis on the quality of life and on the right of an individual to determine whether she wishes to live.

It is from the careful analysis of thousands of responses such as these that Kohlberg has developed a theoretical scheme, roughly paralleling Piaget's stages of cognitive development (see Unit 4), which expresses his view that the development of a moral sense is a sequential, progressive process (see table).

As the table indicates, Kohlberg proposes three broad levels of morality and, within them, discerns six general types. Then, for any particular facet of morality (there are over thirty), he spells out the specific stages, and their guiding principles, which relate to each general type. Our examples refer to the facet "Value of Human Life" and the responses are classified (in order) as stages 2, 4, and 5.

In Kohlberg's view, while social learning obviously conveys the specific contents of moral orientations, it is insufficient to explain the hierarchical nature of a person's progress on the moral scale. He

or culture in which they are raised, and the child-rearing practices to which they are exposed. However, the *sequence* of these stages does not seem to vary.

Piaget (1965), Kohlberg (1969), and many others have noted various dimensions along which moral judgment develops and the approximate ages at which stages of moral development occur. These include:

1. Intentionality. Young children judge an event in terms of its physical consequences, but older children take into account the intentions

Level	Type	Stage
I. Preconventional	1. Punishment and obedience orientation.	1. The value of a human life is confused with the value of physical objects and is based on the social status or physical attributes of its possessor.
	2. Naive instrumental hedonism.	2. The value of a human life is seen as instrumental to the satisfaction of the needs of its possessor or of other persons.
II. Conventional, conforming morality	3. Good-boy morality of maintaining good relations, approval of others.	3. The value of a human life is based on the empathy and affection of family members and others toward its possessor.
	4. Authority maintaining morality.	4. Life is conceived as sacred in terms of its place in a categorical moral or religious order of rights and duties.
III. Autonomous, principled morality	5. Morality of contract, of individual rights, and of democratically accepted law.	5. Life is valued both in terms of its relation to community welfare and in terms of life being a universal human right.
	6. Morality of individual principles of conscience.	6. Belief in the sacredness of human life as representing a universal human value of respect for the individual.

believes that the "stages of moral thinking may not directly represent learning of patterns of verbalization in the culture. Instead, they may represent spontaneous products of the child's effort to make sense out of his experience in a complex social world, each arising sequentially from its predecessors." Thus he invokes biological maturation as the prime mover in moral development, as does Piaget in cognitive development. Moral stage (just as mental age) correlates substantially with chronological age but, as the person grows older, his stage of morality is increasingly independent of age (as is mental ability). Thus growing up does involve moral progression but, just as few adults ever attain genius level, so only a very few of them reach the highest moral stages.

Pursuing this point, later work has caused Kohlberg to modify somewhat his notion of the close tie between biological maturation and moral stage for higher levels. He has proposed that, to reach the highest stage, the individual must undergo life experiences that specifically confront him with

more complex moral dilemmas and with the realities of the social system in which he lives. For example, in one study he found that a sample of draft resistors during the Vietnam War were at about stage 4 when first confronting the choice of resisting the draft but, in the soul-searching that accompanied reaching their eventual decision, they moved toward stage 6—a principled position on the issue. For rare individuals—Kohlberg nominates Socrates and Martin Luther King as examples—a stage 7 may have to be formulated, one which incorporates "a sense of being part of the whole of life and the adoption of a cosmic . . . perspective." By such submerging of the individual self it becomes possible, as these men did, to court death if that is required to live in full accordance with their ethical principles.

L. KOHLBERG. Development of moral character and moral ideology. In M. L. Hoffman & L. W. Hoffman (Eds.), *Review of Child Development Research.* Vol. 1. New York: Russell Sage Foundation, 1964.
L. KOHLBERG. Continuities in childhood and adult moral development. In P. B. Baltes & K. W. Schie (Eds.), *Life-Span Developmental Psychology: Personality and Socialization.* New York: Academic Press, 1973.

of the person who committed the act. For example, an eight-year-old would typically consider it worse to drop four expensive cups accidentally than to smash one of them on purpose. Most fourteen-year-olds would come to the opposite conclusion.

2. Relativism. Young children assume that all acts can be classified unambiguously as right or wrong. Older children seem to lose this absolutist approach; they become more relativistic and accept the notion that the same act may be variously judged. The younger child also assumes that when persons disagree in their moral judgments, one of them must be wrong; they generally assume that the older of the two persons knows best.

3. Independence of sanctions. Younger children tend to judge the gravity of an offense after the fact—by the amount of punishment or other sanctions applied by authority figures. Older children judge the gravity of an offense in terms of the kind of rule that was broken or the seriousness of the harm that was intended. A three-year-old would probably judge as bad a child who had been spanked, regardless of whether the child had earned the spanking in the eyes of adults other than the one administering the punishment. An unfortunate adult analogue is to decide that a person is guilty simply because he has been charged with a crime (and even though he is later acquitted).

4. Use of reciprocity. Many children under the age of twelve or so seem to lack the ability to put themselves in the place of others. They act solely in terms of their own feelings and needs and cannot understand what motivates others to act as they do. Such children are prone to acts of retaliation and reciprocity when injured by another—a hair-pull for a hair-pull, for example. Other children show at quite an early age behavior that is conciliatory or forgiving.

5. Use of punishment for restitution and reform. Young children tend to assume that doers of harmful deeds should be punished severely. Older children tend to favor milder punishments that are designed to restore to the victim his rightful claims and to reform the wrongdoer.

6. Naturalistic views of misfortune. Children under about eight years of age tend to view accidents and misfortunes as punishments willed by God or some omnipotent force. Older children are able to differentiate punishment from natural misfortune.

In general, the young child focuses on specific rules, obeying the letter of the law (which he can understand) more than the spirit of it (which he may not yet comprehend). She perceives rules as absolute. As she matures, however, the child begins to perceive that rules are made by people for everyone's convenience, that rules can be imperfect and in conflict with one another, and that one must decide for herself what rules she regards as being for the general good.

Obviously, the developmental picture just presented is based on observations of Western children growing up in an environment where Western morality is being taught. However, a few investigations of non-Western societies have been carried out and they, generally, have led to similar conclusions. Nevertheless, progress in morality may be subject to specific training experiences.

Investigations by Tracy and Cross (1973) suggest that the development of moral reasoning may be hastened by certain training procedures. They evaluated the moral attitudes of 76 seventh-grade boys and then gave half the boys (the experimental group) an opportunity to role play a part in dilemmas that required ethical reasoning one stage above their current stage of reasoning. Three weeks later, all the boys were given more moral problems to resolve. The boys in the experimental group demonstrated greater maturity of moral judgment than those who were not presented with the possibilities for more mature solutions. Neither intelligence nor socioeconomic class of the boys seemed to affect their ability to advance to a higher stage of reasoning.

Moral judgment is an important aspect, but is not the sole determiner, of moral behavior. It is possible to hold mature views on situations, but to lack the self-control or courage to act in the best interests of another. Similarly, one may demonstrate good-will toward others but hold immature views on the resolution of moral dilemmas. But let us see in the following section some of the many ways that moral behavior and moral judgment are intimately connected.

SOCIALIZATION OF MORAL BEHAVIOR

To behave morally is to demonstrate *internalized* controls on behavior; these controls discourage the commission of harmful acts and encourage the commission of acts that promote the well-being of others. We infer that a control has been internalized when a person repeatedly behaves ethically in the absence of anyone who would punish him if he did otherwise. A person who has internalized most of the rules that his society stresses is said to be socialized.

There is no sharp distinction between internal and external control of behavior. Even an adult who is well socialized with respect to her culture's morality may reflect on the way in which others would evaluate her acts or may be sensitive to the embarrassment of being judged immoral or irresponsible. What characterizes the socialization and internalization of behavioral control is not whether her socializing agents (friends, parents, teachers, etc.) are present in her thoughts, but the kind of behavior she actively considers. If she is concerned with whether or not her friends or parents or teachers would punish her if they knew and disapproved of her behavior, she is not truly socialized; if she is concerned with how her friends or parents or teachers would *evaluate* the morality of her behavior, she is socialized.

How does internalization come about? How does the way a person reasons about morality affect the way he acts and vice versa? How do parents structure their children's moral development?

Much recent research and theorizing about moral development have come to us from developmental psychologists, who treat socialization as a learned process. Other instances of this approach as it relates to personality develop-

ment are to be found in Units 2 and 28. The socialization view begins by asking: How can we make moral behavior so rewarding that a child would learn to act morally instead of being completely self-centered?

Human infants become emotionally attached to any person who treats them regularly in a nurturant way. Consequently, about midway in the first year of life, children with nurturant parents typically have a strong emotional attachment to them. The parents' presence and nurturance is highly rewarding and satisfying; their absence is unpleasant, even disturbing. The words, smiles, and gestures associated with their nurturance take on positive value for the child, and the scolding, frowning, and tenseness that precede withdrawal of nurturance acquire negative value. It may well be that the earliest socialization of behavior occurs through such an instrumental learning process: Desired forms of behavior are rewarded by attention and nurturance and undesired forms are suppressed by withdrawal of approval. But rewarding good behavior and punishing bad behavior is only a small part of moral socialization. Most of the kinds of behavior that we would consider in a moral context do not exist in any form in the very young child.

There is some evidence that internalization is effected by the kind of nurturance the child experiences in his early years. If a warm emotional tie is not formed with an adult during the first year and is not continued through the first few years, the internalization of moral values may not occur at all. This aspect of childrearing may explain some differences in morality between, as well as within, cultures. Crosscultural research suggests that a high incidence of theft with a lack of guilt feelings is prevalent in societies that use severe rather than nurturant socialization practices on young children (see Box 30.3, p. 740).

Functions of Nurturance in Moral Development

Why is nurturance necessary? What else, beyond nurturance, is required for internalization to occur? There are several currently proposed

BOX 30.3

HOW TO RAISE YOUR CHILD TO BE A THIEF

M. Bacon, I. Child, and H. Barry of Yale University examined forty-eight nonliterate societies to see whether there is any relation between the way children are raised and the kind and amount of crime that occurs in these societies.

The societies that were studied included eight African societies, eleven North American Indian societies, five South American Indian societies, sixteen South Pacific societies, and eight Asian societies. These societies were chosen on the basis of their geographical diversity and the availability of information on child-training practices in each. The data needed for this study were obtained from anthropological studies that had been done previously by others.

Each culture was examined to see how it compared with others on frequency of theft and personal crime. Theft was defined as stealing the personal property of others; "property" meant any item on which the particular society placed value—this might include a whale's tooth or a song. Personal crime was defined as intent to injure or kill another and included assault, rape, sorcery, making false accusations, and so forth. The three researchers independently analyzed the information on each society and rated, on a seven-point scale, the relative frequency of each type of crime. Thus, for example, a rating of

4 on theft for a given society would mean that theft occurred there with about average frequency in relation to the rest of the forty-eight societies.

Next, each society was rated on many aspects of its child-training practices. Finally, the relation between these child-training practices and the incidence of crime and theft was determined. Some very strong relations were obtained.

1. Societies in which parents are nurturant (i.e., responsive to the child's needs, affectionate, lacking in severity) tend to have a lower frequency of theft than societies in which parents are severe.
2. Theft is highest in societies that use punitive and anxiety-provoking methods of training children to achieve and to be obedient, responsible, and self-reliant.
3. Both theft and personal crime were very prevalent in societies where boys are raised almost exclusively by their mothers and have little opportunity to develop emotional ties with their fathers.
4. Personal crime is highest in societies in which children are harshly and abruptly forced to be independent.

These results confirm what others have observed about the development of morality in our own culture. A gentle, close relation between the young child and the parent (especially the same-sex parent) fosters the development of morality.

M. K. BACON, I. L. CHILD, & H. BARRY. A cross-cultural study of correlates of crime. *Journal of Abnormal and Social Psychology*, 1963, **66**, 291–300.

explanations that are essentially complementary to one another.

1. Children are more likely to imitate a nurturant adult than a nonnurturant adult. Nurturant behavior is defined as care and consideration for another; as such, it fits the usual definition of moral behavior. Thus the nurturant adult caretaker provides a model of moral behavior and is imitated.
2. The nurturant adult provides the child with an opportunity to see how his behavior can affect the feelings of others. A child must

learn to connect the needs, feelings, and general welfare of others with the pleasurable or distressing consequences for them of his own actions. His earliest recognition of the consequences of his actions probably occurs when his mother or father becomes distressed and shows disapproval or expresses pleasure and gives affection.
3. The love-oriented or nurturant adult offers a strong inducement toward close interaction. He is sought rather than avoided, and this very closeness enhances the potential influence of the other explanations.

Types of Discipline

In addition to nurturance, a love-oriented style of disciplining children seems to be required for extensive internalization of moral controls. This style of discipline involves day-to-day communication with the child—through reasoning, explanation, discussion, verbal disapproval of the child's behavior, inquiry into his motives, suggestion of appropriate ways to act, and praise for moral behavior. The kinds of punishment that might be used include the showing of disapproval, ignoring, and short-term isolation rather than attacklike physical punishment, "bawling out," ridicule, or shaming by public announcement of the transgression.

These two styles of discipline have differing psychological effects. The severe style creates a high level of emotionality in the child, making it unlikely that he will think reflectively about his actions or absorb new information about moral principles. The love-oriented style enables the child to learn and to mature with confidence and flexibility.

A second important difference is in the anxiety level experienced by the child. In love-oriented discipline, the parent warns the child extensively about the kinds of behavior that are to be avoided, the reasons for avoiding them, and the circumstances under which they are especially undesirable. The child has an opportunity to gain a more abstract idea, the spirit, of the moral principle involved and to exercise judgment rather than rigid obedience in relation to that principle. He also understands that his parents' approval will be withdrawn if he disobeys. As a consequence, when the child contemplates committing a transgression, he anticipates the loss of parental affection and experiences anxiety. If temptation is not too great, the anxiety will keep him from misbehaving.

This brief presentation of the socialization approach to learning moral behavior gives us one view of the process. There are others. One is the Freudian conception of the development of conscience (Unit 29); it stresses less manipulable psychodynamic forces. But, as we point out in that unit, the social learning and the psychoanalytic orientations are not necessarily incompatible.

Any description of moral development is, of necessity, oversimplified. Each individual is subjected to so many influences that no one can diagram and account for them all. Some of these influences are physiological for, from the beginning, each individual has a different make-up from every other. One child will be slow, cautious, and seemingly methodical almost from infancy. Another will be quick, impetuous, and impatient—what used to be called high-strung and is now called hyperactive. Myriad influences, of course, are in the environment, not only in the family but in school, on the television screen, and on the street. And, tantalizing as it is, we can neither foretell what effects these influences will have nor explain with hindsight why one child reacts to them so differently from another.

From time to time every child will say, "But gee, Mom, all the other kids do it!" One child may be content to say it and yet, in the long run, accept his parents' values as his own while another, perhaps in the same family, will reject most of the adult standards she has learned and be influenced chiefly by her agemates. Neither child-rearing practices alone, alas, nor the dominant standards of the community can tell us all we need to know about the development of moral judgment and moral behavior.

AGGRESSION

In our discussion of the development of morality it might appear that we were implying that people are distinguished from animals by the extent and complexity of their efforts to raise children to be moral. Indeed, we do believe that morality is a concern of humankind only. But, at the same time, it is appallingly clear that human beings are the most aggressive and destructive creatures on this planet.

We do not mean to imply that aggression is the opposite of morality; actually, some forms of aggression are not generally regarded as immoral. But much aggression is immoral and, therefore, it is not surprising that the same mechanisms underlying the acquisition of moral behavior are believed to underlie also the socialization of aggressive impulses.

Definitions of Aggression

Popular conceptions of aggression include a wide range of events from competitive athletics to cannibalism and warfare. How can we subsume such different situations and their behaviors in a single definition? Here are two reasonable attempts at defining aggression. The first is a behavioral definition: Aggression is any behavior that harms another. The second definition is based on intent: Aggression is any act that is intended to harm another. Like any behavioral definition, the first definition specifies an observable behavioral criterion for deciding whether aggression has occurred: Harm has been inflicted. Simple enough, it would seem. The second definition, however, presents a problem: We cannot observe intentions, so that it is difficult to be sure when aggression, thus defined, has occurred. The choice as to which definition is more useful may seem simple; but consider the following list of events:

1. An infant burps her food all over her mother's good new dress.
2. A burglar is killed by the man whose house he has entered.
3. An angry son purposely fails to write to his mother, who is expecting a letter and will be hurt if none comes.
4. A dentist pulls a screaming child's tooth.
5. A congressman does not protest an escalation of bombing to which he is morally opposed.
6. An executioner presses the button that electrocutes a convicted criminal.

Neither definition of aggression encompasses all these events. The one based on intent seems more adequate but still leaves us with some unsolved problems. The dentist intended to perform a hurt-causing *action* but presumably in a good cause and with no intent to hurt for hurting's sake. Is it an act of aggression to not *act* and thereby intentionally hurt someone, as in the instance of the letter-withholding son or the timid congressman?

Clearly the issue is a complicated one, for aggression is a multidimensional concept. To deal with it scientifically, we must try to understand the different dimensions and the ways in which they are related to one another rather than try to find a single unitary explanation. Some useful distinctions among levels of aggression are presented in Box 30.4.

The Socialization of Aggression

Aggression is often expressed quite blatantly in infancy and early childhood. Most mothers know better than to be shocked or worried if a young child kicks, flails her fists, or screams insults such as "I hate you, you dirty old witch!" While such behavior is not acceptable or pleasant, it is not abnormal; many psychologists believe that aggression is innate. Control and indirect expression of aggression, however, are not inborn—they are learned. The process of learning to control aggression or to express it in ways that are acceptable in one's own culture is called the *socialization of aggression*. Obviously, persons do not cease being aggressive when they reach adulthood. However, as a result of socialization along the way many persons learn to exercise self-control of aggression and indeed most social circumstances require such control. Other individuals remain highly aggressive but learn to express aggression in more subtle ways, through verbal insults, covert coercion, implied demands, and other destructive tactics. Finally, there are those who have remained largely unsocialized and their brutal, aggressive impulses may find frequent expression in the physical injury of others.

There are considerable research data on the question: How is aggression socialized? Let us look at one early study that has greatly influenced later work. Sears, Maccoby, and Levin (1957) pointed out that two important and distinctly different dimensions involved in the socialization of aggression are (1) permissiveness (the extent to which the parent is willing to let the child be aggressive) and (2) severity of punishment (the extent to which the parent punishes the child after he has behaved agressively). Permissiveness refers to a parents' actions *before* a transgression. Does he expect the aggression? Does he give many or few advance warnings that would lead the child to fear to be aggressive? Punishment refers to a parent's actions *after* a transgression. How severely

BOX 30.4

**AGGRESSION AS A
MULTIDIMENSIONAL CONCEPT**

The difficulty of formulating a single precise definition of aggression suggests that aggression is not a
unitary concept. There seem to be many possible

antecedents of aggression and different causes for
different types. Also, aggression may be expressed
in many ways with many possible consequences. S.
Feshbach of UCLA has suggested some useful distinctions among aggressive acts:

> Clearly, the apparent simplicity of the single
> term "aggression" is deceptive.

S. FESHBACH. Dynamics of morality of violence and aggression:
Some psychological considerations. *American Psychologist*,
1971, **26**, 281–292.

Aggression-Related Phenomena	Examples
Hostile aggression (primarily intended to hurt another)	A jealous woman kills her ex-lover. An angered person points out to another his physical unat-tractiveness. A person is purposely omitted from a guest list by someone who wishes to snub him.
Anger (energizes ongoing behavior and serves as a warning)	A man's face flushes and his cheek muscles become tense and move up and down. A woman tightens her lips and glares.
Instrumental aggression (intended to hurt although the aggressor's primary aim is to accomplish something else)	A parent spanks a child to teach him to behave. A man shoots a burglar to protect his family. A cannibal eats a man for good luck.
Assertiveness (legitimate expression of one's own interests; hurting is neither a primary nor a secondary aim, but it may occur)	A senator wins a debate. A scientist defends his theory. A student argues with his instructor about a grade he has received.
Accidents (acts that are neither aggressive nor assertive but that may be misinterpreted as aggression through misunderstanding of intent)	Golfer accidentally hits bystander with golf ball. Nuclear weapon is automatically fired at another country owing to failure of its controlling electronic system.

does he deal with the child who has trans-
gressed?

Since permissiveness does not, by itself,
create anxiety about transgressions (planned or
already committed), we would expect that children with permissive mothers would be more
aggressive than children with nonpermissive
mothers. Similarly, since punishment suppresses behavior, we would expect that the more
severely the mother punishes aggression, the
more the child will avoid being aggressive.
However, this prediction fails to do justice to
the complexity of the situation. Sears et al. obtained mothers' reports on their child-rearing

practices so that families could be classified
as being high or low on the dimensions of permissiveness or punitiveness. Also, mothers reported on the extent of aggressive behavior in
their children. Table 30.1, p. 744, summarizes a
main finding, separated into girls and boys.

We see in Table 30.1 that parents who are
most lenient (group C) tend to have children
who differ very little in level of aggressiveness
from those of parents who are the least lenient
(group B). The parents who raise the least
aggressive children (group A) are those who are
neither permissive nor punitive. These parents
take the attitude that aggression is wrong and

TABLE 30.1 PERCENTAGE OF HIGHLY AGGRESSIVE CHILDREN DIVIDED ACCORDING TO WHETHER THE MOTHER WAS HIGH OR LOW ON PERMISSIVENESS AND PUNITIVENESS FOR AGGRESSION TOWARD PARENTS

Group	Parents' Behavior	Percent Highly Aggressive	
		Boys	Girls
A	Low permissive and low punitive	3.7	13.3
B	Low permissive and high punitive	20.4	19.1
C	High permissive and low punitive	25.3	20.6
D	High permissive and high punitive	41.7	38.1

will not be tolerated; they subtly express this to the child, but they do not punish aggression severely. Such an attitude is, of course, the nurturant style of child-rearing mentioned earlier. The parents who evoked the most aggression (group D) were those who did not convey group A's message effectively. These parents respond as though any form of behavior is acceptable, giving few signals in advance warning the child not to be aggressive. But, when the child does act aggressively, he is severely punished. Why, then, do such children persist in their punishable behavior? Punishment, if it is severe, probably and understandably generates hostility in the child, thus leading to further aggression. Also, the punitive parent unintentionally provides a model of aggressive behavior; the child learns that aggression is a standard way of coping with frustration. Moreover, such parental aggression, if it is consistent and severe enough, may suppress most of the child's aggression in the presence of his parents, but the child will become more aggressive out of the home than children who are not punished severely for fighting (Sears, Whiting, Nowlis, & Sears, 1953).

This brief glimpse refers only to persons within the so-called normal range of behavior. Our news media daily deluge us with graphic illustrations of aggressive behaviors that clearly fall outside of this range and do so because, presumably, such violence somehow fascinates us. The entertainment media pursue the same policy

and with apparent success—as measured by popularity. What the effects are of such intense exposure to violence, especially upon children, remains, despite considerable research, a highly (and continually) debatable question. We will not attempt to summarize the data (often contradictory) and arguments that have accumulated around this issue. At the moment we hopefully lean toward the view that most children (and adults) effectively insulate themselves from, say, television orgies of terror and violence. It is all make-believe and some data suggest that it may even have a cathartic effect, permitting the harmless draining off of unexpressed anger. But for the individual for whom handling aggression is, for personality reasons, a serious problem, viewing violence may exacerbate the problem and threaten self-control.

In Unit 23 we detail the various mechanisms—sometimes adaptive and sometimes not—by which people typically attempt to cope with feelings of frustration and anger and with the often extreme anxiety that can accompany them. On the social-psychological scene perhaps the most relevant mechanism involves **scapegoating**, a mechanism whereby we attribute our frustration to incorrect sources, frequently other groups of people. Entire segments of society who have experienced failure may blame their plight on another segment of the society that is less powerful and fortunate. Scapegoating thus becomes a mechanism for the development and maintenance of bigoted attitudes. (One view of how this may come about is presented in Box 26.1, p. 658.) The more such practices are condoned, the greater the degree of inequity that exists among groups and individuals in any given society.

EQUITY

In one form or another, the following question continues to arise in *all* human societies: How should punishments and rewards be distributed among the members of a group? A related question of great social-psychological interest is: What determines our perception of a just or equitable distribution of rewards and punishments?

Equity refers to justice and impartiality; it especially characterizes any system in which each individual receives his due. While persons may disagree on how to define an individual's "due," a general notion of equity guides much of our social behavior: our decision to share with and to help others, a group leader's allocation of responsibilities and rewards to group members, satisfaction with employment, perception of others as good or responsible, or a decision to participate in a civil-rights movement in an attempt to correct a perceived social wrong. Obviously, the kinds of moral judgments and acts in which a person chooses to engage are affected by the individual's definition and perception of equity and inequity.

Equity Theory

In any relation, whether between two friends, a student and her teacher, two students, two teachers, a patient and his doctor, members of a sports team, employee and employer, or a wife and husband, each individual both *contributes* and *receives* from the exchange. Those things that the individual feels he has given, we will refer to as contributions. Those things that the person feels he has received, we will refer to as benefits. Adams (1965) has defined an equitable relation as one in which an individual's ratio of benefits to contributions is perceived as equal to the other individual's benefit/contribution ratio. To give a simple (and simplified) example: If A is a young doctor in a medical clinic who sees an average of forty patients a week and has an annual salary of $40,000, she would consider her salary an equitable one if another young doctor, B, in the same clinic who sees an average of thirty patients a week, earns $30,000 annually (or, seeing an average of fifty patients a week, earns $50,000 annually). She would consider it inequitable if B sees only ten patients a week but receives $20,000 annually. She would probably be less upset but uncomfortable and sheepish if she learns that B sees 40 patients a week but receives only $30,000 annually. In other words, any time that A's contribution/benefit ratio is unequal to B's contribution/benefit ratio, an inequitable situation is seen as existing.

It is important to bear in mind that contributions are *perceived* contributions, and benefits are *perceived* benefits. But individuals and entire societies may differ in their perception of equity. Japanese society, for example, considers age, education, length of employment, and family size the most important contributions (in the present sense) in determining what a worker should be paid; productivity is of less importance. Women today expect equal pay for equal work, but some male employers and employees feel that a woman's contribution is somehow, automatically, worth less than a man's. One employer may pay his workers less than does another but justify the lower pay on the basis that his plant is more attractive and that he offers more fringe benefits; his employees may not perceive or appreciate these nonsalary benefits. A wife may argue that she manages the household efficiently, yet with little appreciation and an inadequate income from her husband. He, on the other hand, may argue that his income-earning efforts are strenuous and adequate but that his wife fails to recognize this or that she does not budget properly.

Persons tend not to make equity comparisons with persons from quite different social or economic categories. In cases where individuals have had considerable prior experience, their compared object may not be a single individual but an internalized standard based on a composite of the contribution/benefit ratios they have experienced in the past.

Homans (1961) proposed that in situations involving equity considerations people seek "distributive justice—justice in the distribution of rewards and costs between persons." He stresses that the goal is not in achieving complete equity or even in achieving an excess of benefits over contributions, but rather in maintaining a reasonably fair ratio of these factors, usually both for himself and for others.

How do people react when they feel they are not receiving equity? Overt anger, resentment, or at least some experience of tension are frequent responses. But what else may people do?

There are a variety of ways in which to reduce perceived inequity. Some of these actions are honest and objective, some are unrealistic but relatively harmless, and some are irresponsible and harmful (see example in Box 30.5). How does a person respond when he perceives that he is receiving *more* than he feels is his due? He might begin to work harder or perhaps simply to perceive himself as working that much harder. He may forget how much more he is receiving or perceive the other as less able than he. He is, however, unlikely to reduce his own benefits.

BOX 30.5

THE BAGGER RESTORES EQUITY

How do persons act to restore equity when they feel that they are receiving less than their due?

J. V. Clark, a graduate student of business administration at Harvard University, sought answers to this question by studying the behavior of supermarket employees who worked in an inequitable situation.

Cashiering, a full-time supermarket job, brings higher status and better pay than bagging, and the bagger is perceived as working for the cashier. However, in the particular chain of supermarkets studied by Clark, college students who worked part time often bagged for younger, less-educated cashiers; that is, the older and better-educated persons had lower status, received less pay, and took orders from the younger and less-educated persons. Apparently age and education were regarded by these college students as major contribution variables, since they were very explicit about their perception of inequity. How might such inequity be dealt with?

(1) In this particular case, the principal means of reducing inequity was for baggers to reduce the rate at which they filled shopping bags (i.e., to reduce their contributions). One college student explained to the researcher that whenever she was ordered to bag for a lower-status cashier she deliberately bagged more slowly.

Clark went on to examine the relation between work efficiency and cashier-checker equity. Those supermarkets in which there was a high degree of equity within the cashier-bagger pairs needed fewer employees in relation to their volume of sales than did those supermarkets in which many of the cashier-bagger relations were inequitable. Personnel changes within a supermarket that increased equity between cashiers and baggers decreased the operating costs of that store's checkout counters.

(2) One may increase his benefits. Although no such instances were observed in this particular study, the supermarket bagger might have demanded higher pay by persuading his fellow part-time baggers to go out on a wildcat strike. He might also have engaged in thefts from the supermarket. (Theft is perhaps unlikely in the present example.) However, interviews with confidence men and delinquents indicate that many criminals regard society as having been so unfair to them that their own crimes merely serve to even up the score, that is, restore equity.

(3) One may reorganize his perception of contributions or benefits. For example, a bagger might conclude that age and education are not really important after all or that his present salary is not a serious consideration since he will soon have a full-time job and, as a college graduate, will be earning much more than the cashiers can ever hope to earn.

(4) One may leave the situation. A bagger might quit, ask for a transfer, or start to be absent frequently; absenteeism was, in fact, often the solution.

(5) One may attempt to alter the other person's contributions or benefits or to force the other to leave the situation. This could be accomplished by cognitive distortion. For example, the bagger might begin to imagine that the cashier really had greater practical experience. Somewhat more difficult, but still a possibiity, would be to convince the cashier to help with the bagging, to switch jobs once in a while, or to donate some of his pay to the bagger. Finally, a diabolical bagger might find ways of making his cashier's life so miserable that the cashier would quit.

(6) One may change the object of his comparison. Our hypothetical bagger may cease comparing himself with his cashier and concentrate on the fact that all of the baggers are college students his age and receive equal pay.

J. V. CLARK. A preliminary investigation of some unconscious assumptions affecting labor efficiency in eight supermarkets. Unpublished doctoral dissertation, Harvard Graduate School of Business Administration, 1958.

The "Just World" Belief

It is apparent that most persons have internalized some concept of equity and have attempted to maintain a belief in a "just world." We usually succeed in upholding such an image despite the gross inequities that we see daily. How do we manage to do this?

The following example, adapted from various experiments on perception of harmdoing, illustrates some of the mechanisms involved: Imagine that you frequently pass through a rough neighborhood. Policemen are usually around and you feel sure that they will provide protection should you ever need it. You have heard about instances of police brutality, but you also recognize that policemen are often confronted with violent persons so that a forceful response may sometimes be necessary. While you deplore brutality, you regard it as a rare event that does not concern you. One day you see a young man walking down the street; a policeman grabs him by the arm, yanks him backward, hits him in the back of the neck with his club, and pushes him into a waiting police car. Your response to these events will depend partly on the amount of power you feel you have to alleviate this apparent instance of inequity. Imagine the following alternative situations:

1. You are quickly asked by a bystander, who identifies himself as a lawyer for the American Civil Liberties Union, to testify as a witness on behalf of the young man who has been so brutally treated. You believe in justice and equity; hence you agree to testify. You feel deeply concerned about the young man and plan to begin taking a more prominent role in community efforts to improve the training of police.

2. Or you are in such a hurry to get to an appointment that you walk by quickly. You never see the policeman or the young man again. You assume that the young man probably provoked the policeman's response. Perhaps he had pulled a loaded gun, for all you know. You manage to feel somewhat reassured in the knowledge that there *is* justice in the world and that harmdoers *do* get what is coming to them.

In general, when an inequity has occurred but we are unable to correct it, rather than threaten our belief that unjust things cannot happen to decent, innocent persons (such as ourselves), we persuade ourselves that the victim brought it on himself. The social consequences of onlookers' tendencies to restore equity by derogating the victim may be far-reaching. Not only does the victim fail to receive assistance from fellow citizens, but, as a consequence of good citizens' attempts to maintain their perception that the world is just, the victim is further downgraded and blamed. Much of today's prejudice against various minority groups may well be caused by the pervasive need of the majority to justify existing inequities (see Figure 30.2).

We are admittedly, therefore, capable of irrational and irresponsible behavior in the interests of preserving our belief in a just world. As Box 30.6, page 748, describes, those whom

FIGURE 30.2 Will this boy find justice in his lifetime? On the Lower East Side of New York City, volunteer workers range with a mobile truck, advising the poor of their legal rights.

Courtesy, ACTION

BOX ·30.6

WITCHCRAFT AS AN EXPLANATION OF PERSONAL HARM

Belief in witchcraft is an ancient, dishonorable, universal, and (to some extent) contemporary fact of social life. Specific beliefs about witches and witchcraft have varied with time and location. The possibility of witchcraft provides victims of misfortune with a convenient explanation when no other is forthcoming. The kinds of misfortunes that have been explained in terms of witchcraft have varied widely.

According to the earliest definitions of witchcraft, a witch is clearly known by her alleged harmful acts against others, and it was believed that a witch obtained her powers by having formed a pact with the devil. Witchcraft became one of the more serious Christian sins, for it was thought to involve renunciation of God and participation in devil worship—nocturnal Sabbath meetings at which witches worship the devil and have sexual intercourse with him.

These fears became so firmly established that religious and legal actions were taken to cope with witches. In 1484, Pope Innocent VIII issued a decree describing the way in which witches conduct themselves and the procedures that were to be followed in punishing them. The punishment of witches was considered an important function of society because it was believed that the death of the witch would prevent the harm she could cause and even cure persons whom she had already afflicted. Death for witches was considered the only *moral* way of coping with them, for although scratching a witch and drawing her blood was considered the surest way to lift her spell, such countermagic was prohibited by the clergy since it was considered as being itself a kind of witchcraft. The Church of England held similar views on witchcraft, and the witchcraft laws of England reflected those views.

What kinds of persons became witches? The judicial records reveal two essential facts about accused witches: They were *female* and they were

poor. This was easily explained by the authorities in those times: Women are by nature more vulnerable to the temptations of Satan, and so are the poor, since they are eager to escape from grinding poverty by any means.

In rural villages, the inhabitants constantly snooped and minded one another's business in order to discourage nonconformity, temper displays, or cursing. Nonconforming or grumpy, unpleasant old women ("scolds" as they were called) were typically assumed to be witches. In this way, the community exerted powerful control over its potential nonconformists and dissidents. The down-and-out old women who were thus socially isolated and whose complaints were silenced by fear often felt a sense of alienation from the community and a desire for revenge. They had two major ways of retaliating: witchcraft and arson. Setting houses and barns on fire and killing animals were easy means of revenge for the weak against the more fortunate. So prevalent was the belief in witches and so successful was society at allowing conditions of poverty, neglect, and alienation to exist for some of its members that these outcasts not only avenged themselves through witchlike acts—some indeed *imagined they had become witches*! (For a possible explanation of this, see Box 21.6, p. 524.)

However, of the many persons who were accused of witchcraft, most denied the allegations against them and most of them had not been observed committing harmful acts. Why then were such persons accused, and how was their guilt proved?

Persons who believed that they had become the victims of witchcraft usually had a particular suspect in mind. In almost every case on record, the suspect was someone who lived in the so-called victim's community, someone indeed who had previously been wronged *by* the accuser. The accusation of witchcraft was typically a form of double jeopardy: The "witch" was first *abused* by someone more fortunate and then *accused of* witchcraft by the guilt-stricken abuser!

K. THOMAS. *Religion and the Decline of Magic.* London: Weidenfeld & Nicolson, 1971.

society formerly victimized used to be accused of witchcraft. They were seen as bringing trouble on themselves by consorting with the devil, causing illness in humans and animals, and committing other evil deeds. Obviously, in the interests of morality and equity, it was just that all witches be put to death.

But perhaps we should not take too smug a view of our ancestors' irrationalities, for there are many ways in which this same mechanism of just-world inequity operates in modern-day society. We still have witch hunts, though with different definitions of evildoing.

But there may be a chance for progress. The task of analyzing our social and legal institutions to discover what aspects of our culture encourage derogation rather than compensation of a victim has only recently been undertaken by social scientists. Let us now turn to some of their findings.

Factors Influencing the Restoration of Equity

So far, we have focused on two problems of inequity, one in which persons receive less or more than they believe they deserve and one in which persons observe unjust treatment of others, but their feelings of powerlessness to assist the victims are somehow converted into a belief that the unjust treatment is justified after all. We now turn attention to situations in which one individual has harmed another: Under what circumstances will the harmdoer compensate his victim?

There are two basic ways in which a harmdoer may restore her sense of equity: by compensating her victim or by persuading herself that her act was in fact equitable. Several factors in the encounters of everyday life influence the likelihood that a harmdoer will compensate her victim. Compensation is more likely, for example, if she has the resources or if the harmdoer is not forced to justify her behavior in public and can save face through compensation. On the other hand, the harmdoer may derogate his victim, deny personal responsibility for the hurtful action, or minimize the victim's suffering and thus essentially deny that any important inequity has even occurred.

All of us should find these mechanisms recognizable, perhaps more easily if they have been applied to us rather than by us. The broader social issue—how our legal system affects the tendencies of harmdoers to restore equity—is discussed in Box 30.7, page 750.

TOLERANCE OF DISSENT

Throughout this unit, it has been evident that such concepts as morality and equity cannot be defined simply. Most readers might accept the general and abstract definitions we have offered, but there would be considerable disagreement on whether specific actions are moral or equitable. This disagreement should not be surprising to the student of psychology. Each of us has unique sets of motives, ways of understanding and perceiving the behavior of others, attitudes, and prior experiences with respect to any given occurrence that may raise the question of morality or equity. Once one has recognized that disagreements among people regarding morality are inevitable and not easily resolvable, there arise philosophical, legal, and political questions of great importance to an effective society. We cannot deal with these directly here; rather, we will consider a related psychological question: What factors account for an individual's willingness to tolerate dissent, dissent from his own opinions and dissent from the cultural and social norms of his society?

First, we must distinguish between the abstract notion of tolerance of dissent (e.g., Should there be freedom of speech?) and individuals' beliefs about specific instances of dissent (e.g., Do you think that a Nazi should be allowed to make political speeches on television?). The many public opinion polls that provide data on the differences in responses to abstract and concrete questions about tolerance of dissent indicate that over three-quarters of adults in our society today endorse the *concept* of freedom of speech; but less than half of these same adults believe that dissidents of various sorts should be allowed to hold government office or even to make public speeches.

Abstract Concepts of Dissent

Belief in the abstract concept of freedom to dissent is a major social norm in American culture. As such, anyone who is bright enough and old enough to have been exposed to political concepts—and who is a member of mainstream American culture—should be highly responsive to this norm. One study (Gallatin & Adelson, 1971), has shown that American teenagers, on the average, are much more likely than English or German teenagers to consider laws protecting individual freedom (e.g., of speech and reli-

BOX 30.7

EQUITY RESTORATION AND OUR LEGAL SYSTEM

S. Macaulay, a lawyer, and E. Walster, a social psychologist, both of the University of Wisconsin, have examined the basic structures of American law to determine to what extent it socializes the goal of restitution and reconciliation versus self-justification in harmdoers.

As is the case with many complex systems, our system of law turns out to have many kinds of subtle effects on harmdoers' tendencies to restore equity.

Both formally and informally, American law is intended to encourage restoration of equity. The common law of torts (which deals with wrong acts resulting in injury, loss, or damage, e.g., assault and battery, defamation) states that a harmdoer must compensate his victim. Many informal procedures also encourage compensation of the victim. Policemen in many cases will not arrest shoplifters if they return the stolen items; embezzlers are not always prosecuted if they return the amount embezzled.

However, other procedures exist that may discourage compensation and encourage self-justification. *Fault* must be established; if the harmdoer can deny or minimize his role and convince a judge that the victim was partially responsible for his own injury, he can avoid having to provide compensation to the victim. The long time lapse between the injury and a court trial encourages and permits the wrongdoer to find ingenious ways of winning the case, sometimes through distortion of the evidence. Also, the amount of time and money required to win a case may be more than a victim can bear. If the damage is, say, under $1,000, it may not be worth attempting to obtain compensation. If the damage is very great, the victim may find himself willing to accept a smaller settlement quickly, out of court. Exact or willing compensation is rarely given.

Obviously, however, it would be unjust to fail to give both parties the time and opportunity to defend themselves. Other kinds of solutions have been sought. Subsidized legal-aid programs are now available in most cities to serve persons with low incomes. Companies that provide consumer goods and services are more and more carefully scrutinized and regulated to prevent fraud and poor service.

Finally, Macaulay and Walster suggest that complete restoration of equity in all cases is perhaps not a desirable norm for our legal system to attempt to enforce and to socialize. Perhaps it is more reasonable to socialize individuals to be tolerant of the slight injuries that accompany everyday life and to encourage voluntary compensation, turning to the courts only as a last resort. Perhaps our legal system is approaching this goal.

S. MACAULAY & E. WALSTER. Legal structures and restoring equity. *Journal of Social Issues*, 1971, **27**, 173–188.

---

gion) as laws that should not be suspended under any circumstances. Furthermore, this tendency in American teenagers increased with age: Prior to the age of fifteen the American teenagers placed relatively more emphasis on the importance of having irrevocable criminal laws, but by the age of fifteen they were already overwhelmingly more concerned with the overriding importance of having an irrevocable legal guarantee of personal freedom.

Other studies have similarly shown that belief in the abstract concept of freedom of dissent increases with age; increased belief in this concept also goes along with greater intelligence, knowledge of American politics, political involvement, education, and increased exposure to television. One of these studies (Knutson, 1972) deals with determinants of the broader concept of political liberalism (including attitudes toward dissent) and concludes that Maslow's need hierarchy scheme (Unit 19, p. 462) is a useful predictor of this general orientation: People low on Maslow's hierarchy (those most occupied by the satisfaction of lower physiological needs) tend to be dogmatic and illiberal in their narrowly conceived political attitudes. Those most motivated by higher needs (such as self-actualization) show a greater interest—and with a liberal approach—in broad political and ideological issues.

Specific Instances of Dissent

But now let us review attitudes toward *specific instances* of dissent. We start with a bit of self-examination: Suppose you have the authority to determine whether to permit a speech arguing that (1) whites are intrinsically superior to any nonwhite race, or that (2) the free enterprise system must inevitably result in vast social injustice and a sick society, or that (3) unless abortion and infanticide are freely permitted (and even encouraged and subsidized by government) our planet will be disastrously over-populated and perhaps destroyed within 100 years. Probably at least one of these views strikes you as immoral, wrong, inflammatory, in poor taste, dangerous, or frightening. In such a situation, would you, as a decision-maker, consider blocking the free expression of the ideas you find objectionable (see Figure 30.3)?

FIGURE 30.3   Would you support their right of freedom of speech?

A—Photo by George W. Gardner; B—Photo by Irene Stein; C—Photo by UPI; D—Photo by Charles Gatewood.

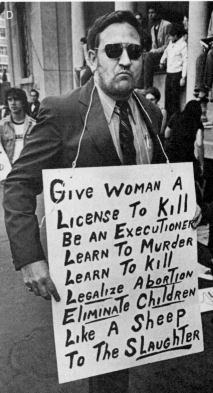

However you yourself answer this question, we all know that many people who consider themselves advocates of free speech would try to prevent the expression of one or more of these specific instances of dissent. Perhaps even most people would have a tendency to do so. Why this apparent contradiction: tolerance for the abstract concept; intolerance of specific instances of dissent?

It may well be that some of the very factors that account for the acceptance of the abstract concept evoke the rejection of the specific instance. To many Americans, for example, the abstract concept of freedom to dissent is part of the socially approved belief system. It is as American as apple pie, Pepsi-Cola, and the Fourth of July. The abstract concept of free speech is part of the whole package—*the established belief system.* But the established belief system also includes (to use our previous example) a belief in the free enterprise system, abhorrence of infanticide, and so forth. Thus the very same socialization and educational forces that bring about the acceptance of the abstract concept produce the rejection of the specific instance.

This possible explanation applies to the liberal person as well as to the conservative person. The liberal, too, has acquired his or her belief in the abstract concept of freedom to dissent as part of the approved liberal belief system. Part of that system includes belief in the equality of races; sponsoring a speech on white supremacy would cause internal conflict. Just as no man is an island unto himself, so few beliefs exist in isolation. The web of beliefs may be irregularly and crazily woven, unfit to catch and hold the truth; but it is a web in which each strand stems from, is strengthened by, or strengthens others.

Despite all this, many people are able to resolve conflicts between abstract and specific instances in favor of the abstract principle. If the polls are to be believed, less than half of the people can do so. One might, therefore, turn our original question around and ask: How is it possible that people can tolerate freedom of

BOX 30.8

WHAT MAKES CHILDREN TOLERANT OF DISSENT?

G. L. Zellman and D. O. Sears, social psychologists at the University of California at Los Angeles, studied tolerance for dissent in fifth- through ninth-grade children. Contrary to commonsense expectations, tolerance for concrete instances of dissent was unrelated to belief in the slogan of freedom of speech, the child's intelligence, and his parents' level of education. However, it was positively related to three measures of self-esteem and to whether the child planned to go to college. The measures of self-esteem were (1) *divergent thinking self-esteem* (the extent to which the child was interested in exploring new ideas on his own), (2) *convergent thinking self-esteem* (the extent of his general knowledge and intellectual ability), and (3) *school work self-esteem* (how capable the child felt of doing well in school). Intolerance of political views different from one's own may partly result from insecurity about one's own thinking. The other factor that was related to tolerance, whether the child planned to go to college, was itself related to self-esteem; children who plan to go to college tend to have higher self-esteem than children who do not plan to go to college. In addition, however, it appears that college-bound children tend to form peer groups that provide mutual support of their tolerance of dissenting views.

G. L. ZELLMAN & D. O. SEARS. Childhood origins of tolerance for dissent. *Journal of Social Issues,* 1971, **27,** No. 2, 109–136.

dissent from their own cherished and firmly held beliefs? The answer to this question, we believe, lies in the intensity of the conflict between the two beliefs, the personality of the believer, the manner in which the belief system was acquired (see Box 30.8), and the structure of the belief system itself. Some of these matters we have already discussed, and some we review next in Unit 31, "Structure and Development of Social Attitudes."

SUMMARY

1. Definitions of moral behavior are necessarily restricted to a given culture at a given time in its history. Even then, considerable variation in what is judged moral and immoral can be found within a culture.

2. One view of morality asserts that people are intuitively aware of and in agreement about what is good behavior (intuitionism). Another theory (emotivism) equates morality with intentional obedience to rules, with no rational basis offered or required for these rules. Prescriptivism, yet another view, insists that the rules be reasonable and, being so, that they are principles universally applicable to all situations.

3. Moral development may be seen as progressing through a series of stages that vary along a number of dimensions: attending to intentions rather than consequences, judging relativistically rather than absolutely, learning to ignore whether sanctions have been applied in reaching a moral judgment, and others.

4. In Western cultures, at least, transitions between moral stages seem to occur at roughly the same ages but may be affected by specific training.

5. Morality is regarded as socialized only when moral principles have been reliably internalized. In this process parental nurturance is a prime factor, in part because it enables the powerful socializing agent of love-oriented discipline. Severe discipline is far less effective in instilling moral behavior.

6. Acquiring morality is to an extent related to learning nonaggressive behavior. Aggressive behavior can be defined on the basis of its hurtful effects or on the aggressor's intent to hurt. Neither definition yields clear-cut classifications.

7. While aggression may or may not be innate, its control must of necessity be learned. The socialization of aggression typically results both in inhibiting its direct expression and in learning its acceptable indirect expression. Involved in this socialization process is parental degree of permissiveness toward aggressive behavior and degree of severity of punishment for its occurrence. Most successful are parents who are neither permissive nor harshly punitive.

8. Psychologically, an equitable relation exists between two people when it is perceived as involving an equal benefits-to-contributions ratio. A variety of actions, some honest and some self-serving, are triggered by a perception of inequity with regard to oneself. When others are subjected to inequity, one's power to affect the situation determines one's response.

9. A harmdoer may reestablish perceived equity through compensation of the victim or through denial that inequity has occurred. Or he may derogate the victim or disclaim personal responsibility.

10. Tolerance of dissent is embraced in the abstract but, for more than half of the persons questioned, is not applied in specific instances. Different factors influence these two levels of belief.

GLOSSARY

emotivism The theory of morality which holds that a moral judgment is simply any kind of comment that is intended to make someone behave in a certain way.

equity Justice and impartiality in human relations, such that an individual perceives his rewards as commensurate with his contributions to a relationship.

intuitionism The theory of morality which holds that man knows intuitively what is moral and good.

prescriptivism The theory of morality which holds that moral principles have more to do with reasoning and with consistency of behavior than with emotion and persuasion.

scapegoating Venting one's aggression on others who are different from oneself, who are weak and unable to retaliate, in response to frustration brought about by one's own lack of ability or by impersonal or unidentifiable causes.

structure and development of social attitudes

DO YOU KNOW...

- *that we learn information more quickly and remember it better when it is in line with our attitudes?*

- *in what sense we can usefully speak of being inoculated against certain attitudes?*

- *whether personal beliefs can to any extent be legislated?*

- *what the effects are of pertending to argue against a point of view you actually believe in?*

- *that mild pressure is better than strong pressure in bringing about a change in attitude?*

- *that people find an opposing point of view more persuasive if they do not think someone is trying to change their minds?*

- *what kinds of people are more easily scared into doing something they would rather not?*

- *why it is that we so exaggerate the extremeness of opposing points of view?*

unit 31

"Ritual group" from Xochipala, circa 1500 B.C., possibly the earliest ceramic sculptures from Mexico.

Photo, The Art Museum, Princeton University

CONTENTS

 We start our study of attitudes with brief accounts of two experiments: The first dramatically illustrates the influence of attitudes on our judgments of other persons; the second illustrates the influence of attitudes on learning and memory. If these studies demonstrate what the experimenters conclude from them, it becomes clear why the concept of attitude has been of such sovereign importance to the social psychologist.

Lambert et al. (1960) reported on a study carried out in Montreal, a community marked by a deep French-English schism. The subjects listened to recorded French and English readings of the same prose passage. They were told to disregard language and to concentrate on voice and style in forming their personality judgments of the speakers. The recordings were made by bilingual speakers, each of whom read both the French and English versions.

Both the English-Canadian and the French-Canadian subjects evaluated the "English speakers" more favorably than the "French speakers" on such traits as height, good looks, intelligence, dependability, ambition, and character. What had happened, according to Lambert, was that the French-Canadians had taken over the attitudes of the English-Canadians in regarding the Englishmen as superior. This attitude then influenced their judgment of the speakers' personalities, even if it reflected negatively upon their own group.

The second study, by Jones and Kohler (1958), examined "the proposition that subjects who hold to one set of beliefs learn plausible statements in favor of those beliefs and implausible statements opposing them better than they learn implausible-favoring or plausible-opposing statements."

The subjects were white college students classified as prosegregationists, antisegregationists, and neutrals on the basis of their scores on a test of this social attitude. All subjects were given twelve statements, printed on individual cards, to read aloud. Three of the statements were plausible prosegregation arguments. For example, "Southerners will have to pay the price

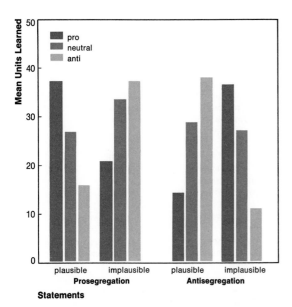

FIGURE 31.1 Differences in learning plausible and implausible statements of attitudes toward segregation by groups differing in initial attitudes. Persons holding definite attitudes on the subject, either pro or con, best learn plausible statements supporting their own view and implausible statements favoring the opposing point of view.

E. E. Jones & R. Köhler. The effects of plausibility on the learning of controversial statements. *Journal of Abnormal Social Psychology*, **57**, 315–320; copyright 1958 by the American Psychological Association, Inc.; adapted by permission.

of lowered scholastic standards if they yield to the pressures to integrate their schools." Three were implausible prosegregation arguments. For example, "If blacks and whites were meant to live together, they never would have been separated at the beginning of history." Three of the statements were plausible antisegregationist arguments, and three were implausible antisegregation arguments. After all twelve statements had been read, the subject was asked to reproduce as many as he could. This procedure was repeated five times.

The results are given in Figure 31.1. The hypothesis of the study is convincingly supported. Both the antisegregationists and the prosegregationists showed better learning for plausible statements compatible with their attitudes and for implausible statements oppos-

ing their attitudes. These findings suggest that we defend our attitudes by bolstering them with sound supporting arguments and weak and irrational opposing arguments.

THE NATURE OF ATTITUDES

How does an **attitude** differ from a fact? Why is it such a powerful determiner of an individual's judgments and actions? How can an attitude endure in the face of facts that would indicate that the attitude was irrational? Is it possible for two persons to share a basic attitude but yet to act upon it in different ways? These are some of the questions that are of interest to social psychologists (and laymen), and they and similar questions will guide our discussion in this unit.

The Components of Attitudes

Most briefly defined, an attitude is a like or a dislike that has behavioral consequences. It can be thought of as consisting of three basic components: a belief, an emotion, and an action-tendency. Example: Suppose that you have a favorable (or unfavorable) attitude toward smoking marijuana, implying, first, that you have certain *beliefs* about marijuana, such as marijuana enhances consciousness (or muddles thinking). Further implied is that your *feelings* about smoking it are positive or negative; perhaps you are pleased when you find it being passed around at a party (or you are disturbed or embarrassed). Finally, your attitude implies that your *behavior* can be predicted: You will probably smoke marijuana occasionally (or would never consider doing so).

So far, a fairly neat concept of attitudes has been presented: Attitudes involve *coherent* sets of beliefs, feelings, and action-tendencies. But be forewarned: It is only under rather restricted circumstances that we can predict one of the components of a person's attitude from knowing the other two. This will become amply clear as we sample the available research on attitudes in this unit. (For a simple starter, see Box 31.1, p. 758.)

BOX 31.1

DO YOU LIKE TO SMOKE?

In 1972, John Swainston at California State University, Hayward, conducted a series of interviews intended to probe persons' attitudes concerning smoking tobacco. (The fact that the probing was successful in getting beneath the comfortable surface of the attitude is clearly evident.) The following interview of a young woman shows that the beliefs, feelings, and action-tendencies that comprise an attitude may be related to one another in a very complex way.

Q: Do you like to smoke?
A: No—sometimes—no—*yesss*, it's a habit.
Q: Why do you smoke?
A: My father gave me my first cigarette at 12 years, it was the thing to do, like most of my friends. Now it's a habit! I'm a nervous smoker, when nervous I smoke more—it's like a security blanket.
Q: What reason can you give why you smoke?
A: Habit—"the need to smoke."
Q: Does the fact that smoking has been connected with cancer and lung disease worry you?
A: Yes and no.
Q: Why yes?
A: *If* there is truth to this, I would hate the thought of not becoming a grandmother.
Q: It is a fact!
A: I've read different reports that say it is not a definite fact but it is more of a theory. But I wouldn't like to look at my lungs!
Q: Would you like to stop smoking?
A: Yes.
Q: How do you think you can stop?
A: I don't know.
Q: Would you seek professional help?
A: Yes—if I could find someone who could help me stop.
Q: Have you looked?
A: No.
Q: Why?
A: Where do you go?
Q: Have you any suggestions for stopping?

A: I have no will-power.
Q: Why?
A: I don't know.
Q: Why?
A: I don't know—it offers me security.
Q: Are you afraid of the consequences of stopping?
A: (No answer; noticeable hostility.)
Q: Do you need this type of security?
A: I must, right?
Q: Why?
A: I don't know, I really don't know.
Q: You said you were familiar with studies that indicate that smoking has not been proven to lead to lung cancer. What evidence do these reports give?
A: I don't remember the details.
Q: Have you been advised to cut down on your smoking?
A: My doctor said I should. My husband is always getting after me for smoking. He keeps nagging me about it.
Q: You said you began smoking at 12? Can you remember what things you liked about it?
A: Irritating my mother.
Q: Oh?
A: I would walk around the house smoking whenever I felt irritated at her. She'd get so mad she wouldn't speak to me.
Q: But your father didn't mind if you smoked?
A: He actually enjoyed it when we sat down together and talked and smoked.
Q: Did you often smoke with your father?
A: Whenever I visited him. My parents are divorced.
Q: Is there anything you enjoy about smoking now?
A: No. Well, yes. I don't know.
Q: Do you like to irritate your husband by smoking?
A: Of course not.
Q: Well, what if you just quit smoking?
A: He'd like it. But I'd feel less womanly . . . less adequate as I went about handling my responsibilities in life.
Q: Less adequate?
A: Look, this is really making me feel anxious. (She lights up a cigarette.)

What consistency can you detect *within* her beliefs, within her feelings, and within her action-tendencies? What consistency can you find *among* her beliefs, feelings, and action-tendencies? Does her attitude strike you as logical?

The belief component The belief component of attitudes may consist of sound factual arguments, generalizations, stereotypes, rationalizations of the person's previous actions, totally unfounded notions that were suggested by someone else, or even assumptions of which the person is unaware. To put it another way, the belief component may consist of reasoned arguments, of vague notions, or of a mixture of both. The belief component may also vary with respect to the *number* of arguments it contains. (Have you ever tried to change someone's attitude by showing him that his belief may be based on incorrect reasoning, only to have him turn about and present a different line of thinking in support of the same belief?) Since the term "attitude" encompasses such a wide range of possible types of belief systems, it is desirable at this point to introduce two concepts pertaining to the *belief structure* of attitudes that may be useful in classifying these varying belief systems.

Bem (1970) has suggested that a helpful way to describe belief structures, presumably *any* belief structure, is in terms of their vertical and horizontal structure. **Vertical structure** *refers to the presence or absence of premises supporting the belief.* Consider, for example, this belief: You should drink at least one glass of milk a day. Young American middle-class children typically learn such beliefs. The statement may be unquestioningly accepted as true and important. Such a belief is called a **primitive belief**. It is so called because it is not based on other, more explicit beliefs, but is given to the believer by someone whose *authority* she accepts. Primitive beliefs have no supporting premises—no vertical structure.

Consider now the same belief, with a vertical structure of supporting premises:

Persons need about 0.8 grams of calcium per day to have strong teeth and bones.
Milk is extremely rich in calcium; a large glass of milk contains about 0.6 grams of calcium.
These nutritional facts are well documented. Therefore, one should drink at least one glass of milk a day.

This is a **higher-order belief,** based on a vertical structure of supporting premises. Its three premises are based on other premises that eventually rest on a primitive (i.e., unexamined) belief; in each of the three supporting beliefs lies implicit and unexamined a belief that any

idea on which most experts (authorities) agree must be true.

One consequence of holding a higher-order belief is that the believer may be responsive to new information pertaining to any of its underlying premises. For example, if a better, tastier, cheaper, and more available source of calcium than milk was discovered, the holder of the higher-order belief just described might change her attitude toward milk and she might even give up drinking milk. But the holder of the primitive belief would not see the relevance of milk drinking to the new discovery. Consequently, she would not be as likely to give up drinking milk, nor would she give up her belief about the body's specific need for milk.

Because many of the beliefs held by young children are primitive, a rational attempt to dissuade the child of her beliefs cannot be effective; the arguments and reasoning are simply not relevant to the child's beliefs. Many attitudes held by adults are also primitive. On complex issues, such as as deciding for which presidential candidate to vote, many persons find it difficult to learn and to organize relevant information into sound arguments for or against the candidate. However, such persons are not necessarily lacking in political attitude. If one has always voted for a certain political party and if his friends and family favor that party's candidate, Herbert Tweedledee, then the action and emotional component of his pro-Tweedledee attitude will probably be strong. Our hypothetical citizen may comfortably maintain a primitive belief that Herbert Tweedledee is a good man and not ever seek strong supporting premises.

However, higher-order beliefs are not necessarily more vulnerable to change or more subject to continual or honest examination (although they are at least available for examination). The belief components of our attitudes often have horizontal as well as vertical structures. **Horizontal structure** *refers to the presence or absence of independent and parallel premises supporting the same belief.* That is, the same surface belief may have not only one but many different sets of vertical supporting arguments. A politically involved person can often give many reasons why one should vote for a given candidate. For example:

Tweedledee will reduce military spending.	Tweedledee has a good voting record on civil rights.	Tweedledee has skill and experience in handling Congress.
Military spending is robbing our country.	Racial equality is essential to a democracy.	This skill is needed if a President is to get his legislation passed.
Therefore, Tweedledee is a good man to elect.	Therefore, Tweedledee is a good man to elect.	Therefore, Tweedledee is a good man to elect.

To weaken one of these premises is not to destroy the belief. To destroy the entire horizontal structure of supporting premises would, of course, destroy the higher-order belief. The individual would then have to (1) change his belief, (2) cling to the belief in its primitive form ("OK, I accept all of your arguments, but I still simply believe Herbert is the best man. I just believe it, that's all."), or (3) scurry about to find new information with which to build new arguments in support of his belief. Which of these things is done depends, in part, upon the emotional and action components of his attitude.

Finally, it should be mentioned that higher-order beliefs may, with the passage of time, revert to primitive beliefs; well-reasoned premises on which they were originally based may fade from memory, leaving only the embraced conclusion.

The emotional component Both positive and negative attitudes, almost by definition, involve our feelings and emotions. The emotional components of our attitudes may be learned through first- or second-hand experience with the objects of those attitudes or even through purely fortuitous associations between the objects and other completely irrelevant events (see Figure 31.2). A child who has a frightening experience the first time he goes to school may learn to fear schools, and this may color all the components of his attitudes (belief systems and action-tendencies) toward school; his fear is based on his own immediate, direct experience with the object of his attitude. But not all emotional colorings are that rational in origin. We ourselves may never have had any contact or direct experience with, say, the Nonsuch People of

Graustark, and yet we may learn to like or dislike them through hearsay, through listening to our neighbors talk about them, or through reading about them. Finally, it has been shown that we can acquire positive or negative feeling tones about entire ethnic groups through sheer, simple, meaningless juxtapositions and associations. Consider the following experiment: Staats and Staats (1958) asked subjects to memorize lists of words. Six of the words were the names of nationalities: Greek, Dutch, French, Italian, Swedish, and German. The rest of the words were positive, negative, or neutral. For one group of subjects, Dutch was always followed in the list by a positive word (e.g., healthy) and Swedish was always followed by a negative word (e.g., failure). This order was reversed for a second group. The rest of the nationality words were always followed by neutral words (e.g., chair). At the end of the experiment, each subject rated how he felt about each nationality name on a seven-point scale ranging from "pleasant" to "unpleasant." As predicted, subjects in the group that paired Dutch with a positive word and Swedish with a negative word rated Dutch as more pleasant than Swedish, and vice versa for the other group. Here we have the ultimate: guilt by word association.

The emotional component can sometimes be the major determinant of the attitude, overriding all else. A striking (and amusing) illustration of this is found in an experiment by Valins (1966), which seems to indicate that a person's judgment can be led astray by misleading cues as to his *own* emotions. Valins showed male subjects slides of seminude women. He pretended to be measuring their heartbeat as they looked at each slide. Actually, the highly amplified heart rate that was audible to both

FIGURE 31.2

Photo by Charles Gatewood

the subject and the experimenter was not that of the subject; it was a recording. And the recording was set so that subjects would hear the heartbeat change markedly when some of the slides, selected at random, were shown. Subjects were to rate each slide for its attractiveness and were told that they could take home the slides they found most attractive. Valins reports that the slides on which there was the greatest change in fake heartbeat tended to be rated most attractive and to be chosen as the ones to be taken home. The subjects still preferred these slides even four weeks after the experiment. Thus, even when a person is "conned" into an emotional state, that emotional state takes over his judgment!

The action-tendency component   It has often been said that racist acts will not cease until

the minds and hearts of men have been changed. And it is true that a change in beliefs and feelings about someone is usually accompanied by a change in behavior toward that person, but this is only generally true. Just as an individual may hold several incompatible beliefs and harbor irrational and indefensible feelings about objects (as in the studies by the Staats and by Valins), so can his behavior be inconsistent with other behavior tendencies or with his beliefs, feelings, and emotions—in a word, with his attitudes. It must be remembered that concrete behavior with respect to a specific object results from the convergence of many factors: the many, different, and incompatible beliefs that accrue to the object; the many, different, and sometimes contradictory feeling tones about the object; and the particular, momentary situation in which the behavior occurs. We must therefore expect to find that what a person believes about, say, pacifism and what he feels about it cannot serve as valid indicators of how he will actually behave toward the occurrence of a war under all circumstances. The guiding principle is this: People are not single-minded; emotions can be ambivalent; and behavior is multidetermined. Nevertheless, the relations among beliefs, feelings, and *actions* are the most important elements in studying attitudes—complex though these elements may be. We will therefore discuss this area in greater detail in a later section of this unit (see *Attitudes versus Actions*, p. 766) after we have laid some necessary groundwork.

THE FORMATION OF ATTITUDES

Among the many determinants of an individual's attitudes, three are of particular importance: the family, the groups with which the individual affiliates, and the personality of the individual.

Family Influences

Young children are dependent on their parents and other family members for many things, including, of course, information about the world they live in. All family members—but we speak only of parents from now on—influence and to some extent control what the child sees and hears and how he interprets this information; they also teach the child what to expect to see and hear.

Obviously, by controlling a child's information, parents can largely determine his specific beliefs and attitudes. Moreover, the way in which parents control their child's access to information affects the child's entire orientation toward new information and ideas and toward society in general. Let us examine a few of the specific ways in which parents may affect the attitudes of their children.

Some parents limit severely the kinds of information with which their children come into contact: They may quite intentionally send the child to a school in which the teachers are known to have attitudes similar to those of the parents; they may restrict the child's viewing of television and movies to those that convey attitudes of which the parents approve; they may determine with whom the child may play and where he may go; parents may even limit the way the child thinks about his own emotions and needs, especially with respect to matters of sexuality and personal autonomy. By punishing the child's early interest in sex, the parent may bring about repression of sexuality in the child (*or* heighten the child's interest in sex); by severely punishing the child when he exerts his will against his parent, the parent may teach the child to keep from consciousness any thoughts of disobeying authority figures (*or* he may learn to be rebellious).

Of course, most parents do not greatly restrict the information to which their children are exposed. Some parents even encourage their children to come in contact with persons having life styles different from those of the parents. It might appear at first glance that, by doing this, these parents relinquish control of their children's attitudes. Not so, since this encouragement is in itself very influential in the development of their attitudes.

There are four major ways in which parental influence can occur: (1) One of the first sets of ideas and life styles to which children are exposed is that of their own parents. (2) The attitude a child learns from exposure to new experiences depends on her interpretation of those experiences. Parents and, occasionally, other family members are the major interpreters for the child, at least until the time that the attitudes and behavior of peers become an important influence. If a child learns from television that Mexican-American farm workers and their allies are demanding the right to form a labor union and are urging that some produce be boycotted in food markets, her first question to her parents may be "Why?" The character of her developing attitudes toward all Mexican-Americans or toward all unions may hinge upon her parents' reply. (3) Parents who present their ideologies to their children but who also encourage their children to seek and consider opposing ideas and attitudes may actually reinforce their own ideas by unwittingly inoculating their children against other ideologies. When existing beliefs are weakly challenged by new information, the person may respond by preparing arguments supporting his original position and by preparing counterarguments against the opposing position. Existing attitudes are thus strengthened and they become all the more resistant to subsequent and more powerful persuasive influences. However, when persons have had no prior exposure to ideas that conflict with their own, their first prolonged exposure to new ideas may result in an inability to defend their existing attitudes, and they may readily accept the new attitudes. McGuire and Papageorgis (1961) compared two means of preventing attitude change: inoculation (exposure of one's attitudes to mild attack) and bolstering (receiving additional support for one's original position). A third group received neither inoculation nor bolstering. All three groups were then subjected to an attack on their initial attitudes. The inoculation group showed far less attitude change than did the group that received support for its attitudes. The support group showed almost as much attitude change as the control group. The effects of such inoculation in childhood are hard to measure or estimate, since these effects are not very apparent until the child has left home and involved himself in other social groups. (4) Parents who encourage their children to explore many and various ideas are passing on to their children an open attitude that may generalize to many other realms of experience. Ideally, the children may learn to explore a wide range of new experiences and to rely on their own intellect to evaluate new possibilities. For a child so raised all matters are regarded as open to inquiry, and censorship and other violations of personal freedom are regarded as undesirable.

Peer-Group Influences

The extent to which peer groups change a person's attitudes depends on many factors, including the extent to which the peer group's attitudes differ from those of the child's parents, the intensity and duration of his exposure to the group, and the extent to which he previously has had an opportunity to examine opposing ideas (inoculation).

When young people leave home and enter a different kind of life—when, for example, they go away to college, or to find a job in another city, or to join a youth commune—usually some of their basic attitudes change. Consider the ways certain kinds of college experiences changed the attitudes of people in your parents' generation. (It might be enlightening to interview them about this.) The impact of college depends of course upon the kind of person and upon the social atmosphere of the college. This point is convincingly brought out in Newcomb's classic Bennington College study (1943). To be fully appreciated this study may require familiarity with early twentieth-century American political history, a period when America was depression-torn, and the world was war-threatened.

At the time of the study (1935–1939) Bennington College was new and geographically isolated. The students, all women, came largely from economically privileged, conservative families. The members of the faculty were predominantly liberal; they were deeply involved in the social issues of the period and felt that their sheltered students ought to face up to political and social realities.

The general trend of attitude change in this college community was from conservatism as freshmen toward liberalism as upperclasswomen. To illustrate: A straw vote of the students during the 1936 presidential campaign revealed a substantial difference between the political preferences of the freshman and of the junior and senior students. As Table 31.1 shows,

TABLE 31.1 PREFERENCES OF STUDENTS AND PARENTS FOR PRESIDENTIAL CANDIDATES IN 1936 CAMPAIGN

	Freshmen		Sophomores		Juniors & Seniors	
	Students	Parents	Students	Parents	Students	Parents
Landon (Republican)	62	66	43	69	15	60
Roosevelt (Democratic)	29	26	42	22	54	35
Thomas, Browder (Socialist, Communist)	9	7	15	8	30	4

T. M. Newcomb. *Personality and Social Change.* Copyright 1943; adapted by permission of Holt, Rinehart and Winston, Inc.

62 percent of the freshmen but only 15 percent of the upperclasswomen voted for Landon, the Republican candidate. Roosevelt, the New Deal Democratic candidate, received only 29 percent of the freshman vote but captured 54 percent of the votes of the upperclasswomen. The votes for the candidates of the American Socialist and Communist parties increased from 9 percent among the freshmen to 30 percent among the juniors and seniors. Table 31.1 reveals that the freshmen voted much as their parents did, whereas the junior and senior students differed remarkably from their parents. Other data also show a trend from freshman conservatism to junior and senior liberalism. Attitudes toward nine specific social and economic issues were measured yearly during the four years of the study. The juniors and seniors were less conservative than the freshmen on all nine issues.

These changes were not found in all students, however. Some students displayed the general trend in heightened form; other students changed not at all; still others reversed the trend. Why did the observed changes occur in some students and fail to occur in others? In seeking an answer, Newcomb studied intensively nineteen conservative and twenty-four liberal seniors.

The liberal seniors were found to be strongly motivated to achieve independence from their families and to achieve status in the college community (at Bennington prestige was accorded liberal students). For these students liberal attitudes served the social-adjustment function. The following interview excerpt is illustrative:

> Of course, there's social pressure here to give up your conservatism. I'm glad of it, because for me this became the vehicle for achieving independence from my family. So changing my attitudes has gone hand in hand with two very important things: establishing my own independence and at the same time becoming a part of the college organism.

The conservative seniors tended to reject the college community or to isolate themselves from it because of fear of disrupting their relationships with their families. The following interview excerpt shows that resistance to change among these students was a self-defensive process.

> I wanted to disagree with all the noisy liberals, but I was afraid and I couldn't. So I built up a wall inside me against what they said. I found I couldn't compete, so I decided to stick to my father's ideas. For at least two years I've been insulated against all college influences.

This excerpt points to one of the most potent sources of resistance to attitude change. Inability to sever a deep, established relationship with an early group may cause the individual to close himself off from new information.

Did these effects last? The follow-up study indicated that twenty years later their attitudes were remarkably unchanged (see Box 31.2 for details).

Personality Factors

The effect of group influences upon attitude development is to produce a relatively high uniformity of attitude among the members of the group. But in the midst of uniformity we also find diversity. A major factor in creating diversity in attitudes, even within the tightest-knit groups, is the existence of personality differences among the individual members. The major functions of attitudes in the individual personality can be grouped into four categories according to their motivational basis.

The instrumental function In seeking to satisfy his needs, the individual develops favorable attitudes toward objects that satisfy his needs or are seen as doing so and unfavorable attitudes toward objects that thwart or punish him.

In a study by Lott and Lott (1960) children played an individual game in the company of fellow group members who were nonfriends. Each group was randomly assigned to conditions in which none, one, two, or all members were rewarded by winning the game and receiving the prize. At the end of the day, each child was asked to indicate his best friends. The rewarded children chose as friends a significantly greater number of their fellow play-group members than did the unrewarded subjects.

BOX 31.2

THE SOCIAL BASES OF PERSISTING ATTITUDES

Political and Economic Progressivism Quartile	Nixon Preferred	Kennedy Preferred	Total
1. (least conservative)	3	30	33
2.	8	25	33
3.	18	13	31
4. (most conservative)	22	11	33
Total	51	79	130

In 1960 and 1961, Theodore M. Newcomb examined the political and economic attitudes of 139 of the 141 Bennington College students whom he had studied as undergraduates between 1935 and 1939. Newcomb's interest in doing the follow-up study was to determine whether his students had maintained their relatively nonconservative attitudes twenty-odd years later or whether they had reverted to relatively conservative attitudes.

As the table shows, the degree of stability of attitudes over the interval of twenty-odd years is startling. Those individuals who, upon graduation, were in the least conservative quartile of the total group preferred John F. Kennedy to Richard M. Nixon by frequencies of 30 to 3; those in the next quartile, by 25 to 8. Twenty years after graduation, 83 percent of the initially less conservative half of the group preferred Kennedy, whereas only 37 percent of the initially more conservative half preferred him.

These findings suggest that the group as a whole is far less conservative twenty years after graduation from college than was to be expected in view of its socioeconomic status. Sixty percent of the group expressed a preference for Kennedy. The percentage of Protestant women college students of the same socioeconomic status who, in 1960, expressed a preference for Kennedy was only 28 percent.

Why this remarkable persistence of nonconservative political attitudes? Newcomb concludes:

> If, therefore, I were to select a single factor that contributed most to these women's maintenance of nonconservative attitudes between the late 1930s and early 1960s, I think it would be the fact of selecting husbands of generally nonconservative stripe who helped to maintain for them an environment that was supportive of their existing attitudes.

T. M. NEWCOMB. Persistence and regression of changed attitudes: Long-range studies. *Journal of Social Issues*, 1963, **19**, 3–14.

This immediate development of friendship attitudes toward the children with whom they happened to be associated in the satisfaction of winning the game is remarkable in view of the fact that their choices of best friends tested *before* the game session were based on prolonged interaction with classmates and had been found to be highly stable.

The self-defensive function As we have seen in Unit 23, self-defensive mechanisms operate by externalizing impulses unacceptable to the self, thus minimizing emotional conflict and anxiety.

It has been proposed that many of our attitudes primarily help us to deal with our inner conflicts and that they have little to do with the actual characteristics of the object to which the attitude is directed. It has been suggested, for example, that anti-Semitism and other forms of ethnic prejudice originate in the individual's personal difficulties with his parents and not in his experiences with members of the ethnic group he dislikes (see Box 26.1, p. 658).

The self-expressive function Many of the attitudes of the individual serve not to protect the self but to proclaim the self. These self-expressive attitudes define the sort of person the individual considers himself to be or aspires to be. The college student who conceives of himself as a political activist may develop a whole syndrome of attitudes—attitudes toward the university administration, the local city government, the faculty, the university curriculum, mode of dress, radical groups off campus, and so on—that serve to express his central values and confirm his self-identity as a political activist.

The social-adjustment function   Our attitudes can serve as social-entrance tickets or social-exit passes. They may facilitate and maintain our relations with members of positively valued groups in increasing our feelings of oneness with persons who are significant to us. Other attitudes—so-called rebel attitudes—may be formed in response to our need to dissociate ourselves from or oppose still other groups or individuals. For example, the hippie son of a middle-class family who aspires to acceptance in a commune will tend to adopt values and attitudes toward material success, dress, or love that, on one hand, will serve as an entrance ticket to that community while, on the other hand, will serve to emphasize his rejection of his middle-class background.

ATTITUDES VERSUS ACTIONS

What is the extent and the manner in which the action-tendency component of an attitude becomes actualized in concrete behavior?

Let us first look at a somewhat puzzling set of results found in a study by Ajzen and Fishbein (1970)—results that help to set the stage for our discussion by pointing to the peculiar complexity of the problem.

Suppose we start by asking you to examine your own attitudes about cooperation. Do you favor being cooperative with others? Would you say that you are a highly cooperative person, mildly so, or not at all? In the light of what you believe your attitude to be, what do you predict: Will you behave cooperatively with other people in a common enterprise, will you be competitive, just how will you respond?

Now let us go to Ajzen and Fishbein. These experimenters asked their subjects to participate in a game in which partners either could cooperate (and thereby each partner would win a certain amount), or one could try to double-cross the other and win a great deal,

unless his partner chose to double-cross him, in which case both players won the least. Players knew these odds. In the course of the game all players were asked to indicate how wise it seemed to cooperate in the specific situation, if each expected his partner to cooperate, and if each thought his partner expected him to cooperate.

Before the game began, players were issued a specific set of suggestions that were intended to manipulate the motivational approach they would adopt. For some players the suggestion stressed that cooperation would bring them the greatest benefit; others were told that self-interest was best served by adopting a competitive approach, that is, by double-crossing their partner. These suggestions were effective in that each group clearly showed more of the kind of behavior they had been told would work best for them.

But—and this is the interesting result—the extent to which a player actually cooperated was determined differently under the two sets of suggestions. Under the competitive instruction the player's decision to cooperate depended more on how *wise* he felt it was to cooperate in the game situation and less on what he guessed his partner expected of him. The cooperative instruction evoked the opposite response: The perception of the partner's expectation was clearly the dominant influence and the attitude toward the wisdom of cooperation was considerably less important. (In neither case did a player's own view of whether or not he expected his partner to cooperate affect his game behavior.) What meaning can be derived from these results? What follows is an interpretation based on the investigators' highly technical treatment of their findings.

In this experiment, we have a finding not anticipated by previous research—that figuring out an opponent's intention to cooperate is not a factor in game behavior, no matter what the instructed attitude. Furthermore, when both have been told that cooperation is the best course, one's personal assessment of the wisdom of that advice becomes relatively unimportant. What does influence behavior is a guess as to what one partner expects the other to do. Conversely, when competition has been advised, one partner may no longer give much weight to his partner's guesses about his behavior. (Perhaps the assumption is that he will naturally expect adoption of the suggested dog-eat-dog approach.) What does matter then is whether one partner believes that this approach is in fact the wise one.

If there is any overriding general theme that might be determined from this complex set of results it is that people tend to view an adversary as gullible. They regard themselves as shrewd, hence worthy of their adversary's attempts to second-guess them; but they do not bother to return the implied compliment.

However, all this involves weaving a tenuous web of inference from the data. Safer ground would be to suggest that relations between attitudes and behavior are indeed highly complex and deserve the considerable research attention they are now receiving. For the research on the relation between attitudes and action, one is tempted to the following maxim: In this area no relation is so complex that good, solid research will not make it even *more* complex.

Fishbein (1967) has suggested a general framework for understanding the relations between consciously held attitudes and the ways a person acts in a specific situation. According to his view, there are three kinds of variables that account for behavior in a social context: (1) one's beliefs about the consequences of acting a given way and his evaluation of those consequences; (2) one's beliefs about what he personally feels he should do and his belief about what society, that is, most other people, says he should do; and (3) his motivation to comply with the dictates of his own conscience and with society's expectations. For the moment this framework only indicates directions that further research can take, but it does encompass the factors that need to be taken into account.

Many persons who hold an attitude that is socially unacceptable do not dare to express it openly either by word or by deed. An interesting question is thus raised: Can an attitude survive if it is not translated into action? What would be the effect on an attitude if one were forced to behave in ways that were directly contrary to that attitude? It is often said that attitudes cannot be legislated, so that laws specifying how one must act toward members of minority groups, for instance, do not affect individuals' underlying racist attitudes. This is another way of saying that racism will not cease until the minds and hearts of men have changed. Is this true? Or *can* laws that govern behavior change basic attitudes? We now examine this issue.

Attitude-Discrepant Action

Suppose that you agreed to prepare and deliver a strong, forceful speech, taking the position that drinking should be prohibited on campus, and you do so. Suppose further that, in reality, you are *opposed* to any prohibition of drinking. What will happen to your personal pro-drinking attitude as a result of behaving in an antidrinking manner?

Goethals and Cooper (1972) have studied the effects of such speech making on the attitude of the speaker. Persons who prepared and delivered a speech to a fellow student (via microphone to an adjacent room), intending to convince him that drinking was evil (though they believed otherwise), consequently modified their own attitude and began to express more antialcohol sentiments. But this effect was observed *only* if they were informed by their fellow student that the speech had indeed convinced him that drinking was bad *and only* when the speaker (who had been given the option of not participating in the experiment when it was described to him) had freely chosen to participate.

What would have happened if the speaker had not intended to give such a speech? Goethals and Cooper sought the answer to this question by asking half of the subjects to give a rehearsal speech on the topic, only later to discover that the microphone had been accidentally left on and thus the speech had been delivered to an audience contrary to the subjects' individual intentions. In this setup, the speaker's attitude did *not* change, even if his speech was convincing and brought about an attitude change in another student.

These results underline some essential principles that govern the effects of counter-attitudinal behavior upon changes in one's own attitude. For such verbalization of an opposing viewpoint to be effective and to cause one to practice (or at least begin to believe) what she has been preaching, it is necessary that (1) one must have freely chosen to perform an action contrary to her own previous attitude, and (2) the action must have been successful in changing someone else's attitude. The general point is that you modify your beliefs when you have been directly responsible for a consequence even if you find it painful and embarrassing. But, if you were forced into the action, then, despite its effectiveness, you do not feel personally responsible, and therefore you can maintain your initial attitude.

Thus, when an individual engages in attitude-discrepant behavior with little external justification, he is apt to change his attitude, making it more consistent with his behavior. As the study described in Box 31.3 illustrates, this principle has important implications for child-rearing, interpersonal relations, and the law. If a person wishes to persuade anyone—a child, a friend, or society as a whole—to change an aspect of its behavior, probably the mildest possible means that will produce the behavioral change should be used. Threats of severe punishment or other dire consequences may force an outward change in *behavior*, but the individual will not change his *attitude* on that issue.,

To return then to the question raised earlier: Can attitudes be legislated? The answer would appear to be a qualified yes. Attitude change can probably be legislated if behavioral compliance can be produced with very little external pressure. Extremely severe threats may modify behavior, but they certainly do not change attitudes. Faced with dictatorial repression, many opponents of a regime may visibly conform and some may go underground, but neither group actually accepts the ideologies of their repressors. On the other hand, threats that are *so* mild that they do not change behavior will not be effective in changing attitudes either.

PERSUASION AND ATTITUDE CHANGE

Studies of the factors influencing the effectiveness of persuasive messages in bringing about attitude change can all be subsumed under the formula of *who* says *what* in which *channel* to *whom* with what *effect*.

The most thoroughly studied factors determining the effectiveness of persuasive communications are those connected with the identity of the communicator (who) and with the nature of the message (what). We can summarize the results of many of these studies in a series of propositions.

The Communicator

1. Communicators regarded by the audience as credible are more effective in inducing immediate change than are untrustworthy communicators (Rhine & Severance, 1970). However, high credibility (as opposed to low credibility) increases attitude change only when the statements of either do not have supporting evidence, that is, when the only support available is the credibility of the communicator (McCrosky, 1970). Evidence can override credibility of the communicator.

2. The advantage of communicators high in credibility over untrustworthy communicators tends to disappear over time. This phenomenon has been called the "sleeper effect." It may result from the dissociation, with the passage of time, of source from content. People tend to remember what was said without spontaneously thinking about who said it (Hovland & Weiss, 1951).

3. Communicators who are perceived as similar in their attitudes to the audience are more effective than communicators who are seen as dissimilar. Anything that the communicator can do to lessen his audience's sense of dissimilarity from him will enhance his effectiveness. Weiss (1957) has shown, for example, that a persuasive attempt preceded by the expression of attitudes (irrelevant to the issue of persuasion) that are known to be similar to those of the audience increases the amount of change in positive attitudes toward the issue

BOX 31.3

SPEAK SOFTLY, AND YOU
WON'T NEED A BIG STICK

Will a person change his attitude to justify his actions? Current theory and recent experiments have suggested that only when a person cannot point to a good reason why he acted contrary to his own attitudes will he change his attitudes; and apparently he will do so in order to justify his *actions*. In view of these finding, J. L. Freedman, a social psychologist at Stanford University, raised the following point: In attempting to mold a child's behavior in accordance with the values of society, our ultimate goal is not obedience in the face of threat, but self-control in the absence of direct pressure. Therefore, might not mild threats be more effective than severe ones? If a child is mildly warned not to do such and so, he has relatively little reason to refrain from that act; if he obeys, he is likely to feel that he has done so of his own accord and adjust his attitudes toward the act accordingly. On the other hand, if severely threatened about committing the act, his reason for not committing the act is clearly external and no attitude change is necessary to justify his behavior.

To test this hypothesis, Freedman gave second-, third-, and fourth-grade children a chance to play with toys that had been forbidden under conditions of either mild or severe threat. He then examined the effects of these threats on how much they later liked—and played with—the forbidden toys. His procedure was as follows:

Each child was told he was participating in a study of toy preference. He was shown five toys: a cheap plastic submarine, an expensive and intriguing battery-operated robot, a baseball glove, a toy rifle, and a toy tractor. He was then asked to indicate his liking of each on a scale ranging from 0 ("very, very bad toy") to 100 ("very, very good toy"). In the two experimental conditions, the child was then told that the experimenter had an errand to run and would have to leave the child in the room with the toys for 10 min. Half of the experimental subjects (Low Threat group) were given a mild threat as follows: "While I'm gone, you can play with the toys if you want. You can play with any of them except the robot. Do not play with the robot. It is wrong to play with the robot." The other half of the experimental children (High Threat group) were given the additional, more severe warning: "If you play with

the robot I'll be very angry and will have to do something about it." In the two parallel control conditions, the children were given similar threats but were not subject to temptation since the experimenter remained in the room and worked on some papers. At the end of the 10-min period the children were again asked to rate the toys and were then excused to return to their class.

The results: In this first phase of the experiment all four groups' preference ratings of the toys changed after having been forbidden to play with the robot; the children rated the robot as less preferred than at their initial contact and the other toys as more preferred than before. However, the greatest change in preference occurred for the Low Threat experimental group; they showed the greatest reduction in liking for the robot and the greatest increase in liking of the other toys. This is in line with Freedman's hypothesis since Low Threat children, in obeying a mild prohibition, rationalized their behavior by downgrading the worth of the taboo robot.

About forty days later, another experimenter came to the school, presumably to administer psychological tests. Each of the children who had participated in the first part of the study was called in, alone, and asked to copy some drawings. When the child was finished, the experimenter told him that, while his drawings were being looked over, he could play with any of the toys that someone else had happened to leave in the room while his drawings were being scored. The experimenter remained present; the toys were, of course, the same ones as before. Some children aked if the robot could be played with, to which the experimenter's reply was that any of the toys could be played with.

In this second phase, when the children had the opportunity to play freely with the robot, two-thirds of the Low Threat subjects chose not to play with it. However, in the High Threat experimental condition about three-quarters of the children later *did* play with the robot.

Thus, on both counts, the Low Threat children —by change first of attitude and later of behavior —indicated that the forbidden toy had simply become less attractive to them; this result appeared to confirm the greater effectiveness of a mild prohibition in giving the child himself a degree of implied freedom to violate it, so that he can himself choose not to do so.

J. L. FREEDMAN Long-term behavioral effects of cognitive dissonance. *Journal of Experimental Social Psychology*, 1965, **1**, 145–155.

of persuasion. Every politician, for example, presents himself as a man of the people, who shares with all Americans love of God and family.

The Message

1. *The acceptance of attitudes opposed by the audience will be promoted if the message is so designed that it evokes minimal counterargument in the audience.* Allyn and Festinger (1961) report a study in which a communicator recommended to an audience of teenagers assembled for a school program that the minimum age for receiving a driver's license should be raised. Before hearing the message, half the subjects were told that the purpose of the program was to study the personality of the speaker. The remaining half of the subjects were told that the speaker "has stated his very strong opinion that teenagers are a menace on the roads and should be strictly controlled by effective new laws." The first group thus did not expect to hear a disagreeing persuasive communication. The results showed that the second group saw the speaker as more biased and were less influenced than the subjects who were not forewarned.

2. *The acceptance of attitudes opposed by the audience will be promoted if arguments containing material desirable to the audience are presented before the undesirable material.* McGuire (1957), who has reported a study that supports this proposition, suggests the following interpretation:

> It would seem that after receiving the earlier undesirable messages, the subject can be thought of as saying to himself, "What this man says appears to be true, but I find it unpleasant and so I am not going to listen to him anymore." The subject . . . who receives earlier desirable messages can be thought of as saying to himself, "This man's comments are pleasant and worth listening to and so I shall pay close attention to him." Thus he receives more of the source's later arguments and as a result is influenced by them . . . even with a presumably "captive" audience, the device of selective self-exposure to information can operate.

3. *When the audience is opposed to the position advocated by the communicator, a communication that presents opposing arguments as well as arguments supporting the position at issue is generally more effective than a communication that presents supporting arguments only* (Hovland et al., 1949).

4. *If the audience, regardless of its initial position, will be exposed to later counterpropaganda, a two-sided presentation will be more effective than a one-sided presentation in creating sustained attitude change.* In a study by Lumsdaine and Janis (1953) subjects who were exposed to a two-sided communication were much more resistant to later counterpropaganda than were those who received a one-sided communication. The authors speculate that a person who has received a two-sided presentation "has been given an advance basis for ignoring or discounting the opposing communication and, thus 'inoculated,' he will tend to retain the positive conclusion." (See also the discussion of the McGuire and Papageorgis study on p. 763 of this unit.)

RESISTANCE TO ATTITUDE CHANGE

From our discussion of attitude change, the reader may have come to think that attitudes are highly labile, changing with docility as new and relevant information is presented. But, alas for the struggling educator or propagandist, the attitudes of people seem to be remarkably obdurate and refractory.

Anchorage in Group Affiliations

Many persons reject new information or resist thinking for themselves because they cherish their groups and seek the approval of persons who are significant in their lives. Then, too, the anticipation of punishment for heterodoxy forces many doubters to adhere to the group line. Assuming attitudes that run counter to group norms inevitably leads to painful disruption of long-established and comfortable patterns of social relations. If the various groups with which the individual affiliates consistently support a particular position on an issue, the attitude of the individual toward that issue is highly unlikely to change even in the face of contradictory information. Indeed, the group affiliations of the individual may serve to stabilize his attitudes by providing him with informational and social support for them (see Box 31.2, p. 765).

Anchorage in Personality Structure

Whether an individual can be persuaded to adopt a new attitude depends also on factors in his own personality such as his self-esteem and anxiety level.

It has been proposed that persons who are highly anxious tend to defend themselves from ideas that are threatening to them and to readily accept any reassuring communication. For somewhat different reasons, the same is thought to be true of persons having high self-esteem. Lehmann (1970) reasoned that, if both of these hypotheses are true and if their effects are to an extent additive, then persons who are high in level of anxiety and high in self-esteem should differ most from persons who are low in level of anxiety and low in self-esteem in their responses to threat or reassurance. To test this hypothesis, he studied the willingness of women who had just given birth to return to the hospital for a medical examination one month later. The women were from an economically depressed area. Various efforts had been made to encourage economically disadvantaged mothers to return for this important medical checkup, but no approach had proved successful. Thus this experiment promised immediately useful data in a real-life situation. Lehmann divided the women into four possible groups (based on their scores on tests of anxiety and self-esteem), as indicated in the following diagram:

Anxiety

		High	Low
Self-Esteem	High	1	2
	Low	3	4

All the women were given information emphasizing the importance of a medical examination shortly after the delivery of their babies. Half of the mothers were given additional *threatening* information stressing the serious consequences of undiagnosed problems, problems that an examination would detect early enough for effective treatment. The other half received *reassuring* information stressing the unlikelihood that any serious problems would arise. Under the reassuring conditions 93 percent of the high-anxious, high–self-esteem mothers (Group 1) returned for their medical checkup, whereas only 47 percent of the low-anxiety, low–self-esteem mothers (Group 4) did so. Groups 2 and 3 had intermediate return rates (64 or 67 percent). This result directly supports the prediction of which groups would show the largest difference in complying with reassuring persuasion. Under the threatening conditions, *every one* of the low-anxiety, low–self-esteem mothers (Group 4) returned, compared with only 60 percent of the high-anxiety, high–self-esteem mothers (Group 1); again the difference is in the predicted direction. It must be remembered that before either threatening or reassuring messages had been delivered very few of the mothers had a positive attitude toward returning for a medical checkup (as indicated by previous failures to so persuade mothers from this same socioeconomic group). In this experiment, then, a generally held negative attitude was apparently changed and behavioral compliance brought about by pandering to certain personality needs: Those with low anxiety and low self-esteem were threatened; those with high anxiety and high self-esteem were reassured.

Some personalities, however, are so constituted that it is very difficult to bring about changes in basic attitudes. These change-resistant personalities were geared to an innately self-protective instrumental function (see p. 765). In the Newcomb study of the 1940s (see p. 763) the Bennington girls who did not show a change in attitudes as they went from freshman to senior year were people who had been independently assessed as having self-defensive personality structures. Katz and Stotland (1959) also found that antiblack attitudes in highly anxious, self-defensive white college girls of the late 1950s were highly resistant to all influences designed to change these attitudes. These girls seemed to need the prop of prejudice.

CONTRAST EFFECTS IN SOCIAL JUDGMENT

What is striking and even disturbing about the steadfastness with which persons maintain their attitudes is that in most cases information that might be reasonably expected to weaken an attitude is known to the individual. The mass media, other persons, and events that occur before one's own eyes present information that the individual cannot escape perceiving, yet simply does not use: How do individuals avoid dealing with this information? One possible way is that in the modern world many of our ideas are based on what we read; however, we are worse at understanding what we read than we think we are. Consequently, we tend to see our expectations confirmed in what we read when, in fact, we have simply misinterpreted the information. Another and more subtle mechanism is that of contrast. From our discussion of perceptual organization (Unit 12), you can see that persons tend to perceive differences (e.g., color or brightness) between two separated areas as more pronounced than they actually are. Contrast effects of the same sort also occur in social judgment; people exaggerate the degree of difference between their own attitudes and opposing views. By regarding the views of one's opponents as more extreme than they really are, one may be able to regard the opponent as less reasonable and therefore less worth heeding.

Just how do we tend to perceive the views of our opponents? Suppose, for example, that someone who has a militaristic attitude is asked to write statements that she believes a peace advocate would endorse. Here are some possible outcomes: (1) She writes statements that a peace advocate would in fact endorse, but she regards them as extreme because they differ

from her own. (2) She writes statements that are less extreme than a peace advocate would endorse because she sees any views that are different from her own as already extreme. (3) She writes statements that are more extreme than even a peace advocate would endorse because she has distorted her opponent's views into a very extreme position that she can easily regard as ridiculous.

Dawes, Singer, and Lemons (1972) performed an experiment using such statement-writing tasks to study the nature of social-contrast effects. People who held militaristic views and people who were peace advocates were asked to write statements that they would expect their opponents to endorse. The third interpretation just described turned out to be the correct one. Both militaristic and peace-advocating people tended to attribute to each other highly exaggerated opinions. Dawes et al. comment that, since the contrast effect involves a significant distortion of reality, it probably contributes to poor communication between opposing sides and even involves the risk of a total communication breakdown. Furthermore, when people misperceive the actual attitudes of their ideological opponents, the chances of cooperating to produce a workable compromise are reduced. Each of these outcomes would tend to reduce the likelihood of subsequent attitude change.

In our discussion of person perception (Unit 32) we note the enormous susceptibility of our view of others to seemingly trivial variations in social contexts. Contrast effects in our judgments of the positions of the other side are yet another instance of such influence. They are of course only one source of the misunderstandings that plague our society, albeit an important one. Such effects, we suggest, are probably more evident in the lack of communication among nations: Owing to possession of even less direct and valid information about each other, the likelihood of greater distortion exists. Perhaps "know thine enemy" has another meaning—one that carries a useful and necessary prescription for peace among men.

SUMMARY

1. Attitudes, which help influence our perceptions of other people, can be analyzed into three components: belief, emotional tone, and action-tendency. These components, however, are only loosely predictive of one another.
2. The belief component can be vertically or horizontally structured (referring to the nature of the premises on which it is based). When it is logically so derived from evidence, the held conclusions are higher-order beliefs; sometimes authority rather than evidence is its basis (primitive beliefs).
3. The emotional component of an attitude may be based on actual and relevant experience with its social object or it may arise from accidental and unrecognized associations with it. A tendency to act on an attitude depends not only on its belief and emotional components (sometimes contradictory) but also on the momentary social situation in which the action would occur.
4. One's family, peer, and other social-group memberships, and underlying personality, all are influential in the process of forming social attitudes. Among the personality-initiated functions served by attitudes is the tendency to favor need-rewarding objects (instrumental), conflict-reducing objects (self-defensive), image-preserving objects (self-expressive), and social objects that provide access to desired group memberships (social adjustment).
5. The relation between consciously held attitudes and attitude-appropriate actions involves one's perception of the consequences of overt action, one's self-expectations, and one's beliefs regarding society's view of such actions.
6. For attitude-discrepant behavior to modify one's own attitudes it must have been freely participated in and effective in changing another's attitude. Being required to behave in an attitude-discrepant manner may also bring about attitude change *if* the requirement has involved moderate rather than severe pressure for behavioral compliance.
7. To the extent that factual evidence is not available to support an attitude the sheer credibility of persons arguing for a change in that attitude has a greater effect, especially if they are perceived as initially holding somewhat similar attitudes, and the intent to persuade is disguised. Balanced presentations, involving opposing points of view, tend to be more effective.
8. Social attitudes are highly resistant to change; group affiliations and the personality function served by attitudes are important sources of such resistance.
9. One way to counteract views running counter to one's own attitudes is to distort and exaggerate the opposing position, thereby making it more easily discreditable. Such contrast effects contribute significantly to personal and societal conflicts.

GLOSSARY

attitude   An enduring system of positive or negative evaluations, feelings, and tendencies toward action with respect to a social object.

higher-order belief   The conclusion reached from a vertically or horizontally structured belief.

horizontal structure   One of several ways the belief component of an attitude can be organized. A belief is horizontally structured when it involves logical derivation from several sets of independent, parallel chains of premises or vertical structures (see **vertical structure**). Any one of the sets of premises is sufficient to support the belief.

primitive belief   A belief based on no supporting premises, characteristically accepted on authority rather than derived from evidence.

vertical structure   One of several ways the belief component of an attitude can be organized. A belief is vertically structured when it involves logical derivation from a set of factual premises. Invalidation of any single premise threatens the validity of the belief.

person perception

DO YOU KNOW...

- *how easily and in what ways we form complete impressions of others even though we have little information to go on?*

- *that we tend to like people we can understand more than those whose personality confuses us?*

- *what we typically do when presented with contradictory information about the same person?*

- *that the first thing we hear about a person dominates the impression we form of him; and under what circumstances this "primacy effect" can be weakened?*

- *the psychological principles behind such adages as "any friend of yours is a friend of mine" and "friends are people who have the same enemies"?*

- *why it is that we sometimes come to hate those whom we have ourselves hurt without reason?*

- *how we come to form distinct beliefs as to another person's intentions and motives?*

unit 32

CONTENTS

What we perceive in the world often depends on much more than what is there to be perceived by means of the biochemistry of sensory receptors and neurons. As we saw in Unit 12, the way we perceive things may depend on such factors as prior experience, expectations, attention, needs, emotions, and the interrelations among the objects perceived. (The poignancy of Figure 32.1 is a result of these factors.) All of them also govern the way in which we perceive (and judge) people, but a number of concepts have been added by the social psychologist in order to help him deal with the particular problem of *person perception*.

Nowhere is the social character of perception more apparent and therefore more exposed to the social psychologist's investigation than in the act of perceiving another human being. In perceiving people all aspects of the self are brought into play, and the resulting experiences reflect a complex blend of our own characteristics and those of the person, the social stimulus. In forming an impression of another, we more or less consciously take note of his physical appearance (including various indications of his social role and class like dress and hair style), his actions, his voice, his expressive movements, and all other cues that may be psychologically informative or meaningful. From such evidence, we formulate (not necessarily on a clearly conscious level) a fairly detailed percept (or concept, rather) of what he is like—his thoughts, his needs, his feelings, his personality. This percept by no means consists of a hodgepodge of discrete and unrelated inferences put together from many separate impressions and observations. On the contrary. A social percept typically represents an integration of all available cues, and there is a strong tendency for it to embody a portrait of a complete person, not just a few features of his personality.

What is our motive for forming coherent impressions of other persons? This question can be answered in a number of ways, each complementary to the others. For one thing, when we must actively cope with the other

FIGURE 32.1

Photo by Michael Gold

person, we are necessarily driven to make sense of her behavior. To do so we must form an overall impression of her personality that hangs together and that then permits us to *predict* her actions and to adapt accordingly. Moreover, the very fact of another person's complexity defines her as a challenging problem to be solved, triggering our need to explore and to understand the new and the unknown.

PERSON PERCEPTION: AN ANALYSIS

A useful way to organize the major factors that affect person perception (and perhaps all perception) is in terms of structure, constancy, and meaning. We impose perceptual structure on a situation or an event by seeing certain of its parts as a unified whole and by ignoring certain of its other parts. We give structure to what we perceive by selecting, attending to, and categorizing. For example, on meeting one of your professors for the first time, you may notice that he wears thin horn-rimmed glasses, almost the

size of granny glasses, and has a lopsided smile and hair that falls in all directions. You see a likable (we hope) eccentric; you may not notice whether he is physically well coordinated, well groomed, or overweight.

And, if you have certain *expectations* of another, you may structure your perception of him so that you find the expected qualities—even when they are not really there. Rubovits and Maehr (1973) gave fake expectations to student teachers about their students. Each teacher was asked to teach a group of four students who were actually of about equal ability; there were two black and two white students in each group. (All of the student teachers were white.) The student teachers were given false information on the intelligence levels of each of their students. Each teacher was told that one of the black and one of the white students had an IQ between 130 and 135 and thus were considered gifted. The teachers were encouraged to be sensitive to their students' levels of ability and to respond accordingly. They tended to interact a good deal with the white "gifted" student, presumably to bring out his full potential. Most of the teachers, however, did not give the black "gifted" student extra attention. Perhaps their existing prejudices—certainly a form of expectation—kept them from believing that a black student could really be gifted.

Another point: Just as the perceived size, shape, or color of a familiar object does not change when we move it nearer or farther away, set it at an odd angle, or change its lighting (see Unit 13), so does such constancy appear in our perception of people. We judge a person as having a rather constant personality or set of traits, which may be manifested in various ways, but remains invariant.

Feldman (1972) gave persons a list of trait descriptions and asked them to indicate which of these traits could be expected to apply to professional persons and which to working-class persons. There was a consensus that, in comparison with working-class people, professional people are many good things: persistent, foresighted, resourceful, ambitious, independent, complex, and intelligent. A single characteristic —a person's occupational category—was sufficient to evoke a highly organized structure that involved a coherent (and complimentary) set of personality traits.

There are other ways in which we jump to conclusions (often incorrect ones) about what a person is like. For example, if we are told that someone is intelligent, industrious, and well educated, we may tend to assume that he is also successful, vigorous, and even likable. That is, we tend to expect that if an individual has certain traits he will have other traits that seem consistent with these. Apparently we are made uneasy by the perception that another person may have what is regarded as an inconsistent set of traits such as energetic, vigorous, resourceful, withdrawn, and silent—though such a combination is possible. Hendrick (1972) found that persons *like* a consistent personality more than an inconsistent one.

Let us now examine some of the ways in which we give constancy, structure, and meaning to our perception of people when we predict the behavior patterns of other people, when we infer their personalities, when we attribute motives to others, and when we perceive *our-*

selves. (A related problem—the judgment of another's emotional state—is treated in detail in Unit 20.)

PREDICTING "THEIR" BEHAVIOR

"I *know* she'd never do a thing like that." "I think I know him well enough to say that he will complete college." We usually believe that we can predict the behavior of persons we know well. If we find we cannot, we question how well indeed we really know them. We may hear a divorced person say (and in so saying imply that his marriage never was a good one) something like, "After all the years I lived with Alice, I never learned to predict what she was going to do. To this day, I don't really understand her." Whatever kind of human interaction we engage in—playing tennis, chatting, or living a married life—we feel pleased and competent when we can predict our partner's behavior and dismayed when we cannot. In fact, Laing, Phillipson, and Lee (1966) have found that marital difficulties arise more often from partners' inability to *understand* one anothers' point of view than from failure to *agree with* the other's point of view.

In a more general work setting, it is believed that a crucial attribute of persons who must conduct complex negotiations with others is the ability to predict the behavior of those with whom they deal. In short, it is satisfying, useful, and sometimes vital to be able to predict accurately the behavior of others. But, unfortunately, given the present state of the art, psychology cannot yet write a "how to" formula for such predictions (see Box 32.1).

Evaluating the Predictions

Consider the problems in evaluating the predictions that we make. We may ask: "Is she honest?" "Will he be successful in his work or in his marriage?" "Is he dependable?" "Will she have enough social or political skill to become a good leader?" Notice how *general* these questions are. What is honesty? (Do we count white-collar crimes?) What is success? How do we measure it? How do we judge whether some-

BOX 32.1

THE PERCEPTIVE PSYCHOLOGIST?

Some people turn to the study of psychology at least partially in order to understand people better. Does this type of training work? This is the question asked by Johan Kremers, a Dutch psychologist at the University of Nijmegen.

Six groups of undergraduate and graduate students majoring in psychology, classics, and the natural sciences were used as judges. These judges predicted how a stimulus person would act in twenty-five different situations on the sole basis of observing him present his views in a 10-min speech on "the place of labor in life." An accuracy score was computed for each judge by counting the number of his predictions that agreed with the true responses.

The stimulus person and the twenty-five to-be-judged situations had been selected through earlier intensive work. Six individuals who had volunteered to serve as the stimulus person filled out a questionnaire (the same one on different occasions, one month apart) that required them to describe their typical behavior in a large number of real-life situations. For example:

You are attending a lecture; the audience consists of more than thirty people. You do not agree with the speaker:
a. Do you stand up and tell him so?
b. Do you remain silent during the lecture and communicate your objections to your neighbors afterward?

The volunteer who showed greatest consistency over time in his questionnaire replies was chosen to serve as the stimulus person, and only those situations in which his replies were *unanimously* confirmed by a number of close acquaintances were later submitted to the student judges.

The true responses were thus indeed impressively documented, so that the students' accuracy scores can confidently be regarded as a measure of their ability to predict at least one other person's behavior. The average numbers of correct predictions for the six groups were as follows:

	Psychology	Classics	Natural Sciences
Undergraduates	14.7	13.3	14.7
Graduates	15.7	14.6	14.1

There are no significant differences among these values, and the very slight superiority of psychology students, overall, can best be regarded as a chance fluctuation. Studying psychology therefore does not offer a royal road to a greater understanding of people, at least not in the terms of this experiment. (It may be too much to ask, however, for a successful prediction of specific bits of behavior from the highly limited and probably very atypical data afforded by a 10-min public oration on a rather abstract topic.) More important, what psychology, as a scientific pursuit, intends is the discovery of general laws relating man's experience and behavior to his biological endowments, his past learning, and his social environments. In this search, the psychologist—and his students—may be a bit ahead.

J. KREMERS. *Scientific Psychology and Naive Psychology.* Nijmegen: Janssen, 1960. Table adapted by permission.

---

one has political skill? The psychologist who wishes to study accuracy in behavior prediction faces the difficult problem of finding an adequate criterion. If we wish to predict the generalized behavioral characteristics of individuals, our task is most difficult. But if we wish to measure the accuracy with which observers predict the concrete, immediate behavior of someone else, for example, how that individual will fill out a questionnaire or what he will say in a specific situation, then the criterion problem is, of course, simplified.

But even when dealing with simpler prediction problems, there are still many conditions under which accuracy may be assessed, and each condition may yield a different result. For example: Are observers being asked to draw on past knowledge of others, to evaluate present behavior of others, or to infer behavior on the basis of selected observations? Are observers being asked to judge how persons in general will act, how specific groups will act, how a certain individual may deviate from typical behavior, or how another individual may act in a specific situation? Are observers being asked to judge friends, strangers, or enemies, persons similar to themselves or persons who are quite different? Ability to predict some kinds of behavior may not generalize to other kinds of situations.

The difficulty of generalizing in person-of-person predictions is well illustrated in the Crow and Hammond (1957) study. These psychologists asked medical students to predict: (1) the personality and ability test scores of psychiatric patients they had observed; (2) the way in which their fellow medical students would rank each other on leadership, cooperation, and likability; and (3) the attitudes their fellow students would express toward medical education. There were fourteen judgments in all; the accuracy scores on each were correlated with one another. Out of a possible 105 correlations among accuracy measures, only three were statistically highly significant. In other words, people who were relatively accurate with one kind of prediction were not necessarily accurate with other kinds. We each have some sensitive areas and some blind spots.

A common blind spot may be ourselves. Ulrich, Stachnik, and Stainton (1963) gave fifty-seven students a personality test, then made up a false analysis of personality based on the test results. Each student received this identical analysis of her personality; she was asked to indicate how accurately it described her. Fifty-three of the students rated the analysis "excellent," three rated it "average," and only one rated it "poor." In fact, many of the students indicated that the analysis gave them new insights into themselves. (Palm-readers have long been aware of this gullibility. Of course, Ulrich's personality analysis and the palm-reader's insights stress the positive!)

The problem of assessing accuracy of person perception has turned out to be more complex than was originally thought. Perhaps because of this, during the last two decades the study of person perception has moved *away* from attention to accuracy and *toward* the study of underlying processes.

IMPRESSION FORMATION

Whatever the reasons underlying our tendency to form a unified organization of another person in **impression formation,** it is clear that such impressions are almost always based on inadequate and incomplete data; or—in perceptual terms—the social stimulus is an ambiguous figure in the sense used in Unit 12, page 265. That is, the stimuli provided by another person can be organized in a number of ways. Often, in order to see a whole picture, the perceiver will invent attributes to fill in any gaps. This invention of attributes operates in accordance with the closure principle in simple perceptual grouping. We have already seen an instance of this in Feldman's study, page 778. Box 32.2 provides us with a classic illustration of this tendency.

Implicit Personality Theory

One factor that determines the content we tend to select (to fill in a sketchy impression) is our general notion of which traits match in people. This general notion constitutes our own, private theory of personality, and it determines, to a considerable extent, how we judge others. Our private theory is almost never examined or stated and is therefore referred to by psychologists as an **implicit theory of personality.** When we know something (but not everything) about another person and we attempt to develop a full and rounded impression of him, we draw the missing material from our implicit theory of personality. Sometimes a single observation about a person is sufficient to evoke a theory of personality, affecting both the judge's perception and behavior.

Apparently, an implicit theory of personality consists of a particular set of descriptive categories (e.g., physical appearance, temperament, intellectual ability, socioeconomic class) and certain assumptions about which characteristics go with other characteristics (e.g.,

BOX 32.2

FORMING IMPRESSIONS OF PERSONALITY—THE ASCH TEST

Here are some terms descriptive of a certain person: energetic, assured, talkative, cold, ironical, inquisitive, persuasive. What is your impression of this person?

S. E. Asch at Brooklyn College, decades ago, in a study which has stood the test of successful replication, posed this question to a large number of college students. He found that the students were readily able to write down a full-bodied impression of the unknown person, with nothing but this series of trait words to go on. For instance, one student wrote the following description:

> He impresses people as being more capable than he really is. He is popular and never ill at ease. Easily becomes the center of attraction at any gathering. He is likely to be a jack-of-all-trades. Although his interests are varied, he is not necessarily well versed in any of them. He possesses a sense of humor. His

presence stimulates enthusiasm and very often he does arrive at a position of importance.

Not only are the given trait terms organized to produce a unified picture of the person, but additional traits are also created in order to give the picture its full character. The person is thus described as possessing a "sense of humor" or as being "not necessaarily well versed" in his varied interests. These traits seem to follow from the overall impression that the original list produced in this particular perceiver, and so they are ascribed to the unknown person.

As Asch summarizes it:

> When a task of this kind is given, a normal adult is capable of responding to the instruction by forming a unified impression. Though he hears a sequence of discrete terms, his resulting impression is not discrete. All subjects . . . of whom there were over 1,000 fulfilled the task in the manner described. . . . Starting from the bare terms, the final account is completed and rounded.

S. E. ASCH. Forming impressions of personality. *Journal of Abnormal and Social Psychology*, 1946, **41**, 258–290.

---

chubby people are easygoing, extremely intelligent people have problems establishing very close relations with others, and lower-class people tend to have crude-looking physical features). Sometimes these implicitly assumed relations among descriptive categories are so dominant as to override observable individual differences. This is nicely illustrated in the study by Dornbusch et al. (1965). These experimenters asked children to evaluate one another. From these evaluations several analyses were made, among them the following: (1) How will two children agree on their evaluation of the same child, and (2) how similar were a single child's evaluations of two *different* children. If descriptions of others are determined primarily by actual characteristics of the individual being described, we would expect most agreement in the first comparison—in which two different children describe a third child. But our ways of perceiving others apparently are not determined

by the actual characteristics of the others: There was only slight matching of the two children's descriptions of the third child. The greatest matching among the descriptions was found in the second comparison. Apparently, the child judge's generalized view of other children was enough to overcome the actual differences among the individuals being judged.

Thus, the nature of the invented content in impression formation is determined by the perceivers' own needs and traits, by her perception of the social role of the stimulus person, and by her private implicit personality theory. If one sees in others only those combinations of qualities she wants or she expects to see, ignoring all other information, the problem of perceiving others in understandable or meaningful ways (albeit inaccurately) is quickly solved.

Frequently, however, conflicting data about a person are hard to ignore. As we learn more and more about a person, our impression can no longer be a simple one but must incorporate new and complex data while preserving a unified picture. Under certain circumstances, unity is no longer possible unless, as already mentioned, we simply ignore evidence that is incompatible with the main impression, which is precisely what many of us do. A simple experimental demonstration of this fact is presented by Gollin (1954).

Gollin presented college students with a motion picture showing a young woman in a number of situations that might evoke contradictory impressions of her true personality. Their task was to create a personality sketch of the woman after viewing the picture. In two enacted scenes, the woman displayed behavior that was easily interpretable as sexually promiscuous; in two other scenes she was shown behaving in a kind and considerate manner (helping another woman who had accidentally fallen, giving money to a beggar). These two general characteristics—promiscuity and helpfulness—quite intentionally did not represent irreconcilable opposites; neither did they immediately and obviously belong together. Actually, a situation was created in which a student could form an impression that integrated the two into a single, unified impression, of a woman, say, who was generous to an extreme. But this type of solution was achieved by only 23 percent of Gollin's subjects. More than twice as many students (48 percent) took what seemed the easier-to-achieve solution in which only one of the two major characteristics was retained, and the other was simply ignored. Both of these groups, in different ways, thus managed a coherent description; the remaining subjects (29 percent) failed to achieve integration. Instead, their impressions faithfully reflected *both* major qualities but showed no attempt to blend the two. Whether it was because they were incapable of doing so, were insufficiently motivated to try, or were simply not aware of a possible conflict is not known. Whatever the reason, this study suggests that impressions are not always unified and that we are quite capable of organizing our perception of a person into two (or more) separate and not necessarily compatible parts.

To a considerable degree, our ability to arrive at an integrated impression of another person depends on how we acquire the bits and pieces of information that we must unify. This outcome was demonstrated by Asch (in another phase of the work reported in Box 32.2, p. 781) and later repeated by Kastenbaum (1951). Their general finding was that, when subjects were asked to form two impressions (ostensibly of two different persons), each based upon internally consistent information, and then asked to combine the two into a single coherent impression, their efforts were not nearly as successful as were those of subjects who *initially* formed a single impression based on *all* the information. Daily (1952) reports a similar finding. In his study, the first group of subjects was asked for their impression of a stimulus person after being given an array of autobiographical information concerning him. A second group of subjects was required to form two impressions: first, when they were halfway through' the presentation of the information and, second, when all the information was in. The concluding impression of the single-stage group, when compared with that of the two-stage group, was found to be not only more coherent but also more accurate.

Functional value and person perception   Part of what determines how we go about organizing an impression based upon only partial information is what we intend to do with that impression. A study by Cohen (1961) illustrates this point. Working with college students, he presented a list of contradictory traits—for example, both ruthless and generous were included—from which they were to form an impression of a person. Half the subjects were told that they were later to communicate their impressions based on these traits to other people. The other half were requested to attend to the facts but were informed that later they would be receiving further information from other people. The first group was thus assigned the social function of transmitting information, the second of receiving it. Under these circumstances the communicators tended to form impressions that conveyed either a consistently good or a consistently bad picture of the person. The receivers, on the other hand, formed impressions that attempted to integrate the contradictory traits into a more complex portrait.

These results may be interpreted as indicating that the communicators were faced with the need to make up their minds about the social object being described and to do so in a way that would lead to efficient transmission of their impressions to others. A clear-cut, even if biased, message satisfied that function best. The receivers were under no such pressure and in fact were implicitly invited to defer final judgment until they had received all the data. They could afford the luxury of complex and comprehensive impressions, and, what is more, this kind of organization was best suited to accommodating new and still unknown information because it provided the most flexible structure.

Culture and implicit personality theory   To a considerable extent, many of us hold the same implicit theory of personality, especially those of us who share the same general culture, because certain traits do, in fact, go with certain other traits for members of the society with which we are familiar. Our implicit theories therefore tend to portray the actual state of affairs in personality organization *among the kinds of people we know.* But when we are confronted with persons who are not—or who we believe are not—part of our own known group, we find that our customary notions of what goes with what may not apply. Under these circumstances we fall back on a set of **stereotypes.**

Stereotyping

People are almost never perceived as isolated individuals. We perceive them as members of this or that aggregate—as our kind or not our kind, as Protestants or Catholics, as Republicans or Democrats, as Russians or Englishmen, as conventional or hippie. And when we see a person as a member of a group, our perception of her personality is influenced by what we believe about her group. In the extreme case we really fail to perceive the person; we see only her group label, then proceed to reel off our well-worn judgment of the group. For not only do we have implicit *personality* theories, we also have implicit *group-personality* theories or *group stereotypes.* And almost all of us operate under

the influence of group stereotypes (see Box 32.3, p. 784).

How we conserve stereotypes   As long as we fail to perceive the true characteristics of a person and in some way distort or eliminate evidence that would challenge our stereotyped image of him, there is no need to modify our implicit group-personality theory. To illustrate: Suppose you believe that the leaders of a certain foreign nation have aggressive and warlike designs against the world and suppose that you listen to one of their diplomats on the podium of the United Nations, appealing for peace and good-will. Under these conditions you will probably perceive all kinds of insincerity in his speech, like cynical smiles and sneering tones. You will interpret what you hear as diplomatic doubletalk, and your original perception of him as an aggressive, warlike person will remain unchanged. His appeal for peace and good-will, inconsistent with your well-established stereotype of him, has thus been altered to permit the original perception of him to remain. Our success in maintaining our stereotype seems to illustrate (at least by analogy) the law of perceptual constancy.

Sometimes, when we cannot reinterpret, that is, distort data that are inconsistent with our stereotype, we adopt a different strategy. Suppose that you firmly believe that Englishmen are insufferable snobs and suppose that you meet an Englishman who is as democratic and homespun as one might wish. It is highly probable that you will set this Englishman apart as an exception—an "exception that proves the rule"—and your very strong percept of Englishmen in general will remain unaltered.

The phenomena of assimilation and contrast (see Units 11 and 12) present yet other analogies for the distortion of our perception of an individual in such a way as to preserve our stereotypes. For example, many Americans believe that the Chinese are inscrutable. When meeting a shy and somewhat bewildered Chinese, we may therefore perceive *him* as mysterious and inscrutable. Here we have an instance of the perceived attributes of an individual being affected by his group membership in the direction of assimilation—shyness becomes inscrut-

BOX 32.3

A FURTHER NOTE ON GENDER
OR
WHEN IS A PERSON NOT A PERSON?
WHEN SHE IS A WOMAN.

Male and female roles have been idealized very differently in our society. The ideal male is seen to be aggressive, successful in a career of his own choosing, and married to a beautiful woman (also of his own choosing) who adores him. The ideal woman is less aggressive, does not choose nor excel in a career, but is able to capture the heart of the ideal male (who had already chosen her). These stereotyped views, simple and even inane as they may be, pervade our culture to such an extent that they have even entrapped experts to assert that women are not exactly people when it comes to mental health norms.

I. K. Broverman, D. M. Broverman, F. E. Clarkson, P. S. Rosenkrantz, and S. R. Vogel surveyed seventy-nine men and women who were clinical psychologists, psychiatrists, and social workers and asked them to describe the personality attributes of the ideally healthy person (sex unspecified), the ideally healthy male, and the ideally healthy female. There was almost perfect correspondence between the clinical descriptions of the ideal *person* and the ideal *male*. However, the ideal female differed in a number of ways from the ideal person. A woman was considered to be *healthy and mature* if (compared to the ideal *person*) she were less competitive, less aggressive, less objective, more submissive, more dependent, more easily influenced, more excitable in minor crises, more susceptible to hurt feelings, more emotional, more conceited about her appearance, and more aversive to mathematics and science. This very same description was used by the experts to characterize an *unhealthy, immature* man or an *unhealthy, immature* person (sex unspecified). That is, the unhealthy, immature male=the unhealthy immature person=the healthy, mature female.

The picture seems clear. We, including the experts, have our group stereotypes, and we operate under the influence of our group stereotypes. If the Broverman findings are reliable, the influence of cultural stereotypes is so strong that our mental health experts have come to believe that for a woman to be considered emotionally healthy, she must deviate from the ideal "person" in the direction of a devalued stereotyped sex role. With such beliefs as guides, professional clinicians may, intentionally or inadvertently, try to help women to adjust to the cultural stereotype. In the Broverman study both men and women clinicians agreed in their downgrading differences for the ideal woman, but this agreement must be carefully assessed in the light of the data in Box 27.1, page 674.

I. K. BROVERMAN, D. M. BROVERMAN, F. E. CLARKSON, P. S. ROSENKRANTZ, & S. R. VOGEL. Sex-role stereotypes and clinical judgments of mental health. *Journal of Consulting and Clinical Psychology*, 1970, *34*, 1–7.

ability. In another example, some Americans believe that blacks are unintelligent. When such Americans meet a black of obvious intellectual achievement, they may tend to *overestimate* his intellectual capacity and see him as an exceptionally bright person. Here we have an instance of the perceived attributes of an individual being affected by his group membership in the direction of *contrast*.

Because these various principles work so well to protect and conserve our stereotypes, a direct confrontation between our stereotyped view of a group and our view of individual human personality is rare. In fact, as we have seen, these two views work well together as long as misperception is allowed to exist. Shyness thus becomes inscrutability, but, once this distortion has taken place, the characteristic of mystery is added, in line with our usual assumptions about which traits are associated with one another. In short, our implicit theory of personality helps to fill in the skeletal impressions that go along with common group stereotypes, impressions that we usually find adequate until we come face to face with a flesh-and-blood member of the group. Then we are seized with the need to round out our impression in order to cope with the fact that a whole person is before us and must be perceptually organized.

Halo Effects

The so-called **halo effect** in person perception refers to the fact that the favorableness (or unfavorableness) of our prime impression of another very often leads us to attribute to him all kinds of good (or bad) traits. It is as if we tended to make first a broad evaluative judgment about a social object and then a halo of specific traits around it. The halo effect is quite common in our everyday social perceptions, extending to groups, institutions, and even abstract concepts. The term "communist" generates a host of evaluative adjectives, whether it is applied to a person, to a political party, or to an ideology. In a sense, the halo effect can be regarded as an instance of stereotyping because it involves a simplification of the world into two groups, the good guys and the bad guys. Once that assignment is set, our implicit theories take over—in this case our notions of good and bad characteristics—and thus a full and rounded impression of a saint or devil is easily generated.

TEMPORAL ORGANIZATION FACTORS

A factor of considerable importance in person perception is the temporal order or sequence in which informational stimuli are received. The critical role of first impressions is a common one in everyday life; the new student, the job applicant, and the blind date are all cautioned to be on their best behavior lest they get off on the wrong foot and forever damage their image.

The first impression, or **primacy effect,** apparently can be detected even over short time intervals. A typical study design is to prepare two descriptions of a hypothetical person that are somewhat contradictory but not hopelessly irreconcilable. Two groups of subjects read both descriptions, but in a different order and then describe what the person is like. Both groups receive the same information but in a different sequence. The usual result is that the first de-

scription overpowers the second and dominates the final impression. The remarkable immediacy of this sort of primacy effect is further demonstrated by experiments showing that the effect can be obtained even when the stimulus material is a short list of descriptive adjectives read in a relatively rapid series. In one such experiment, Anderson and Barrios (1961) asked subjects to give their overall impressions of stimulus persons described only by a series of six adjectives that theoretically had been provided by six different persons who were well acquainted with that person. When the stimulus person was described as "smart, artistic, sentimental, cool, awkward, and faultfinding," he typically received more positive evaluations than when the same description was presented in reverse order: "faultfinding, awkward, cool, sentimental, artistic, and smart." Apparently, in the first instance, we regard an intelligent and artistically gifted person as having the right to be critical, but, in the second case, we are initially put off by a faultfinding individual and may view his being smart and artistic as a trivial asset or perhaps even a pretense. This primacy effect can easily be seen as an instance of the influence of set (created by first impressions) upon all later perceptions (see Unit 12, p. 274).

Though the primacy effect is strong, it is by no means inescapable. Anderson and Hubert (1963) found that the primacy effect is greatly reduced if the subjects, after being exposed to a set of person-descriptive adjectives, are required to recall all of them before going on to report their impressions of the person. This requirement would ostensibly force the subjects to attend about equally to each descriptive item. The obtained reduction in the effect under this instruction therefore suggests that the usual primacy effect is at least somewhat due to subjects' paying increasingly less attention to the later-presented words in the descriptive list.

BALANCE THEORY

In an attempt to explain persons' tendencies to seek harmonious relations with their friends and to exclude from friendship those who are associated with persons they regard as enemies, social psychologists, notably Heider (1958a), have proposed what has come to be known as **balance theory.** According to this theory, we tend to view relations according to the following simple rules: (1) We expect people we like to like one another; similarly, people we dislike should like each other. (2) Anyone not liked by a person whom we ourselves dislike we expect to like; similarly, a friend of a friend of ours should himself be likable. (An important but implicit assumption in balance theory is that persons *like themselves.*) The following diagrams illustrate these rules.

(1)

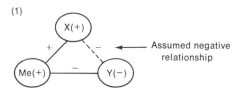

Because I like X and dislike Y, I assume that X dislikes Y (my enemy is my friend's enemy).

(2)

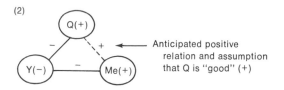

Because Y is my enemy and I know that Y dislikes Q, I assume that I would find Q very likable (my enemy's enemy is my friend).

(3)

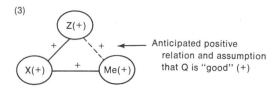

I like X, and X likes Z. Therefore, I assume that I will like Z (any friend of yours is a friend of mine).

By this theory, then, we judge how much we like a person both by her friends and by her enemies. And we are uncomfortable when we find ourselves in an unbalanced relation. For example, Blumberg (1969) found that persons feel more uncomfortable about being liked by someone they dislike than about being disliked by someone they dislike.

Another inference from balance theory is that if a good person (such as you) has a negative relation with another (if, for example, you hurt that other person), then your negative feeling must result from his being bad. An alternate inference, equally compatible with the theory if not with one's self-esteem, is that your negative feeling results from *your* being bad. (The similarity here to equity theory, discussed in Unit 30, p. 745, is worth noting.)

Does it follow from balance theory that chance occurrences may affect interpersonal attitude changes? For example, if you accidentally hurt someone you did not know very well, would you grow to dislike him? Or if you happened to help him, would you like him? Could the person you hurt balance the score by hurting you in return and thereby prevent you from having to dislike him? The notion that an exploiter will justify his wrongdoing is a very old one. The ancient Roman Tacitus observed that "It is a principle of human nature to hate those whom you have injured." The studies which are described in Box 32.4 will help you to evaluate these questions.

ATTRIBUTION OF INTENTIONS AND MOTIVES

Motives and intentions are not directly observable entities. How, then, do we discover the motives or intentions of others? It is widely (and correctly) believed that asking another person, pointblank, what his motives are in a given situation is not a foolproof way of discovering his intentions. Even the more generous among us know that people often make misleading statements about their intentions and motives. Do we all then attempt to *infer* the real motives of others, disregarding what they tell us? Such guesses are one of the ways in which we seek the meaning of the social events we perceive.

BOX 32.4

THE EFFECT OF EXPLOITING ANOTHER ON THE EXPLOITER'S LIKING OF THE VICTIM

If an individual who thinks highly of himself chooses to hurt another, will he begin to think of himself as an exploiter or will he rationalize his exploitations by convincing himself that his victim deserved what he got? K. E. Davis and E. E. Jones performed an experiment to answer this question. Subjects were led to believe that they were participating in two experiments, one involving impression formation and the other concerning the way persons respond to extremely flattering or extremely negative evaluations of their personality. First, the subjects interviewed a confederate (i.e., one of the experimenters who pretended to be another subject) and rated their attitude toward him. Then the subjects entered what they believed to be the second experiment. Half of the subjects were required to read to another person an extremely negative personality evaluation; that is, they were given no choice, hence the exploitation was the fault of the experimenter and not the subject. The other half of the subjects were told that they could read to another person either a very positive or a very negative evaluation, but that the experimenter would appreciate it if the subject chose the negative one. Hence, if the subject did in fact administer the negative evaluation, he was thereby a party to the exploitation. Most of the subjects were successfuly cajoled into reading the negative information; the data from those who insisted on reading the positive information were not used (too bad!). Both of these groups of subjects were told that they would not have an opportunity later to see the victim and explain that the negative statement was not the subject's true opinion. After the subject had read the derogatory statement to the confederate, he was asked to rate the victim's likability, warmth, intelligence, conceit, and adjustment.

The data of interest are the extent to which the subject's liking for the victim changed after the exploitation. The subjects who had *chosen* to read the abusive statement afterward rated their victim on the average 7.7 points lower than their earlier rating of him. The subjects who had been *forced* to read the abusive statement rated their victim on the average only 1.7 points lower than their prior rating. That is, persons who choose to exploit another proceed to lower their opinion of that person far more than do persons who are forced by someone else to do so.

Jones and Davis speculate that neither of these groups of subjects would have had to justify their act by disliking their victim if they knew that they would later have an opportunity to chat with their victim and explain that the abusive statement was merely something they had been asked to read and was not their true opinion. To test this notion, two more groups of subjects were required to perform as the prior two groups had done, except that the members of the second two groups were told that they would see their victim shortly after the experiment and could explain to him what had happened. As predicted, the subjects in the second two groups did not show any significant tendency to become more negative in their assessment of the victim. Apparently, exploitation leads to disliking of the victim by the exploiter only when he chooses to do the exploiting and has no other way of excusing his behavior than by convincing himself that the victim was not a very worthwhile person anyhow.

If this explanation is correct, then we must accept another bizarre notion: If our victim retaliates —hurts us in return for our having hurt him—we will not dislike him. T. Berscheid, D. Boye, and E. Walster performed an experiment to test this prediction. They required a group of subjects to administer electric shocks to a fellow student, while another group was merely told to observe the harmdoing. (No actual shocks, of course, were delivered.) One-half of the subjects in each group were led to believe that the victim would later have an opportunity to shock them; the other half were led to believe that they themselves would not be shocked. The results were as balance theory would predict. When the subject had hurt another, he liked his victim more when he expected retaliation than when he did not. However, the subject who had merely observed the wrongdoing liked the victim less when he anticipated that the victim would shock him than when he believed that he would not be shocked.

K. E. DAVIS & E. E. JONES. Changes in interpersonal perception as a means of reducing cognitive dissonance. *Journal of Abnormal and Social Psychology*, 1960, **61**, 402–410.
E. BERSCHEID, D. BOYE, & E. WALSTER. Retaliation as a means of restoring equity. *Journal of Personal and Social Psychology*, 1968, **10**, 370–376.

When we infer another's intentions ("He is hostile") we feel that we understand the person's behavior and indeed the person himself. Given our tendency to seek perceptual constancy, we are likely to assume that whatever intention or motive we have inferred (correctly or not) is a prevailing aspect of the individual's personality. But how do we gain this sense of certainty about the motives of others? To base our interpretation of a person's intentions solely on observation of her behavior may be misleading indeed. Any bit of behavior may be based on any one of many possible intentions. Consider the following diagram:

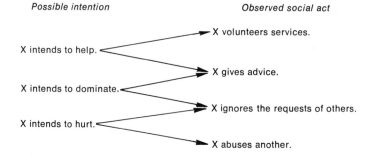

Possible intention   *Observed social act*

X intends to help.   X volunteers services.

X intends to dominate.   X gives advice.

X intends to hurt.   X ignores the requests of others.

                                        X abuses another.

How do we infer which intentions caused which acts? For example, did X give advice because he wanted to help *or* because he wanted to dominate? It is even possible that X's acts were not the result of any of his intentions toward the other. He may have volunteered his services because his wife insisted that he do so. He may have ignored the requests because he did not hear them, and so on.

Heider (1958b) has proposed that we make inferences about the causes and motives of acts in the following way:

First we estimate the extent to which a given individual actually caused an observable situation. Heider distinguishes between three kinds of perceived causation:

1. An event is perceived as *personally caused* if the perceiver believes that the individual intended to cause it and was able to do so; for example, "She purposely pushed the man in front of the train."

2. An event is perceived as *impersonally caused* if the perceiver believes that the individual did something he did not intend to do; for example, "She reached over to embrace him but stumbled and pushed him in front of the train by mistake."

3. An event is perceived as *externally caused* if the perceiver believes that the person was involved in an event that was caused by the environment; for example, "Just as she reached over to embrace him, a gust of wind caught him off balance and he fell in front of the train."

Of these three situations, only the first tells us something about the individual's enduring personality. The other two involve either accidental or environmentally determined acts. We assume that what a person does under strong environmental influences may be very different from what she does on her own accord. If a person you know to be highly honorable reveals secret information, you may assume that he has been cruelly tortured. You thus assume that one's personality has a high degree of constancy. If an individual does something that violates your conception of his personality, you may search hard for, or invent, an environmental cause that explains his behavior in order to avoid violating your own perceived constancy of his personality.

Assuming that you have observed an act that you believe was personally caused, how do you judge the meaning of the act, that is, the individual's intentions or personality? To begin, you would not form any conclusion unless the act were an uncommon one, that is, one that is not in compliance with social norms. For example, suppose that you are in Moscow with two other American tourists. The three of you are not acquainted with each other. One of the other tourists finds that she does not have enough Russian currency to pay for her dinner, so the other lends her one ruble (about $1). You see this as a common act of courtesy; it tells you very little about the lender. But suppose you observe one tourist lending the other 1,000 rubles, without collateral. Such an uncommon act would cause you to wonder about the lender's motives. Is he being extremely generous? Is he foolish? Is he involved in shady dealings? Now that you have observed an uncommon act and tried to formulate plausible inferences about the person's intentions and personality, how do you decide which, if any, of the inferences is correct? According to Jones and Davis (1965), there are two ways.

The first way is to examine the effects of other possible acts in which the person could have engaged under the circumstances and to decide what specific effect might presumably follow from the chosen act that the other possible unchosen acts would not have had. If you can detect such an exclusive effect, you might then infer that that was indeed the effect that the person intended to produce. To return to our example: You have observed that one person lent another 1,000 rubles in a foreign land —a situation in which sources of funds are scanty. You realize that he could just as well have (1) lent her nothing and left her stranded (ungenerous); (2) demanded all of her belongings as collateral (also ungenerous, possibly done for personal gain); (3) helped her to telephone her bank in the United States to have money wired to her (helpful, sensible, somewhat gen-

erous of time, but again not generous of money). Since none of the alternatives you have analyzed involve the extreme generosity of the actual act you then conclude that the lender intended to be extremely generous. With the possibility of alternative (3), which does involve a reasonable amount of generosity and is also sensible, you might conclude that the lender is perhaps lacking in good sense not to have chosen something more like (3).

The second way to decide among your inferences would be to follow the man and observe some of his actions, looking for common possible intended outcomes. Let us return to Moscow. Your curiosity overwhelms you, so for 24 hours you shadow the tourist who lent the money and observe: (1) someone meeting him in a park and handing him a large bundle of money and (2) a policeman checking with his hotel clerk about his whereabouts. Is there a single inference that could be derived from both of these events? Shady dealings, perhaps?

There are, then, several factors that account for the inaccuracy of our judgments about the intentions of another. These include: which acts you see and which you do not see; whether you see any of his uncommon acts; whether you are correct in judging which acts were personally caused and which were externally caused; how good you are at imagining the other possible acts he could have engaged in under the circumstances and the effects of those possible acts.

It is clear that all of us, psychologists, detectives, and real people, have our most difficult moments when we would seek to discover the motive.

SUMMARY

1. All perception is in some sense "social," and, by the same token, general principles of perceptual organization are applicable to such social-perceptual phenomena as forming impressions of other persons. We invariably form such impressions, even though only partial data are typically available to serve as a basis. We fill in the missing information, reconciling contradictory data or excluding it entirely if it cannot be made to fit into a unified and coherent description. Often we do so in line with our expectations, which include our prejudices.

2. This filling in appears to serve a pressing need to predict others' behavior, and this need is largely met even if the predictions are in fact not entirely accurate. Persons regarded as predictable tend to be perceived as more likable than those we find inconsistent, presenting us with an enigma.

3. There are a number of sources for the content added by the perceiver as he rounds out his impression. In part his implicit theory of personality—his ideas as to which psychological traits go with one another—determines which additional characteristics he attributes to the perceived person. Stereotypes also are influential; once the person is tagged as belonging to a specific group possessing certain well-defined (though not necessarily accurately defined) characteristics, a complete personality portrait—the group stereotype—can be made to unfold. In doing this one's generalized judgment as to whether the person or group is bad or good greatly influences the overall impression (halo effect).

4. The order in which information is received by the perceiver is of considerable importance, with earlier (and especially initial) information tending to dominate in the process of impression formation.

5. Unified impressions of others tend to be more likely in the face of contradictory data when we must communicate our impressions to others than when we receive the data with no requirement that we transmit our impressions.

6. In Heider's view (balance theory) we expect people we either like or dislike to like one another; also we tend to dislike anyone liked by those we dislike. Furthermore, we tend to feel friendly to friends of friends.

7. Not only do we form impressions of others' personalities, but we also easily attribute intentions and motives to them. In doing this we make a crucial distinction between their purposive behavior and behavior which we perceive as impersonally caused.

GLOSSARY

balance theory   According to Heider, a set of principles reflecting the tendency to perceive interpersonal relationships as harmonious and, if harmony (or balance) is lacking, to modify person perceptions in such a way as to restore balance. Similar to Festinger's *cognitive dissonance* theory.

halo effect   The tendency, in impression formation, to be influenced by one's general evaluation of the other person and therefore to attribute to him additional characteristics arising from that evaluation.

implicit theory of personality   One's private theory of personality that determines in large part how we fill the gaps in our impressions of others.

impression formation   Forming a unified impression of an individual by adding to the insufficient information that is perceptually given. Assumptions about additional characteristics not directly perceived are based on the perceiver's implicit theory of personality.

primacy effect   The tendency, in impression formation, for the first-received information about another person to dominate one's subsequent handling of additional information and thus his resulting organized impression. Under certain circumstances this tendency can be overcome so that the most recently received information becomes predominant.

stereotype   The social perception of an individual in terms of his group membership rather than of his actual personal attributes. Such perceptions are rarely accurate for the individual, and they may or may not be valid for the group as a whole. Once formed, stereotyped impressions are extremely resistant to change.

the individual in the group

DO YOU KNOW...

- *what kinds of things you tend to do better with an audience and what performances are interfered with if others are around?*

- *whether decisions reached by a group after discussion tend to be more responsible than decisions arrived at individually?*

- *that competition in social situations is significantly reduced if opponents are forced to communicate?*

- *what is meant by "brainstorming"?*

- *why it is that bystanders so infrequently come to the aid of a stranger in serious trouble?*

- *what sorts of personal factors determine how susceptible we are to group pressures to conform?*

- *under what circumstances we are willing to ignore the evidence of our own senses in making a judgment?*

- *that we show signs of physical stress when our "personal space" is invaded by a stranger?*

unit 33

CONTENTS

It is a truism that every person is born into an on-going society and lives out his life as a member of many groups. In the United States, for example, a boy is born into and raised within a family; he is educated in schoolroom groups; he joins neighborhood gangs or plays with groups of friends; on the job he is typically part of a social group. These groups constitute the immediate social environment of an individual, and it is difficult to conceive of any human behavior that is not importantly and continually influenced by this social context. In this sense, all behavior is social behavior, and, in turn, one's social groups become primary determinants of all our psychological functioning.

GROUP INFLUENCES

Viewed developmentally, group influences are fundamental in the transformation of an infant, who indeed starts out very undeveloped socially, into a socialized (i.e., civilized) adult. In this process, the family is of course the most relevant and powerful social group. As is discussed in Unit 30, the family exercises the power of rewarding certain behaviors and punishing others. It also provides opportunities for modeling or imitation: The child learns the forms of mature behavior that the older members of the family follow. Although children in contemporary American society (and in most societies) are greatly influenced by their peers, the family affects the kinds of peer interactions they will have. Aside from their decisive role in selecting the community in which the child develops, parents who are hostile or punitive, for example, tend to have children who are less likely to have good relations with their peers. Through the family and, later, groups, the individual becomes able to cope with problems of living in a complex society. Finally, groups themselves have certain immediate effects on the behavior of the individual.

Effects of Others on Individual Performance

We begin our examination of the effects of the group by considering perhaps the oldest problem in experimental social psychology: **social facilitation.** Studies of social facilitation have been concerned with two specific phenomena: **audience effects** and **coaction effects.** The first concerns the effect on the behavior of the individual of the presence of passive spectators; the second involves the effect on the behavior of the individual of other persons actively and simultaneously engaged in the same activity.

Zajonc, in 1965, reviewed the investigatory work on these problems, much of which was carried out in the 1930s. He proposed that the presence of others—either as passive spectators or as coactors—facilitated the performance of well-learned responses but impaired the learning of new responses. Zajonc was able to show how this proposition interpreted and organized a large number of separate studies of audience and coaction effects. One of these studies on audience effect, conducted during this period of early interest, found that subjects showed considerable improvement on such tasks as simple multiplication and association to familiar words—well-learned cognitive skills—when an audience was present (Dashiell, 1930). When required, however, to learn wholly new material— lists of nonsense syllables—subjects performing in the presence of several spectators, as compared with working alone, required more learning trials to master the lists and made many more errors in the course of the learning process.

Coaction experiments support the same general proposition. For example, F. H. Allport's (1920) pioneer experiment contrasted the performance on a variety of cognitive tasks of subjects who worked either in separate, isolated cubicles or around a common table. Those working alone did better than those working together in groups on a problem-solving test that required that they logically disprove certain classical philosophical arguments. This task called for a new response for the subjects, to say the least, and—as Zajonc suggests —is most effective in solitary conditions. On the other hand, the working-in-group subjects ex-

celled in a number of tasks, again including multiplication and word association, both familiar to the subjects.

Zajonc draws a droll moral, advising the student:

> . . . to study all alone, preferably in an isolated cubicle, and to arrange to take his examination in the company of many other students on stage, and in the presence of a large audience. The results of his examination would be beyond his wildest expectations, provided of course he had learned his material quite thoroughly.

Effects of Group Membership on Risk Taking and Responsibility

It may seem obvious (and even comforting) to expect that groups, with all their collective wisdom and ability to control their members, behave in more responsible and conservative ways than individuals. However, the truth seems to be the precise opposite: Groups seem to behave in riskier and less responsible ways than individuals in the same situation.

One explanation for this is that individuals lose some of their sense of personal responsibility when part of a group. Responsibility becomes diffused among members rather than focused on a single individual. If this explanation is correct, then the more the individual loses his identifiability the more willing he should be to engage in antisocial behavior. Zimbardo (1970) tested this hypothesis by studying the willingness of groups of girls to administer electric shock to an individual unknown to them. Each group of four girls was led to believe that they were participating in a study of their ability to feel empathy with strangers. In one experimental condition, the girls wore their regular attire and self-identifying name tags. In the other, each wore the same uniform (a white laboratory coat) and had a hood on her head. Furthermore, their names were unknown to one another. The groups in which individuals were not identifiable delivered about *twice* as many shocks as did the groups of identifiable individuals. The diffusion of responsibility explanation is too simple, however, to apply to all group decisions; there are many conditions under which groups behave more conservatively than individuals (see Box 33.1).

Competition and Cooperation

One important question about the effects of the group upon the individual is: What are the circumstances in which the individual adopts the goal of the group as her own and voluntarily works with other members to achieve it?

It is apparent that an individual will work for a group goal only if she believes that its achievement promotes her own purposes. Deutsch (1949) approximated this condition in a well-known study. Ten experimental groups were formed, each made up of five college students who were participating in the group as a substitute for part of the regular classwork in a course in introductory psychology. The groups met for one three-hour period each week for six consecutive weeks to work on puzzles and human-relations problems. In five of the groups the students were told that their individual course grades would depend upon how well the group as a whole did in comparison with four similar groups. In these cooperatively organized groups, the individual purpose of each member (attaining a high course grade) was thus linked to the group goal. In the remaining five groups the subjects were told that they would receive different course grades depending upon the quality of their individual contributions to the group's solutions of the problems. In these competitively organized groups, one student could achieve his individual purpose only at the expense of the other students.

As compared with the competitively organized groups, the cooperative group showed the following characteristics:
1. Stronger individual motivation to complete the task of the group.
2. Greater division of labor and greater coordination of effort.
3. More effective communication among members.
4. More friendliness and greater satisfaction with the work of the group.
5. Greater productivity: The cooperative groups solved the puzzles more rapidly and

produced better solutions to the human-relations problems.

Deutsch's work contains one source of possible ambiguity. In his study, the cooperatively organized groups were competing with other groups for high course grades. Cooperation within these groups may then have been affected by the competition between groups.

Julian and Perry (1965) have examined the effects of "pure cooperation," "group competition," and "individual competition" upon productivity and member satisfaction. These investigators compared four-member groups of students formed to work out a laboratory exercise in experimental psychology. In the pure-cooperation conditions, the students were informed that individual grades would be assigned on the basis of the number of team points: Each member of those teams that received 90 percent of the possible points would get an A, 80 percent a B, and so on. In the group-competition conditions, the students were told that individual grades would be determined by the relative standings of the groups; each member of the team producing the best exercise would receive an A, the next best team a B, and so on. In the individual-competition condition, grades were assigned on an individual basis, the best paper receiving an A, the next best a B, and so on.

The quantity of output was measured by the number of words used in developing a research design and in presenting the exploratory material. Quality was judged in terms of the logical orderliness of the hypotheses and research design. Individual and group competition both produced a high quantity and a high quality of performance. The pure-cooperation condition resulted in the lowest level of group performance. In the pure-cooperation condition, however, the students were most satisfied with their relations with other group members.

A caution: It may be that American students have "learned to learn" in individual- or group-competition situations. Competition and rivalry are no strangers to American society. In 1972 Kagan and Madsen tested the behavior of Anglo-American children and children from a rural Mexican town in situations that provided clear choices between a competitive response

BOX 33.1

THE RISKY SHIFT

How much risk will one choose to take? A low-risk decision is one in which an individual chooses a sure but small payoff; a high-risk decision is one in which he gives up the security of the sure but small payoff and takes a chance on a long shot. Some early studies have indicated that the amount of risk persons will take depends in part on whether they reach their decision in a group or alone. In order to test this finding further and to learn why it occurs, problems were constructed in which subjects' responses could vary along a risk dimension and the effects of various kinds of group interactions were studied. The following is a typical problem that has been used in these experiments:

Mr. E. is president of a metals corporation in the United States. The corporation is quite prosperous and Mr. E. has considered the possibility of expansion by building an additional plant in a new location. His choice is between building another plant in the United States, where there would be a moderate return on the initial investment, or building a plant in a foreign country, where lower labor costs and easy access to raw materials would mean a much higher return on the initial investment. However, there is a history of political instability and revolution in the foreign country under consideration. In fact, the leader of a small minority party is committed to nationalizing, that is, taking over, all foreign investments.

Imagine that you are advising Mr. E. Listed below are several probabilities of continued political stability in the foreign country under consideration. Please check the lowest probability that you would consider acceptable in order for Mr. E.'s corporation to build in that country.

The chances are 1 in 10 that the foreign country will remain politically stable.

The chances are 3 in 10 . . .
The chances are 5 in 10 . . .
The chances are 7 in 10 . . .
The chances are 9 in 10 . . .

Place a check here if you think Mr. E.'s corporation should not build a plant in a foreign country, no matter what the probabilities.

To study the effects of group versus individual decision-making on risk-taking behavior, one of two procedures has been used. In the first, subjects are divided into two conditions: (1) they discuss the decision in small groups, then choose; (2) no groups are formed, no discussion is held, and each person just decides individually. The two conditions are then compared. The other procedure requires subjects first to decide individually, then to discuss the problem in a group, after which each subject reaches a second individual decision.

Whichever procedure is employed, the same general result has been typically obtained: Persons reached riskier decisions after a group discussion than after only private consideration of the problem.

But we have not yet told the full story. Other experimenters have succeeded in constructing types of problems that consistently yielded the opposite result: Group decisions were more conservative than individual ones. One such hypothetical problem concerned a decision whether a young man should back out of marrying his fiancée, because they had begun to have more and more quarrels. The decision-makers were given various odds, similar to the choices in the foregoing problem, on a happy marriage.

Examination of the differences between the kinds of problems that tend to produce a risky shift following group discussion and those that tend to produce a conservative shift has provided an interesting clue. The problems that have typically produced risky shifts are ones in which there is a strong element of competition, whether economic or social. In contrast, problems that usually give rise to conservative shifts have been ones in which a person's autonomy is at stake. This clue should lead to further research and eventually to an appropriately more complex formulation of the decision-making process. That both research and complexity are mounting apace is confirmed by the presence in a special issue of a psychological journal of twenty separate reports on "choice shifts in group discussion"; D. G. Pruitt, who bravely endeavors to overview these reports, discusses nearly a dozen distinct theoretical models that remain in contention for achieving better understandings of these choice-shift phenomena.

D. G. PRUITT. Towards an understanding of choice shifts in group discussions. *Journal of Personality and Social Psychology,* 1971, **20**, 495–510.

and a cooperative one. Anglo-American children were enormously more competitive than their Mexican peers, and this cultural difference increased with age. The tendency was so powerful as to lead the Anglo-American children to lose sight of their true self-interest: They preferred the response based on rivalry even when it brought them a lesser reward than if they had behaved cooperatively. (For a glimpse, from this same investigation, of the possible origins of so great a cultural difference, see Box 28.4, p. 703.)

Determinants of competition and cooperation Various kinds of games have been devised for the study of rivalry versus competition. These games have the following characteristics. They provide a way of cooperating that will yield the greatest gain for each party over a number of trials. They also provide ways of double-crossing one's fellow player that will yield the greatest possible gain for an individual on *that* trial, but if each player does his share of double-crossing, the total gain of each over all trials will be far less than would be the case if they had cooperated. Typically, the games are designed for two players, and each pair of contenders has an opportunity to play many times. The purpose of these games is to study the effects of various factors on players' willingness to cooperate. (One version of this game is discussed in Unit 31, p. 766.)

Some generalizations have emerged from these studies: (1) If players have means of keeping their partners from winning, they tend to use those means, thereby reducing their own as well as their partner's winnings. (2) If players are instructed to try to win more than their partners, a very high percentage of players will compete; if instructed to win as much as possible, *ignoring* the partner's amount of winnings, most players will still *compete*; if instructed to be concerned with the partner's welfare, a high percentage of players will cooperate. (3) Communication makes a great difference. Players who are *allowed* to communicate cooperate much more than players who are not allowed to communicate. And players who are *forced* to communicate are most likely to cooperate

(Deutsch and Krauss, 1960; Pruitt and Johnson, 1970).

How are we to interpret these results? Apparently, if both parties decide ahead of time that cooperation will be mutually beneficial, if neither side has weapons or other means of keeping its opponent from winning, and if the players communicate, willingly or under duress, there will be little competition. Unfortunately, all three of these conditions are rarely met in the real world. By the time we begin to worry about our mutual welfare, the situation usually has already been defined as a competitive one. Communication is usually the only hope of reducing competition.

Individual Versus Group Problem Solving

We turn now to the question of the relative efficiency of individual versus group problem solving. The performances of groups—teams, assemblies, committees, commissions, councils, juries—are often assumed to be better than the sum of the achievements of isolated individuals of the same number. Certainly, they are expected to be better than those of a single individual. Two heads are better than one, we are told. But are they?

Work on this problem dates back to 1895 and continues unabated today. Despite this long history, the problem remains unclarified. On one hand, a number of studies suggests that groups are superior to individuals; on the other hand, there are studies that suggest that groups are inferior. For example, in a study by Barnlund (1959), the superiority of a group solution versus pooled individual solutions was clearly established. The task was to choose among several possible conclusions in a series of logical syllogisms. Two parallel forms of a thirty-item syllogism test were constructed. Each subject first worked out his own solutions to all of the syllogisms on one form of the test. Eight or nine weeks later he was placed in a group with other subjects who had reached similar scores on the test. Each group was thus formed of individuals with similar ability. The groups were then given the task of solving through group discussion the thirty syllogisms in the second form of the test. The group solutions were compared with, first, the average individual scores of the members on the first form and, second, a computed majority score arrived at by treating the individual solutions as individual votes in determining the majority decision.

The group solutions were found to be clearly superior in both comparisons. A control group of subjects took the two forms of the test as individuals at two different times. They showed no significant change. The superiority of the discussion group is not then due to practice or familiarity with syllogisms.

Along the same lines, a prominent advertising executive developed and promoted a technique of group problem solving that he called "brainstorming" (see Osborn, 1957). The essence of the technique is an absolute moratorium on all criticism by others on any ideas presented. Osborn claimed that "the average person can think up twice as many ideas when working with a group than when working alone" (but see Box 33.2, p. 800).

The question we raised is seemingly simple and straightforward: What is the relative efficiency of individual versus group problem solving? The evidence suggests that the question is a vastly complex one. It now appears that the answer depends upon such contingent factors as the nature of the task, the distribution of ability among group members, the arrangements for dividing and coordinating the activities of group members, and the scheme for combining individual efforts into a group solution.

GROUPS AND AGGREGATES

Thus far we have used the word "group" loosely to refer to any set of more than one person. Let us now sharpen our definition by distinguishing between groups and aggregates. A group is a set of persons who have the following characteristics:

1. Meet in a face-to-face relation and perceive themselves as a group.
2. Are joined together because each believes that the group will meet some of her needs.
3. Have definite status and role relations with one another and behave according to certain shared norms.

4. Share certain goals.
5. Are interdependent in the sense that certain events affecting one member will probably affect all members.
6. Communicate and otherwise interact with one another over time.

An aggregate is a set of persons who are grouped together for some reason *but who do not share most of the foregoing characteristics.* Some examples of aggregates are persons standing in line to buy tickets, fans at a football game, or inhabitants of a particular block in a city. Of course, the distinction between groups and aggregates is sometimes blurred and an aggregate can become a group; the set of students who sign up for a course may begin as an aggregate but, under certain circumstances, gradually become a group.

Aggregate Relations

In large suburban and urban areas we all participate in many aggregations in which we do not communicate in any way with the other people, let alone share group relations. This is not to say, however, that members of aggregates do not interact in certain lawful ways. Two interesting aggregate phenomena are those of the *familiar stranger* and *bystander intervention*.

The familiar stranger Anyone who regularly takes a bus or train to work has had some familiar strangers in his life. These are the people whom we see almost daily but with whom we do not speak. Milgram (1972) has studied the familiar stranger phenomenon and found that average commuters in a large city report having four familiar strangers. The commuters reported having fantasy relationships with their familiar strangers and wondering about the details of their lives.

The barrier of silence that exists between familiar strangers is so great that when one needs to make a request of another, he would rather make it to an "unfamiliar" stranger than to the previously uncontacted familiar stranger. However, if one meets the familiar stranger in a far-away country or another unexpected place, the two are likely to converse and even to feel a warm surge of friendliness. Similarly, one is more likely to help a familiar stranger in distress than to help an unfamiliar stranger. How does the phenomenon of the familiar stranger come about? Milgram suggests that in complex social environments we simply have not the time or capacity to handle all the possible kinds of personal interactions that exist in our social environment; so self-protectively we enforce a certain psychological distance from people with whom we might otherwise form a closer personal relation.

Bystander intervention Will (unfamiliar) strangers come to one another's aid in case of emergency? Several years ago, a woman named Kitty Genovese was attacked and killed outside her apartment house in New York City at 3 A.M. Her screams brought at least thirty-eight

---

BOX 33.2

BRAINSTORMING

D. W. Taylor, P. C. Berry, and C. H. Block conducted an experiment to test the effectiveness of brainstorming. These investigators compared the problem-solving effectiveness of four-person brainstorming groups with that of so-called nominal groups composed of the same number of individuals working independently. The performance of the nominal groups controlled for the influence of group size per se, and it would equal the level of effectiveness of brainstorming groups if participation in fact neither hinders nor facilitates problem solving. The task of the subjects— Yale University students in an undergraduate course —was to suggest as many solutions as possible to each of three problems, with twelve minutes allowed to work on each. One of the problems was the "education problem":

> Because of the rapidly increasing birthrate beginning in the 1940's, it is now clear that by 1970 public school enrollment will be very much greater than it is today. In fact, it has been estimated that if the student-teacher ratio were to be maintained at what it is today, fifty percent of all individuals graduating from college would have to be induced to enter teaching. What different steps might be taken

to insure that schools will continue to provide instruction at least equal in effectiveness to that now provided?

The rather startling finding—startling in view of Osborn's claims for group brainstorming—was that for each of the three problems, the nominal groups produced an average of twice as many solutions as the real groups. Furthermore, the number of original and qualitatively superior solutions produced by the nominal groups was also found to be greater than the number produced by the real groups. These results mean that brainstorming was far more effective when conducted individually than when conducted in a group.

This study has been criticized on the grounds that the subjects were college students who were not accustomed to working together in brainstorming sessions. The relative ineffectiveness of such ad hoc groups does not necessarily mean that stable, functioning groups are inferior to individuals.

To meet this objection, M. D. Dunnette, J. Campbell, and K. Jaastad repeated the Taylor study with industrial employees as subjects. There were two groups: research scientists and advertising personnel employed by a large corporation. Furthermore, Dunnette and his colleagues modified the design of the previous study in order to allow the subjects to participate in both individual and group brainstorming sessions. The problems were the same as those used by Taylor et al., with the addition of a fourth problem, the "people problem":

> Suppose that discoveries in physiology and nutrition have so affected the diet of American children over a period of twenty years that the average height of

of her neighbors to their windows to watch. The neighbors reported feelings of horror as they watched the attack—which lasted for half an hour! But no one attempted to rescue her or to call the police. Why? The neighbors themselves could not explain their inaction.

One suggested explanation of this inaction is that each bystander assumed that someone else would take care of the situation (see Figure 33.1, p. 802). Perhaps if there had been just a few or only one bystander, help would have been given. Latané and Rodin (1969) did an experiment to examine the effect of the *number* of bystanders upon their individual willingness to help a woman in distress; they predicted that a single bystander would be more likely to give help than would bystanders in groups. When the subjects arrived to participate in the experi-

---

Americans at age 20 has increased to 80 inches and the average weight has about doubled. Comparative studies of the growth of children during the last five years indicate that the phenomenal change in stature is stabilized so that further increase is not expected. What would be the consequences? What adjustments would this situation require?

The table presents the mean total number of different solutions produced by the various groups. These data indicate that individual brainstorming produced more different ideas and solutions than did group brainstorming. Nominal groups of four persons, brainstorming as individuals, produced about one-third more different solutions than did the same persons brainstorming in a group situation. And the quality of the solutions achieved by the individual brainstormers was equal to or greater than that of the group brainstormers.

	Research Personnel		Advertising Personnel	
	Nominal Groups	Real Groups	Nominal Groups	Real Groups
Total (both problems of each set)	140	110	141	97
Thumbs and people problems	78	61	83	60
Education and tourist problems	62	49	58	37

These results should be interpreted with caution, however. The Dunnette et al. study was performed with persons who are accustomed to working together as decision-makers, but their task was contrived. Consequently, the study tells us little about the performance of groups versus individuals in long-term problem-solving tasks. There is, as yet, no conclusive evidence for or against group decision-making, but a number of studies have shown that individuals who are engaged over a long period of time in solving real problems face certain difficulties that may be resolved by a group effort. N. R. F. Maier has summarized their findings as follows:

1. Sometimes no single individual is knowledgeable enough to arrive at a good solution. However, a group of persons who are familiar with different aspects of a problem may supplement one another's knowledge and thus arrive at a good solution.
2. Individuals get into ruts in their thinking. Group members who have different approaches can contribute by knocking one another out of ruts.
3. A decision that is made by a single individual often is rejected by those who are expected to act on it. Group participation in a decision increases the likelihood of its acceptance.
4. A decision that is made by a single individual may be misunderstood by those who are to execute it. Group participation in the decision reduces the possibility of such failure to communicate.

Furthermore, as Box 33.1, page 797, indicated, group participation may affect the riskiness of the ultimate decision.

D. W. TAYLOR, P. C. BERRY, & C. H. BLOCK. Does group participation when using brainstorming facilitate or inhibit creative thinking? *Administrative Science Quarterly*, 1958, **3**, 23–47.
M. D. DUNNETTE, J. CAMPBELL, & K. JAASTAD. The effects of group participation on brainstorming effectiveness for two industrial samples. *Journal of Applied Psychology*, 1963, **47**, 30–37. Table adapted by permission of American Psychological Association.
N. R. F. MAIER. Assets and liabilities in group problem solving: The need for an integrative function. *Psychological Review*, 1967, **74**, 239–249.

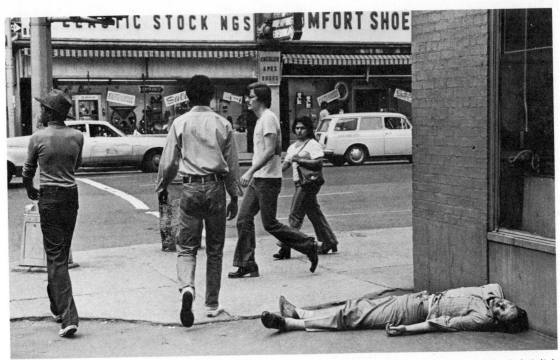

FIGURE 33.1 The man lying on the sidewalk may be drunk or ill—even dead. He is apparently unnoticed, but it is likely that each of the passersby has glanced briefly at him, as the woman at the right is doing. Clearly, no one in this photo is intending to help this man, but, possibly, one of them would if there were no one else around.

Photo by Charles Gatewood

ment they were ushered into a waitingroom by a young woman and given a questionnaire to fill out. In one condition, they worked on the questionnaire alone; in the other condition, two other subjects were present and were also filling out questionnaires. As soon as the subjects had settled down to their task, the young woman walked to an adjoining room and began to work. After a few minutes, the subjects heard a chair fall over in the adjoining room, and the woman began to scream and to say such things as "I . . . can't move . . . it. Oh . . . my ankle. I . . . can't get this thing . . . off me." The main question was, of course, whether the subjects came to the woman's rescue. Of the subjects who were waiting alone, 70 percent came to her aid. Of the subjects who were waiting with two strangers, only 40 percent of the groups came to her aid.

Latané and Rodin speculated that the *degree of concern* shown by the other bystanders is probably also an important determiner of whether a given bystander will decide to offer assistance. To test this hypothesis, they added a third condition to their experiment in which the subject filled out his questionnaire in the presence of one other subject, a confederate who showed no concern whatsoever when the woman began to scream. Under this condition, only 7 percent of the subjects went to the woman's aid.

What powerful forces are working on bystanders that prevent them from aiding a person in distress when other bystanders are present? Although the presence of others, especially unconcerned others, seems to have a negative effect on a bystander's tendency to help someone, the bystanders were either unaware of this effect or unwilling to admit to it in a postexperimental interview. Is the bystander's apparent lack of understanding of his behavior merely the result of feeling defensive about his action (or, rather, inaction)? That may be part of the explanation, but it is not the whole story.

Equity theory (see Unit 30) has also been used to analyze some facets of bystander behavior. Walster and Piliavin (1972) have been concerned with the reactions of the victim who in fact has been helped by a bystander. They observe that gratitude for being helped is by no means the inevitable (nor theoretically expectable) response. The victim, for example, may feel that the help was too little or too late. In any case, he has been placed in a "one down" position and, especially if he will never be able to repay his good samaritan, the resultant inequity may even lead to resentment over having been helped.

The Kitty Genovese case remains a social psychological puzzle. Neither experimental data nor theoretical speculation helps us to understand the inactivity of her thirty-eight neighbors. Perhaps the fate of Kitty Genovese tells us more than we would like to know both of the state of our social order and the state of the art of social psychology.

CONFORMITY TO GROUP PRESSURE

What happens when an individual, in trying to form a judgment on a matter, is confronted with strong pressure from a group in a contradictory direction? And, especially, what happens when she feels that her perceptions are valid, her judgment correct, her solution the right one, and yet there is a consensus of her friends and neighbors against her?

Situational Factors in Conformity

Asch (1956) carried out a series of experimental studies on this question that have become classics in the field. His technique was to make up groups consisting of one genuine subject and various numbers (from three to ten) of other subjects who were actually confederates of the experimenter. These confederates were instructed beforehand to give unanimously wrong judgments at certain points during a series of visual judgments as to which one of three lines projected on a screen before the group was equal in length to a standard line. The purpose was to see how the genuine subject (who gave his judgment as the last one in the group) would respond—whether or not he would yield to group pressure. Would he give an answer contradictory to his own judgment, or would he remain independent of group pressure and respond according to his own views?

The effects of group pressure proved to be very strong. About one-third of all the genuine subjects gave judgments markedly distorted in the direction of the false group consensus. And they did so even though the difference between the correct line and the line picked by the confederates was so large that anyone free from group pressure would never have made a mistake. Furthermore, experimental variations showed that the size of the unanimous group consensus was a significant factor. When the group consisted of only one confederate and a genuine subject, the subject remained completely independent. With two against him, there was appreciable conformity; and, with three against him, the conformity reached a high level. Beyond that point—even with fifteen confederates—there was no increase in conformity. If a partner were introduced who consistently gave the correct answer, this virtually abolished conformity in the subject. Having the social support of *just one other group member* was apparently sufficient to strengthen resistance to an otherwise powerful group pressure. Strength of stimulus structure was also a factor. As the perceptual difference between the correct and false lines was diminished, the amount of conformity greatly increased.

But, clearly, group pressure is not all-powerful. Let us rewrite the second sentence of the previous paragraph without altering its meaning at all: "about two-thirds of all the genuine subjects *resisted* in distorting their judgments in the direction of the false group consensus." Again it appears that some people are, and some people are not, easily swayed by the group. Again we must look to individual factors.

Personal and Social Sources of Conformity

Studies by Crutchfield (1955) show that there are large and consistent individual differences in tendency to conform or to remain independent under such group pressure. The experimental technique he used to measure conformity behavior is described in Box 33.3.

More than 450 persons, varying in age, sex, education, social background, intelligence, and personality characteristics, have been tested in Crutchfield's "standard group pressure" pro-

---

BOX 33.3

THE MEASUREMENT OF CONFORMITY

In work at the University of California's Institute of Personality Assessment and Research, R. S. Crutchfield has developed a technique that reproduces the essential conditions of the Asch group-pressure procedure (see p. 803) but avoids the necessity of confederates and makes all subjects in the group situation genuine subjects. An electrical communication network is used.

Five persons engage in a task in which they express their individual judgments of various kinds of stimuli, for example, determining the relative lengths of lines, choosing the answers to simple arithmetic problems, stating opinions on social issues. The stimuli are presented by slides projected on the wall in front of the group. Each person is seated in his own open cubicle, facing a switchboard. The group members are not permitted to talk directly with one another; they are permitted to communicate only indirectly through these switchboards. Each person indicates his judgment by closing one of the numbered switches on his board and, in so doing, turns on certain signal lights on the switchboards of the other members. Each person in the group can thus see what judgments his fellows reach on each item.

The five subjects are instructed by the experimenter to respond in a preestablished order; that is, one person is designated to give his judgment first, another second, and so on. This order of responding is rotated throughout the session, so that each person responds in each of the five serial positions.

But the subjects are being grossly deceived by the experimenter. Actually, there is *no* electrical connection among their switchboards; all the signals that allegedly show the judgments of their fellow members are really being fed to them by the experimenter. All five subjects always receive the same information; for instance, at a given point each is falsely told that he is answering second, and each is told the same (nonexistent) answer of his (nonexistent) predecessor.

Through this deception, the experimenter can confront the subjects at certain points in the session with deliberately contrived conflicts. He does so by making it appear that all the other four members agree on a false answer. The individual's conformity tendency can thus be measured by determining the number of items on which he expresses agreement with this false group consensus and the number on which he gives the correct answer or the judgment that he privately believes.

The amount of conformity behavior elicited by this technique is remarkably high. On easy perceptual comparisons and simple arithmetical problems, as many as 30 percent of the subjects will conform to the false group consensus. When the arithmetical problem becomes highly ambiguous (it is actually insoluble), as many as 80 percent of the subjects can be induced to accept the clearly illogical answer allegedly agreed upon by the rest of the group. And the conformity tendencies on social issues are equally striking. For example, an expression of agreement or disagreement was called for on the following statement: "Free speech being a privilege rather than a right, it is proper for a society to suspend free speech whenever it feels itself threatened." Among control subjects answering outside the group-pressure situation, only 19 percent expressed agreement. But, among the experimental subjects confronted with a unanimous group consensus purporting to agree with the statement, 58 percent expressed agreement.

As many as fifty different items on which there is such group pressure may be included in a single session. It is easily possible therefore to determine a total conformity score for each individual. These scores can then be used to study the relation of individual differences in conformity behavior to personality factors.

R. S. CRUTCHFIELD. Conformity and character. *American Psychologist*, 1955, **10**, 191–198.

cedure. Included have been samples of military officers, college undergraduates, medical students, and middle-aged alumnae of a women's college. In all these samples the range of individual differences in total conformity scores has been enormous, extending from virtually complete independence on all items exhibited by some persons to virtually complete conformity on all items in other persons.

Many of these persons were tested as part of a larger intensive assessment of their personalities. Analysis of those personality variables found to correlate significantly with conformity scores revealed the following main characteristics of the male individual who is able to withstand group pressure and remain independent:

1. Intelligence, as measured by standard mental tests.
2. Originality, as manifested in thought processes and problem solving.
3. Ego-strength, that is, the ability to cope effectively despite stressful circumstances.
4. Self-confidence and absence of anxiety and inferiority feelings.
5. Optimal social attitudes and behavior such as tolerance, responsibility, dominance, and freedom from disturbed and dependent relationships with other people.

It is also found that, on the average, females are more conforming than males. And there are indications that the basis for conforming or for remaining independent of group pressure in the females lies not mainly in the types of factors listed for the males but in their acceptance or rejection of the culturally stereotyped feminine role of passivity, dependence, and compliance. But, recall, this study was conducted in the 1950s; both the level and correlates of conforming behavior in women may well have changed by now—an area worth further research in the 1970s.

The data also clearly reveal that there are different kinds of conforming behavior. Some persons conform in the group-pressure situation in an expedient way. They express outward agreement with the false group consensus though inwardly they do not believe it to be correct. That they do so is shown by the fact that, when they are tested privately on the

attitude items after the group session, they revert completely to their own initial personal opinions, showing no aftereffects of their compliance to the group consensus. Other subjects seem to conform mainly out of the doubts about their own judgments engendered in them by the contrary group opinion. Thus, they continue to show some of the aftereffects of the group pressure when tested privately even some weeks after the group session.

Those persons who remain independent of group pressure may also be divided into several types. Some of them seem to resist group pressure because they are rebellious and hostile toward other people; they may even move away from their own initial opinion in the direction *opposite* to the group consensus. They are, in a word, deliberate nonconformists. Some other independent subjects may be regarded as true independents. That is, they are able to resist group pressure toward a false answer apparently because of their intelligence, self-confidence, and ego-strength. Subsequent research has shown that one's willingness to conform to group pressure is related to his level of authoritarianism (see Box 26.1, p. 658, for a description of the authoritarian personality). The relation is not direct, however. The person scoring high in authoritarianism will conform when he sees the pressure as coming from a good source— that is, one that satisfies his image of an authority. Otherwise, he tends to be no more conforming than a person scoring low in authoritarianism (Steiner & Vannoy, 1966).

A cautionary epilogue to this conclusion: The demonstration of relations between personality characteristics and conformity in one situation does not establish their existence in different situations. There appears to be only a limited tendency for persons to conform consistently over a variety of situations. The conformity behavior of the individual is determined by more than personality factors alone. Whether or not the individual conforms and how much he conforms seem to be more importantly determined by such factors as the nature of the item being judged, the individual's perception of the particular group situation, the strength of conviction he feels, and his expectations of the consequences of conforming or failing to conform.

Since expectations and perceptions of this sort are presumably based in large part on learned responses to one's social environment, can we predict that age (hence social experience) will affect conformity? Do younger persons conform less owing to their lack of social experience or more owing to their lack of sophistication about matters of consensus and dissent in groups?

Age and conformity Allen and Newtson (1972), using the Crutchfield apparatus described in Box 33.3 (p. 804), studied the conformity behavior of 366 children in grades one, four, seven, and ten. Three different conformity tasks were used: (1) a line-judging task in which a line was presented and subjects were to judge which of nine other lines was of the same length, (2) an opinion task in which subjects were given statements such as "Kittens make good pets," and (3) a delay-of-gratification task in which subjects were given statements such as "I would rather have $1 tomorrow than 50 cents now." The children indicated their responses to the three kinds of tasks by pressing one of five switches. Each switch carried a single label; together they spanned the range of possible responses from "strongly agree" to "strongly disagree." Conformity was generally highest for first-graders, decreasing somewhat with age. It was concluded, however, that the mechanisms of social influence are probably highly similar across all ages and that the observed differences in degree of conformity had more to do with changes in children's conceptions of norms— that is, of what they believe is expected of them by the social group.

It has been shown in many other studies that young children tend to have rigid, oversimplified, ideas about social norms, assuming that the norms to which they are exposed are right and that any violations of those norms are wrong. As children grow older, they begin to realize that norms are not absolute; universal laws are but agreements (sometimes arbitrary ones at that) among groups of people. (Our discussion of the development of moral behavior in Unit 30 touches on this point.) They learn to expect persons to disagree on how to act. Apparently changes of this kind can account for the age differences in the Allen and Newtson experiment; the older children indicated that they were willing to disagree with others because different people can be expected to disagree and should permit one another to disagree.

Another personal factor that has been suggested to account for both the increase in conformity and the recognition of the relativity of norms is change in the individual's social structure. As one grows older, he comes into contact with more and more persons who have backgrounds different from his own. For example, the schoolchild in America often moves from a small, self-contained class in a neighborhood school to a consolidated high school that draws students from many neighborhoods and mixes these students heterogeneously in each of their hourly classes. Many of these children differ from one another in their values and opinions and hence demonstrate to one another the diversity and relativity of social norms. In such a setting, children come to expect to disagree with one another, even though they may still conform when among close friends.

Bronfenbrenner (1970) shows comparative data on this question. Contrasting Russian fifth-graders with their American counterparts, he found considerably more conformity to group social pressure among the Russian children; and the more so if they were living in boarding schools where contact with peers was continual and unrelenting. Furthermore, when confronted with a hypothetical instance of rule-defying misconduct that would become known to their classmates, the Russian children were even less ready to entertain such behavior, the American children *more so*.

But what do we know of the mechanisms of social influence in a conformity situation? We may distinguish between two types of social influence: informational social influence and normative group influence. **Informational social influence** refers to the tendency to accept information obtained from other persons as evidence about reality, even if it conflicts with one's first-hand observations. **Normative social influence** refers to the tendency to conform to the positive expectations of others, behavior for which the person expects to be rewarded by the group.

Informational social influence As we have often suggested in this text, all cognitive activity —imagining, thinking, and reasoning—is an attempt to find meaning and read sense into the information continually impinging upon us from outside. Each of us lives in a complex, constantly changing social environment that places demands upon us to behave correctly—a social environment that provides us with no objective, logical, or empirical tests of correctness. What is the right way to worship God? Which is the best political party? What are the proper standards of sexual behavior? When we face such questions, we tend to seek answers through the acceptance and agreement of others. Consensual validation—what many people agree on as true—provides the individual with evidence that he is behaving in a logical, correct manner.

An experiment by Hood and Sherif (1962) illustrates the operation of informational social influence. In their experiment they made ingenious use of the autokinetic effect, a phenomenon in which a stationary pinpoint of light, exposed in an otherwise completely dark room, will seem to move (see Unit 13, p. 285). The purpose of the experiment was presented to the subjects as a test of visual ability under conditions of low illumination.

Before she made any judgments of the extent of movement of the light, the subject was instructed to wait in the laboratory to allow time for dark adaptation to occur. While waiting she overheard another subject, whom she had never seen, make eighteen judgments of the extent of autokinetic movement. This subject was a confederate of the experimenters. After making her judgments, the subject left the laboratory and did not return. She thus never committed herself in the presence of the confederate.

The experimenter encouraged the subject to make her judgments as she saw the situation. For one-half the subjects, the judgments of the previously overheard confederate had fallen within a range of 1 to 5 in., most frequently at 3 in.; for the remaining half, the judgments of the confederate had been distributed between 6 and 10 in., most of them 8 in. The median judgment of the subjects who overheard the shorter estimates was found to be 4.0 in.; the median judgment of the subjects who overheard the

longer estimates was 6.8 in. Of the first group's judgments, 81 percent fell below 5 in. (the highest estimate overheard), and 70 percent of the second group's values were above 6 in. (the lowest estimate overheard). The "correct" amount of this wholly illusory movement to see was apparently determined by a tendency to agree with the information—or misinformation—provided by another person.

Normative social influence A study by Milgram (1964) illustrates the operation of normative social influence. The purpose of the experiment was explained to the subjects as a study of the effects of punishment upon learning in the context of a collective teaching situation. The basic experimental situation was one in which a team of three teachers (two of whom were confederates of the experimenter) tested a fourth person, the learner (also a confederate of the experimenter), on a verbal-learning task. The teachers were told that the learner must be shocked each time he made an error, the amount of shock being determined by the teachers themselves. In his instructions, the experimenter emphasized that the teachers could stick to one level of shock or raise or lower the level as they wished, the shock administered on any trial being the lowest level suggested by any of the three teachers on that trial. Teachers 1 and 2 (the confederates of the experimenter), according to prearrangement, called for a 15-volt increase each time the learner erred. The naive subject, teacher 3, was always the last person asked to indicate the level of shock to be administered for an error on any trial. On any trial, he could thus effectively control the maximum shock administered to the learner. Under the rules of the experiment, he could hold the shock level down to the initial 15-volt level throughout the entire session, or he could go along with the choices of the two confederates. The naive subject, as teacher 3, administered the shock by depressing the appropriate lever on a shock generator. The shock generator was a seemingly authentic instrument, bearing the fictitious label "Shock Generator, Type ZLB, Dyson Instrument Company, Waltham, Mass. Output 15 volts—450 volts." No subject suspected that the instrument was merely a simulated shock generator which was actually incapable of delivering shocks. (For some considerations regarding the problem of misleading subjects—a frequent and *sometimes* unavoidable practice in social-psychological research—see Box 33.4.)

The learner was strapped in an electric-chair apparatus in a room adjoining the room in which his teachers were seated before the shock generator. His responses were relayed to the teachers through a communication system. According to a prearranged schedule, he made

BOX 33.4

ETHICS AND PSYCHOLOGICAL RESEARCH

It may have impressed (and depressed) the reader that deception seems to be a major tactic in the experimental social psychologist's research. In almost every experiment reviewed in this unit, for example, the dignity or the integrity of either subject or experimenter has been threatened. In the views of many, the experimenter who deceives a subject about the purpose of an experiment (whether explicitly or implicitly) or about the conditions under which the subject is working is thereby demeaning both the subject (who has entered into the experiment in good faith) and himself (insofar as the subject will now have to reassess his evaluation of the experimenter's trustworthiness and of scientists in general). This matter has become of increasing concern to psychologists for two major reasons. First, of course, there is the question of ethics and simple individual dignity or self-regard. By what authority, it is asked, does the experimental psychologist take it upon himself to deceive any person—child, student, volunteer, or paid subject? Second, there is the purely scientific cost of deception. If the deception works and the subject really is deceived, it is obvious that experimentation can work but once; word will soon get around, and the credibility gap between subject and psychologist will widen. This practice risks a long-time erosion of a relationship of trust between experimenters and their subjects— an outcome that would ultimately be fatal to progress in research in human behavior.

Psychologists know all these things and worry much about them. An easy answer might be that one should employ deception *only when* there are no other means for accomplishing the conditions necessary for the experiment and when the experiment is an important one. But who is to say that the experiment is an important one—the experimenter, who is deeply involved in reaping maximum benefits for psychological knowledge? Or should it be the subject who may be minimally involved yet who pays the full cost?

The American Psychological Association has recently endorsed a formal set of ethical principles to govern research with human subjects or, in their words, "participants." It is a carefully drawn document, representing the distillation of several years of consultation with thousands of individual psychologists. It insists on "informed consent" from the participants to the maximum extent possible, and its overriding message is that he must be left in as good or better shape after the experiment than before. But on the critical issue of benefits to science versus costs to the participant, the individual researcher is charged with ultimate responsibility. As the report states:

Almost any psychological research with humans entails some compromise among ethical ideals, some choice of one particular ethical consideration over others. For this reason, there are those who would call a halt to the whole endeavor, or who would erect barriers that would exclude research on many central psychological questions. But for a psychologist, the decision not to do research is itself an ethically questionable solution, since it is one of his obligations to use his research skills to extend knowledge for the sake of ultimate human betterment. . . . in making this judgment, the investigator needs to take account of the potential benefits likely to flow from the research being considered in conjunction with the possible costs to the research participants that the research procedures entail. . . . An analysis following this approach asks about any procedure, "Is it worth it, considering what is required of the research participant, on the one hand, and the importance of the research, on the other?" The decision may rule against doing the research,

thirty errors in the total series of forty trials. In addition, as the shocks administered to him in these error or critical trials became stronger and stronger, he grunted, protested, and demanded to be let out of the experiment. Each complaint of the learner had been prerecorded

---

or it may affirm the investigator's positive obligation to proceed.

Some question whether this kind of cost/benefit analysis is appropriate on a matter of ethics. Diana Baumrind of the University of California is among these:

> Far from avoiding moral dilemmas, the use of a cost/benefit analysis serves to legitimate the loophole known as the "moral dilemma." . . . The cost/benefit analysis becomes particularly onerous when the individual or group calculating the ratio is an interested rather than a disinterested party. . . . For the investigator to equate his own perspective with what is good for mankind . . . in effect dictates to the subject what the investigator thinks *ought* to be done. The subject is "good" if he opts for mankind (as represented by the proposed research) and "bad" if he opts to protect his own interests. It is only one step away . . . to conclude that in the interests of mankind the investigator has the right, indeed, the obligation (provided certain conditions are met), to help the subject come to the "right" decision.

The "moral dilemma," then, is not finally resolved to the satisfaction of all—nor, we suspect, can it ever be. But the APA code of ethics nevertheless remains an extraordinary document, one that is immensely sensitive to the rights of human subjects. It is, as *Science* (the principal organ of the American Association for the Advancement of Science) states, "probably the world's most exhaustive set of ethical principles governing psychological research with human beings."

H. C. KELMAN. Human use of human subjects: The problem of deception in social psychological experiments. *Psychological Bulletin*, 1967, **67**, 1–11.
AD HOC COMMITTEE ON ETHICAL STANDARDS IN PSYCHOLOGICAL RESEARCH. *Ethical Principles on the Conduct of Research with Human Participants.* Washington, D.C.: American Psychological Association, 1973.
D. BAUMRIND. Metaethical and normative considerations covering the treatment of human subjects in the behavioral sciences, paper presented in Symposium in Psychology and Ethics at Loyola University, Chicago, 1973.
C. HOLDEN. APA adopts detailed code on human experimentation. *Science*, 1973b, **179**, 662. Copyright 1973 by the American Association for the Advancement of Science.

on tape, coordinated to a specific shock level. The learner indicated no discomfort until the 75-volt shock was administered, to which he responded with a slight grunt. Similar responses followed shocks of 90 and 105 volts. At 120 volts, the learner shouted to the experimenter that the shocks were becoming painful. On the administration of the 135-volt shock, the learner cried out that he wanted to be released from the experiment, complaining of a heart disturbance (while being strapped into the electric chair in the presence of the three teachers, he had incidentally mentioned that he suffered from a mild heart condition). Cries of this sort continued with rising intensity until, at 180 volts, the learner cried out, "I can't stand the pain." At 285 volts his response to the shock was an agonized scream. At 300 volts, he shouted in desperation that he would no longer give answers to the learning task. Thereafter he remained mute.

A second group of subjects was tested in a control condition in which one naive subject was the sole teacher. He was instructed to administer the shock each time the learner committed an error and was told that, as teacher, he was free to choose any shock level on any of the trials. In all other respects the control experimental conditions were identical.

The results are shown in Figure 33.2. Inspection of the figure indicates that the experimental subjects were mightily influenced by the two confederates, whose suggested shock levels are shown in the "stooge" group curve. Milgram comments:

> Subjects are induced by the group to inflict pain on another person at a level that goes well beyond levels chosen in the absence of social pressures. Hurting a man is an action that for most people carries considerable psychological significance; it is closely tied to questions of conscience and ethical judgment. It might have been thought that the protests of the victim and inner prohibitions against hurting others would have operated effectively to curtail the subjects' compliance.

So it might have been thought. Twenty-seven of the forty experimental subjects continued, however, to administer shocks of in-

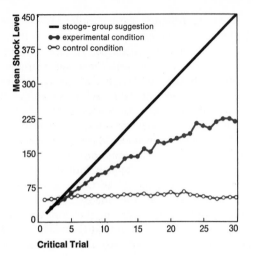

FIGURE 33.2 Mean simulated shock level administered by forty subjects experiencing "stooge" group-suggested levels and by forty subjects not exposed to suggestion.

creasing intensity after the learner had cried out, at 150 volts, that he wanted to be let out of the experiment, complaining of a heart disturbance. Seven of the experimental subjects never stopped yielding, going along with the "stooge" group to the maximum shock level of 450 volts. Among the forty control subjects, only two administered shocks greater than 150 volts.

This experiment shows normative group influence in action, when the group supports cruel treatment of another human being. But group pressure can also have a salutary effect.

A second study by Milgram (1965) illustrates that normative group influence can lead to humane behavior. In this study, both teachers 1 and 2 (again confederates of the experimenter) defied the experimenter, refusing to continue to administer any shock at all to the learner. In these disobedient groups of forty subjects, thirty-six joined in defying the experimenter.

This result, although indicating that normative social influence can also further good, supports the general conclusion of Milgram's earlier experiment. In both instances, the individual goes along with the group, apparently irrespective of his true (though unknown) incli-

nations. Although benign effects of group pressure are certainly less unsettling than are malign ones, it is difficult to draw encouragement from either phenomenon. Serious doubts as to human susceptibility linger, no matter what the direction in which the individual bows to the group.

The Crisis of Conscience

In commenting on the implications of his work, Milgram quotes from Harold J. Laski's (1929) essay "The Dangers of Obedience":

> . . . [C]ivilization means, above all, an unwillingness to inflict unnecessary pain. Within the ambit of that definition, those of us who heedlessly accept the commands of authority cannot yet claim to be civilized men. . . . our business, if we desire to live a life not utterly devoid of meaning and significance, is to accept nothing which contradicts our basic experience merely because it comes to us from tradition or convention or authority. It may well be that we shall be wrong; but our self-expression is thwarted at the root unless the certainties we are asked to accept coincide with the certainties we experience. That is why the condition of freedom in any state is always a widespread and consistent skepticism of the canons upon which power insists.

PERSONAL SPACE

Another set of social norms to which group and aggregate members conform concerns the physical space that one may occupy. Results from this area of study indicate that persons have certain needs for spatial privacy; when these needs are not met, personal ineffectiveness and anxiety may occur. An understanding of this kind of phenomenon is essential if society is to plan for the well-being of persons who live or work in close proximity to others. And, of course, it has implications for group and aggregate behavior.

Territoriality refers to persons' assumptions that they have exclusive rights to certain geographic areas, even if these areas are not theirs by legal right. To take a common example: By the end of the first week of class, most students consider a particular seat to be their territory and will show signs of distress or irritation if someone else sits in that seat. What is interesting, even for the simple example we cited, are the subtle ways in which strangers observe certain implicit territorial rights and the emotional mechanisms that regulate this behavior. We shall return to this in a moment.

Personal space refers not to a geographic area, but to the space surrounding our body, a space that moves with us. Persons regard that space as private and try to prevent others from entering it. For example, persons sitting in a public reading room definitely seek to have at least one empty seat between themselves and the next reader (Sommer, 1969). The phenomenon is also evident in less formal settings (see Figure 33.3).

But personal space does vary with circumstance. Willis (1966) recorded the actual physical distances of pairs of persons when engaged in a natural conversation. Pairs were categorized according to whether they were strangers or acquaintances. Their nose-to-nose speaking distance was measured at the start of conversation. Acquaintances stood closer (about 24 inches, on the average) than did strangers (about 28 inches). There are, of course, many conditions under which personal space must be violated, such as in crowded elevators and waitingrooms. In such settings, it is commonplace for persons to reduce the extent to which they are invaded (and invade others) by closing their eyes, standing back to back, looking down, or holding a newspaper at eye level. Try standing face-to-face with a stranger on a crowded bus and look him straight in the eye. You will probably feel very anxious and even frightened. Your victim may escape from this unexpected confrontation by looking down, moving away, or finding an "interesting" ad on the wall of the bus to read and reread. Or he may respond by glaring, by asking you if something is wrong, or by doing something more openly antagonistic.

FIGURE 33.3

Photo by Marion Bernstein

Our physiological responses to invasions of personal space are similar to the way we feel before embarking on a difficult mission. They include increased sweating, coldness of hands and feet, and increased heart rate and blood pressure. McBride, King, and James (1965) regard these as defensive responses that precede and set off efforts to restore one's personal space. The investigators measured changes in a person's galvanic skin response (a measure of sweating—see Glossary, Unit 22, p. 563) in relation to the direction from which she is approached by another. They found that this response is greatest when an individual is approached directly from the front, intermediate when approached from either side, and least when approached from the rear. They also found that this sweating response is greater when individuals are touched by other persons than when they are touched by inanimate objects. (Our thoughts and emotional responses are also affected by such invasions, as illustrated in Box 33.5.) What is most remarkable about the maintenance of personal space and territoriality is that it is usually regulated at a subconscious level. Among city dwellers, only the more unusual and hard-to-escape invasions ever enter our direct awareness. Nevertheless, minor invasions can cause us to feel vaguely anxious without our realizing the cause of the anxiety.

Contemporary variations of these problems arise in space flights and long submarine voyages in which crew members live for extended periods of time in very close contact with one another. Some studies have been conducted on the relation between patterns of social interaction and ability to complete simulated missions of this kind. Altman, Taylor, and Wheeler (1971) placed pairs of persons in small rooms containing only bunk beds, two chairs, a table, a file cabinet, task equipment, a lamp, a refrigerator, a chemical toilet, and survival rations. Data were collected by audio and video recording and by examination of blood samples taken just before and after the period of isolation. Those subjects who were able successfully to withstand all eight days of this confinement were found to have established bed, chair, and side-of-room territoriality and regularly scheduled social interaction beginning with the first

day of confinement. Those who failed to withstand it had begun to establish territoriality and ground rules for interaction only as a relatively last-minute attempt to make their situation bearable.

The blood samples from these subjects were analyzed for a form of protein-bound iodine (PBI), a measure of stress reaction. Those who were unable to complete the experiment were *initially* much lower in PBI than were the completers, but their post-isolation PBI level was higher than that of the completers. This finding was paralleled by observational and self-reported measures of emotionality. The non-completers seemed, initially, to misread and underestimate the potential stressfulness of the situation they were about to enter. Upon first entering the isolation room, therefore, they experienced little initial stress and did not worry about establishing boundaries for regulating social interaction. However, after a day or so, their level of restlessness and anxiety increased very sharply, but by then it was too late and their efforts to establish territoriality could not restore their sense of equanimity. Apparently, awareness both of the importance of creating personal territory and of doing so early in a potentially intruding situation is crucial to our psychological well-being.

THE INDIVIDUAL'S CONTRIBUTION TO THE GROUP

Thus far, we have dealt mostly with the way in which groups affect individuals. We turn now to the roles played by individuals who are members of groups. Suppose you have just joined a group that has as its function the making of some important decision. Should you handle the decision as you would if there were no group, that is, develop a solution on your own and present it to the group? Should you be a nice person who keeps her mouth shut and accepts whatever the group decides? Many persons in decision-making groups behave in these ways, but this is not *group* behavior. A group has special functions that are not served very well by members who engage in either of these kinds of behavior. We turn now to an examination of group struc-

BOX 33.5

AN INVASION OF PERSONAL SPACE

Suppose that there is a cafeteria in which various persons are seated at tables. The tables are large enough to seat six. There are some vacant tables. When one enters the cafeteria and sits down alone at one of the tables, does her personal space expand so that the entire table becomes temporary territory? Kathy Osmond, an undergraduate student of psychology at California State University, Hayward, decided to find out by performing an informal experiment in which she invaded other people's table space. The following account of her and others' behavioral and emotional reactions provides a clear answer.

On three days, during my afternoon break, I went into the cafeteria next to the place where I work and sat down at a table where someone was already sitting. I had to muster a lot of courage to do this.

My first subject was reading when I sat down. Startled, she looked up, wrinkled her face and stared at me. She half smiled and muttered "Hi." She then pretended to go back to reading, but I doubt that she was concentrating. She wiggled around in her chair and tapped one finger on the table while flipping the pages of the book with her other hand. After a couple of minutes of misery, I explained what I was doing and asked her if she would tell me how she felt. She seemed relieved. She replied:

"I felt so uncomfortable. It just took me so aback that all I could think of was to ignore you and keep reading. I really felt kind of silly. Why should I let your sitting at the same table make me so nervous? I mean, why couldn't I have talked to you instead of pretending to read?"

The second subject was drinking a Coke. I sat down without saying a word. He began to fidget with the ashtray and with his straw. He avoided making eye contact with me until it could no longer be avoided. Then he shrugged his shoulders, laughed and said, "What are you doing?" I explained my mission and asked him how he felt. His comments were as follows:

"I felt funny. I thought you were some crazy 'weirdo.' I didn't know what to say, whether to tell you to get lost or to get up and leave myself."

I asked him why he didn't leave or ask me to leave. He replied, "Oh, I don't know. The whole thing seemed too absurd. I figured, 'Why not?' "

The third subject was also drinking a Coke, and also did a lot of fumbling and fidgeting. Afterwards he remarked:

"I thought you might have thought I was someone you knew or something, so it didn't bother me too much when you first sat down. But later it was obvious that that wasn't the case. It started to bother me and make me mad, but I couldn't say anything."

These events took place between strangers. A friend, of course, would be welcome to sit at one's table. That is, the region of inviolable personal space would become smaller. But it would still exist, as we shall now see. Another undergraduate student of psychology experimented with a mealtime invasion among friends. He and six others share a house, do their own cooking, and regularly have supper together. When one of these suppers was about half over, he began moving his cup, fork, and napkin near another's plate. That person muttered something about doing the dishes, got up, and began to take all the empty dishes out to the kitchen and to wash them. The next evening, the student did the same thing to the person on the other side of him. That person looked at him quizzically for a while, then looked down, and said nothing more during the entire meal. The student who performed this information experiment reported that he found his role extremely stressful and was very relieved when he was able to tell his friends what he had been doing. His friends expressed great relief at receiving his explanation.

Try an experiment on personal space yourself. We are normally unaware of the unwritten rules about personal space though we carefully obey them. But, if you put your mind to the task of becoming aware of these rules, you will be able to discover many of them. Select one of these rules and figure out a way to break it. But use your good sense of moderation by choosing a relatively mild rule and a relatively gentle form of intrusion. Observe how this affects the other persons who are involved. Tell them what you did. Ask them how they felt. Examine your own feelings about the experience. You will all learn a great deal. Go then, and learn!

ture and function and their implications for the behavior of individual group members.

Group Structure and Function

Many group theorists find it useful to think of groups as having two environments and two corresponding sets of functions. The external environment of the group consists of whatever *events or problems the group has been organized to deal with.* If you and others were to work together to change the zoning laws in your neighborhood, your external environment would be your neighborhood and the intellectual and bureaucratic events and problems in obtaining and compiling information, legal forms, and signatures. Accordingly, one function of group members is to participate in obtaining and compiling the information. In addition, however, your group will have to initiate plans and activities that will enable its members to perform this function in an efficient and satisfactory way. To do this, the group must deal with its internal environment. This consists of the *behavior of the group members toward one another,* including behavior dealing with planning, coordinating, and morale maintenance.

Management of the internal environment is a difficult and complicated task at which many groups fail. Members of the group will not work together harmoniously unless they feel that they are accorded an appropriate amount of status and respect by their fellow members and that the group is progressing in its task. Consequently, in addition to concerning themselves with the external environment, group members contribute to the achievement of the group's goal by inviting one another to examine the external problem and to suggest modes of solution, by rewarding one another for constructive contributions, by giving tactful criticism of poor or destructive contributions, and by trying to provide each member with a role in which he can succeed and feel rewarded. Many kinds of obstacles may be encountered in the internal environment, including rivalry or jealousy among members, unwillingness of members to do their share of work, inability to schedule coordinated activities, and disagreement on the way the group's problems should be approached. Be-

cause of these potential problems of internal-environment management, group problem solving is far more complicated than individual problem solving.

Assembly effects, in which the group accomplishes more through cooperation than could have been achieved if individual efforts were merely summed, can be obtained only if the internal environment is managed with great skill. A camel is a horse that was designed by a committee that lacked internal-environment management skills.

Individual Behavior in Groups

One definition that has been given of leadership behavior is that it is any behavior that moves the group closer to its goal. By this definition of leadership, all of the useful members of a group exert some forms of leadership. What are the forms of behavior that move a group closer to its goal? One perspective on these forms of behavior has been provided by Hemphill, who has broken leadership functions down into nine categories, as follows:

1. Initiation—originating, facilitating, or resisting new ideas.
2. Personal exchange among membership—initiating and facilitating social interactions and exchange of personal services with members.
3. Representation—acting on behalf of the group or defending it.
4. Integration—reducing group conflict, encouraging a pleasant group atmosphere, or subordinating individual behavior to group goals.
5. Organization—defining or structuring one's own work, the work of other members, or the working relations between individuals.
6. Domination—restricting the behavior of individuals, decision-making, or expressing opinions.
7. Distribution of information to other group members, seeking information from them, facilitating information exchange, or showing awareness of matters pertaining to the group.
8. Recognition—expressing approval or disapproval of group members.

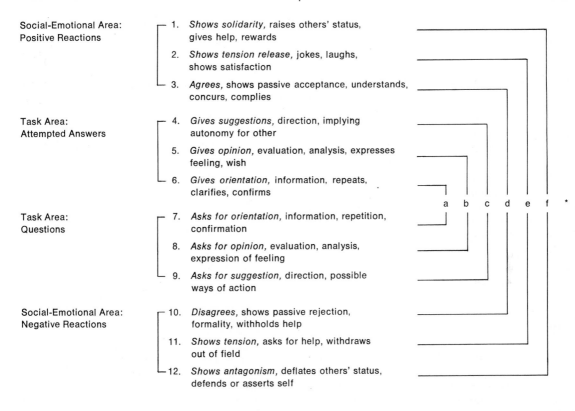

Social-Emotional Area:
Positive Reactions

1. *Shows solidarity*, raises others' status, gives help, rewards

2. *Shows tension release*, jokes, laughs, shows satisfaction

3. *Agrees*, shows passive acceptance, understands, concurs, complies

Task Area:
Attempted Answers

4. *Gives suggestions*, direction, implying autonomy for other

5. *Gives opinion*, evaluation, analysis, expresses feeling, wish

6. *Gives orientation*, information, repeats, clarifies, confirms

Task Area:
Questions

7. *Asks for orientation*, information, repetition, confirmation

8. *Asks for opinion*, evaluation, analysis, expression of feeling

9. *Asks for suggestion*, direction, possible ways of action

Social-Emotional Area:
Negative Reactions

10. *Disagrees*, shows passive rejection, formality, withholds help

11. *Shows tension*, asks for help, withdraws out of field

12. *Shows antagonism*, deflates others' status, defends or asserts self

a b c d e f *

* Key

a. Problems of orientation   c. Problems of control   e. Problems of tension management
b. Problems of evaluation   d. Problems of decision   f. Problems of integration

FIGURE 33.4 Bales' Category System.

From Bales, 1950.

9. Production—setting achievement goals or urging members to achieve more.

There are, of course, other ways of categorizing the kinds of behavior in which group members may engage. Group interaction is an extremely complex process and very difficult to conceptualize or describe. Consequently, you may find it useful to consider another way of categorizing or describing the acts of individual members within a group. Bales (1950) has proposed what may be another useful system, a system that has remained in use over 25 years (Figure 33.4). Note that the Bales system is less specific about the ways in which one may exert *leadership* than is the Hemphill system—that

is not its intent. However, it does provide a more comprehensive scheme within which additional information of other kinds can be effectively encompassed: It includes forms of behavior that all members may engage in but that probably do not move the group closer to its goal; it specifies superordinate categories of task and interpersonal responses; and it further categorizes behavior according to whether it deals with problems of orientation, evaluation, control, decision, tension management, or integration. To increase your understanding of the relation between these two systems for categorizing the behaviors of individuals in groups and the structure and functioning of groups, attempt to answer the following questions for yourself: Which of the Bales and Hemphill categories concern behavior that deals primarily with the external environment of the group? Which of these categories deal primarily with the internal environment of the group? Which of these categories may apply equally to both environments?

Now that we have listed the kinds of things group members do, we turn to the question of how these behaviors are orchestrated in such a way that a functioning group emerges. Which behaviors occur when? What are the consequences of certain patterns of behavior for the other group members and group functioning as a whole?

In the first stages of group formation, certain persons emerge as the informal leaders. The emergent leaders establish their roles, of course, by engaging in a relatively high number of leadership behaviors of the kinds described previously. Put another way, persons who are regarded as leaders by other group members are ones who talk relatively more than other group members. Except in the case of highly talkative group members whose views diverge greatly from those of the rest of the group or whose contributions are almost exclusively of a negative socioemotional variety, *sheer amount of talking in a group is the best single behavioral factor* for indicating whom the group members will consider their leader (see Box 33.6).

BOX 33.6

ONE WAY TO PRODUCE LEADERSHIP

Since group leaders do talk more, A. Bavelas, A. H. Hastorf, A. E. Gross, and W. R. Kite at Stanford University wondered whether the easiest way to make someone a leader might not be simply to ask him to talk more. To test this hypothesis, they gave four-man groups an opportunity to discuss a problem, then asked them to rank one another on leadership ability (from 1 to 4). Following this they trained only the group member who had received the *lowest* average rank on leadership to talk more.

The training procedure was as follows. Each member had before him a box with one green and one red light. Group members were told that each would receive feedback on his performance during a second part of their discussion together; if the red light went on it would mean that he was interfering with the discussion, but if the green light went on that would mean that he was contributing to it. During the subsequent discussion period, the person who had been rated lowest on leadership was positively reinforced (got the green light) whenever he spoke, while the rest of the members received red signals during most of their remarks. After this training session members again rated one another on leadership. Finally, a third discussion session was held in which the signal lights were not used and after which leadership ratings were once more ob-

tained. (In this way it could be determined whether the effects of training could be observed even after reinforcement had been terminated.)

The results were that rewarding "helpful" contributions does increase both a member's talking and the tendency of others to perceive him as a leader. In the first discussion period, the persons who received the lowest leadership ranking (and were subsequently trained) received an average leader rating of only 1.8 (on a scale from 1 to 4); also, at first they spoke an average of 16 percent of the time. After the second period (during which the training had taken place), their average rating rose to 3.3, and they spoke 37 percent of the time. After the third discussion, they fell back slightly to a leadership rating of 2.7 and spoke 27 percent of the time.

Why did this simple technique work so well? The investigators speculate that the leadership change depended on changes in the way the reinforced person perceived himself and was perceived by the other group members. Specifically, the more he regarded the changes in his behavior as *self-caused*, the more he moved into his new leadership role. Similarly, to the extent that his fellow group members perceived his new behavior as spontaneously produced (and not due to the light or to the experimenter), they came to regard him as truly a better leader.

A. BAVELAS, A. H. HASTORF, A. E. GROSS, & W. R. KITE. Experiments on the alteration of group structure. *Journal of Experimental Social Psychology*, 1965, **1**, 55–70.

How many leaders emerge in a particular group? What kinds of things do they say? The results of studies of many kinds of groups indicate that only two people, taken together, usually do about 60 percent of the talking. Moreover, these two leaders tend to communicate *about different things*. One of the leaders usually makes remarks that would be rated as positive social-emotional responses and task-area questions on the Bales category system. She praises the group, tells jokes, and asks for information. She is, in other words, the group's "social leader." The other leader is more task-oriented and directive. His responses fall largely in the task area: attempted-answers categories. That is, he structures the group's tasks, directs the activities of others, and evaluates their responses, criticizing a certain response when he considers that in the best interests of getting the group's task done. He is known as the "task leader."

Aside from the emergence of task and social leaders, in what other ways do groups develop? What sequences of events occur? To answer this question, Bales and Strodtbeck (1951) examined the interaction of twenty-two problem-solving groups using Bales' category system to rate the kinds of responses that were made by group members. The period of time during which each group was to work was divided into three parts. Responses were categorized according to problems of orientation, evaluation, or control. It was observed that most of the orientation responses were made during the first period, most of the evaluation responses were made during the second period, and most of the control responses were made in the third period.

This brief summary of the roles of individuals in the formation of a functioning group provides only a rudimentary outline of what members contribute to groups. Many intriguing questions have not been included here, such as the relation between leader behavior and group performance or the determinants of member compatibility. But these important questions

have been extensively investigated. Also, considerable research has been reported on the effectiveness of leaders using different personal styles in modifying specific kinds of group behavior. [For example, MacDonald (1967) found that bossy leaders get faster results in reducing delinquent behavior, but democratic, group-sensitive leaders were more effective in delinquency reduction in the long run.] It would not be appropriate or possible to review here the enormous body of research, since the findings are more than just complex; they are, unfortunately, often ambiguous and difficult to interpret. There are many reasons for this state of affairs; in a recent review of leadership research, Helmreich, Bakeman, and Scherwitz (1973) provide an assessment of some of the important self-limiting factors that confound and hamper such work. They comment:

> Among the more commonly encountered problem areas are: (a) leaders often have control over important resources which motivate joining and remaining in groups; (b) the relationship between leader and followers is longitudinal—it takes time for group goals, leader abilities, and situational variables to synchronize into a working relationship; (c) most leadership situations are in the context of one or more larger organizations which impose demands and restrictions on leader-member relationships.

At present, it cannot be said that any one kind of leadership is better than another or that specific kinds of persons become the most compatible group members. It is clear that leadership style and combinations of member personalities are important variables in determining group effectiveness and cooperation. However, the effects of these variables depend upon still other factors and other relations. It remains for ingenious future psychologists to disentangle these relations. And this prescription will hold true (for some time to come) for the many unanswered questions we have encountered in our study of the individual in the group —and for all of social psychology.

SUMMARY

1. Human behavior almost inevitably takes place in a social context, so that other persons, directly or indirectly, influence most of our experiences and actions. Social group influences are operative in the development of the individual from infancy onward, initially mediated by the family.

2. Certain social group influences have long been investigated experimentally, including the effects on individuals of spectators (audience effects) and of others simultaneously engaged in the same task (coaction effects). Generally, well-practiced performances benefit from the group context while new ones are interfered with.

3. There is a tendency for groups to behave in riskier and less responsible ways than would the same individuals were they acting alone. But this tendency can be reversed for certain specific social tasks.

4. When engaged in a group task, the individual tends to work for the group goal only if he will personally benefit from its attainment. Experimentally, this requirement is met in cooperatively organized groups in which the individual's reward depends solely upon the group's effectiveness. Individuals in such groups, in comparison with those working in competitively organized groups, typically develop higher morale and show greater productivity.

5. Experimental studies of competition and cooperation in "game" situations suggest the crucial role of communication between opponents: When communication is encouraged, or better, enforced, competition is reduced.

6. Contrary to the generally benign effects of communication in social settings, direct comparisons of the problem-solving performance of groups working *as a unit* (as in "brainstorming") with individuals working alone have shown no consistent advantage for either strategy.

7. A mere collection of people does not make a social group. True groups involve individuals who are psychologically related in specifiable ways; when such relations are absent we speak instead of aggregates. It is among the latter that the phenomenon of the "familiar stranger" can be observed. "Bystander intervention"—or rather the failure of bystanders to help a stranger in distress—is another phenomenon of aggregates.

8. Group pressure generally exerts a powerful effect upon individual judgment, sufficient to influence the person to deny the evidence of his own senses. Adults vary in their susceptibility to such pressure, however; the more intelligent, original, and psychologically mature subjects best withstand its effect. Children tend to be highly conforming but grow less so as they develop. But the nature and extent of such changes in susceptibility depend importantly on the kinds of groups in which they are raised.

9. There are two major mechanisms of social influence in a conformity situation: Information provided by others in the same situation is regarded as reliable evidence for the valid response (informational social influence), and what others do and expect one to do becomes the acceptable behavior in the situation (normative social influence). In either case conforming behavior may be uncritical and betrays a human tendency with disturbing ethical implications for our society.

10. The concepts of territoriality and personal space are supported by considerable experimental evidence pointing to distressing psychological and physiological responses to intrusion by strangers. Early recognition of the need for the provision for the defense of personal space and territory is crucial for a sense of psychological well-being.

11. The behavior of group members toward one another constitutes the internal environment, which critically influences the effectiveness of the group in achieving its goal. Management of this environment so as to ensure proper planning, coordination, and maintenance of individual morale is a challenge often unmet by typical social groups.

12. Analysis of the leadership function in groups can be approached in a number of ways. To a surprising extent, sheer amount of talking is a dominant determinant of whom the group perceives as a leader. Since the role of leader is a multidimensional one, different kinds of leaders, each effective in a particular way, can be detected. Which is to be preferred for a given group depends in part upon the personalities of its individual members.

GLOSSARY

audience effect An instance of social facilitation in which the other persons who are present during the individual's performance are only passive spectators.

coaction effect An instance of social facilitation in which the other persons present are actively and simultaneously engaged in the same performance.

informational social influence When an individual's behavior in a group stituation reflects a tendency to accept information from other persons as evidence about reality. This influence can even overwhelm evidence from one's own senses.

normative social influence When an individual's behavior in a group situation is modified to conform with what he believes the group expects of him and for which it will reward him.

personal space The space immediately surrounding one's body that an individual considers private. The preferred amount of spatial separation between individuals depends, among other things, upon cultural factors and degree of acquaintance.

social facilitation A general term, including audience and coaction effects, for the enhancement of individual performance brought about by the social presence of other persons.

territoriality Refers to the expectation that certain regions should be occupied by oneself and by no others. This sense of territoriality, or exclusive rights to certain areas, is very often without a legal basis.

statistical appendix
psychological measurement

CONTENTS

"Anything that exists can be measured." You may wish to debate this sweeping claim but the usefulness of this appendix does not depend on the truth of this slogan. This appendix *is* indispensable if you are to understand at least some of the steps involved in moving from the psychologist's observations to the drawing of the conclusions (however tentative) that constitute the empirical and theoretical substance of this textbook.

As a starting point, we can agree that people differ in practically everything. The scientific study, analysis, and understanding of many of the problems generated by the fact of such ubiquitous individual differences cannot be undertaken unless we first have a way of *measuring* these individual differences—whether differences of intelligence, abilities, personality, or attitudes. And the scientific usefulness of any measurement hinges upon its reliability and its validity. With good measurement techniques we can discuss rationally some of the bitterly fought social questions of the day. Without these statistical tools we cannot understand the scientific evidence on these problems, and we can only revert to the same dreary prejudices and arguments that have held sway for such a long time.

The word **statistics** is often taken to mean simple enumeration. The number of people killed on our highways annually or the number of births per year are the kinds of things that are usually called "statistics." But enumeration of events comprises only a very small part of statistics. The major part consists of carefully worked-out methods of analyzing numerical data. Statistical methods permit us to summarize such data, to assess their reliability and validity, to generalize from observed events to new events. Statistical methods, properly used, are among the most powerful analytical tools of physics, astronomy, medicine, genetics, psychology, economics, sociology, political science, business, and almost every other human enterprise whose data can be stated in numbers. An understanding of simple statistics is almost as necessary for modern man as is the ability to read and write. And for the study of diversity among humankind, it is, of course, of absolute importance.

QUANTIFYING INDIVIDUAL DIFFERENCES

Our first task is to quantify the degree of individual differences. We need measurement techniques that will give us *numerical* answers to the questions we shall ask about individual differences. The statistical operations that we must perform in order to obtain numerical answers are very much the same whether we are concerned with individual differences in personality or individual differences in height and weight. Let us therefore start our discussion of statistical procedures with the measurement of individual differences in height and weight. This problem is relatively simple because our units of measurement (inches, pounds) are already familiar to us. We can then apply what we learn here to the more complex problems involved in the measurement of intelligence, personality, and attitudes.

Frequency Distribution

Entering the University of Washington in 1923–1924 were 629 freshmen, and in due course they were weighed and measured. Their weights were recorded to the nearest full pound, and their heights to the nearest half-inch. The shortest freshman was 60.5 in. tall; the tallest, 76 in. The lightest weighed 100 lb; the heavyweight tipped the scales at 216 lb. Here, then, are 1,258 numbers—inches and pounds—telling us a story of individual differences. If we are to read and understand this story, we must arrange these numbers in a simple and orderly way. The first step is to arrange them in **frequency tables.**

A frequency table is just what its name implies—a table that tells us how frequently certain values occur. When dealing with large numbers of measurements, it is usually desirable to group the individual values into equal **class intervals** and to specify the number of cases that fall within each given class interval. For example, from the array of data in Table A.1, we can see that heights between 71.5 and 70.5 in. occurred 64 times among the 629 freshmen, whereas heights between 68.5 and 67.5 in. occurred 156 times.

A graph has many perceptual advantages over a table. We can transform frequency tables

TABLE A.1 FREQUENCY DISTRIBUTION OF HEIGHTS OF ENTERING FRESHMEN, UNIVERSITY OF WASHINGTON, 1923–1924

Inches	Number
76.0–75.0	3
74.5–73.5	5
73.0–72.0	43
71.5–70.5	64
70.0–69.0	148
68.5–67.5	156
67.0–66.0	115
65.5–64.5	51
64.0–63.0	33
62.5–61.5	8
61.0–60.0	3
	$n = \overline{629}$

Tables A.1–A.11 adapted by permission from G. I. Gavett, *A First Course in Statistical Methods*; copyright 1925 by McGraw-Hill Book Company, Inc.

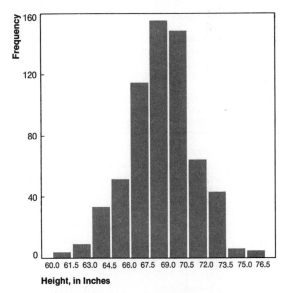

Height, in Inches

FIGURE A.1 Histogram of the distribution of heights among the 629 freshmen entering the University of Washington in 1923–1924.

into frequency graphs. There are two commonly used types of frequency graphs: **histograms** and **frequency curves.**

Figures A.1 and A.2 (p. 824) show how Tables A.1 and A.2 (p. 824) look when made in histograms. Here the measurements are indicated along the horizontal base lines, and frequencies are indicated along the vertical axes. Figures A.3 and A.4 show the same data as fre-

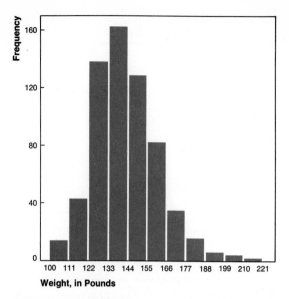

FIGURE A.2 Histogram of the distribution of weights among the 629 freshmen entering the University of Washington, 1923–1924.

TABLE A.2 FREQUENCY DISTRIBUTION OF WEIGHTS OF ENTERING FRESHMEN, UNIVERSITY OF WASHINGTON, 1923–1924

Pounds	Number
220–210	1
209–199	3
198–188	5
187–177	16
176–166	35
165–155	82
154–144	129
143–133	162
132–122	138
121–111	44
110–100	14
	$n = \overline{629}$

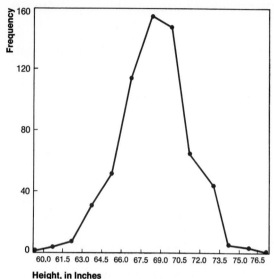

FIGURE A.3 Frequency curve for the data of Table A.1. Each point is placed in the *middle* of the interval.

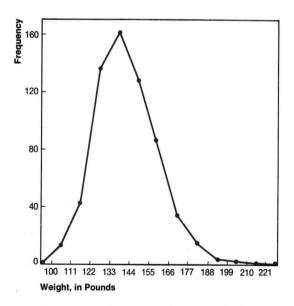

FIGURE A.4 Frequency curve for the data of Table A.2. As in Figure A.3, each point is placed in the middle of the interval.

quency curves (or, technically, "frequency polygons").

The shape of the frequency curve can tell us several interesting things about the nature of the individual differences portrayed. Sometimes the curve looks like an L, sometimes it looks like a rectangle, and sometimes it is so irregular that it defies simple description (see Figure A.5). The shape most commonly found, however, looks somewhat like Figures A.3 and A.4.

The curves in Figures A.3 and A.4 can be described as more or less symmetrical; high toward the middle and tapering off gradually at each end. The curve for freshmen heights

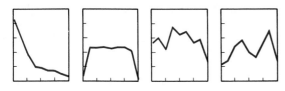

FIGURE A.5 Four infrequently found shapes of distribution curves.

however, is more symmetrical than that for their weights. A curve that departs from the symmetrical shape is called a "skewed curve." Because curves can depart from perfect symmetry to a greater or lesser degree, we can speak of "degree of **skewness**" of a curve. The symmetry, or the degree of skewness of a frequency-distribution curve, plays a very important part in statistical analysis of data.

Almost all measurements of behavior, learning performance, memory, intelligence, or sensory capacity give at least somewhat skewed frequency-distribution curves. This basic fact has significant implications for our understanding of the nature of individual differences among men. For one thing, as we shall soon see, it emphasizes the caution with which we should use such concepts as the average man or average intelligence.

The word "average" is used by many of us as a synonym for "typical," "most frequent," or "representative." All these words refer to some kind of **central tendency**—a middle value between two extremes. When we attempt to give these words exact mathematical meaning, however, we find that they are synonymous only when the distribution curve is symmetrical. These averages can mean quite different things when the distribution curve is skewed—and we have just pointed out that almost all measurements of behavior yield skewed curves.

Mean, mode, median There are three frequently used mathematical measures of central tendency. First, there is the familiar arithmetical **mean.** It is the arithmetical sum of all the values in a distribution divided by the number of cases. Put as a formula, it is written

$$\bar{x} = \frac{\Sigma X}{n}$$

$\bar{x}$ (read as "x-bar") stands for the arithmetical mean, the uppercase Greek capital letter Σ (called "sigma") for "sum of," X for the individual values, and n for the number of cases. The 629 freshmen thus weighed, all told, 89,475 lb. ΣX is therefore 89,475; n is 629; and $\bar{x}$, the arithmetical mean, is found by dividing ΣX by n, which gives us 142.25 lb. Rounding this figure off to the nearest pound, we get 142 lb. The same kind of calculation for freshman heights gives us an arithmetical mean of 68.0 in. If a freshman, Lester Johnson, happened to be 68 in. tall and weighed 142 lb, he would then be of "average" height and weight.

The second measure of central tendency is the **mode.** When we say that Jim McGraw is a freshman of "average height and weight," we may mean that Jim's height is that which occurs most frequently among freshmen and so is his weight. This meaning of "average" (the typical) is quite common. We can get a good estimate of the modes for the freshmen's heights and weights from either the histograms or the frequency curves. The histograms (Figures A.1 and A.2) suggest that the mode for height will fall somewhere in the class interval between 67.5 and 68.5 in. (as can also be seen from Table A.1 and as is represented in Figure A.1 by the bar on the 67.5–69.0 position) and that the mode for weight will be between 133 and 143 lb. But we can obtain a closer approximation of the modes. We assume that they will fall halfway along their respective modal class intervals. This will give us 68.0 in. for height (halfway between 67.5 and 68.5 in.) and 138 lb. for weight (halfway between 133 and 143 lb.)

The third measure is called the **median.** When we say that Tony Morales is of "average" height and weight, we may mean that he is neither short nor tall, nor heavy nor light, but exactly in the middle. For example, if the 629 freshmen were lined up in order of height, with the shortest man at one end and the tallest at the other, Morales would be the 315th man—314 are shorter and 314 taller. His height would be called the "median height." It is a simple matter to array, count up, and find the median of a distribution. Doing so, with our material, we find the median for height (rounded off) to be 68.0 in.

We now have three different "average freshmen" entering the University of Washington in 1923, as indicated in Table A.3. Notice that

TABLE A.3 THE "AVERAGE FRESHMAN" AS A FUNCTION OF THE CENTRAL-TENDENCY MEASURE USED

Measure Used	Height, in.	Weight, lb.
Arithmetic mean (Lester)	68.0	142
Mode (Jim)	68.0	138
Median (Tony)	68.0	141

the average weight varies with the measures used, whereas for height all three measures give the same value. The reason for this difference between weight and height stems from the fact that the distribution curve for height is very close to a true symmetrical shape, whereas for weight the curve is definitely skewed. Figure A.6 makes it clear why the shapes of the distribution curves result in these differences.

The meaning of "average man" or "average intelligence," therefore, may refer to any one of three different measures of central tendency, each with a different value and each mathematically correct. Each measure has certain advantages and certain disadvantages. The arithmetical mean is strongly influenced by the values of the extreme items, whereas the mode and the median are not. And sometimes the extreme values are "unnatural," and their full influence should not be allowed play. For example, suppose four students earn scores of 75, 80, 80, and 85 on an examination. The mean, mode, and median for this group are each 80. Now suppose a fifth student joins the group—a student who has overslept and is late for the examination—and suppose he earns only 15 points. The mean of this group of five is now 67; the mode and median, however, remain at 80. To say that this group of five "averaged" 67 seems a bit misleading. This low average is caused by one man who took the exam under quite different circumstances from the other students. If we wish to get an average that will reflect every score, including the extremes, we

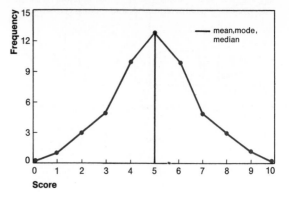

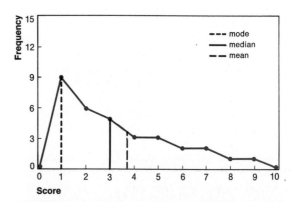

FIGURE A.6 These two curves, one symmetrical and one skewed, indicate the different locations of the three measures of central tendency. Note that in the symmetrical curve the mean, mode, and median must be at the same point (value 5), whereas in the skewed curve they occupy three different points: The mode has a value of 1, the median of 3, and the mean of about 3.8.

use the arithmetic mean; if we wish one that will not be influenced by extreme scores, we use either the mode or the median.

If all we know about a group is its average, our best guess of what the group is like would have to be stated in terms of the average. But doing so can sometimes lead to serious errors. For example, suppose we have two sets of scores from two groups of contestants in a dart-throwing game: 8, 8, 9, 9, 9, 9, 10, 10 (group *A*) and 3, 5, 7, 9, 9, 11, 13, 15 (group *B*). Both distributions are symmetrical, and for both groups the average is 9, whether measured by the mean, the mode, or the median. It is clear, however, that the two groups are dissimilar in one important respect. In the first group the scores cluster closely together; in the second, the individual scores are widely scattered or dispersed. An average is not enough; we must also have information on the degree of dispersion of the scores in the group if we are to appreciate the important respect in which the two distributions differ. Measures of dispersion give us information about extent of individual differences, information that cannot possibly be conveyed by any measure of central tendency.

Measures of Dispersion

For a quick, qualitative impression of the degree of **dispersion**, a look at the frequency-distribution curves is usually enough. For example, in Figure A.7 are these same two distributions with the same averages but different

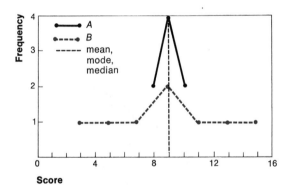

FIGURE A.7 Two distribution curves, both symmetrical, both having the same mean, median, and mode but differing in dispersion. The scores of curve *B* are obviously more scattered (have greater dispersion) than are those of curve *A*.

dispersions. It is obvious that distribution *A* has a smaller dispersion about the average than does distribution *B* and that therefore the average is more representative of *A* than of *B*.

If we wish to state the degree of dispersion more precisely in numerical terms, we must use one of the many available quantitative measures of dispersion. Let us consider some of the more common ones.

Range The **range**, or the distance between the highest and lowest scores, is the simplest numerical measure of dispersion. For our dart-throwing scores, the range for the first set of scores is thus 2 (i.e., 10 minus 8); for the second set it is 12 (15 minus 3). These ranges tell us that the degree of individual differences is greater for the second group than for the first by this measure of dispersion.

For many purposes, and with many distributions, the range is an adequate measure of dispersion and tells us what we wish to know. It is too easily influenced by a single extreme value, however. For example, let us suppose that in 1923 a basketball star, who was 7 ft, 1 in. tall, had decided to enter the University of Washington. Because he would have been only one freshman among 630, he would have affected the mean height very little—in fact, when it was rounded to the nearest inch, not at all. He would, however, have changed the range considerably, as shown in Table A.4.

TABLE A.4 FRESHMEN HEIGHTS WITH AND WITHOUT HYPOTHETICAL BASKETBALL STAR

Measures	With the Star, in.	Without the Star, in.
n (number of students)	630	629
$\bar{x}$ (arithmetic mean)	68.0	68.0
Tallest man	85.0	76.0
Shortest man	60.5	60.5
Range	24.5	15.5

Average deviation We can minimize the influence of a single extreme score by calculating a dispersion measure that takes account of *every* score in the distribution. To do this we first determine by how much each score differs from the group average, and then we can calculate the average of these differences to get a simple measure of dispersion. Let us return to our dart-throwing example.

There are eight scores in each group. The arithmetic mean of each distribution is 9. Now let us see how much each individual's score differs from the arithmetic mean of his group without regard to sign, that is, whether below or above the mean. The values for these individual deviations are listed in the *d* (for deviation) columns of Table A.5, page 828.

TABLE A.5 TWO SETS OF DART-THROWING INDIVIDUAL SCORES AND DEVIATIONS FROM THE MEAN

	Group A		Group B	
	Scores	d	Scores	d
	8	1	3	6
	8	1	5	4
	9	0	7	2
	9	0	9	0
	9	0	9	0
	9	0	11	2
	10	1	13	4
	10	1	15	6
Σ (sum)	72	4	72	24
x̄ (mean)	9		9	

$$A.D. = \frac{\Sigma d}{n} = \frac{4}{8} = .50 \qquad A.D. = \frac{\Sigma d}{n} = \frac{24}{8} = 3.00$$

In group B we find the score of 3 deviates from the group mean by 6 points, the score of 5 by 4 points, and so on. The average deviation for the eight scores in group A is .50 (4 divided by 8). For group B, the average deviation is 3.00. The scores of the second group have a larger average deviation (are more widely dispersed) than the scores of the first group.

The formula for the average deviation is simply

$$A.D. = \frac{\Sigma d}{n}$$

$A.D.$ stands for **average deviation**, Σd for the sum of the individual deviations from the group mean, and n for the total number of cases.

Standard deviation An even more useful—and the most commonly used—measure of dispersion is the **standard deviation.** (In our later discussion of a "normal curve" on p. 840 you will find one instance of the special usefulness of this particular measure of dispersion.) The logic of the standard deviation is similar to that of the average deviation. Again we obtain the individual deviations from the mean. But this time we square each of the deviations, sum the squared deviations, and divide by the number of cases. The reason for squaring the deviations before getting their average lies in certain mathematical considerations that need not concern us here. Because we squared the individual deviations, however, we end with a dispersion measure expressed in squared units instead of in the original units (e.g., in "inches squared"

instead of in "inches"). If we wish to express the dispersion measure in terms of the original units, all we need to do is to take the square root of the result.

This final result, the standard deviation, is usually symbolized by the letters *S.D.* or by the lower-case Greek letter sigma (σ), and its formula is

$$\sigma = \sqrt{\frac{\Sigma d^2}{n}}$$

Returning again to our dart-throwing example, we would calculate the σ as shown in Table A.6.

TABLE A.6 CALCULATION OF STANDARD DEVIATIONS FOR TWO SETS OF DART-THROWING SCORES

Group A			Group B		
Scores	d	d²	Scores	d	d²
8	1	1	3	6	36
8	1	1	5	4	16
9	0	0	7	2	4
9	0	0	9	0	0
9	0	0	9	0	0
9	0	0	11	2	4
10	1	1	13	4	16
10	1	1	15	6	36
Σ=72		4	Σ=72		112
x̄= 9			x̄= 9		
n= 8	Σd²=4		n= 8	Σd²=112	

$$\sigma = \sqrt{\frac{\Sigma d^2}{n}} = \sqrt{\frac{4}{8}} = \sqrt{.50} = .71$$

$$\sigma = \sqrt{\frac{\Sigma d^2}{n}} = \sqrt{\frac{112}{8}} = \sqrt{14} = 3.74$$

The statistics we have learned here can be applied to the measurement of many things—the heights and weights of people, intelligence test scores, reading-ability tests, or personality measurements. Some of these things create special problems, however, and it is to these special problems that we now turn.

UNITS OF MEASUREMENT

If Shirley Cohen weighs 120 lb, Ray Matsumoto 150 lb, and Stan Rudzinski 180 lb, we can make several simple comparisons. We can rank the three and say that Stan is the heaviest, Ray next, and Shirley the lightest. We can make quantitative comparisons and say that Stan weighs 50 percent more than Shirley or that the difference in weight between Stan and Ray is equal to the difference in weight between Ray and Shirley. All this information seems quite obvious. But now let us take a second set of measurements and see what happens.

Suppose that we give intelligence tests to the same three people and find that Stan has a score of 100, Shirley 110, and Ray 120. Again we can rank the three and say that Ray is the most intelligent, Shirley next, and Stan the least intelligent. We can also make a quantitative statement to the effect that Ray has scored 10 points more than Shirley and Shirley 10 points more than Stan. But we *cannot* conclude that Shirley is 10 percent more intelligent than Stan, that Ray is 20 percent more intelligent, or that the amount of difference in intelligence between Ray and Shirley is the same as that between Shirley and Stan! To understand why we cannot reach these conclusions we must consider various problems of measurement.

Absolute Zero

Length is measured with a calibrated ruler of some sort. The numbers on the ruler start, of course, at zero. Suppose we measure the length of three bars and find that one bar extends from 0 to 10 in. along the ruler, another from 0 to 20 in. and the third from 0 to 40 in. The

second bar is twice as long as the first and the third twice as long as the second (Figure A.8).

Let us suppose, however, that we had a ruler whose numbered units did not start at the zero point but at an *unspecified* distance from the zero point, as in Figure A.8. Furthermore, let us suppose that we again measured three bars (different ones, this time) and again found that the first bar ended at the 10-in. mark, the second at the 20-in. mark, and the third at the 40-in. mark. Even with this very strange measuring stick we could still rank the three bars with complete accuracy and say that the second bar was longer than the first and that the third was the longest of all. We could not say, however, that the second bar was twice as long as the first or that the third was twice as long as the second. A little reflection will show that in order to make quantitative comparative statements (e.g., "This is twice as long . . ." or "She is 10 percent brighter than . . ."), we must have measuring instruments that have a real zero starting point.

Most measurement instruments with which we are familiar do have a real zero **(absolute zero)** starting point. A reading of zero on a reliable weighing scale thus literally means "no weight." Not all of our physical measurement instruments are of this kind. For example, on the familiar Fahrenheit or centigrade temperature scale the zero on the thermometer is not the absolute zero of heat, and a temperature of 80 degrees F. is not twice that of 40 degrees F. When we turn to psychological measurement instruments, we find that very few of our tests have a real zero starting point. We have no tests in which a score of zero means that the person has absolutely no intelligence, or absolutely no honesty, cowardice, shyness, or neuroticism. It is even difficult to conceive what zero intelligence or honesty would mean.

Because our mental and personality tests have no absolute zeros, we cannot make ratios of our scores and say that Tony is 10 percent more intelligent than Shirley. Direct comparisons of this sort are not justified. As a result, many problems of psychological measurement arise. But, before turning to some of the suggested solutions to these problems, let us consider a second difficulty with many psychological measuring instruments.

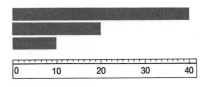

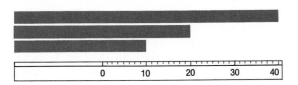

FIGURE A.8 A pictorial representation of the difficulties that exist when we use a measuring instrument that does not have an absolute-zero point of origin (lower figure).

Equal Units

Another important characteristic of the usual physical measuring instrument is that all units are equal in magnitude—an inch is the same length whether it is the first inch on the ruler or the last. This equality permits us to say that the difference in length between 20 and 30 in. is the same as that between 10 and 20.

Suppose, however, that we had a measuring instrument on which there were not **equal units** of measurement—the "inches" becoming progressively longer. Now the distance between 20 and 30 "inches" would be greater than the distance between 10 and 20 "inches."

For no intelligence or personality tests do we know whether the units of measurement are of equal magnitude. For example, in most tests it is essential to add scores from many subtests to arrive at one total score. A reasoning-ability test may consist of verbal-reasoning problems and arithmetic-reasoning problems. We do not know, however, whether or not each arithmetic problem is equal in difficulty to each verbal problem. That is, we do not know whether or not a score of 10 points on the arithmetic problem is equal to a score of 10 points on the verbal problem. Let us assume that Shirley Cohen and Tony Morales have earned the scores shown in Table A.7.

TABLE A.7 HYPOTHETICAL SCORES ON TWO SUBTESTS

	Verbal Problems	Arithmetic Problems	Total
Shirley Cohen	98	22	120
Tony Morales	90	25	115

From these scores it appears that Shirley's general reasoning ability is higher than Tony's (120 versus 115). But this conclusion does not necessarily follow. Quite possibly a difference of 3 points on the arithmetic-reasoning subtest is more significant than is a difference of 8 points on the verbal-reasoning subtest. Therefore Tony's total score may actually indicate a higher reasoning ability than does Shirley's.

In order to meet this and similar problems, several statistical devices have been developed that, within limits, do permit numerical comparisons among scores obtained on different subtests. Almost all these devices require that the original scores (sometimes called **raw scores**) first be changed into **converted scores.** The simplest kind of converted score, the one most commonly used, is the percentile score.

Percentile Score

A **percentile score** tells us a person's standing in relation to the rest of the group. The percentile points divide the total distribution of scores into 100 parts, each containing 1 percent of all the cases. We can then easily transform any raw score into its percentile equivalent by reference to these points. A score with a percentile value of 50 would mean that 50 percent of all the people who took the test scored above that point and 50 percent scored below that point. A percentile value of 90 would mean that only 10 percent scored above that point and 90 percent scored below it.

Percentile scores vary from 0 to 99 *no matter what the range of the raw scores.* As a result, it is possible to compare the performances of different people on quite diverse tests having quite different raw units of measurement.

Despite the undoubted value of percentile scores and other kinds of converted scores (like "standard scores"), we must remember that all comparisons of scores made on psychological tests must be treated with caution. At best the comparisons are relative to the particular group that took the test. When we have neither absolute zero nor equal units of measurement, we cannot make comparisons in absolute terms.

CORRELATION

The description of individual differences not only involves comparing one person with his fellows but also involves comparing two aspects of the same person. For example, what relation exists between being good in arithmetic and being good in music? Do we tend to be good or poor in all abilities, or are most of us good in some things, average in others, and poor in still others? To answer these and other questions, we must have some way of expressing the degree of co-relation of, say, ability in arithmetic with ability in music.

A **correlation plot** is a simple graphic device picturing the relation between two sets of scores.

Let us start with some hypothetical data. Suppose we give ten students three tests—a verbal-reasoning test, an arithmetical-reasoning test, and a maze-learning test—and we also record the students' weights to the nearest pound. Suppose that for the first two tests the score for each student is determined by the number of problems correctly solved, whereas the score for the third test is recorded in terms of the number of errors made before one perfect run through the maze is completed. These hypothetical results are shown in Table A.8.

TABLE A.8 HYPOTHETICAL SCORES ON FOUR SETS OF MEASURES FOR TEN STUDENTS

Student	No. Correct Verbal-Reasoning Test	No. Correct Arithmetical-Reasoning Test	No. Errors Maze Test	Weight, lb.
A	98	24	40	135
B	82	21	46	130
C	90	20	48	160
D	95	26	36	125
E	85	23	42	145
F	100	27	34	165
G	80	22	44	143
H	78	19	50	157
J	102	28	32	140
K	91	25	38	150

Positive Correlation

A **positive correlation** refers to two sets of measures whose values go together. Let us start by taking two sets of the scores from Table A.8: the verbal-reasoning scores and the arithmetical-reasoning scores. To picture the relationship between these two sets of scores, we construct a graph with the verbal-reasoning scores on the horizontal axis, the arithmetical-reasoning scores on the vertical axis. (It does not matter which axis we use for which test.) In this graph (see Figure A.9) a student's score on each test is represented by one point. For example, the point representing student A's performance tells us that he scored 98 on the verbal-reasoning test and 24 on the arithmetical-reasoning test.

An inspection of Figure A.9 shows a clear trend among the ten subjects. The higher the

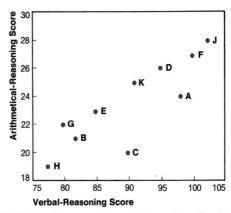

FIGURE A.9 The correlation plot based on the data in Table A.8 and indicating a positive correlation between test scores on arithmetic-reasoning ability and verbal-reasoning ability. Each point represents the scores of the subject on each of the two tests. For purposes of clarity, the subject's "name" (A, B, C, and so forth) has been placed next to the point. Ordinarily the names of the subjects are not indicated.

person's verbal-reasoning score, the higher his arithmetical-reasoning score tends to be. We have here a positive correlation. *Whenever the correlation plot shows a trend from the lower left corner to the upper right corner, a positive correlation exists.* But it will also be noted that there are some exceptions to this trend. Subject C, for example, is definitely out of line. Although she did better than subjects G, B, and E on the verbal test, she did worse than they on the arithmetic test. We can conclude therefore that, although there is a positive correlation, it is not a perfect positive correlation.

Negative Correlation

In Figure A.10, p. 832, data are plotted for the verbal-reasoning test and maze test. Now we find that the higher the score on the verbal test, the fewer the errors on the maze. We have here a **negative correlation** between the two sets of scores. *Whenever the correlation plot shows a trend from the upper left corner to the lower right corner, a negative correlation exists.* But again, we do not have a perfect negative correlation; note, for instance, the scores for subjects A and C.

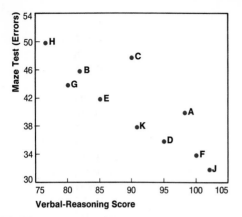

FIGURE A.10 A correlation plot based on the data in Table A.8 and indicating a negative correlation between maze-test errors and verbal-reasoning scores.

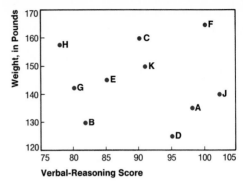

FIGURE A.11 A correlational plot based on data in Table A.8 (indicating a zero correlation between the weight of the subjects and their performance on the verbal-reasoning test). Note that the points do not arrange themselves in any special form but are scattered over the correlational plot. This graph therefore represents a *zero* correlation.

This negative correlation, however, is properly interpreted as indicating a positive relation. In our reasoning test we have recorded the number of solutions achieved, whereas in our maze test we have recorded the number of errors. Obviously, the more errors, the poorer the performance. Therefore this negative correlation between scores really means that a good performance on the maze test is associated with a good performance on the reasoning test; hence, the relation is in fact a positive one. The sign of a correlation (whether positive or negative) merely tells us the relation between the scores on the two tests. The meaning of the correlation depends upon the meaning of the scores.

Zero Correlation

In Figure A.11 we have constructed the correlation plot for the verbal-reasoning test and the body weights of the subjects. The correlation between body weight and verbal-reasoning scores is very close to zero. When the points on the correlation plot do not fall in any specific trend but are found scattered haphazardly, a **zero correlation** exists.

It is clear from the examples we have given that a positive or negative correlation can be something less than perfectly positive or perfectly negative. In many instances we need to know how much less than perfect is

the correlation. This requirement has been satisfied by the development of the **correlation coefficient**—a single index that gives us both the sign and magnitude of the correlation.

By general agreement, it has been decided to call a perfect positive correlation +1.00 and a perfect negative correlation −1.00. The correlation coefficient can thus range from +1.00 to −1.00. For example, a correlation coefficient of +0.14 is low positive; a correlation coefficient of −0.90 is high negative. The size of the correlation refers to the distance from zero (whether positive or negative), not to its positiveness or negativeness. Thus a −0.90 correlation would be considered higher than a +0.14.

Rank-Order Correlation

There are several ways of determining the magnitude of a correlation coefficient. The simplest is the **rank-order correlation coefficient**, the symbol for which is ρ (the Greek letter rho).

The basic logic behind the formula for ρ is readily grasped, and we shall sketch it here through an example.

The first step in obtaining ρ is to rank the subjects in terms of their performances on each of the two tests being analyzed. We then compare the ranks and from that derive the value of ρ. Table A.9 presents the necessary steps for

TABLE A.9 RANK-ORDER CORRELATION BETWEEN VR AND AR TESTS

1	2	3	4	5	6	7
	No. Correct	No. Correct	Rank on	Rank on		
Subject	VR Test	AR Test	VR Test	AR Test	D	D²
A	98	24	3	5	2	4
B	82	21	8	8	0	0
C	90	20	6	9	3	9
D	95	26	4	3	1	1
E	85	23	7	6	1	1
F	100	27	2	2	0	0
G	80	22	9	7	2	4
H	78	19	10	10	0	0
J	102	28	1	1	0	0
K	91	25	5	4	1	1

$$\Sigma D^2 = 20$$

$$\rho = 1 - \frac{6\Sigma D^2}{n(n^2-1)} = 1 - \frac{120}{10(99)} = 1 - \frac{120}{990} = 1 - .12 = +.88$$

getting a ρ for our illustrative data from the verbal and arithmetic tests of Table A.8.

In column 4 we have ranked the performance of the ten subjects on the verbal-reasoning test. The highest score, 102, was earned by subject J, and he is given the top rank of 1; the next best score was 100, earned by F, and she receives the rank of 2; A is ranked 3; and so on. In column 5 we have ranked the ten subjects according to their scores on the arithmetic-reasoning test.

If there were a perfect positive correlation, there would be no difference between the two sets of ranks. For example, subject J, who received rank 1 in the verbal test, would also receive rank 1 in the arithmetic test. The person who received rank 2 in the verbal test would also receive rank 2 in the arithmetic test, and so on down to the one who would be ranked tenth in both lists. If in this case we obtained the differences between the scores of column 5 and those of column 4, we would get a column of zeros.

If the correlation were something less than perfect, however, the differences between the ranks (column 5 minus column 4) would not all be zero. A person receiving the third rank in one test could get the fifth rank in the second test, and so on. The greater the disparities in ranks, the lower would be the positive relation between the two sets of scores. Therefore the

average of the rank differences obviously provides a way of measuring the degree of correlation—the larger the average, the lower the positive correlation.

Again, for various mathematical reasons, we do not deal with the differences among the ranks, but with the squares of these differences. In other words, we square each value in column 6 to give us the values in column 7.

Since a +1.00 is the highest positive correlation possible, to obtain the correlation coefficient we should subtract from 1.00 the average of the differences between the ranks. The higher the average of the differences between the ranks, the lower will be the correlation coefficient.

We arrive finally at the following formula: The size of the correlation should be 1.00 minus the average of the differences between the ranks, or

$$\rho = 1 - \frac{\Sigma D^2}{n}$$

And this logically derived formula is similar in structure to the mathematically derived formula. For various mathematical reasons that need not concern us now, the actual formula is

$$\rho = 1 - \frac{6\Sigma D^2}{n(n^2-1)}$$

Applying this formula, we get a ρ of +0.88 for the correlation coefficient between verbal- and arithmetic-reasoning scores among our ten hypothetical subjects. We have now expressed in numerical terms the positive correlation indicated in Figure A.9.

The same reasoning is involved in the negative rank-order correlation. In a perfect negative correlation the top person in one test would be the worst in the second test; the subject who received a rank of 2 in the first test would receive a rank of 9 in the second, and so on. In this case the differences between the two sets of ranks would be at their maximum. If we subtracted the average of the differences between the ranks from 1.00, we would end as far away from a +1.00 as we could get, that is, at −1.00. For an illustration of a negative correlation, the student is urged to work through the rank-order correlation between the verbal-reasoning test and the maze test, using the data in Table A.8.

Product-Moment Correlation

The correlation coefficient that is most commonly used is the **product-moment correlation coefficient**. The formula for this correlation coefficient (which is symbolized by the letter r) is

$$r = \frac{\Sigma xy}{n\sigma_x\sigma_y}$$

x and y are the deviations of the individual scores from the group means, σ_x is the standard deviation of the scores on test X, and σ_y is the standard deviation of the scores on test Y. An example of how a product-moment correlation coefficient is calculated is given in Box A.1.

As a general rule, the rank-order correlation coefficient is preferred when the number of cases is small (about fifteen to twenty) and when there are few ties in ranks. In other cases the product-moment correlation coefficient is a more desirable measure.

A logical error that is frequently made in the interpretation of the correlation coefficient is the cause-and-effect argument. It is often assumed that, if two variables are highly correlated, one is the cause of the other. A high correlation between two events may, however, mean merely that both events are caused by a third factor, not that one event causes or influences the other. In statistical work the correlation coefficient is often used in problems in which we know there is no causal relationship between the two sets of measurements we are correlating. We shall see some examples in the following pages.

ERRORS OF MEASUREMENT

Whenever we measure anything—the length of a table or the personality of a patient in a mental hospital—our measure suffers from some degree of error. The error may be due to an imperfect measuring instrument, to an imperfect method of applying the instrument, to our careless reading of the instrument or re-

BOX A.1

$$r = \frac{\Sigma xy}{N\sigma_x\sigma_y}$$

The product-moment correlation coefficient was developed by the English mathematician Karl Pearson and is sometimes referred to as "Pearson's coefficient of correlation." Seven steps are involved. Using the hypothetical data of the table, we can demonstrate them:

Subject	Score on X	Score on Y
A	126	120
B	123	100
C	122	60
D	100	50
E	80	25
F	67	23

1. We obtain the group means for test X and test Y, which are 103.0 and 63.0 respectively.
2. Then we determine for each subject the amount by which his score deviates from the group mean. We do this separately for each test. Sub-

ject A, with 126 points, is thus 23 points away from the group mean on the X test. Subject A therefore has an x score of 23. (When the letters are in lower-case type, they refer to deviations from the average.) He is 57 points away from the group mean on the Y test, which gives him a y score of 57.0. In the same manner we obtain the x and y scores for each subject.
3. We then multiply each person's x score by his y score. For example, for subject A we multiply 23 by 57; the product is 1,311.0. We do the same for each of the other five subjects.
4. We then sum all six products, which total 4,347.0 This is the value for Σxy.
5. We then obtain the σs of the x scores and the y scores. They turn out to be 22.8 for the x scores and 36.1 for the y scores.
6. We now multiply the σ of the x scores by the σ of the y scores and by the number of subjects, which gives us a product of 4,938.48. This is the value for $N\sigma_x\sigma_y$.
7. Finally, we divide this last product into the sum of the xy products (step 4). This gives us the product-moment correlation coefficient, which, in this illustration, is +.88.

cording, or to any one of a number of other factors.

Because so much of reasoning in science depends upon the results of measurement, a good deal of concern has been shown for errors of measurement, and we have learned much about their nature, source, and control. For cases in which we have been unable to eliminate them, we have developed techniques that enable us to estimate the degree of error. Knowing the magnitude of our error, we can state the degree of our confidence in any conclusions based on measurements. The study of errors of measurement is one of the basic studies in statistics.

We shall concern ourselves here with two types of error problems: the reliability and the validity of our instruments.

Reliability

No absolutely perfect measuring instrument exists. Even the simplest kind of measuring instrument, the ruler, is not without built-in error. We all know that some measuring instruments give us larger errors than do others, however. A metal ruler, for example, may give us larger errors than a wooden ruler because metal expands or shrinks as the room temperature rises or falls. Obviously, a ruler that expands and shrinks would be unreliable, for, if we used it to measure the same object twice, it might give us two different readings, depending upon the temperature of the room. A reliable ruler would give us the same answer no matter how many times we measured the same object.

This simple consideration gives us the definition of reliable and unreliable measuring instruments. Reliability of a measurement device (including its method of application) can be defined as *the degree to which repeated measurement of the same quantity with the instrument will give the same readings.*

Reliability measured by correlation   Let us suppose that we want to determine the degree of reliability of a new intelligence test. We could administer the test to a group of children and record their scores. One week later we could give them the same test and again record their scores. We would now have two sets of scores

for the same group of children on the same test. If the test and its method of application are reliable, the children should receive the same, or very similar, scores on both occasions. This statement would be true, of course, only if the children's intelligence had not changed during the one-week interval. If the test is not reliable, the children would receive widely different scores at the two testing periods. The correlation coefficient, therefore, gives us a *numerical index expressing the degree of reliability of a test.* When a correlation coefficient is used for this purpose, it is called a **reliability coefficient**.

It is not always desirable, however, to repeat the same test at two different times. It is always possible, for example, that the child may remember what he did the previous week and merely repeat his performance on the basis of memory. In that event, the correlation between the first set of scores and the second would give us a measure of the child's memory rather than of the test's reliability. Or there is the possibility that the child's intelligence itself may actually have changed during the interval, and we would therefore have no way of knowing whether a low correlation between the first and second testing was a result of the change in intelligence or of a lack of testing reliability. Or the child may be bored with the test the second time, so that the low test-retest correlation was caused by lack of motivation rather than by any unreliability of the test or the testing procedure.

Several techniques have been developed in an attempt to avoid these problems in determining the reliability of a test. Among these techniques is one known as **comparable-forms reliability**.

Comparable-forms reliability   Most psychological tests consist of large numbers of items, problems, and questions. Let us assume an arithmetic-reasoning test composed of fifty different arithmetic-reasoning problems. We then proceed to construct another fifty-item test of arithmetic reasoning. The correlation between the two comparable forms would give us the reliability of either form. We can therefore give a group of subjects the first fifty items at one time and, at a later time, the other fifty items. What we have are two comparable forms of the same test.

The comparable-forms method avoids the memory problem and perhaps the boredom problem discussed earlier, but it still leaves the problem of timing. The two forms are given at different times. Many things can happen during the interval to make it difficult to interpret the correlation between the two comparable forms. Partly to meet this problem, the **split-half reliability** method has been developed.

Split-half reliability   The reasoning behind the split-half reliability method is identical with that behind the comparable-forms method. Instead of constructing two comparable forms and giving each form at a different time, we can give our subjects a 100-item test at one sitting and then ourselves split the 100-item test into two 50-item tests. For all practical purposes we have scores on two comparable forms of the test for each subject. Next we correlate the subject's score on all the odd-numbered items with her score on all the even-numbered items; in this way we determine the reliability coefficient of either half and, from this estimate, the reliability of the whole. That is why this method is sometimes call the "odd-even reliability coefficient."

This method has the following advantages over the comparable-forms method: First, both subtests (even and odd) are taken at the same time, under the same conditions of motivation, the same conditions of testing, and the same state of alertness. Second, because we have split the test by the odd-even method, we have ensured comparability of forms—not only in content but also in manner of administration. That is, each subtest contains items that come both early and late in the total sitting so that such factors as fatigue and lagging interest are presumably equated for both subtests.

These and other methods can give us valuable information on the adequacy of a test as a measurement instrument. However, knowing that a test is reliable is not enough to enable us to assess its value as a measurement instrument. *It may be highly reliable and still a very poor measurement instrument because it lacks validity.*

Validity

The terms "reliability" and "validity" are used fairly interchangeably in everyday speech. In measurement theory, however, these terms have different meanings. The statistician, concerned with the question of the reliability of an instrument, asks how consistently the instrument measures whatever it measures. When he is concerned with the question of validity, he asks whether the instrument is measuring what he wants it to measure. An instrument may give consistent measurements (have high reliability), but it may not be measuring what we think it measures (it may have low validity). For example, weekly quizzes in your psychology course may give consistent results in the sense that week after week you earn a 75. The quizzes are reliable indicators. But indicators of what? If your psychology instructor intends them as measures of your understanding of the principles of psychology, he may be wrong. They may be measuring mainly rote memory. Thus, they would have low validity as indicators of psychological understanding.

For many measurement instruments, of course, there are no serious problems of validity. A quiz designed to determine whether you can give a textbook's definitions of specific psychological terms is, by definition, a valid test of whether you can do so. Such a test is said to have **face validity**—it is valid on the face of it!

But most tests that seek to measure more complex phenomena are not that easily validated. For one thing, validity, like reliability, is not an all-or-nothing affair. A test may have degrees of validity. Your quiz grades may be influenced only by your understanding of psychological principles. In that case we would say that the quiz has perfect validity as a measure of understanding of psychological principles. But more probably your score on it is the result of your psychological understanding plus rote-memory ability. The test still has some validity for psychological understanding and some validity for rote-memory capacity, but it is no longer a pure test of either. As with reliability, we must have some way of expressing the degree of the validity of a measuring instrument.

And, again, as with reliability, the correlation coefficient provides us with just such a way.

Validity measured by correlation It is clear that a test is valid to the degree that its measurements correlate with the actual thing it is supposed to measure. For example, suppose we wish to determine the validity of a test designed to measure the ability of students to get high grades in schoolwork. We would give the test to a large number of students and see whether the scores they made on the test correlated highly with the actual grades they received in their schoolwork. Their school grades would, of course, be the final criteria of the validity of the test. If the correlation between the test scores and the criterion scores is high, the test obviously measures what it is intended to measure and it has high validity. If the correlation is low, the test has low validity. When the correlation coefficient is used in this way, it is called a **validity coefficient**.

The difficulty is that frequently we cannot find a criterion with which to correlate the test scores. Suppose we want to measure the validity of an intelligence test. We can get the scores of the test easily enough, but what will serve as our criterion of intelligence? Grades in school? Money earned in adult life? Originality and creativity? Leadership in social affairs? Different people might suggest different criteria, and some of the criteria would themselves pose problems of measurement. For example, even if we all agreed that intelligence refers to originality and creativity, we would still have the problem of finding generally acceptable and quantifiable measures of originality and of creativity to correlate with our intelligence test.

There have been many attempts to solve the criterion problem. Among the more common techniques is the so-called **known-group method** of validity determination.

Known groups and validity There are no easily available criterion scores for originality and creativity. There are, however, certain well-known people whom most of us would regard as highly original and creative. Thus, a group of inventors, scientists, and artists might be picked who exemplify originality and creativity. These people could then be considered as a known group of creative people.

Presumably this known group is more creative than is the average run of men. We would give our test to this known group and also to a large, randomly selected group of people and compare the results. If the test has any validity as a measure of originality and creativity, the average member of the creative group should score higher than the average member of the control group, and the greater the difference between scores, the more valid the test.

Sometimes it is easy to choose the appropriate known group; sometimes it is quite difficult. Nevertheless, in many instances we have no better way of determining the validity of tests than by the known-group method. But, whether we use face validity, correlation with criterion scores, or the known-group method, we must have some information on the validity of a test before we can interpret its results sensibly.

As we have said, a test may have high reliability but low validity in the sense that it turns out not to measure what we intended it to measure. *A test of low reliability cannot have high validity*, however; if a test is capricious in its measurement, now giving a high reading, now a low one, for the same unchanging object, its measurements are being determined by chance factors—in other words, it has low reliability. Unreliable tests cannot consistently correlate highly with any set of criterion scores because what the tests measure is largely error; therefore they must have low validity.

Reliability and validity pertain to errors of measurement and of conceptualization; therefore they arise from an inadequacy in the measurement instrument. But quite aside from this, there is still another major source of error in any investigation that uses measurement. We may make a **sampling error**.

SAMPLING THE "AVERAGE" MAN

Whenever we measure a group of people, we have one of two reasons for choosing them. We may be interested in the particular people themselves, or we may be interested in a specific category of people of which that particular group is supposed to be a **sample**.

In the former instance there are no measurement problems aside from those we have already considered—reliability and validity. If we wish to know what current Berkeley freshmen will score on our scholastic-aptitude test, we measure all the freshmen at Berkeley, and that is all there is to it.

If we want to know what the "American freshman" will score on our test, however, we immediately run into a whole set of measurement problems. We cannot, or do not wish to, test every American freshman. We therefore test a sample of freshmen, and from the results we generalize to the all-American freshman. But how do we know that the results of our sample freshmen correctly portray the American freshman? Perhaps our sample freshmen are brighter than the average American freshman—or duller. As soon as we measure a sample of a group, we introduce the possibility of sampling errors. In scientific investigations we are not primarily interested in the specific individuals we are measuring. For example, when the psychologist studies how quickly a group of sophomores can learn under the recitation method, he is not interested in that specific group of sophomores. He is not even interested in sophomores in general. He is interested in how people—all people, of all colors, of all educational levels, of all cultures—respond to that particular learning method. Most scientific investigations, therefore, are in theory concerned with infinitely large **populations**.

In most studies it would be literally impossible to test and measure every member of the population. We are therefore forced to use a sampling technique. Usually, however, we are being forced to do what is good for us. Even if we had the facilities to test and measure every member of the population in which we are interested, it would be wasteful and foolish. *In many instances we can obtain almost as precise an estimate of a population score by measuring a sample as we can by measuring the total population.* And a sample need not be very large to be a good sample. A group of 3,000 carefully chosen Americans, for example, can be a better

sample of the total population of more than 200 million Americans than can 1 million who are poorly chosen.

Biased and Unbiased Samples

Although the technique of obtaining a good sample is highly sophisticated, the guiding principle is simple. Ideally, in drawing a sample from a large population, we must use a procedure that permits every member of the entire population an equal opportunity to be included in the sample. The result of such a procedure is a **random sample** since it ensures that there has not been a systematic bias in favor of any kind of person. For example, suppose we want to determine the average body weight of all the residents of New York City. To do so, we must first obtain a representative sample of New York residents.

One method, used in the past, was to take the city telephone directory and draw, say, every 500th name. But this method inevitably results in a systematically **biased sample** for it has systematically drawn only those New Yorkers who have telephones and has systematically excluded all those who do not. For our purpose, this group is obviously not a good sample of New Yorkers. It may be, for instance, that New Yorkers who have telephones are in the higher-income brackets, are on a diet fad, eat less, and therefore weigh less than do New Yorkers who have no telephones.

Once we have a systematically biased sample, there is very little we can do to correct the sample mathematically. Whatever measurements we perform on telephone-subscribing New Yorkers cannot safely be generalized to all New Yorkers.

One way to avoid systematic bias would be to write the name of each New Yorker on standard-sized slips of paper, place all the papers in a huge bin, shake the bin vigorously, and then blindly pick out, say, 3,000 names at random. We would then have chosen a random sample of New Yorkers.

Frequently, of course, it is not feasible to use such an ideal random method, so we attempt to approximate the ideal method. We might, for example, take every third city block and choose the members of every tenth family in each block for our sample. This method would give us an approximation of a random sample.

Although we may thus avoid systematic bias or error in our sample, the possibility still remains that our sample would deviate from the population because of unsystematic or chance events. For example, perhaps *just by sheer chance* we might include, say, many more names of women or of older people, proportionally, than there are in the total population of New York City. However, unlike the situation in which there are systematic biases, we can do something about chance errors. We can predict their magnitude. To understand how this prediction is possible, it is necessary to take a rather long detour and discuss **probability.**

Probability

One of the most important mathematical achievements in the field of probability theory was the discovery that **chance events** behave lawfully. That is, if we record all our observations of recurring chance events and draw a distribution curve of these observations, the distribution curve will take the shape of what is called a **normal curve.**

Mutually exclusive events Let us toss a dime in the air. Knowing nothing about the forces that determine how this particular dime will fall at this particular moment, we can say that the probability that we will get a head is 1 out of 2, or, as it is usually written, $h = \frac{1}{2}$ (where h stands for the probability of a head). The same is true, of course, for a tail, that is, $t = \frac{1}{2}$. Because the dime can fall only so that heads *or* tails will show, the two possible occurrences are **mutually exclusive events.** The probability that the coin will fall so that *either* a head or a tail comes up is 1, that is, $\frac{1}{2}h + \frac{1}{2}t = 1$. (Certainty, in probability nomenclature, is represented by the value of 1.) This simple operation is an illustration of an important general probability rule: *The probability of occurrence of two or more mutually exclusive events is obtained by adding the probabilities of the individual events.*

Independent events Now let us throw two dimes at a time. The probability that one dime

will fall heads is $\frac{1}{2}$; the probability that the other dime will fall heads is also $\frac{1}{2}$. What is the probability that both dimes will fall heads? When we have two dimes, the events are *not* mutually exclusive. That is, one dime can show a head, but this does not mean that the other dime cannot also show a head. The falls of the two dimes are **independent events.**

For independent events the following **rule** holds: *The probability of the occurence together of two or more independent events is obtained by multiplying the probabilities of the individual events.* For example, with two coins the probability of getting two heads is found by multiplying $\frac{1}{2}$ (i.e., the probability that one dime will show a head) by $\frac{1}{2}$ (the probability that the other dime will show a head). Thus, on the average, two heads will come up one in four throws and, of course, the odds for two tails are the same.

We can now make a probability prediction. If we were to throw two dimes 10,000 times, we would expect to find that two heads would come up about $\frac{1}{4}$ of the time, or 2,500 times, and that two tails would come up about $\frac{1}{4}$ of the time, or 2,500 times. For the remaining 5,000 throws we would expect one head and one tail. The predicted distribution is shown in Figure A.12, page 840, as a frequency histogram. From this figure it will be seen that the most probable event is one head and one tail, but in 25 percent of the throws we would get two heads and in 25 percent of the throws, two tails.

By similar reasoning, but requiring more complicated mathematics, we can determine the probabilities for three, four, five, or any number of coins. In Table A.10 and Figure A.13, page 840, we present the data for ten coins. The most probable event–the one we would expect to occur 24.6 percent of the time (in 2,460 throws out of 10,000; see Table A.10)—is five heads and five tails. But also by chance we would occasionally expect to find all ten heads showing up, which would occur 0.1 percent of the time (or in 10 out of 10,000 throws). In other words, the chances are 1 in 1,000 that ten heads would show at one throw.

The normal curve Note one very important characteristic of the two histograms shown in

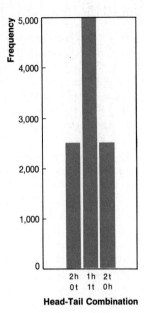

FIGURE A.12 A frequency histogram of the theoretically derived distribution of head-tail combinations that we might expect to find if we flipped two coins 10,000 times.

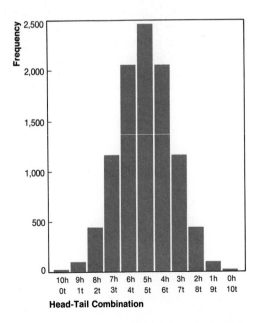

FIGURE A.13 A frequency histogram of the theoretically derived distribution of head-tail combinations that we might expect to find if we flipped ten coins 10,000 times.

TABLE A.10 THEORETICAL EXPECTATIONS OF HEAD-TAIL COMBINATIONS FOR TEN COINS TOSSED 10,000 TIMES

Combinations of H(eads) and T(ails)	Frequency
10h and 0t	10
9h and 1t	98
8h and 2t	439
7h and 3t	1,172
6h and 4t	2,051
5h and 5t	2,460
4h and 6t	2,051
3h and 7t	1,172
2h and 8t	439
1h and 9t	98
0h and 10t	10
	10,000

Figures A.12 and A.13. They are perfectly symmetrical around the most probable event. As the number of coins is increased, the histograms maintain their perfect symmetry, but their shapes gradually change from the sharp, angular shape of the two-coin histogram to the somewhat bell-shaped appearance of the ten-coin histogram. As the number of coins increases, the number of head-tail combinations to be plotted necessarily increases, and the histogram becomes smoother and smoother, ultimately approaching in form the **normal curve.** This eventuality is what we meant by saying that chance events behave lawfully—they give a beautifully smoothed, bell-shaped distribution curve.

Because the normal curve was constructed through the application of mathematical theory, a good deal is known about its mathematical properties. It is these properties that make the normal curve of such great value in estimating sampling errors. The most important of these properties and the one immediately relevant to our problem is the fixed relation that the standard deviation bears to the curve. The relation is such that *the standard deviation measures off constant proportions of the curve from the mean.* An example will clarify this point.

First, let us calculate the standard deviation for the theoretically derived distribution shown in Table A.10 and Figure A.13. Using the formula we have already developed on page 828,

$$\sigma = \sqrt{\frac{\Sigma d^2}{n}}$$

we find that the standard deviation is 1.58. The most probable outcome of a throw of ten dimes will be five heads and five tails, which is the mean of the distribution. Let us therefore start at 5.0 on the base line of Figure A.14 (which portrays the data of Figure A.13 as a smooth curve rather than as a histogram) and measure a distance of 1σ on either side. We arrive at a score of 3.42 on one side and 6.58 on the other. In a perfectly normal curve, exactly 34.13 percent of all cases will be found between the mean value and the value 1σ away from the mean, or—put another way—more than 68 percent of scores fall in the range from −1σ to +1σ.

Let us now mark off another σ distance. We arrive at 1.84 and 8.16. Between 3.42 and 1.84 will be found approximately 13.59 percent of the cases, and the same is true for the interval between 6.58 and 8.16. *The relations between the standard deviation and the distribution of cases in a normal distribution are always present, no matter what the absolute size of the mean or the size of the standard deviation.*

Standard Error

We have now completed our detour and are ready to return to New York City, the weights of its residents, and sampling errors.

Suppose we wish to estimate the mean weight of all New Yorkers from a random sample of only 100 New Yorkers. We have the name and weight of every New Yorker on a separate slip of paper. From this total set of slips we draw 100 at random, and we then calculate the mean weight of the sample of 100. Let us assume that this value is 120 lb. We then calculate the σ of this distribution of 100 cases. Let us assume that σ equals 19.5 lb. With only this information we can now determine how reliable an estimate of the true mean weight of all New Yorkers our sample mean of 120 lb is.

In order to understand how we can do so, let us perform a hypothetical experiment. We must first obtain 10,000 different random samples of the New York population, each sample consisting of 100 cases, and calculate for each sample its mean. We shall thus obtain 10,000 means.

Our first mean, based on our first random sample of 100, we found to be 120 lb. We now throw the 100 slips of paper back into the huge bin that is New York, shake it up again, and draw a new sample of 100 names. Calculating the mean of this new sample, we may find it to be 122 lb. Again we throw the 100 names back, and again we draw a new sample. In this way we build up our total of 10,000 means.

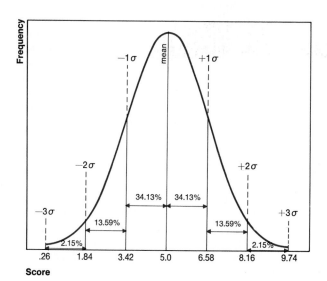

Score

FIGURE A.14 Here the data of the histogram in Figure A.13 are portrayed as a smooth curve with the mean at 5. (The scores here are the numbers of tails; heads would have worked as well.) The percentage values shown are characteristic of every normal distribution curve; thus within the area marked off by +1σ and −1σ will be found 68.26 percent of all the scores in the distribution; within the area marked off by +2σ and −2σ will be found 95.44 percent of all the scores in the distribution; and between the area marked off by +3σ and −3σ will be found about 99.75 percent of all the scores in the distribution. The theoretical normal distribution curve will never hit the base line, although it will continue to approach it. Therefore, no matter how many sigma distances we go from the mean (on both sides), we shall never encompass 100 percent of the cases. Of course, a curve representing actual data does hit the base line on either end because it reflects a limited number of cases.

For each draw of 100 names it is a matter of pure chance which 100 names we get. It is therefore a matter of pure chance (within the limits of all New Yorkers' weights) what the mean weight of each sample will be. It will be recalled that, when we record repeated chance events and throw these observations into a distribution curve, we obtain a normal distribution curve with the most probable value in the center and with the values of the deviant sample means falling on either side of the curve. Therefore we know in advance that, if we were actually to calculate the 10,000 means, they too would distribute themselves in a normal curve.

The standard deviation of such a curve is called the **standard error of the mean** and is symbolized by $\sigma_{\bar{x}}$. The formula for $\sigma_{\bar{x}}$ is

$$\sigma_{\bar{x}} = \frac{\sigma}{\sqrt{n}}$$

In this equation σ is the standard deviation of our sample, and n is the number of cases in our sample. To return to our illustration: As the σ of our sample was 19.5 and the n was 100, the $\sigma_{\bar{x}} = 1.97$ (see Figure A.15).

This standard error of the mean enables us to formulate probability statements about the distance between our sample mean of 120 lb and the true mean of all New Yorkers. Let it be recalled that the curve in Figure A.15 encompasses *all possible* averages obtainable from

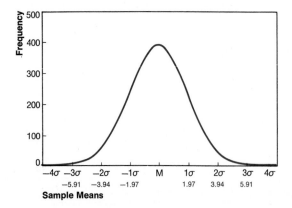

FIGURE A.15 A normal distribution curve representing the theoretically expected distribution of the means of 10,000 random samples of 100 cases each taken from the same population. The standard deviation of one obtained sample is 19.5 and the $\sigma_{\bar{x}}$ is 1.97.

groups of 100 New Yorkers and is a normal distribution curve. As the sigma of this normal distribution curve is 1.97, there are about 68 chances out of 100 (twice 34 percent) that our sample mean is not more than plus or minus 1.97 lb away from the true mean. In statistical language this statement is written as follows: "The mean is 120 ± 1.97."

We can state the probabilities with even more confidence. Because we know that 99.74 percent of all the cases fall within plus and minus 3σ of the mean, we can say that there are over 99 chances out of 100 that our sample mean is not more than plus or minus 5.91 lb away from the true mean.

Precision and size of sample   The level of confidence in the previous example is high (one that any betting man would be willing to risk all on), but the range of ±5.91 lb is pretty wide. Can we reduce this range and still maintain the same level of confidence? There is a relatively simple way to try to do so. When we recall that the standard of the mean is determined by the formula

$$\sigma_{\bar{x}} = \frac{\sigma}{\sqrt{n}}$$

it is clear that by increasing the n (number of cases in our single sample) the $\sigma_{\bar{x}}$ is reduced. For instance, if our sample had 200 cases rather than 100, we would have obtained a standard error of the mean of about 1.30 lb rather than 1.97 lb. With a sample of 200 cases we can state our conclusions with the same degree of confidence but with more precision: That is, there are more than 99 chances out of 100 that our sample mean is not more than plus or minus 3.90 lb (three times the new standard error of the mean) away from the true mean.

While every increase in sample size decreases the standard error of the mean, this increase follows the law of diminishing returns because the n in the $\sigma_{\bar{x}}$ formula is under the square-root sign. That is, an increase in n from 100 to 200 may show a sizable drop in the standard error; an increase of another 100 will show a smaller decrease in the standard error; an increase of another 100 will show a still smaller decrease; and soon the point will be reached at which an additional number of cases will show very little decrease in the size of the standard error of the mean. The determination of what size sample we should use rests mainly upon two considerations: the desired precision of the results and the time, money, and energy available. For some measures we wish a highly precise result, and in such cases we must have a large n; for some measures, however, a less highly precise estimate of the true mean is sufficient.

Everything we have said about the mean of a sample is equally true for other measurements we obtain from samples. We can never be certain that our obtained means are the true means, that our obtained correlation coefficients are the true correlation coefficients, or that our obtained differences between groups are the real differences. With the use of the standard-error statistic we can state the probabilities that our obtained measurements are within a specified distance from the true values. Sometimes the probabilities are high enough so that we are willing to go ahead as if we really did know the truth. And this willingness is essentially what we mean throughout this text when we speak of differences or correlations as "significant." Most scientists will not accept confidence limits of anything less than 95 chances out of 100 before they feel they can go ahead. Such a result is usually labeled "significant at the 5 percent level," by which is meant that if we go ahead, we will have been mistaken 5 out of 100 times. But even when we demand such high odds, we are still speaking of probabilities. The scientist, alas, is forced to be a gambling man. He has no choice.

SUMMARY

1. Statistics refers largely to methods for anlyzing numerical data, and statistical treatment of data obtained from psychological measurement procedures is essentially identical to its applications in other sciences.

2. Frequency distributions and various measures of central tendency and dispersion provide informative descriptive summaries of individual differences in psychological characteristics as they occur in the population.

3. Psychological measurement, like all measurement, depends, of course, upon available scales for quantifying individual differences, and the nature of psychological characteristics almost always prevents the use of scales with absolute zero points and equal units. Typically, our statements about individual differences must be couched in terms of relative values; that is, rather than determining absolute amounts of a given quantity, we can rank individuals only along a given psychological dimension.

4. Even with such relative measurement, however, it remains possible to evaluate the extent of the relation between any pair of variables, and we do so by means of correlation. Correlations tell us the extent to which a change in one characteristic is associated with a change in another, but, by themselves, they cannot specify which is cause and which is effect. That relation is a matter of interpretation; it is a logical or psychological task, not a statistical one.

5. All measurement involves some degree of error. There is the error resulting from inconsistency with repeated measures, either in the instrument or in the characteristic being measured. Here we have a matter of the reliability of measurement. Validity, by comparison, refers to the extent to which the instrument measures what we intend it to measure; if it falls short in this respect, we have an error in validity.

6. Another form of error is sampling error, by which we mean the imperfection arising from the hard fact that we can measure only samples from a population, not all individuals composing it. By assuring that these samples are drawn from the population in an unbiased manner and by applying various principles of mathematical probability, it is possible to estimate the extent of sampling error. From this point we can evaluate the degree of confidence that can be placed in the conclusions reached from a statistical analysis of the data.

GLOSSARY

SOME STATISTICAL SYMBOLS

$\bar{x}$	mean	r	product-moment correlation coefficient
σ	standard deviation	n	number of cases
Σ	sum of	$\sigma_{\bar{x}}$	standard error of the mean
d	deviation		
ρ	rank-order correlation coefficient		

absolute zero   A measuring instrument whose units are numbered from a real zero is said to have an absolute zero as its starting point. Such an instrument is contrasted with a measurement instrument whose numbered units start at some unspecified distance from the zero point. The Fahrenheit and centigrade thermometers and most intelligence and personality scales are illustrations of the latter type of measurement instruments. When a measurement instrument does not have an absolute zero as its starting point, we cannot make direct ratio comparisons of scores; that is, we cannot say that a score of 50 on such an instrument is twice the value of a score of 25 and so on.

average deviation (A.D.)   A measure of dispersion based on the average of the deviations of every score in the distribution from the mean of all the scores of the distribution. The formula for the average deviation is

$$A.D. = \frac{\Sigma d}{n}$$

The average deviation is less influenced by extreme scores than is the range or the standard deviation.

biased sample   The result of a sampling procedure that systematically excludes certain kinds of subjects or systematically underrepresents certain kinds of subjects that should be included. (cf. **random sample**)

central tendency   A middle value between the extremes of a set of measures. There are many different kinds of central-tendency measures. Among the more common are the mean, median, and mode. These three measures of central tendency, even when based on the same scores, need not yield identical values. They will do so only in a perfectly symmetrical frequency curve. Each measure of central tendency has a somewhat different meaning.

chance event   An event that has so many complexly interrelated causes that it is impossible (at the time) to predict the exact nature of the occurrence.

class interval   The range of values treated within one group. For example, if we were to treat all values from 10 to 20 as one group and from 21 to 30 as another group, these ranges would be called "class intervals."

comparable-forms reliability   A method of determining the reliability coefficient for a measuring instrument by obtaining the correlation coefficient between two comparable forms of the same test, administered to the same group of subjects.

converted scores   When a raw score is changed into another kind of score, it is referred to as a converted score. The simplest and the most commonly used converted score is the *percentile score*. (cf. **raw scores**)

correlation coefficient   A single index that gives both the sign and magnitude of a correlation. A correlation coefficient can vary from +1.00 (a perfect positive correlation) to −1.00 (a perfect negative correlation). Two common correlation coefficients are the rank-order correlation coefficient (ρ) and the product-moment correlation coefficient (r).

correlation plot   A graphic device picturing the relation between two sets of scores. In such a graph a person's scores on two different tests are represented by one point. When the scores of a number of people are thus plotted on the graph, we can determine, by inspection, the *sign* of the correlation. When the points on a correlation plot show a trend from the lower left corner to the upper right corner, a *positive correlation* exists; when the trend is from the upper left corner to the lower right corner, a *negative correlation* exists; and when no specific trend is apparent, a *zero correlation* exists.

dispersion   The degree of scatter among the individual scores of a set of scores. If the scores all cluster closely around some measure of central tendency, we speak of a low degree of dispersion; if the scores are widely scattered around the central tendency, we speak of a high degree of dispersion. There are a number of quantitative measures of degree of dispersion, among them the range, the average deviation, and the standard deviation.

equal units   An important characteristic of the usual physical measuring instrument. All units are equal in magnitude; for example, the distance from 4 in. to 7 in. is equal to the distance from 10 in. to 13 in. This chracteristic is to be contrasted with that of many psychological tests (intelligence, personality) in which we do not know whether or not the units of measurement (scores) are of equal magnitude; that is, the difference between a score of 100 and 110 IQ points may *not* be equal to the difference between a score of 110 and 120 IQ points.

face validity Tests that are assumed to be valid simply by definition. For example, a ruler is a valid measuring instrument of length, by definition of what constitutes length.

frequency curve A graphic representation of the data from a frequency table. The measurement values are represented along the horizontal base line of the graph; the number of cases for each value, along the vertical axis. For each class interval a point, in the middle of the interval, is placed at the appropriate height to indicate the frequency of occurrence of cases in that interval. The points are then connected by lines to form a frequency curve. The more technical name for this kind of frequency graph is "frequency polygon."

frequency table An orderly arrangement of discrete values in terms of the frequency of occurrence of the different values. Usually the different values are grouped together into class intervals, and the frequency table presents the number of cases falling into each class interval.

histogram A bar diagram that presents the data from a frequency table. Each class interval is represented by a separate bar, and the height of each bar indicates the number of cases falling within that class interval. The bars are usually arranged so that the bar representing the class interval with the lowest measurement value is at the extreme left of the diagram and the one with the highest measurement value at the extreme right. The histogram is sometimes referred to as a "frequency graph."

independent events Two events are said to be independent when the occurrence of one does not influence, in any degree, the probability of the other's occurrence. For example, when two coins are flipped, the fact that one may fall heads does not influence at all the probability that the other will also fall heads—or tails. The probability of the occurrence of independent events is obtained by multiplying the probabilities of the individual events.

"known-group" method A method for determining the validity of a test by comparing the scores made on the test by a group previously known to be high on a certain trait with the scores of a group known to be lower on that trait.

mean ($\bar{x}$) The arithmetic mean, frequently called the "arithmetic average," is the most commonly used measure of central tendency. It is the arithmetic sum of all the values in a set of data divided by the number of cases. The formula for the mean is written

$$\bar{x} = \frac{\Sigma X}{n}$$

The value of the mean can be strongly influenced by a few extreme values found in the set.

median A measure of central tendency. It refers to that value in an array of values arranged from the lowest to the highest that occupies the middle point. In such an array the median value would thus have as many cases below it as above it. The value of the median is not very strongly influenced by extreme items in the set of values.

mode A measure of central tendency. It refers to the *most frequent* value occurring in a set of values. The terms "most popular" and "most frequent" can be regarded as synonymous. The value of the mode is not at all influenced by a few extreme items in the set of values.

mutually exclusive events Two events, one of which, when it occurs, makes impossible the simultaneous occurrence of the other. For example, when a coin is flipped, the showing of a head makes impossible the simultaneous showing of a tail. The showing of head and the showing of tail are thus mutually exclusive events. The probability of occurrence of two or more mutually exclusive events is obtained by adding the probabilities of the individual events.

negative correlation Inverse relation of the values of two sets of measures. For example, if we found that children who are good in arithmetic are poor in reading and that those who are poor in arithmetic are good in reading, we would have a negative correlation.

normal curve A perfectly symmetrical, bell-shaped frequency curve having certain well-defined mathematical characteristics. Among these are the following: Within the area of the curve marked off by $\pm 1\sigma$ (from the mean) will be found 68.26 percent of all the scores in the distribution; within the area marked off by $\pm 2\sigma$ will be found 95.44 percent; and within the area marked off by $\pm 3\sigma$ will be found 99.75 percent. A distribution curve made up of many chance events will approximate a normal distribution curve.

percentile score One type of converted score expressing a person's score relative to his group in percentile points. A percentile point divides the total distribution of scores into 100 parts, each containing 1 percent of all the cases. A percentile score of 90 thus means that 10 percent of the people in the group scored above that point and 90 percent scored below. Percentile scores vary from 0 to 99, no matter what the range of the raw scores. Percentile scores make it possible to compare the performance of people on diverse tests having quite different raw units of measurement.

population *All* the objects or people of a given class. For example, a population of vocabulary items would refer to all the words in a given language.

positive correlation Direct relation of the values of two sets of measures. For example, if we found that children who are good in arithmetic are also good in reading and that those who are poor in one are poor in the other, we would have a positive correlation.

probability A mathematical theory dealing with the lawful and therefore predictable relations among truly chance events.

product-moment correlation coefficient (*r*) The product-moment correlation coefficient, symbolized by the small letter *r*, is based on the values of the individual deviations and the standard deviations of the two sets of scores. The formula for the product-moment correlation coefficient is

$$r = \frac{\Sigma xy}{n\sigma_x \sigma_y}$$

The product-moment correlation coefficient is sometimes called "Pearson's coefficient of correlation" after its inventor, Karl Pearson, an English mathematician. This coefficient is commonly used where *n* is relatively large.

random sample The result of a sampling procedure permitting every member of the population an equal opportunity to be included. (cf. **biased sample**)

range The simplest numerical measure of dispersion. It is calculated by obtaining the difference between the two extreme (or end) values of a distribution; thus the value of the range is greatly influenced by one extreme score.

rank-order correlation coefficient (*ρ*) A correlation coefficient symbolized by the Greek letter *ρ* (rho) based on a comparison of the ranks of people on two sets of scores. The formula for the rank-order correlation coefficient is

$$\rho = 1 - \frac{6\Sigma D^2}{n(n^2 - 1)}$$

The rank-order correlation coefficient is usually employed where the number of cases (*n*) is relatively small (about fifteen to twenty cases).

raw scores The original scores obtained from a measuring instrument. (cf. **converted scores**)

reliability coefficient Refers to the degree to which repeated measurement of an instrument will give the same or similar readings. This degree is determined by getting the correlation coefficient between two sets of measurements of the same object by the same measuring instrument. The higher the correlation, the more *reliable* the instrument.

sample A portion of a *population*, taken as representative of the whole population. If the sample is truly *random*, conclusions based on it can represent the whole population.

sampling error An error contributing to lack of representativeness of a *sample*. When we measure a sample of subjects and attempt to generalize to the total population, we may make wrong generalizations because our sample was not perfectly representative of the population.

skewness Refers to deviation of the shape of a frequency curve from a normal curve. A skewed curve, therefore, is a frequency curve that departs from the symmetrical normal curve either by having more cases on the right of the mean than on the left, or vice versa. In a skewed curve the values for the mean, median, and mode are not identical.

split-half reliability A method for determining the reliability coefficient for a measuring instrument by obtaining the correlation coefficient between two equal halves of the same test. By splitting a test into two halves, the scores on the odd-numbered items are grouped together to form one subscore and the scores on the even-numbered items to form the second subscore. For this reason the split-half reliability method is sometimes referred to as the "odd-even method."

standard deviation (S.D., σ) A measure of dispersion based on the average of the deviations *squared* of every score in the distribution from the mean of all the scores of the distribution. The formula for the standard deviation is

$$\sigma = \sqrt{\frac{\Sigma d^2}{n}}$$

The standard deviation is the most commonly used measure of dispersion.

standard error of the mean $(\sigma_{\bar{x}})$ The standard deviation of a theoretical frequency curve made up of many sample means. Called the "standard error" because it is useful in estimating the degree to which the obtained sample mean deviates from the true mean of the population. Its formula is

$$\sigma_{\bar{x}} = \frac{\sigma}{\sqrt{n}}$$

statistics The mathematical discipline relating to the analysis of numerical data. Statistical methods are designed to summarize such data, to assess their reliability and validity, to determine the nature and magnitude of relations among sets of data, and to guide us in our attempts to generalize from observed events to new events.

validity coefficient The degree to which the measurements obtained with an instrument correlate with the criterion measures. When we ask whether or not an instrument is *valid*, we ask whether or not it measures what we think it measures. The higher the correlation coefficient between the scores on a test and the criterion scores, the more valid the test.

zero correlation The absence of a relation between two sets of scores. For example, if we found that some children who are good in arithmetic are poor in reading, whereas other children who are good in arithmetic are also good in reading, we would tend toward a zero correlation.

general glossary

ablation technique, 352
absolute threshold, 257
absolute zero, 844
abundancy motives, 464
accommodation, 97, 315, 352
acetylcholine (ACh), 441
acetylcholinesterase (AChE), 441
active theory of sleep, 562
adaptation, 97
adaptation level, 280
adjective checklist, 686
adolescence, 55
adrenal cortex, 562
adrenal medulla, 562
adrenal steroids, 562
adrenocorticotropic hormone (ACTH), 562
affective disorders, 610
agnosia, 441
"aha!" experience, 142
all-or-none law, 74
alpha wave, 74
altered state of consciousness (ASC), 529
amplitude, 257
anal stage, 725
anterior pituitary gland, 562
antidepressant drugs, 562
antidiuretic hormone, 562
antisocial reaction (psychopathic personality), 610
anxiety, 584
anxiety neurosis, 610
aphasia, 441
apparent movement, 315
appreciative emotions, 497
approach-approach conflict, 584
approach-avoidance conflict, 584
aptitude, 188
archetypes, 725
assimilation, 97, 280
association area, 441
association value, 411
asthenic type, 666
attention, 280
attitude, 773
audience effect, 819
auditory (cochlear) nerve, 353
auricle, 353
autistic thinking, 142
autokinetic movement, 315

automatic writing, 529
autonomic nervous system, 562
average deviation (A.D.), 844
avoidance-avoidance conflict, 584
avoidance training, 393
axon, 74
axon terminal, 74

backward conditioning, 371
balance theory, 790
basal ganglia, 74
basilar membrane, 353
basket endings, 353
behavioral disposition, 562
behavior genetics, 25
behavioristic model, 610
behavior therapy, 644
biased sample, 844
binaural cues, 315
binaural interaction, 353
biological clock, 74
bipolar cell, 353
bone conduction, 353
brain, 74
brain stem, 74
brightness, 257

capsule, 353
catecholamine theory of depression, 562
cell body, 74
cell membrane, 74
central mechanism, 353
central nervous system, 74
central tendency, 844
cephalocaudal direction, 55
cerebellum, 74
cerebral hemispheres, cerebrum, 74
chemotherapy, 644
chromosomes, 25
chunking, 411
ciliary muscles, 353
circadian rhythm, 74
class interval, 844
client-centered therapy, 644
closure, 280
clustering, 411
coaction effect, 819
cochlea, 353
cochlear duct, 353

cochlear microphonic, 353
cochlear nuclei, 353
coding, 411
cognitive narrowing, 585
collective unconscious, 725
color blindness, 257
commissure, 74
communicative-thinking stage, 142
comparable-forms reliability, 844
complementary colors, 257
concentrative meditation, 529
concrete operations, 97
conditioned discrimination, 371
conditioned inhibitor, 372
conditioned response (CR), 372
conditioned-response learning, 372
conditioned stimulus (CS), 372
conduct disorders, 610
conduction mechanism, 353
cones, 353
conscious need, 464
conservation, 97
consolidation, 441
constructive alternativism, 666
contour, 281
contrast, 281
convergence, 315, 353
conversion reaction, 610
converted scores, 844
cornea, 353
corpus callosum, 74
correlation coefficient, 844
correlation plot, 844
cortex, 74
counterconditioning, 644
cranial nerve, 74
created image, 142
creative problem solving (productive thinking), 142
cretinism, 562
crossing-over of genes, 25
cross-sectional studies, 55
cue, 725
cultural lag, 464
cultural relativism, 464
"culture-fair" mental tests, 227
cutaneous sensations, 353

decorticate animal, 442
defense mechanisms, 585

bibliography

ABELSON, R. P. & J. D. CARROLL. 1965. Computer Simulation of Individual Belief Systems, *Amer. Behav. Scientist*, 8, 24–30. **154**

AD HOC COMMITTEE ON ETHICAL STANDARDS IN PSYCHOLOGICAL RESEARCH. 1973. *Ethical Principles on the Conduct of Research With Human Participants*. Washington, D.C.: American Psychological Association. **809**

ADAMS, J. S. 1965. Inequity in Social Exchange, in L. Berkowitz (Ed.). *Advances in Experimental Social Psychology*. Vol. 2. New York: Academic Press. **745**

ADAMSON, R. E. 1952. Functional Fixedness as Related to Problem-Solving, *J. Exper. Psychol.*, 44, 288–91. **158**

ADER, R. & P. M. CONKLIN. 1963. Handling of Pregnant Rats: Effects on Emotionality of Their Offspring, *Science*, 142, 411–12. **694**

ADLER, A. 1930. Individual Psychology, in C. Murchison (Ed.). *Psychologies of 1930*. Worcester, Mass.: Clark University Press. **717**

ADORNO, T. W., E. FRENKEL-BRUNSWIK, D. J. LEVINSON & R. N. SANFORD. 1950. *The Authoritarian Personality*. New York: Harper. **659**

AINSWORTH, M. D. 1967. *Infancy in Uganda: Infant Care and the Growth of Love*. Baltimore: Johns Hopkins University Press. **41**

AJZEN, I. & M. FISHBEIN. 1970. The Prediction of Behavior from Attitudinal and Normative Variables, *J. Exp. Soc. Psychol.*, 466–87. **766**

ALDINGTON, R. 1924. A Book of Characters. New York: Dutton. **659**

ALDRICH, C. A. & M. A. NORVAL. 1946. A Developmental Graph for the First Year of Life, *J. Pediat.*, 29, 304–8. **45**

ALEXANDER, F. 1946. Individual Psychotherapy, *Psychosom. Med.*, 8, 110–15. **616**

ALKER, H. A. 1971. A Quasi-Paranoid Feature of Students' Extreme Attitudes Against Colonialism, *Behav. Sci.*, 16, 218–27. **583**

ALLEN, M. G., S. COHEN & W. POLLIN. 1972. Schizophrenia in Veteran Twins: A Diagnostic Review, *Amer. J. Psychiatr.*, 128, 939–45. **605**

ALLEN, V. L. & D. NEWTSON. 1972. Development of Conformity and Independence, *J. Pers. Soc. Psychol.*, 22, 18–30. **806**

ALLPORT, F. H. 1920. The Influence of the Group Upon Association and Thought, *J. Exper. Psychol.*, 3, 159–82. **795**

ALLPORT, G. W. 1937. *Personality*. New York: Holt. **650, 664**

ALLPORT, G. W. & H. S. ODBERT. 1936. Trait-Names: A Psycho-Lexical Study, *Psychol. Monogr.*, 47, Series No. 211. **655**

ALLPORT, G. W. & P. E. VERNON. 1933. *Studies in Expressive Movement*. New York: Macmillan. **653**

ALLPORT, G. W., P. E. VERNON & G. LINDZEY. 1951. *A Study of Values: A Scale for Measuring the Dominant Interests in Personality*. Rev. ed. Boston: Houghton Mifflin. **663**

ALLYN, J. & L. FESTINGER. 1961. The Effectiveness of Unanticipated Persuasive Communications, *J. Abnorm. Soc. Psychol.*, 62, 35–40. **770**

ALTMAN, I., D. A. TAYLOR & L. WHEELER. 1971. Ecological Aspect of Group Behavior in Social Isolation, *J. Appl. Soc. Psychol.*, 1, 76–100. **812**

ALTMAN, J. 1972. Autoradiographic Examination of Behaviorally Induced Changes in the Protein and Nucleic Acid Metabolism of the Brain, in J. Gaito (Ed.). *Macromolecules and Behavior*. 2nd ed. New York: Appleton. **431**

AMBROSE, J. A. 1961. The Development of the Smiling Response in Early Infancy, in B. M. Foss (Ed.). *Determinants of Infant Behavior*. New York: Wiley. **482**

AMERICAN PSYCHIATRIC ASSOCIATION. 1968. *The Diagnostic and Statistical Manual of Mental Disorders*. 2nd ed. Washington, D. C.: American Psychiatric Association. **592**

ANDERSON, N. H. & A. A. BARRIOS. 1961. Primacy Effects in Personality Impression Formation, *J. Abnorm. Soc. Psychol.*, 63, 346–50. **785**

ANDERSON, N. H. & S. HUBERT. 1963. Effects of Concomitant Verbal Recall on Order Effects in Personality Impression Formation, *J. Verb. Learn. Verb. Behav.*, 2, 379–91. **785**

ANSBACHER, H. L. & R. R. ANSBACHER (Eds.). 1964. *Superiority and Social Interest by Alfred Adler*. Evanston, Ill.: Northwestern University Press. **717**

ASCH, S. E. 1946. Forming Impressions of Personality, *J. Abnorm. Soc. Psychol.*, 41, 258–90. **781**

————. 1956. Studies of Independence and Submission to Group Pressure: I. A Minority of One Against a Unanimous Majority, *Psychol. Monogr.*, 7, Series No. 416. **803**

ASCHER, L. M., T. X. BARBER & N. P. SPANOS. 1970. Two Attempts to Replicate the Parrish-Lundy-Leibowitz Experiment on Hypnotic Age Regression. Unpublished manuscript from the Medfield Foundation, Harding, Mass. **39**

ASERINSKY, E. & N. KLEITMAN. 1953. Regularly Occurring Periods of Eye Motility and Concomitant Phenomena During Sleep, *Science*, 118, 273–4. **505**

ATTNEAVE, F. 1954. Some Informational Aspects of Visual Perception, *Psychol. Rev.*, 61, 183–93. **269**

AX, A. F. 1953. The Physiological Differentiation Between Fear and Anger in Humans, *Psychosom. Med.*, 15, 433–42. **488**

BABLADELIS, G. 1972. Birth Order and Responsiveness to Social Influence, *Psychol. Rep.*, 30, 99–104. **700**

BACON, M. K., I. L. CHILD & H. BARRY III. 1963. A Cross-Cultural Study of Some Correlates of Crime, *J. Abnorm. Soc. Psychol.*, 66, 291–300. **740**

BAKER, R. 1965. Observer: Three Arms and a Wire Hanger, *The New York Times* (December 12, 1965), p. D10. **684**

BALES, R. F. 1950. A Set of Categories for the Analysis of Small Group Interaction, *Amer. Soc. Rev.*, 15, 257–63. **815**

BALES, R. F. & F. L. STRODTBECK. 1951. Phases in Group Problem Solving, *J. Abnorm. Soc. Psychol.*, 46, 485–95. **817**

BANDURA, A. 1969. *Principles of Behavior Modification.* New York: Holt. **619, 621**

BARKER, R., T. DEMBO & K. LEWIN. 1941. Frustration and Regression: An Experiment With Young Children, *U. Iowa Stud. Child Welf.*, 18, No. 386. **574**

BARNLUND, D. C. 1959. A Comparative Study of Individual, Majority, and Group Judgment, *J. Abnorm. Soc. Psychol.*, 58, 55–66. **798**

BARONDES, S. H. & H. D. COHEN. 1967. Comparative Effects of Cycloheximide and Puromycin in Cerebral Protein Synthesis and Consolidation of Memory in Mice, *Brain Res.*, 4, 44–51. **436**

BARTLETT, F. C. 1932. *Remembering.* Cambridge: Cambridge University Press. **408**

BATESON, G., D. JACKSON, J. HALEY & J. WEAKLAND. 1956. Toward a Theory of Schizophrenia, *Behav. Sci.*, 1, 251–64. **605**

BATTERSBY, W. S., H.-L. TEUBER & M. B. BENDER. 1953. Problem-Solving Behavior in Men With Frontal or Occipital Brain Injuries, *J. Psychol.*, 35, 329–51. **167**

BAUGHMAN, E. E. 1972. *Personality: The Study of the Individual.* Englewood Cliffs, N. J.: Prentice-Hall. **684**

BAUGHMAN, E. E. & G. S. WELSH. 1964. *Personality: A Behavioral Science.* Englewood Cliffs, N. J.: Prentice-Hall. **651**

BAUMRIND, D. 1973. Metaethical and Normative Considerations Covering the Treatment of Human Subjects in the Behavioral Sciences. Paper presented in Symposium in Psychology and Ethics at Loyola University, Chicago. **809**

BAVELAS, A., A. H. HASTORF, A. E. GROSS & W. R. KITE. 1965. Experiments on the Alteration of Group Structure, *J. Exp. Soc. Psychol.*, 1, 55–70. **816**

BAYLEY, N. 1951. Development and Maturation, in H. Helson (Ed.). *Theoretical Foundations of Psychology.* Princeton: Van Nostrand. **37, 184**

———. 1965. Comparisons of Mental and Motor Test Scores for Ages 1–15 Months by Sex, Birth Order, Race, Geographical Location, and Education of Parents, *Child Develpm.*, 36, 379–411. **41**

———. 1968. Cognition and Aging, in K. W. Schare (Ed.). *Theory and Methods of Research on Aging.* Morgantown, W. V.: West Virginia University Press. **193**

———. 1969. *Bayley Scales of Infant Development.* New York: Psychological Corporation. **185**

BAYLEY, N. & M. H. ODEN. 1955. The Maintenance of Intellectual Ability in Gifted Adults, *J. Gerontol.*, 10, 91–107. **33**

BAYLEY, N., L. RHODES, B. GOOCH & M. MARCUS. 1971. A Comparison of the Growth and Development of Institutionalized and Home-Reared Mongoloids: A Follow-Up Study, in J. Hellmuth (Ed.). *Exceptional Infant.* Vol. 2. Studies in Abnormalities. New York: Brunner-Mazel. **206**

BEECHER, H. K. 1959. *Measurement of Subjective Responses.* New York: Oxford University Press. **473**

BÉKÉSY, G. VON. 1964. Duplexity Theory of Taste, *Science*, 145, 834–835. **252**

BÉKÉSY, G. VON & W. A. ROSENBLITH. 1951. The Mechanical Properties of the Ear, in S. S. Stevens (Ed.). *Handbook of Experimental Psychology.* New York: Wiley. **339**

BELL, R. Q. 1960. Relations Between Behavior Manifestations in the Human Neonate, *Child Develpm.*, 31, 463–77. **49**

BEM, D. J. 1970. *Beliefs, Attitudes and Human Affairs.* Belmont, Calif.: Brooks/Cole. **759**

BENJAMIN, F. S. 1955–1956. Effect of Pain on Simultaneous Perception of Nonpainful Sensory Stimulation, *J. Appl. Physiol.*, 6, 630–4. **253**

BENNETT, E. L., M. C. DIAMOND, D. KRECH & M. R. ROSENZWEIG. 1964. Chemical and Anatomical Plasticity of the Brain, *Science*, 146, 610–19. **431**

BERGER, H. 1929. Über das Elektrencephalogramn des Menschen, *Arch. Psychiat. Nervenkr.*, 87, 527–70. **65**

BERLYNE, D. E. 1960. *Conflict, Arousal, and Curiosity.* New York: McGraw-Hill. **361, 458, 461**

BERSCHEID, E., D. BOYE & E. WALSTER. 1968. Retaliation as a Means of Restoring Equity, *J. Pers. Soc. Psychol.*, 10, 370–6. **787**

BEXTON, W. H., W. HERON & T. H. SCOTT. 1954. Effects of Decreased Variation in the Sensory Environment, *Canadian J. Psychol.*, 8, 70–6. **459**

BION, W. A. 1959. *Experiments in Groups and Other Papers.* New York: Basic Books. **634**

BIRCH, H. G. 1945. The Role of Motivational Factors in Insightful Problem-Solving, *J. Comp. Psychol.*, 38, 295–317. **164**

BIRCH, H. G. & J. D. GUSSOW. 1970. *Disadvantaged Children: Health, Nutrition, and School Failure.* New York: Harcourt. **217**

BLAKEMORE, C. & G. F. COOPER. 1970. Development of the Brain Depends on the Visual Environment, *Nature*, 228, 477–8. **334**

BLATZ, W. E. & D. A. MILLICHAMP. 1935. The Development of Emotion in the Infant, *Univ. Toronto Stud. Child Develpm. Ser.*, 4. **482**

BLEULER, M. & R. BLEULER. 1935. Rorschach's Ink-Blot Tests and Racial Psychology, *Charact. and Pers.*, 4, 97–114. **679**

BLOCK, J. 1961. *The Q-Sort Method in Personality Assessment and Psychiatric Research.* Springfield, Ill.: Charles C. Thomas. **666**

———. 1965. *The Challenge of Response Sets.* New York: Appleton. **677**

BLOCK, J. H. 1968. Further Consideration of Psychosomatic Predisposing Factors in Allergy, *Psychosom. Med.*, 30, 202–8. **695**

BLOCK, J. H., P. H. JENNINGS, E. HARVEY & E. SIMPSON. 1964. The Interaction Between Allergic Predisposition and Psychopathology in Childhood Asthma, *Psychosom. Med.*, 26, 307–26. **695**

BLODGETT, H. C. 1929. The Effect of the Introduction of Reward Upon the Maze Performance of Rats, *U. Calif. Publ. Psychol.*, 4, 113–34. **391**

BLOOM, L. 1970. *Language Development: Form and Function in Emerging Grammars.* Cambridge, Mass.: M.I.T. Press. **114**

BLUM, J. E., J. L. FOSSHAGE & L. F. JARVIK. 1972. Intellectual Changes and Sex Differences in Octogenarians: A Twenty-Year Longitudinal Study of Aging, *Develpm. Psychol.*, 7, 178–87. **194**

BLUM, J. E., L. F. JARVIK & E. T. CLARK. 1970. Rate of Change on Selective Tests of Intelligence: A Twenty-Year Longitudinal Study of Aging, *J. Gerontol.*, 25, 171–6. **194**

BLUMBERG, H. H. 1969. On Being Liked More Than You Like, *J. Pers. Soc. Psychol.*, 11, 121–8. **786**

BOBROW, D. 1964. A Question Answering System for High School Algebra Word Problems, *Proceedings of the Fall Joint Computer Conference*, AFIPS, 26, 591–614. **154**

BOCK, R. D. & D. KOLAKOWSKI. 1973. Further Evidence of Sex-Linked Major-Gene Influence on Human Spatial Visualizing Ability, *Amer. J. Hum. Gen.*, 25, 1–14. **206**

BORING, E. G. 1950. *A History of Experimental Psychology.* 2nd ed. New York: Appleton. **417**

BORING, E. G., H. S. LANGFELD & H. P. WELD (Eds.). 1948. *Foundations of Psychology.* New York: Wiley. **244, 273**

BOUSFIELD, W. E. & C. H. W. SEDGEWICK. 1944. An Analysis of Sequences of Restricted Associative Responses, *J. Gen. Psychol.*, 30, 149–65. **406**

BOWER, T. G. R. 1966. The Visual World of Infants, *Scientific American*, 215, 80–92. **312**

———. 1972. Object Perception in Infants, *Perception*, 1, 15–30. **312**

BRADFORD, L. P., J. A. GIBB & K. D. BENNE. 1964. *T-Group Theory and Laboratory Method.* New York: Wiley. **634**

BREGER, L. & J. L. MCGAUGH. 1965. Critique and Reformulation of Learning-Theory: Approaches to Psychotherapy and Neurosis, *Psychol. Bull.*, 63, 338–58. **621**

BRIDGES, K. M. B. 1932. Emotional Development in

Early Infancy, *Child Develpm.*, 3, 324–41. **480, 482**

BROMILEY, R. B. 1948. Conditioned Responses in a Dog After Removal of Neocortex, *J. Comp. Physiol. Psychol.*, 41, 102–10. **419**

BRONFENBRENNER, U. 1958. Socialization and Social Class Through Time and Space, in E. E. Maccoby, T. M. Newcomb & E. L. Hartley (Eds.). *Readings in Social Psychology.* New York: Holt. **701, 703**

———. 1970. Reaction to Social Pressure from Adults Versus Peers Among Soviet Day School and Boarding School Pupils in the Perspective of an American Sample, *J. Pers. Soc. Psychol.*, 15, 179–89. **806**

BRONSON, G. W. 1972. Infants' Reactions to Unfamiliar Persons and Novel Objects, *Monogr. Soc. Res. Child Develpm.*, 37, Whole No. 3. **483**

BROVERMAN, I. K., D. M. BROVERMAN, F. E. CLARKSON, P. S. ROSENKRANTZ & S. R. VOGEL. 1970. Sex-Role Stereotypes and Clinical Judgments of Mental Health, *J. Consult. Clin. Psychol.*, 34, 1–7. **784**

BROWN, D. R. 1953. Stimulus Similarity and the Anchoring of Subjective Scales, *Amer. J. Psychol.*, 66, 199–214. **271**

BROWN, J. F. 1931. The Visual Perception of Velocity, *Psychol. Forsch.*, 14, 199–232. **289**

BROWN, P. K. & G. WALD. 1964. Visual Pigments in Single Rods and Cones of the Human Retina, *Science*, 144, 45–52. **325**

BROWN, R. 1973. *A First Language.* Cambridge, Mass.: Harvard University Press. **118**

BROWN, R., C. CAZDEN & U. BELLUGI. 1968. The Child's Grammar from I to III, in J. P. Hill (Ed.). *Minnesota Symposium on Child Development.* Vol. 2. Minneapolis: University of Minnesota Press. **118**

BROWN, R. W. & D. MCNEILL. 1966. The "Tip of the Tongue" Phenomenon, *J. Verb. Learn. Verb. Behav.*, 5, 325–7. **128**

BROWN, W. & H. C. GILHOUSEN. 1949. *College Psychology.* Englewood Cliffs, N. J.: Prentice-Hall. **265**

BRUNER, J. S. 1964. The Course of Cognitive Development, *Amer. Psychol.*, 19, 1–16. **95**

BRUNER, J. S. & H. J. KENNEY. 1966. On Multiple Ordering, in J. S. Bruner, R. R. Olver & P. M. Greenfield (Eds.). *Studies in Cognitive Growth.* New York: Wiley. **93**

BRUNER, J. S., R. R. OLVER & P. M. GREENFIELD (Eds.). 1966. *Studies in Cognitive Growth.* New York: Wiley. **92**

BRUNSWIK, E. 1956. *Perception and the Representative Design of Psychological Experiments.* Berkeley: University of California Press. **293, 300**

BUCHWALD, A. M. & R. D. YOUNG. 1969. Some Comments on the Foundations of Behavior Therapy, in C. M. Franks (Ed.). *Behavior Therapy: Appraisal and Status.* New York: McGraw-Hill. **621**

BUCK, R. W., V. J. SAVIN, R. E. MILLER & W. F. CAUL. 1972. Communication of Affect Through Facial Expressions in Humans, *J. Pers. Soc. Psychol.*, 23, 362–71. **489**

BÜHLER, K. 1928. Displeasure and Pleasure in Relation to Activity, in M. L. Reymert (Ed.). *Feelings and Emotions.* Worcester, Mass.: Clark University Press. **458**

BULMER, M. G. 1970. *The Biology of Twinning in Man.* London: Oxford University Press. **14**

BYRNE, D. 1966. *An Introduction to Personality.* Englewood Cliffs, N. J.: Prentice-Hall. **651**

CABANAC, M. & R. DUCLAUX. 1970. Obesity: Absence of Satiety Aversion to Sucrose, *Science,* 168, 496–7. **457**

CAMERON, J., N. LIVSON & N. BAYLEY. 1967. Infant Vocalizations and Their Relationship to Mature Intelligence, *Science,* 157, 331–3. **195**

CAMERON, N. 1963. *Personality Development and Psychopathology.* Boston: Houghton Mifflin. **597**

CAMPBELL, B. A. & N. E. SPEAR. 1972. Ontogeny of Memory, *Psychol. Rev.,* 79, 215–37. **434**

CANCRO, R. 1971. *Intelligence: Genetic and Environmental Influences.* New York: Grune & Stratton. **221**

CANNON, W. B. 1932. *The Wisdom of the Body.* New York: Norton. **454**

CARR, H. A. & M. C. HARDY. 1920. Some Factors in the Perception of Relative Motion, *Psychol. Rev.,* 27, 24–37. **285**

CASON, H. 1930. Common Annoyances: A Psychological Study of Every-Day Aversions and Irritations, *Psychol. Monogr.,* 40, No. 2, 1–218. **475**

CATTELL, R. B. 1946. *Description and Measurement of Personality.* New York: Harcourt. **655**

———. 1963. Theory of Fluid and Crystallized Intelligence: A Critical Experiment, *J. Educ. Psychol.,* 54, 1–22. **33**

CESAREC, Z. & L. NILSSON. 1963. Level of Activation and Figure-Ground Reversal: Inter-Individual Comparisons, *Psychol. Res. Bull.,* 3, No. 6. **272**

CHAMPNEYS, F. E. 1881. Notes on an Infant, *Mind,* 6, 104–97. **101**

CHARLES, D. C. 1953. Ability and Accomplishment of Persons Earlier Judged Mentally Deficient, *Gen. Psychol. Monogr.,* 47, 3–71. **194**

CHESS, S., A. THOMAS, H. G. BIRCH & M. HERTZIG. 1960. Implications of a Longitudinal Study of Child Development for Child Psychiatry, *Amer. J. Psychiat.,* 117, 434–41. **35**

CHOMSKY, N. 1959. A Review of *Verbal Behavior,* by B. F. Skinner, *Language,* 35, 26–58. **116**

CHOWN, S. M. & H. HERON. 1965. Psychological Aspects of Aging in Man, in P. R. Farnsworth (Ed.). *Annual Review of Psychology,* Vol. 16. Palo Alto, Calif.: Annual Reviews. **483**

CHUKOVSKY, K. 1961. *Ot Dvukh Do Pyati.* 15th ed. Moscow: Detgiz. [English translation: Chukovsky, K. *From Two to Five* (translated and edited by M. Morton). 1963. Berkeley/Los Angeles: University of California Press] **119**

CIEUTAT, V. J., F. E. STOCKWELL & C. E. NOBLE. 1958. The Interaction of Ability and Amount of Practice With Stimulus and Response Meaningfulness (m, m') in Paired-Associate Learning, *J. Exper. Psychol.,* 56, 193–202. **400**

CLARK, H. H. 1971. The Chronometric Study of Meaning Components. Paper read at C.N.R.S. Colloque International sur les Problèmes Actuels de Psycholinguistique, Paris. **105**

CLARK, J. V. 1958. A Preliminary Investigation of Some Unconscious Assumptions Affecting Labor Efficiency in Eight Supermarkets. Unpublished doctoral dissertation, Harvard Graduate School of Business Administration. **746**

CLYNES, M. 1970. Biocybernetics of Space-Time Forms in the Genesis and Communication of Emotion. In symposium, "Biocybernetics of the Dynamic Communication of Emotions and Qualities," presented at the meeting of the American Association for the Advancement of Science, Chicago. **490**

COHEN, A. R. 1961. Cognitive Tuning as a Factor Affecting Impression Formation, *J. Pers.,* 29, 235–45. **782**

COLBY, K. M. 1965. Computer Simulation of Neurotic Process, in R. W. Stacy and B. D. Waxman (Eds.). *Computers in Biomedical Research.* New York: Academic. **154**

COLBY, K. M., J. WATT & J. P. GILBERT. 1966. A Computer Method of Psychotherapy, *J. Nerv. Mental Dis.,* 142, 148–52. **154**

COLEMAN, J. S. 1966. *Equality of Educational Opportunity.* Washington, D. C.: U. S. Office of Education. **220**

CONRAD, R. 1964. Acoustic Confusions in Immediate Memory, *Brit. J. Psychol.,* 55, 75–83. **405**

CONROY, R. T. W. L. & J. N. MILLS. 1970. *Human Circadian Rhythms.* London: J. & A. Churchill. **558**

COOK, T. H. 1942. The Application of the Rorschach Test to a Samoan Group, *Rorsch. Res. Exch.,* 6, 51–60. **679**

COREN, S. 1972. Subjective Contours and Apparent Depth, *Psych. Rev.,* 79, 359–67. **265**

CORTÉS, J. B. & F. H. GATTI. 1964. Physique and Self-Description of Temperament, *Amer. Psychol.,* 19, 572. Abstract. **697**

Council Expresses Concern for POW's, Use of Therapy for Political Purposes. 1973. *APA Monitor,* 4, 1. **608**

COURSIN, D. B. 1972. Nutrition and Brain Development in Infants, *Merrill-Palmer Quart.,* 18, 177–202. **217**

COVINGTON, M. V., R. S. CRUTCHFIELD, L. B. DAVIES & R. M. OLTON. 1974. *The Productive Thinking Program.* Columbus, Ohio: Merrill. **150**

COWEN, E. L. 1952a. The Influence of Varying Degrees of Psychological Stress on Problem-Solving Rigidity, *J. Abnorm. Soc. Psychol.,* 47, 512–19. **163**

———. 1952b. Stress Reduction and Problem-Solving Rigidity, *J. Consult. Psychol.,* 16, 425–8. **163**

CRONBACH, L. J. 1960. *Essentials of Psychological Testing.* 2nd ed. New York: Harper. **185**

———. 1970. *Essentials of Psychological Testing.* 3rd ed. New York: Harper & Row. **185**

CROW, W. J. & K. R. HAMMOND. 1957. The Generality of Accuracy and Response Sets in Interpersonal Perception, *J. Abnorm. Soc. Psychol.*, 54, 384–90. **780**

CROWNE, D. P. & D. MARLOWE. 1964. *The Approval Motive: Studies in Evaluative Dependence.* New York: Wiley. **678**

CRUTCHFIELD, R. S. 1955. Conformity and Character, *Amer. Psychol.*, 10, 191–8. **804**

CRUTCHFIELD, R. S., D. G. WOODWORTH & R. E. ALBRECHT. 1955. *Perceptual Performance and the Effective Person.* San Antonio: Air Force Personnel and Training Research Center. **300**

CUMMING, E. & W. E. HENRY. 1961. *Growing Old.* New York: Basic Books. **53**

DAHLSTROM, U. G. & G. S. WELSH. 1960. *An MMPI Handbook: A Guide to Use in Clinical Practice and Research.* Minneapolis: University of Minnesota Press. **676**

DAILEY, C. A. 1952. The Effects of Premature Conclusion Upon the Acquisition of Understanding of a Person, *J. Psychol.*, 33, 133–52. **782**

DAMON, A. 1965. Discrepancies Between the Findings of Longitudinal and Cross-Sectional Studies in Adult Life, Physique and Physiology, *Hum. Develpm.*, 8, 16–22. **34**

DARWIN, C. 1877. A Biographical Sketch of an Infant. *Mind*, 2, 292–4. **101**

——. 1965. *Expression of the Emotions in Man and Animals.* Chicago: University of Chicago Press. Originally published 1872. **487**

DASHIELL, J. F. 1930. An Experimental Analysis of Some Group Effects, *J. Abnorm. Soc. Psychol.*, 25, 190–9. **795**

DAVIDSON, M., R. MCGINNES & R. PARNELL. 1957. The Distribution of Personality Traits in Seven Year Old Children: A Combined Psychological, Psychiatric and Somatotype Study, *Brit. J. Educ. Psychol.*, 27, 48–61. **697**

DAVIS, A., B. B. GARDNER & M. B. GARDNER. 1941. *Deep South.* Chicago: University of Chicago Press. **217**

DAVIS, K. E. & E. E. JONES. 1960. Changes in Interpersonal Perception as a Means of Reducing Cognitive Dissonance, *J. Abnorm. Soc. Psychol.*, 61, 402–10. **787**

DAWES, R. M., D. SINGER & F. LEMMONS. 1972. An Experimental Analysis of the Contrast Effect and Its Implications for Intergroup Communication and the Indirect Assessment of Attitudes, *J. Pers. Soc. Psychol.*, 21, 281–95. **772**

DEFRIES, J. C. 1964. Prenatal Maternal Stress in Mice: Differential Effects on Behavior, *J. Hered.*, 55, 289–95. **17**

DEMENT, W. 1960. The Effect of Dream Deprivation, *Science*, 131, 1705–7. **508**

DENNIS, W. & P. NAJARIAN. 1957. Infant Development Under Environmental Handicap, *Psychol. Monogr.*, 71, 1–13. **212**

DEUTSCH, J. A., M. D. HAMBURG & M. DAHL. 1966. Anticholinesterase-Induced Amnesia and Its Temporal Aspects, *Science*, 136, 1057–8. **433**

DEUTSCH, M. 1949. An Experimental Study of the Effects of Cooperation and Competition Upon Group Process, *Hum. Relat.*, 2, 199–232. **796**

DEUTSCH, M. & R. M. KRAUSS. 1960. The Effect of Threat on Interpersonal Bargaining, *J. Abnorm. Soc. Psychol.*, 51, 629–36. **798**

DICKS, H. V. 1939. *Clinical Studies in Psychopathology.* Baltimore: Wood. **595**

DI GUISTO, E. L., K. CAIRNCROSS & M. G. KING. 1971. Hormonal Influences on Fear-Motivated Responses, *Psychol. Bull.*, 75, 432–44. **544**

DITTMAN, A. I., M. B. PARLOFF & D. S. BOOMER. 1965. Facial and Bodily Expression: A Study of Receptivity of Emotional Cues, *Psychiatry*, 28, 239–44. **487**

DOBELLE, W. H., S. S. STENSAAS, M. G. MLADEJOVSKY & J. B. SMITH. 1973. A Prosthesis for the Deaf Based on Cortical Stimulation, *Annals of Otology, Rhinology, and Laryngology*, 82, No. 4 (July–August), 1–19. **71**

DOBZHANSKY, T. 1967. Changing Man, *Science*, 155, 409–14. **18**

——. 1973. *Genetic Diversity and Human Equality.* New York: Basic Books. **205, 219, 221**

DOLLARD, J. & N. E. MILLER. 1950. *Personality and Psychotherapy: An Analysis in Theories of Learning, Thinking and Culture.* New York: McGraw-Hill. **619, 719**

DOOB, L. W. 1964. Eidetic Images Among the Ibo, *Ethnology*, 3, 357–63. **131**

DORNBUSCH, S. M., A. H. HASTORF, R. E. MAZZY & R. S. VREELAND. 1965. The Perceiver and the Perceived: Their Influence on the Categories of Interpersonal Cognition, *J. Pers. Soc. Psychol.*, 1, 434–40. **781**

DRISCOLL, R., K. E. DAVIS & M. E. LIPETZ. 1972. Parental Interference and Romantic Love: The Romeo and Juliet Effect, *J. Pers. Soc. Psychol.*, 24, 1–10. **xviii, 478–9**

DUFFY, E. 1962. *Activation and Behavior.* New York: Wiley. **495**

DUNCKER, K. 1945. On Problem-Solving (translated by L. S. Lees), *Psychol. Monogr.*, 58, No. 5. **147, 148, 149, 157**

DUNNETTE, M. D., J. CAMPBELL & K. JAASTAD. 1963. The Effect of Group Participation on Brainstorming Effectiveness for Two Industrial Samples, *J. Appl. Psychol.*, 47, 30–7. **801**

DURKIN, H. 1937. Trial-and-Error, Gradual Analysis, and Sudden Re-organization, *Arch. Psychol.*, 30, No. 210. **129**

EBBINGHAUS, H. 1964. *Memory: A Contribution to Experimental Psychology.* New York: Dover. Originally published 1885. **399**

EDWARDS, A. L. 1959. *Edwards Personal Preference Schedule.* New York: Psychological Corp. **676**

EFRON, D. H. (Ed.). 1968. *Psychopharmacology: A Review of Progress, 1957–1967.* Washington, D. C.: U. S. Government Printing Office. **455**

EIBL-EIBESFELDT, I. 1970. *Ethology: The Biology of Behavior.* New York: Holt, Rinehart and Winston. **546**

EIMAS, P. D., E. R. SIQUELAND, P. JUSCZYK & J. VIGORITO. 1971. Speech Perception in Infants, *Science*, 171, 303–6. **103**

EKMAN, P., W. V. FRIESEN & P. ELLSWORTH. 1972. *Emotion in the Human Face.* Oxford: Pergamon. **488**

EKMAN, P., E. R. SORENSON & W. V. FRIESEN. 1969. Pan-Cultural Elements in Facial Displays of Emotion, *Science*, 164, 86–8. **487**

ELSMORE, T. & G. FLETCHER. 1972. Delta⁹-Tetrahydrocannabinol: Aversive Effects in Rat at High Doses, *Science*, 175, 911–12. **519**

ENGEL, B. T. 1972. Operant Conditioning of Cardiac Function: A Status Report, *Psychophysiol.*, 9, 161–77. **387**

EPSTEIN, W. & I. ROCK. 1960. Perceptual Set as an Artifact of Recency, *Amer. J. Psychol.*, 73, 214–28. **275**

ERIKSON, E. H. 1959. Identity and the Life Cycle, *Psychol. Issues*, 1, No. 1. **715**

———. 1963. *Childhood and Society.* 2nd ed. New York: Norton. **715**

———. 1968. *Identity, Youth, and Crisis.* New York: Norton. **715**

ERLENMEYER-KIMLING, L., J. HIRSCH & J. M. WEISS. 1962. Studies in Experimental Behavior Genetics: III. Selection and Hybridization Analyses of Individual Differences in The Sign of Geotaxis, *J. Comp. Physiol. Psychol.*, 55, 722–31. **21**

ERLENMEYER-KIMLING, L. & L. F. JARVIK. 1963. Genetics and Intelligence: A Review, *Science*, 142, 1477–8. **205, 206**

ERNST, G. W. & A. NEWELL. 1969. *A Case Study in Generality and Problem Solving.* New York: Academic. **157**

ERVIN, S. M. 1964. Language and TAT Content in Bilinguals, *J. Abnorm. Soc. Psychol.*, 68, 500–7. **683**

ESCALONA, S. & G. HEIDER. 1959. *Prediction and Outcome.* New York: Basic Books. **49**

ESTES, W. K. 1944. An Experimental Study of Punishment, *Psychol. Monogr.*, 57, No. 263. **382**

———. 1970. *Learning Theory and Mental Development.* New York: Academic. **382**

EYSENCK, H. J. 1970. *The Structure of Human Personality.* New York: Macmillan. **662**

FANTZ, R. L. 1961. A Method for Studying Depth Perception in Infants, *Psychol. Record*, 11, 21–32. **296**

FAVREAU, OLGA E., VICTOR F. EMERSON & MICHAEL C. CORBALLIS. 1972. Motion Perception: A Color-Contingent Aftereffect, *Science*, 176, 78–9. **337**

FEIGENBAUM, K. D. 1963. Task Complexity and IQ as Variables in Piaget's Task of Conservation, *Child Develpm.*, 34, 423–32. **88**

FELDMAN, J. M. 1972. Stimulus Characteristics and Subject Prejudice as Determinants of Stereotype Attribution, *J. Per. Soc. Psychol.*, 21, 333–40. **778**

FELEKY, A. 1922. *Feelings and Emotions.* New York: Pioneer. **486**

FERBER, A., M. MENDELSOHN & A. NUPIER. 1972. *The Book of Family Therapy.* New York: Science House. **634**

FESHBACH, S. 1971. The Dynamics and Morality of Violence and Aggression: Some Psychological Considerations, *Amer. Psychol.*, 26, 281–92. **700, 743**

FISCHER, M., B. HARVALD & M. HAUGE. 1969. A Danish Twin Study of Schizophrenia, *Brit. J. Psychiatr.*, 115, 981–90. **605**

FISHBEIN, M. 1967. Attitude and the Prediction of Behavior, in M. Fishbein (Ed.). *Readings in Attitude Theory and Measurement.* New York: Wiley. **767**

FITZSIMMON, J. T. 1971. The Physiology of Thirst: A Review of the Extraneural Aspects of the Mechanisms of Drinking, in E. Stellar & J. M. Sprague (Eds.). *Progress in Physiological Psychology*, Vol. 4. New York: Academic Press. **557**

FJERDINGSTAD, E. J. (Ed.). 1971. *Chemical Transfer of Learned Information.* Amsterdam: North Holland Publishing Co. **436**

FLAVELL, J. H. 1963. *The Developmental Psychology of Jean Piaget.* Princeton: Van Nostrand. **88**

FLING, S. & M. MANOSEVITZ. 1972. Sex Typing in Nursery School Children's Play Interest, *Child Develpm.*, 1, 146–52. **700**

FLOURENS, P. 1824. *Recherches Expérimentales sur les Propriétés et les Fonctions du Système Nerveux dans les Animaux Vertèbres.* Paris: Librairie de l'Académie Royale de Médecine. **416**

FLUGEL, J. C. 1954. Humor and Laughter, in G. Lindzey (Ed.). *Handbook of Social Psychology.* Reading, Mass.: Addison-Wesley. **481**

FRANKL, V. E. 1962. *Man's Search for Meaning.* Boston: Beacon. **598**

FREEDMAN, D. G. 1972. Genetic Variations on the Hominid Theme: Individual, Sex, and Ethnic Differences, in F. J. Mönks, W. W. Hartup & J. deWit (Eds.). *Determinants of Behavioral Development.* New York: Academic. **50**

FREEDMAN, D. G. & B. KELLER. 1963. Inheritance of Behavior in Infants, *Science*, 140, 196–8. **691**

FREEDMAN, J. L. 1965. Long-Term Behavioral Effects of Cognitive Dissonance, *J. Exp. Soc. Psychol.*, 1, 145–55. **769**

FREEMAN, R. D. & L. N. THIBOS. 1973. Electrophysiological Evidence that Abnormal Early Visual Experience Can Modify the Human Brain, *Science*, 180, 876–8. **334**

FRENKEL-BRUNSWIK, E. & R. N. SANFORD. 1945. Some

Personality Factors in Anti-Semitism, *J. Psychol.*, 20, 271–91. **581**

FREUD, S. 1956. *The Interpretation of Dreams.* New York: Basic Books. Originally published in 1900. **506, 507**

FUNKENSTEIN, D. H., S. H. KING & M. E. DROLETTE. 1957. *Mastery of Stress.* Cambridge, Mass.: Harvard University Press. **485**

GAGNÉ, R. M. & E. C. SMITH. 1962. A Study of the Effects of Verbalization on Problem-Solving, *J. Exper. Psychol.*, 63, 12–18. **139**

GALL, F. J. & G. S. SPURZHEIM. 1810. *Anatomie et Physiologie due Système Nerveux.* Paris: Schoell. **417**

GALLATIN, J. & J. ADELSON. 1971. Legal Guarantees of Individual Freedom: A Cross-National Study of the Development of Political Thought, *J. Soc. Issues*, 27, 93–108. **749**

GALTON, F. 1964. *Hereditary Genius.* New York: Harcourt. Originally published 1869. **130**

GARCIA, J., B. K. MCGOWAN, F. R. ERVIN & R. A. KOELLING. 1968. Cues—Their Relative Effectiveness as a Function of the Reinforcer, *Science*, 160, 794–5. **365**

GARDNER, W. J., J. C. R. LICKLIDER & A. Z. WEISZ. 1960. Suppression of Pain by Sound, *Science*, 132, 32–3. **253**

GARRETT, H. E. 1946. A Developmental Theory of Intelligence, *Amer. Psychol.*, 1, 372–8. **199**

GATES, G. S. 1923. An Experimental Study of the Growth of Social Perception, *J. Educ. Psychol.*, 14, 449–61. **486**

GAVETT, G. I. 1925. *A First Course in Statistical Method.* New York: McGraw-Hill. **823**

GEBER, M. 1958. The Psychomotor Development of African Children in the First Year and the Influence of Maternal Behavior, *J. Soc. Psychol.*, 47, 185–95. **41**

GERGEN, K. J. 1972. Multiple Identity: The Healthy, Happy Human Being Wears Many Masks, *Psychol. Today* (May). **656**

GERGEN, K. J. & B. WISHNOV. 1965. Others' Self-Evaluations and Interaction Anticipation as Determinants of Self-Presentation, *J. Pers. Soc. Psychol.*, 2, 348–58. **656**

GESELL, A. & C. S. AMATRUDA. 1947. *Developmental Diagnosis: Normal and Abnormal Child Development.* New York: Hoeber. **41**

GHISELLI, E. E. 1966. *The Validity of Occupational Aptitude Tests.* New York: Wiley. **186**

GIBSON, E. J. 1969. *Principles of Perceptual Learning and Development.* New York: Appleton. **310**

GIBSON, J. J. 1950. *The Perception of the Visual World.* Boston: Houghton Mifflin. **307, 308**

———. 1963. The Useful Dimensions of Sensitivity, *Amer. Psychol.*, 18, 1–15. **254**

———. 1966. *The Senses Considered as Perceptual Systems.* Boston: Houghton Mifflin. **240**

GIBSON, J. J. & E. J. GIBSON. 1955. Perceptual Learning: Differential or Enrichment?, *Psych. Rev.*, 62, 32–41. **310**

GITTER, A. G., H. BLACK & D. MOSTOFSKY. 1972. Race and Sex in the Perception of Emotion, *J. Soc. Issues*, 28, 63–78. **486, 489**

GLANVILLE, A. D. & K. M. DALLENBACH. 1929. The Range of Attention, *Amer. J. Psychol.*, 41, 207–36. **279**

GLICK, B. S. & R. MARGOLIS. 1962. A Study of the Influence of Experimental Design on Clinical Outcome in Drug Research, *Amer. J. Psychiat.*, 118, 1087–96. **639**

GOETHALS, G. R. & J. COOPER. 1972. Role of Intention and Postbehavioral Consequence in the Arousal of Cognitive Dissonance, *J. Pers. Soc. Psychol.*, 23, 293–301. **767**

GOLDMAN, R., M. JAFFA & S. SCHACHTER. 1968. Yom Kippur, Air France, Dormitory Food and the Eating Behavior of Obese and Normal Persons, *J. Pers. Soc. Psychol.*, 10, 117–23. **456**

GOLDMAN-EISLER, F. 1964. Hesitation and Information in Speech, in A. U. S. de Reuck & N. O'Connor (Eds.). *CIBA Foundation Symposium: Disorders of Language.* Boston: Little, Brown. **110**

GOLDSCHMID, M. L. 1971. The Role of Experience in the Rate and Sequence of Cognitive Development, in D. R. Green, M. P. Ford & G. B. Flamer (Eds.). *Measurement and Piaget.* New York: McGraw-Hill. **91**

GOLDSCHMID, M. L., P. M. BENTLER, R. L. DEBUS, R. RAWLINSON, D. KOHNSTAMM, D. MODGIL, J. G. NICHOLLS, J. REYKOWDKI, B. STRUPCZEWSKA & N. WARREN. 1973. A Cross-Cultural Investigation of Conservation. *J. Cross-cultural Psychol.*, 4, 75–88. **88**

GOLLIN, E. S. 1954. Forming Impressions of Personality, *J. Pers.*, 23, 65–76. **782**

GOTTESMAN, I. I. 1963. Heritability of Personality: A Demonstration, *Psychol. Monogr.*, 77, No. 9. **484, 691**

———. 1966. Genetic Variance in Adaptive Personality Traits, *J. Child Psychol. and Psychiatr.*, 1, 199–208. **484**

———. 1972. Testimony submitted to United States Committee on Equal Education Opportunity (Senator Walter E. Mondale, Chairman). **226**

GOTTESMAN, I. I. & J. SHIELDS. 1972. *Schizophrenia and Genetics—A Twin Study Vantage Point.* New York: Academic Press. **606**

———. 1973. Genetic Theorizing and Schizophrenia, *Brit. J. Psychiatr.*, 122, 15–30. **605**

GOTTSCHALDT, K. 1926. Uber den Einfluss der Erfahrung auf die Wahrnehmung von Figuren, *Psychol. Forsch.*, 8, 261–317. **277**

GOUGH, H. G. 1957. *Manual for the California Psychological Inventory.* Palo Alto, Calif.: Consulting Psychologists Press. **677**

———. 1961. *The Adjective Checklist.* Palo Alto, Calif.: Consulting Psychologists Press. **671, 675**

———. 1962. Clinical Versus Statistical Prediction in

Psychology, in L. Postman (Ed.). *Psychology in the Making.* New York: Knopf. **684**

GOUGH, H. G. & H. S. SANDHU. 1964. Validation of the CPI Socialization Scale in India, *J. Abnorm. Soc. Psychol.,* 68, 544–6. **677**

GOY, R. W. 1970. Experimental Control of Psychosexuality, *Phil. Trans. Roy. Soc. London B,* 259, 149–62. **559**

GRAY, S. W. & R. A. KLAUS. 1965. An Experimental Preschool Program for Culturally Deprived Children, *Child Develpm.,* 36, 887–98. **213**

——. 1970. The Early Training Project: A Seventh Year Report, *Child Develpm.,* 41, 909–24. **213**

GREGG, L. & H. A. SIMON. 1967. Process Models and Stochastic Theories of Simple Concept Formation, *J. Math. Psychol.,* 4, 246–76. **154**

GREGORY, R. L. 1970. *The Intelligent Eye.* New York: McGraw-Hill. **233**

——. 1973. *Eye and Brain: The Psychology of Seeing.* 2nd ed. New York: McGraw-Hill. **321**

GROSS, C. G., C. E. ROCHA-MIRANDA & D. B. BENDER. 1972. Visual Properties of Neurons in Inferotemporal Cortex of the Macaque, *J. Neurophysiol.,* 35, 96–111. **420**

GROSSBERG, J. M. 1964. Behavior Therapy: A Review, *Psychol. Bull.,* 62, 73–85. **621**

GUILFORD, J. P. 1940. *An Inventory of Factors STDCR.* Beverly Hills, Calif.: Sheridan Supply. **662**

——. 1956. The Structure of Intellect, *Psychol. Bull.,* 53, 267–93. **197**

——. 1967. *Nature of Human Intelligence.* New York: McGraw-Hill. **197**

GUILFORD, J. P., R. C. WILSON, P. R. CHRISTIANSEN & D. J. LEWIS. 1951. *A Factor-Analytic Study of Creative Thinking: I. Hypotheses and Descriptions of Tests.* Los Angeles: University of Southern California Report from the Psychology Laboratory No. 3. **682**

GUMPERZ, J. J. & D. HYMES (Eds.). 1972. *Directions in Sociolinguistics: The Ethnography of Communication.* New York: Holt. **104**

GURIN, G., J. VEROFF & S. FELD. 1960. *Americans View Their Mental Health: A Nationwide Interview Survey.* Monograph series No. 4. Joint Commission on Mental Illness and Health. New York: Basic Books. **640**

HAAN, N. 1963. Proposed Model of Ego Functioning: Coping and Defense Mechanisms in Relationship to IQ Change, *Psychol. Monogr.,* 77, No. 8. **214**

——. 1969. A Tripartite Model of Ego Functioning Values and Clinical and Research Applications, *J. Nerv. Ment. Dis.,* 148, 14–30. **583**

HAAN, N. & N. LIVSON. 1973. Sex Differences in the Eyes of Expert Personality Assessors, *J. Pers. Assess.,* 37, 486–92. **674**

HABER, R. N. & R. B. HABER. 1964. Eidetic Imagery: I. Frequency, *Percep. Motor Skills,* 19, 131–8. **131**

HADAMARD, J. 1949. *Psychology of Invention in the Mathematical Field.* Princeton: Princeton University Press. **128, 136**

HADLER, N. M. 1964. Heritability and Phototaxis in *Drosophila melanogaster, Genetics,* 50, 1269–77. **19**

HALEY, J. 1967. Toward a Theory of Pathological Systems, in G. H. Zuk & I. Boszormenyi-Nagy (Eds.). *Family Therapy and Disturbed Families.* Palo Alto, Calif.: Science & Behavior. **631**

HALL, C. S. & G. LINDZEY. 1970. *Theories of Personality.* 2nd ed. New York: Wiley. **709, 718**

HALL, V. C. & R. KINGSLEY. 1968. Conservation and Equilibration Theory, *J. Gen. Psychol.,* 113, 195–213. **91**

HALL, V. C. & G. J. SIMPSON. 1968. Factors Influencing Extinction of Weight Conservation, *Merrill-Palmer Quart.,* 14, No. 3. 197–210. **91**

HAMILTON, E. 1942. *Mythology.* New York: New American Library of World Literature. **xviii**

HAMILTON, M. L. 1973. Imitative Behavior and Expressive Ability in Facial Expression of Emotion, *Develpm. Psychol.,* 8, 138. **486**

HARLOW, H. F. & M. K. HARLOW. 1966. Learning to Love, *Amer. Scientist,* 54, 244–72. **479**

HARLOW, H. F. & S. V. SUOMI. 1970. Nature of Love—Simplified, *Amer. Psychol.,* 25, 161–8. **479**

HARPER, R. A. 1959. *Psychoanalysis and Psychotherapy: 36 Systems.* Englewood Cliffs, N. J.: Prentice-Hall. **615**

HARRELL, T. W. & M. S. HARRELL. 1945. Army General Classification Test Scores for Civilian Occupations, *Educ. Psychol. Meas.,* 5, 229–39. **186**

HATHAWAY, S. R. & J. C. MCKINLEY. 1951. *The Minnesota Multiphasic Personality Inventory Manual.* Rev. ed. New York: Psychological Corp. **676**

HAYES, J. R. (Ed.). 1970. *Cognition and the Development of Language.* New York: Wiley. **116**

HEBB, D. O. 1946. On the Nature of Fear, *Psychol. Rev.,* 53, 259–76. **472**

——. 1949. *The Organization of Behavior.* New York: Wiley. **431**

HEBER, R., R. DEVER & J. CONRY. 1968. The Influence of Environment and Genetic Variables in Intellectual Development, in H. J. Prehm, L. A. Hamerlynch & J. E. Crosson (Eds.). *Behavioral Research in Mental Retardation.* Eugene, Ore.: University of Oregon Press. **207**

HEIDER, F. 1958a. *The Psychology of Interpersonal Relations.* New York: Wiley. **786**

——. 1958b. Social Perception and Phenomenal Causality, in R. Tagiuri & L. Petrullo (Eds.). *Person Perception and Interpersonal Behavior.* Stanford, Calif.: Stanford University Press. **788**

HEIN, A., R. HELD & E. C. GOWER. 1970. Development and Segmentation of Visually Controlled Movement by Selective Exposure During Rearing, *J. Comp. Physiol. Psychol.,* 73, 181–7. **305**

HEINSTEIN, M. 1963. Behavior Correlates of Breast-Bottle Regimes Under Varying Parent-Infant Relationships, *Monogr. Soc. Res. Child Develpm.*, 28 (Series No. 88). **699**

HELD, R. & A. HEIN. 1963. Movement-Produced Stimulation in the Development of Visually Guided Behavior, *J. Comp. Physiol. Psychol.*, 56, 872–6. **305**

HELD, R. & J. REKOSH. 1963. Motor-Sensory Feedback and the Geometry of Visual Space, *Science*, 141, 722–3. **305, 306**

HELMREICH, R., R. BAKEMAN & L. SCHERWITZ. 1973. The Study of Small Groups, in P. H. Mussen & M. R. Rosenzweig (Eds.). *Ann. Rev. Psychol.*, 24, 337–54. **817**

HELSON, H. 1947. Adaptation-Level as a Frame of Reference for Prediction of Psychophysical Data, *Amer. J. Psychol.*, 60, 1–29. **271**

———. 1964. *Adaptation-Level Theory.* New York: Harper. **271**

HELSON, H. & F. H. ROHLES, JR. 1959. A Quantitative Study of Reversal of Classical Lightness-Contrast, *Amer. J. Psychol.*, 72, 530–8. **253**

HENDRICK, C. 1972. Effects of Salience of Stimulus Inconsistency on Impression Formation, *J. Pers. Soc. Psychol.*, 22, 219–22. **778**

HENDRICK, I. 1943. The Discusion of the "Instinct to Master," *Psychoanal. Quart.*, 12, 561–5. **458**

HERON, W., B. K. DOANE & T. H. SCOTT. 1956. Visual Disturbances After Prolonged Perceptual Isolation, *Canad. J. Psychol.*, 10, 13–18. **459**

HESS, E. H. 1956. Space Perception in the Chick, *Sci. Amer.*, 195, 71–80. **306**

———. 1964. Imprinting in Birds, *Science*, 146, 1128–39. **xvii**

HESTON, L. L. 1966. Psychiatric Disorders in Foster Home Reared Children of Schizophrenic Mothers, *Brit. J. Psychiatr.*, 112, 819–25. **604**

HETHERINGTON, E. M. & G. FRANKIE. 1967. Effects of Parental Dominance, Warmth, and Conflict on Imitation in Children, *J. Pers. Soc. Psychol.*, 6, 119–25. **699**

HILGARD, E. R. 1969. Pain as a Puzzle for Psychology and Physiology, *Amer. Psychol.*, 24, 103–13. **473**

HILGARD, J. R. 1932. Learning and Maturation in Pre-school Children, *J. Genet. Psychol.*, 41, 36–56. **49**

———. 1970. *Personality and Hypnosis: A Study of Imaginative Involvement.* Chicago: University of Chicago Press. **509**

HIRSCH, J. 1963. Behavior Genetics and Individuality Understood, *Science*, 142, 1436–42. **19**

HIRSCH, J. & J. C. BOUDREAU. 1958. Studies in Experimental Behavior Genetics: I. The Heritability of Phototaxis in a Population of *Drosophila melanogaster*, *J. Comp. Physiol. Psychol.*, 51, 647–51. **19**

HOCHBERG, J. E. & V. BROOKS. 1962. Pictorial Recognition as an Unlearned Ability: A Study of One Child's Performance, *Amer. J. Psychol.*, 75, 624–8. **309**

HOCHBERG, J. E. & E. MCALISTER. 1953. A Quantitative Approach to Figural Goodness, *J. Exper. Psychol.*, 46, 361–4. **269**

HOLDEN, C. 1973a. Psychosurgery: Legitimate Therapy or Laundered Lobotomy?, *Science*, 179, 1109–12. **638**

———. 1973b. APA Adopts Detailed Code on Human Experimentation, *Science*, 179, 662. **809**

———. 1973c. Altered States of Consciousness: Mind Researchers Meet to Discuss Exploration and Mapping of "Inner Space," *Science*, 179, 982–3. **526**

HOLLINGSHEAD, A. B. & F. C. REDLICH. 1958. *Social Class and Mental Illness: A Community Study.* New York: Wiley. **608**

HOLLISTER, L. 1971. Marihuana in Man: Three Years Later, *Science*, 172, 21–9. **519**

HOLLOWAY, F. A. & R. WANSLEY. 1973. Multiphasic Retention Deficits at Periodic Intervals After Passive-Avoidance Learning, *Science*, 180, 208–10. **381**

HOMANS, G. C. 1961. *Social Behavior: Its Elementary Forms.* New York: Harcourt. **745**

HONZIK, C. H. 1936. The Sensory Basis of Maze Learning in Rats, *Comp. Psychol. Monogr.*, Vol. 13, No. 64. **389**

HONZIK. M. P. 1957. Developmental Studies of Parent-Children Resemblance in Intelligence, *Child Develpm.*, 28, 215–28. **209, 210**

———. 1963. A Sex Difference in the Age of Onset of the Parent-Child Resemblance in Intelligence, *J. Educ. Psychol.*, 54, 231–7. **29, 207**

———. 1972. Intellectual Abilities at Age 40 Years in Relation to the Early Family Environment, in F. J. Mönks, W. W. Hartup & J. deWit (Eds.). *Determinants of Behavioral Development.* New York: Academic. **211**

———. 1973. Predicting IQ Over the First Four Decades of the Life Span. Paper presented at the biennial meeting of the Society for Research in Child Development, Philadelphia. **193, 195**

HONZIK, M. P. & J. W. MACFARLANE. 1973. Personality Development and Intellectual Functioning from 21 Months to 40 Years, in L. F. Jarvik, C. Eisdorfer & J. E. Blum (Eds.). *Intellectual Functioning in Adults.* New York: Springer. **196**

HOOD, W. R. & M. SHERIF. 1962. Verbal Report and Judgment of an Unstructured Stimulus, *J. Psychol.*, 54, 121–30. **807**

HORN, G., S. P. R. ROSE & P. P. G. BATESON. 1973. Experience and Plasticity in the Central Nervous System, *Science*, 181, 506–14. **xvii**

HOVLAND, C. I., A. A. LUMSDAINE & F. D. SHEFFIELD. 1949. *Experiments on Mass Communication.* Princeton: Princeton University Press. **770**

HOVLAND, C. I. & W. WEISS. 1951. The Influence of Source Credibility on Communication Effectiveness, *Pub. Opin. Quart.*, 15, 635–50. **768**

HOWELLS, T. H. 1944. The Experimental Development of Color-Tone Synesthesia, *J. Exper. Psychol.*, 34, 87–103. **254**

HUBEL, D. H. & T. N. WIESEL. 1962. Receptive Fields, Binocular Interaction and Functional Architecture in the Cat's Visual Cortex, *J. Physiol.*, 160, 106–54. **332**

HUDSON, W. 1960. Pictorial Depth Perception in Sub-Cultural Groups in Africa, *J. Soc. Psychol.*, 52, 182–208. **313**

HUMPHREY, G. 1948. *Directed Thinking.* New York: Dodd, Mead. **130**

HUNT, J. & I. UZGIRIS. 1964. Cathexis from Recognitive Familiarity: An Exploratory Study. Paper presented at the annual meeting of the American Psychological Association, Los Angeles. **47**

HUXLEY, A. 1945. *The Perennial Philosophy.* New York: Harpers. **514**

———. 1959. *The Doors of Perception* and *Heaven and Hell.* (Published in one volume.) Harmondsworth, Middlesex: Penguin. **136**

HYDÉN, H. 1972. Some Brain Protein Changes Reflecting Neuronal Plasticity at Learning, in A. G. Karczmar & J. C. Eccles (Eds.). *Brain and Human Behavior.* New York: Springer-Verlag. **437**

HYDÉN, H. & E. EGYHAZI. 1962. Nuclear RNA Changes of Nerve Cells During a Learning Experiment in Rats, *Proc. Nat. Acad. Sci.*, 48, 1366–73. **436**

HYMAN, H. H. & P. B. SHEATSLEY. 1954. The "Authoritarian Personality"—A Methodological Critique, in R. Christie & M. Jahoda (Eds.). *Studies in the Scope and Method of "The Authoritarian Personality."* New York: Free Press. **659**

INDIK, B., S. E. SEASHORE & J. SLESINGER. 1964. Demographic Correlates of Psychological Strain, *J. Abnorm. Soc. Psychol.*, 69, 26–38. **483**

IZARD, C. E. 1971. *The Face of Emotion.* New York: Appleton. **486**

JACKSON, D. D. 1957. The Question of Family Homeostasis, *Psychiatr. Quart. Suppl.*, 31, 79–90. **635**

———. 1960. A Critique of the Literature on the Genetics of Schizophrenia, in D. D. Jackson (Ed.). *The Etiology of Schizophrenia.* New York: Basic Books. **605**

JAENSCH, E. R. 1930. *Eidetic Imagery and Typological Methods of Investigation.* New York: Harcourt. **131, 662**

JAMES, W. 1902. *The Varieties of Religious Experience.* New York: Longmans. **515, 550**

———. 1950. *Principles of Psychology.* New York: Dover. Originally published 1890. **127, 128**

JARVIK, L. F., C. EISDORFER & J. E. BLUM (Eds.). 1973. *Intellectual Functioning in Adults.* New York: Springer. **194**

JARVIK, M. E. & W. B. ESSMAN. 1960. A Simple One-Trial Learning Situation for Mice, *Psychol. Rep.*, 6, 290. **437**

JASPER, H. H. 1941. Electroencephalography, in W. Penfield & T. Erickson (Eds.). *Epilepsy and Cerebral Localization.* Springfield, Ill.: Charles C Thomas. **65**

JENKINS, W. O. & M. K. RIGBY. 1950. Partial (Periodic) Versus Continuous Reinforcement in Resistance to Extinction, *J. Comp. Physiol. Psychol.*, 43, 30–40. **383**

JENSEN, A. R. 1969. How Much Can We Boost IQ and Scholastic Achievement? *Harvard Educational Review*, 39, 1–123. **213, 220**

———. 1972. *Genetics and Education.* New York: Harper. **208, 221**

JONES, E. E. & K. E. DAVIS. 1965. From Acts to Dispositions: The Attribution Process in Person Perception, in L. Berkowitz (Ed.). *Advances in Experimental Social Psychology: II.* New York: Academic. **789**

JONES, E. E. & R. KOHLER. 1958. The Effects of Plausibility on the Learning of Controversial Statements, *J. Abnorm. Soc. Psychol.*, 57, 315–30. **756**

JONES, H. E. & H. S. CONRAD. 1933. The Growth and Decline of Intelligence, *Genet. Psychol. Monogr.*, 13, No. 3. **34, 192, 756**

JONES, M. C. 1924. The Elimination of Children's Fear, *J. Exp. Psychol.*, 1, 382–90. **596**

———. 1965. Psychological Correlates of Somatic Development, *Child Develpm.*, 36, 899–912. **698**

JULIAN, J. W. & F. A. PERRY. 1965. Cooperation Contrasted With Intra-Group and Inter-Group Competition. Paper read at the Midwest Psychological Association Annual Meeting, Chicago. **796**

JUNG, C. G. 1923. *Psychological Types.* New York: Harcourt. **661, 662**

KAGAN, J. 1971. *Change and Continuity in Infancy.* New York: Wiley. **195**

KAGAN, J. & H. A. MOSS. 1962. *Birth to Maturity.* New York: Wiley. **49**

KAGAN, S. 1973. Personal communication. **703**

KAGAN, S. & M. C. MADSEN. 1971. Cooperation and Competition of Mexican, Mexican-American, and Anglo-American Children of Two Ages Under Four Instructional Sets, *Develpm. Psychol.*, 5, 32–9. **703**

———. 1972. Rivalry in Anglo-American and Mexican Children of Two Ages, *J. Pers. Soc. Psychol.*, 24, 214–20. **796**

KALES, A., F. HOEDEMAKER, A. JACOBSON & F. LICHTENSTEIN. 1964. Dream Deprivation: An Experimental Reappraisal, *Nature*, 204, 1337–8. **508**

KALLMANN, F. J. 1946. The Genetic Theory of Schizophrenia, *Amer. J. Psychiatr.*, 103, 309–22. **604**

KANFER, F. H. & J. S. PHILLIPS. 1970. *Learning Foundations of Behavior Therapy.* New York: Wiley. **619**

KANGAS, J. & K. BRADWAY. 1971. Intelligence at Middle Age: A Thirty-Eight Year Follow-Up, *Develpm. Psychol.*, 5, 333–7. **194**

KANNER, L. 1931. Judging Emotions From Facial Expressions, *Psychol. Monogr.*, 41, Series No. 186. **486**

KAPLAN, E. L. 1970. Intonation and Language Acquisition. *Papers and Reports on Child Language Development*, No. 1 (March). Stanford University Committee on Linguistics. **103**

KARLSSON, J. L. 1970. Genetic Association of Giftedness and Creativity with Schizophrenia, *Hereditas*, 66, 177–82. **605**

KASAMATSU, A. & T. HIRAI. 1966. An Electroencephalographic Study on the Zen Meditation (Zazen). *Folio Psychiat. & Neurol. Japonica*, 20, 315–36. **516**

KASTENBAUM, A. 1951. An Experimental Study of the Formation of Impressions of Personality. Unpublished master's thesis, New School for Social Research. **782**

KATZ, D. 1948. *Psychological Atlas.* New York: Philosophical Library. **xxi**

———. 1950. *Gestalt Psychology.* New York: Ronald. **160, 238**

KATZ, D. & E. STOTLAND. 1959. A Preliminary Statement to a Theory of Attitude Structure and Change, in S. Koch (Ed.). *Psychology: A Study of Science.* Vol. 3. New York: McGraw-Hill. **771**

KATZ, I., E. G. EPPS & L. J. AXELSON. 1964. Effect Upon Negro Digit-Symbol Performance of Anticipated Comparison With Whites and With Other Negroes, *J. Abnorm. Soc. Psychol.*, 69, 77–83. **225**

KAUFMAN, H. & M. WILSON. 1970. Information Processing in the Monkey. Paper presented at a meeting of the Psychonomic Society. **405**

KELLOGG, W. N. 1962. Sonar System of the Blind, *Science*, 137, 399–404. **237**

KELLY, G. A. 1955. *The Psychology of Personal Constructs.* (Two volumes.) New York: Norton. **656**

———. 1963. *A Theory of Personality.* New York: Norton. **651, 656**

KELMAN, H. C. 1967. Human Use of Human Subjects: The Problem of Deception in Social Psychological Experiments, *Psychol. Bull.*, 67, 1–11. **809**

KENNEDY, J. M. 1971. Line Representation and Pictorial Perception. Ph.D. Thesis, Cornell. **309**

KESSEN, W., M. M. HAITH & P. H. SALAPATEK. 1970. Human Infancy: A Bibliography and Guide, in P. H. Mussen (Ed.). *Carmichael's Handbook of Child Psychology.* New York: Wiley. **43**

KESSEN, W., E. J. WILLIAMS & J. P. WILLIAMS. 1961. Selection and Test of Response Measures in the Study of the Human Newborn, *Child Develpm.*, 32, 7–24. **49**

KIESLER, D. J. 1966. Some Myths of Psychotherapy Research and the Search for a Paradigm, *Psychol. Bull.*, 65, 110–36. **640**

KIMBLE, G. A. & N. GARMEZY. 1963. *Principles of General Psychology.* 2nd ed. New York: Ronald. **369**

KINTSCH, W. 1970. *Learning, Memory, and Conceptual Processes.* New York: Wiley. **402, 405**

KLAUSMEIER, H. J. & L. J. LOUGHLIN. 1961. Behaviors During Problem Solving Among Children of Low, Average, and High Intelligence, *J. Educ. Psychol.*, 52, 148–52. **171**

KLAUSNER, S. Z. (Ed.). 1969. *Why Man Takes Chances.* Garden City, N.Y.: Doubleday. **461**

KLEITMAN, N. 1963. *Sleep and Wakefulness.* 2nd ed. Chicago: Univ. of Chicago Press. **537**

KLEITMAN, N. & G. CRISLER. 1927. A Quantitative Study of a Salivary Conditioned Reflex, *Amer. J. Physiol.*, 79, 571–614. **370**

KLOPFER, P. H. & J. P. HAILMAN. 1964. Perceptual Preferences and Imprinting in Chicks, *Science*, 145, 1333–4. **xvii**

KLUCKHOHN, C. & H. A. MURRAY. 1948. *Personality in Nature, Society, and Culture.* New York: Knopf. **666**

KLÜVER, H. 1926. An Experimental Study of the Eidetic Type, *Genet. Psychol. Monogr.*, 1, 71–230. **131**

KNAPP, S. & A. J. MANDEL. 1973. Short- and Long-Term Lithium Administration: Effects on the Brain's Serotonergic Biosynthetic Systems, *Science*, 180, 645–7. **553**

KNIGHT, K. E. 1963. Effect of Effort on Behavioral Rigidity in a Luchins Water Jar Task, *J. Abnorm. Soc. Psychol.*, 66, 190–2. **161**

KNUTSON, J. N. 1972. *The Human Basis of the Polity: A Psychological Study of Political Men.* Chicago: Aldine-Atherton. **750**

KOCH, H. L. 1966. *Twins and Twin Relations.* Chicago: University of Chicago Press. **694**

KODLIN, D. & D. J. THOMPSON. 1958. An Appraisal of the Longitudinal Approach to Studies of Growth and Development, *Monogr. Soc. Res. Child Develpm.*, 23, No. 1. **35**

KOFFKA, K. 1928. *The Growth of the Mind.* Translated by R. M. Ogden. New York: Harcourt. **95**

KOHLBERG, L. 1964. Development of Moral Character and Moral Ideology, in M. L. Hoffman & L. W. Hoffman (Eds.). *Review of Child Development Research.* Vol. I. New York: Russell Sage Foundation. **737**

———. 1969. *Stage and Sequence: The Developmental Approach to Moralization.* New York: Holt. **737**

———. 1973. Continuities in Childhood and Adult Moral Development, in P. B. Baltes & K. W. Schie (Eds.). *Life-Span Developmental Psychology: Personality and Socialization.* New York: Academic. **737**

KOHLER, I. 1964. The Formation and Transformation of the Perceptual World, *Psychol. Issues*, 3, Whole Monogr. No. 12. **305**

KÖHLER, W. 1925. *The Mentality of Apes.* New York: Harcourt. **95**

KÖHLER, W. & H. WALLACH. 1944. Figural Aftereffects, *Proc. Amer. Phil. Soc.*, 88, 269–357. **275**

KOHN, M. L. 1959a. Social Class and Parental Values, *Amer. J. Sociol.*, 64, 337–51. **701**

———. 1959b. Social Class and the Exercise of

Parental Authority, *Amer. Sociol. Rev.*, 24, 352–66. **703**

KOLERS, P. A. 1964. Apparent Movement of a Necker Cube, *Amer. J. Psychol.*, 77, 220–30. **301, 303**

———. 1972. Remembering Operations. Paper presented at annual meeting of Eastern Psychological Assn. **304**

KONNER, M. J. 1973. Newborn Walking: Additional Data, *Science*, 178, 307. **49**

KORTE, A. 1915. Kinematoskopische Untersuchungen, *Zeitsch. Psychol.*, 72, 194–296. **287**

KRECH, D. 1967. Psychochemical Manipulation and Social Policy, *Ann. Intern. Med.*, 67 (Part II), 19–24, 61–67. **440**

———. 1968. Brain Chemistry and Anatomy: Implications for Behavior Therapy, in C. Rupp (Ed.). *Mind as Tissue*. New York: Harper. **211**

———. 1969. Psychoneurobiochemeducation, *California Monthly*, University of California Alumni Association (June–July), 14–21. **211**

KRECH, D. & R. S. CRUTCHFIELD. 1958. *Elements of Psychology*. New York: Knopf. **493**

KRECHEVSKY, I. 1935. Measurement of Tension. Paper read at Symposium on Topological Psychology, Bryn Mawr, Pa. **577**

KREMERS, J. 1960. *Scientific Psychology and Naïve Psychology*. Nijmegen: Janssen. **779**

KRETSCHMER, E. 1936. *Physique and Character*. New York: Harcourt. Originally published in German 1921. **661**

KRINGLEN, E. 1967. *Heredity and Environment in the Functional Psychoses*. London: Universitet. **605**

KÜBLER-ROSS, E. 1970. *On Death and Dying*. New York: Macmillan. Paperback edition. **xix**

KUHLMAN, C. K. 1960. Visual Imagery in Children. Unpublished doctoral thesis, Radcliffe College. **135**

LAING, R. D. & A. ESTERSON. 1970. *Sanity, Madness and the Family: Families of Schizophrenics*. 2nd ed. London: Tavistock. **605**

LAING, R. D., H. PHILLIPSON & A. R. LEE. 1966. *Interpersonal Perception: A Theory and a Method of Research*. New York: Springer. **778**

LAMBERT, W. E., R. C. HODGSON, R. C. GARDNER & S. FILLENBAUM. 1960. Evaluational Reactions to Spoken Languages, *J. Abnorm. Soc. Psychol.*, 60, 44–51. **756**

LANGFELD, H. S. 1914. Note on a Case of Chromaesthesia, *Psychol. Bull.*, 11, 113–14. **254**

LASHLEY, K. S. 1929. *Brain Mechanisms and Intelligence: A Quantitative Study of Injuries to the Brain*. Chicago: Univ. of Chicago Press. **419–20**

LASHLEY, K. S. & J. T. RUSSELL. 1934. The Mechanism of Vision. XI. A Preliminary Test of Innate Organization, *J. Genet. Psychol.*, 45, 136–44. **295**

LASKI, H. J. 1929. The Dangers of Obedience, *Harper's Monthly Magazine*, 159, 1–10. **810**

LATANÉ, B. & J. RODIN. 1969. A Lady in Distress: Inhibiting Effects of Friends and Strangers on Bystander Intervention, *J. Exp. Soc. Psychol.*, 5, 189–202. **801**

LAURENDEAU, M. & A. PINARD. 1963. *Causal Thinking in the Child: A Genetic and Experimental Approach*. New York: International Universities Press. **88**

LAZARUS, A. A. 1968. A Plea for Technical and Theoretical Breadth, *AABT Newsletter*, 3 (June), 2. **621**

LAZARUS, R. S. 1968. Emotions and Adaptation: Conceptual and Empirical Relations, in W. J. Arnold (Ed.). *Nebraska Symposium on Motivation*. Lincoln: University of Nebraska Press. **495**

LEE, S. D. & M. K. TEMERLIN. 1970. Social Class, Diagnosis and Prognosis for Psychotherapy, *Psychother. Theory Res. Pract.*, 7, 181–5. **608**

LEEPER, R. W. 1935. A Study of a Neglected Portion of the Field of Learning: The Development of Sensory Organization, *J. Genet. Psychol.*, 46, 41–75. **276**

———. 1965. Some Needed Developments in the Motivational Theory of Emotions, in M. R. Jones (Ed.). *Nebraska Symposium on Motivation*. Lincoln: University of Nebraska Press. **491, 492**

LEHMANN, S. 1970. Personality and Compliance: A Study of Anxiety and Self-Esteem in Opinion and Behavior Change, *J. Pers. Soc. Psychol.*, 15, 76–86. **771**

LEHRMAN, D. S. 1964. Control of Behavior Cycles in Reproduction, in W. Etkin (Ed.). *Social Behavior and Organization Among Vertebrates*. Chicago: University of Chicago Press. **560**

LEIBOWITZ, H. W. 1973. Personal communication. **39**

LERNER, M. 1968. *Heredity, Evolution, and Society*. San Francisco: W. H. Freeman. **22, 23**

LERNER, M. & N. INOUYE. 1969. Personal communication. **19**

LERNER, R. M. & S. J. KORN. 1972. The Development of Body Build Stereotypes in Males, *Child Develpm.*, 43, 908–20. **697**

LESSER, G. H., G. FIFER & D. H. CLARK. 1965. Mental Abilities of Children From Different Social-Class and Cultural Groups, *Monogr. Soc. Res. Child Develpm.*, 30, No. 4. **224**

LEVITSKY, A. & F. S. PERLS. 1970. The Rules and Games of Gestalt Therapy, in J. Fagan & I. L. Shephered (Eds.). *Gestalt Therapy Now*. Palo Alto, Calif.: Science & Behavior. **630**

LEVITT, E. E. 1956. The Water Jar Einstellung Test as a Measure of Rigidity, *Psychol. Bull.*, 53, 347–70. **163**

LEWIN, K. 1935. *A Dynamic Theory of Personality*. New York: McGraw-Hill. **575**

LEWIS, M. K., C. R. ROGERS & J. M. SHLIEN. 1959. Time-Limited, Client-Centered Psychotherapy: Two Cases, in A. Burton (Ed.). *Case Studies in Counseling and Psychotherapy*. Englewood Cliffs, N. J.: Prentice-Hall. **628**

LIBET, B., W. W. ALBERTS, E. W. WRIGHT, JR., & B. FEINSTEIN. 1971. Cortical and Thalamic Activation in Conscious Sensory Experience, in G. Somjen (Ed.). *Neurophysiology Studied in Man.* Reprinted from International Congress Series No. 253. Proceedings of a Symposium held in Paris at the Faculté des Sciences, 20–22 July 1971. Amsterdam: Exerpta Medica. **347, 349**

LIEBERMAN, P. 1967. *Intonation, Perception and Language.* Cambridge, Mass.: M. I. T. Press. **103**

LINDSAY, P. H. & D. A. NORMAN. 1972. *Human Information Processing.* New York: Academic. **403**

LINDZEY, G. 1961. *Projective Techniques and Cross-cultural Research.* New York: Appleton. **679**

LIPSITT, L. P. & H. KAGE. 1964. Conditioned Sucking in the Newborn, *Psychonom. Sci.,* 1, 29–30. **44**

LIVSON, N. 1962. Developmental Changes in the Perception of Incomplete Pictures. Paper read at Institute of Human Development, University of California, Berkeley. **265**

LIVSON, N., D. MCNEILL & K. THOMAS. 1962. Pooled Estimates of Parent-Child Correlation in Stature From Birth to Maturity, *Science,* 138, 818–20. **37**

LIVSON, N. & T. F. NICHOLS. 1956. Discrimination and Reliability in Q-Sort Personality Descriptions, *J. Abnorm. Soc. Psychol.,* 52, 159–65. **673**

LIVSON, N. & PESKIN, H. 1967. Prediction of Adult Psychological Health in a Longitudinal Study, *J. Abnorm. Psychol.,* 72, 509–18. **700**

LOEHLIN, J. C. 1965. A Heredity-Environment Analysis of Personality Inventory Data, in S. G. Vandenberg (Ed.). *Methods and Goals in Human Behavior Genetics.* New York: Academic Press. **484**

LOEVINGER, J. 1966. Models and Measures of Developmental Variation, *Ann. N. Y. Acad. Sci.,* 134, 585–90. **32**

LONDON, P. 1964. *The Modes and Morals of Psychotherapy.* New York: Holt. **620**

———. 1972. The End of Ideology in Behavior Modification, *Amer. Psychol.,* 27, 913–20. **622**

LORENZO, A. J. D. DE. 1963. Studies on the Ultrastructure and Histophysiology of Cell Membranes, Nerve Fibers and Synaptic Junctions in Chemoreceptors, in Y. Zotterman (Ed.). *Olfaction and Taste.* New York: Macmillan. **343**

LOTT, B. E. & A. J. LOTT. 1960. The Formation of Positive Attitude Toward Group Members, *J. Abnorm. Soc. Psychol.,* 61, 297–300. **764**

LOVAAS, O. I. 1966. A Program for the Establishment of Speech in Psychotic Children, in J. K. Wing (Ed.). *Early Childhood Autism.* Elmsford, N. Y.: Pergamon. **621**

LUCHINS, A. S. 1942. Mechanization in Problem-Solving, *Psychol. Monogr.,* Vol. 54, No. 6. **162**

LUMSDAINE, A. A. & I. L. JANIS. 1953. Resistance to Counter-Propaganda Produced by One-Sided and Two-Sided Propaganda Presentations, *Pub. Opin. Quart.,* 17, 311–18. **770**

LUTHE, W. 1963. Autogenic Training: Method, Research, and Application in Medicine, *Amer. J. Psychother.,* 17, 174–95. **511**

LYNCH, H. T. 1971. *International Directory of Genetic Services.* 3rd ed. White Plains, N. Y.: The National Foundation. **23**

MCBRIDE, G., M. G. KING & J. W. JAMES. 1965. Social Proximity Effects on GSR in Adult Humans, *J. Psychol.,* 61, 153–7. **812**

MCCLEARY, R. A. 1966. Response Functions of the Limbic System: Initiation and Suppression, in E. Stellar & J. M. Sprague (Eds.). *Progress in Physiological Psychology,* Vol. 1. New York: Academic Press. **550**

MCCLELLAND, D. C. 1965. Toward a Theory of Motive Acquisition, *Amer. Psychol.,* 20, 321–33. **452**

———. 1973. Testing for Competence Rather Than for "Intelligence," *Amer. Psychol.,* 28, 1–14. **185**

———. *Assessing Human Motivation.* New York: General Learning Press. In press. **452**

MCCLELLAND, D. C., W. DAVIS, R. KALIN & H. WANNER. 1972. *The Drinking Man: Alcohol and Human Motivation.* New York: Free Press. **518**

MCCLELLAND, D. C. & D. WINTER. 1969. *Motivating Economic Achievement.* New York: Free Press. **452**

MCCOLLOUGH, C. 1965. Color Adaptation of Edge-detectors in the Human Visual System, *Science,* 149, 1115–16. **337**

MCCROSKY, J. C. 1970. The Effects of Evidence as an Inhibitor of Counter Persuasion, *Speech Monogr.,* 37, 188–94. **768**

MCGUIRE, W. J. 1957. Order of Presentation as a Factor in Conditioning: Persuasiveness, in C. I. Hovland, *et al.* (Eds.). *The Order of Presentation in Persuasion.* New Haven: Yale University Press. **770**

MCGUIRE, W. J. & D. PAPAGEORGIS. 1961. The Relative Efficacy of Various Types of Prior Belief-Defense in Producing Immunity Against Persuasion, *J. Abnorm. Soc. Psychol.,* 62, 327–37. **763**

MCKUSICK, V. A. 1971. *Mendelian Inheritance in Man.* 3rd ed. Baltimore: The Johns Hopkins Press. **15, 22**

MCNEILL, D. 1966. Developmental Psycholinguistics, in F. Smith & G. A. Miller (Eds.). *The Genesis of Language: A Psycholinguistic Approach.* Cambridge, Mass.: M. I. T. Press. **112, 117**

MACAULAY, S. & E. WALSTER. 1971. Legal Structures and Restoring Equity, *J. Soc. Issues,* 27, 173–88. **750**

MACCOBY, E. E., E. M. DOWLEY, J. W. HAGEN & R. DEGERMAN. 1965. Activity Level and Intellectual Functioning in Normal Preschool Children, *Child Develpm.,* 36, 761–70. **171**

MACDONALD, W. S. 1967. Social Structure and Behavior Modification in Job Corps Training, *Percep. Motor Skills,* 24, 142. **817**

MACFARLANE, J. W. 1938. Studies in Child Guidance: I. Methodology of Data Collection and Organization, *Monogr. Soc. Res. Child Develpm.*, Vol. 3, No. 6. **665**

———. 1964. Perspectives on Personality Consistency and Change From the Guidance Study, *Vita Humana*, 7, 115–26. **704**

MACFARLANE, J. W., L. ALLEN & M. P. HONZIK. 1954. A Developmental Study of the Behavior Problems of Normal Children Between 21 Months and 14 Years, *U. Calif. Publ. Child Develpm.*, Vol. 2. **483, 672**

MACKINNON, D. W. 1938. Violation of Prohibitions, in H. A. Murray (Ed.). *Explorations in Personality.* New York: Oxford. **675**

———. 1962. The Nature and Nurture of Creative Talent, *Amer. Psychol.*, 17, 484–95. **681**

———. 1963. Creativity and Images of the Self, in R. W. White (ed.). *The Study of Lives.* New York: Atherton. **683**

MACLEAN, P. D. 1970. The Limbic Brain in Relation to the Psychoses, in P. Black (Ed.). *Physiological Correlates of Emotion.* New York: Academic Press. **547, 550**

MADDOX, G. L. 1968. Persistence of Life Style Among the Elderly: A Longitudinal Study of Patterns of Social Activity in Relation to Life Satisfaction, in B. L. Neugarten (Ed.). *Middle Age and Aging.* Chicago: University of Chicago Press. **53**

MADSEN, M. C. & S. KAGAN. In Press. Mother-Directed Achievement of Children in Two Cultures, *J. Cross-Cultural Psychol.*, **703**

MAIER, N. R. F. 1933. An Aspect of Human Reasoning, *Brit. J. Psychol.*, 24, 144–55. **166**

———. 1967. Assets and Liabilities in Group Problem Solving: The Need for an Integrative Function, *Psychol. Rev.*, 74, 239–49. **801**

MAIER, N. R. F. & R. J. BURKE. 1967. Response Availability as a Factor in the Problem-Solving Performance of Males and Females, *J. Pers. Soc. Psychol.*, 5, 304–10. **161**

MARK, V. H. & F. R. ERVIN. 1970. *Violence and the Brain.* New York: Harper & Row. **551**

MARKS, W. B., W. H. DOBELLE & E. F. MACNICHOL. 1964. Visual Pigments of Single Primate Cones, *Science*, 143, 1181–2. **325**

MARLOWE, D. & K. J. GERGEN. 1968. Personality and Social Interaction, in G. Lindzey & E. Aronson (Eds.). *The Handbook of Social Psychology.* 2nd ed. Vol. 3. Reading, Mass.: Addison-Wesley. **656**

MASLOW, A. H. 1954. *Motivation and Personality.* New York: Harper. **461, 721**

———. 1962. *Toward a Psychology of Being.* Princeton: Van Nostrand. **512**

———. 1967. A Theory of Metamotivation; The Biological Rooting of the Value Life, *J. Human. Psychol.*, 1, 93–127. **722**

———. 1970. *Motivation and Personality.* 2nd ed. New York: Harper & Row. **722**

MASSERMAN, J. H. 1946. *Principles of Dynamic Psychiatry.* Philadelphia: Saunders. **580**

MASTERS, W. H. & V. E. JOHNSON. 1966. *Human Sexual Response.* Boston: Little, Brown. **557**

MATIN, L. & G. E. MACKINNON. 1964. Autokinetic Movement: Selective Manipulation of Directioned Components by Image Stabilization, *Science*, 143, 147–8. **285**

MEEHL, P. E. 1950. On the Circularity of the Law of Effect, *Psychol. Bull.*, 47, 52–75. **378**

MEICHENBAUM, D. H. 1971. Examination of Model Characteristics in Reducing Avoidance Behavior, *J. Pers. Soc. Psychol.*, 17, 298–307. **626**

MELTON, A. W. 1963. Implications of Short-Term Memory for a General Theory of Memory, *J. Verb. Learn. Verb. Behav.*, 2, 1–21. **410**

MELZACK, R. 1970. Phantom Limbs, *Psychology Today* (October), 63–8. **349**

MELZACK, R. & P. D. WALL. 1965. Pain Mechanisms: A New Theory, *Science*, 150, 971–9. **349**

METZGER, W. 1953. *Gesetze des Sehens.* Frankfurt/ Mainz Kramer. **265**

MICHAEL, R. P. 1971. Pheromones: Isolation of Male Sex Attractants From a Female Primate, *Science*, 172, 964–6. **242**

MICHOTTE, A. 1963. *The Perception of Causality.* New York: Basic Books. Originally published in French, 1954. **290**

MILGRAM, S. 1963. Behavioral Study of Obedience, *J. Abnorm. Soc. Psychol.*, 67, 371–8. **675**

———. 1964. Group Pressure and Action Against a Person, *J. Abnorm. Soc. Psychol.*, 69, 137–43. **807**

———. 1965. Liberating Effects of Group Pressure, *J. Pers. Soc. Psychol.*, 1, 127–34. **810**

———. 1972. The Familiar Stranger: An Aspect of Urban Anonymity, *Division 8 Newsletter*, American Psychological Association (July). **799**

MILLER, G. A. 1951. *Language and Communication.* New York: McGraw-Hill. **111**

———. 1956. The Magical Number Seven, Plus or Minus Two: Some Limits on Our Capacity for Processing Information, *Psychol. Rev.*, 63, 81–97. **405**

———. 1965. Some Preliminaries to Psycholinguistics, *Amer. Psychol.*, 20, 15–20. **116**

MILLER, G. A. & J. C. R. LICKLIDER. 1950. The Intelligibility of Interrupted Speech, *J. Acoust. Soc. Amer.*, 22, 167–73. **111**

MILLER, N. E. 1969. Learning of Visceral and Glandular Responses, *Science*, 163, 434–45. **387**

MILLER, N. E. & A. BANUAZIZI. 1968. Instrumental Learning by Curarized Rats of a Specific, Visceral Response, Intestinal or Cardiac, *J. Comp. Physiol. Psychol.*, 65, 1–7. **387**

MILLER, N. E. & B. R. DWORKIN. 1973. Visceral Learning: Recent Difficulties With Curarized Rats and Significant Programs for Human Research, in P. A. Obrist, *et al.* (Eds.). *Contemporary Trends in Cardiovascular Psychophysiology.* Chicago: Aldine-Atherton. **387**

MILNER, P. M. 1970. *Physiological Psychology*. New York: Holt. **537**

MISCHEL, W. 1971. *Introduction to Personality*. New York: Holt. **719**

MISHKIN, M. 1972. Cortical Visual Areas and Their Interaction, in A. Karczmar & J. C. Eccles (Eds.). *Brain and Human Behavior*. New York: Springer-Verlag. **422**

MOFFITT, A. R. 1968. Speech Perception by Infants. Unpublished doctoral dissertation, University of Minnesota. **103**

MOGAR, R. 1965. Current Status and Future Trends in Psychedelic (LSD) Research, *J. Humanistic Psychol.*, 2, 147–66. **523**

MONEY, J. 1964. Two Cytogenetic Syndromes: Psychological Comparison, Intelligence and Specific Factor Quotients, *J. Psychiatr. Res.*, 2, 223–31. **206**

MONROE, R. 1971. *Journeys Out-of-the-Body*. New York: Doubleday. **508**

MOORE, T. W. 1964. Children of Full-Time and Part-Time Mothers, *Int. J. Soc. Psychiat.*, 2, 1–10. **699**

MORGAN, C. D. & H. A. MURRAY. 1935. A Method for Investigating Fantasies: The Thematic Apperception Test, *Arch. Neurol. Psychiat.*, 34, 289–306. **678**

MOSHER, L. R. & D. FEINSILVER. 1970. *Special Report on Schizophrenia*. National Institute of Mental Health. **601**

MUELLER, N., J. M. KENNEDY & S. TANIMOTO. 1973. Inherent Perceptual Motivation and Detection of Structure, *J. Structural Learning*. **310, 311**

MUIR, DARWIN W. & DONALD E. MITCHELL. 1973. Visual Resolution and Experience: Acuity Deficits in Cats Following Early Selective Visual Deprivation, *Science*, 180, 420–2. **334**

MULLER, J. 1948. The Doctrine of the Specific Energies of Nerves, in W. Dennis (Ed.). *Readings in the History of Psychology*. Translated by W. Brady from *Handbuch der Physiologie*. New York: Appleton. Originally published in German 1838. **70, 76**

MURPHY, G. 1966. Parapsychology, in N. L. Farberow (Ed.). *Taboo Topics*. New York: Atherton. **xx**

MURRAY, H. A. 1943. *Thematic Apperception Test*. Cambridge: Harvard. **681**

NAKAMURA, C. Y. 1958. Conformity and Problem Solving, *J. Abnorm. Soc. Psychol.*, 56, 315–20. **171**

NARANJO, C. & R. ORNSTEIN. 1971. *On the Psychology of Meditation*. New York: Viking. **514, 516, 517**

NEISSER, U. 1967. *Cognitive Psychology*. New York: Appleton. **102, 136, 303, 403, 409**

NEUGARTEN, B. L. (Ed.). 1968. *Middle Age and Aging*. Chicago: Chicago University Press. **52**

———. 1970. Dynamics of Transition of Middle Age to Old Age: Adaptation and the Life Cycle, *J. Ger. Psychiat.*, 4, 71–87. **52**

NEWCOMB, T. M. 1943. *Personality and Social Change: Attitude Formation in a Student Community*. New York: Dryden. **763**

———. 1963. Persistence and Regression of Changed Attitudes: Long Range Studies, *J. Soc. Issues*, 19, 3–14. **765**

NEWELL, A., J. C. SHAW & H. A. SIMON. 1958. Elements of a Theory of Human Problem Solving, *Psychol. Rev.*, 65, 151–66. **153**

———. 1960. Report on a General Problem Solving Program, in *Proceedings of the International Conference on Information Processing*. Paris: UNESCO. **154**

NEWMAN, H. H., F. N. FREEMAN & K. J. HOLZINGER. 1937. *Twins: A Study of Heredity and Environment*. Chicago: University of Chicago Press. **208**

NEYMANN, C. A. & G. K. YACORZYNSKI. 1942. Studies of Introversion-Extroversion and Conflict Motives in the Psychoses, *J. Gen. Psychol.*, 27, 241–55. **661**

NICHOLS, R. C. 1965. The National Merit Twin Study, in S. G. Vandenberg (Ed.). *Methods and Goals of Human Behavior Genetics*. New York: Academic. **691**

NICOLSON, A. B. & C. HANLEY. 1953. Indices of Physiological Maturity: Derivation and Interrelationships, *Child Develpm.*, 24, 3–38. **36**

NISBETT, R. E. 1968. Taste, Deprivation, and Weight Determinants of Eating Behavior, *J. Pers. Soc. Psychol.*, 10, 107–16. **457**

NISSEN, H. W. 1930. A Study of Exploratory Behavior in the White Rat by Means of the Obstruction Method, *J. Genet. Psychol.*, 37, 361–76. **458**

NORMAN, D. A. (Ed.). 1970. *Models of Human Memory*. New York: Academic. **402**

NOWLIS, D. P. & J. KAMIYA. 1970. The Control of EEG Alpha Rhythms Through Auditory Feedback and Associated Mental Activity, *Psychophysiol.*, 6, 476–84. **389**

ODOM, R. D. & C. M. LEMOND. 1972. Developmental Differences in the Perception and Production of Facial Expressions, *Child Develpm.*, 43, 359–70. **486**

OLDS, J. 1961. Differential Effects of Drives and Drugs on Self-Stimulation at Different Brain Sites, in D. E. Sheer (Ed.). *Electrical Stimulation of the Brain*. Austin: University of Texas Press. **549**

OLDS, J., J. F. DISTERHOFT, M. SEGAL, C. L. KORNBLITH & R. HIRSH. 1972. Learning Centers of Rat Brain Mapped by Measuring Latencies of Conditioned Unit Responses, *J. Neurophysiol.*, 35, 202–19. **429**

OLDS, J. & P. MILNER. 1954. Positive Reinforcement Produced by Electrical Stimulation of Septal Area and Other Regions of Rat Brain, *J. Comp. Physiol. Psychol.*, 47, 419–27. **549**

OLTON, R. M. & R. S. CRUTCHFIELD. 1969. Developing the Skills of Productive Thinking, in P. Mussen, J. Langer & M. V. Covington (Eds.). *Trends and*

Issues in Developmental Psychology. New York: Holt. **150**

OLUM, V. 1958. Developmental Differences in the Perception of Causality Under Conditions of Specific Instructions, *Vita Humana*, 1, 191–203. **290**

OSBORN, A. F. 1957. *Applied Imagination.* Rev. ed. New York: Scribner. **799**

OSBORNE, R. T. & C. L. JACKSON. 1964. Factor Structure of the Wechsler Intelligence Scale for Children at Pre-School Level and After First Grade: A Longitudinal Analysis. Paper read at Annual Meeting of American Psychological Association, Los Angeles. **199**

OSLER, S. E. & G. E. TRAUTMAN. 1961. Concept Attainment: II. Effect of Stimulus Complexity Upon Concept Attainment at Two Levels of Intelligence, *J. Exper. Psychol.*, 62, 9–13. **171**

OURTH, L. & K. B. BROWN. 1961. Inadequate Mothering and Disturbance in the Neonatal Period, *Child Develpm.*, 32, 287–95. **484**

OYAMA, T. 1960. Figure-Ground Dominance as a Function of Sector Angle, Brightness, Hue, and Orientation, *J. Exper. Psychol.*, 60, 299–305. **273**

PAHNKE, W. N. 1963. Drugs and Mysticism: An Analysis of the Relationship Between Psychedelic Drugs and Mystical Consciousness. Unpublished doctoral dissertation, Harvard University. **515**

PAIVIO, A., J. C. YUILLE, S. A. MADIGAN. 1968. Concreteness, Imagery, and Meaningfulness Values for 925 Nouns, *J. Exper. Psychol. Monogr.*, 76, 1, part 2. **400**

PAPALIA, D. E. 1972. The Status of Several Conservation Abilities Across the Life-Span, *Human Develpm.*, 15, 229–43. **88**

PAPEZ, J. W. 1937. A Proposed Mechanism of Emotion, *Arch. Neurol. Psychiat. Chicago*, 38, 725–43. **547**

PARKES, C. M. 1965. Bereavement and Mental Illness: Part 2. A Classification of Bereavement Reactions, *Brit. J. Med. Psychol.*, 38, 13–26. **472**

PARRISH, M., R. M. LUNDY & H. W. LEIBOWITZ. 1969. Effect of Hypnotic Age Regression on the Magnitude of the Ponzo and Poggendorff Illusions, *J. Abnorm. Psychol.*, 74, 693–8. **39**

PAVLOV, I. P. 1927. *Conditioned Reflexes.* Translated by G. V. Anrep. London: Oxford. Originally published in Russian. **361**

PENFIELD, W. & T. RASMUSSEN. 1950. *The Cerebral Cortex of Man.* New York: Macmillan. **71**

PERKY, C. W. 1910. An Experimental Study of Imagination, *Amer. J. Psychol.*, 21, 422–52. **132**

PERLS, F. A. 1969. *Gestalt Therapy Verbatim.* Lafayette, Calif.: Real People Press. **633**

PERLS, F., R. E. HEFFERLINE & P. GOODMAN. 1951. *Gestalt Therapy: Excitement and Growth in the Human Personality.* New York: Dell. **629**

PESKIN, H. 1967. Pubertal Onset and Ego-Functioning: A Psychoanalytical Approach, *J. Abnorm. Soc. Psychol.*, 72, 1–15. **698**

———. 1972. Multiple Prediction of Adult Psychological Health from Preadolescent and Adolescent Behavior, *J. Consult. Clin. Psychol.*, 38, 155–60. **700**

PESKIN, H. & N. LIVSON. 1972. Pre- and Post-Pubertal Personality and Adult Psychologic Functioning, *Seminars in Psychiatr.*, 4, 343–53. **698**

PETERSON, L. B. & M. J. PETERSON. 1959. Short-Term Retention of Individual Verbal Items, *J. Exper. Psychol.*, 58, 193–8. **404**

PIAGET, J. 1952. *The Origins of Intelligence in Children.* Translated by Margaret Cook. New York: International Universities Press. Originally published in French, 1936. **85**

———. 1965. *The Moral Judgment of the Child.* New York: Free Press. **737**

PINCHBECK, I. & M. HEWITT. 1969. *Children in English Society.* Vol. I. *From Tudor Times to the Eighteenth Century.* London: Routledge & Kegan Paul. **734**

POSTMAN, L. & L. RAU. 1957. Retention as a Function of the Method of Measurement, *U. Calif. Publ. Psychol.*, 8, No. 3. **401**

PRIBRAM, K. H. 1960. A Review of Theory in Physiological Psychology, *Ann. Rev. Psychol.*, 11, 1–40. **550**

———. 1962. Interrelations of Psychology and the Neurological Disciplines, in S. Koch (Ed.). *Psychology: A Study of A Science*, Vol. 4. New York: McGraw-Hill. **425**

PRICE-WILLIAMS, D., W. GORDON & M. RAMIREZ III. 1969. Skill and Conservation: A Study of Pottery-Making Children, *Develpm. Psychol.*, 1, 769. **89**

PRUITT, D. G. 1971. Towards an Understanding of Choice Shifts in Group Discussions, *J. Pers. Soc. Psychol.*, 20, 495–510. **797**

PRUITT, D. G. & D. F. JOHNSON. 1970. Mediation as an Aid to Face Saving in Negotiation, *J. Pers. Soc. Psychol.*, 14, 238–46. **798**

PYLES, M. K., H. R. STOLZ & J. W. MACFARLANE. 1935. The Accuracy of Mothers: Reports on Birth and Developmental Data, *Child Develpm.*, 6, 165–76. **34**

QUARTERMAIN, D., B. S. MCEWEN & E. C. AZMITIA, JR. 1972. Recovery of Memory Following Amnesia in the Rat and Mouse, *J. Comp. Physiol. Psychol.*, 79, 360–70. **438**

RAAHEIM, K. 1965. Problem Solving and Past Experience, in P. H. Mussen (Ed.). *European Research in Cognitive Development. Monogr. Soc. Res. Child Develpm.*, 30, No. 2. **169**

RANK, O. 1947. *Will Therapy and Truth and Reality.* New York: Knopf. **627**

RAPPOPORT, L. 1972. *Personality Development: The*

Chronology of Experience. Glenview, Ill.: Scott, Foresman. **650**

RATCLIFF, G. & G. A. B. DAVIES-JONES. 1972. Defective Visual Localization in Focal Brain Wounds, *Brain*, 95, 49–60. **427**

RAY, W. S. 1965. Mild Stress and Problem-Solving, *Amer. J. Psychol.*, 78, 227–34. **163, 167**

REICHARD, S., F. LIVSON & P. G. PETERSEN. 1962. *Aging and Personality: A Study of Eighty-Seven Older Men.* New York: Wiley. **53**

RESCORLA, R. A. 1967. Pavlovian Conditioning and Its Proper Control Procedures, *Psychol. Rev.*, 74, 71–80. **367**

RETHLINGSHAFER, D. & E. D. HINCKLEY. 1963. Influence of Judges' Characteristics Upon the Adaptation Level, *Amer. J. Psychol.*, 76, 116–23. **271**

RHEINGOLD, H. L. 1961. The Effect of Environmental Stimulation Upon Social and Exploratory Behavior in the Human Infant, in B. M. Foss (Ed.). *Determinants of Infant Behavior.* New York: Wiley. **482**

RHINE, R. J. & L. J. SEVERANCE. 1970. Ego Involvement, Discrepancy, Source Credibility and Attitude Change, *J. Pers. Soc. Psychol.*, 16, 175–90. **768**

RICHARDS, T. W. & H. NEWBERG. 1938. Studies in Fetal Behavior, *Child Develpm.*, 9, 79–86. **50**

RIGGS, L. A., R. RATLIFF, J. C. CORNSWEET & T. N. CORNSWEET. 1953. Disappearance of Steadily Fixated Visual Test Objects, *J. Opt. Soc. Amer.*, 43, 495–501. **321**

ROBBINS, L. C. 1963. The Accuracy of Parental Recall of Aspects of Child Development and of Child Rearing Practices, *J. Abnorm. Soc. Psychol.*, 66, 261–70. **35**

ROBBINS, W. J., S. BRODY, A. G. HOGAN, C. M. JACKSON & C. W. GREENE. 1928. *Growth.* New Haven: Yale University Press. **40**

ROCK, I. 1965. Adaptation to a Minified Image, *Psychonom. Sci.*, 2, 105–6. **299**

ROCK, I. & S. EBENHOLTZ. 1962. Stroboscopic Movement Based on Change of Phenomenal Rather Than Retinal Location, *Amer. J. Psychol.*, 75, 193–207. **286**

ROCK, I., E. S. TAUBER & D. P. HELLER. 1965. Perception of Stroboscopic Movement: Evidence for Its Innate Basis, *Science*, 147, 1050–2. **302**

ROGERS, C. R. 1942. *Counseling and Psychotherapy.* Boston: Houghton Mifflin. **629**

———. 1951. *Client-Centered Therapy.* Boston: Houghton Mifflin. **629**

———. 1957. The Necessary and Sufficient Conditions of Therapeutic Personality Change, *J. Consult. Psychol.*, 21, 95–103. **629**

ROGERS, C. R. & R. F. DYMOND (Eds.). 1954. *Psychotherapy and Personality Change.* Chicago: University of Chicago Press. **629**

ROGERS, C. R. & B. F. SKINNER. 1956. Some Views Concerning the Control of Human Behavior: A Symposium, *Science*, 124, 1057–1966. **631**

ROSEN, J. M. 1968. *Selected Papers on Direct Psychoanalysis.* New York: Grune & Stratton. **617**

ROSENBLATT, J. S. & L. R. ARONSON. 1958. The Influence of Experience on the Behavioral Effects of Androgen in Prepuberally Castrated Male Cats, *Animal Behav.*, 6, 171–2. **558**

ROSENHAN, D. L. 1973. On Being Sane in Insane Places, *Science*, 179, 250–7. **607**

ROSENZWEIG, M. R., D. KRECH, E. L. BENNETT & M. C. DIAMOND. 1968. Modifying Brain Chemistry and Anatomy by Enrichment or Impoverishment of Experience, in G. Newton & S. Levine (Eds.). *Early Experience and Behavior.* Springfield, Ill.: Charles C Thomas. **433**

ROSENZWEIG, M. R., K. MØLLGAARD, M. C. DIAMOND & E. L. BENNETT. 1972. Negative as Well as Positive Synaptic Changes May Store Memory, *Psychol. Rev.*, 79, 93–6. **434**

ROTHMAN, T. 1972. De Laguna's Commentaries on Hallucinogenic Drugs and Witchcraft in Dioscorides' Materia Medica. *Bulletin of the History of Medicine*, XLVI, 562–7. **525**

RUBIN, Z. 1970. Measurement of Romantic Love, *J. Pers. Soc. Psychol.*, 16, 265–73. **477**

RUBOVITS, P. C. & M. L. MAEHR. 1973. Pygmalion Black and White, *J. Pers. Soc. Psychol.*, 25, 210–18. **777**

SACHS, J. S. 1967. Recognition Memory for Syntactic and Semantic Aspects of Connected Discourse, *Percep. & Psychophys.*, 2(9), 437–42. **107**

———. In press. Memory in Reading and Listening to Discourse, *Memory and Cognition.* **107**

SALES, S. M. & K. E. FRIEND. 1973. Success and Failure as Determinants of Level of Authoritarianism, *Behav. Sci.*, 18, 163–72. **659**

SALTER, A. 1961. *Conditioned Reflex Therapy: The Direct Approach to the Reconstruction of Personality.* New York: Capricorn Books-Putnam. Originally published in 1949. **621**

SAMUEL, A. L. 1963. Some Studies in Machine Learning Using the Game of Checkers, in E. A. Feigenbaum & J. Feldman (Eds.). *Computers and Thought.* New York: McGraw-Hill. **154**

SANDIFER, M. G., C. PETTUS & D. QUADE. 1964. A Study of Psychiatric Diagnosis, *J. Nerv. Ment. Dis.*, 139, 350–6. **606**

SARASON, I. G. & R. E. SMITH. 1971. Personality, in P. H. Mussen & M. R. Rosenzweig (Eds.). *Annual Review of Psychology.* Vol. 22. Palo Alto, Calif.: Annual Reviews. **700**

SARNOFF, I. 1962. *Personality Dynamics and Development.* New York: Wiley. **651**

SATIR, V. 1967. *Conjoint Family Therapy: A Guide to Theory and Technique.* Rev. ed. Palo Alto, Calif.: Science & Behavior. **637**

SAUGSTAD, P. & K. RAAHEIM. 1956. *Problem-Solving as Dependent on Availability of Functions.* Oslo: University of Oslo Library. **169**

SCAMMON, R. E. 1930. The Measurement of the Body in Childhood, in Harris, *et al.* (Eds.). *The Measurement of Man.* Minneapolis: University of Minnesota Press. **42**

SCARR-SALAPATEK, S. 1971. Race, Social Class, & I. Q., *Science,* 174, 1285–95. **222**

SCHACHTER, S. 1968. Obesity and Eating, *Science,* 161, 751–6. **457**

SCHACHTER, S. & L. P. GROSS. 1968. Manipulated Time and Eating Behavior, *J. Pers. Soc. Psychol.,* 10, 98–106. **456**

SCHACHTER, S. & J. E. SINGER. 1962. Cognitive, Social, and Physiological Determinants of Emotional State, *Psychol. Rev.,* 69, 379–99. **493**

SCHAFER, R. & G. MURPHY. 1943. The Role of Autism in a Visual Figure-Ground Relationship, *J. Exper. Psychol.,* 32, 335–43. **266**

SCHAFFER, H. R. & W. M. CALLENDER. 1959. Psychologic Effects of Hospitalization in Infancy, *Pediatr.,* 24, 528–39. **483**

SCHAFFER, H. R. & P. E. EMERSON. 1964. The Development of Social Attachments in Infancy, *Monogr. Soc. Res. Child Develpm.,* 29, Whole No. 1. **483**

SCHEERER, M., E. ROTHMANN & K. GOLDSTEIN. 1945. A Case of "Idiot Savant": An Experimental Study of Personality Organization, *Psychol. Monogr.,* 58, No. 4. **198**

SCHILDKRAUT, J. J. & S. S. KETY. 1967. Biogenic Amines and Emotion, *Science,* 156, 21–30. **552**

SCHLOSBERG, H. 1954. Three Dimensions of Emotion, *Psychol. Rev.,* 61, 81–8. **470**

SCHOENFELDT, L. F. 1968. The Hereditary Components of the Project TALENT Two-Day Test Battery, *Meas. Eval. Guid.,* 1, 130–40. **691**

SCHOFIELD, W. 1964. *Psychotherapy, the Purchase of Friendship.* Englewood Cliffs, N. J.: Prentice-Hall. **640**

SCHUTZ, F. 1965. Sexuelle Prägung bei Anatiden, *Zeitsch. Tierpsychol.,* 22, 50–103. **xvii**

SCOTT, J. P. & J. L. FULLER. 1965. *Genetics and the Social Behavior of the Dog.* Chicago: University of Chicago Press. **21**

SEARLE, L. V. 1949. The Organization of Hereditary Maze-Brightness and Maze-Dullness, *Genet. Psychol. Monogr.,* 39, 279–325. **20**

SEARS, R. R. 1936. Experimental Studies of Projection: I. Attribution of Traits, *J. Soc. Psychol.,* 7, 151–63. **580**

SEARS, R. R., E. E. MACCOBY & H. LEVIN. 1957. *Patterns of Child Rearing.* Evanston, Ill.: Row, Peterson. **742**

SEARS, R. R., J. W. M. WHITING, V. NOWLIS & R. S. SEARS. 1953. Some Child-Rearing Antecedents of Aggression and Dependency in Young Children, *Gen. Psychol. Monogr.,* 47, 135–234. **744**

SEAY, B., B. K. ALEXANDER & H. F. HARLOW. 1964. Maternal Behavior of Socially Deprived Rhesus Monkeys, *J. Abnorm. Soc. Psychol.,* 69, 345–54. **479**

SEM-JACOBSEN, C. W. 1968. *Depth-Electrographic Stimulation of the Human Brain and Behavior.* Springfield, Ill.: Charles C Thomas. **559**

SEM-JACOBSEN, C. W. & A. TORKILDSEN. 1960. Depth Recording and Electrical Stimulation in the Human Brain. In E. R. Ramey & D. S. O'Doherty (Eds.). *Electrical Studies on the Unanesthetized Brain.* New York: Hoeber. **549**

SHAKESPEARE, W. 1597. *Romeo and Juliet* (Act II, Scene 1). **xviii**

SHANNON, C. E. 1951. Prediction and Entropy in Printed English, *Bell Syst. Tech. J.,* 30, 50–64. **108**

SHEALY, C. N., J. T. MORTIMER & N. R. HAGFORS. Dorsal Column Electroanalgesia, *J. Neurosurg.,* 32, 560–4. **349**

SHELDON, W. H. & S. S. STEVENS. 1942. *The Varieties of Temperament.* New York: Harper. **697**

SHELDON, W. H., S. S. STEVENS & W. B. TUCKER. 1940. *The Varieties of Human Physique.* New York: Harper. **697**

SHEPARD, R. N. & J. METZLER. 1971. Mental Rotation of Three Dimensional Objects, *Science,* 171, 701–3. **135**

SHERIF, M. 1935. A Study of Some Social Factors in Perception, *Arch. Psychol. N. Y.,* No. 187. **286**

SHIELDS, J. 1962. *Monozygotic Twins Brought Up Apart and Brought Up Together: An Investigation Into the Genetic and Environmental Causes of Variation in Personality.* London: Oxford. **693**

SHUEY, A. M. 1966. *The Testing of Negro Intelligence.* 2nd ed. New York: Social Science Press. **220**

SHURRAGER, P. S. & E. CULLER. 1940. Conditioning in the Spinal Dog, *J. Exper. Psychol.,* 26, 133–59. **418**

SIEGEL, P. V., S. J. GERATHEWOHL & S. R. MÖHLER. 1969. Time-Zone Effects, *Science,* 164, 1249–55. **538**

SIGUELAND, E. R. & L. P. LIPSITT. 1966. Conditioned Head-Turning in Human Newborns, *J. Exp. Child Psychol.,* 3, 356–76. **44**

SIMMEL, M. L. 1966. Developmental Aspects of the Body Schema, *Child Develpm.,* 37, 83–95. **238**

SIMPSON, G. G. 1966. The Biological Nature of Man, *Science,* 152, 472–8. **13**

SKEELS, H. M. 1966. Adult Status of Children With Contrasting Early Life Experiences, *Monogr. Soc. Res. Child Develpm.,* 31, No. 3. **212**

SKINNER, B. F. 1938. *The Behavior of Organisms.* New York: Appleton. **383**

———. 1948. *Walden Two.* New York: Macmillan. **627**

———. 1953. *Science and Human Behavior.* Paperback. New York: Macmillan. **619**

———. 1971. *Beyond Freedom and Dignity.* New York: Knopf. **627**

SKODAK, M. & H. M. SKEELS. 1949. A Final Followup Study of One Hundred Adopted Children, *J. Genet. Psychol.,* 75, 65–125. **209**

SLOBIN, D. I. 1966. Grammatical Transformations and Sentence Comprehension in Childhood and Adulthood, *J. Verb. Learn. Verb. Behav.,* 5, 219–27. **105**

———. (Ed.). 1971a. *The Ontogenesis of Grammar:*

A Theoretical Symposium. New York: Academic. **116**

——. 1971b. *Psycholinguistics*. Glenview, Ill.: Scott, Foresman. **102, 115**

——. 1972. Cognitive Prerequisites for the Development of Grammar, in C. A. Ferguson & D. I. Slobin (Eds.). *Studies of Child Language Development*. New York: Holt. **113**

——. 1973. On the Nature of Talk to Children, in E. Lenneberg & E. Lenneberg (Eds.). *Foundations of Language Development: A Multidisciplinary Approach*. UNESCO. **117**

SMALL, W. S. 1901. An Experimental Study of the Mental Processes of the Rat, *Amer. J. Psychol.*, 12, 206–39. **385**

SMEDSLUND, J. 1961. The Acquisition of Conservation of Substance and Weight in Children: Extinction of Conservation of Weight Acquired "Normally" and by Means of Empirical Controls on a Balance, *Scand. J. Psychol.*, 2, 85–7. **91**

——. 1968. Conservation and Resistance to Extinction: A Comment on Hall and Simpson's Article, *Merrill-Palmer Quart.*, 14, No. 3, 211–14. **91**

SNYDER, F. W. & N. H. PRONKO. 1952. *Vision With Spatial Inversion*. Wichita: University of Wichita Press. **297**

SOLOMON, R. L. 1964. Punishment, *Amer. Psychol.*, 19, 239–63. **382**

SOMMER, R. 1969. *Personal Space*. Englewood Cliffs, N. J.: Prentice-Hall. **811**

SONTAG, L. W., C. T. BAKER & V. L. NELSON. 1958. Mental Growth and Personality Development: A Longitudinal Study, *Monogr. Soc. Res. Child Develpm.*, 23, No. 2. **214**

SPERLING, G. 1960. Negative Afterimage Without Prior Positive Image, *Science*, 131, 1613–14. **251**

——. 1969. A Model for Visual Memory Tasks, in R. N. Haber (Ed.). *Information Processing Approaches to Visual Perception*. New York: Holt. **403**

SPERRY, R. W. 1961. Cerebral Organization and Behavior, *Science*, 133, 1749–57. **429**

——. 1970. Cerebral Dominance in Perception, in F. A. Young & D. B. Lindsley (Eds.). *Early Experience and Visual Information Processing in Perceptual and Reading Disorders*. Washington, D. C.: National Academy of Sciences. **429**

SPRAGG, S. D. S. 1940. Morphine Addiction in Chimpanzees, *Comp. Psychol. Monogr.*, 15, No. 7. **455**

SPRANGER, E. 1928. *Types of Men*. New York: Stechert. **662**

SROLE, L., T. S. LANGNER, S. T. MICHAEL, M. K. OPLER & T. A. C. RENNIE. 1962. *Mental Health in the Metropolis: The Midtown Manhattan Study*. New York: McGraw-Hill. **591**

STAATS, A. W. & C. K. STAATS. 1958. Attitudes Established by Classical Conditioning, *J. Abnorm. Soc. Psychol.*, 57, 37–40. **760**

STAMPFL, T. G. & D. J. LEWIS. 1967. Essentials of Implosive Therapy: A Learning-Theory-Based Psychodynamic Behavioral Therapy, *J. Abnorm. Psychol.*, 72, 496–503. **620**

STEIN, Z., M. SUSSER, G. SAENGER & F. MAROLLA. 1972. Nutrition and Mental Performance, *Science*, 178, 708–13. **217**

STEINER, I. & J. VANNOY. 1966. Personality Correlates of Two Types of Conformity, *J. Pers. Soc. Psychol.*, 4, 307–15. **805**

STENDLER, C. B. 1950. Sixty Years of Child Training Practices, *J. Pediat.*, 36, 122–34. **698**

STEPHENS, G. J. & J. L. MCGAUGH. 1968. Periodicity and Memory in Mice: A Supplementary Report, *Comm. Behav. Biol., Part A*, 2, 59–63. **438**

STERNBERG, S. 1966. High-Speed Scanning in Human Memory, *Science*, 153, 652–4. **409**

STEWART, K. 1969. Dream Theory in Malaya, in C. Tart (Ed.). *Altered States of Consciousness: A Book of Readings*. New York: Wiley. **508**

STEWART, L. H. 1970. Birth Order and Political Leadership: I. The American Presidents. Paper delivered at the Annual Meeting of the American Psychological Association, Miami, Florida. **700**

STOYVA, J. & J. KAMIYA. 1968. Electrophysiological Studies of Dreaming as the Prototype of a New Strategy in the Study of Consciousness, *Psychol. Rev.*, 75, 192–205. **389**

STRATTON, G. M. 1897. Vision Without Inversion of the Retinal Image, *Psychol. Rev.*, 4, 341–60. **297**

STROSS, B. 1972. Verbal Processes in Tzeltal Speech Socialization, *Anthropol. Linguistics*, 14, 1–3. **113**

STROYMEYER, C. F. 1970. Eidetikers, *Psychology Today* (November). **130**

SULLIVAN, H. S. 1953. *The Interpersonal Theory of Psychiatry*. New York: Norton. **633**

——. 1954. *The Psychiatric Interview*. New York: Norton. **633**

SUPA, M., M. COTZIN & K. M. DALLENBACH. 1944. Facial Vision: The Perception of Obstacles by the Blind, *Amer. J. Psychol.*, 57, 133–83. **237**

SUTTON-SMITH, B. & B. G. ROSENBERG. 1970. *The Sibling*. New York: Holt. **700**

SZASZ, T. S. 1970. *The Manufacture of Madness*. New York: Harper. **589, 606**

——. 1973. *The Second Sin*. New York: Anchor Press/Doubleday. **589**

SZÉKELY, L. 1950. Knowledge and Thinking, *Acta Psychologica*, 7, 1–24. **170**

TANNER, J. M. 1962. *Growth at Adolescence*. 2nd ed. Oxford: Blackwell. **40**

——. 1970. Physical Growth, in P. H. Mussen (Ed.). *Carmichael's Manual of Child Psychology*. New York: Wiley. **37**

TART, C. 1971. *On Being Stoned: A Psychological Study of Marijuana Intoxication*. Palo Alto, Calif.: Science & Behavior Books. **519, 520**

TAYLOR, D. W., P. C. BERRY & C. H. BLOCK. 1958. Does

Group Participation When Using Brainstorming Facilitate or Inhibit Creative Thinking? *Admin. Sci. Quart.*, 3, 23–47. **801**

Techniques and Status of Modern Parapsychology. A Symposium at the 1970 Annual Meeting of the American Association for the Advancement of Science, Chicago. **xx**

TEITELBAUM, P. 1971. The Encephalization of Hunger, in E. Stellar & J. M. Sprague (Eds.). *Progress in Physiological Psychology*. Vol. 4. New York: Academic Press. **556**

TERMAN, L. M. & M. A. MERRILL. 1937. *Measuring Intelligence*. Boston: Houghton Mifflin. **181**

———. 1960. *The Stanford Binet Intelligence Scale: Manual for the Third Revision*. Boston: Houghton Mifflin. **183, 184**

TEUBER, H.-L. 1959. Some Alterations in Behavior After Cerebral Lesions in Man, in E. Bass (Ed.). *Evolution of Nervous Control From Primitive Organisms to Man*. Washington: American Association for the Advancement of Science. **427**

TEUBER, H.-L. & S. WEINSTEIN. 1956. Ability to Discover Hidden Figures After Cerebral Lesion, *Arch. Neurol. Psychiat.*, 76, 369–79. **427**

THOMAS, A., S. CHESS & H. G. BIRCH. 1968. *Temperament and Behavior Disorders in Children*. New York: New York University Press. **699**

THOMAS, A., S. CHESS, H. G. BIRCH, M. E. HERTZIG & S. KORN. 1964. *Behavioral Individuality in Early Childhood*. New York: International Universities Press. **49**

THOMAS, G. J., G. HOSTETTER & D. J. BARKER. 1968. Behavioral Functions of the Limbic System, in E. Stellar & J. M. Sprague (Eds.). *Progress in Physiological Psychology*, Vol. 2. New York: Academic Press. **550**

THOMAS, K. 1971. *Religion and the Decline of Magic*. London: Weldenfeld & Nicholson. **748**

THOMPSON, W. R. 1957. Influence of Prenatal Maternal Anxiety on Emotionality in Young Rats, *Science*, 125, 698–9. **17**

THOMSON, G. H. 1952. Chapter in C. Murchison (Ed.). *A History of Psychology in Autobiography*, Vol. 4. Worcester, Mass.: Clark University Press. **197**

THORNDIKE, E. L. 1898. Animal Intelligence, *Psychol. Monogr.*, 1, No. 8. **197**

———. 1926. *The Measurement of Intelligence*. New York: Bureau of Publications, Teachers College, Columbia University. **180**

THURSTONE, L. L. 1938. *Primary Mental Abilities*. Chicago: University of Chicago Press. **197**

———. 1944. *A Factorial Study of Perception*. Chicago: University of Chicago Press. **266**

TIENARI, P. 1971. Schizophrenia and Monozygotic Twins, *Psychiatria Fennica*, 97–104. **605**

TILLYARD, A. C. W. 1927. *Spiritual Exercises and Their Results: An Essay in Psychology and Comparative Religion*. New York: Macmillan. **515**

TOLMAN, E. C. 1967. *Purposive Behavior in Animals and Men*. New York: Appleton. Originally published 1932. **390**

TOLMAN, E. C. & C. H. HONZIK. 1930. "Insight" in Rats, *U. Calif. Publ. Psychol.*, 4, 215–32. **137**

TOMKINS, S. S. 1962. *Affect, Imagery, Consciousness: Vol. 1. The Positive Affects*. New York: Springer. **494**

TOYNBEE, A. 1961. *A Study of History, Vol. 12: Reconsiderations*. New York: Oxford. **691**

TRACY, J. J. & H. J. CROSS. 1973. Antecedents of Shift in Moral Judgment, *J. Pers. Soc. Psychol.*, 26, 238–44. **738**

TRYON, R. C. 1940. Genetic Differences in Maze Learning in Rats, in National Society for the Study of Education. *The Thirty-ninth Yearbook*. Bloomington, Ill.: Public School Publications. **20**

TUDDENHAM, R. D. 1948. Soldier Intelligence in World Wars I and II, *Amer. Psychol.*, 3, 54–6. **193**

TULVING, E. 1962. Subjective Organization in Free Recall of Unrelated Words, *Psychol. Rev.*, 69, 344–54. **406**

TURNBULL, C. M. 1961. Some Observations Regarding the Experiences and Behavior of the BaMbuti Pygmies, *Amer. J. Psychol.*, 74, 304–8. **299**

TYLER, L. E. 1956. *The Psychology of Human Differences*. New York: Appleton. **217**

ULLMANN, L. P. & J. M. GIOVANNONI. 1964. The Development of a Self-Report Measure of the Process-Reactive Continuum, *J. Nerv. Ment. Dis.*, 138, 38–41. **602**

ULRICH, R. E., T. J. STACHNIK & N. R. STAINTON. 1963. Student Acceptance of Generalized Personality Interpretations, *Psychol. Reports*, 13, 831–4. **780**

UNDERWOOD, B. J. 1957. Interference and Forgetting, *Psychol. Rev.*, 64, 49–60. **407**

UNGER, S. M. 1963. Mescaline, LSD, Psilocybin, and Personality Change, *Psychiatry*, 26, 111–25. **522**

VALINS, S. 1966. Cognitive Effects of False Heart-Rate Feedback, *J. Pers. Soc. Psychol.*, 4, 400–8. **760**

VALVERDE, F. 1967. Apical Dendritic Spines of the Visual Cortex and Light Deprivation in the Mouse, *Exper. Brain Res.*, 3, 337–52. **431**

VANDENBERG, S. G. 1962. The Hereditary Abilities Study: Hereditary Components in a Psychological Test Battery, *Amer. J. Hum. Genet.*, 14, 220–37. **484**

VAUGHN, E. & A. E. FISHER. 1962. Male Sexual Behavior Induced by Intracranial Electrical Stimulation, *Science*, 137, 758–60. **559**

VIGOTSKY, L. S. 1939. Thought and Speech, *Psychiatry*, 2, 29–52. **138**

VOGEL, G., D. FOULKES & H. TROSMAN. 1966. Ego Functions and Dreaming During Sleep Onset, *Arch. Gen. Psychiat.*, 14, 238–48. **501**

WALD, G. 1964. The Receptors of Human Color Vision, *Science*, 145, 1007–16. **246**

WALK, R. D. & S. H. DODGE. 1962. Visual Depth Perception of a 10-Month-Old Monocular Human Infant, *Science*, 137, 529–30. **296**

WALL, P. D. & W. H. SWEET. 1967. Temporary Abolition of Pain in Man, *Science*, 155, 108–9. **349**

WALLACE, R. 1970. Physiological Effects of Transcendental Meditation, *Science*, 167, 1751–4. **516**

WALLACH, H. 1935. Über Visuell Wahrgenommene Bewegungsrichtung, *Psychol. Forsch.*, 20, 325–80. **274**

———. 1940. The Role of Head Movements and Vestibular and Visual Cues in Sound Localization, *J. Exper. Psychol.*, 27, 339–68. **292**

WALLACH, M. A. 1963. Research on Children's Thinking, in *Child Psychology: 62nd Yearbook of the National Society for the Study of Education*. Chicago: University of Chicago Press. **89**

WALSTER, E. & J. A. PILIAVIN. 1972. Equity and the Innocent Bystander, *J. Soc. Issues*, 28, 165–89. **803**

WARDEN, A. & B. SACHS. 1973. Personal communication. **539**

WARDEN, C. J. 1931. *Animal Motivation Studies: The Albino Rat*. New York: Columbia University Press. **573**

WARNER, W. L. & P. S. LUNT. 1941. *The Social Life of the Modern Community*. New Haven: Yale University Press. **217**

WARREN, R. M. 1968. Verbal Transformation Effect and Auditory Perceptual Mechanisms, *Psych. Bull.*, 70, 261–70. **304**

WATSON, J. B. & R. RAYNER. 1920. Conditioned Emotional Reactions, *J. Exp. Psychol.*, 3, 1–14. **596**

WATSON, J. S. 1966. Perception of Object Orientation in Infants, *Merrill-Palmer Quart.*, 12, 73–94. **47**

———. 1972. Smiling, Cooing, and "The Game," *Merrill-Palmer Quart.*, 18, 323–39. **47**

WATSON, J. S. & C. RAMEY. 1969. Reactions to Response Contingent Stimulation in Early Infancy. Revision of paper presented at the biennial meeting of the Society for Research in Child Development, Santa Monica, California. **47**

WECHSLER, D. 1949. *Wechsler Intelligence Scale for Children*. New York: Psychological Corporation. **184**

———. 1958. *The Measurement and Appraisal of Intelligence*. Baltimore: Williams & Wilkins. **184**

WEIL, A. T. 1969. Cannabis, *Sci. J.*, 5a, No. 3, 36–42. **519**

WEIL, A. T., N. E. ZINBERG & J. M. NELSON. 1968. Clinical and Psychological Effects of Marijuana in Man, *Science*, 162, 1234–42. **519**

WEINSTOCK, A. R. 1967. Longitudinal Study of Social Class and Defense Preferences, *J. Consult. Psychol.*, 31, 539–91. **581**

WEISKRANTZ, L., J. ELLIOTT & C. DARLINGTON. 1971. Preliminary Observations on Tickling Oneself, *Nature*, 230, 598–9. **346**

WEISS, W. 1957. Opinion Congruence With a Negative Source on One Issue as a Factor Influencing Agreement on Another Issue, *J. Abnorm. Soc. Psychol.*, 54, 180–6. **768**

WELLER, G. M. & R. Q. BELL. 1965. Basal Skin Conductance and Neonatal State, *Child Develpm.*, 36, 647–57. **489**

WENDER, P. H., D. ROSENTHAL & S. S. KATZ. 1968. A Psychiatric Assessment of the Adoptive Parents of Schizophrenics, in D. Rosenthal & S. S. Katz (Eds.). *The Transmission of Schizophrenia*. London: Pergamon. **605**

WENGER, M. & B. BAGCHI. 1961. Studies of Autonomic Functions in Practitioners of Yoga in India, *Behav. Sci.*, 6, 312–23. **387**

WERNER, H. 1948. *Comparative Psychology of Mental Development*. Chicago: Follett. Originally published 1926. **96**

WERTHEIMER, MAX. 1923. Untersuchungen zur Lehre von der Gestalt, *Psychol. Forsch.*, 4, 301–50. **267**

WERTHEIMER, MICHAEL. 1959. *Productive Thinking*. Rev. ed. New York: Harper. 1st ed. published 1945. **95**

———. 1961. Psychomotor Coordination of Auditory and Visual Space at Birth, *Science*, 134, 1692. **84, 296**

WHEELIS, A. 1973. *How People Change*. New York: Harper & Row. **642**

WHITAKER, H. 1971. Neurolinguistics, in W. O. Dingwall (Ed.). *A Survey of Linguistic Science*. College Park: University of Maryland Linguistics Program. **103**

WHITE, B. W., F. A. SAUNDERS, L. SCADDEN, P. BACH-Y-RITA & C. C. COLLINS. 1970. Seeing with the Skin, *Percep. & Psychophys.*, 7, 23–9. **311, 312**

WHITE, R. W. 1959. Motivation Reconsidered: The Concept of Competence, *Psychol. Rev.*, 66, 297–333. **458**

———. 1964. *The Abnormal Personality*. 3rd ed. New York: Ronald. **595, 603**

WHORF, B. L. 1956. *Language, Thought and Reality*. New York: Wiley. **141**

WICKELGREN, W. A. 1970. Multitrace Strength Theory, in D. A. Norman (Ed.). *Models of Human Memory*. New York: Academic. **410**

WIESEL, T. N. & D. H. HUBEL. 1963. Single-cell Responses in Striate Cortex of Kittens Deprived of Vision in One Eye, *J. Neurophysiol.*, 26, 1003–17. **334**

WIESNER, B. P. & N. M. SHEARD. 1933. *Maternal Behavior in the Rat*. London: Oliver & Boyd. **453**

WIGGINS, J. S., K. E. RENNER, G. L. CLORE & R. J. ROSE. 1971. *The Psychology of Personality*. Reading, Mass.: Addison-Wesley. **651**

WILDE, G. J. S. 1964. Inheritance of Personality Traits: An Investigation into the Hereditary Determination of Neurotic Instability, Extraversion, and Other Personality Traits by Means of a Questionnaire Administered to Twins, *Acta Psychologica*, 22, 37–51. **693**

WILLIS, F. N. 1966. Initial Speaking Distance as a Function of the Speaker's Relationship, *Psychon. Rev.*, 5, 221–2. **811**

WILSON, G. D. & A. H. BRAZENDALE. 1973. Sexual Attractiveness, Social Attitudes, and Response to Risqué Humor, *European J. Soc. Psychol.* **481**

WILSON, M. 1957. Effects of Circumscribed Cortical Lesions Upon Somesthetic and Visual Discrimination in the Monkey, *J. Comp. Physiol. Psychol.*, 50, 630–5. **422**

WILSON, W. A., JR. & M. MISHKIN. 1959. Comparison of the Effects of Inferotemporal and Lateral Occipital Lesions on Visually Guided Behavior in Monkeys, *J. Comp. Physiol. Psychol.*, 52, 10–17. **422**

WINICK, M. 1970. Fetal Malnutrition and Growth Processes, *Hospital Practice*, 33, 33–41. **217**

WOLBERG, L. R. 1954. *The Technique of Psychotherapy.* New York: Grune & Stratton. **618**

WOLLBERG, Z. & J. D. NEWMAN. 1972. Auditory Cortex of Squirrel Monkey: Response Patterns of Single Cells to Species-Specific Vocalizations, *Science*, 175, 212–14. **341**

WOLPE, J. 1958. *Psychotherapy by Reciprocal Inhibition.* Stanford: Stanford University Press. **619**

———. 1969. *The Practice of Behavior Therapy.* New York: Pergamon. **623**

WOODRUFF, D. S. & J. E. BIRREN. 1972. Age Changes and Cohort Differences in Personality, *Develpm. Psychol.*, 6, 252–9. **36**

WORCHEL, P. & K. M. DALLENBACH. 1947. Facial Vision, Perception of Obstacles by the Deaf-Blind, *Amer. J. Psychol.*, 60, 502–53. **237**

YARBUS, A. L. 1967. *Eye Movements and Vision.* New York: Plenum. **306**

YARROW, L. J. 1963. Research in Dimensions of Early Maternal Care, *Merrill-Palmer Quart.*, 9, 101–14. **211**

YARROW, L. J., J. L. RUBENSTEIN, F. A. PEDERSON & J. J. JANKOWSKI. 1972. Dimensions of Early Stimulation and Their Differential Effects on Infant Development, *Merrill-Palmer Quart.*, 18, 205–18. **211**

YARROW, L. J. & M. R. YARROW. 1964. Personality Continuity and Change in the Family Context, in R. Worchel & D. Byrne (Eds.). *Personality Change.* New York: Wiley. **484**

YARROW, M. R., J. D. CAMPBELL & R. V. BURTON. 1970. Recollections of Childhood: A Study of the Retrospective Method, *Monogr. Soc. Res. Child Develpm.*, 35, Whole no. 138. **35**

YOUNG, P. T. 1961. *Motivation and Emotion.* New York: Wiley. **491**

YOUNG, W. C., R. W. GOY & C. H. PHOENIX. 1964. Hormones and Sexual Behavior, *Science*, 143, 212–18. **558**

ZAJONC, R. B. 1965. Social Facilitation, *Science*, 149, 260–74. **795**

ZAPOROZHETS, A. V. 1961. The Origin and Development of the Conscious Control of Movements in Man, in N. O'Connor (Ed.). *Recent Soviet Psychology.* New York: Liveright. **305**

ZELAZO, P. R., N. A. ZELAZO & S. KOLB. 1972. Walking in the Newborn, *Science*, 176, 314–15. **41, 49**

ZELLMAN, G. L. & D. O. SEARS. 1971. Childhood Origins of Tolerance for Dissent, *J. Soc. Issues*, 27, 109–36. **752**

ZIMBARDO, P. G. 1970. The Human Choice: Indivuation, Reason, and Order versus De-indivuation, Impulse, and Chaos, in W. J. Arnold and D. Levine (Eds.). *Nebraska Symposium on Motivation, 1969.* Lincoln: University of Nebraska Press. **795**

———. 1972. Pathology of Prisons, *Society*, 9, No. 4 (April), 4–8. **702**

ZIMBARDO, P. G., G. MARSHALL & C. MASLACH. 1971. Liberating Behavior from Time-Bound Control: Expanding the Present through Hypnosis, *J. App. Soc. Psychol.*, 1, 305–23. **513**

ZIMBARDO, P. G., C. MASLACH & G. MARSHALL. 1972. Hypnosis and the Psychology of Cognitive and Behavioral Control, in E. Fromm & R. E. Shor (Eds.). *Hypnosis: Research Developments and Perspectives.* Chicago: Aldine-Atherton. **493**

ZUBEK, J. P. 1963. Counteracting Effects of Physical Exercises Performed During Prolonged Perceptual Deprivation, *Science*, 142, 504–6. **460**

ZUBEK, J. P. (Ed.). 1969. *Sensory Deprivation: Fifteen Years of Research.* New York: Appleton. **460**

ZWEIGENHAFT, R. 1970. Signature Size: Key to Status Awareness, *J. Soc. Psychol.*, 81, 49–54. **654**

Index

ABOUT THE AUTHORS

DAVID KRECH, Professor Emeritus of Psychology at the University of California in Berkeley, specializes in the study of brain biochemistry and behavior. In 1970 he received the American Psychological Association Distinguished Scientific Contribution Award in recognition of his "productive career in research and teaching." With Richard S. Crutchfield, he is co-author of *Theory and Problems of Social Psychology.*

RICHARD S. CRUTCHFIELD is Professor of Psychology at the University of California in Berkeley, and formerly Director of the Institute of Personality Assessment and Research, which is also at Berkeley. He specializes in the fields of productive thinking and cognition. With David Krech and E. L. Ballachey, he is co-author of *Individual in Society.*

NORMAN LIVSON is Professor of Psychology and Chairman of the Department at California State University at Hayward. He is also a research psychologist with the Institute of Human Development in Berkeley, and has published widely on personality, perceptual, and cognitive development. He has been a consulting editor for *Child Development* and is currently a consulting editor for *Merrill-Palmer Quarterly.*

WILLIAM A. WILSON, JR., Professor of Psychology and Biobehavioral Sciences at the University of Connecticut at Storrs, holds an M.D. from Yale and a Ph.D. from the University of California at Berkeley. His research has been in neuropsychology, and he is an associate editor of the *Journal of Comparative and Physiological Psychology.*

The book was set in Aster and Helvetica types.
It was composed by Cherry Hill Composition, Pennsauken, N.J.
It was printed by Von Hoffman Press, St. Louis, Mo., on Mead Publishers matte paper provided by Allan & Gray Corp., New York. It was bound by Von Hoffman Press.
The color gatefold was printed by Creative Lithographers, New York.

Medical Illustrations: Phillip Johnson

Part Illustrations: Jim Manos

Charts: Anagraphics, Inc., and Graphic Arts International; Ed Malsberg

Frontispiece: "The Proportions of Man" by Leonardo da Vinci

Design: Bill Frost

Cover: John Jeheber

Photo Research: Yvonne Freund